Entrepreneur's

Great Big Book
of Business Lists

Use These Tabs to Navigate This Book

Entrepreneur's

Great Big Book
of Business Lists

All the Things You Need to Know
to Run a Small Business

Courtney Thurman
and Ashlee Gardner

Ep Entrepreneur®Press

Editorial Director: Jere Calmes

Acquisitions Editor: Karen Thomas

Cover Design: Beth Hansen-Winter

Production and Editorial Services: CWL Publishing Enterprises, Inc., Madison, Wisconsin, www.cwlpub.com.

This publication is designed to provide accurate and authoritative information in regard to the subject matter covered. It is sold with the understanding that the publisher is not engaged in rendering legal, accounting, or other professional services. If legal advice or other expert assistance is required, the services of a competent professional person should be sought.

> —From a Declaration of Principles jointly adopted by
> a Committee of the American Bar Association and
> a Committee of Publishers and Associations

ISBN 1-59918-007-3

Library of Congress Cataloging-in-Publication Data

Thurman, Courtney.
  Entrepreneur's great big book of business lists : all the things you need to run a small business / by Courtney Thurman & Ashlee Gardner.
    p. cm.
  ISBN 1-59918-007-3 (alk. paper)
 1. Small business—United States—Management. 2. New business enterprises—United States—Management. 3. Small business—United States—Management—Information services—Directories. 4. Entrepreneurship—United States.
5. Web sites—Directories. I. Gardner, Ashlee. II. Entrepreneur Media, Inc. III. Title.
  HD62.7.T488 2006
  658.1'1—dc22

                                                    2005027241

Printed in Canada

Contents

Preface

Every entrepreneur wants to succeed without making the common mistakes that can threaten a business. However, it's difficult when there are so many hot strategies, methods, and approaches that it can get overwhelming. Ironically, one of the top reasons for business failure is lack of research.

You probably have a closet full of books that contain information on the latest trends in your industry, success stories, and sales secrets. However, even if you get the time to read all those books, you will probably never be able find again in all those books the tips and pieces of advice that seemed so valuable. The purpose of this book is to be a one-stop shop of information in an easy-to-reference guide.

The authors of this book are both graduates of the University of Southern California's Marshall School of Business. Although business school is not a necessity for successful entrepreneurs, we owe much of our personal success to our experiences as Co-Presidents of The USC Entrepreneur Club. Starting a student organization is much like starting a small business. In fact, we saw many small businesses start and flourish; our mission was to make those businesses succeed. In less than two years, The USC Entrepreneur Club went from being an unnoticed "good idea" to becoming the largest student organization in the Marshall School of Business. As a result, we were inspired to develop a tool that could help entrepreneurs from all walks of life to start and grow their businesses, while at the same time provide some tips from young, innovative minds.

Unlike other resource guides, *Entrepreneur's Great Big Book of Business Lists* is compiled with a fresh, young, and innovative perspective and includes contributions from other ambitious members of The USC Entrepreneur Club. You will find insightful approaches that will give your business a competitive edge and also provide you with a basic understanding of normal business practices. The contributing writers come from a variety of backgrounds and cultures; many of them have used these tips and ideas in their own business ventures.

We have used some of the best resources available, including the SCORE (Service Corps of Retired Executives) web site, *Start Your Own Business, Entrepreneur Magazine's Ultimate Start-Up Directory*, the *Start Your Own* series, *Get Smart! 365 Tips to Boost Your*

Entrepreneurial IQ, Accounting and Finance for Small Business Made Easy, Entrepreneur Magazine, and *Entrepreneur.com*.

Our goal is to help you make better decisions for your business, target your customers, and communicate your message more effectively. If you understand yourself, your business, and your customers, you are more likely to make better business decisions that result in more sales.

On a larger scale, *Entrepreneur's Great Big Book of Business Lists* is an anything-about-everything resource guide for entrepreneurs who want to start ventures or expand their businesses. Entrepreneurs are constantly thinking about the current situation in their business life cycle, and this book is a dynamic tool for questions and advice for each phase.

This guide also helps with the many challenges you may be facing, such as running out of money, needing a more consistent customer base, needing to find members for a larger management team or organizational structure, or even needing to buy an appropriate gift for a client. Perhaps your business is doing well and you are looking for ways to grow it and handle the volume and pressure of expanding. *Entrepreneur's Great Big Book of Business Lists* covers a range of business areas and answers the common questions that entrepreneurs ask or should be asking.

In this book you will find lists like:

- Small Business Administration District Offices
- Top Ten Finance Terms You Should Know
- Best Banks for Entrepreneurs by State
- The Great Big List of Venture Capital Firms
- Ten Qualities of Top Salespeople
- Smart Ways to Cut Time Spent on Administrative Duties
- Tips on Consumer Protection Laws
- Tips on Assessing Your Risk Exposure
- Advice on How to Use Civic Marketing
- Tips on How to Manage Your Inventory System

Treat this resource book as a "choose your own adventure" business tool. Use it in whatever ways it works best for your situation. Feel free to skip pages, chapters, or entire sections. Go straight to the parts that are the most appropriate for you.

We have structured this book in two parts. The first part is intended for all businesses, divided into sections that are organized by business category or growth stage. The second part is for specific industries and interests.

Entrepreneur's Great Big Book of Lists provides so many resources that you are sure to save time, money, and stress and be able to focus on running your business. Enjoy— and profit!

—Courtney Thurman and Ashlee Gardner, 2005

Acknowledgments

We would like to thank Entrepreneur Press's Editorial Director, Jere Calmes, for giving us this opportunity and believing in us, and Assistant Acquisitions Editors Jen Dorsey and Karen Thomas, for always taking our calls when we hit the proverbial wall. Thanks also to the President and COO of Entrepreneur Media, Inc., Neil Perlman, and Director of Marketing, Leanne Harvey, for supporting our efforts.

Special thanks to Entrepreneur Media, Inc.'s CEO, Peter Shea, on behalf of The USC Entrepreneur Club for delivering one of the most memorable presentations of a true entrepreneur.

Special thanks also to Bob Magnan of CWL Publishing Enterprises for checking the accuracy of all the entries, web sites, and updating material to make this book as current as possible. He has made a very positive contribution to the quality of the final product. Also thanks to John Woods and Nancy Woods also of CWL for their help in producing the final product.

We also thank our contributing writers for their long hours and dedication:

Ty Martin

Joseph Donelson

Camille Gardner

Nick Kurlas

Tyler Kurlas

Candice Watkins

Michael La Franchi

We would also like to give special thanks to Paul Hogan and Benjamin Kennedy for their involvement. We each thank our family and friends: Paula, Eva, Camille, and Kim Gardner, Eric, Pennie, and Mark Thurman, and especially Robert Kollar and Joseph Donelson. We couldn't have done this without your faith, encouragement, and patience.

The Great Big Book of Business Lists CD

You will find a CD that accompanies this book. On this CD you will find, by section number all the lists in this book plus an additional seven sections that include the following material:

Section 18. Owning and Operating a Health and Wellness Facility

Chapter 1. Getting Started in the Health and Wellness Industry
Chapter 2. Health and Wellness Ideas
Chapter 3. Emerging Trends—What's Hot in Health and Wellness
Chapter 4. The Personal Training Business
Chapter 5. Certifications, Licenses, Permits, and Insurances
Chapter 6. Magazines, Books, and Articles
Chapter 7. More Lists to Check Before Starting Your Business

Section 19. Owning and Operating a Retail Business

Chapter 1. Is Retail for Me?
Chapter 2. Retail Finances and Financial Facts
Chapter 3. The Importance of Retail Locations
Chapter 4. Layout Considerations for Successful Stores
Chapter 5. Pricing Your Products Just Right
Chapter 6. Retail Competition—More than Price Wars
Chapter 7. The Guts of Retail—Inventory Management
Chapter 8. Helpful Retail Resources

Section 20. Owning and Operating a Real Estate Business

Chapter 1. Terms and Fundamentals
Chapter 2. Investing Advice
Chapter 3. Successful Buying and Selling
Chapter 4. Commercial Real Estate
Chapter 5. Inspections and Appraisals
Chapter 6. Residential Real Estate
Chapter 7. Escrow Advice
Chapter 8. Property Management Tips
Chapter 9. Short Sales Advice
Chapter 10. Foreclosure Tips
Chapter 11. Advice for Successful Transactions
Chapter 12. Career Advice

Section 1

Covering the Basics

Chapter 1

Being an Entrepreneur

Seven Habits of Highly Successful Entrepreneurs

Entrepreneurs tend to be involved in every aspect of their business, being bookkeeper, marketer, human resources manager, mediator, customer liaison officer, and cleaner. The smaller the business, the harder it is for the owners to delegate these functions because they dislike spending any money. They fail to realize that if they invest their dollars wisely in accessing the right type of goods and services to grow their business and be more effective, they will see positive changes occur over time. It takes time to build a good "business mindset."

People who grow their businesses successfully do the following:

1. **Highly successful small business owners are great role models.**
   They practice what they preach. They lead from the front.

2. **Highly successful small business owners invest time and money in their team and themselves.**
   They develop their people and themselves through personal and professional development. They utilize outside expertise, as the successful small business owners recognize they do not have all the answers.

3. **Highly successful small business owners are organized.**
   They know how to manage their time and have systems in place, which enables them and their team to work effectively.

4. **Highly successful small business owners are fit and healthy.**
   They understand that having a healthy mind and body improves their productivity and general well-being. They realize that keeping themselves fit and healthy enables them to cope with the pressures of running a business.

5. **Highly successful small business owners have a life.**
   They make time for their personal life a priority because they know it makes them happier and more successful.

6. **Highly successful small business owners look after their clients.**
   They know that clients are the life-blood of their business. Without clients there would be no business. They ensure they continually look after them.

7. **Highly successful small business owners are decisive.**
   They are not afraid to make decisions and take action. They have to if they want to their business to thrive.

Source: Lorraine Pirihi, "7 Habits of Highly Successful Small Business Owners," *The Organised Times*, Vol. 7.12, June 2003, www.office-organiser.com.au/Newsletters/newsletter132.html.

Tips to Help You Do It Instead of Dreaming About It

Here are some smart tips from Valerie Young, author of the *Changing Course* newsletter, on the best way to stop dreaming—and start doing.

Get the point of life. It's short; if you don't do it now, when will you?

Get passionate. Most successful businesses are built on the entrepreneur's passion.

Get a grip on "it." Young says "it" is what scares you—and "it" is different for everyone. Understand that fear comes with the territory.

Get real. Know that it isn't going to be easy.

Get informed. Talk to people, join associations, and read everything relevant.

Get ready. Set a target date, and create a plan to get you there.

Get support. If you have a network, call on them. If you don't, create one.

Get going. Do at least one thing a day to advance your plan.

Source: Rieva Lesonsky, *365 Tips to Boost Your Entrepreneurial IQ.*

Are You a Guerrilla Entrepreneur?

Here, the original guerrilla marketer, **Jay Conrad Levinson**, shares the traits of a great guerrilla.

- Guerrilla entrepreneurs, says Levinson, know the journey is the goal, but they know they are in charge of their businesses, not the other way around.

- Balance is important to guerrillas. They build some free time into their work schedules and respect those leisure hours as much as their work ones.

- Guerrilla entrepreneurs live in the present while remaining well aware of the past and enticed by the future.

- Do you have a plan? Smart guerrillas do—they know who they are, where they're going, and how they're going to get there. And they re-evaluate their plans regularly.

- Finally, Levinson says, guerrilla entrepreneurs are positive and upbeat. Sure, life may be unfair and problems always arise, but it helps to keep your perspective and sense of humor.

Source: Rieva Lesonsky, *365 Tips to Boost Your Entrepreneurial IQ.*

Three Most Common Money Personality Types

What's your money personality? The three most common money personalities are achievers, money masters, and entrepreneurs. This is according to the book, *Your Money Personality* (Kathleen Gurney).

1. **Do you seek challenges and consider money a scorecard?**
   Entrepreneurial types are more interested in making the sale than in managing their money.

2. **If the above doesn't sound like you, maybe you're an achiever.**
   These people are more conservative, know how their money works for them, and trust no one else to take care of their finances.

3. **Or are you a money master?**
   "Value" is the key word here; money masters are bargain hunters, who always demand a cheaper price.

You can change the negative parts of your money personality, but you have to set goals and be honest with yourself.

Source: Rieva Lesonsky, *365 Tips to Boost Your Entrepreneurial IQ.*

Five Tips for Deciding if It's the Right Time to Start Your Business

1. **When real customers are willing to pay real money for your product or service, you have a real business.**
   Start with the fundamentals: Who are you and why should anyone care? If you're not passionate about what you're doing, then why should anyone else be?

   Every great business is built on a great story, so start telling yours to potential customers and see if they buy what you're selling. Testing should always be done with real customers, not with family and friends (who may only tell you what they think you want to hear so they don't hurt your feelings).

2. **Create evangelists for your idea, and make sure they know how, where and why to buy from you.**
   If you've already built a fan base for your new business, you're one step closer to your grand opening. This set of people who support your idea will help you find your early customers.

   What are you offering and how does that stack up to the competition? Start creating a sense of urgency to build demand for your product or service. What can you do to be the "have to have" instead of the "nice to have" in the category you're entering?

3. **If the days (and nights) fly by and you have more ideas than time to address them all, you're moving in the right direction.**
   If you can't shut off the stream of ideas you've got to make your business a success, it's probably time to start acting on them.

4. **When you believe in your core that a bad day on your own is better than a good day at your desk job, you've got nothing to lose.**
   The important thing is to keep moving forward and learn from every experience. You can't wait for the perfect time to launch; you just have to course correct as you get more feedback along the way. Being an entrepreneur means making decisions without perfect information. Get used to it—or find another career path.

5. **If you've made it this far, you owe it to yourself to give it a shot.**
   If I haven't scared you off yet, you may be onto something. How do you get those early customers you can later reference? Ask for the order! People value things they pay for, so always charge a fee. Remember that your enthusiasm and curiosity will inspire others. Never give up on what you believe in.

Source: Paige Arnof-Fenn, "Is It the Right Time to Launch Your Business?," www.entrepreneur. com/article/0,4621,320154,00.html.

The Three-Step Success Plan

What's the path to fame and fortune? Learn from the success of others. Here's how to start your success plan. According to Michael Jefferys, author of *Secrets of the Motivational Superstars*, you must follow three steps:

- First up, you need a written action plan detailing how you intend to achieve your goals. Remember: goals not written down are merely wishes. Your written goals are the road map to your success.

- Never give up! Sure it sounds simple, but a lot of people throw in the towel before they should. To succeed, you must be willing to do whatever it takes.

- And finally, don't delay. You never know how much time you actually have to achieve your dreams, so you better get to it now!

Source: Rieva Lesonsky, *365 Tips to Boost Your Entrepreneurial IQ*.

Entrepreneur Personality Checklist and Essential Qualities

- Are you ready to put your own house, other assets, and collateral on the line?
- Are you a persuasive salesperson?
- Do you possess confidence in yourself as well as in your business concept?
- Are you able and willing to raise a significant amount of money from investors?
- Have you evaluated your strengths and weaknesses?
- Take an EQ test and measure your ability to work with people.

Source: Rieva Lesonsky, *Start Your Own Business.*

There are three essential qualities entrepreneurs all share:

1. **A healthy cynicism:** Successful business owners are not deluded by dreams, fantasies, or illusions about how the world "oughta be."

   They look closely at the world through their five senses, see what is really going on out there, and conform their behavior to the real world. They accept whatever they see at face value, without value judgments, and give people what they want—not what the business owners think they want.

2. **Insecurity:** In business, a little anxiety is a good thing. It helps you spot threats before they become serious and spot opportunities before your competitors do.

   It keeps you awake (often at night) and focused, always asking new questions, always doubting the conventional wisdom. When business owners get too comfortable, decide they finally know what they're doing and start running their businesses on cruise control, that's when failures start to happen.

3. **Chutzpah:** As defined in Leo Rosten's classic book *The Joys of Yiddish*, chutzpah is "gall, brazen nerve, effrontery, incredible guts; presumption plus arrogance such as no other word, and no other language, can do justice to."

Make no mistake. Successful business owners are tough, driven, determined, courageous, persistent, and fiercely aggressive in pursuing their goals.

Source: Cliff Ennico, "Do You Really Have What It Takes?," www.entrepreneur.com/article/0,4621,308119,00.html.

List of Emotional Intelligence Factors
That Complement Entrepreneurship

Emotional Intelligence is a set of acquired skills and competencies that predict positive outcomes at home with one's family, in school, and at work. People who possess these are healthier, less depressed, and more productive at work and have better relationships.

- **Self-Analysis**: Analyzes own emotions in different situations and states.
- **Analysis of Others**: Recognizes how others are feeling in different situations and states.
- **Self-Expression**: Expresses emotions and emotional needs appropriately for the situation.
- **Discrimination**: Recognizes feelings and emotions that point to dishonesty or manipulation.
- **Thinking**: Uses feelings and emotions to redirect or prioritize thinking.
- **Judgment**: Uses feelings and emotions to facilitate judgment and decision making.
- **Sensitivity**: Capitalizes on mood changes to appreciate multiple points of view.
- **Problem Solving**: Uses emotional states to facilitate problem solving and creativity.
- **Symptoms**: Can spot the clues and warning signs of common emotional states.
- **Outcomes**: Perceives the causes and consequences of positive and negative emotions.
- **Complexity**: Understands complex feelings, emotional blends, and contradictory states.
- **Transitions**: Understands transitions among different feelings and emotions.
- **Openness**: Open to pleasant and unpleasant feelings and emotions.
- **Monitoring**: Monitors feelings and emotions and reflects on implications and meaning.
- **Others**: Handles others' feelings and emotions sensitively and effectively.
- **Impression Management**: Pattern of responses consistent with socially desirable responding.
- **Reading People**: Identifies own and other people's feelings and emotions.
- **Using Emotions**: Uses feelings and emotions to facilitate thinking and problem solving.
- **Understanding Emotions**: Understands how emotions operate and affect behavior.
- **Managing Emotions**: Monitors feelings and emotions and knows how to control them.

Source: MySkillsProfile.com, "Rapid Personality + Eq Questionnaire," www.myskillsprofile.com/tests.php?test=23, and "EIQ16 Questionnaire," myskillsprofile.com/eiq16_sample_report.pdf, p. 8.

How to Use Your Subconscious Mind

The programming tool for unleashing the full powers of your subconscious mind is definition of purpose. The clearer your picture of what you want, the more activity you inspire inside your subconscious system. There are three main ways to put this to work, and they all involve writing:

■ **Continually develop your goals in writing.** Paul Meyer, founder of the Success Motivation Institute, says, "If you are not making the progress you'd like to make, it is probably because your goals are not clearly defined." There is power in continually sharpening the definition of your goals on paper. Clarity is power.

■ **Write out your business plan.** A written, detailed business plan combines goal setting, action planning, and problem solving. It makes ideas believable.

■ **Create and use daily checklists.** Have some organization in your day: see where you need to go and what you have done.

These three action steps have great practical value, but they also serve to communicate to your subconscious mind, in an organized manner, the seriousness of your objectives.

Source: Dan Kennedy, *No B.S. Business Success: The Ultimate No Holds Barred Kick Butt Take No Prisoners Tough & Spirited Guide* (Entrepreneur Press, 2004), pp. 188–189.

Advice for Defining Your Business Goals

1. Be specific in what you want for your business.
2. Be optimistic and phrase your goals in a positive manner.
3. Be realistic with your goals.
4. Look at the short term as well as the long term.
5. Consider how much income you want to make during your first year of operation.
6. Consider a balance of life, leisure, and work.
7. Look at which type of setting is most comfortable for you to work in.
8. Watch out for your ego and be honest with yourself and others.

Source: Rieva Lesonsky, *Start Your Own Business.*

Seven Effective Ways to Set Your Goals in Motion

1. **Stop seeking approval from people.**
   You don't need anyone's permission to fulfill your dream. Trust yourself and give yourself permission to succeed. Having support from people whose opinion you value is a wonderful thing but it should not be the criterion for whether you begin acting on fulfilling your goals or not.

   If you really desire to turn your idea into reality, constantly floating it around and seeking the approval of people will waste your time and kill your dream. What will happen to your idea if you don't get the approval of those whose permission you so desperately need? Nothing!

2. **Don't wait for perfection.**
   Waiting for a time when everything is perfect and in place will cause you to lose your enthusiasm and abandon your goal. Conditions may never be as perfect as you desire. You may never have all the money, time, or knowledge you desire to begin working on your goals.

   You must take risks, learn and improve as you go along, and then watch as everything begins to fall in place. If you have to wait for the perfect time to begin working on your goals ..., you will be waiting a long time!

3. **Create time for the goal.**
   Many people have dreams, ideas, or goals, which remain unfulfilled because they are too busy doing everything else but work on the goal! If you have a goal to achieve, you must be ready to invest your time and resources to ensure that it succeeds.

   Making excuses about lacking the time to work on goals that are important to you is a procrastination tactic, which will kill your dream before it has a chance to see the light of day. There is always time to work on what we love and consider important. Create that time and see your dreams begin to unfold!

4. **Decide once and for all!**
   The process of goal achievement, like most things in life begins with a decision. You decide what you want to achieve and then you plan how you intend to achieve it. If achieving your goal is important to you, your inability to make crucial decisions about what you should do, how you should do it, and when you should do it will waste your time and choke your dream. Make up your mind and stop second-guessing yourself. When your mind is made up ..., nothing can stop you from making progress with fulfilling your goals.

5. **Be bold and take the initiative.**
   Be bold! You are the one in charge of turning your dreams to reality. You need to be proactive and actively involved in the process of working on your goals to ensure you achieve them.

Just because you have shared your ideas with others does not necessarily mean that you are no longer responsible for turning them to reality. Don't sit around waiting for others to make suggestions and guide your idea to reality. Don't leave your dream entirely in the hands of others. Nobody cares about your dream like you do.

6. **Invest in your dream.**
No idea is self-funding. Don't be deceived into thinking that people will invest or finance your idea just because it is brilliant. If you are lucky, someone may invest in it, but if you are not, you will have to invest your time, energy, and finances towards activities that will fortify and fulfill your dream.

You may have to invest in the acquisition of knowledge or expertise that will help you achieve your goals. It would be a good idea to keep some money stashed away to finance your goal.

7. **Do one thing at a time.**
Commit yourself only to projects and activities that are connected to your main goal. Whatever you do should directly or indirectly add up to a move toward your main goal. Failure to do this will confuse, overwhelm, sidetrack, and drain your energy.

To get started on achieving your goals, you need to plan for it and make it a priority. If you keep crowding and cluttering your life with what does not matter, you many never, ever achieve your goals.

Remember that you can't do all things, but you can do one thing!

Source: Caroline Jalango, "7 Effective Ways to Set Your Goals in Motion," www.motivation-zone.com/13901.html.

Eight Success Secrets for Entrepreneurs

1. **Success Secret #1: Take 100 percent responsibility for your life.**
In a society where people blame everything from their parents to the government for their failure to get ahead in life, these men and women refused to buy into the mentality that says, "I could succeed if only it weren't for _____." Successful people don't buy into this victim thinking. Taking 100 percent responsibility for your life is one of the most empowering things you can do for yourself.

2. **Success Secret #2: Live your life "on purpose."**
The difference between living your life on purpose and not living it on purpose is like night and day. The latter consists of simply getting through the week with the fewest problems while expending just enough effort to get by. But, when you live your life on purpose, your main concern is doing the job right. You love what you do—and it shows. Your conviction is as evident as it is persuasive. And you will find that people want to do business with you because they sense your commitment to giving your all.

3. **Success Secret #3: Be willing to pay the price for your dreams.**
   Successful men and women find out what it's going to cost to make their dream come true; then they find a way to make it happen. Most important, they don't complain about the work it takes to achieve their dreams. You can get practically anything you want in life—if you are willing to pay the price.

4. **Success Secret #4: Stay focused.**
   Every day, we are bombarded with hundreds of tasks, messages, and people all competing for our time. This is why the ability to focus on your goal is so critical to achieving it. Focusing requires giving up some things in the present because you know the time invested will pay off big-time down the road. Spend as much of your day as you can focusing on achieving your goals and dreams. Focusing is like any habit; the more you do it, the easier it gets.

5. **Success Secret #5: Become an expert in your field.**
   If someone followed you around at your business all day with a video camera to make a how-to tape for people who want to do what you do, would it be a tape you'd be proud of … or embarrassed about? If the latter, make the decision today to work toward being the best in your field. How? By studying the experts. The quickest way to become successful is to find out what the best are doing then do what they do.

6. **Success Secret #6: Write out a plan for achieving your goals.**
   Taking the time to write out an action plan, or map, for how you're going to achieve your goals is one of the best ways to get there faster. Brian Tracy, one of America's most successful business sales trainers and speakers, points out, "Goals that are not in writing are not goals at all. They are merely wishes or fantasies."

7. **Success Secret #7: Never give up.**
   It may sound simple, even obvious, but when you're truly committed to achieving your goal, giving up isn't even an option. You must be willing to do whatever it takes to make it happen.

8. **Success Secret #8: Don't delay.**
   We must remember that we don't have forever. The clock is ticking, there are no time-outs, and sooner or later your number is going to be called. Top achievers know this, but rather than seeing it as something negative or depressing, they use it to spur them on to go after what they want as energetically and as passionately as possible.

Source: Michael Jeffreys, "Power Up," www.entrepreneur.com/Your_Business/YB_SegArticle/0,4621,226997,00.html.

Chapter 2

Entrepreneurial Associations and Memberships

Important General Small-Business Associations

American Management Association

AMA is a global not-for-profit, membership-based association that provides a full range of management development and educational services to individuals, companies, and government agencies worldwide, including 486 of the Fortune 500 companies. Each year, thousands of business professionals acquire the latest business know-how, valuable insights, and increased confidence at AMA seminars, conferences, current issues forums, and briefings, as well as through AMA books and publications, research, and print and online self-study courses.

1601 Broadway
New York, NY 10019
Phone: (212) 586-8100 or (800) 262-9699
Fax: (213) 925-7463
www.amanet.org

The CEO Clubs

The Chief Executive Officers Clubs are a nonprofit organization that creates a nurturing environment for CEOs dedicated to improving the quality and profitability of their enterprises through shared experience and personal growth. Our average club member has $20,000,000 in annual sales. The clubs meet eight times a year for a half-day luncheon program. The morning is spent in roundtables and a speaker usually concludes the program.

295 Greenwich Street, #514 Penthouse
New York, NY 10007
Phone: (212) 925-7911
Fax: (212) 925-7463
www.ceoclubs.org

The Edward Lowe Foundation

The Edward Lowe Foundation is an operating foundation, and we have an approach that is slightly different than the average not-for-profit. Instead of providing grants, we provide services. Instead of providing money directly, we give our time and our expertise. Specifically, we assist groups of second-stage business owners and the organizations that serve them. The purpose of our direct involvement with entrepreneurs is to help them network with their peers, as well as to provide them with ways to gain perspectives and new ideas about their companies. Our web sites and retreat programs complement peer interactions and help entrepreneurs to successfully take their businesses through the second stage.

58220 Decatur Road
P.O. Box 8
Cassopolis, MI 49031
Phone: (800) 232-LOWE
www.lowe.org

Office Business Center Association International

OBCAI is the nonprofit trade association for the Office Business Center Industry. With over 600 member locations worldwide, our member Office Business Centers provide an array of services to their clients. These include office space, phone answering, Internet access, video-conferencing, long distance, calling cards, mobile messaging, desktop publishing, law libraries, computer networking, and more. These centers are located at the world's best business addresses and offer flexible office space.

200 E. Campus View Boulevard, #200
Columbus, OH 43235
Phone: (614) 985-3633
Fax: (614) 985-3601
www.execsuites.org

Independent Insurance Agents of America

The Independent Insurance Agents & Brokers of America (IIABA) is a national alliance of 300,000 business owners and their employees who offer all types of insurance and financial services products. Unlike company-employed agents, IIABA independent insurance agents and insurance brokers represent more than one insurance company, so they can offer clients a wider choice of auto, home, business, life, and health coverages as well as retirement and employee-benefit products. IIABA agents and brokers not only advise clients about insurance, they recommend loss-prevention ideas that can cut costs. If a loss occurs, the independent insurance agent or broker stands with the client until the claim is settled.

127 Payton Street
Alexandria, VA 22314
Phone: (800) 221-7917
Fax: (703) 683-7556
www.independentagent.com

The National Association for the Self-Employed

The National Association for the Self-Employed (NASE) is the nation's leading resource for the self-employed and micro-businesses (up to ten employees), providing a broad range of benefits and support to help the smallest businesses succeed. They secure focused tools and resources that help the self-employed manage and compete more effectively. They represent the interests of the self-employed among legislators in Washington D.C. on key issues that affect their businesses and that give these businesses more equal footing with larger corporations. Lastly, they provide access to benefits that promote the health and financial security of micro-business owners.

P.O. Box 612067, DFW Airport
Dallas, TX 75261-2067
Phone: (800) 232-6273
Fax: (800) 551-4446
www.nase.org

National Association of Professional Employee Organizations

NAPEO, the National Association of Professional Employer Organizations, is the largest trade association, representing more than 325 professional employer organizations nation-wide. NAPEO's members represent more than 70 percent of the industry's revenues and range in size from start-up PEOs to large, publicly held companies with years of success in the industry. NAPEO also embraces a commitment to furthering and protecting the interests of its PEO members at all levels of government through proactive lobbying efforts and timely communications on regulatory and legislative issues of interest.

901 N. Pitt Street, #150
Alexandria, VA 22314
Phone: (703) 836-0466
Fax: (703) 836-0976
www.napeo.org

Small Business Service Bureau

SBSB members are self-employed, in partnerships, family businesses, and home-based businesses and owners involved in every kind of business or trade. Because of the small size of their businesses, SBSB members share a need for products and services custom-designed for them at costs they can afford. SBSB meets this need with an outstanding variety of group programs of their businesses and discounts for members only.

544 Main Street
Worcester, MA 01615-0014
Phone: (800) 343-0939
www.sbsb.com

Recommended Entrepreneur Associations

Young Entrepreneurs Association (YEA)

The Young Entrepreneurs Association is a volunteer-driven non-profit organization whose mandate is to support young people in business. Aimed at business owners 35 and under, YEA provides members an opportunity to learn from each other's experiences and take advantage of peer mentorship as they grow their businesses.

1027 Pandora Avenue
Victoria, BC, Canada V8V 3P6
Phone: (888) 639-3222
www.yea.ca

Entrepreneurs' Organizations (EO)

Entrepreneurs' Organization (EO)—for entrepreneurs only—is a membership organization designed to help business owners from around the world on their path to greater business and personal fulfillment. EO is a global community that enriches members' lives through dynamic peer-to-peer learning and once-in-a-lifetime experiences. We are the catalyst that enables entrepreneurs to learn from each other, leading to greater business success and an enriched personal life.

500 Montgomery Street, Suite 500
Alexandria, VA 22314
Phone: (703) 519-6700
www.eonetwork.org

Los Angeles Venture Association

Los Angeles Venture Association provides forums where entrepreneurs and executives of middle-market companies actively meet and learn from fellow executives, investors, bankers, financial advisors, and other providers of professional services.

13428 Maxella Avenue, #622
Marina Del Rey, CA 90292
Phone: (310) 450-9544
www.lava.org

Association of Small Business Development Centers

The mission of the Association of Small Business Development Centers is to represent the collective interest of our members by promoting, informing, supporting,, and continuously improving the SBDC network, which delivers nationwide educational assistance to strengthen small/medium business management, thereby contributing to the growth of local, state, and national economies.

8990 Burke Lake Road
Burke, VA 22015
Phone: (703) 764-9850
www.asbdc-us.org

Kauffman Center for Entrepreneurial Leadership

EntreWorld is designed to increase your productivity by getting you essential information as quickly and easily as possible. Recognized by *USA Today, Forbes, Inc.,* and *Fast Company* as a premier online resource for small business owners, the EntreWorld search engine delivers the best and most useful information, guidance, and contacts for you, the entrepreneur.

4801 Rockhill Road
Kansas City, MO 64110
Phone: (816) 932-1000
www.entreworld.org

Source: Compiled by authors.

Top Ways to Give Back to Entrepreneurship

Time … talent … treasure. Of these, the two most powerful gifts entrepreneurs can share are time and talent. Money is important but knowledge even more so. There are many different ways you can share your hard-earned knowledge and expertise with entrepreneurs at every stage of development. The choice is up to you.

- **Mentoring.** Mentoring can take many forms and touch many audiences. From high school students to high-growth entrepreneurs, mentors can make a difference in the life of an individual and the success of his or her enterprise. Find out what it takes to help others advance along the path of entrepreneurship.

- **Serving on Boards.** Board service is a structured way of giving advice and counsel to start-up and growth-oriented entrepreneurs and the nonprofit organizations that serve them. You can serve on an informal advisory council or join a board of directors.

- **Evaluating and Incubating Innovation.** The cure for cancer, the next market sensation, or tomorrow's Bill Gates may be hiding within the ivy-covered walls of academia. You can help unleash the power of ideas by working with those on the brink of innovation at America's colleges, universities, and research laboratories.

- **Teaching.** Fifteen years ago, only a handful of colleges offered education in entrepreneurship. Today, entrepreneurship courses are taught in colleges and universities throughout the country and even in high schools. Entrepreneurship education is also booming at community support organizations, such as Small Business Development Centers. You can share your time and expertise through guest lectures, classroom instruction, and panel discussions at any of these venues.

- **Creating Content.** Put your wisdom to work by contributing stories and articles to one of many online or print publications for entrepreneurs. By sharing your story, you not only pass along your experience and ideas, you further the cause of American entrepreneurship.

To become involved, please visit givingback.kauffman.org.

Source: Ewing Marion Kauffman Foundation, "Giving Time & Expertise," givingback.kauffman.org.

Chapter 3

Entrepreneurial Resources

Small Business Administration District Offices

Local SBA Offices

Business hours are typically Monday through Friday from 8 a.m. to 4:30 p.m.

www.sba.gov

Alabama

Alabama District Office
801 Tom Martin Drive, Suite 201
Birmingham, AL 35211
Phone: (205) 290-7101
Fax: (205) 290-7404

Alaska

Anchorage District Office
510 L Street, Suite 310
Anchorage, AK 99501-1952
Phone: (907) 271-4022

Arizona

Arizona District Office
2828 North Central Ave, Suite 800
Phoenix, AZ 85004-1093
Phone: (602) 745-7200
Fax: (602) 745-7210

Arkansas

Arkansas District Office
2120 Riverfront Drive, Suite 250
Little Rock, AR 72202-1794
Phone: (501) 324-5871
Fax: (501) 324-5199

California

Fresno District Office
2719 North Air Fresno Drive, Suite 200
Fresno, CA 93727
Phone: (559) 487-5791
Fax: (559) 487-5636
Toll-free: (800) 359-1833 x 6

Los Angeles District Office
330 North Brand, Suite 1200
Glendale, CA 91203
Phone: (818) 552-3215

Sacramento District Office
650 Capitol Mall, Suite 7-500
Sacramento, CA 95814
Phone: (916) 930-3700
Fax: (916) 930-3737

San Francisco District Office
455 Market Street, Sixth Floor
San Francisco, CA 94105-2420
Phone: (415) 744-6820

Santa Ana District Office
200 W Santa Ana Boulevard, Suite 700
Santa Ana, CA 92701
Phone: (714) 550-7420
Fax: (714) 550-0191
TTYTDD: (714) 550-0655

Colorado

Colorado District Office
721 19th Street, Suite 426
Denver, CO 80202
Phone: (303) 844-2607

Connecticut

Connecticut District Office
330 Main Street, Second Floor
Hartford, CT 06106
Phone: (860) 240-4700

Delaware

Wilmington District Office
1007 N. Orange Street, Suite 1120
Wilmington, DE 19801-1232
Phone: (302) 573-6294

District of Columbia

Washington, DC District Office
1110 Vermont Avenue, NW, Ninth Floor
Washington, DC 20005
Phone: (202) 606-4000

Florida

North Florida District Office
7825 Baymeadows Way, Suite 100B
Jacksonville, FL 32256-7504
Phone: (904) 443-1900

South Florida District Office
100 S. Biscayne Boulevard, Seventh Floor
Miami, FL 33131
Phone: (305) 536-5521
Fax: (305) 536-5058

Georgia
Georgia District Office
233 Peachtree Street, NE, Suite 1900
Atlanta, GA 30303
Phone: (404) 331-0100

Guam
Guam Branch Office
400 Route 8, Suite 302
First Hawaiian Bank Building
Mongmong, GU 96927
Phone: (671) 472-7419
Fax: (671) 472-7365

Hawaii
Hawaii District Office
300 Ala Moana Boulevard
Room 2-235 Box 50207
Honolulu, HI 96850
Phone: (808) 541-2990
Fax: (808) 541-2976

Idaho
Boise District Office
380 East Parkcenter Boulevard, Suite 330
Boise, ID 83706
Phone: (208) 334-1696
Fax: (208) 334-9353

Illinois
Chicago District Office
500 W. Madison Street, Suite 1250
Chicago, IL 60661-2511
Phone: (312) 353-4528
Fax: (312) 886-5688

Springfield District Office
3330 Ginger Creek Road, Suite B
Springfield, IL 62711
Phone: (217) 793-5020
Fax: (217) 793-5025

Indiana
Indiana District Office
429 North Pennsylvania Street, Suite 100
Indianapolis, IN 46204-1873
Phone: (317) 226-7272

Iowa
Cedar Rapids Office
215 4th Avenue SE, Suite 200
Cedar Rapids, IA 52401
Phone: (319) 362-6405

Des Moines Office
210 Walnut Street, Room 749
Des Moines, IA 50309
Phone: (515) 284-4422

Kansas
Kansas District Office
271 W. 3rd Street, N, Suite 2500
Wichita, KS 67202
Phone: (316) 269-6616

Kentucky
Kentucky District Office
600 Dr. Martin Luther King Jr. Place
Louisville, KY 40202
Phone: (502) 582-5971

Louisiana
New Orleans District Office
365 Canal Street, Suite 2820
New Orleans, LA 70130
Phone: (504) 589-6685

Maine
Maine District Office
Edmund S. Muskie Federal Building
Room 512
68 Sewall Street
Augusta, ME 04330
Phone: (207) 622-8274

Maryland
Maryland District Office
City Crescent Building, Sixth Floor
10 South Howard Street
Baltimore, MD 21201
Phone: (410) 962-4392

Massachusetts

Massachusetts District Office
10 Causeway Street, Room 265
Boston, MA 02222
Phone: (617) 565-5590

Michigan

Michigan District Office
477 Michigan Avenue, Suite 515
McNamara Building
Detroit, MI 48226
Phone: (313) 226-6075

Minnesota

Minneapolis District Office
100 North Sixth Street
Suite 210-C, Butler Square
Minneapolis, MN 55403
Phone: (612) 370-2324
Fax: (612) 370-2303

Mississippi

Gulfport Branch Office
Hancock Bank Plaza
2510 14th Street, Suite 101
Gulfport, MS 39501
Phone: (228) 863-4449
Fax: (228) 864-0179

Mississippi District Office
AmSouth Bank Plaza
210 E. Capitol Street, Suite 900
Jackson, MS 39201
Phone: (601) 965-4378
Fax: (601) 965-5629, (601) 965-4294

Missouri

Kansas City District Office
323 W 8th Street, Suite 501
Kansas City, MO 64105
Phone: (816) 374-6701

Eastern Missouri District Office
200 North Broadway, Suite1500
St. Louis, MO 63102
Phone: (314) 539-6600
Fax: (314) 539-3785

Montana

Montana District Office
10 West 15th Street, Suite 1100
Helena, MT 59626
Phone: (406) 441-1081
Fax: (406) 441-1090

Nebraska

Nebraska District Office
11145 Mill Valley Road
Omaha, NE 68154
Phone: (402) 221-4691

Nevada

Nevada District Office
400 South 4th Street, Suite 250
Las Vegas, NV 89101
Phone: (702) 388-6611
Fax: (702) 388-6469

New Hampshire

New Hampshire District Office
JC Cleveland Federal Building
55 Pleasant Street, Suite 3101
Concord, NH 03301
Phone: (603) 225-1400
Fax: (603) 225-1409

New Jersey

New Jersey District Office
Two Gateway Center, Fifteenth Floor
Newark, NJ 07102
Phone: (973) 645-2434

New Mexico

Albuquerque District Office
625 Silver SW, Suite 320
Albuquerque, NM 87102
Phone: (505) 346-7909
Fax: (505) 346-6711

New York

Buffalo District Office
111 West Huron Street, Suite 1311
Buffalo, NY 14202
Phone: (716) 551-4301
Fax: (716) 551-4418

New York District Office
26 Federal Plaza, Suite 3100
New York, NY 10278
Phone: (212) 264-4354
Fax: (212) 264-4963

Syracuse District Office
401 S. Salina Street, Fifth Floor
Syracuse, NY 13202
Phone: (315) 471-9393
Fax: (315) 471-9288

North Dakota
North Dakota District Office
657 Second Avenue North, Room 219
Fargo, ND 58102
Phone: (701) 239-5131

Ohio
Cleveland District Office
1350 Euclid Avenue, Suite 211
Cleveland, OH 44115
Phone: (216) 522-4180
Fax: (216) 522-2038
TDD: (216) 522-8350

Columbus District Office
Two Nationwide Plaza, Suite 1400
Columbus, OH 43215
Phone: (614) 469-6860

Oklahoma
Oklahoma City District Office
Federal Building, 301 NW 6th Street
Oklahoma City, OK 73102
Phone: (405) 609-8000

Oregon
Portland District Office
601 SW Second Avenue, Suite 950
Portland, OR 97204-3154
Phone: (503) 326-2682
Fax: (503) 326-2808

Pennsylvania
Philadelphia District Office
Robert N.C. Nix Federal Building
900 Market Street, 5th Floor
Philadelphia, PA 19107
Phone: (215) 580-2SBA (2722)

Pittsburgh District Office
411 Seventh Avenue, Suite 1450
Pittsburgh, PA 15219
Phone: (412) 395-6560

Puerto Rico and Virgin Islands
Puerto Rico and US Virgin Islands Office
252 Ponce de Leon Avenue
Citibank Tower, Suite 201
Hato Rey, PR 00918
Phone: (787) 766-5572, (800) 669-8049
Fax: (787) 766-5309

Rhode Island
Rhode Island District Office
380 Westminster Street, Room 511
Providence, RI 02903
Phone: (401) 528-4561

South Carolina
South Carolina District Office
1835 Assembly Street, Room 1425
Columbia, SC 29201
Phone: (803) 765-5377
Fax: (803) 765-5962

South Dakota
South Dakota District Office
2329 N. Career Avenue, Suite 105
Sioux Falls, SD 57107
Phone: (605) 330-4243
Fax: (605) 330-4215
TTYTDD: (605) 331-3527

Tennessee
Tennessee District Office
50 Vantage Way, Suite 201
Nashville, TN 37228
Phone: (615) 736-5881
Fax: (615) 736-7232
TTYTDD: (615) 736-2499

Texas
Dallas District Office
4300 Amon Carter Boulevard, Suite 114
Fort Worth, TX 76155
Phone: (817) 684-5500
Fax: (817) 684-5516

Corpus Christi Branch Office
3649 Leopard Street, Suite 411
Corpus Christi, TX 78408
Phone: (361) 879-0017

El Paso District Office
10737 Gateway West
El Paso, TX 79935
Phone: (915) 633-7001
Fax: (915) 633-7005

Harlingen District Office
222 East Van Buren Street, Suite 500
Harlingen, TX 78550
Phone: (956) 427-8533

Houston District Office
8701 S. Gessner Drive, Suite 1200
Houston, TX 77074
Phone: (713) 773-6500
Fax: (713) 773-6550

Lubbock District Office
1205 Texas Avenue, Room 408
Lubbock, TX. 79401-2693
Phone: (806) 472-7462
Fax: (806) 472-7487

San Antonio District Office
17319 San Pedro, Suite 200
San Antonio, Texas 78232-1411
Phone: (210) 403-5900
Fax: (210) 403-5936
TDD: (210) 403-5933

Utah
Utah District Office
125 South State Street, Room 2231
Salt Lake City, UT 84138
Phone: (801) 524-3209

Virginia
Richmond District Office
400 North 8th Street

Federal Building, Suite 1150
Richmond, VA 23240
Phone: (804) 771-2400
Fax: (804) 771-2764

Washington
Seattle District Office
1200 Sixth Avenue, Suite 1700
Seattle, WA 98101-1128
Phone: (206) 553-7310

Spokane Branch Office
801 W. Riverside Avenue, Suite 200
Spokane, WA 92201
Phone: (509) 353-2811

West Virginia
West Virginia District Office
320 West Pike Street, Suite 330
Clarksburg, WV 26301
Phone: (304) 623-5631

Wisconsin
Wisconsin District Office
740 Regent Street, Suite 100
Madison, WI 53715
Phone: (608) 441-5263
Fax: (608) 441-5541

Milwaukee District Office
310 West Wisconsin Avenue, Room 400
Milwaukee, WI 53203
Phone: (414) 297-3941
Fax: (414) 297-1377

Wyoming
Wyoming District Office
100 East B Street
Federal Building
P.O. Box 44001
Casper, WY 82602-5013
Phone: (307) 261-6500

SBA's Small Business Development Centers

The Small Business Administration's Small Business Development Center Program—**www.sba.gov/sbdc**—was developed to assist small businesses through their counseling, training and technical assistance, and services. Some of these services include assistance with financial, marketing, production, organization, engineering, and feasibility analysis. Special SBDC programs include international trade assistance, technical assistance, procurement assistance, venture capital formation, and rural development as well as Small Business Innovation and Research (SBIR) grants from federal agencies.

Alabama
M. William Campbell Jr., State Director
2800 Milan Court, Suite 124
Birmingham, AL 35211-6908
Phone: (205) 943-6750
Fax: (205) 943-6752
E-mail: williamc@uab.edu
Web site: www.asbdc.org

Alaska
Jan Fredericks, State Director
430 West Seventh Avenue, Suite 110
Anchorage, AK 99501
Phone: (907) 274-7232
Fax: (907) 274-9524
E-mail: anjaf@uaa.sbdc.alaska.edu
Web site: www.aksbdc.org

American Samoa
Dr. Herbert Thweatt, Director
American Samoa Community College
P.O. Box 2609
Pago Pago, American Samoa 96799
Phone: 011-684-699-4830
Fax: 011-684-699-6132
E-mail: htalex@att.net

Arizona
Michael York, State Director
2411 West 14th Street, Suite 132
Tempe, AZ 85281
Phone: (480) 731-8720
Fax: (480) 731-8729
E-mail: mike.york@domail.maricopa.edu
Web site: www.dist.maricopa.edu.sbdc

Arkansas
Janet M. Roderick, State Director
2801 S. University Avenue
Little Rock, AR 72204-1099
Phone: (501) 324-9043
Fax: (501) 324-9049
E-mail: jmroderick@ualr.edu
Web site: asbdc.ualr.edu

California - Santa Ana
Ms. Vi Pham, Lead Center Director
Tri-County Lead SBDC
California State University, Fullerton
800 N. State College Boulevard, LH640
Fullerton, CA 92831-3599
Phone: (714) 278-2719
Fax: (714) 278-7858
E-mail: vpham@fullerton.edu
Web site: www.leadsbdc.org

California - San Diego
Debbie P. Trujillo, Regional Director
Southwestern Community College
900 Otey Lakes Road
Chula Vista, CA 91910
Phone: (619) 482-6388
Fax: (619) 482-6402
E-mail: dtrujillo@swc.cc.ca.us
Web site: www.sbditc.org

California - Fresno
Ms. Helen Sullivan, State Director
UC Merced Lead Center
550 East Shaw, Suite 105A
Fresno, CA 93710
Phone: (559) 241-7414

Fax: (559) 241-7422
E-mail: helen.sullivan@ucop.edu
Web site: sbdc.ucmerced.edu

California - Sacramento
Ms. Janice Rhodd, State Director
California State University
Chico, CA 95929-0765
Phone: (530) 898-5443
Fax: (530) 898-4734
E-mail: jrhodd@csuchico.edu
Web site: gsbdc.csuchico.edu

California - San Francisco
Mr. Blake Escudier, State Director
San Jose State University Foundation
210 North 4th Street, Fourth Floor
P. O. Box 720130
San Jose, CA 95129
Phone: (408) 655-9487
E-mail: escudier_b@cob.sjsu.edu
Web site: www.norcalsbdc.org

California - Los Angeles
Steve Jacoby, Director
California State University, Northridge
18111 Nordhoff Street
Northridge, CA 91330-8232
Phone: (818)-677-6397
Fax: (818) 677-6521
E-mail: sjacoby@csun.edu
Web site: www.csun.ed/csunsbdc

Colorado
Kelly Manning, State Director
1625 Broadway, Suite 1700
Denver, CO 80202
Phone: (303) 892-3794
Fax: (303) 892-3848
E-mail: Kelly.Manning@state.co.us
Web site: www.state.co.us/oed/sbdc

Connecticut
Dennis Gruell, State Director
2100 Hillside Road, Unit 1094
Storrs, CT 06269-1094
Phone: (860) 486-4135
Fax: (860) 486-1576

E-mail: dennis.gruell@uconn.edu
Web site: www.sbdc.uconn.edu

Delaware
Clinton Tymes, State Director
1 Innovation Way, Suite 301
Newark, DE 19711
Phone: (302) 831-1555
Fax: (302) 831-1423
E-mail: tymesc@be.udel.edu
Web site: www.delawaresbdc.org

District of Columbia
Henry Turner, State Director
2600 6th Street, NW, Room 128
Washington, DC 20059
Phone: (202) 806-1550
Fax: (202) 806-1777
E-mail: hturner@howard.edu
Web site: www.dcsbdc.com

Florida
Jerry Cartwright, State Director
401 E Chase Street, Suite 100
Pensacola, FL 32502
Phone: (850) 473-7800
Fax: (850) 473-7813
E-mail: jcartwri@uwf.edu
Web site: www.floridasbdc.com

Georgia
Henry Logan, State Director
University of Georgia
1180 East Broad Street
Athens, GA 30602-5412
Phone: (706) 542-6762
Fax: (706) 542-7935
E-mail: HLOGAN@sbdc.uga.edu
Web site: www.sbdc.uga.edu

Guam
Casey Jeszenka, State Director
Pacific Islands SBDC
P.O. Box 5061 - U.O.G. Station
Mangilao, GU 96923
Phone: (671) 735-2590
Fax: (671) 734-2002
E-mail: cjeszenka@hotmail.com

Web site: www.uog.edu/sbdc
(for Guam time, add 15 hours to EST)

Hawaii
Darryl Mleynek, State Director
200 West Kawili Street
Hilo, HI 96720
Phone: (808) 974-7515
Fax: (808) 974-7683
E-mail: darrylm@interpac.net
Web site: www.hawaii-sbdc.org

Idaho
James Hogge, State Director
1910 University Drive
Boise, ID 83725
Phone: (208) 426-1640
Fax: (208) 426-3877
E-mail: jhogge@boisestate.edu
Web site: www.idahosbdc.org

Illinois
Mark A. Petrilli, State Director
Dept. of Commerce and Economic Opportunity
620 E. Adams, S-4
Springfield, IL 62701
Phone: (217) 524-5700
Fax: (217) 524-0171
E-mail: mark_petrilli@illinoisbiz.biz
Web site: www.ilsbdc.biz

Indiana
Debbie Bishop Trocha
One North Capitol, Suite 900
Indianapolis, IN 46204
Phone: (317) 234-2086
Fax: (317) 232-8874
E-mail: dtrocha@isbdc.org
Web site: www.isbdc.org

Iowa
Lars Peterson, Interim State Director
137 Lynn Avenue
Ames, IA 50014-7126
Phone: (515) 292-6351
Fax: (515) 292-0020
E-mail: larsp@iastate.edu
Web site: www.iabusnet.org

Kansas
Wally Kearns, State Director
214 SW Sixth Street, Suite 301
Topeka, KS 66603
Phone: (785) 296-6514
Fax: (785) 291-3261
E-mail: ksbdc.wkearns@fhsu.edu
Web site: www.fhsu.eduk/sbdc

Kentucky
Becky Naugle, State Director
225 Gatton Business and Economics Building
Lexington, KY 40506-0034
Phone: (859) 257-7668
Fax: (859) 323-1907
E-mail: lrnaug0@pop.uky.edu
Web site: www.ksbdc.org

Louisiana
Mary Lynn Wilkerson, State Director
University of Louisiana at Monroe
College of Business Administration
700 University Avenue
Monroe, LA 71209-6435
Phone: (318) 342-5506
Fax: (318) 342-5510
E-mail: wilkerson@ulm.edu
Web site: www.lsbdc.org

Maine
John Massaua, State Director
96 Falmouth Street
P.O. Box 9300
Portland, ME 04104-9300
Phone: (207) 780-4420
Fax: (207) 780-4857
E-mail: jrmassaua@maine.edu
Web site: www.mainesbdc.org

Maryland
Renee Sprow, State Director
7100 Baltimore Avenue, Suite 401
College Park, MD 20740
Phone: (301) 403-8300
Fax: (301) 403-8303
E-mail: Rsprow@mdsbdc.umd.edu
Web site: www.mdsbdc.umd.edu

Massachusetts

Georgianna Parkin, State Director
227 Isenberg School of Management
University of Massachusetts
121 Presidents Drive
Amherst, MA 01001–9310
Phone: (413) 545-6301
Fax: (413) 545-1273
E-mail: gep@msbdc.umass.edu
Web site: msbdc.som.umass.edu

Michigan

Carol Lopucki, State Director
510 W. Fulton Street
Grand Rapids, MI 49504
Phone: (616) 331-7480
Fax: (616) 331-7389
E-mail: lopuckic@gvsu.edu
Web site: www.misbtdc.org

Minnesota

Michael Myhre, State Director
500 Metro Square
121 7th Place East
St. Paul, MN 55010-2146
Phone: (651) 297-5773
Fax: (651) 296-1290
E-mail: michael.myhre@state.mn.us
Web site: www.mnsbdc.com

Mississippi

Walter Gurley, Jr., State Director
B-19 Jeanette Phillips Drive
P.O. Box 1848
University, MS 38677
Phone: (662) 915-5001
Fax: (662) 915-5650
E-mail: wgurley@olemiss.edu
Web site: /www.olemiss.edu/depts/mssbdc

Missouri

Max Summers, State Director
1205 University Avenue, Suite 300
Columbia, MO 65211
Phone: (573) 882-0344
Fax: (573) 884-4297
E-mail: summersm@missouri.edu
Web site: www.mo-sbdc.org/index.shtml

Montana

Ann Desch, State Director
301 S. Park Avenue, Room 114
P.O. Box 200505
Helena, MT 59601
Phone: (406) 841-2747
Fax: (406) 841-2728
E-mail: adesch@state.mt.us
Web site:
commerce.state.mt.us/brd/BRD_SBDC.html

Nebraska

Robert Bernier, State Director
60th and Dodge Street, CBA Room 407
Omaha, NE 68182
Phone: (402) 554-2521
Fax: (402) 554-3473
E-mail: rbernier@unomaha.edu
Web site: nbdc.unomaha.edu

Nevada

Sam Males, State Director
Nazir Ansasri Building 032, Room 411
Reno College of Business
Reno, NV 89557-0100
Phone: (775) 784-1717
Fax: (775) 784-4337
E-mail: males@unr.edu
Web site: www.nsbdc.org

New Hampshire

Mary Collins, State Director
108 McConnell Hall
Durham, NH 03824-3593
Phone: (603) 862-2200
Fax: (603) 862-4876
E-mail: Mary.Collins@unh.edu
Web site: www.nhsbdc.org

New Jersey

Brenda Hopper, State Director
Rutgers-49 Bleeker Street
Newark, NJ 07102-1993
Phone: (973) 353-5950
Fax: (973) 353-1110
E-mail: bhopper@andromeda.rutgers.edu
Web site: www.njsbdc.com/home

Section 1

New Mexico
Roy Miller, State Director
6401 Richards Avenue
Santa Fe, NM 87505
Phone: (505) 428-1362
Fax: (505) 428-1469
E-mail: rmiller@santa-fe.cc.nm.us
Web site: www.nmsbdc.org

New York
Jim King, State Director
SUNY-State University
41 State Street
Albany, NY 12246
Phone: (518) 443-5398
Fax: (518) 443-5275
E-mail: j.king@nyssbdc.org
Web site: www.nyssbdc.org

North Carolina
Scott Daugherty, State Director
5 West Hargett Street, Suite 600
Raleigh, NC 27601
Phone: (919) 715-7272
Fax: (919) 715-7777
E-mail: sdaugherty@sbtdc.org
Web site: www.sbtdc.org

North Dakota
Christine Martin, State Director
UND-118 Gamble Hall
UND, Box 7308
Grand Forks, ND 58202
Phone: (701) 777-3700
Fax: (701) 777-3225
E-mail: christine.martin@und.nodak.edu
Web site: www.ndsbdc.org

Ohio
Holly Schick, State Director
77 South High Street
Columbus, OH 43215-6108
Phone: (614) 466-2711
Fax: (614) 466-0829
E-mail: hschick@odod.state.oh.us
Web site: www.ohiosbdc.org

Oklahoma
Grady Pennington, State Director
517 University
Box 2584, Station A
Durant, OK 74701
Phone: (580) 745-7577
Fax: (580) 745-7471
E-mail: gpennington@sosu.edu
Web site: www.osbdc.org

Oregon
William Carter, State Director
44 West Broadway, Suite 203
Eugene, OR 97401-3021
Phone: (541) 726-2250
Fax: (541) 345-6006
E-mail: carterb@lanecc.edu
Web site: www.bizcenter.org

Pennsylvania
Gregory Higgins, State Director
U-Penn, Vance Hall, 4th Floor
3733 Spruce Street
Philadelphia, PA 19104-6374
Phone: (215) 898-1219
Fax: (215) 573-2135
E-mail: ghiggins@wharton.upenn.edu
Web site: pasbdc.org

Puerto Rico
Carmen Marti, Executive Director
Union Plaza Building, Suite 701
416 Ponce de Leon Avenue
Hato Rey, PR 00918
Phone: (787) 763-6811
Fax: (787) 763-6875
E-mail: cmarti@prsbdc.org
Web site: www.prsbdc.org

Rhode Island
Robert Hamlin, State Director
Bryant College
1150 Douglas Pike
Smithfield, RI 02917
Phone: (401) 232-6111
Fax: (401) 232-6933
E-mail: rhamlin@bryant.edu
Web site: www.risbdc.org

South Carolina
John Lenti, State Director
USC-Dala Moore School of Business
Hipp Building
Columbia, SC 29208
Phone: (803) 777-4907
Fax: (803) 777-4403
E-mail: lenti@darla.badm.sc.edu
Web site: scsbdc.moore.sc.edu

South Dakota
John S. Hemmingstad, State Director
414 East Clark Street
Vermillion, SD 57069
Phone: (605) 677-5287
Fax: (605) 677-5427
E-mail: jshemmin@usd.edu
Web site: www.sdsbdc.org

Tennessee
Greg Sedrick, State Director
615 Memorial Boulevard, Third Floor
Murfreesboro, TN 37132
Phone: (615) 849-9999
Fax: (615) 217-8548
E-mail: gsedrick@mail.tsbdc.org
Web site: www.tsbdc.org

Texas - Houston
Mike Young, State Director
2302 Fannin, Suite 200
Houston, TX 77002
Phone: (713) 752-8444
Fax: (713) 756-1500
E-mail: fyoung@uh.edu
Web site: sbdcnetwork.uh.edu

Texas - North
Liz Klimback, State Director
Bill J. Priest Institute for Economic Development
1402 Corinth Street
Dallas, TX 75215
Phone: (214) 860-5831
Fax: (214) 860-5813
E-mail:emk9402@dcccd.edu
Web site: www.ntsbdc.org

Texas - North-West
Craig Bean, State Director
2579 South Loop 289, Suite 114
Lubbock, TX 79423
Phone: (806) 745-3973
Fax: (806) 745-6207
E-mail: c.bean@nwtsbdc.org
Web site: www.nwtsbdc.org

Texas - South-West
Robert McKinley, State Director
145 Duncan Drive, Suite 200
San Antonio, TX 78226-1816
Phone: (210) 458-2450
Fax: (210) 458-2464
E-mail: rmckinley@utsa.edu
Web site: www.iedtexas.org

Utah
Greg Panichello, State Director
9750 S. 300 E. MCPC 201
Sandy, UT 84070
Phone: (801) 957-3483
Fax: (801) 957-3488
E-mail: Greg.Panichello@slcc.edu
Web site: saltlakesbdc.com

Vermont
Donald Kelpinski, State Director
Vermont Technical College Main Street
Randolph Center, VT 05061-0188
Phone: (802) 728-9101
Fax: (802) 728-3026
E-mail: Dkelpins@vtc.vsc.edu
Web site: www.vtsbdc.org

Virgin Islands
Warren Bush, State Director
8000 Nisky Center, Suite 202
Charlotte Amalie, VI 00802-5804
Phone: (340) 776-3206
Fax: (340) 775-3756
E-mail: wbush@webmail.uvi.edu
Web site: rps.uvi.edu/SBDC

Virginia
Ms. Jody Keenan, Director
Small Business Development Center
George Mason University
4031 University Drive, Suite 200
Fairfax, VA 22030-3409
Phone: (703) 277-7727
Fax: (703) 277-7730
E-mail: jkeenan@gmu.edu
Web site: www.virginiasbdc.org

Washington
Dr. Carolyn Clark, State Director
534 E. Trent, Suite 201
P.O. Box 1495
Spokane, WA 99210-1495
Phone: (509) 358-7765
Fax: (509) 358-7764
E-mail: clrk@wsu.edu
Web site: www.wsbdc.org

West Virginia
Conley Salyor, State Director
1900 Kanawha Boulevard Building, Suite 600

Charleston, WV 25301
Phone: (304) 558-2960
Fax: (304) 558-0127
E-mail: csalyer@wvsbdc.org
Web site: www.wvsbdc.org

Wisconsin
Erica Kauten, State Director
432 North Lake Street, Room 423
Madison, WI 53706
Phone: (608) 63-7794
Fax: (608) 263-7830
E-mail: erica.kauten@uwex.edu
Web site: www.wisconsinsbdc.org

Wyoming
Diane Wolverton, State Director
University of Wyoming, Room 414
Laramie, WY 82071-3922
Phone: (307) 766-3505
Fax: (307) 766-3406
E-mail: DDW@uwyo.edu
Web site: www.uwyo.edu/sbdc

Recommended Credit Services

Dun & Bradstreet
Provides credit-reporting services
(800) 234-3867
www.dnb.com

Equifax
Provides credit-reporting services
(800) 685-1111
www.equifax.com

Experian
Provides credit-reporting services
(800) 682-7654
www.experian.com

First Data Merchant Services Corp.
Provides credit-processing services
6200 South Quebec Street

Greenwood Village, CO 90111
(800) 735-3362, (303) 488-8000
www.firstdata.com

TeleCheck
Provides check-guarantee services
5251 Westheimer
Houston, TX 77056
(800) TELE-CHECK (835-3243)
www.telecheck.com

TransUnion
Provides credit-reporting services
(800) 916-8800
www.transunion.com

National and International Chambers of Commerce

This is a great resource to get your business running and be informed on community news, business trends, and services. Membership entitles you to many benefits and advice on everything from customs to the business climate.

Chamber of Commerce Association
Empire State Building
250 Fifth Avenue, 33rd Floor
New York, NY 10118
Phone: (212) 244-0003
Fax: (212) 244-0240
www.chamber.com

State Chambers of Commerce

Alabama
Business Council of Alabama
2 N. Jackson Street
P.O. Box 76
Montgomery, AL 36101-0076
Phone: (800) 665-9647, (334) 834-6000
Fax: (800) 221-8185, (334) 262-7371
www.bcatoday.org

Alaska
Alaska State Chamber of Commerce
217 Second Street, #201
Juneau, AK 99801-1298
Phone: (907) 586-2323
Fax: (907) 463-5515
www.alaskachamber.com

Arizona
Arizona Chamber of Commerce
1221 E. Osborn Road, #100
Phoenix, AZ 85014-5500
Phone: (602) 248-9172
Fax: (602) 265-1262
www.azchamber.com

Arkansas
Arkansas State Chamber of Commerce
410 S. Cross Street
P.O. Box 3645
Little Rock, AR 72203-3645

Phone: (501) 374-9225
Fax: (501) 372-2722
statechamber-aia.dina.org/default.html

California
California Chamber of Commerce
1201 K Street, 12th Floor
Sacramento, CA 95814-3918
Phone: (916) 444-6670
Fax: (916) 444-6685
www.calchamber.com

Colorado
Colorado Association of Commerce and
Industry
1776 Lincoln Street, #1200
Denver, CO 80203-1029
Phone: (303) 831-7411
Fax: (303) 860-1439
www.businesscolorado.com

Connecticut
Connecticut Business and Industry Association
370 Asylum Street
Hartford, CT 06103-2022
Phone: (860) 244-1900
Fax: (860) 278-8562
www.cbia.com

Delaware
Delaware State Chamber of Commerce
1201 N. Orange Street, #201
P.O. Box 671
Wilmington, DE 19899-0671
Phone: (302) 654-7221
Fax: (302) 654-0691
www.dscc.com

Florida
Florida Chamber of Commerce
136 S. Bronough Street
P.O. Box 11309
Tallahassee, FL 32302-3309
Phone: (800) 940-4879
Fax: (850) 425-1260
www.flchamber.com

Georgia
Georgia Chamber of Commerce
233 Peachtree Street, NE, #200
Atlanta, GA 30303-1500
Phone: (404) 223-2264
Fax: (404) 223-2290
www.gachamber.com

Hawaii
The Chamber of Commerce of Hawaii
1132 Bishop Street, #200
Honolulu, HI 96813-2830
Phone: (808) 545-4300
Fax: (808) 545-4309
www.cochawaii.com

Idaho
Idaho Association of Commerce and Industry
P.O. Box 389
Boise, ID 83701-0389
Phone: (208) 343-1849
Fax: (208) 338-5623
www.iaci.org

Illinois
The Illinois State of Chamber of Commerce
311 S. Wacker Drive, #1500
Chicago, IL 60606-6619
Phone: (312) 983-7100, (800) 322-4722 (within Illinois)
Fax: (312) 983-7101
www.ilchamber.org

Indiana
Indiana Chamber of Commerce
115 W. Washington Street, #850 South
Indianapolis, IN 46204-3407
Phone: (317) 264-3110
Fax: (317) 264-6855
www.indianachamber.com

Iowa
Iowa has no state chamber, but local chambers are listed here:
www.2chambers.comiowa1.htm.

Kansas
Kansas Chamber of Commerce and Industry
835 S.W. Topeka Boulevard
Topeka, KS 66612-1680
Phone: (785) 357-6321
Fax: (785) 357-4732
www.kansaschamber.org

Kentucky
Kentucky Chamber of Commerce
464 Chenault Road
P.O. Box 817
Frankfort, KY 40602-0817
Phone: (502) 695-4700
Fax: (502) 695-6824
www.kychamber.com

Louisiana
Louisiana Association of Business and Industry
3113 Valley Creek Drive
P.O. Box 80258
Baton Rouge, LA 70898-0258
Phone: (225) 928-5388
Fax: (225) 929-6054
www.labi.org

Maine
Maine Chamber and Business Alliance
7 Community Drive
Augusta, ME 04330-9412
Phone: (207) 623-4568
Fax: (207) 622-7723
www.mainechamber.org

Maryland
Maryland Chamber of Commerce
60 West Street, #100
Annapolis, MD 21401-2479
Phone: (410) 269-0642 (toll-free Baltimore)
Phone: (301) 261-2858 (toll-free Washington)
Fax: (410) 269-5247
www.mdchamber.org

Massachusetts
Massachusetts has no state chamber, but local chambers are listed here:
www.2chambers.commassachu2.htm.

Michigan
Michigan Chamber of Commerce
600 S. Walnut Street
Lansing, MI 48933-2200
Phone: (517) 371-2100
Fax: (517) 371-7224
www.michamber.com

Minnesota
Minnesota Chamber of Commerce
30 East 7th Street, #1700
St. Paul, MN 55101-4901
Phone: (800) 821-2230, (651) 292-4650
Fax: (651) 292-4656
www.mnchamber.com

Mississippi
Mississippi Economic Council
666 North Street
P.O. Box 23276
Jackson, MS 39225-3276
Phone: (601) 969-0022
Fax: (601) 353-0247
www.msmec.com

Missouri
Missouri Chamber of Commerce
P.O. Box 149
Jefferson City, MO 65102-0149
Phone: (573) 634-3511
Fax: (573) 634-8855
www.mochamber.org

Montana
Montana Chamber of Commerce
2030 11th Avenue
P.O. Box 1730
Helena, MT 59624-1730
Phone: (406) 442-2405
Fax: (406) 442-2409
www.montanachamber.com

Nebraska
Nebraska Chamber of Commerce and Industry
1320 Lincoln Mall
P.O. Box 95128
Lincoln, NE 68509-5128
Phone: (402) 474-4422

Fax: (402) 474-5681
www.nechamber.com

Nevada
Nevada Chamber of Commerce Association
c/o Greater Reno-Sparks Chamber of Commerce
P.O. Box 3499
Reno, NV 89505-3499
Phone: (702) 686-3030
Fax: (702) 686-3038
207.190.150.43/jsp/rsc/index.jsp

New Hampshire
Business and Industry Association of New Hampshire
122 N. Main Street
Concord, NH 03301-4918
Phone: (800) 540-5388 (in-state toll-free), (603) 224-5388
Fax: (603) 224-2872
www.nhbia.org

New Jersey
New Jersey State Chamber of Commerce
216 W. State Street
Trenton, NJ 08608-1002
Phone: (609) 989-7888
Fax: (609) 989-9696
www.njchamber.com

New Mexico
Association of Commerce and Industry of New Mexico
P.O. Box 9706
Albuquerque, NM 87119-9706
Phone: (505) 842-0644
Fax: (505) 842-0734
www.aci.nm.org

New York
Business Council of New York State Inc.
152 Washington Avenue
Albany, NY 12210-2203
Phone: (518) 465-7511
Fax: (518) 465-4389
www.bcnys.org

North Carolina
North Carolina Citizens for Business and
Industry
225 Hillsborough Street
P.O. Box 2508
Raleigh, NC 27602-2508
Phone: (919) 836-1400
Fax: (919) 836-1425
www.nccbi.org

North Dakota
Greater North Dakota Association State
Chamber of Commerce
2000 Schafer Street
P.O. Box 2639
Bismarck, ND 58502-2639
Phone: (800) 382-1405, (701) 222-0929
Fax: (701) 222-1611
www.gnda.com

Ohio
Ohio Chamber of Commerce
230 E. Town Street
P.O. Box 15159
Columbus, OH 43215-0159
Phone: (614) 228-4201
Fax: (614) 228-6403
www.ohiochamber.com

Oklahoma
The State Chamber Oklahoma's Association of
Business and Industry
330 NE 10th Street
Oklahoma City, OK 73104-3200
Phone: (405) 235-3669
Fax: (405) 235-3670
www.okstatechamber.com

Oregon
Associated Oregon Industries
1149 Court Street, N.E.
Salem, OR 97301-4030
Phone: (503) 588-0050
Fax: (503) 588-0052
www.aoi.org

Pennsylvania
Pennsylvania Chamber of Business and
Industry
One Commerce Square
417 Walnut Street
Harrisburg, PA 17101-1902
Phone: (717) 255-3252
Fax: (717) 255-3298
www.pachamber.org

Rhode Island
Rhode Island has no state chamber, but local
chambers are listed here:
www.2chambers.comrhode2.htm

South Carolina
South Carolina Chamber of Commerce
1201 Main Street, #1810
Columbia, SC 29201-3254
Phone: (803) 799-4601
Fax: (803) 779-6043, (803) 343-3087
www.sccc.org

South Dakota
South Dakota Chamber of Commerce and
Industry
108 N. Euclid Avenue
P.O. Box 190
Pierre, SD 57501-0190
Phone: (605) 224-6161
Fax: (605) 224-7198
www.pierre.org/member.html

Tennessee
Tennessee Association of Business
611 Commerce Street, #3030
Nashville, TN 37203-3742
Phone: (615) 256-5141
Fax: (615) 256-6726
www.tennbiz.org

Texas
Texas Association of Business and Chambers of
Commerce
P.O. Box 2989
Austin, TX 78768-2989
Phone: (512) 477-6721
Fax: (512) 477-0836
www.tabcc.org

Utah

Utah State Chamber of Commerce
c/o Tooele County Chamber of Commerce
201 N. Main Street
P.O. Box 460
Tooele, UT 84074
Phone: (801) 882-0690
Fax: (801) 882-1619
www.tooelechamber.com

Vermont

Vermont Chamber of Commerce
P.O. Box 37
Montpelier, VT 05601-0037
Phone: (802) 223-3443
Fax: (802) 223-4257
www.vtchamber.com

Virginia

Virginia Chamber of Commerce
9 S. 5th Street
Richmond, VA 23219-3890
Phone: (804) 644-1607
Fax: (804) 783-6112
www.vachamber.com

Washington

Association of Washington Business
P.O. Box 658
1414 S. Cherry
Olympia, WA 98507-0658
Phone: (360) 943-1600
Fax: (360) 943-5811
www.awb.org

West Virginia

West Virginia Chamber of Commerce
1314 Virginia Street, East
P.O. Box 2789
Charleston, WV 25330-2789
Phone: (304) 342-1115
Fax: (304) 342-1130
www.wvchamber.com

Wisconsin

Wisconsin Manufacturers and Commerce
501 E. Washington Avenue
P.O. Box 352
Madison, WI 53701-0352

Phone: (608) 258-3400
Fax: (608) 258-3413
www.wmc.org

Wyoming

Wyoming Heritage Foundation and Society
139 W. 2nd Street, Suite 3E
Casper, WY 82601-2465
Phone: (307) 577-8000
Fax: (307) 577-8003
www.casperwyoming.org

U.S. Chambers of Commerce

The Chamber of Commerce of the United States provides you with a voice of experience and influence in Washington, D.C. and around the globe. Members include businesses of all sizes and sectors—from *Fortune* 500 companies to home-based, one-person operations.

U.S. Chambers of Commerce
1615 H. Street, NW
Washington, DC 20062-2000
Phone: (202) 659-6000, (800) 638-6582 (customer service)
www.uschamber.com/sb

World Chambers Network

This is a federative initiative that allows you to benefit of your capacity to "think global and act local." Its mission is to open up global markets and increase sales and trade opportunities for dynamic, entrepreneurial, growing businesses. You can also find out about economic and trade information and company files.

www.worldchambers.com

International Chamber of Commerce

This is the voice of world business championing the global economy as a force for economic growth, job creation, and prosperity. Its activities cover a broad spectrum, from arbitration and dispute resolution to making the case for open trade and the market economy system, business self-regulation, fighting corruption, or combating commercial crime.

International Chamber of Commerce

38 Cours Albert 1er
75008 Paris, France
Phone: +33 1 49 53 29 05
Fax: +33 1 49 53 29 29
E-mail: webmaster@iccebo.org
www.iccwbo.org

International Chambers of Commerce

If doing business abroad, it might be a good idea to visit the chamber of commerce web site for that country.

Argentina
American Chamber of Commerce in Argentina
www.amchamar.com.ar

Australia
American Chamber of Commerce in Australia
www.amcham.com.au

Austria
American Chamber of Commerce in Austria
www.amcham.or.at

Azerbaijan
American Chamber of Commerce in Azerbaijan
www.amchamaz.org

Belgium
American Chamber of Commerce in Belgium
www.amcham.be

Bolivia
American Chamber of Commerce of Bolivia
www.bolivia-us.org

Brazil – Rio
American Chamber of Commerce for Brazil, Rio de Janeiro
www.amchamrio.com.br

Brazil - Sao Paulo
American Chamber of Commerce for Brazil, Sao Paulo
www.amcham.com.br

Bulgaria
American Chamber of Commerce in Bulgaria
www.amcham.bg

Chile
Chilean-American Chamber of Commerce
www.amchamchile.cl

Colombia
Colombian-American Chamber of Commerce
www.amchamcolombia.com.co

Costa Rica
Costa Rican-American Chamber of Commerce
www.amcham.co.cr

Croatia
American Chamber of Commerce in Croatia
www.amcham.hr

Czech Republic
American Chamber of Commerce in the Czech Republic
www.amcham.cz

Cyprus
Cyprus-American Business Association
www.cyaba.com.cy

Denmark
American Chamber of Commerce in Denmark
www.amcham.dk

Dominican Republic
American Chamber of Commerce of the Dominican Republic
www.amcham.org.do

Ecuador – Quito
Ecuadorian-American Chamber of Commerce, Quito
www.ecamcham.com

Egypt
American Chamber of Commerce of Egypt
www.amcham.org.eg

El Salvador
American Chamber of Commerce of El Salvador
www.amchamsal.com

Estonia
American Chamber of Commerce, Estonia
www.acce.ee

France
American Chamber of Commerce in France
www.amchamfrance.org

Georgia
American Chamber of Commerce in Georgia
www.amcham.ge

Germany
American Chamber of Commerce in Germany
www.amcham.de

Greece
American-Hellenic Chamber of Commerce
www.amcham.gr

Guam
Guam Chamber of Commerce
www.guamchamber.com.gu

Guatemala
American Chamber of Commerce in Guatemala
www.amchamguate.com

Haiti
Haitian-American Chamber of Commerce and
Industry
e-mail: hamcham@globelsud.net

Honduras
Honduran-American Chamber of Commerce
www.amcham.hn2.com

Hungary
American Chamber of Commerce in Hungary
www.amcham.hu

India
American Chamber of Commerce in India
www.amchamindia.com

Indonesia
American Chamber of Commerce in Indonesia
www.amcham.or.id

Ireland
U.S. Chamber of Commerce in Ireland
e-mail: amcham@ioi.ie

Israel
Israel-America Chamber of Commerce and
Industry

www.amcham.co.il

Italy
American Chamber of Commerce in Italy
www.amcham.it

Jamaica
American Chamber of Commerce of Jamaica
www.amchamjamaica.org

Japan – Okinawa
American Chamber of Commerce in Okinawa
www.accokinawa.org

Japan – Tokyo
American Chamber of Commerce in Japan
www.accj.or.jp

Jordan
Jordanian American Business Association
www.jaba.org.jo

Korea
American Chamber of Commerce in Korea
www.amchamkorea.org

Kuwait
American Business Council of Kuwait
e-mail: abckuwait@hotmail.com

Latvia
American Chamber of Commerce in Latvia
www.amcham.lv

Lebanon
Lebanese American Business Association
www.dm.net.lblaba

Lithuania
American Chamber of Commerce in Lithuania
www.acc.lt

Luxembourg
American Chamber of Commerce in
Luxembourg
www.amcham.lu

Malaysia
American Malaysian Chamber of Commerce
www.jaring.my/nccim

Mexico
American Chamber of Commerce of Mexico, A.C.
www.amcham.com.mx

Netherlands
American Chamber of Commerce in the Netherlands
www.amcham.nl

New Zealand
American Chamber of Commerce in New Zealand
www.amcham.co.nz

Nicaragua
American Chamber of Commerce of Nicaragua
www.cadin.org.ni

Norway
U.S. Chamber of Commerce in Norway
www.am-cham.com

Pakistan
American Business Council of Pakistan
www.abcpk.org.pk

Panama
American Chamber of Commerce and Industry of Panama
www.panamcham.com

Paraguay
Paraguayan-American Chamber of Commerce
www.pamcham.com.py

People's Republic of China
American Chamber of Commerce in the People's Republic of China
www.amcham-china.org.cn

People's Republic of China, Guangdong
American Chamber of Commerce in Guangdong
www.amcham-guangdong.org

People's Republic of China, Hong Kong
American Chamber of Commerce in Hong Kong
www.amcham.org.hk

People's Republic of China, Shanghai
American Chamber of Commerce in Shanghai
www.amcham-shanghai.org

People's Republic of China, Tianjin
American Chamber of Commerce - Tianjin
www.amchamtianjin.org

Peru
American Chamber of Commerce of Peru
www.amcham.org.pe

Philippines
American Chamber of Commerce of the Philippines
www.amchamphilippines.com

Poland
American Chamber of Commerce in Poland
www.amcham.com.pl

Portugal
American Chamber of Commerce in Portugal
cca.imediata.pt

Romania
American Chamber of Commerce in Romania
www.amcham.ro

Russia
American Chamber of Commerce in Russia
www.amcham.ru

Singapore
American Chamber of Commerce in Singapore
www.amcham.org.sg

Slovak Republic
American Chamber of Commerce in the Slovak Republic
www.amcham.sk

South Africa
American Chamber of Commerce in South Africa
www.amcham.co.za

Spain
American Chamber of Commerce in Spain
www.amchamspain.com

Sweden
American Chamber of Commerce in Sweden
www.amchamswe.se

Switzerland
Swiss-American Chamber of Commerce
www.amcham.ch

Taiwan – Taipei
American Chamber of Commerce, Taipei
www.amcham.com.tw

Thailand
American Chamber of Commerce in Thailand
www.amchamthailand.org

Trinidad and Tobago
American Chamber of Commerce of Trinidad
and Tobago
www.amchamtt.com

Turkey
Turkish-American Business Association
www.amcham.org

Ukraine
American Chamber of Commerce in Ukraine
www.amcham.kiev.ua

United Arab Emirates
American Business Council of Dubai and
Northern Emirates
www.abcdubai.com

United Arab Emirates - Abu Dhabi
American Business Group of Abu Dhabi
www.abgabudhabi.org

Uruguay
Chamber of Commerce Uruguay - U.S.A.
www.zfm.comamchamuru

Uzbekistan
American Chamber of Commerce in Uzbekistan
www.amcham.uz

Venezuela
Venezuelan-American Chamber of Commerce
and Industry
www.venamcham.org

Vietnam – Hanoi
American Chamber of Commerce in Vietnam,
Hanoi
www.amchamhanoi.com

Essential Magazines for Entrepreneurs

Entrepreneur Magazine
Monthly

The small business authority helping to manage and grow your business. It contains great articles, tips, and information on everything an entrepreneur needs to start and grow a business.

Money
Monthly

Whether you're looking to invest, cut taxes, save money, or retire worry-free, *Money* helps you reach your financial goals. Also it provides tips on the hottest stocks and mutual funds.

Business 2.0
Monthly

Business 2.0 informs readers on what is working today in management, technology, marketing, and other areas. *Business 2.0* provides comprehensive industry coverage including emerging technologies, business models, and trends. Also learn strategies of groundbreaking companies and how to put them to use.

The Economist
Weekly

The news and business publication written expressly for top business decision-makers and opinion leaders. Each issue explores the links among domestic and international issues, business, finance, current affairs, science, technology, and the arts.

Fortune
Biweekly

Fortune speaks the language of the street: Wall Street, Silicon Valley, Madison Avenue, and everywhere in between, providing innovative business ideas and in-depth strategies and analysis. *Fortune* offers readers an unparalleled look at a wide range of business and economic news.

BusinessWeek
Weekly

Each issue of *BusinessWeek* features in-depth perspectives on the financial markets, industries, trends, technology, and people guiding the economy. Draw upon *BusinessWeek*'s timely incisive analysis to help you make better decisions about your career, your business, and your personal investments.

Smart Money
Monthly

Smart Money calls itself *The Wall Street Journal* Magazine of Personal Business." It offers investors and affluent consumers expert market analysis, investing strategies, personal finance options, and other tips for financial issues like retirement planning and car leasing. It covers a variety of personal finance topics for upscale readers, including retirement planning, investment strategies, financial planning for education, and related life-style issues.

Inc.
Monthly

Some of the topics included are selling and raising capital, defining your small business opportunity, hiring and training top talent, managing technology, forming clear goals for your business, buying new equipment, and managing employees

To subscribe, go to www.magazines.com or call 1-800-MAGAZINES.

Top-Ranked Entrepreneurial Colleges and Universities 2005

Entrepreneurship programs typically fall into one of three categories: Comprehensive (offering the widest variety of resources), Entrepreneurship Emphasis (a smaller number of entrepreneurship faculty, courses, and initiatives), or Limited Curriculum (only a few faculty teaching a limited number of courses).

#1 The University of Arizona

Karl Eller Center, Berger Entrepreneurship Program
Tuscon, AZ
www.arizona.edu

Program established: 1984
# of faculty: 35
# of courses: 24

Tuition (in state): undergrad $4,096, graduate $4,346
Tuition (out of state): undergrad $13,077, graduate $13,3276

#2 Babson College

Arthur M. Blank Center for Entrepreneurship
Babson Park, MA
www.babson.edu

Program established: 1967
# of faculty: 49
# of courses: 34

Tuition (in state): undergrad $27,247, graduate $29,900
Tuition (out of state): undergrad $27,247, graduate $29,900

#3 Columbia University

Eugene M. Lang Center for Entrepreneurship
New York, NY
www.gsb.columbia.edu

Program established: 1977
# of faculty: 8
# of courses: 15

Tuition (in state): undergrad N/A, graduate $36,296
Tuition (out of state): undergrad N/A, graduate $36,296

#4 DePaul University

Chicago, IL
ent.depaul.edu

Program established: 1982
# of faculty: 16
# of courses: 12

Tuition (in state): undergrad $19,700, graduate $23,400
Tuition (out of state): undergrad $19,700, graduate $23,400

#5 University of Maryland, College Park

Dingman Center for Entrepreneurship
College Park, MD
www.umd.edu

Program established: 1989
# of faculty: 19
# of courses: 18

Tuition (in state): undergrad $26,500, graduate $26,500
Tuition (out of state): undergrad $31,000, graduate $31,000

#6 Massachusetts Institute of Technology

MIT Entrepreneurship Center
Boston, MA
web.mit.edu

Program established: 1960
# of faculty: 19
# of courses: 21

Tuition (in state): undergrad N/A, graduate $32,230
Tuition (out of state): undergrad N/A, graduate $32,230

#7 University of North Carolina at Chapel Hill

Center for Entrepreneurship and Technology Venturing
Chapel Hill, NC
www.eship.unc.edu

Program established: 1986
# of faculty: 24
# of courses: 63

Tuition (in state): undergrad $3,205, graduate $15,325
Tuition (out of state): undergrad $16,303, graduate $30,749

#8 The Ohio State University

Center for Entrepreneurship
Columbus, OH
www.acs.ohio-state.edu

Program established: 1988
# of faculty: 19
# of courses: 14

Tuition (in state): undergrad $6,651, graduate $14,121
Tuition (in state): undergrad $16,638, graduate $25,332

#9 The Pennsylvania State University

University Park, PA
www.psu.edu

Program established: 1992
# of faculty: 24
# of courses: 20

Tuition (in state): undergrad $18,380, graduate $18,380
Tuition (out of state): undergrad $18,380, graduate $18,380

#10 Rensselaer Polytechnic Institute

Troy, NY
www.rpi.edu

Program established: 1985
# of faculty: 30
# of courses: 30

Tuition (in state): undergrad $28,950, graduate $28,950

Tuition (out of state): undergrad $28,950, graduate $28,950

#11 University of South Carolina, Columbia

Faber Entrepreneurship Center
Columbia, SC
www.sc.edu

Program established: 1975
# of faculty:15
or courses: 17

Tuition (in state): undergrad $5,600, graduate $15,000
Tuition (out of state): undergrad $15,000, graduate $25,000

#12 University of Southern California

The Greif Center for Entrepreneurial Studies
Los Angeles, CA
www.marshall.usc.edu/entrepreneur

Program established: 1971
# of faculty: 19
# of courses: 22

Tuition (in state): undergrad $30,000, graduate $30,000
Tuition (out of state): undergrad $30,000, graduate $30,000

#13 Syracuse University

Falcone Center for Entrepreneurship
Syracuse, NY
www.som.syr.edu

Program established: 1992
# of faculty: 30
# of courses: 24

Tuition (in state): undergrad $24,200, graduate $22,260
Tuition (out of state): undergrad $24,200, graduate $22,260

*For a compete list, go to
www.entrepreneur.com/topcolleges.*

U.S. News & World Report's Best Entrepreneurship Programs 2006

1. Babson College (Olin) (MA)
2. Stanford University (CA)
3. University of Pennsylvania (Wharton)

Source: *U.S. News & World Report* www.usnews.com/usnews/edu/grad/rankings/ mba/brief/mbasp06_brief.php.

Recommended Reference Books

AMA Management Handbook, 3rd edition, by John J. Hampton, editor (Amacom, 1994). Descriptions of all business activities that an owner/CEO must control, with guidelines for managing them.

Start Your Business: A Beginner's Guide, 3rd edition, compiled by Vickie Reierson (Oasis/PSI, 1998). Checklists that will protect you from the devil in the details.

Legal Guide for Starting and Running a Small Business, 4th edition, by Fred S. Steingold (Nolo, 2001), or *American Bar Association Legal Guide for Small Business* (Times Books, 2000). Regulations you have to consider to get those details right.

Etiquette Advantage in Business: Personal Skills for Professional Success by Peggy Post and Peter Post (Harper Resource, 1999). A guide to making the best possible impression on the sophisticated professionals with whom you deal.

Entrepreneurial Finance: Finance for Small Business, 2nd edition, by Philip J. Adelman and Alan M. Marks (Prentice Hall, 2001), or *Accounting and Finance for Your Small Business*, by E. James Burton and Steven M. Bragg (Wiley, 2001). Learn to speak the language of small business finance so you'll be able to communicate with your accountant and speak persuasively to lenders and investors.

Anatomy of a Business Plan: A Step-by-Step Guide to Building a Business and Securing Your Company's Future, 5th edition, by Linda Pinson (Dearborn Trade, 2001), or *How to Write a Business Plan*, 5th edition, by Mike P. McKeever (Nolo, 2000). A good business plan not only keeps your efforts focused—it also convinces lenders and investors to do business with you.

Small Business Money Guide: How to Get It, Use It, Keep It, by Terri Lonier and Lisa M. Aldisert (Wiley, 1999). Where to turn for financing.

HR Book: Human Resources Management for Business, by Lin Grensing-Pophal (Self-Counsel, 1999). Selecting, hiring, and dealing with employees.

Thomas Register of American Manufacturers (Thomas, annual). Yellow-Pages style of listings for industrial product suppliers. The 27-volume set is only $29.95 (just the shipping and handling), but you'll need at least eight feet of shelf space for it.

Source: Edward Lowe Foundation, edward-lowe.org.

Useful Government Agencies

Copyright Clearance Center
222 Rosewood Drive
Danvers, MA 01923
Phone: (978) 750-8400
www.copyight.com

Copyright Office
Library of Congress
101 Independence Avenue, SE
Washington, DC 20559-6000
Phone: (202) 707-3000
www.loc.gov/copyright

Department of Agriculture
1400 Independence Avenue, SW
Washington, DC 20250
Phone: (202) 720-7420
www.usda.gov

Department of Commerce
1401 Constitution Avenue, NW
Washington, DC 20230
Phone: (800) 482-2000
Fax: (202) 482-5270
www.doc.gov

Department of Energy
1000 Independence Avenue, SW
Washington, DC 20585
Phone: (800) 342-5363
www.doe.gov

Department of Interior
1948 C Street, NW
Washington, DC 20240
Phone: (202) 208-3100
www.doi.gov

Department of Labor
200 Constitution Avenue, NW, Room S-1004
Washington, DC 20210
Phone: (866) 487-2365
www.dol.gov

Department of Treasury
Main Treasury Building

1500 Pennsylvania Avenue, NW
Washington, DC 20220
Phone: (202) 622-1502
www.ustreas.gov

Export-Import Bank of the United States
11 Vermont Avenue, NW, #911
Washington, DC 20571
Phone: (800) 565-3946 x 3908
www.exim.gov

Federal Communications Commission
445 12th Street, SW
Washington, DC 20544
Phone: (800) 225-5322
www.ftc.gov

Federal Trade Commission
600 Pennsylvania Avenue, NW
Washington, DC 20580
Phone: (202) 326-2222
www.ftc.gov

International Mail Calculator
ircalc.usps.gov

IRS
1111 Constitution Avenue, NW
Washington, DC 20224
Phone: (202) 622-5000
www.irs.ustreas.gov

U.S. Consumer Product Safety Commission
Office of Compliance
4330 East-West Highway
Bethesda, MD 20814
Phone: (301) 504-0990
www.cpsc.gov

U.S. Food and Drug Administration
5600 Fishers Lane
Rockville, MD 20857
Phone: (888) 463-6332
www.fda.gov

U.S. Patent and Trademark Office
Crystal Plaza 3, Room 2C02
Washington, DC 20231
Phone: (800) 786-9199
www.uspto.gov

U.S. Printing Office
Superintendent of Documents
Washington, DC 20402
Phone: (202) 512-1800
www.access.gpo.gov

Securities and Exchange Commission
450 Fifth Street, NW
Washington, DC 20549
Phone: (202) 942-8088
www.sec.gov

Small Business Administration
408 Third Street, SW
Washington, DC 20416
Phone: (800) 827-5722
www.sba.gov

Chapter 4

Resources for Women
and Minorities

Small Business Administration
Women's Business Centers

Alabama

Central Alabama Women's Business Center
Patricia Todd, Executive Director
2 North 20th Street, Suite 830
Birmingham, AL 35203
Phone: (205) 453-0249
Fax: (205) 453-0253
E-mail: Ecsfdn@aol.com
Web site: www.cawbc.org

We provide entrepreneurial counseling and training to women at any stage of small business ownership. Check out our web site for the current program calendar.

Alabama

Women's Business Assistance Center, Inc., WBC of Southern AL
Danette Richards, Program Director
1301 Azalea Road, Suite 201A
Mobile, AL 36693
Phone: (251) 660-2725
Fax: (251) 660-8854
E-mail: wbac@ceebic.org, drichards@ceebic.org
Web site: www.ceebic.org/~wbac

Women's Business Assistance Center, Inc., of Mobile, Alabama, serves current and potential women business owners, with an emphasis on socially and economically disadvantaged women.

Alaska

Women$Finances
Linda Gallagher, Program Director
324 E. 5th Avenue
Anchorage, AK 99501
Phone: (907) 644-9611
Fax: (907) 644-9650
E-mail: lgallagher@ywcaak.org
Web site: www.ywcaak.org/finances.htm

Women$Finances was established in 1995 as a program of the YWCA. It is a micro enterprise training and micro lending program for women entrepreneurs in Anchorage, Alaska. By providing training classes in entrepreneurship, technical assistance, individual mentoring, and seed money for women-owned small businesses, Women$Finances seeks to empower low- and moderate-income single-parent and minority women in Anchorage and surrounding Alaska communities for economic self-sufficiency.

American Samoa

American Samoa Women's Business Center
Tilani Ilaoa, Project Manager
P. O. Box 6849
Pago Pago, AS 96799
Phone: 011/684 699-6570
Fax: 011/684 699-6580
E-mail: nasacwbc1@samoatelco.com

The American Samoa WBC provides comprehensive training programs to fit the specific needs of Native American Samoan women who are socially and economically disadvantaged. Specialized training in agribusiness and village-based business is provided to develop entrepreneurial skills and help women market and export their products.

Arizona

Microbusiness Advancement Center of Southern Arizona (MAC)
Rebecca Wyant, Project Director
10 E. Broadway, Suite 201
P.O. Box 42108
Tucson, AZ 85701
Phone: (520) 620-1241 x 111
Fax: (520) 622-2235
E-mail: rwyant@mac-sa.org
Web site: www.acec-az.org

The Microbusiness Advancement Center is a non-profit organization dedicated to the economic growth of Southern Arizona and the individual professional development of its clients by providing training, resources, referrals, support, and advocacy to those seeking to create, sustain, or grow microbusinesses. MAC offers a variety of programs and services in English and Spanish to assist the small business owner in reaching their entrepreneurial goals: business plan writing, consulting, procurement, informational seminars, microlending, and loan packaging.

Arizona

Self-Employment Loan Fund, Inc.
Sonia Singh, Program Administrator
1601 N. 7th Street, Suite 340
Phoenix, AZ 85006
Phone: (602) 340-8834
Fax: (602) 340-8953
E-mail: carolinenewsom@selfloanfund.org, soniasingh@selfloanfund.org
Web site: www.selfloanfund.org

The mission of Self-Employment Loan Fund, Inc. (SELF) is to promote the self-sufficiency of low-income individuals, especially women and minorities, by encouraging the growth of microenterprise through training, technical assistance, and access to credit. SELF's community programs are designed to alleviate poverty and increase household income throughout Maricopa County, Arizona. SELF is a Women's Business Center and provides a "one-stop shop" for women looking to better their economic situation through self-employment opportunities.

Arkansas

Southern Good Faith Fund ARWBDC
Angela Duran, Program Director
2304 W. 29th Avenue
Pine Bluff, AR 71603
Phone: (870) 535-6233
Fax: (870) 535-0741
E-mail: info@southerngoodfaithfund.org
Web site: www.southerngoodfaithfund.org

The ARWBDC was funded in September 1999 to provide education, training, and technical assistance to women-owned businesses, focusing mainly on those owned by minorities.

California

Valley Economic Development Center
Susan Lentz, Project Director
21515 Soledad Canyon Road #121
Santa Clarita, CA 91350
Phone: (661) 290-3335
Fax: (661) 255-3399
E-mail: slentz@vedc.org
Web site: www.trivalleywbc.org

The Women's Business Center of the Valley Economic Development Center does one-on-one consulting at no cost to client and provides workshops, in-depth consulting and conferences, access to SBA loans and other types of financing, and information for women entrepreneurs.

California

National University Women's Business Center of California
Carolyn Morrow, Co-Directors
4121 Camino del Rio South, Suite 24
San Diego, CA 92108
Phone: (619) 563-7118
Fax: (858) 642-8707
E-mail: cmorrow@natuniv.edu, jloomis@natuniv.edu
Web site: www.wbcc.natuniv.edu

The National University WBC reaches out to women in the San Diego community, which includes many nationalities—Hispanic, European, Asian, Middle Eastern, Native American, and African American. The WBC reaches out to military veterans, spouses of active military personnel, immigrants working in farming, child-care providers, persons in the landscaping industry, and San Diego's 18 Indian reservations. The WBC offers five areas of support to its clients: training through classes and seminars; counseling and mentoring one to one; networking with its Advisory Board, San Diego businesses, NU's students, faculty, and other clients; access to resources and information; and help to access training and obtain financial resources.

California

Pacific Asian Consortium in Employment
Lisa Burton, Project Director
1055 Wilshire Boulevard, Suite 1475
Los Angeles, CA 90017
Phone: (213) 353-3982
Fax: (213) 353-4665
E-mail: ychang@pacela.org, lburton@ltsc.org
Web site: www.pacela.org

PACE is a community development organization that strives to be a conduit for the Pacific Asian community. PACE serves as a resource for identifying, securing, and administering economic solutions to problems of employment, housing, and business development, while serving the community at large.

California

Renaissance Entrepreneurship Center
Janet Lees, Program Director
275 Fifth Street
San Francisco, CA 94103-4120
Phone: (415) 541-8580 x 237
Fax: (415) 541-8589
E-mail: janet@rencenter.org
Web site: www.rencenter.org

Since 1985, Renaissance has been helping economically and socially diverse entrepreneurs throughout the Bay Area to start and grow small businesses. Renaissance offers comprehensive small business training and support services for businesses in all stages of development and all industries. Programs and services include training classes, a business incubator, a financing resource center program providing loan packaging and consultation, topic-specific workshops, access to markets, and computer and internet training.

California

Inland Empire Women's Business Center
Michelle Skiljan, Project Director
202 E. Airport Drive, Suite 155
San Bernardino, CA 92408
Phone: (909) 890-1242
Fax: (909) 880-5901

E-mail: mskiljan@csusb.edu, mbrule@csusb.edu, mstull@csusb.edu
Web site: www.iece.csusb.edu

The Inland Empire WBC is a program of the Inland Empire Center for Entrepreneurship at California State University San Bernardino. The Center targets Riverside and San Bernardino Counties. Inland Empire WBC provides mentoring, advising, long- and short-term training in all areas of business development to women who own or aspire to own businesses. Services are available in English and Spanish. The WBC targets women in the fields of construction, trades, general contracting, and technology.

California

Women's Economic Venture of Santa Barbara
Marsha Bailey, Executive Director
333 S. Salinas Street
Santa Barbara, CA 93103
Phone: (805) 962-6073 x 101
Fax: (805) 962-1396
E-mail: mbailey@wevonline.org, ezavala@wevonline.org, mspaulding@wevonline.org
Web site: www.vevonline.org

Established in 1991, Women's Economic Ventures (WEV) provides training, technical assistance, mentoring, Individual Development Accounts (IDAs), and loans of up to $100,000 to woman-owned businesses in Santa Barbara and Ventura Counties. WEV provides ongoing support for growing businesses through Mastermind Groups, W! (a membership networking organization), workshops, individual business counseling, and Micromentor, an online mentoring project. WEV has offices in Santa Barbara, Camarillo, and Santa Maria, California. All services are provided in English and Spanish.

California

Anew America Community Corporation
Tracey Schear, Director of Programs/WBC Director
1918 University Avenue, Suite 3A

Section 1

Berkeley, CA 94704
Phone: (510) 540-7785 x 302
Fax: (510) 540-7786
E-mail: tschear@anewamerica.org,
jbutler@anewamerica.org
Web site: www.anewamerica.org

AnewAmerica offers a holistic three-year program, the Virtual Business Incubator, that helps
new Americans in the San Francisco Bay Area
establish or expand microbusinesses, build personal assets to sustain their families, and develop the community assets necessary to support
the political, social, and cultural empowerment
of their communities.

California

CHARO Community Development Corporation
Anita Rodriguez, Accounting Manager
4301 East Valley Boulevard
Los Angeles, CA 90032
Phone: (323) 269-0751 x 516
Fax: (323) 343-9484
Web site: www.charocorp.org

Specializing in providing bilingual/bicultural
business services, the CHARO SBA Women's
Center provides all services in both English and
Spanish to enterprises owned by women. The
Center's mission is to harness resources, provide access to capital, and provide economic
opportunities that create wealth and generate
jobs. Services include entrepreneur training, loan
packaging services, business and technical
assistance, financial literacy training, business
incubator, small business contract procurement
center, and access to the computer resource lab.

California

West Company - Fort Bragg Center
Joy Calonico, Project Director
306 East Redwood Avenue, Suite 2
Fort Bragg, CA 95437
Phone: (707) 964-7571
Fax: (707) 964-7576
E-mail: joy@westcompany.org
Web site: www.westcompany.org

West Company - Ukiah Center
Valerie Plummer, Program Manager
367 North State Street, Suite 201
Ukiah, CA 95482
Phone: (707) 468-3553
Fax: (707) 468-3555
Web site: www.westcompany.org

WEST Company serves micro-enterprise owners in rural Northern California, targeting low-
income women and minorities through its
centers in Fort Bragg and Ukiah. WEST
Company provides business planning and
management assistance at every stage of business ownership from feasibility through expansion. Services include business-plan training,
individual consulting, access to capital through
individual microloans, business-network formation, and assistance with business applications
using technology.

California

Women's Initiative for Self-Employment (WISE)
Catherine Riedel, Program Manager
519 17th Street, Suite 110
Oakland, CA 94612
Phone: (415) 247-9473 x 315
Fax: (415) 247-9471
E-mail: criedel@womensinitiative.org,
dpiaino@womensinitiative.org
Web site: www.womensinitiative.org

The Women's Initiative provides business training
and technical assistance in English and Spanish
to low-income women in the San Francisco Bay
Area. The English-language program consists of
a two-week business assessment workshop, a
14-week business skills workshop, and a four-
week workshop on writing a business plan. The
Spanish-language program parallels the English
but in modular format. WI also offers business
support services, including one-to-one consulta-
tions, peer networking and support groups, and
special seminars.

California

Asian Pacific Islander Small Business Program
H. Cook Sunoo, Director
231 East Third Street

Los Angeles, CA 90013
Phone: (213) 473-1603
Fax: (213) 473-1601
E-mail: csunoo@ltsc.org, lburton@ltsc.org
Web site: www.apisbp.org

The mission of the Asian Pacific Islander Small Business Program (API SBP) is to assist the development of small and micro businesses in Los Angeles, with particular focus on Chinatown, Koreatown, Little Tokyo, Thai Town, and Filipino business communities, especially those of low-income immigrants.

Colorado
Mi Casa Resource Center for Women, Inc.
Pueblo
Marta Madrid, Program Manager
505 West Abriendo
Pueblo, CO 81005
Phone: (719) 542-0091
Fax: (719) 542-1006
E-mail: mmadrid@micasadenver.org
Web site: www.micasadenver.org

Denver
Agnes Carroll, Project Director
360 Acoma Street
Denver, CO 80223
Phone: (303) 539-5605
Fax: (303) 595-0422
E-mail: acarroll@micasadenver.org
Web site: www.micasadenver.org

Mi Casa Resource Center for Women provides quality employment and education services that promote economic independence for low-income, predominantly Latina women and Latino youth. Services include educational counseling, job-readiness and job-search training, life-skills development, job placement, nontraditional and computer-skills training, and entrepreneurial training. The center is an SBA Pre-Qual Lender and offers SBA Community Express Loans.

Connecticut
Women's Business Development Center (WBDC)

Fran Pastore, President/CEO
400 Main Street, Suite 500
Stamford, CT 06901
Phone: (203) 353-1750
Fax: (203) 353-1084
E-mail: dbratchell@ctwbdc.org, fpastore@ctwbdc.org, mshannon@ctwbdc.org
Web site: www.ctwbdc.org

The Women's Business Development Center is a not-for-profit organization that promotes economic development through entrepreneurship. The WBDC offers comprehensive business education and increased access to financial resources as essential business tools to economic independence. The WBDC offers myriad programs to meet the needs of aspiring, emerging, and established entrepreneurs. It offers one-to-one counseling, long-term training, workshops, and symposiums on virtually every aspect of owning a small business.

Connecticut
The Entrepreneurial Center
University of Hartford
Jean Blake-Jackson, Director
50 Elizabeth Street
Hartford, CT 06105-2280
Phone: (860) 768-5681
Fax: (860) 768-5622
E-mail: entrectr@hartford.edu
Web site: www.entrepreneurialctr.org

This program serves potential startup and established business owners throughout Connecticut, with special emphasis on women. The Center works in collaboration with the Connecticut Development Authority. The Center offers a series of self-assessment workshops and conducts a comprehensive small business training program. The Connecticut Development Authority provides assistance in accessing capital through its statewide URBANK Entrepreneurial Loan Program.

District of Columbia
Women's Business Center, Inc.
Penny Pompei, Project Director

1001 Connecticut Avenue, NW, Suite 312
Washington, DC 20036
Phone: (202) 785-4922
Fax: (202) 785-4110
E-mail: ppompei@womensbusinesscenter.org
Web site: www.womensbusinesscenter.org

The Women's Business Center offers programs covering owning and managing a business and doing business with the government. Through active mentoring programs, the center reaches a diverse population at all levels of business ownership.

Florida
Alliance Women's Business Center
Ana Leon y Leon, Project Director
625 East Colonial Drive
Orlando, FL 32803
Phone: (407) 428-5860
Fax: (407) 428-5869
E-mail: aleonwbc@allianceflorida.com
Web site: www.allianceflorida.com

The Business Center is part of the Minority/ Women Business Enterprise Alliance, which was formed specifically as a one-stop business resource center to meet the needs of the minority and women business community in Central Florida. It provides entrepreneurial and business development, seminars and workshops, access to capital, management and technical assistance, individual consulting, contract matchmaking, program management, construction services, and community advocacy. The Alliance is a Certified SBA Micro Lender, Community Development Financial Institution (CDFI), National Community Development Agency and Community Development Entity (CDE).

Florida
Florida Women's Business Center
Pamela Morrison, Executive Director
33 SE First Avenue, Suite 102
Delray Beach, FL 33444
Phone: (561) 265-3790
Fax: (561) 265-0806
E-mail: seabron1@tedcenter.org, pamela@ted-
center.org
Web site: /www.flwbc.org

The Florida Women's Business Center is a program within the Center for Technology, Enterprise and Development, Inc. that provides training, resources, referrals, support and advocacy to those seeking to create, sustain, or grow micro businesses. Its services are available to all business concerns, but the center is committed to attracting and serving women, especially those who are socially and/or economically disadvantaged. Training is provided on various business topics, with workshops and seminars on topics such as starting a business, developing a business plan, securing loans, marketing, and financial management.

Florida
Jacksonville Women's Business Center
Sandy Bartow, Executive Director
5000-3 Norwood Avenue
Jacksonville, FL 32208
Phone: (904) 924-1100
Fax: (904) 765-8966
E-mail: Sandy.Bartow@myjaxchamber.com
Web site: www.jaxwbc.com

The Jacksonville Women's Business Center (JWBC) is a program of the Jacksonville Regional Chamber of Commerce that provides services to advance the success of women entrepreneurs. The goal of the JWBC is to positively impact the economy, helping women who control companies and women who want to start businesses. The JWBC provides mentoring, training, consulting, and networking opportunities in a six-county area in NE Florida. A public-private partnership, the JWBC is partially funded by the U.S. Small Business Administration.

Georgia
Women's Business and Enterprise Center
Paola Diaz-Torres, Project Director
Cobb Microenterprise Center
Michael J. Coles College of Business
Kennesaw State University

1000 Chastain Road, # 3305
Kennesaw, GA 30144
Phone: (770) 499-3228
Fax: (770) 499-3636
E-mail: pdiaztor@kennesaw.edu
Web site: www.cobbmicro.org

The Center, a program of the Cobb Micro-enterprise Center, offers women entrepreneurs business and technical assistance and training, including classes in sales and marketing, operations, financial management issues, legal issues, procurement opportunities, and human resource issues as well as access to capital and SBA loan pre-qualification workshops. The Center targets low- to moderate-income women, women with disabilities, and minorities.

Georgia

Women's Economic Development Agency (WEDA)
659 Auburn Avenue, Suite 250
Atlanta, GA 30312
Telephone: (678) 904-2201
Fax: (678) 904-2205
E-mail: inquiries@weda-atlanta.org
Web site: www.weda-atlanta.org

WEDA provides business development, management, and technical assistance to women entrepreneurs throughout 28 counties around Atlanta. WEDA is a bilingual organization and offers its programs and services in both English and Spanish.

Hawaii

Hawaii Women's Business Center
Cherylle Morrow, Acting Executive Director
1041 Nuuanu Avenue, Suite A
Honolulu, HI 96817
Phone: (808) 526-1001
Fax: (808) 550-0724
E-mail: info@hwbc.org
Web site: www.hwbc.org

The Hawaii Women's Business Center (HWBC) was created to support women interested in starting and growing their business and to assist in the economic development and diver-sification of Hawaii. HWBC provides technical assistance and support for women in business through one-on-one counseling, business management training, networking, Business Brown Bag Lunch Series, and quarterly women business owner evening roundtable events.

Illinois

Women's Business Development Center
Kelly Smith, Project Director
8 South Michigan Avenue, Suite 400
Chicago, IL 60603-3306
Phone: (312) 853-3477
Fax: (312) 853-0145
E-mail: wbdc@wbdc.org
Web site: www.wbdc.org

The Women's Business Development Center (WBDC) offers a full-service approach to launching emerging businesses and strengthening existing businesses owned by women in the Chicago area. Services of the WBDC include workshops and one-on-one counseling on all aspects of business development, including marketing, finance, business management, and technology integration.

Indiana

Central Indiana Women's Business Center
Charles Sims, Executive Director
615 N. Alabama Street, Room 219
Indianapolis, IN 46204
Phone: (317) 917-3266, (877) 836-7523
Fax: (317) 916-8921
E-mail: csim@nsibiz.org
Web site: www.nsibiz.org/ciwbc.shtml

The Central Indiana Women's Business Center is a program of the Neighborhood Self-Employment Initiative. The Center provides services to emerging and existing business owners in the 10-county Indianapolis metropolitan area consisting of Marion, Hamilton, Hancock, Shelby, Johnson, Brown, Morgan, Hendricks, Putnam, and Boone counties. Some of the Center's assistance is provided in Spanish. The Center's services include business training classes and workshops, one-on-one business counseling, mentoring, and internet-related training. While the Center's services are available to anyone, we heavily target our efforts toward people who are not in the economic mainstream. This includes the working poor, immigrants, female heads of households, minorities, under- and unemployed, and others who experience barriers to full participation in the mainstream economy.

Indiana
Women's Enterprise,
Leslie Alford, Director
3521 Lake Avenue, Suite 1
Fort Wayne, IN 46805-5533
Phone: (260) 424-7977
Fax: (260) 426-7576
E-mail: info@womensenterprise.org, bojohnson@womensenterprise.org
Web site: www.womensenterprise.org

The mission of Women's Enterprise, a Program of the Fort Wayne's Women's Bureau, is to promote economic development through entrepreneurial assistance and advocacy for women. Our vision is to provide women, including those who are economically and/or socially disadvantaged, with the knowledge and expertise to make informed decisions and actions to improve their financial positions in life. Women's Enterprise promotes the growth of women-owned businesses through programs that offer business counseling, mentoring, training, and technical, financial, and procurement assistance. All services are offered in English and Spanish.

Iowa
Iowa Women's Enterprise Center
Stacie Mitchell, Director of Microenterprise
910 23rd Avenue
Coralville, IA 52241
Phone: (319) 338-2331
Fax: (319) 338-5824
E-mail: smitchell@ised.org
Web site: www.ised.org/EconomicDevelopment/WomenEntCenter.asp

The Iowa Women's Enterprise Center (IWEC) is part of a consortium of major business-development organizations in Iowa and serves every level of woman business owner across the state. The Center serves as the clearinghouse for information and resources for starting a small business in Iowa, providing assistance in business research and planning, acquiring capital, marketing, bookkeeping, and financial management. IWEC can help make a business more profitable, expand into new markets, and maintain its competitive edge, offering e-commerce and technology training, government procurement assistance, acquisition of capital for expansion, growth management consultation, financial management, and marketing assistance.

Kansas
Kansas Women's Business Center
Sherry Turner, Executive Director
8527 Bluejacket Street
Lenexa, KS 66214
Phone: (913) 492-5922
Fax: (913) 888-6928
E-mail: sturner@kansaswbc.com
Web site: www.kansaswbc.com

Kansas Women's Business Center serves the thousands of women business owners in the community and throughout Kansas at every stage of business development. Both aspiring and existing entrepreneurs can access training, access capital, and access resources and networks when they need it most. Programs are designed to support women as they launch and grow their businesses.

Louisiana
Women's Business Resource Center
Patrice A. Williams-Smith, Executive Director
Urban League of Greater New Orleans
2322 Canal Street, Suite 100
New Orleans, LA 70119
Phone: (504) 620-9650
Fax: (504) 620-9659
E-mail: paw_s@bellsouth.net
Web site: www.urbanleagueneworleans.org/womensbusinessresource.htm

The center provides business and entrepreneurial training for women and men, to equip aspiring entrepreneurs with the vital skills to build, operate, and maintain successful businesses.

Maine

Women's Business Center
Marita Fairfield, Senior Program Officer
Coastal Enterprises Inc. (CEI)
36 Water Street
P.O. Box 268
Wiscasset, ME 04578
Phone: (207) 882-7552
Fax: (207) 882-7308
E-mail: mlf@ceimaine.org
Web site: www.ceimaine.org

Coastal Enterprises, Inc., is a private, nonprofit community-development corporation that provides financing and technical assistance to Maine businesses, which in turn provide income, ownership, or employment opportunities to low-income people. The Women's Business Center provides training, management assistance, and access to credit to women across the state who own businesses. Center participants benefit from CEI's capacity to provide access to capital through its SBA.

Maryland

Women Entrepreneurs of Baltimore, Inc. (WEB)
Colette Pichon-Battle, JD, Chief Executive Officer
1118 Light Street, Suite 202
Baltimore, MD 21230
Phone: (410) 727-4921 x 15
Fax: (410) 727-4989
E-mail: cpbattle@webinc.org
Web site: www.webinc.org

Women Entrepreneurs of Baltimore, a nonprofit organization, is an entrepreneurial training program designed to help economically disadvantaged women become self-sufficient through business development. The main components of the WEB Program include: an intensive business-skills training course, mentoring, financing strategy development, community networking, resource sharing, professional business consultation, internet training, government certification and procurement, and information and referral services.

Massachusetts

Center for Women and Enterprise, Inc.

Eastern Massachusetts

Gretchen Dock, Director
24 School Street, Suite 700
Boston, MA 02108
Phone: (617) 536-0700
Fax: (617) 536-7373
E-mail: gdock@cweonline.org
Web site: www.cweonline.org

Central Massachusetts

Jolene Jennings, Director
50 Elm Street, 2nd Floor
Worcester, MA 01609
Phone: (508) 363-2300
Fax: (508) 363-2323
E-mail: jjennings@cweonline.org
Web site: www.cweonline.org

CWE is a non-profit organization dedicated to helping women start and grow their own businesses. It offers education, training, technical assistance, women's business enterprise certification, and access to both debt and equity capital to entrepreneurs at every stage of business development.

Michigan

Grand Rapids Opportunities for Women
Rita VanderVen, Executive Director
25 Sheldon Street, SE
Grand Rapids, MI 49503
Phone: (616) 458-3404
Fax: (616) 458-6557
E-mail: rvanderven@growbusiness.org
Web site: www.growbusiness.org

GROW exists to provide business and economic training to women in transition in West Michigan, to provide the education and resources that will allow them to strive toward their dream of achieving self-fulfillment and positive economic change. It offers four programs: small business readiness and entrepreneurial training, business support services, economic literacy training, and individual development accounts (matched savings accounts).

Michigan

Women's Business Center
Cornerstone Alliance
Jeffrey Noel, Project Director
38 West Wall Street
P.O. Box 428
Benton Harbor, MI 49023
Phone: (269) 925-6100
E-mail: gvaughn@cstonealliance.org
Web site: www.cstonealliance.org/wbc

The WBC is a program that provides women and others from diverse backgrounds, many whom are facing social or economic barriers, with opportunities to develop the skills and acquire the knowledge needed to achieve financial independence. It offers assistance and/or training in finance, management, marketing, procurement, and the internet and addresses specialized topics such as home-based businesses. WBC provides individual business consulting and access to Small Business Administration (SBA) programs and services.

Michigan

Center for Empowerment and Economic Development (CEED)
Michelle Richards, Executive Director
2002 Hogback Road, Suite 12
Ann Arbor, MI 48105
Phone: (734) 677-1400
Fax: (734) 677-1465
E-mail: mrichards@wwnet.net
Web site: www.miceed.org

The Center for Empowerment and Economic Development (CEED) provides business programs and services to assist women and minorities to become economically self-sufficient through business development. CEED is an SBA microloan intermediary for Southeastern Michigan and Michigan's SBA Prequalification Loan Program intermediary, providing loan assistance to women and minorities seeking SBA-guaranteed loans up to

$250,000. CEED's Michigan Women's Business Council offers certification and procurement services to women-owned businesses.

Minnesota

WomenVenture
Stacie Mitchell, Program Director
2324 University Avenue West, Suite 200
St. Paul, MN 55114
Phone: (651) 646-3808
Fax: (651) 641-7223
E-mail: smitchell@womenventure.org, lheglund@womenventure.org, lpadilla@womenventure.org
Web site: www.womenventure.org

WomenVenture's mission is to help women secure economic success and prosperity through consulting and training in business development, career transitioning, training to enter non-traditional occupations, and education and mentoring around economic issues. The WomenVenture Business Center provides technical assistance to women entrepreneurs through one-on-one consulting, business-planning seminars, and workshops. The Center is an intermediary for the SBA Loan Prequalification and Microloan programs.

Minnesota

Minnesota Women's Business Center (The People Connection)
Michelle Landsverk, Project Director
226 East 1st Street
Fosston, MN 56542
Phone: (218) 435-2134
Fax: (218) 435-1347
E-mail: info@thepeopleconnection.org
Web site: www.thepeopleconnection.org/mwbc.htm

The Center assists women in every stage of entrepreneurship with business planning, cash flow projections and analysis, marketing strategies, and technology solutions..

Minnesota

Women's Business Network
Annie Fahrenkrug, Program Director

Northeast Entrepreneur Fund, Inc.
424 West Superior Street
Duluth, MN 55802
Phone: (218) 726-4791, (800) 422-0374
Fax: (218) 726-4792
E-mail: info@entrepreneurfund.org
Web site: www.entrepreneurfund.org

The Women's Business Network serves women entrepreneurs, actual and potential, in eight counties in northeast Minnesota—Aitkin, Carlton, Cook, Itasca, Koochiching, Lake, Pine, and St. Louis counties—and Douglas County in northwest Wisconsin. Its purpose is to help women in the region start, stabilize, or expand their small businesses; identify and address barriers for women who own businesses; raise public awareness of women entrepreneurs; and advocate for women who own businesses.

Missouri

Missouri Women's Business Center
Lori Kravets
Growth Opportunity (GO) Connection, Inc.
4747 Troost Avenue
Kansas City, MO 64110
Phone: (816) 235-6146
Fax: (816) 235-6177
E-mail: lkravets@missouriwbc.com
Web site: www.missouriwbc.com

The Missouri Women's Business Center is a program of GO Connection. It provides business education, advising, access to capital, and mentoring programs for women entrepreneurs. Its mission is to help women build financially sound businesses across each stage of development—start-up, management, and expansion.

Missouri

Women's Business Center
Kendra Martin, Project Director
Grace Hill
2324 N. Florissant Avenue
St. Louis, MO 63106
Phone: (314) 539-9663
Fax: (314) 539-9666
E-mail: kendram@gracehill.org
Web site: www.gracehill.org

The Center serves St. Louis and three counties. The WBC strives to be a centralized service stop for women, mainly African-American, to start or expand their small businesses. Long-term training for start-up and business expansion is provided in cooperation with the local Small Business Development Center (SBDC). In addition, the Center offers one-on-one counseling, marketing and procurement assistance, computer training, loan packaging, and micro-lending. A focal part of the center is outreach and marketing primarily to low- and moderate-income women who are socially and/or economically disadvantaged.

Mississippi

WBC Training and Technical Assistance Program
William Brown, Project Director
Mississippi Action for Community Education Inc.
119 South Theobald Street
Greenville, MS 38701
Phone: (662) 335-3523
Fax: (662) 334-2939
E-mail: mace@tecinfo.com
Web site: www.deltamace.org

Mississippi Action for Community Education Inc. (MACE) administers the Mississippi Women's Business Center. MACE targets disadvantaged persons and under-served communities. The goal of the Women's Business Center is consistent with the organization's mission: "Helping people to help themselves." The WBC educates women on all aspects of business development, including principles of business management, social responsibility, and building wealth consistent with the cultural dynamics of the Delta.

Montana

Business Resource Center (BRC)
Joe Bower, Director
Career Training Institute
347 North Last Chance Gulch
Helena, MT 59601
Phone: (406) 443-0800, (800) 254-6607
Fax: (406) 442-2745

E-mail: jbower@ctibrc.org
Web site: www.ctibrc.org

The Business Resource Center (BRC) provides financial, management, and marketing assistance to new and existing business owners with a focus on women and minorities. The BRC partners with professionals to provide various classes and workshops in the following areas: QuickBooks Pro, marketing, financial, business plan writing, entrepreneurial, government procurement, minority and women business development, and exporting business opportunities. Business planning, consulting, and one-on-one technical assistance are provided at no cost. The BRC works with local lenders to assist loan applications in complying with commercial lending requirements.

Montana

Blackfeet Women's Business Center
Marilyn Parsons, Project Director
Quarters 108 East Government Square
Browning, MT 59417
Phone: (406) 338-7406
Fax: (406) 338-7206
E-mail: info@blackfeetwbc.org
Web site: www.blackfeetwbc.org

The Blackfeet Women's Business Center (BWBC) provides training, counseling, and technical assistance in the areas of finance, management, procurement, and marketing. Although called a "women's center," services are available to all socially and economically disadvantaged persons.

Nebraska

Rural Enterprise Assistance Project (REAP)
Glennis McClure, WBC Director
145 Main Street
P.O. Box 136
Lyons, NE 68038-0136
Phone: (402) 687-2100
Fax: (402) 687-2200
E-mail: reapinfo@cfra.org
Web site: www.cfra.org/reap/womens_business_center.htm

Nebraska's Women's Business Center utilizes the REAP program infrastructure to deliver services to existing and start-up self-employed women across rural Nebraska and is a project of the Center for Rural Affairs. The Center helps rural women in Nebraska through basic business plan training, e-commerce training, one-on-one technical assistance, business plan counseling, networking opportunities, and micro-loans for small businesses that qualify. The WBC service center is "a center without walls." REAP delivers the WBC services across the state with business specialists located throughout Nebraska to provide necessary services to rural small businesses.

Nevada

Nevada Microenterprise Initiative
1600 E. Desert Inn Road, Suite 210
Las Vegas, NV 89109
Phone: (702) 734-3555
Fax: (702) 734-3530
E-mail: info@4microbiz.org
Web site: www.4microbiz.org

They strive to enhance the economic self-sufficiency and quality of life of low- to moderate-income individuals through entrepreneurial training, technical assistance, and access to loans for new and expanding businesses throughout Nevada.

New Hampshire

Women's Business Center, Inc.
Ellen Fineberg, Executive Director
1555 Lafayette Road, 2nd Floor
Portsmouth, NH 03801
Phone: (603) 430-2892
Fax: (603) 430-3706
E-mail: info@womenbiz.org
Web site: www.womenbiz.org

The Women's Business Center, a New Hampshire-based nonprofit, promotes women's business ownership as a means to maximize personal potential and achieve economic independence. It supports entrepreneurial women as they begin and grow their businesses, offering programs and services across southeastern New Hampshire, northern Massachusetts, and southern Maine. The WBC provides educational programming, advocacy, networking, counseling, and mentorship. It provides access to information, networking, and skill development opportunities.

New Jersey

Women's Business Center
Penni Nafus, Project Director
NJ Association of Women Business Owners
White Horse Commercial Park
127 US Highway 206 South, Suite 28
Hamilton, NJ 08610
Phone: (609) 581-2220
Fax: (609) 581-6749
E-mail: wbcnj@njawbo.org
Web site: www.njawbo.org/html/wbc.html

NJAWBO's Women's Business Center of New Jersey positions women business owners for success through education, consulting, resources, and entrepreneurial training.

New Mexico

Women's Economic Self-Sufficiency Team (WESST) Corp.

Albuquerque

700 4th Street, SW
Albuquerque, NM 87102
Phone: (505) 241-0794, (800) GO WESST (469-3778)
Fax: (505) 241-0707
E-mail: albuquerque@wesst.org
Web site: www.wesst.org

Gallup

107 South First Street
Gallup, NM 87301
Phone: (505) 863-3192, (800) GO WESST (469-3778)
Fax: (505) 863-2157
E-mail: gallup@wesst.org
Web site: www.wesst.org

Las Cruces

2907 East Idaho, Suite A
Las Cruces, NM 88011
P.O. Box 444

Las Cruces, NM 88004
Phone: (505) 541-1583, (800) GO WESST (469-3778)
Fax: (505) 647-5524
E-mail: lacruces@wesst.org
Web site: www.wesst.org

Roswell

200 West First Street, Suite 527
Roswell, NM 88203
Phone: (505) 624-9850, (800) GO WESST (469-3778)
Fax: (505) 624-9845
E-mail: roswell@wesst.org
Web site: www.wesst.org

Santa Fe

3900 Paseo de Sol, Suite 322A, Building I
Santa Fe, NM 87507
Phone: (505) 474-6556, (800) GO WESST (469-3778)
Fax: (505) 474-6687
E-mail: santafe@wesst.org
Web site: www.wesst.org

The Women's Economic Self-Sufficiency Team centers assist low-income and minority women throughout New Mexico, typically with long-term training and technical assistance. The centers serve both start-up and expanding businesses and provide training and counseling in both English and Spanish. Counseling and mentoring are offered through professional volunteers, including attorneys, accountants, insurance agents, and benefits counselors. WESST Corp. trainers often travel to clients' businesses. WESST Corp. has the only SBA Microloan Program in New Mexico and is an SBA Loan Prequalification Program intermediary.

New York

Women's Venture Fund, Inc.
240 West 35th Street, Suite 501
Manhattan, NY 10001
Phone: (212) 563-0499
Fax: (212) 868-9116
E-mail: info@wvf-ny.org
Web site: www.womensventurefund.org

The Women's Venture Fund, Inc. is a non-profit organization that targets women entrepreneurs in under-served urban communities. As a multi-service micro-lender, the Women's Venture Fund, Inc. assists these entrepreneurs in pursuing their business aspirations, thereby benefiting themselves, their families and their communities. Unique among micro-lenders, the Women's Venture Fund, Inc. builds on the life experience of each client to develop her self-confidence, expand her understanding of business opportunities, and provide the skills, training, and resources to assume ownership of progressively more complex enterprises

New York
Women's Business Center
Ojeda Hall-Phillips, Director
The Local Development Corporation of East New York
80 Jamaica Avenue, 3rd Floor
Brooklyn, NY 11207
Phone: (718) 385-6700 x 107
Fax: (718) 385-7505
E-mail: ny_wbc@hotmail.com
Web site: www.ldceny.org/ldceny/women.htm

The mission of the Center is to build the wealth and health of the Brooklyn Community through sustainable women's entrepreneurship. The Center addresses the unique issues women face in starting and growing businesses. It provides education, advocacy, and mentoring to current and aspiring women business owners to help them start up and expand their businesses, with special emphasis on underserved African-American and Latina women in Brooklyn.

New York
Women's Entrepreneurial Business Center
ComLinks Community Action Agency
343 West Main Street
Malone, NY 12953
Phone: (518) 483-1261 x 18
Fax: (518) 483-8599
E-mail: info@comlinkscaa.org
Web site: www.comlinkscaa.net/webc/webc.html

The WEBC provides business counseling and technical assistance and training to current and prospective businesses owned and controlled by women. However, the WEBC is not discriminatory and also assists current and prospective male business owners. The WEBC strives to aid women who are socially and economically disadvantaged, of low income (such as women on welfare attempting to become self-sufficient), women whose businesses are located in areas of high unemployment or low income, and prospective business owners.

New York
Women's Business Center
Melinda Sanderson, Executive Director
Canisius College
2365 Main Street
Buffalo, NY 14214
Phone: (716) 888-6650
Fax: (716) 888-6654
E-mail: wbcinfo@canisius.edu
Web site: www.canisius.edu/wbc

The Women's Business Center, a collaborative effort between the Small Business Administration and Canisius College, provides a three-pronged approach to supporting and promoting the success of entrepreneurs and small business owners: training, counseling, and mentoring.

New York
Business Outreach Center Network
Nancy Carin, Executive Director
85 South Oxford Street, 2nd Floor
Brooklyn, NY 11217
Phone: (718) 624-9115
Fax: (718) 246-1881
E-mail: info@bocnet.org
Web site: www.bocnet.org

The Business Outreach Center (BOC) Network is a micro-enterprise/small business development organization that delivers customized business services to underserved entrepreneurs in New York City and Newark, New Jersey, as well as capacity-building services to organizations establishing and operating community and micro-enterprise development programs.

New York
Queens Women's Business Center
Elizabeth Perdomo, Acting Director
Queens Economic Development Corporation
120-55 Queens Boulevard, Suite 309
Kew Gardens, NY 11424
Phone: (718) 263-0546
Fax: (718) 263-0594
E-mail: epd@queensny.org
Web site: www.queenswomen.org/index.php

The mission of Queens Women's Business Center is to foster the growth of women's business ownership in Queens by providing the necessary assistance, targeted resources, and an effective support system in a nurturing environment.

New York
Women's Enterprise Development Center, Inc.
Julie Cantor Peskoe, Associate Director
707 Westchester Avenue, Suite 213
White Plains, NY 10604
Phone: (914) 948-6098
E-mail: jpeskoe@westchester.org
Web site: www.wedc-westchester.org/

WEDC is dedicated to helping women achieve economic self-sufficiency through entrepreneurship in Westchester County and the Lower Hudson Valley. Its core entrepreneurial training program consists of a 15-week course on starting a small business. Classes are offered in English and Spanish. WEDC also provides training and technical assistance to women wishing to expand their businesses through special workshops on topics such as certifying your business; marketing strategies, advanced business planning, and networking events.

New York
Women's Business Resource Center
866 C Hunts Point Avenue
Bronx, NY 10474
Phone: (718) 842-8888
Fax: (718) 620-1153

E-mail: info@hpwbrc.org
Web site: www.hpwbrc.org

The Women's Business Resource Center is a partnership between the Hunts Point Economic Development Corporation and the U.S. Small Business Administration (SBA). The mission of the center is to empower individuals by assisting them to become economically independent through self-employment. It assists women and minorities who own or aspire to own a business in or around the Bronx, to gain the tools, resources, and confidence in order to succeed. It primarily focuses on assisting Latina women.

New York
Women's Business Center of New York State
Donna L. Rebisz, Project Director
200 Genesee Street
Utica, NY 13502
Phone: (315) 733-9848, (877) 844-9848
Fax: (315) 733-0247
E-mail: nywbc@aol.com
Web site: www.nywbc.org

The WBC is dedicated to training and assisting women in business or those who want to start up a business. This Center provides a variety of business skills and ongoing technical assistance to women in 34 counties.

North Carolina
The Women's Center of Fayetteville
Judi Superak, Director
230 Hay Street
Fayetteville, NC 28301
Phone: (910) 323-3377
Fax: (910) 323-8828
E-mail: wcofinfo@wcof.org
Web site: www.wcof.org

The Women's Center of Fayetteville is a non-profit organization that serves as a multi-service resource and advocacy Center, dedicated to helping women and men help themselves through its programs and services. Its mission is to promote growth, productiveness, and well-being through peer counseling, education, information, and advocacy programs. The

Women's Center works with other community agencies to achieve this goal.

North Carolina

Women's Business Center of Western North Carolina
Sharon Oxendine, Director
Mountain Microenterprise Fund, Inc.
29 1/2 Page Avenue
Ashville, NC 28801
Phone: (828) 253-2834, (888) 389-3089 (toll-free)
Fax: (828) 255-7953
E-mail: info@mtnmicro.org
Web site:
www.mtnmicro.org/pages/sba_wbc.html

The Women's Business Center of Western North Carolina, housed at Mountain Microenterprise Fund, is part of the U.S. Small Business Administration's Women's Business Center Program. The WBC provides programs and services that assist entrepreneurs by developing their business skills and encouraging the exchange of information. The WBC offers one-to-one consulting, mentoring, and networking opportunities with other area entrepreneurs and workshops that provide information on the latest topics affecting business owners at every stage of business ownership.

North Carolina

Women's Business Center of North Carolina
Verona P. Edmond, Director
North Carolina Institute of Minority Economic Development
114 West Parrish Street
P.O. Box 1331
Durham, NC 27701
Phone: (919) 956-8889
Fax: (919) 688-4358
E-mail: vedmond@ncimed.com
Web site: www.ncimed.com/wbc

The Women's Business Center of North Carolina (WBC) is a partnership program between the North Carolina Institute of Minority Economic Development and the U. S.

Small Business Administration. The center's mission is to promote economic self-sufficiency for all women of North Carolina through entrepreneurship. The Women's Business Center provides tools and opportunities to help women entrepreneurs achieve their goals. The WBC provides one-on-one counseling, workshops and seminars, business plan development assistance, networking opportunities, and financing assistance.

North Dakota

North Dakota's Women's Business Center
The Center for Technology and Business/Women and Technology
Tara Holt, Director
115 N 2nd Street
Bismarck, ND 58502
P.O. Box 2535
Bismarck, ND 58501-2535
Phone: (701) 223-0707
Fax: (701) 223-2507
E-mail: holt@trainingnd.com
Web site: www.trainingnd.com

The Center provides technology and business education, women-owned business certification, and business assistance and counseling.

Ohio

Cincinnati Business Incubator
1634 Central Parkway
Cincinnati, OH 45202
Phone: (513) 362-2700
Fax: (513) 784-0812
E-mail: info@cbincubator.org
Web site: www.cbincubator.org

Organized in 1989 as the Cincinnati Minority and Female Business Incubator, Cincinnati Business Incubator focuses on the needs of small minority- and women-owned businesses in what is now known as Cincinnati's Empowerment Zone. It provides training, technical assistance, office space, and financial and administrative support, particularly for women and minorities who own small businesses or are starting businesses.

Ohio

Alex Community Development Corporation
Ms. Alexis E. Afzal, CPA, Director
12200 Fairhill Road, 4th Floor
Cleveland, OH 44120
Phone: (216) 707-0777
Fax: (216) 707-0007
E-mail: wbc.alexcdc@sbcglobal.net
Web site: N/A

The Alex Community Development Corporation (Alex CDC) serves small business owners in Cleveland and Cuyahoga County, with a special emphasis on women starting businesses and women looking to grow their businesses. Alex CDC provides training courses, counseling and mentoring, technical assistance, and networking events.

Ohio

Women's Business Center
Ohio Women's Business Resource Network
1393 E. Broad Street, 2nd Floor
Columbus, OH 43205
Phone: (614) 258-4811
Fax: (614) 258-4813
E-mail: info@owbrn.org
Web site: www.owbrn.org

The Center helps women who own businesses with information, business counseling, long-term training, workshops and seminars, strategic business planning, loan packaging, market planning, capital development, and access to SBA programs.

Oklahoma

Women's Business Center
Anne Coleman, Program Director
Institution Programs, Inc.
2709 West I-44 Service Road
Oklahoma City, OK 73112
Phone: (405) 601-1930
Fax: (405) 601-1935
E-mail: N/A
Web site: N/A

The I.P.I. Women's Business Center, operating under the name of the Terry Neese Center for Entrepreneurial Excellence, is a business development center staffed exclusively by entrepreneurs who either currently own a small business or have owned businesses in the past. The staff counsels, free of charge, entrepreneurs wanting to start a business or attempting to expand a business.

Oklahoma

Rural Women's Business Center
Rural Enterprises of Oklahoma, Inc. (REO)
Barbara Rackley, Coordinator
P.O. Box 1335
Durant, OK 74702
Phone: (580) 924-5094, (800) 658-2823
Fax: (580) 920-2745
E-mail: barbara@ruralenterprises.com
Web site: www.rei-rwbc.com

The Rural Women's Business Center is a cooperative agreement between SBA and Rural Enterprises of Oklahoma, Inc. serving women entrepreneurs in the 21 counties of southeastern Oklahoma. The RWBC is committed to assisting rural Oklahoma's enterprising women explore the opportunities of starting a business or expanding and improving an existing business by providing business, technical, and financial assistance.

Oklahoma

Women's Business Center
Betty Olivas, Program Director
Oklahomans for Indian Opportunity (OIO)
3001 South Berry Road, Suite B
Norman, OK 73072
Phone: (405) 329-3737
Fax: (405) 329-8488

The OIO Women's Business Center offers services statewide, with the exception of Oklahoma City. The center provides counseling and technical assistance in all areas pertinent for start-ups and business expansions. The center is an SBA loan prequalification intermediary and offers guidance in loan packaging and makes referrals to SBA lenders. The center's main office is in Norman and has office hours on certain days in the following areas: Durant, Broken Bow, Tahlequah, Lawton, Anadarko, Clinton, El Reno, Pawnee, Ponca City, and Kaw City. Business training is provided in all the locations.

Oregon

ONABEN – A Native American Business Network
Tom Hampson, Executive Director
11825 SW Greenburg Road, Suite B-3
Tigard, OR 97223
Phone: (503) 968-1500, (800) 854-8289
Fax: (503) 968-1548
E-mail: selena@onaben.org, kristi@onaben.org
Web site: www.onaben.org

ONABEN is a nonprofit public-benefit corporation created by Northwest Indian tribes to increase the number and profitability of private enterprises owned by Native Americans. ONABEN offers training, individual counseling, assisted access to markets, and facilitated access to capital for its clients.

Oregon

SOWAC Microenterprise Development Center
33 North Central, Suite 211
Medford, OR 97501
Phone: (541) 779-3992, (866) 608-6094 (toll-free)
Fax: (541) 779-5195
E-mail: sowac@sowac.org
Web site: www.sowac.org

SOWAC Microenterprise Development Center promotes economic development by providing hands-on assistance to help start or expand businesses, through classes, training workshops, roundtable discussion groups, counseling, and loan assistance programs. SOWAC assists entrepreneurs in developing business plans, obtaining financing, and marketing their business throughout Jackson, Josephine, Klamath, and Lake counties.

Pennsylvania

Women's Business Development Center (WBDC)

Sandy Merry, Program Manager
1315 Walnut Street, Suite 1116
Philadelphia, PA 19107-4711
Phone: (215) 790-WBDC (9232)
Fax: (215) 790-9231
E-mail: info@womensbdc.org
Web site: www.womensbdc.org

The Women's Business Development Center fosters business development and business retention. The center enables women to launch new businesses and to run their businesses more successfully. WBDC offers startup, emerging, and established entrepreneurs a unique continuum of supportive services, including planning; entrepreneurial training; individualized business consulting in management, marketing, and financial matters; loan packaging; and procurement and certification assistance.

Pennsylvania

Pennsylvania Women's Business Center
Joan M. Brodhead, Project Director
Community First Fund
30 West Orange Street
P.O. Box 524
Lancaster, PA 17608-0524
Phone: (717) 393-2351, (866) 822-3863 (toll-free)
Fax: (717) 290-7936
E-mail: jbrodhead@pawomensbusinesscenter.com
Web site: www.pawomensbusinesscenter.com

Pennsylvania Women's Business Center, a division of Community First Fund, provides training, consultation, loan capital, and advocacy support to small business enterprises. The goal of the center is to develop more knowledgeable, better prepared business owners. Pennsylvania Women's Business Center offers services in multiple counties with offices in Lancaster, Harrisburg, Reading, and York.

Rhode Island

Center for Women and Enterprise, Inc.
Carol Malysz, Director
132 George M. Cohan Boulevard, 2nd Floor

Providence, RI 02903
Phone: (401) 277-0800
Fax: (401) 277-1122
E-mail: cmalysz@cweprovidence.org
Web site: www.cweonline.org

CWE is a non-profit organization dedicated to helping women start and grow their own businesses. It offers education, training, technical assistance, women's business enterprise certification, and access to both debt and equity capital to entrepreneurs at every stage of business development.

South Carolina

South Carolina Women's Business Center
Haidee Clark Stith, Project Director
South Carolina Manufacturing Extension Partnership
817 Calhoun Street
Columbia, SC 29201
Phone: (803) 461-8900
Fax: (803) 254-8512
E-mail: hstith@scmep.org
Web site: www.scwbc.org

The South Carolina Women's Business Center is supported through the South Carolina Manufacturing Extension Partnership (SCMEP). The SCMEP's mission is to help small to mid-sized manufacturers become more competitive and productive. The WBC offers business development resources for women entrepreneurs throughout the state. The program's services are targeted to support women in manufacturing, including women-owned and managed manufacturers and professional women who seek training and resources to become more effective and successful. Through partnerships with the SBA, the Service Corps of Retired Executives (SCORE), and two universities, the Center offers a variety of training, professional development, and consulting services.

South Dakota

Center for Women Business Institute
Tricia Cole, Director
1101 W. 22nd Street
Sioux Falls, SD 57105

Phone: (605) 331-5000, (800) 888-1047
Fax: (605) 331-6574
E-mail: centerforwomen@usiouxfalls.edu
Web site: www.usiouxfalls.edu/professional-studies/cfw/business/cfw_business.htm

The Center for Women Business Institute provides business counseling, education and training services, and mentoring programs for women in business. In addition, the Center focuses on statewide representation to promote economic development opportunities for women via small business ownership.

Tennessee

National Association of Women Business Owners
Nashville Chapter
P. O. Box 292283
Nashville, TN 37229-2283
Phone: (615) 664-6884
Fax: (615) 256-2706
E-mail: info@ nashvillenawbo.com
Web site: www.nashvillenawbo.com

Nashville NAWBO is an organization that informs, empowers, and promotes women business owners and invites its members to impact the social, political, and economic communities. Its mission is to strengthen the wealth-creating capacity of its members and promote economic development; create innovative and effective changes in the business culture; build strategic alliances, coalitions, and affiliations; and transform public policy and influence opinion makers.

Tennessee

Southeast Women's Business Center
Sandi Brock, Program Director
535 Chestnut Street
Chattanooga, TN 37402
P.O. Box 4757
Chattanooga, TN 37405
Phone: (423) 266-5781
Fax: (423) 267-7705
E-mail: sbrock@sedev.org
Web site: www.sewbc.com

The Southeast Women's Business Center is designed to be a resource for women entrepreneurs to assist with the unique issues they face in starting and growing a business. It assists with all aspects of starting and growing a successful business. The primary focus is to provide services to rural areas throughout the Tennessee River Valley region, including northern Georgia and southwest North Carolina. The Center provides a large range of services, including individual counseling, group training, and access to U.S. Small Business Administration programs such as lending.

Texas

Fort Worth Women's Business Center
1150 South Freeway
Fort Worth, TX 76104
Phone: (817) 871-6025, (817)871-6001
Fax: (817) 871-6031
E-mail: administrativeassistant@fwbac.com
Web site: www.fwbac.com/WBC/index.asp

The Women's Business Center is dedicated to offering women who want to start a business in Fort Worth or Dallas a place to get the help they need to make their businesses successful. It offers free business counseling and mentoring as well as educational workshops in the areas of financing a business, technology, certification, and more.

Texas

Business Investment Growth, Inc. (BiG AUSTIN)
1050 E. 11th Street, Suite 350
Austin, TX 78702
Phone: (512) 928-8010
Fax: (512) 926-2997
E-mail: info@bigaustin.org
Web site: www.bigaustin.org/womens_business_center.htm

BiG AUSTIN's Women's Business Center provides the necessary tools and the unique services required for women to start, grow, and fund their businesses through training, one-on-one counseling, effective roundtable discussions, innovative networking opportunities, and lending programs.

Texas

Women's Business Border Center
Terri Reed, Director
201 E. Main Street, Suite 100
El Paso, TX 79901
Phone: (915) 566-4066
Fax: (915) 566-9714
E-mail: treed@ephcc.org
Web site: www.womenbordercenter.com

The Women's Business Border Center is co-located with the El Paso Hispanic Chamber of Commerce. The WBBC is partially funded by the United States Small Business Administration Office of Women's Business Ownership. It helps women establish businesses, access and develop new markets, master the internet, stabilize their companies, generate sustainable profits, strategize for the future, create jobs, and contribute to the growth and economic development of local businesses owned by women.

Texas

Women's Business Center
Southwest Community Investment Corporation
Nancy Cuellar, Director
2507 Buddy Owens
McAllen, Texas 78504
Phone: (956) 661-6560
Fax: (956) 661-6566
E-mail: cuellarn@scictx.org
Web site: www.scictx.org

The Women's Business Center works in partnership with the Southwest Community Investment Corporation and the Small Business Administration in order to provide business consulting, mentoring, and training opportunities for women entrepreneurs.

Utah

Women's Business Center
Nancy Mitchell, Executive Director
238 South Main Street
Salt Lake City, UT 84111
Phone: (801) 328-5075
Fax: (801) 328-5098
E-mail: nmitchell@saltlakechamber.org

Web site: www.saltlakechamber.org/chamber_info/womens_business/index.htm

The Center is a public/private partnership between the Small Business Administration's Office of Women's Business Ownership and the Salt Lake Chamber of Commerce. It serves aspiring and existing business owners throughout Utah. Through the center's partnership with the chamber, the staff women who own businesses to enter mainstream business and chamber activities. The Center provides counseling, training, networking and mentoring opportunities, business-plan writing, and loan packaging for both women and men. In addition, assistance with marketing, management, finance, technology, and government contracting is available.

Virginia

New Visions, New Ventures, Inc.
Jennifer Pierce, Director Development
801 East Main Street, Suite 1102
Richmond, VA 23219
Phone: (804) 643-1081
Fax: (804) 643-1085
E-mail: programinfo@nvnv.org
Web site: www.nvnv.org/businesscenter.html

The Women's Business Center at New Visions, New Ventures offers programs and other services to entrepreneurs who want to start, strengthen, or expand home-based or small businesses. Services include training, business counseling, access to capital, mentoring and networking, and computer and internet access.

Virginia

Women's Business Center of Northern Virginia
Barbara Wrigley, Executive Director
7001 Loisdale Road, Suite C
Springfield, VA 22150
Phone: (703) 778-9WBC (9922)
Fax: (703) 768-0547
E-mail: info@wbcnova.org
Web site: www.wbcnova.org

The Women's Business Center of Northern Virginia is a program of the Community

Business Partnership, Inc., funded to help any woman in the Northern Virginia area who is interested in starting a business or expanding her small business. It offers free and low-cost training programs, free one-on-one technical counseling, marketing assistance, access to those who can make loans, help in getting special certifications to do business with all levels of government, a resource library, computers and Internet access, and more.

Vermont

Vermont's Women's Business Center
Linda Ingold, Director
660 Elm Street
Montpelier, VT 05602
Phone: (802) 229-2181, (800) 266-4062 (toll-free)
Fax: (802) 229-2141
E-mail: lingold@cvcac.org
Web site: www.vwbc.org

The Vermont Women's Business Center offers entrepreneurial counseling, technical training, and networking opportunities statewide for women of all economic levels. Working with providers throughout the state, it provides resources and referral services for women at all stages of small business development paying particular attention to assistance with writing business plans and ongoing support for women already in business.

Washington

Northwest Washington Women's Business Center
c/o Greater Marysville Tulalip Chamber
8825 34th Ave NE, Suite C
Marysville, WA 98271
Phone: (425) 954-4040
Fax: (425) 745-5563
E-mail: info@nwwbc.org
Web site: www.nwwbc.org

The Women's Business Center was established by the Community Capital Development and the Small Business Administration to provide women entrepreneurs in Snohomish, Skagit,

Whatcom, Island, San Juan, and Kitsap counties entrepreneurial training and business counseling. It also runs programs that serve the Latino business community, Native American entrepreneurs, and rural business owners.

Washington
Women's Business Center
Community Capital Development Program
1437 South Jackson Street, Suite 302
P.O. Box 22283
Seattle, WA 98144
Phone: (206) 325-9458, (206) 324-4330 x 100
Fax: (206) 325-4322
E-mail: info@seattleccd.com
Web site: www.seattleccd.com/wbc/index.htm

The Women's Business Center, part of Community Capital Development, helps women succeed in business by providing them with training, counseling, and mentoring. The primary focus is to foster entrepreneurial women; however, the Center works with any entrepreneur who would like to start a business or who has recently started one.

Washington
Inland Northwest Women's Business Center
827 W. First Street, Suite 121
Spokane, WA 99201
Phone: (509) 747-2821
Fax: (509) 744-1120
E-mail: info@inwbc.org
Web site: www.inwbc.org

Founded by The Inland Northwest Community Access Network and partially funded by the Small Business Administration, the WBC offers five core services: free business counseling for those who have a business idea, who are launching a business, or who are established in business and want to tap into the next level of success; ongoing workshops on various topics; use of the SAFECO computer lab in the Center; basic web design and web hosting for a reduced fee; and open access to the WBC resource center.

Wisconsin
Wisconsin Women's Business Initiative Corporation
Wendy K. Werkmeister, President
Milwaukee
2745 North Dr. Martin Luther King Jr. Drive
Milwaukee, WI 53212
Phone: (414) 263-5450
Fax: (414) 263-5456
Madison
South Central Region Office
2300 S. Park Street
Madison, WI 53713
Phone: (608) 257-5450
Fax: (608) 257-5454
E-mail: info@wwbic.com
Web site: www.wwbic.com

The Wisconsin Women's Business Initiative Corporation (WWBIC) is a nonprofit economic development corporation providing business education, classes, one-on-one assistance, and access to capital. It focuses on women, low-income individuals, and people of color. WWBIC provides more than 300 training sessions on various business topics throughout the state. It is the state's largest microlender and a Certified Community Development Financial Institution (CDFI).

Wisconsin
Western Dairyland Women's Business Center
Eau Claire
418 Wisconsin Street
Eau Claire, WI 54701
P.O. Box 540
Eau Claire, WI 54702-0540
Phone: (715) 836-7511
Fax: (715) 836-7580
Independence
23122 Whitehall Road
P.O. Box 125
Independence, WI 54747
Phone: (715) 985-2391, (800) 782-1063
Fax: (715) 985-3239
E-mail: info@ successfulbusiness.org
Web site: www.successfulbusiness.org

The Women's Business Center (WBC) specializes in providing services to assist women entrepreneurs. Special efforts are made to assist economically and socially disadvantaged women. It provides intensive group and one-on-one business training and technical assistance that helps women grow their business ideas and develop business management skills. The Center's primary service area is Buffalo, Eau Claire, Jackson, and Trempeleau counties in Western Wisconsin.

West Virginia

Women's Business Center
Region 1 Workforce Investment Board, Work 4WV Region 1, Inc.
Tara Elder, Project Director
201 Grey Flats Road, 2nd Floor
Beckley, WV 25801
Phone: (800) 766-4556 or (304) 255-4022
Fax: (304) 252-9584
E-mail: telder@r1workforcewv.org

The Region 1 WorkForce Women's Business Center nurtures the spirit of women to lead, learn, and become business leaders. Through one-to-one counseling, peer mentoring, and step-by-step training, the Region 1 WBC prepares women of all socioeconomic levels to make educated informed decisions about pursuing the dream of business ownership. Training consists of orientations, first steps, a business plan writing course, a marketing series, a human resource series, and more.

Wyoming

Wyoming Women's Business Center
P.O. Box 764
Laramie, WY 82073
University of Wyoming Campus
Education Annex Building, Rooms 155 and 158
13th and Lewis Streets
Laramie, WY 82071
Phone: (307) 766-3084, (888) 524-1947 (toll-free within WY)
Fax: (307) 766-3085
E-mail: wwbc@uwyo.edu
Web site: www.wyomingwomen.org

The Wyoming Women's Business Center strives to advance financial self-sufficiency by promoting economic justice and equality throughout Wyoming. The Center promotes economic independence through successful business ownership. As Wyoming's only SBA Intermediary lender, the WWBC provides access to capital, training and technical assistance, and statewide networking opportunities to women, people of color, and low-income individuals.

10 Venture Capital Firms for Woman Entrepreneurs

1. Capital Across America
414 Union Street, Suite 2025
Nashville, TN 37219
Phone: (615) 254-1515
Fax: (615) 254-1856
Web site: www.capitalacrossamerica.org

2. The Capital Fund for Entrepreneurs, Inc.
c/o KCSourceLink
4747 Troost Avenue
Kansas City, MO 64110
Phone: (816) 561-4646, (816) 235-6500
Fax: (816) 235-6590
Web site: www.kcsourcelink.com

3. Isabella Capital
312 Walnut Street #3540
Cincinnati, OH 45202
Phone: (513) 721-7110
Fax: (513) 721-7115
Web site: www.fundisabella.com

4. Inroads Capital Partners
1603 Orrington Avenue, #2050
Evanston, IL 60201
Phone: (847) 864-2000
Fax: (847) 864-9692
Web site: www.inroadsvc.com

5. New Vista Capital
161 East Evelyn Avenue
Mountain View, CA 94041
Phone: (650) 864-2553
Fax: (650) 864-2599
Web site: www.nvcap.com

6. Telecommunications Development Fund
1850 K Street, NW, Suite 1075

Washington, DC 20006
Phone: (202) 293-8840
Fax: (202) 293-8850
Web site: www.tdfund.com

7. Viridian Capital
220 Montgomery Street, #946
San Francisco, CA 94101
Phone: (415) 391-8937
Fax: (415) 391-8937
Web site: viridiancapital.com

8. Wired Partners
8447 Ridge Road
Medina, WA 98039
Phone: (425) 709-7137
Fax: (425) 709-6886
E-mail: reneed@oz.net
Web site: N/A

9. Women First Capital Fund
P.O. Box 7505
Portland, ME 04112
Phone: (207) 828-1077
E-mail: N/A
Web site: N/A

10. Women's Fund Capital Growth
1054 31 Street, NW
Washington, DC 20007
Phone: (202) 342-1431
Fax: (202) 342-1203
Web site: www.wgcf.com

Source: Profit Dynamics Inc., "Resources for Women Entrepreneurs," www.capital-connection.com/womenvcs.html.

Helpful Business Resources for Women and Minorities

Advancing Women

Featuring a Business Center with articles and business resources as well as a section on workplace issues concerning women, this site is designed to give you all the basics of starting and running a business.
www.advancingwomen.com

Business and Professional Women's Foundations

The BPW Foundation's mission is to empower working women to achieve their full potential and to partner with employers to build successful workplaces. The BPW Foundation is supported by foundations, corporations, BPW/USA members, and other individuals who share a common belief in equity for working women.
www.bpwusa.org

Catalyst

Catalyst is the leading research and advisory organization working with businesses and the professions to build inclusive environments and expand opportunities for women at work. As an independent, nonprofit membership organization, Catalyst conducts research on all aspects of women's career advancement and provides strategic and web-based consulting services globally. With the support and confidence of member corporations and firms, Catalyst remains connected to business and its changing needs.
www.catalystwomen.org

Center for Women's Business Research

The premier source of information, research, and resources for women entrepreneurs. Access leadership development resources to grow your business as well as marketing advice and consulting services to help you reach women-owned businesses.
www.womensbusinessresearch.org

SBA's Online Women's Business Center

Practical information for women entrepreneurs. Get tips on starting, financing, and running your business. Get a list of SBA Women's Business Centers around the country.
www.onlinewbc.gov

Springboard Enterprises: Women's Capital Connection

Great tips for those seeking financing. This nonprofit organization is dedicated to increasing women's participation in financial markets as investors and as entrepreneurs.
www.springboardenterprises.org

Women's Business Enterprise National Council

Get certified as a woman-owned business here.
www.wbenc.org

WomenBiz.gov

For certified women-owned businesses, stop here to find out how to bid on a government contract.
www.womenbiz.gov

Digital Woman

Digital Women® provides an international online community for women in business, businesswomen, and all women around the world. Inside you will find free business resources and tools including information about grants for women, loans for women, payday loans, cash advance loans, free business tips, work-at-home business ideas, free marketing and sales tips, how to write a mission statement, free daily planner, how-to business articles for women, and an opportunity to join and promote your business right here.
www.digital-women.com

Motivation Zone

Helps women who are interested in a career in business. Gives them motivational goals and helps with career choices.
www.motivationzone.com

Franchise Woman

Franchisewoman.com recognizes the fast and powerful growth of women-owned businesses and has been established to propel this women's "franchise building" economy forward even further. We are committed to finding the right "franchise fit" for both dealers and franchisees. Franchisewoman.com provides information on resources and a franchise directory of companies specifically targeting women entrepreneurs.

www.franchisewoman.com

U.S. Women's Chamber of Commerce

The U.S. Women's Chamber of Commerce™ has established a new generation of leadership for women. To take that last great step that transforms women from "influenced" to "influential," the USWCC is implementing important strategic shifts, focusing on targeted issues, providing education and access, and creating strong connections and advocacy.

www.sblink.us/html/uswcc-main.aspx

The Women's News

This web site keeps women informed with what kind of policies and trends that are arising in the U.S. small business or corporate sector. They also explore other areas or interest such as health, leisure, and world events.

www.thewomensnews.com

Women's Calendar

This is a place to post or view events that are happening for women.

www.womenscalendar.org

Womans-Net

An online networking community for woman in business, Womans-Net strives to offer the highest quality products and services on the market today. Since May 2000, we have provided superior service to our customers and have assisted them in achieving their work-at-home goals.

womans-net.com

Women's Business Development Center

The Women's Business Development Center (WBDC) has offered a full-service approach to launching emerging businesses and strengthening existing businesses owned by women in the Chicago area. Since inception, the WBDC has been on the forefront of economic development policy and program development to strengthen and accelerate the growth of women owned businesses nationally. Services of the WBDC include workshops and one-on-one counseling on all aspects of business development, including marketing, finance, business management, technology integration, and more.

www.wbdc.org

Diversity Information Resources

Diversity Information Resources continues its mission to create products and services providing supplier diversity information.

www.diversityinforesources.com

Federal Money Retriever

This site features a grants and loans database, pre-Application Wizard, and a Guide to Federal Funding. Recommended by *The Wall Street Journal*, the *American Library Association*, *Entrepreneur* Magazine, and the *Chronicle of Philanthropy*.

www.fedmoney.com/grants/11802.htm

Minority and Women Business Development (MWBD)

This site is maintained by the City of Charlotte and Mecklenburg County, North Carolina.

www.charmeck.nc.us/cibss/mwbd

Minority Bank Deposit Program

The Minority Bank Deposit Program (MBDP) is a voluntary program to encourage federal agencies, state and local governments, and the private sector to use MBDP participants as depositaries and financial agents.

www.fms.treas.gov/mbdp

Minority Franchising

Franchising directory listing over 1,000 franchisors, attorneys, consultants, and service providers, with detailed profiles on each company.
www.minorityfranchising.com

National Minority Supplier Development Council Inc.

The primary objective of the National Minority Supplier Development Council is to provide a direct ink between corporate America and minority-owned businesses.
www.nmsdcus.org

ODA Minority Business Development Center

The ODA Minority Business Development Center provides a wide array of business assistance and services to minority businesses. The MBDC is funded by the U.S. Department of Commerce MBDA.
odabdc.org

Small, Disadvantaged, and Minority Business - HUD

The Small, Disadvantaged and Minority Business (SDMB) Community is a vital and important part of our country's economic health and well-being. Government officials who recognize this importance have spoken repeatedly on the need to bring more economic opportunity to the SDMB Community.
www.hud.gov/offices/cio/sdb/index.cfm

Surveys of Minority-Owned and Women-Owned Business Enterprises

U.S. Census Bureau—1997 Economic Census, Surveys of Minority-Owned and Women-Owned Business Enterprises provide valuable economic data on business owners' race, ethnicity, and gender.
www.census.gov/csd/mwb

Office of Small and Disadvantaged Business Utilization (OSDBU)

The Department of Transportation's Office of Small and Disadvantaged Business Utilization is responsible for the development and implementation of activities directed at ensuring small, woman-owned and minority, disadvantaged business participation.
osdbuweb.dot.gov

Supplier Diversity for the New Millennium M/WBE Directory

Informative database of Minority and Women Business Enterprises (M/WBEs) and contacts within *Fortune* 1000 companies. Free to register and use. E-procurement resource that maintains a national database with up-to-date information as well as all the data necessary for expanding M/WBEs on a national basis.
www.div2000.com

U.S. Department of Commerce, Minority Business Development Agency

Specifically created to encourage the creation, growth, and expansion of minority-owned businesses in the United States. MBDA's programs form a national business service network that effectively addresses the special needs of minority entrepreneurs throughout the United States.
www.mbda.gov

The Capital Connection: Resources for Woman Entrepreneurs

The resources throughout the Capital Connection web site are appropriate for women. However, there are several venture capital companies, loan sources, publications, and web sites that are targeted specifically for women.
www.capital-connection.com/womenvcs.html

Suggested Magazines and Publications for Women and Minorities

Equal Opportunity Publications, Inc.
Equal Opportunity Publications, Inc., with its expertise in diversity recruitment, brings to the internet a new communications station that specializes in connecting employers committed to the recruitment of a diversified work force (minorities, women, and people with disabilities) with career seekers.
www.eop.com

Family Business Magazine
The Guide for Family Companies. Written expressly for family company owners and advisers. Focuses on issues—business and human dynamic—special to family enterprises. Offers practical guidance and tried-and-true solutions for business stakeholders.
www.familybusinessmagazine.com

Indian Country Today
The world's largest Native American Indian news source, shipped internationally.
www.indiancountry.com

Women's News Bureau
Women's News Bureau is a source of local, national, and international news of interest to women in business.
www.womensnewsbureau.com

Minority Business Entrepreneur
MBEMAG is the web site of *Minority Business Entrepreneur* (MBE) magazine, a bimonthly publication for and about minority and women business owners. We focus on affirmative action and contracting issues. We also offer information on *Women's Business Exclusive*, a newsletter exclusively for women business owners.
www.mbemag.com

Minority Business News
America's monthly news source for information about minority business enterprise and diversity.
www.minoritybusinessnews.com

Next Step Online
Next Step Online is the premier site for diversity-related information, products, and services.
www.nextstepmag.com

Source: www.abusinessresource.com.

Recommended Associations for Women and Minorities

National Association for Female Executives
The National Association for Female Executives (NAFE), the largest women's professional association and the largest women business owners' organization in the country, provides resources and services—through education, networking, and public advocacy—to empower its members to achieve career success and financial security.
www.nafe.com

American Association of University Women
The AAUW Educational Foundation is the world's largest source of funding exclusively for graduate women. Each year the Foundation provides about $4 million in fellowships, grants, and awards for outstanding women around the globe and for community action projects. The Foundation also funds pioneering research on women, girls, and education, and international symposia. The AAUW Legal Advocacy Fund is the nation's largest legal fund focused solely on sex discrimination in higher education. The Legal Advocacy Fund provides funds and a support system for women seeking judicial redress for sex discrimination in higher education.
www.aauw.org

National Association of Women Business Owners

NAWBO is the only dues-based national organization representing the interests of all women entrepreneurs in all industries. NAWBO's strength comes from the diversity of its membership—all sizes from sole proprietorship to hundreds of employees, every industry from construction, importers, and retailers to service providers, and in all areas of the country. www.nawbo.org

National Women's Studies Association

This organization is committed to support and promote feminist teaching, research, and professional and community service at the pre-K through post-secondary levels. Integral to this commitment is understanding the political ramifications in our teaching, research, and service. NWSA is committed to the creation and growth of women's studies institutional units dedicated to teaching, research, scholarship, and community activism, and especially committed to the efforts of programs and departments to realize the research and scholarship missions of NWSA. www.nwsa.org

Women's Business Enterprise National Council

The Women's Business Enterprise National Council (WBENC), founded in 1997, is the nation's leading advocate of women-owned businesses as suppliers to America's corporations. WBENC works to foster diversity in the world of commerce with programs and policies designed to expand opportunities and eliminate barriers in the marketplace for women business owners. WBENC works with representatives of corporations to encourage the utilization and expansion of supplier/vendor diversity programs. www.wbenc.org/excellence

Chapter 5

Using the Internet

Popular Entrepreneurial Online Newsletters

Small Business Yahoo
The Yahoo! Small Business Newsletter is a monthly e-mail that focuses on helping you grow your business online. Topics include search engine marketing and other online marketing best practices, small business success stories, product tips and tricks, and more. Stay informed of all the Yahoo Small Business news. **smallbusiness.yahoo.com**

Forbes
Forbes has over 35 different newsletters to choose from. They focus more on investment and corporations. They have newsletters ranging from oil and trade to Dow theory forecasts and investing news. **www.forbes.com**

Growthink
Growthink's newsletter provides great tips on writing business plans. They have a keen understanding of the perspective investor, bank, or business partner. **growthink.com/businessplan**

Entrepreneur.com
This site offers newsletters on various industries within entrepreneurship, such as starting a business, sales and marketing, growing a business, e-business and technology, and franchise news. **www.entrepreneur.com**

U.S. Chamber of Commerce
U.S. Chamber of Commerce Newsletter encompasses small business news, economic reports, access to resources and toolkits, and analysis of the issues that are impacting you and your bottom line. Their tips on products and services can lower your business costs, while tools and resources help you maximize opportunities for profit. **www.uschamber.com/sb**

Small Business Association
The Small Business Advocate is a monthly or bi-monthly newsletter that details economic developments and regulatory trends related to small business as well as the latest initiatives of the Small Business Administration's Office of Advocacy. **www.sba.gov/advo/newsletter.html**

BNET
BNET newsletters offer selected headlines, white papers, and blog posts to keep you current with trends and thought leadership in your industry and/or job. Some of the newsletters available are supply chain and operations, leadership and strategy, finance, medical and health care, retail, financial services, human resources, marketing and sales, government, and manufacturing. **bnet.com**

Online Entrepreneur Resource Centers

These are excellent web sites that are easy to navigate through to keep up with current trends and find information about a specific industry or area of business.

- Entrepreneur.com
- Business.com
- SmallBusiness.yahoo
- Inc.com
- SBA.gov
- Morebusiness.com
- Ceoexpress.com
- Bizlink.com
- Entrepreneurs.about.com
- Bet.com
- Businessnation.com
- Forbes.com

- Entreworld.org
- Startupjournal.com

- Abusinessresource.com

Source: Compiled by author Ashlee Gardner.

Online Statistics Sites

Bureau of Labor Statistics

www.bls.gov

The Bureau of Labor Statistics (BLS) is the principal fact-finding federal agency in the broad field of labor economics and statistics. The BLS collects, processes, analyzes, and disseminates essential statistical data to the American public, the U.S. Congress, other federal agencies, state and local governments, business, and labor. The BLS also serves as a statistical resource to the Department of Labor.

Cyber Atlas

www.clickz.com/stats

ClickZ Stats checks the accuracy of counts by comparing them with regional growth patterns and other projections to provide the most accurate and up-to-date statistics on the internet, using population available online.

Fed Stats

www.fedstats.gov

FedStats is the new window on the full range of official statistical information available to the public from the federal government. Track economic and population trends, education, health care costs, aviation safety, foreign trade, energy use, farm production, and more. Access official statistics collected and published by more than 100 federal agencies without having to know in advance which agency produces them.

Stat-USA

www.stat-usa.gov

The function of Stat-USA is to deliver vital economic, business, and international trade information produced by the U.S. government to you so you can make decisions that may affect your business, your career, your community, or your personal finances. Information is produced by hundreds of offices and divisions of the government. It is almost impossible for individuals to find out what is available, much less obtain it and use it. Stat-USA scours the government information vaults, assembles that information in one location, and delivers it to you using the most advanced computer technologies available.

U.S. Census Bureau

www.census.gov

The Census Bureau serves as the leading source of quality data about the nation's people and economy. We honor privacy, protect confidentiality, share our expertise globally, and conduct our work openly. We are guided on this mission by our strong and capable workforce, our readiness to innovate, and our abiding commitment to our customers

Source: www.onlinewbc.gov/links.html.

Chapter 6

Entrepreneur.com's Best Web Sites for Small Business

Best Web Sites for B2B Services

Alibaba.com
You can buy or sell just about anything on this site. An international smorgasbord of companies offer their wares from all over the world.
www.alibaba.com

CEOExpress
This free site features dozens of links to newspaper, investment and business news sites—everything a CEO could possibly need—all in one place. And it's surprisingly easy to navigate. You can also subscribe to their paid service, CEOExpressSelect, for some added features.
www.ceoexpress.com

Ecountries
This site offers great links to international news and international business services, like market research in foreign countries and translation services.
www.ecountries.com

Hushmail.com
Keep private e-mails private using this free encryption service. Subscribers can upload documents onto their secure servers. Hush Secure Forms lets visitors to your site submit secure forms directly to you.
www.hushmail.com

World Language
Buy language courses, dictionaries, translation software—all you need to communicate in more than 700 languages.
www.worldlanguage.com

Best Web Sites for Comparison Shopping

BizRate.com
Check out customer ratings of online merchants before buying from them. This site offers rate comparisons on millions of products offered by thousands of online merchants in 20 popular product categories, like electronics and health and beauty.
www.bizrate.com

Gomez
Find out just how satisfied your customers are with your site by taking the Internet Channel Effectiveness quiz. By registering on the site, you can also read market research for free.
www.gomez.com

LowerMyBills.com
Find the lowest rates for just about any service, from credit cards to phone service. This comprehensive site makes it easy to pick the best service for you and your business.
www.lowermybills.com

MySimon.com
Compare prices for a variety of products, including computers and software, office supplies, and even travel. A powerful search tool helps you locate the product you're looking for in a snap.
www.mysimon.com

PriceSCAN.com
Check out the Computers section of the site for a bevy of computer-related products and set your maximum price for new and refurbished products. You'll also find consumer products, including home and health and beauty products.
www.pricescan.com

Best Web Sites for E-Commerce and Technology

Alldomains.com
Check to see if your favorite domain name is taken on this site. They also offer corporate services for protecting your name and trademark.
www.alldomains.com

Cisco Small-Medium Business Network Solutions and Services
Make sure your network is up and running,

and read technology white papers and solution guides on this site.
www.cisco.com/en/US/netsol/networking_solu-tions_small_medium-sized_businesses.html

LinkShare
Partner with the web's top 500 e-tailers by adding their links to your consumer site when you register on this site.
www.linkshare.com

Overstock.com
Save up to 80 percent on all sorts of retail and computer-related products.
www.overstock.com

Webdeveloper.com
Pick up great web development tips on this site and subscribe to the free newsletter.
www.webdeveloper.com

Yahoo! Small Business Center
Read technology news, access online tools, and check out Yahoo!'s business resources.
smallbusiness.yahoo.com

eBay
Search for goods or sell yours on the world's best-known auction site.
www.ebay.com

Best Web Sites for Legal Help

Coollawyer.com
Get legal forms online, research legal topics and even incorporate online.
www.coollawyer.com

Cornell Law Library
Produced by Cornell Law School, this site will let you search current law by source, jurisdiction, or subject.
www.law.cornell.edu

FindLaw
One of the most popular legal resources on the web, this site features business-related topics such as employer rights, intellectual property,

and product liability.
www.findlaw.com

LawCrawler
An offshoot of FindLaw, Law Crawler is a powerful legal search engine that will sift through legal web sites, news, documents, dictionaries, and U.S. government sites to find the legal information you're looking for.
lawcrawler.findlaw.com

LegalZoom
Produce legal documents online without the help of a lawyer on this site. Co-founded by Robert Shapiro, it features sections on copyright, trademark, corporations, and even taxes. For more complicated matters, you can also find a lawyer on the site.
www.legalzoom.com

RSiCopyright.com
Find out how to copyright your work or get reprint rights and sign up for the news-clipping service to find out whenever you or your company are mentioned in news articles. It's free for registered users of the site.
www.rsicopyright.com

Best Web Sites for Government

SBA
The government agency to contact in all small-business matters. Obtain loan information and find out how to get help in starting your business.
www.sba.gov

SBA and Palo Alto Software
This site is brought to you by the SBA and business-plan software-maker Palo Alto Software and features a variety of sample business plans in a range of industries.
www.bplans.com/samples/sba.cfm

SBA's Online Women's Business Center
Practical information for women entrepreneurs. Get tips on starting, financing, and running

your business. Get a list of SBA Women's Business Centers around the country.
www.onlinewbc.gov

The Catalog of Federal Domestic Assistance
Search for government grants gratis on this site.
www.cfda.gov

U.S. Business Advisor
Created by the SBA, this site features a variety of topics for entrepreneurs, including taxes, international trade, and business development. Click on Agencies and Gateways for links to federal agencies' web sites.
www.business.gov/busadv

U.S. Chamber of Commerce
Find out how the Chamber is lobbying the federal government or duking it out in the courts, or simply get in on special member discounts and benefits. Click on Resources, then Small Business Tools for information specific to small businesses. Find local chapters on the site as well.
www.uschamber.org

U.S. House of Representatives
Know what's going on in our government, track bills that affect your business, and get contact information for your local congressperson.
www.house.gov

U.S. Senate
Know what's going on in our government, track bills that affect your business, and get contact information for your local congressperson.
www.senate.gov

Best Web Sites for Insurance

Independent Insurance Agents and Brokers of America
Find a broker or keep abreast of industry news and research. You can also read IA Magazine online for free.
www.iiaa.net

InsWeb
Search for quotes for all types of insurance, including health and life insurance.
www.insweb.com

Insurance Information Institute
This site provides a wealth of information on what you should look for before signing an insurance policy as well as industry statistics and directories. There's also a handy glossary of insurance terms.
www.iii.org

eHealthInsurance.com
Get individual coverage or compare a selection of health plans geared at small businesses.
www.ehealthinsurance.com

Best Web Sites for Inventions

Inventor's Digest
Read the magazine or find out where upcoming trade shows are taking place. This site gives inventors information on how to protect or promote their inventions, as well as a variety of other topics.
www.inventorsdigest.com

Inventors Headquarters
Find patent help, an inventor's agent, or even a mentor. This site is dedicated to helping inventors take their inventions to the next level.
www.inventorshq.com

U.S. Patent and Trademark Office
All the information you ever wanted to know about patents and trademarks is in this government site. You can search for existing patents or check on the status of your filing.
www.uspto.gov

United Inventors Association
Advice and support for inventors. A subscription to *Inventors' Digest* is included in your membership when you join. Browse through their bookstore for additional information.
www.uiausa.com

Best Web Sites for Management

Bain & Co.
Get access to expert advice for free by reading the well-written, informative articles on the publication portion of this web site.
www.bain.com

Get More Done
This site will help you figure out where you spend your time—and how to better manage it.
www.getmoredone.com

Knowledge@Wharton
The University of Pennsylvania's Wharton School provides a searchable database of business research, plus a wide variety of articles and an analysis of current business issues.
www.knowledge.wharton.upenn.edu

MeansBusiness
This site features a variety of business topics as well as a searchable database of concept book summaries. Think of this site as the Cliffs Notes of business books for the busy entrepreneur.
www.meansbusiness.com

Society for Human Resource Management
Learn how to better manage your employees and get info on workplace trends.
www.shrm.org

WorkingWounded
Want to know how to be the world's best boss? Employees go here to vent, so what better place to get their point of view?
www.workingwounded.com

Best Web Sites for Money and Finance

Bankrate
With debt advisors and small-business advisors, as well as a slew of information on borrowing, credit, and other financial matters, this site is great for managing your business and personal finances.
www.bankrate.com

Freerealtime
Keep track of the markets in real time.
www.freerealtime.com

Garage Technology Ventures
Looking for venture funding? Garage venture capitalists offer more than money. Check out their online resources and even submit your business plan to them online.
www.garage.com

Green Sheet
Find out what's going on in the payment-processing industry and how it affects your business. Get breaking business news here as well.
www.greensheet.com

Overstock.com
Although it's geared more toward consumers, this site does have a great section on electronics and computers.
www.overstock.com

Quicken
Manage all your finances online. Whether you update your portfolio or set up online payments, the service integrates with your Quicken software. It also features a variety of handy financial calculators.
www.quicken.com

Salary.com
Make sure you're offering competitive salaries. Check out the HR Edition for business owners for tips on compensation packages. For more in-depth information, you can purchase compensation market studies.
www.salary.com

SmartMoney.com
This site lets you track your stocks using its customizable stock-watch feature. You'll also find breaking financial news and in-depth tend information.
www.smartmoney.com

StatusFactory
Never worry about late bills again. Pay all your bills online, get e-mail reminders, and even archive your bills on this site.
www.statusfactory.com

Best Web Sites for News, Weather, and More

CNN
Get breaking international, national, and business news.
www.cnn.com

ExecutivePlanet.com
Get tips on business etiquette localized to different countries. If you're an international business traveler, this site is a must.
www.executiveplanet.com

MSN
Shop, read news headlines, check your e-mail—this portal has a little bit of everything.
www.msn.com

Mediabistro
Get tips on how to pitch magazine editors and reporters, and keep abreast of personnel changes at the nation's leading publications.
www.mediabistro.com

Salon
Read news feeds and well-written opinion articles on topics ranging from politics and business to technology and international relations.
www.salon.com

Slate
Too busy to read the paper every day? Read a digest of the day's news from the nation's leading newspapers on this site.
www.slate.com

SustainableBusiness.com
Keep abreast of environmental news and see how you can make your business environmentally friendly. There are even business opportu-

nities posted on the site.
www.sustainablebusiness.com

The New York Times
Well-written news that's relevant, whatever part of the country you're in. Check out the Business and Technology sections.
www.nytimes.com

The World Time Server
Find out exactly what time it is in any corner of the world.
www.worldtimeserver.com

Weather.com
If you do any sort of traveling, this site is a must. Brought to you by The Weather Channel.
www.weather.com

World News Network
A portal with links to the world press, this site is a great place to get the international perspective on breaking world news.
www.worldnews.com

Best Web Sites for Research Tools

Gartner Research
Great site for checking out market research on trends and technology. Some research can be accessed for free; others require a subscription.
www4.gartner.com/Init

Hoovers Online
Find market research and breaking business news on this site. Sign up for a free newsletter.
www.hoovers.com

KnowX.com
Search public records for bankruptcies and get background information on business owners/officers and corporate records before you do business with them. Quite a few are free; those for sale range in price from $1.50 to $123 for comprehensive D&B business reports.
www.knowx.com

OneLook Dictionaries

This site lets you search for the meaning of any word using more than 900 online dictionaries. You can even translate the word into other languages.
www.onelook.com

Refdesk.com

Find random facts and search the Merriam-Webster thesaurus or dictionary for free.
www.refdesk.com

Reporter's Desktop

Search for just about anything or anyone in one spot.
www.reporter.org/desktop

Thomas Register of American Manufacturers

Search for manufacturers in the U.S. and Canada on this free site.
www.thomasregister.com

Best Web Sites for Sales and Marketing

Guerilla Marketing

Read Guerilla Marketing articles online, order marketing books, and even get a marketing coach on this site, brought to you by marketing guru Jay Conrad Levinson.
www.gmarketing.com

MarketingAngel.com

This site features a searchable database of marketing articles from Kimberly L. McCall, marketing whiz and *Entrepreneur* columnist.
www.marketingangel.com

MarketingProfs.com

Get expert advice for your marketing strategy from marketing professors and professionals. This site has a ton of articles on every aspect of marketing.
www.marketingprofs.com

Reveries Magazine

This site features many links to news articles related to consumer and marketing trends.
www.reveries.com

Salesforce.com

Take this CRM service for a free 30-day test drive; it promises sales-force automation as well as customer service and support.
www.salesforce.com

SellingPower.com

This site provides selling skills and motivation for your sales force—and sales management skills for you.
www.sellingpower.com

Small Business Now

More than 60 articles on marketing for small businesses.
www.smallbusinessnow.com

Best Web Sites for Search Engines

Alexa

Search the web's top 500 sites by subject on this site, powered by Google and brought to you by Amazon.
www.alexa.com

AnyWho

Find any person or business with this site. Brought to you by the folks at AT&T, it also features a reverse lookup option so you can find out who called you just by having the number.
www.anywho.com

Google

Try this site and you'll be hooked. Google can find just about anything.
www.google.com

Northern Light

Search a variety of publications from this site using its Northern Light search engine. The search is free; the articles will probably cost you since they mostly come from for-pay sites.
www.northernlight.com

Yahoo!
Use the search engine, Yellow Pages, maps, and free e-mail or just read the news. This portal is the home page to many people.
www.yahoo.com

Best Web Sites for Taxes

CCH Inc.
Get tax tips and other small-business information from this site.
www.cch.com

IRS
Go straight to the source for IRS news and to obtain updated tax forms and publications.
www.irs.gov

Small Business Taxes and Management
Read tax articles, IRS news releases, and special reports.
www.smbiz.com

The Tax Prophet
All you ever wanted to know about taxes, tax scams, estate planning, and even employee stock options.
www.taxprophet.com

Best Web Sites for Technology

Download.com
Download all sorts of software, tools, and even games from this CNet site.
www.download.com

FierceWireless
Get wireless industry updates e-mailed to you daily by signing up on this site.
www.fiercewireless.com

News.com
Get breaking tech news on this CNET site, including new gadget releases, mergers, and other industry news.
www.news.com

NewsLinx
A round-up of the day's tech headlines from tech news services around the country.
www.newslinx.com

TheFeature
For news on the mobile technology industry, this site has message boards, in-depth articles, and breaking technology news.
www.thefeature.com

Webopedia
From Internet.com comes this online encyclopedia of Internet and tech terms. It's easy to use and features links to Internet.com content.
www.webopedia.com

Wired
Keep abreast of technology news on this site, which includes breaking industry news.
www.wired.com

Best Web Sites for Travel

Cheap Tickets
This site sells tickets cheap, but make sure you're aware of any restrictions.
www.cheaptickets.com

Expedia
Sign up for their Fare Tracker and be notified when your fare drops. Easy-to-use search features make this site a travel must.
www.expedia.com

Hotels.com
Cheap hotel rooms on an easy-to-use site—what more can you ask for? You choose the neighborhood and the number of stars, and the site does the rest.
www.hotels.com

MapQuest.com
Accurate maps and door-to-door directions will ensure you never get lost again. It even estimates how long it will take you to get there so you can plan accordingly.
www.mapquest.com

OneTravel.com
Nothing glitzy here, just low prices and lots of travel news.
www.onetravel.com

Orbitz
The flight and travel deals displayed prominently on this site sure make the mind wander, but its low prices are real for car, hotel, plane, and even cruise reservations.
www.orbitz.com

Quikbook
Book hotel rooms online at discounted rates on this easy-to-use site.
www.quikbook.com

Travelocity
Keeping an eye out for that dream fare to your favorite destination is a breeze—Travelocity will e-mail you when it's on sale. Search by best fare and even get a credit card that earns travel points.
www.travelocity.com

WebFlyer
Are you a frequent-flier junkie? WebFlyer offers tools for tracking points and will notify you of special rewards incentives.
www.webflyer.com

Planning Your Venture: Map It Out

Chapter 7

Conceptualizing and Brainstorming

SCORE's Five Tips for Developing Policies for Your Business

1. Think ahead. Establish policies before you need them. Doing so helps avert crises and awkward situations, and helps solve problems before they arise.

2. Determine what policies you need. Some you'll want early in your business include a mission statement and compensation, performance evaluation and employee policies.

3. Get input from key employees, as well as from members of your advisory board, your board of directors, and/or your professional advisors and consultants.

4. Communicate policies to everyone in your business.

5. Review policies on a regular basis—once a year, for example—and revise them as necessary.

Source: SCORE, www.score.org/business_tips.html.

Six Steps to Starting Your Business

When you are beginning your venture, it is very easy to get confused with all the different resources and areas to research for your business. Here is a six-step process used by SBA to make your process a little more focused.

Step 1: Begin with a business plan. This is the blueprint for you and for anyone else interested in investing or joining your business.

Step 2: Solidify a location. You can get some help from the Regional Chambers of Commerce.

Step 3: Choose and form a business structure. Find a legal representative and an accountant before making final decisions. The choices are:

- sole proprietorship
- corporation
- limited liability company
- general partnership
- limited liability partnership

Step 4: File your tax and employer identification documents. Also check whether your business requires special licenses and permits.

Step 5: Use the "Starting a Business Checklist" (next).

Step 6: Have fun on your entrepreneurial journey!

Source: SBA, *Starting a Business Handbook*.

Starting a Business Checklist

- Choose a business.
- Research the business idea.
- What will you sell?
- Is it legal?
- Who will buy it and how often?
- Are you willing to do what it takes to sell the product?
- What will it cost to produce, advertise, sell, and deliver?
- With what laws will you have to comply?
- Can you make a profit?
- How long will it take to make a profit?
- Write a business plan and marketing plan.
- Choose a business name.
- See if the business name is available for use as a domain name.
- Register the domain name even if you aren't ready to use it yet.
- Choose a location for the business.
- Check zoning laws.
- File partnership, corporate, or limited liability company papers with the Secretary of State's office.
- File state tax forms with your state Department of Revenue or Treasury Department.
- Check your state licensing authorities to get any required business licenses or permits.
- Contact the Internal Revenue Service for information on filing your federal tax schedules.
- Apply for a seller's permit or resale license, if necessary in your state if you are going to sell tangible personal property. Examples of tangible personal property include property such items as furniture, giftware, toys, antiques, clothing, cars, etc.
- Contact your State Board of Equalization or its equivalent to see if you are responsible for any fuel, alcohol, tobacco, or other special taxes and fees.
- Apply for an employer identification number with your state Department of Labor, Department of Employment, or its equivalent if you will have employees.
- Find out about workers' compensation if you will have employees.
- Register or reserve any federal trademark or service mark.
- Register copyrights.

- Apply for patent if you will be marketing an invention.
- Order any required notices (advertisements) of your intent to do business in the community.
- Have business phone or extra residential phone lines installed.
- Check into business insurance needs.
- Get adequate business insurance or a business rider to a homeowner's policy.
- Get tax information such as record-keeping requirements, information on withholding taxes if you will have employees, information on hiring independent contractors, facts about estimating taxes, form of organization, etc.
- Open a bank account for the business.
- Have business cards and stationary printed.
- Purchase equipment or supplies.
- Order inventory, signage, and fixtures.
- Get an e-mail address.
- Get your web site set up.
- Have sales literature prepared.
- Call for information about Yellow Pages advertising.
- Place advertising in newspapers or other media if your type of business will benefit from paid advertising.
- Call everyone you know and let them know you are in business.

Source: SBA, *Starting a Business Handbook.*

Six Creative Brainstorming Techniques

1. **Suspend criticism.** All ideas, no matter how crazy they may seem, should be encouraged and recorded without comment or criticism from the group. The general goal of brainstorming is to collect as many ideas as possible, making quantity much more important than quality at this initial stage.

2. **Postpone evaluation.** Brainstorming sessions are not the time or place to evaluate the merits of the ideas suggested. So don't suspend the process to evaluate the projected results of any single idea.

3. **Build on others' ideas.** At their best, brainstorming sessions are fast-paced and fun. Participants should try to build each consecutive idea on the previous ones. This can sometimes result in surprising twists and turns.

4. **Pose an initial question.** Suppose you had created a product for small businesses

and were looking for a new marketing approach. The facilitator might open the brainstorming session by posing a question such as "What do small business owners want?" Participants would then throw out ideas, such as "to save time" or "to increase sales." Or you might select a feature of your new product, one-button operation, for example, and open with a question such as "How does one-button operation help small business owners?"

5. **Use word association.** This method involves brainstorming lists of words and then finding linkage between key words on each list. For example, imagine you want to create a new slogan for a hair gel product. You could start with the root word "gel" and use word association to come up with a list of ideas, such as "flexible hold." Then you could brainstorm another list beginning with "flexible." In the end, you might have four or five lists of ideas based on word association. To build your slogan, you'd choose a word from each of the lists and creatively link them together.

6. **Identify a challenge.** Even the most difficult questions can be tackled by brainstorming, provided you have the right group of people. When I was called in by an auto parts manufacturer to find ways to use the company's roll-forming expertise to produce additional products, we gathered together a large group of experienced workers from throughout the plant for brainstorming. As the facilitator, I began by posing a simple challenge—list anything made from rolled metal not presently manufactured by the company. In short order, the group turned out dozens of viable product ideas. Later, management evaluated all the ideas to determine which products offered the greatest potential.

Source: Kim T. Gordon, "Creative Brainstorming Techniques," www.entrepreneur.com/article/0,4621,304962,00.html.

Tips for Choosing the Name of Your Business

Be sure that your company's name conveys the proper message.

- What does your company's name communicate? Your business's name should reinforce key elements of your business. Are you upscale, convenient, or a bargain? Your name should tell the tale.

- Is your name too cute or obscure to mean anything to strangers? Avoid meaningless initials or cute names that only you understand. And if you're planning to expand, don't limit your business by using a geographic name.

- Is your name suggestive, which is more abstract, or is it descriptive, telling something about your business, such as what it does or where it is?

- How about your competitors? What approach do they take? Make sure your name distinguishes you from the pack.

Source: Rieva Lesonsky, *365 Tips to Boost Your Entrepreneurial IQ.*

Tips for Getting Unstuck During Creative Problem-Solving

Are you a creative thinker? Too many people think they're not, but almost anyone can learn to think creatively. Next time you just can't think of a new way to solve a problem, try these tips:

- **Think like a child.** Remember: childhood is the breeding ground of creative thinking.

- **Pay attention!** Great ideas are all around you. Don't hesitate to steal solutions from others and tailor them to your needs.

- **Ask everyone you know for input.** You never know who or what can spark your creativity.

- **Don't force your ideas.** If your mind is truly blank, take a break. Do something else—or do nothing at all. Getting a fresh perspective may be all you need to get you going.

Above all, have fun. Too many of us think business has to be all work, but adding an element of play can really get those creative juices flowing.

Source: Rieva Lesonsky, *365 Tips to Boost Your Entrepreneurial IQ.*

Rules for Brainstorming

Brainstorming sessions can boost creativity. But too often people think it's a free-form process. But the best free-thinking comes from having a plan. Follow these rules and let the juices flow:

- Before you start, make sure you define the problem or issue you're going to discuss.

- During the session, make sure someone writes down all ideas as they surface.

- Once you get started, everyone must suspend judgment. Reserve criticism for after the session.

- Encourage people to build on the ideas of others. Remember: few ideas have a single author.

- The idea is to push the envelope—invite unconventional thinking. In fact, often the wilder the idea, the better.

And don't sweat the details. During brainstorming, quantity is more important than quality.

Source: Rieva Lesonsky, *365 Tips to Boost Your Entrepreneurial IQ.*

Tips for Goal-Setting

Every entrepreneur has—or should have—goals. But do you know how to effectively achieve them?

- **Put them in writing.** This sounds simple but is often the difference between goals that remain dreams and those that become accomplishments.

- **Challenge yourself.** Sure, you must always be true to yourself. But to reach new heights, you have to push beyond your previous limits.

- **Distinguish between long- and short-term goals.** Short-term goals are the building blocks for your long-term vision. They should not read like a to-do list.

- **Focus on the goal, not the journey.** It's too easy to lose sight of your goals when life has a nasty habit of interfering. Sometimes it helps to post your goals where you can see them often.

- **Be flexible about how you will achieve your goals.** Trust your intuition and never expect for it to happen the "right" way.

Source: Rieva Lesonsky, *365 Tips to Boost Your Entrepreneurial IQ.*

Chapter 8

Hot Businesses

Hot Trends 2005

The reasons why people buy are just as important as what they buy. Read on to find out the eight trends that are leading people to their next purchase and understand people's buying behaviors.

1. Authenticity

Who wants to serve Velveeta to guests when you can offer handcrafted cheese made from local, organic dairy milk? Why wear clothes from the mall when you can purchase the handiwork of a local designer—U.S.-made and sweatshop-free? Buying products with an aura of authenticity allows people to take control of their purchases so they truly know what they're getting. They can be unique and shop at businesses they feel akin to politically, ethically, and aesthetically.

How can a company tout its authenticity? You can make like Apple Computer, Levi Strauss & Co., and Mercedes-Benz and use real customers in your ads. Brag about your use of local ingredients and materials, traditional and artisanal methods, or environmentally and socially responsible practices. If you do it right, your customers will then boast to friends about how authentic they are for patronizing your authentic business.

2. Age 35

How can you reach a 19-year-old undergrad, a 31-year-old on the career path, and a 47-year-old who's raising a toddler—with just one message? Market to all of them as if they're 35. From using botox to erase any physical signs of aging to shopping at the same stores as their kids to postponing their retirements, boomers refuse to grow older. If you targeted them at their true ages, they'd balk.

But surprisingly, younger people are also generation hopping. They're rejecting the belly- and booty-baring fashions of late and—gasp!—embracing sensible, preppy outfits. It's a backlash that may reflect the current conservative climate (thanks a lot, Janet and Justin) or that the latest generation has grown up with different aspirations. Kids now save for iPods and video games. Your teenage niece can code a web site better than you.

So with the more mature seeking a return to their youthful selves and young people looking to the future, age 35 has become a golden median, as a recent *Los Angeles Times* article explored. Target this age group and you may end up hooking more customers than you ever anticipated.

3. Multitasking and Memory Loss

In our jam-packed society, it seems the only thing there's a lack of is time. Whether this overextension of our lives is self-inflicted is an argument for another article, but multitasking seems here to stay. People are watching TV while surfing the net, driving while chatting on their cells, and checking their e-mail on PDAs during meetings. TV series are having shorter seasons, and popular magazines like *Maxim* and *Star* pack plenty of blurbs, lists, and photos for quick digestion.

While an obvious opportunity for aging boomers and rampant multitaskers will be memory aids (both pharmaceutical and herbal), courses, and guides, we wouldn't be surprised if consulting firms dealing with the negative effects of multitasking skyrocket in the near future.

4. Obesity

The widening of Americans isn't news anymore, but this is an incredibly vast market still worthy of entrepreneurial exploration. Health care, food service, apparel manufacturing and retailing, medical device manufacturing and retailing—all these industries are touched by what many consider a national health crisis.

There seem to be two sides to this trend: helping people lose weight and helping heavier people live more comfortably.

5. The Third Place

While it's a no-brainer that teens ditch their parents as often as possible, many young adults are also in the same boat. With 56 percent of men and 43 percent of women aged 18 to 24 still living at home, according to the 2000 Census, an escape from the house is more a necessity than a luxury. Businesses that position themselves as what Starbucks' Howard Schultz calls "third places" (home and work are the first two places) may become popular destinations.

Starbucks and Barnes & Noble have built their businesses around providing customers a comfortable environment to wile away the hours. Wi-Fi has been a huge advantage in drawing in students, businesspeople, and home-office dwellers; smart businesses like Panera Bread and Starbucks tout this by including it in their location search on their web sites and by offering information in their stores.

Other big businesses are trying to get in on this act, too. McDonald's is building a flagship restaurant in Chicago, slated to open in 2005, that will feature wireless access and will encourage customers to hang around in a relaxed atmosphere. Coca-Cola is targeting teens with its new Red Lounges—mall-based stores designed to let teens learn about new music, games, and movies ... while they drink lots of Coke.

It's no longer wise to get people in and out of your business as quickly as possible. Give them a reason to stay and you'll also give them a reason to come back.

6. Snobization

Middle-class Americans are turning into a bunch of snobs. Premium jeans labels like Diesel and Miss Sixty are showing up on small-town derrières. Day spas, once considered a luxury, are popping up all over the place. And don't get us started again about food connoisseurs.

Starbucks is often cited as the originator of what Reinier Evers, founder of trend agency Trendwatching.com, calls "snobmoddities": everyday items that have been turned into chic, luxury must-haves. These items aren't always expensive. Instead, says Evers, they're small indulgences. "[These purchases] are only mind-blowing compared to some of the prices we're still used to from back in the day."

You can see accessible luxuries at Target with Todd Oldham dorm décor and Michael Graves sleek kitchenware. And often, people wear a $15 shirt so they can afford a pair of $100 jeans.

"We live in a consumption society and a meritocracy," says Evers. "Thus our identity is shaped by the things we consume. So the more luxury items we can purchase and show the rest of the world, the higher we rank in society."

The $400 billion luxury market is expected to grow 15 percent per year, according to strategy and management consulting firm The Boston Consulting Group, until it hits $1 trillion in 2010. Figure out how you can repurpose your products and services in a luxurious yet mostly affordable fashion, and you could be the next to cash in on this sky-rocketing market.

7. Uniqueness

Being unique is a tough gig these days. Mass production, large chains, and the quest for convenience often dictate uniformity. But even though it takes a little more work, consumers are shopping niche stores, looking for customizable options, and wearing their interests and beliefs on their sleeves. No one industry explores this consumer quirk more than T-shirt designers. While major chains are still selling pseudo-vintage tees, people looking to "outcool" their friends are hunting for truly unique items: overtly political tees; designs from favorite bloggers from CafePress.com; remixed designer tees that are ripped up, laced up, and bejeweled; religious designs, especially Judaica; and truly vintage wear from eBay. While apparel sales fell 5.1 percent last year, according to market research firm The NPD Group, T-shirt sales rose 2.2 percent, making up $17 billion in a $166 billion market.

Consumers desiring uniqueness are closely related to those seeking accessible luxury and authenticity in their wares. Part of the fun of ordering an expensive bottle of vinegar from a regional producer is knowing you'll wow your friends at your next dinner party. It's the cachet of being an early adopter, combined with the need to never be wearing the same outfit as someone else at a party. In a world of big-box retailers, it's up to the entrepreneur to fill this need.

8. Life Caching

Today's boomers and seniors cherish the grainy super-8 films, fading Polaroids, and locked diaries of their childhoods. But future generations will instead hoard memory cards full of blog entries, digital photos, and the first web sites they ever built. As we learn to click to save every moment of our lives, data will become the stuff that memories are made of. "Life caching will become a given," says Reinier Evers, whose company coined the term. "Consumers will come to expect [that] they can relive every experience they've ever had and have instant access to any life collection they've ever built."

Memory making has been big business for a while. Scrapbooking has been one of the hottest trends in recent years—the $2.5 billion industry has doubled since 2001, according to the Hobby Industry Association, and is still growing. But businesses that can provide creative solutions to both physical and digital life caching are the ones that stand to gain from this trend. One million Memory Maker Photo Bracelets (a bracelet that wearers can insert several photos into) were sold in six months. MyPublisher.com allows users to create coffee-table books from their digital photos. Nokia's Lifeblog service lets users download and arrange their cell-phone-created content-messages, photos, videos, notes, and audio clips.

"Entrepreneurs can offer this space [for life caching], taking on the gatekeeper role," explains Evers. "On a grander scale, start thinking about how you can provide consumers with the means to capture everything. This includes entrepreneurs who already offer 'experiences.' What are you doing to help [customers] capture and store these experiences?"

Source: Laura Tiffany, "Hot Trends for 2005," www.entrepreneur.com/artcle/0,4621,318062,00. html.

Top Ten Franchises in 2005

#1 Subway

325 Bic Drive
Milford, CT 06460
Phone: (800) 888-4848, (203) 877-4281
Fax: (203) 783-7329
www.subway.com
Year began: 1965 Franchising since: 1974
Headquarters size: 650 employees
Franchising department: 20 employees
U.S. franchises: 18,280
Canadian franchises: 2,032
Foreign franchises: 2,742

Costs:
Total investment: $70K–220K
Express/kiosk option available
Franchise fee: $12.5K
Ongoing royalty fee: 8%
Term of agreement: 20 years, renewable

Qualifications:
Net worth requirement: $30K–90K
Cash liquidity requirement: $30K–90K

Business Experience:
General business experience

#2 Curves

100 Ritchie Road
Waco, TX 76712
Phone: (800) 848-1096, (254) 399-9285
Fax: (254) 399-9731
www.buycurves.com
Year began: 1992 Franchising since: 1995
Headquarters size: 50 employees
Franchise department: 40 employees
U.S. franchises: 7,860
Canadian franchises: 726
Foreign franchises: 800

Costs:
Total investment: $36.4K–42.9K
Franchise fee: $39.9K
Ongoing royalty fee: 5%
Term of agreement: 5 years, renewable

Qualifications:
Net worth requirement: $75K
Cash liquidity requirement: $50K

Business Experience:
Financially stable

#3 The Quiznos Franchise Co.

1475 Lawrence Street, #400
Denver, CO 80202
Phone: (720) 359-3300
Fax: (720) 359-3399
www.quiznos.com
Year began: 1981 Franchising since: 1983
Headquarters size: 300 employees
Franchise department: 30 employees
U.S. Franchises: 2,961
Canadian franchises: 289
Foreign franchises: 50

Costs:
Total investment: $208.4K-243.8K
Franchise fee: $25K
Ongoing royalty fee: 7%
Term of agreement: 15 years, renewable
Renewal fee: $1K

Qualifications:
Net worth requirement: $125K
Cash liquidity requirement: $60K

Business Experience:
Industry experience
General business experience

#4 Jackson Hewitt Tax Service

7 Sylvan Way
Parsippany, NJ 07054
Phone: (800) 475-2904
Fax: (973) 496-2760
www.jacksonhewitt.com
E-mail: franchisedev@jtax.com
Year began: 1960 Franchising since: 1986
Headquarters size: 322 employees
Franchising department: 19 employees
U.S. franchises: 4,330

Costs:
Total investment: $51.7K-85.4K
Express/kiosk option available
Franchise fee: $25K
Ongoing royalty fee: 15%
Term of agreement: 10 years, renewable

Qualifications:
Net worth requirement: $100K-200K
Cash liquidity requirement: $50K

#5 The UPS Store

6060 Cornerstone Court W.
San Diego, CA 92121
Phone: (877) 623-7253
Fax: (858) 546-7492
www.theupsstore.com
E-mail: usafranchise@mbe.com
Year began: 1980 Franchising since: 1980
Headquarters size: 300 employees
Franchising department: 84 employees
U.S. franchises: 4,201
Canadian franchises: 271
Foreign franchises: 1,213

Costs:
Total investment: $138.7K-245.5K
Franchise fee: $29.95K
Ongoing royalty fee: 5%
Term of agreement: 10 years, renewable
Renewal fee: 25% of current franchise fee

Qualifications:
Net worth requirement: $150K
Cash liquidity requirement: $50K

Business Experience:
General business experience
General computer skills

#6 Sonic Drive-In Restaurants

300 Johnny Bench Drive
Oklahoma City, OK 73104
Phone: (800) 569-6656, (405) 225-5000
Fax: (405) 225-5963
www.sonicdrivein.com
Year began: 1954 Franchising since: 1959
Headquarters size: 200 employees
U.S. franchises: 2,384
Foreign franchises: 7

Costs:
Total investment: $710K-2.3M
Express/kiosk option available
Franchise fee: $30K
Ongoing royalty fee: 1-5%
Term of agreement: 20 years, renewable
Renewal fee: 10 years for $6K

Qualifications:
Net worth requirement: $1M

Section 2

Cash liquidity requirement: $500K

Business Experience:
Industry experience
General business experience
If no industry experience, must have an operating equity partner

#7 Jani-King

Description: Janitorial Services

16885 Dallas Parkway
Addison, TX 75001
Phone: (800) 552-5264
Fax: (972) 991-5723, (972) 239-7706
www.janiking.com
E-mail: info@janiking.com
Year began: 1969 Franchising since: 1974
Headquarters size: 100 employees
Franchise department: 100 employees
U.S. franchises: 9,023
Canadian franchises: 540
Foreign franchises: 1,369

Costs:
Total investment: $11.3K–34.1K+
Franchise fee: $8.6K–16.3K+
Ongoing royalty fee: 10%

Qualifications:
Net worth requirement: Varies
Cash liquidity requirement: Varies

#8 7-Eleven Inc.

2711 N. Haskell Avenue, Box 711
Dallas, TX 75221
Phone: (800) 255-0711
Fax: (214) 841-6776
www.7-eleven.com
Year began: 1927 Franchising since: 1964
Headquarters size: 1000 employees
Franchise department: 18 employees
U.S. franchises: 3,899
Foreign franchises: 21,240

Costs:
Total investment: Varies
Franchise fee: Varies
Ongoing royalty fee: Varies
Term of agreement: 15 years, renewable

Qualifications:
Net worth requirement: Varies

Business Experience:
General business experience
Retail experience, customer service skills

#9 Dunkin' Donuts

130 Royall Street
Canton, MA 02021
Phone: (781) 737-3000
Fax: (781) 737-4000
www.dunkin-baskin.com
Year began: 1950 Franchising since: 1955
U.S. franchises: 4,418
Canadian franchises: 90
Foreign franchises: 1,711

Costs:
Total investment: $255.7K–1.1M
Express/kiosk option available
Franchise fee: $40K–80K
Ongoing royalty fee: 5.9%

Qualifications:
Net worth requirement: $1.3M
Cash liquidity requirement: $750K

Business Experience:
Industry experience
General business experience
Marketing skills

#10 RE/MAX Int'l. Inc.

P.O. Box 3907
Englewood, CO 80155-3907
Phone: (800) 525-7452, (303) 770-5531
Fax: (303) 796-3599
www.remax.com
Year began: 1973 Franchising since: 1975
Headquarters size: 350 employees
Franchising department: 10 employees
U.S. franchises: 3,614
Canadian franchises: 580
Foreign franchises: 1,285

Costs:
Total investment: $20K–200K
Franchise fee: $10K–25K
Ongoing royalty fee: Varies

Term of agreement: 5 years, renewable
Renewal fee: Varies

Qualifications:
Business Experience:
Industry experience

General business experience
Marketing skills

Source: Rieva Lesonsky and Maria Anton-Conley, *Entrepreneur Magazine's Ultimate Book of Low-Cost Franchises 2005/2006.*

Top Ten Global Franchises

#1 Subway

325 Bic Drive
Milford, CT 06460
Phone: (800) 888-4848, (203) 877-4281
Fax: (203) 783-7329
www.subway.com
Year began: 1965 Franchising since: 1974
Headquarters size: 650 employees
Franchising department: 20 employees
U.S. franchises: 18,280
Canadian franchises: 2,032
Foreign franchises: 2,742

Costs:
Total investment: $70K-220K
Express/kiosk option available
Franchise fee: $12.5K
Ongoing royalty fee: 8%
Term of agreement: 20 years, renewable

Qualifications:
Net worth requirement: $30K-90K
Cash liquidity requirement: $30K-90K

Business Experience:
General business experience

#2 Curves

100 Ritchie Road
Waco, TX 76712
Phone: (800) 848-1096, (254) 399-9285
Fax: (254) 399-9731
www.buycurves.com
Year began: 1992 Franchising since: 1995
Headquarters size: 50 employees
Franchise department: 40 employees
U.S. franchises: 7,860
Canadian franchises: 726
Foreign franchises: 800

Costs:
Total investment: $36.4K-42.9K
Franchise fee: $39.9K
Ongoing royalty fee: 5%
Term of agreement: 5 years, renewable

Qualifications:
Net worth requirement: $75K
Cash liquidity requirement: $50K

Business Experience:
Financially stable

#3 Quiznos Franchise Co.

Description: Quick service sandwich shop

1475 Lawrence Street, #400
Denver, CO 80202
Phone: (720) 359-3300
Fax: (720) 359-3399
www.quiznos.com
Year began: 1981 Franchising since: 1983
Headquarters size: 300 employees
Franchise department: 15-30 employees
U.S. franchises: 2,961
Canadian franchises: 289
Foreign franchises: 50

Costs:
Total investment: $208.4K-243.8K
Franchise fee: $25K
Ongoing royalty fee: 7%
Term of agreement: 15 years, renewable
Renewal fee: $1K

Qualifications:
Net worth requirement: $125K
Cash liquidity requirement: $60K

Business Experience:
Industry experience
General business experience

#4 Kumon Math and Reading Services

Description: An after-school educational program specializing in math and reading

300 Frank W. Burr Boulevard, 5th Floor
Teaneck, NJ 07666
Phone: (866) 633-0740, (201) 928-0444
Fax: (201) 928-0044
www.kumon.com
E-mail: franchise@kumon.com
Year began: 1958 Franchising since: 1958
Headquarters size: 400 employees
Franchise department: 12 employees
U.S. franchises: 1,352
Canadian franchises: 341
Foreign franchises: 21,800

Costs:
Total investment: $10K–30K
Franchise fee: $1K
Ongoing royalty fee: $30+/student/mo.
Term of agreement: 2 years, renewable

Business Experience:
General business experience
Marketing skills
Good math, reading, and communications skills

#5 KFC Corporation

Description: Fast-food chicken restaurant

1441 Gardiner Lane
Louisville, KY 40213
Phone: (866) 298-6986
Fax: (502) 874-8848
www.yumfranchises.com
Year began: 1930 Franchising since: 1952
U.S. franchises: 4,227
Canadian franchises: 715
Foreign franchises: 5,275

Costs:
Total investment: $1.1M–1.7M
Express/kiosk option available
Franchise fee: $25K
Ongoing royalty fee: 4%
Term of agreement: 20 years, renewable
Renewal fee: $4.9K

Qualifications:
Net worth requirement: $1M
Cash liquidity requirement: $360K

Business Experience:
Industry experience
General business experience
Marketing skills

#6 The UPS Store

Description: Business, communications, and postal service centers

6060 Cornerstone Court W.
San Diego, CA 92121
Phone: (877) 623-7253
Fax: (858) 546-7492
www.theupsstore.com
E-mail: usafranchise@mbe.com
Year began: 1980 Franchising since: 1980
Headquarters size: 300 employees
Franchising department: 84 employees
U.S. franchises: 4,201
Canadian franchises: 271
Foreign franchises: 1,213

Costs:
Total investment: $138.7K–245.5K
Franchise fee: $29.95K
Ongoing royalty fee: 5%
Term of agreement: 10 years, renewable
Renewal fee: 25% of current franchise fee

Qualifications:
Net worth requirement: $150K
Cash liquidity requirement: $50K

Business Experience:
General business experience
General computer skills

#7 RE/MAX Int'l. Inc.

P.O. Box 3907
Englewood, CO 80155-3907
Phone: (800) 525-7452, (303) 770-5531
Fax: (303) 796-3599
www.remax.com
Year began: 1973 Franchising since: 1975
Headquarters size: 350 employees
Franchising department: 10 employees

U.S. franchises: 3,614
Canadian franchises: 580
Foreign franchises: 1,285

Costs:

Total investment: $20K-200K
Franchise fee: $10K-25K
Ongoing royalty fee: Varies
Term of agreement: 5 years, renewable
Renewal fee: Varies

Qualifications:

Business Experience:
Industry experience
General business experience
Marketing skills

#8 Domino's Pizza LLC

Description: Pizza

30 Frank Lloyd Wright Drive
P.O. Box 997
Ann Arbor, MI 48106
Phone: (734) 930-3030
Fax: (734) 930-4346
www.dominos.com
Year began: 1960 Franchising since: 1967
Headquarters size: 350 employees
Franchise department: 75 employees
U.S. franchises: 4,348
Foreign franchises: 2,605

Costs:

Total investment: $141.4K-415.1K
Express/kiosk option available
Franchise fee: to $3.3K
Ongoing royalty fee: 5.5%
Term of agreement: 10 years, renewable

Qualifications:

Net worth requirement: $200K
Cash liquidity requirement: $50K

Business Experience:

Industry experience
Successful experience in food service/retail management; entrepreneurial/equivalent experience

#9 Jani-King

Description: Janitorial services
16885 Dallas Parkway

Addison, TX 75001
Phone: (800) 552-5264
Fax: (972) 991-5723, (972) 239-7706
www.janiking.com
E-mail: info@janiking.com
Year began: 1969 Franchising since: 1974
Headquarters size: 100 employees
Franchise department: 100 employees
U.S. franchises: 9,023
Canadian franchises: 540
Foreign franchises: 1,369

Costs:

Total investment: $11.3K-34.1K+
Franchise fee: $8.6K-16.3K+
Ongoing royalty fee: 10%

Qualifications:

Net worth requirement: Varies
Cash liquidity requirement: Varies

#10 GNC Franchising Inc.

Description: Vitamin and nutritional product services

300 Sixth Avenue
Pittsburgh, PA 15222
Phone: (800) 766-7099, (412) 338-2503
Fax: (412) 402-7105
www.gncfranchising.com
E-mail: livewell@gncfranchising.com
Year began: 1935 Franchising since: 1988
Headquarters size: 600 employees
Franchise department: 28 employees
U.S. franchises: 1,314
Foreign franchises: 737

Costs:

Total investment: $132.7K-182K
Franchise fee: $40K/30K
Ongoing royalty fee: 6%
Term of agreement: 10 years, renewable
Renewal fee: Current franchise fee

Qualifications:

Net worth requirement: $100K
Cash liquidity requirement: $65K

Source: "Top 10 Global Franchises for 2005,"
www.entrepreneur.com/franzone/listings/top-global/0,5835,,00.html.

Top Nine Senior-Oriented Businesses to Start

1. Senior Care Consultant
2. Non-Medical Home Care
3. Senior Meal Delivery
4. Senior Clothing and Products
5. Senior Transportation
6. Senior Concierge
7. Adult Day Care
8. Tech Training
9. Online Dating

Source: Karen E. Spaeder, "9 Senior Businesses to Start," www.entrepreneur.com/article/0,4621,318357,00.html.

Top Teen-Oriented Businesses to Start

There are more than 32 million teens aged between 12 and 19 years old. They need places to go and spend their parents' discretionary income.

1. Teen Grooming Products—projected to bring in $8 billion in sales by 2008
2. Teen Hangouts—with all the free time teens have they need places to go, such as music shops, movies, and their kind of clothing stores
3. Financial Aid/ College Planning—families spend at least over $5 billion a year in researching and applying to colleges

Source: April Y. Pennington, "The Hottest Teen Business for 2005," www.entrepreneur.com/article/0,4621,318067,00.html.

Top 45 Pet-Related Businesses to Start

1. **Doggie Wash.** The business is similar to a coin-operated car wash, except instead of washing the car, you wash your dog. Additionally, you can sell related products such as pet foods, books, pet toys, treats, walking collars, and leashes as a way to increase sales and profits.

2. **Mobile Dog-Wash Service.** After outfitting a van or enclosed trailer with a water

tank and some other basic equipment, marketing with promotional fliers, and moving to a densely populated urban center, you can build wealth with a mobile dog-wash service.

3. **Dog-Walking Service.** A dog-walking service is perfectly suited for the person who has the time, patience, and a love for dogs. Best of all, this business venture can be initiated for less than $100.

4. **Online Talented Pet Directory.** The concept is to create a portal that brings animal owners and trainers together with the film production industry via your web site. Your revenue stream can be generated by a yearly listing fee.

5. **Pet Taxi.** The main requirements for operating a pet taxi service is to have suitable transportation such as a van or station wagon and a good communications system to enable you to quickly respond to customers' calls for pet pickup and delivery.

6. **Dog Run Sales and Installations.** A business that focuses on manufacturing and retailing predesigned and constructed dog runs can be started by anyone regardless of experience. The profit potential is endless since this type of product is also suited to internet marketing and mail-order sales.

7. **Custom Collar and Leash Manufacturing.** With somewhere in the neighborhood of one to two million dog collars and leashes sold each year in North America, starting this business can prove very profitable.

8. **Pet Grooming.** A pet grooming service is very inexpensive to start and has the potential to be extremely profitable, as pet grooming for medium-sized dogs now costs in the range of $30 to $80 per visit. Check out www.nauticom.net/www/ndga, the National Dog Groomers Association of America.

9. **Best Walking Trails Book.** Harnessing the power of the internet can enable you to write books about the best pet-walking trails for every community across North America. By asking site visitors about the best pet walking trails, you can compile information for a "best pet-walking trails" book.

10. **House Safety Service for Pets.** Starting a business that focuses on securing households to prevent pet injuries can be a very personally rewarding and profitable.

11. **Engraved Pet Tags.** After sourcing blank tags in bulk and purchasing basic metal-engraving equipment, you can earn income while retaining flexibility in working hours, operating location, and expansion potential.

12. **Pet Day Care.** Dogs like people, are social creatures and need to have contact with people as well as other dogs to become better behaved. A doggie day care is the perfect place for pets to learn important and beneficial socialization skills.

13. **Pet Memorials.** After selecting certain styles of monuments and hiring an artist to draw designs, the only part of the memorial that needs to be customized is the pet's name and possibly a date.

14. **Online Pet Memorials.** Visitors to the site could select the style of memorial for their

pet as well as typing in exactly what they want to say on the memorial. By paying immediately on the site, customers will have their orders shipped promptly.

15. **Online Specialty Pet Foods.** By either producing your own recipes for pet foods or locating a manufacturer, you can start at home and expand gradually from the profits generated. Check out www.appma.org, the American Pet Products Manufacturers Association.

16. **Everything for Birds.** This type of business would sell products related to bird watching, feeding, and ownership, but not birds themselves. The profit potential is terrific, as the markups that can be applied are in the range of 100 to 200 percent.

17. **Pet Trick Books and Videos.** You can work with established pet trainers to produce your own pet trick videos and sell the videos through retail merchant accounts, mail-order catalogs, and the internet.

18. **Pet Emergency Kits.** The kits should include simple products and medications that can assist in a pet emergency. The kits can be sold to pet-related businesses on a wholesale basis, as well as directly to consumers via mail order and the web.

19. **Portable Sunshades for Pets.** Not only can these handy little shades potentially save some dogs' lives, they also make a dog's day at a park a whole lot more comfortable. Check out www.avma.org, the American Veterinary Medical Association.

20. **Specialty Fish Sales.** The only requirements to start this business in motion are to purchase large breeding tanks or construct breeding ponds. Some tropical fish breeds sell for as much as $100 each.

21. **Dog Saddle Bags.** Dog saddle bags can be manufactured with comical messages printed on them and feature various compartments that can be utilized for carrying items like water, dog biscuits, and balls.

22. **Interior and Exterior Pet Fencing.** The business is preassembling fencing that can be used inside and outside the home, as well as easily packaged and transported for the occasion when pet and owner are on vacation.

23. **Petting Zoo.** Although special handling skills and investment capital may be necessary, a petting zoo business can be both a personally and financially rewarding business to own and operate. Check out www.pettingzoofarm.com, a directory service listing nationwide petting zoos and industry information.

24. **Pet Food Store.** More than one billion dollars' worth of pet food is sold every year in North America; thus opening your own pet food store may just put you on the road to financial freedom. Check out www.appma.org, the American Pet Products Manufacturers Association.

25. **Pet Food Bowls.** The key to success in this type of business is for the pet food bowls to be interesting, made from a unique construction material, and perhaps service a specific need, such as bowls that are higher than normal for dogs with arthritis.

26. **Pet Name Books.** Writing a pet name book is almost guaranteed not to make you rich, but it is guaranteed to be a whole lot of fun.

27. **Tropical Fish and Aquarium Rentals.** By renting tropical fish and aquariums to dentist waiting rooms, restaurants, and business offices, you can generate gigantic profits.

28. **Packaged Catnip.** Starting a business that produces catnip or purchases it in bulk and wholesales the catnip in smaller quantities is a homebased business venture that just about anyone can tackle. Check out www.appma.org, the American Pet Products Manufacturers Association.

29. **Kennel.** The investment needed to establish a dog kennel from the ground up can easily exceed $150,000, making this business venture one that should be tackled only by a seasoned business pro with experience in the industry. Profit potential range is $25,000 to $150,000 per year. Check out www.abka.com, the American Boarding Kennels Association.

30. **Pet Toys.** Designing, manufacturing, and wholesaling pet toys could put you on the path to financial freedom, as most people will spare no expense when it comes to the happiness of their pets.

31. **Pet Travel Kits.** This business opportunity can be started for less than a few thousand dollars, and selling a mere 5,000 car kits for pets per year with a gross profit of $5 each will generate income of $25,000.

32. **Pet Furniture Covers.** Put your sewing experience to work for you and start making made-to-order furniture covers for pet owners. This type of specialized service can be marketed through pet stores, furniture stores, and veterinarians.

33. **Online All for Dogs Web Site.** Develop a portal to bring dog lovers together with retailers of products for dogs and service providers that specialize in services for dogs via a specially designed web site.

34. **Play Center for Dogs.** More and more communities are banning dogs from parks and beaches, making it a chore to find an off-leash area for dogs. Start a play center and charge customers an hourly fee for using the facility.

35. **Pet-Grooming Kits.** Pet-grooming kits can be sold to pet store retailers nationally on a wholesale basis, as well as directly to consumers via the Internet and mail order.

36. **Breed Books.** Starting a business that publishes and distributes breed-specific pet books will require a substantial investment and planning, but the financial rewards could be well worth the effort. Check out the American Kennel Club and the Kennel Club of America, www.kennelclubofamercia.com.

37. **Pooper Scooper Service.** As crazy as this may sound, how difficult would it be to find 200 customers willing to pay a mere $30 each per month to ensure that all little treasures have been cleaned up and removed on a weekly basis from their yards? Check out www.pooperscooper.com, a directory listing hundreds of pooper scooper services in North America.

38. **Pet Breeder.** If you have a keen interest in a particular breed of animal and you also have a keen interest in ensuring that the animal is sold to a caring family, this is the business for you. Check out the American Kennel Club (www.akc.org).

39. **Online Pet Breeders Directory.** A web site that features a directory of pet breeders nationwide is a very straightforward online enterprise to initiate, and a yearly posting fee could gain you some extra income.

40. **Pet Mats.** You can purchase the mats in bulk and silkscreen the customer's pet name in bright colors. Sell the mats directly to consumers via a sales kiosk that can be set up at malls and flea markets.

41. **Pet Fairs.** A pet fair trade show business can feature retailers of pets, pet clothing, pet toys, pet foods, and just about any other product or service that is related to pets.

42. **Online Pet Fairs.** The concept behind this type of online business is to provide small business owners within the pet industry an affordable alternative to the high cost associated with developing and marketing their own online presence.

43. **Online All-for-Cats Web Site.** This type of "mega site for cats" will have to be indexed by types of products, types of services, and geographic area. Income is earned by charging retailers and service providers an annual fee for being featured on the web site.

44. **Online Pet Adoption.** Sometimes pet owners are forced to give their cherished pets up for adoption, and you can help by developing a web site that is focused on finding good families for good pets.

45 **Invisible Pet Fencing.** An underground wire loop with a low-voltage transmitter ensures that pets don't get too close to the boundaries. Promote your business through groomers, kennels, and trainers. Check out www.contain-a-pet.com, manufacturers and distributors of invisible fencing products, also have certified dealer territories available.

Source: James Stephenson, *Entrepreneur Magazine's Ultimate Start-Up Directory*.

Top 13 Businesses to Start

1. eBay Drop-off Stores

2. Kids' Plus-Size Clothing

3. Search Engine Optimization

4. Performance Apparel

5. Functional Food (with vitamins and minerals to enhance health)

6. Financial Planning for Baby Boomers

7. Concierge Physician Businesses

8. Hispanic Marketing

9. Technology Security Consulting

10. Peer Support Groups

11. Wine Business

12. Staffing Services

13. Niche Health and Fitness

Source: staff of Entrepreneur magazine, "13 Hot Businesses for 2005," www.entrepreneur.com/article/0,4621,318045-4,00.html.

Top 20 Part-Time Businesses to Start

1. Espresso Cart

2. Plant Leasing and Maintenance

3. Personal Chef

4. T-Shirt Design

5. Office and Home Organizer

6. Luggage Rental

7. Antiques

8. Color Consultant

9. Mobile Window Tint

10. Handyman

11. Medical Transcription

12. Records Search

13. Custom Jewelry and Accessories

14. Computer Tutor

15. Restaurant Delivery

16. Personal Trainer

17. Wallpaper Hanging

18. Yoga and Tai Chi Instructor

19. Home Inspection

20. Mobile Home-Entertainment Services

Source: Carla Goodman, "25 Part-Time Business Ideas," www.entrepreneur.com/article/0,4621,311229,00.html.

Top Five Homebased Businesses

1. **Alternative Energy Installation.** To get started view energy.sourceguides.com

2. **Online Auction.** To get started view www.auction-sellers-news.com

3. **Daily Money Management.** To get started view www.aadmm.com

4. **Tutoring.** To get started view www.ntatutor.org

5. **Virtual Assistance.** To get started view www.assistu.com

Source: Paul Edwards and Sarah Edwards, "Top 5 Homebased Businesses for 2005," www.entrepreneur.com/article/0,4621,319154,00.html.

2005 Hot 100 Fastest-Growing Businesses in America

1. Huron Consulting Group
Chicago, IL
www.huronconsultinggroup.com
Financial and operational consulting
Founder(s): Gary E. Holdren
Began: 2002
2004 Sales: $173.9M
Initial Investment: $22.8M

Success Secret: Everything must start with good people. I don't think there's any possible way we could have been so successful so quickly if it weren't for the quality of the people we have.

2. Badger State Ethanol
Monroe, WI
www.badgerstateethanol.com
Ethanol production facility
Founder(s): Gary L. Kramer, John L. Malchine
Began: 2000
2004 Sales: $92.1M
Initial Investment: $23.6M

Success Secret: Surround yourself with competent, dedicated, and caring people.

3. Compass Energy Services Inc.
Richmond, VA
www.compassenergy.net
Natural gas, coal, and oil sales and services/energy procurement outsourcing

Founder(s): Barry M. Koski, Christopher J. Ziegler, George A. Minor, James E. Johnson, Joseph C. Lyne Jr., Steven S. Baum
Began: 2002
2004 Sales: $43.3M
Initial Investment: $150K

Success Secret: You can't do it all yourself. Utilize the advice of many people, both internal and external, with expertise and experience in a lot of areas to help build your business.

4. Liquidity Services Inc.
Washington, DC
www.liquidityservicesinc.com
Sales and marketing of surplus and wholesale goods
Founder(s): William P. Angrick, III, Benjamin R. Brown, Jaime Mateus-Tique
Began: 2000
2004 Sales: $75.9M
Initial Investment: $12.5M

Success Secret: Three key ingredients to a successful business are people, product, and profit, in descending order of importance.

5. Fortinet Inc.
Sunnyvale, CA
www.fortinet.com
Network security
Founder(s): Ken Xie, Michael Xie

Began: 2000
2004 Sales: $55.3M
Initial Investment: $93M

Success Secret: Understand the requirements of your customers, believe in what you are developing, work hard, and surround yourself with a strong team.

6. Infologix Inc.

Warminster, PA
www.infologixsys.com
Mobile wireless computing services
Founder(s): David Gulian, Richard Hodge, Craig Wilensky, Cosmo Dinacola, Al Ciardi
Began: 2001
2004 Sales: $43.3M
Initial Investment: $200K

Success Secret: Stay focused on the big picture and the long-term goals.

7. Ionic Media

Sherman Oaks, CA
www.ionicmarketing.com
Marketing and media-buying agency
Founder(s): Michael Kubin, Jeff Bender
Began: 2003
2004 Sales: $22.6M
Initial Investment: $50K

Success Secret: Experience. This is the third company in the media planning and buying business that we've had, and if the combined experience of the two partners can't make us successful, then nothing will.

8. Media Storm

Norwalk, CT
www.mediastorm.biz
Advertising agency
Founder(s): Tim A. Williams, Craig C. Woerz
Began: 2001
2004 Sales: $36.5M
Initial Investment: $90K

Success Secret: Develop a core competency and stick to it.

9. Adjoined Consulting

Miami, FL

www.adjoined.com
Management consulting, technology integration, and outsourcing firm
Founder(s): Rodney Rogers
Began: 2000
2004 Sales: $50.1M
Initial Investment: $25M

Success Secret: When in doubt, attack.

10. SeamlessWeb Professional Solutions Inc.

New York, NY
www.seamlessweb.com
Online food ordering and billing
Founder(s): Jason Finger, Paul Appelbaum, Todd Arky, Stefanie Finger
Began: 2000
2004 Sales: $49.7M
Initial Investment: $345K

Success Secret: If I had eight hours to chop down a tree, I'd spend six hours sharpening an axe. — Abraham Lincoln

11. Capital Media Group

Columbus, OH
www.capitalmedia-group.com
Wholesale distribution of data media supplies
Founder(s): Tony Somers, Nate Williams, Andy Haenszel, John Roth, Bill Kleeh, Doug Broshar, Larry Pangalangan
Began: 2003
2004 Sales: $10.1M
Initial Investment: $170K

Success Secret: Getting the first order is easy. It's in getting the second, third, and fourth orders that good companies are separated from the mediocre ones.

12. Ovation Pharmaceutical Inc.

Deerfield, IL
www.ovationpharma.com
Pharmaceuticals
Founder(s): Jeffrey S. Aronin
Began: 2000
2004 Sales: $38.8M
Initial Investment: $152M

Success Secret: Believe in yourself. Very often,

Section 2

people will doubt and challenge you. Be flexible but firm in your convictions and your vision.

13. Netezza Inc.
Framingham, MA
www.netezza.com
Data warehouse appliance sales
Founder(s): Jit Saxena
Began: 2000
2004 Sales: $35.9M
Initial Investment: $69M

Success Secret: A successful company is all about the value of human capital. Top-notch talent can turn a good product and opportunity into greatness.

14. Martin Capital
Clayton, GA
www.martincap.com
Real estate financing and development
Founder(s): J. Ashley Martin
Began: 2001
2004 Sales: $30.1M
Initial Investment: $30K

Success Secret: Work hard. Good things don't come easy. Think about your decisions. Make sure you have thought about potential outcomes, and be prepared for all of them.

15. Louisiana Lumber
Slidell, LA
Lumber and building materials
Founder(s): James C. Shoemake, Wes Wyman
Began: 2001
2004 Sales: $23.9M
Initial Investment: $700K

Success Secret: Hire the right people in the beginning.

16. Sceptor Industries Inc.
Kansas City, MO
www.sceptorindustries.com
Biosafety and biosecurity equipment
Founder(s): Richard S. Jarman
Began: 2001
2004 Sales: $18.7M
Initial Investment: $2.5M

Success Secret: Understand your niche in the market and be better at it than anyone else.

17. Debt XS LP
Addison, TX
www.debtxs.com
Debt negotiation
Founder(s): Ken Talbert
Began: 2002
2004 Sales: $15.9M
Initial Investment: $25K

Success Secret: As an entrepreneur, it's easy to hear yes, but you should listen to no when the idea isn't right for the company.

18. Southampton Group LLC
Charlotte, NC
www.southamptongroup.com
Residential builder
Founder(s): Jim Merrill, Jim McKinney, Paul Christenbury
Began: 2001
2004 Sales: $16.5M
Initial Investment: $20K

Success Secret: Always follow the golden rule—treat your customers and employees like you would want to be treated. Build every home as if it were your own!

19. SUNRx Inc.
Cherry Hill, NJ
www.sunrx.com
Pharmacy benefit administrator
Founder(s): Gerard J. Ferro
Began: 2001
2004 Sales: $17.8M
Initial Investment: $2.4M

Success Secret: Most people do not plan to fail, but fail to plan! Success is easier with a plan; planning is easier with a superior product.

20. BillBoard Video Inc.
Dallas, TX
www.billboardvideo.com
LED advertising products/services
Founder(s): William Y. Hall
Began: 2000

2004 Sales: $26M
Initial Investment: $10.5K

Success Secret: The key to success in business and life is building and maintaining relationships.

21. Phoenix Group Holdings LLC
Warren, NJ
www.phoenixmsolutions.com
Medical education for pharmaceutical industry
Founder(s): Tracy Doyle, Angela Fiordilino, Michelle Cicchini
Began: 2002
2004 Sales: $14.7M
Initial Investment: $10K

Success Secret: Prepare for business adolescence, accept growing pains, and take the steps to move to the next level. Always surround yourself with people smarter than you.

22. CaseStack Inc.
Santa Monica, CA
www.casestack.com
Logistics outsourcing
Founder(s): Daniel Sanker, Polly Rebich
Began: 2000
2004 Sales: $25.4M
Initial Investment: $9M

Success Secret: Life is too short to work with dullards.

23. Parts Source LLC
Twinsburg, OH
www.mypartssource.com
Mechanical parts replacement for hospitals
Founder(s): A. Ray Dalton
Began: 2001
2004 Sales: $19.3M
Initial Investment: $250K

Success Secret: Always deliver excellent customer service, and you will always make a profit.

24. Belle Marmick Inc.
North Hollywood, CA
Wholesale flooring
Founder(s): Michael Cope

Began: 2001
2004 Sales: $19.1M
Initial Investment: $60K

Success Secret: Work hard, and never get complacent.

25. Myrtle Beach Building Supply
Conway, SC
Retail building materials
Founder(s): Bobby Smith, Tripp Nealy, Joe Jenkins
Began: 2002
2004 Sales: $13.7M
Initial Investment: $1M

Success Secret: Understand what cash flow is and where it comes from, protect your capital, have a sales mentality, and watch and learn to recognize change in your business and your customer base.

26. ProEthic Pharmaceuticals Inc.
Montgomery, AL
www.proethic.com
Pharmaceuticals
Founder(s): Carl Whatley Jr., Jim Harwick, Benjamin Stakely
Began: 2001
2004 Sales: $16.8M
Initial Investment: $100K

Success Secret: Hire employees who are smarter than you.

27. SkillStorm Inc.
San Diego, CA
www.skillstorm.com
IT services and staffing
Founder(s): Hany Girgis
Began: 2002
2004 Sales: $11.3M
Initial Investment: $20K

Success Secret: To achieve things you never have before, you must do things you've never done before.

28. VSA Construction Services LLC
Jessup, MD
www.vsaconstruction.com

Section 2

Civil, utility, and specialty construction
Founder(s): Richard Vance, Bob Sharps
Began: 2002
2004 Sales: $10.6M
Initial Investment: $765K

Success Secret: Complete each project by undercommitting and overdelivering.

29. Avondale Partners LLC
Nashville, TN
www.avondaleonline.com
Investment banking firm
Founder(s): R. Patrick Shepherd, Richard W. Henderson, Philip D. Krebs, Jeffrey C. Nahley, Raymond H. Pirtle Jr., Steven S. Riven
Began: 2001
2004 Sales: $15.2M
Initial Investment: $300K

Success Secret: Hire the smartest people you can; pass on people you don't like or don't trust.

30. Reprise Media
New York, NY
www.reprisemedia.com
Search engine marketing firm
Founder(s): Peter Hershberg, Joshua Stylman
Began: 2003
2004 Sales: $7.6M
Initial Investment: $200K

Success Secret: Make quick, informed, strategic decisions, and then make execution your number-one priority. Don't get mired in planning.

31. Gestalt
Camden, NJ
www.gestalt-llc.com
Technology services
Founder(s): William Loftus, Mark Whelan, John Loftus, David Perme
Began: 2001
2004 Sales: $15.8M
Initial Investment: $200K

Success Secret: Building a great company is an endurance event, not a sprint.

32. Archibald's Inc.
Kennewick, WA
www.archibalds.biz
Pre-owned auto sales
Founder(s): John C. Archibald, Daniel J. Archibald
Began: 2001
2004 Sales: $13.6M
Initial Investment: $150K

Success Secret: Always put yourself in the other person's shoes. Treat everyone that you come in contact with just like you would a friend or a loved one.

33. Ascent Construction Inc.
Centerville, UT
General contractor
Founder(s): Brad L. Knowlton, J. Scott Johnson, Ron Bagley
Began: 2000
2004 Sales: $18.2M
Initial Investment: $500K

Success Secret: Find out what you love to do, then formulate a plan to get paid to do it.

34. Structure Networks Inc.
Tustin, CA
www.structurenetworks.com
IT staffing and consulting
Founder(s): Alex Salottolo
Began: 2001
2004 Sales: $12.3M
Initial Investment: $3K

Success Secret: Never let success overtake you. The minute you do, it can slip away.

35. marketRx Inc.
Bridgewater, NJ
www.marketrx.com
Sales and marketing services for pharmaceutical companies
Founder(s): Jaswinder S. Chadha, Phil Brennan, Navdeep Chadha
Began: 2000
2004 Sales: $16.7M
Initial Investment: $13.9M

Success Secret: Fail fast. It's important to constantly experiment and evaluate success and failure quickly. Try many things, and keep what works.

36. YESTech Inc.

San Clemente, CA
www.yestechinc.com
Optical and X-ray inspection systems
Founder(s): Richard Amtower, Don Miller, Owen Sit, Garrett Zopf, Troy Johnson, Robert Un, Richard DePalma
Began: 2002
2004 Sales: $7.2M
Initial Investment: $642.5K

Success Secret: Recognize that the major differentiating quality between companies is the quality of the employees.

37. American Community Bank & Trust

Woodstock, IL
www.amcombank.com
Community bank
Founder(s): Charie A. Zanck, Andrew T. Hartlieb, Rick M. Francois
Began: 2000
2004 Sales: $16.4M
Initial Investment: $19.1M

Success Secret: Be vigilant in preserving and promoting your core values.

38. Lumber One

Van Buren, AR
www.lumberone.org
Lumber
Founder(s): Stephen Gann, William Dodson, Dennis Joyce
Began: 2002
2004 Sales: $8.96M
Initial Investment: $500K

Success Secret: Make every decision that involves other people as if, by sunrise tomorrow, it will be known in 1) the front page of your local paper, 2) the marquee in your parking lot, 3) your mother's breakfast table. Do this, and you'll be okay.

39. Anteo Group

Atlanta, GA
www.anteogroup.com
IT staffing and consulting
Founder(s): Dion DeLoof, James Yeagle
Began: 2002
2004 Sales: $8.6M
Initial Investment: $400K

Success Secret: Hire the right people! Since we are in the people business, it is imperative that we hire the right type of person who handles our internal culture as well as our clients' cultures.

40. Kurtzman Carson Consultants LLC

Los Angeles, CA
www.kccllc.com
Financial and technology services firm specializing in corporate restructuring
Founder(s): Jonathan A. Carson, Eric S. Kurtzman
Began: 2001
2004 Sales: $11.8M
Initial Investment: $200K

Success Secret: Focus on core competencies, and profits will follow.

41. Kitchens Direct of Sarasota Inc.

Sarasota, FL
www.kitchensdirectofsarasota.com
Cabinet and countertop sales and installation
Founder(s): Tony J. Zanoni, Karl Susmann, Jim Powers
Began: 2001
2004 Sales: $12M
Initial Investment: $27K

Success Secret: Treat staff and customers as if they are special, because they are your lifeline to success.

42. LG&P In-Store Agency

Paramus, NJ
www.lginstore.com
Brand and retail marketing agency
Founder(s): Rob Gerstner, David Lloyd
Began: 2001

2004 Sales: $9.4M
Initial Investment: $90K

Success Secret: Manage cash with your life.

43. PointRoll Inc.
Fort Washington, PA
www.pointroll.com
Online marketing services and technology
Founder(s): Jules Gardner
Began: 2000
2004 Sales: $13.7M
Initial Investment: NA

Success Secret: Walk the walk before you talk the talk. Earn your credibility. Keep your options open, and never, never give up.

44. Mobius Partners
San Antonio, TX
www.mobiuspartners.com
Computer reseller
Founder(s): Jay Uribe, Junab Ali
Began: 2000
2004 Sales: $12.1M
Initial Investment: $30K

Success Secret: Work hard, and the rewards will come in time.

45. Business Flooring Specialists
Richland Hills, TX
www.bfsflooring.com
Flooring sales and installation
Founder(s): Jeff Bennett, Dale Walton
Began: 2003
2004 Sales: $4.9M
Initial Investment: $400K

Success Secret: Start with a solid business philosophy, strategy, and plan, then deliver it with perfection.

46. Professional Builders Supply LLC
Raleigh, NC
Building-materials distribution
Founder(s): Van Isley
Began: 2003
2004 Sales: $4.5M
Initial Investment: $900K

Success Secret: Take care of your employees, and they will, in turn, take care of your customers.

47. Talisman International LLC
Washington, DC
www.talisman-intl.com
Litigation assistance and computer network security consulting
Founder(s): Michael J. Hutsell, Arthur J. Wacaster, Thomas H. Heitman, Hugh L. Thompson Jr., O. Niel Skousen, John A. Olshinski
Began: 2002
2004 Sales: $7.4M
Initial Investment: $79K

Success Secret: We only accept work in areas where we are well qualified, and we always do high-quality work.

48. UltraCade Technologies
San Jose, CA
www.ultracade.com
Video game manufacturer
Founder(s): David Foley
Began: 2002
2004 Sales: $5.9M
Initial Investment: $2.5M

Success Secret: Plan for the best-case scenario and prepare for the worst-case scenario.

49. Q Staffing Services
Fullerton, CA
www.qstaffingservices.com
Temporary staffing
Founder(s): Robert J. Gaynor
Began: 2001
2004 Sales: $8.7M
Initial Investment: $30K

Success Secret: Underpromise, and overdeliver.

50. WebXites LP
Houston, TX
www.webxites.com
Web site design, hosting, e-mail, and online marketing
Founder(s): Gene McCubbin

Began: 2001
2004 Sales: $8.4M
Initial Investment: $500K

Success Secret: Familiarity breeds contempt. Leaders must always maintain the proper example in all their actions and show bravery, honesty and integrity in every effort they undertake.

51. Kelle's Transport Services

Salt Lake City, UT
www.kellestransport.com
Transportation services/long-haul trucking
Founder(s): Kelle Simon
Began: 2002
2004 Sales: $6.9M
Initial Investment: $45K

Success Secret: Treat your employees like they are your customers.

52. Vocera Communications

Cupertino, CA
www.vocera.com
Wireless communications
Founder(s): Robert Shostak, Paul Barsley, Randy Nielsen
Began: 2000
2004 Sales: $12.1M
Initial Investment: $37.3M

Success Secret: Listen to your customers' needs, and then provide a product that they find they cannot live without.

53. Innovation Ads Inc.

New York, NY
www.innovationads.com
Interactive direct-marketing services
Founder(s): Iain Grae, Michael Lastoria
Began: 2002
2004 Sales: $5.5M
Initial Investment: $0

Success Secret: Execution. Have the discipline to follow through with what you say, and take responsibility for your successes or failures—do not just manage expectations.

54. Laminates R Us Inc.

Coral Springs, FL
www.laminatesrus.com
Laminate wood flooring sales and installation
Founder(s): Ken Baer, Pattie Capezza
Began: 2001
2004 Sales: $7.4M
Initial Investment: $900

Success Secret: Take an ordinary business and approach it in an extraordinary way.

55. Equity Consultants LLC

Richfield, OH
www.equityconsultants.com
Mortgage company
Founder(s): Goran Marich, Ryko Marich
Began: 2002
2004 Sales: $6.3M
Initial Investment: $75K

Success Secret: Set big goals and expect big things from your staff. People will rise to your standards and expectations.

56. Panther Technologies Inc.

Medford, NJ
www.panthertech.com
Environmental remediation contractor
Founder(s): Peter J. Palko, John Twomey, Robert Foley
Began: 2000
2004 Sales: $10.8M
Initial Investment: $80K

Success Secret: Make decisions based on your comfort level, and don't let others sway you.

57. Ritchey Enterprises Inc.

Atlanta, GA
General contractor
Founder(s): Jeffrey H. Ritchey
Began: 2003
2004 Sales: $3.1M
Initial Investment: $3K

Success Secret: Focus on finding great people to work for and to work with; build relationships based on integrity and core values.

58. US Environmental Inc.

Downingtown, PA
www.usenv.com
Environmental services
Founder(s): Richard L. Weaver, James M. Hoff
Began: 2000
2004 Sales: $10.6M
Initial Investment: $100K

Success Secret: Build and maintain relationships with customers, vendors, and employees. These relationships are key to any company's success.

59. Sourcery

New York, NY
www.sourceryonline.com
Product design and sourcing agency
Founder(s): Scott Milstein, Noah Ross
Began: 2002
2004 Sales: $4.9M
Initial Investment: $300K

Success Secret: Stay the course. You are never as good as you think you are when things are going well, and never as bad when things are going poorly.

60. Homeland Solutions Inc.

Carlsbad, CA
www.hsiteam.com
Technical infrastructure design and installation
Founder(s): Lou Wilburn, Frank Gomez, Kyle Hoover, Brett Pollack
Began: 2003
2004 Sales: $3.8M
Initial Investment: $150K

Success Secret: Spend adequate time to ensure executive and management roles and responsibilities are clearly defined and documented.

61. Texas Air Composites

Cedar Hill, TX
www.texasaircomposites.com
Aircraft component repair and overhauling
Founder(s): Randy Haran, Michael Haran, Glen Daugherty, Ed Schauer, Russ Oonk
Began: 2000

2004 Sales: $10.2M
Initial Investment: $220K

Success Secret: Establishing and ownership culture that enables employees to feel, think, and act like owners. If employees feel like they have a voice in the direction of the company, the sky's the limit.

62. Sunlight Saunas

Lenexa, KS
www.sunlightsaunas.com
Infrared saunas
Founder(s): Jason L. Jeffers, Connie J. Zack, Aaron M. Zack
Began: 2001
2004 Sales: $6.8M
Initial Investment: $200K

Success Secret: Never settle for anything less than the best. If you cannot be the best, or don't have the desire to be the best, do not do it.

63. Commerce West Bank

Irvine, CA
www.cwbk.com
Commercial banking
Founder(s): Ivo A. Tjan
Began: 2001
2004 Sales: $6.6M
Initial Investment: $10.5M

Success Secret: It's not the mileage of the car, but where the car has been that is most important.

64. Nanosys Inc.

Palo Alto, CA
www.nanosysinc.com
Nanotechnology
Founder(s): Larry Bock
Began: 2001
2004 Sales: $6.8M
Initial Investment: $55M

Success Secret: The key to having a good business is to be in a good business. You have to give to get. Help without being asked, and help without keeping a scorecard.

65. Apex Mortgage Services LLC
Columbus, OH
www.apexmortgage.cc
Residential and commercial mortgage broker
Founder(s): Brenton T. Cline, Zachary G. Swartz
Began: 2003
2004 Sales: $3.8M
Initial Investment: $110K

Success Secret: Treat your employees with the utmost respect: 90 percent of your assets walk out the door every night—do whatever you can to ensure they come back the next morning.

66. The Alaris Group Inc.
Edina, MN
www.alarisgroup.com
Medical and disability case management firm
Founder(s): Nancy J. Caven, Christine Delich, Kandise Garrison, Jane Petersen, Cheryl San Martin
Began: 2000
2004 Sales: $9.5M
Initial Investment: $2K

Success Secret: The culture we promote is one of support and affirmation, which allows us to attract and employ the best of the best.

67. Exhale Enterprises Inc.
New York, NY
www.exhalespa.com
Spa
Founder(s): Annbeth Eschbach
Began: 2001
2004 Sales: $5.6M
Initial Investment: $40M

Success Secret: Always evolve, but do so within the context of being true to your core values.

68. Axiom Legal
New York, NY
www.axiomlegal.com
Legal services firm
Founder(s): Mark Harris, Alec Guettel
Began: 2000
2004 Sales: $8.9M
Initial Investment: $5.3M

Success Secret: Remember that business is a human construct: interact with colleagues and clients as human beings, not as instruments of growth and profitability.

69. Techlink Northwest
Bellevue, WA
www.techlinknw.com
Technical staffing
Founder(s): Donn Harvey, Debra Harvey
Began: 2001
2004 Sales: $5.7M
Initial Investment: $40K

Success Secret: To work *on* the business, not *in* the business. —Michael Gerber

70. MNM Distribution Corporation
Houston, TX
www.mnmdistribution.com
Wholesale and retail goods distributor
Founder(s): Moses Musallam
Began: 2002
2004 Sales: $5.4M
Initial Investment: $105K

Success Secret: Be aggressive, and take risks, but make sure they're calculated risks.

71. Advance Med LLC
Cedar Park, TX
www.advancemed.org
Health–care staffing
Founder(s): John Clements, Erick Barnett, Kaine Smith
Began: 2001
2004 Sales: $5.9M
Initial Investment: $100K

Success Secret: Move on. Whether you just lost or gained a large client, you have to always be looking for new clients.

72. The Perishable Specialist Inc.
Miami, FL
www.theperishablespecialist.com
Customs broker specializing in perishable goods
Founder(s): Frank A. Ramos
Began: 2002

Section 2

2004 Sales: $5.1M
Initial Investment: $100K

Success Secret: Maintain a PHD mentality—Poor, Hungry, and Driven.

73. Cybera Inc.
Nashville, TN
www.cybera.net
Private, broadband wide-area networking solutions
Founder(s): Cliff Duffy
Began: 2001
2004 Sales: $6.5M
Initial Investment: $5.8M

Success Secret: Everyone told me not to start during a slump in the industry, but since I did, I had little competition and gained a head start over future competitors.

74. TCP Communications LLC
Beverly, MA
www.tcpcommunications.com
Communication towers
Founder(s): Paul McGinn
Began: 2002
2004 Sales: $3.8M
Initial Investment: $1.1M

Success Secret: Have great employees, and keep focused on the core elements of the business.

75. Glacier Computer LLC
New Milford, CT
www.glaciercomputer.com
Rugged mobile computer systems
Founder(s): John Geary, Dan Poisson, Don Berch, Ron D'Ambrosio
Began: 2000
2004 Sales: $7.2M
Initial Investment: $250K

Success Secret: Be consumed by customer service. Problems are going to happen; responding to them quickly will allow your customers to mentally move past them. As obvious as this is, your competitors aren't doing it.

76. Crestwood Technology Group
Tuckahoe, NY

www.ctg123.com
Wholesale electronic components
Founder(s): Claire McGarvey, Denise Gilchrist, Katherine Saviano
Began: 2000
2004 Sales: $6.3M
Initial Investment: $4.8K

Success Secret: Respect, respond to, and care for your clients in a manner that is greater than you would expect for yourself.

77. American Steel Corporation
Mesa, AZ
www.americansteelcorporation.com
Steel fabrication and erection
Founder(s): Tim Williamson
Began: 2001
2004 Sales: $5.8M
Initial Investment: $100K

Success Secret: Don't lose sight of your bread and butter.

78. 4 Star Electronics
San Clemente, CA
www.4starelectronics.com
Electronic components distributor
Founder(s): Duane Wilson, Josh Wilson, Jake Wilson
Began: 2001
2004 Sales: $5.2M
Initial Investment: $200K

Success Secret: Always stay one step ahead of your competitor.

79. Data Partners Inc.
Fort Myers, FL
www.data-partners.com
Provider of marketing lists, demographics, and analytics
Founder(s): Brigid Berry, Jody Pelfrey
Began: 2002
2004 Sales: $3.9M
Initial Investment: $75K

Success Secret: Once you stop having fun, it's time to find something else to do.

80. Delta Consulting Group Inc.

Occoquan, VA

www.delta-cgi.com

Engineering, accounting, and management consulting

Founder(s): Jeffrey E. Fuchs, J. Mark Dungan

Began: 2000

2004 Sales: $6.9M

Initial Investment: $30K

Success Secret: Fill your company with intelligent, hardworking, and dedicated employees.

81. Jenkco Inc.

Fontana, CA

www.jenkco.com

Computer distributor

Founder(s): Shawn Jenkins, Greg Rowney

Began: 2003

2004 Sales: $2.2M

Initial Investment: $15K

Success Secret: Do not be afraid of change. Take a chance, and believe in your ability.

82. American Realty Professionals Inc.

Conyers, GA

www.americanrealtypro.com

Real estate brokerage

Founder(s): Shane Mask, Traci Mask

Began: 2002

2004 Sales: $2.9M

Initial Investment: $150K

Success Secret: Value long-term relationships over short-term profits.

83. DZP Marketing Communications

New York, NY

www.dzpusa.com

Advertising and marketing

Founder(s): John Barker, Brian Diecks

Began: 2003

2004 Sales: $1.9M

Initial Investment: $78K

Success Secret: You can't pay rent with receivables. Cash flow is king.

84. Investor Relations Int'l.

Los Angeles, CA

www.irintl.com

Investor-relations services

Founder(s): Haris Tajyar

Began: 2002

2004 Sales: $3.5M

Initial Investment: $10K

Success Secret: It takes about 20 years to build a reputation and five minutes to ruin it. If you think about that, you'll do things differently. — Warren Buffett

85. Crown Partners

Dayton, OH

www.crownpartners.com

Consulting and systems integration

Founder(s): Richard Hearn, Dave Bennett, Mark Kennedy

Began: 2001

2004 Sales: $5.1M

Initial Investment: $6K

Success Secret: Most partners are only good for dancing. Pick partners that you have a history with (successes and failures).

86. GetActive Software

Berkeley, CA

www.getactive.com

Provider of relationship-management products for membership organizations

Founder(s): Sheeraz Haji

Began: 2000

2004 Sales: $6.1M

Initial Investment: $9M

Success Secret: Hire the smartest, most talented individuals you can find, and keep them happy. Surround yourself with people who will help ensure the success of your clients and your business while making you look good in the process.

87. IO Integration Inc.

San Francisco, CA

www.iointegration.com

Systems integration

Founder(s): Eric Rewitzer, Mike Holt, Nige Oswald, Brian Anderson

Began: 2001

2004 Sales: $3.8M
Initial Investment: $150K

Success Secret: Persistence, follow-up, and effort.

88. Sierra Logic
Roseville, CA
www.sierralogic.com
Silicon storage solutions
Founder(s): Bob Whitson, Margie Euashenk, Bryan Cowger, Joe Steinmetz
Began: 2001
2004 Sales: $4.4M
Initial Investment: $200K

Success Secret: Always trust your intuition.

89. Quest Builders Group Inc.
New York, NY
www.questbuildersgroup.com
Construction management
Founder(s): Raymond Murray, Patrick J. Fitzpatrick
Began: 2000
2004 Sales: $5.2M
Initial Investment: $10K

Success Secret: It is better to do less work efficiently than more work by the seat of your pants.

90. American Broadband Inc.
Uniontown, PA
www.american-bb.com
Private network service provider
Founder(s): Stephen John, Andy Newton, Paul Bullington, Eric Daniels
Began: 2002
2004 Sales: $2.2M
Initial Investment: $5.1M

Success Secret: You can't be all things to all people. Focus on what you do best, and perform beyond people's expectations.

91. Measurable Solutions
Clearwater, FL
www.measurablesolutions.com
Executive training
Founder(s): Jeff F. Lee, Shaun Kirk

Began: 2001
2004 Sales: $4M
Initial Investment: $0

Success Secret: Promote broadly to all potential public, and internally make sure everyone's purposes align with the goals of the group.

92. Expression Analysis
Durham, NC
www.expressionanalysis.com
Genetic testing services
Founder(s): Steven Casey, Donald Holzworth
Began: 2001
2004 Sales: $3.3M
Initial Investment: $1.2M

Success Secret: Customer service: We do not differentiate ourselves on price—we provide a higher level of service and quality. For us to compete with academic institutions that have captive audience mentalities, we must show our clients the value of our services, which justifies our higher commercial pricing.

93. Shearer & Associates
Huntsville, AL
www.shearerassociates.us
Facilities and security engineering
Founder(s): Robert F. Shearer
Began: 2000
2004 Sales: $4.3M
Initial Investment: $32K

Success Secret: Take good care of your people. Be open and honest, with no secrets.

94. Mel's Tire LLC
Emporia, KS
Retail tires and suspension; auto and light truck repairs
Founder(s): Melvin Reed, Joseph Dreier, Allen Mize, Todd Preisner
Began: 2002
2004 Sales: $2.6M
Initial Investment: $312.5K

Success Secret: If you treat people the way you would like to be treated and give great service, they will come back.

Section 2

95. Business Vitals LLC
Columbia, SC
www.businessvitals.com
Information security consulting and outsourcing
Founder(s): Jeff Brewer
Began: 2001
2004 Sales: $3.1M
Initial Investment: $50K

Success Secret: Surround yourself with capable people, people of integrity, and people who aren't afraid to tell you what they think.

96. Excel Occupational Health Clinic PC
Bedford Park, IL
www.excelhealth.net
Occupational and sports medicine practice
Founder(s): Joe Laluya, Ed Pillar
Began: 2001
2004 Sales: $3.1M
Initial Investment: $350K

Success Secret: Become an expert in a focused area, and people will seek you out for that expertise.

97. ExtenData Solutions LLC
Englewood, CO
www.extendata.com
Mobile computing and automated data collection solutions
Founder(s): Steve Sager
Began: 2002
2004 Sales: $2.9M
Initial Investment: $400K

Success Secret: Surround yourself with good people, and good things will happen.

98. Auctionpay Inc.
Portland, OR
www.auctionpay.com
Fundraising solutions and services for nonprofit organizations
Founder(s): Jeff Jetton
Began: 2001
2004 Sales: $3.2M
Initial Investment: $200K

Success Secret: Make really good decisions, and recover quickly from the bad ones.

99. Brand Resources Group
Atlanta, GA
www.brandresourcesgroup.com
Communications consulting
Founder(s): Jane L. Barwis
Began: 2001
2004 Sales: $3M
Initial Investment: $20K

Success Secret: You can do anything if you put your mind to it. This is not only the best business advice; it's also great life advice.

100. Big Island Grill
Kailua Kona, HI
Restaurant
Founder(s): Bruce Goold, Maile Goold
Began: 2002
2004 Sales: $1.97M
Initial Investment: $60K

Success Secret: We keep our customers happy by serving good food with good service at affordable prices.

Source: Entrepreneur and PricewaterhouseCoopers, "2005 Hot 100," www.entrepreneur.com/hot100/listings/0,6868,296117-2005-0,00.html.

Chapter 9

Researching and Doing Your Homework

Lists of Business Entities to Form

Anyone who operates a business, alone or with others, may incorporate. This is also true for anyone or any group engaged in religious, civil, non-profit, or charitable endeavors. You do not have to be a business giant to be able to have the financial and other benefits of operating a corporation. Given the right circumstances, the owner(s) of a business of any size can benefit from incorporating.

General Corporation

This is the most common corporate structure. The corporation is a separate legal entity that is owned by stockholders. A general corporation may have an unlimited number of stockholders, who, due to the separate legal nature of the corporation, are protected from the creditors of the business. A stockholder's personal liability is usually limited to the amount of investment in the corporation and no more.

Advantages

- Owners' personal assets are protected from business debt and liability.
- Corporations have unlimited life, extending beyond the illness or death of the owners.
- Tax-free benefits such as insurance, travel, and retirement plan deductions.
- Transfer of ownership facilitated by sale of stock.
- Change of ownership need not affect management.
- Easier to raise capital through sale of stocks and bonds.

Disadvantages

- More expensive to form than proprietorship or partnerships.
- More legal formality.
- More state and federal rules and regulations.

Close Corporation

There are a few minor, but significant differences between general corporations and close corporations. In most states where they are recognized, close corporations are limited to 30 to 50 stockholders. In addition, many close corporation statutes require that the directors of a close corporation must first offer the shares to existing stock-holders before selling to new shareholders.

This type of corporation is particularly well suited for a group of individuals who will own the corporation with some members actively involved in the management and other members involved only on a limited or indirect level.

S Corporation

With the Tax Reform Act of 1986, the S Corporation became a highly desirable entity for corporate tax purposes. An S Corporation is not really a different type of corporation. It is a special tax designation applied for and granted by the IRS to corporations that have already been formed. Many entrepreneurs and small business owners are partial to the S Corporation because it combines many of the advantages of the sole proprietorship, partnership, and the corporate forms of business structure.

S Corporations have the same basic advantages and disadvantages of general or close corporations with the added benefit of the S Corporation special tax provisions. When a standard corporation (general, close, or professional) makes a profit, it pays a federal corporate income tax on the profit. If the company declares a dividend, the shareholders must report the dividend as personal income and pay more taxes.

S Corporations avoid this "double taxation" (once at the corporate level and again at the personal level) because all income or loss is reported only once, on the personal tax returns of the shareholders. However, like standard corporations (and unlike some partnerships), the S Corporation shareholders are exempt from personal liability for business debt.

S Corporation Restrictions

To elect S Corporation status, your corporation must meet specific guidelines. As a result of the 1996 Tax Law, which became effective January 1, 1997, many of these qualifying guidelines have been changed. A few of these changes are noted below:

- Prior to the 1996 Tax Law, the maximum number of shareholders was 35. The maximum number of shareholders for an S Corporation has been increased to 75.

- Previously, S Corporation ownership was limited to individuals, estates, and certain trusts. Under the new law, stock of an S Corporation may be held by a new "electing small business trust." All beneficiaries of the trust must be individuals or estates, except that charitable organizations may hold limited interests. Interests in the trust must be acquired by gift or bequest—not by purchase. Each potential current beneficiary of the trust is counted toward the 75-shareholder limit on S Corporation shareholders.

- S Corporations are now allowed to own 80 percent or more of the stock of a regular C corporation, which may elect to file a consolidated return with other affiliated regular C corporations. The S Corporation itself may not join in that election. In addition, an S Corporation is now allowed to own a "qualified subchapter S subsidiary." The parent S Corporation must own 100 percent of the stock of the subsidiary.

- Qualified retirement plans or Section 501(c)(3) charitable organizations may now be shareholders in S Corporations.

- All S Corporations must have shareholders who are citizens or residents of the United States. Nonresident aliens cannot be shareholders.

- S Corporations may only issue one class of stock.

- No more than 25 percent of the gross corporate income may be derived from passive income.

■ An S Corporation can generally provide employee benefits and deferred compensation plans.

■ S Corporations eliminate the problems faced by standard corporations whose shareholder-employees might be subject to IRS claims of excessive compensation.

■ Not all domestic general business corporations are eligible for S Corporation status. These exclusions include:

- A financial institution that is a bank;

- An insurance company taxed under Subchapter L;

- A Domestic International Sales Corporation (DISC); or

- Certain affiliated groups of corporations.

Keep in mind: these lists of qualifying S Corporation aspects are not all-inclusive. In addition, there are specific circumstances in which an S Corporation may owe income tax. For more detailed information about these changes and other aspects regarding S Corporation status, contact your accountant, attorney, or local IRS office.

How to File as an S Corporation

To become an S Corporation, you must know the mechanics of filing for this special tax status. Your first step is to form a general, close, or professional corporation in the state of your choice. Second, you must obtain the formal consent of the corporation's shareholders. This consent should be noted in the corporation's minutes. Once the filing is approved, your company must complete Form 2553, Election by a Small Business Corporation. This form must be filed with the appropriate IRS office for your region. Please consult the IRS' instructions for Form 2553 to determine your proper deadline for completing and submitting this form.

Limited Liability Company (LLC)

LLCs have long been a traditional form of business structure in Europe and Latin America. LLCs were first introduced in the United States by the state of Wyoming in 1977 and authorized for pass-through taxation (similar to partnerships and S Corporations) by the IRS in 1988. All 50 states and Washington, DC have now adopted some form of LLC legislation for both domestic and foreign (out-of-state) limited liability companies.

Many business professionals believe LLCs present a superior alternative to corporations and partnerships because LLCs combine many of the advantages of both. With an LLC, the owners can have the corporate liability protection for their personal assets from business debt as well as the tax advantages of partnerships or S Corporations. It is similar to an S Corporation without the IRS's restrictions.

Advantages

■ Protection of personal assets from business debt.

■ Profits/losses pass through to personal income tax returns of the owners.

- Great flexibility in management and organization of the business.

- LLCs do not have the ownership restrictions of S Corporations, making them ideal business structures for foreign investors.

Disadvantages

- LLCs often have a limited life (not to exceed 30 years in many states).

- Some states require at least two members to form an LLC.

- LLCs are not corporations and therefore do not have stock—and the benefits of stock ownership and sales.

As with the S Corporation listing, these lists are not inclusive. For more detailed information, please be sure to speak with a qualified legal and/or financial advisor.

Important Note Regarding the Federal Taxation of LLCs

Before January 1, 1997, the Internal Revenue Service determined whether a limited liability company would be taxed "like a partnership" or "like a corporation" by analyzing its legal structure or by requiring the members to elect the tax status on a special form. As of January 1, 1997, the IRS simplified this process.

Now if a limited liability company has satisfied IRS requirements, it can be treated as a partnership for federal tax purposes. As such, LLCs are required to file the same federal tax forms as partnerships and take advantage of the same benefits. However, this is still a highly technical area, and if you require further information, it is recommended that you communicate with the Internal Revenue Service or consult a competent professional such as a qualified tax accountant or attorney.

Source: The Company Corporation, www.morebusiness.com/getting_started/incorporating/ d934832501.brc.

Tips on When to File an Employer Identification Number (EIN)

An EIN is a nine-digit number assigned to sole proprietors, corporations, partnerships, estates, trusts, and other entities for tax filing and reporting purposes. The information you provide on this form will establish your business tax account. The list below is a listing of who must file an EIN.

- If you pay wages to one or more employees, including household employees

- Use EIN to use on any return, statement, or other document, even if you are not an employer.

- You are a withholding agent required to withhold taxes on income, other than wages, paid to a nonresident alien.

- You file Schedule C, Profit or Loss From Business (Schedule C-EZ), Net Profit Form

Business, or Schedule F, Profit or Loss Farming, or Form 1040, U.S. Individual Income Tax Return and are required to file excise, employment, alcohol, tobacco, or firearms taxes.

Source: SBA, *Starting a Business Handbook.*

SCORE's Five Tips for Using Colleges and Universities to Help Your Business

1. Volunteer your company to be a business school case study. You'll learn much about your company in the process and get good ideas for the future.

2. Obtain management and technical assistance from one of more than 50 Small Business Development Centers. Check the U.S. Small Business Administration web site at www.sba.gov for locations.

3. Participate in special programs. Many colleges and universities sponsor venture capital forums, entrepreneurship centers, and family business programs.

4. Work with the business school to offer internships to graduate students.

5. Find out what expertise is on a business school's staff. You may find just the right person to hire as a consultant or serve on your board.

Source: SCORE, www.score.org/business_tips.html.

Six Guidelines for Conducting Start-up Research

1. **Find the one.** Pick one person to oversee all your market research—it's a full-time job. If you have one person at the helm, you can ensure there's a linear and constant flow of information.

2. **Play both ways.** Do both quantitative and qualitative research. Quantitative looks at a general group to find major trends. Qualitative looks at more personal issues to find the whys of major trends.

3. **Use the net.** It's an incredible way to get real-time feedback. Which flavor do customers like best: raspberry or lemon? Conduct a flash poll on your site—you'll get instant results.

4. **Choose wisely.** If you decide to use a market research firm, be selective. Just like any other vendor selection, even if you're a small company, you have every right to do an RFP and ask for references. Your company's future is at stake. Be mindful of how long that research firm has been covering your market.

5. **Don't treat research as gospel.** You can't take everything an analyst says as the be-

all, end-all of information. Ask questions. Understand the methodology of the researchers. Is the analyst looking at both sides—what vendors and customers are saying—before making an analysis?

6. **Make a commitment.** Market research is a vital part of any business plan, but don't forget about it once you've opened your doors. Do a great deal of broad, quantitative research in the planning stages to learn your market, then modify it into more targeted research within your customer base in order to define and launch your new company. Finally, broaden the scope again. Get feedback from your customers, and find out how you can best improve.

Don't forget to benchmark yourself against the right set of companies out there and monitor the competition, and make sure that, no matter what type of business you're in, you're among the best of the best.

Source: Nichole L. Torres, "The Search Is On," www.entrepreneur.com/article/ 0,4621,278410,00.html.

Top Places to Find General Trends in Business

Don't we all wish we had insight so we could better grow our business? Well, predicting trends isn't necessarily as hard as it appears.

- First, look to yourself, your friends, family, and colleagues. What grabs your attention will likely captivate theirs as well. Are you spending more time in the garden? Dressing more casually? Or ordering more by mail? These are all clues.

- Next, look around you. What are Americans watching on TV? What are the most popular movies? Reading magazines and newspapers—and not just your local ones— often leads to insights you can build ideas on.

- Futurist Watts Wacker says you can hone your predictive skills by merely listening more, especially to people whose points of view are different than yours.

Source: Rieva Lesonsky, *365 Tips to Boost Your Entrepreneurial IQ.*

| Chapter 10 |

Conducting Market Research

How to Get on Target

You need market research to hit the mark with prospects. But if costly surveys and focus groups aren't in the financial picture, try these creative, budget-friendly ways to get to know your clients' target audience. Isabella Trebond, a marketing consultant who specializes in start-up business planning and copywriting, shares some tips.

Step 1: Define Your Target Customers

Your "target customers" are those who are most likely to buy from you. Resist the temptation to be too general in the hopes of getting a larger slice of the market. That's like firing 10 bullets in random directions instead of aiming just one dead center of the mark—expensive and dangerous.

Try to describe them with as much detail as you can, based on your knowledge of your product or service.

Here are some questions to get you started:

- Are your target customers male or female?

- How old are they?

- Where do they live? Is geography a limiting factor for any reason?

- What do they do for a living?

- How much money do they make? This is most significant if you're selling relatively expensive or luxury items. Most people can afford a carob bar. You can't say the same of custom murals.

- What other aspects of their lives matter? If you're launching a roof-tiling service, the target customers probably own their homes.

Step 2: Decide if You Have a Market

Before you commit hours to researching what your customers want from you, it makes sense to find out whether you have a viable target market.

The cheapest and simplest way to do this is through "secondary data," or information someone else has already gathered for you. Usually, this takes the form of various statistics and can only answer closed-ended questions: How many? When? Where? Your own questions will depend on your customer profile and become more tightly targeted based on what you find out as you go.

You can find answers in a number of ways:

1. **Reference librarians:** Most are delighted to help you research. Often, they'll practically do it for you. These days, they can look up a lot of what you need on computer databases, and you have a decent chance of walking away with all your answers. Printouts may cost several cents per page.

2. **The local field office of the Department of Commerce:** It should supply you with free or nearly free information on population, demographics, housing, the economy, market trends, surveys of current businesses, and more.

3. **The business libraries of local universities:** These often have more specific information on business trends than a public library. Ask the librarian for help.

4. **Your local SBA branch or Small Business Development Center:** It has a multitude of publications and business literature full of advice and market forecasts.

Once you've got all the answers, it's time for a judgment call: Do you have a working market?

Only you can decide if 14 competitors are too many for 19,000 target customers, or if you want to gamble on the fact that your target customer spent 30 percent more last year than three years ago. If you don't like the numbers, at least you've just saved yourself from a potential financial disaster. Now you're armed with a much better grasp of market conditions to revamp your business idea or marketing direction and return to Step 1.

Step 3: Get to Know Your Marketing

Once you decide you have a viable market, it's time to find out more about it. Keep your mind open to any information, but also keep a list of primary research questions handy, such as:

- **Who influences your customers and how?** Spouses, neighbors, peer groups, professional colleagues, children, and the media can all affect buying decisions. Look for hints that one or more of these are a factor for you.

- **Why do they buy?** Distinguish between the features and the benefits your product or service offers. Features describe what it is; benefits are what your customers get out of it. The latter is why your customers pay you. Are they looking for a status symbol, a savings in time or energy, a personal treat, or something else?

- **Why should customers choose you and not your competition?** What can you offer that the competition doesn't?

- **How do your customers prefer to buy?** Many businesses benefit from the broader market provided by the internet and mail order, while others do better with a physical presence. Don't assume you fall into one category or the other; customers may surprise you.

Keep those questions in mind as you take the following research steps:

1. **Read, read, read.** Articles, interviews, and survey results published in trade periodicals reflect specialist knowledge of your market. Publications that focus on your business type are invaluable for forecasting upcoming trends and identifying customers' needs. But ads, letters to the editor, and other "extras" can be even more revealing. Study the ads (full- and half-page ones as well as the classifieds) of businesses similar to yours; watch for features your competitors most want to empha-

size or de-emphasize. Readers' letters often contain information on what your customers like or dislike about certain products or companies. Editorial pieces frequently highlight hot trends, which should have a bearing on your marketing plan.

2. **Tap the internet.** Newsgroups and discussion lists on the internet debate every imaginable topic. Chances are, some of them partially match your customer profile. They may be talking about the type of product or service you offer—or can be encouraged to do so. Best of all, everything they've ever said has been archived.

You can also take it one step further and start your own thread to initiate a more tightly focused discussion.

3. **Check out the competition.** You can learn about what to do and not to do by studying your competitors. Visit their web sites and look at their prices, guarantees, testimonials, and special offers. If they offer newsletters, get on their mailing lists. You'll get free information on improvements, new product lines, trends, and even customer responses.

Try calling or e-mailing them to ask about their rates and services. If they have stores, visit and browse them. Write down your impressions as soon as you've hung up or left the building. Keep a record of each one, and ask what all or most of them have in common, why you think that is, and how you can set yourself apart.

4. **Get students involved.** Call or visit the web sites of local business colleges as well as the faculty of business departments at universities and colleges in your area. Find out who teaches classes on marketing, preferably small-business marketing. Try to persuade them that your business would make a great real-life market research project.

Source: Isabella Trebond, "On Target," www.entrepreneur.com/article/0,4621,316421,00.html.

Researching Your Market—Primary Research

Whether you're just starting out or if you've been in business for years, you should always stay up-to-date with your market information. Here are the best methods for finding your data.

The purpose of market research is to provide relevant data that will help solve marketing problems a business will encounter. This is absolutely necessary in the start-up phase.

Primary Research

When conducting primary research using your own resources, you must first decide how you will question your target group of individuals. There are basically three avenues you can take: direct mail, telemarketing, or personal interviews.

1. **Direct Mail.** If you choose a direct-mail questionnaire, be sure to do the following in order to increase your response rate:

- Make sure your questions are short and to the point.
- Make sure questionnaires are addressed to specific individuals and they're of interest to the respondent.
- Limit the questionnaire's length to two pages.
- Enclose a professionally prepared cover letter that adequately explains what you need.
- Send a reminder about two weeks after the initial mailing. Include a postage-paid self-addressed envelope.

Unfortunately, even if you employ the above tactics, response to direct mail is always low, sometimes less than five percent.

2. Phone Surveys

Phone surveys are generally the most cost-effective, considering overall response rates; they cost about one-third as much as personal interviews, which have, on average, a response rate of only ten percent. Following are some phone survey guidelines:

- At the beginning of the conversation, your interviewer should confirm the name of the respondent if calling a home, or give the appropriate name to the switchboard operator if calling a business.
- Pauses should be avoided, as respondent interest can quickly drop.
- Make sure that a follow-up call is possible if additional information is required.
- Make sure that interviewers don't divulge details about the poll until the respondent is reached.

As mentioned, phone interviews are cost-effective but speed is another big advantage. Some of the more experienced interviewers can get through up to ten interviews an hour (however, speed for speed's sake is not the goal of any of these surveys), but five to six per hour is more typical. Phone interviews also allow you to cover a wide geographical range relatively inexpensively. Phone costs can be reduced by taking advantage of cheaper rates during certain hours.

3. Personal Interviews

There are two main types of personal interviews:

- **The group survey.** Used mostly by big business, group interviews can be useful as brainstorming tools resulting in product modifications and new product ideas. They also give you insight into buying preferences and purchasing decisions among certain populations.
- **The depth interview.** One-on-one interviews where the interviewer is guided by a small checklist and basic common sense. Depth interviews are either focused or non-directive. Non-directive interviews encourage respondents to address certain topics with minimal questioning. The respondent, in essence, leads the interview. The focused interview, on the other hand, is based on a pre-set checklist. The

choice and timing of questions, however, is left to the interviewer, depending on how the interview goes.

When considering which type of survey to use, keep the following cost factors in mind:

- **Mail.** Most of the costs here concern the printing of questionnaires, envelopes, postage, the cover letter, time taken in the analysis and presentation, the cost of researcher time, and any incentives used.

- **Telephone.** The main costs here are the interviewer's fee, phone charges, preparation of the questionnaire, cost of researcher time, and the analysis and presentation of the results of the questioning.

- **Personal interviews.** Costs include the printing of questionnaires and prompt cards if needed, the incentives used, the interviewer's fee and expenses, cost of researcher time, and analysis and presentation.

- **Group discussions.** Your main costs here are the interviewer's fees and expenses in recruiting and assembling the groups, renting the conference room or other facility, researcher time, any incentives used, analysis and presentation, and the cost of recording media such as tapes, if any are used.

Source: Laura Tiffany, "Researching Your Market," www.entrepreneur.com/article/ 0,4621,291713,00.html.

Researching Your Market—Secondary Research

Secondary data is outside information assembled by government agencies, industry and trade associations, labor unions, media sources, chambers of commerce, etc., and found in the form of pamphlets, newsletters, trade and other magazines, newspapers, and so on. It's termed secondary data because the information has been gathered by another, or secondary, source. The benefits of this are obvious—time and money are saved because you don't have to develop survey methods or do the interviewing.

Here are different types of secondary research resources:

1. Government statistics are among the most plentiful and wide-ranging public sources of information. Start with the Census Bureau's helpful *Hidden Treasures—Census Bureau Data and Where to Find It!* In seconds, you'll find out where to find federal and state information. Other government publications that are helpful include:

   - *Statistical and Metropolitan Area Data Book.* Offers statistics for metropolitan areas, central cities, and counties.

   - *Statistical Abstract of the United States.* Data books with statistics from numerous sources, government to private.

   - *U.S. Global Outlook.* Traces the growth of 200 industries and gives five-year forecasts for each.

2. Don't neglect to contact specific government agencies such as the Small Business Administration (SBA). They sponsor several helpful programs, such as SCORE and Small Business Development Centers (SBDCs), which can provide you with free counseling and a wealth of business information. The Department of Commerce not only publishes helpful books like the *U.S. Global Outlook*, it also produces an array of products with information regarding both domestic industries and foreign markets through its International Trade Administration (ITA) branch. The above items are available from the U.S. Government Printing Office.

3. One of the best public sources is the business section of public libraries. The services provided vary from city to city, but usually include a wide range of government and market statistics, a large collection of directories including information on domestic and foreign businesses, as well as a wide selection of magazines, newspapers, and newsletters.

4. Almost every county government publishes population density and distribution figures in accessible census tracts. These tracts will show you the number of people living in specific areas, such as precincts, water districts, or even 10-block neighborhoods. Other public sources include city chambers of commerce or business development departments, which encourage new businesses in their communities. They will supply you (usually for free) with information on population trends, community income characteristics, payrolls, industrial development, and so on.

5. Among the best commercial sources of information are research and trade associations. Information gathered by trade associations is usually confined to a certain industry and available only to association members, with a membership fee frequently required. However, the research gathered by the larger associations is usually thorough, accurate, and worth the cost of membership. Two excellent resources to help you locate a trade association that reports on the business you're researching are *Encyclopedia of Associations* (Gale Research) and *Business Information Sources* (University of California Press) and can usually be found at your local library.

6. Research associations are often independent but are sometimes affiliated with trade associations. They often limit their activities to conducting and applying research in industrial development, but some have become full-service information sources with a wide range of supplementary publications such as directories.

7. Educational institutions are very good sources of research. Research there ranges from faculty-based projects often published under professors' bylines to student projects, theses, and assignments. Copies of student research projects may be available for free with faculty permission. Consulting services are available either for free or at a cost negotiated with the appropriate faculty members. This can be an excellent way to generate research at little or no cost, using students who welcome the professional experience either as interns or for special credit. Contact the university administration departments and marketing/management studies departments for further information. University libraries are additional sources of research.

Section 2

Source: Laura Tiffany, "Researching Your Market: Secondary Research," www.entrepreneur. com/article/0,4621,291713-2,00.html.

Top Five Fee-Based Web Sites for Market Research

1. **MarketResearch.com** aggregates the needs of individual consumers of market research and allows you to buy market research "by the slice." They even provide assistance finding the relevant research.

2. **BizVida.com** does custom research or can sell you prepackages research. They charge by the project but have free content you can access for registering.

3. *The Wall Street Journal* may have relevant articles in its archives. For about $7 a month, you can access the archives and purchase individual articles.

4. **HBS Working Knowledge** is a portal of Harvard Business School that includes a variety of useful articles and services.

5. **Forrester Research** publishes research reports on the technology sector. Their research can be pricey, but you can buy reports online and they're generally considered a reputable source of market intelligence.

Source: Stever Robbins, "Finding Market Research Sources," www.entrepreneur.com/article/0,4621,292412,00.html.

List of Places for Internet Statistics

comScore
comScore Networks is a global information provider and consultancy to which leading companies turn for consumer behavior insight that drives successful marketing, sales, and trading strategies.
www.comscore.com
5 Penn Plaza, 14th Floor
New York, NY 10001
Phone: (212) 497-1700
Fax: (212) 497-1701

Nielsen NetRatings, Inc.
Provides the industry's global standard for Internet and digital media measurement and analysis, offering technology-driven Internet information solutions for media, advertising, e-commerce, and financial companies that enable customers to make informed decisions regarding their internet strategies.
www.nielsen-netratings.com
120 West 45th Street, 35th Floor

New York, NY 10036
Phone: (212) 703-5900
Fax: (212) 703-5901

Internet Stats
Get stats in any industry—one of the best resources on the net.
www.internetstats.com

netCraft
Get monthly stats and latest news for your market research projects.
www.netcraft.com

StatMarket
Launched in 1999, StatMarket provides valuable market share data on which browser versions, operating systems, and screen resolutions web surfers are using worldwide
www.websidestory.com
10182 Telesis Court
San Diego, CA 92121
Phone: (858) 546-0040
Fax: (858) 546-0480

Source: Compiled by Contributing Writer Candice Watkins.

SCORE's Five Tips on Simple Market Research

1. Ask your customers for suggestions. Provide cards for them to fill out (with name and address) and leave in a fish bowl.

2. Analyze the rich information you already have—such as invoices, customer credit applications, and salespeople's reports. See what these items tell you about sales and customers.

3. Use your trade associations. Read their studies and journals or call them when you need information.

4. Ask the government. Agencies ranging from the U.S. Bureau of the Census to local economic development offices can provide a wealth of market information.

5. Create an advisory board and seek members' observations and opinions regularly.

Source: SCORE, www.score.org/business_tips.html.

Market Research Resources

Click Z Network. Get the latest news, trends, stats about the latest online market trends and research.
www.clickz.com

Jupiter Research. JupiterResearch provides unbiased research, analysis, and advice, backed by proprietary data, to help companies profit from the impact of the internet and emerging consumer technologies on their business.
www.jupiterresearch.com
Phone: (800) 481-1212
E-mail: researchsales@jupitermedia.com

Market Research. MarketResearch.com is an aggregator of global business intelligence representing the most comprehensive collection of published market research available on demand. Strategy starts with the most relevant, current, and credible research.
www.marketresearch.com
38 East 29th Street, 6th Floor
New York, NY 10016
Phone: (800) 298-5699
E-mail: customerservice@marketresearch.com

Free Demographics. FreeDemographics.com is the industry's leading free web site for business professionals at all levels seeking to perform quick and reliable market analyses in an easy-to-use web environment. Your free subscription provides complete access to historic and present U.S. Census data.
www.freedemographics.com

ResearchInfo. If you are involved in, or have any interest in the marketing research field, this site will become your source for information on the market research industry.
www.researchinfo.com

Market Research Organizations and Associations

Marketing Research Association. MRA promotes excellence in the opinion and marketing research industry by providing members with a variety of opportunities for advancing and expanding their marketing research and related business skills.
1344 Silas Deane Highway, Suite 306
Rocky Hill, CT 06067
Phone: (860) 257-4008
Fax: (860) 257-3990
E-mail: email@mra-net.org
www.mra-net.org

ESOMAR—The World Association of Research Professionals. ESOMAR's mission is to promote the use of opinion and market research for improving decision making in business and society worldwide through seminars and conferences, professional publications, training and education, promotion of codes of professional and ethical conduct and guidelines of best practice, and representation of the research industry to international bodies.
E-mail@esomar.org
US Rep: Daphne Chandler, daphne@globalfocus.com
www.esomar.org

American Association of Public Opinion Research. AAPOR is an association of about 1,600 individuals who share an interest in public opinion and survey research. Members work in a wide variety of settings, including academic institutions, commercial firms, government agencies, and non-profit groups, as both producers and users of survey data.
P.O. Box 14263
Lenexa, KS 66285-4263
Phone: (913) 310-0118
Fax: (913) 599-5340
E-mail: aapor-info@goamp.com
www.aapor.org

American Statistical Association (ASA). ASA's mission is to support excellence in statistical practice, research, journals, and meetings; work for the improvement of statistical education at all levels; promote the proper application of statistics; anticipate and meet the needs of members; use statistics to enhance human welfare; and seek opportunities to advance the statistics profession.
1429 Duke Street
Alexandria, VA 22314-3415
Phone: (703) 684-1221
Fax: (703) 684-2037
E-mail: asainfo@amstat.org
www.amstat.org

CMOR—Promoting and Advocating Survey Research. CMOR is a nonprofit organization that works on behalf of the survey research industry to improve respondent cooperation in research and to promote positive legislation and prevent restrictive legislation that could impact the survey research industry.
1285 Silas Deane Highway
P.O. Box 123
Wethersfield, CT 06109
Phone: (860) 571-6838
Fax: (860) 257-3990
E-mail: info@cmor.org

Source: Compiled by Contributing Writer Candice Watkins.

List of Survey Services

InSight Express. InsightExpress is the world's leading provider of fully automated market research. Its patented technology and proven methodology successfully leverage the power of the internet to deliver timely, affordable, and reliable research conducted among targeted audiences, customers, and employees.

InsightExpress, LLC
1351 Washington Boulevard
Stamford, CT 06902
Phone: (203) 359-4174
Fax: (203) 359-4718
info@insightexpress.com

Zoomerang. Zoomerang is the premium global online survey software that businesses, organizations, and individuals use to create professional, customized surveys.

Zoomerang
One Belvedere Place
Mill Valley, CA 94941
E-mail: zsamplesales@zoomerang.com
www.zoomerang.com

OpinionLab, Inc. Has a proven system to monitor and improve the online user experience based on continuously listening to visitors across your entire web site.

OpinionLab, Inc.
513 Central Avenue, Suite 300
Highland Park, IL 60035
Phone: (847) 681-6100
Fax: (847) 681-6101
www.opinionlab.com

OpinionPower. OpinionPower.com is a place where you can make surveys by yourself, quickly and easily. You type in the question and they do the rest of the work.

Dan Ferro, President
E-mail: dan@opinionpower.com
www.opinionpower.com

SurveyHost. Whether your online survey is short and simple, or large and complex, SurveyHost's experienced team of web survey designers can help make your web survey a success. All you need to do is provide the questions and they'll take care of the rest!
Apian Software, Inc.
Phone: (800) 237-4565 x 2, (206) 547-5321
E-mail: sales@apian.com
www.surveyhost.com

Top Market Research Companies

Greenfield Online. Greenfield Online serves the online data collection needs of the largest research companies in the industry and help companies get closer to their consumers by gathering consumer feedback. We serve the needs of more than 300 marketing research firms and are considered one of the leading online panel companies in the industry.

Greenfield Online
21 River Road
Wilton, CT 06897
www.greenfieldonline.com

The Gallup Organization. Has studied human nature and behavior for more than 70 years. Gallup employs many of the world's leading scientists in management, economics, psychology, and sociology. Gallup performance management systems help organizations boost organic growth by increasing customer engagement and maximizing employee productivity through measurement tools, coursework, and strategic advisory services.

The Gallup Organization
Corporate Headquarters
901 F Street, NW
Washington, DC 20004
www.gallup.com

ACNielsen. Offers an integrated suite of market information gathered from a wide range of sources, advanced information management tools, sophisticated analytical systems and methodologies, and dedicated professional client service to help our clients find the best paths to growth.

770 Broadway
New York, NY 10003
Phone: (646) 654-5000
Fax: (646) 654-5002
www.acnielsen.com

Gartner. Offers the combined brainpower of more than 1,200 research analysts and consultants who advise executives in 75 countries every day. We publish tens of thousands of pages of original research annually and answer more than 215,000 client questions every year.

56 Top Gallant Road
P.O. Box 10212
Stamford, CT 06902 USA
Phone: (203) 316-1111
Fax: (203) 967-6878
www.gartner.com

Harris Interactive Inc. The 13th-largest market research firm in the world, this is a Rochester, NY-based global research company that blends premier strategic consulting with innovative and efficient methods of investigation, analysis, and application.
135 Corporate Woods
Rochester, NY 14623-1457
info@harrisinteractive.com

Source: Compiled by Contributing Writer Candice Watkins.

Chapter 11

Specifically for Nonprofits

List of Places for Web Design

CYBER-NY

Web development and online marketing solutions uniquely tailored to the needs of non-profit organizations and foundations.

nonprofit.cyber-ny.com

Capitol Web Design

Leverage the power of the internet for your nonprofit organization.

www.CapitolWebDesign.com

Singularity Design

Experts' web design for nonprofits.

www.singularitydesign.com

Altrue

Professional web design and development firm for nonprofit web sites, church web sites, and volunteer web pages.

www.altrue.com

Organic-Design.net

Provider of web site design and development services to socially responsible companies and nonprofits.

organic-design.net

R & R Web Design

Specializing in web site design, search engine optimization, and web site maintenance for profit and nonprofit clients.

r-rwebdesign.com

Red Acorn Design

Web designers and developers providing web hosting and design discounts for nonprofit organizations.

www.redacorn.org

Common Mistakes Made by Nonprofits

Form 990

It is a relief for many organizations to learn that IRS Form 990, the annual "Return of Organization Exempt From Income Tax," is not required when gross receipts are less than $25,000. It might be a better idea to file a "blank" Form 990 than to not file at all:

1. In some cases, the IRS deletes organizations that do not file from their annual list of qualified charities (Pub. 78).

2. The annual 990 is a very good way to notify the IRS of changes in your organization's address, etc.

3. Filing a blank Form 990 gives your organization a "paper trail." When a new president or treasurer takes office, he or she will be able to tell at a glance that IRS filings are all up-to-date.

4. Most important, the normal IRS three-year "statute of limitations" is triggered by the filing of a return. If your group does not file a 990 or 990EZ, the three-year period never starts, the statute never closes, and there is no limit on how far back the IRS can go in an audit situation.

Employment Taxes

It is never a good idea to ignore a Form 941, "Employer's Quarterly Federal Tax Return," sent to you by the IRS. If you do not need to file the return, because you had no payroll for the quarter or because you have no employees, complete the return anyway and send it in (keeping a copy for your own records).

There are times, of course, when workers really are independent contractors. Many organizations overlook the need to report compensation of $600 or more to the IRS. Awards, fees, and similar payments must be reported on Form 1099-MISC, which must be sent to the recipient no later than January 31, and to the IRS, with a Form 1096 transmittal, no later than February 28.

Public Charity Status

Public charities are supposed to receive at least one third of their support from the general public. Some organizations find themselves relying heavily on donations from founders or board members, or going back year after year to the same foundations or corporations, for income that may not count as "public" support.

Unrelated Business Income

The IRS considers newsletters produced by nonprofits income to be advertising unrelated to exempt purposes, and therefore taxable. Up to $1,000 in unrelated income can be earned without having to pay tax, but an organization that receives at least $1,000 in advertising or other unrelated receipts must file Form 990-T, and pay any tax due.

For more information, visit www.IRS.gov.

Source: "Common Mistakes Made by New 501(c)(3) Organizations," members.aol.com/irs-form1023/misc/commis.html.

Nonprofit Resource Centers

FirstGov.gov
FirstGov.gov, the official U.S. gateway to all government information, is the catalyst for a growing electronic government. Our work transcends the traditional boundaries of government and our vision is global—connecting the world to all U.S. government information and services.

www.firstgov.gov.business/nonprofit.shtml

Internal Revenue Service
The Internal Revenue Service is the nation's tax collection agency and administers the Internal Revenue Code enacted by Congress.

www.irs.gov/charities/index.html

Idealist (Action Without Borders)
On this site you will find:

- Over 47,000 nonprofit and community organizations in 165 countries, which you can search or browse by name, location, or mission.

- Thousands of volunteer opportunities in your community and around the world, and a list of organizations that can help you volunteer abroad.

- Volunteers who want to work with you by looking through the Volunteer Profiles created by individuals on the site board.

Organizations can post job openings, volunteer opportunities, events, internships, campaigns, and resources in the knowledge that these postings will be seen by over 294,000 Idealist subscribers from around the world, as well as thousands of people visiting the Idealist site daily.

www.nonprofits.org

Nonprofit Resource Center
Here you can find virtually everything you need to know about how to form, manage, and maintain your nonprofit organization.

www.not-for-profit.org

Small Business Administration
This new area of SBA's web site is designed to help nonprofit organizations by presenting nonprofit information pertinent to small businesses, as well as to providing access to online Federal information and services. The site is linked to official federal departments and agencies that contain information about grants, regulations, taxes, and other services.

www.sba.gov/nonprofit

NonProfitExpert.com

The Center for Non Profit Creation will be happy to assist you in the process from start to finish, acting as your agent, filling out all the paperwork with the IRS as well as incorporating within your state. This is a one-stop site for people interested in starting or already owning a nonprofit.

www.nonprofitexpert.com

NPO Regulations

Here is a glossary of terms. Some of the terms here are specifically defined in state statutes and therefore the exact definition may vary among states. For this reason, it is critical to consult the appropriate state code when determining matters of law

www.muridae.com/nporegulation/glossary.html

About

About offers extensive material and articles by experts on nonprofits.

nonprofit.about.com

Source: Compiled by author.

Ten Rules for Fundraisers

Here are some tips to make you a better fundraiser.

1. Ask for a gift; don't wait. Another will ask if you don't.
2. Be professional and look professional.
3. Be accountable—personally and for your nonprofit.
4. Be honest. Listen to your heart; it's more honest than your mind.
5. Speak with conviction for your cause.
6. If you can't, recruit someone who can.
7. A prospect is simply a donor without motivation. You provide motivation.
8. A donor is a fundraiser who has yet to share their conviction with a friend. Ask them to.
9. A good fundraiser, then, is a friendly motivator. It's that simple.
10. A successful fundraiser has thick skin, a soft heart, exceptional hearing, a quick mind, a slow tongue, and no shame—at least when it comes to asking for a gift!

Source: Robert DeMartinis, "Ten Rules for Being a Good Fundraiser," nonprofit.about.com/od/fundraising/a/ten_rules.htm.

Agency-Specific Nonprofit Resource Centers

Department of Defense
www.defenselink.mil/other_info/nonprft.html

Department of Education
www.ed.gov/NPAdvisor/index.html

Department of Labor
www.dol.gov/dol/audience/aud-nonprofit.htm

Department of the Interior
www.doi.gov/non-profit/index.html

Department of Transportation
www.dot.gov/business.html

Department of Veterans Affairs
www.va.gov/oaa/nonprofitcorp/default.asp

Environmental Protection Agency
www.epa.gov/epahome/nonprof.htm

Health and Human Services
www.hhs.gov/grants/index.shtml

Housing and Urban Development
www.hud.gov/groups/grantees.cfm

Internal Revenue Service
www.irs.ustreas.gov/charities/index.html

Mailing and Shipping Solutions
www.usps.com/business/welcome.htm

For more information, visit www.firstgov.gov/Business/Nonprofit.shtml.

FAQ on Tax-Exempt Status

How do we get a tax ID number?

Use IRS Form SS-4 to obtain an EIN (Employer Identification Number), an identifying number for all federal tax purposes, whether you plan to have employees or not. You can apply for an EIN separately if you need one immediately, for banking, for instance, or attach a completed Form SS-4 to your application for tax-exempt status. **Note:** This number does not, in any way, indicate whether or not your organization is exempt from tax!

What form do we file to get our tax-exempt status?

Organizations seeking 501(c)(3) status (generally, charitable, educational, scientific, and religious organizations) file IRS Form 1023. Other groups, such as social welfare organizations, labor unions, professional associations, or social clubs, use Form 1024.

How much will it cost to get our tax-exempt status?

The IRS has charged a nonrefundable processing fee for exemption applications since 1987. There is currently a two-tier fee schedule. Organizations whose gross receipts have averaged, or will average, not more than $10,000 per year pay $150. Larger organizations pay $500. A new IRS Revenue Procedure announcing the fees comes out each January; if you are submitting your application late in the year, there may be some benefit to getting it in before January 1.

Other costs you might incur when setting up a new nonprofit organization include incorporation, charitable solicitation, and other registration fees to state and local authorities, and fees to have your articles of incorporation, bylaws, and exemption application professionally prepared.

How long will it take to get our tax-exempt status?

The IRS is currently (March 1999) saying that it takes an average of 120 days to process an application. Roughly a quarter to a third of the applications they receive do not require further development and are processed in six to ten weeks. The balance of the applications they receive take closer to five or six months—hence the "average" 120 days.

What is the deadline for applying for tax-exempt status?

A new charitable, educational, scientific, or religious organization must submit its application to the IRS by the end of the 27th month after the end of the month in which the organization was created. There is no similar deadline for non 501(c)(3) groups.

Can we ask for donations before we get our tax-exempt status?

If your charitable, educational, scientific, or religious organization submits its application to the IRS by the deadline described above and is approved, the "effective date" of your group's tax-exempt status will be the day it was created. This means that contributions that your organization received after incorporation, but before the IRS issued your exemption letter will be deductible.

Because there is, of course, a chance that your application for tax-exempt status will be turned down, it is only fair to let your potential donors know that you do not actually have IRS approval yet—"501(c)(3) application pending."

What are the chances of having our exemption application approved?

Recent statistics show the IRS approving tax-exempt status for a little more than 70 percent of the applications they receive, and denying tax-exempt status for less than 1 percent of the applications they receive. The other 29 percent or so are mostly organizations that become discouraged by the numerous questions the IRS asks and give up before they actually get a ruling.

Does a small organization really need to apply?

Tax law does not require a 501(c)(3) application when an organization normally has gross receipts less than $5,000 per year. A small organization may want to apply anyway to save donors possible inconvenience in an audit, to be able to apply for grants, or to obtain a bulk mailing permit. An organization that no longer qualifies for this low-gross-receipts exception must submit its application to the IRS within 90 days of the end of the year in which average gross receipts exceed $5,000.

Can we pay salaries to our board members? Can we rent a building owned by a board member or purchase equipment from a board member?

Tax law always permits the payment of reasonable compensation for goods or services actually rendered. If the IRS finds that amounts received by insiders are unreasonably high, however, they can fine both the insider who received the payment and the board members who approved the payment. In extreme cases, they can take away the organization's tax-exempt status.

It is a good idea, therefore, to fully document the board's decision-making process when any kind of payment will be made to an insider. Place copies of all relevant information (salary surveys, job description, résumés, prior salary history, real estate appraisals, rent "comparables") in the minutes and never let a board member vote on his or her own compensation or on the compensation of anyone related to him or her.

Source: "Frequently Asked Questions on Tax-Exempt Status," members.aol.com/irsform1023/misc/faq.html.

Tips on Funding Sources

You can find funding for your nonprofit through these sources:
- Foundations
- Grants
- Donations
- Direct Mail
- Fundraising

Discussed below are quick references to foundations, grants, and donations.

Foundations

Choosing a Foundation

Look at geographic proximity, matching goals and missions. Look to those foundations that are located in you state and then national that fit interests of your nonprofit.

Foundation Finder, from The Foundation Center—A quick and easy tool for you to search by name for basic information about foundations within the universe of more than 70,000 private and community foundations in the U.S.:

lnp.fdncenter.org/finder.html

Here's another resource to find a community foundation near you:

www.communityfoundationlocator.org/search/index.cfm

Grants

Things That Characterize a Good Proposal:

Absolute adherence to guidelines. Clarity, simplicity, brevity. For state and federal programs, you'll probably have to use the jargon they used in the RFP; for foundations and corporation grant programs, use plain language and define any specialized terminology you can't avoid using. Include all documents requested in the guidelines. Make sure your budget makes sense. Explain any apparent peculiarities in it.

Grant Information

www.gen.umn.edu/grants/tools.html

Writing a Grant Proposal: Tips and Application Forms

cpmcnet.columbia.edu/research/writing.htm

Yahoo's Collection of Grant-Making Foundations

dir.yahoo.com/Society_and_Culture/Issues_and_Causes/Philanthropy/Organizations/Grant_Making_Foundations

Grants and Related Resources: National Grant Makers

www.lib.msu.edu/harris23/grants/priv.htm

Search the Entire Collection of Over 600 Proposal Abstracts

www.tgcigrantproposals.com

Donations

To be deductible, charitable contributions must be made to qualified organizations. Qualified organizations include, but are not limited to, federal, state, and local governments and organizations organized and operated only for charitable, religious, educational, scientific, or literary purposes, or for the prevention of cruelty to children or animals. Organizations can tell you if they are qualified and if donations to them are deductible.

For a contribution of $250 or more, you can claim a deduction only if you obtain a written acknowledgment from the qualified organization. The written acknowledgment required to substantiate a charitable contribution of $250 or more must contain the following information:

- Name of the organization;

- Amount of cash contribution;

- Description (but not value) of non-cash contribution;

- Statement that no goods or services were provided by the organization, if that is the case;

- Description and good faith estimate of the value of goods or services, if any, that organization provided in return for the contribution; and

- Statement that goods or services, if any, that the organization provided in return for the contribution consisted entirely of intangible religious benefits, if that was the case.

Source: Compiled by author and www.nonprofitexpert.com.

Nonprofit Online Newsletters

Nonprofit Issues

Nonprofit law you can use—for nonprofit executives and their professional advisors. Can also search through cases, ruling, and legislation.

nonprofitissues.com

Blackbaud

Blackbaud is pleased to provide a variety of information to our clients and the nonprofit community in the form of weekly, monthly, and quarterly newsletters. These newsletters are free to all nonprofit professionals.

www.blackbaud.com/resources/newsletters.aspx

Network for Good Nonprofit Newsletter

Network for Good's Nonprofit Newsletter keeps your organization up-to-date on upcoming events, suggests ways to fundraise and recruit volunteers, and provides useful information about topics that are important to nonprofits.

www.networkforgood.org/npo/newsletter/subscribe.aspx

PULSE!

This free bimonthly e-mail newsletter from the Alliance for Nonprofit Management is devoted primarily to helping nonprofit organizations increase their effectiveness and impact.

www.allianceonline.org/publications

Philanthropy News Network Online

"The nonprofit news and information resource" is all about philanthropy and nonprofits.

pnnonline.org

501(c)(3) Monthly Letter

This monthly newsletter features articles by leaders in the nonprofit world on such topics as fundraising, grants, computerization, communication, and more.
www.501c3monthlyletter.com

FirstGov

This site lists electronic newsletters from federal departments and agencies. Many of these are about 7–10 days later than the *Federal Register* announcements.
apps.gsa.gov/FirstGovCommonSubscriptionService.php

Source: Compiled by author.

Advice on Laying the Foundation

Consider these questions if you are planning on forming a nonprofit:

1. How many owners will your company have and what will be their roles?
2. Are you concerned about the tax consequences of your business structure?
3. Do you want to consider having employees become owners in the company?
4. Can you deal with the extra costs that come with selecting a complicated business structure?
5. How much paperwork are you prepared to deal with?
6. Do you want to make decisions in the company?
7. Are you planning to go public?
8. Do you want to protect your personal resources from debts or other claims against your company?
9. Are family succession issues a concern?

Source: Rieva Lesonsky, *Start Your Own Business.*

Nonprofit Associations by State

Alabama

The Nonprofit Resource Center of Alabama
Contact: George Elliott, Executive Director
3324 Independence Drive, Suite 100
Birmingham, AL 35209
Phone: (205) 879-4712
Fax: (205) 879-4724
E-mail: george@nrca.org
Web: www.nrca.info

Alaska

The Foraker Group
880 H Street #100
Anchorage, AK 99501
Phone: (907) 743-1200, (877) 834-5003 (toll-free)
Fax: (907) 276-5014
Web: www.forakergroup.org

The Foraker Group is a nonprofit organization dedicated to improving the leadership and management skills of professionals and volunteers working in Alaska's nonprofit and tribal organizations.

Arizona

Alliance of Arizona Nonprofits
Contact: Tim Delaney, Interim Executive Director
c/o Center for Leadership, Ethics, and Public Service
1404 W. Gardenia
Phoenix, AZ 85021
Phone: (602) 870-9061
E-mail: info@arizonanonprofits.org
Web: www.arizonanonprofits.org

Arkansas

Nonprofit Resources, Inc.
Contact: Bonnie Johnson
500 Broadway, Suite 403
Little Rock, AR 72201-3342
Phone: (501) 374-8515
Fax: (501) 374-6548

California

California Association of Nonprofits

Contact: Florence Green, Executive Director
520 South Grand Avenue, Suite 695
Los Angeles, CA 90071
Phone: (213) 347-2070
Fax: (213) 347-2080
E-mail: info@canonprofits.org
Web: www.canonprofits.org

Colorado

Colorado Association of Nonprofit Organizations
Contact: Barbara Shaw, Executive Director
225 E. 16th Avenue, Suite 1060
Denver, CO 80203
Phone: (303) 832-5710
Fax: (303) 894-0161
E-mail: canpo@canpo.org
Web: www.canpo.org

Colorado Nonprofit Association
455 Sherman Street, Suite 207
Denver, CO 80203
Phone: (303) 832-5710
Fax: (303) 894-0161
E-mail: info@coloradononprofits.org
Web: www.coloradononprofits.org

Connecticut

Connecticut Association of Nonprofits
Contact: Ron Cretaro, Executive Director
90 Brainard Road
Hartford, CT 06114
Phone: (860) 525-5080
Fax: (860) 525-5088
E-mail: rcretaro@ctnonprofits.org
Web: www.ctnonprofits.org

Connecticut Nonprofit Cabinet
c/o CT Association of Human Services
110 Bartholomew Avenue, Suite 4030
Hartford, CT 06106
Contact: Doug Fazzina
Phone: (860) 951-2212
Fax: (860) 951-6511

Delaware

Delaware Association of Nonprofit Agencies
Contact: Connie Hughes, President and CEO
100 West 10th Street, Suite 102
Wilmington, DE 19801
Phone: (302) 777-5500
Fax: (302) 777-5386
E-mail: dana@delawarenonprofit.org
Web: www.delawarenonprofit.org

District of Columbia

Center for Nonprofit Advancement
Contact: Betsy Johnson, Executive Director
1666 K Street, NW, Suite 440
Washington, DC 20036
Phone: (202) 457-0540
Fax: (202) 457-0549
E-mail: info@nonprofitadvancement.org
Web: www.nonprofitadvancement.org

Florida

Florida Association of Nonprofit Organizations
Contact: Marina Pavlov, President
7480 Fairway Drive, #206
Miami Lakes, FL 33014
Phone: (305) 557-1764
Fax: (305) 821-5528
E-mail: fanoinfo@fano.org
Web: www.fano.org

Georgia

Georgia Center for Nonprofits
Contact: Karen Beavor, Executive Director
The Hurt Building, 50 Hurt Plaza SE, Suite 220
Atlanta, GA 30303
Phone: (404) 688-4845
Fax: (404) 521-0487
E-mail: info@gcn.org
Web: www.nonprofitgeorgia.org

Hawaii

Hawai'i Alliance of Nonprofit Organizations
Contact: John M. Flanagan, President & CEO
33 South King Street, Suite 501
Honolulu, HI 96813
Phone: (808) 529-0454
Fax: (808) 529-0477
E-mail: jflanagan@hcsc-hawaii.org
Web: www.hcsc-hawaii.org

Idaho

Idaho Nonprofit Development Center
ParkCenter Pointe
1509 Tyrell Lane, Suite A
Boise, Idaho 83706
Phone: (208) 424-2229
Fax: (208) 424-2294
E-mail: info@idahononprofits.org
Web: www.idahononprofits.org

Illinois

Donors Forum of Chicago
Contact: Valerie Lies, President
208 South LaSalle Street, Suite 740
Chicago, IL 60604
Phone: (312) 578-0090
Fax: (312) 578-0103
E-mail: valerie@donorsforum.org
Web: www.donorsforum.org

Indiana

Indiana Association of Nonprofit Organizations
Contact: Harriet O'Connor, President
10 West Market Street, Suite 1720
Indianapolis, IN 46204
Phone: (317) 464-5324
Fax: (317) 464-5146
E-mail: hoconnor@npteam.org

Iowa

Iowa Nonprofit Resource Center
130 Grand Avenue Court
Iowa City, IA 52242
Phone: (319) 335-9765, (866) 500-8980 (toll-free)
Fax: (319) 335-7614
E-mail:law-nonprofit@uiowa.edu
Web: nonprofit.law.uiowa.edu

Kansas

Kansas Nonprofit Association
Contact: Herb Callison, Executive Director
P.O. Box 47054
Topeka, KS 66647
Phone: (785) 266-6886
Fax: (785) 266-2113
E-mail: knap@inlandnet.net
Web: www.ksnonprofitassoc.net

Kentucky
Kentucky Nonprofit Leadership Initiative
Contact: Danielle Clore, Director
University of Kentucky
314 Garrigus Building
Lexington, KY 40546
Phone: (859) 257-2542
Fax: (859) 323-2715
E-mail: emailus@kynonprofits.org
Web: www.kynonprofits.org

Louisiana
Louisiana Association of Nonprofit
Organizations
Contact: Melissa Flournoy, President and CEO
P.O. Box 3808
Baton Rouge, LA 70821
Phone: (225) 343-5266
Fax: (225) 338-9470
E-mail: contactus@lano.org
Web: www.lano.org

Maine
Maine Association of Nonprofits
Contact: Scott Schnapp, Executive Director
565 Congress Street, Suite 301
Portland, ME 04101
Phone: (207) 871-1885
Fax: (207) 780-0346
E-mail: manp@nonprofitmaine.org
Web: www.nonprofitmaine.org

Maryland
Maryland Association of Nonprofit
Organizations
Contact: Peter Berns, Executive Director
190 West Ostend Street, Suite 201
Baltimore, MD 21230
Phone: (410) 727-6367
Fax: (410) 727-1914
E-mail: vbvinson@mdnonprofit.org
Web: www.marylandnonprofits.org

Massachusetts
Massachusetts Council of Human Service
Providers
Contact: Michael Weekes, President
250 Summer Street, Suite 1
Boston, MA 02210
Phone: (617) 428-3637
Fax: (617) 428-1533
E-mail: mweekes@providers.org
Web: www.providers.org

Michigan
Michigan Nonprofit Association
Contact: Sam Singh, President
1048 Pierpont, Suite 3
Lansing, MI 48911
Phone: (517) 492-2400
Fax: (517) 492-2410
E-mail: singhsam@mnaonline.org
Web: www.mnaonline.org

Michigan League for Human Services
Contact: Ann Marston, President & CEO
1115 South Pennsylvania, Suite 202
Lansing, MI 48912
Phone: (517) 487-5436
Fax: (517) 371-4546
E-mail: amarston@mlan.net
Web: www.milhs.org

Minnesota
Minnesota Council of Nonprofits
Contact: Jon Pratt, Executive Director
2314 University Avenue West #20
St. Paul, MN 55114
Phone: (651) 642-1904
Fax: (651) 642-1517
E-mail: info@mncn.org
Web: www.mncn.org

Mississippi
Mississippi Center for Nonprofits
Contact: Mark McCrary, Executive Director
612 North State Street, Suite B
Jackson, MS 39202
Phone: (601) 968-0061
Fax: (601) 352-8820
E-mail: mcn@msnonprofits.org
Web: www.msnonprofits.org

Missouri
Midwest Center for Nonprofit Leadership
University of Missouri-Kansas City
5100 Rockhill Road
Bloch School, Room 310
Kansas City, MO 64110
Phone: (816) 235-2305, (800) 474-1170 (toll-free)
Fax: (816) 235-1169, (816) 235-5727
E-mail: mcnl@umkc.edu
Web: bsbpa.umkc.edu/mwcnl

Greater Kansas City Council on Philanthropy
P.O. Box 5813
Kansas City, MO 64171-0813
4747 Troost, #201
Kansas City, MO 64110
Phone: (816) 235-6259
Fax: (816) 235-5727
Web: www.kcphilnet.org

Nonprofit Services Consortium
1415 Olive Street, Suite 200
St. Louis, MO 63103
Phone: (314) 436-9580
Fax: (314) 621-6224
E-mail: Valerie@nonprofitservices.org
Web: www.nonprofitservices.org

Montana
Montana Nonprofit Association
432 Last Chance Gulch, Suite E
P.O. Box 1744
Helena, MT 59624
Phone: (406) 449-3717
Fax: (406) 449-3718
E-mail: info@mtnonprofit.org
Web: www.mtnonprofit.org

Nebraska
Nebraska Association of the Midlands
Contact: David Catalan, Executive Director
115 South 49th Avenue
Omaha, NE 68132
Phone: (402) 561-7580
Fax: (402) 561-7599
E-mail: dcatalan@mail.unomaha.edu
Web: www.nonprofitam.org

Nevada
Nevada Association of Nonprofits
Contact Lamar Marchese, President of Board
c/o Nevada Public Radio
1289 Torrey Pines Drive
Las Vegas, NV 89146
Phone: (702) 258-9895
Fax: (702) 258-5646
E-mail: lamar@knpr.org

New Hampshire
New Hampshire Center for Nonprofits
Contact: Linda Quinn, Executive Director
10 Ferry Street, Suite 310
The Concord Center
Concord, NH 03301
Phone: (603) 225-1947
Fax: (603) 228-5574
E-mail: info@nhnonprofits.org
Web: www.nhnonprofits.org

New Jersey
Center for Non-Profit Corporations
Contact: Linda Czipo, Executive Director
1501 Livingston Avenue
North Brunswick, NJ 08902
Phone: (732) 227-0800
Fax: (732) 227-0087
E-mail: center@njnonprofits.org
Web: www.njnonprofits.org

New Mexico
NGO New Mexico—Association of Nonprofit
Organizations
P.O. Box 5398
Santa Fe, NM, 87502
Phone: (505) 466-3540
Fax: (505) 351-1031
E-mail: aegan@cybermesa.com
Web: www.ngonm.org

New York
Council of Community Services of New York
State
Contact: Doug Sauer, Executive Director
272 Broadway
Albany, NY 12210
Phone: (518) 434-9194

Section
2

Fax: (518) 434-0392
E-mail: dsauer@ccsnys.org
Web: www.ccsnys.org

Nonprofit Coordinating Committee of New York
Contact: Jonathan Small, Executive Director
1350 Broadway, Suite 1801
New York, NY 10018-7802
Phone: (212) 502-4191
Fax: (212) 502-4189
E-mail: jsmall@npccny.org
Web: www.npccny.org

North Carolina
North Carolina Center for Nonprofits
Contact: Trisha Lester
1110 Navaho Drive, Suite 200
Raleigh, NC 27609-7322
Phone: (919) 790-1555
Fax: (919) 790-5307
E-mail: info@ncnonprofits.org
Web: www.ncnonprofits.org

North Dakota
North Dakota Association of Nonprofit
Organizations
P.O. Box 1091
1605 E Capitol Avenue
Bismarck ND 58502
Phone: (701) 258-9101, (888) 396-3266 (toll-free)
Fax: (701) 255-2411
E-mail: ndano@btinet.net
Web: www.ndano.org

Ohio
Ohio Association of Nonprofit Organizations
100 E. Broad Street, Suite 2440
Columbus, OH 43215-3119
Phone: (614) 280-0233
Fax: (614) 280-0657
E-mail: info@oano.org
Web: www.ohiononprofits.org

Oklahoma
Oklahoma Center for Nonprofits
923 N. Robinson, Suite 400
Oklahoma City, OK 73102-2203
Phone: (405) 236-8133

Fax: (405) 272-0436
E-mail: info@centerfornonprofits.us
Web: www.centerfornonprofits.us

Oregon
Technical Assistance for Community Services
(TACS)
1001 SE Water Avenue, Suite 490
Portland, OR 97214
Phone: (503) 239-4001
Fax: (503) 236-8313
E-mail: info@tacs.org
Web: www.tacs.org
Nonprofit Helpline: (503) 233-9240, (888) 206-3076 (toll-free in Oregon, Washington, and Alaska)

Technical Assistance for Community Services provides support and services to nonprofits statewide, but it is not a nonprofit association.

Pennsylvania
Pennsylvania Association of Nonprofit
Organizations (PANO)
777 East Park Drive, Suite 200
Harrisburg, PA 17111
Phone: (717) 236-8584
Fax: (717) 236-8767
E-mail: info@pano.org
Web: www.pano.org

Rhode Island
The Rhode Island Foundation
One Union Station
Providence, RI 02903
Phone: (401) 274-4564
Fax: (401) 331-8085
Web: www.rifoundation.org

South Carolina
South Carolina Association of Nonprofit
Organizations
Contact: Erin Hardwick, Executive Director
P.O. Box 11252
Columbia, SC 29211
Phone: (803) 929-0399
Fax: (803) 929-0173
E-mail: info@scanpo.org
Web: www.scanpo.org

South Dakota
South Dakota State Association
Contact: Christine Yackley, Executive Director
28670 181st Street
Pierre, SD 57501-5926
Phone: (605) 264-5350
E-mail: yack@sullybuttes.net

Tennessee
Center for Nonprofit Management
44 Vantage Way, Suite 230
Nashville, TN 37228
Phone: (615) 259-0100
Fax: (615) 259-0400
E-mail: Info@cnm.org
Web: www.cnm.org

Texas
Texas Association of Nonprofit Organizations
(TANO)
Barry Silverberg, Executive Director
5930 Middle Fiskville Road, Box 51
Austin, TX 78752
Phone: (512) 223-7076
Fax: (512) 223-7210
E-mail: info@tano.org
Web: www.tano.org

Utah
Utah Nonprofits Association
Contact: Diane Hartz Warsoff, Executive
Director
260 S Central Campus Drive, Room 214
Salt Lake City, UT 84112-9154
Phone: (801) 581-4883
Fax: (801) 585-5489
E-mail: DWarsoff@utahnonprofits.org
Web: www.utahnonprofits.org

Vermont
Vermont Alliance of Nonprofit Organizations
Contact: Jane Van Buren, Executive Director
299 North Winooski #3
Burlington, VT 05401
P.O. Box 8345
Burlington, VT 05402
Phone: (802) 862-0292
Fax: (802) 862-3549

E-mail: info@vanpo.org
Web: www.vanpo.org

Virginia
Virginia Network of Nonprofit Organizations
Contact: Katie Campbell
PMB# 339
2711 Buford Road
Richmond, VA 23235-2433
Phone: (804) 794-8689
E-mail: info@vanno.org
Web: www.vanno.org

Coalition of Virginia Nonprofits
Karin Talbert
1011 East Main Street, Suite 400
Richmond, VA 23219
Phone: (804) 228-4509
E-mail: info@cvnp.org
Web: www.cvnp.org

Washington
Executive Alliance
P.O. Box 22438
Seattle, WA 98122-0438
Phone: (206) 328-3836
Fax: (206) 323-1017
E-mail: info@exec-alliance.org
Web: www.exec-alliance.org

Northwest Nonprofit Resources
Contact: Sandy Gill
P.O. Box 9066
Spokane, WA 99209
Phone: (509) 325-4303
Fax: (509) 325-4260
E-mail: sgill@nnr.org
Web site: www.nnr.org

West Virginia
Community Development Partnership of West
Virginia
1045 Bridge Road
Charleston, WV 25314
Phone: (304) 342-3754
Fax: (304) 342-1639
E-mail: info@cdpwv.org
Web: www.cdpwv.org

Section
2

Wisconsin

Wisconsin does not have a formal state association. However, these resources may be helpful:

The Nonprofit Center of Milwaukee
2819 West Highland Boulevard
Milwaukee, WI 53208-3217
Phone: (414) 344-3933
Fax: (414) 344-7071
E-mail: info@nonprofitcentermilwaukee.org
Web: www.nonprofitcentermilwaukee.org

Donors Forum of Wisconsin
759 N. Milwaukee Street, Suite 515
Milwaukee, WI 53202
Phone: (414) 270-1978
Web: www.dfwonline.org

Donors Forum membership is open to grant
makers residing or giving primarily in
Wisconsin.

University of Wisconsin nonprofit resource
page: grants.library.wisc.edu/organizations/wis-
consinresources.html

Wyoming

Wyoming Nonprofit Support
Initiative/Wyoming Association of Nonprofit
Organizations
Contact: Lisa E. Johnson, Coordinator
3896 Road 162
Lagrange, WY 82221
Phone: (307) 834-2293
Fax: (307) 834-2294
E-mail: lisa@compasswy.net

Source: "Nonprofit State Associations,"
www.nonprofitexpert.com/nonprofit_state_asso
ciations.htm.

Chapter 12

Choosing a Location

Tips to Finding the Best Location

The Types of Locations

The type of location you choose depends largely on the type of business you're in, but there are enough mixed-use areas and creative applications of space that you should give some thought to each type before making a final decision. For example, business parks and office buildings typically have retail space so they can attract the restaurants and stores that business tenants want nearby. Shopping centers are often home to an assortment of professional services—medical, legal, accounting, insurance, etc.—as well as retailers. It's entirely possible some version of nontraditional space will work for you, so use your imagination.

1. **Home-based:** This is the trendiest location. Then they move into commercial space as their business grows. Others start at home with no thought or intention of ever moving. You can run a home-based business from an office in a spare bedroom, the basement, the attic—even the kitchen table. On the plus side, you don't need to worry about negotiating leases, coming up with substantial deposits, or commuting. On the downside, your room for physical growth is limited and you may find accommodating employees or meetings with clients a challenge.

2. **Retail:** Retail space comes in a variety of shapes and sizes and may be located in enclosed malls, strip shopping centers, freestanding buildings, downtown shopping districts, or mixed-use facilities. You'll also find retail space in airports and other transportation facilities, hotel lobbies, sports stadiums, and a variety of temporary or special event venues.

3. **Mobile:** Whether you're selling to the general public or other businesses, if you have a product or service that you take to your customers, your ideal location may be a car, van, or truck.

4. **Commercial:** Commercial space includes even more options than retail. Commercial office buildings and business parks offer traditional office space geared to businesses that do not require a significant amount of pedestrian or automobile traffic for sales. You'll find commercial office space in downtown business districts, business parks, and sometimes interspersed among suburban retail facilities. One office option to consider is an executive suite, where the landlord provides receptionist and secretarial services, faxing, photocopying, conference rooms, and other support services as part of the space package. Executive suites help you project the image of a professional operation at a more affordable cost than a traditional office and can be found in most commercial office areas.

5. **Industrial:** If your business involves manufacturing or heavy distribution, you'll need a plant or warehouse facility. Light industrial parks typically attract smaller manufacturers in nonpolluting industries as well as companies that need showrooms in addition to manufacturing facilities. Heavy industrial areas tend to be older and poorly

planned and usually offer rail and/or water port access. Though industrial parks are generally newer and often have better infrastructures, you may also want to consider any freestanding commercial building that meets your needs and is adequately zoned.

Source: "Choosing a Location for Your Business," www.entrepreneur.com/article/ 0,4621,265091,00.html, from Rieva Lesonsky, *Start Your Own Business.*

Top 25 Large Cities for Doing Business in America

Sustained growth in the Southeast left formerly hot cities such as San Francisco, New York City, and Boston behind.

1. Atlanta. "Hotlanta" is precisely that, the hottest of the hot economies of the country. Pummeled in the early days of the 2000 recession, the sprawling Georgia metropolis has roared back, mostly on the basis of its strong service sector, pro-business culture, and a relatively affordable housing environment in comparison with other big-time cities.

2. Riverside-San Bernardino. California's premier hot spot has been criticized as the epitome of urban sprawl and for creating mostly "crummy jobs." But it's also been the Golden State's economic Energizer Bunny: the low-cost haven keeps on growing in population, attracting emigrants from the coast.

3. Las Vegas. At first hurt by the downturn in tourism after 9/11, the Nevada metropolis has gotten its groove back. Although tourism remains the linchpin, the area is creating jobs in high-end sectors and even manufacturing, in large part because of an exodus from more expensive locales on the Western Seaboard.

4. San Antonio. Largely unnoticed amidst the mega-hype surrounding media favorite Austin, this more affordable Texas city has benefited from steady population growth, a diversifying economy, and a strong military presence.

5. West Palm Beach. This part of Florida is getting crowded, so relatively low prices could soon be a thing of the past. Right now, the perceived

high quality of life and reasonable housing prices make this area an almost irresistible lure.

6. Southern New Jersey, New Jersey

7. Fort Lauderdale-Hollywood-Pompano Beach, Florida

8. Jacksonville, Florida

9. Newark, New Jersey

10. Suburban Maryland-D.C., Maryland

11. Orlando, Florida

12. Phoenix, Arizona

13. Washington MSA, District of Columbia

14. Tampa-St. Petersburg-Clearwater, Florida

15. San Diego, California

16. Nassau-Suffolk, New York

17. Richmond-Petersburg, Virginia

18. New Orleans, Louisiana

19. Austin, Texas

20. Northern Virginia, Virginia

21. Middlesex-Somerset-Hunterdon, New Jersey

22. Miami-Hialeah, Florida

23. Orange County, California

24. Oklahoma City, Oklahoma

25. Albany-Schenectady-Troy, New York

Source: Joel Kotkin, "Top 25 Cities for Doing Business in America," www.inc.com/magazine/20040301/top25.html.

Top 25 Midsized Cities for Doing Business in America

With job bases from 150,000 to 450,000, the midsize cities include a strong showing from the Inland Empire, driven by escapees from the California coast.

1. Green Bay. The Packers may provide name recognition to this Wisconsin city, but locals swear to the quality of life, a diversified economy, and a hardworking, skilled labor force. It lacks the population-driven growth of Sunbelt cities such as Las Vegas or Atlanta, but it is an excellent place to start and expand a business.

2. Madison. Cold weather didn't stop Wisconsin from packing a one-two punch among midsized cities. Madison is peculiarly well suited for the service-driven economic expansion. As state capital and locale of one of the region's top universities, its population is exceptionally well educated.

3. Sarasota. This may well be Florida's "next big thing," an affordable coastal region that attracts many skilled, middle-class emigrants from the north. A sizable tech work force has made this among the fastest-growing areas for information-based industries. And there's always the beach.

4. Fresno. California's economy is driven by real estate affordability and population growth, but here it's particularly spurred on by Latino and Asian immigration. A key issue, as in other growth centers, will be creating a bigger high-end service, manufacturing, and information sector.

5. Bakersfield. Like Fresno, but with perhaps stronger prospects. Sprawl has made the old Merle Haggard Okie capital a distant suburb of pricey Los Angeles, and people actually commute over the mountains. A good choice for firms seeking to expand close to southern California, without the price tag.

6. **Reno**, Nevada

7. **Albuquerque**, New Mexico

8. **Tucson**, Arizona

9. **Vallejo-Fairfield-Napa**, California

10. **Modesto, California**

11. **Stockton, California**

12. **Fort Myers-Cape Coral, Florida**

13. **Corpus Christi**, Texas

14. **Syracuse**, New York

15. **Springfield, Missouri**

16. **Monmouth-Ocean**, New Jersey

17. **Westchester County**, New York

18. **Harrisburg-Lebanon-Carlisle, Pennsylvania**

19. **Baton Rouge, Louisiana**

20. **Daytona Beach, Florida**

21. **Jackson, Mississippi**

22. **Lancaster, Pennsylvania**

23. **Portland, Maine**

24. **Boise City**, Idaho

25. **Akron, Ohio**

Source: Joel Kotkin, "Top 25 Cities for Doing Business in America," www.inc.com/magazine/ 20040301/top25.html.

Top 25 Small Cities for Doing Business in America

Small cities (job bases up to 150,000) have suffered from years of dwindling population. Their affordability is reversing the trend.

1. Montpelier. With classic Yankee humility, George Malek, executive vice president of the Central Vermont Chamber, could not bring himself to boast about his region's top ranking. He cited instead his city's burgeoning insurance industry and the advantages of being a state capital and home to several small colleges.

2. Missoula. Montana's nice scenery and the local university go a long way in a small place. Missoula's population has almost doubled in the past 30 years, and many newcomers have started businesses. Financial and professional business services, as well as information, have all made solid gains.

3. Casper. With 66,000 people in this Wyoming region, Casper is small even by small-town standards. But its business services industries—in particular, financial services—made strong showings. Another sign that professional service sectors are declustering from traditional urban centers.

4. Rockland County. Although not cheap by Midwestern or Southern standards, its housing prices are bargain basement compared with areas closer to New York City. Population growth has been three times the New York average since 2000, while information and business services have shown solid growth.

5. Sioux Falls. This South Dakota small city is picking up population, a far cry from the out-migration of years past. There's a skilled work force for financial and professional services and an emerging information and biological sciences sector. Both are attracting investment dollars.

6. **Waco, Texas**

7. **Burlington, Vermont**

8. **Dutchess County, New York**

9. **Anchorage, Alaska**

10. **Manchester, New Hampshire**

11. **Bismarck, North Dakota**

12. **Bryan-College Station, Texas**

13. **Danbury, Connecticut**

14. **Altoona, Pennsylvania**

15. **Fargo-Moorhead, North Dakota**

16. **Las Cruces, New Mexico**

17. **La Crosse, Wisconsin**

18. **Newburgh, New York**

19. **Albany, Georgia**

20. **Medford, Oregon**

21. **Utica-Rome, New York**

22. **Lake Charles, Louisiana**

23. **Bristol, Virginia**

24. **Fort Smith, Arkansas**

25. **Enid, Oklahoma**

Source: Joel Kotkin, "Top 25 Cities for Doing Business in America," www.inc.com/magazine/20040301/top25.html.

Entrepreneur.com's Best Cities for Entrepreneurs

Four criteria are used to rank the cities: Entrepreneurial Activity (based on the number of businesses five years old or younger), Small-Business Growth (based on the number of businesses with fewer than 20 employees that had significant employment growth from January 2002 to January 2003), Job Growth (change in job growth over a three-year period through January 2003), and Risk (bankruptcy rates). Large cities have populations of over 1 million; midsized cities have populations between 350,000 and 1 million.

Best Cities Overall

1. Minneapolis/St Paul, MN/WI
2. Washington, DC
3. Atlanta, GA
4. Fort Lauderdale, FL
5. Salt Lake City, UT
6. West Palm Beach, FL
7. Norfolk, VA
8. Miami, FL
9. Charlotte/Gastonia/Rock Hill, NC/SC
10. Orlando, FL

East

1. Washington, DC
2. Baltimore, MD
3. Monmouth/Ocean, NJ
4. Boston, MA/NH
5. Middlesex/Somerset/Hunterdon, NJ
6. Providence/Fall River/Warwick, RI/MA
7. New York, NY
8. Bergen/Passaic, NJ
9. Nassau/Suffolk, NY
10. Philadelphia, PA/NJ

West

1. Las Vegas, NV
2. San Diego, CA
3. Sacramento, CA
4. Orange County, CA
5. Riverside, CA
6. Oakland, CA
7. San Jose, CA
8. Seattle, WA
9. Portland/Vancouver OR/WA
10. San Francisco, CA

South

1. Atlanta, GA
2. Fort Lauderdale, FL
3. West Palm Beach, FL
4. Norfolk, VA
5. Miami, FL
6. Charlotte/Gastonia/Rock Hill, NC/SC
7. Orlando, FL
8. Jacksonville, FL
9. Tampa, St. Petersburg/Clearwater, FL
10. New Orleans, LA

Mountain

1. Salt Lake City/Ogden, UT
2. Denver, CO

Southwest

1. Phoenix/Mesa, AZ
2. San Antonio, TX
3. Austin/San Marcos, TX
4. Houston, TX
5. Dallas, TX
6. Fort Worth/Arlington, TX

Midwest

1. Minneapolis/St Paul, MN/WI
2. Louisville, KY/IN
3. Oklahoma City, OK
4. Kansas City, MO/KS
5. Columbus, OH
6. St. Louis, MO/IL
7. Milwaukee, WI
8. Indianapolis, IN
9. Cincinnati, OH
10. Chicago, IL

Source: *Entrepreneur*, October 2003, D&B research by Nipa Basu and Henry Lawrence.

Location, Location, Location—Checklist

We all know how important a business's location is to its success. So whether you're looking for your first place or moving up, here's a general checklist of factors to consider:

- Proximity to your customer base, suppliers, and employees
- Affordable rent—watch out for hidden costs
- Available and affordable parking
- Ease of entry and exit
- Is the space functional for your needs?
- Utility costs—these can vary widely from city to city
- Accessible transportation
- Appearance of area, building, or shopping center
- Growth potential of site
- Zoning regulations
- City's future plans for the area

The importance of each item will vary with the type of business, but make sure you get what you need for your company.

Source: Rieva Lesonsky, *365 Tips to Boost Your Entrepreneurial IQ.*

SCORE's Five Tips on Choosing a Location for Your Business

1. Find out if local zoning laws permit your kind of business at the site that you desire.
2. Make sure the site has adequate public services—such as water and sewer services, trash collection, adequate drainage, and police and fire protection.
3. Determine if there's adequate, affordable transportation. Can your employees get to work? If you're a manufacturer, are trucking services available?
4. Consider the surrounding community. If you're a high-end retailer, for example, are there sufficient high-income households nearby to support your business?
5. Look at the other businesses in the area. Decide whether or not having direct competitors will be helpful.

Source: SCORE, www.score.org/business_tips.html.

Tips on Finding a Franchise Location

The topic of finding a good location and then negotiating a favorable lease is one that all franchisees face when they are in a site-based franchise system. Because most new franchisees do not have any experience in finding a location, they can experience significant anxiety if the proper assistance is not available from the franchise company.

- Most site-based franchises have support available to help with this issue, but that support varies from company to company.

- One of the critical issues to address in your research of prospective franchise offerings is the amount and type of such real estate support.

- There is usually a team approach to finding the location and negotiating and finalizing the lease. The team consists of you, the franchisor, a local commercial real estate broker, and a good lease attorney.

- Most franchisors provide you with specific selection criteria for finding a good site. This information covers topics such as the demographic characteristics and population density, traffic and parking parameters, and the importance of site visibility to the success of your business. They often provide other helpful information, such as the type of tenant mix that is preferable in a shopping center you are considering or which side of a busy street you should be located on.

- Most franchise systems assume you'll do most of the legwork in terms of locating a prospective site, based on the selection criteria they have provided. In many cases, the franchisor requires that they have consent to any site and may ask you to provide them with information (often including pictures or videos) about the site prior to consenting.

- Some franchisors send one of their operations support staff out to your market to personally verify the acceptability of the site prior to consent.

- After you have found one or more acceptable potential locations, you will move on to lease negotiations. This is where you determine the economics of the locations you have found and also any other considerations that might be important to your specific business.

- The economics of a location revolve primarily around the rent. Another possible factor: percentage rent clauses that escalate your rent as your business grows over time.

- There are also commonly clauses requiring you to pay for common area maintenance, real estate taxes, landlord insurance, and other expenses. You need to work with the franchisor and the local real estate broker to make sure these other expenses are reasonable.

- The franchisor and the broker should also help you identify financial assistance available from the landlord. This commonly comes in the form of free rent allowances and tenant improvement allowances. This can represent a significant amount of money, so make sure you pursue this area.

- When the prescribed terms of the lease have been agreed to, you will typically have the lease reviewed by the lease attorney. This is a specialized area of the law, and you need to make sure you're dealing with an attorney who is experienced in reviewing leases.

- The franchisor should also have support materials to assist you and the lease attorney in the lease review process, such as sample language for "use" clauses that need to be included in the lease, or suggestions for language restricting competing use by other businesses in the center. The franchisor will typically also have language suggestions relating to other normal and standard clauses in lease contracts.

- In some cases, the franchisor may even have a suggested lease document they would like you to propose to the landlord. Keep in mind, though, that your bargaining power with landlords is often not as strong as theirs, so you typically have to work from their standard lease document.

- Throughout this entire process, you are the main player. The rest of the team, including the franchise company personnel, should be your support system to help you get the best site on the most favorable terms possible.

- When you are investigating any franchise company, always ask the existing franchisees about their experiences with the real estate process. Ask about each of the factors mentioned above and find out whether they had any other unforeseen problems.

- Finally, make sure to find out how long the entire process took them from start to finish and whether their time frame was normal and met their expectations. This type of research takes time, but will arm you with the knowledge you need to avoid unpleasant surprises when you become a franchisee.

Source: Jeff Elgin, "Choosing a Great Franchise Location," www.entrepreneur.com/article/0,4621,316187,00.html.

22 Questions to Ask When Deciding on the Best Retail Location

1. Is the facility located in an area zoned for your type of business?
2. Is the facility large enough for your business? Does it offer room for all the retail, office, storage, or workroom space you need?
3. Does it meet your layout requirements?
4. Does the building need any repairs?
5. Do the existing utilities—lighting, heating, and cooling—meet your needs or will you have to do any rewiring or plumbing work? Is ventilation adequate?

6. Are the lease terms and rent favorable?

7. Is the location convenient to where you live?

8. Can you find a number of qualified employees in the area in which the facility is located?

9. Do people you want for customers live nearby? Is the population density of the area sufficient for your sales needs?

10. Is the trade area heavily dependent on seasonal business?

11. If you choose a location that's relatively remote from your customer base, will you be able to afford the higher advertising expenses?

12. Is the facility consistent with the image you'd like to maintain?

13. Is the facility located in a safe neighborhood with a low crime rate?

14. Is exterior lighting in the area adequate to attract evening shoppers and make them feel safe?

15. Will crime insurance be prohibitively expensive?

16. Are neighboring businesses likely to attract customers who will also patronize your business?

17. Are there any competitors located close to the facility? If so, can you compete with them successfully?

18. Is the facility easily accessible to your potential customers?

19. Is parking space available and adequate?

20. Is the area served by public transportation?

21. Can suppliers make deliveries conveniently at this location?

22. If your business expands in the future, will the facility be able to accommodate this growth?

Source: Karen E. Spaeder, "How to Find the Best Location," www.entrepreneur.com/article/ 0,4621,318054,00.html.

Chapter 13

Writing the Business Plan

Ten Reasons Why You Need a Strong Business Plan

1. **To Attract Investors:** Before investors can decide whether or not to back your business financially, they will need to know as much as possible about how the business will operate and how their investment will be spent.

2. **To See if Your Business Ideas Will Work:** By writing a business plan and outlining each aspect of your business, you can determine if your idea is actually viable.

3. **To Outline Each Area of the Business:** A business plan will provide an overview of all aspects of the business. You will be able to detail the who, what, where, when, and why of your day-to-day business operations, costs, and projected profitability.

4. **To Set up Milestones:** By forecasting where your business will be in six months, one year, or five years, you are not only letting potential investors know your plans, but also setting up realistic milestones for yourself and your employees.

5. **To Learn About the Market:** Researching, analyzing, and writing about the market not only provides you with an overview for the business plan, but gives you greater insight into the overall market.

6. **To Secure Additional Funding or Loans:** Your business plan can demonstrate that you have met goals and illustrate the company's growth and need for additional funding.

7. **To Determine Your Financial Needs:** The process of writing your business plan will force you to analyze your financial picture.

8. **To Attract Top-Level People:** Your business plan will give talented people an overview of your business.

9. **To Monitor Your Business:** A business plan should serve as an ongoing business tool that you can use to monitor your progress.

10. **To Devise Contingency Plans:** While business plans often include some contingency plans, by virtue of having the document available, you can see how and where you can make such changes relatively quickly if, and when, necessary.

Source: "10 Reasons Why You Need a Strong Business Plan," www.allbusiness.com/articles/BusinessPlans/1716-1746-1767.html.

Tips for Writing Your Business Plan

Do you really need a business plan? You bet your business you do. Whether you're seeking capital or devising a road map for success, you need a business plan. Though you may have started your business without one, it's never too late to plot your business's fortunes.

- Start by defining your business. How does your product or service fit within your industry? And what makes your company unique?

- Then, define your customer. Focus in as narrowly as possible, by age, gender, ethnicity, and income.

- A market plan is next. Tell how you plan to get your product or service to market. Also, assess your competition and recognize their strengths and weaknesses.

- When you're done writing your plan, you need to boil it down to a one- or two-page executive summary. Even though this goes at the front of your plan, it should be the last thing you write.

If you need help writing your plan, try Mark Henricks, *Business Plans Made Easy: It's Not as Hard as You Think!* (Entrepreneur Press).

Source: Rieva Lesonsky, *365 Tips to Boost Your Entrepreneurial IQ.*

Eight More Tips for Writing Your Business Plan

These suggestions come from Daniel McGilvery, who heads up the Business Planning Services division of vFinance, an investment banking firm.

1. **Use lots of graphics.** "People's attention spans are getting shorter by the day, and investors are accustomed to the high-end graphic tools used in PowerPoint presentations," McGilvery explains, recommending that you sprinkle color graphs and charts, pull quotes, text boxes, and other visual aids liberally throughout your plan, "punching" and breaking up the text as much as possible.

2. **Highlight the plan's executive summary section.** "Sometimes we spend as much time writing the executive summary as we do the entire rest of the plan," McGilvery says, explaining that most investors will not read beyond a poorly drafted executive summary that doesn't grab them.

3. **Focus on the section of the plan that describes your market strategy.** "Of the many factors that will determine your chances of success, your marketing strategy is very high on the list. It's also one of the weakest components of most business plans."

4. **Eliminate the risk factors section altogether.** "Investors will conduct a very thorough risk assessment on their own—the only exception would be if there are risks that the investors would not normally uncover in their due diligence."

5. **Make sure the "pro forma" financial information in the plan is tailored to your business.** For example, if you're a manufacturer, you don't want to use the same pro formas as a clothing retailer would, because you have production, inventory, and capital expenses that they don't.

Section 2

6. **Fine-tune and polish your management's resumes.** Be sure to include information about your professional advisors. "When investors see a responsible law firm or accounting firm name, it enhances your credibility," explains McGilvery.

7. **Request funding in stages.** Where years ago you would ask for $3 million upfront, you're much better off asking for $1 million at a time in three stages, because, McGilvery says, "Investors want to see you producing a revenue stream with the smallest possible investment."

8. **Don't forget to spell-check.** Typographical errors in a business plan are the kiss of death.

Source: Cliff Ennico, "Smart Tips for Writing Your Business Plan," www.entrepreneur.com/article/0,4621,311598,00.html.

SCORE's Five Tips for Writing a Business Plan for a Loan

1. Begin with a statement of purpose. You should be able to explain your business in 25 words or less.

2. Tell how your business will work and why it will be successful. List the owners.

3. Fill in the business details. Describe its products or services, the customers, the market, and the competition. List the managers and their credentials.

4. Supply three years of projected financial statements. Include income, loss, and cash-flow projections.

5. Provide supporting documents, such as references from creditors and potential clients and suppliers, evidence of insurance, and the like.

Source: SCORE, www.score.org/business_tips.html.

Create a Picture of Your Business's Mission Statement

1. Why are you in business?

2. Who are your customers?

3. What image of your business do you want to convey?

4. What is the nature of your product or service?

5. What level of service do you provide?

6. What roles do you and your employees play?

7. What kind of relationships will you maintain with suppliers?

8. How do you differ from competitors?

9. How will you use technology, capital, processes, products, and services?

10. What underlying philosophies or values guided your responses to previous questions?

Source: Rieva Lesonsky, *Start Your Own Business.*

Five Things to Include in an Executive Summary

The statement should be kept short and businesslike, probably no more than half a page. It could be longer, depending on how complicated the use of funds may be, but the summary of a business plan, like the summary of a loan application, is generally no more than one page. Within that space you'll need to provide a synopsis of the entire business plan. Key elements that should be included are:

1. **Business concept:** Describes the business, its product, and the market it will serve. It should point out just exactly what will be sold, to whom, and why the business will hold a competitive advantage.

2. **Financial features:** Highlights the important financial points of the business including sales, profits, cash flows, and return on investment.

3. **Financial requirements:** Clearly states the capital needed to start the business and to expand. It should detail how the capital will be used, and the equity, if any, that will be provided for funding. If the loan for initial capital will be based on security instead of equity within the company, you should also specify the source of collateral.

4. **Current business position:** Furnishes relevant information about the company, its legal form of operation, when it was formed, the principal owners, and key personnel.

5. **Major achievements:** Details any developments within the company that are essential to the success of the business. Major achievements include items like patents, prototypes, location of a facility, any crucial contracts that need to be in place for product development, or results from any test marketing that has been conducted.

Source: "Executive Summary," www.entrepreneur.com/article/0,4621,270366,00.html.

SCORE's Five Tips on Building a Sound Business Plan

1. Write a business plan with a complete financial and marketing plan.

2. Your marketing strategy should be built around your strengths, your competitors' weaknesses, and your customers' desires.

3. Test the reality of your business—know why it will work and how you will make it work. Think your business through step by step.

4. Allow at least two hours every week for thinking and planning. Do not allow anything to interfere with this time. You run the business. Don't let it run you.

5. Establish an annual operating plan. Review it and update it monthly with appropriate employees.

Source: SCORE, www.score.org/business_tips.html.

Eight Biggest Mistakes to Make in Your Business Plan

1. **Putting it off.** Don't wait to write a plan until you absolutely have to. Too many businesses make business plans only when they have no choice in the matter. Unless the bank or the investors want a plan, there is no plan.

2. **Cash flow casualness.** Cash flow is more important than sales, profits, or anything else in the business plan, but most people think in terms of profits instead of cash. When you and your friends imagine a new business, you think of what it would cost to make the product, what you could sell it for, and what the profits per unit might be. We are trained to think of business as sales minus costs and expenses, which equals profits. Unfortunately, we don't spend the profits in a business. We spend cash. So understanding cash flow is critical. If you have only one table in your business plan, make it the cash flow table.

3. **Idea inflation.** Plans don't sell new business ideas to investors. People do. The plan, though necessary, is only a way to present information. Investors invest in people, not ideas.

4. **Fear and dread.** Doing a business plan isn't as hard as you think. You don't have to write a doctoral thesis or a novel. There are good books to help, many advisors among the Small Business Development Centers (SBDCs), business schools, and software available to help you (such as Business Plan Pro and others).

5. **Spongy, vague goals.** Leave out the vague and the meaningless babble of business phrases (such as "being the best") because they are simply hype. Remember that the objective of a plan is its results, and for results, you need tracking and follow-up. You need specific dates, management responsibilities, budgets, and milestones. Then you can follow up. No matter how well thought out or brilliantly presented, it means nothing unless it produces results.

6. **One size fits all.** Tailor your business plan to its real business purpose. Business plans can be different things: they are often just sales documents to sell an idea for a new business. They can be detailed action plans, financial plans, marketing plans, and even personnel plans. They can be used to start a business, or just run a business better.

7. **Diluted priorities.** Remember: strategy is focus. A priority list with three or four items is focus. A priority list with 20 items is something else, certainly not strategic, and rarely if ever effective. The more items on the list, the less the importance of each.

8. **Hockey-stick shaped growth projections.** Have projections that are conservative so you can defend them. When in doubt, be less optimistic

Source: Tim Berry, "Common Business Plan Mistakes," www.bplans.com/dp/article.cfm/35.

SCORE's Five Tips on Developing a Marketing Plan

1. Determine specific goals and the time frame in which you want to achieve them. Communicate the goals to your employees.

2. Decide what tools can best help you meet your goals and how they will be used. These can include the internet, newsletters, direct mail, special events, trade shows, advertising, and more.

3. Come up with a budget that reflects your goals.

4. Delegate responsibility for implementing each segment of the plan.

5. Monitor the results and make adjustments as necessary.

Source: SCORE, www.score.org/business_tips.html.

Glossary of Business Plan Terms

What They Say:

1. We conservatively project …

2. We took our best guess and divided by two …

3. We project a ten percent margin.

4. The project is 98 percent complete.

5. Our business model is proven …

6. We have a six-month lead.

7. We only need a ten percent market share.

8. We are the low-cost producer.

9. We have no competition.

10. We seek a value-added investor.

What They Really Mean:

1. We read a book that said we had to be a $50 million company in five years, and we reverse-engineered the numbers.

2. We accidentally divided by 0.5.

3. We did not modify any of the assumptions in the business plan template we downloaded from the internet.

4. To complete the remaining two percent we will take as long as it took to create the initial 98 percent but will cost twice as much.

5. If you take the evidence from the past week for the best of our 50 locations and extrapolate it for all the others.

6. We tried not to find out how many other people have a six-month lead.

7. So do the other 50 entrants getting funded.

8. We have not produced anything yet, but we are confident that we will be able to do so.

9. Only IBM, Microsoft, and Netscape have announced plans to enter the business.

10. We are looking for a passive, dumb-as-rocks inventor.

Source: William A. Sahlman, "How to Write a Great Business Plan," *Harvard Business Review*, July–August 1997, p. 106.

Financial Statement Tips

Keep these numbers in order while you are developing your business.

1. **Working capital.** Working capital is the capital you have available to work with today. This is determined by subtracting current liabilities from current assets. A rule of thumb says you should have $1.50 to $2 of current assets for every $1 of current liabilities.

2. **Revenues.** Know your sales on a monthly, quarterly, and year-to-date basis. Compare these with your plan to see if you are behind or ahead.

3. **Gross profit.** Revenues less the direct costs of producing your product is your gross profit. In most cases, there should be 50 percent or more of your sales volume left over after you subtract your direct costs (cost of goods sold).

4. **Profit margin.** Subtract the total of your general and administrative expenses from your gross profit, then divide that number by your sales. This number will tell you how profitable the business is. If the number is negative, you are losing money. Make sure the number is as good as or better than others in your industry. If the typical profit margin in your industry is 12 percent and yours is five percent, you are

not managing your business as well as your competitors. Find out what you need to do to improve that margin.

5. **General and administrative expenses.** There are typically three biggies over which the business owner has a great deal of control. Know these numbers, and be prepared to adjust them to the current business environment.

6. **Compensation.** This is often one of the largest expenses for any business. When business slows, you need to be positioned to reduce compensation quickly and decisively. This isn't always fun, but it's a decision that a business owner who knows the numbers must make.

7. **Marketing expenses.** The largest marketing expense is often advertising. You should be able to turn up or slow down your sales by adjusting your advertising expenditures. If there does not appear to be a correlation between advertising and sales, then there may be something wrong with your advertising strategy. The important point is that if you do not compare your advertising expenses and sales, how will you know the effectiveness of your advertising?

8. **Research and development.** R&D effectiveness is not as easy to quantify as advertising. However, the savvy manager sets a budget based on anticipated costs necessary to achieve a certain goal. Be certain to periodically measure your progress by comparing the amount spent with the proximity to the goal. Like compensation and marketing, this is a variable number that must be monitored and adjusted quickly to meet current needs.

Source: Bill Fiduccia, "Know Your Numbers," www.entrepreneur.com/article/0,4621,293752,00.html.

SCORE's Five Tips for Making the Most of Your Business Plans

1. Take the long view and do long-term planning. Map out where you want to be five years from now and how you plan to get there.

2. Write the plan yourself. You will learn more about your business by doing so.

3. Think of your plan as a living document. Review it regularly to make sure you are on track or to adjust it to market changes.

4. Share the plan with others who can help you get where you want to go—such as lenders, key employees, and advisors.

5. Understand that you might pay a price in the short run to obtain long-term business growth and health.

Source: SCORE, www.score.org/business_tips.html.

SCORE's Five Tips for Effective Business Planning

1. Clearly define your business idea and be able to succinctly articulate it. Know your mission.

2. Examine your motives. Make sure that you have a passion for owning a business and for this particular business.

3. Be willing to commit to the hours, discipline, continuous learning, and the frustrations of owning your own business.

4. Conduct a competitive analysis in your market, including products, prices, promotions, advertising, distribution, quality, and service, and be aware of the outside influences that affect your business.

5. Seek help from other small businesses, vendors, professionals, government agencies, employees, trade associations, and trade shows. Be alert, ask questions, and visit your local SCORE office.

Source: SCORE, www.score.org/business_tips.html.

Finding Example Business Plans Online

These following resources offer sample business plans that you can use to get basic ideas on format and structure of typical business plans.

More Business.com
www.bplans.com/samples/mbus.cfm

Small Business Administration
www.sba.gov/managing/strategicplan/sampleplan.html

Entreprenur.com
www.entrepreneur.com/businessplan/a-z/

Business Resource Software, Inc.—Center for Business Planning
www.businessplans.org

Try *Business Plan Software: Business Plan Pro*, 2006 edition, from Palo Alto Software: www.paloalto.com/ps/bp.

Check www.entrepreneur.com for books on writing business plans, including *Creating a Successful Business Plan*, by *Entrepreneur Magazine*.

Where to Go for Help Developing a Business Plan

1. **Organizations.** Get professional help and free business plan coaching from Small Business Service Centers such as the following:

   - Small Business Administration Small Business Development Centers, which provide free consulting (sba.gov/sbdc)

   - Kauffman Center for Entrepreneur Leadership (www.entreworld.com)

   - The Service Corps of Retired Executives (SCORE), a nonprofit group of mostly retired businesspeople who volunteer to provide counseling to small businesses at no charge (www.score.org)

   - National Business Incubation Association, a national organization for business incubators, which are organizations set up to nurture young firms and help them survive and grow (nbia.org)

   - Chambers of Commerce, organizations throughout the United States devoted to providing networking, lobbying, training, and more (www.uschamber.com)

2. **Take a class at a local school on entrepreneurship.** A great thing about this is you have access to the school's database and can do all the researching you need for free and ask the librarian to point you in the right direction for your researching.

3. **Buy a business plan book and look at templates from Entrepreneur.com to help you along the journey.** Try using Business Plan Pro 2006 to help you structure and format your business plan. Some helpful books include:

   - *Business Plans for Dummies* by Paul Tiffany, and Steven D. Peterson

   - *Business Plans Kit for Dummies* (with CD-ROM) by Paul Tiffany and Steven D. Peterson

   - *Creating a Successful Business Plan* from Entrepreneur Press

   - *The Ernst & Young Business Plan Guide* by Eric S. Siegel, Brian R. Ford, and Jay M. Bornstein

   - *Rule's Book of Business Plans for Startups* by Roger C. Rule

   - *Start Your Own Business* by Rieva Lesonsky

   - *The Successful Business Plan: Secrets and Strategies* by Rhonda Abrams

   - *Writing a Convincing Business Plan* by Arthur R. DeThomas and Lin Grensing-Pophal

   - *Perfect Phases for Business Proposals and Business Plans* by Don Debelak

4. **Hire a business consultant** such as Growthink.com or MyBusinessAnalyst.com, which charge a fee for their services. Look for referrals, look for a company fit, check references, and get any estimates for work in writing.

For more information: Laura Tiffany, "Get Help With Your Plan," www.entrepreneur.com/article/0,4621,287379-1,00.html.

Chapter 14

Business Partners
and Acting the Part

Five Common Traps in Starting a Business with Your Spouse

Avoid these five common traps so both your business and marriage can thrive.

1. **Misplacing your priorities**: Your relationship should always come first. Don't let the business become more important than the marriage.

2. **Overworking**: Don't fall into the all-work-and-no-play trap. It proves deadly to both the business and the relationship.

3. **Poor communication**: Couples must talk openly and frequently about both business and personal issues.

4. **Forgetting the big picture**: It's all too easy to get bogged down in daily minutiae. But don't lose sight of your business or personal goals.

5. **Conflicting personalities**: In business, it's actually better to think differently than the same. Consider your differences opportunities to grow your business.

Source: Rieva Lesonsky, *365 Tips to Boost Your Entrepreneurial IQ.*

Survival Strategies for Entering a Partnership

Shared Goals. Achieving success will require you and your partners to agree on what success looks like. The most frequent objectives of small-business owners are to be profitable and have highly satisfied customers. But clearly, entrepreneurs may have other goals relating to size, growth, innovation, risk-taking, and the cultivation of respect and recognition within their industry and community.

Different Roles. One of the most obvious reasons for partnering with others is to enlarge the skill mix of ownership. While you can hire someone with almost any skill, you can't hire individuals with the same level of commitment to success as owners. The time-honored division of labor into "outside activities," like sales and business development, and "inside activities," like operations and management, still makes sense for many businesses. More recently, having a technology-savvy partner can offer huge advantages for many types of firms. Even if partners play similar functional roles—as is often the case in small, professional service firms—it's useful to have partners who cater to different types of clients. Skill differences are among the most healthy and productive differences that business partners can have.

Compatible Tastes. Business owners make hundreds of decisions about how to run their business: whether to operate a formal or informal office environment, whether to have many meetings or few, whether to have an open floor plan or individualized

Section 2

offices, whether or not to have company outings, how frequently and how best to conduct employee reviews, the type and number of administrative staff, and so forth

Effective Decision-Making. One of the most reliable predictors of partnership success or failure is whether partners improve the decision-making process. Partners with shared objectives and a shared understanding of how to reach those objectives make better decisions as a group than they would on their own because they benefit from the diversity of knowledge all the partners bring to the process.

Share (and Often Share Alike). While you might suspect that compensation is one of the most difficult partnership issues, in many cases, it may be among the simplest. Unless there's a good reason to do otherwise, partners should receive a fixed share of profits (and in many cases, an equal share of profits).

Trust—but Verify. As Milton Friedman, Ayn Rand, and generations of economists have pointed out, people pursue their own self-interests. That's as true of great business partners as it is of anyone else. But business partnerships work in spite of self-interest because partners have mutual interests (shared goals). But shared goals aren't enough. Trust and transparency are equally important.

Don't Sign on with Your Best Friend. Beyond a shared vision of success, shared tastes, and complementary skills, successful partners are often individuals who like and respect each other enough to be good friends even if they weren't in business together. But in order to maintain your objectivity about a business relationship—and continue to have the flexibility to change or end the relationship if necessary—it's best not to partner with your innermost circle of friends.

Source: Paige Arnof-Fenn, "The Partner Track," www.entrepreneur.com/article/ 0,4621,322335,00.html.

Tips on Finding the Perfect Business Partner

Being someone's friend or relative is one of the worst reasons I can think of for making that someone your business partner, says author Cliff Ennico. Generally, once someone becomes your business partner, there is only one way to get rid of them legally if things don't work out. You must buy them out for the fair value of their interest in the business. That can be an expensive proposition, especially if it needs to be done when the business has not yet established itself and doesn't have the cash flow to support a partner buyout.

- **Are you a visionary, or an operations person?** Successful partnerships combine those two kinds of people.
  - A visionary is a strategic, "big picture" thinker who understands the business model, the market, and the overall business plan.
  - An operations person is someone who rolls up their sleeves, wades up to their

hip boots in the details, and executes the strategy that the visionary comes up with.

You are either one or the other—it is almost impossible to be both. Once you have determined if you are a "visionary" or an "operations person," look for your opposite number. That way your business is more likely to strike the right balance between strategy and tactics.

- **Do you have all the skills you need on board to make the business work?** Your partners should complement your set of business skills, not duplicate them. Keep in mind that you can acquire someone's skills without making them a partner. If a particular skill, such as contract negotiation or bookkeeping, is not critical to the success of your business, you may be better off hiring a lawyer, accountant, or consultant to do it for you and keeping ownership of your business.

- **Can you communicate directly and honestly with this person, without pulling any punches?** Communication between partners can often get rough; disagreements and arguments break out all the time. It is difficult to criticize someone harshly, yet sometimes you must be cruel with your business partners in order to do the right thing for your business. Sometimes the most successful business partnerships are those where the partners do not socialize outside the office.

- **Is your business partner willing to hang around for the long haul?** This is the critical test of a business partner. Many people are happy to help out with a business during its start-up phase, only to lose interest later on when something more attractive comes along, a life-changing event occurs, or the going is getting tougher and the business isn't as much "fun" as it used to be.

If you are not sure if someone is committed to the long-term success of your business, make them an employee or independent contractor, with perhaps an "option" to acquire an interest in your business at a date two or three years down the road ... provided, of course, they are still working for you at that time and you continue to be satisfied with their performance.

Source: Cliff Ennico, "Picking the Right Partner," www.entrepreneur.com/article/0,4621,298643,00.html.

Tips on How Entrepreneurs See the World

Point #1: The entrepreneur is a systems thinker.

She sees everything as a system. She sees the business she intends to create as a system. She sees the end game she's going to produce—in other terms, the exit strategy—as a systems opportunity. She sees everything as an opportunity to create synergy among how the business attracts a customer, how the business converts that customer into cash flow, and how the business continuously fulfills the promise it makes to its customers to turn those customers into clients.

Point #2: The entrepreneur is a visionary.

That means before he ever gets down into doing it, he's primarily one who sees the business visually. To him, the business is first and foremost a vision, a picture that has shape, size, colors, form. And all of that is seen as signs, and floors, and walls, and people, and how the look, the color and style of their dress, the napkins, the windows, the logo, the stationary, the inventory, the trucks, the cars—everything you can see in a business is a significant component of the completed visual system.

Point #3: The entrepreneur is a marketing maniac.

To the true entrepreneur, the entire business is the fulfillment of the promise the entrepreneur makes. "On time, every time!" is such a promise. "When you care enough to give the very best!" is such a promise. "The lowest prices ... guaranteed!" is such a promise. The promise, the promise, the promise.

You get to make one promise to your customer to grab his or her attention, and only one promise. And that promise has got to define you in the world, in your customers' mind.

The entrepreneur is responsible for seeing that promise and understanding why and how his company must operate in such a deliberate way as to keep that promise, every single time. The entrepreneur is a marketing maniac. His passion, his persistence, his dogged determination to invent a company that makes and keeps a promise that defines it in the world as preferentially unique—that is his reason for being.

Point #4: The entrepreneur is a fanatic for detail.

If the entrepreneur can't see it, it doesn't exist. The entrepreneur sees his or her company as though it were a product, a widget, a thing, just like a computer or an automobile or a chair is a thing. And every thing in the world is made up of details. Every thing in the world is constructed, thoughtfully, patiently, intentionally, piece by piece by small, often unobservable pieces.

The entrepreneur is fascinated by how those pieces fit together to make up his or her extraordinarily functional, wonderfully visual, and emotionally satisfying business. See the pieces. See how they fit together. Every little part of a business either contributes to that business' success—or to its failure. Every great entrepreneur knows that businesses fail because of all the little things that don't work. That explains his fanaticism. Make it work! Make it work better than any other business!

Source: Michael Gerber, "The Entrepreneur's Point of View," www.entrepreneur.com/article/0,4621,320210,00.html.

Three Exercises to Awaken the Entrepreneur Inside You

The First Exercise

Stop thinking about what you want to do. Stop doing what you're doing. Go to a place—any place will do—where activity ceases, where there is no itinerary, no schedule, no agenda, no responsibility, no work of any kind, no expectation, no result you've set for yourself, no goals, no objectives, no action plans whatsoever. Go to such a place to empty your mind.

And that's the first exercise to awaken the entrepreneur in you: to empty your mind. To dream and to create, there needs to be both space and energy. The entrepreneur in us wants to play with the idea of things, without constraint. To write without purpose, to imagine without an end game, to live fully and completely in the moment of his or her experience, now. Not in the past nor in the future, but now.

To prepare yourself for this exercise, try sitting down where you are, closing the door, telling everyone who might bother you to give you ten minutes without a disturbance of any kind. Unplug the phone, turn off your computer, sit down, face a wall, close your eyes, place your hands in your lap, breathe deeply, and just stay there, just like that.

You must do this first exercise every single day!

The Second Exercise

Get a blank piece of paper. You have nothing in mind. Sit with the blank piece of paper, and let whatever comes to mind go to the paper. Whether it be a sentence, or just three seemingly unrelated words. Whether it be an entire paragraph, a thought, a concern, a conclusion, let it write itself down. The key here is to let "It" speak. To let "It" say what "It" wants to say. To let "It" have the room to breath.

Do it for only ten minutes. Do it once a day. And save those pieces of paper, with the date on the top right-hand corner. Save them in a box, or a file folder, and know that that box or file folder is a sacred place. Because your dreamer has created it. Your entrepreneur has become vulnerable. Your creator has expressed himself or herself, and you've been a witness to it.

The Third Exercise

Maintaining an entrepreneurial journal is a daily process. Buy yourself a journal, prefer-ably with leather covers, a rich-looking journal, a journal that impresses you because it looks so rich, so permanent, so significant. Write in that journal what you learned that day. Write in that journal what you felt that day. Write in that journal anything that came to mind that day, as you sat with a blank piece of paper, as you sat in your chair facing the wall for ten minutes with absolutely no interruption at all, as you felt your feelings come up, your feelings of being blocked, your feelings of being ashamed, your feelings of excitement, your feelings of despair ... whatever came up that day, record it, even though you may not think you're an accomplished writer—or even if you think you are. Your entrepreneurial journal is not about the writing; it's about the recording. This is your life, and if you don't take it seriously, who will? This third exercise will feed your first exercise and your second exercise, and you will know it.

Believe me, you will know it.

Source: Michael Gerber, "Awakening the Entrepreneur Within You," www.entrepreneur.com/article/0,4621,321024,00.html.

Starting Your Business

Avoiding the Pitfalls

Three Most Common Mistakes When Starting

1. **Underestimating the amount of money and time it takes to start a business.** The money part is tricky, but it doesn't have to be a puzzle. That's what business plans are for.

2. **Commitment.** Of course it'll depend on the type of business you're starting and whether you plan to start the business full time or on the side. For example, if you want to start a part-time business selling jewelry on eBay—jewelry that you already make for fun—that's a far different story from someone who wants to start a restaurant and has to devote the time to finding start-up capital, employees, a location, and equipment. But large or small, a business tends to consume time, and large chunks of it, so be prepared to handle that reality.

3. **Failing to enlist professionals who can walk you through start-up.** There are certain things you might be able to figure out on your own—marketing materials, for instance—by reading good books and articles, but you don't want to mess around with things like figuring out how to structure your company (sole proprietorship, corporation, etc.), what licenses and permits to get, and so on. Even if you get just a little input from an attorney and an accountant, you're probably better off than if you attempt to think of every legal and tax question in the book.

Source: Karen Spaeder, "Biggest Start-Up Mistakes to Avoid," www.entrepreneur.com/article/0,4621,308530,00.html.

Three Myths in Small Business Planning

Here are three myths that need to be dispelled about strategic planning for small business.

1. It has to be formal.
Not so. The value of a strategic plan for your small business is in putting the ideas on paper, creating action steps that will get you where you want to go, and implementing those action steps.

2. I'm too small.
Not so. Even a one-person business can benefit from a strategic plan. A strategic plan can help you make decisions about time management and budget. You can use your strategic plan to help you determine whether to attend an event or advertise in a publication. It's a check-and-balance tool.

3. A strategic plan is like a ball and chain.
Not so. It's your plan. Too many small business owners feel like once it's on paper, it can't be changed. Wrong! Your plan should be an active document that gets reviewed and updated at least monthly, if not weekly. You're the business owner, you wrote it,

you know what's happening in your market—adjust as necessary.

Source: Denise O'Berry, "Small Business Planning—Three Myths," ezinearticles.com/?Small-Business-Planning----Three-Myths&id=6118.

Ways to Avoid Giving Away Free Consulting

In most cases, arrange to meet with your potential clients for about 30 minutes, to see if you are a match; that is, can you offer a service to them and do they need it? Try to give something free to each potential client so they get a sample of your services. Giving one or two pieces of information away for free is OK; however, 30 minutes' worth is not.

Client Interviews (Get-to-Know Session)

When meeting with a potential client, your goal is to uncover a need they may have that matches a service you provide. How can you do this?

- Ask open-ended questions, that is, ask questions that will evoke a conversation. For example, an open-ended question may start with the words: "Tell me" or "What is …" or "When do …," etc. Open-ended questions will enable the client to give you more than just a yes or no answer, thus giving you more details about what they need.

- After hearing a series of problems that you can solve through your services, it is important to state that you have solutions to their problems. Do not offer the solution here, but suggest that there are solutions and that by working with you, they can resolve these problems.

- Make it clear to the client during the conversation that this is your work and you charge a fee for such a consultation. This area seems to be most sensitive with your friends and family.

- Keep your boundaries clear—you charge for your services. Make a policy about consulting to your friends/family.

To summarize, it is your responsibility to avoid giving away free service.

- Probe the potential client through questioning to find out about their needs and problems.

- Once you have heard their needs and problems, mention that you have solutions for them.

- Be clear throughout the conversation that this is your career and you would be happy to work with them.

- Have a policy in place for friends and family in the event they want your services for free. Once you have mastered this skill, you will increase your confidence in asking the right questions during the process of earning new clients.

Source: Michael Losier, "How to Avoid Giving Away Free Consulting," www.ezinearticles.com/?How-to-Avoid-Giving-Away-Free-Consulting&id=22652.

Surviving Seasonal Sales Slumps

1. **Save your money.**
   People have an all-too-common inclination to spend, spend, spend when the coffers are full. Rule No. 1 of seasonal businesses: don't do that.

2. **Keep yourself busy during the slow times.**
   These are suggestions from Mike Marchev, a motivational speaker and author:

   - **Strengthen client relationships.** "Call people you already know, arrange a meeting with them, and brainstorm. It re-energizes your batteries."

   - **Play catch-up—or don't.** "That can be anything from straightening up your desk or [organizing] your files to reading or remembering why you went into business in the first place—and that is to enjoy a Thursday afternoon. Now, that doesn't mean go play golf every day. [But if] there's a slow time, don't beat yourself up. Enjoy the afternoon."

   - **Call associates in a similar situation.** "[When they say,] 'Boy, I hope you're busier than I am because I'm really dead,' then you can say, 'Gee, I'm dead, too. I feel better already.'"

   - **Write a book.** "If you're a home-based entrepreneur, regardless of your [industry,] you want to be known as the expert in what you do. Every entrepreneur should have a goal to put their knowledge into a book. Because once you become an author, it puts you into a different category. You must know what you're talking about—you wrote the book. So that's a perfect downtime activity."

3. **Stay afloat through diversification.**
   "A person who feels they have a slump should look at it from a different angle or find a niche they haven't reviewed before," says Gillian Christie, whose firm, Christie Communications Inc., is headquartered in Santa Barbara, California, and focuses on ethically minded clients. "It's really a wonderful exercise in creativity. Just think and play with ideas. Study and read a lot of industry publications outside your category so you're familiar with what's going on in other industries."

4. **Make your decision.**
   With a seasonal business, you have several options. You can remain busy year-round through diversification, you can focus on other activities like writing a book, or you can plan carefully and take some extra time off for yourself.

Source: Laura Tiffany, "Surviving Seasonal Sales Slumps," www.entrepreneur.com/article/ 0,4621,293270,00.html.

Seven Investor Presentation Pitfalls

1. **Missing the "a-ha!"** "The thing that really kills an entrepreneur's case is not nailing down their story—not getting to the 'a-ha!' very quickly in the presentation," says J. Neil Weintraut, a general partner at San Francisco venture capital firm 21st Century Internet Venture Partners. "Instead of [explaining] that you have a Java-enabled spreadsheet, for example, tell me upfront why [your business] changes people's lives. We're looking for something that will knock consumers' socks off."

2. **Having an unclear market focus.** "Some [entrepreneurs] come in and say they're going after a trillion-dollar market," says Weintraut. "Glad to hear the market is that big, but how does it connect with your business? What's the market [segment] you're going after?"

   Here's a solution. Break your target market into highly specific segments. For example, let's say your company targets the small-business market. There are 25 million small businesses in the United States, and the SBA defines them as companies with fewer than 500 employees. However, a one-person start-up has vastly different needs than a 100-employee company. Therefore, you would break your market into segments, like one to four employees, five to nine employees, and so forth. Then you would focus on the one or two segments that will benefit most from your product or service.

3. **Being fluffy.** "You often hear people say, 'We have a great management team.' But don't declare that! Just give me the facts and let me come to my own conclusion," says Weintraut. Be specific about your credentials and those of your team members. In what specific ways did you help your former company be more successful? Did you help boost sales by 25 percent, for example? Advises Weintraut, "Say something like 'I was the VP of business development who contributed to the success of company X in this way.' "

4. **Having poor team dynamics.** "You bring your team but don't let them say anything. What does that tell you? What kind of team is this?" poses Rich Shapero, managing partner at Woodside, California, VC firm CrossPoint Venture Partners. "These are good signals. Is this entrepreneur a good leader? Can he really motivate people? We care not only about the individual who started the company or is running it but also about the other people and the chemistry between them."

   Andreas Stavropoulos, a director at Redwood City, California, VC firm Draper Fisher Jurvetson, agrees. "The team dynamic is very important," he says. "People get so focused on trying to deliver the message just the right way, they don't realize that through their interactions, they're stepping on their partners' toes or cutting them off. That can be even more important than what they're actually saying."

5. **Being underprepared.** "What we see in a fair number of situations is that the entrepreneur doesn't have the [presentation] staged—they don't know what they're going

to do," says Shapero. "So they come in and start talking casually about the business, and I'm always mystified because I think, 'Good God! This was a tough appointment for you to get. I'm assuming you have planned what you're going to do. What I'm seeing is that you don't have a clue!' That's pretty scary."

So how do you ensure you're prepared? Stavropoulos suggests building a presentation of no more than 10 to 20 PowerPoint slides, organized around the main points of your business model. But you should also be flexible enough to deviate from your intended structure to accommodate investor questions. "We like our questions answered directly—at the point when [we ask] the question," says Stavropoulos. "People who say, 'Well, let me just get through my presentation' put the presentation itself, more than the content, above the substance."

6. **Having unrealistic expectations.** Don't expect to walk out of your first presentation with a check. "That's where a lot of entrepreneurs get confused," says Shapero. "You're not going to convince the investor in [the first presentation] to invest. Instead, your objective is to give investors a high-level overview that is compelling enough to capture their interest [and allow you] to go to the next level of detail."

7. **Lacking common sense.** Shapero must have seen it all. He's even had entrepreneurs bring their kids to the presentation. Another tip: "Turn cell phones off! Don't wait for it to ring to realize it's on," he says. Of course, you would know better.

Source: Sean M. Lyden, "7 Investor Presentation Pitfalls," www.entrepreneur.com/article/0,4621,285913-2,00.html.

Five Common Budgeting Mistakes

1. **Overstating projections.** Enron was not the first company to overpromise and underdeliver, and, unfortunately, it won't be the last. Investors are occasionally fooled by numbers in the short term, but in the end the funded company almost always gets hurt. Realistic budgets and projections may lengthen your search for funding, but when the money does arrive, it will be honest money, and you should then have a profitable plan to follow for several years to come.

2. **Ignoring your immediate budgetary needs.** On the other hand, if your plan shows that you need $50,000 to take a product to market, don't ask for only $30,000. Potential investors and bankers will only wonder why they should give you money for a project that will fail without additional funding. This was the sad lesson of the dotcom bubble. Companies burned through their initial seed money without coming close to profitability and then gave up. Investors have become more savvy and would rather spend $50,000 in a smart fashion than throw $30,000 out the window.

3. **Assuming that the existence of revenue is indicative of being cash-flow positive.** In virtually every transaction, there is a lag time between the finalization of the deal

and the completed cash collection. This is a fact of business and should not be a problem, assuming you are prepared. Unfortunately, many businesses aren't and run into serious cash-flow problems because they spend money they don't yet have. Perhaps what's most troubling is many of these purchases could easily have been delayed for 30 days, when the available money is finally in the bank. A little wisdom, discretion, and foresight can go a long way toward corporate survival.

4. **Forgetting about Uncle Sam.** End-of-the-day balances can often appear larger than they really are. Sales tax on revenues and employee withholdings may sit in your account temporarily but will ultimately be owed to the government. Your balance sheets should not count these finances as holdings; otherwise you run the risk of budgeting for future projects and costs that you will not be able to afford.

5. **Mismanaging the advertising timeline.** It seems so elementary: advertising leads to sales. However, many budgets show advertising costs as a percentage of sales in the same period. To be truly effective, an advertising/marketing campaign will have to be initiated at least one period before sales can be expected. When the additional out-of-pocket costs are taken into account, a healthy advertising budget is needed before any revenue can be assumed. Failure to budget the appropriate items in a strategic time frame will underutilize finances needed to achieve these sales goals and can lead to overspending in later months.

Source: Ian Benoliel, "5 Common Budgeting Mistakes," www.entrepreneur.com/article/0,4621,297437,00.html.

Chapter 16

Developing Your Brand Image

Tips for Your Business Image Checkup

First impressions are important for businesses, but many entrepreneurs don't bother to check theirs. So let's take the time to give your business an image checkup.

- If you have a sign, take a look at it. Does it grab attention and convey a sense of quality and stability? Does it say too much or not enough?
- Remember, neatness counts. How crowded are your display shelves?
- If you have plants, make sure they're green and healthy.
- Are your brochures and other literature relevant and current?
- How is your packaging? This includes bags, envelopes, stationery, and business cards.
- Is your logo up-to-date and professional-looking?
- Are your mailings clear and concise? Check your paper and printing as well as your message.

Don't put this off. Check your business image sometime this month and once a year thereafter.

Source: Rieva Lesonsky, *365 Tips to Boost Your Entrepreneurial IQ.*

Four Important Tips for Developing a Brand Image

1. **Be uniquely valuable.** The first step is to ask a series of basic questions, such as "What do we do that benefits our customers? What's our company's ultimate goal? How is what we offer unique?" Ultimately, the relationship you build between your brand and your customers will be based on the value your company offers. And the bottom line is that perceived value is what creates loyal customers who will choose your product or service over others—even when they're tempted with cheaper offers elsewhere.

2. **Stand out from the pack.** So how can you differentiate from your competition? To help find the answer, it's a great idea to conduct a competitive analysis. It doesn't have to be complex. Just gather together the marketing materials from your chief competitors, including their ads and brochures. Examine the materials carefully and look for the key selling points and the basic "promises" they make.

3. **Drive your core message home.** Ideally, your core message may come down to a single idea, which will become the focus of all your external communications. Advertising, public relations, collateral tools, and even the message you use when networking should all revolve around this central theme. For some companies, par-

ticularly those focused on consumer products, a single slogan may embody the essence of their brand.

4. **Live up to your promise.** Branding isn't just something that's achieved when a prospect encounters your marketing. It's about creating and meeting expectations, and its success rests on your customers' total experience with your brand.

It may surprise you to learn that each time a customer visits your web site, he or she is undergoing a branding experience. In essence, your site is your brand, and everything visitors encounter there—from the site design and depth of products or services offered to their satisfaction with your online customer service and shipping policies—positively or negatively impacts your company or brand image.

Source: Kim T. Gordon, "Branding Made Simple," www.entrepreneur.com/article/ 0,4621,318050,00.html.

Eight Image-Building Tips

To convey an image of professionalism and stability, you'll need a family of top-quality tools that work together.

1. **Choose a great company name.** Your company needs a name that's descriptive and easily recognizable, such as "Jones Public Relations." If the name you've started out with isn't working, change it.

2. **Answer professionally.** Answer the phone clearly and distinctly with the company name, followed by your own name, to help the caller remember it, such as "Jones Public Relations. This is Sally Jones."

3. **Record a professional-sounding message.** The way your phone is answered when you're unavailable says a lot about your concern for customer satisfaction. One simple solution is using voice mail from your local phone company. For less than $10 per month, voice mail allows your callers to leave you a message even when you're on the line. Whether you use voice mail or an answering machine, make sure your outgoing message is upbeat, short, crisp, and professional.

4. **Become an expert at describing what you do.** Write down a single, clear sentence that describes what your company does. Then memorize it and repeat it in every contact with prospects, from networking to cold calls. Being able to describe your business in a consistent, memorable fashion is a great way to position your company in your prospects' minds.

5. **Start with a stationery package.** To stand out, coordinate two-color business cards (black ink plus a second color) with letterhead and matching envelopes. Add a distinctive logo with help from your printer or a graphic designer. Then use your logo on all your printed materials to maintain a consistent visual image.

6. **Create a company brochure.** This single tool must convey that your company is solid and stable, communicate the benefits of selecting your company, and create a distinct visual image. Examine your principal competitors' brochures to assess the formats they use and their key selling points. When developing your own brochure, production quality is critical to the success of the piece—and to your professional image. So be certain your company brochure can stand up to those of your largest competitors in terms of design, readability, and paper quality.

7. **Polish your forms.** Print invoices, contracts, and estimates on letterhead or preprinted forms, so every communication your prospects and customers receive from your business conveys a consistent, professional image.

8. **Tie in presentation tools.** If you need presentation folders or proposal covers, have them printed at the same time you print your brochure. A large portion of printers' charges are for "inking" the press. If your materials use the same kind of paper and ink colors, printing them together will save money.

Source: Kim T. Gordon, "8 Image-Building Tips," www.entrepreneur.com/article/ 0,4621,317690,00.html.

How to Dare to Be Different

Are you ready to develop your own differentiation strategy? Here are four steps to get you started.

1. **Evaluate competitive messages.** Your first step is to gather and evaluate the marketing materials of your chief competitors, including their ads, brochures, and web site content. Don't be surprised if you see a lot of "me too" marketing. There's simply a lot of bad marketing out there, and the fact that many of your competitors have no differentiation strategy will work to your advantage.

    At least some of your competitors—usually the category leaders—will make promises that resonate with their target audiences. Carefully review the benefit statements your competitors make, and determine what claims set them apart.

2. **Find what makes you unique.** For a companywide differentiation strategy, consider what separates you from the competitors you've evaluated. Whether you market a product or operate a service business, such as an accounting firm or a power-washing company, it's essential to clearly differentiate through your marketing how what you offer is of unique value.

    Your point of differentiation may relate to the way your product or service is provided, priced, or even delivered. The most important thing to discover is the principal benefit you offer that is uniquely valuable to customers and gives you a competitive advantage.

3. **Tell the world.** Your next step is to create a new marketing message that communicates your product or service's unique value. This message should become the core of your entire marketing campaign. To successfully gain a competitive advantage, consistently drive this point of differentiation home until it becomes integral to your brand image.

4. **Keep your promise.** Effective differentiation has everything to do with customer satisfaction, which builds loyalty and often trumps price as a primary consideration of consumers. As long as your company can sustain its ability to differentiate in a way that consistently meets consumer expectations, customers may reject lower-cost competitors in favor of what you have to offer.

Source: Kim T. Gordon, "Dare to Be Different," www.entrepreneur.com/article/0,4621,320499,00.html.

Tips for Developing the Right Brand Image

Scott Bedbury, who helped build both Nike and Starbucks into brand leaders before launching Brandstream, his own branding consultancy, shares helpful hints on how to get the right brand image. Whether you are starting a company, changing your company, or revitalizing your brand, the following will steer you in the right direction:

1. **Where do I start?**
   Find the answers to why the brand is starting out. What does the brand stand for? What should it resonate with customers? What are its core values? Just as important, are they still relevant? Probe consumers about the product category that you're in. How do they feel about your competitors? What does your product or service provide them with? What are the tangible benefits, and, perhaps more important, what are the emotional benefits? Think of this as a brand audit, and don't bring your personal prejudices to the table. Listen and learn.

2. **How do I keep the brand cohesive with different products?**
   One solution: think like Plato. You may not think of the great Greek philosopher as a brilliant marketer, but he understood a fundamental principle that lies at the heart of a great brand: the concept of essence. Plato believed that deep within everything concrete is the idea of that thing. Plato, in other words, was the first to articulate the importance of a brand's essence.

3. **My brand is boring. It doesn't create excitement in my customers or in my employees. (And it's been a long time since it excited anyone on Wall Street.)**
   Because of the clutter of offerings in the marketplace, brands need more than customer awareness or surface-level connection. Brands need to connect on a deeper psychological level. They need to respect and acknowledge the customers' emotions—feelings such as the yearning to belong, the need to feel connected, the hope to transcend, and the desire to experience joy and fulfillment.

4. My brand does not connect with my customers.

The good news is that even a dead brand can be revived or completely reinvented. Think of Banana Republic. It started out as a clothing retailer with a gimmick: Wouldn't it be fun to buy safari clothing and shop in a store that has fake palm trees, shipping crates for props, and a piece or two of a Jeep? Well, maybe for a while. But the half-life of even the best, most narrowly defined concept is painfully brief, and that version of Banana Republic soon enough became an endangered species. But still, there was something there, something within the notion of "business casual" that had potential for resuscitation. The Gap acquired Banana Republic and reinvented it, this time as a more upscale retailer offering everything from essential sweaters to aromatherapy products to knockoff Donna Karan crepe suits.

5. My brand is stuck in the past.

It happens to the best brands. In fact, it almost always happens to the best brands. They take off like a comet, only to plateau. They make gradual improvements, but they need transformation.

For instance, look at Nike. Consumers already knew all that they needed to know about fitness. Most were not happy about the shape they were in. Few had the time to be serious athletes. So why rub their noses in it? They just needed a little encouragement, an optimistic challenge. "Just Do It" was a watershed moment for Nike. It established a broad communication platform from which we could talk to just about anyone. It wasn't only about world-class athletics; it was about fundamental human values shared by triathletes and mall walkers alike. It wasn't a product statement either. It was a brand ethos. Nike had found a way to respect its past while embracing its future. "Just Do It" was a much-needed re-expression of timeless Nike values.

6. My brand is too narrow.

Use creative outlets and partners to reach more customers with your brand. For example, Starbucks serves United Airlines with their coffee, and also have their own ice cream in thousands of grocery stores. Brand extension is the key and can be accomplished by cobranding, seeking different distribution channels, and also product line extensions.

7. My brand is immature.

Raising a great brand is like raising a great kid. And that means you need to be patient. Great brands take steady guidance, a long view, and uncompromising values. When raising a brand, be consistent and committed. The shuffling of brand responsibilities and the management churn within organizations can easily produce a troubled brand. It takes time for a brand to develop its own values and personality. Good brand stewards, like good parents, build values into their brands that help them grow and endure. Great brands outlive their creators—just like kids. And if you do your job right, they can make you proud.

8. My brand has been reduced to a commodity.

If that's what has happened to your product, then here's what you don't do: don't throw money at the problem. Even the best advertising can't create something that isn't there.

First, set your sights high. Great brand builders don't just reinvent the product; they see themselves as protagonists for an entire category. That's what Nike did with sneakers, Starbucks did with coffee, and Southwest Airlines did with flying.

Second, elevate your product. If you want to be more than a commodity, offer a unique product that is unique and so much better than the rest of the field that it can't be considered a commodity. Is Krispy Kreme just a doughnut?

Third, offer more than the product. Create an experience around it and pay attention to the details. Everything matters.

Fourth, remember that the company is the brand. Customers are looking through the product to your values and how you do business. Today, the difference between similar products may be corporate reputation.

9. **My brand isn't cool.**
Given where the world is going, I recommend that companies be more concerned with their karma than with being cool. As a society, our concerns about the effects that globalization has on cultures and the environment will only intensify, and the bar for corporate behavior will rise. I expect that we'll look to our most trusted brands, big and small, to help reduce the enormous gap that exists between profits and benevolence.

It's a new brand world out there. We are just starting to see the issues and opportunities associated with brand karma. However it evolves, I do know that strong karma will develop after years of doing the right thing: being honest and principled and being respectful of customers, employees, and the environment. Brands like Nike and Starbucks took lightning bolts early on because they were highly visible, global, and influential—and because they care. These companies aren't perfect, but I'm confident that they will help write a much-needed new chapter on brand management. They will prove that big doesn't have to be bad, that profits are only one measure of success, and that great brands can use their unique superhuman powers for good.

Source: Scott Bedbury, "Nine Ways to Fix a Broken Brand," www.fastcompany.com/magazine/55/brokenbrand.html.

How to Write Ads That Build Brands

Before we get started, let me warn you: this is going to hurt a little. Creating branding ads that resonate with your audience is certainly not the easiest thing you'll ever do. However, following my tips will help you simplify the process.

The keys to successful brand writing are these:

1. **Find out what your customers are saying about you.** Bad ads are filled with phrases you like to say about yourself. Good ads are filled with what your customers say about you when you're not around. To be successful, your branding ads must sharply echo "the word on the street" about your company. Jeff Bezos, the CEO of Amazon, got it right when he said, "It has always seemed to me that your brand is formed primarily, not by what your company says about itself, but what the company does." You'll discover the truth behind your brand when you can explain why customers come back to you.

2. **Substantiate your claims.** Overstatement is passé. Today's customers are equipped with a sensitive hype-meter whose needle jumps at the slightest sign of "big talk." So be sure to offer proof to back up what you say, even if that proof lies only in the customers' past experience or in their long-held assumptions. Branding isn't just about the facts: people buy brands with their hearts as well as their heads. Brand loyalty is built on the fact that our purchases remind us—and tell the world around us—who we are.

3. **Double the verbs; whack the adjectives.** Search for evocative words. Sniff out overused phrases. Stimulate customers' minds with thoughts more interesting than the ones they were previously thinking.

   Count the verbs in this famous branding ad I wrote a few years ago:

   "You are standing in the snow, five and one half miles above sea level, gazing at a horizon hundreds of miles away. It occurs to you that life here is very simple: You live, or you die. No compromises, no whining, no second chances. This is a place constantly ravaged by wind and storm, where every ragged breath is an accomplishment. You stand on the uppermost pinnacle of the earth. This is the mountain they call Everest. Yesterday it was considered unbeatable. But thatt was yesterday. Rolex believed Sir Edmund Hillary would conquer Mount Everest, so for him they created the Rolex Explorer. In every life there is a Mount Everest to be conquered. When you have conquered yours, you'll find your Rolex waiting patiently for you to come and pick it up at Justice Jewelers. I'm Woody Justice, and I've got a Rolex for you."

4. **Link your "first mental image" and "last mental image."** The psychological principles of primacy and recency mean that in any list the first few words and the last few words will be the easiest to remember. Great ads focus on a single point and contain that point in both the opening and closing statements of the ad. When possible, link your last mental image to your first mental image, and you'll elevate customers' ability to recall your ad. The Rolex ad was focused on you and your accomplishments. The watch was merely a symbol of those accomplishments. "You are standing in the snow …. I've got a Rolex for you."

5. **Be consistent.** The consistent use of the same colors and fonts is often called "branding," but true branding extends far beyond a visual style signature. The brand essence you've translated visually must now be translated into an auditory style signature in your radio and TV ads, as well as throughout your store. Does the audi-

tory style signature of what your customer hears while "on hold" agree with the balance of your brand essence?

Brands are built on consistency, and the roots of consistency are patience and attention to detail. It's going to take a lot longer to build your brand than you feel it should. Here's the bottom line: if you think you're going to be able to measure brand progress at the end of 12 short months, you're dreaming. Brand development isn't measured in months, but in years. Twenty-four months is the soonest you can hope to begin seeing fruit from any brand orchard you might plant today.

Source: Roy H. Williams, "How to Write Ads That Build Brands," www.entrepreneur.com/article/0,4621,319796,00.html.

Tips on Finding the Right Name

1. **Look two steps ahead, not one.**
   First and foremost, you should identify the long-term business objectives, with the intent to create a name for tomorrow and not just for today. Spend enough time analyzing the market, identifying opportunities for differentiation, and setting the appropriate strategic naming objectives to be used for the name-evaluation process.

2. **Think creatively.**
   The key in name creation is to think outside the box and not be tempted to play in the comfort zone of your competition. Look for inspiration outside your category and learn from completely unrelated brands. Names created in this way have the advantage of being more readily available from a trademark perspective since they go beyond the common category descriptors into fresher territory.

3. **Avoid the "my wife said" syndrome.**
   When it comes to evaluating the names, avoid subjectivity. Do not evaluate the names based on a like/dislike basis, but more on a "fit to concept" scale.

4. **Don't forget the legal battle.**
   Names should always be prescreened for legal availability to avoid the risk of falling in love with a specific name, since it probably isn't available.

5. **Listen to your target audiences.**
   Test the old name alongside new alternatives. The key in name research is to listen carefully for things that can be overcome (e.g., neutral name, reminders of different category, etc.) and for things that can't (e.g., negative associations, inappropriate meanings). In addition, pay attention to key languages for linguistic issues. Even if you are solely U.S.-based, we live in a very diverse country and cannot ignore key languages such as Spanish, French, etc.

6. **Don't ask for everybody's opinion.**
   When it comes to final name selection, it is not a democracy. The final name should

be selected by a small team of the key decision makers, who have a good understanding of the business and strategic objectives. In addition, in the case where senior management is not involved in the development process, make sure to build in
enough time to strategically introduce your new name choice and gain their
approval.

7. **Let everybody know the smart, strategic vision behind the name.**
   Your internal audiences are the most critical for the success of a name. Employees
   are the ones who will "live" the brand on an everyday basis and they should feel
   good about it. The goal is to effectively use internal communications to raise
   employee morale and excitement about the name, by building awareness, generating
   acceptance, and sustaining commitment.

Source: Yannis Kavounis, with additional editing and research from Julie Cottineau and Lizzy
Stallard at Interbrand Corporation, "Successfully Navigating a Name Change," www.brand-
channel.com/papers_review.asp?sp_id=108.

Five Ways to Build Intelligent BRANDwidth

1. **Develop a beneficial cobranding deal with a good partner**—someone who brings
   something of value to the table that you don't have. Starbucks's deal with United
   Airlines put Starbucks coffee on United flights worldwide and allowed both sides to
   achieve important brand objectives.

2. **Reach out for a brand extension.** *Time* magazine had a very popular section in the
   back of the book that featured interesting people. A brand extension turned that section into *People* magazine. *People* magazine was a dazzling success—so much so that
   it launched its own brand extension: *Teen People* magazine.

3. **Leap into new distribution channels.** Putting Starbucks on United flights cobranded
   the cup of coffee. Putting whole-bean and ground coffees into more than 30,000
   grocery stores created a complementary channel for an existing product.

4. **Jump into new product categories.** Think about Ralph Lauren's line of paints,
   which are now sold in home-improvement stores. The company unearthed a new
   category and a new distribution channel. Martha Stewart started with a cookbook.
   Today she has a whole range of household products. Starbucks became the maker
   of the best-selling coffee ice cream in grocery stores around the nation in less than
   six months.

5. **Create a new subbrand.** Nike is a big brand—but Air Jordan is a tremendously successful subbrand. Toyota is a big brand—but Lexus is such a successful subbrand
   that most car buyers don't even think of it as the child of a parent company (which
   may be the best compliment you can pay any subbrand).

Source: Scott Bedbury, "Nine Ways to Fix a Broken Brand," www.fastcompany.com/magazine/

Top Branding Companies

Core Brand

Core Brand focuses on helping companies understand, craft, measure, and leverage the essence of their corporate brands.

470 West Avenue
Stamford, CT 06902
Phone: (203) 327-6333, (888) 969-2726 (toll-free in U.S.)
Fax: (203) 353-8180
Web: www.corebrand.com

Rob Frankel

Rob Frankel has been called the best branding expert on the planet, creating brands and producing revenue for start-ups and Fortune 1000 companies alike. His web site offers tools, tips, and advice on branding.

Phone: (888) ROBFRANKEL (762-3726) (toll-free in North America)
E-mail: rob@robfrankel.com
Web: www.robfrankel.com

Bolt

Bolt's vision is to be an extension of their clients, focused and experienced in their market, and dedicated to their success by designing the most powerful and complete brand solutions for their customers.

1415 S. Church Street, Suite 5
Charlotte, NC 28203
Phone: (888) GET BOLT (438-2658)
E-mail: bolt@boltgroup.com
Web: www.boltgroup.com

Fresh!

Fresh! is a award-winning creative studio specializing in design, branding, and communications. The firm helps organizations increase their revenues and improve their operations by defining, connecting with, and motivating their target audiences.

3520 Long Beach Boulevard, Suite 214
Long Beach, CA 90807
Phone: (562) 595-0555
Fax: (562) 595-0527
E-mail: info@freshgraphics.net
Web: www.freshgraphics.net

Brand Institute, Inc.

Brand Institute is a full-service brand identity consultancy dedicated to the strategic and innovative development of brand nomenclature and identity solutions.

200 S.E. 1 Street, 12th Floor
Miami, FL 33131
Phone: (305) 374-2500
Fax: (305) 374-2504
Web: www.brandinstitute.com

Small Business Branding

Small Business Branding is a weblog written by Michael D. Pollock, as part of Solostream, "a web-based media company run by solopreneurs for solopreneurs."

P.O. Box 446
Plainfield, CT 06374
Phone: (860) 748-4902
E-mail: savvysolo@gmail.com
Web: www.smallbusinessbranding.com

BrandSolutions, Inc

A leading brand consulting and research firm with extensive brand building experience and a proven strategic brand process.

8222 Overlake Drive W.
Medina, WA 98039
Phone: (425) 637-8777
Fax: (425) 637-8778
Web: www.brand.com

Brains on Fire

Help companies create and sustain excitement about who they are and why they are here, through corporate branding, corporate identity, identity revitalization, etc.

148 River Street, Suite 100
Greenville, SC 29601
Phone: (864) 676-9663

E-mail: firestarter@brainsonfire.com
Web: www.brainsonfire.com

T3 The Think Tank

T3's Think Tank brand development process is a fast-track method to uncover core truths, hidden strengths, and potential vulnerabilities of a brand.

T3 Austin
1806 Rio Grande
Austin, TX 78701
Phone: (512) 499-8811
Fax: (512) 499-8552
T3 New York
80 8th Avenue, 20th Floor
New York, NY 10011

Phone: (212) 404-7045
Fax: (212) 404-7049
Web: www.t-3.com

MC Brandworks

MC Brandworks, a division of Medelia Communications, creates new brand identities and evolves existing brands.

3709 NE 214th Street
Aventura, FL 33180
Phone: (305) 918-0750
Fax: (305) 918-0650
E-mail: info@medelia.com
Web: www.mcbrandworks.com

Source: Compiled by author.

Section
3

Chapter 17

Finding Support

Tips for Selecting an Incubator

Incubators usually offer a low-cost, nurturing environment for entrepreneurs to nurse their fledgling enterprises. But before you jump into an incubator, get answers to these questions:

- **What is the incubator's mission?** Does the management want to revitalize a certain area in the community, or are they more interested in out-of-state or international activities?

- **What experiences have other tenants had?** Talk to current incubator residents as well as alumni and ask their opinions.

- **What is the incubator's track record?** How many jobs have been created? How many companies have survived once they've left?

- **What are its standard operating procedures?** Are some services free? How long can you stay? Will your rent increase as your business grows? Does the incubator collect royalties?

- **Do you like the facilities?** Does your space meet your needs? Are there regular seminars, training programs, and expert assistance?

Source: Rieva Lesonsky, *365 Tips to Boost Your Entrepreneurial IQ.*

International Incubator Associations and Organizations

NBIA—National Business Incubation Association
USA
nbia.org

ADT—Association of German Technology and Business Incubation Centers
Germany
www.adt-online.de

ANPROTEC—Brazilian Association of Science Parks and Incubators
Brazil
www.anprotec.org.br

BIIA—Business Innovation and Incubation Australia Inc.
Australia
www.businessincubation.com.au

CABI—Canadian Association of Business Incubators
Canada
www.cabi.ca

Dutch Incubator Association
Netherlands
www.dutchincubator.nl

ENTERWeb: Enterprise Development Website
www.enterweb.org

European Business and Innovation Centre Network
www.ebn.be

France Incubation
France
www.franceincubation.com

International Association of Science Parks
www.iasp.ws

Israeli Technology Business Incubators
Israel
www.incubators.org.il

JANBO—Japan Association of New Business Incubation Organization
Japan
www.janbo.gr.jp

Polish Business and Innovation Centres Association
Poland
www.sooipp.org.pl

UK Business Incubation
United Kingdom
www.ukbi.co.uk

Source: compiled by author.

Top Qualities to Look for in a Mentor

It's never easy going it alone, but start-up entrepreneurs may find it particularly hard flying solo. The solution? Find a mentor. Start your search for a mentor by thinking about all the successful people you know. Next, figure out what you expect from a mentor. A mentor should:

- **Have your best interest at heart.** You should feel free to share sensitive information with your mentor and be confident he or she won't betray your trust.

- **Speak honestly.** You don't need someone who is worried about sparing your feelings. A mentor should be able to objectively tell you what he or she thinks.

- **Get to know you.** A mentor does you no good if he or she is not aware of your skills and talents. A good mentor should also have a solid working knowledge of your industry.

Most importantly, listen to your mentor. He or she is there to help you, so let your mentor play the role.

Source: Rieva Lesonsky, *365 Tips to Boost Your Entrepreneurial IQ.*

Building Your Advisory Board

1. **Understand the types of boards.**

   First, a simple explanation of the type of boards you can create is critical to address. An actual "board of directors" is a fiduciary body, which carries significant legal weight and liability. Its members, who are usually compensated, are the final arbiters of corporate governance in a business. For the typical entrepreneur of a private company, this is not the norm and is rarely required.

   The second, far more common association is the "board of advisors." This group carries no fiduciary responsibility to shareholders, but simply serves as a mentoring organization for the management team. We will assume that this structure is your desired outcome.

2. Develop the profile.

You must have a clear vision of the type of individual you require for each seat.

After the skill set is clearly identified, you must next focus on the personality of the individuals being sought. You must recruit only those individuals who motivate and inspire you and, of course, in whom you can trust.

3. Develop the list.

After the profiles of the ideal candidates are developed, it is time to focus on identifying the right individuals.

First, develop the list of potential candidates. Do this by sitting down with individuals who are leaders in your field or community, and simply ask for recommendations. Think about your lawyer, accountant, and banker for referrals.

When adding names to your target list, be sure to balance your desire to recruit well-known leaders with your need to have ready access.

Lastly, when developing your list, be sure to have at least three names for every board seat, because many will be either unwilling or unable to commit.

4. Create the "ask."

You've got your target list. Now you need to start recruiting.

First, prioritize your three names for each seat from most desired to least. Obviously, begin with the most desired for each.

When creating your "ask," you are basically creating your sales pitch. In doing so, remember that most individuals who agree to board service do not do so for the money or stock. They simply get excited about the opportunity to assist an energetic entrepreneur, and perhaps to mingle with other advisors who are likely to have common interests.

When creating your pitch, focus on your need and desire to learn and grow as a businessperson and entrepreneur.

Lastly, in your "ask," create a brief synopsis of your business concept and model as well as the time commitment that you are expecting from each member. Do not expect that the prospective board member will read your entire plan; just focus on the elevator pitch for now. Remember that this is more about you than your business.

5. Ask.

You have what you need, now call. This is where the referrals you gained while building your list are critical.

If possible, have the individual who referred you call and notify your prospect about who you are and why you will be calling. If this is not possible, create an e-mail explaining yourself and your purpose.

After the initial contact is made, follow up, follow up, and follow up. This is a sales process. It may take many attempts to "get on the radar screen" of the targeted individual. He or she will respect you for your tenacity and ambition.

If an individual rejects your offer, always ask for a referral to another prospective member.

6. **Coda**.

How many advisors are optimal? Between three and five, since it's the common belief smaller boards are more productive. The more critical factor, however, is that you have a board.

Building an advisory board is not a terribly difficult process, but it does carry a tremendous benefit when done with thought and clear structure. Strong, active boards can often be a determining factor in the long-term success of your business. Its members can open doors for you that could not have been opened on your own.

But, as with anything else, your return will be a derivative of your planning for the process. Identify the characteristics and personality types, the structure, and the commitment. Then focus on how you plan to ask

Source: Greg Moran, "Building the Entrepreneurial Advisory Board," entreworld.org/Content/EntreByline.cfm?ColumnID=699.

List of Areas for Which You Can Hire a Management Consultant

Management consultants are either sole practitioners who work with a small support staff or members of a consulting firm who work with professional colleagues and a large support staff. They may be generalists able to work with top management on a wide range of concerns or specialists.

- research and development
- physical distribution
- financial planning and control
- sales and marketing
- human resources management and labor relations
- administration
- strategic and business planning
- manufacturing information
- technology
- wage and salary administration
- incentive compensation
- organizational planning and development

Source: Institute of Management Consultants, *How to Hire a Management Consultant and Get the Results You Expect.*

Deciding if You Really Need a Consultant

There are no hard and fast rules for deciding to bring in a management consultant. Common situations suggesting that a consultant may provide help include:

1. Management believes that performance could be better but is not sure what to do to gain improvements.

2. Management does not have the specific knowledge and skills necessary to solve the problems it has identified.

3. Management has the necessary knowledge and skills but not the time or personnel to solve problems.

4. Management's efforts have not produced the desired long-term improvements.

5. Management requires an independent, third-party opinion, either to confirm a decision or to provide alternatives.

Often a situation will require that a consultant be retained until in-house capabilities are enhanced by a permanent staff

Source: Institute of Management Consultants, *How to Hire a Management Consultant and Get the Results You Expect.*

Tips on How Consultants Charge for Their Services

A management consultant's fee will be influenced by a number of factors, including the client's need for special knowledge and experience; how much competition for clients there is; the consultant's reputation; and, if known, the benefit to the client of a successful outcome.

In a typical engagement a consultant may charge a portion of the total fee when the project begins and throughout the project (including any adjustment) until acceptance of the final report. Management consultants who have previously engaged in projects that resemble yours will generally quote a flat fee. Occasionally this fee is payable in advance, but more commonly it is paid according to a benchmark-related schedule.

When the management consultant serves in a purely advisory or coaching capacity, it is traditional to charge a flat fee for each advisory session, board of directors meeting, or private session.

Sometimes the consulting arrangement will involve a not-to-exceed figure or a figure that when reached triggers a joint evaluation of results-to-date and an estimate of the time needed to reach a satisfactory conclusion.

Source: Institute of Management Consultants, *How to Hire a Management Consultant and Get the Results You Expect.*

Chapter 18

Building Your Office

Part One. Products

SCORE's Five Tips on Obtaining a Lease

1. **Be prepared to negotiate.** The landlord's printed lease will most likely favor the landlord.

2. **Match the lease to your business's needs.** If location is important, you'll want a longer lease—or a shorter one with options to renew.

3. **Understand who pays what—such as utilities, repairs, insurance, and even taxes.** You may want to pay slightly higher rent for eliminating these items.

4. **Be aware that your negotiating power is stronger in a market where lots of commercial space is available.**

5. **Remember that a lease is a legal document.** Have your attorney review it before you sign.

Source: SCORE, www.score.org.

Questions to Ask Before Signing a Location Lease

Ready to sign a lease? Before you do, ask yourself these questions:

- Does the lease state the square footage of your space?
- Must the landlord provide a detailed list of expenses to support rent increases?
- Do you have the right to audit the landlord's books and records?
- If your use of the building is "interrupted," does the lease define available remedies, such as rent abatement or cancellation?
- If the landlord doesn't make requested repairs, can you pay for them and deduct the cost from your rent?
- Does the lease define how disputes will be handled?

Before you sign your lease, make sure you get what you want. And remember, everything is negotiable.

Source: Rieva Lesonsky, *365 Tips to Boost Your Entrepreneurial IQ.*

Web Sites for Buying Computers

BizRate shopping search
comparison shopping site
www.bizrate.com

TigerDirect.com Business to Business
"world leader in corporate computing"
biz.tigerdirect.com

eBay
online marketplace for buying and selling computers
www.ebay.com

Newegg.com
the widest selection of IT and consumer brands for computer hardware, software and electronics.
www.newegg.com

Circuit City
www.CircuitCity.com

Source: compiled by the author.

Where to Find Computer Hardware Security

Tryten Technologies: Security Hardware
Tryten manufactures a line of security solutions to prevent the theft of computers, laptops, monitors, projectors, and other valuable enterprise assets—from portable security cable locks to Ultra-Strength Computer Enclosures.
999 3rd Avenue, Suite 3800
Seattle, WA 98104–4023
Phone: (206) 625–0440
Fax: (206) 508–9165
E-mail: info@tryten.com
Web: www.tryten.com

Network Liquidators: Network Security Hardware
Provides new, used, refurbished, and open box new network security hardware from leading manufacturers, including Cisco, Compaq, and F5 Network.
14400 Carlson Circle
Tampa, FL 33626
Phone: (813) 852–6400
Web: www.networkliquidators.com

Nalpeiron
This company provides hardware and software protection.
One Embarcadero Center, Suite #500
San Francisco, CA 94111
Phone: (800) 939-0602
Web: www.nalpeiron.com

Optrics Engineering: Server Security Hardware
NetBotz environmental monitoring appliances protect hardware and information.
1740 S. 300 West #10
Clearfield, UT 84015
Phone: (877) 386-3763 (toll-free)
Fax: (801) 705-3150
E-mail: info@netbotz.ca
Web: www.netbotz.ca

Source: compiled by author.

Part Two. Services
Tips for Getting the Best Phone Rates

Understand your calling patterns.
Before you start comparing programs, you need to understand your company's calling profile. The best way to do so is to examine a recent phone bill. Break out where the calls went, when they were made, and how long they lasted. Use this analysis and information about your total call volume to direct your comparison of programs, focusing on rates that apply to the majority of your calls.

Remember to negotiate.
Once you have determined the best program for your company, it is time to make a deal. Depending on the size of your account, you will have varying leverage to negotiate below the published rates. Often, it is simplest to agree upon specific discounts, such as calls to a branch office or within your state. Any adjustments you agree upon should be made in writing to avoid annoying fights down the road.

Avoid signing up for long-term contracts.
Carriers often offer lower rates to entice customers to sign up for a multiple-year contract. While signing up for long terms of service can also help you obtain low rates, we recommend that you avoid plans that lock you in for more than 12 months. Because the industry is changing rapidly, you will want to keep your options open to take advantage of lower rates in the future.

Watch out for monthly minimums.
Make sure to build in a cushion when signing up for service that requires a monthly call minimum. If you fail to meet this minimum, most programs will simply bill your company the difference. To be safe, your calling volume should be at least 15 percent above a given threshold.

Review tour long-distance services.
Like spring cleaning, it can be useful to take stock of your telecommunications holdings on a yearly basis. Instead of giving long distance sales reps the cold shoulder, ask them to fax you the program specifics, and file the information. Programs can be reviewed all at once at a later time.

Source: Mie-Yun Lee, "Get the Best Phone Rates," www.entrepreneur.com/article/ 0,4621,304105,00.html.

List of Places for Business Phone Systems

Business Phones Direct
They sell new and like-new telephone systems at competitive market prices. They also purchase used telephones and telephone systems against fair market value.
6107 Obispo Avenue
Long Beach, CA 90805
Phone: (562) 424-0072, (866) 777-PHONE (7466)
Fax: (562) 424-5620
Web: www.businessphonesdirect.com

The Phone Resource
They partner with hundreds of local telephone installers to offer installation along with the purchase.
P.O. Box 797
Gibsonia, PA 15044
Phone: (866) 222-9344
E-mail: info@thephoneresource.com
Web: www.thephoneresource.com

American Telephone Headquarters
On their web site you can browse their inventory and purchase phones, components, and even entire systems online. They also provide information about all of their products, including brochures, manuals, compatibility charts, software feature lists, and technical tips and suggestions.
P.O. Box 1303
West Caldwell NJ 07007
Phone: (800) 475-0989
Fax: (973) 808-2472

E-mail: sales@athq.com
Web: www.athq.com

A Telephone System

They have Lucent/Avaya business phone systems, office phones, voice mail, headsets, conference phones, and all telephone equipment.
Phone: (866) 272-8292
Fax: (914) 479-1133
E-mail: info@atelephonesystem.com
Web: atelephonesystem.com

Associated Engineering Systems

They offer a range of systems, including telecommunications, security, closed circuit television, access control, fire alarm, nurse call, paging, and sound. They also offer services such as design, consulting, sales, installation, service, and maintenance.
625 Hazelvalley Drive
St. Louis, MO 63042
Phone: (314) 839-9100
Fax: (314) 839-8813
E-mail: info@aesstl.com
Web: www.aesstl.com

BLS Communications

BLS Communications Northwest Inc. is a nationwide business communications systems service provider specializing in managed services for Fortune 1000 companies. Over 1,200 affiliated BLS service providers install, program, and service communications and data network systems by major manufacturers such as Avaya and Nortel Systems.
25797 Conifer Road, #217
P.O. Box 1091
Conifer, CO 80433
Phone: (303) 838-1657
Fax: (303) 838-1678
E-mail: info@blscomm.com
Web: www.blscomm.com

Source: compiled by the author.

Tips for Selecting Cell Phone Providers

The one question you have when it comes to cell phones is "Which carrier should I sign up with?" As a wireless expert, I get asked that question all the time—and I'll tell you the answer, but before I do, understand that as I write this, on my desk are an AT&T cell phone, a Verizon wireless phone, and a Sprint PCS wireless phone. They are there for one simple reason: I am conducting an experiment to find out who offers the best cell phone service.

Cell phones, as you know, remain maddening tools. Today I called my girlfriend in Santa Rosa, California, a few miles away, on my Verizon phone, and the signal broke off just as she answered. Yesterday I called a friend in Los Angeles on the AT&T phone, and within three minutes, the signal snapped. The day before, I'd called my sister in New Jersey on the Sprint phone, and the same thing happened.

No, it's not you. The real problem is that the industry is still building out its network, and there are simply lots of kinks.

Which bring us back to your question: What carrier deserves your allegiance? If you really want to know the answer, ask your neighbors. Don't ask experts like me, don't believe phone company advertising, and definitely don't believe the sales spiels in the cell phone stores. It's easy enough for experts to gather up data about numbers of subscribers, the percent of the country each carrier covers, and so forth, but at day's end, all that matters is the quality of the signal where you are. I could tell you that in most ways, I believe AT&T wireless is the best, with the most reliable signal, but what if that's true only of southwest Santa Rosa?

When you talk to your neighbors, ask what carriers they use, where signals are dropped and at what times of day, and so forth. And do note, system performance varies greatly with time of day. In hilly San Francisco, which I visit often, cell phone performance is notoriously bad, but it's unspeakably awful around 6 p.m. on Friday. Place a call Saturday at 9 a.m., however, and usually it's a great signal, even in San Francisco.

Make a checklist. Where will you make most of your calls? At what time of day? Know how you will use your phone, and from there, it's easy to quiz your neighbors. That's the big secret that will let you pick your ideal carrier. Happy calling!

Source: Robert McGarvey, "Choosing a Cell Phone Provider," www.entrepreneur.com/article/0,4621,289069,00.html.

Preparing for Web Conferencing

Plan Ahead
Before the conference ensure that there are no time zone conflicts. Notify all participants of the date, time, and duration of the conference. Provide any printed materials or e-mail documents needed in advance. Provide any security information to attendees in advance, such as login information or passwords. Check that no one will be blocked from access by firewall software. Make sure everyone has the right tools necessary to participate.

Web Camera: Angles, Focus, and Movement
Make sure to adjust the web camera so that you are centered in the screen and leave some head room (approximately ten percent). Adjust the focus on the web camera before the web conference begins so that you can be seen clearly and don't have to fuss with it

once the web conference starts. It's important to remember that you should not make any sudden or quick movements; it is distracting and will be seen as just a big blur.

Microphones, Speakers, and Headphones

Avoid feedback; play with the position of mike and speakers or headphones to get the best sound. If you are using a headset mike and earphones, ensure they aren't blocking your face. Avoid shuffling papers or moving things while speaking or others are speaking. Do not eat or drink, as those noises may be picked up and broadcast. Turn off TVs and radios and close any doors to eliminate background noise.

Clothing: Dress for Success

It is better to wear solid colors, not wild or fancy patterns. Muted colors such as grays and blues, not bright reds or yellows. This is not the time to be wearing your bathrobe or "work naked." Dress that same as you would were you attending a meeting onsite.

Lighting Concerns

Avoid glare from open windows and place light in front rather than behind. Light from behind puts you in shadows. Also don't aim lights directly at web camera. If you are in a low-light area and relying on your laptop light, be sure to aim the light properly so that you can still see the keyboard and be seen in the web conference. This is where having two laptop lights comes in handy.

Telephones

If you are using a telephone for the conference, try and use a headset model so that the phone isn't blocking your face. It will also be more comfortable to have a headset, rather than holding the phone for the duration. You may need to speak a little more loudly than normal to be heard properly by other web conference participants.

Test the Software

Get used to how the software works before using it for a conference. Many programs have free trials; take advantage of that trial period to get accustomed to the software. Learn what tools you can use and learn how to use whiteboards and other interactive elements to improve the quality of your web conference.

Make Your Web Conference a Success

Practice before any conferences to ensure that you can be seen and heard clearly. Do practice runs of any presentations that will be included in the conference. Set a specific end time for the conference (generally one hour max). Stay on topic and limit questions to what is being discussed. Schedule Q & A time and adhere to it. Keep slides or presentations on the simple side—no fancy transitions. Let participants know in advance if the conference is being recorded.

Source: Catherine Roseberry, "Before You Participate in a Web Conference," mobileoffice.about.com/od/webbased/bb/webconference.htm?terms=web+conference.

Chapter 19

Finding Suppliers
and Distributors

Tips on How to Get Big Merchants to Notice You

Inventors of just one product typically won't have a lot of luck selling it to mass merchants, so they often turn to private labeling. They find another company that does sell to mass merchants and offer their product to that company to sell under its name.

Keys to Success

The major appeal of private labeling to private-label buyers is that they can generate a little extra profit without a lot of extra work. And if sales don't work out, the private-label buyer just stops buying your product.

You can form successful relationships with private-label buyers by:

1. **Making things easy**: Ask the buyer for a purchase order, and state that you'll supply the product in the buyer's package, or that you'll modify your package to the buyer's specifications. If necessary, you can also offer training to the buyer's salespeople, and you can even offer to maintain a web site for the product. If you are selling to a retailer, you might want to offer a display, and you could even show a diagram of what complementary products yours should be displayed next to.

2. **Providing top-notch service**: Provide marketing support, such as attending trade shows, doing publicity releases, actively working a web page, or offering layouts for ads or brochures. You can also offer to provide customer service for handling product problems, to take care of product returns, and to suggest product improvements.

3. **Paying attention to your product's packaging**: Your private-label buyer is probably not going to invest any money in marketing. So potential buyers need to see your product and immediately realize its benefit. If you have a consumer product, take time to package your product so it sells itself. The packaging and design of a product are important if your private-label agreement is with a retailer.

4. **Understanding the competition**: Companies take on private-label products primarily for competitive reasons. To sell the concept effectively, you need to know your target company's competitors and how your product improves the company's position in relation to them. Being familiar with the competition is also important if retailers are the final stop in the targeted distribution channel.

To find potential private-label partners, do an internet search for "private label," and you'll find hundreds of companies that market private-label products in dozens of ways. Also check out the Private Label Manufacturers Association (www.plma.com), which hosts trade shows and offers information for potential private-label manufacturers.

What You'll Need

Before you approach a company for a private-label contract, make sure you've taken these five steps:

1. **Protection**: Companies buying private-label products usually aren't overly concerned about your patent status. But you do run the risk that the company might decide to make the product or that a competitor might quickly introduce the same product. If you have enough money, you can apply for a utility patent before approaching the company. If your funds are limited, apply for a provisional patent, which gives you a one-year leeway until you have to apply for a utility patent.

2. **Prototypes**: Inventors need a "looks like, works like" prototype before landing a private-label agreement. A company wants to not only see, but also test your product before deciding to go ahead. If you can't make the prototype, you can get a contract manufacturer to make it for you at a low cost—provided you sign an agreement to give them the business if you get the sale.

3. **Research**: When you approach a company with a private-label proposal, show them that their target customers like and need your product. This can be shown by having surveys of potential customers, or interviews or supporting letters from influential users.

4. **Manufacturing**: You're responsible for providing the product in a private-label agreement, either by making the product yourself or by having a contract manufacturer make it. No matter how low your margin is, start with a contract manufacturer to ensure the agreement gets off to a good start. You can switch to your own manufacturing operation once sales are secure.

5. **Key Contacts**: Key contacts who can get you in the door of your target customers include salespeople, marketing personnel, regional sales managers, and top executives. You can meet these contacts by attending industry trade shows or association meetings.

Up, Up and Away

Private-label marketing can help you generate quick sales, but it does so at a price.

1. The extra discounts cut into your profits.

2. You have your product promoted under someone else's name.

3. Your agreement probably restricts the distribution outlets you can sell through.

All these factors work against you in launching your own larger business. One of the reasons most private-label products are accessories or complementary products is that it's hard to build a powerful company out of those types of products. Often, inventors sell the product themselves in their major markets and use private-label sales in smaller markets. The success and staying power of your agreement will increase as you become better known to people involved with the product.

Source: Don Debelak, "Private Matters," www.entrepreneur.com/article/0,4621,316841,00.html.

Six Steps to Find Suppliers

Here are six suggestions from Jim Daigle, whose company, Energy $aver$ of America in Houma, Louisiana, manufactures and distributes building insulation made from recycled aluminum film and polyethylene.

1. **Get referrals.** "Sometimes it's a crapshoot to pick the right suppliers," Daigle says. "I always ask for referrals and check them out. I also ask for samples before I sign a contract."

2. **Don't be cheap.** "Price is the last thing anyone should use to pick a supplier," Daigle says. "You'll get ripped off every time." While you shouldn't ignore price completely, a more important consideration is the supplier's ability to consistently and promptly deliver the goods or services you need. "Quality is the number-one thing I look for," Daigle says.

3. **Ask questions.** New business owners often struggle because there's so much they don't know, says Tim Cottrill, owner of Bookery Fantasy, a comic book and collectibles shop in Fairborn, Ohio. "You have to talk with others in your industry, but if they're in your market, they might not want to share information," Cottrill says. "Try going to another geographic area to pick someone's brain."

   Mary Maxwell, owner of Heart Enterprises in Roseville, California, says questioning is the only way to learn. "I couldn't find all the supplies I wanted," says Maxwell, who makes custom Victorian lampshades and teaches others to make them, "so I kept asking questions. I'd send drawings of beads or other items to manufacturers and ask if they could make them. Sometimes it would take me a year to find someone."

   The public library's reference section is a good place to find answers and leaf through the Thomas Register of American Manufacturers (www. thomasregister.com), a directory you can use to discover who makes thousands of different products. Libraries also have directories of trade groups and trade publications that can lead you to vendors.

4. **Go to trade shows.** Contact trade associations and read trade publications for information about trade shows where potential suppliers gather in abundance, says Jeffrey Lauer, owner of Kitchen and Bath Distributors Inc., a Forestville, Maryland, supplier of cabinets, countertops, and other products for builders and remodelers. Lauer found one of his cabinet suppliers at the National Kitchen and Bath Show, held primarily in Chicago and Atlanta. "These shows are important to gain knowledge of the industry," says Lauer, "and that knowledge leads you to vendors."

5. **Let customers help.** The comic book industry has gone through tremendous consolidation in recent years, driving thousands of retailers out of business and reducing comic book distribution to one major company, Cottrill says. "My store also deals in old comic books, which I can buy directly from the public," he says. "I can fall back on [individual sellers] if I can't get something from the distributor."

6. **Do it yourself.** When Maxwell couldn't find all the products she wanted to make her lampshades, she got so frustrated, she made her own frames for a while with the help of a welder friend—until she found a wire rack company that was willing to weld the frames for her.

Maxwell became so good at finding suppliers of Victorian lampshade products, she was able to turn that knowledge into a profit center. She created a catalog of 160 frames, 28 bead styles, lamp bases, fabrics, and other supplies she sells to people worldwide. The catalog has grown to include more than 300 products and accounts for more than half the revenues of Heart Enterprises.

Source: Jan Norman, "How To: Find Suppliers," www.entrepreneur.com/article/ 0,4621,229271,00.html

Nine Steps to Find Distributors

Distributors can be as difficult to entice as retail buyers. Winning them over takes time, research, and hard work. Here are nine steps to success:

1. **Get your product market-ready.** "Most new manufacturers aren't prepared to go to market," says Joseph Coen, president of ASKCO Marketing Services in Kure Beach, North Carolina. Before going to market, manufacturers must resolve issues ranging from the most appealing packaging to the best way to ship their products, he says. They also must find a price consumers will pay that still means good profit margins for retailers, distributors, and, of course, themselves.

   "The product needs to have a point of difference," Coen says. "If the product is lotion, the only difference is the fragrance and maybe a few ounces per bottle. The manufacturer must create a perceived difference with packaging or marketing."

   New manufacturers must prepare sales materials that tell retailers the product's benefits and its statistical information, such as how much space it needs in the warehouse and on the shelf. Production capacity is also a major issue, Coen says: "You can't sell to Wal-Mart unless you're ready to manufacture millions of units."

2. **Understand whom you're selling to.** Most manufacturers don't sell directly to the consumers who eventually use their products. Instead, the manufacturer's marketing strategy must aim at sales through dealers or distributors.

   Most manufacturers, distributors, and independent sales reps deal with a narrow range of products. They know each other and refer work to each other. A distributor or sales rep wants to carry products that sell in high volume. If you can't promise huge sales, you might have to lure distributors with high profit margins.

3. **Target your market.** One way to focus your marketing is with targeted mailing lists, which you can often find through trade associations. If you use such lists for direct-

mail advertising campaigns, plan to send out at least three separate mailings, then follow up with phone calls, advises John Metscher, a business analyst with the Central Ohio Manufacturing Small Business Development Center in Columbus, Ohio. "One mailing is a waste of money. Don't give up; you'll be surprised at the results," says Metscher. He also recommends advertising in carefully selected trade journals targeted at the industries most suited to your product.

Section 3

4. **Create demand.** The manufacturer—not the distributor or retailer—must make consumers want to buy a product. That can involve cooperative advertising campaigns with retailers, display stands, signs, fliers, brochures, and other marketing materials, Coen says.

5. **Prove your product will sell.** A new company may have to prove its product will sell before distributors and major retailers take notice, says Ronn King, co-founder of Site-b in Spokane, Washington, which makes a paint-stirring device called the Squirrel Mixer. He first started selling the device by mail order and to a few local retail stores to prove consumers would buy it. "Distributors' sales forces started seeing the Squirrel Mixer in several stores and asked them about it," King says. "Even then, the distributors didn't call us. We had to call them."

6. **Ask questions.** Many new manufacturers don't even know where to look for distributors and sales representatives. King found many of his by asking questions. He asked retail buyers for names of distributors, he called manufacturers of similar products and asked who their distributors and sales representatives were, and he studied industry magazines for names and ads.
Many trade groups have distributors and reps as members. The *Encyclopedia of Associations* (Gale Research) lists thousands of associations; look for it in your local library.

7. **Attend trade shows.** "Take an exhibit booth, either by yourself or in partnership with another company with complementary products," Metscher says. As with other marketing efforts, choose a trade show targeted to your market.

At the show, collect business cards from prospective distributors or sales reps, then follow up after the show is over. Even if you can't afford your own booth, attend the shows that target your industry. "Shows are good places to network and identify the people and companies that will buy your products," Metscher says.

8. **Select distributors and sales reps carefully.** Ask others in your industry for referrals to good sales reps and distributors. When considering reps, ask for their credentials and references. Look for reps and distributors who carry similar but noncompeting products and who sell to the same geographic territory and type of retailer who carries your type of product.

Distributors usually buy some of your product and store it at their warehouses. Good ones fill orders quickly and accurately and help build a market for your product. Independent sales reps don't buy your product, but they should aggressively sell your product in markets you can't reach.

Section 3

Section 4

Financing Your Business

Chapter 20

Buying and Maintaining Your Equipment

Tips for Entrepreneurs Who Aren't Tech Savvy

Not all entrepreneurs are tech savvy. What's worse, a lot don't want to be. What follows is a look at the underlying factors—three truths—that provide a framework to help entrepreneurs take charge of the ever-important technology upon which their businesses depend.

Truth #1: Technology is simpler than you think.

Entrepreneurs should make it a practice to spend a few minutes each day getting a tech "education," not so much to find the answers as to be able to ask the right questions. You can get a tech education by being alert to tech trends. Read newspapers and journals, listen to talk shows, attend forums, and surf the best of the relevant web sites, such as howstuffworks.com. Occasionally, pick up the manual for the new piece of equipment you just bought and do more than just flip through it. These small investments of time every day will enhance your decision-making process in the technology area—and your company will benefit.

Truth #2: Technology equals people.

In the heat of the entrepreneurial battle, nothing quite equals a failed computer system or a network collapse to make even the most resourceful entrepreneur feel utterly alone. While the number of automated voices on tech company phone lines and hotlines is increasing, the fact remains that people are behind technology every step of the way.

When considering software, for example, you can discuss your needs with designers engaged by the vendors from whom you might buy. You can nail down information about tech support, such as whether you will have access to a human being when problems with a product arise.

With technology, ironically, it's all about people. Make sure you do your part. Treat the people you deal with as human beings, not as handy targets for venting about the problems you've encountered with your equipment. If you are respectful, you will reap the reward of gaining their knowledge.

Truth #3: Technology is interconnected.

When building companies, entrepreneurs must always keep the big picture in mind. In no area is that more apparent than in technology. As your company grows, you must remember that the list of contacts on your desktop must be able to make its way to the new inventory control system and eventually onto the sophisticated network. In short, you must make sure that the hardware and software you select when upgrading can work with what you already have.

Some questions to ask when buying, using, or maintaining your various technological items include the following:

- Is the new device compatible with the machines to which it will be connected?
- Do you have enough software?

- Is the new component more advanced than the pieces you have and thus limited in its usefulness?

- What are the costs of supplies and maintenance?

Technology can no longer be ignored, even in pursuit of the more visionary aspects of company building. The truth is that you, the entrepreneur, have a stake in making technology work for your company.

Source: Brian J. Nichelson, "Tips for Entrepreneurs Who Aren't Tech Savvy," www.startupjournal.com/howto/entreworld/20031003-entreworld.html.

SCORE's Five Tips on Technology Planning

1. Create a master plan for technology, just as you would draw up a business plan, a budget, or a marketing plan.

2. Design the plan so that it supports your business strategy and goals. Use it to guide technology-buying decisions.

3. Think of technology purchases as investments, not costs. And, remember: when you have an overall plan, your company avoids wasting money on unnecessary purchases or quick fixes.

4. Start by determining your company's needs. Look at what problems need to be solved and how technology can help.

5. Get expert help to guide you. Check your Yellow Pages under "Computers-System Designers and Consultants," or ask your local chamber of commerce. As always, get references.

Source: SCORE, www.score.org/business_tips.html.

Tips for Buying a Personal Computer

A business-class PC should include the following specifications. Minimum configurations should have enough headroom to run the latest software for three years. Better-configuration systems from brand-name manufacturers might still have resale value for up to five years.

CPU: 2.4 GHz Pentium 4 or Athon XP 2100+ with at least 512 KB of on-chip cache

Display: 15-inch LCD capable of 1024x768 dpi or 17-inch LCD capable of 1280x1024 dpi

Free Bays: one or two free internal 3.5-inch bays; one or two free 5.25-inch external bays

Free Slots: at least two full-sized PCI slots

Graphics: 1280x1024 dpi capable graphics adapter either built in or as a PCI card compatible with a 4X or 8X Advanced Graphics Port (AGP) and 32 MB video memory

Hard Drive: 80 GB serial ATA with 7200RPM

Memory: minimum 512 MB of 266GHz or faster DDR (double data rate) SDRAM

Modem: 56K board or software modem

Optical Drive: 32X Combo DVD-ROM/CD-RW rewritable, 4X DVD-R/CD-RW, or 48X CD-R/CD-RW

Ports: at least six USB 2.0 ports distributed in front and back

Price: between $1,000 and $1,500, depending on feature combination

System Bus: 400MHz or 533MHz frontside bus

Source: Rieva Lesonsky, *Start Your Own Business.*

Tips on Buying a Printer

Low-cost does not mean low-end. This new generation of printers comes loaded with features previously found only in expensive machines. When you're ready to buy, keep these pointers in mind:

1. Ask about the minimum computer requirements needed for the printer you're considering.
2. Don't purchase pricey options you don't need and won't use.
3. Know your RAM requirements, particularly if you print spreadsheets or graphics.
4. Always get a product demonstration and check the warranties. Ask about tech support hotlines.
5. If you're in the market for more high-end equipment but cash is a problem, don't forget to check out any equipment financing options.

Source: Rieva Lesonsky, *365 Tips to Boost Your Entrepreneurial IQ.*

Seven Steps to Keeping a Healthy Macintosh Computer

These tips come from Michael Chesney, founder of ChesTech Corp. in Fairfield, Connecticut, and a franchisee of CM IT Solutions.

1. **Repair your disks.** "Running a Mac on a hard drive with a damaged file system could eventually lead to a catastrophic disk failure," says Chesney, "so to prevent this,

the 'Disk Utility' feature should be executed at least once a month." To exercise Disk Utility, boot from the Mac OS X Install CD 1 and use the Installer menu to open the Disk Utility. Click on the First Aid Tab, select the hard drive, then repair the hard drive until there are no problems.

2. **Keep up with your permissions repair.** "By doing this, you install files in the correct place, and you won't be denied access," says Chesney, who adds that this also guarantees that parts of an installation that should be locked are definitely locked. Here are the clicks, in order: Utilities; Disk Utility; First Aid Tab; select Mac OS X partition; Repair Disk Permissions.

Warning: The following two tips require that users be comfortable with Unix shell commands. If you're not, there are commercially available software programs that can accomplish the following:

3. **Update your prebinding.** "Over time, when applications are installed on a Mac, the computer may become sluggish or slow, particularly after a large application, such as an iDVD, is installed," says Chesny, "which requires updating the prebinding." Updating the prebinding causes Mac OS X to verify that all application files are correctly linked together. "By default, the Mac OS X installer handles this, but occasionally installers from other vendors may overlook this," Chesney explains. To update the prebinding, open a Terminal (shell), type "sudo update_prebinding-root / –force," type the root password, and return again. When the scrolling messages stop, the command's been completed. Then reboot your computer to make sure the prebinding has taken properly.

4. **Stay on top of your forced periodic maintenance tasks.** According to Chesney, "The Mac OS X has some maintenance tasks that are programmed to execute during the middle of the night, but if the Mac is turned off during those hours, these maintenance tasks aren't executed." While Chesney says not running these tasks will not harm the Mac, running them will free up disk space. To manually run these tasks, open a Terminal (shell) and type the following, in order:

"sudo periodic daily"

"sudo periodic weekly"

"sudo periodic monthly"

5. **Remember to always select "Shut down" from the "Special" menu when you're ready to turn your computer off.** Failing to do so could result in a monitor with "ghost images" that remain on screen even after the document's been closed.

6. **Rebuild your desktop once a month to get rid of all kinds of invisible, unnecessary stuff that hinders your computer.** Rebuilding isn't as hard as you think: just hold down the "apple" and "option" keys simultaneously as you start your computer, and answer "yes" when you're asked if you want to rebuild the desktop.

Section
4

7. **Last, but not least, leave ten percent of your hard drive empty at all times.** This will help ensure that you're getting optimal performance out of your Mac.

Source: Cliff Ennico, "7 Steps to a Healthy Macintosh," www.entrepreneur.com/article/ 0,4621,317254,00.html.

Spring Computer Cleaning Tips

Once a year, think spring—spring cleaning, that is, and time to clean your computer. Here are some smart pointers:

1. Dust the outside of your CPU case and keyboard. Use an antistatic spray on your monitor to keep it easy to read.

2. Take the CPU case off and blow compressed air into any parts that may have gotten dusty.

3. Turn your keyboard upside down over a trashcan and gently shake it to loosen any grit inside.

4. Don't forget your mouse. Remove the cover that holds the mouse's ball in place. Using that handy can of compressed air—or your finger—remove any grime on the mouse ball and inside the compartment. Make sure you pay close attention to the rollers.

5. Lastly, don't forget what's in your computer as well. Don't go too crazy, but get rid of any unwanted files. Do not delete any files ending with .dat, .dll, .exe, .eni, or .sys. You can always make archive copies of files you don't want cluttering up your hard drive.

Source: Rieva Lesonsky, *365 Tips to Boost Your Entrepreneurial IQ.*

SCORE's Five Tips on Leasing Equipment

1. Keep in mind that leasing equipment instead of buying it can help you manage your company without tying up funds needed for working capital. You can use the equipment to make money while you are paying for the lease.

2. Use leasing to help you meet objectives that might otherwise be out of reach. Instead of giving a deserving employee a raise, one cash-strapped entrepreneur instead more cheaply leased a new car for the employee.

3. Be aware that monthly payments are often tax-deductible and may offer a larger tax break than you would get if the equipment were depreciated.

4. Do the math. Leasing is a form of borrowing, and usually the interest rate is higher than that of a commercial bank.

5. To find a lessor, look in the Yellow Pages under "Equipment Leasing" or "Leasing Services." Some banks offer leasing services.

Source: SCORE, www.score.org/business_tips.html.

The Pros and Cons of Leasing Equipment

Section 4

When making a decision between leasing and purchasing, you need to know the advantages and disadvantages of leasing.

Advantages

- **Minimum cash layout.** Through leasing you don't finance the entire cost of whatever you are leasing; you pay only for what you use and always without a large initial capital outlay.

- **Less stringent financial requirements.** Lessees usually find it easier to obtain financing to lease an asset than to obtain credit to purchase.

- **No equipment obsolescence.** You can ensure that your equipment is always up-to-date by negotiating a short-term lease and exchanging the equipment when the lease runs out.

- **Built-in maintenance.** Depending on the terms of the lease, maintenance can be included on the lease, thereby reducing the working capital expenses.

- **Tax advantage.** Lease payments show up as expenses, not as debt on the balance sheet.

- **Greater payment flexibility.** Not only can leases be spread over a longer period than a loan, thus reducing monthly payments, they can also be structured to account for variations in cash flow, especially for companies that experience seasonal fluctuations in sales.

- **Expert advice available from the lessor.** This is especially true if the lessor is the manufacturer.

Disadvantages

- **No ownership.** Since lessees do not own their property, they do not accrue tax benefits associated with ownership. In addition, lessees don't build equity in the property, unless a lease-to-purchase option agreement is added to the lease.

- **Higher long-term cost.** While leases generally offer lower monthly payments, since they do not offer significant tax benefits and provide no equity in the leased property, the ultimate cost at the end of the lease is often higher than if you purchased the item or property.

- **Non-cancelable lease contract.** Some leases have non-cancelable clauses in the contract or else charge a severe penalty for early termination of the lease.

Source: *Entrepreneur Magazine's Ultimate Small Business Advisor.*

Important Questions on Leasing Equipment

Section
4

Sometimes it's smarter to lease rather than buy equipment. How do you know? Once you find a potential leasing company, ask the salesperson—and yourself—these questions:

- What equipment do I need and how long will I need it?
- How much can I afford to pay monthly?
- Can I show my financial advisor a sample copy of the lease?
- How is this lease terminated?
- Are there buyout options? Are they negotiable?
- Can I upgrade at no cost? Are there time limits?
- How flexible is the payment schedule?
- Do you service and/or repair the equipment?

Once you get your answers, don't jump at the first lease offered. Shop around, do your homework, and consult your financial advisor.

Source: Rieva Lesonsky, *365 Tips to Boost Your Entrepreneurial IQ.*

SCORE's Five Tips on Vendor Financing

1. Know that vendors can sometimes play a significant role in financing a new business. Partners in one start-up persuaded vendors to give them net-30 terms in order to stock a retail store. They made enough money to pay the vendors back in 30 days.

2. If you need financing for equipment or supplies, ask your suppliers first. They may be willing to work out an arrangement with you to keep you as a customer.

3. If you haven't established vendor relationships, shop around. Your trade association may be able to point you to suppliers that offer financing.

4. Check the vendor's credentials and reputation before you sign an agreement. Look for stability.

5. Keep in mind that a number of major suppliers own financial companies that can help you, such as GE Small Business Solutions (www.gesmallbusiness.com) and IBM Global Financing (www.financing.ibm.com).

Source: SCORE, www.score.org/business_tips.html.

Top Ten Business Technology Tips

1. **Invest in scalable technology**. Think about where you see your business in the next two or three years. What you invest in now may be suitable for the size of your company, but if you intend to grow quickly, you will need technology that grows as your business does.

2. **Keep it simple.** It's important for a computer to be fast, but for other specifications, keep it simple. Most computers off the shelf come with standard packages such as word processing, spreadsheets, accounts packages, database software, e-mail, and access to the web. If you need particular software, choose the package and install it yourself.

3. **Choose a supplier that has an established user base.** If you need support or if you experience any problems with your technology, choose a supplier that has a solid user base and offers a support line. If your technology systems fail, time and money will be wasted.

4. **Justify every penny you spend.** A good PC will not cost you a fortune, but you get what you pay for. Don't go over your budget, as the technology changes so fast.

5. **Decide exactly what you need before you buy.** If you don't want to go for an off-the-shelf model, decide exactly what you need and price each item up to compare. Remember to factor in the time it will take you to set everything up.

6. **Get recommendations.** It can be difficult knowing which product or manufacturer to go for, so ask a range of people for their recommendations. See if you can test out the equipment so you get a better idea of what would be most suitable.

7. **Don't buy without a warranty.** Make sure that any equipment you buy comes with a warranty or a guarantee. It's all too easy for things to go wrong, and paying for repairs if you don't have a warranty can often end up costing more than buying another product.

8. **Provide IT training.** If you invest in new technology and your staff don't know how to use it, you are wasting your money. Provide good training from the start, as this will pay off many times over by increasing overall efficiency and output.

9. **Look after your company data.** Don't let the hard drive on your PC become clogged up with data, as this will slow down your computer's performance. Get into the habit of deleting files you no longer need. Always remember to back up information you want to keep.

10. **Be firm with IT consultants.** If there is more than one of you involved in the business, you will need to set up a network. An IT consultant can give you advice on the best way to set this up. Be firm with what you want from your IT on a day-to-day basis and don't get sidetracked if your IT consultant starts to explain other services.

Source: SmallBusiness.co.uk, "Top 10 Technology Tips," www.smallbusiness.co.uk/5.4/business-technology/dont-miss/20786/top-10-technology-tips.thtml.

Tips on When to Outsource Technology

How to be sure you are getting the best outsource partner for your money? How to be certain that your IT functions will be handled properly? Some things are easy. Check references. Make sure their advertised skills meet your needs. But there are other more subtle items to take into account.

1. **The big picture:** Before outsourcing an IT function, look at your firm's goals and culture. What business objectives are you trying to achieve by outsourcing this particular function? How will sending this function to an outside party impact the workflow within the company? Clear answers to these questions can help guide a business owner toward the most appropriate vendor.

2. **Look beyond the dollar signs:** Price is a consideration, of course, but it cannot be the only yardstick by which to gauge competing service providers. In the case of web hosting, for example, "when you over-prioritize price, you run the risk of ending up with a host that will provide you with a connection to the Internet and little else in terms of support," cautions Chris Kivlehan, president of Web hosting service InetU.

3. **Buy the expertise:** A valuable outsource partner will do more than lighten the load. Such a partner will lend expertise to ensure an optimum blend of in-house and outsourced functions. In the case of network management, for instance, an outsourcer should "provide a small business with an operational, tactical, and strategic view of their network environment," said Doug Lane, services marketing manager for Vanguard Managed Solutions. "This allows for quality recommendations to ensure network availability, reduction of total cost of ownership, optimization of network assets for meeting business needs, and support of future growth."

4. **On the cutting edge?** Make sure your service provider is keeping current. "IT is very dynamic, so it can be difficult to intelligently know what's happening in IT," said Jeremy F. Shapiro, professor emeritus of operations research and management at MIT. The best vendors can provide not just services, but also "state-of-the-art knowledge about IT needs and developments."

5. **Values and philosophy:** Does this vendor value its employees? What is the average length of employment of the staff? "A company that retains its employees must treat them well and value them," said Chris Stephenson, founder of iCorps Technologies. "This will impact the delivery to clients. Happy employees result in happy clients."

6. **Meet the team:** Before signing anything, meet the people who will actually service your account. "Good outsourcers will have a dedicated team servicing the customer, led by the controller who acts as the 'go to' person," said Dale Hoyer, president of

Franchise Services Company (FSC), which provides full-service, outsourced accounting, payroll and management reporting services to the restaurant and retail industries. "Do yourself a favor and meet the members of the outsourcer's team that would be working on your behalf."

7. **Know what you are buying:** "As you get closer to making a decision, it is important to agree upon a set of service level expectations or objectives," said Hoyer. What matters most is to agree in advance on the service to be delivered and especially on the measures that will be used to determine satisfactory performance.

8. **Chain of command:** Along these same lines, know who is talking to whom. "The last thing that you can afford to have are layers of contacts, especially when time means money. Finding a provider or consultant that provides one point of contact and even better, one person, is any business's best bet," said Valerie Brown, vice president of knowledge management for WSI Internet Consultants & Education. Make sure you know in advance how the chain of communication will work.

9. **Big or small?** This one is a judgment call. A local small shop can sometimes give greater attention to its clients. Its services may cost less and it will perhaps be more eager to please. A bigger firm may cost more, but it also will typically have a greater depth of expertise and a broader set of resources. Both sides have their advocates. What's important is to know that they are different and to be mindful of those distinctions when comparing offers.

10. **The language barrier:** It's important to remember that even an outsourced IT function does not go away entirely. In most instances the small-business owner still will have to maintain some involvement. That means you'll need a partner who can give it to you plain and simple, said Bill Jelen, a spreadsheet expert known internationally as "Mr. Excel" (www.mrexcel.com/MrExcel.com).

Source: Adam Stone, "Ten Points to Ponder Before You Outsource," www.smallbusinesscomputing.com/webmaster/article.php/3319531.

Business Loans and Terms

Top Ten Finance Terms to Know

1. **Return on investment (ROI):** The only way to think about your business is with an ROI perspective. The entrepreneur has committed capital investment into a certain combination of assets, from which the company generates sales. Those sales cover the costs of operations and hopefully produce a profit. That profit, divided by the total funds invested in the company (the assets), equals the ROI to the entrepreneur. Think of it this way: Would you work all those hours and take on all that responsibility if your ROI were only six percent annually? The stronger the profit picture compared with the total funds employed in the enterprise, the higher the ROI.

2. **Internal rate of return (IRR):** Every decision enacted by the entrepreneur must be viewed in terms of its internally generated return to the company. Unlike the simple division used to find the ROI, the IRR compares the net expected returns over the useful life of a project being reviewed by management with the funds spent on that project. All projects must meet a certain IRR in order to be acceptable for investment by the company. If a project cannot meet a minimum IRR, then don't invest in it.

3. **Fixed asset base:** This is the long-term base of the company's operation strategy, represented by all the equipment, machinery, vehicles, facilities, IT infrastructure, and long-term contracts the firm has invested in to conduct business. From a finance perspective, these assets are the revenue generators. When the entrepreneur decides to invest in a certain fixed asset configuration, that becomes the base from which the company functions week in and week out, doing business and servicing its customers.

4. **Working capital:** Current assets are those short-term funds represented by cash in the bank, funds parked in near-term instruments earning interest, funds tied up in inventory, and all those accounts receivable waiting to be collected. Subtracting the company's current liabilities from these current assets shows how much working capital (your firm's truest measure of liquidity) is on hand and its ability to pay for decisions in the short-term. For example, if the firm has $500,000 in current assets and $350,000 in current liabilities, then $150,000 is free and clear as working capital, available for spending on new things as needed by the company.

5. **Cost of capital:** This is the true cost of securing the funds that the business uses to pay for its asset base. Some funds are from debt (less risky to the creditors, so it has a lower cost of capital to the firm), and some funds come from equity (more risky to the investors, so these have a higher cost of capital). The combination of lower-cost debt capital with higher-cost equity capital produces the next item in this list.

6. **Weighted average cost of capital (WACC):** The average is between debt and equity. This is the firm's true annual cost to obtain and hold onto the combination of debt and equity that pays for the fixed asset base. Every time the owners contemplate investing in a new project, the IRR for that project must be at least equal to the WACC of the funds used to do that project; otherwise it makes no sense taking on

that new project, because its return cannot even cover the cost of the capital employed to make the project happen.

7. **Risk premium:** Entrepreneurs must understand that every decision they consider has an inherent level of risk associated with it. If project A is far riskier than project B, there should be a clear risk premium that could accrue to the firm if project A is enacted. But with that risk premium return, there will also be a risk premium cost to the company for the use of the funds. Business owners always have to decide whether the risk premium of additional potential return is commensurate with the additional risk costs that come with doing that investment project.

8. **Systematic risk:** Some risks facing the company are not unique to that business in that market, but are faced by all firms operating in the broader, general marketplace. These so-called "systematic" risks (such as changes in interest rate levels, the performance and direction of the U.S. economy, or the availability of certain types of skilled labor) cannot be avoided.

9. **Nonsystematic risk:** The risks that are entirely unique to your company, products, buyers, promotional programs, billing, pricing, IT system, and so on are nonsystematic risks specific to your firm. Although there's little you can do to avoid or mitigate exposure to systematic risk, it is possible to use various diversification strategies to offset risks that are unique to your business. When working with risk premium, systematic risk, and nonsystematic risk, the rule is that the expected return on the business operations will always be directly related to the amount of risk taken on: lower-risk decisions come with lower expected returns, and higher-risk decisions come with higher expected returns.

10. **Option premium:** On virtually every partnership contract, vendor deal, distributor arrangement, equipment lease or financing, personnel hire, and investment decision, there will likely be some kind of option offered to one party by the other. Entrepreneurs must always place a dollar value on any option premium they offer or have offered to them in these various deals. (A "call" is an option to buy something at a future date; a "put" is an option to sell something at a future date.) The value of having an option—to either buy or sell, agree or disagree, accept certain terms or let them expire—should always be determined prior to signing any deal or contract or term sheet, and that value should always be treated as a tangible benefit when negotiating decisions with parties inside and outside the firm.

Source: David Newton, "Top 10 Finance Terms," www.entrepreneur.com/article/0,4621,317217,00.html.

When Should You Get a Loan?

Some entrepreneurs have never borrowed a dime, and believe it or not, that can hinder your business's growth. Bankers and other financial advisors say there are four crucial times when small businesses should seek a loan:

1. When it's time to hire new employees.
2. When you're trying to increase long-term sales.
3. When you want to increase your market share.
4. When you'd like to take advantage of suppliers' early payment discounts.

If this sounds like you or if you simply need money to pay bills, pay off creditors, or improve cash flow, a loan may be your answer. But it's important not to take on too much debt, so consult a financial advisor.

Source: Rieva Lesonsky, *365 Tips to Boost Your Entrepreneurial IQ.*

Tips on Asset-Based Loans

Definition or Explanation: Asset-based loans are usually from commercial finance companies (as opposed to banks) and are offered on a revolving basis and collateralized by a company's assets, specifically accounts receivable and inventory.

Appropriate for: Companies that may be rapidly growing, highly leveraged, in the midst of a turnaround, or undercapitalized. In addition, asset-based financing works only for companies with proven accounts receivable and a demonstrated track record of turning over their inventory several times each year.

Supply: Overall, the supply of asset-based financing is vast. A large number of commercial finance companies, as well as many banks, have massive pools of capital to lend to businesses. However, for smaller asset-based loans, those of $500,000 or less, the market is considerably smaller. Most asset-based lenders would prefer to make larger loans because the cost to monitor an asset-based loan is generally the same whether it is large or small.

Best Use: Financing rapid growth in the absence of sufficient equity capital to fund receivables and inventory. Asset-based loans can also be used to finance acquisitions.

Cost: More expensive than bank financing since asset-based lenders generally have higher expenses than bankers. Still, pricing is competitive among asset-based lenders. Small asset-based loans can be pricey, though, running 12 percent to 28 percent.

Ease of Acquisition: Comparatively easy if your company has good financial statements, good reporting systems, inventory that is not exotic, and, finally, customers who have a track record of paying their bills. If you don't have any of these, your path to an asset-based loan will be challenging.

Funds Typically Available: $100,000 and greater.

Source: "Asset-Based Loans," www.entrepreneur.com/article/0,4621,261890,00.html, from *Where's the Money? Sure-Fire Financing Solutions for Your Small Business*, by Art Beroff and Dwayne Moyers.

Questions a Banker Will Ask

1. Can the business repay the loan? (Is cash flow greater than debt service?)
2. Can you repay the loan if the business fails? (Is collateral sufficient to repay the loan?)
3. Does the business collect its bills?
4. Does the business control its inventory?
5. Does the business pay its bills?
6. Are the officers committed to the business?
7. Does the business have a profitable operating history?
8. Does the business match its sources and uses of fund?
9. Does the business control expenses?
10. Is there any discretionary cash flow?
11. What is the future of the industry?
12. Who is your competition and what are their strengths and weaknesses?

Source: Small Business Administration, "Finance Basics."

Building Your Business Credit Report

Business credit scores range on a scale from 0 to 100, with 75 or more considered an excellent rating. Personal credit scores, on the other hand, range from 300 to 850, with a score of 680 or high considered excellent. The mistake many business owners make is using their personal information to apply for business credit, leases, and loans. By doing so, they risk having a lower personal credit score.

The average consumer credit report gets just one inquiry per year and has 11 credit obligations, typically broken down as seven credit cards and four installment loans. Business owners are not your average consumer, however, because they carry both personal and business credit. This typically doubles the number of inquiries made to their personal credit profile and the number of credit obligations they carry at any given time, all of which negatively impact their personal credit score. By using their personal credit history to get business credit, they're not able to build their business score, which could help them attain critical business credit in the future. The following are the basic steps you need to take to establish your business credit profile and score.

1. **Form a corporation or LLC to operate your business under and obtain an FIN or EIN from the IRS. You can apply for an EIN at the IRS web site.** Form a corporation or LLC, as opposed to structuring your business as a sole proprietorship or partnership, because with a sole proprietorship or partnership, your personal credit information could be included on your business credit report—and vice-versa. Corporations and LLCs, on the other hand, afford business owners liability protection, and you can build a business credit profile that's separate from your personal debts.

2. **Register your company with the business credit bureaus.**

3. **Comply with the business credit market requirements.** It's extremely important for businesses to meet all the requirements of the credit market in order to ensure a higher likelihood of credit approval. The red flags include such simple things as not having a business license or a phone line. You can research the list of business credit market requirements at iBank.com.

4. **Prepare financial statements and a professional business plan.** These documents are often required by many credit grantors.

5. **Find companies willing to grant credit to your business without a personal credit check or guarantee.**

6. **Manage your debt so you don't fall into trouble making your payments, which will negatively affect your credit score.**

7. **Make monthly payments to credit grantors to keep your business credit profile active.**

Source: David Gass, "The ABCs of Business Credit," www.entrepreneur.com/article/0,4621,320634,00.html.

Self-Assessment Checklist Before Approaching a Financer

You must be able to answer yes to all the questions below to avoid difficulties in obtaining financing. Evaluate the needs of your business and take advantage of local business assistance centers.

- Do you have a good personal credit history?
- Have you filed all income tax returns?
- Are your income taxes paid?

Section 4

- Does the business have the ability to repay a loan?
- Does your business have a positive net worth?
- Is your business not carrying too much debt?
- Do you have enough of your money in the business?
- Do you have collateral to secure a business loan?
- Are you willing to personally guarantee a loan?
- Does your business have qualified managers and advisors?
- Do you have experience in running your own business?

Source: Small Business Administration, "Finance Basics."

Things to Include in a Written Loan Proposal

When applying for a loan, you must prepare a written loan proposal. Make your best presentation in the initial loan proposal and application. First impressions last! There are many different loan proposals and you may want to contract your commercial lender to determine which format is best for you. Include these items below:

Description of the business:

- Type of organization
- Date of information
- Location
- Product or service
- Brief history
- Proposed future operation
- Competition
- Customers
- Suppliers

Management Experience: Resumes of all management.

Personal Financial Statements: Financial statements must not be older than 90 days and make sure to attach a copy of last year's federal income tax return to the financial statements.

Loan Repayment: Describe briefly how the loan be repaid, including repayment sources and time requirements.

Existing Business: Provide financial statements for the last three years, plus a balance sheet, profit and loss statement, and reconciliation of net worth.

Proposed Business: Provide a projection of future operation for at least one year or until positive cash can be shown. Include earnings, expenses, and reasoning for these estimates.

Collateral: List real property and other assets to be held as collateral.

Other items:

- lease
- franchise agreement
- purchase agreement
- articles of incorporation
- plans, specifications
- copies of licenses
- letters of reference
- letters of intent
- contracts
- partnership agreement

Source: Small Business Administration, "Finance Basics."

Tips for Doing Your Homework Before Dialing for Investors

When it comes to raising money, many business owners skip the preparation stage and launch right into dialing for dollars. Before you look for investors, make sure you:

- **Write a business plan.** After you prepare the plan, write a two-page executive summary. This part will be well read.

- **Have your accountant prepare historical financial statements.** Investors like these prepared by an independent outside party.

- **Line up your references.** Investors may want to talk to your suppliers, customers, potential partners, or professional advisors.

- **Figure out your sizzle.** When you're asked what you do, you want your answer to be clever and memorable.

- **Meet and greet.** Once you've isolated your investor prospects, you'll want personal introductions to as many as possible.

Source: Rieva Lesonsky, *365 Tips to Boost Your Entrepreneurial IQ.*

# Chapter 22

Section 4

Personal Finance

Tips for the Entrepreneurial Retirement Plan

Do you have a retirement plan? Today, as we live longer and longer, it's more important than ever to plan our financial futures. And entrepreneurs are finally able to participate.

- One of the best ways to plan your future is to set up a Simplified Employee Pension-Individual Retirement Account (SEP-IRA).

- SEP-IRA accounts are for very small businesses with few employees. You're eligible for opening a SEP-IRA even if you operate a part-time business or if you're structured as a sole proprietorship, an S corporation, or a partnership.

- One of the immediate advantages of a SEP-IRA is tax savings. Contributions are tax-deductible for the year in which they are made.

- You can contribute nothing or as much as 15 percent of your net profits or $24,000 a year, whichever is less.

To learn more about your options, consult a financial advisor.

Source: Rieva Lesonsky, *365 Tips to Boost Your Entrepreneurial IQ.*

Section 4

Building Your Personal Credit Report

Payment History Tips

- Pay your bills on time. Delinquent payments and collections can have a major negative impact on your score.

- If you have missed payments, get current and stay current. The longer you pay your bills on time, the better your score.

- Be aware that paying off a collection account will not remove it from your credit report. It will stay on your report for seven years.

- If you are having trouble making ends meet, contact your creditors or see a legitimate credit counselor. This won't improve your score immediately, but if you can begin to manage your credit and pay on time, your score will get better over time.

Amounts Owed Tips

- Keep balances low on credit cards and other "revolving credit." High outstanding debt can affect a score.

- Pay off debt rather than moving it around. The most effective way to improve your score in this area is by paying down your revolving credit. In fact, owing the same amount but having fewer open accounts may lower your score.

- Don't close unused credit cards as a short-term strategy to raise your score.

- Don't open a number of new credit cards that you don't need, just to increase your available credit. This approach could backfire and actually lower your score.

New Credit Tips

- Do your rate shopping for a given loan within a focused period of time. FICO® scores distinguish between a search for a single loan and a search for many new credit lines, in part by the length of time over which inquiries occur.

- Re-establish your credit history if you have had problems. Opening new accounts responsibly and paying them off on time will raise your score in the long term.

- Note that it's OK to request and check your own credit report. This won't affect your score, as long as you order your credit report directly from the credit-reporting agency or through an organization authorized to provide credit reports to consumers.

- Apply for and open new credit accounts only as needed. Don't open accounts just to have a better credit mix; it probably won't raise your score.

- Have credit cards—but manage them responsibly. In general, having credit cards and installment loans (and paying timely payments) will raise your score. Someone with no credit cards, for example, tends to be higher risk than someone who has managed credit cards responsibly.

- Note that closing an account doesn't make it go away. A closed account will still show up on your credit report, and may be considered by the score.

Source: "Improving Your FICO® Score," www.myfico.com/CreditEducation/ImproveYourScore. aspx.

SCORE's Five Tips on Paying Yourself

1. Don't pay yourself so much that you cripple your company or so little that you trigger IRS scrutiny and penalties.

2. Understand how your company's legal structure affects your compensation and taxes. Your salary and bonuses are taxed one way; distributions to you as a shareholder are taxed another.

3. Find out what the market rates are for CEOs in your industry and your size of business. Your trade association can help.

4. Seek advice from the best accountant and lawyer you can find.

5. If you were paid little or nothing in the first years of your business, don't be ashamed of compensating yourself well when the business is successful. You've earned it.

Source: SCORE, www.score.org/business_tips.html.

Nine Things to Do to Obtain a Small Business Loan

To get approval for your small business loan application, you must be able to meet the lending criteria set down. Some organizations are more risk-averse than others and will therefore have more stringent criteria. To vastly increase your chances of a successful funding application, you will need to present the following information:

1. The reason for the loan. The lender will be looking for something that fits within the normal range and expertise of your business. The amount may cover a number of items, so you will need to cover each.

2. The amount required and the repayment term of the small business loan you want (e.g., $10,000, term five years, payable quarterly).

3. Details of how you will repay the amount borrowed. For example, "From the increase in profits of reduced running costs of the Whizzbang Go4It."

4. Details of security you will be able to offer to the lender. This will act as reassurance for the lender. If you're not prepared to put up some aspect of security, then why should they?

5. You will need to include your business plan, which will serve to answer essential questions relating to management capabilities, information about the market you operate in, what kind of business you are in, etc.

6. Three years' financial statements. You will need to present quality financial information from your accounting software, preferably signed off by your accountant or tax advisor.

7. Latest set of management accounts. Again, produced from your accounting software.

8. Accounts receivable (debtors) and payable (creditors) aging reports.

9. Principals' financial statements. Particularly required if some form of security is necessary.

If you are a new company, the emphasis is going to be on your business plan and the security (collateral) you or your business can provide against the loan.

Source: Neil Best, "9 Things You Must Do To Maximize Your Chances of Obtaining a Small Business Loan," www.morebusiness.com/running_your_business/financing/Estory-14777.brc.

SCORE's Five Tips on Being Creative in the Search for Funding

1. Contact your state, county, and local development departments. Many offer funding programs to foster business within a certain geographic area.

2. Take advantage of organizations aimed at helping you. The National Organization of Women Business Owners offers special funding programs for women entrepreneurs, for example, and the National Minority Supplier Development Council has an arm that works with minority entrepreneurs.

3. Call on the community banks in your area. These smaller banks pride themselves on helping small business owners.

4. Find out of there are any revolving loan fund (RLF) programs for which you might qualify. They provide "gap financing" that your bank won't or can't offer. Your banker should know of any RLFs available.

5. Visit www.sba.gov/financing, the finance section of the U.S. Small Business Administration's web site. It provides details on the SBA's many funding programs. Perhaps you qualify for one.

Source: SCORE, www.score.org/business_tips.html.

Advice on Accepting Credit Cards

Pros for accepting credit cards:

1. Credit cards increase the probability, speed, and size of customer purchases.

2. Customers carry these around because they are convenient and it will be easier to get refunded for returned or exchanged merchandise.

3. You can increase sales by enabling customers to make impulse buys when they don't have enough money in their wallet.

4. It improves your cash flow because you receive the money in a few days rather than waiting for a check to clear or an invoice to come due.

5. Credit cards provide a guarantee that you will be paid, without the risks involved in accepting personal checks.

Be aware of credit card fraud with these steps:

1. Check the signature on the charge slip against the one on the back of the card. This may seem basic, but you'd be surprised how often it is neglected.

2. Verify the card's expiration date.

3. Check the frequently updated bulletin listing canceled card numbers.

Some fees you can expect to pay (some negotiable):

1. Start-up fee around $100

2. Equipment costs of $250-$1,000, depending on whether you buy or lease the equipment

3. Monthly statement fee of $4 to $20

4. Transaction fee of 5 to 50 cents per purchase

5. The discount rate, the actual percentage you are charged per transaction based on projected card sales volume, the degree of risk, and a few other factors

6. Charge-back fees, up to $15 per return transaction

7. Miscellaneous fees, including per-transaction communication costs of five to 12 cents for connection to the processor, a postage fee for sending statements, and a supply fee for charge slips

A Word About Accepting Debit Cards

Debit cards are becoming more widely accepted in businesses. Debit cards are less expensive than credit cards or checks and are not vulnerable to employee theft like cash.

Source: Rieva Lesonsky, *Start Your Own Business.*

Advantages and Disadvantages of Extending Credit

Cash and carry is the most efficient way to do business. It eliminates the need for credit checks and costly monitoring of receivables, and it minimizes the chances of operating losses. By their nature certain types of businesses need to offer credit, such as construction and clothing manufacturers. Offering credit can:

Advantages of offering credit:

■ It can encourage customers to spend more, which can result in increased sales—if receivables are turned to cash.

■ It can increase customer goodwill and build good customer relations.

■ It can make your customers less sensitive to price and more focused on the services you offer.

Disadvantages of offering credit:

■ Credit costs you money. Customers might not pay. Statistics indicate that 97-98 percent of all credit bills in America are paid on time. However, the remaining 2-3 percent can sink a small business.

■ Credit costs you cash. When you offer credit, you're selling an item you've already paid for on the premise that you'll be paid by the buyer tomorrow. It may lead into a cash flow problem if they do not pay you on time.

■ Credit costs you time. You spend time making credit decisions, time you could spend making other decisions on other aspects of the business.

Source: Andi Axman, *Entrepreneur Magazine's Ultimate Small Business Advisor.*

SCORE's Five Tips on Budgeting

1. Think of a budget as a useful tool—a written financial plan that helps you set goals and measure progress.

2. Start by coming up with a sales revenue target. Make it your best estimate.

3. Based on experience, estimate your cost of goods sold (e.g., 70 percent of sales) and subtract it from the sales revenue to come up with your estimated gross margin.

4. Forecast variable expenses (items such as travel and commissions that vary according to the level of sales) and fixed expenses (items like taxes and rent that stay the same, regardless of sales). Subtract these expenses from your gross margin to arrive at your estimated net income (before federal taxes).

5. Break your annual budget into quarters and monitor your progress every three months to detect problems and make corrections.

Source: SCORE, www.score.org/business_tips.html.

Small Business Banks

Eight Ways to Find the Best Bank for You

Not all banks make it appoint to reach out to small businesses. These are some tips to find out if your bank is directly catering to your small business needs.

1. **Meet the commercial lenders or relationship managers you might be working with.** Large banks are often divided into two sectors: commercial banking and retail banking. Retail banking usually focuses on personal accounts. Commercial banking is often segmented into three parts: small business (less than $3 million in sales), midmarket ($3 million to $20 million in sales), and large business (more than $20 million in sales). Occasionally, large banks will attach their small-business lending unit to the retail banking division. The point? Find out which bank department best fits your company's needs. Then you're ready to meet with the right people.

2. **Find out if the bank classifies your industry as undesirable.** This isn't common knowledge among a bank's staff. You'll have to get it directly from the small-business banker. He or she may feel uncomfortable with the subject matter, so make it easy by saying something like "In your bank's loan policy manual, in the section titled 'Undesirable Loans,' is my industry listed?"

3. **The bank must understand your industry—no exceptions.** Every industry has certain characteristics not commonly understood. When bankers don't understand how an industry operates, they don't understand how they'll be repaid. And when bankers don't understand how they'll be repaid, they decline loan requests.

4. **Make sure the bank is small enough.** Only then will a banker take time to spell out the requirements. You should be able to ask questions—and get answers—about loan-to-cost, cash-coverage ratios, how they calculate the debt-to-income ratio of entrepreneurs, and more.

5. **Determine if the bank is large enough to accommodate your needs.** Every bank has a legal lending limit based on its equity. So a bank with less than $100 million in assets may not be able to accommodate a small manufacturer with $5 million to $10 million in sales.

6. **Make sure loan requests for your business are underwritten locally.** Here's why. Let's say a business in Jacksonville, Florida, delivers its loan application to the local branch. Several days later, it receives a letter of decline in the mail. When the business owner later questions the branch manager, he or she learns that all small-business loans are actually processed in Tampa, Florida, and that there's no one there to answer questions.

7. **The bank must be looking for smaller customers.** These days, a growing number of niche banks aim to deal exclusively with small businesses. It also helps to ask around and find out which banks other entrepreneurs are using.

8. **Start with the bank that handles your deposits.** But if it turns out not to be friendly to your business's needs, it's time to move on to one that is.

Source: Wallace Weeks, "Making The Cut," www.entrepreneur.com/article/ 0,4621,276972,00.html.

SCORE's Five Tips for Finding and Keeping a Bank

1. **Understand the basics.** Large or small, banks are interested in the same fundamentals—such as cash flow, collateral, and the viability of your business.

2. **Sell the bank on your company.** Provide solid information on its financial history and your business plan, and information about the kinds of loans you need and the terms you want.

3. **Look for a good fit.** Let prospects know what kind of a relationship you want with a bank.

4. **Ask the right questions.** Find out where decision making takes place, how many people you will have to deal with, and if the bank is open to meeting with you and your advisors fairly regularly.

5. **Commit time and energy to developing your relationship with the bank you choose.** Get to know more than one person at the institution so that if your bank is merged or acquired, someone familiar with your business will probably still be there.

Source: SCORE, www.score.org/business_tips.html.

SCORE's Five Tips on Approaching Your Bank

1. Understand that your primary responsibility is the proper use of capital and that you are in business to make a profit.

2. Test the economics of your product or service. Make sure that it is profitable and that the gross profit percent is in line with that of the industry.

3. Know how you will finance your business. Visit lenders (banks) prior to seeking financing to gather information. Ask your lenders what they will want to see before you apply for a loan.

4. Develop a personal financial evaluation. Determine your net worth and your annual, personal cash flow needs.

5. Develop realistic financial forecasts for income statements, cash flow, and balance sheets for three years. Forecast monthly for the first year.

Source: SCORE, www.score.org/business_tips.html.

Best Banks for Entrepreneurs, by State

Alabama

1. Community Bank
Blountsville, AL
(205) 429-1000

1. Farmers & Merchants Bank
Piedmont, AL
(256) 447-9041

1. First National Bank of Central Alabama
Aliceville, AL
(202) 373-6367

2. First Lowndes Bank
Fort Deposit, AL
(334) 227-8301

2. Small Town Bank
Wedowee, AL
(256) 357-4936

2. Traders & Farmers Bank
Haleyville, AL
(205) 486-5263

3. First National Bank
Hamilton, AL
(205) 921-7435

3. Town-Country National Bank
Camden, AL
(334) 682-4155

4. Alabama Trust Bank National Association
Sylacauga, AL
(256) 245-6099

4. Camden National Bank
Camden, AL
(334) 682-4215

4. Commercial Bank of Demopolis
Demopolis, AL
(334) 289-3820

4. First Citizens Bank
Luverne, AL
(334) 335-3346

4. First Metro Bank
Muscle Shoals, AL
(256) 386-0600

4. Peachtree Bank
Maplesville, AL
(334) 366-2921

Alaska

First National Bank Alaska
Anchorage, AK
(800) 856-4362

Arizona

1. Sunstate Bank
Casa Grande, AZ
(520) 836-4666

2. Bank of America, N.A.
Phoenix, AZ
(602) 973-7216

2. Stockmen's Bank
Kingman, AZ
(928) 757-7171

3. Union Bank of Arizona
Gilbert, AZ
(480) 926-2265

Arkansas

1. Arvest Bank-Yellville
Yellville, AR
(870) 449-7101

2. Bank of Salem
Salem, AR
(870) 895-2591

3. Community Bank
Cabot, AR
(501) 843-3575

4. Commercial Bank & Trust
Monticello, AR
(870) 367-6221

4. First National Bank of Eastern Arkansas
Forrest City, AR
(870) 633-3112

4. First Service Bank
Greenbrier, AR
(501) 679-7300

5. DeWitt Bank & Trust
DeWitt, AR
(870) 946-3531

5. Diamond State Bank
Murfreesboro, AR
(870) 285-2172

5. Southern State Bank
Malvern, AR
(501) 332-2462

6. Allied Bank
Mulberry, AR
(479) 997-1154

6. Bank of Paragould
Paragould, AR
(870) 236-7000

6. Bank of Pocahontas
Pocahontas, AR
(870) 892-5286

6. First National Bank
Ashdown, AR
(870) 898-2761

6. Fordyce Bank & Trust Company
Fordyce, AR
(870) 352-3107

6. Union Bank of Mena
Mena, AR
(479) 394-2211

California

1. North Valley Bank
Redding, CA
(530) 226-2920

2. Community Commerce Bank
Los Angeles, CA
(323) 888-0065

3. Bank of the Sierra
Porterville, CA
(559) 782-4300

3. Innovative Bank
Oakland, CA
(888) 960-0700

3. Wells Fargo Bank
San Francisco, CA
(415) 437-1582

4. Bank of Marin
Corte Madera, CA
(415) 927-2265

4. Butte Community Bank
Chico, CA
(530) 891-9000

4. Plumas Bank
Quincy, CA
(530) 283-6800

4. Six Rivers Bank
Eureka, CA
(707) 443-8400

4. Tri Counties Bank
Chico, CA
(530) 893-8861

Colorado

1. First National Bank of Las Animas
Las Animas, CO
(719) 456-1512

1. Park State Bank and Trust
Woodland Park, CO
(719) 687-9234

1. Wells Fargo (formerly Bank of Grand Junction)
Grand Junction, CO
(970) 257-4888

2. Bank of Durango
Durango, CO
(970) 259-5500

2. Pine River Valley Bank
Bayfield, CO
(970) 884-9583

Section 4

3. First National Bank in Trinidad
Trinidad, CO
(719) 846-9881

4. Citizens State Bank of Ouray
Ouray, CO
(970) 325-4478

4. Colonial Bank
Aurora, CO
(505) 671-9000

4. Dolores State Bank
Dolores, CO
(970) 882-7600

4. First National Bank of Lake City and Creede
Lake City, CO
(970) 944-2242

4. Kit Carson State Bank
Kit Carson, CO
(719) 962-3273

Connecticut

1. First City Bank
New Britain, CT
(860) 224-3865

2. Valley Bank
Bristol, CT
(860) 582-8868

Delaware

1. MBNA America
Wilmington, DE
(302) 453-9930

2. Chase Manhattan Bank
Wilmington, DE
(302) 576-1030

2. Citibank Delaware
New Castle, DE
(302) 323-3900

District of Columbia

Adams National Bank
Washington, DC
(202) 772-3600

Florida

1. First National Bank of Alachua
Alachua, FL
(386) 462-1041

1. Suntrust Bankcard
Orlando, FL
(407) 237-4882

2. Destin Bank
Destin, FL
(850) 837-8100

2. Drummond Community Bank
Chiefland, FL
(352) 493-2277

2. First National Bank of Wauchula
Wauchula, FL
(863) 773-4136

3. First State Bank
Sarasota, FL
(941) 929-9000

3. Highlands Independent Bank
Sebring, FL
(863) 385-8700

3. Perkins State Bank
Williston, FL
(352) 528-3101

4. Capital City Bank
Tallahassee, FL
(850) 671-0661

4. Citrus & Chemical Bank
Bartow, FL
(863) 533-3171

4. Columbia County Bank
Lake City, FL
(386) 752-5646

4. The Citizens Bank of Perry
Perry, FL
(850) 584-4411

Georgia

1. Farmers & Merchants Bank
Lakeland, GA
(229) 482-3585

1. Security Bank of Bibb County
Macon, GA
(478) 722-6200

2. Bank of Dudley
Dudley, GA
(478) 277-1500

2. Citizens Bank of Effingham
Springfield, GA
(912) 754-0754

2. First State Bank
Stockbridge, GA
(770) 474-7293

2. Planters First Bank
Cordele, GA
(229) 273-2416

3. Bank of Ellaville
Ellaville, GA
(229) 937-2507

3. Citizens Bank of Washington County
Sandersville, GA
(478) 552-5116

3. Community Banking Company of Fitzgerald
Fitzgerald, GA
(229) 423-4321

3. First State Bank of Blakely
Blakely, GA
(229) 723-3711

3. State Bank of Cochran
Cochran, GA
(478) 934-4501

Hawaii

First Hawaiian Bank
Honolulu, HI
(808) 525-7000

Idaho

Farmers & Merchants State Bank
Meridian, ID
(208) 888-1416

Illinois

1. Bank of Pontiac
Pontiac, IL
(815) 842-1069

1. Bradford National Bank
Greenville, IL
(618) 664-2200

1. First National Bank of Ottawa
Ottawa, IL
(815) 434-0044

1. Germantown Trust & Savings Bank
Breese, IL
(618) 523-4202

1. Peoples National Bank of Kewanee
Kewanee, IL
(309) 853-3333

1. Peotone Bank and Trust
Peotone, IL
(708) 258-3231

2. Anna National Bank
Anna, IL
(618) 833-8506

2. First National Bank of Pana
Pana, IL
(217) 562-3961

2. First Neighbor Bank, N.A. (formerly First National Bank in Toledo)
Toledo, IL
(217) 849-2701

2. National Bank of Petersburg
Petersburg, IL
(217) 632-3241

2. Peoples Bank & Trust
Pana, IL
(217) 562-2137

Section 4

Section 4

2. Trustbank
Olney, IL
(618) 395-4311

Indiana

1. Friendship State Bank
Friendship, IN
(812) 667-5101

1. Markle Bank
Markle, IN
(260) 758-3111

2. DeMotte State Bank
DeMotte, IN
(219) 987-4141

2. First State Bank
Brazil, IN
(812) 238-6000

2. Fowler State Bank
Fowler, IN
(765) 884-1200

2. State Bank of Oxford
Oxford, IN
(765) 385-2213

3. Bank of Wolcott
Wolcott, IN
(219) 279-2185

3. First State Bank of Middlebury
Middlebury, IN
(574) 825-2166

3. Heritage Community Bank
Columbus, IN
(812) 375-5192

3. The Farmers Bank
Frankfort, IN
(765) 654-8731

Iowa

1. Decorah Bank & Trust
Decorah, IA
(563) 382-9661

1. Farmers State Bank
Jesup, IA
(319) 827-1050

1. Libertyville Savings Bank
Libertyville, IA
(641) 693-3141

2. Central State Bank
Muscatine, IA
(563) 263-3131

2. Cresco Union Savings Bank
Cresco, IA
(563) 547-2040

2. Freedom Security Bank
Coralville, IA
(319) 688-9005

2. Maquoketa State Bank
Maquoketa, IA
(563) 652-2491

3. Bank Iowa
Red Oak, IA
(712) 623-6960

3. Great Western Bank (formerly Security State Bank)
Red Oak, IA
(712) 623-9809

3. Houghton State Bank
Red Oak, IA
(712) 623-4823

3. Northstar Bank
Estherville, IA
(712) 362-3322

3. Peoples Trust & Savings Bank
Adel, IA
(515) 993-5680

Kansas

1. First National Bank
Independence, KS
(620) 331-2265

1. Union State Bank
Everest, KS
(785) 548-7521

2. Bankers Bank of Kansas, N.A.
Wichita, KS
(316) 681-2265

2. Citizens State Bank
Gridley, KS
(620) 836-2888

3. Emprise Bank
Iola, KS
(620) 365-6921

3. Farmers State Bank of Mcpherson
Mcpherson, KS
(620) 241-3090

3. First National Bank of Southern Kansas
Mount Hope, KS
(316) 661-2471

3. First National Bank of Wamego
Wamego, KS
(785) 456-2221

3. First State Bank
Norton, KS
(785) 877-3341

3. Peoples Bank & Trust
Mcpherson, KS
(620) 241-2100

3. Rose Hill Bank
Rose Hill, KS
(316) 776-2131

Kentucky

1. Bank of Columbia
Columbia, KY
(270) 384-6433

1. Peoples Bank & Trust Company of Hazard
Hazard, KY
(606) 436-2161

1.Peoples Bank of Fleming County
Flemingsburg, KY
(606) 845-2461

2. Farmers National Bank of Danville
Danville, KY
(859) 236-2926

2. First National Bank of Columbia
Columbia, KY
(270) 384-2361

2. Town Square Bank
Ashland, KY
(606) 929-9700

3. Bank of Edmonson County
Brownsville, KY
(270) 597-2175

3. The Farmers Bank
Hardinsburg, KY
(270) 756-2166

3. Kentucky Banking Centers
Glasgow, KY
(270) 651-2265

3. South Central Bank
Glasgow, KY
(270) 651-7466

Louisiana

1. Jeff Davis Bank & Trust
Jennings, LA
(337) 824-3424

2. Farmers-Merchants Bank & Trust Co.
Breaux Bridge, LA
(337) 332-2115

3. Delta Bank
Vidalia, LA
(318) 336-4510

4. City Savings Bank and Trust Co.
DeRidder, LA
(337) 463-8661

4. Feliciana Bank & Trust Co.
Clinton, LA
(225) 344-8890

5. Franklin State Bank
Winnsboro, LA
(318) 435-3711

5. Southern Heritage Bank
Jonesville, LA
(318) 339-8505

6. Citizens Progressive Bank
Columbia, LA
(318) 649-6136

6. First Louisiana National Bank
Breaux Bridge, LA
(337) 332-5960

6. Gibsland Bank & Trust Co.
Gibsland, LA
(318) 843-6228

6. Saint Martin Bank & Trust Company
Saint Martinville, LA
(337) 845-4711

6. Vermillion Bank & Trust Company
Kaplan, LA
(337) 643-7900

Maine

Franklin Savings Bank
Farmington, ME
(800) 287-0752

Maryland

1. Patapsco Bank
Dundalk, MD
(410) 285-1010

2. Peoples Bank of Kent County
Chestertown, MD
(410) 778-5500

3. Bank of the Eastern Shore
Cambridge, MD
(410) 228-5800

4. Bank Annapolis
Annapolis, MD
(800) 582-2651

4. NBRS Financial
Rising Sun, MD
(800) 562-9301

4. Peninsula Bank
Princess Anne, MD
(410) 651-2404

5. Community Bank of Tri-County
Waldorf, MD
(301) 645-5601

5. Hebron Savings Bank
Hebron, MD
(410) 749-1185

5. Provident State Bank
Preston, MD
(410) 673-2401

Massachusetts

1. Enterprise Bank & Trust Company
Lowell, MA
(978) 459-9000

2. Bank of Western Massachusetts
Springfield, MA
(413) 781-2265

3. Bank North (formerly Cape Cod Bank and Trust)
Hyannis, MA
(508) 362-1944

3. Capital Crossing Bank
Boston, MA
(617) 880-1050

Michigan

1. First National Bank & Trust Co. of Iron Mountain
Iron Mountain, MI
(906) 774-2200

1. Hillsdale County National Bank
Hillsdale, MI
(517) 439-4300

2. Independent Bank
Bay City, MI
(989) 892-3511

2. Peninsula Bank of Ishpeming
Ishpeming, MI
(906) 485-6333

3. Firstbank-West Branch
West Branch, MI
(989) 345-7900

4. Firstbank
Mount Pleasant, MI
(989) 773-2600

4. Michigan Heritage Bank
Farmington, MI
(248) 538-2525

5. First National Bank of America
East Lansing, MI
(517) 351-2665

5. Firstbank-Alma
Alma, MI
(989) 463-3131

5. Huron National Bank
Rogers City, MI
(517) 734-4734

5. Independent Bank West Michigan
Rockford, MI
(616) 866-4471

5. Isabella Bank and Trust
Mount Pleasant, MI
(989) 772-9471

5. Peoples State Bank of Munising
Munising, MI
(906) 387-2006

Minnesota

1. Heritage Bank
Spicer, MN
(320) 796-0215

1. Kasson State Bank
Kasson, MN
(507) 634-7022

2. First National Bank
Bagley, MN
(218) 694-6233

2. Northland Community Bank
Northome, MN
(218) 897-5285

2. Pine River State Bank
Pine River, MN
(218) 587-4463

3. Community Bank Minnesota Valley
Jordan, MN
(952) 492-5599

3. Farmers & Merchants State Bank
Blooming Prairie, MN
(507) 583-6688

3. Northwestern Bank, N.A.
Dilworth, MN
(218) 287-2311

3. Paragon Bank
Wells, MN
(507) 553-2265

3. Prinsburg State Bank
Prinsburg, MN
(320) 978-6351

3. Wadena State Bank
Wadena, MN
(218) 631-1860

Mississippi

1. First State Bank
Waynesboro, MS
(866) 408-3582

2. Bank of Holly Springs
Holly Springs, MS
(662) 252-2511

2. Bank of New Albany
New Albany, MS
(662) 534-8171

2. First National Bank of Pontotoc
Pontotoc, MS
(662) 489-1631

3. Mechanics Bank
Water Valley, MS
(662) 473-2261

3. Merchants & Marine Bank
Pascagoula, MS
(228) 762-3311

**Section
4**

3. Omnibank
Mantee, MS
(662) 456-5341

3. Pike County National Bank
McComb, MS
(601) 684-7575

4. Farmers & Merchants Bank
Baldwyn, MS
(662) 365-1200

Missouri

1. First Community Bank
Poplar Bluff, MO
(573) 778-0101

2. Century Bank of the Ozarks
Gainesville, MO
(417) 679-3321

2. Community State Bank
Bowling Green, MO
(573) 324-2233

2. First Missouri State Bank
Poplar Bluff, MO
(573) 785-6800

2. First National Bank
Malden, MO
(573) 276-2257

2. Kearney Trust Company
Kearney, MO
(816) 628-6666

2. O'Bannon Bank
Buffalo, MO
(417) 345-2251

2. Southern Missouri Bank of Marshfield
Marshfield, MO
(417) 859-1292

2. Southwest Missouri Bank
Carthage, MO
(417) 358-9331

3. First National Bank
Mountain View, MO
(417) 934-2033

3. Perry State Bank
Perry, MO
(573) 565-2221

Montana

1. First Citizens Bank of Butte
Butte, MT
(406) 494-4400

2. First State Bank
Thompson Falls, MT
(406) 827-7000

3. Citizens State Bank
Hamilton, MT
(406) 363-3551

4. Heritage Bank
Great Falls, MT
(406) 727-6106

4. Lake County Bank
Saint Ignatius, MT
(406) 745-3123

5. Flint Creek Valley Bank
Philipsburg, MT
(406) 859-3241

5. Montana First National Bank
Kalispell, MT
(406) 755-9999

5. Three Rivers Bank of Montana
Kalispell, MT
(406) 755-4271

5. United Bank, N.A.
Absarokee, MT
(406) 328-4742

Nebraska

1. Commercial State Bank
Wausa, NE
(402) 586-2266

1. Dakota County State Bank
South Sioux City, NE
(402) 494-4215

1. Otoe County Bank & Trust
Nebraska City, NE
(402) 873-3388

2. Gothenburg State Bank & Trust Co.
Gothenburg, NE
(308) 537-7181

2. Midwest Bank
Pierce, NE
(402) 329-6221

2. Saline State Bank
Wilber, NE
(402) 821-2241

3. Centennial Bank
Omaha, NE
(402) 891-0003

3. Community Bank
Alma, NE
(308) 928-2929

3. Farmers & Merchants Bank
Milford, NE
(402) 761-7600

4. Farmers & Merchants State Bank
Wayne, NE
(402) 375-2043

4. First National Bank in Ord
Ord, NE
(308) 728-3201

4. Wahoo State Bank
Wahoo, NE
(402) 443-3207

4. York State Bank & Trust
York, NE
(402) 759-3124

Nevada

1. First National Bank
Ely, NV
(775) 289-4441

2. BankWest of Nevada
Las Vegas, NV
(702) 248-4200

2. Red Rock Community Bank
Las Vegas, NV
(702) 948-7500

New Hampshire

First Colebrook Bank
Colebrook, NH
(603) 237-5551

New Jersey

1. Panasia Bank
Fort Lee, NJ
(201) 947-6666

1. The Bank
Woodbury, NJ
(856) 845-0700

2. Skylands Community Bank
Hackettstown, NJ
(908) 850-9010

3. Harvest Community Bank
Pennsville, NJ
(856) 678-4555

3. Newfield National Bank
Newfield, NJ
(856) 692-3440

4. 1st Colonial National Bank
Collingswood, NJ
(856) 858-1100

4. Union Center National Bank
Union, NJ
(908) 688-9500

New Mexico

1. Citizens Bank of Clovis
Clovis, NM
(505) 769-1911

2. Valley Bank of Commerce
Roswell, NM
(505) 623-2265

3. First National Bank of Las Vegas
Las Vegas, NM
(505) 425-7584

3. Portales National Bank
Portales, NM
(505) 356-6601

3. Western Commerce Bank
Carlsbad, NM
(505) 887-6686

New York

1. National Bank of Geneva
Geneva, NY
(315) 789-2300

2. Atlantic Bank of New York
New York, NY
(800) 435-1769

3. Bath National Bank
Bath, NY
(607) 776-3381

3. First National Bank of Groton
Groton, NY
(607) 898-5871

3. Solvay Bank
Solvay, NY
(315) 468-1661

3. Suffolk County National Bank
Riverhead, NY
(631) 727-4712

4. Adirondack Bank
Saranac Lake, NY
(518) 891-2323

4. Bank of Castile
Castile, NY
(585) 493-2576

4. Canandaigua National Bank & Trust
Canandaigua, NY
(585) 394-5520

4. Capital Bank & Trust Co.
Albany, NY
(518) 434-1212

4. Cattaraugus County Bank
Little Valley, NY
(716) 938-9128

4. Ellenville National Bank
Ellenville, NY
(845) 647-4300

4. National Bank of Coxsackie
Coxsackie, NY
(518) 731-6161

4. Savannah Bank, N.A.
Savannah, NY
(315) 365-2896

4. Steuben Trust Company
Hornell, NY
(607) 587-9122

North Carolina

1. Four Oaks Bank & Trust Company
Four Oaks, NC
(919) 963-2177

2. Catawba Valley Bank
Hickory, NC
(828) 431-2300

2. Surrey Bank & Trust
Mount Airy, NC
(336) 719-2310

2. Yadkin Valley Bank & Trust Company
Elkin, NC
(336) 526-6301

3. Bank of Granite
Granite Falls, NC
(828) 496-2027

3. Carolina First (formerly MountainBank)
Hendersonville, NC
(828) 697-3222

3. Farmers & Merchants Bank
Granite Quarry, NC
(704) 279-7291

North Dakota

1. Bank Center First
Bismarck, ND
(701) 223-2265

2. First United Bank
Park River, ND
(701) 284-7244

2. Stutsman County State Bank
Jamestown, ND
(701) 253-5600

3. United Community Bank of North Dakota
Leeds, ND
(701) 466-2232

4. First State Bank of North Dakota
Arthur, ND
(701) 967-8914

4. State Bank of Bottineau
Bottineau, ND
(701) 228-2204

4. U.S. Bank
Fargo, ND
(701) 280-3500

4. United Valley Bank
Cavalier, ND
(701) 780-9757

5. Farmers State Bank
Elgin, ND
(701) 584-2525

5. Sargent County Bank
Forman, ND
(701) 724-3216

Ohio

1. Sutton Bank
Attica, OH
(419) 426-3641

2. Savings Bank
Circleville, OH
(740) 474-3191

2. Vinton County National Bank
McArthur, OH
(740) 596-2525

3. 1st National Community Bank
East Liverpool, OH
(330) 385-9200

3. Hocking Valley Bank
Athens, OH
(740) 592-4441

3. Union Bank Co.
Columbus Grove, OH
(419) 659-2141

4. First Federal Bank (formerly Commercial Bank)
Delphos, OH
(419) 695-1055

5. Farmers & Merchants Bank
Caldwell, OH
(740) 732-5621

5. Farmers & Merchants State Bank
Archbold, OH
(419) 446-2501

5. First National Bank
Sycamore, OH
(419) 927-6392

5. Merchants National Bank
Hillsboro, OH
(937) 393-9850

5. Ohio Heritage Bank
Coshocton, OH
(740) 622-8311

Oklahoma

1. First American Bank
Purcell, OK
(800) 522-1262

1. Pauls Valley National Bank
Pauls Valley, OK
(405) 238-9321

2. Community State Bank
Poteau, OK
(918) 647-8101

2. First National Bank & Trust Co.
Weatherford, OK
(580) 772-5574

2. Firstbank
Antlers, OK
(580) 298-3368

Section
4

2. Welch State Bank
Welch, OK
(918) 788-2265

3. Bank of Union
Union City, OK
(405) 483-5308

3. Chickasha Bank & Trust Company
Chickasha, OK
(405) 222-0550

4. American Exchange Bank
Henryetta, OK
(918) 652-3321

4. Bank of Cushing & Trust Company
Cushing, OK
(918) 225-2010

4. Bank of Western Oklahoma
Elk City, OK
(580) 225-3434

4. Liberty National Bank
Lawton, OK
(580) 357-5800

Oregon

1. Columbia River Bank
The Dalles, OR
(877) 272-3678

2. Community Bank
Joseph, OR
(800) 472-4292

3. Albina Community Bank
Portland, OR
(503) 445-2150

Pennsylvania

1. Community Bank & Trust Company
Clarks Summit, PA
(570) 586-6876

2. Mercer County State Bank
Sandy Lake, PA
(724) 376-7015

2. Old Forge Bank
Old Forge, PA
(570) 457-8345

3. Community Banks
Millersburg, PA
(717) 692-4781

3. County National Bank
Clearfield, PA
(800) 492-3221

4. Elderton State Bank
Elderton, PA
(724) 354-2111

4. Fidelity Deposit & Discount Bank
Dunmore, PA
(570) 342-8281

5. CSB Bank
Curwensville, PA
(800) 494-3453

6. Bank of Lancaster County
Strasburg, PA
(717) 560-5800

6. First National Community Bank
Dunmore, PA
(570) 348-4817

6. Jersey Shore State Bank
Jersey Shore, PA
(570) 398-2213

6. The Dime Bank
Honesdale, PA
(570) 253-6000

Rhode Island

Washington Trust Co.
Westerly, RI
(401) 351-6240

South Carolina

1. Enterprise Bank of South Carolina
Ehrhardt, SC
(803) 267-4351

2. Anderson Bros. Bank
Mullins, SC
(843) 464-6271

2. Palmetto State Bank
Hampton, SC
(803) 943-2671

3. Capitalbank
Greenwood, SC
(864) 941-8212

3. Conway National Bank
Conway, SC
(843) 248-5721

4. Citizens Bank
Olanta, SC
(843) 396-4314

4. Horry County State Bank
Loris, SC
(843) 756-6333

South Dakota

1. Peoples State Bank
De Smet, SD
(605) 854-3321

2. Citibank
Sioux Falls, SD
(605) 331-2626

3. Merchants State Bank
Freeman, SD
(605) 925-4222

4. First Fidelity Bank
Burke, SD
(605) 775-2641

4. First State Bank of Roscoe
Roscoe, SD
(605) 287-4451

4. Peoples State Bank
Summit, SD
(605) 398-6111

5. American Bank & Trust
Wessington Springs, SD
(605) 539-1222

5. Campbell County Bank
Herreid, SD
(605) 437-2294

6. Great Plains Bank
Eureka, SD
(605) 284-2633

Tennessee

1. Citizens Bank
Carthage, TN
(615) 256-2912

1. First Bank of Tennessee
Spring City, TN
(423) 365-8400

1. Wayne County Bank
Waynesboro, TN
(931) 722-5438

2. First National Bank of Manchester
Manchester, TN
(931) 728-3518

2. Macon Bank & Trust Co.
Lafayette, TN
(615) 666-2121

2. Peoples Bank
Clifton, TN
(931) 676-3311

3. Bank of Crockett
Bells, TN
(731) 663-2031

3. Peoples Bank & Trust Co. of Pickett County
Byrdstown, TN
(931) 864-3168

4. Citizens Bank
Lafayette, TN
(615) 666-2196

4. People's National Bank of Lafollette
Lafollette, TN
(423) 562-4921

Section
4

Texas

1. First Financial Bank (formerly Peoples State Bank)
Clyde, TX
(325) 893-4211

1. First National Bank
Hughes Springs, TX
(903) 639-2521

2. City National Bank
Sulphur Springs, TX
(903) 885-7523

2. Fidelity Bank of Texas
Waco, TX
(254) 755-6555

2. First National Bank
Newton, TX
(409) 379-8587

2. First National Bank
George West, TX
(361) 449-1571

2. First State Bank
Louise, TX
(979) 648-2691

2. Peoples National Bank
Paris, TX
(903) 785-1099

3. Community National Bank
Hondo, TX
(830) 741-3066

3. First National Bank of Albany Breckenridge
Albany, TX
(325) 762-2221

3. Round Top State Bank
Round Top, TX
(979) 249-3151

Utah

1. Associates Capital Bank
Salt Lake City, UT
(801) 453-1378

1. Pitney Bowes Bank
Salt Lake City, UT
(801) 832-4440

1. Universal Financial Corporation
Salt Lake City, UT
(801) 453-1380

2. Advanta Bank Corporation
Draper, UT
(801) 523-2909

2. American Express Centurion Bank
Salt Lake City, UT
(801) 945-3000

Vermont

Peoples Trust Company of St. Albans
St. Albans, VT
(802) 524-3773

Virginia

1. Grayson National Bank
Independence, VA
(276) 773-2811

1. New Peoples Bank
Honaker, VA
(276) 873-6288

1. Powell Valley National Bank
Jonesville, VA
(276) 346-1414

2. Benchmark Community Bank
Kenbridge, VA
(434) 676-8444

2. Highlands Union Bank
Abingdon, VA
(276) 628-9181

3. Bank of Northumberland
Heathsville, VA
(804) 529-6158

4. Bank of the James
Lynchburg, VA
(434) 528-9106

4. First and Citizens Bank
Monterey, VA
(540) 468-2430

5. First Virginia Bank
Falls Church, VA
(703) 241-3505

5. Peoples Community Bank
Montross, VA
(804) 493-8031

Washington

1. Americanwest Bank
Spokane, WA
(509) 467-9084

1. Community First Bank
Kennewick, WA
(509) 783-3435

1. Whidbey Island Bank
Oak Harbor, WA
(360) 675-5968

2. Bank of the Pacific
Aberdeen, WA
(888) 366-3267

2. State National Bank
Garfield, WA
(509) 635-1361

3. Hometown National Bank
Longview, WA
(360) 414-0716

3. Islanders Bank
Friday Harbor, WA
(360) 378-2265

West Virginia

1. Poca Valley Bank
Walton, WV
(304) 577-6611

2. Community Bank of Parkersburg
Parkersburg, WV
(304) 485-7991

2. Traders Bank
Spencer, WV
(304) 927-3340

3. Calhoun City Bank
Grantsville, WV
(304) 354-6116

4. Bank of Mingo
Naugatuck, WV
(304) 664-3535

5. Bank of Romney
Romney, WV
(304) 822-3541

5. Union Bank
Middlebourne, WV
(304) 758-2191

Wisconsin

1. Northern State Bank
Ashland, WI
(715) 682-2772

2. Fortress Bank of Westby
Westby, WI
(608) 634-3787

3. Community Bank
Superior, WI
(715) 392-8241

3. Community Bank of Central Wisconsin
Colby, WI
(715) 223-3998

3. Laona State Bank
Laona, WI
(715) 674-2911

3. Premier Community Bank
Marion, WI
(715) 754-2535

3. Reedsburg Bank
Reedsburg, WI
(608) 524-8251

3. Royal Bank
Elroy, WI
(608) 462-8163

Section 4

4. First National Bank Manitowoc
Manitowoc, WI
(920) 684-6611

5. Peoples State Bank of Bloomer
Bloomer, WI
(715) 568-1100

5. Shell Lake State Bank
Shell Lake, WI
(715) 468-7858

Wyoming

1. Bank of Star Valley
Afton, WY
(307) 885-0000

2. Hilltop National Bank
Casper, WY
(307) 265-2740

3. Bank of Commerce
Rawlins, WY
(307) 324-2265

4. Cowboy State Bank
Ranchester, WY
(307) 655-2291

Source: Best Banks for Entrepreneurs,
www.entrepreneur.com/bestbanks.

Finding Venture Capital Firms

Great Big List of Venture Capital Firms

1. @Ventures
2. 1st Source Capital Corp.
3. 1to1 Ventures
4. 2i Capital
5. 3i
6. 3i Deutschland GmbH
7. 3i Group plc
8. 3M Company
9. 4C Ventures
10. A.B. Asesores Electra S.A.
11. A.M. Pappas & Associates
12. AAM Capital Partners, L.P.
13. AAVIN Equity Partners, L.P.
14. Abell Venture Fund
15. Aberdeen Asset Managers Ltd.
16. Abingworth Management Limited
17. ABN AMRO Bank N.V.Investor Relations (HQ 9141)
18. ABN AMRO Capital
19. ABN AMRO Capital (USA) Inc.
20. ABN AMRO Private Equity
21. ABRY Partners Inc.
22. ABS Capital Partners
23. ABS Ventures
24. Abundance Venture Capital
25. Acacia Venture Partners
26. Academy Funds
27. Accel Partners
28. Accenture Technology Ventures
29. Access Capital Corp.
30. Access Venture Partners
31. Acer Technology Ventures
32. ACF Equity Atlantic (Canada)
33. ACF Equity Atlantic Inc.
34. Achenbaum Capital Partners, LLC
35. ACI Capital Co. Inc.
36. Acorn Ventures Inc.
37. Acuity Ventures
38. Ad-Ventures, LLC.
39. Adams Capital Management, Inc.
40. Adams Street Partners, LLC
41. Adobe Ventures IV, L.P.
42. Advance Capital Partners, L.P.
43. Advance Property Fund
44. Advanced Technology Ventures
45. Advanta Partners, L.P.
46. Advantage Capital Partners
47. Advent International Corporation
48. Aegis Capital
49. Aerostar Capital, LLC
50. Affarsstrategerna Sverige AB
51. Affiliated Managers Group
52. Affinity Capital Management
53. Agave Capital
54. Agilent Ventures
55. Agility Capital
56. Agio Capital Partners I, L.P.
57. Agio Capital Partners, L.P.
58. AgriCapital Corp.
59. Aim High Enterprises, Inc
60. Akers Capital LLC
61. Albemarle Private Equity Ltd.
62. Alchemy Partners LLP
63. Alden Ventures LLC
64. Alexander Hutton Venture Partners
65. Alfa Capital
66. All American Capital
67. Allegheny Financial Group Ltd.
68. Allegiance Financial Group, Inc.
69. Allegis Capital, LLC
70. Allegra Capital Partners
71. Allen & Buckeridge Pty Ltd.
72. Alliance Global Investments
73. Alliance Technology Ventures
74. Alliance Ventures
75. Allied Capital Corporation
76. Alloy Ventures
77. Allstate Private Equity
78. Almasa Capital Inc.
79. Almeida Capital
80. Alpha Capital Partners Ltd.
81. Alpha Group
82. Alpine Technology Ventures
83. Alta Communications
84. Alta Communications
85. Alta Partners

86. Alta-Berkeley Associates
87. Altira Group LLC
88. Altos Ventures
89. AltoTech Ventures
90. AM Fund
91. AM Private Investments Inc.
92. Amadeus Capital Partners Limited
93. AmBex Venture Group
94. Ambient Advisors, LLC
95. America 1st,LLC
96. American Capital Strategies
97. American River Ventures
98. American Securities Capital Partners, LLC
99. Amerimark Capital Group
100. Ameritech Venture Capital
101. AMP Asset Management Australia Ltd.
102. Ampal-American Israel Corporation
103. Ampersand Ventures
104. Amphion Capital Management, LLC
105. Amsterdam Pacific Securities, LLC
106. Anderson Pacific Corporation
107. Andrew W. Byrd & Co., LLC
108. Angel Strategies, LLC
109. Antares Capital Corporation
110. Antares Leveraged Capital Corp.
111. Anthem Capital, L.P.
112. Apax Partners & Co. Ventures Ltd.
113. Apax Partners Israel
114. Apax Partners, Inc.
115. Apex Venture Partners
116. Applied Materials Ventures
117. APV Technology Partners
118. Arbor Partners, LLC
119. Arcadia Management, LLC
120. Arch Development Partners LLC
121. ARCH Venture Partners
122. ARCIS Group
123. Arcturus Capital
124. Ardesta
125. Arete Corporation
126. Argonaut Partners, LLC
127. Argos Soditic S.A.
128. Argosy Partners
129. Ark Capital Management
130. Ark Venture Partners
131. Artificial Life Ventures Inc.

132. Ascension Health Ventures, LLC
133. Ascent Venture Management Inc.
134. Asia Capital Management Limited
135. Aspen Ventures
136. Asset Management Company
137. Astellas Venture Capital LLC
138. Astrina Capital LLC
139. Ata Invest Inc.
140. Athena Technology Ventures
141. Atlantic Advisory Group
142. Atlantic Bank Mezzanine Fund
143. Atlas Venture
144. Auda Advisor Associates, LLC
145. August Capital Management, LLC
146. Aurora Capital Group
147. Aurora Funds
148. Austin Ventures
149. Autodesk Ventures
150. Av Tech Ventures
151. Avalon Invest
152. AVI Capital, L.P.
153. AXA Private Equity
154. Axiom Venture Partners, L.P.
155. B4 Ventures
156. BA Venture Partners
157. Baccharis Capital Inc.
158. Bachow & Associates Inc.
159. Bahr International Inc.
160. Bain Capital Inc.
161. Baird Capital Partners
162. Baker Capital Corp.
163. Ballast Point Venture Partners
164. Band of Angels
165. BankAmerica Corp.
166. Baring Americas Partners LLC
167. Baring Communications Equity
168. BaseCamp Ventures
169. Batterson Venture Partners, LLC
170. Battery Ventures
171. Bay BG Bavarian Venture Capital Corp.
172. Bay City Capital
173. Bay Partners
174. Bayview Capital Management, LLC
175. BCE Capital Inc.
176. BCM Technologies, Inc.
177. BD Ventures, LLC

178. Bedrock Capital Partners
179. Beecken, Petty & Co.
180. Behrman Capital, LP
181. Ben Franklin Technology Partners
182. Benchmark Capital
183. Benelux Venture Partners
184. Benvest Capital Inc.
185. Berenson Minella Ventures
186. Beringea Limited
187. Berkeley International Capital Corp.
188. Berkshire Partners, LLC
189. Bertelsmann Ventures
190. Berthel Fisher & Company
191. Bessemer Venture Partners
192. BEV Capital
193. BG Affiliates LLC
194. BG Media
195. Big Sky Partners
196. BioAdvance Ventures
197. BioVeda Capital
198. BioVentures Investors
199. Bison Capital
200. Black Enterprise/Greenwich Street Capital, LLC
201. Blacksmith Capital
202. Blue Chip Venture Company
203. Blue Point Capital Partners
204. Blue Rock Capital, LP
205. Blue Water Capital, LLC
206. Bluegrass Capital Corp.
207. Blueprint Ventures
208. BlueStar Ventures, L.P.
209. Bluestem Capital Partners
210. Bluestream Ventures
211. BNY Capital Partners, L.P.
212. Boston Capital Ventures
213. Boston Financial & Equity Corp.
214. Boston Millennia Partners
215. Boston University Community Technology Fund
216. Boston Ventures Management Inc.
217. Boulder Ventures Ltd.
218. Bradford Equities Management, LLC
219. Brait South Africa Limited
220. Branford Castle Inc.
221. Brantley Partners
222. Brazos Private Equity Partners, LLC

223. Brentwood Associates
224. Brentwood Private Equity
225. Brentwood Venture Capital
226. Brera Capital Partners, LLC
227. Bridge Technology Group, LLC
228. Broadband Venture Partners, LLC
229. Broadmark Capital Corp.
230. Brockway Moran & Partners Inc.
231. Brooks, Houghton & Co. Inc.
232. Brookwood Partners
233. Brown Brothers Harriman & Co.
234. Brown, Gibbons, Lang & Co., LP
235. Bruckmann, Rosser, Sherrill & Co., LLC
236. Bruml Capital Corp.
237. Bure Equity AB
238. Burrill & Company
239. Butler Capital Corp.
240. Butler Capital Partners France
241. C & C Vencap Corp.
242. C&T Access Ventures
243. Cahill, Warnock & Co., LLC
244. CAI Managers & Co., L.P.
245. Calgary Enterprises Inc.
246. California Technology Ventures
247. Calvert Social Venture Partners, L.P.
248. Cambridge Research BioVentures
249. CambridgeLight Partners
250. Camp Ventures
251. Canaan Partners
252. Candover Partners Ltd.
253. Capital Access Partners
254. Capital For Business, Inc.
255. Capital International Inc.
256. Capital Investments Inc.
257. Capital Partners
258. Capital Resource Partners
259. Capital Southwest Corporation
260. Capital Valley Ventures, LLC
261. Capital Z Partners Ltd.
262. CapitalSouth Partners, LLC
263. CapiTech
264. Capitol Health Partners, L.P.
265. Capitol Partners, LLC
266. CapMan Plc
267. Capricorn Holdings, LLC
268. Capricorn International Ltd.

Section
4

361. Continental Illinois Venture Corp.
362. Continental SBIC
363. Continental Venture Capital Ltd.
364. Convergence Partners
365. Convergent Capital
366. Convergent Capital, LLC
367. Copernicus Capital Partners
368. Cordova Ventures
369. Core Capital Partners
370. Cornerstone Capital Holdings
371. Cornerstone Equity Investors, LLC
372. Corning Innovation Ventures
373. Corpfin Capital
374. Cortec Group Inc.
375. Crabtree Partners
376. Crates Thompson Capital Inc.
377. Credit Suisse First Boston Private Equity
378. Crescendo Ventures
379. Crescent Capital Investments, Inc.
380. Crescent Private Capital, L.P
381. Crest Communications Holdings, LLC
382. Crosbie & Company Inc.
383. Cross Atlantic Capital Partners
384. Cross Atlantic Partners, Inc.
385. Cross Pacific Technology Partners, LLC
386. CrossBow Ventures
387. CrossBridge Venture Partners
388. Crosslink Capital, Inc.
389. Crosspoint Venture Partners
390. Crown Capital Corp.
391. Crystal Internet Venture Fund, L.P.
392. CSK Venture Capital Co. Ltd.
393. Custer Capital, Inc.
394. CVC Capital Partners
395. CVC Investment Managers Ltd.
396. CVC Opportunity Equity Partners
397. CW Group, Inc.
398. Cypress Advisors, L.P.
399. Daedalus Capital, LLC
400. Dain Rauscher Wessels
401. Dakota Capital Partners, LLC
402. Dansk Kapitalanlaeg Aktieselskab
403. Darby Overseas Investments Ltd.
404. Darr Global Holdings Inc.
405. Data Return Leadership
406. Davis, Tuttle Venture Partners

407. DBS Capital Investments Ltd.
408. De Novo Ventures
409. Defta Partners
410. Delphi Ventures
411. Delta Partners
412. Delta Ventures Ltd.
413. Demir Yatirim Menkul Degerler A.S.
414. Desai Capital Management Inc.
415. Desco Capital Partners
416. Deutsche Bank
417. Deutsche Bank SPM SpA
418. Deutsche Beteiligungs AG
419. Development Australia Fund
420. DFW Capital Partners
421. Diamond State Ventures, L.P.
422. DigitalVentures
423. Dilmun Investments
424. Dimeling, Schreiber & Park
425. Direct Capital Private Equity Ltd.
426. Discovery Capital Corp.
427. DN Partners, LLC
428. DNJ Capital Partners, LLC
429. Doll Capital Management Co., LLC
430. Dolphin Equity Partners
431. Domain Associates, LLC.
432. Dominion Ventures Inc.
433. Dorset Capital
434. Doughty Hanson & Co.
435. Doyle & Boissiere, LLC
436. Dragonfly Capital
437. DragonVenture
438. Draper Atlantic Management, LLC
439. Draper Fisher Jurvetson
440. Draper Fisher Jurvetson Gotham Ventures
441. Draper Richards, L.P.
442. Dresdner Kleinwort Capital
443. Dresner Capital Resources Inc.
444. Drysdale Enterprises
445. Dubin Clark & Co.
446. Duchossois TECnology Partners, LLC
447. Duff Ackerman & Goodrich, LLC
448. Duke Street Capital
449. DynaFund Ventures
450. Dynasty Capital
451. E*Capital Corporation
452. e.Lilly Ventures

453. E.M. Warburg, Pincus & Co., LLC
454. Early Stage Enterprises
455. Earlybird
456. East River Ventures
457. East River Ventures, L.P.
458. Eastman Chemical Company
459. Eastman Kodak Co.
460. EBRD Regional Venture Fund
461. ECentury Capital
462. ECI Ventures Ltd.
463. EDB Investments Pte Ltd.
464. Edelson Technology Partners
465. EDF Ventures
466. Edgewater Capital Partners, LP
467. Edison Venture Fund
468. eFund
469. Egan & Talbot Capital Ltd.
470. Egan Managed Capital
471. EGL Holdings
472. EIF Management Holdings, LLC
473. El Dorado Ventures
474. Elderstreet DrKC Ltd.
475. Emerald Capital Group
476. Emerging Markets Partnership
477. Emigrant Capital
478. Empire Ventures
479. Encompass Ventures Management Co.
480. Endeavor Capital Management
481. EnerTech Capital Partners
482. Eno River Capital
483. Enterprise Equity (NI) Ltd.
484. Enterprise Partners
485. Enterprise Ventures Ltd.
486. Envest Ventures
487. Eos Partners SBIC, L.P.
488. EPTAVenture S.r.l.
489. Equita Management GmbH
490. Equity Partners Pty Ltd.
491. Equity Ventures Ltd.
492. Equus Capital Corp.
493. EQY
494. Essex Woodlands Health Ventures
495. Ethos Private Equity
496. Euclid SR Partners
497. European Acquisition Capital Ltd. EAC Group
498. European Bank for Reconstruction and

Development
499. European Investment Fund
500. Euroventures Management AB
501. Evercore Partners Inc.
502. Excel Partners S.A.
503. Facilitator Fund
504. Fairfax Partners
505. Fairmont Capital, Inc
506. Fannie Mae
507. Far East National Bank
508. FCP Investors Inc.
509. Fenway Partners Inc.
510. FHL Capital Corporation
511. Fidelity Capital
512. Fidelity Ventures
513. Financial Technology Ventures
514. Finansa Ltd.
515. Fincor Finance
516. Finnfund
517. Firemark Group Inc.
518. Firemark Investments
519. FireStarter Partners, LLC
520. First Analysis
521. First Atlantic Capital Ltd.
522. First Capital Group Management Co.
523. First Isratech
524. First New England Capital, L.P.
525. First Reserve Corp.
526. FLAG Venture Partners
527. Flagship Ventures
528. Flatiron Partners
529. Fluke Venture Partners
530. Flynn Ventures
531. Focus Capital Group
532. Focus Ventures
533. Fogel International
534. Fond Rizikového Kapitálu
535. FondElec Group Inc.
536. Forest Hill Partners
537. Forge Medical Ventures Inc.
538. Forrest Binkley & Brown
539. Fortis Private Equity NV
540. Forward Ventures
541. Foster Management Co.
542. Foundation Capital
543. Founders Equity Inc.

544. Four Seasons Venture A/S
545. Fox Paine & Co., L.P.
546. Frazier & Company
547. Freddie Mac
548. Freeman Spogli & Co.
549. Fremont Group
550. Fremont Partners
551. Fremont Ventures
552. Friedman Billings Ramsey & Co.
553. Friedman Billings Ramsey Group, Inc.
554. Friedman Fleischer & Lowe, LLC
555. Frontenac Company
556. Frontier Capital, LLC
557. Fry Consultants Inc.
558. Frye-Louis Capital Management Inc.
559. Fulcrum Management Inc.
560. Fulcrum Venture Capital Corp.
561. Funk Ventures
562. Furman Selz Investments, LLC
563. G-51 Capital Management, LLC
564. G.A. Herrera & Co., LLC
565. Gabriel Venture Partners, L.P.
566. Gaebler Ventures
567. Galen Associates
568. Garage.com
569. Garnett & Helfrich
570. Gateway Associates, L.P.
571. Gazelle TechVentures
572. GBS Venture Partners Ltd.
573. Gefinor Ventures
574. Gemini Capital Ltd.
575. Gemini Investors, LLC
576. Gemini Israel Venture Funds Ltd.
577. General Alliance Corp. Ltd.
578. General Atlantic Partners, LLC
579. General Catalyst Partners
580. Generation Partners
581. GENES GmbH Venture Services
582. Genesis Partners
583. Geneva Merchant Banking Partners
584. Geneva Venture Partners
585. Genevest Consulting Group S.A.
586. Genstar Capital, L.P.
587. Geocapital Partners, LLC
588. George K. Baum Merchant Banc, LLC
589. Gerken Capital Associates
590. Gilbert Global Equity Capital, LLC
591. GIMV
592. Giza Venture Capital
593. Glencoe Capital, LLC
594. Glenthorne Capital Inc.
595. Glick Morganstern Capital Group
596. Global Partner Ventures
597. Globespan Capital Partners
598. GMG Capital Partners
599. Goldner Hawn Johnson & Morrison Inc.
600. Golub Associates Inc.
601. Grace Venture Partners
602. Graham Partners Investments, L.P.
603. Granite Ventures, LLC
604. Gray Ventures
605. Grayson & Associates Inc.
606. Great Hill Equity Partners
607. Gresham Rabo Management Ltd.
608. Greylock
609. Grotech Capital Group
610. Grove Street Advisors
611. Growth Capital Partners Inc.
612. GrowthWorks
613. GrowthWorks Capital Ltd.
614. GRP Partners
615. Gruppo Levey & Capell Inc.
616. Gryffindor Capital Partners LLC
617. Gryphon Ventures
618. GS Capital Partners Inc.
619. GSCP Inc.
620. GSM Industriebeteiligungen
621. GTCR Golder Rauner, LLC
622. GTI Capital
623. Guide Ventures
624. Gulfstar Group Inc.
625. H&Q Asia Pacific Ltd.
626. Haddington Ventures, LLC
627. Halder Holdings B.V.
628. Halpern, Denny & Co.
629. Hambrecht & Quist Capital Management
630. Hamilton Apex Tech Ventures LP
631. Hamilton Robinson LLC
632. Hampshire Equity partners
633. Hannover Finanz GmbH
634. Hanover Partners Inc.
635. HarbourVest Partners, LLC

636. Harlingwood Equity Partners
637. Harris & Harris Group, Inc
638. Harvest Partners Inc.
639. HDS Australia R&D Pty Ltd.
640. Healthcare Capital Partners Ltd.
641. HealthCare Ventures
642. Heartland Capital Partners, L.P.
643. Hellman & Friedman LLC
644. Heritage Partners Inc.
645. HG Capital, LLC
646. Hibernia Capital Corporation
647. Hibernia Capital Partners Ltd.
648. Hickory Venture Group
649. HIG Capital Management
650. High Street Capital
651. Highland Capital Partners
652. HMS Group
653. HMS Hawaii Management, LLC
654. HO2 Partners
655. Holland Venture III B.V.
656. Hook Partners
657. Horizon Holdings, LLC
658. Horizon Partners Ltd.
659. Horizonte Venture Management GmbH
660. Hotung Group
661. Housatonic Partners
662. Houston Partners
663. Howard Industries Inc.
664. HRJ Capital
665. HT Capital Advisors, LLC
666. Humana Venture Capital
667. Hummer Winblad Venture Partners
668. Hunt Private Equity Group
669. Huntington Holdings Inc.
670. Huntington Ventures
671. Hydro-Québec CapiTech
672. Ibero-American Investors Corp.
673. idealab! Capital Partners
674. IDG Ventures
675. IEG Venture Management
676. IGNITE Group
677. Ignition Partners
678. IMH Industrie Management Holding Treuhand GmbH
679. iMinds Ventures
680. Impact Venture Partners
681. Imperial Capital Group
682. Impulsora del Fondo Mexico S.A.de C.V.
683. Inclusive Ventures, LLC
684. Incyte Capital
685. Index Ventures
686. Indiana Business Modernization & Technology Co.
687. Indosuez Ventures
688. Industri Kapital Ltd.
689. Industrial Growth Partners
690. Industrifinans A/S
691. Industry Ventures
692. Infinity Capital
693. Inflection Point Ventures
694. Information Technology Ventures
695. InnoCal Venture Capital
696. Innovacom
697. Innovation Works, Inc.
698. Innovationsagentur GmbH
699. InnovationsKapital AB
700. InroadsCapital Partners, L.P.
701. Insight Venture Partners
702. Institutional Capital Corporation
703. Institutional Venture Partners
704. Instituto Aragones de Fomento
705. Integra BioHealth Inc.
706. Intel 64 Fund, LLC
707. Intel Capital
708. Intelligent Systems Corporation
709. Inteq Ltd.
710. Inter-American Investment Corp.
711. International Mergers & Acquisitions Inc.
712. Internet Capital Group
713. Internode
714. Interprime Capital
715. Intersouth Partners
716. InterWest Partners
717. invencor, inc.
718. Inventech Investment Co. Ltd.
719. INVESCO Private Capital
720. InveStar Capital, Inc
721. InvestCare Partners Limited Partnership
722. Investcorp
723. Investeringsmaatschappij voor Vlaanderen
724. InvestLinc Capital

Section 4

725. Investment Fund for Central and Eastern Europe
726. Investment Partners of America
727. Irwin Ventures, LLC
728. Isabella Capital LLC
729. IT-Partners N.V.
730. ITU Ventures, LLC
731. IVP-Institutional Venture Partners
732. J.H. Whitney & Co.
733. J.L. Albright Venture Partners
734. J.M. Galef & Co. Inc.
735. J.P. Morgan Partners
736. J.W. Childs Associates, L.P.
737. Jack Augsback Associates Inc.
738. JAFCO Ventures
739. Japan Asia Investment Co., Ltd
740. JatoTech Ventures
741. Jefferson Capital Partners Ltd.
742. JEGI Capital
743. Jerusalem Venture Partners
744. JK&B Capital
745. JMI Equity Fund
746. JMP Securities
747. Johnston Associates Inc.
748. JZ International
749. Kaiser Permanente Ventures
750. Kalkhoven, Pettit and Levin Ventures LLC
751. Kansas City Equity Partners
752. Kansas Technology Enterprise Corp.
753. Kansas Venture Capital, Inc.
754. Kasten Group, LLC
755. KB Partners, LLC
756. KBL Healthcare Ventures
757. Kennet Venture Partners Ltd.
758. Kenson Ventures LLC
759. Kestrel Venture Management
760. Key Venture Partners
761. Keystone Capital, Inc.
762. Kidd & Company, LLC
763. Kilmer Capital
764. Kinetic Ventures, LLC
765. Kisco Corporation
766. Kleiner Perkins Caufield & Byers
767. Klesch & Company Ltd.
768. Kline Hawkes & Co.
769. KLM Capital Group
770. Knight Ridder Ventures
771. Knightsbridge Advisers Inc.
772. Knoll Capital Management
773. Kodiak Venture Partners
774. Koor Corporate Venture Capital
775. KPS Special Situations Funds
776. Kula Fund Limited
777. Labrador Ventures
778. Lafayette Equity Fund, L.P.
779. Lancet Capital
780. Larkspur Capital Corporation
781. Latterell Venture Partners
782. LaunchCyte
783. Lawrence Financial Group
784. Lazard Technology Partners
785. Leapfrog Ventures
786. Leasing Technologies International Inc.
787. LeBonfante International Investors Group
788. Legg Mason Merchant Banking
789. Lehman Brothers Merchant Banking
790. Leo Capital Holdings, LLC
791. Leonard Green & Partners
792. Levensohn Capital Management, LLC
793. Levine Leichtman Capital Partners Inc.
794. Levy Trajman Management Investment Inc.
795. Lewis Hollingsworth, L.P.
796. LF International Inc.
797. LFE Capital
798. Liberty Bidco Investment Corp.
799. LibertyView Equity Partners
800. Life Science Ventures
801. Lighthouse Capital Partners
802. Lightspeed Venture Partners
803. Linsalata Capital Partners
804. Lion Selection Group Ltd.
805. Littlejohn & Co.
806. LJH Global Investments, LLC
807. Lloyds TSB Development Capital Ltd.
808. Lombard Investments Inc.
809. LongueVue Capital, LLC
810. Longworth Venture Partners, L.P.
811. Lovett Miller & Co., Incorporated
812. Lubar & Co
813. Lucent Venture Partners
814. Lynwood Capital Partners, Inc.
815. Lyric Capital Partners

816. M.D. Sass & Company Inc.
817. M/C Venture Partners
818. Mac Investment
819. Macadam Capital Partners
820. Macquarie Direct Investment Ltd.
821. Madison Dearborn Partners, LLC
822. Madrona Investment Group, LLC
823. Malmöhus Invest AB
824. Mandeville Partners
825. Manitou Ventures
826. Marathon Venture Capital Fund Ltd.
827. Marcus & Millichap Venture Partners
828. Markpoint Venture Partners
829. Marlborough Capital Advisors
830. Marquette Venture Partners
831. Marwit Capital Corp.
832. Maryland Technology Development Corporation
833. Mason Wells Biomedical Fund
834. Massachusetts Technology Development Corp.
835. Maton Venture
836. Matrix Capital Markets Group Inc.
837. Matrix Partners
838. MAVA Investment Ltd.
839. Maveron, LLC
840. Max Capital Partners, LLC
841. Mayfield Fund
842. McCown, De Leeuw & Co. Inc.
843. McKenna Gale Capital Inc.
844. MCM Capital Partners, L.P.
845. MDS Capital Corp.
846. MDT Advisers, a division of Harris Bretall Sullivan
847. Medallion Capital Inc.
848. Medica Venture Partners
849. Medical Imaging Innovation & Investments, L.P.
850. Mediphase Venture Partners
851. MedVenture Associates
852. Mellon Ventures
853. Memhard Investment Bankers Inc.
854. Menlo Ventures
855. Mercapital Servicios Financieros S.L.
856. Meridian Venture Partners
857. Merit Energy Co.

858. MeriTech Capital Partners
859. Meriturn Partners
860. Merlin Biosciences Ltd.
861. Merrill Lynch Private Equity Partners
862. Metapoint Partners
863. Mid-Atlantic Venture Funds
864. Middlefield Capital Fund
865. MidMark Associates Inc.
866. Midwest Mezzanine Funds
867. Milestone Partners
868. Milestone Venture Partners
869. Mille Capital Corp.
870. Miller Capital Corp.
871. Minnesota Investment Network Corporation
872. Mission Ventures
873. Mitsui & Co. Venture Partners, Inc.
874. MJ Whitman Management, LLC
875. MM Venture Partners
876. Mobius Venture Capital
877. Mohr, Davidow Ventures
878. Momentum Funds Management Pty Ltd.
879. Monitor Clipper Partners Inc.
880. Montreux Equity Partners
881. Monument Advisors, Inc
882. Monument Capital Partners
883. Monumental Venture Partners
884. Morgenthaler
885. Motorola Ventures
886. Mountaineer Capital LP
887. MPM Capital
888. MTI Partners Ltd.
889. N.C. Technological Development Authority Inc.
890. Nanyang Management Pty Ltd.
891. Nassau Capital, LLC
892. National City Equity Partners
893. Nazem & Company
894. NCIC CapitalFund
895. NeoCarta Ventures
896. NeSBIC Groep B.V.
897. NeuroVentures Capital
898. Nevada Ventures, L.P.
899. New Century Holdings Inc.
900. New England Business Exchange
901. New England Partners

Section 4

902. New Enterprise Associates
903. New Horizons Venture Capital
904. New Millennium Partners, L.P.
905. New Vantage Group
906. New World Ventures
907. New York Community Investment Company (NYCIC)
908. Newbury Ventures
909. Newbury, Piret & Co.
910. NewCap Partners Inc.
911. Newlight Associates, L.P.
912. Newport Capital
913. Newton Technology Partners
914. NewVista Capital, LLC
915. Next Century Partners
916. Next Generation Fund
917. NextGen Partners
918. NextPoint Partners, L.P.
919. Nexus Group, LLC
920. NGEN Partners
921. NIF Ventures USA, Inc.
922. NJTC Venture Fund
923. Noble Financial Group
924. Nokia Venture Partners, L.P.
925. Nordic Wireless AB
926. Noro–Moseley Partners
927. North American Funds
928. North Atlantic Capital Corp.
929. North Bridge Venture Partners
930. North Castle Partners
931. North Coast Technology Investors, L.P.
932. North Hill Ventures, L.P.
933. NorthEast Ventures
934. Northern Venture Managers Ltd.
935. Northwood Ventures
936. Norwest Equity Partners
937. Norwest Venture Partners
938. Novak Biddle Venture Partners
939. Novus Ventures, L.P.
940. Nth Power
941. NYBDC Capital Corp.
942. Oak Investment Partners
943. Oaktree Capital Management, LLC
944. Odeon Capital Partners
945. OEM Capital Corp.
946. Olympic Venture Partners

947. Olympus Advisory Partners
948. ONSET Ventures
949. Opportunity Capital Partners
950. Orchid Asia Holdings
951. Oresa Ventures
952. Origin Partners
953. ORIX Venture Finance
954. Osprey Ventures, L.P.
955. Outlook™ Ventures
956. Ovation Capital Partners, L.P.
957. OVP Venture Partners
958. Oxford Bioscience Partners
959. PA Early Stage
960. Pacific Century Group Ventures
961. Pacific Corporate Group Inc.
962. Pacific Horizon Ventures
963. Pacific Mezzanine Fund, L.P.
964. Pacific Venture Group
965. Pacifica Fund
966. Palisade Capital Management, LLC
967. Palladium Equity Partners, LLC
968. Palo Alto Venture Partners
969. Palomar Ventures
970. Pantheon Ventures Ltd.
971. Parallax Capital Partners, LLC
972. Partech International
973. Parthenon Capital Inc.
974. Pecks Management Partners Ltd.
975. Pegasus Capital
976. Pencarrow Private Equity
977. Peninsula Capital Partners
978. Pequot Ventures
979. Petra Capital Partners, LLC
980. Pfingsten Partners, LLC
981. Philadelphia Commercial Development Corp.
982. Phillips-Smith-Machens Venture Partners
983. Phoenix Growth Capital Corp.
984. Phoenix Partners
985. PICA Corporation
986. Pierce Financial Corp.
987. Pinecreek Capital
988. Pinetree Capital Ltd
989. Pinnacle Equity Capital
990. Piper Jaffray Ventures
991. Pitango Venture Capital

992. Plantagenet Capital Management, LLC
993. PNC Equity Management Corp.
994. POD Holding, Inc.
995. Polaris Venture Partners
996. PolyTechnos Venture-Partners GmbH
997. Portage Venture Partners, LLC
998. Posco Bioventures Inc
999. Pouschine Cook Capital Management, LLC
1000. Power Project Financing
1001. PPM Stimulans
1002. Prairie Capital
1003. Prelude Venutres Limited
1004. PRIMEDIA Ventures
1005. Primus Venture Partners, Inc.
1006. Prism Capital
1007. Prism Venture Partners
1008. Private Equity Investors Inc.
1009. Priveq Capital Funds
1010. Procuritas Partners KB
1011. Progress Investment Management Co.
1012. Prolog Ventures
1013. Prometheus Partners, L.P.
1014. Propel Partners
1015. ProQuest Investments
1016. Prospect Partners, LLC
1017. Prospect Street Ventures
1018. Prospect Venture Partners
1019. Providence Equity Partners Inc.
1020. Psilos Group Managers, LLC
1021. Putnam Lovell Capital Partners, Inc.
1022. QTV Capital
1023. Quad-C Management, Inc.
1024. Quaestus Management Inc.
1025. Quester Capital Management Ltd.
1026. QuestMark Partners
1027. Questor Management Co.
1028. Radius Ventures
1029. RAF Ventures
1030. Ralph Wilson Equity Fund, LLC
1031. Rand Capital Corporation
1032. Raymond James Capital Inc.
1033. RayvonVC
1034. RBC Technology Ventures Inc.
1035. Red Rock Ventures
1036. Redleaf Venture Management, LLC

1037. Redmont Venture Partners, Inc.
1038. Redpoint Ventures
1039. Rein Capital, LLC
1040. Relational Investors, LLC
1041. Research Triangle Ventures
1042. Retail & Restaurant Growth Capital, L.P.
1043. RFE Investment Partners
1044. Rho Ventures
1045. Rice Sangalis Toole & Wilson
1046. Richards Industries Inc.
1047. Richards Investment Capital
1048. Richland Ventures
1049. Ridge Ventures
1050. Ridgewood Capital
1051. Riggs Capital Partners
1052. Riordan, Lewis & Haden
1053. Riordan, Lewis & Haden
1054. River Capital Equity Partners
1055. River Cities Capital Fund, L.P.
1056. Riverside Company
1057. Riverside Partners
1058. RiverVest Venture Partners
1059. Robin Hood Ventures
1060. Rock Maple Ventures, L.P.
1061. Rocket Ventures
1062. Rockmont Capital Partners, Ltd.
1063. Rocky Mountain Capital Partners, LLP
1064. Roser Ventures, LLC
1065. Rosewood Capital
1066. Rosewood Stone Group Inc
1067. Rothschild Quantico Capital
1068. RoundTable Healthcare Partners
1069. RoyNat Inc.
1070. RP&C International Inc.
1071. RRE Ventures
1072. Ruppert Ventures
1073. Rustic Canyon Partners
1074. RWI Group, L.P.
1075. Ryan Partners
1076. Salix Ventures
1077. Samsung Venture Investment Corp.
1078. Sanderling
1079. Sandler Capital Management
1080. Santa Barbara Technology Incubator
1081. Saratoga Partners
1082. Saugatuck Capital Company

Section 4

1083. SBV Venture Partners
1084. Schneider Electric
1085. Schroder Investment Management
1086. Scottish Equity Partners
1087. SCP Private Equity Partners
1088. Scripps Ventures
1089. Seaflower Ventures
1090. SeaPoint Ventures
1091. Seaport Capital
1092. Seed Capital Company Ltd.
1093. Seidler Equity Partners, LP
1094. Selby Venture Partners
1095. SembCorp Industries Ltd
1096. Sentinel Capital Partners
1097. Sequel Venture Partners
1098. Sequoia Capital
1099. Sevin Rosen Funds
1100. SG Capital Partners, LLC
1101. Shalom Equity Fund
1102. Shawmut Capital Partners
1103. Shelter Capital Partners
1104. Shepard Ventures
1105. Sherpa Partners
1106. Sherpalo
1107. Shipley Raidy Capital Partners
1108. Shrem, Fudim, Kelner & Co. Ltd.
1109. SI Ventures
1110. Siemens Corp.
1111. Siemens Venture Capital Inc.
1112. Sienna Ventures
1113. Sierra Ventures
1114. Sigma Partners
1115. Signal Equity Partners, L.P.
1116. Signal Lake
1117. Signature Capital, LLC
1118. Silicom Ventures
1119. Silicon Alley Venture Partners
1120. Silicon Valley BancVentures
1121. Silver Brands Inc.
1122. Silver Lake Partners, L.P.
1123. Siparex Ingenerie et Finance
1124. SJF Ventures
1125. Skandia Investment
1126. Skyline Ventures
1127. Skymoon Ventures
1128. Skypoint Capital Corporation

1129. SmartForest Ventures
1130. Smedvig Capital
1131. Soc. de Promocion y Desarrollo Talde S.A.
1132. Sofinnova Ventures, Inc.
1133. Softbank Venture Capital
1134. Solera Capital, LLC
1135. Solstice Capital
1136. Sonera Corporation
1137. Sonostar Ventures LLC
1138. Sony Strategic Venture Investment
1139. Sorrento Ventures
1140. Source Capital Corp.
1141. South Atlantic Venture Funds
1142. Southeast Interactive Technology Funds
1143. Southeastern Technology Fund
1144. Southern Cross Group
1145. Space Center Ventures, Inc.
1146. SpaceVest
1147. Spectrum Equity Investors
1148. Spencer Trask Holdings Inc.
1149. Split Rock Partners
1150. Spray Venture Partners
1151. Spring Capital Partners, L.P.
1152. Sprout Group
1153. Square One Ventures
1154. SR One
1155. SSM Ventures
1156. Staenberg Venture Partners
1157. Stanford Investment Group Inc.
1158. Star Ventures Management
1159. Start-up Australia Pty Ltd.
1160. STARTech
1161. StarVest Management Co.
1164. Starwood Capital Group, LLC
1163. Steamboat Ventures, LLC
1164. Steps Ventures
1165. Sterling Investment Partners
1166. Sterling Partners
1167. Sterling/Carl Marks Capital
1168. Still River Fund
1169. Stone Canyon Venture Partners
1170. Stonehenge Capital Corp.
1171. Stonington Partners Inc.
1172. Storm Ventures
1173. Strategic Advisory Group Inc.
1174. Stratus Investimentos Ltda.

1175. Sucsy, Fischer & Company
1176. Summer Street Capital Partners
1177. Summit Partners
1178. Sumnet Communications
1179. Sutter Hill Ventures
1180. SV Investment Partners
1181. SV Life Sciences
1182. Svoboda, Collins LLC
1183. Swander Pace Capital
1184. Sweetwater Partners
1185. Synopsys Inc.
1186. T-Venture of America, Inc.
1187. T. Rowe Price Threshold Fund Inc.
1188. TA Associates, Inc.
1189. Tall Oaks Capital
1190. Tamar Venture Capital Ltd.
1191. Tamir Fishman & Co.
1192. Tangent Fund Management, LLC
1193. TAT Capital Partners Ltd.
1194. TCW/Crescent Mezzanine, LLC
1195. TD Capital Communications Partners
1196. TDH
1197. Techfarm Ventures
1198. Technocap Inc.
1199. Technology Crossover Ventures
1200. Technology Funding
1201. Technology Partners
1202. Technology Venture Partners Pty Ltd.
1203. TechnoStart GmbH
1204. Techstock Inc
1205. Techxas Ventures
1206. Telecom Partners, LLC
1207. Telecommunications Development Fund
1208. TeleSoft Partners
1209. Telos Venture Partners
1210. Tenex Greenhouse Ventures, LLC
1211. Teuza Management & Development Ltd.
1212. Texas Growth Fund
1213. Texas Pacific Group
1214. Thales Corporate Ventures
1215. Thayer Capital Partners
1216. The Angels' Forum
1217. The Audax Group
1218. The Aurora Funds, Inc.
1219. The Bayer Group
1220. The Blackstone Group

1221. The Boeing Company
1222. The Cambria Group
1223. The Capital Network Inc.
1224. The Catalyst Group
1225. The Centennial Funds
1226. The Compass Group International, LLC
1227. The Courtney Group, Inc.
1228. The Crossroads Group
1229. The Dow Chemical Company
1230. The Edgewater Funds
1231. The Exxel Group S.A.
1232. The Grosvenor Funds
1233. The Halifax Group
1234. The Hopkins Capital Group
1235. The McLean Group, LLC
1236. The North Dakota Development Fund
1237. The Oxford Technology VCTs
1238. The Parkside Group
1239. The Pembroke Group
1240. The Shelley Group
1241. The Sterling Group Inc.
1242. The Tech Coast Angels
1243. The Venture Capital Fund of New England
1244. The Vertical Group
1245. Thomas Cressey Equity Partners
1246. Thomas Weisel Partners, LLC
1247. Thompson Clive & Partners Ltd.
1248. Three Arch Partners
1249. Three Cities Research Inc.
1250. TI Ventures
1251. Tianguis Ltd.
1252. Ticonderoga Capital
1253. Timberline Venture Partners
1254. Timeline Ventures
1255. TL Ventures
1256. Tondu Corporation
1257. Top Technology Ventures Ltd.
1258. Topspin Partners, L.P.
1259. Total Technology Ventures, LLC
1260. Toucan Capital Corp.
1261. Trans Cosmos USA
1262. Transition Partners Ltd.
1263. Trautman Wasserman and Company Ltd.
1264. Trellis Partners
1265. Trenwith Securities, LLC
1266. TRF Urban Growth Partners

Section 4

1267. Tri-State Investment Group
1268. Tribune Ventures
1269. TriCapital Corporation
1270. Trident Capital
1271. Trillium Capital Partners
1272. Trinity Ventures
1273. Triton Venture Partners, L.P.
1274. Trivest Inc.
1275. TriWest Capital Partners
1276. TSG Equity Partners, LLC
1277. Tuckerman Capital
1278. Tudor Ventures
1279. Tuerk & Associates
1280. Tullis-Dickerson & Co., Inc.
1281. Tully & Holland, Inc
1282. Turkven Private Equity
1283. TVM Techno Venture Management
1284. U.S. Trust Private Equity
1285. U.S. Venture Partners
1286. UBS Capital
1287. UNC Partners Inc.
1288. Unison Capital Inc.
1289. UOB Venture Management Pte Ltd.
1290. Updata Capital Inc.
1291. Updata Venture Partners
1292. UPS Strategic Enterprise Fund
1293. Utah Ventures
1294. UV Partners
1295. Valletta Investment Bank Ltd.
1296. Valley Ventures, L.P.
1297. Value Added Capital, LLC
1298. Van Reekum Ventures Pty Ltd.
1299. Vanguard Ventures
1300. Vantage Partners, LLC
1301. VantagePoint Venture Partners
1302. Vaxa Capital Partners, L.P.
1303. VC Advantage Funds
1304. VCM Venture Capital Management
1305. Veber Partners, LLC
1306. Vector Capital
1307. Vencon Management Inc.
1308. Venglobal Capital
1309. Venrock Associates
1310. Ventana Growth Funds
1311. Ventech Inc.
1312. Venture Associates Ltd.

1313. Venture Capital Fund of America
1314. Venture Capital Fund of New England
1315. Venture Capital Partners Pty Ltd.
1316. Venture Corporation of Australia Pty Ltd.
1317. Venture Investment Management Company, LLC
1318. Venture Investors
1319. Venture Investors LLC
1320. Venture TDF China LLC
1321. Ventures Medical Associates
1322. Ventures West Management Inc.
1323. Venturion Capital LLC
1324. Veritas Capital Inc.
1325. Veritas Venture Capital Management Ltd.
1326. Versant Ventures
1327. Vertex Management II Pte Ltd.
1328. Vertex Management III Ltd.
1329. Vertex Management Inc.
1330. Vertical Systems Group, Inc.
1331. Vesbridge Partners
1332. Vestar Capital Partners
1333. Vestor Partners, L.P.
1334. Village Ventures
1335. Virginia Capital
1336. Visa International
1337. Vision Capital
1338. Vivo Ventures (formerly Bio Asia)
1339. Vortex Partners, L.P.
1340. Voyager Capital
1341. VS&A Communications Partners, L.P.
1342. VSP Capital
1343. vSpring Capital
1344. W.I. Harper Group
1345. Wafra Partners
1346. Wakefield Group
1347. Walden Capital Partners, L.P.
1348. Walden Group of Venture Capital Funds
1349. Walden International
1350. Walden International Investment Group (S) Pte Ltd.
1351. Wales Fund Managers Ltd.
1352. Wall Street Venture Capital
1353. Wand Partners Inc.
1354. Warburg Pincus
1355. Wasatch Venture Fund
1356. Washington Capital Ventures

1357. Wasserstein Ventures
1358. Watermill Ventures
1359. Waterside Capital
1360. Waud Capital Partners, LLC
1361. Waypoint Ventures
1362. Weiss, Peck & Greer
1363. Wellspring Capital Management, LLC
1364. West Midlands Enterprise Ltd.
1365. WestBridge Ventures
1366. Western America Capital
1367. Western NIS Enterprise Fund
1368. Western States Investment Corp.
1369. Western Technology Investment
1370. Weston Presidio
1371. Weston Presidio Capital
1372. WestSphere Equity Investors, L.P.
1373. Wheatley Partners
1374. White Pines Ventures, LLC
1375. Wicks Group of Companies, LLC
1376. William Blair Mezzanine Capital Partners
1377. Willis Stein & Partners
1378. Willowridge Incorporated
1379. Wind Point Partners
1380. Windamere Venture Partners, LLC
1381. Windjammer Capital Investors, LLC
1382. Windward Holdings
1383. Windward Ventures

1384. Winfield Capital Corp.
1385. Wingate Partners
1386. Winston Partners Group, LLC
1387. Wolf Ventures
1388. Women's Growth Capital
1389. Woodbridge Group Inc.
1390. Woodside Fund
1391. World Equity Group, Inc.
1392. World Investments Inc.
1393. WorldView Technology Partners
1394. WRF Capital
1395. XMLFund
1396. Y.L.R. Capital Markets Ltd.
1397. YAS Broadband Ventures
1398. Yasuda Enterprise Development Co., Ltd.
1399. Yellowstone Capital Inc.
1400. Yozma Management & Investments
1401. Zephyr Internet Partners
1402. Zero Stage Capital Co.
1403. ZS Fund, L.P

Source: Venture Capital Resource Directory, www.vfinance.com/ent/ent_3.asp?ToolPage=ven caentire.asp. vFinance updates its Venture Capital Resource Directory regularly and its web site (www.vfinance.com) features a Search for Capital.

Section 4

Top Venture Capital Firms for Early-Stage Companies

Firm and Number of Deals in 2004

15 Maryland Technology Development Corporation
Columbia, MD

12 Draper Fisher Jurvetson
Menlo Park, CA

12 Ignition Partners
Bellevue, WA

11 Austin Ventures
Austin, TX

9 Mobius Venture Capital
Palo Alto, CA

9 Versant Ventures
Menlo Park, CA

8 ARCH Venture Partners
Chicago, IL

8 Enterprise Partners Venture Capital
La Jolla, CA

8 MPM Capital
Boston, MA

8 Tech Coast Angels
Laguna Hills, CA

8 Venrock Associates
New York, NY

7 Angels Forum & the Halo Fund
Los Altos, CA

7 Band of Angels
Menlo Park, CA

7 **Intel Capital**
Santa Clara, CA

7 **Mayfield Fund**
Menlo Park, CA

7 **Noro Moseley Partners**
Atlanta, GA

7 **Rho Ventures**
York City, NY

7 **Village Ventures**
Williamstown, MA

6 **Altira Group**
Denver, CO

6 **Benchmark Capital**
Menlo Park, CA

6 **Domain Associates**
Princeton, NJ

6 **General Catalyst Partners**
Cambridge, MA

6 **Highland Capital Partners**
Lexington, MA

6 **Insight Venture Partners**
New York, NY

6 **New Enterprise Associates**
Baltimore, MD

6 **Novak Biddle Venture Partners**
Bethesda, MD

6 **Redpoint Ventures**
Menlo Park, CA

6 **Sequoia Capital**
Menlo Park, CA

6 **Sevin Rosen Funds**
Dallas, TX

6 **U.S. Venture Partners**
Menlo Park, CA

5 **Alloy Ventures**
Palo Alto, CA

5 **Appian Ventures**
Denver, CO

5 **Bay Partners**
Cupertino, CA

5 **Edison Venture Fund**
Lawrenceville, NJ

5 **Flagship Ventures**
Cambridge, MA

5 **Frazier Healthcare and Technology Ventures**
Seattle, WA

5 **Hummer Winblad Venture Partners**
San Francisco, CA

5 **InterWest Partners**
Menlo Park, CA

5 **Kleiner Perkins Caufield & Byers**
Menlo Park, CA

5 **North Bridge Venture Partners**
Waltham, MA

5 **Oak Investment Partners**
Westport, CT

5 **Oxford Bioscience Partners**
Boston, MA

5 **Polaris Venture Partners**
Waltham, MA

5 **Three Arch Partners**
Portola Valley, CA

4 **Accel Partners**
Palo Alto, CA

4 **Allegis Capital**
Palo Alto, CA

4 **Alta Partners**
San Francisco, CA

4 **ArrowPath Venture Capital**
Redwood City, CA

4 **August Capital Management**
Menlo Park, CA

4 **Aurora Funds**
Durham, NC

4 **Bessemer Venture Partners**
Larchmont, NY

4 **Canaan Partners**
Rowayton, CT

4 **Draper Atlantic Venture Fund**
Reston, VA

4 Greylock
Waltham, MA

4 Innovation Works
Pittsburgh, PA

4 Intersouth Partners
Durham, NC

4 Kline Hawkes & Co.
Brentwood, CA

4 Lightspeed Venture Partners
Menlo Park, CA

4 Maryland Dept. of Business & Economic
Development
Baltimore, MD

4 Menlo Ventures
Menlo Park, CA

4 Mohr Davidow Ventures
Menlo Park, CA

4 Morgenthaler Ventures
Menlo Park, CA

4 New Jersey Technology Council
Mount Laurel, NJ

4 OVP Venture Partners
Kirkland, WA

4 Palomar Ventures
Santa Monica, CA

4 Partech International
San Francisco, CA

4 Red River Ventures
Addison, TX

4 Storm Ventures
Menlo Park, CA

4 Sutter Hill Ventures
Palo Alto, CA

4 Techno Venture Management
Boston, MA

4 The Venture Capital Fund of New England
Wellesley Hills, MA

4 Walden International
San Francisco, CA

3 Advanced Technology Ventures
Waltham, MA

3 Advent International PLC
Boston, MA

3 Alexandria Real Estate Equities
Pasadena, CA

3 Ampersand Ventures
Wellesley, MA

3 Atlas Venture
Waltham, MA

3 Battery Ventures
Wellesley, MA

3 Buerk Dale Victor
Seattle, WA

3 Burrill & Company
San Francisco, CA

3 C&B Capital
Atlanta, GA

3 CMEA Ventures
San Francisco, CA

3 Care Capital
Princeton, NJ

3 Charles River Ventures
Waltham, MA

3 Citizens Capital
Boston, MA

3 Clayton Associates
Franklin, TN

3 Columbia Capital
Alexandria, VA

3 Council Ventures
Nashville, TN

3 Crosslink Capital
Francisco, CA

3 De Novo Ventures
Menlo Park, CA

3 Doll Capital Management
Menlo Park, CA

3 Draper Fisher Jurvetson Gotham Venture
Partners
New York, NY

3 Globespan Capital Partners
Boston, MA

3 Granite Ventures
San Francisco, CA

3 Grayhawk Venture Partners
Phoenix, AZ

3 HLM Venture Partners
Boston, MA

3 JK&B Capital
Chicago, IL

3 Kleiner Perkins Caufield & Byers
Menlo Park, CA

3 Longworth Venture Partners
Waltham, MA

3 Menlo Ventures
Menlo Park, CA

3 Mid-Atlantic Venture Funds
Bethlehem, PA

3 New England Partners
Boston, MA

3 Norwest Venture Partners
Palo Alto, CA

3 Oak Investment Partners
Westport, CT

3 Pennsylvania Early Stage Partners
Wayne, PA

3 Pequot Capital Management
Westport, CT

3 Prism Venture Partners
Westwood, MA

3 Prospect Venture Partners
Palo Alto, CA

3 Sanders Morris Harris
Houston, TX

3 Sequoia Capital
Menlo Park, CA

3 Sprout Group
New York, NY

3 Stonehenge Capital Company
Baton Rouge, LA

3 Thomas, McNerney & Partners
Minneapolis, MN

3 Trident Capital
Palo Alto, CA

3 Valley Ventures
Tempe, AZ

3 Venture Strategy Partners
San Francisco, CA

3 Virginia's Center for Innovative Technology
Herndon, VA

3 Voyager Capital
Seattle, WA

3 WI Harper Group
San Francisco, CA

3 Woodside Fund
Redwood City, CA

3 vSpring Capital
Salt Lake City, UT

2 ABS Capital Partners
Baltimore, MD

2 Apax Partners
New York, NY

2 Apex Venture Partners
Chicago, IL

2 Austin Ventures
Austin, TX

2 Benchmark Capital
Menlo Park, CA

2 Blue Chip Venture Company
Cincinnati, OH

2 Carmel Ventures
Herzeliya, Israel

2 ComVentures
Palo Alto, CA

2 Core Capital Partners
Washington, DC

2 Delta Capital Management
Cordova, TN

2 El Dorado Ventures
Menlo Park, CA

2 Frontier Capital
Charlotte, NC

2 **Greylock**
Waltham, MA

2 **Highland Capital Partners**
Lexington, MA

2 **Hispania Capital Partners**
Chicago, IL

2 **Ignition Partners**
Bellevue, WA

2 **MedVenture Associates**
Emeryville, CA

2 **Minnesota Investment Network Corp.**
Saint Paul, MN

2 **Miramar Venture Partners**
Corona del Mar, CA

2 **New Enterprise Associates**
Baltimore, MD

2 **Northwood Ventures**
Syosset, NY

2 **Norwest Venture Partners**
Palo Alto, CA

2 **Pacesetter Capital Group**
Richardson, TX

2 **Primus Venture Partners**
Cleveland, OH

2 **Rho Ventures**
New York, NY

2 **Salix Ventures**
Nashville, TN

2 **Sigma Partners**
Menlo Park, CA

2 **Sorenson Capital Partners**
Sandy, UT

2 **Spectrum Equity Investors**
Menlo Park, CA

2 **Steamboat Ventures**
Burbank, CA

2 **Stonehenge Capital Company**
Baton Rouge, LA

2 **Tech Coast Angels**
Laguna Hills, CA

2 **Technology Crossover Ventures**
Palo Alto, CA

2 **The Carlyle Group**
Washington, DC

2 **U.S. Venture Partners**
Menlo Park, CA

2 **Updata Venture Partners**
Reston, VA

2 **VantagePoint Venture Partners**
San Bruno, CA

2 **Wasatch Venture Fund**
Salt Lake City, UT

2 **Westbury Partners**
Westbury, NY

Source: "Top 100 Venture Capital Firms,"
www.entrepreneur.com/listings/vc100/deals.

Top Venture Capital Firms for Late-Stage Companies

Firm and Number of Deals in 2004

6 **Insight Venture Partners**
New York, NY

5 **Edison Venture Fund**
Lawrenceville, NJ

5 **Kleiner Perkins Caufield & Byers**
Menlo Park, CA

5 **Oak Investment Partners**
Westport, CT

4 **Kline Hawkes & Co.**
Brentwood, CA

3 **Advent International PLC**
Boston, MA

3 **Ampersand Ventures**
Wellesley, MA

3 **Battery Ventures**
Wellesley, MA

3 **Citizens Capital**
Boston, MA

3 **Clayton Associates**
Franklin, TN

3 **Columbia Capital**

Alexandria, VA

3 Menlo Ventures
Menlo Park, CA

3 Sequoia Capital
Menlo Park, CA

2 ABS Capital Partners
Baltimore, MD

2 Apax Partners
New York, NY

2 Apex Venture Partners
Chicago, IL

2 Austin Ventures
Austin, TX

2 Benchmark Capital
Menlo Park, CA

2 Blue Chip Venture Company
Cincinnati, OH

2 Carmel Ventures
Herzeliya, Israel

2 ComVentures
Palo Alto, CA

2 Core Capital Partners
Washington, DC

2 Delta Capital Management
Cordova, TN

2 El Dorado Ventures
Menlo Park, CA

2 Frontier Capital
Charlotte, NC

2 Highland Capital Partners
Lexington, MA

2 Hispania Capital Partners
Chicago, IL

2 Ignition Partners
Bellevue, WA

2 MedVenture Associates
Emeryville, CA

2 Minnesota Investment Network Corp.
Saint Paul, MN

2 Miramar Venture Partners
Corona del Mar, CA

2 New Enterprise Associates

Baltimore, MD

2 Northwood Ventures
Syosset, NY

2 Norwest Venture Partners
Palo Alto, CA

2 Pacesetter Capital Group
Richardson, TX

2 Primus Venture Partners
Cleveland, OH

2 Rho Ventures
New York, NY

2 Salix Ventures
Nashville, TN

2 Sigma Partners
Menlo Park, CA

2 Sorenson Capital Partners
Sandy, UT

2 Spectrum Equity Investors
Menlo Park, CA

2 Steamboat Ventures
Burbank, CA

2 Stonehenge Capital Company
Baton Rouge, LA

2 Tech Coast Angels
Laguna Hills, CA

2 Technology Crossover Ventures
Palo Alto, CA

2 The Carlyle Group
Washington, DC

2 U.S. Venture Partners
Menlo Park, CA

2 Updata Venture Partners
Reston, VA

2 VantagePoint Venture Partners
San Bruno, CA

2 Wasatch Venture Fund
Salt Lake City, UT

2 Westbury Partners
Westbury, NY

Source: "Top 100 Venture Capital Firms,"
www.entrepreneur.com/listings/vc100/deals-
expansion/0,7327,,00.html.

Questions to Test Your Eligibility for Venture Capital

Every entrepreneur dreams about finding venture capital. But most don't ever get it. Do you have a shot? Answer the following questions and find out:

- Are you a technology company?
- Is your business capable of being a market leader?
- Do you have a clear distribution channel?
- Do much will it take to build your business?
- Are your margins "fat" enough?
- How fast can you grow?

Most venture capital firms:

- Invest in high-tech firms.
- Rarely finance a company that is trying to take on a market leader (but they do make exceptions for businesses capable of producing breakthrough technologies).

Give yourself a big plus if:

- You've got a clear and easy way to sell your product or service.
- If your business can be built for less than $10 million.
- If your business will generate margins of 50 percent.
- If your business can grow to $25 million in five years.

Doesn't sound like you? There are more places than ever for entrepreneurs to seek funding.

Source: Rieva Lesonsky, *365 Tips to Boost Your Entrepreneurial IQ.*

SCORE's Five Tips on Finding Angel Investors and Venture Capitalists

1. Do some research. Identify the most likely candidates by asking your accountant, banker, and lawyer.
2. Keep an open mind—potential investors may be anywhere. According to *Success* magazine, one entrepreneur found an angel investor among the motorcyclists he rides with on weekends.
3. Surf the web. Good places to start are www.nvca.org, the web site of the National Venture Capital Association, and www.mavf.com, the site of Mid-Atlantic Venture Funds, a venture capital firm in Bethlehem, PA.

4. Make presentations at venture capital forums or fairs. Your local university business school or Small Business Administration office should have information on such events.

5. Check your library or the web for such references as *Pratt's Guide to Venture Capital Sources* and *The Directory of Buyout Financing Sources*, both published by Thomson Financial Securities Data at www.tfsd.com.

Source: SCORE, www.score.org/business_tips.html.

Chapter 25

Different Sources of Funding

Finding Money to Fund Your Venture

It is important to consider all of your options before making a decision. Here are some places to start looking for capital.

Personal Savings: This is the primary source of funding for new business owners.

Friends and Relatives: Through this option, money is often listed interest-free or at a low interest rate, which can be very helpful when starting your business.

Banks and Credit Unions: The most common of funding, banks and credit unions, will provide a loan if you can show that your business proposal is sound.

Angel Investors and Venture Capital Firms: These individuals and firms help expanding companies grow in exchange for equity or partial ownership.

Source: Small Business Administration, "Finance Basics."

U.S. Federal Grant Web Sites

- **Federal Register:** www.gpoaccess.gov/fr/index.html
- **Developing a Federal Grant Proposal:** www.cfda.gov/public/cat-writing.htm
- **Nonprofit Gateway for Federal Departments and Agencies for Grants:** www.nonprofit.gov or firstgov.gov/Business/Nonprofit.shtml
- **Catalogue of Federal Domestic Assistance:** www.cfda.gov
- **FirstGov:** www.FirstGov.gov
- **FedGrants:** www.fedgrants.gov (Click on "Applicant") Federal Grant Topics has links to agencies that fund under a common topic–grants.gov
- **Federal Government Gateway for Nonprofits:** www.nonprofit.gov
- **Administration for Children and Families, Families and Youth Services Bureau grant programs:** www.acf.hhs.gov/programs/fysb/grant.htm
- **Bureau of Health Professions Grants Page:** bhpr.hrsa.gov
- **Centers for Disease Control and Prevention (CDC) Funding Opportunities:** www.cdc.gov/od/pgo/funding/funding.htm
- **Corporation for National Service (CNS, AmeriCorps, Senior Corps):** www.cns.gov
- **Department of Agriculture:** www.usda.gov/nonprofi.htm
- **Department of Agriculture (USDA) National Research Initiative Competitive Grants Program:** www.reeusda.gov/nri/
- **Department of Commerce (USDOC) Home Page:** www.doc.gov

- **Department of Commerce (Nonprofit Gateway to National Telecommunication and Information Administration (NTIA)**: www.ntia.doc.gov/ntiahome/gateway/non-profit/gateway.htm

- **Department of Defense**: www.defenselink.mil/other_info/nonprft.html

- **Department of Education Federal Register links**: www.ed.gov/news/fedregister/index.html

- **Department of Education: Grants and Contracts Information for States and School Districts**: www.ed.gov/fund/landing.jhtml?src=rt and www.ed.gov/offices/OCFO/gcsindex.html

- **Department of Education Grants**: www.ed.gov/about/offices/list/ocfo/grants/grants.html

- **Department of Education**: Safe and Drug-Free Schools Grants: www.ed.gov/about/offices/list/osdfs/news.html?exp=0

- **Department of Education**: Office of English Language Acquisition, Language Enhancement, and Academic Achievement for Limited English Proficient Students (formerly Bilingual Education and Minority Language Affairs): www.ed.gov/about/offices/list/oela/index.html?src=mr

- **Department of Education**: Office of Educational Research and Improvement (OERI) Funding: www.ed.gov/offices/OERI/funding.html

- **Department of Education**: Office of Elementary and Secondary Education (OESE) Programs and Funding: www.ed.gov/about/offices/list/oese/programs.html

- **Department of Education**: Office of Special Educational and Rehabilitation Services Programs (OSERS): www.ed.gov/about/offices/list/osers/osep/index.html?src=mr

- **Department of Education**: Office of Vocational and Adult Education (OVAE): www.ed.gov/about/offices/list/ovae/index.html?src=mr

- **Department of Energy (DOE), Office of Science Grants and Contracts**: www.er.doe.gov/production/grants/grants.html

- **Department of Health and Human Services (HHS)**: www.hhs.gov/grants/index.shtml and hhs.gov/grantsnet

- **Department of Health and Human Services, Head Start Bureau**: www2.acf.dhhs.gov/programs/hsb/

- **Department of Housing and Urban Development (HUD)**: www.hud.gov/groups/grantees.cfm

- **Department of the Interior**: www.doi.gov

- **Department/Office of Justice Funding Links**: www.ojp.usdoj.gov/fundopps.htm

- **Department/Office of Justice, Faith-Based and Community-Based Initiatives**: www.ojp.usdoj.gov/fbci/

Section
4

- **Department of Justice (DOJ) Grant Information:** www.usdoj.gov/10grants/index.html
- **Department of Labor (DOL) Contracting and Grant Program Overview:** www.dol.gov/oasam/grants/prgms.htm
- **Department of Labor Education and Training Administration (ETA):** www.doleta.gov
- **Department of Transportation Grants:** www.dot.gov/ost/m60/grant/
- **Department of Transportation (DOT) Home Page:** www.dot.gov
- **Department of Transportation (DOT) Nonprofit Links:** www.dot.gov/business.html
- **Department of Veterans Affairs:** www.va.gov/oaa/nonprofitcorp/default.asp
- **Environmental Protection Agency Resources for Nonprofits:** www.epa.gov/epa-home/nonprof.htm
- **Environmental Protection Agency Research Grants:** es.epa.gov/ncerqa/grants/
- **Environmental Protection Agency Grant Writing Tutorial:** www.epa.gov/seahome/grants.html
- **Faith-Based Organizations Catalogue:** www.whitehouse.gov/government/fbci/grants-catalog-index.html
- **Federal Acquisition Jumpstation for Procurement and Acquisition Links:** nais.nasa.gov/fedproc/home.html
- **Federal Communications Commission (FCC):** www.fcc.gov
- **General Services Administration:** gsa.gov/nonprofit
- **Health Resources and Services Administration (HRSA) Preview of Grants for 2004:** www.hrsa.gov/grants/preview/default.htm
- **Institute of Museums and Libraries Services (IMLS):** www.imls.gov/grants/index.htm and a tutorial for preparing grants at e-services.imls.gov/project_planning/
- **Internal Revenue Services (IRS):** www.irs.ustreas.gov/charities/index.html
- **National Aeronautics and Space Administration (NASA) Grants Information:** genesis.gsfc.nasa.gov/grants/grants.htm
- **National Archives and Records Administration (NARA), Federal Register and CFDA:** www.gpoaccess.gov/nara/index.html
- **National Clearinghouse for Alcohol and Drug Information (NCADI) Grants:** www.health.org/about/funding.aspx
- **National Endowment for the Arts (NEA) Grants:** www.nea.gov/grants/index.html
- **National Endowment for the Humanities (NEH):** www.neh.gov/grants/index.html
- **National Institutes of Health (NIH):** grants1.nih.gov/grants/ and grants1.nih.gov/grants/funding/funding.htm
- **NIH Office of Extramural Research:** grants1.nih.gov/grants/oer.htm

- **National Institute of Allergy and Infectious Diseases:** www.niaid.nih.gov/ncn/ grants/default_grants.htm and www.niaid.nih.gov/ncn/grants

- **National Institutes of Health Tutorial and Application Course:** www.niaid.nih.gov/ ncn/grants/default.htm

- **National Oceanic and Atmospheric Administration (NOAA) Grants:** www.rdc.noaa.gov/~grants/

- **National Science Foundation (NSF):** www.nsf.gov/home/grants.htm

- **Small Business Administration (SBA) and Nonprofits:** www.sba.gov/nonprofit

- **Social Security Administration (SSA) Acquisition and Grants:** www.ssa.gov/oag/

- **Substance Abuse and Mental Health Services Administration (SAMHSA):** www.samhsa.gov/funding/funding.html, www.samhsa.gov/grants/grants.html, and www.samhsa.gov/grants/tamanual/tamanual_frame.html

- **Substance Abuse and Mental Health Services Administration (SAMHSA), Focus on Partnerships and Funding** (information on kinds and sources of support, tips on making your case to funders, and additional resources for more information): www.preventionpartners.samhsa.gov/

- **NonProfitExpert.com:** www.nonprofitexpert.com/Default.htm and www.nonprofitexpert.com/federal_grants.htm

- **The Grantsmanship Center Daily List of Federal Grants** (free registration required): www.tgci.com/funding/fedToday.asp

Source: Donald A. Griesmann, "U.S. Federal Grants Web Sites," www.nonprofits.org/if/idealist/ en/FAQ/QuestionViewer/default?category-id=84&item=63&section=19&sid=38344545-141- hzEAi.

SCORE's Five Tips on Financial Packages

1. Understand that loans and venture capital often come in packages—that is, each may have several sources of funds and one piece of financing may depend on another.

2. Recognize that even government programs may require several sources. Under the federal 504 loan program, funds might come from a certified development company and one or more banks.

3. Expect to come up with some cash yourself. A down payment or demonstration of willingness to risk some of your own capital may be required.

4. Be sure you understand what's expected of you. For example, does a government program expect you to employ a certain number of workers within a certain time period?

5. Be patient. When more than one financing institution is involved, there's more paperwork, and each institution must give its approval.

Source: SCORE, www.score.org/business_tips.html.

SCORE's Five Tips on State and Local Funding

1. Don't overlook city, county, or state governments when you seek capital. Many economic development offices have funding-assistance programs for qualified small firms.

2. Understand the purpose and the requirements of the program you're interested in. It may call for raising matching funds or creating jobs.

3. Be modest in making projections. For example, don't inflate the number of jobs you think you can generate in hopes of getting a larger grant.

4. Take advantage of "in-kind" credits. Like cash, these can be used as matching funds. In one case, a state program counted a company's $200,000 local property tax abatement as part of the matching requirement.

5. Remember that having a good business plan and strong management team in place will help you make your case.

Source: SCORE, www.score.org/business_tips.html.

List of Additional Sources of Capital

When in a pickle and you need to round up some extra cash, whether short term or long term, here are a few sources of capital to keep in mind:

- credit cards
- customer financing
- employee stock ownership (ESOP)
- factoring accounts receivables
- home equity loans
- mergers and acquisitions
- purchase order financing
- state-specific economic development programs (search your individual state)
- strategic planning

Source: Small Business Administration, "Finance Basics."

Types of SBA Loans

The Small Business Administration has a portfolio of business loans, loan guarantees, and disaster relief worth more than $45 billion, along with a venture capital portfolio of $12 billion. The SBA is the nation's largest single financial backer of small businesses. Here are some types of SBA loans—although the financing programs vary depending on the borrower's needs.

7(a) Guaranteed Loan Program

This loan is generally used for business start-ups and to meet various short- and long-term needs of existing businesses, such as equipment purchase, working capital, leasehold improvements, inventory, or real estate purchase. These loans are generally guaranteed up to $75,000. The guaranteed loans are similar to those for standard bank loans. As for interest rates, if the loan has a term of seven years or more, the SBA allows the lender to charge as much as 2.75 percent above the prevailing prime rate. If the loan has less than seven years, the surcharge can be as much as 2.25 percent.

504 Local Development Company Program

This loan program provides long-term, fixed-rate financing to small businesses to acquire real estate, machinery, or equipment. The loans are administered by Certified Development Companies (CDCs) through commercial lending institutions. These loans are typically financed 50 percent by the bank, 40 percent by the CDC, and ten percent by the business.

The MicroLoan Program

This loan offers anywhere from a few hundred dollars to $25,000 for working capital or the purchase of inventory, supplies, furniture, fixtures, machinery, and/or equipment to businesses that cannot apply to traditional lenders because the amount they need is too small. Proceeds may not be used to pay for real estate or debts. According to the SBA, the average loan size is close to $10,000, with 37 percent going to minority-owned companies and 45 percent awarded to woman-owned companies.

Please go to www.sba.gov for more information.

Source: Andi Axman, *Entrepreneur Magazine's Ultimate Small Business Advisor*.

List of Other SBA Loan Programs

- State Business and Industrial Development Corporations (SBIDCs) offer long-term loans of up to 20 years for expansion of a small business or the purchase of capital equipment.

- 504 CDC Loans provide fixed-asset financing through Certified Development Companies (CDCs). They enable small businesses to create and retain jobs.

- Community Adjustment and Investment Program Loans are intended to create new,

sustainable jobs and preserve existing jobs in businesses at risk as a result of changing trade patterns with Canada and Mexico.

■ Energy and Conservation Loans are for small businesses engaged in engineering,
manufacturing, distributing, marketing, and installing or servicing products to conserve the nation's energy resources.

■ Export Working Capital Programs provide short-term loans to small businesses for
export-related transactions.

■ Export-Import Bank provides working capital for small companies to finance export
and foreign marketing operations.

■ Small Business Innovation Research Program offers an opportunity for small businesses to benefit from more than $1 billion in federal grants or contracts. It pro-
motes research and development for American-owned small businesses with 500 or
fewer employees.

Source: Andi Axman, *Entrepreneur Magazine's Ultimate Small Business Advisor.*

List of Things to Use as Collateral to Secure a Loan

■ Land and/or buildings

■ Machinery and/or equipment

■ Real estate and/or chattel mortgages

■ Warehouse receipts for marketable merchandise

■ Personal endorsement of a guarantor (a friend or family member who is willing to
pay off the loan if you are unable)

■ Accounts receivable

■ Savings accounts

■ Life insurance policies

■ Stocks and bonds

Source: compiled by the author.

Government Agencies Offering Financing
to Small Businesses

Congress requires that federal agencies set aside 23 percent of their contracts for small
businesses. Here are some agencies that make loans to small businesses:

- **Farmers Home Administration (FmHA) of the U.S. Department of Agriculture.** Applicants must be residents of cities or areas with a population of 50,000 or less, outside of major metropolitan areas. FmHA loans are guaranteed long-term loans backed 90 percent by the FmHA. They can be used as a source of start-up or working capital, new equipment purchase, refinancing, or expansion.

- **Economic Development Administration (EDA) of the Department of Commerce.** This agency makes loans and loan guarantees to new and existing businesses in depressed areas (regions with high unemployment and low-to-average income levels). Loans may not be granted to cover working capital or to purchase fixed assets.

- **Department of Energy (DOE).** This agency offers a loan program geared toward firms developing methods to increase domestic energy efficiency through conservation, alternate energy sources, or new methods of energy utilization.

- **Department of Housing and Urban Development (HUD).** It has several programs for the construction of commercial and residential buildings to rehabilitate needy areas of targeted cities. Funds are channeled through local officials in cities and towns, who make loans or grants to entrepreneurs to develop properties.

- **Department of the Interior (DOI).** This agency has a program through which it makes grants for the restoration of rundown properties that have been declared historic sites by a state agency.

Source: Andi Axman, *Entrepreneur Magazine's Ultimate Small Business Advisor.*

Section
4

Section 5

Organizing Your Business

Filing Your Taxes

Common Overlooked Deductions

- **Your car:** If you use a car in your business, you can deduct the business cost of the car, plus operating and maintenance expenses that pertain to business activities. You can take this deduction based on either actual costs or the IRS' "standard mileage rate," whichever gives you the greater deduction.

- **Personal assets:** Depending on the percentage of use that pertains to your business, some of your personal assets may become business tax deductions. This can be accomplished in part or in total, depending on the situation. For example, if your home computer is used 60 percent for your business, 60 percent of its cost and operating expenses can become business tax deductions.

- **Your home:** The home office is the portion of your home that's used for business purposes. In order to qualify for this deduction, your home office must be used for your business on both an exclusive and regular basis. If you qualify, you may deduct depreciation and other indirect expenses of operating your home on a pro-rata basis.

- **Your family:** Sometimes you can convert family activities into tax-deductible expenditures for your business. For instance, if you don't qualify as an employee of your business, you may be able to create deductible family medical coverage for your spouse, your children, and yourself by hiring your spouse in your business. Also, you can hire your children to do legitimate work for your business—depending on the type of work, your kids can begin earning wages from around age eight up until they have a "real" job and are on their own. This actually allows you to shift income away from your business to your children, who are typically in a lower tax bracket or who may not have any tax liability on the dollars they're paid. Another option: rather than supporting your parents using after-tax dollars, hire your parents to perform legitimate work for your business.

- **Travel:** Travel expenses—such as airline tickets, taxi fares, baggage, shipping, your car or a rental car, overnight lodging, 50 percent of the cost of meals, and other selected expenses—are tax-deductible when you travel on business. When you combine personal travel with business, the expenses must be prorated between the two, with the exception that the full cost of the round-trip airfare is tax-deductible as a business expense. Also, you can deduct the travel expenses of an employee, partner, or customer who travels with you on business

- **Entertainment:** You can deduct 50 percent of your business-entertainment expenses. These expenses include business meals, as well as the cost of attending entertainment where you discuss relevant business topics with a customer or client. This may also include the cost of tickets for you and your customers to attend sporting events, concerts, and other forms of entertainment (excluding country club dues).

- **Retirement:** For you to qualify as a participant in a tax-deductible retirement plan funded by your business, you must have earned income each tax year in which you wish to participate. Earned income consists of your share of the business's profits plus wages paid to you by your business. Dollars used to fund your retirement plan are tax-deductible to your business and grow tax-free until you retire.

Source: David Meier, "Commonly Overlooked Tax Deductions," www.entrepreneur.com/article/ 0,4621,294385,00.html.

List of Contributions You Can Deduct

Section 5

- Generally, you can deduct your contributions of money or property that you make to, or for the use of, a qualified organization. A gift or contribution is "for the use of" a qualified organization when it is held in a legally enforceable trust for the qualified organization or in a similar legal arrangement.

- The contributions must be made to a qualified organization and not set aside for use by a specific person.

- If you give property to a qualified organization, you generally can deduct the fair market value of the property at the time of the contribution.

- Your deduction for charitable contributions is generally limited to 50 percent of your adjusted gross income, but in some cases 20 percent and 30 percent limits may apply.

- The total of your charitable contributions deduction and certain other itemized deductions may be limited. See the instructions for Form 1040 for more information.

Source: Internal Revenue Service, www.irs.gov/publications/p526/ar02.html#d0e491.

List of Contributions You Cannot Deduct

There are some contributions you cannot deduct. There are others you can deduct only part of.

You cannot deduct as a charitable contribution:

1. A contribution to a specific individual
2. A contribution to a nonqualified organization
3. The part of a contribution from which you receive or expect to receive a benefit
4. The value of your time or services
5. Your personal expenses
6. Appraisal fees

7. Certain contributions of partial interests in property

Detailed discussions of these items follow.

Contributions to Individuals

You cannot deduct contributions to specific individuals, including:

■ Contributions to fraternal societies made for the purpose of paying medical or burial expenses of deceased members.

■ Contributions to individuals who are needy or worthy. This includes contributions to a qualified organization if you indicate that your contribution is for a specific person. But you can deduct a contribution that you give to a qualified organization that in turn helps needy or worthy individuals if you do not indicate that your contribution is for a specific person.
Example: You can deduct contributions earmarked for flood relief, hurricane relief, or other disaster relief to a qualified organization. However, you cannot deduct contributions earmarked for relief of a particular individual or family.

■ Payments to a member of the clergy that can be spent as he or she wishes, such as for personal expenses.

■ Expenses you paid for another person who provided services to a qualified organization.
Example: Your son does missionary work. You pay his expenses. You cannot claim a deduction for your son's unreimbursed expenses related to his contribution of services.

■ Payments to a hospital that are for a specific patient's care or for services for a specific patient. You cannot deduct these payments even if the hospital is operated by a city, state, or other qualified organization.

Contributions to Nonqualified Organizations

You cannot deduct contributions to organizations that are not qualified to receive tax-deductible contributions, including the following.

1. Certain state bar associations if:

   a. The state bar is not a political subdivision of a state,

   b. The bar has private, as well as public, purposes, such as promoting the professional interests of members, and

   c. Your contribution is unrestricted and can be used for private purposes.

2. Chambers of commerce and other business leagues or organizations.

3. Civic leagues and associations.

4. Communist organizations.

5. Country clubs and other social clubs.

6. Foreign organizations other than:

a. A U.S. organization that transfers funds to a charitable foreign organization if the U.S. organization controls the use of the funds or if the foreign organization is only an administrative arm of the U.S. organization, or

b. Certain Canadian, Israeli, or Mexican charitable organizations. See Canadian charities, Mexican charities, and Israeli charities under Organizations That Qualify to Receive Deductible Contributions.

7. Homeowners' associations.

8. Labor unions. But you may be able to deduct union dues as a miscellaneous itemized deduction, subject to the 2%-of-adjusted-gross-income limit, on Schedule A (Form 1040). See Publication 529, *Miscellaneous Deductions*.

9. Political organizations and candidates.

Section 5

Contributions from Which You Benefit

If you receive or expect to receive a financial or economic benefit as a result of making a contribution to a qualified organization, you cannot deduct the part of the contribution that represents the value of the benefit you receive. These contributions include:

- **Contributions for lobbying.** This includes amounts that you earmark for use in, or in connection with, influencing specific legislation.

- **Contributions to a retirement home that are clearly for room, board, maintenance, or admittance.** Also, if the amount of your contribution depends on the type or size of apartment you will occupy, it is not a charitable contribution.

- **Costs of raffles, bingo, lottery, etc.** You cannot deduct as a charitable contribution amounts you pay to buy raffle or lottery tickets or to play bingo or other games of chance. For information on how to report gambling winnings and losses, see Deductions Not Subject to the 2% Limit in Publication 529.

- **Dues to fraternal orders and similar groups.** However, see Membership Fees or Dues under Contributions from Which You Benefit (web site below).

- **Tuition, or amounts you pay instead of tuition, even if you pay them for children to attend parochial schools or qualifying nonprofit day-care centers.** You also cannot deduct any fixed amount you may be required to pay in addition to the tuition fee to enroll in a private school, even if it is designated as a "donation."

- **Contributions connected with split-dollar insurance arrangements.** You cannot deduct any part of a contribution to a charitable organization if, in connection with the contribution, the organization directly or indirectly pays, has paid, or is expected to pay any premium on any life insurance, annuity, or endowment contract for which you, any member of your family or any other person chosen by you (other than a qualified charitable organization) is a beneficiary.

Example: You donate money to a charitable organization. The charity uses the money to purchase a cash value life insurance policy. The beneficiaries under the insurance policy include members of your family. Even though the charity may eventually get some benefit out of the insurance policy, you cannot deduct any part of the donation.

Value of Time or Services

You cannot deduct the value of your time or services, including:

■ Blood donations to the Red Cross or to blood banks, and

■ The value of income lost while you work as an unpaid volunteer for a qualified organization.

Personal Expenses

You cannot deduct personal, living, or family expenses, such as the following items.

■ The cost of meals you eat while you perform services for a qualified organization, unless it is necessary for you to be away from home overnight while performing the services.

■ Adoption expenses, including fees paid to an adoption agency and the costs of keeping a child in your home before adoption is final. However, you may be able to claim a tax credit for these expenses. Also, you may be able to exclude from your gross income amounts paid or reimbursed by your employer for your adoption expenses. See Publication 968, *Tax Benefits for Adoption*, for more information. You also may be able to claim an exemption for the child. See Adoption in Publication 501, *Exemptions, Standard Deduction, and Filing Information*, for more information.

Appraisal Fees

Fees that you pay to find the fair market value of donated property are not deductible as contributions. You can claim them, subject to the 2%-of-adjusted-gross-income limit, as a miscellaneous itemized deduction on Schedule A (Form 1040). See Deductions Subject to the 2% Limit in Publication 529 for more information (web site below).

Partial Interest in Property

Generally, you cannot deduct a contribution of less than your entire interest in property. For details, see Partial interest in property under Contributions of Property (web site below).

Contributions of Property

If you contribute property to a qualified organization, the amount of your charitable contribution is generally the fair market value of the property at the time of the contribution. However, if the property has increased in value, you may have to make some adjustments to the amount of your deduction. See "Giving Property That Has Increased in Value" (web site below).

For information about the records you must keep and the information you must furnish with your return if you donate property, see "Records To Keep and How To Report" (web site below).

Source: Internal Revenue Service, www.irs.gov/publications/p526/ar02.html#d0e1042.

SCORE's Five Tips on How to Start Filing Taxes Correctly

1. Consult a tax advisor, even if you are a start-up. A professional can save you both money and valuable time and keep you from running afoul of the Internal Revenue Service.

2. Pay estimated federal and state taxes four times a year. Your tax advisor can help you determine how much to set aside ahead of time for each payment.

3. Keep good records of both income and expenses. Save all receipts.

4. Ask your tax advisor about special deductions you can take as a small-business owner—such as allowances for health insurance, long-term care insurance, or self-employment tax.

5. Schedule a "tax tune-up" at least once a year. Update your tax advisor on your situation and your goals and get his or her advice on planning your tax strategy for the coming year.

Source: SCORE, www.score.org/business_tips.html.

Tips for Taking Advantage of Tax Laws

At the end of every year, do you wonder if you'll end up paying too much in taxes? CPA Sandy Botkin says many new entrepreneurs don't take full advantage of the tax laws. Try his tips:

- If you own two cars, alternate your use of each car from month to month.

- If you have children under age 18, you can hire them at fully deductible wages and owe no Social Security or federal employment taxes if your company is a sole proprietorship or partnership in which both partners are parents of the children. But don't cheat—they must perform actual work for your business.

- You may remember that dry cleaning and laundry expenses during a business trip are deductible. But you can also deduct your first dry-cleaning bill after returning home—however, only for the clothes dirtied while traveling.

Source: Rieva Lesonsky, *365 Tips to Boost Your Entrepreneurial IQ.*

Section 5

Ten Small Business Tax Tips

The following tax tips suggest ten ways you, as a small business owner, can implement strategies to minimize your business' income tax liability and make your business life tax deductible. (For details, visit www.thesmallbusinessadvantage.com/taxTips.html.)

Tax Tip #1: Your Car. Deduct the entire cost of purchasing, operating, and maintaining your car that is applicable to business usage.

Tax Tip #2: Your Equipment. Create a special equipment deduction of up to $100,000 every year.

Tax Tip #3: Your Family. Pay your children tax-free dollars that your business can deduct.

Tax Tip #4: Your Travel. Deduct 100 percent of all business travel, including round-trip airfare—even when your trip is not all business.

Tax Tip #5: Your Entertainment. Deduct 50 percent of your meals, concerts, season tickets to sporting events, and other entertainment costs that are either directly related to or associated with a business purpose.

Tax Tip #6: Your Home. Write off a portion of your home, plus 100 percent of your other business deductions.

Tax Tip #7: Your Retirement. Invest dollars pretax and let them grow tax-deferred. Invest dollars after-tax and let them grow tax-free forever.

Tax Tip #8: Your Form of Organization. Select the proper form of organization to minimize your business and personal income tax liability, as well as sheltering you (as the owner) from personal liability exposure.

Tax Tip #9: Yourself. Create tax-deductible fringe benefits, such as health care, insurance, and transportation.

Tax Tip #10: Your Strategic Issues. Use certain current year tax deductions to reduce prior and future years' taxable income.

Source: "Tax Tips," www.thesmallbusinessadvantage.com/taxTips.html.

SCORE's Five Tips on Understanding Home-Office Deductions

1. Take advantage of every legal opportunity to reduce your taxes. Recent changes in the law benefit business owners who use their homes as an administrative and management base but work at other locations—such as plumbers, general contractors, and health-care professionals.

2. Ask your tax professional to analyze your business regularly so you don't miss important deductions.

3. Document deductible items. These usually include such costs as computers and other equipment, telephone charges, furnishings, and prorated portions of rent, utilities, home insurance, and homeowner association fees.

4. If you are a homeowner, discuss with your tax advisor whether or not to take a depreciation deduction for the office space. Sometimes it pays; sometimes it doesn't.

5. For detailed information, visit www.toolkit.cch.com, the web site of CCH Inc., a business information services company based in Illinois. Or, go to the Internal Revenue Service Web Site, www.irs.ustreas.gov, and download IRS Publication 587, *Business Use of Your Home*.

Source: SCORE, www.score.org/business_tips.html.

Section 5

Chapter 27

Complete Guide
to Office Software

Accounting/Financial/Tax

BusinessEssentials Pro
OS: Windows 98/NT 4.0 (SP 6) or higher/2000/Me/XP
Price: $299
Publisher: MYOB
Phone: (800) 322-6962
Product Description: Software suite that includes accounting components and business productivity applications. Includes Premier Accounting (formerly MYOB Plus), an accounting application with complete sales and purchases, inventory tracking, customer management, and payroll features. Additional features include tools for conducting performance evaluations, employee training, and attendance tracking.
Publisher site: www.myob.com
Download Available

Money 2005 Small Business
OS: Windows 98 SE/2000 (SP 3)/XP
Price: $89.95
Publisher: Microsoft
Phone: (800) 426-9400
Product Description: Software for managing personal and small-business finances. Features include cash-flow management, tax planning, inventory tracking, and payroll. Also allows you to create invoices, automatically categorize business and personal income and expenses, and manage accounts receivable and payable.
Publisher site: www.microsoft.com/money
Download Available

Peachtree Premium Accounting 2005
OS: Windows 98 SE/NT 4.0/2000/Me/XP
Price: $500
Publisher: Best Software
Phone: (800) 247-3224
Product Description: Full-featured accounting and business management software with robust inventory tools, including serialized inventory management. Includes features for archiving past company data for use in future reports as well as the ability to run consolidated financial statements for multiple companies. Industry-specific versions are available, including manufacturing, distribution, accounting, and nonprofit.
Publisher site: www.peachtree.com

QuickBooks Premier 2005
OS: Windows 98 SE/2000/XP
Price: $500
Publisher: Intuit
Phone: (888) 246-8848
Product Description: Financial management software with business planning tools. Allows you to forecast income and expenses, track inventory, and create purchase orders and

Section 5

invoices. Remote-access subscription service available for accessing your data over the web.
Publisher site: www.quickbooks.com

Quicken 2005 Premier Home & Business

OS: Windows 98/2000/Me/XP
Price: $89.95
Publisher: Intuit
Phone: (888) 246-8848
Product Description: Suite for managing personal and business finances. Includes a Business Center where you can see unpaid invoices, upcoming bills, and predict cash flow all in one place.
Publisher site: www.quicken.com

Simply Accounting 2005 Basic

OS: Windows 98 SE/NT 4.0/2000/Me/XP
Price: $49
Publisher: Best Software
Phone: (800) 773-5445
Product Description: Designed for smaller businesses and start-ups with simple accounting requirements. Offers core accounting functions for product- and service-based companies, including an optional payroll service. Also offers daily updates on key business information.
Publisher site: www.simplyaccounting.com
Download Available

TaxCut Complete Home & Business

OS: Windows 95/98/NT 4.0/2000/Me/XP
Price: $69.95
Publisher: H&R Block
Phone: (800) 457-9525
Product Description: Includes two software programs for filing both personal and business tax returns. Includes forms for preparing self-employment, corporate, partnership, estate, payroll, and nonprofit returns, and tools for calculating home-office and business expense deductions.
Publisher site: www.taxcut.com

TurboTax Business for Tax Year 2004

OS: Windows 98/2000/Me/XP
Price: $99.95
Publisher: Intuit
Phone: (888) 246-8848
Product Description: Software to help you file corporation, partnership and fiduciary income taxes. Includes tools for preparing and printing W-2 and 1099-MISC forms for employees and contractors.
Publisher site: www.turbotax.com

Source: *Entrepreneur's Complete Guide to Software*, 2005 Edition, www.entrepreneur.com/features/softguide/category/0,6570,Accounting~Financial,00.html.

Backup

Acronis True Image 8.0
OS: Linux, Windows 95/98/2000/Me/XP
Price: $49.99
Publisher: Acronis
Phone: (877) 825-0953
Product Description: Software that creates an exact disc image (including all computer data, operating system, and programs) for backup and disc cloning. Also lets you create an online system disk backup.
Publisher site: www.acronis.com
Download Available

Alohabob PC Backup
OS: Windows 95/98/2000/Me/XP
Price: $49.95
Publisher: Eisenworld
Phone: (888) 392-5642
Product Description: Allows you to rank the importance of critical files, and search for and select files to be backed up. Files can be saved to CDs, DVDs, USB drives, ZIP drives, and separate hard-drive partitions on your PC.
Publisher site: www.eisenworld.com

Backup Now! 4 Deluxe
OS: Windows 9x/NT/2000/Me/XP
Price: $79.99
Publisher: NTI
Phone: (949) 421-0720
Product Description: Offers both full image and individual file/folder backup for networked and stand-alone PC users. Features include remote backup and recovery, DVD+R (16x and DL) support, e-mail backups, and the ability to schedule full and incremental backups. Backup Now! can also be used as a cloning utility when setting up new computers.
Publisher site: www.ntius.com
Download Available

Backup Platinum 2.0
OS: Windows 95/98/NT/2000/Me/XP/Server 2003
Price: $67 per license
Publisher: SoftLogica
Phone: (888) 364-6797
Product Description: Copies data to a variety of storage media, including hard drives, USB drives, CDs, and DVDs, FTP servers or local networks. Offers disk spanning to split

Section 5

large backups across several optical discs, and allows users to schedule automatic backups.
Publisher site: www.backup-platinum.com
Download Available

BounceBack Professional 6.0
OS: Mac OS X, Windows 98/2000/XP
Price: $79
Publisher: CMS Products
Phone: (800) 327-5773
Product Description: Hard drive-based backup and recovery software. Includes QuickRestore feature to restore single files, folders, or the entire contents of a hard drive, as well as the ability to recover multiple versions of the same file. Also offers automatic scheduled backups and incremental backups.
Publisher site: www.cmsproducts.com

Data Rescue PC 1.0
OS: DOS file systems, Windows 95/98/NT/2000/Me/XP/3.x/Server 2003
Price: $129 (single user), $249 (unlimited-use license)
Publisher: Prosoft Engineering
Phone: (877) 477-6763
Product Description: Data recovery utility designed to safely store files when PC problems strike. It allows you to select files you wish to recover and save them to an external storage device or second internal hard drive.
Publisher site: www.prosofteng.com

Norton Ghost 9.0
OS: Windows 2000/XP
Price: $69.95
Publisher: Symantec
Phone: (800) 441-7234
Product Description: Data backup and recovery application that can back up data without restarting your OS. Can clone your hard drive for system recovery. Backups and disc images can be stored on multiple types of media, including network servers, hard drives, CDs, and DVDs.
Publisher site: www.symantec.com

Retrospect Single Server 7
OS: Windows 98/NT 4.0/2000/Me/XP/Server 2003
Price: $699
Publisher: EMC Dantz
Phone: (800) 225-4880
Product Description: Automated backup software for desktops, notebooks, servers, and networks. Features on-site/off-site media rotation, self-adjusting backup operations, support for tape libraries and disaster-recovery features.
Publisher site: www.dantz.com
Download Available

Undelete 5.0 Professional
OS: Windows NT/2000/XP/Server 2003
Price: $39.95
Publisher: Executive Software
Phone: (800) 829-6468
Product Description: File-recovery application that provides data protection for stand-alone and networked PCs. A $299 server version includes remote installation features.
Publisher site: www.executive.com
Download Available

Source: *Entrepreneur's Complete Guide to Software*, 2005 Edition, www.entrepreneur.com/features/softguide/category/0,6570,Backup,00.html.

CD/DVD Authoring

CD & DVD-Maker7 Titanium Suite
OS: Windows 98/2000/Me/XP
Price: $79.99
Publisher: NTI
Phone: (949) 421-0720
Product Description: Software for saving data to recordable and rewritable CDs and DVDs. Includes disc spanning (for organizing and archiving data across a series of discs when a single disc does not provide enough capacity) and offers support for 16X DVD+R and double-layer DVDs.
Publisher site: www.ntius.com

DVD MovieFactory 4 Disc Creator
OS: Windows 98 SE/2000/Me/XP
Price: $99.99
Publisher: Ulead
Phone: (800) 858-5323
Product Description: Leads you through the process of creating CDs and DVDs with a wizard-style work flow. Includes tools for editing videos and backing up data, as well as support for double-layer DVD+R discs and 16X burning.
Publisher site: www.ulead.com
Download Available

MyDVD Studio 6
OS: Windows 2000/XP
Price: $69.99
Publisher: Sonic Solutions
Phone: (415) 893-8000
Product Description: Software for authoring, burning, creating, and sharing data, video, and photos on CD and DVD.
Publisher site: www.sonic.com

Nero 6 Ultra Edition
OS: Windows 98/2000/Me/XP
Price: $99 (boxed version), $69 (downloaded version)
Publisher: Ahead Software
Phone: (888) 309-4212
Product Description: Software suite for capturing, editing, and burning video and audio to CDs and DVDs. Includes tools for creating multimedia slideshows and a drag-and-drop feature for saving data to discs.
Publisher site: www.nero.com
Download Available

Source: *Entrepreneur's Complete Guide to Software*, 2005 Edition, www.entrepreneur.com/features/softguide/category/0,6570,CD~DVD%20Authoring,00.html

Communication

AIM for Palm and Pocket PC
OS: Palm OS 3.52 and higher, Pocket PC 2002, Windows Mobile 2003
Price: $19.95
Publisher: AOL
Phone: (800) 827-6364
Product Description: Mobile version of AOL's Instant Messenger. Allows you to exchange IMs with other AIM users, whether they're connected via desktop PC or PDA. A version for mobile phones running the Symbian Series 60 OS is also available.
Publisher site: www.aim.com
Download Available

Eudora 6.2
OS: Mac OS 9/OS X or higher, Windows 95/98/Me/NT/2000/XP
Price: $49.95
Publisher: Qualcomm
Phone: (800) 238-3672
Product Description: E-mail client with built-in protection against spam and e-mail scams. Includes tools for organizing long e-mail threads into manageable messages.
Publisher site: www.eudora.com
Download Available

IM+ Mobile Instant Messenger
OS: Palm OS 4 and higher, Pocket PC 2002, Windows Mobile 2003
Price: $29.95 (Windows), $24.95 (Palm OS)
Publisher: Shape Services
Product Description: Mobile IM application. Allows you to connect to a variety of IM services—including AOL, ICQ, Jabber, MSN, and Yahoo!—from one client.
Publisher site: www.shapeservices.de

Live Communications Server 2005
OS: SQL Server 2000, Windows Server 2003
Price: $1,199 (server plus five users)
Publisher: Microsoft
Phone: (800) 426-9400
Product Description: Secure collaboration and IM solution for businesses. Allows remote users to connect over a VPN.
Publisher site: www.microsoft.com
Download Available

Lotus Instant Messaging and Web Conferencing 6.5.1
OS: OS/400 V5.x, Windows NT/2000/XP
Price: $47.59 per user
Publisher: IBM
Phone: (888) 746-7426
Product Description: Formerly known as Lotus Sametime. Allows you to connect instantly with co-workers and share presentations and applications in real time. Offers web conferences with integrated audio.
Publisher site: www.lotus.com

Lotus Notes 6.5
OS: Mac OS X, Windows 95/98/NT/2000/Me/XP
Price: $89.82 per user
Publisher: IBM
Phone: (888) 746-7426
Product Description: Complete e-mail and collaboration suite, featuring integrated IM tools. Includes calendar, scheduling' and collaboration tools.
Publisher site: www.lotus.com

Onemail
OS: Palm OS, Pocket PC 2002, Windows CE/Mobile 2003
Price: $29.95
Publisher: Brightex Technology Limited
Product Description: Retrieves your web-based e-mail from your PC for display on Windows Mobile- and Palm OS-based devices. Works with Hotmail, MSN, and Yahoo! Mail. No e-mail reader is required.
Publisher site: www.net.worth.com.hk/onemail/main.htm
Download Available

Outlook 2003
OS: Windows 2000/XP
Price: $109 or $49 (Office System Small Business Edition price)
Publisher: Microsoft
Phone: (800) 426-9400
Product Description: Complete system for managing your digital communications, contacts, and calendar. Includes spam-filtering and search tools.
Publisher site: www.microsoft.com
Download Available

Section 5

Thunderbird 1.0
OS: Linux, Mac OS X, Windows 98/Me/2000/XP
Price: free
Publisher: Mozilla
Product Description: E-mail client that supports all POP3 and IMAP e-mail accounts, as well as AOL and HTML mail. Includes spam filters, support for newsgroup access, and an RSS newsreader. Offers advanced e-mail sorting features, including customized views of your inbox based on personalized settings.
Publisher site: www.mozilla.org
Download Available

Trillian 3.0
OS: Windows 98/2000/Me/XP
Price: free
Publisher: Cerulean Studios
Phone: (203) 775-6310,
Product Description: Unified IM client that lets you connect to users of various interoperable IM services, including AOL Instant Messenger, ICQ, Microsoft MSN Messenger, and Yahoo! Messenger. A $25 Pro version adds video messaging.
Publisher site: www.ceruleanstudios.com

WebIS Mail 2.0
OS: Pocket PC 2002, Windows Mobile 2003
Price: $24.95
Publisher: Web Information Solutions
Product Description: Application for managing your e-mail from your Windows Mobile-based handheld. Can be synchronized with your desktop or with mailboxes on POP3 or IMAP servers.
Publisher site: www.webis.net
Download Available

Source: *Entrepreneur's Complete Guide to Software*, 2005 Edition, www.entrepreneur.com/features/softguide/category/0,6570,Communication,00.html.

Connectivity/Networking

GoToMyPC Pro 4.1
OS: Windows 95/98/2000/Me/NT 4.0/XP/Server 2003
Price: $67.80 per month (four-PC plan)
Publisher: Citrix
Phone: (888) 646-0016
Product Description: Remote-access application that includes administrative functionality. Connects users to their PCs from any internet-based computer or handheld device.
Publisher site: www.citrix.com
Download Available

Management Suite 8.5
OS: Linux, Mac OS 9.2.2/10.2.x/10.3.x, Novell NetWare, Solaris, Windows 95/98 SE/NT 4.0/2000/XP/2000 Server/Server 2003
Price: $89 per managed node (minimum 10 nodes)
Publisher: LANDesk
Phone: (800) 982-2130
Product Description: Systems management software that offers automated, centralized control over your IT assets, including desktop PCs and mobile devices. Lets you automate the installation of software, security patches, and updates.
Publisher site: www.landesk.com
Download Available

Observer 10.1
OS: Windows 2000/XP/Server 2003
Price: $995
Publisher: Network Instruments
Phone: (800) 526-7919
Product Description: Network monitoring and troubleshooting tool that offers real-time analysis. Includes support for 802.11a/b/g wireless, and long-term network trending and reporting.
Publisher site: www.networkinstruments.com
Download Available

PCAnywhere 11.5
OS: Windows 98/NT 4.0/2000/Me/XP
Price: $200 (single user), $800 (five user licenses)
Publisher: Symantec
Phone: (800) 441-7234
Product Description: Remote-control software that allows help-desk staff to diagnose and correct PC problems from a distance. Offers remote file transfer capabilities and AES encryption for security.
Publisher site: www.symantec.com

Server Nanny Standard
OS: Windows 2000/XP/Server 2003
Price: $249
Publisher: Xenos Software
Phone: (888) 755-5611
Product Description: Network monitoring software. Detects and alerts you to problems with web servers, database servers, environmental conditions, and applications. Can also perform automated corrective actions.
Publisher site: www.servernanny.com
Download Available

sitekeeper 3.5
OS: Windows 95/98/NT/2000/Me/XP/Server 2003
Price: $199.75 (five licenses)
Publisher: Executive Software

Phone: (800) 829-6468
Product Description: Automated systems management software that helps keep software and patches up-to-date. Includes Patchkeeper for centralized patch management, PushInstaller for networkwide software deployment, and Inventory for tracking inventory and licenses.
Publisher site: www.executive.com
Download Available

Small Business Suite 6.5
OS: Linux, Novell NetWare 6.5
Price: $475 (five user licenses)
Publisher: Novell
Phone: (800) 321-4272
Product Description: Software for building and maintaining a small-business network. Includes Netware 6.5, Groupwise 6.5 (e-mail and collaboration application), ZenWorks for Desktops 4 (management), Nterprise Branch Office 1.02 (provides network services to branch offices), and Novell BorderManager 3.8 (network security).
Publisher site: www.novell.com

Source: *Entrepreneur's Complete Guide to Software*, 2005 Edition, www.entrepreneur.com/features/softguide/category/0,6570,Connectivity~Networking,00.html.

Contact Management/CRM

ACT! 2005
OS: Windows 2000/XP/Server 2003
Price: $230
Publisher: Best Software
Phone: (877) 228-2005
Product Description: Software for managing customer and vendor relationships. Designed for individuals and small teams of up to 10 users. A $400 Premium Workgroup version supports database collaboration for up to 50 users.
Publisher site: www.act.com
Download Available

Business Contact Manager
OS: Windows 2000/XP
Price: included with Office Small Business Edition 2003 ($449)
Publisher: Microsoft
Phone: (800) 426-9400
Product Description: Free add-on for Outlook 2003 that keeps track of accounts, contacts and sales opportunities without purchasing a full-scale CRM solution.
Publisher site: www.microsoft.com

Goldmine Business Contact Manager 7.0

OS: Windows 98/2000/Me/XP
Price: $180
Publisher: FrontRange Solutions
Phone: (800) 776-7889
Product Description: Contact management suite with integrated sales and relationship-management tools. Includes appointment tracking, to-do lists, and an opportunity manager. Synchronizes with Palm- and Pocket PC-based handhelds.
Publisher site: www.frontrange.com/goldmine

Maximizer Enterprise 8

OS: Windows 98 SE/NT 4.0/2000/Me/XP/2003
Price: $489
Publisher: Maximizer Software
Phone: (800) 804-6299
Product Description: CRM software that includes features for sales, marketing, customer service, and support. Includes accounting integration (an accounting link for QuickBooks is available for $99), reporting and analytic features, anti-spam and Do-Not-Call legislation compliance, and integration with Outlook.
Publisher site: www.maximizer.com

Section 5

Prophet 2004

OS: Windows 2000/XP
Price: $150
Publisher: Avidian Technologies
Phone: (877) 284-3426
Product Description: Sales management software that works inside Microsoft Outlook, allowing you to use a single application to manage all your customer communications.
Publisher site: www.avidian.com

QuickBooks Customer Manager 2.0

OS: Windows 98 SE/2000/XP
Price: $79.95
Publisher: Intuit
Phone: (888) 246-8848
Product Description: Organizes all your customer data in one place, including contact information, files, correspondence, projects, appointments, and financial transactions. Synchronizes financial transactions, contact information, and appointments with QuickBooks, Outlook, and Outlook Express.
Publisher site: www.quickbooks.intuit.com

SalesLogix 6.2

OS: Windows 98/2000/XP
Price: $795 per user
Publisher: Best Software
Phone: (800) 643-6400
Product Description: CRM software for small to midsize businesses. Includes sales, marketing, customer-service, and support automation features.
Publisher site: www.saleslogix.com

Smart Contact Manager Pro 4.1
OS: Windows 98 SE/NT/2000/XP
Price: $180
Publisher: Surado Solutions
Phone: (800) 478-7236
Product Description: Includes tools for contact management, sales force automation and marketing campaign management. Synchronizes with Pocket PC 2002 and Windows Mobile 2003 handhelds.
Publisher site: www.smartcontactmanager.com

Source: *Entrepreneur's Complete Guide to Software*, 2005 Edition, www.entrepreneur.com/features/softguide/category/0,6570,Connectivity~Networking,00.html.

Database

Access 2003
OS: Windows 2000 SP3/XP or later
Price: $229
Publisher: Microsoft
Phone: (800) 426-9400
Product Description: Software for building simple or complex databases for organizing, accessing, and sharing information. Supports a variety of data formats, including ODBC, OLE, and XML.
Publisher site: www.microsoft.com
Download Available

Alpha Five Version 6
OS: Windows 98/NT/2000/Me/XP
Price: $349
Publisher: Alpha Software
Phone: (800) 451-1018
Product Description: Relational database application that allows professionals and novices to build desktop and web-based databases without writing any code.
Publisher site: www.alphasoftware.com
Download Available

AskSam Professional 5
OS: Windows 95/98/98 SE/NT/2000/Me/XP
Price: $395
Publisher: askSam Systems
Phone: (800) 800-1997
Product Description: Free-form database designed to manage disorganized information. Turns all of your documents—including e-mail messages, spreadsheets, text files, and web pages—into searchable documents.
Publisher site: www.asksam.com

DataBase Professional
OS: Windows 95/98/NT/2000/Me/XP
Price: $69.95
Publisher: Avanquest
Phone: (650) 212-9300
Product Description: Database software includes network setup and administrator security features. Also allows backup and restore functionality, and contact management features, including the ability to output information to labels and envelopes.
Publisher site: www.avanquest.com

FileMaker Pro 7
OS: Mac OS X, Windows 98/NT 4.0/2000/Me/XP
Price: $299
Publisher: FileMaker
Phone: (800) 325-2747
Product Description: Database and information management software that lets you import, store and export any kind of file or document, including Microsoft Excel, PowerPoint and Word files, digital images, video, and music. Includes web features to allow remote users to access your database online.
Publisher site: www.filemaker.com
Download Available

HanDBase Professional
OS: Palm OS 3.0 or higher, Pocket PC 2000 or higher, Windows CE 3.0 or higher
Price: $39.99
Publisher: DDH Software
Phone: (877) 334-4608
Product Description: Mobile relational database for Palm OS and Windows Mobile PDAs. Includes multi-user syncing so that two or more users can enter data into a single database, as well as the ability to sync with PCs and servers.
Publisher site: www.ddhsoftware.com

MySQL Database Server Pro 4.1
OS: FreeBSD, HP-UX, IBM AIX, Linux, Mac OS X, Novell NetWare, SGI Irix, Solaris, Windows
Price: $595 per server
Publisher: MySQL
Phone: (425) 743-5635
Product Description: Open-source database management system. Includes full-text indexing and searching, as well as support for SSL transport layer encryption for security.
Publisher site: www.mysql.com
Download Available

Oracle Database 10g Standard Edition One
OS: HP Tru64/UX, IBM AIX, Linux, Mac OS X, Solaris, Sun Microsystems, Windows NT
Price: $149 per user (minimum five users)
Publisher: Oracle
Phone: (800) 633-0615
Product Description: Single-processor version of Oracle's database software for simpler

installation and management. Fully compatible with the complete Oracle database family. Includes automated web application development tools.
Publisher site: www.oracle.com
Download Available

SmartList To Go 3.0
OS: Palm OS 3.5 and higher
Price: $49.99
Publisher: DataViz
Phone: (800) 733-0030
Product Description: Allows you to create, view, and manage databases on your Palm OS PDA. Offers synchronization with Microsoft Access and the ability to store databases on expansion cards to save internal memory.
Publisher site: www.dataviz.com
Download Available

Visual CE Professional 9.0
OS: Pocket PC 2000/2002, Windows CE/Mobile 2003
Price: $399
Publisher: Syware
Phone: (617) 497-1300
Product Description: Relational database for Windows Mobile PDAs. Features drag-and-drop controls, an unlimited number of forms, and synchronization with desktop PCs and servers. Data can be shared with desktop software, including Lotus Approach, Microsoft Access, and Oracle.
Publisher site: www.syware.com
Download Available

abcDB Professional Database 6.0
OS: Pocket PC 2002, Windows Mobile 2003
Price: $19.89
Publisher: PocketSOFT.ca
Product Description: Software for creating and managing databases on your Windows Mobile-based handheld. Features integration with Microsoft Access. Also allows you to access and modify Microsoft Pocket Outlook data from within the application.
Publisher site: www.pocketsoft.ca
Download Available

Source: *Entrepreneur's Complete Guide to Software*, 2005 Edition, www.entrepreneur.com/features/softguide/category/0,6570,Database,00.html.

Desktop Publishing/Graphic Design/Image Editing

Acrobat 7.0 Professional
OS: Mac OS X (10.2.8 or 10.3), Windows 2000/XP/XP Tablet PC edition

Price: $449
Publisher: Adobe
Phone: (800) 833-6687
Product Description: Allows you to create and control Adobe PDF documents. Transforms electronic or paper files, including websites, drawings, and e-mail messages, into PDFs that can be shared with others using the free Acrobat reader.
Publisher site: www.adobe.com
Download Available

CorelDraw Graphics Suite 12
OS: Windows 2000/XP
Price: $399
Publisher: Corel
Phone: (800) 772-6735
Product Description: Graphics software suite includes three applications: CorelDraw 12 for illustration and page layout, Corel Photo-Paint 12 for digital imaging, and Corel RAVE 3 for motion graphics creation.
Publisher site: www.corel.com
Download Available

Creative Suite 2 Premium Edition
OS: Mac OS X, Windows 2000/XP
Price: $1,199
Publisher: Adobe
Phone: (800) 833-6687
Product Description: Suite of graphics and imaging applications for print and web publishing. Includes Acrobat 7.0, GoLive, Illustrator, InDesign, and Photoshop.
Publisher site: www.adobe.com

PagePlus 10
OS: Windows 98/2000/Me/XP
Price: $130
Publisher: Serif
Phone: (800) 557-3743
Product Description: Software for designing and creating documents, including business cards, newsletters, posters, and magazines. Includes page wizards for layout assistance; can input 3-D objects.
Publisher site: www.serif.com

Paint Shop Pro 9
OS: Windows 98 SE/2000/Me/XP
Price: $129
Publisher: Corel
Phone: (800) 772-6735
Product Description: Software for creating and editing digital images, graphics, and digital art. Includes automatic fixing tools to correct digital images.
Publisher site: www.corel.com
Download Available

Section 5

PhotoImpact 10
OS: Windows 98 SE/2000/Me/XP
Price: $89.99
Publisher: Ulead
Phone: (800) 858-5323
Product Description: Image-editing suite with digital photography, graphic design, and web-page creation tools. Includes painting, drawing, and cloning tools.
Publisher site: www.ulead.com
Download Available

Print Shop Pro Publisher 20
OS: Windows 98/2000/Me/XP
Price: $69.99
Publisher: Broderbund
Phone: (800) 395-0277
Product Description: Software for creating print and multimedia projects, including business cards, newsletters, and presentations. Includes a small-business center.
Publisher site: www.broderbund.com

Publisher 2003
OS: Windows 2000/XP
Price: $169
Publisher: Microsoft
Phone: (800) 426-9400
Product Description: Software for designing, creating, and publishing business and marketing materials for print, web, or e-mail.
Publisher site: www.microsoft.com
Download Available

QuarkXPress 6.5
OS: Mac OS X (10.3 and higher), Windows 2000/XP
Price: $945
Publisher: Quark
Phone: (800) 676-4575
Product Description: Page layout software for creating advertisements, newsletters. books, and more for both print and website production. Allows you to manipulate images from within the software. Includes XML and PDF support.
Publisher site: www.quark.com
Download Available

Ventura 10
OS: Windows 2000/XP
Price: $699
Publisher: Corel
Phone: (800) 772-6735
Product Description: Page layout and desktop publishing software that transforms long, complex documents into formatted, visually rich publications. Includes support for PDF and XML.
Publisher site: www.corel.com

Source: *Entrepreneur's Complete Guide to Software,* 2005 Edition, www.entrepreneur.com/features/softguide/category/0,6570,Desktop%20Publishing~Graphic%20Design~Image%20Editing,00.html.

Office Suites

Lotus SmartSuite 9.8
OS: Windows 95/98/NT 4.0/2000/Me/XP
Price: $235
Publisher: IBM
Phone: (888) 746-7426
Product Description: Includes Lotus 1-2-3, Lotus Approach, Lotus FastSite, Lotus Freelance Graphics, Lotus Organizer, Lotus SmartCenter, and Lotus Word Pro. Features compatibility with Microsoft Office file formats.
Publisher site: www.lotus.com

Office 2004 for the Mac Professional Edition
OS: Mac OS X (10.2.8 or higher)
Price: $499
Publisher: Microsoft
Phone: (800) 426-9400
Product Description: Includes the Entourage e-mail client and personal information manager, Excel, PowerPoint, and Word. Professional Edition includes Virtual PC for Mac Version 7 with Windows XP Professional.
Publisher site: www.microsoft.com/mac
Download Available

Office System 2003 Small Business Edition
OS: Windows 2000/XP
Price: $449
Publisher: Microsoft
Phone: (800) 426-9400
Product Description: Includes 2003 versions of Excel, Outlook (including Business Contact Manager), PowerPoint, Publisher, and Word. Upgrade from previous versions is $279.
Publisher site: www.microsoft.com/office

StarOffice 7 Office Suite
OS: Linux Kernel (2.2.13 or higher), Solaris 8, Windows 98/NT/2000/Me/XP
Price: $59.95 (download)
Publisher: Sun Microsystems
Phone: (800) 786-0404
Product Description: Office suite based on open standards. Includes word processing, spreadsheet, presentation, drawing, and database applications.
Publisher site: www.sun.com

Section 5

WordPerfect Office 12
OS: Windows 98 SE/NT 4.0/2000/XP/Server 2003
Price: $299
Publisher: Corel
Phone: (800) 772-6735
Product Description: Office suite standard edition includes WordPerfect for word processing, Quattro Pro for spreadsheets, Presentations, and Address Book. Professional edition adds Paradox database application. Features compatibility with Microsoft Office file formats.
Publisher site: www.corel.com
Download Available

Source: *Entrepreneur's Complete Guide to Software*, 2005 Edition, www.entrepreneur.com/features/softguide/category/0,6570,Office%20Suites,00.html.

Presentation

Captivate
OS: Windows 2000/XP
Price: $499
Publisher: Macromedia
Phone: (800) 457-1249
Product Description: Formerly known as RoboDemo, Captivate allows you to create interactive simulations and software demonstrations. It can record on-screen actions to create an interactive Flash simulation. Content can be viewed by any browser (including Mac applications) with Flash Player 6 or later installed.
Publisher site: www.macromedia.com
Download Available

Keynote 2.0
OS: Mac OS X (10.2 or later)
Price: $79
Publisher: Apple
Phone: (800) 692-7753
Product Description: Allows Mac OS users to create presentations that can be shared with users in other platforms. Presentations can be exported to PDF, PowerPoint, and QuickTime. Includes support for multiple graphics formats, including Adobe Photoshop, Illustrator, and PDF, as well as flash files.
Publisher site: www.apple.com/keynote

PowerPoint 2003
OS: Windows 2000/XP
Price: $229
Publisher: Microsoft
Phone: (800) 426-9400
Product Description: Software for creating, presenting, and collaborating on presentations.

Includes multimedia support, allowing you to add images, audio files, photos, and full-screen video to your presentations.
Publisher site: www.microsoft.com/powerpoint
Download Available

Presenter 1.44
OS: Windows 98/2000/Me/XP/Server 2003
Price: $19.95
Publisher: Powerbullet
Product Description: Application for creating multipage, multimedia, animated Flash presentations. A freeware version offering limited customization is also available.
Publisher site: www.powerbullet.com
Download Available

Producer 2003
OS: Windows 2000/XP
Price: free
Publisher: Microsoft
Phone: (800) 426-9400
Product Description: Free add-on that enhances the multimedia features in PowerPoint 2003. Allows you to add audio and video to presentations that can be viewed in a web browser.
Publisher site: www.microsoft.com/producer
Download Available

Xcelsius X4
OS: Windows 2000/XP/Server 2003
Price: $195
Publisher: Infommersion
Phone: (866) 923-5748
Product Description: Allows you to transfer the contents of an Excel spreadsheet into an interactive Macromedia Flash file, enlivening number-intensive presentations. Numbers can be transferred to charts, tables, and maps.
Publisher site: www.infommersion.com
Download Available

Source: *Entrepreneur's Complete Guide to Software*, 2005 Edition, www.entrepreneur.com/features/softguide/category/0,6570,Presentation,00.html.

Project Management

FastTrack Schedule 8
OS: Windows 95/98/NT 4.0/2000/Me/XP, Mac OS 9.1, OS X 10.1.3
Price: $299
Publisher: AEC Software

Phone: (800) 346-9413
Product Description: Software for organizing, tracking, and managing multiple projects. Allows you to create schedules, track progress and costs, and communicate status and goals.
Publisher site: www.aecsoft.com
Download Available

Groove Virtual Office Professional Edition

OS: Windows NT 4.0 (SP 5 or higher)/2000/XP
Price: $179
Publisher: Groove Networks
Phone: (877) 747-6683
Product Description: Collaboration software that allows you to create virtual work spaces for sharing files and project information. Allows real-time collaboration through IM, voice and text chat, and live document editing. Also lets you conduct virtual meetings.
Publisher site: www.groove.net
Download Available

MindManager X5 Pro

OS: Windows NT 4.0 (SP 6)/2000/XP/XP Tablet PC Edition
Price: $349
Publisher: Mindjet
Phone: (877) 646-3538
Product Description: Application designed to give structure to notes taken during meetings, brainstorming sessions, and project planning sessions. Offers integration with Microsoft Office to allow sharing of results. Compatible with Microsoft Office 2000, XP, and 2003.
Publisher site: www.mindjet.com
Download Available

Office Tracker 7.0

OS: Windows 98/NT/2000/XP/Server 2003
Price: $695 (single user), $1,295 (10-user license)
Publisher: Milum
Phone: (800) 257-2120
Product Description: Scheduling software that allows you to track appointments, group meetings, and use of conference rooms and facilities. Includes a web client that can be used to share schedules across different PCs and platforms, including Linux and Mac.
Publisher site: www.officetracker.com
Download Available

Project Standard 2003

OS: Windows 2000/XP
Price: $599
Publisher: Microsoft
Phone: (800) 426-9400
Product Description: Application for planning and managing projects. Includes tools to organize and track tasks and resources. Offers complete integration with Office System 2003.

Publisher site: *www.microsoft.com/project*
Download Available

ShareDirect Pro
OS: Windows 2000/XP/Server 2003
Price: $99.95 per year
Publisher: Laplink
Phone: (800) 527-5465
Product Description: Allows you to share files and folders with other users by transforming Windows Explorer into a direct peer-to-peer application. Files are shared by designation and invitation only. Can bypass firewalls.
Publisher site: *www.laplink.com*
Download Available

Source: *Entrepreneur's Complete Guide to Software*, 2005 Edition, www.entrepreneur.com/features/softguide/category/0,6570,Project%20Management,00.html.

Security/System Suites

Anti-Virus Small Business Suite
OS: Windows 98/NT 4.0/2000/Me/XP/Server 2003
Price: $490 (five users)
Publisher: F-Secure
Phone: (888) 432-8233
Product Description: Designed to protect network, file and e-mail servers, as well as desktop PCs and notebooks, from viruses and other threats. Includes anti-virus and firewall client for desktops, anti-virus protection for file and e-mail servers, and a policy manager for central management.
Publisher site: *www.f-secure.com*
Download Available

Client Security 3.0
OS: Windows 98/2000/Me/XP
Price: $320 (5 users)
Publisher: Symantec
Phone: (800) 441-7234
Product Description: Offers small businesses protection against viruses, hackers, and blended threats. Includes firewall and anti-virus software, protection for desktops and servers, and centralized management tools.
Publisher site: *www.symantec.com*
Download Available

Exchange Edition 2.0
OS: Microsoft Exchange Server
Price: $599 (up to 10 users)
Publisher: Cloudmark

Section 5

Phone: (415) 543-1220
Product Description: Server-based application designed to fight spam, fraud, and other e-mail threats. Uses Cloudmark's community-based, peer-to-peer filtering model to identify and fight spam.
Publisher site: www.cloudmark.com
Download Available

Section 5

IHateSpam 4
OS: Windows 98/NT 4.0/2000/Me/XP
Price: $19.95 per license
Publisher: Sunbelt Software
Phone: (888) 688-8457
Product Description: Designed to eliminate unsolicited e-mail messages. Works with Eudora, Hotmail, Outlook, and Outlook Express e-mail clients.
Publisher site: www.sunbelt-software.com
Download Available

Internet Security Suite 2005
OS: Windows 98/2000/Me/XP
Price: $69.99
Publisher: McAfee
Phone: (972) 963-8000
Product Description: Provides protection against internet-borne threats, such as worms, viruses, and spam. Includes VirusScan 2005, software-based firewall, SpamKiller and Privacy Service.
Publisher site: www.mcafee.com

Norton Internet Security 2005
OS: Windows 98/2000/Me/XP
Price: $69.95
Publisher: Symantec
Phone: (800) 441-7234
Product Description: Designed to protect computers against online threats, including worms, viruses, hackers, spam, and identity theft. Includes AntiSpam, Norton AntiVirus, Personal Firewall, and Privacy Control.
Publisher site: www.symantec.com
Download Available

PC-cillin Internet Security 2005
OS: Windows 98/2000/Me/XP
Price: $49.99
Publisher: Trend Micro
Phone: (408) 257-1500
Product Description: Protects against hackers, internet-based threats, worms, viruses, Trojan horses, privacy threats, phishing attacks, and spam. Includes firewall, anti-virus, anti-spyware, anti-spam, and privacy protection components. Also includes protection for wired and wireless networks.
Publisher site: www.trendmicro.com

Platinum Internet Security 2005

OS: Windows 98/NT/2000/Me/XP
Price: $79
Publisher: Panda Software
Phone: (818) 543-6901
Product Description: Security suite includes anti-virus, firewall, anti-spam, anti-spyware, and anti-phishing applications. Also includes TruPrevent Technologies, designed to protect against unknown viruses and threats.
Publisher site: www.pandasoftware.com
Download Available

Postini Perimeter Manager Enterprise Edition 5.2

OS: Runs on any platform
Price: $6 to $30 per user per year ($2,500 minimum)
Publisher: Postini
Phone: (888) 584-3150
Product Description: Hosted e-mail security system that protects against viruses and spam. Also guards against directory-harvest attacks, often used by spammers to gather e-mail addresses.
Publisher site: www.postini.com
Download Available

Zone Alarm Security Suite 5.5

OS: Windows 98 SE/2000 Pro/Me/XP
Price: $69.95
Publisher: Zone Labs
Phone: (877) 365-9663
Product Description: Includes firewall and anti-virus software, privacy protection, and protection against e-mail threats, including spam and phishing attacks. Also features protection for IM applications.
Publisher site: www.zonelabs.com
Download Available

Source: *Entrepreneur's Complete Guide to Software*, 2005 Edition, www.entrepreneur.com/features/softguide/category/0,6570,Security~System%20Suites,00.html.

Utilities

Alohabob PC Relocator Business Professional Edition

OS: Windows 95/98/NT/2000/Me/XP
Price: $1,000
Publisher: Eisenworld
Phone: (888) 392-5642
Product Description: Data migration tool. Allows you to move applications, applications settings, system settings, user profiles, files, and folders to new PCs. Professional Edition

includes a 12-month unlimited-usage license.
Publisher site: www.eisenworld.com
Download Available

CalliGrapher 7.4
OS: Pocket PC 2000/2002, Pocket PC Phone Edition 2002/2003, Windows CE 3.0 and higher/Mobile 2003
Price: $29.95
Publisher: PhatWare
Phone: (650) 559-5600
Product Description: Handwriting-recognition software for Pocket PC devices. Uses fuzzy logic and neural net techniques to recognize symbol strings and words from its integrated dictionary. Also supports custom user dictionaries.
Publisher site: www.phatware.com
Download Available

CoolCalc
OS: Pocket PC 2000/2002, Windows Mobile 2003
Price: $19.95
Publisher: Applian
Phone: (415) 480-1748
Product Description: A 12-in-1 programmable calculator. Includes loans, money, dates, conversions, and more, as well as the ability to create customized calculators.
Publisher site: www.applian.com
Download Available

Desktop DNA Professional
OS: Windows 95/98/NT/2000/Me/XP
Price: $69.95
Publisher: Computer Associates
Phone: (888) 423-1000
Product Description: Automates the process of moving to a new PC by transferring application and system settings, mailboxes, toolbars, and bookmarks. Transfers data via removable media, network connections, and Ethernet or USB cables (not included).
Publisher site: www.ca.com

Diskeeper Professional Edition 9
OS: Windows 95/98/NT/2000/Me/XP/Server 2003
Price: $49.50
Publisher: Executive Software
Phone: (800) 829-6468
Product Description: Disk defragmentation software designed to prevent system crashes and slowdowns. Includes "Set It and Forget It" feature for automatic defrags.
Publisher site: www.executive.com
Download Available

GoToMyPC PocketView
OS: Pocket PC 2002/2002 Phone edition, Windows CE 4.x/Mobile 2003/2003 Phone edition

Price: included as part of GoToMyPCPro ($67.80 per month for a four-PC monthly plan)
Publisher: Citrix
Phone: (888) 646-0016
Product Description: Allows you to connect to your desktop PC from your Windows-based PDA. Provides remote access to desktop applications, files, and networks. Offers 128-bit encryption.
Publisher site: www.gotomypc.com
Download Available

JETCET Print
OS: Pocket PC 2002, Windows Mobile 2003
Price: $8.95
Publisher: WESTTEK
Phone: (425) 861-8271
Product Description: Allows users to print Pocket Word files, digital images, contact information, tasks, appointments, and e-mail attachments. Integrates with Westtek's ClearVue document viewers.
Publisher site: www.westtek.com
Download Available

Norton PartitionMagic 8.0
OS: Windows 95/98/NT/2000/Me/XP
Price: $69.95
Publisher: Symantec
Phone: (800) 441-7234
Product Description: Organizes your hard drive by creating, resizing, copying, and merging disk partitions. Allows you to separate your operating system, applications, documents, and backup files to reduce the risk of data loss. Also lets you run multiple OSes simultaneously.
Publisher site: www.symantec.com

Pocket Controller-Professional 4.12
OS: Pocket PC 2000/2002, Windows CE/Mobile 2003
Price: $29.95
Publisher: Soft Object Technologies
Phone: (905) 624-9828
Product Description: Remotely connect to your Windows Mobile-based PDA from your desktop. Allows you to enter data into your mobile device using your desktop or notebook computer.
Publisher site: www.soti.net
Download Available

ThunderHawk 2.0
OS: Pocket PC 2000/2002, Windows Mobile 2003
Price: $49.95 per year
Publisher: Bitstream
Phone: (800) 522-3668
Product Description: Optimizes web pages for viewing on your Windows Mobile-based PDA. Allows you to view full HTML pages wirelessly, and includes a zooming feature so

Section 5

you can adjust the resolution.
Publisher site: www.bitstream.com
Download Available

Voice Command
OS: Pocket PC Phone Edition, Windows Mobile 2003-based Pocket PC
Price: $39.99
Publisher: Microsoft
Phone: (800) 426-9400
Product Description: Allows you to control your Windows Mobile PDA or smartphone through voice commands. You can dial phone numbers, search contacts and calendar entries, and operate Windows Media Player.
Publisher site: www.microsoft.com
Download Available

VoiceCentral 3.0
OS: Pocket PC 2000/2002, Windows Mobile 2003
Price: $29.95
Publisher: Fonix
Phone: (801) 553-6600
Product Description: Lets you operate your Windows Mobile-based handheld by speaking. Launch, utilize, and close applications, dial contacts, listen to e-mail, access your calendar and tasks, and respond to messages via recorded audio files.
Publisher site: www.fonix.com

Source: *Entrepreneur's Complete Guide to Software*, 2005 Edition, www.entrepreneur.com/features/softguide/category/0,6570,Utilities,00.html.

Web Browsers

Contribute 3.0
OS: Mac OS (10.2.8 and later or 10.3.4), Windows 98 SE/2000/XP
Price: $149
Publisher: Macromedia
Phone: (800) 526-0509
Product Description: Content-creation tool designed to allow nontechnical users to publish information to websites and corporate intranets. Offers integration with other Macromedia applications, including Dreamweaver MX 2004.
Publisher site: www.macromedia.com
Download Available

Firefox 1.0
OS: Linux, Mac OS X, Windows 98/2000/Me/XP
Price: free
Publisher: Mozilla Foundation

Product Description: Open-source web browser includes a pop-up ad blocker and built-in security features. Also includes tabbed browsing, allowing you to view more than one web page in a single window.
Publisher site: www.mozilla.org
Download Available

FrameMaker 7.1
OS: Sun Solaris (2.6 and higher), Windows 98 SE/2000/XP
Price: $799 (Windows), $1,329 (UNIX/Solaris)
Publisher: Adobe
Phone: (888) 724-4508
Product Description: Software for publishing content in print, on the web, and as ODF documents. Offers XML files handling and support for print vector graphics.
Publisher site: www.adobe.com
Download Available

Section 5

FrontPage 2003
OS: Windows 2000/XP
Price: $199
Publisher: Microsoft
Phone: (800) 426-9400
Product Description: Tool for designing, creating, publishing, and maintaining a dynamic website. Includes e-commerce tools.
Publisher site: www.microsoft.com/frontpage
Download Available

Internet Explorer 6
OS: Windows 2000/XP
Price: free
Publisher: Microsoft
Phone: (800) 426-9400
Product Description: Microsoft's web browser features built-in search tools, the ability to find and return to previously visited pages, and the ability to save web pages in a list of favorites.
Publisher site: www.microsoft.com
Download Available

Netscape 7.2
OS: Linux Kernel 2.2.14, Mac OS X 10.1.x/10.2.x and later, Windows 98/98 SE/NT 4.0/2000/Me/XP
Price: free
Publisher: America Online
Phone: (866) 541-8233
Product Description: Web browser includes tabbed browsing for viewing multiple web pages in one window, a password manager, an HTML editor, and an e-mail program.
Publisher site: www.netscape.com
Download Available

Opera Browser
OS: FreeBSD, Linux, Mac, OS/2, Psion, Solaris, Windows 95/98/NT/2000/Me/XP
Price: $39
Publisher: Opera Software
Product Description: Can import bookmarks, contacts and e-mails from other applications. Includes an e-mail program. A free, ad-supported version is available. Mobile version is available for PDAs and smartphones.
Publisher site: www.opera.com
Download Available

Safari
OS: Mac OS X
Price: free
Publisher: Apple
Phone: (800) 692-7753
Product Description: Default web browser for Mac OS X. Supports personal certificate authentication and 128-bit encryption for accessing secure sites; features the ability to resume interrupted downloads.
Publisher site: www.apple.com/safari
Download Available

Studio MX 2004 with Flash Professional
OS: Mac OS 10.2.6, Windows 98 SE/2000/XP
Price: $999
Publisher: Macromedia
Phone: (800) 457-1774
Product Description: Web-development suite includes the latest versions of Dreamweaver, Fireworks, Flash, and FreeHand.
Publisher site: www.macromedia.com
Download Available

Source: *Entrepreneur's Complete Guide to Software*, 2005 Edition, www.entrepreneur.com/features/softguide/category/0,6570,Web%20Browsers,00.html.

Where to Find Time Clock Software

Time Clock Plus
www.timeclockplus.com/products/products.aspx

Replicon
www.replicon.com/lp/lpk_time_clock_software.asp

Celayix Software
www.celayix.com

Qqest Software
www.qqesttime.com

# Chapter 28

Wireless and Handheld Business Software

Antivirus/Backup/Security

AntiVirus for Handhelds
OS: Palm OS 3.5/4.x/5, Pocket PC 2002, Windows Mobile 2003
Price: $39.95
Publisher: Symantec
Phone: (800) 441-7234
Product Description: Real-time virus protection for Windows Mobile- and Palm OS-based handhelds. Offers automatic updates, either through a wireless connection or when connected to your PC.
Publisher site: www.symantec.com
Download Available

BackupBuddy 2
OS: Palm OS 2.x and higher
Price: $29.95
Publisher: Blue Nomad Software
Fax: (650) 249-3466
Product Description: Protects the contents of your PDA by storing all changes made to your device since your last backup in a database on your PC. Can restore copies of programs, data files, and settings.
Publisher site: www.bluenomad.com
Download Available

Mobile Anti-Virus
OS: Pocket PC 2000/2002, Symbian OS Series 60, Windows Mobile 2003
Price: $11.77 (six-month subscription)
Publisher: F-Secure
Phone: (888) 432-8233
Product Description: Protection for smartphones and Windows Mobile-based PDAs. Scans all files when they are saved, copied, downloaded or synchronized, and also scans all files on memory cards.
Publisher site: www.f-secure.com
Download Available

PC-cillin for Wireless
OS: Palm OS 3.1/4.x, Pocket PC, Psion Revo/Revo Plus
Price: free with desktop version
Publisher: Trend Micro
Phone: (877) 268-4847
Product Description: Automatic, real-time scanning to protect wireless devices from threats that are downloaded from the internet, sent via e-mail, beamed wirelessly, or acquired during synchronization.
Publisher site: www.trendmicro.com

visKeeper 2.0
OS: Pocket PC 2000/2002, Windows Mobile 2003
Price: $20
Publisher: Sfr GmbH
Product Description: Uses a visual, not text, password to protect your data and documents. The program locks the computer, displays a picture of your choice, and will not allow access to your data until you have entered the correct visual password.
Publisher site: www.viskeeper.com
Download Available

Source: *Entrepreneur's Complete Guide to Software*, 2005 Edition, www.entrepreneur.com/features/softguide/detail/1,5804,,00.html?mode=wl&sCat=Antivirus/Backup/Security.

Section 5

Communication

AIM for Palm and Pocket PC
OS: Palm OS 3.52 and higher, Pocket PC 2002, Windows Mobile 2003
Price: $19.95
Publisher: AOL
Phone: (800) 827-6364
Product Description: Mobile version of AOL's Instant Messenger. Allows you to exchange IMs with other AIM users, whether they're connected via desktop PC or PDA. A version for mobile phones running the Symbian Series 60 OS is also available.
Publisher site: www.aim.com
Download Available

IM+ Mobile Instant Messenger
OS: Palm OS 4 and higher, Pocket PC 2002, Windows Mobile 2003
Price: $29.95 (Windows), $24.95 (Palm OS)
Publisher: Shape Services
Product Description: Mobile IM application. Allows you to connect to a variety of IM services—including AOL, ICQ, Jabber, MSN, and Yahoo!—from one client.
Publisher site: www.shapeservices.de

Onemail
OS: Palm OS, Pocket PC 2002, Windows CE/Mobile 2003
Price: $29.95
Publisher: Brightex Technology Limited
Product Description: Retrieves your web-based e-mail from your PC for display on Windows Mobile- and Palm OS-based devices. Works with Hotmail, MSN, and Yahoo! Mail. No e-mail reader is required.
Publisher site: www.net.worth.com.hk/onemail/main.htm
Download Available

WebIS Mail 2.0
OS: Pocket PC 2002, Windows Mobile 2003
Price: $24.95
Publisher: Web Information Solutions
Product Description: Application for managing your e-mail from your Windows Mobile-based handheld. Can be synchronized with your desktop or with mailboxes on POP3 or IMAP servers.
Publisher site: www.webis.net
Download Available

Source: *Entrepreneur's Complete Guide to Software*, 2005 Edition, www.entrepreneur.com/features/softguide/detail/1,5804,,00.html?mode=wl&sCat=Communication.

Section 5

Database

HanDBase Professional
OS: Palm OS 3.0 or higher, Pocket PC 2000 or higher, Windows CE 3.0 or higher
Price: $39.99
Publisher: DDH Software
Phone: (877) 334-4608
Product Description: Mobile relational database for Palm OS and Windows Mobile PDAs. Includes multi-user syncing so that two or more users can enter data into a single database, as well as the ability to sync with PCs and servers.
Publisher site: www.ddhsoftware.com

SmartList To Go 3.0
OS: Palm OS 3.5 and higher
Price: $49.99
Publisher: DataViz
Phone: (800) 733-0030
Product Description: Allows you to create, view, and manage databases on your Palm OS PDA. Offers synchronization with Microsoft Access and the ability to store databases on expansion cards to save internal memory.
Publisher site: www.dataviz.com
Download Available

Visual CE Professional 9.0
OS: Pocket PC 2000/2002, Windows CE/Mobile 2003
Price: $399
Publisher: Syware
Phone: (617) 497-1300
Product Description: Relational database for Windows Mobile PDAs. Features drag-and-drop controls, an unlimited number of forms, and synchronization with desktop PCs and servers. Data can be shared with desktop software, including Lotus Approach, Microsoft Access, and Oracle.

Publisher site: www.syware.com
Download Available

abcDB Professional Database 6.0
OS: Pocket PC 2002, Windows Mobile 2003
Price: $19.89
Publisher: PocketSOFT.ca
Phone: (780) 628-2212
Product Description: Software for creating and managing databases on your Windows Mobile-based handheld. Features integration with Microsoft Access. Also allows you to access and modify Microsoft Pocket Outlook data from within the application.
Publisher site: www.pocketsoft.ca
Download Available

Source: *Entrepreneur's Complete Guide to Software*, 2005 Edition, www.entrepreneur.com/features/softguide/detail/1,5804,,00.html?mode=wl&sCat=Database.

Financial

Cash Organizer 2004 Deluxe
OS: Pocket PC 2000/2002, Windows Mobile 2003
Price: $29.95
Publisher: Inesoft
Product Description: Software for tracking and analyzing expenses. Allows you to plan for upcoming expenses and income. Includes integration with Microsoft Outlook for accessing contact information.
Publisher site: www.inesoft.com
Download Available

Checkbook
OS: Palm OS 3.0 and higher
Price: $19.95
Publisher: Ultrasoft
Product Description: Financial management software for Palm OS PDAs. Designed for users who don't use a desktop financial software application. Allows you to track transactions, analyze spending, and manage recurring bills.
Publisher site: www.ultrasoft.com

Money 2005 for Windows Mobile-based Pocket PCs
OS: Pocket PC 2002, Windows Mobile 2003
Price: included with desktop version
Publisher: Microsoft
Phone: (800) 426-9400
Product Description: Synchronizes your personal and business financial information between your desktop PC and your Windows Mobile PDA. Investment information can be synced with your desktop or downloaded directly from the internet.
Publisher site: www.microsoft.com

Pocket Quicken
OS: Palm OS 3.0 or higher, Pocket PC 2000/2002, Windows Mobile 2003
Price: $34.95
Publisher: LandWare
Phone: (800) 526-3977
Product Description: Mobile companion to Intuit's desktop Quicken application. Financial tracking software that offers simplified data entry and access to account balances, transactions, and budgets.
Publisher site: www.landware.com
Download Available

PocketMoney
OS: Palm OS 2.0 and higher, Pocket PC 2000/2002, Windows Mobile 2003
Price: $30
Publisher: Catamount Software
Phone: (510) 658-5244
Product Description: Tracks finances on your Windows Mobile- or Palm-based PDA. Tracks spending, checking accounts, savings accounts, credit cards, and petty cash.
Publisher site: www.pocketmoney.com
Download Available

Source: *Entrepreneur's Complete Guide to Software*, 2005 Edition, www.entrepreneur.com/features/softguide/detail/1,5804,,00.html?mode=wl&sCat=Financial.

Office Applications

ClearVue Suite
OS: Pocket PC 2002, Windows Mobile 2003
Price: $29.95
Publisher: Westtek
Phone: (425) 861-8271
Product Description: Collection of document viewers that can open Microsoft Word, Excel and PowerPoint files on your Pocket PC without any conversion. Can also open and view image files. Individual viewers are available for $8.95 each.
Publisher site: www.westtek.com
Download Available

Documents To Go Premium Edition 7
OS: Palm OS 5.0 or higher
Price: $49.99
Publisher: DataViz
Phone: (800) 733-0030
Product Description: Offers word processing, spreadsheets, presentations and support for PDFs and image files on your PDA. You can view and edit existing files or create new documents. Includes support for Microsoft Outlook.

Publisher site: www.dataviz.com
Download Available

Quickoffice Premier

OS: Palm OS 3.0 or above
Price: $39.95
Publisher: Mobile Digital Media
Phone: (800) 991-7360
Product Description: Mobile Office suite for opening and editing native Microsoft Office files on your Palm OS PDA. Includes Quickword, Quicksheet, and Quickpoint for editing Word, Excel, and PowerPoint files, respectively. Also features QuickThesaurus and QuickSpellcheck.
Publisher site: www.quickoffice.com
Download Available

RepliGo 2.0

OS: Palm OS 3.5 and higher, Pocket PC 2002, Windows Mobile 2003
Price: $29.95
Publisher: Cerience
Phone: (970) 282-3850
Product Description: Converts documents from your PC for viewing on your PDA. Allows you to view Microsoft Word, Excel, PowerPoint, Project, Visio, and PDF files as well as web pages in their original formats.
Publisher site: www.cerience.com
Download Available

TextMaker

OS: Pocket PC 2000/2002, Windows Mobile 2003
Price: $49.95
Publisher: SoftMaker Software
Product Description: Full-featured Word processor for Windows Mobile-based PDAs. Includes a multilingual spell-checker; support for graphics, footnotes, and tables, and the ability to view Microsoft Word documents in their original format.
Publisher site: www.softmaker.com
Download Available

WordSmith for Palm OS

OS: Palm OS 3.0 and higher
Price: $29.95
Publisher: Blue Nomad Software
Phone: (650) 249-3466
Product Description: Word processor, electronic book-reader, and enhanced memo pad for Palm PDAs. Features a spell-checker and thesaurus, and integration with Microsoft Word.
Publisher site: www.bluenomad.com
Download Available

Source: *Entrepreneur's Complete Guide to Software*, 2005 Edition, www.entrepreneur.com/features/softguide/detail/1,5804,,00.html?mode=wl&sCat=Office+Applications.

Time Management

AllTime
OS: Palm OS 3.5 and higher
Price: $39.95
Publisher: Iambic
Phone: Fax: (408) 736-2022
Product Description: Software for tracking time, expenses, and mileage on your Palm PDA. Tracks time during meetings, phone calls, and billable hours.
Publisher site: www.iambic.com
Download Available

Time Recorder
OS: Pocket PC 2000/2002, Windows Mobile 2003
Price: $15
Publisher: Owlseeker Solutions
Product Description: Time-tracking application includes a timer mode. Allows you to record time spent on certain tasks and view a breakdown by day or by project.
Publisher site: www.owlseeker.demon.co.uk
Download Available

TimeBiller
OS: Pocket PC 2002, Windows Mobile 2003
Price: $40
Publisher: Fann Software
Phone: (817) 548-2199
Product Description: Time-tracking and billing tool. Allows you to track multiple clients and projects, and link clients with projects, tasks, and contacts.
Publisher site: www.fannsoftware.com
Download Available

Titrax 4.0
OS: Any Palm OS
Price: free
Publisher: Titrax
Product Description: Time-tracking utility. Allows you to track the amount of time spent on a given project in a day.
Publisher site: www.titrax.com

Source: *Entrepreneur's Complete Guide to Software*, 2005 Edition, www.entrepreneur.com/features/softguide/detail/1,5804,,00.html?mode=wl&sCat=Time+Management.

Utilities

CalliGrapher 7.4

OS: Pocket PC 2000/2002, Pocket PC Phone Edition 2002/2003, Windows CE 3.0 and higher/Mobile 2003
Price: $29.95
Publisher: PhatWare
Phone: (650) 559-5600
Product Description: Handwriting-recognition software for Pocket PC devices. Uses fuzzy logic and neural net techniques to recognize symbol strings and words from its integrated dictionary. Also supports custom user dictionaries.
Publisher site: www.phatware.com
Download Available

CoolCalc

OS: Pocket PC 2000/2002, Windows Mobile 2003
Price: $19.95
Publisher: Applian
Phone: (415) 480-1748
Product Description: A 12-in-1 programmable calculator. Includes loans, money, dates, conversions, and more, as well as the ability to create customized calculators.
Publisher site: www.applian.com
Download Available

GoToMyPC PocketView

OS: Pocket PC 2002/2002 Phone edition, Windows CE 4.x/Mobile 2003/2003 Phone edition
Price: included as part of GoToMyPCPro ($67.80 per month for a four-PC monthly plan)
Publisher: Citrix
Phone: (888) 646-0016
Product Description: Allows you to connect to your desktop PC from your Windows-based PDA. Provides remote access to desktop applications, files, and networks. Offers 128-bit encryption.
Publisher site: www.gotomypc.com
Download Available

JETCET Print

OS: Pocket PC 2002, Windows Mobile 2003
Price: $8.95
Publisher: WESTTEK
Phone: (425) 861-8271
Product Description: Allows users to print Pocket Word files, digital images, contact information, tasks, appointments, and e-mail attachments. Integrates with Westtek's ClearVue document viewers.
Publisher site: www.westtek.com
Download Available

Pocket Controller-Professional 4.12
OS: Pocket PC 2000/2002, Windows CE/Mobile 2003
Price: $29.95
Publisher: Soft Object Technologies
Phone: (905) 624-9828
Product Description: Remotely connect to your Windows Mobile-based PDA from your desktop. Allows you to enter data into your mobile device using your desktop or notebook computer.
Publisher site: www.soti.net
Download Available

ThunderHawk 2.0
OS: Pocket PC 2000/2002, Windows Mobile 2003
Price: $49.95 per year
Publisher: Bitstream
Phone: (800) 522-3668
Product Description: Optimizes web pages for viewing on your Windows Mobile-based PDA. Allows you to view full HTML pages wirelessly, and includes a zooming feature so you can adjust the resolution.
Publisher site: www.bitstream.com
Download Available

Voice Command
OS: Pocket PC Phone Edition, Windows Mobile 2003-based Pocket PC
Price: $39.99
Publisher: Microsoft
Phone: (800) 426-9400
Product Description: Allows you to control your Windows Mobile PDA or smartphone through voice commands. You can dial phone numbers, search contacts and calendar entries, and operate Windows Media Player.
Publisher site: www.microsoft.com

VoiceCentral 3.0
OS: Pocket PC 2000/2002, Windows Mobile 2003
Price: $29.95
Publisher: Fonix
Phone: (801) 553-6600
Product Description: Lets you operate your Windows Mobile-based handheld by speaking. Launch, utilize, and close applications, dial contacts, listen to e-mail, access your calendar and tasks, and respond to messages via recorded audio files.
Publisher site: www.fonix.com

Source: *Entrepreneur's Complete Guide to Software*, 2005 Edition, www.entrepreneur.com/features/softguide/detail/1,5804,,00.html?mode=wl&sCat=Utilities.

Business Travel

Seven Simple Ways to Maximize Tax Deductions for Travel

1. Allocate travel expenses between business and non-business. Prorate your business and non-business expenses to identify the business expenses that are tax-deductible. If your travel is all business, you can deduct all the travel-related expenses. If your travel is part business and part non-business, you can prorate your expenses between business and non-business to identify business expenses that are tax-deductible.

2. Do not prorate the travel costs of getting to and from your business destination. Even though your entire travel activities were not business (only), you do not have to prorate the travel costs of getting to and from your business destination. Even though you engaged in non-business activities on your travel, you can deduct the entire cost of getting to and from your business destination—if your travel takes you to your business destination in a reasonably direct fashion.

3. Deduct costs associated with travel outside the United States. Even if you did not spend your entire time on business, you can deduct the entire cost of your travel outside the United States—if you meet any of the following three exceptions:

   ■ You were outside the United States no more than one week (seven consecutive days).

   ■ You were outside the United States and less than 25 percent of the time was spent on non-business (personal) travel.

   ■ You can establish that a personal vacation was not a major consideration, even if you have substantial control over arranging the travel.

4. Deduct travel expenses for another individual. You can deduct the travel expenses for an individual who travels with you on a business trip under any of the following circumstances:

   ■ He or she is an employee of your business.

   ■ You traveled with any of the following business associates, with whom it is reasonable to expect that you will actively conduct business: customer, client, supplier, agent, partner (co-owner of the business), or a professional advisor.

5. Deduct the cost of travel associated with your attending a business convention. You can deduct your travel expenses when you attend a convention—if you can show that your attendance benefits your business. Note: You cannot deduct the travel expenses of your family. The convention or seminar must have scheduled a minimum of six hours during the day (and you must have attended at least two-thirds of those activities—more than four hours).

6. Deduct up to $2,000 each year for attending cruise ship conventions that are directly related to your business. To do this, you must meet all of the following conditions:

- The ship must be registered in the United States.

- All ports must be in the United States or one of its possessions.

- You must submit two supporting statements with your tax return.

- You must spend at least 51 percent of your (waking) time attending the seminar.

7. Qualify a day as a business day. You can qualify a day for business, and therefore for a business tax deduction, if your primary activity was business. A good rule of thumb is that your business activity be at least four hours in length, during normal working hours.

Source: David Meir, "Travel-Related Tax Deductions," www.entrepreneur.com/article/ 0,4621,307376,00.html.

Section 5

Five Online Resources to Find Legit Hotel Ratings

TripAdvisor.com
Pick a destination, and this site ranks the hotels there based on star ratings provided by its members. With more than 1 million travel reviews on over 140,000 hotels and resorts, over 90,000 restaurants and nearly 60,000 attractions, TripAdvisor.com is by far the most popular travel review site. Another perk: to round out its hotel reviews, it provides links to online guidebook content and recent articles about each hotel.

Hotelchatter.com
This campy site groups hotels into "Hotel Heaven" or "Hotel Hell," reveals where celebrities have bedded down in "Celebrity Scoop," and offers a daily newsletter and blog with a lot of attitude—and a lot of good information. Much of the information on the site comes from members who send in their news, tips, and reviews.

HotelShark.com
The editors at HotelShark.com parse incoming reviews, advising hopeful contributors that "excessive giddiness, or gratuitous profanity, meets with our suspicion. We take seriously opinions that are thoughtful, specific, and sincere." You'll find many detailed reviews for popular, well-traveled destinations like New York City and San Francisco, but the number of reviews thins out for second-tier cities like Atlanta and Dallas.

Travel.yahoo.com
If you want to read consumer reviews, look in the "Travel Guides" section of this site. Yahoo!'s hotel reviews are similar to what you'll find at TripAdvisor, but they tend to be shorter and lean toward the positive. You'll also find links to other online guidebook reviews and articles about each hotel. Yahoo! provides helpful maps that display restaurants and attractions in each hotel's neighborhood.

CitySearch.com
Choose the city, then click on the "Hotels" tab for reviews. CitySearch posts editorial

reviews (claiming they're written independently of advertising on the site), plus user commentary and reviews.

Source: Chris McGinnis, "Seeing Stars," www.entrepreneur.com/Magazines/ Copy_of_MA_SegArticle/0,4453,322390,00.html.

15 Great Travel Books

Here is an eclectic combination of travel resource books. The topics range from road maps to common mistakes when traveling.

1. *202 Tips Even the Best Business Traveler May Not Know* by Christopher J. McGinnis
2. *Fly Free as Easy as 1-2-3!* by David Crandall
3. *Discount Airfares: The Insider's Guide, How to Save Up to 75% on Airline Tickets* by George E. Hobart
4. *Fly Free, Stay Cheap!: 'How-To' Strategies and Tips for Free Flights and Cheap Travel* by Vicki Mills
5. *62 Natural Ways to Beat Jet Lag* by Charles B. Inlander and Cynthia K. Moran
6. *Organize Your Business Travel: Simple Routines for Managing Your Work When You're Out of the Office* by Ronni Eisenberg
7. *The Unofficial Business Traveler's Pocket Guide: 249 Tips Even the Best Business Traveler May Not Know* by Christopher J. McGinnis
8. *Wendy Perrin's Secrets Every Smart Traveler Should Know* by Wendy Perrin
9. *Pack It Up: A Book for the Contemporary Traveler* by Anne McAlpin
10. *The Packing Book: Secrets of the Carry-on Traveler* by Judith Gilford
11. *Keeping Your Family Close: When Frequent Travel Pulls You Apart* by Elizabeth M. Hoekstra
12. *The Smart Woman's Guide to Business Travel* by Laurie D. Borman
13. *101 Stupid Things Business Travelers Do to Sabotage Success* by Harry Knitter
14. *The Business Traveler's World Guide* by Philip Seldon and Dale Strand
15. *Rand McNally Road Atlas: United States, Canada, Mexico*

Source: "15 Travel Tomes," www.entrepreneur.com/article/0,4621,289169,00.html.

15 Ways to Tackle Your Trip Overseas

1. **Avoid hot spots.** They're everywhere you don't want to be. "Know which cities are safe to walk around in at night," advises Atlanta media consultant and business trav–

eler James Caruso. Check with the government's Consular Information Sheets and the U.S. Centers for Disease Control to steer clear of any dangerous areas.

Insider tip: Private organizations such as Kroll Associates (800 824-7502) also offer reports on global hot spots.

2. **Know your airlines.** Code-sharing can confuse even the most seasoned travelers. This is when your ticket is issued through one carrier, but the flight is shared with another carrier and may even use the other airline's plane. This usually doesn't make a lot of difference unless you're counting on a particular service or amenity. For example, you might pack a power adaptor that fits the outlets on a U.S. carrier but end up on its European code-share partner without the correct plug. Or, if you're counting on a favorite meal on a particular flight, you might have to go without.

Another downside to code-sharing is that sometimes there are dramatic price differences between tickets for the same flight. Terry Trippler, a consumer advocate with OneTravel.com, a bargain travel web site, found that for one particular flight, a ticket that cost $1,050 if you bought it through Continental was just $209 if you bought it through code-share partner Northwest.

Insider tip: 1travel.com gives you the lowdown on airline rules and regulations.

3. **Phone home first.** Rent a cell phone before you leave. Depending on which country you're traveling to, using a rented cell phone is probably less expensive than using the phones at your hotel. Checking with an expert before you leave will also ensure you'll have the right cellular for the country you're in.

Insider tip: Most of Europe and Asia is on the GSM (global system for mobile communications) network and their phones operate on a frequency that is incompatible with the majority of U.S. mobile phones.

4. **Use the web.** The internet is an excellent resource for business intelligence. Whether it's a pre-trip briefing using financial data from a service such as Dow Jones Interactive or a random internet search for the best restaurants in an international city, logging on beforehand can help prevent problems. "You'll know what to do before you get there," says Malcolm Kaufman, president of online business travel service ontheroad.com. The internet is also a must-have tool for making lightning-fast airline, hotel, and car rental bookings when your travel agent is unavailable.

Insider tip: Web sites such as TheTrip.com can even help you track a flight.

5. **Brush up on the language.** New programs can help you learn to speak like a native. Berlitz Passport to 31 Languages, a CD-ROM tutorial that helps you grasp the essential elements of 31 major languages, is a great crash course. With the help of a microphone plugged in to your PC, the multi-CD set compares your speech with that of a native and lets you hone your pronunciation until you sound like you fit in. The set costs about $30.

Insider tip: For more in-depth language study, Berlitz also offers CDs that teach you a single language.

Section 5

6. **Hedge your bets.** Offset the risks of travel with adequate insurance. Traveling may be expensive, but insurance to protect you and your business in case you get sick on the road generally isn't. Figure on spending about $100 per year for the most comprehensive coverage. "People often don't buy insurance, and then they get hit with a large bill—anywhere from $30,000 to $50,000—if they need to be airlifted out of a country and brought back to the United States for medical attention," says Jeffrey G. Jones, director of the Traveler's Health Center at St. Francis Hospital and Health Centers in Indianapolis.

Insider tip: Insuring your entire company or family is often cheaper than buying coverage for an individual.

7. **Get your shots.** This will keep you from getting sick on the road and having to use that travelers' insurance. Researching a country's endemic diseases is extremely important, says Bruce Taylor, manager of clinical services for online pharmacist Soma.com. "Because certain immunizations require more than one dosage to ensure effectiveness, travelers should allow at least 30 days before their trip to secure all necessary shots or medications."

Insider tip: If you've never been a frequent flier, it's a good idea to see your doctor for a checkup, even if you're traveling to a well-developed country.

8. **Pack like a pro.** If you're going to live out of your suitcase, at least make it livable. Buy a durable carry-on bag and invest in industrial-strength luggage. Never put all your important travel documents in a single bag; spread the risk among all your luggage. Bob Morgan, a professor emeritus at Gardner-Webb University in Boiling Springs, North Carolina, and a seasoned business traveler, suggests folding shirts and blouses into gallon-size freezer bags. "They won't get as wrinkled as they would be if you just folded them and put them in your suitcase," he says.

Insider tip: Stuff your socks in your shoes. It conserves space.

9. **Stay sane on the plane.** Don't board a flight without the following items: a carry-on bag packed with a sleeping mask, earplugs, saline solution (if you wear contact lenses), moisturizer, lip balm, pain reliever, bottled water, a snack, and, of course, something to keep you busy (a book or paperwork). Cabin air is bone dry, so above all, don't leave out the liquids, warns Ron Welding of the Air Transport Association. "Drink lots of fluids," he advises. "And stay away from caffeine and alcohol." They both dehydrate you.

Insider tip: Try noise-canceling headphones. They really work.

10. **Behave.** International airlines are cracking down on passengers who misbehave. Virgin Atlantic Airways chairman Richard Branson has supported a plan to blacklist potentially dangerous "air rage" passengers from flights, and Vereinigung Cockpit E.V., the German pilots' association, recently suggested parceling out nicotine gum to smokers who get cut off from their cigarettes. The group also wants to limit the number of alcoholic drinks served to passengers.

Insider tip: Book a seat next to the bulkhead, where there's less chance of an in-flight incident.

11. **Get connected.** Don't suffer without e-mail while you're on the road. A few years ago, you could afford to take a break from your inbox but no longer. The Europe Access Pack from 1-800-Batteries all but guarantees you'll make a connection. The package includes 20 telephone adaptors and six grounded power adaptors, plus an in-line telephone coupler, a modular dual telephone adaptor, a two-line adaptor, and an RJ11 retractable phone cable. Use them anywhere from Austria to Russia. The whole kit costs $230.

    Insider tip: Too thrifty to buy the package? Pack a screwdriver and make the connections yourself. (You'll want to practice before you leave.)

12. **Stay connected.** Make sure your laptop remains in peak condition during your trip. Symantec's Mobile Essentials 2.0, for instance, is a nifty application that helps you connect to the Internet while you're away from the office. It handles complex and time-consuming tasks, such as troubleshooting, with ease and reduces your setup time significantly. At a cost of about $70, the current release will probably save you lots of headaches.

    Insider tip: A little know-how will make these kinds of programs unnecessary. However, if time is short, they're indispensable.

13. **Remember your ATM card.** Accepted in nearly every major international city, ATM cards are safer than carrying cash and less cumbersome than travelers' checks. "Using credit cards or ATM cards also helps you avoid the sky-high commissions banks charge to exchange your currency," says Paolo Mantegazza, president and CEO of tour operator Globus & Cosmos. In addition, he notes, ATM cards can help save you money by securing that day's exchange rate and allowing you to withdraw exactly the currency you need.

    Insider tip: Your bank can furnish you with a list of locations where your ATM card will be accepted.

14. **Don't worry about the euro.** You won't notice much of a change—for now. Travelers heading to Europe shouldn't give a second thought to the new currency being used in paperless transactions. "While the euro will mean significant changes in Europe, for business travelers using [credit] cards, it'll be business as usual," assures Mike Sherman of Visa International. He says his company's payment system has been handling euro transactions since January 1999. For all intents and purposes, he says, the process of paying in euros on a credit card is now seamless.

    Insider tip: Euro notes and coins were put into circulation January 1, 2002. [This article was published in August 1999. The euro is now in use in Austria, Belgium, Finland, France, Greece, Germany, Ireland, Italy, Luxembourg, Netherlands, Portugal, and Spain.]

15. **Don't forget the chambers of commerce.** There are 85 U.S. Chambers of Commerce around the world that can help make your international trips successful.

Section 5

"The chambers of commerce offer a number of insights and services for companies that want to go global," says John Howard of the U.S. Chambers of Commerce. The chambers will help a U.S. business owner get settled in his or her new country and give start-ups advice on everything from customs to the business climate. Call (800) 649-9719 for more information.

Insider tip: A U.S. Chamber of Commerce is often an entrepreneur's first contact in a foreign city. The community of expatriates found there often becomes a de facto social club for travelers.

Source: Christopher Elliot, "Around The World In 15 Ways," www.entrepreneur.com/article/0,4621,230528-1,00.html.

List of Airlines and Web Sites

A

Air Canada
www.aircanada.com

Air China
www.airchina.com

Air France
www.airfrance.com

Air India
airindia.com

AirTran Airways
www.airtran.com

Alaska Airlines/Horizon Air
www.airtran.com

America West Airlines
www.americawest.com/awa/

American Airlines
www.aa.com

Asiana Airlines
us.flyasiana.com

ATA Airlines
www.ata.com

B

British Airways
ba.com

C

Cathay Pacific
www.cathaypacific.com

China Airlines
www.china-airlines.com

Continental Airlines
www.continental.com

D

Delta Air Lines
www.delta.com

E

Emirates
www.emirates.com

F

Finnair
www.finnair.com

Frontier Airlines
www.flyfrontier.com

G

Ghana Airways
www.ghanaairways-us.com

Gulf Air
www.gulfairco.com

H

Hawaiian Airlines
www.hawaiianair.com

Hooters Air
www.hootersair.com

I

Icelandair
www.icelandair.com

Iran Air
Iranair.co.ir

J

Japan Airlines
www.japanair.com

Jet Blue
www.jetblue.com

K

KLM Royal Dutch Airlines
www.klm.com

Korean Air
www.koreanair.com

L

Lufthansa
www.lufthansa-usa.com

M

Malaysia Air
www.emalaysiatravel.com

Mexicana Airlines
www.mexicana.com

Midway Airlines
www.midwayair.com

Midwest Express Airlines
www.midwestairlines.com

N

Northwest Airlines
www.nwa.com

P

Pan American Airlines
www.flypanam.com

Philippine Airlines
www.philippineairlines.com

Q

Qantas Airlines
www.qantas.com.au/index.html

R

Royal Brunei Airlines
www.bruneiair.com

S

Singapore Airlines
www.singaporeair.com

Sky West Airlines
www.skywest.com

South African Airways
ww2.flysaa.com/saa_home.html

Southwest Airlines
www.southwest.com

U

United Airlines
www.united.com

U.S. Airways
www.usairways.com

V

Virgin Atlantic Airways
www.virgin-atlantic.com

Source: "Airline Sites," ww.entrepreneur.com/
article/0,4621,289036,00.html.

Great Places to Dine Solo

The following restaurants cater to or have special programs for solo diners, according to Marya Charles Alexander, editor and publisher of *Solo Dining Savvy*.

Boston

Durgin Park
340 Faneuil Hall Marketplace
Boston
(617) 227-2038

Chicago

Gordon
500 N. Clark Street
Chicago
(312) 467-9780

Dallas

City Cafe
5757 Lovers Lane
Dallas
(214) 351-2233

Los Angeles

Pacific Dining Car
1310 W. Sixth Street
Los Angeles
(213) 483-6000

New Orleans

Emeril's
800 Tchoupitoulas Street

New Orleans
(504) 528-9393

New York

The Library at the Regency Hotel
540 Park Avenue
New York
(212) 759-4100

San Francisco

One Market Restaurant
1 Market Street
San Francisco
(415) 777-5577

Seattle

Union Square Grill
621 Union Street
Seattle
(206) 224-4321

Washington

Red Sage
605 14th Street N.W.
Washington, DC
(202) 638-4444

Source: Karin Moeller, "Table for One," www.Entrepreneur.com/article/ 0,4621,228363,00.html.

Best Nationally Ranked Cheap Places to Eat

1. Cheeseboard Pizza
1512 Shattuck Avenue
Berkeley, CA

A hugely popular Berkeley institution draws throngs with its artisanal organic pizza.

2. The Cosmic Cantina
1920 1/2 Perry Street
Durham, NC

Fast, cheap, and tasty: Duke students and young professionals flock to this Durham institution all day (and night).

3. Crif Dogs
113 St. Marks Place
New York, NY

Kick it with cheap chili dogs and video games on St. Marks.

4. Dunbar's Creole Cooking
4927 Freret Street
New Orleans, LA

Unassuming dining spot sets higher standard for Creole comfort food.

5. Grant Central Pizza
451 Cherokee Avenue, SE
Atlanta, GA

Charming neighborhood Italian joint serves cheap, delicious pizza and pasta.

6. Magnolia Cafe South
1920 S. Congress Avenue
Austin, TX

A 24-hour Austin dining institution serving home-style favorites in a casual, bohemian setting.

7. Penny's Noodle Shop
3400 N. Sheffield Avenue
Chicago, IL

Bold Asian flavors and bargain prices make this neighborhood joint hot with the locals.

8. Skyline Chili
8635 Colerain Avenue
Cincinnati, OH

A local favorite since 1949, this is the birthplace of Cincinnati-style chili and the three-way.

9. Tommy's Thai
3410 E. Colfax Avenue
Denver, CO

This remodeled Congress Park favorite still serves up simple, tasty, inexpensive Thai food.

10. Versailles
1415 S. La Cienega Boulevard
Los Angeles, CA

Cuban-style food is a hit with the masses, thanks to an almost-legendary garlic chicken dish.

Source: "Best Cheap Eats: 2003 National Winners," www.bestofcitysearch.com/2003/national/restaurants/cheap_eats/index.html.

Online Flight-Booking Agencies

Hotwire
www.hotwire.com

Hotwire provides low prices without any time-consuming bidding. Hotwire has partnered with airlines to allow access to empty seats at unpublished discount prices.

Priceline
www.priceline.com

Priceline.com pioneered a unique new type of e-commerce through which consumers named the price they're willing to pay for airline tickets, hotel rooms, rental cars, and more.

Travelocity.com
www.travelocity.com

At Travelocity you can book flights, hotel reservations, cruises, car rentals, and more. Travelocity also handles international reservations, to and from any country.

ebookers.com
www.ebookers.com

ebookers is Europe's leading 24-hour travel service. European travelers may make reservations here for international flight, hotel, and car reservations.

Expedia
www.expedia.com

Expedia offers worldwide flight booking, plus complete destination information and links to hotel, cruise, and car rental booking entities.

TravelNow.com
www.travelnow.com

Travelnow.com offers a large selection of hotels worldwide as well as flight, car, rail, and cruise reservations.

CheapTickets
www.cheaptickets.com

CheapTickets provides consumers access to a large selections of low fares, accommodations, customizable vacation packages, cruises, rental cars, condo rentals, and last-minute trips.

Orbitz
www.orbitz.com

Orbitz makes it easy to find low fares on more than 455 airlines. It also offers a selection of hotel rates (including discounted OrbitzSaver SM rates), preferred rates from a comprehensive selection of car rental companies, and special deals on cruises available only to online customers.

Travelzoo
www.travelzoo.com

Travelzoo Inc. features sales and specials available directly from more than 300 travel companies.

Source: compiled by author.

Entrepreneur.com's List of Car Rental Agencies

Ace Rent a Car
www.acerentacar.com

Alamo Rent a Car
www.alamo.com

AutoRentalDiscount.com
www.autorentaldiscount.com

Budget Rent-a-Car
www.budget.com

Dollar Rent-a-Car
www.dollarcar.com

Enterprise
www.enterprise.com

Hertz
www.hertz.com

National Car Rental
www.nationalcar.com

Payless Car Rental
www.paylesscarrental.com

Rent-A-Wreck
www.rent-a-wreck.com

Rentadeal.com
www.rentadeal.com

Thrifty Car Rental
www.thrifty.com

U-Save Auto Rental
www.usave.net

Source: "Rental Car Web Sites," www.entrepreneur.com/article/0,4621,288669,00.html.

13 Low-Cost Car Rental Web Sites

ComparisonTravel.com
www.comparisontravel.com

Priceline
www.priceline.com

Expedia
www.expedia.com

Hotwire
www.hotwire.com

Travelocity.com
www.travelocity.com

BookingBuddy.com
www.bookingbuddy.com

AirportRentalCars
www.airportrentalcars.com

CheapTickets
www.cheaptickets.com

all-cheap-travel.com
www.all-cheap-travel.com

IncredibleTravelDeals.com
www.incredibletraveldeals.com

TripMania.com
www.tripmania.com

MyTravelGuide
www.mytravelguide.com

SideStep
www.idestep.com

Source: compiled by author.

How to Watch out for Hidden Car Rental Costs

Car rental companies generally charge four types of basic rates:

1. A daily rate with a mileage charge

2. A daily rate with a limited number of free miles per day

3. A daily rate with unlimited mileage

4. A rate that has free mileage over an extended period.

Most firms offer economy, compact, intermediate, and deluxe cars—rates vary according to the size and style of the vehicle. Special promotional rates are often available, especially over weekends, but they should be specifically requested in advance.

Watch out for these additional charges:

- Being charged an extra fee if a car is returned to a different city or location than where it was picked up.

- Check details about the insurance policy. Usually, if a rental car is damaged the renter may be responsible for the first several hundred dollars (the deductible); the renter may even have to buy the car. You can absolve yourself from this liability by purchasing a Collision Damage Waiver or Loss Damage Waiver. Although these are optional, some rental companies insist that you purchase CDW or LDW as regulations vary from state to state. Your personal auto insurance may already provide coverage for damage to rental cars, so it may be unnecessary. You may also want to consider the cost of purchasing other kinds of coverage, like personal accident insurance, personal effects coverage, or additional liability insurance.

- The next rental budget buster is gasoline. Make sure you are familiar with the car rental company's policy on gasoline when you check in. Some companies charge you a flat rate for gas upon renting the car and expect you to return with the gas tank empty. Most, however, will levy a charge based on the firm's gas rates for filling the gas tank when the car is returned, if it is not already full. If this is the case, be sure to fill the tank before returning the car—gas prices are usually cheaper at gas stations.

- In addition to the daily rental rate, taxes are also charged. These vary from state to state. For international car rentals, taxes often raise the original rate price by 10 to 30 percent. International rentals are also subject to a possible value added tax.

- At a few airport rental locations, some car rental companies may also tack on an "airport surcharge" fee of about 10 percent of the rental rate in addition to normal taxes.

- Be sure to read the rental agreement carefully to see what the rental rate covers. Look for possible restrictions. If a car rental firm is offering a low rate, make sure that the agreement's restrictions do not outweigh the cost savings.

Source: "Car Rentals: The Hidden Costs," www.morebusiness.com/running_your_business/ profitability/d930585175.brc.

Entrepreneur.com's Business Travel Awards

These awards were created 12 years ago to give entrepreneurs the best travel suppliers that offer the best travel products and services for entrepreneurs at the most affordable prices.

Airlines

Best Low-Fare Airline Value
AirTran Airways
www.airtran.com
(800) AIR-TRAN

Best Major Airline Value
Southwest Airlines
www.southwest.com
(800) I-FLY-SWA

Hotels

Best Budget Hotel Value
Holiday Inn Express
www.hiexpress.com
(800) HOLIDAY

Best Midprice Hotel Value
Hampton Inn & Suites and Hampton Inn
www.hamptoninn.com
(800) HAMPTON

Best Upscale Hotel Value
W Hotels

www.whotels.com
1(877) W-HOTELS

Best Hotel Value in Chicago
Hilton Garden Inn Chicago/Downtown
www.hiltongardenchicago.com
(312) 527-1989

Best Hotel Value in New York City
Affinia Dumont
www.affinia.com
(212) 481-7600

Best Hotel Value in San Francisco
Courtyard by Marriott Downtown
www.marriott.com
(415) 947-0700

Car Rental and Online Deals

Best Site for Hotel/Car Rental Rate Deals
Priceline.com
www.priceline.com

Best Car Rental Value
Enterprise Rent-A-Car
www.enerprise.com

Best Site for Airfare Deals
SideStep.com
www.sidestep.com

Best Site for Travel Advice

USAToday.com/travel
www.usatoday.com/travel

Travel Must-Haves

Luggage
Hatman's Mobile Traveler—easy airport travel
www.hartmann.com/shop

The Commute Bag—messenger bag with protective pouch for laptop
www.timbuk2.com

Gadgets
Eagle Pack-it Compressor Set—creates 80 percent more packing space
www.magellans.com

Bucky Shades—ultimate lightweight eye mask for traveling on planes
www.bucky.com

Source: Entrepreneur's Business Travel Awards," www.entrepreneur.com/travelcenter.

Section
5

Chapter 30

Managing Your Business

Four Bookkeeping Tips

When setting up your bookkeeping system, keep these four points in mind:

1. **Competency.**
   To run a small business efficiently, you must become familiar with your bookkeeping system as well as the financial report it generates. Even if you hire a bookkeeper, it is crucial that you understand the numbers. Successful entrepreneurs are proficient in all areas of their business. Most community colleges offer basic training in financial statements. Sign up for a class so you can make sure you have control of your finances and make sure the money is going in the right places.

2. **Computerization.**
   Don't let your lack of computer skills keep you from automating your bookkeeping system. You have to think long term here. A manual system might suffice in the early stages, but it will become more difficult when you grow and it can become very costly as well.

3. **Consistency.**
   When deciding on a computer software package for your bookkeeping system, don't just consider the price. The important issues are:

   - The track record of the software system itself
   - The track record of the software manufacturer
   - The amount of technical assistance provided by the manufacturer.

4. **Compatibility.**
   Before you make a final bookkeeping software decision, check to see if the system is compatible with the other software you plan to use in your venture.

Source: Rieva Lesonsky, *Start Your Own Business.*

Smart Steps Before Hiring a Payroll Service

No business is too small to use a payroll service. Even a company with fewer than five employees can benefit from outsourcing its payroll. But before you hire a payroll service, take these smart steps:

- Check out the service's reputation. Ask for references from clients, accountants, and bankers.

- Ask about the specific services available. Some companies help with payroll deductions and direct deposits.

- Make sure the service knows about all the federal and state government requirements and regulations. Good services give you brochures to keep you informed.

- Rates are based on your number of employees and how often they're paid. It costs more to handle weekly payrolls than biweekly ones.

Still hesitant? You can handle payroll yourself with special payroll software, but then it's your responsibility to keep up with changing regulations.

Source: Rieva Lesonsky, *365 Tips to Boost Your Entrepreneurial IQ.*

Pros and Cons of Outsourcing Your Human Resources

Deciding which HR functions to offload and which firm to outsource to can be quite a challenge. This buyer's guide will help you to easily navigate through the process.

What is HR outsourcing?

HR outsourcing services generally fall into four categories: PEOs, BPOs, ASPs, and e-services. The terms are used loosely, so a big tip is to know exactly what the outsourcing firm you are investigating offers, especially when it comes to employee liability.

- **PEOs.** A Professional Employer Organization (PEO) assumes full responsibility of your company's human resources administration. It becomes a co-employer of your company's workers by taking full legal responsibility of your employees, including having the final say in hiring, firing, and the amount of money employees make. The PEO and business owner become partners, essentially, with the PEO handling all the HR aspects and the business handling all other aspects of the company. By proper definition, a service is a PEO only when it takes legal responsibility of employees.

- **BPOs.** Business Process Outsourcing is a broad term referring to outsourcing in all fields, not just HR. A BPO differentiates itself by either putting in new technology or applying existing technology in a new way to improve a process. Specifically in HR, a BPO would make sure a company's HR system is supported by the latest technologies, such as self-access and HR data warehousing.

- **ASPs.** Application service providers host software on the web and rent it to users—some ASPs host HR software. Some are well-known packaged applications (People Soft) while others are customized HR software developed by the vendor. These software programs can manage payroll, benefits, and more.

- **E-services.** E-services are those HR services that are web-based. Both BPOs and ASPs are often referred to as e-services.

What can you get?

When you outsource HR functions, some services go with the "all-or-nothing" approach, requiring that they handle all your HR functions or none at all. Others offer their services "à la carte," meaning you can pick and choose from the services they offer.

Typical services include:

- **Payroll administration**: Produce checks, handle taxes, and deal with sick time and vacation time.

- **Employee benefits**: Health, medical, life, 401(k) plans, cafeteria plans, etc.

- **HR management**: Recruiting, hiring, and firing. Also background interviews, exit interviews, and wage reviews.

- **Risk management**: Workers' compensation, dispute resolution, safety inspection, office policies and handbooks.

Some services are full-service and will provide these as well as additional services like on-call consultants, who will come in to train or even settle a dispute. Online services tend to be limited in their offerings, but you'll get added options like web access, which will allow you to view information (like benefits packages) and even make changes to such information online. Most will give you and your employees access to view their benefits plans, enroll in benefits, read policies, and make changes to current data.

Pricing

There are no clear-cut price ranges with HR outsourcing. The fees range greatly among services, as well as within the services. Aspects like number of employees, the options you choose to use, and even geography will affect your overall cost.

- A PEO typically charges 4 percent to 8 percent of each employee's pretax salary per month. The monthly range can be as little as $20 per employee to as much as $200.

- A typical package with an online service, including insurance, 401(k) and workers' compensation, costs $75 to $130 per employee per month with an upfront setup fee of about $2,000.

If you think this sounds expensive, do a cost comparison of an outsourcing program you are investigating and the average salary and maintenance of an in-house HR director or staff. Contracts with HR outsourcing firms will usually run a year. But you should work in a clause in which you can give 30 days' notice to break the contract if you are dissatisfied with the services or don't need the services anymore.

Advantages

What are the biggest advantages to outsourcing your HR needs?

- Does your business allow you the time to personally deal with federal and state employment laws? A big reason businesses turn to HR services is that they don't have the time or expertise to deal with this. And if you choose to go with a PEO, you can pass the legal responsibility of your employees onto them.

- You may also save money. You can usually count on a reduced benefits rate when outsourcing to HR services. Because they buy so often from vendors, they usually get a discounted rate that they pass on to you.

- If you opt for an online service (ASP/e-service), you don't have to purchase software, install it, and worry about configuring it. An ASP business model is hosting software, so you don't have to bother with additional software or installation.

Downsides

So what are some key things you'll have to give up if you favor outsourcing to hiring a full-time, in-house HR department?

- There are some definite drawbacks to not having an HR manager in-house. An in-house HR person handles perks that you can't necessarily count on an outsourcing service to carry out—like looking into group offerings, building employee incentive programs, even taking care of recognition for employees' birthdays. And employees may want someone in-house—an impartial co-worker they can trust and see daily—to turn to if they have a work-related problem or dispute with another co-worker.

- Because an in-house HR person interacts daily with your employees, he or she will likely have more of an interest in your employees.

- Also, in the case of using a PEO, giving up the right to hire and fire your employees may not be desirable for your particular business. Most PEOs insist that they have the final right to hire, fire, and discipline employees.

- And if you decide to use an e-service, the same issues you'd have with any ASP remain. When everything is stored and handled online, there are concerns about security as well as potential crashes, both of which can be detrimental to your business.

Common complaints about HR outsourcing range from payroll mix-ups to payroll not being deposited on time and denied medical claims.

Should you consider outsourcing?

- If you have fewer than 100 employees, the answer is yes. At this size, you often don't have the resources for an in-house HR staff, so outsourcing is just right for you.

- If you have at least 12 employees, consider a PEO. Most PEOs take on only businesses with at least a dozen employees. Get recommendations and references for PEOs, and consider one that is part of the NAPEO (National Association of Professional Employment Organizations). The NAPEO is committed to educating PEOs. If a PEO is a member, it's a good sign that it is committed to being the best in the field.

- If you're even smaller, online services are the way to go. These services are tailored to work with all sizes of businesses, even the smallest. You don't have to give up legal responsibility just yet, and you'll be able to easily access your information online. And since the charge is usually by user, you won't be overpaying.

- If you're uncertain about outsourcing everything but know you don't have the staff or experience to keep it in-house, try outsourcing only certain parts, such as payroll and benefits. You can also purchase HR software right off the shelf to support any in-house efforts.

Whatever you decide, make sure to keep your employees in the loop. They will appreciate knowing that you are seeking the most affordable solution for the business while doing your best to meet their needs.

Source: Mie-Yun Lee, "Outsource Your HR," www.entrepreneur.com/article/
0,4621,305528,00.html.

Ten Tips for Effective Meetings

1. Avoid meetings. Test the importance and ask if the meeting is really necessary.
2. Prepare goals before the meeting begins.
3. Challenge each goal. Save tasks that require a team effort.
4. Prepare an agenda.
5. Inform others and send the agenda for participants to look over and arrive prepared.
6. Assume control: address the most important issue and don't get distracted with minor details.
7. Focus on the issue: don't get distracted with jokes and unrelated stories. Save them for social occasions, when they will be appreciated.
8. Be selective. Invite those who will be contributing to the goals.
9. Budget time in relation to the importance of the issue.
10. Use structured activities in your meetings to ensure equal participation and engagement.

Source: Steve Kaye, "Ten Tips for Effective Meetings," www.sideroad.com/Meetings/effective-meetings.html.

Tips for Boosting Your Bottom Line

No matter what stage your business is in, one thing's for sure: money matters. Here are some money-saving ideas to boost your business's bottom line:

1. Cut your advertising costs by piggybacking your ad materials with other mailings, including invoices, reminder notices, and thank-you notes.
2. If you wait until the last minute, you can often buy cheaper ad space in local newspapers and magazines.
3. You can fax for less by not using a cover sheet, sending faxes in standard rather than fine mode, and waiting until the rates go down to transmit.
4. Market research needn't be pricey. Set up a suggestion box for your customers to use and get their names and addresses for your mailing list.

Source: Rieva Lesonsky, *365 Tips to Boost Your Entrepreneurial IQ.*

Tips on Writing Deadbeat Clients Off

Getting paid can be a problem for home-based business owners. Some clients may think you're too small or not professional enough to go after them for unpaid bills. How do you make sure you'll be paid for your work?

Determine from the beginning what your payment policies will be by asking yourself these questions:

1. Will you accept checks, credit card payments, or cash only?

2. Is payment due upon completion of a project, or will you bill monthly for ongoing work?

3. Will you offer a discount for early payment? How much?

4. Will you require a deposit? How much? Is it refundable and, if so, in what situations?

5. Will you do a credit check before accepting a client?

Here are some things you can do to help ensure you get paid for the work you do:

- Clarify your payment policies before starting any work for a client. In the case of medical billing, where it's ongoing work, determine the volume of work you'll be doing for each client. If it's extensive, perhaps you should bill every week or every two weeks instead of monthly. Sometimes it's easier for a client to pay smaller amounts than one big bill. It's also easier on your cash flow.

- For a business that has out-of-pocket expenses, asking a client to make a deposit at least large enough to cover these expenses is a reasonable business practice.

- Put it in writing! Have a contract with your client that spells out who's responsible for what, how billing will be done, and the consequences of slow or nonpayment of an invoice.

- Know your rights. Find out what you'd have to do to collect on a bad debt by calling your local bar association or small claims court.

Let's say you've done all that and a client still refuses to pay you. What do you do?

- First, document your efforts to collect the invoice. How many times and when have you called? How many letters or past due invoices have you sent and when? What was the response?

- If you're able to speak with the client (either in person or by phone), ask the reason for nonpayment. Are they dissatisfied with your work? Are they having cash-flow problems? Could they make a partial payment and arrangements for the balance?

- If you get no response from your efforts to contact the client, send a certified letter requesting a return receipt, reiterating that the amount is past due and that previous attempts to reach the client have been unsuccessful. Most courts require this type of attempt before you can go forward with legal action.

- If the letter isn't signed for and gets returned to you, or is received but no payment or contact is made, your next step is to take legal action either in small claims court (if the amount is less than the limit for small claims court in your area, which you can find by contacting your local district court office) or by contacting a collection agency or lawyer. Having a signed contract and a log of your attempts to collect will elp your case.

Source: Beverley Williams, "How to Collect Payments," www.entrepreneur.com/article/ 0,4621,279117,00.html.

Tips on How to Land New Clients Fast

First, set your attitude toward success by doing three things:

- **Be bold.** Don't take anyone's advice about not doing something that will make people pay attention to you (as long as it's legal, of course).

- **Be creative.** Start-up time is your most creative. In fact, when business owners who've been around awhile ask me what they can do to add new zest to their businesses, I ask them to tell me what they did when they launched—and do it again.

- **Give up your fears, doubts, and insecurities.** You'll love yourself better when you do!

Next, take action:

1. Make a web site that gives you credibility your prospects will appreciate. For tips, visit my web site at www.websitecopywriters.com.

2. Dash off to a quick printer for fast business cards. Don't worry about making something perfect.

3. Unless you're hiding from the law, add your photograph to your business card. It tells prospects you're for real. Have a professional photographer take your photo, because you need to look your best.

4. Create a verbal "30-second commercial" that says something powerful about your business. As an example, here's mine: "I'm Pete Silver, and I'm in the business of helping small businesses get new clients fast without blowing lots of money on unnecessary expenses. As a former journalist, I know how to use free publicity in the media for my clients, and I write websites and other materials that persuade prospects to BUY. My website is MarketYourBusiness.com."

5. Distribute your card everywhere you can: bulletin boards at supermarkets, universities, public libraries, and anywhere else people congregate who possibly could be your clients.

6. Contact local groups and offer to give a free 20-minute informative speech, and guarantee them you won't try to sell your service or product—and stick to it. Merely

by not selling, you will interest your audience in getting your card, and using the next technique I will give you, you'll get their names for follow-up.

7. Tell members of your audience that you're going to have a free drawing. They should all put their business cards in a box, and you'll draw the winning card. If they don't have business cards, they can write down their names, e-mail addresses, and phone numbers on a blank card you supply, and then the drawing takes place. It could be something you normally sell. If that's not possible, offer a bookstore gift card.

8. Practice the art of "give a card, get a card" with everyone you meet—except double your odds. First, ask them for two cards and say that if you run into a prospect for their service, you'll give out the extra card for them. Then offer them three of your own cards and explain that since you're a start-up, you'd appreciate the same favor in return!

9. Read your local newspaper and see who writes about new businesses. Write up as complete a backgrounder as possible about your business and deliver it to that person—along with your photograph. When it appears in the newspaper, quickly reprint it to distribute as a flier everywhere you can.

Source: Pete Silver, "How to Land New Clients Fast," www.entrepreneur.com/article/0,4621,319564,00.html.

Section 6

Operating Your Business

Chapter 31

Creating an Image

Tips for Creating a Positive Image

Your company's image is your business's calling card. Here's how to make the message a positive one:

- First, create a one- or two-sentence positioning statement describing what sets you apart from your competition. Keep it short, simple, and snappy, and then communicate it in some form in all your marketing materials.

- Don't scrimp when crafting your marketing message. If you don't have the talent, pay for a professional to design your logo and marketing materials. You need these to represent you professionally and persuasively.

- Use public relations to spread the word. Don't overlook community newspapers or local radio stations when sending out press releases.

Finally, remember: your goal is to build positive awareness of your business.

Source: Rieva Lesonsky, *365 Tips to Boost Your Entrepreneurial IQ.*

Tips on Choosing an Online Newsletter Provider

Advantages of using an outside service provider over sending your own e-news out are:
- It is much less labor-intensive.
- You won't be accused of spamming by your ISP.
- Distribution is fast and won't hog your computer's resources.
- You get reports on bounces and user response.

Before you start searching for the right provider, you need to define what you're looking for. Common features you'll want to include are the ability to easily move your database of e-mails and names in and out, opt-in setup, reader-tracking information, bounce management, ability to segment your list, and personalization.

You'll also need to estimate number of recipients and distribution frequency to ballpark service provider fees. Here are a few tips:

1. Solicit recommendations on e-newsletter service providers from colleagues, based on your own parameters.

2. Research other providers and get additional input on those recommended. I'm considering the following providers as a result of my research:

   - **Intelli Contact**—User-friendly and fairly priced. Very focused on ensuring deliverability to e-news subscribers. www.intellicontact.com/index.pl

   - **Constant Contact**—Also easy and fairly priced with a few less features. Good customer support. www.constantcontact.com

- **BrontoMail**—More expensive but offers other tools such as e-survey distribution to e-news subscribers. Very service-oriented. www.brontomail.com

3. Focus on these critical factors:

- **Ease of Use**—It should be straightforward and fairly quick to import your mailing database, manage your list online, create and send e-newsletters, and review results.

- **Deliverability**—Ask prospective providers what they do to ensure the highest probability of e-news receipt. Ideally, they will maintain a strict anti-spam policy, build relationships and feedback loops with major ISPs, and get on white lists (lists of approved e-mail addresses) to ensure your e-news is delivered. Ask what kind of information you get on bounces and how bounces are handled. You'll want to know which e-mail addresses are hard bounces (the address no longer exists) and which are soft bounces (undeliverable at the present time).

- **Reliability**—Make sure your provider has a track record of reliable service. Ask for references or statistics to prove it. Your organization has too much to lose if something happens—your e-mail list gets copied or your newsletter goes out looking very different from the way you previewed it.

- **Flexibility**—You may want to switch from text to HTML format at some point, to send both for different purposes, or to segment your e-mail addresses by state or title.

- **Tracking**—One of the greatest benefits of e-newsletters is generation of quantifiable results. Make sure your e-newsletter provider tracks how many people (and who) get it, open it, and/or click through to your web site.

- **Pricing**—Usually a monthly fee based on size of your list and/or number of e-mails sent. Some providers also charge a modest one-time setup fee. Constant Contact charges $50/month for 2,500–5,000 readers to whom you can send an unlimited number of e-mails. Intelli Contact charges $25/month for unlimited e-mails to 2,501–5,000 readers. BrontoMail charges $150/month for up to 5,000 readers.

Source: Nancy Schwartz, "Selecting the Best E-News Service Provider," nancyschwartz.com/select_email_newsletter_provider.html.

Seven Tips for Publishing a Monthly Newsletter

1. **Re-examine why are you publishing.**
   If you've published for a while (say, at least four issues), you've established a track record with your readers. But what are you getting in return?

   Most e-newsletters are a cross between a branding tool and a lead-generating tactic. Evaluate which yours is. And which marketing tactic is more important to you right now. If you're not generating a significant number of leads with each issue, you might consider cutting back to bimonthly (every two months) or even quarterly. You'll get more ROI out of your e-newsletter if you continue to publish it, rather than run out of steam after four or five issues.

2. Assign a point person.

Designate an inside point person to keep track of all the details. Whether or not you are using a web-based service to deliver your e-newsletter, you need at least one staff member whose job responsibility includes "getting the newsletter out."

This can be a junior staffer who is meticulous as well as a good writer and editor. Ideally, he or she will have a basic knowledge of HTML.

3. Take stock of your editorial resources.

Do you have a CEO who's got a real touch when it comes to writing? His or her informal musings about hot topics in your industry—or a personal note—can create the "voice" of your newsletter.

On the other hand, if no one in your group has the ability to write clearly, informally, and succinctly (key to successful online content), outsource. Hire an outside editor and feed him or her article ideas on an ongoing basis.

4. Planning your next issue.

The best time to plan the content of your next issue is immediately after sending out the current one. You're "in the groove," so to speak, and able to think most clearly about your publication.

Within hours of hitting Send you'll know what attracted the most interest from your readers—and whether your subject line inspired a click to open the issue.

This is where your content formula comes into play. Ideally, you have a formula for a mix of articles, topics, departments, letter from the CEO, quizzes, etc. Be prepared to change it.

If click-through reporting tells you that the number-two article is the most popular, analyze why. Make that the lead next time. If you ask for reader feedback on a certain topic and get a flood of responses, you have the basis for an article in the next issue.

5. Calendarize the process.

But it's easy to let the weeks go by and realize that your next issue is "due out" next week. Before panic sets in, turn to your point person and ask him or her to come up with a publishing calendar. Or hand the task to an outside editor. This should include deadline dates for:

- collecting article ideas
- getting reprint permission, if necessary
- turning ideas into rough drafts
- dropping the copy into your HTML template with placeholder titles
- editing and cutting within the HTML (the copy is almost always too long)

- writing final article titles and a draft subject line
- sending test issues to your internal "newsletter approval" group
- checking every link
- printing out to do a final proof for typos
- sharpening the subject line one last time before you publish (yes, do this last; it's key!)

You'll note that a number of the tasks above are not dissimilar to what your web team does before revising your home page and reposting it.

6. **Keep an idea file for each issue.**
   The best time to plan future issues of your newsletter (other than right after sending) is when you're not thinking about your newsletter at all. You may be responding to e-mail, looking for information on the web, speaking to a colleague on the phone, etc.

   If a URL on another site sparks an idea, immediately cut and paste it into a "running ideas" file on your hard drive. If it's an e-mail from a potential contributor, do the same. Better yet, put ideas into folders named April '03 or May '03. If you've got a shared drive, your point person will have access to them as well.

7. **Apply the newsworthy test the day before publishing.**
   Finally, apply the newsworthy test. Has something come up that will be of keen interest to your readers? A new regulation, a connection to world events? If so, add a blurb in your CEO or publisher's note to reflect this. Making your newsletter "newsworthy" adds huge credibility.

Source: Debbie Weil, "7 Tips for Publishing a Monthly E-newsletter," www.office.com/templates/page3.asp?docid=85.

Top Ways a Small Business Can Be Socially Responsible

Entrepreneurs can do good and make profits, too. Make social responsibility an important part of your marketing message. Sixty percent of customers will actually switch retail employees if the store is involved in a good cause.

- Pick a cause relevant to your customers. For instance, a book chain in Texas promotes literacy. Restaurant owners have banded together to fight hunger.
- Involve your customers too. If they donate a used item, you can give them a discount on a new one.
- Be prepared to say no. Once the word gets out about your charitable efforts, you'll likely get many requests for help, but it's better to do one project very well than to spread yourself too thin.

Remember, it's a win-win situation. You win, but so does your community.

Source: Rieva Lesonsky, *365 Tips to Boost Your Entrepreneurial IQ.*

# Chapter 32

Supplies and Utilities

Four Important Qualities of an Impressive Business Card

All business cards should contain the vitals: your name and title, your company's name, street and e-mail address, phone and fax numbers, and your logo. More information than this gets crowded and can detract from your professional image.

When ordering, keep these factors in mind:

- **Weight**: Most business cards are printed on 80-pound cover stock.
- **Finish**: Of the three available, the smooth finish is the most popular.
- **Color**: Today, two-color cards dominate. Most catalogs offer from 5–15 standard colors to choose from.
- **Quantity**: Setup is what costs, so it generally pays to order more cards rather than fewer.

Source: Rieva Lesonsky, *365 Tips to Boost Your Entrepreneurial IQ.*

Section 6

Tips on Finding an Internet Service Provider (ISP)

Your business needs to have a web site to be competitive. You can design your site yourself, but chances are you'll need to find an internet service provider (ISP).

Here are some questions to ask prospective ISPs:

- How much server space will I have? You'll need to know if your use of graphics will be limited.
- How much access will I have to my site? This is especially important if you plan to update your site regularly.
- What kind of tech support do you provide? As a small-business owner, without a support staff, you'll need all the help you can get.
- How do you handle failures? Make sure the ISP has a backup system in place.
- How long have you been in business? You need stability, so look for an ISP that has been around for a year or so.

Source: Rieva Lesonsky, *365 Tips to Boost Your Entrepreneurial IQ.*

Tips for Companies Looking for Uniforms

Types of Uniforms

Most uniforms are made from a blend of polyester and cotton fabrics. While uniforms have traditionally been associated with plain, matching, single-color shirts and pants, you can generally get whatever you want. In recent years, more firms are opting for coordinating shirts and pants that match but are of different colors. "Executive wear," such as Oxford-type shirts and dress pants, is also gaining in popularity.

Uniforms can also be worn over regular street clothes. Garments such as lab coats, smocks, aprons, or vests promote a more consistent image without requiring each person to be outfitted in the same clothes.

Most uniforms require regular washing and do not require ironing. The life expectancy of these garments is three to five years with regular wear.

Buying vs. Renting

Firms can choose either to buy or to rent uniforms. Buying is generally the less expensive option. Not surprisingly, about 80 percent of uniforms are bought rather than rented.

However, buying uniforms means that you will need to manage cleaning and maintenance. You will have to either trust your workers to keep up their uniforms or hire an industrial launderer to deal with the garments.

A uniform rental firm supplies and cleans uniforms. Working with a service may be preferred in situations where employees may not wash their uniforms on a regular basis. In addition, renting can be a better option for companies that have a high turnover rate. That way, the firm will not have to pay for uniforms that are no longer needed.

About Uniform Vendors

Uniforms are sold through retail outlets, direct sales, and mail order catalogs. Generally, the offerings do not vary very much among vendors. However, some vendors specialize in a particular type of uniform, such as lab coats, which can mean better prices for the buyers.

Vendors can also differ in terms of their service levels. For example, firms can vary in terms of their turnaround time for delivery, availability of custom embroidering of logos and/or names, and handling of emergency requests for uniforms.

Choosing a Rental Firm

Each week, uniform rental companies provide employees with up to five changes of work clothes and pick up a set of uniforms from the previous week for cleaning.

These services generally require a minimum order of garments to be delivered each week. Services also typically require a minimum two-year commitment, with three- and four-year terms becoming quite common.

Generally, it will be cheaper for a uniform rental firm to handle your account if you are located nearby or along a route already being served. In addition, it can be more cost-effective to work with a firm that already supplies the same garments to other firms. That way, the rental service can better manage their inventory and can obtain better pricing from uniform manufacturers.

Pricing

Purchasing five or six sets of uniforms, which should each last three to five years, will cost approximately $150-$250. Note, however, that this figure does not incorporate the cost of cleaning or repairs.

Most uniform rental services bill a flat rate based on a negotiated contract. Generally, rates are based on the number of garment changes provided for each worker; this usually ranges from $1 to $1.50 per day's worth of clothing. This rate remains the same regardless of whether garments are returned for cleaning, with an additional per-piece rate typically charged when uniform delivery goes above a contracted maximum. Altogether, uniform rental will cost between $200 and $300 per employee per year.

Special Tips

Avoiding uniqueness can save money.

When choosing garments from a rental firm, it is more economical to choose those that can also be used by other businesses. That way, when you have turnover or need additional garments, replacement uniforms can come from the rental service's used garment inventory.

Good News for Logos

A recent technology allows small patches to be heat-sealed onto clothing. Logos printed on these patches can be removed with little problem, so clothing can be easily reused.

Source: Mie-Yun Lee, "Making Uniform Decisions," www.entrepreneur.com/article/0,4621,298167,00.html.

List of Convenient Small Packaging and Postal Services

Thomas Net
www.thomasnet.com
They provide a listing of different packaging and delivery companies by state.

J & J Packaging
www.jjpackaging.com

They are an established "brick and mortar" manufacturer of paperboard packaging, thermoplastic packaging, and full-service contract packaging. In addition, they offer complete inventory and supply chain solutions. This combination of products and services allows them to produce all the components for a packaging project as well as inventory, pack, and deliver complete packaged goods.

Contract Packaging
www.contract-packaging.com
Contract packaging and packaging design services, including fulfillment services, packaging companies, custom packaging, electronic packaging, and pharmaceutical packaging.

United States Postal Service
www.usps.com

FedEx
www.fedex.com

United Parcel Service
www.fedex.com

Freightworld
www.freightworld.com/postal.html

Pak Mail
www.pakmail.com

Overnite
www.overnite.com

Human Resources

SCORE's Five Tips on How to Recruit Workers in a Tough Labor Market

1. **Get referrals from employees.** Consider giving bonuses to employees whose referrals are hired.

2. **Ask your suppliers.** They can recommend good salespeople who have called on them or competent technical people who have serviced their equipment.

3. **Approach retirees and other good people who have worked for you before.**

4. **Post an ad on the internet.** Some small business owners experience success in recruiting through such employment sites as CareerBuilder, Monster Board, and Career Mosaic.

5. **Consider unconventional sources.** People with disabilities often make excellent employees. One business owner turned to non-violent first offenders, who were not sent to prison, but had graduated from a Marine-style boot camp program instead.

Source: SCORE, www.score.org/business_tips.html.

SCORE's Five Tips for Training on a Budget

1. Form a training "co-op." The American Society for Training and Development suggests teaming up with other companies to offer courses.

2. Take advantage of training offered by the manufacturers of equipment that you buy. Have training included in the purchase agreement.

3. Find out if your employees can take part in training programs that major customers have for their own employees.

4. Encourage employees to participate in educational opportunities offered by their unions or professional associations.

5. Train one employee to train others. The American Society for Training and Development (ASTD) suggests sending one employee for training and sharing what he or she learns with the rest of your staff.

Source: SCORE, www.score.org/business_tips.html.

Five Differences Between Interns and Employees

Thinking of hiring a free intern? Be careful. Your interns may look like employees, which can get you into a lot of trouble. The Labor Department has set five criteria for distinguishing interns from employees:

1. Training must consist of experiences similar to those offered in vocational school.

2. Interns cannot replace regular employees, and they must work under close observation and supervision.

3. At the end of the internship, the intern is not necessarily entitled to a job. If he or she is, the internship looks like a training program, and the intern would be entitled to a fair wage.

4. Both you and the intern must acknowledge that he or she is not entitled to wages.

5. The training must be primarily for the intern's benefit. That means no coffee-making or errand-running. Interns are not gofers or secretaries—they are there to learn.

And remember, interns have the same legal rights as employees. It's smart to cover them under a workers' compensation package.

Source: Rieva Lesonsky, *365 Tips to Boost Your Entrepreneurial IQ.*

SCORE's Five Tips on What Makes Online Training Valuable

1. Online training can be an affordable alternative. Companies can save up to two-thirds of what classroom-based courses cost.

2. More and more traditional training vendors are offering online courses. More choices means competitive rates.

3. Students can ask tutors and instructors questions, and get a personalized response in minutes. In addition, many online training classes provide instant responses to quizzes—providing the employer quick results.

4. Online courses are as easy as self-tutorials; they provide click-through instructions.

5. Training content is flexible up until the very moment the student sits in front of the monitor. This makes altering content to address a new technology situation a snap.

Source: SCORE, www.score.org/business_tips.html.

SCORE's Five Tips on Ethics Training

1. Know that a strong ethics program can protect your company's reputation and enhance profits. Employees need to understand what's expected of them.

2. Begin by creating a statement of values and a code of ethics for your company, involving employees in the process.

3. Set up a training process. Having managers (including the CEO) train direct reports can be very effective.

4. Keep in mind that some employees may need special training because certain jobs, such as purchasing, expose them to more ethical lapses.

5. A good source of information is www.bsr.org, the web site of the organization Business for Social Responsibility.

Source: SCORE, www.score.org/business_tips.html.

Tips on Building Employee Loyalty

In a tight job market, it's essential that entrepreneurs build employee loyalty. Here are some smart ways to build a loyal work force:

- As obvious as it sounds, treat your people well. Create a friendly work environment where communication is frequent and comfortable.

- Employees like to know the results of what they do. When you get feedback from customers, be sure to share that with your staff—the good and the bad.

- Challenge your people. Let your workers try new tasks, perhaps even new jobs within your company. The more challenged employees are, the longer they tend to stay.

- Train your staff. Studies show that employees who received training were more likely to be with their same employer five years later.

Source: Rieva Lesonsky, *365 Tips to Boost Your Entrepreneurial IQ.*

SCORE's Five Tips on Building a Senior Management Team

1. Start with part-timers. You may not be able to afford a full-time chief financial officer at first, but chances are you can find one who will gladly work part time.

2. Look for volunteers. The SCORE association is one place to start and may help you establish a volunteer advisory board. Also check with your local business schools.

3. Consider outsourcing your management team. Check the Yellow Pages under Employment Agencies, Employee Leasing, Executive Search Consultants, and Management Consultants.

4. Check references and backgrounds, just as you would for a full-time employee. Look for a good fit.

5. Treat part-time and volunteer executives just as you would full-time, paid senior managers. Make them a part of your team.

Source: SCORE, www.score.org/business_tips.html.

SCORE's Five Tips on Employee Performance Reviews

1. Concentrate on what you and the employee can achieve together in the future. Don't use performance reviews just as a means of telling workers everything they're doing wrong.

2. Strive for consistency and fairness. Apply performance criteria to all employees, not just a few.

3. Encourage employees to evaluate themselves and to discuss their own strengths. Your view of an employee and the employee's view of himself or herself should match fairly well. Otherwise, it's a warning signal.

4. Be honest about poor performance, but not brutal. Document your observations in writing.

5. If you're small enough that constant communication and feedback are taking place, you may be able to avoid performance reviews. But don't send the message that performance isn't critical.

Source: SCORE, www.score.org/business_tips.html.

SCORE's Five Tips on Helping Employees Take Pride in Their Work

1. Employees are your most important assets, so hire the best, provide training and growth opportunities, and recognize good performance.

2. Have a meaningful, concise, and realistic job description for each employee. Make sure you review it with the employee and that it is understood.

3. Be sure employees know what is expected of them. Establish high standards of performance ethics.

4. Offer specialized training or skills enhancement to your current employees. Promoting from within encourages and motivates your greatest assets—your current workforce.

5. Create a new employee referral bonus program. Describe your needs in title and duties and offer a reward for your "most wanted."

Source: SCORE, www.score.org/business_tips.html.

SCORE's Five Tips on Promoting from Within

1. Understand your advantage. In a small company, you are in a better position to know what people's abilities and interests are than in a large company.

2. Develop a nose for hidden talent. Find out what skills people use when they're not at work and determine if those skills can be put to use in your company—in a higher position.

3. Create career paths for employees. Your people need opportunities to grow.

4. Consider the work that you outsource. Can that work be brought inside, creating an advancement opportunity for one of your employees?

5. If an employee needs outside training for a higher-level job, pay for it. That will be cheaper than recruiting a new employee.

Source: SCORE, www.score.org/business_tips.html.

SCORE's Five Tips on Where to Publicize for New Hires

1. Write and place "sizzling" help wanted ads. Write ads with a marketing perspective as to what will bring you prime prospects. Place them in trade journals and in professional association job banks and newspapers.

2. Post job openings at colleges and trade schools. Let educational institutions know about your company and its hiring goals. Schedule personal visits as needed.

3. Place magnetic signs on your car, truck, or van. Take your advertising with you wherever you go. Showcase the phrase "Now Hiring" in large print with your phone number.

4. Advertise on radio or cable television; rates can be very reasonable. Or sponsor a promotional event.

5. Consider outdoor advertising or even bus bench ads. You can reach a wide audience.

Source: SCORE, www.score.org/business_tips.html.

How to Get Your Prospect to Accept Your Offer

OK, you've conducted all the interviews and you've found a job candidate you'd like to offer the position to. Now how do you get the person to accept the job?

- Be sure your compensation package is competitive. Remember, salary is not necessarily the most important factor, so include as many perks as you can afford.

- People like to work where employees are positive, creative, and happy. Would you want to work at your company?

- Treat the candidate with courtesy and respect. Just as you judge them in the interview, they are judging you.

- Introduce the candidate to current employees. This allows them to check out the people they'll be working with.

- Always be on the lookout for good workers, even if you have no job openings. You never know when you will have to fill a position, and it's best to be prepared before you really have to be.

Source: Rieva Lesonsky, *365 Tips to Boost Your Entrepreneurial IQ.*

SCORE's Five Tips on Where to Find Employee Training

1. Check out the Internet for convenient, cost-effective web-based courses. Start with internet service providers like America Online or the education sections of such portals as Netscape and Yahoo!

2. Contact state and local development agencies. Some of them offer training programs in order to attract and keep businesses.

3. Investigate programs offered by local universities, community colleges, and adult-education programs.

4. Hire teachers or consultants to provide training at your place of business or off-site. Get references first.

5. Ask corporations. Many offer instruction on the software they market or the equipment they manufacture.

Source: SCORE, www.score.org/business_tips.html.

SCORE's Five Tips on Employee Orientation

1. Don't ignore new-employee orientation. The first days on the job are a wonderful "teachable moment."

2. Concentrate on showing a new employee how his or her work will contribute to the success of the company.

3. Help the new employee gain a complete understanding of your products or services and how your company differs from its competitors.

4. Make sure newcomers are introduced to all their co-workers.

5. School newcomers in the corporate culture. Make sure, for example, that they don't mistake a casual dress code for a casual attitude toward work.

Source: SCORE, www.score.org/business_tips.html.

SCORE's Five Tips for Developing Employees

1. Take the attitude that training is really employee development. That will help you think more strategically about what your employees need to learn.

2. Recognize that formal training programs are only part of the picture. Most real training occurs on the job.

3. Help employees develop problem-solving skills and the ability to think by giving them work that will stretch them.

4. Set an example. Your own pleasant attitude and good work habits will influence your workers.

5. Understand that when you give employees an opportunity to grow, their job satisfaction and your ability to retain them as employees both increase substantially.

Source: SCORE, www.score.org/business_tips.html.

How to Evaluate Temporary Personnel Services

Workers supplied by a temporary service firm are quickly available. Usually they can start the day after a request is made, and sometimes the same day. Although the rate paid to a temporary service firm is higher than pay to permanent employee, the costs of recruiting and training and of idle periods are much less. Base the temporary services by the criteria listed below.

- **Reliability:** Is the service well established, with a history of success and financial stability?

- **Recruiting:** The firm with an aggressive recruiting program is more likely to have the most skilled and reliable employees.

- **Testing and evaluation:** How does it test and evaluate personnel?

- **Training programs:** Does the company train personnel in modern office methods, word processing, records management, and other important skills?

- **Quality control:** Does the company check the quality of work of its temporary employees?

Source: Small Business Administration, *Human Resources Handbook.*

Pros and Cons of Employee Leasing

Employee leasing is similar to employing temporary personnel, but involves permanent employees. An employer transfers employees to the payroll of a leasing firm that, in turn, leases them back to the employer. The leasing firm becomes the legal employer and its responsible for the payroll and leave; record-keeping benefits, and services; and participation in hiring, evaluation, and firing.

Pros:

- Saving time and money
- Improved employee benefits
- Help with personnel policies and employee handbooks
- Records uniform and easily audited

Cons:

- Leasing company exercises certain control over employee policies
- Employer retains responsibility for productivity and conduct
- Labor union contracts or state law might keep certain employers from leasing certain employees
- Most leasing firms require the value of one full payroll in an escrow or trust account in addition to regular payroll costs

Source: Small Business Administration, *Human Resources Handbook*.

SCORE's Five Tips to Get Great Talent for Less Money

1. Consider immigrants. Many are talented people who will accept less pay because they don't speak English. (But pay them fairly!)
2. Keep an eye out for displaced "Mommy Trackers"—smart women who've left corporate executive positions to start a family or be closer to their children. They can make excellent part-time executives.
3. Investigate employee-leasing and temporary-help services.
4. Offer internships and part-time challenges to graduate students and upper-level undergrads. They want to get experience and can bring excellent knowledge and skills.
5. Get referrals from employees—and don't be afraid to hire relatives of good workers. You can save substantially on recruiting costs this way.

Source: SCORE, www.score.org/5_tips_fc_8.html.

SCORE's Five Tips for Getting the Most out of Training

1. Make sure your employees understand ahead of time the reasons for training. What problems will it solve?

2. Put yourself in their shoes. Tell them how they will benefit.

3. Make it interesting. Hire a competent trainer or, if you do it yourself, find ways to engage your employees' attention—such as including videotapes or role-playing.

4. Be clear about expectations. Focus on the behavioral changes or improvements that you are looking for.

5. Measure the results. Training without follow-up is ineffective. Keep repeating your message and show appreciation to employees who keep trying to meet the expectations.

Source: SCORE, www.score.org/business_tips.html.

SCORE's Five Tips on Where to Go to Gain Referrals

1. Hold an open house or an in-house job fair. Invite schools, county or state job developers, and others in the community to attend.

2. Contact Urban League, Youth Employment Programs, and Private Industry Council in your area. These are wonderful training organizations that offer free placement assistance.

3. Go online and search the Internet. Post your openings on free and fee-based bulletin boards such as Monster.com, Careerpath.com, or pdqcareers.com.

4. Contact local government job banks for free referrals. All states have aggressive welfare-reform goals and may be a source of employees.

5. Call the Veterans Administration and Rehabilitation Agency. They can refer some very capable people.

Source: SCORE, www.score.org/business_tips.html.

Hiring and Firing Employees

Advice on Finding Top-Quality Employees

In a tight job market, it's harder than ever for entrepreneurs to find top-quality employees. Sure, you can place an ad in the classifieds, but don't expect this to bring you the best job candidates. Here are some better techniques:

- Tap into your personal and professional networks. Tell everyone you know, from your vendors to your next-door neighbor, about your job opening.

- Establish an employee referral program. If you have employees, ask them to recommend people they know. Offer cash bonuses if the referral results in a hiring.

- Contact school placement offices. Include local colleges and universities, as well as trade and vocational schools.

- Post notices at senior citizen centers. Retirees needing extra income often make productive workers.

- Use an employment agency. The time you save in the search is probably worth the fee you'll pay.

Source: Rieva Lesonsky, *365 Tips to Boost Your Entrepreneurial IQ.*

SCORE's Five Tips on Hiring Immigrants

1. Understand the benefits. Immigrants are often well educated, intelligent, loyal, and dedicated.

2. Follow the law. Contact your U.S. Citizenship and Immigration Services (USCIS) (formerly Immigration and Naturalization Service) field office for information and required forms. For locations, visit the USCIS web site at uscis.gov.

3. Keep things simple. Limit the number of languages spoken to reduce the need for interpreters.

4. Expect a community to develop among those who speak the same language. It's OK. They can help and support each other and assist in interpretation.

5. Encourage your employees to learn English. Send them to courses offered locally or provide classes on-site.

Source: SCORE, www.score.org/business_tips.html.

SCORE's Five Tips on Hiring Quality and Reliable People

1. Examine your own skills carefully. Know your own strengths and weaknesses and hire to complement your skills, not duplicate them.

2. Ensure yourself plenty of applicants by casting a broad net. Interview applicants in a structured way by asking all applicants for a job the same questions.

3. Draw applicants to your web site by placing the web address in all advertisements.

4. Use an 800 phone or fax number as a toll-free way for applicants to contact you.

5. Offer a signing bonus—anything from $25 to $2,500 could be an incentive to help bring on a fence-sitting applicant. This is a common practice for "super starts."

Source: SCORE, www.score.org/business_tips.html.

SCORE's Five Tips on Hiring Smart

1. Hire slowly. Be willing to invest time and energy in your hiring decisions.

2. Be clear in your own mind what the job requires and measure candidates' qualifications against the requirements of the job.

3. Consider how well a candidate will fit in with your corporate culture. Are his or her attitudes compatible? Is he or she cooperative?

4. Narrow the pool to serious candidates. Ways of weeding out non-contenders include announcing that drug testing is required of all new employees or asking applicants to write a brief essay on why they want the job.

5. Do brief phone interviews with eight or ten top candidates to reduce the pool further. Then do longer in-person interviews with two or three finalists.

Source: SCORE, www.score.org/business_tips.html.

Most Common Illegal Questions Asked When Interviewing

Equal Employment Opportunity Commission (EEOC) guidelines, as well as federal and state laws, prohibit asking certain questions of a job applicant, either on the application form or during the interview. What questions should you sidestep? Basically, you can't ask about anything not directly related to the job, including:

- Age or date of birth (if interviewing a teenager, you can ask if he or she is 16 years old)

- Sex, race, creed, color, religion, or national origin
- Disabilities of any kind
- Date and type of military discharge
- Marital status
- Maiden name (for female applicants)
- If a person is a citizen (however, you can ask if he or she has the legal right to work in the United States)

Other questions you should avoid include:

- How many children do you have? How old are they? Who will care for them while you are at work?
- Have you ever been treated by a psychologist or psychiatrist?
- Have you ever been treated for drug addiction or alcoholism?
- Have you ever been arrested? (You may, however, ask if the person has been convicted if it is accompanied by a statement saying that a conviction will not necessarily disqualify an applicant for employment.)
- How many days were you sick last year?
- Have you ever filed for worker's compensation? Have you ever been injured on the job?

Source: Rieva Lesonsky, *Start Your Own Business.*

Tips for Hiring Your First Employee

Ready to hire your first employee? First, bone up on the law so you don't inadvertently ask illegal questions. Then, before you start your search, make sure you do the following:

- Write a job description that clearly outlines the duties and responsibilities of the position.
- Establish a salary range and a benefits package.
- Use an "official" job application form. And once the interview process begins, make sure the information on the form matches that on the candidate's resume.
- Prepare your interview questions in advance, and ask all the candidates the same questions. Take notes during the interview so you can more accurately assess later.
- Ask open-ended questions in the interview. You want to encourage the candidate to talk, not just answer yes or no.

Finally, don't spill the beans: find out as much as you can about them before you share details about the job.

Source: Rieva Lesonsky, *365 Tips to Boost Your Entrepreneurial IQ.*

SCORE's Five Tips on Developing an Employee Handbook

1. Some company policies have to be in writing—such as policies on sexual harassment and discipline—so that employees know what is expected of them. These can form the basis of an employee manual.

2. Draft your employee handbook yourself or assign someone else in the company to do it. Then have it reviewed and fine-tuned by your lawyer.

3. Include a disclaimer stating clearly that the manual is in no way a legal contract.

4. Visit the Online Women's Business Center at www.onlinewbc.org, and click on "Management" and then "How to Write a Policies & Procedures Manual" for an excellent model for an employee handbook. You can adapt the policies to suit the needs of your business.

5. Make sure every employee receives a copy of the handbook and signs a statement saying they've read it. Review it every six months or so and update it as needed.

Source: SCORE, www.score.org/business_tips.html.

Tips for Hiring Your Sales Force

Are you looking for people to sell your goods? Who you hire can make a big difference in how your company grows.

- Don't rely solely on resumes. Good sales people should be able to sell themselves without pieces of paper.

- In the first phone contact, if the applicant doesn't ask for an appointment, stop right there. If they won't ask for an interview now, they're not likely to ask for orders later.

- Determine if the person sounds like someone you'd like to spend time with. If not, it's probable your customers won't want to, either.

- Pay attention to whether or not the applicant listens. If the person is too busy talking to listen to you, he or she is not going to listen to your customers.

- At the end of your phone call, say you plan to talk to other candidates. If someone says, "You don't need to talk to anyone; I'm your person," you may not need to look further.

Source: Rieva Lesonsky, *365 Tips to Boost Your Entrepreneurial IQ*.

Ten Qualities of Top Salespeople

Top salespeople:

1. **Are entrepreneurial.** They see themselves running their own business within a business. "They're highly motivated, focused, and organized," says Joe Galvin, vice president and research director of CRM strategies for research firm Gartner Inc.

2. **Have developed a process.** "They've figured out a process that has been successful for them to maintain their success," Galvin says. "Then they execute against it."

3. **Think about clients, not quotas.** "The best salespeople focus on the customer," says Skip Miller, founder and president of M3 Learning Corp., a sales management firm in Los Gatos, California. "It's always about the customer."

4. **Sell solutions.** Great salespeople see themselves selling more than just widgets; they sell solutions. They tailor their sales pitches to offer a clear solution that solves the customer's problem.

5. **Get customers thinking.** Great salespeople can make customers see value early on so they're selling themselves on the solution. They're able to find "the catalyst for the customer to move forward," says Sam Reese, CEO and president of sales development company Miller Heiman, with headquarters in Reno, Nevada. Stellar salespeople can also find this catalyst early in the sales process. "Closing a sale starts really early in the process."

6. **Aren't afraid to get creative.** "You have to be creative. It's almost like putting on a show for customers," says Michael Minelli, New York City–based media and entertainment business manager for SAS Institute Inc., the world's largest privately held software company. "You're talking with them, finding out what their vision is, then demonstrating [value] back to them."

7. **Are on the move.** The great salespeople "are still going out and seeing customers and prospects," Reese says. "They're crafting clear, valid business reasons to meet."

8. **Know when to move on.** Great salespeople don't waste time on dead ends. They're experts at targeting their resources.

9. **Stay current.** They keep up with products, clients, trends, and what the competition is doing.

10. **Love what they do.** Top-grade salespeople are passionate about their work. If selling isn't fun anymore, incorporating tips one through nine might help you and your sales reps get your mojo back.

Source: Chris Penttila, "Have You Got It?", www.entrepreneur.com/article/0,4621,309867–3,00.html.

Tips on When It Is the Right Time to Hire

Do you know when it's the right time to hire? Ask yourself these questions, and see if you've waited too long:

- Are you turning down assignments because you don't have time to do them?
- Have you missed some deadlines? Are you satisfied with the work you're doing?
- Do you spend more than half your time on clerical tasks?
- Are you consistently working more than 10 hours a day, plus weekends?
- Are your family and friends complaining about your lack of attention or participation?
- Have you needed to hire a temp worker or subcontract out some assignments?
- Do you often feel stressed, overworked, or overwhelmed? Is your health suffering?
- Have you wondered if your business is worth the effort?

Source: Rieva Lesonsky, *365 Tips to Boost Your Entrepreneurial IQ.*

Section 6

Alternatives to Hiring Your First Employee

Think you're ready to hire your first employee? Before you take on the costs and hassle of hiring permanent employees, consider these alternatives.

- If your need is seasonal or project-based, consider hiring temporary employees from a service. While temps might cost more on an hourly basis, in the long run you'll save time, energy, and money.
- Independent contractors are another good source of help. But be careful here. This is a hot area for the IRS. Make sure your independent contractors are truly independent. Not sure? Contact the IRS for a free booklet.
- Consider college students; they often work for free or low wages if they can earn class credit. Ask local colleges if they have an internship program you can participate in.

Remember, full-time employees cost more than just their wages. Before you hire, make sure you truly have to.

Source: Rieva Lesonsky, *365 Tips to Boost Your Entrepreneurial IQ.*

Four Questions When Interviewing Candidates

You should have a number of questions to ask prospective employees. But here are four basic questions you should ask in every job interview:

1. What's the greatest asset you'll bring into this company? This question is a great icebreaker and sets the interviewee at ease.

2. What's your greatest weakness? Asking this still surprises many and the answer is key to how the candidate thinks on his or her feet.

3. What was your favorite and least favorite job? Look here for the candidate's ability to objectively evaluate a situation rather than subjectively react to it.

4. And the ever-popular "Where do you see yourself in five years?" The right answer here should reflect a wish list of increased responsibilities.

Source: Rieva Lesonsky, *365 Tips to Boost Your Entrepreneurial IQ.*

Should You Hire Your Family Members?

Did you know that most small businesses in America are family-owned? But it's usually not as easy as it sounds to hire family members. Before you take the plunge, ask yourself:

- Does this person have the necessary experience to do the job?
- Would this person be more valuable to the business in the long term if he or she first got a job elsewhere?

Here are some tips:

- Once you hire a family member, make sure you clearly define his or her role and areas of responsibility.
- Make sure the person is capable of handling the job and that his or her attributes are evident to other employees.
- If conflicts arise—and they will—make sure you deal with the issue at hand. Keep emotions and family history out of the discussion.
- If you want to keep your business on track, it's vital that family employees are treated just like the rest of your staff. That means their salary, hours, and vacation time are within company guidelines.

Source: Rieva Lesonsky, *365 Tips to Boost Your Entrepreneurial IQ.*

# Chapter 35

Watching Your Costs

Four Cost-Saving Tips

There are lots of way for entrepreneurs to save money. Here of some you may not have thought of:

1. Buy recycled laser printer cartridges. Suppliers can be found in the Yellow Pages. And while we're talking about laser cartridges, use the draft mode on your printer for all internal communications and less important documents.

2. Get together with other entrepreneurs in the area to form buying alliances. Bulk purchases are generally less expensive.

3. Buying computers and other equipment by mail can often cost lots less. But check out the mail order company's warranty and support policies before you buy.

4. Furniture can be found at bargain basement prices at used furniture stores, furniture rental chains, and auctions or estate sales. But make sure desk chairs are ergonomically designed, or you'll end up spending more in the long run.

Source: Rieva Lesonsky, *365 Tips to Boost Your Entrepreneurial IQ.*

Tips for Minimizing Your Energy Costs

You can save a lot of money on your bottom line just by watching your energy costs.

1. Adjust your thermostats. Don't pay for heating or air conditioning when your building is not occupied.

2. Use water-flow restrictors in sink faucets.

3. Turn off all lights when they're not needed. Also, turn off equipment that's not being used.

4. When replacing computers, copiers, printers, etc., buy energy-efficient equipment.

5. Keep your exterior doors closed as much as possible.

6. Encourage your employees to be energy-conscious. Try offering them a small reward or other incentive for energy-saving ideas.

Source: Rieva Lesonsky, *365 Tips to Boost Your Entrepreneurial IQ.*

Tips for Keeping Your Travel Expenses in Line

Are you traveling more and enjoying it less? These tips help entrepreneurs on the go keep their travel expenses in line.

1. If you are departing from or traveling to an area with multiple airports, shop around for the best fares.

2. When you rent a car, price all the options. Sometimes local car-rental companies offer lower rates. Does your credit card automatically provide you with increased insurance coverage? Don't pay for services you don't need.

3. Always ask for the best price, especially when making hotel reservations. If there's a chance your trip might be canceled, reserve your hotel room with a credit card that guarantees your money back.

4. Unless you are truly strapped for cash, don't use frequent flier miles to travel on business. Remember, business trips are tax-deductible, so it's best to charge your trip to your business credit card.

Source: Rieva Lesonsky, *365 Tips to Boost Your Entrepreneurial IQ.*

Section 6

More Cost-Saving Tips for the Road Warrior

Being an entrepreneurial road warrior doesn't have to cost you a fortune. Try these money-saving tips:

- When calling from a hotel or pay phone, ask about charges. If they're too high, ask to be connected to your regular long-distance carrier.

- If you use a charge card to call from hotels, don't hang up between calls. Just press the pound key and dial your account number. This avoids the connect surcharges many hotels charge.

- You should always shop around for the best rates on hotel rooms. And make sure to ask about any discounts or specials.

- The same applies to car rentals—ask for discounts. Don't pay for collision coverage if you don't have to. Check your credit card agreement; many include car rental insurance if you use that card to rent the car.

Source: Rieva Lesonsky, *365 Tips to Boost Your Entrepreneurial IQ.*

Smart Postal Pointers

Even in this era of instant communications, entrepreneurs can't avoid using the mail. And don't think your business is too small to get mailing discounts.

- **Clean up.** The post office can clean your mailing list—for free! They'll correct addresses, note incomplete addresses, and add ZIP-plus-4 codes so you'll be eligible for bar-code discounts.
- **Bulk up.** If you mail in bulk, consider purchasing a standard-mail permit. Although the permit costs around $85 a year, you'll pay substantially less than first-class rates.
- **Shop around.** Delivery rates vary among carriers. Compare rates and ask about small-business discounts.
- **Mail early.** In many cases, this results in one- to two-day delivery—all for the price of a first-class stamp!

Source: Rieva Lesonsky, *365 Tips to Boost Your Entrepreneurial IQ.*

Ways to Minimize Your Printing Expenses

Printing costs are one of those necessary evils—it's an unavoidable expense. But don't pay more than you have to.

- **Proof thoroughly**—at least three times. And never sign the proof until you're sure. If you've approved a "mistake," you'll have to pay the cost of reprinting.
- **Evaluate your forms.** Are they are efficient and functional as possible? Can you combine a few forms into one? Can your six-part form shrink into four parts?
- **Order smart.** Only print what you can use in a reasonable time. Ordering too much not only ties up your money, but you also risk your materials becoming obsolete.
- **Seek advice.** Ask your printer if there's anything you can do to reduce costs.

Finally, price should not be your sole criterion. Consider quality, consistency, service, and support before you choose a printer.

Source: Rieva Lesonsky, *365 Tips to Boost Your Entrepreneurial IQ.*

Smart Bootstrapping Tips

Interested in starting a business on a budget? Who isn't? And bootstrapping can be one the smartest ways to get started. Before you do, though, follow these bootstrapping tips:

- Realize some businesses are easier to bootstrap than others Service businesses, particularly home-based ones, are easier to start up than manufacturing or retail operations.

- If possible, run your business part time at the start. This way, you still have your job income to fall back on, which also allows you to redirect monies back into the company. Again, this favors service entrepreneurs.

- Once you get started, keep your overhead low. If you're a home-based entrepreneur, stay there as long as possible.

- As you try to get your cash flowing, negotiate with vendors and suppliers to get payment extensions.

- Maximize the resources you have. Make do with what you've got until no longer serves your purpose.

Source: Rieva Lesonsky, *365 Tips to Boost Your Entrepreneurial IQ.*

Free Public Relation Strategies

In the spirit of guerrilla marketing, here are five types of free marketing using PR:

1. **Writing articles:** Writing about how to do something is always something of value to readers. Writing articles gives you instant credibility. Submitting online, as well as offline, provides another good chance to get your name in print at no cost. Not a writer? Write down 10 questions you think your prospects might have about a particular area of your expertise and write out the answers to those questions. This can be an article. Lists are great articles and can be top-ten lists, checklists, mistakes made, and so on.

2. **Free reports:** Offering a free report online is a good way to get an e-mail from prospects so you may market to them later. You can do the same thing offline to get contact information. Offering the report offline is a good way to get a prospect to call or contact you. The information gained from the exchange can then be used for subsequent marketing over and over again.

3. **Online forums:** Participating in online newsgroups and forums is another way to get your name in front of a prospective buyer. Participating by answering and asking questions will position you as an expert and a resource for others. Many online forums will let you put an e-mail signature with a link to your web site or an affiliate web site.

Section 6

4. **Letters to the editor:** A little-known secret that's a good follow-up to a press release is a letter to an editor. This is free PR. Many times, a letter to the editor has a better chance of getting published than the actual press release. You'd be surprised how many people read this column in publications. You can even write a letter to the editor about someone else's PR. Don't ignore this one.

5. **Hosting an event:** Hosting an event for your business or at your business can be the equivalent to getting an article published in a targeted publication. The event can take the form of an open house or a ribbon-cutting ceremony. Publicizing the event is news in the eyes of an editor, a producer, or a target market member. Not only can you publicize the announcement of the event, but you can also invite the media and publicize the event itself. Another kind of event is a seminar or presentation of some type. Again, the same PR leverages can occur.

Source: Al Lautenslager, "Free PR Tactics," www.entrepreneur.com/article/0,4621,318428,00.html

Low-Cost Advertising Strategies

Print Ads

The design and layout of your print ads—whether for daily or weekly newspapers, free shoppers, direct mail, or coupon inserts—will be handled at no charge through the publication or direct mail house doing the distribution.

Weekly subscription papers add color to their pages for special editions and, since they're using it anyway, will sometimes add the same color to your ad at no charge if you ask. Tell your reps to notify you whenever free color, which under normal circumstances can be cost-prohibitive, is available.

Radio and TV (Almost) Freebies

Radio and TV stations may need your products or services as much as you need them, and they don't want to pay cash either! They will trade dollar-for-dollar advertising for office machines and maintenance, cleaning and decorating services, office supplies, delivery service, office furniture, news and station vehicles (and the supplies and maintenance that go along with those vehicles, such as fuel, cleaning, tires, oil changes, repairs, painting), printing, office and/or client party planning and catering ... the list is endless.

■ Contact the general sales manager at each of your local stations by phone. Ask the receptionist for the contact's name before the call is put through, and come right to the point when you get him or her on the line.

Promotional advertising (found more often, but not exclusively, on radio) is slightly different than straight trade advertising in that you get produced commercials plus live promotional announcements attached to a special station event.

- Perfect candidates for this kind of advertising include catering companies, travel agencies, health spas, boutiques, specialty gift companies, and bakeries.

What other freebies should you expect to receive?

- Every radio and TV station will provide you with no-charge copywriting. Many actually employ full-time copywriters, and some provide the service through their media reps.

- Production of your radio commercials should be free, unless you're taking a "dub," or copy of the produced commercial, to use on another station as well. You can even get around this charge by providing each station you're going to advertise on with a script and letting each produce its own version of your commercial.

- You may be able to include the cost of producing your TV commercial as part of the trade or promotional advertising. If producing a full 30-second commercial takes up too much of your trade balance, have a 15-second ad produced instead. They're less expensive to make and run, so you should be able to have the commercial made and still run it with some frequency.

Source: Kathy J. Kobliski, "Advertising on the Cheap," www.entrepreneur.com/article/0,4621,283038,00.html.

Seven Low-Cost Ways to Reward Your Employees

Here are some tips for rewarding employees even on a tight budget:

1. **Personally thank an employee for a specific job well done.** Specify what was good about it and why you appreciate it, which tells the employee you pay attention. For example, say, "Thank you, Jim, for organizing that project so well. You made it very clear what should happen, when, and why."

2. **Put that specific praise in a letter or thank-you note.** When you take the time to write something down, you clearly value it. This makes the praise even more meaningful. When appropriate, copy the employee's manager on your praise letter. Sharing the praise with management lets the employee know you support his or her success at your company.

3. **Provide as much information as possible about the company.** Share as much as you can about how the company is doing, where it's making money, where it's losing money, how its products are doing in the marketplace, what new initiatives are being considered and why, and how the employee can best contribute to these efforts.

4. **At every opportunity, include your employees in the decisions you make.** In many cases, your employees understand a side of an issue that you may not. If you need to create a more efficient delivery system, ask your delivery men and women

how they would improve the current system. If you want to improve work flow for support staff, discuss with your secretaries and clerical workers how to best keep the work flowing. Use their ideas, and give them credit for them.

5. **Give employees the opportunity to learn as many new skills as they are able to.** Most people like to learn, to grow, and to improve their marketability, and the more skills you enable your employees to learn, the more they will value their position with you. Cross-train whenever possible so employees know each other's jobs. An added benefit is that employees who understand the realities of one another's positions are more willing to cooperate and feel more like members of the same team.

6. **Celebrate successes.** Celebrate an employee's successful completion of a project, a salesperson's landing a big client, your company's improved sales figures, your organization's successful year-end. After a particularly tense week, bring doughnuts and coffee and gather everyone together to applaud a hard-working team. Provide balloons and noisemakers for a rousing chorus of cheers for the completion of a difficult project. Don't be afraid to be goofy in your celebration; it's a refreshing change from hard work.

7. **Provide free time and flexibility.** Set aside an hour here and there for employees who have delivered an extra level of work. Make it clear that the free time is a reward for a specific accomplishment, such as finishing a challenging project or delivering month-end reports early. Alternatively, you can reward all your employees together, for example, by letting them leave an hour early to miss rush-hour traffic on a day of expected heavy traffic. Give extra time for lunch to an employee or team who has worked through lunch to deliver something to a client. Allow time off for personal or family responsibilities.

Source: Scott Miller, "How to Reward Employees When Your Budget Is Tight," www.entrepreneur.com/article/0,4621,297355,00.html.

Tips for Maintaining Your Utility Bills

Let's talk about bills—specifically, your utility bills. Sure you're busy; what entrepreneur isn't? But make the time to check your bills.

- Your phone bill is a good place to start. Before you dial a vendor, a supplier, or even a customer, check the toll-free directory to see if the company has a toll-free number. Shop all the local and long-distance phone companies for the best deal.

- Cellular phone bills are often riddled with errors. Make sure you're charged only for calls that you made and ones that actually went through.

- You can lower your electricity bills as well. Turn off machines when they're not in use. And use fluorescent lights; they not only conserve energy but also cost less to use. Today, many utility companies offer special rates to small businesses. Call yours to find out if you qualify.

Chapter 36

Etiquette

Section 6

Lunch Meeting Protocol

Use your lunch hour for lunch dates with current clients or potential customers. Here are a few helpful hints for truly "fine dining":

- Make it clear you are hosting the meal, but offer your guests a choice of dates and times.
- Chose a restaurant where you feel comfortable and the environment is conducive to doing business.
- Make reservations, and show up at least 15 minutes early so you can greet your guests.
- Don't jump into talking shop. Wait until most of the meal is over.
- Let your guests order first, and follow their lead when you order. Also, don't order food that is difficult or messy to eat.
- Leave your cell phone at the office, or at least turn it off during the meal.
- Limit your intake of alcohol.
- Don't fuss over your order or hassle the server. You don't want to leave a bad impression.

Source: Rieva Lesonsky, *365 Tips to Boost Your Entrepreneurial IQ.*

Top Ten Business Etiquette Tips

Good manners can be one of your most important assets. Just in case your career fate is in the hands of someone who is a stickler for proper manners, it might be wise to read and practice the following ten business etiquette tips:

1. **Know how to introduce your spouse.** Do not say, "This is my wife, Mary." Say instead, "This is Mary, my wife." Why? When you put the description before the name, it implies that your spouse belongs to you, which is demeaning. The description after the name suggests an independent person who just happens to be married to you.

2. **Do not become the office clown.** A few people do this out of nervousness. Some do it merely to be liked, as it achieved that end in the past. But gaining a reputation as the office jokester can be detrimental to your long-term career. The reasoning is simple: coworkers are less likely to take you and your ideas seriously. If this advice contradicts your naturally jovial personality, here is an option. Maintain a low-key office persona during working hours and a lighter, less business-like persona after hours.

3. **Do not get intoxicated at business-related functions.** This is one of the biggest out-of-office blunders. Using profanity in the office is the only other blunder that tops this. For the record: if you care about your career and the way you are perceived by others, never—repeat, never—do either.

4. **Do not give your boss a gift.** Unless you have a personal relationship with your boss, do not give him or her a gift for holidays or birthdays. It is inappropriate, can be seen as apple-polishing, and puts the employer in an awkward situation. In general, try to downplay exchanging personal gifts in your office. An option is to create an office fund for purchasing birthday flowers or taking the employee to lunch.

5. **Do not correct your boss in public.** If a mistake was made, explain it in private. An exception: if you are in a meeting and your boss makes a major error in his or her statements, you can speak up gently with something like "The last figure I got was $2 million, not $4 million, Jim."

6. **Rise and shake hands during business introductions.** In a business situation, when anyone enters the room and is being introduced, stand and shake hands. Contrary to popular belief, it does not matter who puts their hand out first. Another sidebar: before a staff meeting starts, wait in the conference room for the person who called the meeting to arrive; remain standing until that person enters and let him or her take the best seat.

Section 6

7. **Avoid sexual harassment.** Play it safe and err on the side of caution. Some men still feel obligated to tell a female colleague or client how nice she looks since she changed her hairstyle or how attractive an outfit looks on her. However, such comments denigrate your business relationship. Save such compliments for personal friends.

8. **Mind your mealtime manners.** When calling to extend a breakfast or lunch invitation, you should clearly and immediately establish yourself as the host. When it's time to pay the bill, the rule is simple: the host pays. The host should give the guest a choice of dates (e.g., How about next week? Monday or Wednesday?), a choice of restaurants, and a choice of times (Would you prefer 12:30 or 1:00?). Never discuss business until after your guest has had the chance to order.

9. **Know when to use someone's first name.** The general rule is that you always defer to authority by using an honorific (Mr., Ms., Mrs., or Dr.) until you are given permission to use a first name. It is always inappropriate to call prospective clients by their first name until they give you permission to do so. Additionally, even if you are on a first-name basis with your boss, always introduce your boss to someone as Mr., Ms., Mrs., etc., and include his or her title (e.g., This is Mr. John Doe, vice president of Operations). At that point, your boss can tell the person to use his or her first name, if so desired.

10. **Never use profanity in any business situations.** This one is normally considered the biggest breach of business etiquette, especially when it is aimed at people. There are few things that so touch us with instinctive revulsion as the use of profanity.

Remember: having good manners costs nothing, but it buys everything.

Source: Joe Hodowanes, "Top 10 Business Etiquette Tips," www.ocjobsite.com/job-articles/business-etiquette.asp.

Get Informed About E-Mail Etiquette

Keep e-mail formatting simple. Don't be tempted to use bold, italic, underline, colored text, or other formatting features. If everyone used the same e-mail program, then light doses of formatting would be helpful. Unfortunately, what you see on the screen when you're writing an e-mail message is not at all what the people on the receiving end will see when they open your message. Turn HTML formatting off. Don't use special font faces or sizes. Don't use fancy signatures (sign-offs). Resist the temptation. Over the long run, you'll be better read for it.

Never use ALL CAPS. You'd be surprised how many people think that hitting that Caps Lock key makes their messages seem important or easy to read. In fact, using all capital letters makes messages much harder to read. Most people experienced on the internet also consider all caps to be rude.

Include the previous message "thread." Most e-mail programs automatically include the text of previous messages in an ongoing thread, or back and forth interchange of messages under a given subject. People have strong opinions on this point. (And if an important client is one of them, then modify what I'm about to say for that person.) There's only one smart way to handle an ongoing thread of business e-mail. Never delete the previous message text, and place your response at the very top of the file. When you're responding to a long set of questions or comments, however, you should intersperse your responses after the specific points or questions of the previous message. When you're responding to a message that's more than a week old, you might want to remind the person of the gist of his or her last message in your response.

Note: America Online doesn't automatically include the previous message on e-mail responses, which makes it a very bad e-mail system to use in a business setting. If you're an America Online subscriber, you may want to look into an alternative e-mail provider.

When to use "Reply to All." Whenever you receive a message sent to multiple people, start by thinking about who you want to respond to. If your response doesn't need to be read by everyone on the distribution list, then please save those other people some time, and respond to the original sender only. But watch for the opposite mistake. It's easy to forget to click "Reply to All" and just click "Reply." You may think your answer is going out to everyone on the list, but in fact, it's only going to the original sender. That can cause real confusion. It would be nice if e-mail packages required you to make the decision of whether to reply to all or just reply to sender after you've written your message. But they make you decide this first. So, make a habit of double-checking whom you're sending to before you press the "Send" button.

Source: Scott Finnie, "E-Mail Etiquette," www.entrepreneur.com/Your_Business/YB_SegArticle/0,4621,276224,00.html.

International Business Etiquette Protocols

Keep these areas of protocol in mind when traveling overseas. For details on business ethics protocols in a particular country, visit www.executiveplanet.com.

Let's Make a Deal—negotiating tactics, the value of connections, recommended business card style and content, business card protocol, sitting and presenting yourself in meetings, language for brochures and promotional material, pace of business, preferred presentation styles, final agreements, thinking styles, adherence to company policy, etc.

Prosperous Entertaining—typical mealtimes throughout the day, best venues for business entertaining, punctuality for social events, dinner table seating etiquette, mealtime etiquette, importance of alcohol, toasting, guidelines for hosting a banquet/social event, what foods should be served or avoided, accepting and declining invitations, and more business etiquette info, etc.

Appointment Alert!—typical vacation times, recommended appointment times, length of the lunch hour, signals that indicate beginning or end of an appointment, best arrival time (early, late, right on time), etc.

Gift Giving—recommended gifts, gifts to avoid, good and bad colors for wrapping paper, how to present a gift to individuals and groups, guidelines for receiving gifts, etc.

First Name or Title?—using titles such as "Doctor," naming conventions to avoid, when to use first names, etc.

Public Behavior—how to greet strangers and introduce yourself, the rules for men shaking hands with women, acceptable demeanor, rules for eye contact, gestures and expressions to avoid, etc.

Business Dress—generalities, specific dress requirements for men and women, what visitors should wear to social functions, etc.

Conversation—welcome and unwelcome topics of conversation, the role of compliments, the tone of voice to be used, whether your hosts are physical or more reserved, etc.

Source: Executive Planet Inc., www.executiveplanet.com.

Chapter 37

General Management

Tips for Basic E-Mail Management

Is your e-mail killing your productivity? Then it's time for some basic e-mail management. Checking e-mail, reading e-mail, and answering e-mail can take up hours of time if you let it.

1. **The first rule** of e-mail management is to let your e-mail program manage your e-mail as much as possible. E-mail management starts with setting up and using filters. If you're using an e-mail program such as Outlook, you can configure e-mail rules to send your spam directly to the trash—meaning that you don't waste your time reading and deleting it.

2. **The second rule** of e-mail management is to not respond to your e-mail on demand. You don't need to see every piece of e-mail the second it arrives. If you're using an e-mail program that announces the arrival of new e-mail, turn off the program's announcement features, such as making a sound or having a pop-up screen announce the arrival of e-mail.

3. **The third rule** of e-mail management is closely related to the second rule: don't read and answer your e-mail all day long. You may get anywhere from a handful to hundreds of e-mails each day that need to be answered, but they don't need to be answered immediately, interrupting whatever else you're doing. Instead, set aside a particular time each day to review and answer your e-mail. Schedule the hour or whatever time it takes you to answer the volume of e-mail you get, and stick to that schedule as regularly as possible.

4. **The fourth rule** is to not answer your e-mail at your most productive time of day. What time of day is your most productive? Scheduling less demanding tasks such as checking, reading, and answering e-mail outside of your "best" working time will help you make the most of your working day—and that's good e-mail management.

Source: Susan Ward, "Basic Email Management," sbinfocanada.about.com/cs/management/qt/email1.htm.

How to Stop Reshuffling Paper

Are ever-growing stacks of paperwork interfering with your productivity? When you sit down to work, do you find yourself buried beneath a stack of paperwork and never being able to lay your hands on the one piece of paper you need for the task at hand?

Remind yourself that there are really only two types of paper: paperwork that needs to be dealt with immediately and paperwork that doesn't.

■ So instead of handling each piece of paperwork many times, as you shuffle it from stack to pile, search for it, look at it again, and stick it into another growing stack, handle each piece of paper as few times as possible.

- If the piece of paper falls into the first category, paperwork that needs to be dealt with immediately, and is something that can be responded to in three minutes or less, respond to it right then.

- If the piece of paper falls into the first category, but is something that will require a longer response, place the paperwork in your Current file or inbox.

- Follow up by scheduling the time you will respond to the paperwork in your Current file (within the next three days if possible). Ideally, you should be clearing your Current file every two days.

- If the piece of paper falls into the second category, something that doesn't need a response, such as a receipt or information that doesn't call for any action on your part, file the piece of paper right away in the appropriate place.

- Filing paper the first time around takes only a few seconds. But if you just toss the paperwork into a anonymous pile to be dealt with "later," those seconds will turn into minutes and maybe even hours of paper filing, as you're forced to reread and sort through your old paperwork before you can file it.

- If you're going to waste time, there are plenty of more pleasant ways to do it than rereading and filing old papers. So when a piece of paperwork lands on your desk, deal with it on the spot.

Source: Susan Ward, "Stop Shuffling Paper," sbinfocanada.about.com/cs/management/qt/ paperwork.htm.

Four Tips for Handling Receipts

1. **Establish a simple routine for dealing with paper (including receipts!) as soon as it comes into your hands and stick to it.**
   For instance, have a Day-Timer® that you take everywhere. When you buy something, put the receipt into the flap in your Day-Timer®. When you get back to the office, immediately put the receipt into the appropriate folder. That way, you never have to think about where you might have put a receipt, and never have to waste time looking for one that's gone astray.

2. **When you get a receipt, look at it, and fill in missing or faded receipt information on the spot.**
   Even if you've paid with a credit card, not every machine will fill in all the receipt information you'll need later clearly. And handwritten receipts are worse. There's nothing more frustrating then trying to decipher a date or a product long after the fact when you've finally gotten around to the data entry stage. Dates are particularly annoying, as different countries use different dating conventions. Is 01–08–01 January 8 or August 1? Solve this problem by writing the month on receipts when you get them.

3. **If you must fold a receipt, fold it so that the printed side is uppermost.**
That way, it will be easier to find the receipt if you ever have to look for it. When you fold a receipt so that the printed side is hidden, all receipts look alike, and you'll have to unfold them all to find the receipt you want.

4. **Don't let the data entry pile up.**
If you have a bookkeeper, deliver your receipts on a weekly or monthly basis. If you're the one doing it, schedule time every week to do the necessary data entry, and stick to that schedule. If you don't, you'll just put it off, and your piles of receipts will become even more unappealing. You'll always find something more important or interesting to do if you don't force yourself to do it!

Following these four receipt tips will make it much easier to always be able to lay your hands on the exact receipt you need.

Source: Susan Ward, "Four Tips for Handling Receipts," sbinfocanada.about.com/cs/management/qt/handlereceipts.htm

Using Invoices That Encourage Action

Having the money you're owed sitting in someone else's bank account can seriously interfere with your business's cash flow. If many of the clients or customers you invoice are slow payers, maybe it's time to look at your invoices; they could be contributing to your collections problem.

- Does the invoice you're sending out encourage action or inaction? For example, many invoices are simply marked, "Payable upon receipt." Invoices so labeled are saying to your customers or clients, "Pay me when it's convenient for you," instead of "Pay me now." Those inclined to be slow payers will find the built-in excuse especially convenient; we've all heard the line, "The check's in the mail"!

- Worse, some invoices have boxes such as "current," "30 days," "60 days," "90 days," and "over 90 days" that broadcast the aging of the account that's due.

- Using an invoice that's formatted this way is also broadcasting to those inclined to be slow payers that you're willing to serve as a creditor; there's no reason to pay you right away.

- Instead of using invoices that encourage inaction, use invoices that encourage prompt payment. All of the invoices you send out should state a specific date of payment, such as "Due on November 30, 2001," rather than "Payable upon receipt" or "Due in 30 days." People are much more likely to pay attention to a specific payment date, and you eliminate the possibility of misunderstanding or loose interpretation.

- You can also encourage prompt payment of invoices by offering an incentive to pay on time. Many businesses, for instance, offer a small discount for paying within ten days of an invoice date. A discount of two percent for payment within ten days is common.

■ Don't let your invoices contribute to collections problems and make your prompt payers feel as if they're being unfairly treated. Using invoices that state specific dates that payment is expected and offer an incentive to pay promptly encourages action— and will help get the money you're owed flowing into your bank account.

Source: Susan Ward, "Use Invoices That Encourage Action," sbinfocanada.about.com/cs/management/qt/actioninvoices.htm

Tips on How to Get the Most out of Seminars and Meetings

Here are some tips for examining seminars or meetings in advance:

1. Find out all you can about the speaker before signing up for his or her seminar, including past seminars, his or her personality type, how long the person usually speaks, what his or her main expertise is, etc.

2. See if that person is just repeating something that may be in print, which you possibly could purchase at much less cost, getting the same information. However, live is always more exciting, if the person is a dynamic speaker.

3. Ask other people if they have heard or seen anything on this topic, to be up to date before you attend. You might even find the same information from the same source the speaker is bringing it in from. Also, there may be cassette tapes, CDs, or even videos available at a much lower price, from the same speaker. Many speakers just repeat themselves everywhere they go and also market themselves in print and on tapes heavily, which is how they make most of their money.

4. Always, always, take a note pad and possibly a cassette tape recorder (if allowed) and be prepared to take many notes and examples, because the more times you repeat something, the faster you learn it. Repetition is the best way.

Source: Jerry Cunningham, "Tip 18: Getting The Most Out of Meetings/Seminars," sbinfocanada.about.com/library/biztips/bl_biztips_18.htm.

Tips on Determining Your Personal ROI

Running your own small business means wearing many different hats, but all the myriad tasks associated with running a business don't have equal value, especially if we look at them in terms of our personal return on investment (ROI).

Think of all the different business-related tasks you perform in a single week. List them if you need to, or look at your records to determine how much time you're spending on different types of tasks.

- One way to determine your personal return on investment is to simply look at the bottom line. Tally the number of hours you spent in that particular week on book-keeping tasks. Now think about how you make your profit. What do you charge to deliver the service you provide or how much product would you sell in that time frame?

- Another way of determining our personal return on investment is to look at the "human" cost. How are those hours spent on the particular task affecting the things that are important to you, such as your family life, lifestyle, or even health?

Determining your personal return on investment can help you see which business-related tasks you could or should be delegating—and free some of your time to do more of the things that you find more profitable and enjoyable.

Source: Susan Ward, "Determining Your Personal Return on Investment," sbinfocanada.about.com/cs/management/qt/personalroi.htm.

How to Form an Advisory Board

- Determine the type of individual who fits the company culture. Identifying the commitment, structure, characteristics, and personality type is the first step toward forming a well-rounded board.

- Decide on the number of advisors. For smaller companies, expect about three to five advisors. Smaller boards are more productive.

- Make a list of potential candidates. Ask people in the community for recommendations. Your lawyer, accountant, and banker may provide referrals.

- Look at the skill set of your prospects. Do they complement each other?

- What type of personalities do your prospects have?

- Have your prospects served on advisory boards? If so, what kinds and for how long?

- Create a pitch for your business, to describe it briefly and specify what you expect of board members and how much time will be required..

- Call, using any referrals. If possible, ask the person who referred you to call and tell your prospect who you are and why you will be calling. If not possible, create an e-mail introducing yourself and explaining your purpose.

- Follow up on the initial contact. Be persistent.

- If a prospect declines your request, ask him or her to suggest another prospect.

Source: Greg Moran, "Building the Entrepreneurial Advisory Board," www.eventuring.org.

Three Things That Encourage Employee Turnover

Surveys consistently show that more than 40 percent of people who quit do so because they feel they weren't appreciated for their contributions. These surveys show that lack of appreciation, lack of teamwork, and the perception that the company doesn't care about employees are consistently the highest-rated reasons for low job satisfaction.

1. Employees feel lack of appreciation, which is in itself a negative. There are many managers who are very nice people, but who manage almost exclusively by negative reinforcement—not because of what they do but because of what they don't do.

2. When you give out positives—whether it is a pat on the back or a raise in pay—if you give them equally to all performers, then you end up punishing the best performers. Most employees think that it's not fair that they work hard every day, while others do just enough to get by—yet the consequences, pay, benefits, perks, and praise are the same.

3. Employees feel negative about the workplace when managers frequently fail to deal effectively and efficiently with problem performers.

Source: Aubrey C. Daniels, "How to Prevent Employee Turnover," www.entrepreneur.com/article/0,4621,307637,00.html.

How to Prevent Employee Turnover

Provide workers with responsibility—and then let them use it. Most surveys show that the greatest source of employee pride and satisfaction is the feeling of accomplishment that comes from having—and exercising—responsibility. Yet many business owners, consumed by fears of a shrinking bottom line, have turned micromanagement into an art form. Unfortunately, few things employers do cause more employee dissatisfaction. Here's the real bottom line: if you can't trust your employees to be able to think and act on their own, you probably shouldn't have hired them.

Show respect. Frustrated by a faltering economy, diminishing markets, and meddling investors, many business owners look close to home for someone to blame—all too often, that's their own employees. The result? A growing number of employees feel like they're being viewed as the enemy, not as loyal partners. It's little wonder so many workers seem ready to jump ship at the first sign of opportunity. On the other hand, companies that truly value their employees earn more than gratitude—they win greater dedication and productivity as well. So be sure to show your employees how much you respect and value them. Tell them how much you appreciate them, throw them a pizza party, recognize an employee of the month—do anything you can to show them how much you care.

Recognize the whole person. Employees are more than 9-to-5 robots who turn off at night and can't wait until the starting bell rings the next morning. All workers have lives, interests, and friends and family outside the office—and most are constantly struggling to balance increasingly hectic schedules. While companies can't sacrifice unduly to the whims of a single individual, making concessions where possible—allowing a long lunch break to attend a child's school event, for instance, or permitting a sales executive to fly out on Monday morning instead of Sunday night—can pay huge dividends in the long run.

Mark out a clear path to growth. Some employees are content to remain where they are in an organization, but most want to grow in their careers over time. While annual performance reviews were originally designed to promote this goal, too often they have become empty, "Dilbertized" rituals, more embarrassing than ennobling. By contrast, business owners who wish to increase worker satisfaction tend to look past formalities and establish genuine growth paths for all their employees, not just their senior executives.

Source: "Improve Your Employees' Job Satisfaction," www.entrepreneur.com/article/0,4621,314871,00.html, from the HP *Technology at Work* e-newsletter.

Ten Management Lessons from a Young Entrepreneur

Scott Smigler, 22, is one young entrepreneur who has learned some important lessons from his pursuit of entrepreneurship. Smigler started Exclusive Concepts Inc., a company that provides professional web design and online marketing solutions to growing businesses, when he was only a freshman in high school. Smigler ran the company by himself at first, slowly building a reputation with his clients and gaining more business through word-of-mouth. As he put himself through college, he ran the business out of his dorm room until May 2002. Now, in December 2003, he has offices in Burlington, Massachusetts, and a staff of five, and expects to bring in sales of $300,000 in 2003. Between working full-time on his business, maintaining a 3.7 GPA as a finance major at Bentley College in Waltham, Massachusetts, and running the Entrepreneurship Society he co-founded at his school, Smigler took some time out of his 90-hour week to offer entrepreneurs—of any age—some advice: ten of the most important lessons he's learned from starting and running his own business.

1. It's all about perseverance. Implementing your dream is never as easy as you think it will be—it can take years to develop. Make sure you're organized and stay focused. And understand that you can't reach the highest levels of success without taking risks and maintaining the strength of mind needed to persevere through the difficult times.

    "I know there are so many people right now, especially my age, who are looking to start and develop their own business," says Smigler. "It's such an intimidating process once you've broken through the first layer and you have to worry about insurance and payroll and making sure your accounting is perfect. So many people allow themselves to get intimidated by it; they're not willing to follow their dreams. It's very important for people to really sit down and recognize exactly what they want out of life—and their business life—and just go for it."

2. Understand the value of mentorship and teamwork. A small company doesn't have all the resources it will need internally. So it's essential to have a network of advisors, mentors, and other people who can help you work through the problems you encounter—whether those problems are related to finances, marketing, whatever.

3. Stick to your niche. "I've learned that I can only make money when I stay focused on what my company does best," Smigler says. "This isn't to say I don't pursue avenues where I can expand my business. Ultimately, the needs of my customers will dictate the services I offer. Everything I do has to be based on a very strong customer-service focus. We know a lot about our clients because we spend a lot of time knowing exactly what they need."

4. Stay on top of news that affects your clients. Major events happen almost every day that will affect your customers. In order to ensure the best for them, you must be up-to-date on the latest market trends and implement them so your company consistently offers the best services and your clients receive the best there is to offer. "Even on the busiest of days," says Smigler, "my entire staff and I are required to monitor late-breaking news. Knowledge separates you from your competitors."

5. Communication is key. While you think your clients understand what you say, often they don't. Be sure to always speak clearly and follow up with concise e-mails. You must also pace their expectations with the reality of the project. Part of the communication process involves documenting the understanding between your company and the client so that in the event of a misunderstanding, you have an agreement to fall back on. Not only does the client need to know what they can expect from you, it's essential that the client understand your expectations of them. Success is a two-way street.

"Search-engine marketing and web development can be very intimidating to a lot of people," says Smigler. "My clients tell me over and over again that what makes a huge difference to them is that I take the time to explain things clearly and that I'm patient with them. They know they're not just getting a cookie-cutter solution."

6. Capitalization is crucial. Everything is more expensive than you'll anticipate. In your budgeting process, you need to plan for things you haven't anticipated but that will more than likely happen. In addition, don't be a penny-pincher: don't be afraid to spend money when you believe the return will warrant the risk.

7. Communicate unwavering honesty and integrity. Above everything else, you must be truthful. Dishonesty is a sign of weakness, not to mention a poor business strategy. If your clients know you'll always be truthful with them and "tell it like it is," they'll never have any reason to doubt you. Your reputation as an excellent service provider takes years to develop—but it can be destroyed in a minute.

"My family pushes the simplicity of life that comes from honesty and character and integrity," Smigler says. "One of the big things that makes [our company] different is our clients really do trust us."

8. Stay on top of the curve. The environment of business changes rapidly, and education is a critical factor to success. "There was a time when I was tempted to drop out of college and devote all my time to managing my growing company," Smigler says. "I recognized that it wouldn't be a smart strategy for the long term. It's possible to grow a company while being successful in school."

9. Take ownership in your clients' success. When you undertake the commitment to provide products or services for a company, you must work at it as diligently as they expect you to. Keep your customers' needs in mind at all times. And remember: if you're able to help your clients become successful, they will make you successful, because what goes around, comes around.

10. Never stop marketing. Never forget that anyone can be a prospective client. Constantly look to build on your existing relationships, as well as acquire new ones. You need to catch the customers at the moment they have a need. By staying in front of them on a regular basis, you become known to them, so when they do have a need, they'll be more inclined to give you the business without shopping around. The value of a referral is always more than the value of a cold lead.

Source: Sarah Pierce, "10 Management Lessons from a Young Entrepreneur," www.entrepreneur.com/article/0,4621,312349,00.html.

Section 6

Time Management

Section 6

Smart Ways to Cut Time Spent on Administrative Duties

Entrepreneurs complain that administrative tasks consume too much of their time. First, take an inventory of how you spend your time. List your activities and then evaluate them, keeping the following in mind:

- Be sure the task is essential. If it doesn't get done, will your business suffer?

- Can you systemize the task? By creating a step-by-step formula to get it done, you'll likely come up with the most efficient way to handle it.

- Delegate. Do you have a staff person to hand off the job to? If not, is it worth hiring a part-timer, using a temp worker, or outsourcing the work?

- If you decide to outsource, can you combine several related tasks and give yourself even more time?

It's important to remember time spent on trivial tasks takes time away from income generation.

Source: Rieva Lesonsky, *365 Tips to Boost Your Entrepreneurial IQ.*

Section 6

Five Steps for Making Your Office More Effective

Here are five steps for setting up your office for maximum effectiveness.

- **Remove.** "I can't get my drawer open." Sound familiar? Whatever your situation, the first step is to remove everything—take out all the pens, pencils, clips, twisties, sugar packs, tea bags, photos, keys, and dried-up candy.

- **Sort.** As you remove items, sort according to like items. Sorting shows that you have 87 pens and 830 clips. You might ask yourself, "Do I really need so many?"

- **Eliminate.** After you've discovered that 54 pens don't even work or that the sugar packets are rock-hard, then you can eliminate the items directly into the trash or into a box labeled "to go elsewhere."

- **Contain.** Now comes the step most people leave out. Stop and think: if you put all that stuff back into the drawer, it will soon be a jumbled mess again. Instead, keep those groups sorted and separated at all times by first containing them. If you put each group in a drawer divider or shallow box before placing them back in the drawer, they'll stay in one place.

- **Assign.** Don't just stick the containers in the drawer. Assign them a place. Unassigned items simply float from place to place.

Now you're probably wondering where to start with your filing system. Your first step is to empty your file drawers one at a time. Start with the file drawer in your desk.

Remove each file and sort it on the floor using a nifty filing system that I call FileMAP:

- **Main:** These are the files you're currently working on.

- **Archive:** These are files you haven't looked at and never will look at, but you might need them someday.

- **Personal:** These are your personal files. This would include your 401(k), taxes, and so on.

Source: Sue McMillin, "Organize Your Organization Process," www.entrepreneur.com/article/0,4621,299444,00.html.

Tips to Avoiding Procrastination

Here are several ways to help you jump-start your next project and avoid a last-minute time crunch:

- First, use a to-do list—whether on paper, in an electronic organizer, or on your PC—to record everything you need to do.

- Give each task on your list a priority, either by listing the more important tasks at the top or by using a numeric system (No. 1 for high-priority tasks, No. 2 for less important tasks, and so on).

- Refer to your list often while you're working, and if you're still having trouble getting started, work on a quick No. 3 or easy task. After completing a simple task, you'll be ready to tackle bigger ones.

- Reward yourself for completing various aspects of a project. A reward may be as simple as taking a walk around the block or reading part of your favorite magazine.

- Don't beat yourself up. Realize that you're not the only person who has trouble getting started on various projects.

If you're still having trouble getting started, use one of these methods to make your tasks a bit more manageable and fun:

- **Elephant.** The old saying, "How do you eat an elephant? One bite at a time," is still true. Break your project into smaller tasks.

- **Ten Minutes.** Promise yourself you'll work on a project for ten minutes and then quit if you're tired or bored. Chances are at least 30 minutes will pass and you'll have made progress.

- **Best for Last.** Handle a few tasks first and, as a reward, save the easiest task or the one you want to do the most for last.

- **Game Playing.** Challenge yourself to handle one task in less than 30 minutes. Then move on to another task and shorten the amount of time you give yourself. Make it a game to see how quickly you can tackle tasks you've been putting off.

■ **Public Announcement.** Be brave and tell others about your plans. If you fail to complete a task you've committed to in front of witnesses, not only do you have to face yourself, you have to face others.

Source: Lisa Kanarek, "The Time Is Now," www.entrepreneur.com/article/0,4621,272528,00.html.

Section 6

Chapter 39

Office and Store Management

SCORE's Five Tips on Creating an Office Where You Can Work

1. Locate your office in a quiet location where you won't be distracted with passersby. Locate your office in a space you love.

2. If you have to share an office, make space for two desks and two sets of files and supplies.

3. Situate the workspaces to allow each person maximum quiet and minimal distractions.

4. Project your office's needs for the next year and acquire equipment and furnishings accordingly.

5. Your office will grow. Purchase systems and furniture that will allow for growth or add-ons.

Source: SCORE, www.score.org/business_tips.html.

Section 6

Evaluating a Business Opportunity

You can tell if something is a business opportunity by looking at the general criteria listed below.

- A business opportunity involves the sale or lease of any product, service, equipment, and so on that will enable the purchaser-licensee to begin a business.

- The licenser or seller of a business opportunity declares that it will secure or assist the buyer in finding a suitable location or provide the product to the purchaser-licensee.

- The licenser-seller guarantees an income greater than or equal to the price of licensee-buyer pays for the product when it is resold and that there is a market present for the product or service.

- The initial fee paid to the seller to start the business opportunity must be more than $500.

- The licenser-seller promises to buy back any product purchased by the licensee-buyer in the event that it cannot be sold to a prospective customer of the business.

- Any product or services developed by the seller-licenser will be purchased by the licensee-buyer.

- The licenser-seller of the business opportunity will supply a sales or marketing program for the licensee-buyer that many times will include the use of a trademark.

Source: Andi Axman, *Entrepreneur Magazine's Ultimate Small Business Advisor.*

Tips for Organizing Your Home Office

Is your home-based business a mess? According to industry experts, paperwork can be a home-based business owner's biggest burden. Here are some smart ways to unclutter your workplace:

- First, sort all your paperwork by category, and put it into clearly marked file boxes. Don't keep what you don't need.

- Organize your work space. How many file cabinets do you really need? What can be boxed and stored elsewhere?

- Items you use every day should be within easy reach; everything else should be put away.

- At the end of your workday, always put things back where they belong. Remember: staying organized is like any good habit—the more you practice it, the easier it becomes.

Source: Rieva Lesonsky, *365 Tips to Boost Your Entrepreneurial IQ.*

Six Steps to an Organized Office

If you find yourself spending more than 30 seconds to locate an important document in your office, it may be time to clean. Working in the comfort of your home, you may be less inclined to be strict about office organization. Follow these steps to organization:

Step 1. Arm yourself with supplies. Before you begin to clear out your office, go shopping for office supplies that you will need to aid your reorganization. Purchase hanging and file folders, new pens, pads, self-stick notes, cleaning solutions, and lots of garbage bags.

Step 2. Get mentally prepared. Cleaning out your office includes throwing stuff away. Get into the mind-frame of "when in doubt, throw it out."

Step 3. Take your time. To give your office a thorough cleaning, be prepared to spend the whole day throwing out, wiping down, and re-organizing. If you can't devote at least five hours to tidying your work space, save the task for later.

Step 4. Empty it out. Take everything out of each drawer, from each file cabinet, and off each shelf. Wipe down all of your drawers, cabinets, and desk space with a rag. Then focus on what you have removed. Go through the contents of each drawer and throw out what you don't need or use.

Step 5. Reorganize. Create a place for everything. Some people find it useful to dedicate each desk drawer to a specific function—e.g., a communication drawer to hold all writing utensils, paper, printer cartridges, and pads.

Step 6. Clean and organize often. Get into the habit of cleaning out and reorganizing your office on a regular basis. It will reduce the time you spend reorganizing in the future, and it will help to make your daily work life more efficient.

Source: "Six Steps to an Organized Office,"morebusiness.com/running_your_business/management/d914862919.brc.

Common Types of Business Opportunity Ventures

Business opportunity ventures, like franchises, are businesses where the seller makes a commitment of continuing involvement with the buyer. The Federal Trade Commission describes the most common types of business opportunity ventures as follows:

- **Distributors.** This involves an independent agent entering into an agreement to offer and sell the product of another, without being entitled to use the manufacturer's trade name as part of the agent's trade name.

- **Rack Jobbing.** This involves selling another company's products through a distribution system of racks in stores. The rack jobber maintains the inventory, moves the merchandise around to attract the customer, and does the bookkeeping. The agent presents the store manager with a copy of the inventory sheet, which indicates what has been sold, and the distributor is paid by the store or location that has the rack, less the store's commission.

- **Vending Machine Routes.** This is similar to rack jobbing, although the financial investment is greater. The businessperson must buy the machines and the merchandise being sold in them. The vending machine operator typically pays the location owner a percentage based on sales.

For more information on the FTC and business opportunities, visit www.ftc.gov/bcp/online/pubs/alerts/bizopalrt.htm.

Source: "Types of Business Opportunities," www.entrepreneur.com/article/0,4621,291618----2-,00.html, from *The Small Business Encyclopedia* (Entrepreneur Magazine Group).

Tips for Choosing a Business Opportunity

- Make an honest evaluation of yourself and your abilities.
- Be enthusiastic about the business you'll be operating.
- Be knowledgeable about the product or service you will be involved with.
- Make a market evaluation of the product or service to be offered.
- Analyze the market trends.

- How many buyers have been in the business and for what period of time?
- Check the skills required to run the business properly.
- Calculate the business opportunity's profitability and financial leverage ratios.
- Determine how much time you need to earn what you do now.
- Check with current operators to see what they are doing now.
- Get the history of the offering company's operation.
- Learn about the service personnel at the parent company.
- Examine the financial standing of the parent company.
- Evaluate the policies and plans of the company with the associations and business groups with which the parent company or seller is involved.
- Find out whether complaints against the company have been registered with the Better Business Bureau.
- Get a status report on the firm from Dun & Bradstreet.
- Have your attorney or CPA evaluate the company.
- Visit the licenser-seller's office at your earliest convenience.

Source: Andi Axman, *Entrepreneur Magazine's Ultimate Small Business Advisor.*

Employee Management

How to Boost Morale in the Office

Just make sure a declining economy doesn't pull your sales staff's morale down with it. Consider these attitude-enhancing tips.

- **Stay positive.** If your salespeople smell fear, they'll start to worry.
- **Have a plan.** When the economy takes a dive, sales are tougher to find and your sales team will need new ideas. Plan promotions and specials to get things moving. Investigate new markets or launch new products. Active people are positive people.
- **Get out in the field.** Schedule ride-alongs with salespeople to visit key clients. Use this time to hear their problems and ideas. In tough times, we all need to be heard.
- **Rev 'em up!** In a soft market, salespeople are getting beaten up every day. It's your job to inject a positive attitude into their lives. Leave them encouraging voice mails or pager text messages.
- **Be a cheerleader.** Make a big deal out of every sale. Celebrate successes to motivate your team to keep on winning.
- **Set realistic goals.** Reset your goals to reflect the tougher market. Consistently missing goals lowers morale.

Source: Kimberly L. McCall, "Cheer Up!," www.entrepreneur.com/article/0,4621,292904,00.html.

Recommended Acts of Appreciation to Your Employees

Do you take the time to thank your employees? Most entrepreneurs consumed with growing their businesses don't do it often enough. Try incorporating "little acts of appreciation" into your daily business routine, says Rosalind Jeffries, author of *101 Recognition Secrets*.

- Instead of giving workers birthday cards at the office, why not mail them to their homes?
- After a job particularly well done, handwrite or e-mail a congratulatory note.
- Make sure to give special recognition to employees who do good deeds in or out of the office.
- Food treats can also serves as a general morale booster. Try serving hot chocolate on cold winter days or providing Popsicles® to beat the summer swelter.

These gestures may sound trivial, but, as Jeffries reminds us, one of the greatest human needs is to be appreciated.

Source: Rieva Lesonsky, *365 Tips to Boost Your Entrepreneurial IQ.*

SCORE's Five Tips on Supporting Your Sales Staff

1. Make sure sales representatives have adequate training. They should have a thorough understanding of how your products or services can help potential customers.

2. Develop an annual sales plan. It should include sales and gross-profit goals and plans for increasing sales to current customers and developing new ones. See that sales reps implement the plan and modify it as necessary.

3. Make everyone in your company understand that they are part of the selling team. Courteous treatment of customers, quick responses to telephone calls and e-mails, and pleasant demeanors go a long way toward supporting the sales staff.

4. Offer meaningful incentives. One company told salespeople they could go home at 2 p.m. the rest of the month once they hit their monthly goals; the first sales rep to sell more than $50,000 would get the last two days of the month off. Result: broken sales records.

5. Encourage salespeople to put a lost sale in perspective. Getting angry yourself only adds to their frustration. Help them concentrate on making the next sale.

Source: SCORE, www.score.org/business_tips.html.

SCORE's Five Tips on Teaching Employees to "Own" Their Work

1. Include them in long- and short-term planning efforts.

2. Ask for their input on projects for which they are held responsible.

3. Include them on top-level discussions, conferences, and meetings when appropriate.

4. Allow them to byline the work they wrote or to speak at the presentation they helped prepare.

5. Help them to become more vested in the work by asking for their opinion. Ask what, if anything, should be done to make the next project easier.

Source: SCORE, www.score.org/business_tips.html.

SCORE's Five Tips for Hands-on Leadership

1. Be there. Entrepreneurs warn that a successful business can slip when an owner is not there at least part of every day, keeping in touch with how things are going.

Section 6

2. Set an example for working hard. One wholesale bakery owner sometimes sleeps on the couch in his office so he can be there when the early shift comes in at 4 a.m.

3. Don't confuse "hands-on" managing with micro-management. Set objectives and offer guidance, but don't make employees do every little thing your way. Gauge what they do by the results.

4. Understand your business down to the last detail. The founder of a toy-store chain visits the stores and spends time doing each job (selling, clerking, etc.) and observing customers' reactions.

5. Stay in touch with "stakeholders"—including customers, employees and suppliers.

Source: SCORE, www.score.org/business_tips.html.

SCORE's Five Tips on How to Empower Your Employees

1. **Organize an orientation session.** Answer the most frequently asked questions and walk employees through solving problems common to your business.

2. **Provide employees with the history behind procedures and policies.** Background is essential for good decision making.

3. **Furnish the necessary resources.** Whether it is a list of your contacts or where to find appropriate forms, give your employees the opportunity to succeed.

4. **Teach employees where to turn when they can't solve a problem.** Always going to the president should not be the solution.

5. **Learn to delegate.** Delegating tasks will build confidence and teach employees the necessary steps to follow in your business

Source: SCORE, www.score.org/business_tips.html.

Tips for Employee Empowerment

A lot has been said about how empowering employees can help businesses grow, but here are some more tidbits of information.

- Empowerment is merely giving your staff the authority to make decisions, like letting them hire new employees, and rewarding them for making great choices.

- Entrepreneurs often have difficulty delegating any task and incorrectly believe only they are capable of making the right call.

- Empowerment is popular with workers. It not only boosts job satisfaction, but it also reduces absenteeism and creates job loyalty, which decreases job turnover and improves customer service.

- Employee empowerment saves you money. It also frees you up to do what you do best ... all of which can end up giving your business a strong competitive advantage.

Source: Rieva Lesonsky, *365 Tips to Boost Your Entrepreneurial IQ.*

SCORE's Five Tips on Effective Leadership

1. Communicate clearly and routinely. Lay out your company goals and principles in a mission statement and keep sharing your vision with your employees.

2. Involve employees in setting objectives. Give them feedback on how they are progressing toward meeting those targets.

3. Give your people authority; then hold them accountable. But don't go after them personally when things go wrong. Find out first if the process is at fault.

4. Be accountable yourself. Install an advisory board or executive team to help you make good strategic decisions and give you feedback on your own performance.

5. Be trustworthy and extend trust to your employees. That will help you earn their loyalty and strengthen your company.

Source: SCORE, www.score.org/business_tips.html.

Section 6

SCORE's Five Tips on Exemplary Leadership

1. Give employees their freedom. Communicate the goals and let them figure out how to reach those goals. They want control over their working lives.

2. Create an environment that encourages energy and spirit. That leads to happy customers.

3. Strive to help employees feel that when they have achieved the business's goals, they have also achieved their own personal goals.

4. Create a sense of meaningful purpose. Most workers want to feel they are engaged in something "larger than themselves."

5. Recognize that leadership means responsibility and stewardship. "Leadership is not rank, privileges, titles, or money," said the late management thinker Peter F. Drucker.

Source: SCORE, www.score.org/business_tips.html.

SCORE's Five Tips on Cultivating Confident Employees

1. Ask them to be responsible for progressively larger projects.
2. Use them as examples (in their presence) when describing to others how to do something.
3. Give them feedback at various times during a project—not just at its completion.
4. Send a note of praise to them or, better still, to their direct boss.
5. Ask for their opinions and advice on matters not necessarily related to their normal duties.

Source: SCORE, www.score.org/business_tips.html.

Tips for Avoiding Sexual Harassment

Are you safe from sexual harassment charges? You may think you are, but these days business owners can't be too careful. Here are some ground rules to help keep you out of trouble:

- Don't touch your employees without permission.
- Don't treat employees as potential dates. Whatever you do, never get involved with someone who works for you.
- Don't demean others, especially in reference to their gender.
- Don't make suggestive comments.
- Watch your language; what amuses some can offend others.
- Make sure your company has a written sexual harassment policy and that all employees know what to do if they're harassed.
- Take all complaints seriously, and launch an immediate investigation.

You have to worry about more than yourself. Make sure your employees are not harassing each other, either. But remember: it's your business—you set the tone.

Source: Rieva Lesonsky, *365 Tips to Boost Your Entrepreneurial IQ.*

Eight Ways to Charm Your Employees

Here are some suggestions for creating good relationships, loyalty, and rapport in the workplace.

1. Watch how you're standing. Men enjoy standing side by side when speaking to one another. Women enjoy facing each other while talking to one another. Women: when

approaching a man, slowly position your torso at an angle to his torso to make him comfortable. Men: to make a woman comfortable, slowly move your torso so you're standing face to face with her to make her comfortable.

2. In your mind's eye, picture a spotlight on anyone you're speaking to. Every time you speak, the spotlight turns off of them and onto you. So do your best to keep them, not you, in the spotlight. Don't regale them with your tales of your experiences. Instead, use active-listening skills—stay with them and explore their comments.

3. Avoid touching yourself when speaking to others. Do your best to keep your hands still. Don't play with your hair or jewelry, wring your hands, or touch your face. By touching yourself, you're indicating your need to comfort yourself; unconsciously that makes the other person feel you're not paying attention to him or her.

4. Smile while you're talking. It's great to smile when you're listening to someone, but it's equally powerful to smile at someone while you're speaking to them.

5. Subtly mirror people's gestures when you're speaking to them. If they sit back in their chair, sit back in yours. If they fold their hands, fold yours. You must be subtle or you'll get caught. Learn to be very graceful in your mirroring and move very slowly, as if you're making natural movements and not copying them.

6. Talk 20 percent of the time and listen 80 percent of the time. Let people talk about their favorite subject: themselves. When people are speaking, ask them questions, nod affirmatively as they speak, and avoid interrupting them until they've finished talking and then ask them another question. When you're listening, you're in control of the conversation because you can guide the conversation anywhere you want it to go without volunteering anything about yourself or your own opinions.

7. Avoid offering unsolicited advice in public or in private. Generally, people will become defensive and stop talking when you offer them advice they didn't ask to hear. Offering advice makes a listener think they're wrong and that they've made a mistake by volunteering their viewpoint. Instead, say, "That's one way of looking at it," or "Let's take the learning experience from that and take it to the next level."

8. Offer sincere flattery every day to work associates, clients, and vendors. Most people enjoy being thanked for a job well done, but comment only on their behavior and not them personally. Be specific with your flattery, or it will fall flat. Give flattery in a timely manner—don't wait too long to deliver it. Be sensitive to the fact that some people like public flattery and some prefer to receive theirs privately. Some people need frequent flattery and some have difficulty with hearing any flattery at all.

Source: Phyllis Davis, "8 Ways to Charm Your Employees," www.entrepreneur.com/article/0,4621,301297,00.html.

Section 6

SCORE's Five Tips on What Employees Want from You as a Leader

1. Employees want to trust you and you to trust them. Begin by being trustworthy and extending trust.

2. Employees want good two-way communication. Begin by being a good listener.

3. Employees want to be challenged. Set forth your vision and goals clearly and then let your workers exercise their creativity and authority in meeting your goals.

4. Employees want accountability. Not only should you hold them accountable for their own performance but you should measure your own performance as well.

5. Employees want recognition. Offer praise and express appreciation at every opportunity.

Source: SCORE, www.score.org/business_tips.htm.

Key Steps for Successful Delegation

One of the hardest tasks for entrepreneurs is delegation. But if you want to grow your business, use these tips:

1. **Change your attitude.** This means giving up your belief that only you can do it the right way. In other words, you need to consciously decide to give up some control.

2. **Identify tasks.** Break each job you plan to delegate into individual steps so you can explain them easily.

3. **Set limits.** Share your expectations. Explain the deadline and the quality of work that's required.

4. **Let go.** Once you explain what you want, let your workers decide how they'll tackle the task. Remember: different is not necessarily worse.

5. **Make it a habit.** Once you're comfortable delegating small jobs, try assigning larger ones. Most employees respond well to tackling greater responsibilities.

Source: Rieva Lesonsky, *365 Tips to Boost Your Entrepreneurial IQ.*

Must-Have Skills for Leading a Sales Team

1. **Clarity:** Clearly articulating expectations to your sales team is essential. Frank Bell, 38, is founder and CEO of Intellinet Corp., a provider of IT services in Atlanta. Bell names

vision and clarity as the top traits he needs to effectively lead his sales force of seven. According to Bell, whose company made $10 million in sales in 2003 and projected $12.5 million for 2004, "Clarity is essential for the sales team to understand which clients are strategic and what types of deals we are best positioned to deliver."

2. **Consistency:** All employees, including sales reps, operate best in an environment where they know what's expected of them. Elements of consistency include a simple compensation model, regular sales meetings and performance reviews, and unwavering communication. For Eric Ansley, 34, president of Aaxis Technologies Inc. in Washington, DC, consistency is the premier characteristic he requires to manage the five-person sales team in his $1.8 million business. "Creating a selling environment where good selling practices occur every day is a key to success," says Ansley, who strives to make it a habit to do such things as team cold-calling sessions and sales meetings.

3. **Urgency:** Grant Mazmanian is president of Pinnacle Group International, a company in Media, Pennsylvania, that provides behavioral assessments for small-company sales teams. Mazmanian likens the urgent sales manager to Merlin, the magician of Arthurian lore who could foresee the future because he lived his life in reverse. Urgent sales managers are already at "Z," working their way back to "A," and they prioritize all that has to be accomplished to meet objectives, such as quarterly sales goals. A manager with the urgency trait is always five blocks ahead of his or her sales reps, waiting for them to catch up.

4. **Empathy:** This may well be the trickiest trait to master. Empathy for your fellow human can make for stronger relationships with reps—as long as it's tempered with attention to bottom-line performance requirements. Show your reps that you do care about their lives outside of the office, but expect them to do their jobs.

5. **An eye for good talent:** Be urgent, be empathic—but if you haven't hired the right reps, all your brilliant skills may be for naught. Ansley cites hiring top-notch talent as his biggest challenge. "In our early days," he says, "we were eager to hire people just to get them out in the market." He laments that rush to fill positions and says he should have been more selective at the outset of his business.

Source: Kimberly L. McCall, "Leading the Pack," www.entrepreneur.com/article/0,4621,315190,00.html.

Section 6

Chapter 41

Be Environmentally Conscious

Environmental Protection Agency FAQ

Do I need an environmental permit for my business? Permits for business are usually administered at the state or local community level. Contact your State Environmental Agency for assistance with this matter.

How do I register a pesticide? EPA's Office of Pesticide Programs has prepared a Pesticide Registration Kit. You can access this Kit and other pesticide registration information on the web at www.epa.gov/pesticides/regulating/registering.

Where can I find toxic release inventory (TRI) data? Visit EPA's Toxics Release Inventory web page at www.epa.gov/tri/. The EPCRA (Emergency Planning and Community Right-to-Know Act) Hotline answers TRI-related questions. The EPCRA Hotline toll free number is (800) 424-9346. In the DC area, please call (703) 412-9810. Also, the TDD is (800) 553-7672.

How can I report an environmental emergency? Environmental emergencies such as oil and chemical spills should be reported immediately to the National Response Center at (800) 424-8802. For more information on environmental emergencies, visit EPA's Concerned Citizens' Environmental Emergencies page.

How can I submit a comment on proposed environmental regulations? Comments on proposed rules should be submitted to the EPA docket for the regulatory area that oversees the rule. Many dockets accept comments via e-mail. Consult our list of EPA dockets for the address, telephone number, and e-mail address for the docket you may wish to contact.

Where can I get information on loans, grants, financial and paperwork assistance, and start-up advice for starting a new business? You can access this information on the U.S. Small Business Administration Web site at www.sba.gov/regions/states.html.

Is it OK for me to link to the EPA web site from my web site? EPA is happy to have anyone link to our site from personal or organizational web sites, as long as EPA endorsement or approval is not implied. For the same reason, we do not provide links from our site back to yours.

Source: Environmental Protection Agency, www.epa.gov/smallbusiness.

Small Business Environmental Resource Centers

Environmental Resource Center
www.ercweb.com
(919) 469-1585

Environmental Resource Center offers consulting, training, and product-related services. Environmental consulting services are offered in the areas of hazardous waste management, toxic substances, impact assessment, and compliance auditing. Its safety consulting services include audits and the development of plant-specific compliance programs. Its training services include both open-enrollment and on-site courses throughout the country. The ERC also offers reference products designed to help maintain compliance with environmental and safety regulations.

Environmental Business and Legal Reports
enviro.blr.com
(800) 454-0404

The goal of this subscription site is to provide the most comprehensive state and federal environmental compliance information on the web. A basic subscription includes all federal content and the content of one state. Additional states and multi-user licenses can be purchased at discounted prices.

Community Environmental Health Resource Center
www.cehrc.org
(202) 543-1147

CEHRC offers local organizations a spectrum of services related to identifying housing-related environmental health hazards, including access to hazard assessment tools and training in using them, technical assistance, strategy advice, and sub-grants. CEHRC also provides opportunities and mechanisms for groups to cooperatively develop and sharpen local strategies and share information, skills, and experiences in support of each other's work.

U.S. Environmental Protection Agency, Small Business Gateway
epa.gov/smallbusiness
(800) 368-5888

Source: compiled by author.

Small Business Environmental Protection Agency FAQ

1. **Where may I dispose of my household wastes, solvents, paints, and paint cans?**
   Check with your local authorities (town, county, state) for directions on how to dispose correctly of household wastes, solvents, paints, and paint cans.

2. **What am I required to do when the property owners next door, ex-employers, or competitors have discarded objectionable waste on their property and it has led to groundwater and air contamination? What if I have reports of alleged illegal or offensive releases or dumping and local authorities have ignored these situations?**

Check with your local authorities (state, region). States are typically the agencies authorized to operate programs for clean air, groundwater, and solid waste. Regional EPA offices will have information about current Superfund investigations and potential new ones. Contact these regional offices with reports of alleged illegal or offensive releases or dumping in cases where local authorities have not responded.

3. **I have concerns about local dumping and air pollution incidents caused by companies and/or individuals. What should I do?**

First, contact your local authorities (town, county, state). If you are not satisfied, then check with your regional EPA office. For web site/contact information on EPA's regional offices, see www.epa.gov/epahome/whereyoulive.htm.

4. **How do I dispose of ammonia properly?**

Check with your local authorities (town, county, state).

5. **How do I dispose of paint stripper properly?**

Check with your local authorities (town, county, state).

6. **How do I dispose of biodegradable diapers and beverage cans/bottles properly?**

Check with your local authorities (town, county, state). You may also need to check your city's waste management program.

7. **What is the best concrete form release compound/shot for blasting concrete I can use?**

Check with your local building authority to see what they can identify. Check to see if any there are conditions included in the building permit.

8. **What do I need to do to test the air and make sure that I am in compliance with local air regulations?**

Check with your state and Clean Air Act Small Business Assistance Program (SBAP) offices. You can locate a Key Contact Listing for Ombudsman and SBAP offices at www.smallbiz-enviroweb.org/sba/sba.html. There are also links to State Environmental Agencies and Small Business Assistance Programs.

9. **How do I transport hazardous and nonhazardous wastes properly?**

The generator must prepare EPA Form 8700-22, Uniform Waste Manifest. The transporter must also comply with DOT Hazardous Materials Transportation Regulations. The DOT Hazardous Materials Hotline can be reached at (800) 467-4922.

10. **I am starting up a small business (e.g., pharmacy, recycler, chemical compounder, auto body shop, gas station). Where can I find general environmental guidance, requirements, and liability information? What do I need to do for existing properties? What do I need to consider when purchasing an abandoned site for the new business?**

To find out about general environmental guidance/requirements/liability information, first check with your local licensing bureau, and then your state. When considering the purchase of an abandoned site for new business, check with the state. They can provide you with previous use information, such as whether the site had been formerly used as a gasoline station or for similar activities. Make a final check with your EPA region to see if there is any record of contamination for the abandoned site on file.

11. **Are there grants for buying additional equipment for pollution prevention or for meeting EPA rules and regulations?**

There are no grant programs for normal business operations. However, if you are involved with developing a new pollution prevention system, it is possible that you may be able to apply for funding for demonstration of that system. There are a number of possible routes.

One is to apply through the Assistance Application Kit, which can be obtained from the EPA SBO, or directly from EPA's Grant Operations Branch. To obtain the kit directly from EPA's Grant Operations Branch, call or write:

Grant Operations Branch (MC 3903R)
U.S. Environmental Protection Agency
1200 Pennsylvania Ave.
Washington, DC 20460
(202) 564-5305
(202) 564-5359

Another route is through EPA's Small Business Innovation Research Program (SBIR). The EPA Office of Research and Development's National Center for Environmental Research and Quality Assurance announces program solicitations each fall. The solicitation includes a program description, definitions, proposal preparation instruction and requirements, method of selection and evaluation criteria, considerations, submission of proposals, scientific and technical information sources, and research topics. Program Solicitations are posted on the web at es.epa.gov/ncer/sbir (Enviroene).

For larger firms, Project XL may provide certain opportunities. This program, created by President Clinton in 1995 with his Reinventing Environmental Regulation initiative, is designed to provide regulated sources with the flexibility to develop alternative strategies to replace or modify certain regulatory requirements as long as they produce greater environmental benefits. Eight projects have been selected to be in the first group of XL pilots. EPA is interested in selecting 50 projects to be part of the XL pilot. Information on EPA's Project XL is posted on the web at es.epa.gov/partners/xl/xl.html (Enviroene).

Finally, EPA provides grants through state agencies for funding of small community projects, such as wastewater treatment programs and other public service programs.

12. **Will EPA support the development of my new process that affords improved environmental control (e.g., soil decontamination, lower air emissions)?**

See information about the Assistance Application Kit from EPA's Grant Operations Branch, above in Question 11.

13. **Are there tax credits for expenses incurred in meeting EPA requirements?**

There is currently no EPA program for such tax credits. Check with the IRS for further information.

14. **Where can I get information on loans, grants, financial and paperwork assistance, and start-up advice for starting a new business?**
EPA SBO can provide you with a listing of SBA district offices. You can also access this information on the U.S. Small Business Administration web site at www.sba.gov/regions/states.html.

15. **Can I receive funding for completed or planned cleanups, conceived research projects, or starting an environmentally oriented business?**
If the property becomes a Superfund site, the federal government may be able to go back to the original owners for cleanup funding. See information about funding opportunities under EPA's SBIR program in Question 11. Check with your state for other programs. Also, please note that when purchasing property, you should ensure that as part of the purchase agreement, the previous owner indicates that the property is free of impediments from contaminants and pollution.

Section 6

16. **Where can I get a copy of the *Small Quantity Waste Generator Handbook*?**
You can obtain a copy of the *Small Quantity Waste Generator Handbook* directly from EPA SBO, including an Addendum with updates and specific state contacts for waste programs.

17. **Can someone help me fill out and submit various EPA forms and documents (e.g., Form 8700-12—Notification of Regulated Waste Activity, Material Safety Data Sheets)?**
A copy of Form 8700-12 and Instructions are found in the EPA document, *Understanding the Hazardous Waste Rules—A Handbook for Small Businesses*. EPA SBO can provide this document.

A Material Safety Data Sheet is prepared by the manufacturer of the product and is provided to the buyer. The Occupational Safety and Health Administration (OSHA) is the responsible federal agency.

18. **Where can I find the publication that I need or information about an organization that can help me?**
EPA SBO can help you find the publication you need or information about organizations. Also, see Question 19.

19. **How can I get a copy of an EPA or other publication that I am interested in?**
First, look at EPA SBO's list of publications, which can be obtained by calling EPA SBO, or can be accessed from EPA SBO's home page at www.epa.gov/sbo/pubs.htm. Second, the National Center for Environmental Publications and Information (NCEPI), a central repository for all EPA documents in paper and/or electronic format available for free, can be accessed at www.epa.gov/ncepihom/ or call (800) 490-9198. Other sources of EPA technical and public information can be found at www.epa.gov/epahome/publications.htm.

Finally, you can search a database for federal, state, and other publications and fact sheets on the Small Business Environmental Home Page. The database can be accessed at www.smallbiz-enviroweb.org/pub_video/pubs_videos.html.

20. **How can I be added to the EPA SBO mailing list?**
Simply call EPA SBO or send your name, address, and phone number to EPA SBO by letter, fax, or e-mail.

21. **Where can I find telephone numbers for other hotlines, EPA employees, and other government agencies (headquarters, regions, states)?**
This type of information can be found in EPA SBO's Update Newsletters, download-able from the EPA SBO home page, www.epa.gov/sbo/newslet.htm. Also, hotline information can be found at www.epa.gov/epahome/hotline.htm. Web site and con-tact information for state environmental agencies, state small business assistance programs, EPA headquarters and regions, and trade associations can be found on the Small Business Environmental home page, www.smallbiz-enviroweb.org.

Source: Environmental Protection Agency, www.epa.gov/sbo/faq.htm.

Section 6

Tips on How to Save Water in Your Business

General:

- Designate a water efficiency coordinator.
- Develop a mission statement and a plan.
- Educate and involve employees in water efficiency efforts.

Equipment:

- Install ultra-low flow toilets or adjust flush valves or install dams on existing toilets.
- Install faucet aerators and high-efficiency showerheads.
- Use water-conserving icemakers.
- As appliances and equipment wear out, replace them with water-saving models.
- Eliminate "once-through" cooling of equipment with municipal water by recycling water flow to cooling tower or replacing with air-cooled equipment.

Practices:

- Detect and repair all leaks.
- Minimize the water used in cooling equipment in accordance with manufacturers' recommendations. Shut off cooling units when not needed.

Kitchens and Laundries:

- Turn off dishwashers when not in use. Wash full loads only.

- Scrape rather than rinse dishes before washing.
- Use water from steam tables to wash down cooking areas.
- Do not use running water to melt ice or frozen foods.
- Handle waste materials in a dry state whenever possible.
- Wash only full loads of laundry or select the appropriate washing cycle provided on the washing machine. Use a rinse water recycle system. Consider purchasing high-efficiency equipment.

Outside:

- Wash vehicles less often; use a commercial car wash that recycles water.
- If you have a swimming pool, consider a new water-saving pool filter.
- Lower pool water level to reduce amount of water splashed out.
- Use pool filter backwash for landscape irrigation.
- Use a pool cover to reduce evaporation when pool is not being used.
- Sweep or blow paved areas to clean, rather than hosing off.

Source: Environmental Protection Agency, www.epa.gov/OW-OWM.html/water-efficiency/comtips.htm.

Section 6

Chapter 42

Interior Design

Tips for Selecting Colors for Your Store and Office

At some point, almost all entrepreneurs can use a lift—and one of the best ways to get it is by painting your office walls. Appropriate colors can make your work environment more comfortable and productive. Inappropriate colors can be distracting and increase anxiety.

So how do you choose the right color? Well, first remember that no color conveys the same feelings to everyone. But there are some common perceptions:

- Reds, oranges, and yellows are earthy, friendly, and approachable.
- Dark blue is refined, authoritative, and classic.
- Blue-greens are more relaxing than yellow-greens.
- Bright colors are energetic and enthusiastic, while muted shades are more conservative, casual, and demure.
- Light colors are considered friendly, casual, and feminine. Dark hues are dramatic, authoritative, and masculine.

Source: Rieva Lesonsky, *365 Tips to Boost Your Entrepreneurial IQ.*

Tips on How to Maximize Elbow Room in Your Office

Susan Sherman, an interior design professional in Clayton, North Carolina, suggests:

- Design your workspace with you in the center. You should be able to perform multiple tasks within reasonable reach.
- If you purchase furniture, be sure it offers flexible spaces and cubbyholes for various items and equipment.
- Keep a small amount of supplies close at hand. Store the rest out of the way.
- Force yourself to stay organized. Whether you use cardboard boxes or file cabinets, take the time at least once a week to put everything in its place.
- To cut down on excess paper, scan and file documents on your computer. Be sure to make a backup copy on disk. Then get rid of the original paper version.
- Look up. Shelves that reach the ceiling can help compensate for lack of floor space.
- If you need bookshelves, make them only as deep as necessary. Unless you store a lot of three-ring binders or other large books, a depth of eight inches should work. This will leave more floor space.
- Use the tops of filing cabinets to hold peripherals such as printers and scanners. Don't allow piles of papers to collect on these otherwise useful surfaces.
- If you're buying a new computer and are really squeezed for space, consider a lap-

top. They take up far less desk or table space than a full-size PC and have the obvious advantage of being portable. Downside: typing on a laptop keyboard can be tiring; make sure you choose one that's big enough for you.

■ How can you use wall space? Shelves, hanging files, pencil sharpeners, telephones, fans, and lights can all be affixed to the wall instead of taking up precious floor or esk space.

Source: Lynn H. Colwell, "Elbow Room," www.entrepreneur.com/article/0,4621,265944,00.html.

Tips on Going from Drab to Fab

Thom Filicia, designer and spokesperson for Xerox and Entrepreneur's Makeover Contest, has plenty of ideas for entrepreneurs looking to revitalize drab and uninspiring corporate environments:

■ Encourage natural light. If that's not possible, use dimmers, desk lamps, and other lighting solutions for "creating an atmosphere where people don't mind working extra hours."

■ Incorporate elements from the home. An open and comfortable kitchen, for instance, "becomes the same thing it is in the house—a place where people gather," says Filicia. "They have coffee, they talk, you have informal meetings." And think about installing wall-to-wall carpeting: "It's acoustical, it's comfortable, it's inviting," he continues. When employees have to work late, "they kick their shoes off. The overhead lights go off, and the lamps come on."

■ Hang mirrors. "It's a little bit more exciting, it brings in light, it reflects the views," says Filicia. "If you have two windows, now you have four windows. It changes the whole environment. It makes it feel more energized."

■ Don't be afraid to experiment. "Playing with different ideas and concepts is a wonderful thing," he says. "Just because you designed it today doesn't mean you have to live with this for the rest of your life." That goes for painting the walls, too: "Color is one of the best things to explore with because it's only paint."

■ Think of design as another vehicle for expressing your personality and ideas. "If you have this beautiful environment that people walk into and are really taken by, I think that's a huge [business] advantage," Filicia says. "Someone walks in and goes, 'You know what? This person is very interesting to me.'"

Source: Charlotte Jensen, "Office Space," www.entrepreneur.com/article/0,4621,317529-2,00.html

Office Ergonomics Checklist

If you answer "no" to any of the questions below, you should reconsider how your office space is designed.

1. Does the workspace allow for full range of movement?
2. Are mechanical aids and equipment available?
3. Is the height of the work surface adjustable?
4. Can the work surface be tilted or angled?
5. Is the workstation designed to reduce or eliminate
   - bending or twisting at the wrist?
   - reaching above the shoulder?
   - static muscle loading?
   - full extension of the arms?
   - raised elbows?
6. Are the workers able to vary posture?
7. Are the hands and arms free from sharp edges on work surfaces?
8. Is an armrest provided where needed?
9. Is a footrest provided where needed?
10. Is the floor surface free of obstacles and flat?
11. Are cushioned floor mats provided for employees required to stand for long periods?
12. Are chairs or stools easily adjustable and suited to the task?
13. Are all task elements visible from comfortable positions?
14. Is there a preventive maintenance program for mechanical aids, tools, and other equipment?

Source: National Institute for Occupational Safety and Health, www.cdc.gov/niosh/ eptbtr5c.html.

Section 6

Section 7

Protecting Your Business

Section
7

Chapter 43

Legal Protection

Section 7

Tips for Keeping Your Legal Costs Down

Are your legal costs out of control? Here are some tips to help lower your legal fees:

1. First—and most obvious—choose the right lawyer. You'll want to match his or her skills with your needs. And it helps if the lawyer has other small business clients.

2. Determine the best fee structure for your business. Will the lawyer charge you by the hour, on a contingency, or on a fixed-fee basis?

3. For legal tasks, use paralegals instead of attorneys. This alone can save you thousands of dollars.

4. Don't call your attorney just to chat. Usually those "small tasks" turn into billable hours, which can add up.

5. Finally, don't accept—negotiate. Ask for prompt-payment discounts. Even a seemingly small discount of five percent can, over time, be significant.

Source: Rieva Lesonsky, *365 Tips to Boost Your Entrepreneurial IQ.*

SCORE's Five Tips for Employers to Implement

1. A policy that states that the company is an equal opportunity employer and strongly enforces a nondiscrimination policy.

2. A strong sexual harassment policy detailing what is not accepted at your place of business.

3. A policy about phone and/or e-mail communications.

4. Expectations of employees.

5. Include how your company plans to monitor or take action on all of the stated policies.

Source: SCORE, www.score.org/business_tips.html.

Tips for Developing a Personal Will

Do you have a will? If you're like most entrepreneurs, the answer is no. But not having a will is one of the biggest mistakes small business owners make. No matter your age or the size of your business, you can't afford to put off writing your will.

- It's important to understand the basics of estate planning and taxes.
- Books and software are available to help you draft your will.

- You need to name your beneficiaries
- You need to specify whom you want to run your company.
- Before you finalize the document, make sure you review it with an estate attorney.

Still not convinced you need a will? Think about this: if something were to happen to you, your business could be in for a bumpy transition, and your family could lose everything you've worked so hard to build.

Source: Rieva Lesonsky, *365 Tips to Boost Your Entrepreneurial IQ.*

SCORE's Five Tips on Consumer Credit Basics

1. Know the laws. If you must grant credit directly to consumers, familiarize yourself with both federal and state consumer credit statutes.

2. Tell the truth. The Truth in Lending Act requires you to disclose exact credit terms, such as the monthly finance charge and annual interest rate.

3. Follow correct procedures for handling billing mistakes. If you don't, you may have to give the customer a $50 credit even if your billing was right.

4. Don't discriminate on the basis of race, color, religion, national origin, age, sex, or marital status when granting credit.

5. For detailed information on consumer credit laws, visit www.nolo.com, a web site specializing in legal matters.

Source: SCORE, www.score.org/business_tips.html.

Five Situations When You Need to Hire an Attorney

1. **Written agreements:** Do your lease agreements and purchase contract indicate the specific duties and expectations of each party?

2. **Licensing and ordinances:** Do you need to be licensed or bonded? Is liability insurance required?

3. **Business structure:** Should you incorporate or stay a sole proprietorship?

4. **Employer-employee relations:** Are you familiar with the laws that govern hiring employees? Do you need an employee handbook?

5. **Partnership:** If you don't have a partnership agreement in place, you could lose your business.

Source: Rieva Lesonsky, *365 Tips to Boost Your Entrepreneurial IQ.*

SCORE's Five Tips on Advertising Legally

1. Don't engage in false, misleading, or deceptive advertising. Make sure your claims are accurate.

2. Obtain written permission to use photographs, endorsements, or quoted matter. Remember that some material is protected by copyright.

3. Don't use words and phrases like "free" and "easy credit" unless they're true. Easy credit, for example, means you offer credit to poor risks without charging them more for it.

4. Remember that consumers can sue you for deceptive advertising, and federal, state, and local governments can take action against you.

5. For more information, visit www.nolo.com, a web site from Nolo.com, Inc., a self-help legal publisher in Berkeley, CA.

Source: SCORE, www.score.org/business_tips.html.

Section 7

Tips on Consumer Protection Laws

Advertising Compliance

- Don't promise more than a product will deliver. For example, if your product will remove some but not all types of stains, list only those that it will affect.

- Be sure the visual image you show in your ad truly reflects what you're offering for sale.

- If you're using someone's picture or written endorsement or quoting from someone's copyrighted work, be sure you get his or her permission in writing.

- Don't knock your competitors.

- Have sufficient quantities of advertised items in stock or state, "Quantities are limited."

- Be careful about advertising something as "free."

- If you advertise credit terms, you should provide all details, such as down payment amount, terms of repayment, annual interest rate, and so on.

Product Pricing and Return Policies

- Using vocabulary such as "regular" or "reduced" prices is fine if you can prove that you offered the merchandise at a particular price for a specified period of time before "reducing" it.

- If you offer merchandise for sale at a price that's higher than $25 at a location other than your normal place of business, such as at a flea market or a business expo, you should give customers a written receipt or copy of the sales contract and a notice of their right to cancel the sale within three days.

- Other than the "three-day rule," you aren't required by law to give any refunds on sales, but you may want to do so anyway to promote good customer relations. If you have a refund policy, you should post the written policy conspicuously in your location.

- If you do business by mail order, you need to become familiar with the Federal Trade Commission's mail order rule.

Warranties

- Express warranties are statements or promises about a product or about a promise to correct defects or malfunctions in a product. They can be either oral or in writing.

- Written warranties don't need to be called warranties or be part of a formal written contract to be legally treated as warranties. Any statements in product literature or in advertisements may be considered a warranty.

- Implied warranties don't stem from anything said either orally or in writing or anything done by the seller. They're automatically assumed whenever a product is sold. These implied warranties automatically guarantee that the product is fit for ordinary use and any special uses the seller is aware of.

Source: Carlotta Roberts, "What You Need to Know About Consumer Protection Laws," www.entrepreneur.com/article/0,4621,284044,00.html.

Section 7

SCORE's Five Tips if Military Duty Calls

1. Employees have the right to use their vacation time or personal days during their service; they may also opt for unpaid leave.

2. You are not obligated to pay employees who are absent on account of military duties, unless your company policy says you will.

3. If your company does have a paying policy for military service time, you cannot require employees to use their vacation or paid leave time.

4. You must extend the same benefits to employees who are absent for military service as you do to employees who are on nonmilitary leaves of absence.

5. You may temporarily fill vacancies left by military employees absent for service. However, upon their return, military employees are entitled to the same positions they left.

Source: SCORE, www.score.org/business_tips.html.

SCORE's Five Tips for Avoiding Legal Problems

1. Arm yourself with basic knowledge of business law so that you're alert to your company's obligations and rights.

2. Practice prevention. Have your attorney review contracts and agreements before they're signed.

3. Get your attorney's opinions on documents you have drafted—such as employee policies—before you put them in place. You want to make sure they meet the requirements of the law.

4. Familiarize yourself with trademark and patent laws so that you don't violate them. Learn how to apply for a trademark or copyright should you need to do so.

5. Understand the law as it pertains to your organizational structure. Your legal obligations as a C corporation, for example, will differ from those as a sole proprietor.

Source: SCORE, www.score.org/business_tips.html.

SCORE's Five Tips for Protecting Yourself from Employee Lawsuits

1. Obey the laws regarding employees. Don't discriminate in hiring, for example, or permit sexual harassment.

2. Hire carefully. Look for people with a strong work ethic and avoid hiring those who feel life owes them something.

3. Adopt strong employment policies. Communicate them clearly to employees and enforce them.

4. Keep good records on employee mistakes, even when they're not firing offenses. Document your own actions and the reasons behind your employment decisions.

5. Consider buying employment-practices liability insurance (EPLI).

Source: SCORE, www.score.org/business_tips.html.

SCORE's Five Tips on Resolving Disputes

1. Consider adopting an alternative dispute resolution (ADR) program as a way to resolve employer-employee conflicts. It can be less costly and time-consuming than litigation.

2. Understand that ADR uses such tools as mediation and arbitration and is conducted in private.

3. To find help in setting up an ADR program, look in the Yellow Pages under "Mediation Services." Ask other small business owners or your local chamber of commerce for referrals.

4. Remember that ADR programs work best when you have a clearly written ADR policy that employees see as fair. Start by maintaining an open-door policy that encourages employees to bring grievances to their managers without fear of retribution.

5. Visit www.chorda.com, the web site of Chorda Conflict Management Services. The site includes a *Nation's Business* article, "A Working Alternative for Settling Disputes," which provides a thorough discussion of ADR.

Source: SCORE, www.score.org/business_tips.html.

Section
7

Business Insurance and Licensing

Section 7

SCORE's Five Tips to Be Sure You're Adequately Insured

1. Assess your company's insurance needs. Property-casualty coverage isn't enough. Consider a broad range of coverage, from business interruption and consequent loss of revenue to product liability and wrongful termination.

2. Shop around. Ask several agents to evaluate your insurable risks and listen to their ideas.

3. Don't buy on price alone. Check www.ambest.com or your library for the insurance provider's standing with A.M. Best Co., a company that rates insurers.

4. When you are expanding, ask your agent if you need an endorsement to your policy.

5. Search the internet for more small-business insurance information. A good place to start is www.iiaa.org, the site of the Independent Insurance Agents & Brokers of America.

Source: SCORE, www.score.org/business_tips.html.

Tips on Assessing Your Risk Exposure

Insurance is one of those things that you probably don't think about but should. Many entrepreneurs are underinsured. To adequately assess your risk exposure, ask yourself these questions:

- What would it cost to replace your equipment and supplies and to recover your records in the event of a disaster?
- Do you work with clients' materials on-site that you'd have to replace if something happened to them?
- If you maintain an inventory, what is its dollar value?
- If you weren't able to operate your business for any length of time, what would it cost in lost revenue?
- Do clients visit your office?
- Do you take equipment to other locations, such as to clients' offices, to exhibits, or on the road?
- Does your work leave you vulnerable to professional liability claims?
- Do your customers require you to carry certain levels of insurance?

Source: Rieva Lesonsky, *365 Tips to Boost Your Entrepreneurial IQ.*

Types of Insurance for Your Business

Liability Insurance

- **Liability Insurance**—Customers, employees, repair people, and anyone else who comes into contact with your business can hold you liable for your degree to take proper care.

- **Automotive Liability**—Be certain that all employees with an active driver's license in your state are listed on the policy.

- **Product Liability**—In manufacturing and in certain sectors of retail trade, you have assumed product liability; you are responsible for knowing if a product is defective.

- **Workers' Compensation**—Workers' compensation mandates unlimited medical coverage during the course of employment for job-related injuries incurred on company property or in pursuit of employee livelihood.

Comprehensive Property Insurance

- **Comprehensive Property Insurance**—Make sure to get a policy written on an all-risk basis rather than on a named-peril basis.

Replacement Cost Property Insurance

- **Replacement Cost Property Insurance**—This will replace your property at current prices, regardless of what you paid for it, and thus protect against inflation.

- **Coinsurance**—The owners of the building can actually share the potential loss with the insurance company if they are willing to share the premium costs. These terms are crucial if you are in a leasing agreement.

Special Coverage

- **Care, Custody, and Control**—This is a must for the service industries, particularly those with customer goods in their control anytime during the business transaction. Should an accident happen, the insurance company would reimburse you and the customer.

- **Consequential Losses**—This clause should be inserted into a standard property or fire insurance property. For an extra premium, you can ensure the extra expenses of obtaining temporary quarters, relocation, and incidental expenses.

Business Interruption

- **Business Interruption**—This reimburses the business owner for future profits lost and fixed charges as a result of damage due to perils specifically accounted for in the policy. Weather damage is the most common.

Section 7

- **Profit Insurance**—This covers future profits and the loss of products already manufactured but destroyed before they could be sold.
- **Credit Insurance**—This is used if your business extends credit to another party, person, partnership, or corporation.
- **General Coverage**—Covers losses incurred during the one-year policy caused from sales made during the year prior to starting date.
- **Forward Coverage**—Covers the insured for losses resulting from accounts that were created by sales made during the policy term.
- **Money and Securities Insurance**—This additional coverage covers the peak cash-holding periods during the business day such as closing, after lunch, or payday.
- **Glass Insurance**—This is a comprehensive policy that insures breakage of plate glass, neon signs, and showcases from any source except fire or nuclear reaction.
- **Electronic Equipment**—This insurance protects against fire, theft, malicious damage, accidental damage, mechanical breakdown, or electrical breakdown.
- **Power Interruption**—This insurance is available on the machinery contract to provide coverage for losses from interruption of electricity, gas, heat, or other energy from public utilities.
- **Rain**
- **Temperature Damage**
- **Transportation**—This indemnifies your materials in transit.
- **Fidelity Bonds**—Protect your company from losses incurred by employee theft.
- **Surety Bonds**—Protect your company against losses insured as a result of the failure of others to perform on schedule.
- **Title Insurance**—You should request it for real estate purchases.
- **Water Damage**—Different from flood insurance, this insurance covers risks from leaking pipes, backed-up toilets, bursting water tanks, and a leaking roof.
- **FAIR Plan Program**—This insurance provides coverage for looting, fire, vandalism, building, glass, and inventory if damage occurs during a riot or group demonstration.

Source: Andi Axman, *Entrepreneur Magazine's Ultimate Small Business Advisor.*

Steps Before Talking with an Insurance Representative

- Make a list of risks that your business faces.
- Evaluate your liabilities from your customers' point of view.
- Chart the customers' path as they come into contact with your shop—across the sidewalk, through the door, under the ceiling fan, up to your counter, etc.

Section 7

- Decide the most economical way to handle the possible losses, considering the following avenues:

  - Assumption means assuming the risk and the accompanying financial burdens.

  - Avoidance means removing the cause of risk. An organized safety program that implements suggestions from employees and insurance safety representatives can also help to eliminate potentially dangerous situations.

  - Loss reduction is the transfer of the risk to another party. Know what your potential liabilities are.

  - Self-insurance entails setting aside a specified amount of money into a reserve fund each year to cover any losses incurred.

Source: Andi Axman, *Entrepreneur Magazine's Ultimate Small Business Advisor.*

Tips for Picking an Insurance Agent

Hunting for an insurance agent? Don't go into the search unarmed. Before you sign on the dotted line, ask your agent for some answers.

- How long as the agency been around? If it's new, find out if the principals have extensive industry experience.

- Is the agent familiar with your industry? What are his or her background, experience, and education?

- Does the agent actually listen to you and address your concerns? Or do you feel like you're getting a cookie-cutter presentation?

- Will you be "just a client"? Clients get sold insurance. Instead look for an agent who wants to be your partner—one who helps you analyze your risks.

- Check references. Sure, that's obvious, but busy entrepreneurs frequently don't bother.

- How comfortable do you feel? Remember: you are entrusting this person with the future of your business.

Source: Rieva Lesonsky, *365 Tips to Boost Your Entrepreneurial IQ.*

Tips for Keeping Business Insurance Costs Low

Every entrepreneur needs insurance, but not everyone can afford it. Here's how to keep a lid on insurance costs:

1. When shopping for insurance, make sure you contact your trade association. Many offer discounted group rates to their members.

2. Don't automatically renew your policies. Periodically check your needs, and always get several bids before renewing.

3. Many entrepreneurs scrimp on disaster coverage. Don't! Make sure you're protected or you could lose your business.

4. Consider raising your deductibles. Usually, this lowers premiums.

5. Check your workers' comp insurance classification rate to make sure you're getting the proper discount.

6. Sponsor a wellness program for your workers. Healthy employees can cut your health-claim costs significantly.

Source: Rieva Lesonsky, *365 Tips to Boost Your Entrepreneurial IQ.*

Tips for Filing an Insurance Claim

Though we all hope it never happens, someday you may have to file an insurance claim. Here are some tips that may ease the process:

1. Immediately report any incidents—accidents, theft, fire, or other damage—to your agent or insurance carrier.

2. Make sure you protect your property from further damage; temporary repairs are covered in most policies.

3. If possible, save any damaged property. Your claims adjuster may want to see it.

4. Most policies ask for at least two repair estimates; find out what kind of estimate documentation your carrier requires.

5. The insurance company needs proof of loss, so document everything, including financial data before and after the incident.

6. Most important? Keep your agent informed. You never know when you'll need his or her help.

Source: Rieva Lesonsky, *365 Tips to Boost Your Entrepreneurial IQ.*

Tips for Good Insurance Habits

Are your business insurance costs out of control? You can keep your expenses down if you practice these good insurance habits.

■ Review your insurance needs and coverage annually. If your business is growing rapidly, you may want to check it more frequently.

- Ask your insurance agent to help you reduce your risks. Have him or her visit your premises and point out where you can make improvements.

- Check out new insurance products. Make sure your agent keeps you up-to-date on any new types of coverage you may need.

- No business is too new—or too small—for insurance. And if you're home-based and think your homeowner's insurance is adequate, you're in for a big unpleasant surprise.

- You'd better shop around. Sure, you're busy, but a few hours of research now can save you thousands of dollars on premiums or claims later.

Source: Rieva Lesonsky, *365 Tips to Boost Your Entrepreneurial IQ.*

How Signage Is Regulated

Signage is regulated through the following two categories of codes.

Building and Electrical Codes

The construction, installation, and operation of any permanent business sign will need to conform to all applicable building and electrical codes. Because compliance with these codes requires specialized technical expertise, a business owner should specify that conformity to these codes is the responsibility of the sign company that builds and installs a business sign. This responsibility would extend to the sign company's subcontractors.

Local Zoning or Sign Codes

Nearly every local government regulates the display of business signs. Such regulations are found either in the local zoning code or a separate "sign code." Most codes will contain the following provisions regarding business signs:

A. Regulation of the size, number, and location.

B. Permit application requirements and review procedures.

C. Provision for a "variance."

D. Treatment of "nonconforming" signs.

A. Regulation of the Size, Number, and Location of Signs

A local zoning or sign code will normally regulate the location, number, size, etc. of business signs.

B. Permit Applications and Approvals

The permit process usually begins when the sign company or business owner obtains an application from a zoning or building official in the local government office. While applications normally require the applicant to submit information related to the construction and installation of the sign, and the site where it will be installed, requirements will vary from community to community.

The application must be filled out completely and accurately. In most communities, the application fee must be paid in full before the application will be reviewed.

There are two basic procedures for local government review of a sign permit application: administrative approval, which stresses quantitative criteria, and design review, which goes beyond quantitative criteria to consider qualitative guidelines.

C. Provision for a Variance

A variance is a "flexibility" device that allows a local government to provide a property owner with relief from the normal application of a restriction in the zoning code, such as minimum lot or building size or setback requirements. And it also applies to relief from a sign code provision. In effect, a variance works like a special code section or exception, specifically enacted by the local government on behalf of a specific property or property interest.

D. Treatment of Nonconforming Signs and Amortization Provisions

Local governments commonly revise sections of zoning ordinances and sign codes from time to time. Less frequently, a local government will enact a comprehensive revision that replaces an existing zoning or sign code in its entirety. In either case, there will normally be a number of building lots, structures, or uses (including signs) that were in compliance with or conformed to the old code, but are out of conformance or compliance under the new code. A sign in this category becomes a "legal non-conforming" sign.

Source: Small Business Administration, www.sba.gov/starting/signage/regulated.html.

List of Typical Licenses

Requirements vary from state to state, from city to city, and for different types of businesses, but here's a checklist of the most common types of legal regulations and requirements that new businesses must take into consideration:

1. **Federal Employer Identification Number:** If you plan on hiring employees, you need to let the IRS know by filing Form SS-4 (available from your local IRS office). You may also need to register with your state's Department of Labor.

2. **Federal licenses and permits:** Most small businesses won't need any federal licenses or permits, but there are some exceptions: interstate trucking companies, businesses that will be offering investment advice, and businesses involved with meat preparation.

3. **Seller's permit:** If you'll be purchasing wholesale merchandise for resale, your state will probably require you to register for a seller's permit or sales tax permit. Check with your state's Equalization Board, Sales Tax Commission, or Franchise Tax Board.

4. **State licenses and permits:** Call your state's Department of Commerce to see if your

type of business will need a state license. Among those that probably will are building contractors, auto mechanics, hairdressers, and private investigators. Restaurants that serve alcohol will also require a state liquor license.

5. **Local regulations:** Again, local licensing requirements vary. Phone your city or county clerk's office for information about exactly what you'll need. If you'll be preparing food, you'll also need to call the governing health department. And, if you'll be doing any remodeling to a commercial space, check building codes to find out if you'll need to get a building permit.

6. **Business name:** If you'll be doing business under a name other than your own, you'll need to file a fictitious name certificate or a "Doing Business As" (DBA). Usually, this is done at the county level. Some states may also require you to publish a notice of the business name in your local newspaper.

7. **Zoning laws:** Don't sign a lease without first checking that the space is properly zoned for the use you have in mind. Some cities require all new businesses to get a zoning compliance permit before they begin operating. If you work from your home, verify local zoning ordinances covering homebased businesses. Don't assume that just because your neighbor is working from home, it's fine for you to do so, too. If you live in a condominium or planned community, make sure homebased businesses fall within the community's bylaws.

If you're not sure which agency in your city or state to contact for specific questions about what your business will require, start with unofficial sources of information. The Small Business Administration (SBA), your local chamber of commerce, trade associations, and even other businesspeople should be able to point you in the right direction. Even better is to consult an attorney who has worked with your type of business.

Source: Carolyn Z. Lawrence, "License & Registration, Please," www.entrepreneur.com/article/0,4621,226665,00.html.

Chapter 45

Fraud Protection

Section
7

Tips for Protecting Against Check Fraud

More than one million bad checks enter the banking system every day. Protect your business by following these tips:

1. Store your checks in a secure area.

2. Track check numbers so you'll notice missing checks.

3. Evaluate your check-issuing process, and conduct an audit to detect any risk areas.

4. Everyone hates to do it, but you must reconcile your bank statements as soon as possible.

5. Add several security features to your checks. Your checks should indicate that they are protected, and you should inform your bank of the security measures that you've taken. If the bank pays a check that doesn't include your security features, you are not responsible for the loss.

Source: Rieva Lesonsky, *365 Tips to Boost Your Entrepreneurial IQ.*

Tips for Protecting Against Phone Fraud

Many entrepreneurs think they're too small to worry about fighting phone fraud. If this sounds like you, watch out—because you're wrong and, if you're not careful, it will cost you. Here's how it works:

■ Using default passwords programmed by the manufacturer, phone hackers can easily break into unused voice-mail boxes and rack up thousands of dollar in toll charges. Make sure all phone extensions, whether in use or not, are password-protected.

■ Be especially careful when using long-distance calling cards. Thieves known as "shoulder surfers" observe callers as they punch in their account numbers in public or other unsecured areas.

■ The best way to protect your business from phone fraud is to analyze your bills as soon as they arrive. Look for unusual calling patterns, excessive calls to certain areas, and be particularly alert to calls to the 809 area code in the Caribbean.

Source: Rieva Lesonsky, *365 Tips to Boost Your Entrepreneurial IQ.*

Tips on Protecting Against Gift Certificate Fraud

Do you offer gift certificates to your customers? Many entrepreneurs don't because the potential of fraud scares them. With the right precautions, anyone can take advantage of this great sales tool.

- Don't buy generic gift certificates from stationery or office supply stores. These are too easily duplicated. Invest in custom-designed certificates.

- Avoid cash refunds. State on the certificate that if more than $5 worth of change is due, it will be issued as another certificate.

- Keep a log. Record the certificate number, date of sale, and dollar amount. Make sure you note when the certificate is redeemed.

- Use security features like an embossed logo or watermark to prevent photocopying.

Does this sound like a lot of trouble? It's really not, and certificates are a great way for you to expand your client base.

Source: Rieva Lesonsky, *365 Tips to Boost Your Entrepreneurial IQ.*

Section 7

Tips from the Securities and Exchange Commission (SEC)

Many busy entrepreneurs try to augment their business's earnings by investing online. But be careful: web scams abound. The Securities and Exchange Commission (SEC) offers the following warning tips:

- Investigate before investing. Don't trust what you read. Consult a trusted financial advisor, broker, or attorney.

- Check the company out with your state securities regulator and the SEC. Are there complaints?

- Don't assume the offering is what it's claimed to be or the backers are who they say they are.

- Ask the online promoter where the firm is incorporated. Verify that information with that state's secretary of state. Is a current annual report on file?

- Get written financial information, such as a prospectus, annual report, or offering circular, and compare it with the online information.

- Be wary of get-rich-quick promises or offers to share "insider" information. Don't trust words like "guarantee," "high return," and "limited offer."

Source: Rieva Lesonsky, *365 Tips to Boost Your Entrepreneurial IQ.*

Top Five Most Common Business Scams

Scam artists are getting more and more adept at exploiting the weaknesses of small businesses. While some of these business scams are golden oldies, they're still putting money into scammers' pockets—and taking it out of the pockets of many small business owners. The best defense against scams is awareness and vigilance. Here are five of the most common small business scams and how to avoid them.

1. **Advance Fee Loan Scams.**
   Whether it's offered in a newspaper ad, on the internet, or by e-mail, this scam offers money at reasonable rates—if you send them money. They may say they need the money for insurance purposes or to get the money across the border. Whatever the reason, you'll never see that money again—or the money they were supposedly going to loan your business.

   How to Avoid This Scam: Be aware that it is illegal in both Canada and the U.S. to ask for money upfront for a loan. If you're asked to pay anything before you've received an agreed-on loan, walk away.

   Related Scam: Bogus Equipment Leasing Deals—Your company gets a letter saying that you're pre-approved for leasing. All you have to do is send in your first (or your first and last months') payment. The scam is that you never receive the equipment you were expecting to lease.

2. **Fraudulent Billing Scams.**
   Your business receives an invoice for goods or services that you haven't ordered. The hope of the scammers sending these out is that your business will just pay up. Easy money for them. Easy loss for you.

   How to Avoid This Scam: Examine your invoices carefully. Educate your staff about phony invoices. Set up your payables system so that at least two people must authorize any payments.

   Related Scam: The Surprise Check—Your business receives a check for a small amount. The catch is that the check is actually a "promotional incentive." If you cash it, the company will claim that you've agreed to whatever terms are printed on the back of the check, and start the billing process immediately.

3. **Business Identity Theft.**
   Identity theft itself is the fastest-growing fraud in North America, according to the Better Business Bureau, and business identity theft is growing apace. Just as someone can steal your personal identity, your business's identity can be stolen. Once it's stolen, the thieves can use your business name and financial information to open a bank account and run up expenses.

   How to Avoid This Scam: Take steps to protect your business data. Shred all your discarded paper, including anything that has your business name on it. Be careful when responding to e-mail asking you to do such things as verify your account. Be wary about information you give out over the phone.

Related Scam: Phishing—internet "come-ons" that trick consumers and small businesses into providing bank or other financial information.

4. Work-at-Home Scams.

Preying on people who want to have homebased businesses, these scams offer the opportunity to "make big bucks" working at home. Sometimes the ads say all you have to do is own a computer. Other times, the work-at-home scam involves stuffing envelopes or assembly work. The scam is simple; you pay for the information or the materials you supposedly need. Rather than being the key to making money, what you get is useless.

How to Avoid This Scam: Don't bite. These are not profitable opportunities; the only ones who make money from them are the scammers. If it seems too good to be true, it is. You never have to send money to get information about legitimate business opportunities.

5. Credit Card Scams.

Fraudulent use of credit cards is also on the rise. In the standard credit card scam, someone will call and place an order, offering to pay with fraudulently obtained credit card information. The business fills the order, but later is informed that the credit card was stolen and the amount of the transaction will be charged back to the business's account.

How to Avoid This Scam: Always use due diligence to ensure that orders are legitimate. Be particularly leery of overseas callers, new callers placing large orders, and/or callers requesting rush shipping. If you are suspicious, ask the customer for the name of the credit card's issuing bank and its toll-free customer service number, which is printed on the back of all credit cards. Tell the customer you will check with the bank and call him or her back.

Sick Scam Twist: Overseas credit card thieves are using the TTY phone service for the deaf and posing as hearing-impaired callers. These scammers use the TTY relay operator to place an order for multiple high-end items.

Hopefully the information in this article will help your business avoid these particular scams. If your business is the victim of a scam, do take the time to report it to your local police and your local Better Business Bureau. Reporting scams is the first step to alerting others and putting the scammers out of business.

Source: Susan Ward, "The 5 Most Common Business Scams and How to Avoid Them," sbinfocanada.about.com/od/scams/a/commonscams.htm.

Section 7

Ethical Business Practices

Basic Traits of a Good Leader

- **Emotional stability.** Good leaders must be able to tolerate frustration and stress. Overall, they must be well adjusted and have the psychological maturity to deal with anything they are required to face.

- **Dominance.** Leaders are often times competitive and decisive and usually enjoy overcoming obstacles. Overall, they are assertive in their thinking style as well as their attitude in dealing with others.

- **Enthusiasm.** Leaders are usually seen as active, expressive, and energetic. They are often very optimistic and open to change. Overall, they are generally quick and alert and tend to be uninhibited.

- **Conscientiousness.** Leaders are often dominated by a sense of duty and tend to be very exacting in character. They usually have a very high standard of excellence and an inward desire to do one's best. They also have a need for order and tend to be very self-disciplined.

- **Social boldness.** Leaders tend to be spontaneous risk-takers. They are usually socially aggressive and generally thick-skinned. Overall, they are responsive to others and tend to be high in emotional stamina.

- **Tough-mindedness.** Good leaders are practical, logical, and to-the-point. They tend to be low in sentimental attachments and comfortable with criticism. They are usually insensitive to hardship and overall are very poised.

- **Self-assurance.** Self-confidence and resiliency are common traits among leaders. They tend to be free of guilt feelings and have little or no need for approval. They are generally secure and are usually unaffected by prior mistakes or failures.

- **Compulsiveness.** Leaders are controlled and very precise in their social interactions. Overall, they are very protective of their integrity and reputation and consequently tend to be socially aware and careful, abundant in foresight, and very careful when making decisions or determining specific actions.

Beyond these basic traits, leaders of today must also possess traits that will help them motivate others and lead them in new directions. Leaders of the future must be able to envision the future and convince others that their vision is worth following. To do this, they must have the following personality traits:

- **High energy.** Long hours and some travel are usually a prerequisite for leadership positions, especially as your company grows. Remaining alert and staying focused are two of the greatest challenges you will have to face as a leader.

- **Intuitiveness.** Rapid changes in the world today and information overload result in an inability to "know" everything. In other words, reasoning and logic will not get you through all situations. In fact, more and more leaders are learning to the value of using their intuition and trusting their "gut" when making decisions.

Section 7

- **Maturity.** To be a good leader, personal power and recognition must be secondary to the development of your employees. In other words, maturity is based on recognizing that more can be accomplished by empowering others than by ruling others.

- **Team orientation.** Business leaders today put a strong emphasis on teamwork. Instead of promoting an adult/child relationship with their employees, leaders create an adult/adult relationship that fosters team cohesiveness.

- **Empathy.** Being able to "put yourself in the other person's shoes" is a key trait of leaders today. Without empathy, you can't build trust. And without trust, you will never be able to get the best effort from your employees.

- **Charisma.** People usually perceive leaders as larger than life. Charisma plays a large part in this perception. Leaders who have charisma are able to arouse strong emotions in their employees by defining a vision that unites and captivates them. Using this vision, leaders motivate employees to reach toward a future goal by tying the goal to substantial personal rewards and values.

Source: "Leadership Traits," Small Business Administration, www.sba.gov/managing/leadership/traits.html.

How to Incorporate Ethics into Your Business

1. **Set priorities.** The first—and perhaps simplest—thing you can do to delineate your company's values is to create a clear mission statement. What's your highest priority? "Whenever we have to make a tough judgment, we refer to our mission statement," says Charlie Wilson, founder of SeaRail International Inc. "Putting things down on paper helps set in stone what your standards are."

2. **Start now to create company policies and procedures that guide you.** When you're just starting out, writing a policy manual may seem premature. In reality, now's the best time to start crafting policies that will guide you as you grow.

   Use procedures that help you with the kinds of dilemmas you face each day. In Iris Salsman's public relations business, Salsman Lundgren Public Relations Inc. in St. Louis, credibility is key. "We're asking the media to portray [clients] as certain kinds of people," Salsman says. "If they aren't that kind of person, [the discrepancy] affects our reputation." Salsman performs careful client interviews and investigates online and with contacts to make sure the story a prospective client tells is in line with the client's reputation. "We're not saying we won't accept a client who's had problems in the past," says Salsman, "but we don't want to be taken by surprise."

3. **Get advice.** Your industry's trade association may have a code of ethics that will help you establish your own company's policies and procedures.

   When faced with an individual dilemma, Wilson consults fellow business owners in the Greater Houston Partnership (similar to a chamber of commerce). "Sometimes you don't know what's best," he says. "That's when it helps to turn to your peers."

4. **Avoid hypocrisy.** Suppose you have no compunction about lying to clients, you cook the books, and—worst of all—you have no interest in changing your evil ways. Go with that. But don't promote yourself to clients as a paragon of virtue. "People are a lot more observant than you realize," says Wilson. "You can't lie about being ethical."

Source: Gayle Sato Stodder, "Do the Right Thing," www.entrepreneur.com/article/0,4621,229018-1,00.html.

Different Types of Ethics Consulting

Here are some general considerations from the Ethics Resource Center. You can go to www.ethics.org for consulting on the areas of ethics listed below.

Ethics Program Assessment
An Ethics Program Assessment (EPA) examines an organization's current ethics program to maximize its effectiveness and expand its reach.

An EPA measures the program against minimum requirements set forth by the Federal Sentencing Guidelines. But perhaps more important than these minimum requirements, the EPA compares the organization with best practices from similarly situated organizations.

Ethics Climate Assessment
Climate Assessments (OEA) are a systemic examination of an organization's ethics effectiveness and are used to help our clients develop a comprehensive ethics program. Generally, OEAs are conducted when an organization is just beginning to develop a new ethics program or is interested in a complete revision or revitalization of an existing one.

We study the organization's environment, resources, history, strategic focus, work processes, formal and informal systems, outputs, and communications. Together, these components provide a complete picture of the organization's ethical climate and direct our conclusions and recommendations.

Infrastructure Development
Many times, organizations have a clear agenda for their ethics program, but they need direction on where or how to begin. We can help an organization develop or improve an existing ethics infrastructure to ensure maximum effectiveness and sustainability.

Our goal is to help craft a living ethics program—one that can be managed by the organization's employees. We will help the organization craft (or update) its:

■ values and credo statements., ■ codes of conduct,

- ethics policies, and
- employee handbooks.

Ethics Communications

At the heart of any such program is a communications strategy. Typically that strategy has several simultaneous components. Some of the most common and effective ethics communications components are discussed below. Stated compliance standards and procedures must be communicated to employees.

- Create effective systems for ensuring that all employees (or members in the case of associations and professions) understand the standards and procedures and their responsibilities under those standards

- Supplement any "acknowledgment form" used to document distribution and acceptance of responsibility with a more detailed briefing/training so employees understand:
  - Why this is important,
  - What is required/expected of them,
  - How to seek guidance,
  - How to report concerns,
  - Safeguards afforded them, and
  - Their personal responsibilities.

Code and Documentation Review

Companies with existing codes find it valuable to seek outside assessment of their codes and comparison with ERC's Organization Ethics Model.

The Organizational Ethics Model consists of 12 basic components that are essential to the continued monitoring, evaluation, and refinement of an ongoing ethics initiative. Most of the components are process-oriented—that is, they relate to defining "how" the ethics initiative is implemented and ensuring that it is consistent with organization's vision and mission.

Source: The Ethics Resource Center, "Communications," www.ethics.org/communications.html.

Eight Rationalizations for Ethical Compromise

1. I have to cut corners to meet my goals.

2. I lack the time/resources to do what is right.

3. My peers expect me to act this way.

4. My superiors want results, not excuses.

5. I don't think it is really wrong or illegal.

6. Others would think that it is a good choice.

7. No one will ever know the difference.

8. I am afraid to do what I know is right.

Source: Michael G. Daigneault, "Ethics & Professionalism: Why Good People Do Bad Things," www.ethics.org/resources/article_detail.cfm?ID=30.

List of Ethics Resource Centers and Associations

CFA Institute: Code of Ethics and Standards of Professional Conduct
www.cfainstitute.org/standards/ethics/code/index.html

This section of the CFA Institute site is designed to provide "guidance to users as to what constitutes fair and ethical business practices." Translations are available for this Code in more than a dozen languages.

Better Business Bureau (BBB): Promoting Fairness and Integrity in the Marketplace
www.bbb.org

In 1912, the first BBB was founded; today, this system is supported by 250,000 local business members throughout the world. The goal of the Better Business Bureau is to "promote and foster the highest ethical relationship between businesses and the public through voluntary self-regulation, consumer and business education, and service excellence."

Business for Social Responsibility (BSR)
www.bsr.org

BSR, a global nonprofit organization, works to "create a just and sustainable world by working with companies to promote more responsible business practices, innovation and collaboration." It helps members be successful and operate successful businesses while upholding the highest ethical standards of professional behavior. Links to free reports on a variety of issues plus other resources are available at this site.

The Caux Roundtable
www.cauxroundtable.org

The Caux Roundtable is an organization composed of senior business leaders from around the world, including Europe, Japan, and North America. These leaders are individuals who "believe that business has a crucial role in developing and promoting equitable solutions to key global issues." One document provided on this site that serves as a guide to all businesses interested in responsible conduct is "The Principles for Business."

The Center for Ethics, Capital Markets, and Political Economy

www3.iath.virginia.edu/cecmpe/

This Center is a nonprofit organization established in 1994 to be an arena to foster discussion and a resource center for ethics information for "persons who believe that moral concerns should be taken into account in economic and political thinking." Services provided by the Center include sponsoring a working paper series, offering seminars, publishing "Ethics Behind the News," and providing other research materials.

CorpWatch: Holding Companies Accountable
www.corpwatch.org

CorpWatch is an organization that keeps an eye on corporations expanding into global markets and provides resources on these issues. The organization's mission is to "counter corporate-led globalization through education and activism" and "to foster democratic control over corporations by building grassroots globalization—a diverse movement for human rights, labor rights and environmental justice."

Council for Ethics in Economics
www.businessethics.org

This is an association of leaders in business, higher education, religion, and other areas who work together "to strengthen the ethical fabric of business and economic life ... by identifying and responding to emerging issues important to the pursuit of business ethics."

The Defense Industry Initiative (DII) of Business Ethics and Conduct
www.dii.org

DII is a "consortium of U.S. defense industry contractors which subscribes to a set of principles for achieving high standards of business ethics and conduct." Links to ethics training resources plus other resources of interest can be found at this site.

Ethics Officer Association (EOA)
www.eoa.org

This is "a non-consulting, member-driven association exclusively for individuals who are responsible for their company's ethics, compliance, and business conduct programs."

European Business Ethics Network (EBEN)
www.eben-net.org

The objective of EBEN is "to promote business ethics education and training as well as improving practices."

Financial Executives International (FEI): Code of Ethics
www.fei.org/about/ethics.cfm

FEI is considered to be the "professional association of choice for corporate financial executives." This organization strongly encourages all its members to practice the highest level of professional and ethical conduct.

Financial Planning Association (FPA): Code of Ethics

www.fpanet.org/member/about/principles/Ethics.cfm

The Code of Ethics for FPA consists of seven principles intended to guide members in the practice of professional ethics in the field of financial planning. FPA was formed on January 1, 2000 as the result of the merger of the International Association for Financial Planning (IAFP) and the Institute of Certified Financial Planners (ICFP).

Institute for Business, Technology & Ethics (IBTE)
www.ethix.org

IBTE was founded in 1998 to study the connections and relationships among business, ethics, and technology. The mission of this organization is to "promote good business through appropriate technology and sound ethics." Sections of the IBTE web site to note are the Tools for Better Business and the Ethics Forum.

Institute for Global Ethics (IGE)
www.globalethics.org

This organization is "dedicated to promoting ethical action in a global context." The site provides numerous resources and articles.

Institute of Business Ethics (IBE): Code of Ethics
www.ibe.org.uk/codesofconduct.html

The code of ethics section of the web site goes beyond stating the IBE code. It also provides tips for making codes effective, information on content included in a code of ethics policy, and links to various company codes of ethics.

International Business Ethics Institute (IBEI)
www.business-ethics.org

IBEI is a private, nonprofit organization that was founded in response to the growing demand for business ethics programs and resources. This organization focuses on increasing public awareness and dialogue about international business ethics issues and assisting companies in establishing effective ethics programs.

National Association of Insurance and Financial Advisors (NAIFA): Code of Ethics
www.naifa.org/about/ethics.cfm

NAIFA is a national, nonprofit organization that was founded in 1890 as the National Association of Life Underwriters (NALU). It is the oldest and largest organization in the insurance and finance fields. Its Code of Ethics outlines the ethical duty of members to their clients, their companies, and the profession.

The Netcheck Commerce Bureau
www.netcheck.com

Netcheck was established in 1995 to "promote ethical business practices worldwide and to increase consumer and corporate confidence in purchasing products and services on-line on the Internet." It was one of the first alternatives to the Better Business Bureau. This service is designed for consumers as well as online businesses.

The Society for Business Ethics (SBE)
www.societyforbusinessethics.org

SBE is "an international organization of scholars engaged in the academic study of business ethics and others with interest in the field." The Ethics Links section of this site provides access to other associations and resource centers.

The Society of Corporate Compliance and Ethics
www.corporatecompliance.org/index.htm

SCCE is a nonprofit organization "dedicated to improving the quality of corporate governance, compliance and ethics." This site provides information about SCCE membership and events as well as resources, such as newsletters, books, and training kits (some for free).

UN Global Compact
www.unglobalcompact.org

The Global Compact is based on ten principles taken from The Universal Declaration on Human Rights, The International Labour Organization's Declaration on Fundamental Principles and Rights at Work, and The Rio Declaration on Environment and Development. Businesses are encouraged to participate in the Compact in order to become good corporate neighbors in this global environment.

U. S. Office of Government Ethics (OGE)
www.usoge.gov

In 1978, the Office of Government Ethics (OGE) was established as the result of the Ethics in Government Act. An agency within the Executive Branch, it acts to prevent and resolve conflicts-of-interest situations that may occur with government employees. The resources found on the OGE site include ethics documents and publications, computer and web-based training modules, laws and regulations, and international resources

Source: compiled by Sharon Stoerger, "Business Ethics," www.web-miner.com/ busethics.htm#orgs.

Developing a Code of Ethics in Your Business

When you are developing your ethics policy, you must decide what it is you want your company to stand for, put it in writing, and enforce it. According to Kenneth Blanchard and Norman Vincent Peale, authors of *The Power of Ethical Management*, you can base your policy on five fundamental principles:

- **Purpose.** A purpose combines both your vision and the values you would like to see upheld in your business. It comes from the top and outlines specifically what is considered acceptable or unacceptable in terms of conduct in your business.

- **Pride.** Pride builds dignity and self-respect. If employees are proud of where they work and what they are doing, they are much more apt to act in an ethical manner.

- **Patience.** Since you must focus on long-term vs. short-term results, you must develop a certain degree of patience. Without it, you will become too frustrated and will be more tempted to choose unethical alternatives.

- **Persistence.** Persistence means standing by your word. It means being committed. If you are not committed to the ethics you have outlined, then they become worthless. Stand by your word.

- **Perspective.** In a world where there is never enough time to do everything we need or want to do, it is often difficult to maintain perspective. However, stopping and reflecting on where your business is headed, why you are headed that way, and how you are going to get there allows you to make the best decisions, both in the short term and in the long term.

A company policy is a reflection of the values deemed important to the business. As you develop your ethics policy, focus on what you would like the world to be like, not on what others tell you it is.

Source: Small Business Administration, www.sba.gov/managing/leadership/ethics.html.

# Chapter 47

In Case of an Emergency

How to Prepare for an Emergency

Many entrepreneurs believe that preparing for disaster is too expensive or time-consuming. But that's not necessarily true, say crisis-management experts. The most important steps for surviving a crisis cost little or nothing. Being unprepared, however, can be the costliest strategy of all. Here are some tips to keep in mind to get your business prepared.

People First

- Every effective disaster-recovery program begins with a simple step, explains John Laye, an adjunct instructor at the Federal Emergency Management Agency's Emergency Management Institute. Companies should hold seminars for employees on how to prepare themselves and their families for potential disasters, and to set up emergency response teams of four or five employees—at least one team for every floor of the building the company occupies—trained in CPR, first aid, basic firefighting, and evacuation procedures. Much of this information and training is available for free from the American Red Cross and local fire departments, Laye adds.

- Laye recommends running practice drills twice a year—more often if your business has a high turnover rate—to improve your emergency response teams' ability to go it alone if you are caught in a natural disaster. "In an earthquake or tornado," he says, "this practice really pays off because the fire department isn't coming,"

Business Second

- "Gather your managers in some quiet place and say 'OK, you come to work one morning and, for whatever reason, the building is wrapped in yellow caution tape and you can't get in,'" says Laye. "Ask them, 'Who are your key people, and what do they need to keep the business running?'" The next step? Ask your managers to predict what could go wrong and how the company should respond in each case, says Bruce Blythe, CEO of Crisis Management International.

- After the initial meetings, establish a crisis-management team, selecting members with expertise in all areas of the company. Unlike the emergency response teams, which serve to ensure employee safety, the crisis team deals with the aftermath of the event—how to keep the business going and back to normal as quickly as possible.

Communication, Always

- Spread word to employees if something happens. This can be as simple as a prerecorded message on a toll-free number that tells people not to show up that day, or as complex as an automated system that calls members of a facility's emergency crew and asks a series of questions to evaluate their fitness for duty.

For more information, please go to the Institute for Crisis Management, www.crisis-experts.com.

Source: Daniel Tynan, "In Case of Emergency," www.entrepreneur.com/article/0,4621,307161-2,00.html.

List of Emergency Resource Centers

Here is a list of domestic and international emergency management companies and web sites.

Ready.gov
www.ready.gov

Ready.gov is a commonsense framework designed to launch a process of learning about citizen preparedness. One of the primary mandates of the U.S. Department of Homeland Security is to educate the public, on a continuing basis, about how to be prepared in case of a national emergency—including a possible terrorist attack.

Federal Emergency Management Agency (FEMA)
www.fema.gov

FEMA is a formerly independent agency that became part of the new Department of Homeland Security March 1, 2003. It is tasked with responding to, planning for, recovering from, and mitigating against disasters.

DisasterHelp
www.disasterhelp.gov

This web site is an initial deployment that will become part of a larger initiative aimed at greatly enhanced disaster management on an interagency and intergovernmental basis. The major objective of the initial deployment is to demonstrate the basic functions and to field-test the presentation.

American Red Cross
www.redcross.org

The Red Cross offers domestic disaster relief and services in five other areas: community services that help the needy; support and comfort for military members and their families; the collection, processing, and distribution of lifesaving blood and blood products; educational programs that promote health and safety; and international relief and development programs.

Emergency Preparedness Information Exchange (EPIX)
epix.hazard.net

The purpose of EPIX is to facilitate the exchange of ideas and information among Canadian and international public and private sector organizations about the prevention of, preparation for, recovery from, and/or mitigation of risk associated with natural and socio-technological disasters.

U.S. Department of Housing and Urban Development (HUD)
www.hud.gov

HUD can provide critical housing and community development resources to aid disaster recovery. HUD's Disaster Recovery Teams are located in offices throughout the country.

Institute for Business & Home Safety (IBHS)

www.ibhs.org/business_protection

IBHS is a nonprofit association that engages in communication, education, engineering, and research. Its mission is to reduce deaths, injuries, property damage, economic losses, and human suffering caused by natural disasters.

CBS News Disaster Links

www.cbsnews.com/digitaldan/disaster/disasters.shtml

CBS news disaster links contains updated web sites for quick reference. Here is an extensive site with over 700 web sites with disaster and emergency information and resources.

Source: Small Business Administration, www.sba.gov.

Emergency Business Survival Checklist

- **Stock up on emergency supplies and information.** The American Red Cross offers several comprehensive guides on what to do before disaster strikes.

- **Create a list of all your employees and how to reach them.** Distribute copies to emergency team leaders.

- **Set up a remote call-forwarding service with your phone provider.** In the event of a crisis, you can quickly reroute all calls to a new location.

- **Identify places that can be used as temporary relocation facilities.** Make arrangements with hotel chains or conferencing facilities before a crisis so your company and your employees have priority if space becomes scarce.

- **Back up all computer data every night and store it in a secure, off-site location.** Online backup offers several advantages for small businesses, including the ability to access your data from remote locations; @backup (www.backup.com) and Connected TLM (www.connected.com) offer a wide range of data storage services.

- **Make emergency arrangements with a service provider.** If your business relies heavily on computers for its day-to-day operations, arrange with providers such as Agility Recovery Systems (www.agilityrecovery.com) or Sungard Availability Services (www.recovery.sungard.com) to have replacement systems available within a specified number of hours.

- **Document duties and responsibilities for each job.** That way, someone can step in when a key employee is incapacitated.

- **Consider business interruption insurance.** For more information, visit the

Insurance Information Institute's site (www.iii.org).

■ **Think about hiring a crisis-management or business continuity consultant.** The Service Core of Retired Executives has 389 offices in the United States that offer crisis-management counseling to small businesses. You can find the one nearest you at www.score.org.

Source: Daniel Tynan, "Better Safe than Sorry," www.entrepreneur.com/article/0,4621,307161-5,00.html.

SCORE's Five Tips on Preparing for Disaster Recovery

1. Recognize that your business can suffer a natural disaster. Small businesses the world over have been affected by disasters such as hurricanes, tornadoes, floods, earthquakes, tsunamis, volcanic eruptions, and fire.

2. Develop your recovery plan before disaster strikes. Make sure everyone in your company is familiar with the plan and knows what steps to take in emergencies.

3. Have adequate insurance. You'll need coverage not only for property damage and loss (including inventory), but also for business interruption.

4. Draw up a list of telephone numbers for all employees. Assign certain employees to call others if disaster strikes. That way, you can learn who is all right and who needs help, and you can quickly communicate instructions about your business.

5. Don't forget your computer system. Keep backup programs and duplicate records (accounts receivable, client information, and the like) at a different, safe site.

Source: SCORE, www.score.org/business_tips.html.

List of State Emergency Management Phone Numbers

Alabama Emergency Management Agency
www.ema.alabama.gov
(205) 280-2200

Alaska Emergency Management
www.ak-prepared.com
(907) 428-7000

Arizona Division of Emergency Management
www.dem.state.az.us
(602) 244-0504

Arkansas Department of Emergency Management
www.adem.state.ar.us

(501) 730-9750

California Office of Emergency Management
www.oes.ca.gov
(916) 845-8500

Colorado Division of Emergency Management
www.dola.state.co.us
(720) 852-6600

Connecticut Office of Emergency Management
www.ct.gov
(860) 566-3180

DC Emergency Management Agency
dcema.dc.gov
(202) 727-6161

Delaware Emergency Management Agency
www.state.de.us/dema/index.htm
(302) 659-3362

Florida Division of Emergency Management
www.floridadisaster.org
(850) 413-9900

Georgia Emergency Management Agency
www2.state.ga.us/GEMA/
(404) 635-7205

Hawaii Emergency Management Agency
www.scd.state.hi.us
(808) 733-4300

Idaho Bureau of Homeland Security
www.bhs.idaho.gov
(208) 422-3429

Illinois Emergency Management Agency
www.state.il.us/iema/
(217) 785-9890

Indiana Department of Homeland Security
www.in.gov/dhs/
(317) 232-3834

Iowa Homeland Security and Emergency Management
www.iowahomelandsecurity.org
(515) 281-3231

Kansas Division of Emergency Management
www.accesskansas.org/kdem/
(785) 274-1911

Kentucky Division of Emergency Management
kyem.ky.gov
(800) 255-2587

Louisiana Office of Homeland Security and Emergency Preparedness
www.loep.state.la.us
(225) 925-7500

Maine Emergency Management Agency
www.state.me.us/mema/
(207) 626-4503

Maryland Emergency Management Agency
memaportal.mema.state.md.us
(410) 517-3600

Massachusetts Emergency Management Agency
www.mass.gov/mema
(508) 820-2000

Michigan State Police
www.michigan.gov
(517) 332-2521

Minnesota Homeland Security and Emergency Management
www.hsem.state.mn.us
(651) 296-2233

Mississippi Emergency Management Agency
www.msema.org/index.htm
(601) 352-9100

Missouri State Emergency Management Agency
www.sema.state.mo.us/semapage.htm
(573) 526-9101

Montana State Emergency Management Agency
www.state.mt.us
(406) 444-2700

Nebraska Emergency Management Agency
www.nebema.org
(877) 297-2368

Nevada Division of Emergency Management
dem.state.nv.us
(775) 687-4240

New Hampshire Office of Emergency Management
www.nhoem.state.nh.us
(603) 271-223

Section 7

New Jersey Office of Emergency Management
www.state.nj.us/njoem
(609) 882-2000

New Mexico Office of Emergency Management
www.dps.nm.org/emergency
(505) 827-9000

New York State Emergency Management Office
www.nysemo.state.ny.us
(518) 457-2200

North Carolina Division of Emergency Management
www.dem.dcc.state.nc.us
(919) 733-3867

North Dakota Department of Emergency Services
www.nd.gov/des
(701) 328-8100

Ohio Emergency Management Agency
ema.ohio.gov/ema.asp
(614) 889-7150

Oklahoma Department of Emergency Management
www.ok.gov/oem
(405) 713-1475

Oregon Emergency Management
egov.oregon.gov/OOHS/OEM
(503) 378-2911

Pennsylvania Emergency Management Agency
www.pema.state.pa.us
(717) 651-2001

Rhode Island Emergency Management Agency
www.riema.ri.gov
(401) 946-9996

South Carolina Emergency Management Division
www.scemd.org
(803) 737-8500

South Dakota Office of Emergency Management
www.oem.sd.gov
(605) 773-3231

Tennessee Emergency Management Agency
www.tnema.org
(615) 741-9303

Texas Division of Emergency Management
www.txdps.state.tx.us/dem/
(512) 424-2138

Utah Emergency Services and Homeland Security
cem.utah.gov
(801) 538-3400

Vermont Emergency Management
www.dps.state.vt.us/vem/
(802) 244-8721

Virginia Department of Emergency Management
www.vaemergency.com
(804) 897-6510

Washington Emergency Management Division
www.emd.wa.gov
(800) 562-6108

West Virginia Office of Emergency Services
www.state.wv.us/wvoes
(304) 558-5380

Wisconsin Emergency Management
emergencymanagement.wi.gov
(608) 242-3232

Wyoming Office of Homeland Security
wyohomelandsecurity.state.wy.us
(307) 777-4900

Section 7

Small Business Administration Disaster Offices

The Small Business Administration (SBA) helps people recover from disasters and rebuild their lives by providing affordable, timely, and accessible financial assistance to homeowners, renters, and businesses.

The Buffalo Customer Service Center covers the entire United States and its territories (SBA Regions I through X). The Field Operations Center–East comprises SBA Regions I through V; the Field Operations Center–West comprises SBA Regions VI through X. The Processing and Disbursing Center covers the entire United States and its territories. The breakdown of SBA Regions by states can be found at www.sba.gov.

U.S. Small Business Administration (U.S. and its territories–SBA Regions I through X)
Disaster Assistance Customer Service Center
130 South Elmwood Avenue
Buffalo, NY 14202
(800) 659-2955

U.S. Small Business Administration (U.S. and its territories–SBA Regions I through X)
Disaster Assistance Processing and Disbursement Center
14925 Kingsport Road
Ft. Worth, TX 76155-2243
(800) 366-6303

U.S. Small Business Administration
Field Operations Center–East
One Baltimore Place, Suite 300
Atlanta, GA 30308
(800) 359-2227

SBA Regions I (Maine, New Hampshire, Vermont, Massachusetts, Rhode Island, Connecticut), **II** (New York, New Jersey, Virgin Islands, Puerto Rico), **III** (Pennsylvania, Maryland, Delaware, Virginia, West Virginia), **IV** (Kentucky, Tennessee, North Carolina, South Carolina, Georgia, Florida, Alabama, Mississippi), **V** (Ohio, Michigan, Indiana, Illinois, Wisconsin, Minnesota)

U.S. Small Business Administration
Field Operations Center–West
P.O. Box 419004
Sacramento, CA 95841-9004
(800) 488-5323

SBA Regions VI (Arkansas, Louisiana, Oklahoma, Texas, New Mexico), **VII** (Iowa, Missouri, Nebraska, Kansas), *VIII* (North Dakota, South Dakota, Montana, Wyoming, Colorado, Utah), **IX** (Nevada, Arizona, California), **X** (Idaho, Washington, Oregon, Alaska, Hawaii, Guam)

Section 7

Chapter 48

Software and Internet Protection

Section 7

Five Steps for Setting up a Spam Defense

1. Make sure your employees are aware of "phishing" attacks. Phishing is a high-tech scam that uses spam, pop-up messages, or counterfeit web sites to deceive users into disclosing credit card numbers, bank account information, Social Security numbers, passwords, or other sensitive information. The message may pop up while you're online or take the form of an e-mail notification that says you need to "update" or "validate" your individual or company account information.

2. Educate employees on the how-tos of secure e-mail usage. Make sure your employees know they should avoid filling out forms in e-mail messages that ask for personal financial information or passwords. This affects all employees, especially those who book travel reservations, deal with human resources issues, or make purchases for your business. Legitimate companies won't ask for this information via e-mail.

3. Protect your business from being "phished." Authentication on your site removes phishers' profit motives—if they can't abuse stolen passwords and identity information, they'll stop stealing them. Other ways to protect your company are to use digital signatures to sign outbound mail and provide signature verification at the gateway or e-mail client.

4. Let your employees have some control. Look for a spam-filtering solution that lets users sort through their own junk mail, so they can determine exactly what is spam and what is other mail that might accidentally end up in the trash bin (such as e-mail newsletters and marketing messages). Also, have a procedure in place so employees can report spam and you can in turn report it to your ISP or the feds at www.ftc.gov.

5. Choose an e-mail security solution that's right for you. Because small businesses may not have the money to afford dedicated IT resources, they often require a different type of solution to support their security infrastructure. Since you may not be able to afford the upfront investment in technology to help meet these challenges, you should look to solutions that don't require an IT resource, are easy to use, and are specifically designed with small businesses in mind.

Source: Karl Jacob, "5 Steps for Setting up a Small-Business Spam Defense," www.entrepreneur.com/article/0,4621,319335,00.html.

Eight Steps to Minimize Credit Card Fraud for Merchants

Here are some tips to minimize your risk of credit card fraud from Internet ScamBusters™:

1. Begin taking a few extra steps to validate each order. Don't accept orders unless complete information is provided (including full address and phone number). We also now require address verification for all of our credit card orders.

2. Be wary of orders with different "bill to" and "ship to" addresses. We now require anyone who uses a different "ship to" address to send us a fax with his or her signature and credit card number authorizing the transaction.

3. Be especially careful with orders that come from free e-mail services—there is a much higher incidence of fraud from these services (hotmail.com, juno.com, usa.net, etc.). Many businesses won't even accept orders that come through these free e-mail accounts anymore. That's because it's so easy for a scamster to open a free, anonymous e-mail account in another person's name and then send you, the merchant, an order using the fake e-mail account and a fraudulent credit card number.

   Since there are so many free e-mail services, how do you know if the order you receive is from one of these free e-mail services? You can check a list of 700+ of these free e-mail services (www.antifraud.com/redflag.htm).

   You can also find an excellent article published at this same site (www.antifraud.com) that provides a good (although not foolproof) suggestion for verifying e-mail addresses: check every e-mail address by typing "www" in front of the domain name of the e-mail address into your browser.

   For example, if you got an order addressed from audri@scambusters.org and you typed www.scambusters.org, you'd get to the ScamBusters web site, which is a legitimate web site. Or, if you got an order from sallysmith@netcom.com, you'd type in www.netcom.com and you'd be at a legitimate ISP. On the other hand, the article suggests that if you got an order from joesmith@cyberdude.com and typed in www.cyberdude.com, you'd find yourself at a site that offers 150+ free e-mail domains. (We're not saying cyberdudes, juno, hotmail, etc. are not legitimate. Rather, we're suggesting that orders that come from these free e-mail services warrant additional care and attention.)

   What precautions should you take with orders from free e-mail accounts? We recommend sending an e-mail requesting additional information before you process the order. More specifically, ask for a non-free mail address, the name and phone number of the bank that issued the credit card, the exact name on credit card, and the exact billing address. Often, you won't get a reply. If you do, you can easily verify the information (which you should take the time to do).

4. Be especially wary of orders that are larger than your typical order amount and orders with next-day delivery. Crooks don't care what it costs, since they aren't planning on paying for it anyway.

5. Pay extra attention to international orders. Do everything you can to validate the order before you ship your product to another country. We won't ship international orders that have different "bill to" and "ship to" addresses.

6. If you're suspicious, pick up the phone and call the customer to confirm the order. Believe us, it will save you a lot of time and money in the long run.

7. Consider using software or services to fight credit card fraud online. We haven't tried

any of these services. However, we have heard positive reviews from colleagues who have used Cybersource (www.cybersource.com) and ClearCommerce Corporation (www.clearcommerce.com).

8. If you (as a merchant) do have the misfortune of being scammed by a credit card thief, you should contact your merchant processor immediately and inform them of the situation. In our case, our merchant provider was able to give us the name and number of the cardholder's bank and we were then able to contact the cardholder and inform them that their card number had been stolen. (Many people aren't even aware that their account number has been stolen.) You should also want to contact your bank and the authorities as well. (As we mentioned, the authorities will probably take a report, but may not do much else depending on the dollar amount of the fraud.)

Source: Audri Lanford and Jim Lanford, "Eight Sure-Fire Strategies Any Business Owner Can Use to Reduce Credit Card Fraud," www.scambusters.org/Scambusters23.html.

Tips for Setting up a Password-Protected Site

Password-protected, subscription-based web sites are an excellent way to offer high-quality, fee-based content to a paying audience. Here are some tips to get you going:

- Most web server software packages include password-protection mechanisms, so if you're running your own web server, you can get started right away without buying anything else. But, if you're like most of us who use a hosting service, you don't run your own web server.

- If you don't run your own server but you use a hosting company or get web space from your ISP, then this is the next most logical place to look for password functionality. It's possible that your provider may offer you this service at no extra charge or for a low cost. If it does, chances are it's preconfigured and you won't have to do a lot of complicated programming. The web host to which you pay your monthly fee for hosting your web site is the one that runs the web server, and they have the facilities there to add password protection to your site. So check to see if your hosting service offers this functionality—although the free, ad-supported, or low-budget hosting companies probably do not.

- If your provider can't give you this, there are still other options. There are products and services available that let you add this functionality, such as HTML Password Pro and HTMLock (www.atrise.com), which can add password protection to your hosted site.

- For the most secure configuration, deploy your own web server and add a firewall with VPN (virtual private network) capabilities and a strong authentication mechanism. A firewall is a piece of hardware or software that sits between your server and the Internet, protecting your internal network and keeping the bad guys out. A VPN is a piece of technology that makes private tunnels in the public internet, which means that anything going between you and your subscribers is absolutely protected from prying eyes.

■ For most secure implementations, you need stronger authentication than just a password. This is where technology like smart cards and two-factor authentication comes in. In this type of authentication scheme, a user has to have a physical card or token into which they enter a personal identification number (PIN). The card then generates a one-time-only password that is synchronized with your web server. The end user enters this one-time password into a web interface to gain access to your system. The great thing about this model is that even if someone does steal the password, it's useless to the thief because the password becomes invalid after a single use. While this is probably more than you would need for a subscription-based newsletter, it is widely used in more sensitive applications.

Source: Dan Blacharski, "Setting up a Password-Protected Site," www.entrepreneur.com/article/0,4621,304782,00.html.

Essential Computer Backup Strategies

For large businesses, the answer to backing up data can be expensive and complicated. It can involve tapes, off-premises servers, and other complicated technologies. For smaller businesses, here are some options (as of February 2005):

■ Burning CDs and DVDs is reliable and inexpensive; it also requires the most consistent effort of the options to keep up to date.

■ GoDaddy.com's secure offsite storage service ($9.95 for 1GB per year, expandable up to 10GB of storage) lets you synchronize files on your computer with your "Online File Folder." Because you're always working on the latest version, you can access, share, and manage files and folders right from your desktop or from any computer with an internet connection.

■ Google's gmail.com (2.5 GB for free) and Yahoo.com's supersized e-mail account (2GB for $19.99 per year) allow you to stash your important files via e-mail. The downside: you have to consistently e-mail them to yourself, so if you're pressed for time, this one's not your best choice.

■ Tiny USB drives are the ideal solution for transporting files and even some small programs. Two drives (512MB and 1GB) plug into any USB port without installation software, and they're selling at very low prices these days. However, tech experts have expressed concern about the vulnerability of the drives to shocks and other hazards that could render the data useless, and because they're so tiny, they can be easily misplaced.

- Maxtor's popular "OneTouch II" external hard drives (250GB and 300GB each, starting around $250 street) connect via FireWire or USB to your PC or Mac. For PC users, it also creates historical backup versions with full system restore to a point in time, something that's unique to this way of backing up. And if it's lost or stolen, Maxtor DriveLock protects the contents of your drive.

- If you don't have as much stuff, you can use an inexpensive Iomega Zip drive. With some 50 million Zip drives sold, ranging from 100MB to 750MB storage each, their durable disks are able to take a fair amount of abuse. So when that next hurricane comes into town and you're packing up stuff to leave, you could stuff one small Zip disk in your pocket—or 519 regular floppies. Some choice. Today's Zip drives come with free Iomega Sync to automatically back up and synchronize your file revisions.

- Tape drives are primarily aimed at the needs of network administrators and, for the requirements of most small businesses, don't offer the affordability, convenience, and "anywhere access" most of the other choices give you.

Source: Pete Silver, "Essential Computer Backup Strategies," www.entrepreneur.com/article/0,4621,320214,00.html.

Section 7

Five Things You Should Know About Security, Privacy, and Encryption

1. A relatively simple solution is to design security into products from the beginning rather than having to come up with retrofits on top of them to fix problems that may arise. We know we have a problem and now we need to focus on design.

2. Lots of people who look at security problems seem to focus on web servers. But at the same time we have to look at desktop products—products that people use every day—like web browsers and e-mail. A problem in one of them can potentially affect everyone.

3. Security and product quality are of secondary importance to people writing code. For them it's a waste of time. They're more interested in creating great new features in the software. Security is really about getting people to do the right thing, not to be lazy.

4. In the future, much more of our lives is going to be recorded in computers. We're seeing all sorts of ways in which what used to be anonymous transactions suddenly become recorded in order to make our lives work better. The E911 system is just another example of the technology that's being developed out there in order to watch us more. Police are going to start using this as an inexpensive tracking system to watch where we go. There are a lot of possibilities for this technology beyond what's being stated.

5. If we had to pay ten cents per e-mail sent, or even five cents, then the spam problem would disappear because the spammers couldn't afford to do what they do. They're taking advantage of the fact that it's easy and cheap to send. Be very careful and check off all the boxes so you don't get all the extra stuff.

Source: Richard Smith, "10 Things You Should Know About Security, Privacy and Encryption," www.edge.org/3rd_culture/smith/smith_index.html.

Intellectual Property

Section 7

Nine Common Myths and Misunderstandings About Patents

1. **The first thing to do with a new idea is to get a patent.**
   Wrong. Mere ideas are not patentable. Only useful products and processes can be patented, and you have to be able to describe it with such completeness as to enable others to make or practice and use it.

2. **If my product has not been on the market before, I can patent it.**
   Wrong. That's not enough. If it has been described in a prior printed publication anywhere in the world, it is not patentable. Moreover, merely being different is not enough—it has to be an unobvious improvement over what is known to the public.

3. **Having a patent stops others from copying or imitating my product.**
   Wrong. Patents are not self-enforcing. You have to identify and pursue copiers, and a patent infringement lawsuit takes years and costs hundreds of thousands of dollars, win or lose.

4. **Getting a patent is something I can do quickly, at low cost.**
   Wrong. The U.S. Supreme Court has characterized a patent as one of the most difficult documents to write. Getting a patent is a highly specialized undertaking that requires the services of a patent attorney or agent. And, it takes a couple of years and costs thousands of dollars, even if no complications are encountered.

5. **Having a patent is necessary to be able to sell my product.**
   Wrong. Most products on the market are not and never were patented, and in most cases any applicable patents have expired.

6. **Having a patent will ensure the success of my product.**
   Wrong. Fewer than one patented product in a hundred ever makes it to the marketplace.

7. **Having a patent will ensure that I will be able to sell my idea or license it to a big company.**
   Wrong. Big companies have many specialists developing new products, and the likelihood that a private inventor without that expertise might come up with something they haven't thought of is unusual. Besides, your product would have to be a good fit for all three major company divisions—manufacturing, engineering, and sales/marketing—before a big company would have any interest.

8. **I can get a non-disclosure agreement, which will give me adequate protection without a patent.**
   Wrong. Non-disclosure agreements are not all alike, but to be enforceable they must be limited in time and scope. Typically they expire in a year or two, and they cover only specifically disclosed subject matter. Besides, for a manufacturing company, signing such an agreement in advance is like signing a blank check—you simply cannot expect that.

9. **Describing my idea in a registered mail letter to myself will protect me.**
   Wrong. Such documents are useless. They are not even admissible in evidence in the Patent Office or in the courts.

So is there anything I can do, without major expense, for at least a measure of protection?

You can file a provisional application in the U.S. Patent and Trademark Office. No search, no claims, and no special format requirements apply, so you can do it yourself provided that you make a complete enough disclosure to enable others to practice the invention by using only ordinary skill in the field to which the invention pertains. For a private inventor or small business, the only cost is a government fee of $100. For more information, visit www.uspto.gov/web/offices/pac/provapp.htm.

A provisional application is not a patent and can never become a patent. It does not enable you to stop others from imitating or copying. What it does is give you an official priority date in the Patent and Trademark Office for the material that it contains. And, it holds that date for up to one year, enabling you to test your invention, do market research, have a patentability search, see if you can find prospective licensees, and get other information to help you make the cost/benefit decision on whether it's worth making an $8,000 to $10,000 commitment to go after a patent. Unless you file a complete application within that year, the provisional application dies and will never be opened to public access.

Having a provisional application on file enables you to mark your invention "Patent Pending," but only while either the provisional or a follow-on complete application is alive. However "Patent Pending" does not mean that others cannot make or sell copies. It is like a "Keep Off the Grass" sign: it has no teeth.

Source: John Pederson, "10 Common Myths & Misunderstandings about Patents," www.score.org/myths_patents.html.

The Three Types of Patents

There are three types of patents:

- Utility patents may be granted to anyone who invents or discovers any new and useful process, machine, article of manufacture, or composition of matter, or any new and useful improvement thereof.

- Design patents may be granted to anyone who invents a new, original, and ornamental design for an article of manufacture.

- Plant patents may be granted to anyone who invents or discovers and asexually reproduces any distinct and new variety of plant.

Source: U.S. Patent and Trademark Office, www.uspto.gov/smallbusiness/patents/types.html.

SCORE's Five Tips on Researching Your Invention or Idea Before You Patent

1. An idea, without knowledge of how to make it work, is not patentable. You must be able to present an illustrated description of a specific useful product, which achieves the desired objective, in sufficient detail to enable others to make and use it.

2. Even then, not every invention is patentable. The U.S. Patent and Trademark Office Web site at www.uspto.gov sets forth applicable requirements and procedures.

3. A patent takes one and a half years or more to obtain, expires within 20 years, and is not renewable. Total costs are typically $8,000 or more, about 50-50 government and attorney fees.

4. Beware of invention promotion scams. Read the Federal Trade Commission's warnings on such scams at www.ftc.gov.

5. U.S. patents have no effect elsewhere, but a U.S. patent can be used to block importation of infringing products from abroad. Foreign patents are harder and more costly to obtain.

Source: SCORE, www.score.org.

SCORE's Five Tips on Patents

1. If your company has an invention that you think is patentable, take steps at once. You may lose your right to patent it if you offer it for sale or disclose it publicly without patent protection.

2. Make sure your product or invention is not infringing on someone else's patent. Your library can help you conduct a patents search.

3. Be prepared to establish the novelty of your idea. Keep good records of its development—including dates, drawings, etc.—and round up witnesses.

4. Hire a patent attorney or agent. Look in the Yellow Pages under "Patent Attorneys." Get references.

5. Consider patenting your method of doing business. According to *Success* magazine, Amazon.com owns the patent on the one-click shopping-cart strategy and successfully defended it in court against Barnes & Noble.

Source: SCORE, www.score.org.

Questions to Ask Before Hiring a Patent Attorney

Before you run to the patent attorney, you can assess the profit potential of your new ideas by asking yourself the following questions:

- What are the advantages of this idea? Is there a real need for it?
- Do I know exactly what problems my idea will solve?
- Is this an original idea or an adaptation of an existing one?
- What are my anticipated short-term results?
- What are my anticipated long-term gains?
- Are there any faults or limitations to my idea?
- Could this idea create any problems?
- How simple—or complex—will it be to execute this idea?
- Are there variations to this idea? Do I have alternatives?
- Is this idea saleable? Will people want it? Can they afford to pay for it?
- Who are my competitors, and what are their plans?

Source: Rieva Lesonsky, *365 Tips to Boost Your Entrepreneurial IQ.*

Advice for Hiring a Patent Attorney

So many people have great ideas but don't know how to protect them. How do you find a patent attorney you can trust? Tomima Edmark, inventor of the Topsy Tail, shares her advice:

- Get names from other business owners. Or ask your local or state bar association for referrals.
- Once you get the names of some potential attorneys, find out who some of their clients are and how long they've been practicing—look for at least three years of experience.
- Make sure their area of specialization is relevant to your invention and that they file about 12 patent applications a year.
- Finally, ask for the cost range of the last ten applications they filed.
- Most important, if you're not comfortable with a lawyer, keep looking until you are.

Source: Rieva Lesonsky, *365 Tips to Boost Your Entrepreneurial IQ.*

Section 8

Sales

Entertaining

Best Power Lunch Restaurants

Atlanta

1. South City Kitchen
1144 Crescent Avenue NE
Atlanta, GA
Southern favorites get edgy updates at this ever-popular eatery.

2. Cafe Lily
308 W Ponce De Leon Avenue, Suite B
Decatur, GA
Creative Mediterranean specialties shine at this comfortable bistro.

3. Bone's Restaurant
3130 Piedmont Road
Atlanta, GA
The city's standard-bearing steakhouse serves up superior beef to Buckhead's wheeling-and-dealing set.

4. City Grill
50 Hurt Plaza SE
Atlanta, GA
Fine dining, Southern style, draws crowds to a landmark downtown building.

5. Chops
70 West Paces Ferry
Atlanta, GA
This Buckhead mainstay offers great seafood and killer steaks.

Boston

1. Turner Fisheries Restaurant & Bar
10 Huntington Avenue
Boston, MA
The Back Bay's swankiest seafood emporium provides fresh fish and a blow to its diners' expense accounts.

2. Stephanie's on Newbury
190 Newbury Street
Boston, MA
Warm indoor expansion adds extra layer of comfort to Boston's queen of sidewalk dining.

3. Legal Sea Foods
255 State Street
Boston, MA
This waterside location of the world-famous seafood chain keeps tourists happy.

4. The Capital Grille
359 Newbury Street
Boston, MA
A serious, superb steakhouse attracts high rollers and local celebs to the foot of Newbury St.

5. Radius
8 High Street
Boston, MA
One of Boston's true destination restaurants continues to impress with an outstanding take on modern French cuisine.

6. Bravo
465 Huntington Avenue (Museum of Fine Arts)
Boston, MA
Classy museum restaurant boasts exemplary modern American fare, plus an evolving art exhibit.

7. Restaurant L
234 Berkeley Street
Boston, MA
Inventive, Asian-tinged modern cuisine combines with a sleek atmosphere to yield Boston's most stylish culinary experience.

8. Bristol Lounge
200 Boylston Street
Boston, MA
The Four Seasons Hotel's lounge is the destination for an upscale date spot.

9. Houston's
60 State Street
Boston, MA
A rarity among the tourist traps in Quincy Market: uniformly excellent American cuisine.

10. Armani Cafe
214 Newbury Street

Boston, MA
Besides eye candy, this stylish eatery serves surprisingly good Italian food.

Chicago

1. Italian Village
71 W. Monroe Street
Chicago, IL
For more than 75 years, this old-school hangout has been one of Chicago's favorite Italian eateries.

2. The Capital Grille
633 N. St. Clair Street
Chicago, IL
Subdued Streeterville steakhouse draws a heavy-hitting corporate crowd for red meat in sophisticated surroundings.

3. Joe's Seafood, Prime Steak & Stone Crab
60 E. Grand Avenue
Chicago, IL
A Miami legend puts some welcome swank into Chicago's steak-and-seafood scene.

4. Kinzie Chophouse
400 North Wells Street
Chicago, IL
This River North spot draws a Merchandise Mart crowd for salads, sandwiches, and steaks.

5. The Berghoff Restaurant
17 W. Adams Street
Chicago, IL
Hearty German cuisine served in a historic Loop building has made this a Chicago classic.

6. Blackbird
619 W. Randolph Street
Chicago, IL
Hyper-trendy scene and inspired cuisine make this Randolph Street's hottest restaurant.

7. Catch 35 Seafood Restaurant
35 W. Wacker Drive
Chicago, IL
Exciting, Asian-influenced seafood for the expense-account set.

8. Harry Caray's Restaurant
33 W. Kinzie Street
Chicago, IL
Nostalgic Italian restaurant pays homage to the dearly departed Cub announcer.

9. Nine Steak House
440 W. Randolph Street
Chicago, IL
Flashy, fabulous Randolph Street steakhouse impresses with accomplished cuisine and glitzy atmosphere.

10. Frontera Grill & Topolobampo
445 N. Clark Street
Chicago, IL
Two excellent restaurants—one casual and buzzing, the other sophisticated and sedate—with a reputation for Chicago's finest Mexican food.

Cleveland

1. Hyde Park Grille
123 Prospect Avenue
Cleveland, OH
Pay homage to your favorite sports hero by ordering a beefy tribute and savoring it in this art-deco building.

2. Johnny's Downtown
1406 W. 6th Street
Cleveland, OH
The meal and deal choice of the Cleveland power hungry. Think of it as the culinary catwalk for the big dogs.

3. Lockkeepers
8001 Rockside Road
Valley View, OH
Fine modern American food, a vast wine roster in refined, historic Thornburg Station overlooking the Ohio & Erie Canal.

4. Don's Lighthouse
8905 Lake Avenue
Cleveland, OH
Totally devoted to the catch of the day.

Section 8

5. Nighttown
12387 Cedar Road
Cleveland, OH
Put on the red light and enjoy American food, live jazz, and stiff drinks.

6. Century
1515 W. Third Street
Cleveland, OH
Graceful railroad designs and exceptional seafood ensure the elegant experience one expects from Ritz-Carlton.

7. Gilly's Donuts
12409 Mayfield Road
Cleveland, OH
Ranked #5 in Best Comfort Food in 2004.

8. John Q's Steakhouse
55 Public Square
Cleveland, OH
Prime beef and a prime location elevate this spot beyond its common-man name.

Denver

1. The Capital Grille
1450 Larimer Street
Denver, CO
The Rat Pack would have fit right in at this elegant, clubby LoDo steakhouse.

2. Marlowe's
501 16th Street
Denver, CO
A downtown hot spot for steaks, seafood, and swift service.

3. Tamayo
1400 Larimer Street
Denver, CO
Rich color and brilliant flavors from central Mexico make this one of LoDo's top dining spots.

4. The Palm
1201 16th Street
Denver, CO
Upscale steakhouse rewards high-profile patrons by immortalizing their likenesses in colorful caricatures.

5. 240 Union
240 Union Boulevard
Lakewood, CO
Popular West Denver eatery serves up fresh seafood, fantastic pasta, and gourmet pizza.

Houston

1. Spencer's for Steaks and Chops
1600 Lamar
Houston, TX
Stylish steakhouse featuring beef, lamb, seafood, and an extensive wine list.

2. Americas
1800 Post Oak
Houston, TX
South American fare with a Caribbean/Mexican twist served up in a striking setting.

3. La Griglia
2002 W. Gray Street
Houston, TX
A sparkling display of playful New Italian dining in the River Oaks shopping center.

4. Truluck's Steak & Stone Crab
5919 Westheimer Road
Houston, TX
Crowds swarm this upscale diner that features steak, stone crabs, and good times.

5. Brennan's of Houston
3300 Smith Street
Houston, TX
In a classic New Orleans-style abode, this local landmark serves upper-crust Cajun-Creole cuisine.

6. Mark's American Cuisine
1658 Westheimer Road
Houston, TX
A chic temple of top-notch nouveau American cuisine, complete with a private dining chamber.

7. Quattro
1300 Lamar Street
Houston, TX
Four Seasons restaurant features fashionable American-Italian dining in Euro-sleek style.

Section 8

8. Bank Jean-Georges
220 Main Street
Houston, TX
Chef Jean-George Vongerichten's operation in downtown's Hotel Icon is expansive, expensive, and excellent.

Los Angeles

1. The Ivy
113 N. Robertson Boulevard
Los Angeles, CA
Dealmakers who'd rather die than live in a two-room cottage gladly pay a lot to eat in one.

2. Spago Beverly Hills
176 N. Canon Drive
Beverly Hills, CA
The chef is more famous than the glossy clientele, but it's the sparkling cuisine that deserves top billing.

3. Maple Drive
345 North Maple Drive
Beverly Hills, CA
Beverly Hills mainstay catches up to the millennium with a seasonally changing menu.

4. The Grill on Hollywood
6801 Hollywood Boulevard
Hollywood, CA
Settle down for a costly taste of yesteryear at Hollywood and Highland's retro chophouse.

5. Buffalo Club
1520 Olympic Boulevard
Santa Monica, CA
Swinging supper club with old-school glamour and classic steakhouse cuisine.

6. Michael's
1147 3rd Street
Santa Monica, CA
The rabble-rouser of the early '80s restaurant scene is aging gracefully.

7. Ciao Trattoria
815 W. Seventh Street
Los Angeles, CA
Businesspeople, hotel guests, and concertgoers

dine on Italian specialties in a landmark downtown building.

8. Cafe Del Rey
4451 Admiralty Way
Marina del Rey, CA
Sublime harbor views vie with inspired haute cuisine at this posh Marina spot.

9. Foodies
11701 Wilshire Boulevard
Los Angeles, CA
Generic mini-mall decor belies business and family popularity and the New American fare.

Miami

1. The Capital Grille
444 Brickell Avenue
Miami, FL
Where Brickell fat cats come to sip gin and tonics and slice into aged cuts of beef.

2. Herbets Restaurant and Caterers
3900 NW 79th Avenue, Suite 124
Miami, FL

3. Coral Gables Palm Restaurant
4425 Ponce De Leon Boulevard
Coral Gables, FL

4. Joe's Stone Crab
11 Washington Avenue
Miami Beach, FL
You won't leave crabby after a bout with the famously fresh, sweet-tasting crustaceans.

5. Porcao
801 Brickell Bay Drive
Miami, FL
Stake your claim to all the meat you can eat at this busy Brazilian churrascaria.

6. Azul
500 Brickell Key Drive
Miami, FL
Understated elegance meets haute world cuisine on the edge of Biscayne Bay.

7. Christy's
3101 Ponce De Leon Boulevard

Section 8

Coral Gables, FL
Old-fashioned steakhouse follows only two
trends: excellent beef and stellar service.

8. Shula's Steak House
7601 Miami Lakes Drive
Miami Lakes, FL
Ex-Miami Dolphins football coach Don Shula
scores a touchdown with this upscale steakhouse.

9. 1220 at the Tides
1220 Ocean Drive
Miami Beach, FL
There's a new source of excitement on South
Beach, and it's this sleek contemporary
American restaurant.

New York

1. The Four Seasons
99 E 52nd Street
New York, NY
A New York dining landmark for movers and
shakers.

2. Downtown Atlantic Restaurant & Bakery
364 Atlantic Avenue
Brooklyn, NY
Brooklyn-centric eatery attempts classy
American fare, but the plain ol' burger is still
the best.

3. Burger Joint
118 W 57th Street
New York, NY
A hidden hall in Le Parker Meridien's lobby
transports New Yorkers to hamburger heaven.

4. Del Frisco's Double Eagle Steak House
1221 Avenue of the Americas
New York, NY
A Texas-sized steakhouse with chain-restaurant
roots.

5. Jean Georges
1 Central Park W
New York, NY
Jean Georges' four-star magical mystery tour
remains the city's culinary measuring stick.

6. Lever House Restaurant
390 Park Avenue
New York, NY
Cutting-edge decor and New American fare
deserving of all the hype, in midtown's modern
landmark.

7. Oceana
55 East 54th Street
New York, NY
Plush midtown power den boasts pampering
service and extraordinary seafood.

8. Michael's Restaurant
24 W 55th Street
New York, NY
Manhattan media's favorite power-lunch spot.

9. River Cafe
1 Water Street
Brooklyn, NY
The cuisine lives up to—but never outshines—
one of New York's truly stunning settings.

10. Fred's at Barney's New York
660 Madison Avenue, 9th Floor
New York, NY
Pricey American cafe favorites popular with the
ladies who lunch and Midtown execs.

Philadelphia

1. The Capital Grille
1338 Chestnut Street
Philadelphia, PA
A big-money, big-portioned, big-ego dining
experience.

2. Saloon
750 S. Seventh Street
Philadelphia, PA
Old boys' club serves up rich dishes with unde-
niable Bella Vista class.

3. The Grill
10 S. Broad Street
Philadelphia, PA
In the shadow of City Hall, customers can experience refined dining at the Ritz-Carlton.

4. Twenty21
2005 Market Street
Philadelphia, PA
A handy, upscale business-dining arena on
Commerce Square.

San Francisco

1. Boulevard
1 Mission Street
San Francisco, CA
A mainstay in San Francisco's upscale dining
scene, featuring seasonal California cuisine and
a prime bay view.

2. Aqua
252 California Street
San Francisco, CA
After a decade, this impressive destination still
turns out exquisite seafood in a plush setting.

3. One Market Restaurant
1 Market Street
San Francisco, CA
Upscale California cuisine, elegant decor, and
superb waterfront views have made this restaurant an Embarcadero favorite.

4. Moose's
1652 Stockton Street
San Francisco, CA
This North Beach institution known for its seasonal California cuisine never goes out of style.

5. Jeanty at Jack's
615 Sacramento Street
San Francisco, CA
One of the Wine Country's favorite chefs brings
his signature French cuisine to a classic
Financial District venue.

6. Laurel Court Restaurant & Bar
950 Mason Street
San Francisco, CA
Steep yourself in history and sophistication in
this famous hotel dining room.

7. Careme Room
625 Polk Street
San Francisco, CA

Feast on a range of international dishes prepared by California Culinary Academy students.

8. Balboa Cafe
3199 Fillmore Street
San Francisco, CA
Classic San Francisco style and a sophisticated
Marina bar scene converge at this American
eatery.

Seattle

1. Metropolitan Grill
820 Second Avenue
Seattle, WA
A second home to Seattle's power players, this
beloved institution serves up surefire steak dinners.

2. Seastar Restaurant and Raw Bar
205 108th Avenue NE
Bellevue, WA
A worthy destination for dressed-up seafood in
the heart of Bellevue.

3. The Hunt Club at the Sorrento
900 Madison Street
Seattle, WA
Victorian elegance and a regional menu bring
an elegant spark to hotel dining.

4. Dahlia Lounge
2001 4th Avenue
Seattle, WA
Seattle's new crop could learn a thing or two
from Tom Douglas' sage experimentation and
mass appeal.

5. SkyCity at the Needle
400 Broad Street
Seattle, WA
The slowly rotating dining room showcases the
region's every highlight, from Queen Anne to
Mount Rainier.

6. Earth & Ocean
1112 4th Avenue
Seattle, WA
Beautiful food served to beautiful people in the
hip and luxurious W Hotel.

7. Bis On Main

10213 Main Street
Bellevue, WA
Comfortably elegant bistro draws Bellevue's moneyed boomers for wining, dining, and networking.

8. Von's Grand City Cafe

619 Pine Street
Seattle, WA
This downtown spot's vibe makes it easy for the after-work crowd to relax.

9. Brooklyn Seafood, Steak & Oyster House

1212 2nd Avenue
Seattle, WA
Old Seattle-style upscale saloon pulsing with tourists and locals lured by oysters and booze.

10. The Georgian

411 University Street
Seattle, WA
Refined hotel dining ideal for celebrations and special occasions.

St. Louis

1. J. Buck's

101 S Hanley Road
St. Louis, MO
This swank restaurant is all dressed up, but has no pretensions.

2. 1111 Mississippi

1111 Mississippi Avenue
St. Louis, MO
Another converted warehouse adds itself to the list of sexy city eateries.

3. Portabella Restaurant

15 N. Central Avenue
Clayton, MO
Exceptional house-made pastas and elegant atmosphere perfect for intimate dining.

4. The Crossing

7823 Forsyth Boulevard
St. Louis, MO
Clayton mainstay boasts exceptional New American cuisine in charming surroundings.

5. Sqwires

1415 S. 18th Street
St. Louis, MO
Upscale without the attitude, this Lafayette Square hot spot offers tantalizing American food, an attractive young crowd, and even shopping.

6. Luciano's Trattoria

172 Carondelet Plaza
Clayton, MO

7. Kemoll's Italian Restaurant

1 Metropolitan Square
St. Louis, MO
St. Louis' glam Italian.

8. Cardwell's

8100 Maryland Avenue
St. Louis, MO

Source: Best of CitySearch, www.bestofcity-search.com.

Forbes' Best Business Restaurants by Region

Atlanta

Bacchanalia
3125 Piedmont
Phone: (404) 365-0410

Seeger's
111 W. Paces Ferry Road

Buckhead
Phone: (404) 846-9779

City Grill
50 Hurt Plaza
Phone: (404) 524-2489

Ritz-Carlton Buckhead Dining Room
Ritz-Carlton Buckhead
3434 Peachtree Road, NE
Phone: (404) 237-2700

Boston

The Federalist
15 Beacon Street
Phone: (617) 670-1500

Grill 23 & Bar
161 Berkeley Street (Stuart Street)
Phone: (617) 542-2255

Chicago

Charlie Trotter's
816 W. Armitage Avenue
Phone: (773) 248-6228

Ritz-Carlton Dining Room
Ritz-Carlton Hotel
160 E. Pearson Street
Phone: (312) 573-5223

Morton's of Chicago
Newberry Plaza Location
1050 N. State Street
Phone: (312) 266-4820
9525 W. Bryn Mawr Avenue

Rosemont Location
9525 W. Bryn Mawr Avenue
Phone: (847) 678-5155

Westchester Location
1 Westbrook Corporate Center
Phone: (708) 562-7000

Cleveland

Johnny's Bar on Fulton
3164 Fulton Road
Phone: (216) 281-0055

Johnny's Downtown
1406 W. Sixth Street
Phone: (216) 623-0055

Sans Souci
Cleveland Renaissance Hotel
24 Public Square
Phone: (216) 696-5600

Denver

Papillon Café
250 Josephine Street
Phone: (303) 333-7166

Palace Arms
Brown Palace Hotel
321 17th Street
Phone: (303) 297-3111

Del Frisco's Double Eagle Steakhouse
Denver Tech Center
8100 E. Orchard Road
Phone: (303) 796-0100

Houston

Churrascos
2055 Westheimer
Phone: (713) 527-8300

Rotisserie for Beef & Bird
2200 Wilcrest
Phone: (713) 977-9524

Goode Co.
5109 Kirby Drive
Phone: (713) 522-2530
8911 Katy Freeway
Phone: (713) 464-1901

Los Angeles

The Ivy
133 N. Robertson Boulevard
West Hollywood
Phone: (310) 274-8303

Spago
176 North Canon Drive
Beverly Hills
Phone: (310) 385-0880

The Palm
9001 Santa Monica Boulevard
West Hollywood
Phone: (310) 550-8811

The Grill
9560 Dayton Way
Beverly Hills
Phone: (310) 276-0615

Miami

Joe's Stone Crab
11 Washington Street
Miami Beach
Phone: (305) 673-0365

The Palm
9650 E. Bay Harbor Drive
Bay Harbor Islands
Phone: (305) 868-7256

Norman's
21 Almeria Avenue
Coral Gables
Phone: (305) 446-6767

Blue Door
Delano Hotel
1685 Collins Avenue
South Beach
Phone: (305) 674-6400

New York

The Four Seasons
99 East 52nd Street
Phone: (212) 754-9494

21 Club
21 West 52nd Street
Phone: (212) 582-7200

Le Bernardin
155 West 51st Street
Phone: (212) 489-1515

Chanterelle
2 Harrison Street
Phone: (212) 966-6960

Sparks Steak House
210 East 46th Street
Phone: (212) 687-4855

San Francisco

Aqua
252 California Street
Phone: (415) 956-9662

Gary Danko
800 Northpoint Street
Phone: (415) 749-2060

Seattle

Rover's
2808 E. Madison Street
Phone: (206) 325-7442

Fullers
Sheraton Hotel & Towers
1400 Sixth Avenue
Phone: (206) 447-5544

Dahlia Lounge
1904 Fourth Avenue
Phone: (206) 682-4142

Metropolitan Grill
818 Second Avenue
Phone: (206) 624-3287

Georgian Room
Four Seasons Olympic Hotel
411 University Street
Phone: (206) 621-7889

St. Louis

Tony's
410 Market Street
Phone: (314) 771-5777

Section 8

Ritz-Carlton Grill
Ritz-Carlton Hotel
100 Carondelet Avenue

Clayton
Phone: (314) 719-1484

Washington, DC

The Palm
1225 19th Street NW
Phone: (202) 293-9091

Kinkeads
2000 Pennsylvania Avenue NW
Phone: (202) 296-7700

Galileo
1110 21st Street NW
Phone: (202) 293-7191

Old Ebbit Grill
675 15th Street NW
Phone: (202) 347-4800

Source: Forbes.com,
www.forbes.com/2001/08/16/0816feat.html.

Best Business Dining by Metro City

Atlanta

1. Vinny's on Windward
5355 Windward Parkway
Alpharetta, GA
Italian-inspired dishes please at this higher-end restaurant north of the city.

2. Bone's Restaurant
3130 Piedmont Road
Atlanta, GA
The city's standard-bearing steakhouse serves up superior beef to Buckhead's wheeling-and-dealing set.

3. Atmosphere
1620 Piedmont Avenue
Atlanta, GA
Satisfyingly rich French fare in a picturesque, romantic setting.

4. City Grill
50 Hurt Plaza SE
Atlanta, GA
Fine dining, Southern style, draws crowds to a landmark downtown building.

5. Chops
70 West Paces Ferry
Atlanta, GA
This Buckhead mainstay offers great seafood and killer steaks.

6. Canoe
4199 Paces Ferry Road NW
Atlanta, GA
Deftly conceived New American cuisine thrives in a picturesque riverside setting.

7. Cafe Lily
308 W Ponce De Leon Avenue, Suite B
Decatur, GA
Creative Mediterranean specialties shine at this comfortable Decatur bistro.

8. The Capital Grille
255 East Paces Perry Road
Atlanta, GA
Stunning city views set this by-the-book steakhouse apart from the Buckhead pack.

9. Fogo de Chao
3101 Piedmont Road
Atlanta, GA
Fast-paced steakhouse brings the flavors of a Brazilian cookout to Buckhead.

10. South City Kitchen
1144 Crescent Avenue NE
Atlanta, GA
Southern favorites get edgy updates at this ever-popular eatery.

Section 8

Los Angeles

1. Spago Beverly Hills
176 N Canon Drive
Beverly Hills, CA
The chef is more famous than the glossy clientele, but it's the sparkling cuisine that deserves top billing.

2. Cafe Del Rey
4451 Admiralty Way
Marina del Rey, CA
Sublime harbor views vie with inspired haute cuisine at this posh Marina spot.

3. Ciao Trattoria
815 W Seventh Street
Los Angeles, CA
Businesspeople, hotel guests, and concertgoers dine on Italian specialties in a landmark downtown building.

4. Morton's—The Steakhouse
735 S Figueroa Street
Los Angeles, CA
USDA prime beef, elegant tableside service, and mammoth martinis.

5. Restaurant Halie, LLC
1030 East Green Street
Pasadena, CA
Escape hectic Old Town to this hidden gem with affordable American fare.

6. Tangier Lounge
2138 Hillhurst Avenue
Los Angeles, CA
There's a full-blown scene at this exotic Eastside spot—the delicious food is merely a bonus.

7. Buffalo Club
1520 Olympic Boulevard
Santa Monica, CA
Swinging supper club with old-school glamour and classic steakhouse cuisine.

8. Ivy at the Shore
1535 Ocean Avenue
Santa Monica, CA
Slightly more reclusive seaside sibling to paparazzi-filled Robertson Boulevard location caters to millionaire beach bums with families in tow.

9. Water Grill
544 S. Grand
Los Angeles, CA
This exquisite downtown destination elevates impeccably fresh seafood to new heights.

10. Jer-ne Restaurant + Bar
4375 Admiralty Way
Marina Del Rey, CA
Marina views and Asian-fusion cuisine enliven a Ritz-Carlton dining experience.

Las Vegas

1. Cili
5160 Las Vegas Boulevard S
Las Vegas, NV
Solid Pacific Rim cuisine and refined tropical elegance make for a breezy meal overlooking the Bali Hai golf course.

2. Ruth's Chris Steak House
3900 Paradise Road
Las Vegas, NV
Sophisticated American chain serves up corn-fed USDA prime cuts and New Orleans-style appetizers and sides.

3. Charlie Palmer Steak
3960 Las Vegas Boulevard S
Las Vegas, NV
Wine enthusiasts and carnivores unite at this posh steakhouse.

4. El Coqui Caribbean Restaurant
2210 Paradise Road
Las Vegas, NV

5. Del Frisco's
3925 Paradise Road
Las Vegas, NV
Upscale steakhouse boasts aged USDA prime cuts; family-style side dishes, extensive wine list, and Southern hospitality.

6. McCormick & Schmick's

335 Hughes Center Drive
Las Vegas, NV
Clubby corporate restaurant draws seafood lovers with fresh daily catches and posh atmosphere.

7. Firefly* on Paradise, Tapas Kitchen and Bar

3900 Paradise Road
Las Vegas, NV
Late-night bistro off the Strip features Spanish tapas and live entertainment.

New York

1. Dylan Prime

62 Laight Street
New York, NY
A hip steakhouse catering to fondue-eating 20-somethings.

2. Gotham Bar and Grill

12 E 12th Street
New York, NY
This highly praised, elegant destination perseveres with pure and vigorous flavors.

3. Del Frisco's Double Eagle Steak House

1221 Avenue of the Americas
New York, NY
A Texas-sized steakhouse with chain-restaurant roots.

4. Lever House Restaurant

390 Park Avenue
New York, NY
Cutting-edge decor and New American fare deserving of all the hype, in midtown's modern landmark.

5. Suspenders

111 Broadway
New York, NY
Owned by retired firemen, this dark wood-filled American restaurant serves families hearty breakfasts, lunches, and dinners including BBQ ribs, burgers.

6. Le Bernardin

155 W. 51st Street
New York, NY
Revered old-line French favorite dishes out elegant seafood with class and consistency.

7. The Four Seasons

99 E. 52nd Street
New York, NY
A New York dining landmark for movers and shakers.

8. Lasaro's

29 East 30th Street
New York, NY
Savor live music alongside traditional old-world Cuban recipes and seafood dishes at this midtown eatery.

9. Andavi

91 Christopher Street
New York, NY
Italian classics and romance go hand in hand in this West Village trattoria and wine bar.

Source: Best of CitySearch, www.bestofcitysearch.com.

Section 8

Best Nationally Ranked After-Work Bars

1. 111 Minna Street Gallery
111 Minna Street
San Francisco, CA
An edgy SoMa art gallery by day; uber-hip club by night.

2. Brit's Pub
1110 Nicollet Avenue
Minneapolis, MN
Whatever the weather, this downtown pub is a perennial favorite.

3. Falling Rock Tap House
1919 Blake Street
Denver, CO
A popular LoDo watering hole with a huge beer selection and laid-back atmosphere.

4. Kaz Bar
333 Dearborn
Chicago, IL
Moroccan-inspired surroundings, lush fare, and live music attract downtowners and out-of-towners to this House of Blues Hotel lobby lounge.

5. Little Woodrow's Neighborhood
2301 W Alabama Street
Houston, TX
This quintessential Texas bar aims to please the beer-loving sports fan.

6. Moon and Sixpence British Pub
2014 NE 42nd Avenue
Portland, OR
Laid-back conversation pub offers a diverse selection of brews and whiskeys.

7. Nic's Restaurant and Martini Lounge
453 N Canon Drive
Beverly Hills, CA
Larry Nicola's cool supper club and martini lounge proves he just can't lose.

8. P.J. Clarke's
915 Third Avenue
New York, NY
A lively crowd enjoys the best of the old and the new in this renovated New York pub and restaurant.

9. Treehouse Pub
7 Kings Circle NE
Atlanta, GA
One of the coziest watering holes in town offers a busy after-work scene and intimate patio.

10. Vox Populi
755 Boylston Street
Boston, MA
One of Boylston Street's most popular after-work destinations serves modern American cuisine in an excellent people-watching locale.

Source: Best of CitySearch,, www.bestofcity-search.com/2003/national/bars_&_nightlife/after-work_drinks/index.html.

Best After-Work Bars by Metro City

Atlanta

1. Smokers Paradise
4090 Johns Creek Parkway
Suwanee, GA
This cigar lounge/wine bar is a suburban cigar shop that thinks like a bar, with a cozy lounge and a wide selection of cigars, beers, and wines.

2. Twist
3500 Peachtree Road
Atlanta, GA
Midtown meets Buckhead with a sleek setting and sophisticated menu that takes mall dining to a new level.

3. Fado Irish Pub
3035 Peachtree Road NE
Atlanta, GA
Buckhead pub does Ireland to the extreme.

4. Treehouse Pub
7 Kings Circle NE
Atlanta, GA
One of the coziest watering holes in town offers a busy after-work scene and intimate patio.

5. Barcelona
11705 Medlock Bridge Road
Duluth, GA
Spanish cuisine like no other in the city, served in smart, glamorous surroundings.

6. Halo
817 W Peachtree Street NW
Atlanta, GA
Striking and spacious lounge gives Midtowners a downtempo scene for stylish cocktails.

7. Front Page News
1104 Crescent Avenue
Atlanta, GA
A booming Big Easy-style bar scene and a serious Sunday brunch grab headlines on Crescent Avenue.

8. Righteous Room
1051 Ponce De Leon Avenue NE
Atlanta, GA
This funky Titan of the Atlanta bar scene wins big with a solid beer list, great snacks, and a killer jukebox.

9. Gilbert's Mediterranean Cafe
219 10th Street NE
Atlanta, GA
Chic neighborhood restaurant offers superb Mediterranean cuisine at moderate prices.

10. Manuel's Tavern
602 N Highland Avenue
Atlanta, GA
Home to politicos and plumbers, this friendly half-century-old tavern is an Atlanta institution.
Boston

1. Bar 10
10 Huntington Avenue
Boston, MA
Westin Hotel bar with understated decor and a crowd that's anything but.

2. Tia's on the Waterfront
200 Atlantic Avenue
Boston, MA
Large outdoor patio entices after-work drones and searching singles with a magnificent waterfront view.

3. The Rack
24 Clinton Street
Boston, MA
Haven for young professionals and athletes who like pop music, microbrews, martinis, and pool.

4. Lucky's
355 Congress Street
Boston, MA
A sizzling subterranean lounge heats up Fort Point Channel with retro cool.

5. Cask 'n Flagon
62 Brookline Avenue
Boston, MA
Located behind the Green Monster, a true Fenway landmark serves as a popular meeting spot before or after a game.

6. Sidney's Grille
20 Sidney Street
Cambridge, MA
The Hotel @ MIT's house restaurant serves contemporary American fare in style.

7. Sunset Cantina
916 Commonwealth Avenue
Boston, MA
The Sunset Grill empire moves its popular menu closer to the city limits with fantastic success.

8. Vox Populi
755 Boylston Street
Boston, MA
One of Boylston Street's most popular after-

work destinations serves modern American cuisine in an excellent people-watching locale.

9. 33 Restaurant & Lounge
33 Stanhope Street
Boston, MA
A decor as stylish as the well-dressed clientele meshes with an eclectic, international menu of contemporary cuisine.

10. Aqua Bar and Grill
120 Water Street
Boston, MA
An after-work hot spot with a sizzling roof deck in the Financial District.

Chicago

1. Kaz Bar
333 Dearborn
Chicago, IL
Moroccan-inspired surroundings, lush fare, and live music attract downtowners and out-of-towners to this House of Blues Hotel lobby lounge.

2. Cactus Bar & Grill
404 S. Wells Street
Chicago, IL
Rowdy South Loop hot spot with a south-of-the-border spirit and spicy after-work crowds.

3. Justin's
3358 N. Southport Avenue
Chicago, IL
Lakeview haunt for fans of sports and summertime beer gardens.

4. Metro Deli & Cafe
210 S. Canal Street
Chicago, IL

5. Chicago West
270 Main Street
Sugar Grove, IL

6. Kinzie Chophouse
400 North Wells Street
Chicago, IL
This River North spot draws a Merchandise Mart crowd for salads, sandwiches, and steaks.

7. Rock Bottom Restaurant & Brewery
1 W. Grand Street
Chicago, IL
A casual brew pub with great beer, a collegiate atmosphere, and an alluring rooftop deck.

8. Coq d'Or
140 E. Walton Place
Chicago, IL
Distinguished locals and visitors share swanky after-work sips at this Prohibition-era bar in the Drake Hotel.

9. The Capital Grille
633 N. St. Clair Street
Chicago, IL
Subdued Streeterville steakhouse draws a heavy-hitting corporate crowd for red meat in sophisticated surroundings.

10. Melvin B's
1114 N. State Street
Chicago, IL
Gold Coast hangout that's lively and legendary for its patio, truly one of the most popular in the city.

Cleveland

1. Harpo's Sports Cafe
5777 Smith Road
Brook Park, OH
Family-friendly vibes make this a sports bar even bench jockeys can love.

2. Great Lakes Brewing Company
2516 Market Avenue
Cleveland, OH
The place for homemade gourmet beer and equally imaginative food.

3. Wright Place
34300 Chardon Road
Willoughby, OH

4. Blind Pig Speakeasy
1228 W. Sixth Street
Cleveland, OH
When it comes to attitude, this bar is a Warehouse District wallflower.

5. Winking Lizard Gateway
811 Huron Road
Cleveland, OH
This longtime Cleveland favorite caters to a mixed crowd with its many munchies and good beer selection.

6. The Treehouse
820 College Avenue
Cleveland, OH
Stumped for a place to begin your Tremont pub crawl? Try this trendy, Irish-flavored watering hole.

7. D'Vine Wine Bar
836 W. St. Clair Avenue
Cleveland, OH
Heavenly choices for the palate in the form of a wide selection of vintages.

8. Harpo's Sports Cafe
19654 W. 130th Street
Cleveland, OH
Sports for mere mortals, screens for giants.

9. Panini's Grill of Willoughby
37333 Euclid Avenue
Willoughby, OH

10. John Q's Steakhouse
55 Public Square
Cleveland, OH
Prime beef and a prime location elevate this spot beyond its common-man name.

Denver

1. Giggling Grizzly
1320 20th Street
Denver, CO
A Colorado-themed bar with a collegiate crowd.

2. Govnr's Park
672 Logan Street
Denver, CO
Capitol Hill's most popular sports bar serves up some great group-sized drinks.

3. My Brother's Bar
2376 15th Street
Denver, CO
The edge-of-downtown location and tree-shaded patio of this burger haven are a welcome respite from LoDo.

4. Rock Bottom Restaurant & Brewery
1001 16th Street
Denver, CO
An ever-popular spot for consistently good meals and top-notch craft beer.

5. Bull and Bush Brewery
4700 Cherry Creek South Drive
Denver, CO
America's first true sports bar gleams with rustic British revelry.

6. Rio Grande Mexican Restaurant
1525 Blake Street
Denver, CO
Food takes a backseat to the potent margaritas and the crowd that loves them.

7. Falling Rock Tap House
1919 Blake Street
Denver, CO
A popular LoDo watering hole with a huge beer selection and laid-back atmosphere.

8. Celtic Tavern
1801 Blake Street
Denver, CO
Lively spirits served with a thick brogue.

9. The Keg Steakhouse and Bar
1890 Wynkoop Street
Denver, CO

Houston

1. McGonigel's Mucky Duck
2425 Norfolk Street
Houston, TX
This homey club is Houston's premier destination for those with a yen for folk, Irish, and Celtic music.

2. Slainte Irish Pub
509 Main Street
Houston, TX
Festive two-story tavern's drink specials, games, and music attract a diverse downtown crowd.

Section 8

3. Lounge at Benjy's
2424 Dunstan Street
Houston, TX
Posh little Rice Village joint cuts a space-age, bachelor-pad groove.

4. Red Lion Pub
2316 S. Shepherd
Houston, TX
This British pub lays claim to authentic English tradition.

5. Cafe Adobe
2111 Westheimer Road
Houston, TX
Margaritas pack in after-work partiers, while the Tex-Mex menu provides some local flavor.

6. Nick's Place Italian Sports Bar & Pizzeria
2713 Rockyridge Drive
Houston, TX
Combination sports bar-Italian eatery with food as good as mamma used to make.

7. Brian O'Neill's
5555 Morningside Drive
Houston, TX
An Irish heart beats proudly within this Rice Village pub.

8. Sambuca
909 Texas Street
Houston, TX
A thriving bar scene, slick dining, and cool tunes make this one of downtown's most reliable hot spots.

9. Taco Milagro
2555 Kirby Drive
Houston, TX
When the sun shines, the patio at this gourmet Mexican eatery teems with successful, attractive singles.

10. Sherlock's Baker St. Pub & Grill
10001 Westheimer Road
Houston, TX
It's not on Baker Street, but the attraction of this relaxed little bar is elementary.

Los Angeles

1. Father's Office
1018 Montana Avenue
Santa Monica, CA
Where heaven is served in a bun and a pint glass.

2. Cat & Fiddle
6530 W. Sunset Boulevard
Los Angeles, CA
Enjoy live music and pub grub at this Brit-themed bar.

3. Normandie Room
8737 Santa Monica Boulevard
West Hollywood, CA
An eclectic mix, minus homophobes or hetero-phobes, combines with good music for a laid-back atmosphere.

4. Roof Bar at the Standard Downtown
550 S. Flower Street
Los Angeles, CA
Sip and dip at this chic poolside lounge atop the hip downtown Standard hotel.

5. Red Rock
8782 Sunset Boulevard
West Hollywod, CA
Come for the scenery and stay for the action at this red-hot Sunset Strip party spot.

6. Red Lion Tavern
2366 Glendale Boulevard
Los Angeles, CA
Dirndl-clad waitresses, Bavarian fare, and live oompah music make every day Oktoberfest.

7. The Abbey
692 N Robertson Boulevard
West Hollywood, CA
West Hollywood gay coffeehouse and bar provides both relaxed fun and atypically cosmo-politan atmosphere.

8. Ye Olde King's Head
116 Santa Monica Boulevard
Santa Monica, CA
Authentic teas, pints, and fish and chips at this lively British pub by the beach.

9. Cabo Cantina
8301 W. Sunset Boulevard
Los Angeles, CA
Cheap margaritas and no-frills Mexican food fuel a spring break-style party.

10. Senor Fred
13730 Ventura Boulevard
Sherman Oaks, CA
Authentic Mexican fare and a bordello-like setting give sleepy Sherman Oaks a shot of gusto.

Miami

1. Houston's
201 Miracle Mile
Miami, FL
Roomy banquettes and hefty portions typify this polished American grill that's popular for business deals and special occasions.

2. Tobacco Road
626 S. Miami Avenue
Miami, FL
A reputation for great blues and debauchery stretching back more than 80 years.

3. Wet Willie's
760 Ocean Drive
Miami Beach, FL
Margarita mecca with rooftop bar, Mexican bar bites, and a reputation for noise and revelry.

4. Gordon Biersch Brewery Restaurant
1201 Brickell Avenue
Miami, FL
Visual flair and fusion fare distinguish this upscale beer hall from smaller microbreweries.

5. Cafe Tu Tu Tango
3015 Grand Avenue
Coconut Grove, FL
Appetizer-sized portions and nightly entertainment make this a great place for groups.

6. Monty's on the Beach
300 Alton Road
Miami Beach, FL

7. Globe Cafe & Bar
377 Alhambra Circle
Coral Gables, FL
This elegant bar is a "Cheers" for the young, urban Cuban-American set.

8. Tantra
1445 Pennsylvania Avenue
Miami Beach, FL
Erotic cuisine and exotic atmosphere make dining a feast for all your senses.

9. Purdy Lounge
1811 Purdy Avenue
Miami Beach, FL
Find fun and games, funky decor, and well-priced drinks at this hip yet laid-back spot.

10. Playwright Irish Pub & Restaurant
1265 Washington Avenue
Miami Beach, FL
Laid-back but not divey, this pub is a good spot to grab a pint and a bite.

New York

1. Brite Bar
297 10th Avenue (at 27th Street)
New York, NY
Lite-Brite toys and locally brewed "energy" vodka stir up a lively vibe at this 10th Avenue lounge.

2. Ship of Fools
1590 2nd Avenue
New York, NY
Drinking is not a spectator sport at this bar where TVs nearly outnumber patrons.

3. Proof
239 3rd Avenue
New York, NY
Part lounge, part sports bar—it aims for the best of both without offending anyone.

4. People
163 Allen Street
New York, NY
Upscale, attitude-free drinking den woos Lower East Side singles.

Section 8

5. Nice Guy Eddie's
5 Avenue A
New York, NY
An all-female bar staff draws crowds to this dark East Village haunt.

6. Fat Black Pussycat
130 W. 3rd Street
New York, NY
This cool kitty's frat-bar face cloaks a romantic hideaway.

7. Patio Lounge
179 5th Avenue
Brooklyn, NY
A serene green setting, plus beachy cocktails and comfy couches.

8. Dylan Prime
62 Laight Street
New York, NY
A hip steakhouse catering to fondue-eating 20-somethings.

9. Dip
416 3rd Avenue
New York, NY
With bar, lounge, dinner, pool, and fondue—it tries to be all things to all people.

Philadelphia

1. Eulogy Belgian Tavern
136 Chestnut Street
Philadelphia, PA
Glitzy Old City gets a basic Belgian bar.

2. McGillin's Old Ale House
1310 Drury Street
Philadelphia, PA
This friendly family-run tavern is one of the city's oldest watering holes.

3. Azure
931 N. 2nd Street
Philadelphia, PA

4. Tir Na Nog
1600 Arch Street
Philadelphia, PA
Direct from New York, this Irish-inspired bar and restaurant brings New American fare—with an Emerald Isle twinkle—to Philly.

5. Monk's Cafe
264 S. 16th Street
Philadelphia, PA
Beer geeks, foodies, and everyday folks make this cozy Belgian-themed brasserie a perennial favorite.

6. McFadden's
461 N. Third Street
Philadelphia, PA
Happy hour hot spot for those who've graduated from Delaware Avenue.

7. Irish Pub
2007 Walnut Street
Philadelphia, PA
Maybe it's not the most authentic Irish bar in town, but don't tell that to the crowds of students who flock here.

8. Trappe Tavern
416 Main Street
Schwenksville, PA

9. Marathon Grill
2001 Market Street
Philadelphia, PA
A small local chain is the favored lunchtime choice for everyone in the office.

10. Twenty21
2005 Market Street
Philadelphia, PA
A handy, upscale business-dining arena on Commerce Square.

San Francisco

1. Levende Lounge and Restaurant
1710 Mission Street
San Francisco, CA
Romantic Mission spot toes the line between club and restaurant.

2. Blondie's Bar & No Grill
540 Valencia Street
San Francisco, CA
Singles on the make head to this Mission main-

stay for mammoth martinis and prime patio seating.

3. WISH
1539 Folsom Street
San Francisco, CA
A SoMa DJ lounge serving exceptional cocktails to a packed house.

4. Tony Niks
1534 Stockton Street
San Francisco, CA
An elegantly appointed, retro lounge ticking to the time of the Eisenhower hour.

5. Nova
555 Second Street
San Francisco, CA
A cozy bar near the Giants' ballpark serving infused vodkas and comfort food with a twist.

6. 111 Minna Street Gallery
111 Minna Street
San Francisco, CA
An edgy SoMa art gallery by day; uber-hip club by night.

7. Voda
56 Belden Place
San Francisco, CA
A hip, affordable vodka lounge nestled among European restaurants in the Financial District.

8. Zebulon
83 Natoma Street
San Francisco, CA
A casual SoMa loft dishing cocktails and cuisine in airy surroundings.

9. Royal Exchange
301 Sacramento Street
San Francisco, CA
An old-school Financial District bar and grill with strong drinks, gigantic burgers and fine brews.

10. Lush Lounge
1092 Post Street
San Francisco, CA
Theatrical decor and throwback cocktails at a friendly Tenderloin bar.

Seattle

1. The People's Pub
5429 Ballard Avenue NW
Seattle, WA
German fare finds a home on Seattle's most happening street.

2. Zig Zag Cafe
1501 Western Avenue
Seattle, WA
The finely crafted cocktails are the draw at this classy downtown escape.

3. Tini Bigs Lounge
100 Denny Way
Seattle, WA
The young, hip, and single gather for a '50s cocktail culture with '90s attitude.

4. Metropolitan Grill
820 Second Avenue
Seattle, WA
A second home to Seattle's power players, this beloved institution serves up surefire steak dinners.

5. BluWater Bistro
1001 Fairview Avenue N
Seattle, WA
Dock the boat and drop in for a waterfront view and icy drinks.

6. Fado Irish Pub
801 1st Avenue
Seattle, WA
Go green and sip a mighty fine pint at this friendly Irish pub.

7. Chandler's Crabhouse
901 Fairview Avenue N
Seattle, WA
With a gorgeous view and a bar designed for post-work parties, this updated classic draws in a new crowd of fun seekers.

8. Morton's—The Steakhouse
1511 Sixth Avenue

Section 8

Seattle, WA
USDA prime beef, elegant tableside service, and mammoth martinis.

9. Dragonfish Asian Cafe
722 Pine Street
Seattle, WA
Great deals on dim sum and drinks for passionate Pan-Asian fans.

10. Elliott Bay Brewery & Pub
4720 California Avenue SW
Seattle, WA
West Seattle microbrewer with broad-age appeal and standard pub fare.

St. Louis

1. J. Buck's
101 S. Hanley Road
St. Louis, MO
This swank restaurant is all dressed up, but has no pretensions.

2. Fast Eddie's Bon-Air
1530 E. 4th Street
Alton, IL
This perpetually jammed bar and restaurant caters to a blue-collar crowd in for the cheap eats and live music.

3. Hacienda
9748 Manchester Road
St. Louis, MO
Authentic fixings and a breezy patio are the star attractions at this agreeable Mexican restaurant.

4. Trainwreck West Port Plaza
314 Westport Plaza
St. Louis, MO

5. Blueberry Hill
6504 Delmar Boulevard
St. Louis, MO
St. Louis natives from Bob Costas to Chuck Berry have found their thrill—and an unbeatable burger—right here.

6. Grappa Grill
1644 Country Club Plaza Drive
St. Charles, MO
Munch on Italian and American eats while kicking back on a nice patio at this St. Charles favorite.

7. Milo's Tavern
5201 Wilson Avenue
St. Louis, MO

8. Cafe Eau
212 N. Kingshighway Boulevard
St. Louis, MO
Pleasant, contemporary room lures the beautiful set to socialize over reasonably priced bistro fare.

9. Trailhead Brewing Co.
921 S. Riverside Drive
St. Charles, MO

10. Rue 13
1313 Washington Avenue
St. Louis, MO
Washington Avenue's latest debut serves sushi.

Source: Best of CitySearch, www.bestofcitysearch.com.

Best Nationally Ranked Steakhouses

1. Brook's Steak House
6538 S. Yosemite Street
Greenwood Village, CO
Where high-rollers and the business crowd indulge on the city's top beef.

2. Delmonico Steakhouse at the Venetian
3355 Las Vegas Boulevard S
Las Vegas, NV

Celebrity chef Emeril Lagasse serves an elegant experience at this Creole-influenced, upscale steakhouse.

3. Golden Ox Restaurant and Lounge
1600 Genessee Street
Kansas City, MO
This historical restaurant-lounge is definitely a beef-eater's paradise.

Section 8

4. Grill 23 & Bar
161 Berkeley Street
Boston, MA
Upscale country-club atmosphere plus world-class beef equals the city's premier steakhouse experience.

5. Harris'
2100 Van Ness Avenue
San Francisco, CA
In-house dry aging and an old-boys' club setting guarantee diners a juicy rib eye to remember.

6. Manny's Steakhouse
1300 Nicollet Avenue
Minneapolis, MN
An unabashedly masculine vibe pervades this handsome old-school steakhouse.

7. Metropolitan Grill
820 Second Avenue
Seattle, WA
A second home to Seattle's power players, this beloved institution serves up surefire steak dinners.

8. Morton's—The Steakhouse
1050 N. State Street
Chicago, IL
USDA prime beef, elegant tableside service, and mammoth martinis.

9. Sparks Steakhouse
210 E. 46th Street
New York, NY
A quintessentially masculine retreat where well-aged, char-fired steaks meet a top-notch wine list.

10. Taste of Texas Restaurant
10505 Katy Freeway
Houston, TX
Choose your own cut and enjoy a hearty meal with the family at this simple, satisfying steakhouse.

Source: Best of CitySearch, www.bestofcitysearch.com/2003/national/restaurants/steakhouse/index.html.

Section 8

Seven Most Common Business Gift-Giving Mistakes

The most common gift-giving mistakes are:

1. Giving gifts that hint of a need of change or self-improvement.
2. Spending too much or too little effort, money, or creativity.
3. Taking clues from retailers rather than the recipient.
4. Waiting till the last minute to shop.
5. Giving gifts with strings attached.
6. Giving gifts without taking into consideration the preferences of the recipient.
7. Giving gifts only when they are expected.

Source: Creatively Corporate, www.creativelycorporate.com/misc/mistakes.shtml.

Eight Business Gift-Giving Guidelines

In today's corporate world, gift giving is an integral part of doing business. The selection of a gift can communicate several messages: power, sophistication, knowledge, and interest. Gifts, whether business or personal, can help define and cement relationships. Careful consideration should be given in the choice of a gift because the gift can enhance or harm a corporate image. The goal of a corporate gift is to send a favorable message—not to have the gift get lost in the shuffle. The right gift can give great momentum to a business relationship, whether it is with an employee or a client. Some helpful guidelines to follow include:

1. Before searching for a gift, check to see if the recipient company has a gift policy.
2. Ask yourself what you want the gift to say about your company and about yourself.
3. Ask yourself if the gift will be interpreted in a favorable light.
4. Do not give gifts prohibited by the recipient's ethnic, moral, religious, or political beliefs.
5. Make sure the timeliness of the gift is appropriate.
6. Take careful consideration in the selection of the gift.
7. Make sure the gift fits within your personal and corporate budget guidelines.
8. Have fun and don't be afraid to be creative.

Source: Creatively Corporate, www.creativelycorporate.com/misc/tips.shtml.

Six Business Gift-Presentation Tips

Although the wrapping and presentation of the gift is the final touch for the presenter, it is the first impression for the recipient. So keep in mind that the presentation of the gift is just as important as the gift itself. The following are a few guidelines to follow when presenting gifts:

1. Choose a wrapping paper that is appropriate for the occasion and recipient. Select a pattern size to correspond with package size: large, bold patterns should be used only with large gifts.
2. The gift should be beautifully wrapped. The detail and the creativity of the gift-wrapping will be the first impression of the presentation.
3. Attach a card with the business gift. A few words of sentiment would be more appreciated than a simple signature. Never just enclose a business card without writing a small note.
4. Gifts should be presented in person. This conveys to the recipient that he or she is a valued friend. Also, this allows the giver to see and hear the recipient's reactions to the gift.

5. If a gift is expensive or personal in nature, always present it in private.

6. When choosing the setting of the presentation of the gift, be sure it relates to the occasion and the recipient.

Source: Creatively Corporate, www.creativelycorporate.com/misc/presentation.shtml.

Top 150 U.S. Golf Courses

1. Pebble Beach
Pebble Beach, CA

2. Pinehurst #2
Pinehurst, NC

3. Spyglass Hill
Pebble Beach, CA

4. Cog Hill #4 (Dubsdread)
Lemont, IL

5. River Course (Blackwolf Run)
Kohler, WI

6. Pumpkin Ridge (Ghost Creek)
Cornelius, OR

7. The Cascades
Hot Springs, VA

8. Monument (Troon North)
Scottsdale, AZ

9. Pine Barrens (World Woods)
Brooksville, FL

10. Harbour Town
Hilton Head Island, SC

11. Ocean Course
Kiawah Island, SC

12. Mauna Kea
Kohala Coast, HI

13. Stadium Course (TCP Sawgrass)
Ponte Vedra Beach, FL

14. Pasatiempo
Santa Cruz, CA

15. Challenger-Champion (Bay Hill)
Orlando, FL

16. Black Course (Bethpage)
Farmingdale, NY

17. Sandpines
Florence, OR

18. Karsten Creek
Stillwater, OK

19. Sugarloaf
Kingfield, ME

20. Links Course (Wild Dunes)
Isle of Palms, SC

21. The Prince
Princeville, Kauai, HI

22. Coeur D'Alene
Coeur D'Alene, ID

23. La Cantera
San Antonio, TX

24. Fazio Course (Barton Creek)
Austin, TX

25. Blue Monster (Doral)
Miami, FL

26. Fazio Course (Treetops)
Gaylord, MI

27. White Columns
Alpharetta, GA

28. Great Waters (Reynold's Plantation)
Greensboro, GA

29. Lake Course (RTJ–Grand National)
Opelika, AL

30.Tidewater
N. Myrtle Beach, SC

31. **Pine Meadow**
Mundelein, IL

32. **Pinon Hills**
Farmington, NM

33. **Links Course (Pelican Hill)**
Newport Coast, CA

34. **Championship (Tanglewood Park)**
Clemmons, NC

35. **Ocean Course (Pelican Hill)**
Newport Coast, CA

36. **Gailes (Lakewood)**
Oscoda, MI

37. **Otter Creek**
Columbus, IN

38. **North Woodlands**
Sunriver, OR

39. **Kemper Lakes**
Long Grove, IL

40. **Woodside/Lakeside (Cantigny)**
Wheaton, IL

41. **Spanish Bay**
Pebble Beach, CA

42. **Brickyard Crossing**
Indianapolis, IN

43. **Crosswater Course**
Sunriver, OR

44. **Mountain Course**
La Quinta, CA

45. **TPC Stadium Course (PGA West)**
La Quinta, CA

46. **Sentry World**
Stevens Point, WI

47. **The Dunes**
Myrtle Beach, SC

48. **Pinehurst #7**
Pinehurst, NC

49. **Wailua**
Lihue, Kauai, HI

50. **Ram Rock**
Horseshoe Bay, TX

51. **Smith Course (Treetops)**
Gaylord, MI

52. **Hominy Hill**
Colts Neck, NJ

53. **Kiva Dunes**
Gulf Shores, AL

54. **Rolling Oaks (World Woods)**
Brooksville, FL

55. **Kiele Course (Kauai Lagoons)**
Kalapaki Beach, Kauai, HI

56. **The Quarry**
San Antonio, TX

57. **Plantation Course (Kapalua Bay)**
Maui, HI

58. **Talon (Grayhawk)**
Scottsdale, AZ

59. **Bluffs on Thompson Creek**
St. Francisville, LA

60. **South Course (Torrey Pines)**
La Jolla, CA

61. **Caledonia**
Pawleys Island, SC

62. **South Course (Boulders)**
Carefree, AZ

63. **Gold Course (Golden Horseshoe)**
Williamsburg, VA

64. **Thoroughbred**
Rothbury, MI

65. **The Falls Course (RTJ-Magnolia Grove)**
Mobile, AL

66. **Desert Canyon**
Orondo, WA

67. **Pole Creek**
Winter Park, CO

68. **Links Course (RTJ-Grand National)**
Opelika, AL

69. Indian Canyon
Spokane, WA

70. SunRidge Canyon
Fountain Hills, AZ

71. Copperhead (Innisbrook)
Tarpon Springs, FL

72. Edgewood Tahoe
Stateline, NV

73. High Pointe
Williamsburg, MI

74. Meadow Valleys (Blackwolf Run)
Kohler, WI

75. Mountain Course (Ventana Canyon)
Tucson, AZ

76. Jackson Hole
Jackson, WY

77. Missouri Bluffs
St. Charles, MO

78. Heather (Boyne Highlands)
Harbor Springs, MI

79. Dunmaglas
Charlevoix, MI

80. Tokatee
Blue River, OR

81. Robert Trent Jones (Treetops)
Gaylord, MI

82. Greenbrier Course
White Sulphur Springs, WV

83. Elk Ridge
Atlanta, MI

84. Breckenridge GC
Breckenridge, CO

85. Crumpin-Fox
Bernardston, MA

86. Keystone Ranch
Dillon, CO

87. Gold Course (Sagamore Resort)
Bolton Landing, NY

88. Samoset
Rockport, ME

89. Shaker Hills
Harvard, MA

90. Sherling/Canyon (RTJ-Cambrian Ridge)
Greenville, AL

91. The Challenge at Manele
Lanai, HI

92. Walking Stick
Pueblo, CO

93. East Course (The Broadmoor)
Colorado Springs, CO

94. Emerald Dunes
W. Palm Beach, FL

95. Genoa Lakes
Genoa, NV

96. Richter Park
Danbury, CT

97. Blue-Championship
New Seabury, MA

98. East/West (Sawgrass CC)
Ponte Vedra Beach, FL

99. Champions (Bryan Park)
Brown Summit, NC

100. Legend (Legend Trail)
Scottsdale, AZ

101. The Champion (PGA National)
Palm Beach, FL

102. The Monster (Concord Resort)
Kiamesha Lake, NY

103. Aviara (Four Seasons)
Carlsbad, CA

104. Eaglesticks
Zanesville, OH

105. Plantation (Pinehurst Plantation)
Pinehurst, NC

106. North Course (Mauna Lani)
Kohala Coast, HI

Section
8

107. **Taos CC**
Rancho de Taos, NM

108. **Edinburgh**
Brooklyn Park, MN

109. **La Purisima**
Lompoc, CA

110. **Plantation/Seaside**
Sea Island, GA

111. **Pines-Lakes/Woods (Grand View)**
Nisswa, MN

112. **Links at Key Biscayne**
Key Biscayne, FL

113. **Legacy Ridge**
Westminster, CO

114. **Duke University**
Durham, NC

115. **University of Michigan**
Ann Arbor, MI

116. **Rock Hollow**
Peru, IN

117. **Old White (Greenbrier)**
White Sulphur Springs, WV

118. **Teton Pines**
Jackson, WY

119. **Raptor (Grayhawk)**
Scottsdale, AZ

120. **Burnt Pines (Sandestin Beach)**
Destin, FL

121. **Apple Rock**
Horseshoe Bay, TX

122. **The Orchards**
Washington, MI

123. **South Course (University of New Mexico)**
Albuquerque, NM

124. **Linville GC**
Linville, NC

125. **Taconic**
Williamstown, MA

126. **Blackthorn**
South Bend, IN

127. **Dunes Course (Riverdale GC)**
Brighton, CO

128. **Simi-ah-moo**
Blaine, WA

129. **TPC at The Woodlands**
Woodlands, TX

130. **Masters (Bear Creek Golf World)**
Houston, TX

131. **South Course (Eagle Ridge)**
Gelena, IL

132. **Sandpiper**
Goleta, CA

133. **Nicklaus Course (PGA West)**
La Quinta, CA

134. **Stoney Creek**
Wintergreen, VA

135. **The Bear (Grand Traverse)**
Acme, MI

136. **Pine Needles**
Southern Pines, NC

137. **Hawthorne Valley**
Snowshoe, WV

138. **South Course (La Costa Resort)**
Carlsbad, CA

139. **Canyon/Meadow (Foxhollow)**
Lakewood, CO

140. **New Course (Grand Cypress)**
Orlando, FL

141. **George W. Dunne**
Oak Forest, IL

142. **Bay Course**
Kapalua, Maui, HI

143. **Sedona Golf Resort**
Sedona, AZ

144. **Osprey Ridge (Walt Disney World)**
Lake Buena Vista, FL

145. Legend Course (Shanty Creek)
Bellaire, MI

146. Heather Glen
Little River, SC

147. Palmer Course (Geneva National)
Lake Geneva, WI

148. The Vineyard
Cincinnati, OH

149. Tide/Timber/Trail
Port Ludlow, WA

150. The Experience at Koele
Lanai City, Lanai, HI

Source: Golf-Travel.com, www.golf-travel.com/HR_Index_150Courses101to50.html.

Tips on Business Entertainment Deductions

Which Entertainment Expenses Are Not Deductible?

Certain costs are so personal in nature that they can't be deducted at all on your tax return, even if they're incurred in connection with your business. And other expenses seem distant from the business or excessive. In order to be deductible, expenses must be ordinary and necessary to your business.

Here are some expenses that you cannot deduct:

- Dues for clubs whose purpose is social, athletic, or pleasure
- Facilities used in connection with entertainment, such as an athletic facility, a hunting lodge, a yacht, a fishing camp, a swimming pool, a tennis court, or a dining room

There is an exception to this rule for businesses that provide entertainment to the general public and charge a fee for its use. For example, a fitness facility that is open to the public and charges monthly dues for its use.

- Lavish or extravagant expenses
- Excluded portion of meals and entertainment (50 percent of the total cost)

Which Entertainment Costs Are Partially Deductible?

You can deduct 50 percent of most expenses (including taxes and tips) that are normally associated with business entertainment, such as:

Entertaining customers at your place of business, a restaurant, or other location

- Attending a business convention or reception, business meeting, or business luncheon at a club

Entertainment includes any activity generally considered to provide entertainment, amusement, or recreation. Examples include entertaining guests:

- At nightclubs
- At social, athletic, and sporting clubs
- At theaters

- At sporting events
- On yachts
- On hunting, fishing, vacation, or similar trips

You can deduct 50 percent of meal expenses, whether or not the meal is part of other entertainment or is consumed separately. Meal expenses include the cost of food, beverages, taxes, and tips.

Good news: transportation to and from a business meal or entertainment is fully deductible.

If you're an employee or a self-employed consultant and your employer or your client reimburses you for your expenses, the 50 percent limitation is imposed on the employer or client, not on you.

You Must Prove That the Expense Is for Business

To be deductible, the expense must meet one of two tests: the directly related test or the associated test.

To pass the *directly related* test, you must show that:

- The main purpose of the combined business and entertainment was the active conduct of business.
- You engaged in business with the person during the entertainment period.
- You had more than a general expectation of getting income or some other specific business benefit at some future time.

To pass the *associated* test, you must show that:

- The entertainment is associated with your trade or business (there's a clear business purpose).
- The entertainment directly precedes or follows a substantial business discussion.

Example of Directly Related Test: A Recruiting Lunch

The main purpose is to discuss the recruit's background and experience, and to observe behavior in social situations away from the office. Usually, discussions center on the job for which the recruit is interviewing and the extent to which his or her skills will fit that job. Therefore, you have an expectation of obtaining a better understanding of the recruit's fit within your company, with the possible result of a job offer.

Example of Associated Test: A Golf Game

A sales rep meets with potential customers in the morning and then accompanies his prospects for a round of golf in the afternoon. The golf is associated with the rep's trade or business because the purpose is to establish a personal relationship with the customer in order to facilitate doing business in the future. It also directly follows a substantial business discussion (the sales meeting in the morning).

You do not have to discuss business during the entertainment, to pass the associated test. But you or your employee must be present when the food or beverages appear.

Some Limits

You do not need to make sure that the time spent in business is equal to or greater than the time spent entertaining.

If you entertain both business and non-business individuals at the same time, you must allocate the cost between the two. For example, you host a barbeque for four business customers and five personal friends. You are allowed a deduction related to 5/10 (one-half) of your barbeque expenses.

If you purchase tickets for an entertainment event, you can deduct only the face value of those tickets. If you pay more than the face value, the excess is nondeductible, unless you are participating in a fundraiser for a charitable organization where the entire proceeds go to the charitable organization and volunteers perform substantially all the event's work.

If you rent a skybox or other private luxury box for more than one event at the same sports arena in the same year, you generally can't deduct more than the price of a non-luxury box seat ticket multiplied by the number of people attending the events. If food and beverages are separately stated in the price of the skybox, you can deduct these expenses in addition to the cost of the skybox (subject to the 50 percent limitation).

You generally can't deduct entertainment expenses for spouses of customers. However, you can deduct these costs if you can show that you had a clear business purpose rather than a personal or social purpose for providing the entertainment. If your spouse attends the entertainment because the customer's spouse is also attending, your spouse's expenses are also deductible.

Which Entertainment Costs Are Fully Deductible?

Certain costs are not considered entertainment and are fully deductible if they are ordinary and necessary business expenses.

- Transportation costs are fully deductible if they are business related.
- Reimbursed costs are fully deductible by you, but when you take the deduction, you must also include your reimbursements in your taxable income.
- Costs incurred in providing food that is available to the general public can be deducted.
- If you sell meals or entertainment in your business, the associated cost is deductible.

How Should I Calculate and Deduct These Costs?

You should first reduce your entertainment costs by the nondeductible part of the expenses (for example, the lavish or extravagant expenses). Then deduct 50 percent of the cost.

Take the deduction on the form or schedule where you deduct your other business expenses. For example, self-employed individuals report their entertainment expenses

Section 8

on Form 1040, Schedule C, Profit or Loss from Business. If the expenses relate to a rental, the expenses are reported on Form 1040, Schedule E, Supplemental Income & Loss.

Source: TurboTax.com, www.turbotax.com/articles/DeductingBusinessEntertainment-Expenses.html.

Building Rapport

Section 8

SCORE's Five Tips for Pleasing Customers

1. Teach employees to answer the phone with smiles on their faces. Phone experts say that customers will hear the smile in the employees' voices.

2. Hire people who love people.

3. Require that employees speak clearly and slowly enough to be understood—especially on the phone. Nothing turns off customers more quickly than impatient, sullen, or indifferent employees.

4. Make sure employees have a thorough understanding of your products and services so they can answer customer questions.

5. Give employees leeway to meet customer needs. Does a vegetarian in your restaurant want a meatless meal? Be sure waiters know they can make substitutions.

Source: SCORE, www.score.org/business_tips.html.

SCORE's Five Tips on Building Customer Relationships

Section 8

1. Make sure your employees know that courtesy and friendliness are not enough. What customers really want is effective, efficient help.

2. Introduce your clients to your customer service representatives. Meeting a customer face-to-face instead of just on the phone can motivate employees.

3. Thank customers for their referrals. One real estate agent sends a fruit basket to clients who refer other homebuyers or sellers to him.

4. Encourage employees to go the extra mile. One dry-cleaning employee couldn't find a customer's garment immediately because it was missing the usual identification and price information. To make up for the inconvenience, she let the customer have the order free.

5. Don't lose the human touch. If most of your business is done via technology, you have to try even harder to make customers feel valued.

Source: SCORE, www.score.org/business_tips.html.

SCORE's Five Tips on Getting to Know Your Customers

1. Determine what you need to know. For example, what do they like or dislike about your product or service? How do they feel about the way your company handles complaints? Are they repeat customers? Why or why not?

2. Use one or more survey methods to measure customer satisfaction, such as direct mail, telephone calls, or focus groups (groups of six to ten people who share their ideas about your product or service).

3. Hire an outside market research firm to develop questions and interpret findings, unless you have an experienced person in-house.

4. Have employees keep ongoing written records of customer compliments and complaints. Review these at staff meetings.

5. Once you know what your customers want, make the adjustments and improvements necessary to keep them coming back.

Source: SCORE, www.score.org/business_tips.html.

Tips for Building Rapport Before the Sales Presentation

What makes a successful sales presentation? Before you actually get down to business, build rapport with your prospect.

Section 8

- To do that, you need to do some homework. Do you have a colleague in common? Or maybe you share a passion for golf. Has the prospect's company accomplished something of note recently? Find out so the rapport is genuine.

- One you start your pitch, ask lots of questions, and make sure they require more than yes-or-no answers.

- Learn to listen. Experts say you should be listening at least 50 percent of the time.

- Once you get the sale, be sure to follow up. Send a thank-you note, call to make sure they're happy, and develop a schedule for future communications.

Source: Rieva Lesonsky, *365 Tips to Boost Your Entrepreneurial IQ.*

SCORE's Five Tips on Good Vendor Relationships

1. Get to know your suppliers. Use new technology for communication, but don't forget the personal touch of a phone conversation.

2. Consider your vendors as a part of your team and treat them as such.

3. Make sure they understand your needs and expectations.

4. Show appreciation for good service or for a new product that's just right for you.

5. Pay on time. If you can't, let your vendors know right away and work out a payment plan. That's when knowing them personally will be invaluable.

Source: SCORE, www.score.org/business_tips.html.

Making the Pitch

Section 8

Tips for Dealing with the Skeptical Consumer

It's inbred: most consumers are skeptical. So it's your job to convince your customers that they need your product or service.

1. **Acknowledge the customers' fears.** Telling them not to worry is not enough; you have to directly address their fears.

2. **Ask questions.** Too many entrepreneurs believe the customers will think this a waste of time, but you can't soothe their worries if you don't know what they are.

3. **Promise to follow up.** And make sure that you keep that promise. Find out how the customers would like you to stay in touch—by phone, letter, or a face-to-face meeting.

4. **Emphasize value.** Many consumers fear being overcharged. Combat this by stressing the value of your product or service.

5. **Most important, communicate.** The key to serving your customers well is to meet their expectations.

Source: Rieva Lesonsky, *365 Tips to Boost Your Entrepreneurial IQ.*

Six Common Sales Myths

Myth #1: Only Someone Who Talks a Good Game Can Sell. In reality, fast talkers don't really do very well in the world of sales. They have a bad reputation because their prospects can sense the pressure, the insincerity, and the lack of concern and compassion. A good listener will outsell a fast talker any day of the week.

Myth #2: Sales Is a Numbers Game. Sales work is about people, not numbers. It's about research, information, and relationships. No, sales is not a numbers game.

Myth #3: To Succeed in Sales, You Must Have Thick Skin. Yes, we all have to (graciously) call on internal reservoirs of strength to deal with inevitable setbacks. But that's not the same thing as developing an outer persona that is offensively aggressive.

In the name of thick skin, a lot of salespeople have adopted a persona that is, in a word, insufferable. Their attitude seems to be "I succeed, you fail, see you around!" Professional sales result in win–win situations.

Myth #4: Sales Has Its Unavoidable Ups and Downs. Sales becomes a roller coaster ride only if you let the process drive you instead of the other way around. It has ups and downs only if you don't have goals. Almost every industry is vulnerable to seasonal shifts. Like most other inconveniences, these shifts can be avoided with proper planning.

Myth #5: You Have to Be Good at Handling Rejection to Be in Sales. Out of the millions of sales professionals in the United States, I'll warrant that every one of them has heard "no thanks" much more often than the average individual. Rejection is a bad thing only if you make a conscious choice not to learn anything from the situation. Otherwise, rejection is an opportunity for growth!

Myth #6: Sales Is a Dead-End Career with Little Promotional Opportunity. Did you know that 85 percent of the company leaders and entrepreneurs in America today were once salespeople? They carried sample cases, made cold calls, dialed for dollars, did product demonstrations, and handled objections. Sales is a dead-end job, all right—especially when you consider that the end may be at the very top of an organization.

Source: Tony Parinello, "6 Common Sales Myths," www.entrepreneur.com/article/0,4621,310776,00.html.

Tips for Leaving Good Voice Mails

This technology has simplified our lives, but it's also created a barrier to reaching prospects. Follow these tips to make the most of voice mail:

1. First, clearly state who you are and why they should be interested in talking to you. Then, "tease" them with the offer of some good news. This increases the odds of them returning your call.

2. Be polite, but don't sound condescending. Use the words "please" or the phrase "I'd appreciate it if you would call me."

3. Use a fax in conjunction with your voice-mail message. Either have your fax remind them to check their voice mail for an important message or leave a message that you'll be faxing them with items of interest.

4. When you call, leave your phone number twice, one at the beginning and again at the end of the call. Practice saying your number slowly enough to be understood.

Source: Rieva Lesonsky, *365 Tips to Boost Your Entrepreneurial IQ.*

Crafting Your 15-Second Elevator Speech

Here are two big mistakes you can make when you are put on the spot.

Trap 1: The Laundry List. The most common of the two traps is to try and list every product and service you provide. Here's your solution. Like everything else in branding, your 15-second elevator speech should convey the essence of what you do, not just be a descriptive phrase. It should stress the benefits of what you provide, not the features.

You should look for the solution or benefits your products and services provide and then figure out how you can sum that up in two to three sentences.

Trap 2: The Sweeping Statement. Once you realize the laundry list approach doesn't work, you may be tempted to simply summarize. Make it a goal to develop a one- to two-sentence statement that sums up the benefits of what your company offers. Avoid dry, purely descriptive statements. Instead, go for the "wow" factor. What is it you do that your customers truly appreciate, demand, and are willing to pay top dollar to obtain? To help you figure that out, think of the last customer you had who just raved about your products or services.

Source: Phil Davis, "Crafting Your 15-Second Elevator Speech," www.entrepreneur.com/article/ 0,4621,321578,00.html.

SCORE's Five Tips for Finding Your First Customer

1. Define the types of businesses or industries you want to serve, and how your new business can help them. This should be an integral part of your business plan.

2. Go where your prospective customers are. Many trade and professional groups are open to vendors such as you. This creates opportunities for spreading your name through advertising and face-to-face networking.

3. Position yourself as an expert by writing brief articles on issues that affect your prospective customers. Offer them free of charge to newspapers and trade publications. Be sure to follow their editorial guidelines and focus on providing helpful information, not making a sales pitch.

4. Offer your services to local community and charitable groups. You get free visibility in return for your pro bono work, and your fellow volunteers may prove to be potential customers.

5. Network with other businesses in your industry or specialty. They may need help with backlogs and overflow business, or with specialized services they're unable to offer.

Source: SCORE, www.score.org/business_tips.html.

Hot Sales Tips and Secrets

Need some hot sales tips? Sales expert and author Barry Farber shares his top sales secrets.

- Farber says customers expect you to know their business—and their competition—as well as you know your own. Use annual reports, trade publications, chamber of commerce directories, and prospects' own marketing materials for research.

- Answer objections with words like "feel." Farber says not to argue when a prospect says, "I'm not interested." Instead, say, "I understand how you feel," and explain your company's advantages and ask for an appointment.

- Once you've made a sale, ask for feedback. Farber advises new entrepreneurs to ask prospects, "What do I need to do to maintain and grow our relationship?"

- Even if your clients have complaints, always give clients the chance to let you solve the problem.

Source: Rieva Lesonsky, *365 Tips to Boost Your Entrepreneurial IQ.*

Common Mistakes When Writing Pitch Letters

As an entrepreneur, you'll probably have to write hundreds of pitch letters. Here's what not to include:

- **Overly solicitous greetings:** Try to stick with "Dear." It may not be original, but it's not silly or clichéd.

- **Exaggerations:** Don't send your prospects a snow job; you're sure to lose credibility if you do. Try to say something nice about the prospect's business, but strive to be believable.

- **Dramatic punctuation:** Don't overuse exclamation points, underlines, italics, and bold typefaces. And limit your use of fonts; remember: it's a letter, not an ad.

- **Too much information:** Don't waste prospects' time giving them data they don't need. Tell prospects what you can do for them and why they should chose you instead of a competitor.

- **Odd closings:** Keep it simple, not desperate. You are, after all, trying to sound sincere.

Source: Rieva Lesonsky, *365 Tips to Boost Your Entrepreneurial IQ.*

Four Tips for Winning Sales Letters

1. **Pretend you're the customer.** Imagine yourself as the reader of your letter, and write what the customer wants to know, not what you want to say.

2. **Organize your letter.** Good sales letters need an introduction, a body, and a conclusion. First, tell why you're sending the letter. Then make your sales pitch in the body of the letter, and bring all your points together at the end.

3. **Make it easy to read.** Write conversationally, using short sentences and paragraphs. And edit and re-edit your letter. Typos and grammatical errors destroy your credibility.

4. Most important, ask your readers to take action. State what you want them to do, whether it's to call, visit, or send for more information.

Source: Rieva Lesonsky, *365 Tips to Boost Your Entrepreneurial IQ.*

Tips for Becoming a Good Listener

It's important to let people you're talking to know you really heard them. Here are some techniques you can use:

1. Don't just nod your head. Ask pertinent questions that allow the talker to expand or clarify what he or she is saying.

2. Resist the natural temptation to make your point when the other person is still making theirs. If you're busy thinking about what you're going to say next, you're probably not really listening.

3. If it's appropriate, take notes. This physically demonstrates that you're paying attention.

4. If follow-up attention is required, don't forget to do so in a timely manner.

Finally, it may help to think of it this way: listening is something you do for yourself; hearing is something you do for the other person.

Source: Rieva Lesonsky, *365 Tips to Boost Your Entrepreneurial IQ.*

Section
8

Tips for Developing a Closing-the-Deal Handshake

Here's something most entrepreneurs don't even think about, but it can make a big difference in how you're perceived. It's your handshake, and here's some info about it:

- Experts say how you shake hands says a lot about who you are and how you feel about yourself.

- To send a positive message, extend your hand with the thumb up and open. Wrap your fingers around the other person's hand and shake once or twice from the elbow, not the shoulder. This results in a firm handshake that it is neither too weak nor too strong.

- At networking events, make sure you keep your right hand free so you'll always be ready to shake hands. That means carrying your briefcase or purse in your left hand. At cocktail parties, hold your glass in your left hand, so your right one doesn't get cold or wet.

- In our culture, handshakes mean a lot. Make sure you do it every time you're introduced to someone and at the beginning and end of every meeting.

Source: Rieva Lesonsky, *365 Tips to Boost Your Entrepreneurial IQ.*

25 Super Sales Secrets

1. **Sell benefits, not features.** The biggest mistake entrepreneurs make is in focusing on what their product or service is. Rather, it's what it does that's important, according to Brian Tracy, president of Brian Tracy International in Solana Beach, California, and the author of several books, including *Advanced Selling Strategies* and *Great Little Book on Successful Selling*. Tracy advises, "Always concentrate on how your product will benefit your customer."

2. **Sell to the people most likely to buy.** Your best prospects have a keen interest in your product or service and the financial resources to purchase it. They are the ones who will buy most quickly.

3. **Differentiate your product.** Why should a customer buy from you and not from your competitor? Come up with at least three features that will give a customer reason to buy from you.

4. **Get face to face.** Spending huge sums of money on print-media advertising or direct mail is one of the least effective ways for first-time entrepreneurs to build up their business. There is no shortcut to the personal approach. Get one-on-one with your customer—if not in person, at least by phone.

5. **Focus on the second sale.** Nearly 85 percent of all sales are produced by word of mouth. They're the result of someone telling a friend or associate to buy a product or service because the customer was satisfied. Ask yourself, "Will this be such a satisfactory experience that my customer will buy from me again or tell his or her friends?"

6. **Build rapport.** Before discussing business, build rapport with your prospect. To build rapport, do some homework. Find out if you have a colleague in common. Has the prospect's company been in the news lately? Is he or she interested in sports?

7. **Ask a broad range of questions.** Ask questions that require more than a "yes" or "no" response, and that deal with more than just costs, price, procedures, and the technical aspects of the prospect's business. Most importantly, ask questions that will reveal the prospect's motivation to purchase, his or her problems and needs, and his or her decision-making processes. Don't be afraid to ask a client why he or she feels a certain way.

8. **Probe deeper.** If a prospect tells you, "We're looking for cost savings and efficiency," will you immediately tell him how your product meets his need for cost savings and efficiency? A really smart salesperson won't, says Linda Richardson, president of The Richardson Company, a leadership- and sales-training company in Philadelphia, and author of *Stop Telling, Start Selling: Using Customer Focus Dialogue to Close Sales*. He or she will ask more questions and probe deeper: "I understand why that is important. Can you give me a specific example?" Richardson suggests, "Ask for more infor-

mation so you can better position your product and show you understand the client's needs."

9. **Learn to listen.** Salespeople who do all the talking during a presentation not only bore the prospect, but also generally lose the sale. You should be listening at least 50 percent of the time. You can improve your listening skills by taking notes, observing your prospect's body language, not jumping to conclusions, and concentrating on what your prospect is saying.

10. **Follow up.** Write thank-you notes, call the customer after the sale to make sure he or she is satisfied, and maintain a schedule of future communications. "You have to be in front of that client and always show attention and responsiveness," Richardson says. "Follow-up is critical."

11. **Write out your sales presentation.** Making a sales "isn't something you do on the fly," warns Shari Posey, president of Executive Insights, an audio-tape production company in Long Beach, California. Think about the six major selling points of your product or service. Develop leading questions to probe your customer's reactions and needs to each selling point.

12. **Write down objections.** Show your prospects you are truly listening to what they are saying by writing down their objections. In this way, you can specifically answer their objections by showing how they will benefit from your product or service. It could be, for instance, by saving money, raising productivity, increasing employee motivation, or increasing their company's name recognition.

13. **Offer a first-time incentive.** Offer your prospect something significant, so if they do like your product or service, they'll be inclined to make a decision now, rather than wait a few days or put off the decision indefinitely. First-time incentives might include "Ten percent off with your purchase today" or "With today's purchase, you'll receive one free hour of consultation."

14. **Offer a 100-percent guarantee.** Let your customers know their satisfaction is guaranteed. "A good return policy minimizes customer objections and shows that you believe in your product or service," says Posey. Product guarantees should be unconditional and should not include hidden clauses, like "guaranteed for only 30 days." You can use a guarantee even if you're selling a service: "Satisfaction guaranteed. You'll be thrilled with our service or we'll redo it at our expense."

15. **Close with two choices.** Rather than ask, "How does this sound?" give your prospect a choice. For example, if you're selling educational books to preschool owners, ask if they want to purchase the book series or the book and tape series together. When they state their choice, write the order. "Your prospect is not likely to stop you," Posey explains, "because mentally they realize they've committed and they've said 'yes.'"

16. **Target your material toward a specific audience.** These days, it's not possible to understand and meet the needs of every potential customer. Show you are a specialist. "You have a selling advantage and come across as believable when your sales

Section 8

materials are tightly targeted to specific audiences," according to Bob Bly, an independent copywriter and consultant in Dumont, New Jersey, and the author of *The Copywriter's Handbook*.

17. **Use testimonials.** People might not believe your product or service can do what you say it will. You can overcome this disbelief by having a past or present customer praise you and your company. Testimonials are usually written in the customer's own words, are surrounded by quotation marks, and are attributed to the individual. They can be used in sales letters, brochures, and advertisements.

18. **Write from the customer's point of view.** "Start your copy with something that engages the prospect, and what most people are interested in is themselves," Bly advises. The agency would get better results if it wrote something that directly interests the prospect. "That's something business owners who provide benefits to their employees can relate to."

19. **Use questions.** A great way to engage your prospect is to pose questions in the headlines of your sales literature. "Every car-wash owner should know these seven business-success secrets. Do you?" Or, "Why haven't satellite-dish owners been told these facts?"

20. **Turn a negative into a positive.** If you are new in business and haven't sold many products or signed up many clients for your services, don't despair. You can phrase your situation this way: "Not one widget buyer in a thousand has ever experienced the advantages of this new XYZ widget."

21. **Know your customers' business.** Customers expect you to know their business, customers, and competition as well as you know your own product or service. Study your customer's industry. Know its problems and trends. Find out who his or her biggest competitors are. Some research tools include the company's annual report, trade publications, chamber of commerce directories, and the company's own brochures, newsletters, and catalogs.

22. **Organize your sales presentation.** The basic structure of any sales presentation includes six key points: build rapport with your prospect, introduce the business topic, ask questions to better understand your prospect's needs, summarize your key selling points, and close the sale. "Always begin the process by first visualizing a successful outcome," says Barry J. Farber, a sales, management, and motivation speaker and author of several books, including *12 Clichés of Selling and Why They Work*.

23. **Take notes.** Don't rely on your memory to remind you of what's important to your prospect. Ask upfront if it's OK for you to take notes during your sales presentation. Write down key points you can refer to later during your presentation.

24. **Answer objections with "feel, felt, found."** Don't argue when a prospect says, "I'm not interested," "I just bought one," or "I don't have time right now." Simply say, "I understand how you feel. A lot of my present customers felt the same way. But when they found out how much time they saved by using our product, they were amazed."

Then ask for an appointment.

25. Ask for feedback. If you want to improve your sales presentation or your relations with your customers, ask them what you need to do to maintain and increase their business. "Many customers have minor complaints but will never say anything," says Farber. "They just won't buy from you again. If you ask their opinion, they'll be glad to tell you, and to give you the chance to solve the problem."

Source: Carla Goodman, "25 Super Sales Secrets" (Shari Posey, Linda Richardson, Barry Farber, Bob Bly, and Brian Tracy), www.entrepreneur.com/article/0,4621,299184–1,00.html.

Ten Laws of Sales Success

Law 1: Keep your mouth shut and your ears open. This is crucial in the first few minutes of any sales interaction. Remember:

1. Don't talk about yourself.

2. Don't talk about your products.

3. Don't talk about your services.

4. And above all, don't recite your sales pitch!

Law 2: Sell with questions, not answers. Remember this: nobody cares how great you are until they understand how great you think they are.

Forget about trying to "sell" your product or service and focus instead on why your prospect wants to buy. To do this, you need to get fascinated with your prospect; you need to ask questions (lots and lots of them) with no hidden agenda or ulterior motives.

Law 3: Pretend you're on a first date with your prospect. Get curious about them. Ask about the products and services they're already using. Are they happy? Is what they're using now too expensive, not reliable enough, too slow? Find out what they really want. Remember: you're not conducting an impersonal survey here, so don't ask questions just for the sake of asking them. Instead, ask questions that will provide you with information about what your customers really need.

Law 4: Speak to your prospect just as you speak to your family or friends. There's never any time that you should switch into "sales mode" with ham-handed persuasion clichés and tag lines. Affected speech patterns, exaggerated tones, and slow, hypnotic-sounding "sales inductions" are never acceptable in today's professional selling environments. Speak normally (and of course, appropriately), just as you would when you're around your friends and loved ones.

Law 5: Pay close attention to what your prospect isn't saying. Is your prospect rushed? Does he or she seem agitated or upset? If so, ask, "Is this a good time to talk? If it's not, perhaps we can meet another day." Most salespeople are so concerned with what they're going to say next that they forget there's another human being involved in the conversation.

Law 6: If you're asked a question, answer it briefly and then move on. Remember: this isn't about you; it's about whether you're right for them.

Law 7: Only after you've correctly assessed the needs of your prospect do you mention anything about what you're offering. I knew a guy who pitched a mannequin (I'm not kidding)! He was so stuck in his own automated, habitual mode, he never bothered to notice that his prospect wasn't breathing. Don't make this mistake. Know with whom you're speaking before figuring out what it is you want to say.

Law 8: Refrain from delivering a three-hour product seminar. Don't ramble on and on about things that have no bearing on anything your prospect has said. Pick a handful of things you think could help with your prospect's particular situation, and tell him or her about it. (And if possible, reiterate the benefits in his or her own words, not yours.)

Law 9: Ask the prospect if there are any barriers to him or her taking the next logical step. After having gone through the first eight steps, you should have a good understanding of your prospect's needs in relation to your product or service. Knowing this, and having established a mutual feeling of trust and rapport, you're now ready to bridge the gap between your prospect's needs and what it is you're offering.

Law 10: Invite your prospect to take some kind of action. This principle eliminates the need for any "closing techniques" because the ball is placed on the prospect's court. A sales close keeps the ball in your court and all the focus on you, the salesperson. But you don't want the focus on you. You don't want the prospect to be reminded that he or she is dealing with a "salesperson." You're not a salesperson; you're a human being offering a particular product or service. And if you can get your prospect to understand that, you're well on your way to becoming an outstanding salesperson.

Source: Len Foley, "The 10 Laws of Sales Success," www.entrepreneur.com/article/ 0,4621,312252,00.html.

Tips on How to Get Corporate and Government Clients

Step One: Feasibility Study
It is entirely possible there are corporate entities and government agencies that could become direct customers for you. What seems even likelier is that there are suppliers to these groups that you should be seeking out as well.

- Do your homework and be direct.
- Identify up to ten diverse companies and three to four government agencies procuring minority contracts that you'd like to do business with.

- Read up on them; find out who the purchasing agents are and investigate where they post their RFPs (requests for proposals).

- Before responding, read the RFPs and learn what will be required of you.

- Write them a short e-mail or letter, or call and simply have them answer the question as to whether or not they have RFPs to respond to or what their requirements are to do business with you.

- Learn what will be expected from you in terms of meeting their demand for product, delivery, and service.

Step Two: Strategic Plan

Have a business plan or update an old business plan. Make sure all the information is current.

Step Three: Communication Tactic

The final step in the process, whether you're going solo or launching a strategic alliance, is to map out, very precisely and deliberately, a tactical plan for communication. How will you get the word out, and what is the word?

- You may want to consider focusing on one industry at a time and, within that industry, a handful of particular organizations or companies.

- You'll want to make as many impressions as you can. You want to be seen on the internet and in their industry publications. You'll also want to develop some strategic marketing letters, join their association for access to members and opportunities for exposure, and establish yourself or a company spokesperson as an expert on your topic.

Section 8

These resources will help you further:

- *How to Write an Effective Proposal to Government*: This document provides tips on writing proposals to do business with the government. (www.homebiz.ca/BIC/HowTo/lesson5.htm)

- Gtracts: This firm works with companies that are seeking opportunities for government contracts and has worked with companies to find and secure opportunities. (www.gtracts.com/events.htm)

Source: Robert Wallace, "How to Get Government and Corporate Clients," www.entrepreneur.com/article/0,4621,310810,00.html.

Improving Your Sales

Section 8

SCORE's Five Tips on Superior Customer Service

1. Educate your customers about your products and services. If you own a hobby shop, for example, you can keep customers coming back by helping them develop knowledge of their own hobbies.

2. Make sure items are delivered in good condition. Call the customer after delivery and if a piece is not right, offer to fix it or replace it.

3. Offer your customers personal attention, even if they don't buy anything. Engage them in pleasant conversation and find out why they're not buying. Make use of what you learn.

4. Go out of your way to meet customer needs. One interior designer got draperies made for a client in a hurry so they would be ready for an at-home wedding.

5. Show appreciation. Make sure employees always thank customers for their business. Consider sending occasional handwritten thank-you notes.

Source: SCORE, www.score.org/business_tips.html.

SCORE's Five Tips to Make Customers Come to You

1. Determine who your customers are and what their wants or needs are. Know how your product or service satisfies their wants or needs.

2. Instill and practice the concept of continuous quality improvement and quality customer service as a way of life in your business.

3. Make sure you select the proper medium to carry out your message and choose the proper location within that medium.

4. Direct your message to where your prospects are listening, viewing, or reading.

5. Create a forum or place of business that is unique is some way. Make customers feel different while they are doing business with you.

Source: SCORE, www.score.org/business_tips.html.

SCORE's Five Tips for Improving Sales

1. Educate your customers. Entrepreneurs whose businesses are ahead of the curve need to help customers understand the value of their products or services.

2. Put prospect identification on the front burner. Keep developing sales leads and cultivating the people or organizations most likely to become your customers.

3. Make an offer the customer can't refuse. One professional association offered $250 off on next year's annual conference if members signed up and paid now. Only $50 was not returnable if the member could not actually attend.

4. Don't give up. Persistence pays off—as long as it's friendly and helpful and not over-bearing.

5. Show customers that you are an asset to them. Prove that you can improve their businesses or enhance their lives.

Source: SCORE, www.score.org/business_tips.html.

Five Questions to Assess Your New Prospects

Don't know how much time to devote to new prospects? Try the RADAR System, developed by sales trainer Jeffrey Hansler. The key to RADAR is asking questions, and if done right, it will tell you if the prospect is worth spending time with.

Here's how RADAR works:

1. **Rapport:** Is the prospect answering any questions honestly?

2. **Acknowledged interest:** Does the prospect see that he has a problem, and is he interested in solving it?

3. **Decision:** Find out who the decision makers are.

4. **Acknowledged funds:** How much energy, time, and money is the prospect willing to invest?

5. **Risk coefficient:** Has the prospect ever purchased a similar product or service? "Yes" means the prospect has a positive risk coefficient, and you have a good chance of landing the account. If not, make sure this person is worth the extra time you're going to have to invest.

A two-minute RADAR conversation with the prospect should give you your answer.

Source: Rieva Lesonsky, *365 Tips to Boost Your Entrepreneurial IQ.*

Section 8

SCORE's Five Tips on Forecasting the Future

1. Develop meaningful sales forecasts in terms of basic business units. Predict weekly sales for the first few months and monthly sales for the first year. Consider possible scenarios, such as a ten-percent rise or fall in sales.

2. Develop profiles for your products or services, customers, and markets.

3. Know how customers will buy from you.

4. Plan how you will make your product or service available to them—wholesale, retail, direct, or internet.

5. Develop a plan or strategy to follow if your sales forecasts completely miss your predictions.

Source: SCORE, www.score.org/business_tips.html.

Hot Tips for Getting Past "No"

As an entrepreneur, you hear the word "no"—a lot. It just goes with the territory. But as the saying goes, "It's not you; it's them."

Here's some insight:

■ When prospects object to a sales pitch, it means they're afraid. They fear making a mistake or looking foolish. It's your job to help them overcome their fears.

■ Start by saying, "Let's explore your concerns." Then isolate their true objection.

Here's how:

■ **Offer them a choice.** For example, ask, "Is it the delivery time or the financing you're concerned about?"

■ **Be direct.** Find out specifically what they want to think about.

■ **Be flexible.** Every sale should end up in a win-win deal, so you may need to compromise. Waive the delivery fee, offer some additional merchandise, or provide marketing support.

■ **Keep track.** Write down the answers to the objections you hear most often so you'll be prepared with the best response.

Source: Rieva Lesonsky, *365 Tips to Boost Your Entrepreneurial IQ.*

Section 8

SCORE's Five Tips on Educating Outside Salespeople

1. Put yourself in their shoes. For example, understand what a retail clerk selling your product needs to know to help a customer.

2. Provide support materials. These can range from inexpensive fact sheets to videos that provide refresher training.

3. When a product is complicated, do on-site training with sales associates.

4. Make sure you or a knowledgeable member of your staff is available to answer questions from sales associates—via telephone or e-mail.

5. Get feedback from outside salespeople so that you can improve training as you introduce new products.

Source: SCORE, www.score.org/business_tips.html.

Seven Steps for Generating New Opportunities

Step 1: Focus on your core product. Prospects buy when they trust your value is applicable to them and believe your company is stable. Keep this statement in mind as we go through the rest of the seven steps, because internalizing this mantra is the key to a solid plan.

Step 2: Keep your pitch simple. What every company needs is a simple "elevator pitch." That's a short, concise message that can communicate your message to a prospect in 30 seconds or less. It explains the value your product or service provides so the prospect understands why it's applicable to them.

Step 3: Stay true to who you are. Knowing who you are and what gets you excited (and what bores you to tears) will help you reach your goals. Stay true to who you are and what you do best. Hand off those tasks that will blow you off course because you don't like doing them, so you don't! Stretch and grow your capabilities in alignment with your interests and expertise

Step 4: Map it. Mapping your capabilities with your target clients' needs is an excellent way for you to determine your service strategy. One common trait among many entrepreneurs is the urge to "cast a wide net" by being all things to all companies. In almost every case, however, a small business flourishes because it has a narrower service offering.

Step 5: Utilize marketing tools that work best for you. When deciding on a marketing strategy, implement one that fits your personality and the customers you serve. Identify the top two marketing tools you've used in the past that have worked for your company. Decide what will yield the best return on your efforts. Each tool should lead to a revenue-producing result in one way or another.

Step 6: Implement a plan of action. Establish goals that can be reviewed at three and six months. At incremental points within each three-month period, keep checking your plan to see if you're meeting your goals

Step 7: Exercise the plan. Just do it: complete the daily actions, and then do something extra to accelerate your success plan. If you approach your plan and get butterflies in your stomach, either get over it or substitute an action that you're comfortable with so you stay on course. Don't let unplanned tasks waste precious time that should be applied toward reaching your goal.

Source: Linda Kazares, "7 Steps for Generating New Business Opportunities," www.entrepreneur.com/article/0,4621,311646,00.html.

Seven Ways to Boost Online Sales During the Holidays

1. **Communicate with past customers.** While the explosion of spam has reduced the open rates for some types of solicitations, e-mail campaigns to in-house lists are still top producers. November is a great time to send e-mail to your opt-in list of customers and prospects. For best results, it should be instantly recognizable as coming from you, a valued source of information.

2. **Be easy to find.** If you're not already using pay-per-click advertising on the major search engines, this may be an excellent time to start. And if you're a veteran of paid search, consider adding additional keyword pairs, participating in local search opportunities, and fine-tuning your ads.

3. **Advertise your site.** To build holiday traffic, place ads on sites that reach your best prospects. To maximize click-through rates, look for ad units (not necessarily banners) that are surrounded by editorial. And to increase sales from those who respond to your ads, direct click-through to specific landing pages where shoppers can find exactly what they're looking for, instead of your main page.

4. **Deepen your content.** Product research is a top priority, particularly for female shoppers online. Take time now to add in-depth content, from product reviews, photographs, size charts, and maps to pages on your company background and executive bios. It's essential to have enough information on your site to persuade shoppers to complete their transactions there—rather than move on to other sites to further their research.

5. **Make shopping easy.** Saving time and convenience are two of the primary reasons shoppers use the internet. So visitors to your site must find what they're looking for quickly and easily. Adding an on-site search facility has been shown to prompt consumers to buy more often and spend more per purchase. Also, offer quick checkout for repeat buyers and consider adding live online customer service during peak hours so customers with questions can have them answered immediately—while they're actively shopping on your site.

6. **Reduce cart abandonment.** Most shopping carts are abandoned because of "surprises" such as added tax and shipping costs, which are factored into the price of a product only once a user makes the decision to buy. To eliminate this problem, simply supply these prices upfront. You may even choose to offer free shipping, which has proven to be a strong sales incentive. Offering multiple payment options can also translate to more sales

7. **Protect customers' privacy.** Keeping personal information secure is a top priority for many online shoppers. Is your privacy policy displayed prominently on your site? For maximum sales this holiday season, it pays to reassure customers that the personal information they choose to share with you will be used only to enhance their shopping experience.

Source: Kim T. Gordon, "Ring up Holiday Sales," www.entrepreneur.com/article/0,4621,317378,00.html.

Seven Ways to Turn a Profit Online

There are seven ways to generate revenue on the web:

1. **Sell your own products.** The main advantage to selling your own products is that you ultimately control how much profit you make on every sale and you therefore have the potential for the biggest profit margin. You know exactly what each product costs, and you can try out different price points to see what works the best.

2. **Sell your own services.** It's easy to get started selling a service online, but your revenue potential, in most cases, is limited. When you sell a service, you're essentially selling a relationship with yourself. And this requires that you spend more time and effort establishing your credibility and developing rapport with your visitors than is typically required on a site selling a physical product.

3. **Drop ship products.** Drop shipping lets you sell quality, brand-name products on your site for a hefty profit, while the drop shipper takes care of fulfilling the order. They warehouse the stock, pack the orders, and ship them out to your customers.

4. **Recommend affiliate products.** As one of the company's "affiliates" or promotion partners, you earn a commission each time someone you've referred to their site makes a purchase. To advertise their wares, you might post a banner on your site that links to the affiliate program's site, or you might publish an article about the company and its products in your newsletter.

5. **Sell ad space.** Once your site has lots of highly targeted traffic or a large, targeted opt-in list, you may be able to sell advertising. Advertisers are willing to buy ads when they're being directed at large numbers of their target market. Selling ad space can be a great additional profit stream, but it's unlikely to keep your business afloat on its own.

6. **Create a joint venture with like-minded businesses.** Joint ventures are all about related businesses teaming up and combining skills, products, services, and resources to create new streams of income and profit. One great way to profit through joint ventures is to seek out products or services that would benefit your visitors, and then approach the companies that provide those products or services.

7. **Start an affiliate program.** With your own affiliate program, you can recruit an army of people (your affiliates) who will recommend your product on their web site for a percentage of any sale they refer. You have the power to exponentially increase your income as more and more affiliates sign up and you continue to teach your existing affiliates how to increase their commission checks (and your income).

Source: Corey Rudl, "7 Ways to Turn a Profit Online," www.entrepreneur.com/article/0,4621,309042,00.html.

Sales Calls

Section 8

Tips on How to Do Your Homework Before You Call

What's the biggest sales mistake entrepreneurs make? Most entrepreneurs don't do their homework. Here are some tips:

- Research, says Brian Tracy, one of the nation's best sales trainers, is critical to successful selling.
- Before you do business with someone, you have to understand his or her business. Only then will you be prepared to meet his or her needs.
- Research is not as intimidating as it used to be. Tracy recommends you turn first to the internet.
- The internet is a powerful tool that makes it almost easy to dig for information about companies and their industries.
- If you're not "net adept," try the library. Or simply call the company directly.
- How you choose to research the companies you are going to call is not important; just make sure you do it.

Source: Rieva Lesonsky, *365 Tips to Boost Your Entrepreneurial IQ.*

SCORE's Five Tips on Ways to Sell Your Products or Services

1. Try direct mail. Buying or renting a good mailing list helps you reach the people most interested in your product.
2. Partner with another business and sell each other's products or services. If you're a caterer, for example, join forces with a wedding planner.
3. Use your web site as a marketing tool. Sell items directly on the site or use the site to educate customers about your product or service.
4. Test coupons—in the Yellow Pages, in your local newspaper, or on your web site. Or, participate in a cooperative direct mail program like those offered by Val-Pak, Carol Wright, and other advertisers.
5. Offer a seminar and use it to sell—such as a cooking class if you make food products, or a meeting on long-term care insurance if you are a financial planner.

Source: SCORE, www.score.org/business_tips.html.

Tips on Using the National "Do Not Call" Registry

Who must access the registry?

- Sellers: people selling directly to consumers via telephone
- Telemarketers: people who call consumers on behalf of sellers
- Service providers: people who provide assistance to sellers and telemarketers (such as list brokers and service bureaus)

Please note: Exempt organizations, such as non-profits, charities, pollsters, and certain others, may voluntarily access the registry but aren't required to do so.

Must I register, even if I don't make cold calls?

Yes! Many companies that don't make cold calls mistakenly believe the regulations don't pertain to them. What they don't realize is that the regulation covers past customers. Under the new law, companies are allowed to call past customers for only 18 months after the conclusion of business, unless the customer gives written permission to the company to continue calling them. Also, unless a business relationship is established or written permission obtained, companies are permitted to call consumers for only 90 days after the consumers have contacted the companies with an inquiry about their products or services. There's also a provision for penalizing companies that call consumers, even if they're not on the list, if the company hasn't signed up to access the registry but is required to do so.

What does it cost to access the registry?

Registration, as well as access to up to five area codes, is free. After that, the annual cost is $25 per area code, up to a maximum of $7,375 annually for the entire U.S. database. (Incidentally, the registry covers all 50 states, the District of Columbia, Puerto Rico, the U.S. Virgin Islands, Guam, North Mariana Islands, American Samoa, and all toll-free numbers.)

What are the fines for noncompliance?

Fines of up to $11,000 per call can be levied against companies that don't comply.

Where can I go for help and information?

For more information on regulations and frequently asked questions and to sign up for access to the registry, there are two web sites you can access. There's also an e-mail help desk. The two sites provide plenty of useful information, although some links are in legalese. Spanish translations are available by clicking the "En Español" link on each site.

- The official government site is https://www.donotcall.gov. To register your company, click on the link for Sellers and Telemarketers (https://telemarketing.donotcall.gov). (You may also call this toll-free number, 888 382-1222, from the number you wish to register.)
- The Federal Trade Commission's web site (www.ftc.gov/bcp/rulemaking/tsr/index.html) also provides detailed information about the Do Not Call registry.

Section 8

Now that we've covered some basics, let's discuss how to make the registry work for you. Several obvious options emerge for companies that must deal with this law and its ramifications:

1. Ignore the list and call everyone.

2. Stop prospecting by telephone and call no one, whether they're on the list or not.

3. Check the list and call only those who aren't listed. This option assumes that you either won't prospect those listed via any method or will just send them standard mailing pieces.

Let's examine the first three options to see how a fourth is unique—and preferable.

Option 1: Ignore the list and call everyone. If a consumer is adamant about not being called at home, why would a company think its call is welcome? Choosing this option tells potential customers you don't care about them. Additionally, you can be fined pretty heavily if consumers report you.

Option 2: Stop prospecting by telephone and call no one, whether they're on the list or not. Not every consumer is listed on the registry, so if a consumer doesn't mind being called at home, why wouldn't a company call? The registry can actually be used to screen out non-customers, saving you time and money by helping you contact only those people predisposed to talk to salespeople by telephone. While this option won't hurt your reputation, it definitely hurts sales.

Option 3: Check the list and call only those not listed. This option respects consumers' wishes while taking advantage of the opportunity to sell to those willing to accept calls. However, this option doesn't differentiate you in any way from your competition and it doesn't inform those on the list that their wishes were respected.

Option 4: Check the list and call only those not listed. In addition, create a special campaign to contact those who are listed. This option offers all the benefits of Option 3, plus one more. Ask yourself this question: If a consumer on the list doesn't get a call from you, how does he know you're respecting his wishes? If you simply ignore him or send him standard mailings, he doesn't know that you're going out of your way to follow his no-contact request. Furthermore, you look just like everyone else sending out mailings, the amount of which will certainly increase due to this law. Send out a mailing to consumers on the list that clearly states:

"We saw your name on the Do Not Call registry and respect your wishes. We will not call you. However, we do have a valuable service that you may be interested in. If you'd like to do business with a company that respects your wishes even before we begin working together, PLEASE CALL US. We would love to help you with all your (fill in your company's product or services) needs."

Source: Sandy Geroux, "What You Really Need to Know About the National 'Do Not Call' Registry," www.entrepreneur.com/article/0,4621,312090,00.html.

Advice for Improving Cold Calls

No one really likes to make cold calls, but for most startup entrepreneurs, they're a necessary evil. Follow these smart steps to turn your cold calls into hot sales:

- Analyze your feelings and realize fear is usually the anticipation of negative results. So instead of thinking about possible rejection, think about the business you'll gain if you make the sale.

- Develop a market focus. Your calls are more likely to result in sales if you target folks who have an interest in your product or service—and the money to pay for it.

- Don't sell your products or service; sell its benefits. Show people what you can do for them, and they're more likely to buy.

- Be a good listener. In fact, listen more than you talk. This way, you'll learn what the prospect's needs really are and how you can fill them.

- Learn to accept "no." Not everyone wants what you're selling. Don't take the rejection personally—just make the next call.

Source: Rieva Lesonsky, *365 Tips to Boost Your Entrepreneurial IQ.*

Tips on Conquering Your Fear of Cold-Calling

One of the most common sales fears is the fear of cold-calling. If this fear plagues you, too, here's how to overcome it.

First, you need to understand that if someone doesn't buy from you, he or she is not rejecting you; the person is just turning down your ideas. Don't take rejection personally.

When you're ready to make a sales call, remember these three key facts:

1. Believe in your product or service. If you truly do, you shouldn't hesitate to interrupt someone to tell them about it. Think of your call as the chance to help someone benefit from your solution.

2. Don't overprepare. It's better to just take the plunge and make the call. You can't answer the potential customer's objections if you don't have the chance to hear them.

3. Maintain a winning attitude. Remember, if you don't expect to be successful, you won't be.

Source: Rieva Lesonsky, *365 Tips to Boost Your Entrepreneurial IQ.*

SCORE's Five Tips for Great Telephone Customer Service

1. Never let the telephone ring more than twice before answering. The last thing a customer wants to do is wait, no matter how routine the call may be. Greet your caller in a warm, professional manner.

2. Document everything that happens with the customer's call, including time and date; a description of the question, problem, or request; actions taken; and any follow-up contact. Keep the information on file, particularly for your regular customers.

3. If you're short of time and the service call is not urgent, politely explain the situation to the customer and get his or her contact information, including a convenient time when you can call back and discuss the issue at length.

4. If you need to use automated answering system, your customer service line should be one of the first options. Limit any subsequent menus for routing calls by specifying as few selection options as possible.

5. Always follow up with the customer to make sure the issue was addressed to his or her satisfaction. You may receive some valuable suggestions for improving your service or—even better—a happy customer who will refer your business to others.

Source: SCORE, www.score.org/business_tips.html.

Advice on Sales Pitching and Active Listening

Many people mistakenly believe that to be a good salesperson, you need to be a good talker. On the contrary, you need to be a good listener. The hardest part is fighting your instinct to jabber away when you should be keeping your mouth closed and your ears open. Here are three smart tips to improve your listening skills:

1. Follow the 70/30 Rule. Listen 70 percent of the time, and talk the remaining 30 percent.

2. Don't interrupt. It is usually tempting to interrupt because you feel you need to say something vitally important. Before you speak, ask yourself if what you're about to say is really necessary at that very moment.

3. Ask a question—and then shut up! This forces you to listen. You can practice by pretending to be a TV interviewer.

Remember, the key to sales is finding out what your prospects problems are and then offering solutions. The best way—and the only way—to do that is to listen.

Source: Rieva Lesonsky, *365 Tips to Boost Your Entrepreneurial IQ.*

# Chapter 55

Sales Presentations and Meetings

Section 8

Recommended PowerPoint® Tips and Techniques

1. Start with the end in mind.
2. Use the AutoContent Wizard to help you figure out what to say.
3. Stick with what works. Use a template.
4. Use the Outline view to write content quickly.
5. Use images to liven things up.
6. Present your data in a chart.
7. Create your own template for repeated presentations.
8. Color-coordinate your materials.
9. Make your presentation available on the web.
10. Practice, practice, practice. Use Rehearse Timings.

For more info on how to use PowerPoint, visit www.Extras4PowerPoint.com.

Source: Katherine Murray, "10 Tips for Creating Effective Presentations in PowerPoint 2002," www.microsoft.com/office/previous/xp/columns/column08.asp.

Ten Reasons to Plan a Business Event

1. **Grand Openings**—A grand opening is one of the best reasons to stage a special event. No one thinks twice about why you're blowing your own horn. What you do want them to think about is what a great time they had at your event.

2. **Entertainment**—Just keep in mind that the novelties and entertainment shouldn't last so long or be so distracting that no one finds the time or inclination to do business with you. Think of these events as the appetizer, with your product or service as the main course.

3. **Novelty Attractions**—Time, space, and popular appeal are three things to consider if and when you host or sponsor a one-time special attraction.

4. **Holidays**—Some of the most common and easily developed special events are based on holidays or times of year. For example, during the Christmas season, Santa's Workshop can be found in thousands of communities, not just the North Pole.

5. **Seasons**—When planning an event tied to a holiday or season, make originality your motto.

6. **Celebrity Appearances**—Celebrities don't have to be nationally known names. Think about local celebrities in your community who might be willing to be part of your special event.

7. **Co-sponsoring**—You can partner with complementary businesses to host an event, or you can take part as a sponsor of an established charity or public cause. Sporting events, fairs, and festivals have proved to be popular event choices with good track records for achieving companies' marketing goals.

8. **Anniversary Celebrations**—Staying in business for a number of years is something to be proud of, so why not share the achievement with others?

9. **Games**—Be sure your prizes are first-rate and that you get the word out in a timely and professional manner.

10. **Contests**—From naming a mascot to guessing the number of jelly beans in a jar, contests are a proven means of attracting attention.

Source: "Special Events," www.entrepreneur.com/article/0,4621,268962,00.html, from Rieva Lesonsky, *Start Your Own Business*.

Choosing Your Words During a Presentation

Every time you speak, you have a chance to make or break your business. That's why it's so important to choose your words with care. So says Donald Weiss, author of *Why Didn't I Say That?*, who recommends the following:

- Eliminate the "ahs" and "uhs" from our vocabulary. They make the speaker sound unsure and ill at ease.

- Use active sentences, such as "We need to fix this now!" instead of the more passive "This is in need of some attention."

- Be aware that how people speak is just as important as what they say.

- Don't talk too loudly—or too fast. People are more apt to listen when spoken to in a relatively slow, lower tone of voice.

- Be aware of how you sound. Powerful speech patterns can strengthen your image and influence.

Source: Rieva Lesonsky, *365 Tips to Boost Your Entrepreneurial IQ*.

Six Tips for Your Sales Presentations

Even using the most sophisticated presentation technology won't help you make the sale if you haven't polished your presentation skills. Here are six smart ways to come across like a pro:

1. **Stay loose.** If you feel tight, you'll likely come across as cold or unsure of yourself.

2. **Connect with your audience.** Make sure you talk to them in terms they understand.

Watch them, and address their concerns on the spot.

3. **Use body language to project confidence.** Stand or sit solidly, don't sway or waver, but don't be stiff either.

4. **Speak up.** Make sure your tone conveys conviction and authority. And don't forget to project so listeners can clearly hear you.

5. **Don't hide your passion.** Your enthusiasm and energy will help you make your case. And clients want to know you will feel strongly on their behalf.

6. **Most important, relax—and don't forget to smile.** Remember, you are communicating with real people who are seeking to make a connection with you In other words, be yourself.

Source: Rieva Lesonsky, *365 Tips to Boost Your Entrepreneurial IQ.*

Tips to Make Great Presentation Materials

You're about to make a big presentation. You're ready, but are your materials? Here's how to make sure everything comes together:

1. **Don't overdo it.** If you use every flying bullet and unique effect that comes with your presentation software, you'll drive your audience crazy. For maximum impact, keep these features to a minimum. Remember: you don't want to distract your viewers.

2. **Think big.** Display text in at least 24-point type. Use serif fonts for large titles only; use sans serif in the main body of your presentation.

3. **Be organized.** Every presentation needs some kind of structure. One basic yet effective structure includes an introduction or agenda, key point, a closing, and some recommendations.

4. **Spell it out.** Avoid just making statistics—tell your audience exactly what they mean.

Source: Rieva Lesonsky, *365 Tips to Boost Your Entrepreneurial IQ.*

Tips for Preparing a Meeting with Prospective Clients

Meetings—everyone hates them, but you can't grow your business without them. Here's how to prepare for an effective meeting with sales prospects:

- **Do your homework.** Find out what the prospects' needs are before you meet with them. Then make a list of all the ways your product or service can benefit them.

- **Set realistic goals.** Meeting costs can easily add up to hundreds of dollars. So make sure each meeting moves the prospects closer to a positive buying decision.

- **Prepare quality materials.** You need a coordinated package of professional-looking printed materials, including business cards, letterhead, brochures, and other presentation tools. Make sure your materials not only look good, but are also well-written.

- **Rehearse your presentation.** Practice how you'll use your materials, particularly if you're doing a computer presentation.

Source: Rieva Lesonsky, *365 Tips to Boost Your Entrepreneurial IQ.*

15 Tips for Becoming a Great Speaker

1. **Give yourself plenty of time to prepare.** Too many people wait until the last minute to work on their speeches, and once they've finished writing their rough drafts, they have no time to edit and revise.

2. **Organize your thoughts.** A good speech is built on an intriguing introduction, a substantive body, and a memorable conclusion. If you use generalized statements, be sure to follow them with specific examples and facts. Supporting your points with evidence, anecdotes, and data strengthens your message and reinforces your position as an expert.

3. **Be a ruthless editor.** Eliminate anything that is not truly necessary to make your talk more interesting. Keep sentences simple, work from an outline if possible, highlight key points, and make sure the type is large enough for you to read easily.

4. **Know your audience.** Knowing as much as possible about your audience enables you to tailor your comments and message to their needs. Once you know what the background, number, gender mix, level of experience, and overall attitude of the audience are likely to be, you can create examples specifically for them.

5. **Use nerves to your advantage.** A bit of nervousness gets your adrenaline going and puts some extra punch in your presentation. If stage fright paralyzes you, keep two things in mind. First, the more you practice, the more confident and relaxed you will be. Knowing your subject (not the same thing as memorizing) allows you to focus on delivery. Second, realize you are bringing something of value to the audience.

6. **Prepare and rehearse more than you think you need to.** Go through your presentation at least six to eight times—first in front of an imaginary audience, then in front of a few people whose opinions and feedback you trust.

7. **Do a voice check.** Have someone help you assess your vocal quality and delivery. Is your pitch at a natural level? Do you use inflection to give variety to how you sound, or does the word "monotone" come to mind?

8. **Do a body check.** Your hands should be naturally at your sides or held comfortably at your waist. When you gesture, do so upwardly and openly, and make sure the gesture is appropriate for your talk. Keep your eye contact distributed throughout the room.

Section 8

9. **Check out the site ahead of time.** Arrive early so you have time to prepare and relax. Never just show up and wing it. Too often there are surprises that could sabotage your presentation.

10. **Make the most of the podium.** Don't hide behind it and read your script. Step to one side of the podium for a while, then back to the center; later, step to the other side. Moving in front of the podium is also an effective way to emphasize a point or relate more directly with the audience.

11. **Watch your language.** Use "we" and "you" frequently to make your talk seem like more of a dialogue. Don't talk down to your audience. Use stories and anecdotes to help get your message across.

12. **Be creative.** Inject your personality into the speech; have some fun with it. Make your gestures and facial expressions a bit bolder than usual.

13. **Anticipate questions, and think about your answers ahead of time.** Repeat questions before you answer for those in the audience who may not have heard them.

14. **Let the audience know where you're headed.** The old advice, "Tell them what you're going to tell them; tell them; then tell them what you told them," applies here. Before you start, briefly tell the audience the key points you'll be covering, then be sure to recap at the end of your talk.

15. **Remember why you're doing this.** The goal of public speaking is to give something of benefit to the audience, to share information, to advance your company's position, and, if possible, to entertain.

Source: Leann Anderson, "Speak Up," www.entrepreneur.com/article/0,4621,227022,00.html.

Tips for Running Sales Meetings

You can prepare and prepare for a meeting with sales prospects, but all the preparation in the world won't help if you can't run a meeting like a pro.

- **Be observant.** Notice the "stuff" in the prospect's office, and talk about any mutual passions you have. These can range from sports memorabilia to photographs or even music.

- **Ask qualifying questions.** New business meetings aren't about pitching product. It's a conversation, where you get the opportunity to learn your prospect's needs and present your solutions for solving them.

- **Offer good solutions.** At the end of the meeting, summarize your solutions to their needs, and answer any final questions they may have.

- **Take action.** If you've prepared properly, it's now time to ask for what you want. If it's hard for you to close the deal, you may not have given the prospect sufficient reason to buy. If so, ask why. And tackle their objections so they feel comfortable making the deal.

Source: Rieva Lesonsky, *365 Tips to Boost Your Entrepreneurial IQ.*

Tips for Conquering Your Fear of Public Speaking

Are you like most Americans, who rank public speaking as their greatest fear? Learning to speak effectively can only boost your business.

- Step one is to promote yourself as an expert in your field. Start out speaking to business and civic groups. Volunteer to speak at conference or industry trade shows, or offer free seminars. The key is to get experience speaking in front of groups of people.

- Once you get the opportunity to speak in public, make sure you do it well. Preparation is key.

- Know your audience; it helps you personalize your message.

- Don't ramble; make sure you organize your thoughts.

- Rehearse, rehearse, rehearse. Practice does make perfect.

Not sure why you should do this? Once you fine-tune your public speaking, you'll be better at conducting meetings, making sales presentations, and negotiating with clients, suppliers, and bankers.

Source: Rieva Lesonsky, *365 Tips to Boost Your Entrepreneurial IQ.*

Section 8

Tips for Preparing for Radio and TV

More and more business owners are taking to the airwaves—as the spokespersons for their businesses on radio and TV. Could you be next? Before you hit the air, consider the following:

- Remember: not everyone is cut out to be on the air. Some people have weak voices; others may not photograph well. Get a brutally honest assessment of how you look and sound before you buy air time.

- If you need help, take a speech class at a local college. Or hire a coach to help you.

- Local TV or radio stations can help you prepare your spot. But first find out what your costs will be. Remember: the ads need to be written and produced.

- If you're filming a TV spot, make sure you look good. Dress appropriately and get your hair and makeup done professionally.

- And finally, practice, practice, practice. You're not trying to be slick, but you should come across as professional. Most important, though, be yourself.

Source: Rieva Lesonsky, *365 Tips to Boost Your Entrepreneurial IQ.*

Tips for an Effective Speaking Voice

It's not only what you say but how you say it that affects your business and your credibility. Even if you sound like Betty Boop or Elmer Fudd, with awareness and practice, you can develop an effective speaking voice, says motivational speaker Don Abbott.

- Step one—you must breathe! Remember to pause every now and then.
- If you talk nonstop, you'll sound anxious and secure.
- Don't forget to enunciate. Make sure your pronunciation is correct or you'll sound uneducated.
- Pace yourself. Talking too slowly can be as ineffective as speaking too quickly.
- If you're nervous, fess up! Tell the crowd you're a little uptight and you'll put them—and yourself—at ease.
- Remember, practice makes perfect. Once you get the drill down, you'll feel—and sound—more confident.

Source: Rieva Lesonsky, *365 Tips to Boost Your Entrepreneurial IQ.*

Chapter 56

Closing the Deal

Section
8

Three Tips for Selling Retail

1. **Beat a cold greeting.** Many retail salespeople struggle with the "I'm just browsing" rebuff. Kathy Williams, a salesperson in Charlotte, North Carolina, for Chico's, a chain of women's clothing stores, asks, "Have you shopped with us before?" Williams wants to know why a shopper came into the store. "If a customer says, 'I'm just looking,' well, what is she looking for?" Williams says. "You're just trying to trigger what's of interest to her."

2. **Think for the customer.** Once Williams triggers an interest, she starts a dressing room and selects an outfit based on that one item. Chico's doesn't put mirrors in its dressing rooms, which puts Williams front and center with the customer. "I don't consider myself a salesclerk. I'm a wardrobe consultant," she says. "I take the thinking out of it for them." Williams takes notes on each customer after a sale, and then follows up with a call or a handwritten note.

3. **Attack the sack.** Williams sees opportunity in returns, a philosophy she calls "attacking the sack." She finds out what didn't work for the customer and finds a solution, which could be another color, another size, or another look. "Nine times out of ten, if they bought once, they'll buy again," she says. "A lot of times, they end up buying more merchandise. They may return $300 [worth] and buy $500."

Source: Chris Penttila, "The Art of the Sale," www.entrepreneur.com/article/0,4621,309867-1,00.html.

Three Tips for Selling B2B

1. **Remember: it's about someone else's job.** According to Michael Minelli, a New York City-based media and entertainment business manager for SAS Institute Inc., "One of the key challenges is the implication to someone's career. They're so emotionally attached [to the purchase], it's a hard sell. If you can't show how you'll increase revenue and decrease operating costs, you're out of the game. You have to pull [buyers] into the process so they can articulate how this will add value."

2. **Focus on first quarter.** "With B2B," says Minelli, "you're asking the customer at every step for a 'go' or 'no-go' decision, and sales cycles are much longer—months on end. First and second quarters are the magic months. You have to make it happen then if you're going to close lengthy sales cycles within a fiscal year."

3. **Don't sell a need; sell a vision.** Ask a lot of questions: How does this potential customer generate revenue? What is important to them? Where does our solution fit? "Customers don't care if you make your quota," he says. "They're concerned about their side of the equation. You have to find compelling reasons why this is good for their company."

Source: Chris Penttila, "The Art of the Sale," www.entrepreneur.com/article/0,4621,309867-1,00.html.

Three Tips for Selling Wholesale

1. **Have a buyer's mind-set.** A retail buyer's biggest fear is using limited funds to buy something that does not sell. "Larger retailers aren't going to tell you what they're looking for," notes Chuck Bond, founder of COKeM International Ltd., a wholesaler of software, video games, and accessories in Plymouth, Minnesota. "You have to tell them 'Here's what you're looking for.'"

2. **Customize.** Retailers are competitive, and they don't want the same thing as the next retailer. Customize programs as well as product displays for each of your customers. Bond says, "You have to bring them a margin opportunity or a theme sales opportunity."

3. **Give them R-E-S-P-E-C-T.** A lot of buyers don't want samples and long-winded pitches. "Respect their time. Don't have your own agenda," Bond says. "I've seen too many salespeople fail by only thinking about their own agenda."

Source: Chris Penttila, "The Art of the Sale," www.entrepreneur.com/article/0,4621,309867-2,00.html.

SCORE's Five Tips for Building Your Referral Business

1. Referrals always begin with providing your current customers with prompt, reliable, quality service. They'll be happy to spread the word on your behalf—often without your having to ask.

2. Ask your current customers if they know of any colleagues who are looking for the kind of service you provide. Follow up with a call or letter to those businesses. Make sure you get your customers' permission to cite them as a referral source.

3. If a customer compliments you on your work, ask them to put it in writing for use as a testimonial in your marketing materials. Again, make sure you have their permission to use their name for that purpose.

4. Always acknowledge a customer's referral with a thank-you note or phone call. If you send a card, consider including a coupon to popular restaurant or discount on a future purchase.

5. Many retail and service businesses lend themselves well to formal referral incentive programs with cash, gifts, or discounts. Make sure these "rewards" fit in your budget, and that you have clear rules and guidelines (e.g., only one referral reward per customer during a defined period).

Source: SCORE, www.score.org/business_tips.html.

Five Tips for Business-to-Business Selling

1. **Listen well.** Let your customers talk so you can learn their needs and determine how your products or services can help them.

2. **Learn as much as you can about your prospects' industry.** You may come up with ideas to help them that they haven't thought of before.

3. **Make yourself a part of their team.** Demonstrate that you are there to help them increase their bottom line.

4. **Emphasize the benefit of your products or services.** Show how you can help customers cut costs, increase profits, or beat the competition.

5. **Follow up.** Keep customers coming back by making sure your products or services work well for them. If not, show concern and fix things cheerfully.

Source: SCORE, www.score.org/business_tips.html.

Three Tips for Selling Technology

1. **Distinguish between purchase price and total cost of ownership.** Today's technology customers look at the total cost of ownership, from initial price and support to downtime and depreciation. "With technology, there are multiple factors to price outside of dollars spent on day one," says Alan Mayer, formerly a top phone-based sales rep for Dell and now a field account executive. "The price is just one element of the sale."

2. **Stay flexible and knowledgeable.** No two technology sales are the same. Stay flexible, respond to questions quickly, and keep up-to-date on products.

3. **Understand value from the customer's perspective.** Get an idea of each customer's time frame and goals, and whether they're working within a budget, so you can propose products and a financing plan. "Realize that value is perceived," Mayer says. "You won't know what the hot button is until you engage the customer. Meet customer needs where they want to be met."

Source: Chris Penttila, "The Art of the Sale," www.entrepreneur.com/article/0,4621,309867-3,00.html.

Three Tips for Selling Solutions

1. **Don't compete, collaborate.** Salespeople from different departments should work together to meet the needs of one shopper. They should be empowered to problem-

solve. "It's a team approach that amazes customers," says Garrett Boone, co-founder of The Container Store, a Dallas-based retailer of shelving and organizational supplies.

2. **Engage the customer.** Salespeople are trained to notice the types of products customers are looking at or already have in their shopping carts. "We're trying to engage them in a way that says, 'I can see you need help,'" Boone says, "and I'm not going to ask a dumb question like 'Do you need help?'"

3. **Remember the man in the desert.** Employees are versed in a philosophy called "the man in the desert." A man crawls through the desert gasping for water and finds a retailer who gives him a drink. Then the man crawls away and finds the store, where he gets water, food, and help in finding his family. Translation: always offer customers a comprehensive solution. If a customer is looking at wrapping paper, she'll probably need a box, a bow, some tissue paper, and a greeting card to go with it.

Source: Chris Penttila, "The Art of the Sale," www.entrepreneur.com/article/0,4621,309867-2,00.html.

Three Tips for Selling a Service

1. **Don't talk, listen.** Spend more time listening than talking. Listening is so basic, it's overlooked. But it's the first step to respect.

2. **Develop trust.** Ask the customer very targeted questions: "What is the competition doing that you want done better? What would you use our service for?" Your goal is to build trust.

3. **Make a difference.** Find a cost-effective answer for each customer. Provide solutions. Then, when you've shown them how to grow their business, sales are easier.

Source: Chris Penttila, "The Art of the Sale," www.entrepreneur.com/article/0,4621,309867-1,00.html.

Five Strategies for Closing a Large Deal

1. **Sell from the top down.** You'll probably have to keep trying, but top-level executives will be able to give you a clear overview of the company's needs and concerns, as well as direct you to the person who handles your type of product or service.

2. **Become mayor of the account.** Candidates running for political office toil to meet as many voters as possible. When you're in the running for an account, you've got to do the same thing. Write a note of thanks to everyone you meet, and include some information that might interest them. You never know what their influence on the decision-maker might be or when they might be in the decision-making position themselves.

3. **Use referrals to build contacts.** The best way to get into a large account is via a positive reference from someone who can testify to the quality of your company's product or service. Often, the smartest question you can ask is "Do you know anyone else in your industry that might benefit from my product or service?"

4. **Be relentless.** Be relentless in your pursuit of an account—not by constantly calling to make a sale, but by building a relationship that will pay off over time.

5. **Stand out from the crowd.** Large accounts are bombarded with new vendors. If you want to impress the top gun, load up with ammunition that separates you from the competition. You do need to have two or three major points that demonstrate your unique value, and you should do your homework so that your information is heavily focused on their goals and challenges.

Source: Barry Farber, "Big Deal," www.entrepreneur.com/article/0,4621,316760,00.html.

# Chapter 57

Customer Satisfaction and Retention

Section
8

Ten Smart Ways to Keep Your Customers

1. Always stress the benefits—not the features—of your product or service.
2. Exceed your customers' expectations.
3. Don't focus solely on price. Instead, point out the total value of your products or services.
4. Send customers and clients thank-you notes after making the sale.
5. Ask your customers for feedback—and follow their advice.
6. Give something extra to customers who bring you referral business.
7. Try to greet regular customers by name.
8. Keep in touch with your best customers.
9. Use special discounts to commemorate holidays and customers' birthdays.
10. Remember the golden rule, and always treat customers the way you want to be treated.

Source: Rieva Lesonsky, *365 Tips to Boost Your Entrepreneurial IQ.*

Nine Tools for Building Customer Loyalty

1. **Thank-you notes:** This is a no-brainer, but you'd be surprised at how many entrepreneurs neglect to write thank-you notes—especially when they get really busy. Take the time to show your customers that you genuinely appreciate their business. They'll remember your thoughtfulness because most of your competition won't send out thank-you notes.

2. **Postcard mailings:** If you target consumers, send out monthly mailings that make good refrigerator fodder, such as "Quote of the Month," "Recipe of the Month," or useful tips on such topics as time-management, gardening, or anything else that interests the bulk of your customers. Avoid being too promotional here. Just provide the kind of information that customers will want to hang on their fridge. The added benefit to you is that whenever guests visit your customers' homes, they'll see your name, potentially leading to conversations about your business.

3. **E-mail updates:** Think of your e-mail update as a press release that you send to your customers. Providing them with regular product, service, and customer updates via e-mail at least once per month will convey a sense of positive momentum. This keeps customers in the loop and, over time, gets them excited to be involved with you and motivates them to pass on referrals.

4. **Getting together over coffee or lunch:** Try to spend face time in a non-sales envi-

ronment with your customers. Ask about their family, hobbies, personal goals, and so forth. When you show customers that you really care about them on a personal level, they're yours for life.

5. **Birthdays, anniversaries, and other special occasions:** These occasions are very important to your customers and their families and friends. Be among the few who actually remember a customer's special days and that customer will never forget you!

6. **Follow up on well-being:** For example, if you find that a customer's wife has been sick, call periodically just to find out how she's recovering.

7. **Pass referrals:** One of the most powerful ways to encourage loyalty in customers is to pass them referrals. When you get a chance, scroll through your customer database and think through people you know who might add value to your customers.

8. **Entertaining at your home:** Throw a party for your best customers. You'll be amazed at how much rapport and goodwill you can build with people when you get them in your home environment.

9. **Post-sale feedback:** Demonstrate that you care about the quality of your service. Call customers and ask them questions like:

- Are you pleased with the service you received?
- What did you like most about working with us?
- What would you like to see improved?

Source: Sean M. Lyden, "9 Tools for Building Customer Loyalty," www.entrepreneur.com/article/0,4621,302675,00.html.

Section 8

How to Keep Apathy from Costing You Clients

Why do most small businesses lose customers? According to guerrilla marketing guru Jay Conrad Levinson, it's apathy. Misguided entrepreneurs believe that once they've made the sale they can stop their marketing efforts, when that's when marketing should begin. Follow-up is essential to keeping customers. Here's an abbreviated version of Levinson's follow-up calendar:

- Within two days of making the sale, send your customers a thank-you note.
- 30 days later, send another note or call to find out if the customer has any questions.
- Within 90 days, send buyers another note, telling them about related products or services.
- After nine months, ask for the names of three people you can add to your mailing list.
- On the one-year anniversary of the sale, send a card, perhaps with a discount included.

According to Levinson, it costs six times more to sell something to a new customer than to an existing one.

Source: Rieva Lesonsky, *365 Tips to Boost Your Entrepreneurial IQ.*

Six Tips for Customer Satisfaction

Wat's the key to small-business success? Well, one important component, obviously, is keeping your customers satisfied.

1. Find out what your customers want. Don't guess—ask them through surveys, focus groups, any way you can.

2. Dazzle them with services so remarkable they'll tell their friends and colleagues. Nothing works like word-of-mouth marketing.

3. Be responsive. Don't make your customers wait for service, not on the phone or in your store. Take care of their needs immediately.

4. Never deceive your customers. Eventually, they'll find out, and they'll never come back to you.

5. Reward your clients. Offer frequent-buyer programs, volume discounts, or other incentives that show you appreciate their business.

6. If it's wrong, make it right. Even if the mistake is not your fault, fix it!

Source: Rieva Lesonsky, *365 Tips to Boost Your Entrepreneurial IQ.*

Section 8

Smart Tips to Increase Customer Satisfaction

1. Go out of your way for loyal customers. Do them a favor: locate a hard-to-find item or, if your staff is tied up, do the work yourself.

2. Underpromise and overdeliver. Do they need it in two weeks? Give it to them in one.

3. Offer your best customers a benefit they didn't even know existed. Did they miss your coupon in the paper? Give them the discount anyway.

4. Follow up, especially after a big order or a major project. Are they satisfied, or is there something else you can do for them?

5. Above all, be honest. Don't oversell goods or services. Show them you have their best interests at heart, and you'll have a customer for life.

Source: Rieva Lesonsky, *365 Tips to Boost Your Entrepreneurial IQ.*

Is Your Problem Client Worth Keeping?

Entrepreneurs generally work very hard at keeping every client. But this is not always the best way to grow your business. When the client is a nuisance, sometimes it's better to end your relationship.

How do you know when the client just isn't worth it? It may be time to say goodbye when your client:

1. Doesn't respect or appreciate your work,

2. Makes excessive demands on you or your staff,

3. Has unrealistic expectations of what you can do for him or her,

4. Isn't willing to pay a fair price for your services, or

5. Considers you a disposable vendor instead of a valued partner.

If you are ready to split, be sure to have a termination plan. Make the transition as smooth as possible and maintain a professional attitude throughout the process.

Source: Rieva Lesonsky, *365 Tips to Boost Your Entrepreneurial IQ.*

Section 8

Section 9

Chapter 58

Effective Advertising Techniques for Your Business

Section
9

Section
9

How to Test Your Sales Materials

Follow these tips to make sure your sales materials are up to snuff:

- Target your sales materials to your audience. The materials should show you're a specialist with a vast knowledge of your field.
- Use testimonials in your sales letters, brochures, and advertisements. These should be written by satisfied customers.
- Write your sales copy from the customer's point of view. Remember: most people are interested in helping themselves.
- Use questions in your copy. This is a great way to engage prospects' attention and pique their interest.

Source: Rieva Lesonsky, *365 Tips to Boost Your Entrepreneurial IQ.*

SCORE's Five Tips on Advertising Basics

1. Be consistent in your ad message and style, including business cards, letterhead, envelopes, invoices, signs, and banners.
2. Newspapers and radio and TV stations are helpful in producing the advertising that you will be running with them.
3. While word-of-mouth advertising has been around a long time, it usually falls short of being able to attract the number of customers needed to be successful in business.
4. Promote benefits rather than features. A benefit is the emotional satisfaction your product or service provides, or a tangible performance characteristic.
5. Know your competitors. Knowing everything about your competitors is just as important as knowing everything about your own business.

Source: SCORE, www.score.org/business_tips.html.

SCORE's Five Tips on How to Advertise, Cheap!

1. Advertising is expensive, so know why you are advertising and what you want to accomplish. Evaluate your advertising carefully and measure its effectiveness.
2. Develop appropriate sales promotion tools such as flyers, brochures, and signs. Carefully review each item for its effectiveness and evaluate what these tools say about your business.

3. Signage should be a major part of your marketing strategy. Signs are a vital part of small businesses and can be the most efficient, effective, and consistent device for generating revenue.

4. Every small business should be listed under the appropriate heading in the Yellow Pages, but not every business needs to buy expensive display ads. Be judicious.

5. Get involved in your community. Join the chamber of commerce, business organizations, service clubs, and charities. Network yourself and keep your antennae up.

Source: SCORE, www.score.org/business_tips.html.

SCORE's Five Tips on Effective News Releases

1. Make sure your signs are newsworthy. Good topics include the announcement of a major new client, a celebrity appearance at your store, and community service performed by your company.

2. Create news and put out a press release about it. Speak at a seminar, for example, or provide expert comment on developing news events.

3. Get your releases to the right people. Find out who at your radio and TV stations and newspaper will be the most interested in your news.

4. Capture editors' attention by putting the news in the first paragraph. Then add the necessary details.

5. Make your releases look crisp and professional—that means no smudgy type. Include the name and phone number of a contact person. Then, answer media queries promptly.

Source: SCORE, www.score.org/business_tips.html.

Four Tips for Choosing a Slogan

To win the name game in the marketing world, you must make sure your prospects and customers do more than remember hearing your slogan—they have to associate it with your brand name, not your competitor's. To make sure your slogan or tag line hits home, follow these four tips:

1. **Evoke your key benefit.** Great slogans not only are built around a brand's core promise—they also establish an exclusive connection in customers' minds. You and your in-house marketing staff or advertising agency must create a slogan that evokes your key benefits and reflects the unique experience your product or service delivers.

2. **Test with prospects and customers.** Qualitative research is essential before putting your marketing resources squarely behind a newly developed slogan. It's important to speak to potential customers as well as current ones to avoid skewing the outcome. If you query only your current customers, you may never figure out how to appeal to those who never considered your previous marketing messages very compelling. Phone surveys (particularly for B2B marketers) and focus groups can be used to test proposed slogans as well as uncover or verify information about the benefits your prospects and customers expect to realize when they use your product or service.

3. **Include your company name.** Evidence suggests slogans fare better when it comes to customer recall if they incorporate the company or product name. Wolf Group New York, an ad agency with such clients as Häagen-Dazs and Miracle-Gro, tested consumer recognition of 19 tag lines that were part of successful, long-running advertising campaigns backed by hundreds of millions of dollars. Each of the top-five brands in the survey included the product or advertiser's name, while none of the bottom ten did.

4. **Stick with it.** Never adopt a new slogan as a quick fix or as part of a temporary campaign. Success requires committing to a slogan or tag line for several years—perhaps even decades—and incorporating it into all your marketing materials as a part of the company logo. If you want to protect your business's marketing investment in the new slogan, you should consider trademarking it. At the U.S. Patent and Trademark Office web site (www.uspto.gov), you can fill out a trademark application, search the trademark database, and research general information about trademarks.

Whatever you do, just remember that a great slogan is like a partner in a happy marriage—it will share your company's name and be your marketing partner for many years to come. So consider your options carefully.

For help with creating slogans, go to www.adslogans.com.

Source: Kim T. Gordon, "Slogan's Heroes," www.entrepreneur.com/article/0,4621,290043,00.html.

Tips for When Your Ad Falls Flat

Is your ad working? If you didn't get the response you were expecting, don't panic. First ask yourself these questions:

- Is it a good ad in the wrong place? Check your media plan. Did you find the medium that best targeted your audience?

- Was the offer too weak? How does it stack up to your competitors' ads? And don't forget to test your offer, find what works best for you, and stick with that message until it stops working for you.

Section 9

- Are there sales barriers? Do prospects know where to reach or find you? Did you provide a toll-free phone number? Do you have a web site where customers can find out more information and place an order? If they call, are they stuck in voice-mail hell?
- Are you consistent? Smart marketers build up awareness of their products or services by advertising with some degree of frequency.

Source: Rieva Lesonsky, *365 Tips to Boost Your Entrepreneurial IQ.*

Questions to Answer Before Going to a Web Developer

If you want an accurate assessment of what your web site will cost, you must have a clear idea about what you need. Take some time to answer these questions before you talk to a developer.

1. **How will your web site function?**
   - As an online store where product is sold?
   - As an online brochure to inform the consumer about your company or services?
   - As an online community?

2. **What will your web site look and feel like? What will be its corporate culture? Will it be light and fun, or high-tech-looking, or businesslike and professional?**

3. **How many pages and what specific pages do you need for your web site?**
   Here are some typical pages to think about for starters:
   - Home
   - About
   - Products/Services
   - Order
   - Contact
   - Resources
   - Free Newsletter

4. **What is your budget?**
   Be reasonable. If you have only $500, you won't get too much out of your web site. There are affordable designers who can design a small business web site ranging in price from $700 to $2,500.

5. **What is your deadline for project completion?**
   Are you pressed for time or do you have several weeks to play with? If you need your site in a hurry, you may be able to get it sooner by paying a "rush fee."

6. **Will you require any specialized programming, such as a shopping cart, a data-**

base, or a contact form?

If you need these items, make sure your web developer has the skills to meet these requirements.

7. **What level of assistance do you need in development?**

   By knowing in advance how much and what kind of help your project requires, you can confirm that the developer you're considering can (and will) provide the level of service you need.

   - Do you need full site design and concepting?

   - Do you have the concept and just need it created into HTML pages?

   - Do you just need some new graphics and a web site makeover?

   - Do you have a logo or will they need to create one?

8. **What guidance can you provide the developer?**

   Find web sites that you like, list the URLs, and note what you like and why it appeals to you. Show this to the designer to give him or her a better idea about what you are looking for, so he or she can more easily provide a quote and conceptualize a graphic design to match your vision.

Source: Kristie Tamsevicius, "Top 10 Things to Look for When Hiring a Web Developer," www.soho.org/Technology_Articles/hiring_web_developer.htm.

Top Ten Things You Need to Know When Working with a Graphic Designer

Designers are individuals, and every designer has a slightly different working method. There are several things that most professional designers do have in common, though. Here are a few things you can expect when you work with a graphic designer.

1. **Expect to sign a contract before work.**

   A contract protects the designer and you. It will spell out who owns what, how long the estimate is good for, payment terms, etc. Some designers call contracts by another name, such as terms and conditions, to make it seem a little less scary. Designers who don't require you to sign a contract most likely haven't been in business very long; that's not necessarily a bad thing, but it is a clue to the designer's level of professionalism.

2. **Expect to pay a deposit before work.**

   Many people believe that designers just make things pretty. A good designer tries to communicate your message, and that takes research. While your designer is researching your job, he or she cannot take on new work or promote their business. A deposit isn't payment for future work—it's a payment for the work that is going on right now.

3. Expect to pay more for rush jobs.

People often have unrealistic ideas of how long it takes to get something designed. There's a lot of research and legwork involved in designing. If your job is a rush, you can expect to pay more—especially if it requires weekend work. Not all designers treat rush jobs the same, so it's a good idea when you hire a designer to discuss what constitutes a rush job and what extra fees rush jobs might incur. Just because your job isn't a rush now doesn't mean it won't become one.

4. Expect to pay more when you make changes.

Changes that you make, that aren't errors on the part of the designer, are usually called author's alterations (AAs). You can expect to be billed extra for any AAs you request, so it's a good idea to go over your copy carefully before submitting it to your designer. If you change the actual specifications of the job (job specs), you can also expect additional charges. A professional designer will let you know what extra fees you are incurring before they begin to work on your changes.

5. Expect to be charged by the project, not by the hour.

Most professional designers charge by the project. They may break it down for you so that you can see where all your money is going, but they usually don't charge by the hour.

6. Expect that you will get an agreed-upon number of concepts.

Every designer's worst nightmare is customers who will "know it when they see it." That's why it pays to do your homework ahead of time: if you really know what you want, like, and need, your designer is more likely to come up with something that works for you. Whatever price you agree upon will only include a limited number of initial design concepts; if you need more, the price will go up.

7. Expect to do your homework first.

It's truly critical that you spend some time thinking about what you really need. Who is your target market? What's special about your company? Why your company and not some other company? While it's true your designer should spend time discussing this with you, you'll get better results if you think about these issues before you meet with designers.

8. Expect to pay more for files.

Most design projects are for a one-time use: a brochure, an ad, a postcard. When the designer quotes a price for you, they're assuming that you will use the design for only that one project. If you want to take that graphic from your brochure and use it in an ad, for instance, it will cost you more because you're using it for two projects. If you know that you want to use the design for several different projects, let the designer know; the designer will then price your job accordingly.

9. Expect GIGO (garbage in, garbage out).

Designers are not miracle workers. If you hand a designer your 72-dpi, digital camera photos for a brochure that will be printed, your photos will most likely end up looking fuzzy in print. Yes, the designer can improve the photos somewhat, but there's a limit to how much such photos can be improved. The same is true if you give the designer already printed material to scan, torn photos, blurry photos, scratched photos .... You get the idea.

10. **Expect that you will give final approval for the job.**
When all is said and done, this is your job; final approval (and responsibility) rests with you. While your designer will certainly proofread your work, most likely they will also have you proofread it and sign a form that says the work is approved. Don't sign off on the job unless you're completely satisfied. If you sign off and find a mistake later, it will cost you more money to fix the error.

Source: Judy Litt, "Top 10 Tips for Working with a Designer," graphicdesign.about.com/od/businesstips/tp/workingdesigner.htm.

Top Ten Things to Look for When Choosing a Web Developer

1. **Experience**
An experienced designer will have more skills to create a sophisticated looking and functioning web site. He or she will have more tools and tricks and knowledge to help you achieve your business goals.

First, do you like the designer's own business web site? Next, here are some questions to consider for a potential web developer:

- Can I see your design portfolio?

- How long have you been doing web site design?

- How many web sites have you developed?

- What areas of web development do you specialize in?

- Do you know how to hand-code HTML or do you only use an HTML editor? (Hand coding can allow for an extra level of precision that may be difficult to achieve with various HTML editors.)

- Do you know Javascript?

- Can you do database work?

- Do you have a professional graphic design team or do you create the graphics yourself?

- Will you help market our web site?

The whole process of interviewing the designer will not only give you the answers to those questions, but gives you insight as to who the designer is, his or her level of expertise, and how well you can work together.

2. Top-Quality Customer Service

Equally important to experience is quality customer service. After all, what good is having a top designer if he or she is too busy to answer your e-mails and jump in during an emergency? Ask for a list of references—and call them! Don't be afraid to ask them if their web developer is responsive to their needs and assists them in a timely manner.

3. Professional, Original Web Site Graphics

Anyone can put words on a page and create links. But only a skilled designer will have a good sense of page layout, know how to create a good color scheme, and be able to create tasteful graphics that will enhance the web site. Take a look at other sites the designer has created. Do they demonstrate a considerable range of "styles" or do they use templates? Do the web sites feature original web graphics? If you want a one-of-a-kind web site to brand your business, you must insist on original graphics for your web site. Can the designer create "extras" such as flash, animation, or mouse-over effects?

4. Marketing Savvy

Here are some questions to ask your designer to determine what level of marketing assistance he or she will provide you:

- Will you help create meta tags for our web site?

- Will you register our site with the search engines?

- What search engines do you submit to?

- Do you mass-submit or will you hand-submit our site to the important search engines?

Note: If designers claim to be experts in search engine positioning, check first to see how highly listed their web site is: it's the proof in the pudding for their techniques!

5. Creativity

One thing you'd better know upfront is how involved your web developer will be in the creative process. Unless you are an experienced marketer, you probably will need at least a little help writing web copy and planning the layout of your web site. Will your web developer help you develop content?

Writing for the web is a little different from writing for a print marketing piece. By using someone with experience in writing web copy, you can ensure that the message, like the look of your site, is geared to sell. Also, be aware of over-creative know-it-all designers who won't listen to your input. It's your web site; you should have creative input. The key is to finding a developer who will listen to your suggestions and work with your ideas and advice when planning your site.

6. Pricing

The cost of a professionally designed small business web site can run anywhere from $500 to $5,000. To ensure you don't overspend your budget, you need to get a written estimate. Depending on the complexity or your project, you may even have to pay to get an estimate. To get a complete picture of all costs involved, have the designer break out costs for domain name, hosting services, graphics, web development, and marketing fees separately.

Will you be required to put down a deposit? Some firms may ask for half of estimated fees up front as a deposit. What methods of payment do they accept? Will they accept credit cards or do you have to pay by cash or check?

Do they charge a flat rate or by the hour? Typical hourly web development fees can range from $30 to $200 per hour. But beware: cheaper is not always better! Whatever the hourly rate, make sure it is justified by the amount of experience and skill set they bring to the table. While a designer who charges $30 an hour might seems like a deal at first, it might take them twice as long to accomplish a task.

What items will cost you extra? If there are items that will not be included in the estimate which will be additional, make sure to get the a la carte pricing. And finally, find out what the costs will be to maintain the site. If you will be updating your site frequently, this ongoing cost is an important one to keep in mind.

7. Communication Skills

How easy is your designer to talk to? Do you trust the person? Can you understand what he or she is explaining to you or is it techno-babble? Does the developer take time to listen to your needs? If you are going to have a good long-term working relationship, it's crucial that you feel comfortable with one another and can communicate clearly.

8. Time Frame to Completion

Ask how long the web development process will take. And then you may want to ask their references how close they came to completing the project on target. A simple web site could be developed in one or two weeks, while a larger, more intense site could take several weeks or months. Knowing what to expect can help you manage your expectations.

9. Full Range of Services

Does the developer offer a full range of web site services? Will he or she help you acquire a domain name, set up a web hosting account, market your web site, write copy, and/or provide CGI and database programming?

Working with a developer who can handle all these details will save you time, money, and frustration. You can rely on their expertise to handle some of the more technical questions that may arise. If they don't provide these services, then ask if they have companies that they recommend. Be sure to get prices from those vendors too so that the total web sites costs don't sneak up on you.

10. Availability

Is he or she a full-time web developer or is web design a moonlighting job? A full-time developer will probably be able to complete your site in a shorter time frame than someone who is squeezing you into his or her spare time. What are the developer's hours? Is he or she open to you calling with questions? Can the developer

Section
9

start your project right away? If you need maintenance down the road, how soon can you expect changes after you submit them?

Source: Kristie Tamsevicius, "Top 10 Things to Look for When Hiring a Web Developer," www.soho.org/Technology_Articles/hiring_web_developer.htm.

Four Tips to Make Your Ads Stick!

These methods will make your next campaign memorable:

1. **Engage prospects.** The more time someone spends with your ad, the more likely he or she is to remember it. The best ads get the advertiser or brand into the minds of prospects as they consider different possibilities.

   How can you get prospects to spend more time with your ads? According to Philip W. Sawyer, director of Starch Communications, a Harrison, New York, testing firm specializing in readership studies, the most memorable print ads have messages that grab the reader. Those ads include headlines that contain a benefit and a strong visual focal point, such as a close-up of a model looking directly at you. One large photo works best in magazines; in newspapers, you can use multiproduct visuals.

2. **Add color and contrast.** For magazine readers, high-contrast images also boost recognition. When Starch Communications tested two identical ads for Stolichnaya vodka—one with a white background and another with a black background—twice as many people remembered seeing the version with the black background, even though everything else in the ad was the same.

   Testing also shows that, on average, larger ads in print media are more memorable. However, a creative ad in a small space can be more memorable than a so-so one that takes up a full page.

   Some colors enhance memorability in print media—including sky blue, golden yellow, and shades of blue-green. Red is a good spot color in newspapers, where Sawyer says color increases recognition by 20 percent. But there's new information about four-color ads in magazines: A few years ago, color ads earned 24 percent higher recognition scores than black-and-white ads. Now, full-page black-and-white campaigns are breaking through the clutter, and four-color ads have lost their advantage.

3. **Communicate frequently.** Repetition is important to memorability. At the Washington University School of Medicine in St. Louis, psychologist Mark E. Wheeler conducted a study of memory in which a word was paired with a picture or sound many times over several days to test subjects' recognition rates. He says exposure to information in different contexts helps you remember it. So when you see a message in different formats, such as a print ad, a billboard, and a TV commercial, he says, "You associate the different impressions, and that helps you retrieve the information when you need it."

4. Use memorable benefits. Ads that grab and hold a prospect's attention are those that immediately communicate a benefit that answers the question, "What's in it for me?" The bottom line, says Sawyer, is that features aren't memorable—benefits are. "If you have a headline that states a benefit, people will read it, remember it, clip it out of the magazine or newspaper, and hold onto it. And that's the trump card for everything."

Source: Kim T. Gordon, "Total Recall," www.entrepreneur.com/article/0,4621,311562,00.html.

Great Tips for Creating a Headline

In the beginning, most entrepreneurs not only run their businesses but serve as advertising copywriters as well. Here are some tips to help you write the most important part of an ad—the headline.

- **Offer a benefit.** Does your business save your customers money, time, energy, or what? Tell readers immediately why they should be interested in what you're selling.

- **Remember: in most cases, the shorter the headline, the better.** In no case should the headline exceed 20 words.

- **Make your message simple.** The headline should focus on one benefit; address any others in the ad copy.

- **Know your market.** Target the headline to a specific audience. If it's too broad, it won't mean anything to anyone.

- **Avoid all capital letters.** They're harder to read. And avoid fancy typefaces—unless you're trying to make a point, don't use strange fonts.

- **Be provocative.** Make readers want to keep reading. Effective headlines grab attention and compel prospects to read on.

Source: Rieva Lesonsky, *365 Tips to Boost Your Entrepreneurial IQ.*

Ten Tips to Get the Clicks

How do you write online ads that generate results? First, you need to choose a specific objective for your campaign. Once this is established, the following copywriting tips will help summarize, strengthen, and sharpen your ad's message:

1. **Lead with a question.** Want to write better online ads? Looking to ramp up your click-through rate? See how engaging this technique can be in getting potential customers' attention?

2. **Create a lyrical rhythm.** Well-written online ads follow a catchy word flow from

frame to frame. The number of syllables chosen to convey the message is deliberate, like haiku. The pacing of the words is energetic, like a roadside Burma Shave ad. And the idea builds to a payoff, like a well-told joke (frame 1 is the setup, frame 2 the fill-in, and frame 3 the punchline).

3. **Keep it single and simple.** The more ideas you force your online ad to communicate, the more muddled it will be. Choose one easily digestible point and drive it home with as few words as possible.

4. **Show, don't tell.** If an image can get your idea across instead of words, use it. Your message will be communicated quickly, easily, and memorably.

5. **Write visually.** Online ads offer infinite choices of entertaining visual techniques that can enhance and sell your message (words and images shrinking, dissolving, stretching, morphing, zooming in, crawling, etc.). Keep these tricks in mind as you compose your text, and include them as suggestions for your designer.

6. **Make an offer.** When it comes to calls to action, offers rule. Free downloads, free demos, free white papers, free info kits, free shipping—pretty much anything free (or other incentives, such as percentage- or dollar-off savings) will get a potential customer clicking faster and more consistently than an uninspiring and ambiguous "Click here!" button.

7. **Justify the click.** If your online ad isn't offer-driven, continue its message by making the call to action specific to what the user would receive if he or she clicked the banner. For instance, "Click for more info!" or "Click to see it in action!" or "Click to get started!"

8. **Drive home the benefits.** Enumerate the enticing and absolutely essential benefits (e.g., save money, improve productivity, lose weight, etc.) that your brand promises.

9. **Nix the tricks.** Online ads using cute come-ons ("Catch the monkey and win $20!") may boost site traffic, but they can only work once. You also run the risk of alienating scads of potential customers who will never visit your site again.

10. **Test as the user.** Once your campaign has been conceived, imagine the mind-set of a potential customer who's viewing a web page where your online ad will appear. Reread each idea and ask yourself, "Is this ad's message communicated credibly, simply, and irresistibly enough to compel a user to leave the site that he or she is in and click to my site?"

Source: Barry Zeger, "10 Tips to Get the Clicks," www.entrepreneur.com/mag/article/ 0,1539,294137,00.html.

Top 12 Advertising Mistakes to Avoid

1. **The quest for instant gratification:** The ad that creates enough urgency to cause people to respond immediately is the ad most likely to be forgotten immediately once the offer expires. It is of little use in establishing the advertiser's identity in the mind of the consumer.

2. **Trying to reach more people than the budget will allow:** For a media mix to be effective, each element in the mix must have enough repetition to establish retention in the mind of the prospect. Too often, however, the result of a media mix is too much reach and not enough frequency. Will you reach 100 percent of the people and persuade them ten percent of the way? Or will you reach ten percent of the people and persuade them 100 percent of the way? The cost is the same.

3. **Assuming the business owner knows best:** The business owner is uniquely unqualified to see his company or product objectively. Too much product knowledge leads him to answer questions no one is asking. He's on the inside looking out, trying to describe himself to a person on the outside looking in. It's hard to read the label when you're inside the bottle.

4. **Unsubstantiated claims:** Advertisers often claim to have what the customer wants, such as "highest quality at the lowest price," but fail to offer any evidence. An unsubstantiated claim is nothing more than a cliché the prospect is tired of hearing. You must prove what you say in every ad. Do your ads give the prospect new information? Do they provide a new perspective? If not, prepare to be disappointed with the results.

5. **Improper use of passive media:** Nonintrusive media, such as newspapers and Yellow Pages, tend to reach only buyers who are looking for the product. They are poor at reaching prospects before their need arises, so they're not much use for creating a predisposition toward your company. The patient, consistent use of intrusive media, such as radio and TV, will win the hearts of relational customers long before they're in the market for your product.

6. **Creating ads instead of campaigns:** It is foolish to believe a single ad can ever tell the entire story. The most effective, persuasive, and memorable ads are those most like a rhinoceros: they make a single point, powerfully. An advertiser with 17 different things to say should commit to a campaign of at least 17 different ads, repeating each ad enough to stick in the prospect's mind.

7. **Obedience to unwritten rules:** For some insane reason, advertisers want their ads to look and sound like ads. Why?

8. **Late-week schedules:** Advertisers justify their obsession with Thursday and Friday advertising by saying, "We need to reach the customer just before she goes shopping." Why do these advertisers choose to compete for the customer's attention each

Thursday and Friday when they could have a nice, quiet chat all alone with her on Sunday, Monday, and Tuesday?

9. **Overconfidence in qualitative targeting**: Many advertisers and media professionals grossly overestimate the importance of audience quality. In reality, saying the wrong thing has killed far more ad campaigns than reaching the wrong people. It's amazing how many people become "the right people" when you're saying the right thing.

10. **Event-driven marketing**: A special event should be judged only by its ability to help you more clearly define your market position and substantiate your claims. If one percent of the people who hear your ad for a special event choose to come, you will be in desperate need of a traffic cop and a bus to shuttle people from distant parking lots. Yet your real investment will be in the 99 percent who did not come! What did your ad say to them?

11. **Great production without great copy**: Too many ads today are creative without being persuasive. Slick, clever, funny, creative, and different are poor substitutes for informative, believable, memorable, and persuasive.

12. **Confusing response with results**: The goal of advertising is to create a clear awareness of your company and its unique selling proposition. Unfortunately, most advertisers evaluate their ads by the comments they hear from the people around them. The slickest, cleverest, funniest, most creative, and most distinctive ads are the ones most likely to generate these comments. See the problem? When we confuse response with results, we create attention-getting ads that say absolutely nothing.

Source: Roy H. Williams, "Top 12 Advertising Mistakes to Avoid," www.entrepreneur.com/article/0,4621,308364,00.html.

Nine Questions to Answer Before Planning Advertising

1. **What does your client have to say that matters to the customer?** Most ads are written under the assumption that the reader, listener, or viewer has a basic level of interest and is paying close attention to the ad. But customers tend to ignore all ads that do not speak directly to them. Your first task is not media selection; it's message selection.

2. **Can you say it persuasively?** Most ads are ineffective because the writer was trying to say too much, include too much, and be too much. Fearful of leaving someone out, these writers write vague, all-encompassing ads that speak specifically to no one. "We Fix Cars" is a terrible headline for an ad.

3. **Are you speaking to a felt need?** Let's say the "We Fix Cars" auto mechanic has a great deal of affection for older BMW 2002s. He knows that 2002 owners love their cars like few drivers on the road and that the only weakness of the 2002 is its evil Solex carburetor. Every 2002 owner knows this, too. So he writes the headline,

"BMW 2002 Owners: Aren't You Tired of Fooling with That Solex by Now?" In the body of the ad, he talks about the fabulous new Weber two-barrel carburetor now available for BMW 2002s, raves about how it dramatically increases performance and reliability, explains that he keeps these new Weber carburetors in stock at his shop, then names the price at which he will install and adjust that carburetor for you. He closes the ad by saying, "You'll rocket out of here in a completely different BMW than the one you drove in." If a list of BMW owners in your area is available for a direct-mail card (such as the list from the local BMW club), then a direct-mail card or flier would be the way to go. But if no such list is available, the newspaper might be a second choice. In either case, you'd want to include a large picture of a BMW 2002 to serve as a recall cue and help gain the attention of your target customer.

4. **How long is your time horizon?** Some ads build traffic, some build relationships, and others build your reputation. If you don't have the financial resources to launch a true branding campaign focused on building relationships and reputation among potential customers, you're going to have to settle for traffic-building ads until you can afford to begin developing your brand. To what degree do you have financial staying power?

5. **What is the urgency of your message?** If you need an ad to produce immediate results, your offer must have a time limit. This technique will simultaneously work for and against you. On one hand, customers tend to delay what can be delayed, so limited-time offers generate traffic more quickly since the threat of "losing the opportunity" is real. On the other hand, customers have no memory of messages that have expired; short-term messages are erased from our brains immediately. Therefore, it's extremely difficult to create long-term awareness with a series of limited-time-offer, short-term ads.

6. **What is the impact quotient of your ad?** How good your ad must be depends on the quality of the competitors' ads. A .22-caliber pistol is a weapon against an opponent with a peashooter. But aim that pathetic pistol at an opponent holding a machine gun, and you can kiss your silly butt goodbye. How powerful is the message of the opposition? If your competitor carries a machine gun, don't go where he goes. In other words, don't use the media he uses.

7. **How long is the purchase cycle?** How long it will take your advertising to pay off is tied to the purchase cycle of your product. Ads for restaurants work more quickly than ads for sewing machines, because a larger percentage of people are looking for a good meal today than are looking for a machine that will let them make their own clothes. Likewise, an ad for a product we buy twice per year will produce results faster than an ad for a product we buy only once a year. Remember: a customer first has to be exposed to your ad often enough to remember it, then you have to wait for that customer to need what you sell. How soon will he or she likely need it?

Source: Roy H. Williams, "Building a Successful Advertising Plan," www.entrepreneur.com/article/0,4621,315431,00.html.

Advice on Using Third-Party Advertisements

Robert McGarvey and Melissa Campanelli share how you can use third-party ads on your web site and make more money for your company. Alleviate your start-up costs and debt with their tips, which you can find in their book, *Start Your Own e-Business*, from Entrepreneur Press.

Can you generate cash by putting third-party advertisements on your web site? You bet! Smarter than chasing down individual advertisers (and trying to collect!), join a net ad network, an intermediary that brings web sites and advertisers together. Some ad networks to join are the following:

- Burst! Media
  www.burstmedia.com

- 24/7 Real Media
  www.247realmedia.com

- MaxWorldwide
  www.maxworldwide.com

- ValueClick
  www.valueclick.com

- Advertising.com
  www.advertising.com

Find many more by going to Yahoo! at www.yahoo.com and clicking on "Business" (Business and Economy), "Business to Business," "Marketing and Advertising," "Internet," and then "Advertising." Also, check out MediaPost's Ad Network Watch at www.media-post.com/signin.cfm.

Literally dozens of companies want your business. Before signing any deals, check references, asking the following questions. Is payment prompt? Are advertisers as promised? Can you ban certain kinds of ads from your site? The model doesn't always work, so be careful.

Source: Robert McGarvey and Melissa Campanelli, *Start Your Own e-Business*.

Three Questions for Advertising Effectiveness

To save money, many new business owners handle their own advertising. But it's important to ensure you're effectively spreading the message. So before you release your ad, make sure you can answer "yes" to the following three questions:

- **Does your ad create a sense of immediacy?** Response diminishes over time, so make sure your ad includes a call to action. Use powerful phrases like "act quickly," "call now!" or "limited-time offer."

- **Have you hit as many "hot buttons" as possible?** People have diverse tastes. Keep the old saying, "Different strokes for different folks," in mind when writing your ad.

- **Have you evaluated other ads?** Check out all types of ads and emulate their strengths. Remember: nothing is more wasteful than reinventing the wheel.

Source: Rieva Lesonsky, *365 Tips to Boost Your Entrepreneurial IQ.*

Five Cardinal Rules of Logo Design

John Williams, founder and president of LogoYes.com, the world's first do-it-yourself logo design web site, gives the following guidelines for creating the best logo for your company.

Your logo reaches everyone who has any contact with you and is the first impression someone will have of your company. Because of its potential impact, your logo must offer a favorable impression of your business.

1. Your logo should reflect your company in a unique and honest way. Sounds obvious, but you'd be surprised how many business owners want something "just like" a competitor. If your logo contains a symbol—often called a "bug"—it should relate to your industry, your name, a defining characteristic of your company, or a competitive advantage you offer.

   What's the overriding trait you want people to remember about your business? Consider an abstract symbol to convey a progressive approach—abstracts are a great choice for high-tech companies. Or maybe you simply want an object that represents the product or service you're selling. Be clever, if you can, but not at the expense of being clear.

2. Avoid too much detail. Simple logos are recognized faster than complex ones. Strong lines and letters show up better than thin ones. Clean, simple logos reduce and enlarge much better than complicated ones.

   But although your logo should be simple, it shouldn't be simplistic. Good logos feature something unexpected or unique without being overdrawn.

3. Your logo should work well in black and white (one-color printing). If it doesn't look good in black and white, it won't look good in any color. Also keep in mind that printing costs for four-color logos are often greater than those for one- or two-color jobs.

4. Make sure your logo's scalable. It should be aesthetically pleasing in both small and large sizes, in a variety of mediums. A good rule of thumb is the "business card/billboard rule": your logo should look good on both.

5. Your logo should be artistically balanced. The best way to explain this is that your logo should seem "balanced" to the eye—no one part should overpower the rest. Color, line density, and shape all affect a logo's balance.

And once you commit to your logo design, be sure you have it in all three of these essential file formats: EPS for printing, JPG and GIF for your web site. Essentially, these file conversions render your logo as a single piece of art, so it's no longer a symbol with a typeface. Which brings us to the most important rule in logo design.

Never, ever redraw or alter your logo! If you want to animate it for your web site, fine. But don't change its essence. Reduce and enlarge it proportionally. And if you become tired of your logo, that's good. Because that's usually about the time it's starting to make an impression on everyone else!

Source: John Williams, "5 Cardinal Rules of Logo Design," www.entrepreneur.com/article/0,4621,319992,00.html.

Three Tips for a Radio Campaign

1. **Grab attention.** Right from the start, a great spot should grab and hold the listener's attention. Comedy is a common technique. With clever writing, the product itself can be the antidote to a comedic situation, for example. Many successful spots use sounds such as an unusual voice or compelling music to get people's attention. The key is to understand your target audience and fit your musical choices to their preferences.

2. **Keep them listening.** The best radio spots make you want to listen all the way through. For that, an audience must be able to relate to the story. Listeners will also pay more attention to your spot if it's part of a campaign. They'll associate each new ad with the previous ones and listen for the latest twist, helping to extend your brand message more successfully than if you were to run unrelated spots.

3. **Reward the audience.** Radio isn't a direct-response medium, although some advertisers mistakenly use it that way. While most listeners probably won't recall a telephone number at the end of a spot or a complicated call to action, what they will remember is how what's being advertised is going to make their lives better. Your spot should close with a solid payoff—the resolution of a humorous situation or some final bit of information that helps listeners take advantage of what you offer.

Source: Kim T. Gordon, "Turn It Up," www.entrepreneur.com/article/0,4621,312394,00.html.

Four Tips for Cable TV Advertising

A small business owner of a flower shop asked for advice on how to get started in TV advertising. Here are a few tips:

1. Bad advertising is about your company—its product or service.

2. Good advertising is about your customers and how your product or service will change their world. Consequently, guard against using "I," "we," "me," "my," and "our" too often in your ads. Replace those words with "you" and "your" and watch how much better these new ads work.

3. Your customers aren't really buying flowers. They're buying the reaction of someone important to them. So don't focus on the flowers. Focus on the reaction of the person who will receive them.

4. Don't get hung up on reaching the right people with your message. I've never seen a business fail because they were reaching the wrong people. But I've seen thousands who have failed because they were saying the wrong things in their ads.

Source: Roy H. Williams, "The Keys to Cable Ad Success," www.entrepreneur.com/article/0,4621,304954,00.html.

Important Aspects to Consider Before Becoming a Sponsor

As your business grows, you're likely to be approached to sponsor some type of industry or community event. Because events often attract attendees with specific profiles and interests, this can be a great way to reach targeted clients and customers. Before you say yes to a sponsorship, first take these steps to protect your investment:

- Examine the event's track record. Look for one that's been around a while and has an established audience. If the event is new, make sure the producer is reputable.

- Get details about expected attendance—how many and who they are.

- Check references. Ask current sponsors about their experiences.

- Ask if sponsorship packages can be customized.

- Look for promotional opportunities. Find out how the event will be marketed, and see if co-op advertising is available.

- Be unique. Will you get industry exclusivity?

Most important, get it in writing. Make sure your agreement is itemized. Have your attorney review the contract to be safe.

Source: Rieva Lesonsky, *365 Tips to Boost Your Entrepreneurial IQ*.

Section 9

Three Simple Rules When Picking Newspapers for Advertising

Rule No. 1: Select newspapers that reach your target audience with the least waste. This rule is easy to apply. Since advertising costs are often based on circulation, just examine the readership breakdown for each publication to see whether it efficiently reaches your customers. For example, a major metropolitan daily with hundreds of thousands of readers may offer too much "wasted circulation" for a single retail operation that draws business from its immediate neighborhood.

Rule No. 2: Select the newspapers your target audience reads for information on what you market. In some cases, rule No. 2 can completely override rule No. 1. Suppose you're choosing between a local, neighborhood newspaper and the major, market-wide daily. The small, local paper offers little wasted circulation when compared with the major daily. But if your customers are reading the market-wide newspaper for information on what you sell, you'll have to pay for the wasted circulation in order to reach them when they're predisposed to respond positively to your message.

Rule No. 3: Select newspapers you can afford to advertise in with enough frequency to penetrate. Newspapers are rarely a one-shot medium, so you'll need to run a consistent campaign. It's better to advertise with sufficient frequency in one paper, rather than just a few times each in several publications.

Source: Kim T. Gordon, "Choosing the Best Newspapers for Your Marketing Campaign," www.entrepreneur.com/article/0,4621,313967,00.html.

Section 9

Four Choices to Make When Selecting Newspapers for Advertising

Now that you know the basic framework for selecting the right newspapers for your campaign, here's how to make sense of all the choices:

- **Free vs. paid:** There are free newspapers of all types and descriptions in many communities nationwide. Some are excellent advertising vehicles; others are not. Many media buyers will tell you that people are more likely to read the publications they pay for. So all other aspects being equal, it's often a better choice to select newspapers that go to paid subscribers.

- **Audited vs. unaudited:** A newspaper that's audited, such as by the Audit Bureau of Circulation, can guarantee that its circulation figures are accurate and you'll get what you pay for. By comparing audits over time, you can tell if a newspaper's circulation is trending up or down. If a newspaper is unaudited, ask to see a sworn publisher's statement regarding circulation. Any publication unwilling to provide this form of verification is not a safe bet.

- **Bulk distribution vs. delivered:** When newspapers are distributed in bulk, such as the ones available for free in convenience stores and gas stations, there's significantly less control over who actually picks them up and reads them. While the publishers can guarantee the number of papers being distributed, it's more difficult to determine who they actually reach. However, many bulk-distributed publications meet special communications needs or are well targeted for unique purposes.

- **Market-wide vs. neighborhood:** One way to tell if a neighborhood paper is valued when compared with a market-wide paper is to try to determine which one people are most likely to read. Look at the household penetration of the major daily. If it's very high, then chances are that smaller, neighborhood papers have to fight much harder to secure readers by supplying special editorial or advertising sections, including classifieds. Evaluate the neighborhood paper by looking at other advertisers in your category. If they're advertising consistently, that's an indication they're getting results—and it's likely you will, too.

Source: Kim T. Gordon, "Choosing the Best Newspapers for Your Marketing Campaign," www.entrepreneur.com/article/0,4621,313967,00.html.

Seven Ways to Attract Transactional Customers

Here's how to write ads that trigger instant traffic:

1. Begin with a product that has wide appeal. Transactional ads don't create desire; they merely capitalize on a desire that's already there.

2. Reduce the price below what is considered the typical discount. The more desirable the item and the lower the price, the faster the traffic will come.

3. Explain why you're offering the price reduction. Your volume of quick-response traffic will be directly tied to the credibility of your desperation.

4. Create urgency by having a time limit. "Everyday low prices" may be a reasonable brand position in the long term, but it's no reason to rush to your store today.

5. Discount a highly respected brand that isn't usually discounted. A low price is unimpressive when there's a question about the quality.

6. Use specifics, which are more believable than generalities. Avoid ambiguous claims such as "up to 70 percent off" and vague disclaimers like "on selected items."

7. Schedule a high frequency of repetition for your TV or radio ads or use a second color (like red) in key lines of your newspaper ad, to support the perception of urgency.

Leverage these seven factors and you'll increase your store traffic quickly. But be aware:

the more often you use these tips, the less well they'll work.

You'll know your company is addicted to transactional advertising when customers begin asking, "When does this go on sale?" The price of this strategy is that you train your customers to wait for the next sale. Their sense of urgency is diminished with every new "Sale!" ad you write. In the end, the brand you're building will be weak. A number of studies on customer loyalty have clearly indicated customers who switch to you for reasons of price alone will switch away to a competitor for the same reason.

Source: Roy H. Williams, "Wow Customers with Your Ads," www.entrepreneur.com/article/0,4621,317810,00.html.

Types of Advertising Media

Roy H. Williams—author of *The Wizard of Ads*, *Secret Formulas of the Wizard of Ads*, *Magical Worlds of the Wizard of Ads*, *Accidental Magic*, and *Free the Beagle*—offers the following summary of your advertising options.

1. **Outdoor advertising/billboards:** Reach more people for a dollar than any other media, but are limited to a picture and no more than eight words.

2. **Radio:** Reaches the second-most people for a dollar, but cannot be targeted geographically and can only be loosely demographically targeted. But if people will drive significant distances to buy your product, or if you're selling a "we come to you" service, this is likely your best bet.

3. **Cable television:** Offers the impact of moving images as well as spoken words. Can easily be geographically targeted. But your ad will likely look homemade.

4. **Broadcast television:** Big prestige. Big bucks. But able to target psychographic profiles. Buy specific shows; never buy a rotator.

5. **Newspapers:** Reach customers who are in the market to buy today. Unfortunately, people not currently in the market for your product or service are less likely to notice your ad than if it had appeared in another medium.

6. **Magazines:** Expensive, but high impact with tight targeting. Little waste. Weakness is infrequency of repetition.

7. **Direct mail:** Highly targeted, all the way down to the level of the individual. But shockingly expensive to do right.

8. **Yellow Pages:** Essentially a service directory for the customer who has not yet made up his or her mind. Very foolish for retail businesses.

Source: Roy H. Williams, "Selecting the Most Effective Advertising Media," www.entrepreneur.com/article/0,4621,311248,00.html.

Improving Your Marketing

Section 9

Section 9

Five Steps to a Simple Marketing Plan

Section 1: Situation Analysis

This introductory section contains an overview of your situation as it exists today and will provide a useful benchmark as you adapt and refine your plan in the coming months. Begin with a short description of your current product or service offering, the marketing advantages and challenges you face, and a look at the threats posed by your competitors.

Section 2: Target Audience

All that's needed here is a simple, bulleted description of your target audiences. If you're marketing to consumers, write a target-audience profile based on demographics, including age, gender, and any other important characteristics. If you're marketing B2B, list your target audiences by category (such as lawyers, doctors, shopping malls) and include any qualifying criteria for each.

Section 3: Goals

In one page or less, list your company's marketing goals for the coming year. The key is to make your goals realistic and measurable so that you can easily evaluate your performance. You'd be in a much better position to gauge your marketing progress with a goal such as "Increase sales of peripherals 10 percent in the first quarter, 15 percent in the second quarter, 15 percent in the third quarter and 10 percent in fourth quarter."

Section 4: Strategies and Tactics

This section will make up the bulk of your plan. You should take as much space as you need to give an overview of your marketing strategies and list each of the corresponding tactics you'll employ to execute them. Your tactics section should include all the actionable steps you plan to take for advertising, public relations, direct mail, trade shows, and special promotions.

Section 5: Budget Breakdown

The final section of your plan includes a brief breakdown of the costs associated with each of your tactics. If you find the tactics you've selected are too costly, you can go back and make revisions before you arrive at a final budget.

Source: Kim T. Gordon, "Write a Simple Marketing Plan," www.entrepreneur.com/article/0,4621,306980,00.html.

Section 9

Ten Design Disasters for Marketing Materials

1. Don't enlarge your logo so it's the main focus of the page. People are interested in what you're selling, not who you are. In fact, the smaller your logo, the more established your company will appear. Check out ads by pros like Nike or Hewlett-Packard.

2. Don't place your logo in the text of your piece. Of course it's fine to use the name of your company in the text of any of your marketing materials, but inserting your actual logo into a headline or body copy is design suicide.

3. Don't use every font at your disposal. Choose one or two fonts for all your materials to build brand equity. Your font choices should be consistent with your image and your industry. For example, a conservative industry means a conservative font.

4. Don't use color indiscriminately. More color doesn't necessarily make something more appealing. Often it just makes it loud and off-putting. Most, if not all, your text should be the same color, preferably black for readability. For a unique look, try duotone photographs or print in two colors.

5. Don't be redundant. Don't repeat the name of your industry or product in your company name and your tagline and your headline. Potential customers know your industry. Restating it implies you don't.

6. Don't choose low-quality or low-resolution photography. A photo may look great in an album, but unless it features balanced lighting and good composition, it's not print-worthy. Photos need to be at least 300 dpi. And yes, people can tell the difference.

7. Don't fill up every inch of white space on the page. White space, or negative space, brings focus to what's important and gives the eye a rest. You may have a lot to say, but cramming it all in creates chaos and minimizes impact. Your piece will end up visually overwhelming. Think less, not more.

8. Don't focus on the details of your product or service; instead, focus on how it benefits your audience. Unless your product is extremely technical, make your offering relevant to your audience by emphasizing its benefits, not its features.

9. Don't do exactly what your competitors are doing. When you're positioning your product, it's good to know your competition. But don't copy them. Find out what your customers want and are attracted to. Stand out without sticking out.

10. Don't change design styles with every marketing piece you create. Strive for a consistent look and feel, keeping the same fonts and logo placement. If you use photos in one ad, don't use illustrations in another. If you place your logo in the middle of one brochure, don't place in at the top-right corner in another.

Source: John Williams, "What Not to Do When Designing Marketing Pieces Yourself," www.entrepreneur.com/article/0,4621,320242,00.html.

Six Ways to Make Time for Marketing

1. **Make marketing a priority.** You must commit to making time for marketing—whether to attend networking events, put together a brochure and business card, research prospects on the Web, or write a proposal. Without a strong commitment, you'll find yourself consistently putting off your marketing efforts, which could haunt you a month or two from now.

2. **Plan ahead to diffuse crises.** It's hard to market your business when you must spend the bulk of your day dealing with urgent matters. Anticipate potential problems and do what you need to do to diffuse them ahead of time. When you're proactive in managing your time, you reduce the number of unexpected crises that you'll have to face in the next week, freeing you up to devote more time to your marketing initiatives.

3. **Cut the fat.** A common mistake new entrepreneurs make is not focusing on their most important tasks. As a result, they're spending hours upon hours working but aren't really getting anything done. So, create time for marketing by evaluating your schedule to see where you can "cut the fat."

4. **Consolidate your activities when possible.** Plan ahead to accomplish tasks in a single trip. Bulk group-related activities together. If you have client and prospect meetings outside the home office, try to cluster them within the same vicinity.

5. **Avoid telephone interruptions.** Break the habit of answering the phone every time it rings. Schedule time for answering and making phone calls and checking your voice mail. This way, you can get more done without the stress created from the phone ringing off the hook.

6. **Cultivate positive thinking.** Negative emotions like worry, frustration, and anxiety waste time and cause you to panic. And it's hard to market your products or services when you're stuck in panic mode. Say no to anxiety and "rescript" worries into proactive and positive thoughts.

Source: Sean M. Lyden, "Find Time for Marketing," www.entrepreneur.com/article/ 0,4621,299091,00.html.

Four Fresh Ways to Target Your Market

1. **Reach college students.** The more than 15 million students in colleges nationwide spend $200 billion on products and services each year, according to the National Center for Education Statistics. Now there's a down-and-dirty way to reach them—with ads posted in laundry rooms on college campuses. For information, contact Washboard Media (www.encompassmediagroup.com) and OnPoint Marketing (www.onpointmarketing.com).

2. **Hit the links.** If golfers are your target, trying advertising on the sides and backs of hospitality carts—mobile units selling beverages and golfing supplies that stop once every hour at each group of golfers. Sports Cart Media (www.sportscartmedia.com) offers hospitality cart signage on nearly 1,000 golf courses, with seven advertising spaces available on each cart.

3. **Pump them up.** Local business owners in select markets have a new form of advertising available to them via the nearest gas pump. DirectCast Network (www.direct-castnetwork.com) has embedded computer chips in gasoline pump handles that play a mix of advertisements, information, and entertainment when a nozzle is placed in a fuel tank.

4. **Get in the swim.** Take corporate sponsorship of sports facilities one step further with logos and ads in and around public swimming pools. You can place signage on scoreboards, timing clocks, starting blocks, walls, and supporting pillars—and even on the bottom of the pools. Contact your local community pools, aquatic centers, and universities concerning sponsorship.

Source: Kim T. Gordon, "Best Places for Your Marketing Message," www.entrepreneur.com/article/0,4621,314532,00.html.

Six Tips to Boost Your Marketing Strategies

Do your marketing strategies need a boost? Guerrilla marketing guru, Jay Conrad Levinson offers these smart tips:

1. Don't just network—build relationships. Send notes to people you've just met to indicate you would like to talk again.

2. Make sure your ads answer every consumer's No. 1 question: What's in it for me?

3. Give something to your best customers. Gifts work best as a follow-up to a sale or a referral, on a holiday, or for the customer's birthday.

4. Personalize your faxes. And add an easy-response device, such as "To order, sign here and fax back."

5. Know the best ways to reach a prospect. A letter followed by a phone call is tops. Next best is a referral, then a cold call.

6. Always communicate with your customers, even when you're not trying to sell them anything. That's why you build relationships.

Source: Rieva Lesonsky, *365 Tips to Boost Your Entrepreneurial IQ.*

17 Practical No-Cost Promotions

1. Ask your previous customers to write a letter of referral that you can show to prospects and post on your web site. My research has shown that as they give you these letters, their own referrals to you will also increase.

2. Create a one-page newsletter and distribute it wherever you go. Your cost will be just pennies, and you'll be able to tell people more about what you do in a newsletter than you could in a brochure. Visit OnePageNewsletters.com (www.onepagenewsletters.com) for more ideas and promotional strategies on this powerful marketing strategy.

3. Put on an educational seminar at a public place such as your local library. Keep it educational so attendees won't feel they're being sold to. Then offer a private 30-minute one-to-one session to your attendees afterward to get better acquainted.

4. Write letters to the editors of local newspapers and business publications. And be sure you mention your web site.

5. You do have a web site, don't you? Even though it's not free, if you forgo just one of your specialty coffees per month you can cover the cost.

6. Ask for introductions from your accountant, your lawyer, and even your clergy. People who know people are golden for your marketing.

7. Circulate to meet as many people as possible, gathering business cards as you go. Then hit the phone and e-mail to follow up immediately. Almost no one follows up these days, and you'll be noticed for your thoroughness.

8. Triple the number of business cards you hand out. Give each person you meet one card to keep, and two to give to others they meet who might need your service. Merely the suggestion of this will get them thinking—and will sometimes result in real referrals.

9. Ask people you meet how their businesses are doing. Then ask, "Could what I do be helpful to your business at this time?"

10. Publish your own blog. Blogger.com, owned by Google, is totally free. By linking to your own site, you'll also boost your Google rankings.

11. Offer to speak to local civic groups. Most meet weekly, so they need 50 speakers per year. I've posted names of civic organizations on my web site, MarketingTalks.com (www.marketingtalks.com).

12. Team up with a colleague whose business complements yours and do joint promotions. As a copywriter and marketing consultant, I team up with graphic designers to mutually spread the word about our services.

13. Add a "tell a friend" button to your web site to encourage visitors to direct others to your site.

Section 9

14. At every public meeting, make a commitment to say something useful. I know this works; it's how I found my lawyer!

15. Write thank-you letters to businesses you frequent. A quick print shop owner posted my letter above his self-service photocopier. His customers read my letter and called to ask me to write for their businesses.

16. Make a bold flier and post it everywhere your prospects might lurk, such as Laundromats, supermarkets, or community centers. Be sure to create tear-off tabs at the bottom so readers can take your phone number. Microsoft Publisher includes this form in its free template collection.

17. Create a dramatic handout with information about what you offer. Mine was entitled "The 21 Most Common Direct Mail Mistakes and How to Overcome Them." Be sure your name, phone, e-mail, web site, and basic description are at the bottom of the document so readers can contact you.

Source: Pete Silver, "17 Practical No-Cost Promotions," www.entrepreneur.com/article/ 0,4621,317481,00.html.

Seven P's of Marketing

1. **Product**—First, develop the habit of looking at your product as though you were an outside marketing consultant brought in to help your company decide whether or not it's in the right business at this time.

2. **Prices**—Develop the habit of continually examining and re-examining the prices of the products and services you sell to make sure they're still appropriate to the realities of the current market.

3. **Promotion**—The third habit in marketing and sales is to think in terms of promotion all the time. Promotion includes all the ways you tell your customers about your products or services and how you then market and sell to them.

4. **Place**—The fourth P in the marketing mix is the place where your product or service is actually sold. Develop the habit of reviewing and reflecting upon the exact location where the customer meets the salesperson. Sometimes a change in place can lead to a rapid increase in sales.

5. **Packaging**—Develop the habit of standing back and looking at every visual element in the packaging of your product or service through the eyes of a critical prospect. Remember: people form their first impression about you within the first 30 seconds of seeing you or some element of your company. Small improvements in the packaging or external appearance of your product or service can often lead to completely different reactions from your customers.

6. **Positioning**—You should develop the habit of thinking continually about how you

are positioned in the hearts and minds of your customers. How do people think and talk about you when you're not present? How do people think and talk about your company? What positioning do you have in your market, in terms of the specific words people use when they describe you and your offerings to others?

7. **People**—Develop the habit of thinking in terms of the people inside and outside of your business who are responsible for every element of your sales and marketing strategy and activities.

Source: Brian Tracy, "The 7 Ps of Marketing," www.entrepreneur.com/article/ 0,4621,315531,00.html.

Three Rules for Niche Marketing

1. **Meet their unique needs.** The benefits you promise must have special appeal to the market niche. What can you provide that's new and compelling? Identify the unique needs of your potential audience, and look for ways to tailor your product or service to meet them.

2. **Say the right thing.** When approaching a new market niche, it's imperative to speak their language. In other words, you should understand the market's "hot buttons" and be prepared to communicate with the target group as an understanding member—not an outsider. In addition to launching a unique campaign for the new niche, you may need to alter other, more basic elements, such as your company slogan if it translates poorly to another language, for example.

3. **Always test-market.** Before moving ahead, assess the direct competitors you'll find in the new market niche and determine how you will position against them. For an overview, it's best to conduct a competitive analysis by reviewing competitors' ads, brochures, and Web sites and looking for their key selling points, along with pricing, delivery, and other service characteristics.

Source: Kim T. Gordon, "3 Rules for Niche Marketing," www.entrepreneur.com/article/0,4621,297662,00.html.

Three Marketing Mistakes to Avoid

1. **A pinch of this, a pinch of that.** This mistake is often made by entrepreneurs with big appetites and small budgets. They want to try a little bit of everything—advertising in multiple magazines and newspapers, online ads on a variety of sites, and a list of special events. But with limited budgets, they end up with a tiny presence in each. To maximize results from your marketing program, narrow your media choices and consistently run larger ads with enough frequency to get noticed.

2. **Tossing out the rule book.** If you think most rules were made to be broken, you may want to think again. Sometimes thinking outside the box can produce surprisingly positive results, but generally not at the expense of tried-and-true rules for effective marketing. Thanks to the billions of dollars businesses invest in advertising every year, all aspects of it have been studied.

3. **Focusing only on what's happening inside your business.** Some entrepreneurs get so inner-focused that they lose sight of all else, while others are constantly listening, looking, and learning from the changing marketing environment outside their own companies. Entrepreneurs who are too inner-focused often become complacent.

Source: Kim T. Gordon, "3 Marketing Mistakes to Avoid," www.entrepreneur.com/article/ 0,4621,311668,00.html.

Four Steps to Making Money in Mail Order Marketing

Can you still make money in the crowded mail order field? Yes—if you follow these four steps to mail order success:

1. **Know your niche.** You should bring a special knowledge, insight, or talent to your mail order specialty.

2. **Hit the books.** Immerse yourself in other companies' catalogs. Are they too long, too short? Do photos or illustrations work best? Make sure you also check out their order-processing methods.

3. **Find a list broker—fast.** Don't wait until you've printed your catalogs to pick your list broker. You need to incorporate the proper tracking codes, ensure your design is appropriate to your audience, and print the right number of catalogs.

4. **Know the code.** Make sure you take advantage of postal discounts.

Here's a bonus tip: Be patient; mail order empires are not built overnight.

Source: Rieva Lesonsky, *365 Tips to Boost Your Entrepreneurial IQ.*

Tips for Successful Mail Order Marketing

Building successful mail order enterprises is one way small entrepreneurs can grow their businesses.

- Study the competition to help you learn what's hot and what to avoid.

- Join a trade association, and pay attention to industry experts. Many predict annual trends based on extensive—and expensive—research.

- Don't try to be a one-product wonder; it rarely works. Develop piggyback products to broaden your appeal.

- Consider selling products outside your industry that would interest your customers. For example, florists could sell floral books, stationery, or even jewelry in addition to flowers.

- Watch your costs. Catalog expenses are rising. Make sure postage and handling costs are covered. And don't overlook the internet as an additional or alternative way to sell products.

Source: Rieva Lesonsky, *365 Tips to Boost Your Entrepreneurial IQ.*

Tips for Proper Marketing Timing

To get the most for your marketing dollar, make sure you properly time your efforts.

- Try to ensure that your direct-mail package arrives Tuesday, Wednesday, or Thursday.

- When relevant, tie your message to what's going on in the world.

- Don't launch your marketing too soon. Make sure you have worked all the bugs out, that your salespeople know all the facts, and that you can deliver on what you promise.

- If you're in retail, wait a month before you have your grand opening celebration. This way, you will be more practiced.

- Don't waste time telemarketing when nobody's there. Find out the best time to call.

- Never rush through creating your marketing materials. The key words to keep in mind here? Economy and quality. Remember: when it comes to marketing, speed can kill.

Source: Rieva Lesonsky, *365 Tips to Boost Your Entrepreneurial IQ.*

SCORE's Five Tips for Low-Cost Marketing

1. **Make yourself stand out.** Nancy Michaels, owner of a marketing communications firm in Concord, MA, sends greetings and gifts at odd holidays, like Chinese New Year and the Fourth of July, instead of at Christmas and Hanukkah.

2. **Create a memorable title for yourself.** The business cards of one husband-and-wife team refer to them as "Dad" and "Mom" because their furniture store is named after their children.

3. **Write educational articles** for trade journals, newspapers, and other publications

that reach your audience. They'll get your name before the public and add to your credibility.

4. **Don't underestimate the market value of your name.** By using their names over and over to promote their talents, Oprah Winfrey and Martha Stewart have turned small businesses into enormous enterprises.

5. **Make sure the name of your company is legible.** Some logos use such fancy lettering that the company name is unreadable.

Source: SCORE, www.score.org/business_tips.html.

Five Cheap Ways to Market Your Small Business

1. **Talk with your clients.** It's amazing how much money businesses spend to gather market information and attract new clients when they have a wealth of opportunity and information in their current client base. One of the best ways to increase revenue is to talk with current customers.

   When you assess perceptions, choose five to ten clients and contact them to ask if they'd participate in a phone interview. Here's how it works:

   1. Send a letter asking permission to have someone contact them about your company.
   2. Have the interviewer call and ask value-based questions such as:
      - What problems were you trying to solve or what challenges were you facing when you considered the services of Company ABC?
      - How important were Company ABC's services in solving your problems or addressing your challenges?
      - What did you value most about this company's work?
      - What other products or services do you wish they offered that could help you with other business challenges?
   3. After conducting all the interviews, compile the information to discover trends and themes.
   4. Send a thank-you letter to every client who participated. Include key lessons from the interviews and explain the specific changes you plan to make to your business based on this information.

      The important part here is to use what you learn. If you don't make changes to your business, then you've wasted everyone's time.

   Keys to success: The conversation with your customers is just that—a conversation. Don't fire questions at them; instead, have the interviewer engage in a conversation and gather as much valuable data as possible.

2. **Creatively package your marketing campaigns.** A postcard is one way to market your business. But how about putting a small box together with a fork, a knife, a spoon, and a custom-printed napkin that invites your prospect to "have lunch on us"? Think outside the box, and your marketing campaigns will have more impact.

Keys to success: Set a clear objective for your marketing campaign, and identify how you'll measure its success. Then follow up to measure the results and adjust the program if necessary.

3. **Get the word out with publicity.** Think you can't do PR or publicity without employing the services of a high-priced firm? Although a good firm brings tremendous contacts and experience, most small companies can do enough PR on their own to spark the public's interest.

Keys to success: In one word, leverage. Though it does happen, don't expect one story placement to generate thousands in revenue. Your success depends on leveraging each press release, each article, and each published mention. Remember: PR is more cost-effective and more credible than advertising.

4. **Leverage existing relationships.** Most people know at least 200 people. Do the math: if you know 200 people and they each know 200 people, that's 40,000 potential contacts! Spend time developing relationships with the people you already know—clients, colleagues, people you meet through professional networking organizations, friends, and even family.

Keys to success: Educate, don't sell. The key here is to build relationships. Start from the perspective of giving more than you ask, and your network will become your most valuable marketing tool.

5. **Commit to e-mail marketing.** Marketing through e-mail is flexible, cost-effective, easy to measure (assuming you put the right tracking in place), and high impact. Remember: this is a marketing campaign. So be sure to think it through, develop an appropriate message, create a piece that reflects your brand, know your objectives, and make sure the information is valuable for your market, or people will quickly unsubscribe.

Keys to success: Don't be seen as a "spammer"! Send e-mail only to those people who have given permission. When someone asks to be removed, respond immediately.

Source: Susan LaPlante-Dube, "5 Cheap Ways to Market Your Business," www.entrepreneur.com/article/0,4621,315529,00.html.

Section 9

Top Nine Ways to Give Yourself the Technology Edge

Are you taking advantage of today's technology to help market your business? Here are nine smart ways to give yourself the technology edge.

1. Fax or e-mail coupons or discount offers to prime customers.

2. Host an online forum or chat session with potential and existing clients.

3. Create a customer fax-request ordering system.

4. Use online advertising to reach people and markets previously beyond your geographical boundaries and your budget.

5. Create customer databases loaded with client information, including special dates, orders, and preferences.

6. Check your competitor's web sites regularly.

7. Be creative. Use graphic software to create fliers, brochures, and newsletters.

8. Stay in touch—no matter where you are—with e-mail, pagers, cell phones, and voice mail.

9. Post your message on as many free message boards as appropriate.

Source: Rieva Lesonsky, *365 Tips to Boost Your Entrepreneurial IQ.*

Eight More Marketing Mistakes to Avoid

1. **Putting all your eggs in one basket.** If your entire marketing budget is used on just one method of promoting your business, you won't realize the highest return on your investment. Diversifying your efforts will increase the frequency and reach of your messages and stretch your marketing dollars.

2. **Not measuring results.** Measuring the results of your marketing efforts allows you to reinvest in vehicles that are working—and ditch those that aren't. Try tactics like surveys, coded coupons, in-store response cards, or focus groups to find out how well your messages are being received.

3. **Firing before you take aim.** If you find yourself throwing money at every promotional opportunity, take a step back and realize the benefits of planning. Set objectives, define the audience you wish to reach, and set your budget over the next six to 12 months.

4. **Eliminating marketing efforts when things get tight.** When cash flow slows, advertising, direct mail, and other forms of marketing are the easiest expenses to reduce, right? But cut these, and you eliminate the very activities that will bring in new customers to turn your business around.

5. **Not getting help when you need it.** If you find you're too busy to handle your marketing efforts or that your materials aren't looking as professional as they should, it's time to call in the reinforcements. Hire a full- or part-time employee, a marketing or public relations agency, or an independent business consultant, but make sure you're getting the message out in a manner that reflects your business.

6. **Fixing programs that aren't broken.** If your advertising campaign or direct-mail program is producing results, don't change it just for the sake of changing it. Once you see returns slow down, look for new approaches, but always test them before implementing changes on a full scale.

7. **Allowing ego to get in the way of common sense.** Ego tempts very bright people to do very dumb things. Your marketing decisions should be based on factors that will positively impact some area of your business—usually its bottom line. Hiring an expensive multinational agency for a small account, sacrificing valuable frequency for full-page advertising, and buying blanket mailing lists without matching criteria to your customer profile are all examples of an ego that's sabotaging effectiveness.

8. **Relying on hunches.** It came to you in the shower: the Big Idea for promoting your business. So you put all your marketing dollars into, for instance, painting your delivery trucks with neon colors. Before you blow your money on hunches, however, you need to do your homework. Talk to your customers and others who may have done something similar. Then test your theory by trying a small-scale version of the Big Idea.

Source: Gwen Moran, "To Err Is Dangerous," www.entrepreneur.com/article/0,4621,231005,00.html.

Section 9

Tips for Using Coupons as a Marketing Tool

All of us have clipped coupons at one time or another. But did you know that these simple pieces of paper could be one of the most powerful marketing tools?

- Coupons are merely incentives to do business with you. But with them, you can achieve several goals. Are you introducing a new product or service? Do you need to increase your repeat business?

- Coupons help you fend off competitors, reinforce a current ad campaign, or even soften the blow of a price increase.

- Direct mail is not your only choice for distribution. Consider running coupons in local newspapers or even on the internet.

- Coupons are more than words on a piece of paper. Be sure your coupons are clear, stating precisely what the offer is, how long it lasts, and how many customers can redeem them.

Most importantly, most entrepreneurs report that coupons increase their business significantly.

Source: Rieva Lesonsky, *365 Tips to Boost Your Entrepreneurial IQ.*

Tips on Giving Free Gifts

Do you bribe your customers? You might quickly answer, "Of course not." But free gifts can be great marketing tools.

- Free gifts like T-shirts, caps, coffee mugs, scratch pads, and mouse pads can be really effective.
- Giving those away can generate leads, boost store traffic, and increase awareness of your business.
- When considering free gifts, first figure out who you want to reach and how much money you have to spend. Then focus on the gift and the message you want to print on it.
- Are freebies worth it? Experts say 40 percent of recipients remember the name of the company that sent the gifts and about one-third still use the gifts six months later.
- Best yet, free gifts can increase your average order by 300 percent.

Source: Rieva Lesonsky, *365 Tips to Boost Your Entrepreneurial IQ.*

Advice for Using Civic Marketing

"Civic marketing"—the kind practiced by people like Ben & Jerry—is one of the newest business buzzwords. But even the smallest businesses can use community outreach as a low-cost, high-impact marketing tool. Here's some information about it:

- The benefits of civic marketing are plentiful: it raises community awareness of your business, builds customer and employee loyalty, helps you stand out from your competitors, and positions you as a community leader.
- Select your causes carefully. Look for ones truly meaningful to your community, your industry, or your target market.
- Depending on your situation, you can donate money, time, or resources. Some business owners encourage their employees to volunteer at the charity or cause of their choice. Others may establish scholarships for high school or college students.
- Whatever your involvement, don't forget to use public relations campaigns, promotional signs, or in-store displays to let the community know what you're up to.

Source: Rieva Lesonsky, *365 Tips to Boost Your Entrepreneurial IQ.*

SCORE's Five Tips for Sprucing up a Tired Image

1. Identify who your customers and other stakeholders are and what they want from you. Through interviews or questionnaires, have them help you evaluate your image.

2. Pinpoint the strengths and weaknesses of your current image. What misconceptions or negative perceptions need to be corrected?

3. Devise a strategy. It could include changing your company's name and logo, changing your product mix, or even dropping some customers and courting others.

4. Get expert help. Image makeovers usually call for professionals who can help you devise and implement a new concept.

5. Follow up to make sure the makeover is doing its job. Are sales up? Are you attracting the customers you want?

Source: SCORE, www.score.org/business_tips.html.

Section
9

Chapter 60

Trade Shows

Section 9

Online Trade Show Resource Centers

TSNN.com

www.tsnn.com

This is a great resource if you are looking for suppliers or venues, whether you want to exhibit or to attend. Easy to navigate and find trade shows nearest you.

tradeshowspecialist.com

www.tradeshowspecialist.com

This web site contains helpful information on everything: trade show display booths, online trade, trade show displays, and trade show gifts.

Tradeshow Week

tradeshowweek.com

This site features a tradeshow directory that is consistently updated, an exhibit hall directory, and a newsletter to keep you informed on trade show news.

GearMX, Inc.

www.gearmx.com

This company works with organizations to build high-traffic exhibits and coordinate trade shows. These consultants advise your staff on any improvements needed and follow up with detailed show reports to help you plan your next event. They work on a per-project basis to develop a trade show management package that fits your organization's budget and time constraints.

Source: compiled by author.

Section 9

List of Places to Find Trade Show Displays

Displays2Go: Trade Show Displays

www.displays2go.com

Manufacturer of trade show displays. Stock selection includes portable presentation boards, pop-up display walls, and folding display stands.

Quality One Engineering, Inc.: Trade Show Displays

www.showbooth.com

Designs and manufactures trade show booths, displays, and fixtures since 1990. Servicing all of southern California.

Industrial Export Express: Display Crating and Shipping

www.crating.net

Offers corporate and industrial crating nationwide, including heavyweight packaging and certified export crating designed to ensure safe arrival.

TradeShowJoe.com: Displays

www.tradeshowjoe.com

Sells, rents, and services a variety of new and used portable and custom trade show displays and trade show display accessories.

Displayit: Event and Trade Show Displays

www.exhibitstogo.com

Provides trade show exhibits and trade show displays, including pop-up, portable, counters, kiosks, screens, flooring, lighting, and truss systems.

Tradeshow Supermarket: Trade Show Displays

www.tradeshowsupermarket.com

Supplies displays for trade shows, including pop-up displays, panel displays, modular displays, tabletop displays, podiums, counters, and banners.

Above & Beyond Balloons: Inflatable Trade Show Displays

www.balloons.biz

Manufactures inflatable balloons, blimps, kiosks, and tents to increase sales and visibility at outdoor and indoor trade shows. Ships worldwide.

Source: compiled by author.

Tips for Attending Trade Shows

One of the best methods for new entrepreneurs to market their wares is to exhibit at trade shows. But the costs of attending can add up considerably, so before you go, ask yourself these questions:

- Have I set specific goals for participating in this show? Make sure you know what you hope to accomplish at the show, including how many leads you need to get, how many sales you must generate, and how many connections you need to make.

- Is this the right show to meet my needs? You'll want to make sure the show audience fits the profile of your best customer. For example, if you only distribute regionally, is a national show a waste of time and money?

- Am I ready for this show? You should always market to attendees before you get there. Mail a flier, postcard, or coupon to current customers and past show attendees. Your goal is to make it worth their while to stop by your booth.

Source: Rieva Lesonsky, *365 Tips to Boost Your Entrepreneurial IQ.*

Helpful Trade Show Prep Tips

The key word here is "prepared." The last thing you want to do is just throw together a booth with a tablecloth on it, set out your products, prop up your feet, and expect buyers to rush over and gush. Plus, there are a lot of details to consider—paperwork to fill out, travel arrangements to be made, and so on.

- It's imperative, then, that you are organized and prepared for anything that comes your way. Keep track of everything, down to the person you talked to at the convention center who told you what you need to do to become an exhibitor.

- Make sure you are in close contact with the event sponsor, taking care to read through the exhibitors' manual carefully and follow whatever guidelines the sponsor has set forth.

- Trade shows themselves are easy to find; nearly every major city hosts at least one show relevant to a particular retailer. Contact your local chamber of commerce or convention and visitors' bureau to find out about upcoming events in your area.

- You can also find them via online searches; use the trade show finder tool at *Tradeshow Week* magazine online (www.tradeshowweek.com).

- As for your display, unless you're skilled in graphic design or visual merchandising, we would recommend getting help from an exhibit designer. They will know what kind of signage you need and how to display your product. But don't let your display speak for itself—you need to talk to people about your product, demonstrate if necessary, answer any questions, collect business cards, and network.

- Get help with the exhibit so you will have adequate staff on hand so that somebody acknowledges every person who visits your booth.

- And when the show is over, it's not really over—you've got all those leads to follow up on in a timely fashion.

Source: Karen E. Spaeder, "Attending a Trade Show," www.entrepreneur.com/article/0,4621,292174,00.html.

The Dos and Don'ts to Ensure an Effective Trade Show Display

1. **Get there early.** Even though you have most likely been given the dimensions of your space, it's a great idea to survey the hall before you set up your tradeshow displays. Many have been caught off guard when they arrived and were forced to scramble at the last minute.

2. **Survey your neighbors.** Look around your area at the types of trade show displays others are setting up. Will yours be lost in the crowd? If so, make adjustments to bring more attention to your booth. Have someone standing in front of your area to greet visitors—instead of behind a counter. Offer free samples or a drawing. Visit a nearby store and buy lots of colorful, helium balloons to use in your booth.

3. **Have a backup plan.** Nothing strikes fear in the heart of an exhibitor like hearing, "I'm sorry—the shipper must have lost your boxes." Now what?! Trade show displays from Showbooth.com are lightweight, easy to transport, and affordable. Carry an extra display in your car or check it as baggage when you fly to your new destination. This way you can be sure your event will go off without a hitch.

4. **Have professionally designed displays.** "Homemade-looking" trade show displays do little to impress show visitors. They also present a cheap image of you and your company. Go all out with professionally designed tradeshow displays in order to gain attention and draw traffic to your booth. Showbooth.com offers graphic-design services for tradeshow displays.

5. **Use a variety of sizes.** Let your imagination go wild! To create an eye-catching booth, choose several sizes of tradeshow displays. Use one for a backdrop, add pop-up displays on tabletops, and create an entranceway or border for your booth with banner stands. The more creativity you use, the more traffic you'll stop.

Source: Showbooth.com, "Dos and Don'ts to Ensure the Effectiveness of Your Tradeshow Displays," www.showbooth.com.

Section 9

Nine Tips for Getting the Most out of Exhibiting at Trade Shows

1. **Set goals for the show.** "Develop clear goals for participation at each exhibition and write them down," says Casey Seidenberg, director of promotions and events for Guru.com. "It's important to remember what your ultimate goals are for the show so that appropriate decisions can be made. It's too easy to get busy and lose site of the big picture."

2. **Read the exhibitor manual, cover to cover.** In it, you'll find a wealth of information: forms to set up booth services (furniture, electricity, carpet, and so on), show hours, sponsorship opportunities, and hotel and airfare discounts. Contact the event sponsor or exposition company if you have questions.

3. **Watch those deadlines!** "Miss a deadline, and costs go up significantly," says Sheryl Sookman, a principal at The MeetingConnection. Setting up show services on-site is expensive, and you'll spend lots of valuable time standing in line. Complete and submit your paperwork early for substantial discounts.

4. **Pack important paperwork in your luggage, not with the booth.** This includes contracts, service orders, and shipment tracking numbers. Take a backup copy of electronic presentations and make sure you have the contact numbers for any vendors you used in connection with the show.

5. **Take your tools.** Create a show toolbox labeled "open first," and ship it with your booth. Include such items as office supplies, tools you need to set up the exhibit, a small first aid kit, preprinted shipping labels, snacks, and water. Don't forget plenty of business cards.

6. **Individually label each box.** Include your company name, contact information, and booth number. Without proper identification, it's highly unlikely the loading dock will be able to identify your shipment and deliver it to your booth. If it can't be identified, it can't be delivered.

7. **Staff the booth; work the show.** Working a trade show booth is exhausting. Set up shifts of three or four hours each and give everyone time to take breaks (preferably away from the booth). You should also schedule time for your staff to walk the floor and check out the competition, make contacts, and see what's new in your industry.

8. **Don't let your leads get cold!** Immediately contact leads and thank them for dropping by your booth. Your prompt handling of requests for additional information will show potential clients you value their time and provide quality customer service.

9. **Evaluate your success.** Did you reach your goals? Was this the right audience? Note your successes and brainstorm for ideas while the show is still fresh in your mind.

Source: Donna Curry, "Show 'Em What You Got," www.entrepreneur.com/article/0,4621,277400,00.html.

Section 9

Direct-Mail Marketing

Section 9

Seven Steps to a Direct-Mail Campaign

Once you've outlined your target market, a direct-mail campaign has seven key steps.

1. **Develop a mailing list.** Put your description of the targets on this list in writing, so you know exactly to whom you're mailing. If you're mailing to a larger-sized list (more than 20,000), you'll probably want to provide your letter shop with Cheshire labels: unglued labels that are affixed to your mailing piece with special glue. These labels require machine application at the mailing house. For smaller quantities, you might just provide self-sticking labels. Your list supplier will provide you the labels in whatever format you want.

2. **Create a mailing piece.** You don't just mail out a brochure to your list. That gets too expensive, and your brochures weren't designed for it. You need to create a direct-mail piece with a strong offer that will spur the recipient to action. All direct mail leads to the "call to action": what do you want the recipient to do next? Mail back the business reply card? Call the 800 number? Fill out the order form and fax it to your number?

   Your goal is to get action. You don't want a direct-mail piece to inform. That's what your brochures are for. You want action!

3. **Code your response vehicle.** Whatever way you ask recipients to respond, make sure you code your mailing. All you have to do is assign each mailing a batch number, such as 03062103: 0306 is the month/year of the mailing, 21 is the identifier for the particular mailing you used, and 03 is the identifier for the particular offer. Coding provides a simple device for revealing just who has responded to which mailing and which offer. It makes individual responses much more valuable, since you can easily tabulate the codes to see what's working the best for you.

4. **Test the campaign.** Even a modest campaign of a few thousand pieces can run up the budget with mailing and duplication costs. So you should always test-mail a portion of your mailing list and check the results. No one can predict the response rate you'll get; there are just too many variables.

   What percentage of your mailing makes for a reliable test? Again it varies, but most authorities would tell you to test ten percent of your list and no fewer than 250 pieces. This will give you enough of a spread across the variables to make the results worth something. Before you do your test, you should decide what response rate will support your going ahead with the planned major mailing. This will depend on your budget. Writers on direct mail duck the issue of response rates because there are so many variables—and because no one really knows how to predict response. Experience suggests that if your rate is less than two percent, something is wrong. Either your list is wrong or your offer is too weak. If you get a response rate above seven percent for a mass mailing (without giving away the farm), you've done very, very well.

Section 9

5. **Run the campaign.** Keep your mailing pace in line with your ability to handle the potential responses. Your test mailing will give you some sense of the rate of customer response. Use that as a gauge for how many pieces you should mail in a given week. Mail only those pieces you can support with your sales effort.

6. **Handle customer responses.** You can't handle the fulfillment end of a direct-mail campaign without considerable planning. If you're asking respondents to request additional information, what are you going to send them? How soon do you want to mail the information out? What else will you do with the responses? In other words, how will you make maximum use of the names you've spent so much time to acquire?

   If you're a company with distributors or sales offices, it's common to pass along the names of prospects so that follow-up can be handled on the local level. The quicker the response the better, since your speed in dispatching information can quite justifiably be viewed as reflective of your commitment to customer service. Why should respondents have to wait for materials?

7. **Analyze the results of the campaign.** This is perhaps the most important, and underrated, aspect of the campaign. Did the final results match what you expected from the test? What parts of the demographics responded better than expected? Are there subsets of your target audience that you can focus on in future mailings?

   Every direct-mail campaign you run should contribute not just to your sales figures but also to enhancing your customer database. In very real terms, it represents the future of your business.

Source: Jack Ferreri, "Direct Marketing 101," www.entrepreneur.com/article/ 0,4621,317818,00.html.

Secrets to Making Your Direct-Mail Marketing More Effective

Knowing these secrets to success can help you avoid some direct-mail pitfalls.

1. **Converse first.** If your mailing is going to require a team effort—printer, list broker, mailing house, graphic designer, and writer—be sure to consult in detail with each person at the project's onset. Discuss your goals and invite feedback. Ask the mailing house whether the list should arrive on disk or on labels. And make sure your graphic designer knows the size and weight restrictions for the postage classification you need to meet before he or she starts designing.

2. **Buy from a broker.** Because selecting the right list is the single most important element in your direct-mail effort, consult a reputable list broker. To find a broker, one good resource is the *Standard Rate and Data Service* (SRDS) direct-mail book, which

can be found in many libraries. You can also ask your local chamber of commerce or post office for recommendations. A knowledgeable broker will be able to help you find a list that will meet your criteria with minimal waste. Be sure to ask what the "deliverability guarantee" is—in most cases, it's 93 percent. Find out whether you'll be compensated if your return rate from incorrect addresses is higher than that.

3. **Use the list ethically.** Most lists are rented for one-time use (although you can usually pay for multiple uses) and have minimum purchase requirements. Don't even think about poaching the list to use more than once—most are salted with dummy names that allow list companies to track who's mailing without authorization.

4. **Be careful with creativity.** It's important to be creative when you're competing for a prospect's attention. But if your piece is an eighth of an inch too big or a fraction of an ounce too heavy for the standard Postal Service weight and size classifications, you could end up wasting big bucks in extra postage. Be creative—but run unusual sizes or shapes by your local post office first.

5. **Be benefits-oriented.** Too many direct-mail pieces get bogged down in details that don't sell the prospect. Be clear, show your prospects what's in it for them, and make sure your response mechanism is easy to understand.

6. **Testing 1-2-3.** Test different lists, mailing pieces and offers, and don't be afraid to try new approaches. Jack Rein, owner of Rein Associates, a direct-mail marketing consulting firm in Little Silver, New Jersey, cites a Columbia House example: by changing its offer from 10 records for $1.99 plus free shipping and handling to 10 records for a penny, plus $1.98 shipping and handling, the direct-music seller increased its response rate by 23 percent.

7. **Check your timing.** Rein suggests sending local, first-class mailings on Monday. Most pieces will reach prospects on Tuesday, the lightest mail day of the week. Different industries have different times of the year that work best for them; check with your trade association or list broker for recommended times.

Source: Gwen Moran, "Postal Power," www.entrepreneur.com/article/0,4621,230458,00.html.

10 Direct-Mail Marketing Secrets

1. Develop a visual sense for what works and what doesn't. You have an abundance of learning materials right inside your mailbox. The next time you go through your mail, take a minute to examine what's there, what catches your attention, what attracts you, and what repels you. Do you have examples of previous campaigns you've sent out? Or pieces from your competitors that you can learn from? "Junk mail" has a unique style—learn to recognize it and think about how you can create the opposite.

Section 9

2. Don't insult your prospects' intelligence by using cheesy tag lines or see-and-say visuals. Believe it or not, "FREE MONEY" doesn't attract much attention in the inundated world of today's consumers. So avoid using bold with italics, ALL CAPS, and multiple exclamation points (!!!!), as these are the clichéd visual cues of junk mail.

3. Don't assume your audience knows everything. An educated consumer is one who's more willing to make a purchase. Your headline should draw attention to your body copy, which is your most powerful selling tool. Ignore what people say about how no one reads anymore—if compelled by a good headline and provoking imagery, a potential customer will want more information immediately. Directing them to a web site or phone number is asking a lot of your audience, so instead include essential information right on the mail piece. When writing copy, start from the beginning, be direct, and include as much information as you can in five sentences or less.

4. Use what you know. If you know your customers inside and out, by all means, use that information in your mail piece. Meeting your potential customers where they are is a great way to attain trust quickly.

5. "You Won't Believe This Amazing Offer!" At least that part's true, when it comes to your prospects—people are much more skeptical these days. So do something completely unusual with your direct-mail piece: tell the truth. Exposing your weaknesses make your strengths seem even greater and (yes, believe it) creates a sense of honesty and trust.

6. Ask and you shall receive. Know exactly what action you want your mail piece to elicit, and then ask for it. Then ask again. This is known in the world of direct mail as the call to action, and it's the consumers' cue for getting what they want. If there's no call to action, your direct-mail piece is just creating brand recognition. Is there a number to call? Don't just list the number—ask them to make the call. Is there a web site to visit? A response mail required? Ask, suggest, and entice your audience to respond to your piece.

7. Consider the medium. What will your message be delivered on? Postcards are an effective medium for most products, because they cut down a barrier (the envelope) between the consumer and the message. However, some direct mail is more appropriate when crafted as a letter, especially those that involve high-dollar sales and financial services.

8. Use color wisely. Color will always catch more attention than black and white, but when it comes to color, more is not necessarily better. Additional colors may cost more money to produce—and too many colors can make a piece confusing and cluttered, so it's important to find what's best for your project. Begin by choosing one or two main colors and one or two supporting colors based on the feelings they elicit. Warm colors are exciting and energizing; cool colors are relaxing and refreshing. Bright colors speak loudly; dull colors suggest quietly. Think about your product, corporate image and your audience when choosing color. Metallic colors are a great option for one- or two-color jobs.

Section
9

9. Personalize your pieces. You've seen them: "[your name here], you've got to check out this deal!" Personalization can enhance a consumer's inclination to read your direct-mail piece by creating a sense of familiarity. It also emphasizes their importance to your business.

   When it comes to personalizing a direct-mail piece, there are a lot of options, ranging from addressing it to a specific consumer or including his or her name in the letter portion to printing his or her name in the art area on the postcard or letter. Some of these options can get pricey, so if you think it's appropriate for your mailer, talk with your printer about your personalization options so you'll know what options fit your budget.

10. Determine the best way to mail it. When it comes to mailing your direct-mail pieces, you have options regarding the postage you purchase. Think about your customers and the value of your product, as well as time sensitivity. Will presort (formerly bulk rate) arrive in time? Do your potential customers care about first-class postage or not? Are you eligible to receive special, not-for-profit postage rates? And don't forget to consider the type of postage for your direct-mail piece. You can use first-class or presort stamps or you can print the first-class or presort postage directly on the piece. (This is known as the indicia.) In pieces that are highly personalized and look official, a stamp can increase response rates because consumers infer a human touch. On postcards, indicia work just as well as stamps and don't cost anything to apply to the mail piece.

Source: Mark Risley, "10 Direct Mail Secrets," www.entrepreneur.com/article/ 0,4621,322602,00.html.

Great Tips for Direct-Mail Marketing Success

Let's get direct—with direct marketing. Sometimes the best way to increase your sales is to go straight to the source. Here are some suggestions on how to make direct marketing work for you:

- Why not send old customers who you haven't heard from in the past six months a discount coupon? Bargains are usually great motivators.

- If you want to poll your customers, it's traditional to give a monetary incentive. Sending the unexpected usually increases response—try a two-dollar bill for a change.

- Acknowledge your customers' birthdays or other special occasions with a special offer. It may sound sentimental, but customers love the attention, and that translates into increased sales.

- Direct-marketing guru Jerry Fisher recommends you send a "lumpy" mailer. Few, says Fisher, can resist opening an envelope with a lump or small box in it.

Why bother with direct marketing? Because it is especially designed to get people to stop ogling and start ordering.

Source: Rieva Lesonsky, *365 Tips to Boost Your Entrepreneurial IQ.*

Direct-Mail Tips to Increase Response Rate

Direct-mail marketing is popular with entrepreneurs nationwide, who rely on it to sell products and generate leads. But with an average two-percent response rate, the difference between a good package and a great one can mean the difference between spending a fortune and earning one.

1. Use five components: an envelope, a letter, an order form, optional inserts, and a return envelope. For a small test, mail 2,500 to 5,000 pieces. Mail to the same list at least three times.

2. "The envelope is your 'handshake,'" says Don Dailey, president of Dailey Direct Inc., a Gaithersburg, Maryland, graphic design firm specializing in direct marketing. "A teaser on the envelope is vital."

3. Your letter should explain the benefits of your product or service, followed by the features.

4. Be sure your letter includes a "Johnson box"—the sentence or headline before the salutation that highlights your marketing hook—and a P.S. "The second thing people read in a letter is the P.S.," says Dick Goldsmith, president of the New York City direct-mail production agency The Horah Group. It should contain some aspect of the offer that makes the recipient want to read on.

5. Make your order form clear, brief, and easy to fill out. Include a fax number.

6. Include a toll-free number on every page, because you never know which component your prospect will keep.

7. "Avoid a monochromatic package," warns Dailey. Keep your carrier envelope and letter stock consistent, but for the rest, use different textures, sizes, or colors.

8. At the same time, says Dailey, "Don't overdesign. Some of the best packages are simple-looking."

9. "Lack of a single focus is one of the biggest mistakes entrepreneurs make," says Dailey. If you have a good offer, it should lead the package. If you have a one-of-a-kind product, make that the lead.

10. The more pieces you include, the better, as long as each explains an additional benefit. Include brochures to explain complex services. Use coupons for offers.

11. Testing is vital and should be ongoing. If you're serious about using direct mail to build your business, use it continually.

Source: Kim T. Gordon, "Copy Right," www.entrepreneur.com/article/0,4621,268488,00.html.

Recommendations on Mailing List Databases

Info USA
Access to over 14 million businesses and 200 million residents to add to your mailing lists.
Phone: (800) 321-0869
E-mail: help@infousa.com
Web: www.infousa.com

American List Counsel Lists
Access to millions of national businesses and residential contacts.
4300 U.S. Highway 1, CN-5219
Princeton, NJ 08543
Phone: (866) 767-1154
Web: www.alclists.com

The List Company
Delivers your target consumers to you by demographic characteristics and others.
11906 Arbor Street
Omaha, NE 68144
Phone: (877) 247-4770
Fax: (402) 778-0124
E-mail: info@tlclists.com
Web: www.tlclists.com

AmeriList Mailing List Company
Accurate responsive business and consumer mailing list and sales leads.
978 Route 45, Suite L 2
Pomona, NY 10970
Phone: (845) 362-6737, (800) 457-2899
Fax: (845) 362-6433,
Web: www.amerilist.com

B2B Marketing Database
Unlimited access to U.S. businesses, sales leads, mailing lists, and more.
P.O. Box 541034,
Omaha, NE 68154
Phone: (402) 334-1824
Fax: (402) 991-7701
Web: www.goleads.com

Source: Compiled by Contributing Writer Candice Watkins.

Section 9

Top Mailing List Hosts and Solution Centers

Bravenet

www.bravenet.com

Build mailing lists or send newsletters. Keep your visitors up-to-date with your site changes or product news. Send HTML or plain text messages and manage your list subscribers in a Mailing List control panel.

Topica

www.topica.com

The Online Marketing and Sales Solution integrates e-mail marketing and automation tools with performance-based advertising services, data integration, and online conversion capabilities.

G-Lock Software

www.glocksoft.com

Create different kinds of mailing lists, newsletters, subscribe lists. Prevent spam. Keep the database clean.

Mailloop

www.mailloop.com

Mailloop is an all-in-one e-mail marketing and management solution. This software provides everything for setting up, managing, and sending e-mail promotions, newsletters, and auto responders to the e-mail list you have or plan to build.

Spark List

www.sparklist.com

This company provides e-mail list hosting.

L-Soft

www.lsoft.com

L-Soft created LISTSERV, which set the industry standard for e-mail list management software. It allows you to easily manage opt-in e-mail lists, such as e-mail newsletters, announcement lists, and discussion groups.

Lyris

www.lyris.com

Services include List Manager, List Hosting, and an E-mail Advisor.

iMakeNews

www.imninc.com

An application service provider that delivers e-communications solutions for boosting business performance by using e-newsletters, HTML e-mail, micro-sites, and blogs, with tracking and analytics.

Cooler Email

www.cooleremail.com

A state-of-the-art, user-friendly, do-it-yourself e-mail newsletter tool.

Section 9

Mail Chimp

mailchimp.com
The easy way to send e-mail marketing. It tracks opens and clicks.

Managing Mailing Lists, by Alan Schwartz (Reilly & Associates, 1998)

This comprehensive guide is for anyone who wants to run or manage a mailing list, including the system administrator who needs to ensure that user-owned mailing lists run as trouble-free as possible.

Email Addresses

www.emailaddresses.com
The best e-mail resource on the Web, with reviews of hundreds of free e-mail services and for-fee e-mail services, advice on using e-mail, a guide to setting up your own e-mail service, and more.

The Email Universe Network

emailuniverse.com/list-lingo
"The Newbie's Guide to Email List Terminology."

List Server Mailing Lists

"Creating and Using List Server Mailing Lists"
www.public.iastate.edu/~majordomo/psg211.html

Source: compiled by Contributing Writer Candice Watkins.

Section 9

Develop an Online Presence

Section 9

Ways to Make Your Web Site Globally Friendly

A web site is important to building an international business, but remember that not all nations use the same equipment or web standards. Here are some smart ways to make your web site globally friendly:

1. Keep images to a minimum. Not only can they slow the downloading process, but in many cases, images developed for the American marketplace may not be relevant or global users may misunderstand them.

2. Make sure your site is easy to navigate. Don't try to dazzle the user with cleverness. Provide clear instructions and text guidelines.

3. Use international formats for dates, times, and currencies. For instance, instead of 3:30 p.m., say 15:30.

4. Develop an e-mail response form that includes automated options, such as radio buttons. This minimizes the amount of translation needed.

5. Make it easy for customer to request information via e-mail.

Source: Rieva Lesonsky, *365 Tips to Boost Your Entrepreneurial IQ.*

Four Fatal Web Site Design Mistakes

Fatal Mistake #1: Trying to "dazzle" customers instead of trying to sell to them. A lot of new business owners want their sites to be as eye-catching as possible. They think that by including a lot of flashy graphics and nifty animation effects, they'll capture their visitors' attention.

- Graphics should be used only to support the main purpose of your site: to get people to buy what you have to sell.

- Anything that distracts visitors from your copy is guaranteed to lose you sales. So if a graphic doesn't directly relate to your product or service, then it shouldn't be on your site.

- You also don't want to chase your visitors away with long, unnecessary Flash presentations and splash pages.

- The best way to drive sales is to design a simple, clean site using only two or three colors and one or two fonts throughout the entire site. Avoid using colored or patterned backgrounds—you might think they look cool, but they make it really difficult to read your sales copy.

Fatal Mistake #2: Making your site too large. One of the worst mistakes people can make is building massive, multipaged sites that take forever to load.

- Wherever possible, try to reduce the number of files on your web pages. The more files a page has, the longer it'll take to load—especially if they're large graphics files.

- Use colored text instead of graphics to grab attention. If you must use a graphic, make sure it's a small file.

- You need only 72 dpi (dots per inch) for screen resolution. And most graphics only need to be 256 colors or less.

Fatal Mistake #3: Designing confusing navigation. Some Web designers like to show off their skills by creating new and different ways to navigate through a multipage site. Sometimes they hide links beneath icons or images, so that users can't find the links unless they mouse over the graphics. This may be very clever, but it certainly doesn't help people find what they're looking for.

Fatal Mistake #4: Burying essential information too deep within the site. Web surfers are impatient! They don't want to spend a lot of time trying to find what they're seeking on your site.

Source: Corey Rudl, "4 Fatal Website Design Mistakes," www.entrepreneur.com/article/0,4621,316156,00.html.

Top Ten Things Customers Look for on Your Web Site

1. Contact information, such as phone numbers, e-mail addresses, and physical location

2. Product information, which means in-depth information on the products or services you provide, including prices

3. Samples of your products or previous work

4. Support, including product information, troubleshooting help, FAQs, etc.

5. The ability to shop, so they can purchase products online or at least find a physical location where your products are being sold

6. Company information, such as background information on the business and the management team

7. News and announcements, including press releases and updated product or service enhancements

8. Employment opportunities

9. An easy way to get back to your home page, the place where all paths begin in the customer's mind

10. Simple navigation that makes all these other items easy to find

Source: Matthew Krabbenhoft, "10 Things Your Site Must Have," www.entrepreneur.com/article/0,4621,320595,00.html.

12 Ways to Increase Online Sales

Test everything; assume nothing! You never know what strategy or angle is going to work best for you until you test it. Testing is the only way to discover what works and what doesn't on your web site. Keep that in mind as you try the following dozen possibilities.

1. Offer just one product or service on your home page. It's all about focus. Instead of trying to please everyone who visits your site by offering a large range of products with minimal detail about each one, if you offer just one product—or one set of related products—you can really focus on one key set of benefits and answer all the possible questions and doubts your visitors might have about your product. And you don't have to stop selling your other products; you can always offer them to your customers from other web pages or by using follow-up offers.

2. Reposition your opt-in offer to boost your opt-ins and build a bigger list of loyal subscribers. Your opt-in offer is your tool for gathering your customers' e-mail addresses and building your e-mail list, which allows you to regularly keep in touch with your subscribers, build relationships of trust and loyalty, and sell them your products or services. If you don't use a long sales letter, test placing your opt-in offer in as prominent a position as possible on your home page—the top left of a page is where visitors' eyes are often drawn first. The more sign-up opportunities you provide, the more subscribers you're likely to get. Test it and see.

3. Add impact to your promotions with hover ads. I'm sure everyone's familiar with pop-ups, the small windows containing a special offer or other information that sometimes pop up when you visit a web site. But that was before we discovered a very impressive technology that actually lets you use ads that behave like pop-ups but that aren't pop-ups—so they don't get blocked. They're called hover ads, and they're well worth testing on your site.

4. Feature different benefits in your headline. Your headline has a huge impact on your sales. It's often the first thing visitors to your site see, so it must grab their attention and compel them to read your sales letter. A successful headline should highlight a problem your target audience faces and stress the main benefit of your product or service in solving this problem.

5. Establish a problem in your copy and show how you can solve it. In the first few paragraphs that appear on your home page, you need to go into more detail about the problem you introduced in your headline—showing your audience that you relate to them. (Only when your visitors feel you understand their problem will they feel confident that you can solve it.) Once the problem is established, you can then begin introducing your product or service as the solution to this problem. By emphasizing exactly how your product or service will solve your visitors' problem, you're guaranteed to see a boost in sales.

Section 9

6. Add credibility to your copy, so your visitors trust you more. It's vital for your sales copy to establish your credibility. There are several ways you can do this effectively. One of the best ways to establish your credibility is to include customer testimonials in your sales letter. These should be excerpts from genuine e-mails or letters from customers expressing how your product or service helped solve the particular problem they faced. This last point is important: a customer testimonial that states how your product benefited them is much more effective than one that just says something like "Your product is great!"

7. Focus on your site visitors, not yourself. The most successful sales copy focuses on the reader. Too often, business owners neglect this simple golden rule. Look carefully at your sales copy. Is it filled with references to "I," "me," and "we"? Instead of using sentences like "I designed my time-management software with the busy homeowner in mind," try "Your new time-management software will free up hours of time for you to spend with your family." So try searching for "I," "me," and "our" in your sales copy and replace them with "you" and "your."

8. Instill urgency in your copy—and convince readers they need to buy now! It's very important that your sales copy instill a sense of urgency in your visitors, compelling them to buy now. The best place to do this is toward the end of your sales letter, near the call to action (when you ask for the sale). Here are a few of the most effective ways to create a sense of urgency. Try testing each one against your current copy:

   - Offer a limited-time price discount where visitors must buy before a certain date in order to qualify for the discount.

   - Offer additional bonuses for free if visitors buy within a certain time frame.

   - Offer only a limited quantity of your products or services.

   - Offer a limited quantity bonus.

9. Remove any references to "buying" from the top fold. (That's the part of the screen that's visible without scrolling.) People usually go online looking for free information. If you start your sales pitch too early in your copy, you may end up losing them before you've had the chance to hook them. Try removing references to "buying," "cost," and "sale" from the top fold and compare the results with results from the copy you're using now. Remember: don't mention anything to do with making a purchase or spending money until after your reader is interested in your product and trusts you enough to buy from you.

10. Boost your product's desirability by adding images. Images of your products make them seem more tangible and "real" to your visitors and are a powerful sales tool. Test placing images near the top of the page vs. placing them near the call to action at the bottom (where you're asking for the sale).

11. Grab the attention of "scanners" by changing the formatting and appearance of your copy. Very few visitors to your site will read every word of your sales copy from start

to finish. Most will "scan" your copy as they scroll down the page, reading only certain words and phrases that jump out at them or catch their eye.

That's why you need to test highlighting your key benefits to find the right combination that will grab the attention of people who scan rather than read online. These include the following:

- Use bold, italics, and highlighting (sparingly) to emphasize the most important benefits of your offer.

- Vary the length of your paragraphs so the page doesn't just look like a block of uniformly formatted text.

- Add sub-headlines that emphasize your key messages and compel your visitors to read the paragraphs that follow.

- Leave the right-hand side of your text ragged: that's easier to read than justified text that uses the whole width of the page.

- Center important—but short—chunks of text or sub-headlines to further draw them out of the main body of text.

- Use bullet lists (like this one) to emphasize key points.

12. Fine-tune your follow-up process to maximize sales and attract more repeat business. Following up with your customers and subscribers using auto responders (automated e-mails) is crucial to generating more sales as it often takes several contacts before someone buys from your site. In your follow-up e-mails to new subscribers who haven't bought from you yet, you can restate your offer and ask for the sale again. Try sending an immediate follow-up after new subscribers sign up, giving them a reason to return to your site the same day they subscribe.

Source: Derek Gehl, "12 Ways to Increase Online Sales," www.entrepreneur.com/article/ 0,4621,322588,00.html.

Ten Tips for Creating Online Ads That Perform

Do you want a better response from your online ads? Of course! Here are ten tips that will help you improve your ads—and your response rate.

1. Define the goals of your advertising campaign. That may be to produce 100 transactions. It may be to generate 1,000 visitor sessions. It may be to produce 500 leads. Whatever it is, clearly define your objective.

2. Identify the most effective sites for achieving your goals. Sites that are most relevant to your product or service will more than likely be your best bet, but also consider larger sites or networks that can target the audience you're trying to reach. They can be very cost-effective. If you have multiple products or services that appeal to various target markets, you'll have to consider sites that reach all those various segments.

3. Craft your message to fit the needs of the audience you're targeting. That comes down to understanding the audience of the sites you're advertising on. The message you use on a technology site to appeal to technologically savvy customers won't have the same appeal for visitors on a small-business site.

4. Formulate the specific promotional messages that correspond to your goals. Those promotional messages should concentrate on the major selling points of your product or service and have a strong call to action. For instance, "Get a FREE Trial Issue of *Entrepreneur* magazine. Sign up Today and Download Our FREE Report, '23 Tips for Closing a Sale.' Click here for your FREE Trial Issue!"

5. Make the desired action clearly visible. That doesn't mean the desired action should necessarily blink, bounce, or do flips, but it should be visible within an accepted format for the media you're using. In the case of the internet, underlined text links, "click here," text-entry boxes, and pull-down menus are all ways you can make the desired action clearly visible.

6. Use rich media to expand your message. Static ads can be effective, but they're one-dimensional in terms of response. Animated ads can be effective, but like static ads, they're also one-dimensional in terms of response. Use HTML, DHTML, Javascript, layered ads, etc. to add more depth to your creative and expand the capabilities for response.

7. Maximize the use of your space when using rich media. If you have limited space in your ad, use HTML to create an animated message in one portion of the ad and a pull-down menu or text-entry box in the rest of the space, depending on your goals. With DHTML, you can use simple scripting to take a confined area and have it expand upon mouseover or click, giving you more room to communicate a desired action such as a sign-up form, quote check, etc. As more and more sites start to provide larger ad units for advertisers, use the space to your advantage by including simple Javascript forms to promote a desired action or have text links that depict categories potential customers can choose from. There are numerous resources on the internet to help you understand and build rich creative through the use of scripting. One such resource is Builder.com (builder.com.com).

8. Don't restrict the response when using rich media. Each portion of your creative should have a function. For instance, if you're using an HTML ad with a pull-down menu, make sure the other portions of your ad have a function such as a link. Having just the pull-down menu active restricts the ability of your potential customers to respond.

9. Design the ad so it looks like it belongs on the sites where you're advertising. For instance, you may want to use the site's font faces in your text, color schemes in your background, and font color choices overall, and to emulate images where appropriate. Try to conform to the environment so potential customers visiting the site don't gasp in shock when they see your ad.

10. Produce multiple versions of each ad. Create three or four versions of each ad, changing the promotional message, call to action, font faces, and color schemes. This is especially important if you're doing price testing or gauging reaction to specific promotions. By splitting your advertising buy among the various versions of your creative, you can then start to optimize your buy based on the message that works best.

Finally, don't be afraid to experiment. One of the beauties of the internet is that you can gauge reaction to your ad right away. You can then make adjustments based on the initial reaction. Don't be one of those marketers who settle for poor response from their advertising creative. Make it work for you!

Source: Charles Fuller, "Creating Online Ads That Perform," www.entrepreneur.com/article/0,4621,303357,00.html.

Five Dos and Five Don'ts of Search Engine Optimization

The Dos

1. Ask relevant sites to link to your site. In the past, scoring a high ranking with a search engine was all about positioning your keywords in "prime real estate" positions in your text and site coding. All that has changed, however, because now search engines place a huge amount of importance on the number of sites that link to yours. But it's not just the quantity of links that matters; it's also the quality. Search engines look at how relevant the links are, that is, how much the content of the linking site has in common with the content on your site.

2. Pay attention to keyword inclusion and placement. Keywords may no longer be the sole determining factor of a site's ranking, but they're still pretty important. The most useful places to include them are:

   - In your domain name—only make sure your keywords are in the root of your URL, not the stem. For example, if your main keyword phrase is "cell phones," try to get a domain name such as "www.cell-phones.com" instead of "www.mobileusa.com/cell-phones." Some search engines will actually penalize sites for including key words in the stem of a URL.

   - In the title tags in your source code

   - In the meta description of your site. This is much less important than it used to be, but it can't hurt.

   - In your meta keyword tags

3. Create content-rich information pages to direct traffic to your site. An easy way to boost the number of pages that link to your site is to create some pages yourself.

   Be sure the information relates to the content on your site and has your keywords placed in advantageous positions. This will boost the ranking of your pages with the search engines and ensure they get lots of traffic—which they can then redirect to your site.

4. Submit your site to online directories. Be sure to submit your site to important directories such as Yahoo!, the Open Directory Project, and About.com, as well as smaller directories. Your listing on these directories will help your ranking with the major search engines.

5. Multiply and conquer. Create a community of related sites that link to each other. Why stop at only one information page? The more content-rich sites that point to your site, the better. You can also boost the number of links that point to your site by dividing it into several separate sites that all link to each other. This works especially well if you sell a number of different products or services. If you build a different site to focus on each of your products and services, then you can also concentrate the use of specific keyword phrases on each site. That's another great way to boost your search engine ranking.

The Don'ts

1. Beware of irrelevant links. Yes, it's a good idea to get a lot of different links pointing to your site, but the search engines like only relevant links. If they find sites that have nothing in common with the content on your site linked to your web site, they'll lower your relevancy rating.

2. Beware of irrelevant keywords. Search engines hate finding irrelevant keywords on your site—especially in your meta tags. If they catch you using keywords that have nothing to do with the actual content of your site, they'll penalize you for it.

3. Don't "keyword-stuff" your meta tags. In the past, people used to repeat their keywords in their meta tags over and over again. This used to get them a high ranking with the search engines—but not any more. Search engines are on to this trick and will punish you for it by dropping your ranking.

4. Don't create "link farms." Link farms are the evil cousins of the information pages we discussed above. In the past, some spammers used to build multiple "doorway" sites that existed only to multiply the number of links pointing to their sites. Unlike content-rich information pages, these doorway pages would usually only include a string of keyword terms that would earn them a high ranking with the search engines. The search engines have caught on to this tactic, however, and will drop you from their listings if they find you using it.

5. Avoid "free for all" link pages. Don't bother placing links to your site on pages where everyone and their cousin are invited to put up a link. Such sites have extremely low relevancy ratings and will cost you points with the search engines.

Source: Corey Rudl, "The Dos and Don'ts of Search Engine Optimization," www.entrepreneur.com /article/sbc/0,6136,317788,00.html.

Top Four Paid Online Advertising Techniques

1. Get your site listed on the major pay-per-click search engines. Without a doubt, pay-per-click (PPC) search engines are still the best value for your advertising dollar. If you want to get listed on a PPC search engine, bid on keywords that relate to the content of your site. If you're the highest bidder on a given keyword, your site will be the first listing that appears at the top of the "results" page when someone performs a search for that keyword.

   And getting listed on a PPC search engine is the easiest way to get listed at the top of the major search engines fast. Plus, when you're in the top three listings on Overture (the industry leader in PPC search, www.overture.com), your site will be featured as a "sponsored listing" on highly trafficked sites such as Yahoo!, Altavista, CNN.com, InfoSpace, and MSN.com.

   If you monitor the click-through and sales-conversion rates of the keywords you're bidding on, there's no way you can lose money. Just be sure to keep your bids lower than your visitor worth, and you'll be set.

2. Place text ads in popular e-zines and online trade journals. E-zines are popping up everywhere on the internet these days, all catering to very different niche markets. And just like offline magazines, a lot of them need to sell advertising in order to stay profitable.

   The cost of running an e-zine ad can vary anywhere from $20 to $100 per ad, depending on the e-zine and the type of ads they publish. It's generally safe to assume that more popular e-zines charge more for their ads. To learn more about which e-zines are going to be the best places for you to advertise, here are a couple sites to check out:

   - EzineAdAuction.com (www.ezineadauction.com)
   - EzineArticles.com (ezinearticles.com)

3. Get your site listed on paid inclusion directories and portals. A great way to get your site seen by a lot of people—and boost your ranking with the free search engines—is to buy a listing on paid directories or portal sites.

   A directory is an indexed listing of sites that's managed by human editors (as opposed to the free search engines, which are entirely run by computers). Some directories are free, while others charge anywhere from $10 to $100 for a listing. Do some research to discover which directories are popular with your niche market before deciding where you want your site to be listed.

4. Post a banner, classified, or pop-up ad on industry "hot sites." Whenever you come across sites that are popular with your niche market, do whatever you can to get your site listed on them. If they sell classified ads on their site, buy one. You can even submit your ad to classified ad web sites and databases automatically using software

like Power Submitter (www.becanada.com). You can also pay these industry hot sites to place a banner ad or pop-up on their site.

Source: Corey Rudl, "Top 4 Paid Online Advertising Techniques," www.entrepreneur.com/article/0,4621,319298–1,00.html.

Ten Tips to Improve Online Survey Response

1. Clearly define the purpose of your survey. Effective surveys have focused objectives that are easily understood. For a survey to be successful, you need to spend time upfront to identify, in writing, the following objectives:

   ■ What is the goal of this survey?

   ■ What do you hope to accomplish with this survey?

   ■ How will you use the data you are collecting?

   ■ What decisions do you hope to be able to provide input to from the responses to this survey?

2. Keep the survey short and focused. Keeping it short and focused helps with both the quality and quantity of the responses you'll get. It's generally better to focus on a single objective than try to create a master survey that covers multiple objectives.

   Shorter surveys generally have high response rates and lower abandonment among survey takers. It's human nature to want things to be quick and easy—once a survey taker loses interest, he or she simply abandons the survey, leaving you with the task of determining how to interpret the partial data or whether to use it at all.

   Make sure each of your questions is focused on helping to meet your stated objective. Don't toss in 'nice to have' questions that don't directly provide answers that will help you reach your goals.

3. Keep the questions simple. When crafting your questions, make sure you get to the point and avoid the use of jargon. If you're asking something like "When was the last time you used our RGS?" you're probably going to get a lot of unanswered questions. Don't assume your survey takers are as comfortable with your acronyms as you are.

   Try to make your questions as specific and direct as possible. Compare "What has your experience been working with our HR team?" and "How satisfied are you with the response time of our HR team?" The second is much more likely to garner useful responses.

4. Used closed-ended questions whenever possible. Closed-ended questions make it easier to analyze results and can take the form of yes/no, multiple choice, or a rating scale. Open-ended questions are great supplemental questions and may provide useful qualitative information and insights. However, for collating and analysis pur-

poses, close-ended questions are best. One warning: make sure your closed-ended questions don't force survey takers into choosing a "less bad" answer.

5. Keep rating scale questions consistent. Questions that offer rating scales—for example, a scale of 1 to 5—are a great way to measure and compare sets of variables. But if you elect to use rating scales, you need to keep them consistent throughout your survey. Use the same number of points on the scale for each question, and make sure the meanings of high and low remain the same. Switching your rating scales around throughout the survey will only confuse survey takers, leading to untrustworthy responses.

6. Make sure your survey flows in a logical order. Begin with a brief introduction—don't reveal the survey objective. Next, start with the broader-based questions, later moving to those that are narrower in scope. It's usually better to collect demographic data and ask any particularly sensitive questions at the end (unless you're using this information to screen out survey participants). If you're requesting contact information, put those questions last.

7. Pretest your survey. Before launching your survey, be sure to pretest it with a few members of your target audience to help you uncover glitches and unexpected question interpretations. Also, to make sure it's not too long, time a few of your test subjects as they take the survey. Ideally the survey should take no more than five minutes to complete. Six to ten minutes is acceptable, but you'll probably see significant abandonment rates occurring after 11 minutes.

8. Schedule your survey by taking the calendar into account. When you're planning your e-mail blast date—the e-mail that asks people to visit your site to take the survey—keep in mind that Tuesdays, Wednesdays, and Thursdays are the best days to do it: you'll generate more responses than if you send it out on one of the other four days. You want to catch people's attention, and you won't do that on Friday, when your survey respondents are most likely gearing up for the weekend, on Saturday or Sunday, when the last thing on people's minds is a customer survey, or Monday, when most people are wading through a loaded in-box.

9. Offer an incentive for responding. Depending on the type of survey you're conducting and your survey audience, offering an incentive can be very effective in improving your response rates. People like the idea of getting something in return for their time—incentives typically boost response rates by an average of 50 percent.

10. Consider using reminders. While not appropriate for all surveys, sending out reminders to those who haven't yet responded can often provide a significant boost to your response rates.

Source: Dana Meade and Paula Rivers, "Boosting Your Online Survey Responses," www.entrepreneur.com/article/0,4621,319023,00.html.

Advice for Launching Your E-Mail Campaign

Reaching people by e-mail is still a relatively new marketing method. Before you launch your campaign, keep these tips in mind:

- Get a good list. List sources can be found in the Yellow Pages, in books, or online. Opt-in lists are lists of people who are interested in receiving information.

- Keep your message short and concise. E-mail readers want to know upfront what they're reading, or they won't bother to continue. Keep it to one screen length.

- Be clear. E-mail readers tend to be more suspicious. If your message is vague, it will quickly get deleted.

- Get to the point. Ask prospects to talk some sort of action; this doesn't mean do a hard sell—just don't waste their time.

- Start now! E-mail still generates interest and curiosity, so get started before it becomes ordinary junk mail.

Source: Rieva Lesonsky, *365 Tips to Boost Your Entrepreneurial IQ.*

Tips for More Effective E-Mails

- When writing a message, leave the recipient field blank as long as possible. This prevents accidentally sending your message prematurely.

- Most e-mail packages allow you to include the sender's original message in your reply. This helps remind the person of what you are replying to.

- If you have more than one e-mail account, try to have your mail forwarded to the account you use the most. This can save you considerable time.

- Answer your e-mail. Many companies don't. If you've told people they can get in touch with you via e-mail and you don't respond, you're making an unprofessional impression that will badly reflect on your business.

Source: Rieva Lesonsky, *365 Tips to Boost Your Entrepreneurial IQ.*

Eight Common Misconceptions About Business Web Sites

1. **"If I build it, they will come."** Marketing your site may not be as easy as it seems. You'll need economical ways to direct traffic to your site on a national—or international—level. Perhaps the most obvious way is to advertise on search engines like Google and Overture, but this can get expensive. Unfortunately, it can take months

or even years for your URL to turn up near the top of organic searches. Investigate other ways to get eyes to your site, like affiliate programs, e-mail newsletters, and partnering.

2. **The more you offer, the more you'll sell.** Trying to be all things to all people rarely works. It may seem logical that the more things you have for sale online, the more people you'll attract. But even if you attract them, will they buy? The "general" aspect of your offering will communicate that the value of your product or service is equal to that of others—so price becomes the only issue and branding becomes more difficult.

3. **The best way to generate sales is to copy the competition.** It can be tempting to copy your competitors in everything from marketing strategies and positioning to sales offers and design choices. Remember the adage that imitation is the sincerest form of flattery? This means that when you imitate, you're not just reminding your audience about your competitors—you're suggesting they're better!

4. **Your home page should explain everything about your business or you'll lose visitors.** You've got about three seconds to hook visitors—not bore them with visually overwhelming text. Grab their attention by being concise, clear, and compelling.

5. **Once I get my site up and running, sales will skyrocket.** Yes, your potential customer pool has grown exponentially—but so has your competition's. How will you stand out? How will you locate the people most likely to buy your product or service and get them to visit your site?

6. **Web sites should be slick, with lots of bells and whistles.** On the internet, functionality is king. High-tech gimmicks may look great, but they load slowly. It's best to find a good balance between form and function.

7. **Building a web site is easy—I'll just buy a how-to book.** Whether or not you can do it yourself depends on the type of site you want and your own experience and skills. For example, will you require shopping cart functionality or database programming? Building a web site is deceptively complex and requires a variety of skill sets, from HTML savvy to good artistic taste. You might want to think about hiring a web design pro.

8. **Everybody else has a site, so I should, too.** Determining the real purpose of your site is crucial. Is it to sell your product? Increase awareness of your business? Provide information to drive local sales? Add credibility? Despite what some critics say, creating an "online brochure" is a legitimate reason to build a site. However, that's a very different purpose than selling directly over the internet.

Source: John Williams, "8 Common Misconceptions About Business Websites," www.entrepreneur.com/article/0,4621,322598,00.html.

Section 9

Tips on Avoiding Legal Issues for Your Web Site

Are you planning a web site? There are some legal issues you should be concerned about, so heed these tips.

- First of all, naming your site is like naming your business. You'll need to conduct a search looking for conflicts and then register your name.

- If you plan to use text, music, or graphics on your site, find out who owns the rights to the material and get permission to use it.

- Have you hired someone to design your site? Establish upfront the ownership of the product.

- Are you planning to sell your product online? Then make sure your product liability insurance covers online transactions.

- E-commerce rules are constantly changing. Be aware of consumer privacy regulations and observe them.

If you're feeling overwhelmed, don't worry; you can always find an experienced consultant to help you.

Source: Rieva Lesonsky, *365 Tips to Boost Your Entrepreneurial IQ.*

Section 9

Tips to Help You with Pay-per-Click Advertising

Pay-per-click (PPC) search engines can be a powerful, instant source of qualified traffic for your web site—provided you do your homework and invest a bit of time in managing your campaign.

1. Figure out what you can afford to bid. This might sound obvious, but it needs to be said: don't bid more than you can afford! A lot of businesses make this mistake.

   Before you pay for advertising of any sort, calculate the value of a single visitor to your site. Once you know what one visitor is worth, you'll know the maximum amount you can afford to pay per click.

2. Being "No. 1" isn't always best. You don't always need to be ranked first for certain keywords to attract visitors. Sure, it helps if your ad appears in the top ten results. But people click on listings featured on the second and even third page of results for competitive keywords.

   So run some tests. Vary your bids so that your listing appears higher and lower on the page and see what effect the ranking has on your profits. You may actually find that for more costly keywords, a slightly lower ranking is more profitable.

3. Bid on low-cost variations and common misspellings of particular keywords.

Frequently, you'll see businesses bidding as much as $5.00 per click for popular keywords—while nobody is bidding on common misspellings and similar keywords that cost just pennies per click. Use Wordtracker (www.wordtracker.com) to locate keywords that relate to your business and are frequently searched by your market, but that none of your competitors are bidding on.

4. Bid on highly targeted phrases with less traffic. Rather than bid on a handful of general keywords, which tend to be more expensive because they get the highest number of searches, bid on dozens—or even hundreds—of highly targeted keywords, which tend to be cheap. For example, instead of bidding on "pet supplies," you might bid on "red dog leash," "oversize dog kennel," and "cat toys with bells." You're sure to see better sales conversions on the more targeted keywords because they attract more qualified buyers. And since no one is bidding on these keywords, your advertising costs associated with this traffic are extremely low.

Another benefit of this strategy is that you can direct these qualified visitors to a page that gives them exactly what they're looking for. In the above example, your listing for the keyword, "oversize dog kennel" could link directly to your dog kennel catalog page, rather than to just the home page of your pet supply store.

5. Bid on keywords in the lesser-known PPC search engines. Overture and Google are the PPC industry leaders, but some of the smaller PPC search engines are worth checking out as well. The most popular ones are:

- Findwhat (www.findwhat.com)

- Kanoodle (www.kanoodle.com)

- Enhance Interactive (www.enhance.com)

- LookSmart (www.looksmart.com)

- Espotting (for the UK and Europe) (www.espotting.com)

These engines won't get you the same exposure you might get with Overture and Google AdWords, but you can still generate a respectable amount of traffic with them. And best of all, they're much cheaper.

6. Create separate ads for each product or service you sell. This is an extremely effective strategy, but very few businesses are using it. Write ads specific to each keyword and phrase you bid on. For example, instead of writing an ad for "sporting goods," write one for "quality leather soccer balls," another for "discount ladies' tennis shoes," and so on.

These customized ads will attract more attention (and clicks!) from qualified buyers. And of course, you'll be able to convert more of these visitors to buyers if you direct them to a page on your site with the exact product or service they're searching for.

7. Get listed in relevant specialty PPC search engines. Did you know that there are specialty PPC search engines that target different markets such as brides, pet owners, antique collectors, car owners, and so on? Check out PayPerClickSearchEngines.com

Section 9

(www.payperclicksearchengines.com) to see if there are any relevant to your business that might be worth getting listed in.

Source: Corey Rudl, "Pay-per-Click Tips for Attracting Traffic," www.entrepreneur.com/article/0,4621,316859,00.html.

51 Secrets to eBay Success

These tips for successful selling on eBay come from the following panel of experts.

- Marsha Collier (eBay User ID: marsha_c), PowerSeller, eBay University instructor, and author of *eBay for Dummies*, now in its fourth edition

- David Early (eBay User ID: 66cvette), PowerSeller and creator of MarketPlacePro, software that enables individuals to sell products and manage their businesses online

- Jim "Griff" Griffith, dean of eBay Education, author of *The Official eBay Bible*, and host of eBay Radio

- Steve Lindhorst (eBay User ID: listingrover), instructor at eBay University, owner of a small business on eBay, and dealer assistant who helps car dealerships list inventory on eBay

- Christopher Spencer (eBay User ID: borntodeal), Gold Power-Seller and president of The Spencer Company, which has listed more than 80,000 items on eBay

Do Your Homework

1. Set aside a day to browse the entire eBay site. Use the eBay Navigation Bar as your anchor—it's located on the top of every eBay page. Make a note of the pages you'll need in the future, such as the "Services" page, which contains a treasure trove of tools and services.—J.G.

2. Get step-by-step guidance. Visit www.ebay.com/education. It teaches everything you need to know to sell on eBay and offers interactive audio tours that show you exactly how to create a listing.—C.S.

What to Sell?

3. Sell what you know first. If you're into fashion, sell that; if you're into golf, sell golf equipment; and so on.—M.C.

4. Be observant. Watch for opportunities to obtain items (in quantity if possible) at a low price for resale. Often, they're right under your nose, such as merchandise your local retailer would liquidate. Make an offer to clear out the retailer's old or damaged stock.—S.L.

5. Don't start out with just one product or product line. An effective way to build a customer base on eBay is to offer at least two separate types of items, between which

you can cross promote and drive customers from one to the other.—J.G.

6. Spend time on eBay browsing outside your normal categories. Find out what's hot at www.ebay.com/sellercentral.—S.L.

7. Become a Trading Assistant and sell other people's items for a commission. As a Trading Assistant, you won't have the expense of building inventory, and you can build your business on eBay very quickly without having to spend a lot of capital.—C.S.

8. Take some calculated risks. Being too careful can cost you. Do a little research on eBay, and trust your gut when you find potentially salable items.—S.L.

9. If you're not familiar with the product you're trying to sell, educate yourself before you write the description. If you describe the item incorrectly, buyers may be leery of bidding. Even worse, buyers could decide not to bid on any of your future items if they're under the impression that you don't know what you're selling. The more correct information you have and use, the more credible you'll become in the buyers' eyes.—D.E.

Getting Set Up

10. Become a verified member of eBay through their ID verification process. Getting verified will help get you past a lot of the restrictions placed on new sellers.—C.S.

11. Choose your eBay User ID wisely. Pick a name that's descriptive, easy to remember, and instantly identifiable with your niche. Your User ID will become your business identification—the name that people in the eBay universe will learn to search for when they want to buy your products.—D.E.

12. According to eBay, you can have more than one User ID name, as long as all your names refer to the same e-mail address. So if you want to sell cars in addition to Hummel figurines, you might choose another User ID that would be more pertinent to your new product line, such as "Mustangsrock" or "Supeduphotrods."—D.E.

13. Organize. If you're selling from home, set up a dedicated space with areas for inventory storage, packing materials, photographing, and, of course, a desk for your computer and printer. The best businesses are orderly and organized.—J.G.

14. Set up a designated area within your business location used only for photography. You can use household lighting and inexpensive cloth or paper backdrops.—J.G.

15. When taking pictures of the items you're selling, choose a camera with good macro-lens and auto-focus features, and make sure it easily interfaces with your computer. Get great lighting tips from eBay community boards.—C.S.

Create Your Listing

16. Listings formatted with HTML look more professional than plain, unformatted text. Use the HTML editor built into both eBay's "Sell Your Item" form and eBay's free Turbo Lister. With the HTML editor, you can format description text quickly and easily.—J.G.

17. When you write your title, don't use all capital letters. Uppercase and lowercase letters are easier to read and will help people quickly see what you're selling.—M.C.

Section 9

18. When creating your listings, provide a complete and specific item description with as many clear, detailed photos as possible. You cannot overdescribe or overrepresent your item. Not sure what information to include along with your item description? See the next tip.—J.G.

19. Clearly list your terms and conditions, as well as shipping, returns, warranty, and guarantee policies. You can use an existing template to help separate the terms and conditions into sections and highlight them with bullet points, so people can read them easily.—C.S.

20. Develop a listing schedule. Before you place a listing, consider the best times for starting and ending an auction for your particular product. For example, if you had American flags to sell, you would probably want the listing to end several days before the Fourth of July, rather than just after it—thus allowing you enough time to ship your product to your buyers in time for the holiday. If you're working in a niche area, pay attention to the days and times your items do the best, and start keeping a listing schedule. Then stick to it. Your clientele will learn when you list items, and you will get much better results from your listings.—D.E.

21. For advanced users, use Seller's Assistant Pro. It will help you put your listings together offline, then load them onto the site using its bulk-loading feature. There's a free trial; then the service costs $24.99 per month.—C.S.

While You're Selling

22. Feed the frenzy. You can feed a bidding frenzy on your item by using a low opening bid price and no Reserve, which should attract more bidders at the outset. The more people bidding on your listing, the more likely that two or more of them will get drawn into a personal bidding war. At that point, winning the item becomes almost as important as the product they want to buy, and these bidders might eventually pay more than they intended to pay to beat out the competition. This can lead to you getting much more for your product than you expected.—D.E.

23. Don't get stuck in a rut. If an item isn't selling as well as it once did, take a look at your photos, title, and description to see if they can be freshened up.—S.L.

24. Just because you're moving merchandise on eBay doesn't mean you're making a profit. If you can't sell an item with enough of a profit margin, it's probably not worth your time and effort to sell that item.—M.C.

25. Once you are notified of a sold item, you should promptly respond using the eBay checkout system. Give buyers an invoice with their total including shipping (which you can calculate using eBay's shipping rate calculator).—C.S.

Ship It

26. Once the buyer has paid, arrange for shipping as soon as possible. Make sure you pack the item securely. For more tips on packing and shipping, check out eBay's packing and shipping community help board.—C.S.

27. Be reasonable with shipping and handling costs. These costs often make the difference for buyers choosing between your listing and the competition's. One sure way to get buyers to move on to another listing is to bait them with a low price and then spring high shipping and handling costs on them.–S.L.

28. Have a regular shipping day or days. State those dates in your listings so people know when to expect their packages.–S.L.

29. Use the built-in postage service from PayPal, the eBay company that allows you to accept online payments from credit cards or bank accounts. The service allows you to purchase postage and print labels from both UPS and the USPS using your PayPal account; it's a big time-saver.–C.S.

30. Schedule courier pickups through the USPS web site. It's free and your regular mail carrier will come to get your packages. All you have to do is pay the postage and you won't have to wait in long lines at the post office. You can even insure the packages without having to go through a lot of hassles.–C.S.

31. Once the item is shipped out, track the package and make sure it has been delivered. Follow up with a quick e-mail to the buyer, asking for feedback and whether the item was satisfactory.–C.S.

Customers First

32. Provide prompt, punctual, and courteous responses to any questions your customers might have. People will probably want to do business with you again if they receive a pleasant response from you.–C.S.

33. Never forget that the customer is king. When in doubt, always think like a buyer. If you do, you will be able to better anticipate what buyers want and plan your business accordingly.–J.G.

34. Treat your customers like you would treat guests in your home. Be kind and understanding. Be willing to help them when there are problems.–S.L.

35. Eliminate the roadblocks to selling your products. If a buyer wants to use PayPal to buy your product and you can't accept a PayPal payment, that's a problem. It's a roadblock to selling your item, making a profit, and moving on to the next sale. Take down the roadblocks! This is my golden rule of retail: make sure customers who come in the door have a way to pay, and customers who leave have a smile and a full shopping cart. The point is simple: sell your item, collect the money, and ship the product.–D.E.

36. Communicate as soon as possible with all buyers who e-mail you. If you make a mistake and something's not sent when it should have been, let the customer know the truth. Don't ignore questions or complaints.–S.L.

37. Schedule time once a week for posting feedback–no more than 15 minutes. You have to do it to be successful. Create a couple of generic feedback statements, such as "Great buyer, quick payment, great trans," check the spelling, then cut and paste

these generic statements into your feedback submissions. People don't care what you say, as long as it's positive–D.E.

38. Leave emotion out of feedback. Keep it strictly business.–S.L.

Money Matters

39. Use QuickBooks or other accounting software to help you keep your books in order for yourself and for your tax specialist. QuickBooks allows you to input your inventory and gives you reports telling you your average profit per item, as well as how many items you sell each week. The program also gives you statistics, your markup, and a lot of other helpful data.–M.C.

40. Open a premier or business PayPal account. Many buyers limit their eBay shopping to those sellers who offer PayPal. Using PayPal makes tracking sales, invoicing, and bookkeeping much easier.–J.G.

41. Pennies count. Keep track of expenses. The difference in listing fees between starting an item at $9.99 and at $10.00 is 25 cents. That adds up to $25 if you're listing 100 items per week. Also pay attention to hidden costs like shipping supplies and postage.–S.L.

Competitive Edge

42. Once you've settled on regular inventory, use eBay Keywords, a pay–per–click banner advertising service, to draw people into your store. See https://ebay.admarketplace.net/ebay/servlet/ebay.–M.C.

43. Watch your competition. Search them out on eBay. Follow their sales. Determine their best business practices and adopt them. For example, if your competition is offering goods similar to yours at about the same price, consider driving customers to your items by offering free shipping on some or all of them.–J.G.

44. Don't be afraid to put some items away and wait for your competition to sell out. Profits definitely rise when you're the only source of a popular item.–S.L.

45. Cultivate your customer database–it's a gold mine. You can use it to market any of your new items directly to qualified customers. For example, you could send a monthly newsletter to your database to describe your new products or to give these customers discounts. But before you proceed with any marketing campaign using your buyers' e-mail addresses, be sure you understand and comply with the national spam laws.–D.E.

46. Cross-promote with your e-mail signature. It should read something like "If you need additional products or services, please visit my Storefront at storefront.com."–D.E.

Growing Your Business

47. Don't open an eBay store until you've had a number of transactions on the site and you're comfortable with the way eBay works.–M.C.

48. When you open an eBay store, be sure you take advantage of eBay's cross-promotion tools. These tools allow you to choose which merchandise is featured in your store, so you can choose items that might be of interest to somebody already buying one of your listed items.–M.C.

49. Once you become a power seller, consider using a service like Endicia.com, which allows you to print your own postage and delivery confirmations on one label and gives you a separate expense line for your postage.–M.C.

50. Don't limit yourself to buyers in the United States. Many brands that are popular and easy to come by in the United States are practically impossible to get elsewhere. For example, a friend of mine bought some OshKosh B'Gosh baby clothes at a local garage sale and sold them on eBay to an eager mother in Australia for a nice profit. And I bought model airplane engines that are made in Germany at a local swap meet and was surprised to find my biggest demand for these engines came from buyers in Germany.–D.E.

51. Remember this simple rule for non-U.S. buyers: don't accept foreign currency; specify that you'll accept U.S. dollars only. If a buyer sends you $20 Canadian and you were expecting $20 American, you just lost about $8, depending on the current rate of exchange. Always specify "U.S. funds only." And consider the additional shipping charges that may apply before you agree to ship the product outside of the country.–D.E.

Source: Gisela M. Pedroza, "51 Secrets to eBay Success," www.entrepreneur.com/article/sbc/0,6136,317792,00.html.

Public Relations

Smart Publicity Pointers on a Budget

You don't need a big budget to get a lot of attention for your business. Try these smart publicity pointers:

- **Write a column**. Approach your local newspaper, and offer to write a column—for free—on your area of expertise or about business in general.

- **Speak up**. Volunteer to talk to business, civic, and educational groups. Again, speak about what you know best, but don't try to sell anything. Your growing reputation will take care of that.

- **Get personal**. Include a very short personal message—one or two lines—when you send out your literature.

- **Join up**. Find the groups that are important to you—the local chamber or industry association—and join. Then make sure you show up for meetings.

- **Be a good neighbor**. Sponsor a Little League team or donate time, money, or goods to a local cause. A few hundred dollars can go a long way toward gaining good will.

Source: Rieva Lesonsky, *365 Tips to Boost Your Entrepreneurial IQ.*

Secrets to Putting Together Media Kits

"Media kits are essential tools for any business that wants to gain exposure in print, on television and radio, or even through internet sources," says Alan Seko, vice president of Axsys Resource Public Relations in Salt Lake City. "In addition to providing important information, the kits help establish a company's credibility." After all, reporters want to know that the sources they cite are reliable and will be around for a while after their stories are published or aired. And, best of all, media kits are relatively inexpensive.

He says the basic elements of a good media kit are the following:

1. A one- or two-page fact sheet. Fact sheets provide quick overviews of companies in an easy-to-read format, and typically include information such as a description of products or services, company history, key personnel, the number of employees, the number of offices and locations, statistical information (number of products produced, sales, number of clients), any other notable company facts, and information for reaching a contact person.

2. Biographies of key individuals. If possible, keep them to one page and focus on information that's pertinent to your company.

3. A list of products and services. When applicable, include retail prices and outlets, or other information on how consumers can acquire your goods and/or services.

4. Photograph(s). Depending on your specific business, you might want to include professional photos of your product(s), your service(s) (or somehow depict the service being delivered), your facility, and/or your key people.

5. A news release. Ideally, the release should be specific to the reporter's needs or it may be about any timely or event of interest to the reporter.

Always include a cover letter, which should either make reference to the fact that the kit was requested or, if you haven't had any previous contact, pitch a specific story. Keep in mind that more is not necessarily better. Reporters don't have time to wade through pages of material looking for the information they need, so make sure everything you include in your kit has a reason for being there.

Let the media kit work for you in other ways. Seko says he's adapted Axsys's media kit to use as a tool to attract new investors. The client can also use it as a recruiting device for top employee talent, to support loan applications, or on any other occasion when there's a need to showcase your company in a positive way.

Source: Jacquelyn Lynn, "Your Public Face," www.entrepreneur.com/article/ 0,4621,276533,00.html.

SCORE's Five Tips on Establishing a Presence in Your Community

1. Create an advisory board representative of your customers (even if they're kids) and publicize it. Listen to the board's ideas.

2. Publish a newsletter about your business for customers and potential customers. Send it via regular mail or e-mail and post it on your web page.

3. Make your values clear. One couple promotes their commitment to family—sometimes closing their store early to attend soccer games when their children or employees' children are competing.

4. Make donations that represent your business. If you have a garden supply business, for example, contribute seeds and simple tools for a community garden.

5. Serve as a volunteer in your community and encourage your employees to follow suit. Let them contribute some hours on company time.

Source: SCORE, www.score.org/business_tips.html.

Tips for the Holiday Season and the Entrepreneur

The holidays are the season not only to be jolly but to be creative as well. They are a great time to cement business relationships. Try these tips to get the most out of the holiday season:

- Make a list—lots of them. Make sure your card or gift list includes loyal clients, colleagues who've referred business to you, former customers you'd like to win back, and valuable employees.

- Party on. Be creative; you needn't spend a lot on a holiday bash. Rent an unusual location, such as a skating rink or a boat. Be sure to manage the alcohol intake of the partygoers.

- Stand out in the crowd. Your invitation or card will be one of many received by clients, so be creative. If you can't afford a professional, try hiring an art student to design your cards.

- Deck the walls. Help your employees and customers get in the mood by decorating your office or shop. Be sure you don't overdo it; you want festive, not gaudy.

- Be card smart. Your cards will stand out if you use a personal touch. Consider using a photo of your staff—it shows the real people behind your business.

- Give gifts that keep on giving. Make a lasting impression by sending thoughtful, creative gifts rather than the standard food baskets or pen sets. Think about your clients' likes and try tickets to a ballgame or show or books about their hobbies and interests.

- Remember, charity begins—well, you know where. While money is always appreciated, you should think about donating time, products, or services to worthy local causes. Encourage your employees to do the same.

- Don't forget to say thanks. Acknowledge invitations, cards, and gifts. Make it personal, but be sure to remind them how your business will continue to meet their needs in the coming year.

Source: Rieva Lesonsky, *365 Tips to Boost Your Entrepreneurial IQ.*

30 Reasons to Write a Press Release

If you're not sure about what you should cover in a press release, consider these ideas to see if any apply to your business:

1. Starting a new business
2. Introducing a new product
3. Celebrating an anniversary

Section 9

4. Announcing a restructuring of the company

5. Offering an article series for publishing

6. Opening up branch or satellite offices

7. Receiving an award

8. Receiving an appointment

9. Participating in a philanthropic event

10. Introducing a unique strategy/approach

11. Announcing a partnership

12. Changing the company or product name

13. Earning recognition of the company, product, and/or executives by a publication

14. Announcing that you're available to speak on particular subjects of interest

15. Issuing a statement of position regarding a local, regional, or national issue

16. Announcing a public appearance on television, on radio, or in person

17. Launching a web site

18. Making free information available

19. Reaching a major milestone

20. Obtaining a new, significant customer

21. Expanding or renovating the business

22. Establishing a unique vendor agreement

23. Meeting some kind of unusual challenge or rising above adversity

24. Restructuring your business or its business model

25. Setting up a customer advisory group

26. Announcing the results of research or surveys you have conducted

27. Announcing that an individual in your business has been named to serve in a leadership position in a community, professional, or charitable organization

28. Sponsoring a workshop or seminar

29. Making public statements on future business trends or conditions

30. Forming a new strategic partnership or alliance

Source: Al Lautenslager, "30 Reasons to Write a Press Release,"www.entrepreneur.com/article/0,4621,294808,00.html.

SCORE's Five Tips for Effective News Releases

1. Make sure they're newsworthy. Good topics include the announcement of a major new client, a celebrity appearance at your store, and community service performed by your company.

2. Create news and put out a press release about it. Speak at a seminar, for example, or provide expert comment on developing news events.

3. Get your releases to the right people. Find out who at your radio and TV stations and newspaper will be the most interested in your news.

4. Capture editors' attention by putting the news in the first paragraph. Then add the necessary details.

5. Make your releases look crisp and professional. That means no smudgy type. Include the name and phone number of a contact person, and answer media queries promptly.

Source: SCORE, www.score.org/business_tips.html.

Tips on Choosing a PR Firm for Your Business

Because most small businesses don't have huge advertising budgets, it is important to spend your dollars wisely. That means working with an agency that can really meet your needs and with which you feel comfortable. Not all advertising agencies can deliver everything they claim. There are lots of companies vying for your precious money, so carefully consider the following issues before committing to any contractual agreement.

1. Define your objective in hiring an ad agency. What do you want to achieve? What should be different after the agency goes to work for you? What kind of working relationship do you prefer?

2. Check out sources. Consider work you've seen or heard that has impressed you. Call friends and colleagues you trust and get their recommendations. Attend professional or trade association meetings, and talk to members who have used agencies before. Seek out their opinions and note whose names come up often (both pro and con). Watch for articles about ad agencies in area papers, trade magazines, and related publications (such as chamber of commerce newsletters).

3. Once you have a list of candidates, screen them by phone. Ask about their backgrounds, projects they've worked on, the results they've had, their fees, and anything else important to you. Then set up interviews with the three or four firms that impress you the most.

4. Interview the finalists. Find out the following:

- Do they have experience working with your industry? What is their track record when working with companies like yours? Do they understand your business and the nuances of what you do? If not, are they willing to research the information they need?

- Is there chemistry? You can tell if there is a good "fit" with an ad agency. A good agency will express interest in getting to know you as an individual and learning more about your company. The people will be good listeners and quick learners. They will make good suggestions and react quickly to your questions and opinions. They should demonstrate the ability to anticipate what is best for your business and be prepared to disagree with you if they feel you're on the wrong track.

- Do they show originality and creativity? Based on the agency's previous work, do you feel these people understand how best to "sell" your product or service? If you operate a home health-care agency, for example, you probably don't want an ad campaign that features technology over tenderness. Sensing your clientele, the agency should know enough about you to put together the appropriate message.

- Are they reliable and budget-conscious? No amount of chemistry and creativity can make up for a missed deadline or an estimate that's way off. Be sure the agency has not only the creative skills needed but also the time and commitment to devote to your needs. Whether you're the biggest or smallest client in their stable, you should be able to count on consistent attention to detail. They should be available to answer your questions and be accountable for delays and expenses.

The local chapter of the Public Relations Society of America (PRSA) (www.prsa.org) can provide a list of members available for hire. Because PRSA members agree to abide by a code of ethics, you are likely to find firms and individuals you can trust.

Source: Leann Anderson, "Star Makers," www.entrepreneur.com/article/0,4621,227097,00.html.

Ten Differences Between Advertising and Public Relations

1. Paid Space or Free Coverage

Advertising: The company pays for ad space. You know exactly when that ad will air or be published.

Public Relations: Your job is to get free publicity for the company. From news conferences to press releases, you're focused on getting free media exposure for the company and its products/services.

2. Creative Control vs. No Control

Advertising: Since you're paying for the space, you have creative control on what goes into that ad.

Public Relations: You have no control over how the media presents your information, if they decide to use your info at all. They're not obligated to cover your event or publish your press release just because you sent something to them.

3. Shelf Life

Advertising: Since you pay for the space, you can run your ads over and over for as long as your budget allows. An ad generally has a longer shelf life than one press release.

Public Relations: You submit a press release about a new product only once. You submit a press release about a news conference only once. The PR exposure you receive is circulated only once. An editor won't publish your same press release three or four times in his or her magazine.

4. Wise Consumers

Advertising: Consumers know when they're reading an advertisement that it's intended to sell them a product or a service.

"The consumer understands that we have paid to present our selling message to him or her, and unfortunately, the consumer often views our selling message very guardedly," Paul Flowers, president of Dallas-based Flowers & Partners, Inc., said. "After all, they know we are trying to sell them."

Public Relations: When people read a third-party article written about your product or view coverage of your event on TV, they're seeing something you didn't pay for with ad dollars and view it differently than they do paid advertising.

"Where we can generate some sort of third-party 'endorsement' by independent media sources, we can create great credibility for our clients' products or services," Flowers said.

5. Creativity or a Nose for News

Advertising: In advertising, you get to exercise your creativity in creating new ad campaigns and materials.

Public Relations: In public relations, you have to have a nose for news and be able to generate buzz through that news. You exercise your creativity, to an extent, in the way you search for new news to release to the media.

6. In-House or out on the Town

Advertising: If you're working at an ad agency, your main contacts are your co-workers and the agency's clients. If you buy and plan ad space on behalf of the client, like advertising agency BBH's Media Director Barry Lowenthal does, then you'll also interact with media salespeople.

Public Relations: You interact with the media and develop a relationship with them. Your contact is not limited to in-house communications. You're in constant touch with your contacts at the print publications and broadcast media.

Section 9

7. **Target Audience or Hooked Editor**

Advertising: You're looking for your target audience and advertising accordingly. For example, you wouldn't advertise a women's TV network in a male-oriented sports magazine.

Public Relations: You must have an angle and hook editors to get them to use info for an article, to run a press release, or to cover your event.

8. **Limited or Unlimited Contact**

Advertising: Some industry pros, such as Flowers & Partners Account Executive Trey Sullivan, have contact with the clients. Others, like copywriters or graphic designers in the agency, may not meet with the client at all.

Public Relations: In public relations, you are very visible to the media. PR pros aren't always called on for the good news.

If there's an accident at your company, you may have to give a statement or on-camera interview to journalists. You may represent your company as a spokesperson at an event. Or you may work within community relations to show that your company is actively involved in good work and committed to the city and its citizens.

9. **Special Events**

Advertising: If your company sponsors an event, you wouldn't want to take out an ad giving yourself a pat on the back for being such a great company. This is where your PR department steps in.

Public Relations: If you're sponsoring an event, you can send out a press release and the media might pick it up. They may publish the information or cover the event.

10. **Writing Style**

Advertising: Buy this product! Act now! Call today! These are all things you can say in an advertisement. You want to use those buzz words to motivate people to buy your product.

Public Relations: You're strictly writing in a no-nonsense news format. Any blatant commercial messages in your communications are disregarded by the media.

Source: Apryl Duncan, "10 Differences Between Advertising and Public Relations," advertising.about.com/od/careersource/a/10advpr.htm.

Eight Secrets for Powerful Press Releases

1. **Select the right media for your particular story.** Always begin by creating a "press list." This is a list of media that reach large numbers of your target audience and are looked to as reputable sources of information. Then select different media from your press list to receive various types of stories.

Before you decide what type of information to send, get copies of each publication to learn what kind of information will be most relevant to that publication's readers. For example, if your firm wins a local award, your release may be of interest to your hometown newspaper, but if you invent a breakthrough medical product, you should target general-business, consumer, and medical trade press with your story.

2. **Send your press release to a specific person.** Major media outlets receive hundreds or even thousands of press releases daily. To keep yours from being lost in the shuffle, take the time to research the name of a specific editor, news director, or journalist to receive it. If you've followed Rule No. 1 and become familiar with the newspapers, magazines, and broadcast news stations you're targeting, it will be easy to identify the individuals who typically handle stories like yours.

   Press releases may be distributed by mail, fax, or e-mail. You'll find that journalists at technology publications, among others, typically prefer releases via e-mail. In general, faxing conveys an immediacy that traditional mail does not. However, many journalists still prefer to receive releases via traditional mail, so it's always a good idea to ask what the preferred method is.

3. **Spotlight a newsworthy angle.** The majority of press releases sent to the news media don't turn into stories. Those that do have one thing in common: they meet the specific needs of a publication or broadcast outlet's readers, viewers, or listeners. To be newsworthy, your release has to contain beneficial information, identify a trend, shed new light on a timely or relevant issue, or contain information about an upcoming event.

4. **Write a headline that states a benefit.** The media will evaluate your press release with one thing in mind: how the information it contains will benefit or interest their readers or viewers. In order for your release to stand out, your headline must instantly communicate why your information is relevant.

   If the headline benefit is quantifiable, so much the better. For example, "New Tax-Checking Software Reduces Errors by 10 Percent" is a better headline than "Herr Technology Introduces New Tax-Checking Software."

5. **Make sure the copy doesn't sound like an ad.** Too many press releases read like thinly disguised advertisements. To be effective, your release must stick to the facts, avoiding broad claims and hyperbole. Tone down the sales language in your release, and focus on clear communication. Use testimonials, expert quotes, and statistics to give weight to your claims.

6. **Keep your layout simple.** A straightforward presentation is best. Avoid the temptation to "dress up" your layout with artful typefaces that can make your release look like an advertising flier. Stay away from headlines or text in all capital letters, which slows the reader down. Instead, make your release clean and easy to read.

7. **Give the media an incentive to respond.** If your public relations arsenal includes studies, booklets, or product samples, don't send them along with your initial release.

Mention the tools in your release; then send them later to journalists who contact you for more information. This helps you build a better-qualified press list and reduces your costs.

8. **Always follow up by telephone.** While most journalists say they hate follow-up phone calls, these calls are a necessary element in a successful public relations program. With the crush of releases sent to every outlet, telephone follow-up ensures your information gets into the right hands. Phone contact also allows you to elaborate on how your story will benefit the journalist's readers or viewers.

Building relationships with the media takes patience. Each time you contact a member of the media, ask if you've called at a good time. Be sensitive to deadline pressures and note the best times to call back.

Regularly send appropriate stories to each medium and be sure to follow these eight rules to make your releases stand out from the crowd. Soon, you'll find your business getting the kind of publicity you've only dreamed of.

Source: Kim T. Gordon, "8 Secrets for Powerful Press Releases," www.entrepreneur.com/article/ 0,4621,309578,00.html.

Seven Free Types of PR Avenues

Alfred J. Lautenslager—an award-winning marketing and PR consultant, direct-mail promotion specialist, principal of marketing consulting firm Marketing Now, and president and owner of The Ink Well, a commercial printing and mailing company—offers some suggestions for ways to do PR beyond sending out press releases.

1. **Writing articles:** Articles don't have to be long; they just need to be informative. Share your experience. Cite your wisdom. Tell a story. Make a list. These are all things you can write an article about. Everyone is more of an expert in one particular area than another. Writing about how to do something is always something of value to readers. Writing articles gives you instant credibility, too. Submitting online, as well as offline, provides another good chance to get your name in print at no cost. Be sure to put your contact information in a contact resource box at the end of the article.

2. **Newsletters:** Writing a newsletter is another way to keep your name top-of-mind. This can be online or offline. Online newsletters are often referred to as e-zines; offline newsletters are printed and mailed. Both contain content valuable to your target market and many times advertise your products and services. It's always been said that your best prospect is a current customer. Advertising to current customers is your best bet to get more business. E-zines are e-mails to your permission-based e-mail database. The cost of this is nothing, yet the return potential is infinite.

3. **Public speaking:** Speaking in front of an audience usually makes you an expert. People like to buy from experts. If they're in your audience, then they'll remember

your expertise and come to you when they need the product or service. Chambers of commerce are also good targets, but so are all the service clubs that need luncheon speakers. Speaking is free, and it's just like making a sales call to many people at one time.

4. **Free reports:** Offering a free report online is a good way to get an e-mail from prospects so you may market to them later. This is the whole basis of permission-based marketing or opt-in lists. You can do the same thing offline. You can increase the response of a direct-mail program from one percent to double-digit percentage returns. The free reports can be a dressed-up article, a list, a survey that you've done, or some research-based information. Use your imagination here.

5. **Radio:** Radio is expensive, you say? Not if you are being interviewed or calling in on a talk show. Getting interviewed is free, except for your continual follow-up with producers. Calling in is free, but sometimes it's hard to relay contact information. Both of these work, especially when supplemented with other marketing strategies.

6. **Online forum participation:** There are many online newsgroups or forums for a particular subject area. Participating in these is another way to get your name out. Advertising is not usually permitted. Participating by answering and asking questions will position you as an expert and a resource for others. Many online forums will let you put an e-mail signature with a link to your site or message with another site linked. Take full advantage of this; these links get clicked often when of interest to the forum participants.

7. **Letters to the editor:** A little-known secret that's a good follow-up to a press release is a letter to an editor. This is free PR. Many times a letter to the editor has a better chance of getting published than the press release. Sometimes you'll get a press release published with editorial comments from the editor. The letter to the editor is a great place to respond to editorial comments as well as to further state a position. You'd be surprised how many people read this column in publications. This is also another way to become friends with the editor. If the editor sees you enough and matches you with a newsworthy press release, then your chances of getting a press release in print increase.

These are just some of the many free PR avenues that can increase the top-of-mind awareness with your target customers and prospects. As always, it's best to do this as part of an overall marketing plan with measurement and follow-up.

Source: Al Lautenslager, "Take Advantage of Free PR," www.entrepreneur.com/article/0,4621,309223,00.html.

Section 9

Five Ways to Promote Your Business Beyond Press Releases

1. **Events:** These can be open houses, celebrity visits, clearance sales, "meet the owners" events, or other events that give you a reason to invite customers and prospects to your place of business. The most important invitee of all for effective PR is the media. This includes newspaper officials and reporters, editors, management, and similar titles from radio and TV stations.

2. **Fact sheets, newsletters, and brochures for customers and prospects:** This almost sounds more like part of the marketing plan vs. the PR plan, but these marketing vehicles can be tailored to support PR and one-time situations and enhance media relations.

3. **A PR firm:** You can make your company seem more newsworthy and media-friendly by hiring a PR agency. This doesn't have to be done on an ongoing basis. This should be done only if it's part of your overall plan and the budget is in line with your company financials.

4. **FAQ development:** Radio and TV people, believe it or not, sometimes have trouble selecting topics to fill their airtime and finding good people to interview. Compile a list of answers to anticipated questions or questions that make your point. These FAQs can also be included in your media kits, posted on your web site, and distributed when meeting with customers and prospects.

5. **Speaking engagements:** Nothing gets the word out more than the spoken word. When you speak to a group, you are the center of attention, competing with no one for share of mind. Speaking is a great form of PR.

Source: Al Lautenslager, "PR Is More Than Just Press Releases," www.entrepreneur.com/article/0,4621,310647,00.html.

How a Press Release Gets You Free Publicity

What Is a Press Release?

A press release or a news release, as it is also called, is a condensed article that is written in a journalistic style. A press release is not a sales document, a resume, or an advertisement. The purpose of the news release is to highlight what is interesting and newsworthy about your company or organization. This can include announcing product releases, new services, or drama within your market.

What Are the Costs?

Press releases are relatively inexpensive to prepare and distribute. Compare the price of a full-page ad from a major news publication—generally tens of thousands of dollars. Even local papers typically charge several thousand dollars. For less than a few hundred dollars, you can receive better, more comprehensive coverage than paid advertising. Research shows that most news releases generate a higher return than even high-powered ad campaigns.

Free Publicity

When members of the news media feature your story pulled from your press release, it generates free publicity. Frequently, your story can show up not only in one major newspaper, but in two or three, as well as in news talk shows carried on major networks such as NBC or CBS. If you are looking to publicize in local markets only, releases can be directed to those local publications and hit the news feeds of editors who write for your specific industry. If you are looking for global coverage, news releases are the best marketing tools. In a sense, a press release is a gift that just keeps giving.

News releases not only reach journalists but they also capture potential customers and/or investors, which means that your products and/or services can be both funded and made more profitable simply based on the media attention your release receives. Whatever your target audience may be, news releases offer you a way to become known to the public without a significant investment. Even large corporations that spend millions of dollars on ad campaigns continue to use news releases to maintain public interest, which results in higher revenue.

Added Benefits for Sending a Press Release

Another advantage to sending out news releases is that there is always demand. All news organizations—including magazine editors, broadcast editors, and industry-specific editors—use press releases to develop the bulk of their published news stories. From a consumer standpoint, editors who report on your news release are considered disinterested parties, meaning that your announcement was chosen because of public demand for relevant and useful information. Often, paid advertising is suspect in the customers' eye because companies are more interested in their products selling than what is in the best interest of their customers.

To sum up, the benefits to sending out news releases include:

- low cost
- increased visibility for your company
- high demand for press releases
- added credibility for your organization
- new customers
- new investors
- free publicity

This free publicity generated from your news release is all the better because the media has given its stamp of approval, which adds credibility and value to your company or organization.

Go to entrepreneur.prwebdirect.com/pressreleasebenefits.php for more information or for help writing press releases.

Source: PR Web™, "How Can a Press Release Help You Get Free Publicity?," entrepreneur.prwebdirect.com/pressreleasebenefits.php.

SCORE's Five Tips on Using PR to Your Advantage

1. Public relations should be an important part of your marketing effort. Use it to promote special events such as grand openings and to build the image of your business in the public eye.

2. Get involved in your community. Join the chamber of commerce, business organizations, service clubs, and charities. Network yourself and keep your antennae up.

3. Gain third-party credibility by sending the media news releases. Limit copy to one page, if possible, and send releases to local and regional media when you have an important story to tell.

4. Maintain relations with the markets you serve. By following the trends and news that affect your market, you will become the "town expert." The public and the media will come to you for your opinion or to learn about marketplace trends.

5. Sponsor a radio or TV public service announcement (PSA) for a local charity. This will give you name recognition and show community support.

Source: SCORE, www.score.org/business_tips.html.

Six Steps to Winning Publicity

1. **Make a contact list.** Most entrepreneurs have more than one type of story to tell. For example, one story might be of interest to trade press in your industry or even consumers, while a story about your company's affiliation with a local charity would be most interesting to your local business press. Develop a media contact list with help from print publications and online sources including Bacon's MediaSource (www.bacons.com) and Gebbie Press (www.gebbieinc.com), which both provide a free searchable database of media links.

2. **Don't waste editors' time.** The media are interested only in stories that will help them sell more issues or increase ratings—in other words, they want stories that are compelling to their readers, viewers, or listeners. Either tailor a story specifically for that outlet or wait until the right opportunity presents itself.

3. **Establish relationships with key journalists.** Instead of taking the "blast" approach to media relations, it's often better to take the time to develop relationships with select members of the media and provide them with exclusive materials or story ideas.

4. **Send great materials.** Sometimes it's smart to send your media relations list something other than the standard release or media alert. One way to win publicity is to provide quality materials that take some of the work out of covering your story, such as by sending product photographs to magazines, e-mailing links to online high-tech product demos, or providing a page of tips writers can use as story background or as a springboard to your interview.

5. **Take the time to follow up.** Entrepreneurs new to publicity often overlook the fact that media relations is about building relationships with members of the media. It's vital to tailor stories appropriately, send top-notch materials, and then follow up by phone or e-mail. If your current story pitch doesn't meet his or her needs, find out what will so you can better tailor your next pitch.

6. **Be ready with more.** The best thing that can happen in your follow-up call with a journalist is that you'll spark an interest in learning more about you, your company, or its products and services. So be prepared to send a full media kit or any supporting materials the media outlet may require. After you've made your first few follow-up calls, you'll have a clear idea of what this kit should contain.

Source: Kim T. Gordon, "6 Steps to Winning Publicity," www.entrepreneur.com/article/ 0,4621,320576,00.html.

SCORE's Five Tips on Hiring a Public Relations Firm

1. Be clear on what you want from a public relations effort. Some things a PR firm can do for you are to get you positive exposure in the media, create and conduct special events, and help you build and maintain a solid reputation.

2. Be realistic about what a PR firm cannot do. It cannot whitewash an unethical business or cover up fraud or other illegal activities.

3. Interview a number of firms. Get their ideas on how they can help you and seriously consider those with the best ideas.

4. If you are looking for only local publicity, hire a local firm. But if you want a national program, your PR firm can be anywhere.

5. Once you've hired a company, keep your account executive fully informed about your business. Treat him or her as part of your strategic team.

Source: SCORE, www.score.org/business_tips.html.

Section
9

Product and Service Management

Testing Your Product

Section 10

717

Five Key Criteria for New Products Before Going to Market

When is a good product a good idea? Obviously, when the orders flood in. So how do you know before you hit the market? Product expert Don Debelak says good products must satisfy five key criteria before they go to market.

1. Is the product easy to distribute? Entrepreneurs need easy-to-penetrate distribution networks open to small companies.

2. Is the technology simple? Most products go through several prototypes and product changes. The more complex the technology, the more expensive it is to get to market.

3. Is the item unique? Store buyers and consumers tend to break brand loyalty only when faced with the new and different.

4. Are the product's benefits obvious?

5. Can the product be sold for four to five times its manufacturing cost? There are a lot of people ahead of the inventor who need to be paid, so you need to make sure there's money left for you.

Source: Rieva Lesonsky, *365 Tips to Boost Your Entrepreneurial IQ.*

New Product Expectations for a Manufacturer

As the manufacturer, you are expected to:

- Make a quality product.
- Create a demand for your product through marketing efforts and provide the marketing materials.
- Be able to fill all orders the distributor gets.
- Offer incentives to the distributor's sales team.
- Not undercut your distribution network. In other words, if a customer calls you directly, pass that call on to your distributor.
- Provide technical support and customer service.

Source: Rieva Lesonsky, *365 Tips to Boost Your Entrepreneurial IQ.*

New Product Expectations for a Distributor

Frequently, new product entrepreneurs don't fully understand the role they play and what they should expect from their distributors. You should expect your distributor to:

- Respond quickly when you pass on leads.
- Store your products prior to sale.
- Fill customers' orders quickly and accurately.
- Help build a market for your products.

Source: Rieva Lesonsky, *365 Tips to Boost Your Entrepreneurial IQ.*

**Section
10**

Inventory

Section 10

Tactics to Drive Sales Before Having Product Inventory

Here's a shocker for most of you: you don't necessarily need inventory to take orders for your products. Here are some tactics to drive sales without products:

- Use a prototype. Design a flier or brochure that describes your product; then approach catalogs, retailers, distributors, and manufacturer's reps seeking orders. You can also exhibit your prototype at trade shows—or even flea markets—and take orders for future delivery.

- Advertise or send out direct mail and see how many orders you receive. Make sure you offer customers an option to cancel the order if it can't be delivered within 30 days.

- If possible, produce a small quantity of products made with low-volume production techniques. Don't worry if this costs you a bit more. Consider it an investment that will tell you if you have a product worth selling. Then, if it works, you can increase your production schedule.

Source: Rieva Lesonsky, *365 Tips to Boost Your Entrepreneurial IQ.*

Tips on How to Manage Your Inventory System

A good inventory tracking system will tell you what merchandise is in stock, what is on order, when it will arrive, and what you've sold. There are two types of inventory systems: *dollar-control systems* and *unit-control systems*.

- Dollar-control systems show the cost and gross profit margin on individual inventory items. A basic method of dollar control begins at the cash register with sales receipts listing the product, quantity sold, and price. You can compare sales receipts with delivery receipts to determine your gross profit margin on a given item. You can also use software programs to track inventory by type, cost, volume, and profit.

- Unit-control systems use methods ranging from simply eyeballing shelves to using sophisticated bin tickets—tiny cards kept with each type of product that list a stock number, description, maximum and minimum quantities stocked, cost (in code), selling price, and any other information you want to include. Bin tickets correspond to office file cards that list a stock number, selling price, cost, number of items to a case, supply source and alternative source, order dates, quantities, and delivery time. Retailers make physical inventory checks daily, weekly, or as often as practical—once a year at the minimum.

Computerized Inventory Control

While manual methods may have their place, most entrepreneurs these days find that computerizing gives them a far wider range of information with far less effort. Inventory software programs now on the market let you track usage, monitor changes in unit dollar costs, calculate when you need to reorder, and analyze inventory levels on an item-by-item basis.

Point-of-Sale (POS) software records each sale when it happens, so your inventory records are always up to date. Better still, you get much more information about the sale than you could gather with a manual system. By running reports based on this information, you can make better decisions about ordering and merchandising.

With a POS system:

- You can analyze sales data, figure out how well all the items on your shelves sell, and adjust purchasing levels accordingly.

- You can maintain a sales history to help adjust your buying decisions for seasonal purchasing trends.

- You can improve pricing accuracy by integrating bar-code scanners and credit card authorization ability with the POS system.

Features to consider in a POS system include the following:

- **Ease of use:** Look for software with a user-friendly graphical interface.

- **Entry of sales information:** Most systems allow you to enter inventory codes either manually or automatically via a bar-code scanner. Once the inventory code is entered, the systems call up the standard or sales price, compute the price at multiple quantities, and provide a running total. Many systems make it easy to enter sales manually when needed by letting you search for inventory codes based on a partial merchandise number, description, manufacturing code, or vendor.

- **Pricing:** POS systems generally offer a variety of ways to keep track of pricing, including add-on amounts, percentage of cost, margin percentage, and custom formulas. For example, if you provide volume discounts, you can set up multiple prices for each item.

- **Updating product information:** Once a sale is entered, these systems automatically update inventory and accounts receivable records.

- **Sales tracking options:** Different businesses get paid in different ways. For example, repair or service shops often keep invoices open until the work is completed, so they need a system that allows them to put sales on hold. If you sell expensive consumer goods and allow installment purchases, you might appreciate a loan calculator that tabulates monthly payments. And if you offer rent-to-own items, you'll want a system that can handle rentals as well as sales.

- **Security:** In retail, it's important to keep tight control over cash receipts to prevent theft. Most of these systems provide audit trails so you can trace any problems.

- **Taxes:** Many POS systems can support numerous tax rates—useful if you run a mail order business and need to deal with taxes for more than one state.

Section 10

Source: "Tracking Inventory," www.entrepreneur.com/article/0,4621,265115,00.html, excerpted from Rieva Lesonsky, *Start Your Own Business*.

Tips on How to Value Your Inventory

What is the effect of valuation inventory on the P&L?

Your P&L and balance sheets are interconnected. How you value inventory determines costs of sales and therefore profit. The formula is as follows:

Costs of sales = (beginning inventory) + (inventory purchases) - (ending inventory)

Ending inventory depends on how you value inventory on your balance sheet. Therefore, the lower the inventory, the higher the costs of sales, which results in lower profit. Conversely, a higher inventory valuation results in lower cost of sales and higher profits.

What are the different valuation methods?

The three main valuation methods are:

1. **First-in-first-out (FIFO):** This means your cost of sales is determined by the cost of the items you purchased the earliest. Inventory is composed of the cost of the items you purchased the latest.

2. **Last-in-first-out (LIFO):** This means your cost of sales is determined by the cost of the items you purchased the latest. It should be noted that, depending on your industry, LIFO may not be allowed for tax purposes.

3. **Weighted average cost (WAC):** This means that your cost of sales is determined by the average cost of the items you purchased determined at the time of sale.

Source: Ian Benoliel, "How to Value Your Inventory," www.entrepreneur.com/article/0,4621,303291,00.html.

Section 10

Tips on Keeping Up with Inventory on eBay

Storing Your Inventory

Space in your home. If you are homebased and your merchandise doesn't take up a lot of room, you may have adequate storage space in your home. Designate a large closet or a room for your products. Many homebased eBay sellers work from their garages.

Self-storage facilities. You can rent space equivalent to anything from a large closet to an extra garage at a self-storage facility. Many offer options ranging from air-conditioned space, indoor access, loading docks, and more. Some operators will accept deliveries on your behalf if you can't be there to sign for them yourself.

Commercial warehouse space. If you maintain a sizeable inventory and your items tend to be heavy, you may need a commercial warehouse facility with a shipping dock. You'll find this type of commercial space in industrial (light and heavy) parks and mixed-use commercial areas. Some offer only warehouse space; others have small offices and even showrooms adjacent to the warehouse. Gary Neubert (eBay User ID: gatorpack) has a 5,000-square-foot warehouse with a loading dock. After they closed their retail shop, Ron and Sheri Walker (eBay User ID: beansantiques) turned their building into what they call an "eBay factory" with a computer room, storage areas, and packing stations.

Public (commercial) storage. A viable option to your own commercial space is a public warehouse. Public warehousing companies can essentially function as your shipping department. In addition to storage, their services include pick-and-pack operations, packaging, and labeling, and they will arrange for shipping on the carrier you specify. Public warehousing prices are based on usage: you pay only for the space and labor you use. Contract warehousing is similar in terms of services, but you pay fees whether or not you use space and services. Find public warehouse companies in your local telephone directory or through an internet search.

Remember that the more storage space you have, the easier it is to purchase off-season inventory that you hold until the time is right to sell. However, always remember to calculate storage costs into your cost of selling those items. Assign specific areas for items "to be listed," "listed," "sold, waiting for payment," and "ready to pack and ship."

Tracking Your Inventory

Your own inventory management system doesn't have to be as high-tech or complex, but it does have to be as serious. At any given moment, you need to know what you have on hand, what you've purchased that's on the way, what you need to buy, what's up for auction, what's available in your eBay store and on your web site, what's been sold, and what's been shipped.

For small, low-volume sellers, a simple index card system or spreadsheet will be sufficient. Serious eBay sellers track this information electronically. Most auction management software packages include inventory tracking.

Source: Jacquelyn Lynn and Charlene Davis, "Keeping Up With Your eBay Inventory," www.entrepreneur.com/article/0,4621,321115,00.html, excerpted from *Make Big Profits on eBay*.

Chapter 66

Pricing Your Product or Service

Section
10

Tips for Setting Your Price

Do you charge enough for your products or services? Many new entrepreneurs don't. When setting prices, keep these tips in mind:

- What's the going rate? Find the acceptable rate in your industry, both the high and the low end. Ask colleagues and check with your trade association. Average that rate with your experience and expertise.

- Are you a recognized expert in your field, or are there only a few people who do what you do? If so, then you can charge more. However, the more competition you have, the more competitive your prices have to be.

- How busy are you? If you have more work than you can handle, it might be a good time to raise rates. Sure, you'll lose some business, but the business you keep will be more profitable.

- How valuable are you to your clients and customers? If you provide products or services essential to your clients, then you can probably charge more.

Source: Rieva Lesonsky, *365 Tips to Boost Your Entrepreneurial IQ.*

Three Steps for Determining Price

Pricing is an important aspect of every business because price is used to create financial projections, establish a breakeven point, and calculate profit and loss. Establishing a good price point from the beginning is vital, because it's much easier to lower prices than to raise them. Though price may be determined by any number of factors, basically there are three ways to establish the price for your product:

1. Perform a comparative analysis on similar products sold by competitors. Are the features and benefits similar to your product's features and benefits? If so, use the price of the competing product as a possible price point for your product. If your product is of superior quality and has more features and benefits, then you might be able to justify a higher price and still be competitive. If your product is inferior, then your price point will be lower.

2. Calculate the total cost to produce and deliver your product. Use this amount to figure in an acceptable margin of profit to calculate the final price.

3. Use what I call "The David Copperfield Method." Named after the famous magician who made the Statue of Liberty disappear on national TV, this method of pricing simply means that you pull the price out of thin air. Believe it or not, many companies use this method to establish pricing. It's also the reason many companies disappear.

   It's easier to understand the allure of the Copperfield Method when you realize that more often than not, product pricing comes down to one thing: perception.

Perception—or, as it is more commonly referred to in business, perceived value—is one factor most entrepreneurs use to determine product pricing. After all, our products are our children. We create them, nurture them, grow them, and love them. And often we perceive their value to be much greater than the market perceives it to be.

Source: Tim W. Knox, "Secrets to Pricing Your Product," www.entrepreneur.com/article/0,4621,314970,00.html.

Market Planning Checklist

Before you launch a marketing campaign, answer the following questions about your business and your product or service.

- Have you analyzed the total market for your product or service? Do you know which features of your product or service will appeal to different market segments?
- In forming your marketing message, have you described how your product or service will benefit your clients?
- Have you prepared a pricing schedule? What kinds of discounts do you offer and to whom do you offer them?
- Have you prepared a sales forecast?
- Which media will you use in your marketing campaign?
- Do your marketing materials mention any optional accessories or added services that consumers might want to purchase?
- If you offer a product, have you prepared clear assembly and operating instructions if required? What kind of warranty do you provide? What type of customer service or support do you offer after the sale?
- Do you have product liability insurance?
- Is your packaging likely to appeal to your target market?
- If your product is one you can patent, have you done so?
- How will you distribute your product?

Source: Rieva Lesonsky, *Start Your Own Business.*

Section 10

Tips for Raising Prices

How's your bottom line? If it's not a large as you'd like, maybe it's time to raise prices. One of the easiest ways to increase profits is to boost prices.

- Don't initiate an immediate across-the-board price hike. Instead, use a niche-pricing technique: find the areas within your business where you can support an increase.

- Price is based on a perceived value, so you have to find the places where you are undervaluing your product or service.

- To do this, study costs—your and your competitors'. Then analyze your competitive advantages and disadvantages. This is not an easy process, but it's well worth the effort.

- Once you identify the areas where you've undervalued your product or service, adjust those prices accordingly.

- Make sure you give your customers advance notice, explain the increase, and focus on value, not price.

Source: Rieva Lesonsky, *365 Tips to Boost Your Entrepreneurial IQ.*

Four Pricing Methods

1. **Cost-Plus Pricing.** Many manufacturers use cost-plus pricing. The key to being successful is making the "plus" figure not only cover all overhead but also generate the percentage profit you require. If your overhead figure is not accurate, you risk profits that are too low.

2. **Demand Pricing.** Demand pricing is determined by the optimum combination of volume and profit. This is used for businesses that charge different prices, such as retailers, discount chains, wholesalers, or direct marketers. A wholesaler might buy greater quantities than a retailer, which results in a lower unit price. Demand pricing is difficult to master because you must correctly calculate beforehand what price will generate the optimum relation of profit to volume.

3. **Competitive Pricing.** Competitive pricing is used when there is an established market price for a particular product or service. To use competitive pricing effectively, know the prices each competitor has established. Should you charge a higher price then your competitors, have a reason to do so, such as quality customer service or a warranty policy.

4. **Markup Pricing.** This pricing method is used by manufacturers, wholesalers, and retailers. A markup is calculated by adding a set amount to the cost of a product. This pricing method gets confused with new businesses. They often confuse markup (expressed as a percentage of cost) and gross profit (expressed as a percentage of selling price).

Source: Andi Axman, *Entrepreneur Magazine's Ultimate Start-Up Advisor.*

Section 11

Growing Your Business

Section
11

Chapter 67

Networking

Section 11

Top Ways to Improve Your Networking Skills

Networking—everyone talks about it. But do you know how to do it right? Networking expert Dee Helfgott says networking is people connecting with people—exchanging ideas, information, and resources. Try her networking tips:

- Prepare a 30-second introduction of who you are, what you do, and how your business benefits others. It should be long enough to convey information but short enough so it's not a sales pitch.

- Volunteer for a small role on a committee of an important organization or association. This gives you visibility and will gain you respect.

- Listen more than you talk. That's the best way to get information that may help you.

- Don't forget to network outside your group. You never know who knows someone who may need your product or service.

Source: Rieva Lesonsky, *365 Tips to Boost Your Entrepreneurial IQ.*

Tips on Effective Networking

Many consider networking so simple anyone can do it, but don't listen to them. You have to learn to network the right way.

- Develop a plan. Networking is more than saying hello. It's the smart way to build long-lasting business relationships.

- Decide who your best prospects are and where you're likely to find them. Then go where they are: committees, conferences, meetings, or associations.

- Learn to make small talk. Ask open-ended questions.

- Don't forget to listen!

- Don't think of networking as just a sales opportunity. Instead, consider it a mission—a chance to learn something. The sales will come later.

- Always follow up. If you don't, you've wasted your time, not to mention your energy and money.

- Most important, be prepared. Networking opportunities can—and do—crop up unexpectedly.

Source: Rieva Lesonsky, *365 Tips to Boost Your Entrepreneurial IQ.*

Four More Networking Tips

Do you network? Many entrepreneurs claim they don't have time. But networking may be vital to your success, so make the time. To get the most out of networking, try these suggestions:

- Make sure your name is printed boldly on your nametag, which should be on your right shoulder for easy visibility.

- If you attend an event with someone you know, split up. This is not the place to talk with friends or employees.

- If you don't know anyone in the room, stand in the food or bar line. There are usually plenty of people there to start conversations with.

- This is not the time to be shy. Smile, extend your hand, and introduce yourself, but don't interrupt when other are speaking.

Remember the purpose of networking: meet as many people as possible, and don't forget to follow up with a letter or phone call.

Source: Rieva Lesonsky, *365 Tips to Boost Your Entrepreneurial IQ*.

Tips for Getting over Your Networking Shyness

1. **Set clear goals.** What do you want to accomplish in your business? What income level do you want to achieve? By simply taking the time to define your goals and write them down, you intensify your desire to overcome your shyness.

2. **Turn your focus away from yourself.** When you're at a networking event, instead of feeling embarrassed about "forcing yourself" onto the other person, simply switch the focus of the conversation to that person. Ask questions like:

   - Are you a member?

   - How have you benefited from your membership?

   - Do you attend regularly?

   - Are you on any committees?

   - What business are you in?

   - How did you get into your business (or career path)?

   The irony is that when you allow people to talk about themselves, they'll be more likely to enjoy the conversation with you—and naturally view your business in a positive light.

3. **Practice, practice, practice.** A key step to overcoming shyness is preparation and practice. Write down in advance the questions you think will stimulate and sustain

conversations. Try role-playing with someone you feel comfortable with, perhaps a spouse, friend, coach, or even a sales trainer.

4. **Learn from your mistakes—don't fear them.** Often shyness comes from a fear of making a fool of yourself. Diminish that fear by focusing on what you can learn from networking situations, whether good or bad. When you take time to assess your approach, you'll position yourself to be more successful with your interactions with people.

5. **Reward yourself when you've done well.** If you make it to a networking event and speak with, say, five or six new people and stay as long as you planned, give yourself a reward. Perhaps it's a new book, a dinner out—whatever motivates you. Withhold the reward if you don't meet your goal.

Source: Sean M. Lyden, "Get over Your Networking Shyness," www.entrepreneur.com/article/ 0,4621,296695,00.html.

Golden Rules for Networking

1. **Spread out your contacts.** Regardless of the type of relationship with your clients, regular contact is generally good. Two short meetings or phone calls are more beneficial than one long session. Each meeting becomes an opportunity to strengthen the relationship and to enhance your visibility and recognition.

2. **Schedule predictably.** Stay in touch with your clients regularly. Train them to expect to hear from you at certain times. For example, if you usually contact certain customers during the first week of every quarter, they will come to expect it and will budget time for you. If they don't hear from you, they may actually call on their own to see how you are doing.

3. **Make each contact lead to the next.** Before concluding a meeting or telephone conversation, schedule the date of your next contact. In written correspondence, close by stating the date your customer should expect to hear from you again: "I'll send you a note or e-mail by the end of the quarter." Having made the commitment, you're more likely to follow through.

4. **Assume responsibility for making contact.** You can't control whether clients will contact you, but you can control when you contact them. Take the initiative; stay in touch with your customers. This is especially important for your most important clients. By staying in touch with them, you are much more likely to head off potential problems down the road.

5. **Invite them to networking events.** One way of making sure to stay in contact with your customers is to invite select ones to some of the networking events that you go to. This is a great way to meet with them periodically while getting you out of your cave to network and to meet other people.

Section 11

6. **Stick to your plan.** As you achieve success in establishing routines with your sources, some of them may begin taking initiative with contact. Don't let this interfere with your contact schedule—that is, when they initiate the call, don't count it as one of the contacts you've scheduled.

Source: Ivan Misner, "The Golden Rule of Networking: Stay in Touch with Your Clients," www.entrepreneur.com/article/0,4621,306665,00.html.

Seven Relationship-Building Strategies for Your Business

1. **Communicate frequently.** For best results, it's important to communicate frequently and vary the types of messages you send. The exact frequency you choose will depend on your industry and even seasonality, but for many types of businesses, it's possible to combine e-mail, direct mail, phone contact, and face-to-face communication to keep prospects moving through your sales cycle without burning out on your message.

2. **Offer customer rewards.** Customer loyalty or reward programs work well for many types of businesses, from retail to cruise and travel. The most effective programs offer graduated rewards, so the more customers spend, the more they earn. This rewards your best, most profitable clients or customers and cuts down on low-value price switchers—customers who switch from program to program to get entry-level rewards.

3. **Hold special events.** With the renewed interest in retaining and up-selling current customers, company-sponsored special events are returning to the forefront. Any event that allows you and your staff to interact with your best customers is a good bet, whether it's a springtime golf outing, a summertime pool party, or an early fall barbecue.

4. **Build two-way communication.** When it comes to customer relations, listening can be every bit as important as telling. Use every tool and opportunity to create interaction, including asking for feedback through your web site and e-newsletters, sending customer surveys (online or offline), and providing online message boards or blogs. Customers who know they're heard instantly feel a rapport and a relationship with your company.

5. **Enhance your customer service.** One of the best ways to add value and stand out from the competition is to have superior customer service. Customers often make choices between parity products and services based on the perceived customer experience. This is what they can expect to receive in the way of support from your company after a sale is closed.

6. **Launch multicultural programs.** It may be time to add a multilingual component to your marketing program. For example, you might offer a Spanish-language transla-

Section 11

tion of your web site or use ethnic print and broadcast media to reach niche markets. Bilingual customer service will also go a long way toward helping your company build relationships with minority groups.

7. **Visit the trenches.** For many entrepreneurs, particularly those selling products and services to other businesses, it's important to go beyond standard sales calls and off-the-shelf marketing tools in order to build relationships with top customers or clients. There's no better way to really understand the challenges your customers face and the ways you can help meet them than to occasionally get out in the trenches.

Source: Kim T. Gordon, "7 Relationship-Building Strategies for Your Business," www.entrepreneur.com/article/0,4621,312509,00.html.

Ten Commandments of Networking

1. **Have the tools to network with you at all times.** These include an informative name badge, business cards, brochures about your business, and a pocket-sized business card file containing cards of other professionals to whom you can refer new business.

2. **Set a goal for the number of people you'll meet.** Identify a reachable goal based on attendance and the type of group. If you feel inspired, set a goal to meet 15 to 20 people, and make sure you get all their cards. Don't leave until you've met your goal.

3. **Act like a host, not a guest.** A host is expected to do things for others, while a guest sits back and relaxes. Volunteer to help greet people. If you see visitors sitting, introduce yourself and ask if they would like to meet others. Act as a conduit.

4. **Listen and ask questions.** Remember that a good networker has two ears and one mouth and uses them proportionately. After you've learned what another person does, tell them what you do. Be specific but brief.

5. **Don't try to close a deal.** These events are not meant to be a vehicle to hit on businesspeople to buy your products or services. Networking is about developing relationships with other professionals.

6. **Give referrals whenever possible.** The best networkers believe in the "givers gain" philosophy—what goes around comes around. If I help you, you'll help me and we'll both do better as a result of it. In other words, if you don't genuinely attempt to help the people you meet, then you are not networking effectively.

7. **Exchange business cards.** Ask each person you meet for two cards—one to pass on to someone else and one to keep. This sets the stage for networking to happen.

8. **Manage your time efficiently.** Spend ten minutes or less with each person you meet, and don't linger with friends or associates. If your goal is to meet a given

number of people, be careful not to spend too much time with any one person. When you meet someone interesting with whom you'd like to speak further, set up an appointment for a later date.

9. **Write notes on the backs of business cards you collect.** Record anything you think may be useful in remembering each person more clearly. This will come in handy when you follow up on each contact.

10. **Follow up!** You can obey the previous nine commandments religiously, but if you don't follow up effectively, you will have wasted your time. Drop a note or give a call to each person you've met. Be sure to fulfill any promises you've made.

Source: Ivan Misner, "The 10 Commandments of Networking," www.entrepreneur.com/article/ 0,4621,302801,00.html.

Tips for Remembering People's Names

Attitude

I'm bad with names. I can only remember faces. I always forget people. I don't think I'll ever improve my memory for names. I feel guilty when I ask the person to repeat their name again and again.

Change your attitude! You can't continue to make excuses and apologize to people if you forgot their names. If you tell yourself you're terrible with names, you're always going to be terrible—it's a self-fulfilling prophecy. Moreover, if you apologize to people, you only remind them that you're terrible!

Focus

I failed to focus on the moment of introduction. I was too busy worrying about the correct handshake. I was overly self-conscious about my first impression with the new client. I thought about me and not about them.

Forget about you. Focus on them. This is the foundation of customer loyalty. Smile and make eye contact as soon as they say their name. Repeat it back to them within four seconds. Don't worry: when you do remember their name, you will make a good first impression.

The Name Itself

I forgot their name because it's complicated. I forgot their name because it's too long. I forgot their name because it's derived from a culture different than my own.

Ask them about the spelling, origin, or context of their name. The longer and more unusual a name, the easier it will be to inquire further. As such, this not only allows them to repeat their name, but you appeal to their personal interests. It shows them you care about their personal information, flatters them, and makes them feel valued. Usually, they will be glad to tell you about their name.

Section 11

Memory

I forgot a customer's name within ten seconds of introduction. I drew a complete mental blank. I was humiliated.

This occurs because a person's name is the single context of human memory most apt to be forgotten. So, widen other areas of your memory circuit and repeat the name out loud in the beginning, during, and at the end of the conversation. When you speak the name, hear the name, and listen to yourself say the name, you will remember it.

Assumption

I assume someone will tell me their name. I assume my coworker will introduce me. I assume names aren't a big deal.

Be the first to ask. Go out of your way to find out people's names. Take your colleague aside and tell them to introduce you to the person clearly and properly. When they do introduce you, be certain to make eye contact with your new associate. This forces you to concentrate on his or her face and name and block out noises and distractions.

Substitution

I accidentally put the wrong names with the wrong people. I confused people's faces. I saw someone's name as an arbitrary fact, and did not turn it into a meaningful representation of them.

Look at people's facial features when they tell you their name. Dramatize those features and make a memorable connection between the person and their name. The crazier the connection, the easier the name will be to remember.

Overload

I was introduced to several customers at the same time. My brain was overloaded. Five names went in one ear and out the other. My memory for names has diffused.

Ask the person who introduced you to quietly repeat everyone's name in your ear. Then, go around the group and say their names to yourself while you look at their faces. Say them over and over again in your head during the conversation. Do this several times. If all else fails, write the names down, look at their business cards, and/or visualize the person's face while you consult your notes.

You know how it feels when someone makes an effort to remember your name. That warm sense of appreciation rings in your ear and resonates like a bell down to your heart.

Source: Scott Ginsberg, "Why Can't I Remember Your Name?," www.businessknowhow.com/growth/forgetful.htm.

Five Ways to Encourage Your Employees to Network

1. Include networking in the job description for each and every employee. Often, if a new hire knows upfront that he or she is expected to incorporate networking into the job, it will happen.

2. Have clear and reasonable expectations. If your company manufactures a very obscure product, your staff might have a hard time bringing in tons of referrals. However, keep in mind that people are more important in the networking process than the type of product being sold.

3. Teach your staff how to network effectively for the company. Hold focus groups where you role-play ways to ask for referrals from other customers, friends, and family. Bring in local networking experts for in-house trainings. The bottom line: until you teach people how to do something effectively, expecting them to do it well—or even at all—is unrealistic.

4. Motivate your staff to bring referrals to the company. Set up a bonus system that makes it obvious that employees will be developing connections in the community while passing out business cards and fliers for the company. You might even establish a "networker of the month" status for the staff, using a reserved parking spot or an overnight hotel stay somewhere fun as a reward.

5. Be sure your staff sees you practicing your networking skills. Often, we as entrepreneurs don't share with our staff the amount of time and energy we put into building and maintaining our businesses utilizing word-of-mouth marketing. One way to change this is to track how much business you brought in, as well as the staff's numbers.

Source: Ivan Misner, "5 Ways to Encourage Employees to Network," www.entrepreneur.com/article/0,4621,315310,00.html.

Section 11

Teamwork

Section 11

Six Ways Others Can Promote Your Business

1. **They can provide you with referrals.** The kind of support you'd most like to get from your contacts is referrals—the names of specific individuals who need your products and services. They can also give prospects your name and number.

2. **They can introduce you to prospects.** Your contacts can help you build new relationships faster by introducing you in person to people they think need your products and services. Furthermore, they can provide you with key information about the prospects. They can also tell the prospects a few things about you, your business, how the two of you met, some of the things you and the prospects have in common, and the value of your products and services.

3. **They can endorse your products and services.** By telling others, in presentations or informal conversations, what they've gained from using your products or services, your sources can encourage others to use your products or services.

4. **They can display your literature and products in their offices and homes.** If these items are displayed well—such as on a counter or bulletin board in a waiting room—visitors will ask questions or read the information. Some may take your promotional materials and display them in other places, increasing your visibility.

5. **They can distribute your information.** Your contacts can help you distribute marketing materials. For instance, a dry cleaner might attach a coupon from the hair salon next door to each plastic bag he or she uses to cover customers' clothes.

6. **They can publish information for you.** Your contacts may be able to get information about you and your business printed in publications to which they subscribe and in which they have some input or influence. These support activities are also things you can do to help your contacts promote their businesses and generate referrals. Helping your sources achieve their goals goes a long way toward building effective and rewarding relationships.

Source: Ivan Misner, "6 Ways Others Can Promote Your Business," www.entrepreneur.com/article/0,4621,302125,00.html.

Ten Ways to Become a Hands-on Leader with Your Salespeople

1. **Know your ideal prospects.** CEOs who sell hate wasting time, so they target the people and groups most likely to buy from them. CEOs who are successful in sales have no qualms about calling another organization's top person to find out whether there's a potential fit between their companies. It's also helpful to identify all the sales that are taking too long to close.

2. **Understand that other CEOs use similar criteria to buy and sell.** Find out what the target CEO is buying and what the selling criteria are before approaching him or her.

3. **Have the final say.** Even when they delegate, successful CEOs are the final approvers of every initiative with which they come into contact. Their employees are charged with the task of conducting the fact-finding process and making decisions and recommendations, which the CEO must approve.

4. **Model the ideal sales process consistently for your organization.** No one plays the role of a model salesperson better than the head of the company.

5. **Establish personal visibility within the marketplace and the community as a whole.** Try becoming visible in your community of potential and existing customers. Volunteer your time to a professional organization and get on the mailing lists of associations whose members can purchase your products.

6. **Personally monitor changes in your marketplace.** Sure, this is extra work. But it pays off—and it's already part of your job description. Ask yourself, "How does this information affect our selling process?"

7. **Build on interpersonal relationships to secure one-on-one loyalty from customers.** Bob Posten, CEO of Landis Strategy & Innovation, puts it this way: "I had to get real about what I was doing for my customers. I had to use what I was selling. [Only] then was I able to articulate what I did to my prospects and customers."

8. **Have a crystal-clear understanding of your vision.** Many would say that Howard Putnam, former CEO of Southwest Airlines, stands out as the ultimate "champion of vision." Putnam says, "Vision is critically important when it comes to training customers on what your mission statement really means."

9. **Make intelligent decisions quickly and independently.** Joel Ronning, CEO of Digital River, an e-commerce outsourcing provider in Eden Prairie, Minnesota, makes decisions for his company based on this equation: "Experience plus intelligence equals intuition." To this, Ronning adds a degree of fearlessness and puts the element of time in front of every decision. Follow his lead. Look at opportunities in your sales forecast and ask yourself these questions: When does an outcome need to take place? What has to happen to get the results that you, your prospects, and your customers want?

10. **Stay focused.** Isn't it amazing what the power of focus can accomplish? In your own business, you have the opportunity to take the power of focus and use it to change everything.

Source: Tony Parinello, "Higher Power," www.entrepreneur.com/article/0,4621,301654,00.html.

Section
11

Tips That Make Your Team Work

Here is some advice on teamwork from six pros:

Ray Oglethorpe
President, AOL Technologies
America Online Inc.
Dulles, Virginia

What's the secret to a great team? Think small. Ideally, your team should have seven to nine people. If you have more than 15 or 20, you're dead: the connections between team members are too hard to make.

Size is the key. Have the smallest number of people possible on each team. Another rule: no delegates. You don't want people who have to take the team's ideas back to someone else to get authorization. You want the decision makers.

Jon Katzenbach
Senior Partner
Katzenbach Partners LCC
New York, New York

Teams work when they are created for the right reasons, and when they are created in the right way. The organization that I think does the best job of meeting these requirements is the U.S. Marine Corps. Most people think of the USMC as a command-and-control organization. But when they put a team together, it's in the right place for the right reasons. The corps is extremely disciplined about assessing whether it really needs a team for the task at hand. The notion that a team is always better is misleading, yet all too often, that's the path that managers choose.

The critical decision for any manager or leader who wants to get higher performance from a small group of people is determining whether the group should try to work as a team, or whether they should be satisfied with what I call "single-leader unit" discipline. Single-leader units are intrinsically faster and more efficient than teams. Tasks are more clearly defined by one leader, and members work on their own much of the time.

Michael Leinbach
Shuttle Launch Director
John F. Kennedy Space Center
Kennedy Space Center, Florida

Where I work, having a well-functioning team can be a matter of life or death. The most critical element of a successful shuttle-launch team is an open channel of communication from each member to the team leader.

With my team, I make sure that everyone knows to inform me immediately if there's a glitch in his or her work—any glitch—even if it's just something that's marginally off, but still within normal specs.

Section 11

But there are a couple of human factors that can work against us. People tend to be intimidated by those who hold leadership positions. And often people don't want to stand out. It takes about four months to prepare for each mission. By the time the launch date arrives, everyone wants it to go. It's natural not to want to be the person who gets the mission scrubbed.

Martha Rogers
Partner
Peppers and Rogers Group
Bowling Green, Ohio

You can't say, "teams work because of this" or "teams don't work because of that"—because it depends. But if you're looking for one quality that most good teams share, I'd have to say that it's the culture of the company in which the team exists. Is the culture one that rewards groups? Is it one that rewards individuals? Or is it a culture where no one gets rewarded? Look around. Watch how people act and interact, regardless of whether they're on a team. Do people do things for one another? Do they pick up coffee for others when they're going out? If the culture is full of give and take—if it's supportive and trusting—there's a good chance that you'll see successful teams at work.

People from different parts of a company are going to have disparate styles, expectations, and reward systems. The best teams have leaders who recognize those differences. Communism has fallen all over the world, and it doesn't work for teams either.

Tony DiCicco
Former Head Coach
U.S. Women's World Cup Champion Soccer Team and gold-medal-winning 1996 U.S. Women's Olympic Soccer Team
Wethersfield, Connecticut

To have a successful team, you must have a shared culture. My team's culture is largely built on fitness, intensity in training, individual respect, and respect for the group—both on and off the field. You know you have a good team member when she arrives at training camp fit and ready to play. That kind of preparation shows respect—for herself and for her fellow team members.

A long-term team must have a way for new people to join in successfully. To survive, new players have to buy into the team's culture. However, your current team members can't be afraid of new talent or new ideas.

The natural inclination is to protect what you have and not allow a new star to rise to the top. Team members have to fight against that. The bottom line is that new talent can force everyone to play at a higher level.

Janine Bay
Director of Vehicle Personalization for Automotive Consumer-Services Group
Ford Motor Co.
Dearborn, Michigan

Section 11

A team should be made up of people who have different opinions about things, people who approach their work in different ways. Diversity is one of the keys to a successful team. But I'm sure that on every good team, a member has gone home at the end of a day thinking, "This isn't going to work."

So my advice is this: bring in a facilitator. Someone from the outside—an unbiased third party—may have insights about what's working, what's not, and why you are just too close to the project to see clearly. A facilitator may be just what team members need to make the most of their diversity and to help them overcome any personal agendas or conflicts.

Source: Regina Fazio Maruca, "What Makes Teams Work?," www.fastcompany.com/online/40/one.html.

Real Tools for Virtual Teams

Figuring out how to "stay in touch" is one of the big challenges for colleagues who have to work together, even though most of them work in different places. And staying in touch doesn't just mean communicating—it means sharing documents, organizing calendars, and clarifying who's doing what by when.

How solid are web-based tools that claim to address these and other teamwork challenges? Does using those tools require more work than they're worth?

Here are two places to provide you with virtual tools:

eRoom.net (www.eroom.net)
Utility: * * * *
Usability: * * * *
The service, which seems ideal to meet the needs of teams within companies (as opposed to, say, a group of free agents), is designed to help people who are working together on a specific project. Its digital workspace—or, in the spirit of the company's name, its virtual room—offers lots of useful features. Teams can share documents, compare schedules, or conduct threaded discussions.

HotOffice (www.hotoffice.com)
Utility: * * *
Usability: * * * 1/2
Online conferencing may be its least impressive feature. HotOffice's most impressive feature is its ability to manage documents. It allows users to upload documents to a personal file, to a folder dedicated to a project or a department, or to the company. It also offers some amazing ways to control who has access to which documents. Users can also check out documents, which then makes them unavailable to other users in HotOffice, so that no more than one member can modify a document at the same time. It also integrates the workspaces of individuals with a shared work area—without compromising privacy. One downside to HotOffice: your computer must be constantly con-

nected to the Net, since the service lacks offline capability.

Source: Gina Imperato, "Real Tools for Virtual Teams," www.fastcompany.com/online/36/first-site.html.

Being on a Team: Pros and Cons

With effective direction and facilitation from the right team leader, team building can be a very productive and cost-effective process. To help ensure success, the team needs to consider five crucial success factors:

1. Clear identification and ownership of the team goal.
2. Clear definition and acceptance of each person's role and responsibilities.
3. Clear delineation of team processes, such as decision-making, conflict resolution, communication, and participation.
4. Clear opportunities to build trust between participants.
5. Clear acceptance of each other's strengths and limitations in a manner that encourages positive working relationships.

Pros

- Teams combine various employee skills, ideas, knowledge bases, and perspectives.
- Teams usually increase individual productivity and workplace satisfaction. Simply being on a team can be a key source of employee motivation, status, and pride for having been selected to participate.
- Team output is generally higher in quality and quantity than individual performance.

Cons

- Teams may take longer to achieve a goal than an individual would.
- Teams grow through predictable stages that are time-consuming, such as member selection, organization, socialization, and creation of final products or ideas.
- Key resources (time, money, people, and equipment) are restricted to the team and not available to others.
- Some of the team members may lack interest, necessary skills or abilities, or motivation. They may have been appointed or self-appointed to the team for political reasons or merely to enjoy themselves while others do the work. This "social loafing" can be a source of tension among productive team members.
- People dynamics can complicate the team process, replete with conflicts, group pressure to reach a fast or unanimous conclusion, and taking risky stances.

Source: David G. Javitch, "How to Foster Effective Teamwork," www.entrepreneur.com/article/0,4621,308367,00.html.

# Chapter 69

Stay a Step Ahead of Your Competition

Section 11

Ten Questions to Ask Yourself About Your Competitor

Do you know your competition? Here are ten questions every entrepreneur should be able to answer:

1. Who are my competitors?
2. What are their financial resources?
3. How do they market their products or services?
4. How many employees do they have?
5. Where are they located?
6. How do they treat their customers?
7. What are their pricing strategies?
8. What are their main strengths, and can I meet—or exceed—them?
9. What are their biggest weaknesses, and how can I do better?
10. How will they react to my entry into their territory?

Source: Rieva Lesonsky, *365 Tips to Boost Your Entrepreneurial IQ.*

Tips for Researching the Competition

Do you know what your competitors are up to? You should—or you could end up losing business to them. Here are some smart ways to check the competition:

- **Request information.** Call for a price list, a brochure, or other marketing information. Evaluate how you were treated on the phone, how the request was processed, and how long it took to get answers.
- **Order something.** Have a friend order something from your competition and from your company. Compare and contrast the two experiences.
- **Pay a visit.** Note the differences between your business and theirs.
- **Compare everything.** Think price, packaging, marketing, selection, quality, delivery, and attitude.

When the comparisons are over, be ready to react. Implement any necessary changes as soon as possible.

Source: Rieva Lesonsky, *365 Tips to Boost Your Entrepreneurial IQ.*

Seven Ways to Research Your Competitors

1. Examine the number of competitors on a local and, if relevant, national scale. Study their strategies and operations. Your analysis should supply a clear picture of potential threats and opportunities, and of the weaknesses and strengths of the competition facing your new business.

2. When looking at the competition, try to see what trends have been established in the industry you want to enter and whether there's an opportunity or advantage for your business.

3. Use the library, the internet, and other secondary research sources—such as government data, reference books, and industry associations—to dig up as much as you can on competitors, their tactics, and their goals.

4. Read articles on the companies you'll be competing with. If you're researching publicly owned companies, contact them and get copies of their annual reports. These show not only how successful a company is, but also what products or services it plans to emphasize in the future.

5. Role-play. Get in the trenches and put yourself in your competitors' shoes. Visit their stores and assess their strategies and operations through a consumer's eyes.

6. Never underestimate the number of competitors out there. Keep an eye out for potential future competitors as well as current ones.

7. Don't limit yourself to the obvious definitions of competition and you'll be less likely to get sideswiped by an unexpected rival.

Source: Rieva Lesonsky and the staff of *Entrepreneur*, "Know Thy Enemy," www.entrepreneur.com/article/0,4621,309514,00.html.

Section 11

Tips for Creating a Board of Advisors

No entrepreneur knows everything. So to be sure you cover all your bases, why not create a board of advisors?

- How you stock your advisory board depends on your business's needs and your own expertise, but it's generally a good idea to include a lawyer, an accountant, a marketing expert, and a financial advisor.

- When recruiting your board, make sure you ask the most successful people you can find, even if you don't know them well.

- Be very clear about your needs and be sure to let them know you don't expect them to take an active management role or assume any liability.

- It's smart to meet with your board monthly, whether as a group or individually. And remember that it's advice they're offering, not instructions. You are still the ultimate decision maker.

Source: Rieva Lesonsky, *365 Tips to Boost Your Entrepreneurial IQ.*

25 Ways to Innovate Your Business

1. **Why you need to be the innovator.** "Radical innovation in established companies, whether large or small, tends to go in cycles," says Mark Rice, co-author of *Radical Innovation: How Mature Firms Can Outsmart Upstarts.* "When the leadership of the company says, 'That's important, but we also need to look to the future and see the innovative products and services that are going to create the future of this company,' then there's a corresponding response from the [employees] to start looking to the future."

2. **Get real.** Don't overestimate your product or service, don't underestimate your competitors, and never exaggerate consumer demand for what you're doing. That leads to delusion, not creativity.

3. **Incubate your ideas.** Atlanta-based BrightHouse is hired by big-name clients like Coca-Cola, The Home Depot, and McDonald's to do the creative thinking for them—to the tune of half a million for a 10-week brainstorming session. For every BrightHouse project, founder Joey Reiman builds in three to four weeks of incubation, "where all we do—literally—is think." In fact, he's written a book on the subject, *Thinking for a Living.* "What happens when you ponder?" asks Reiman. "You have more insight, more discovery, more compassion, more wonder. And the results all lead to, of course, more profits."

4. **Rebel against the status quo.** "Conformity to the status quo is a real enemy of creativity," says Mike Vance, former dean of Disney University (The Walt Disney Company's training program).

   "The real beginning point for creativity is emptying your mind—pushing out the ideas you know to be true," says Raymond Gleason, a professor of strategy and creativity at George Fox University in Newberg, Oregon. "The more successful a businessperson is, the more resistance there can be to doing this. But if you don't, you cannot be really creative."

Everyday Tips

5. **Carry a notebook.** "You never know when an idea will occur to you—an idea for a new business or a better way of doing what you're presently doing. As you drive, watch TV, eat lunch, ideas pop into your head. Unless you write them down, you will not remember them," says Kathleen R. Allen, a professor of entrepreneurship at the University of Southern California in Los Angeles.

6. **Think opportunistically.** "Wherever you go, really pay attention," Allen advises. "Most of us navigate through our world on autopilot, but when we start paying attention—when we start questioning what we are seeing and why—good ideas can occur to us."

7. **Think in opposites.** "Everybody says recessions are bad—but haven't they been good for some businesses? The past recession gave birth to a huge outsourcing industry, for instance," says Allen. "For every idea—for every sacred cow—there is an opposite idea, and, sometimes, exploring the opposite is where entrepreneurs will find the best ideas."

8. **Reinvent the wheel.** "Ask yourself how you can put a new twist on an old product or service." Take any product, and come up with 50 unexpected uses for it. "Keep in mind that sometimes the most creative uses [involve] literally smashing the product and coming up with something entirely new," says Allen.

9. **Challenge your ruts.** "We do the same things, the same way, every day. This is a primary barrier to creativity," Allen warns. "Often we need to feel a little uncomfortable—we need to experience new things—to get creative sparks." Eat in different restaurants. Listen to different music. Alone, none of these steps may trigger creative ideas, but taken together, "anything we do that forces us out of our normal environment will let us see things in new, different ways."

Inspiring Creativity in Your Employees

10. **Start laughing.** "Humor can really foster creativity," says Vance. "Humor is the unmasking of the hypocritical, and what makes us laugh often is seeing how things are screwed up—then, sometimes, seeing how we can fix them. Whenever I go into a company and don't hear much laughter, I know it's not a creative place."

11. **Make it easy for employees to be creative.** The more requirements you have about submitting ideas, the less people will participate, and the fewer ideas you'll receive. The best way to stimulate creativity is to simply allow people to verbally share their ideas with you, which should be easy since your company is small.

12. **Positively reinforce all ideas.** This doesn't mean you'll accept every idea, but you should make sure you reinforce the activity of coming up with ideas. You can be excited about the number of ideas presented even if all of them aren't acceptable or "on target."

13. **React to ideas ASAP.** How quickly you respond to ideas has the most influence on the number of ideas people will produce. If an idea or other creative work sits on your desk for a week before you respond to it, you'll have deflated creative energy.

14. **Let employees outside their box.** Give employees experiences that are far removed from their usual activities. Variation is the mother of creativity. The more varied the experiences you can give people, the more creative they'll be.

15. **Give 'em time off.** Reiman encourages paid sabbaticals. Employees cut out early on Fridays during the summer, and during the incubation period, "the five bastions of thinking" are highlighted. Says Reiman, "We have this notion that there are five places

left in the world to really think: the john, the shower, the car, the gym, and church or temple." Get your team together in a place of relaxation to capture that "Aha!" moment.

Brainstorming Meeting Techniques

16. **Draw a crowd.** Reiman invites a diverse crowd into his brainstorming sessions—say, an astrologist, a physicist, and a psychologist to discuss life insurance. When inviting employees, include both the lowest employees on the company ladder and the highest in your management team. Twelve people is an optimum number for the group, though BrightHouse has facilitated successful ideations with as few as seven people and as many as 16. The mix is most important.

17. **Use prompts.** The prompt can be anything: a word, an object, a fantasy, a color. The theory behind this technique is that by using something unusual to launch your thinking, you'll generate ideas you wouldn't otherwise. You never know what will work or what will spark another idea that might work. Remember: in this generating stage, the ideas that come to you don't have to be realistic. You want to go for volume. Quality control comes later.

18. **Word association.** This method involves brainstorming lists of words and then finding linkage between key words on each list. In the end, you might have four or five lists of ideas based on word association. To build your slogan, you'd choose a word from each of the lists and creatively link them together.

19. **Be playful.** "Some of our best ideas happen when darts are flying," says Evelyn Girard, co-owner of the Forum Conference & Educational Center, a meeting facility in Cleveland, who frequently enlists toys as helpers during in-house strategy sessions. "With toys in our hands, creative ideas really get flowing," she says.

20. **Get in the zone.** "Every business needs a ... space designed to nurture creativity," says Vance. Supplies needn't be costly or elaborate—a chalkboard, a meeting table, a coffee pot, maybe a stereo, possibly toys, and "anything else that stimulates creative juices in you and your team," adds Vance.

21. **Suspend criticism and postpone evaluation.** The general goal of brainstorming is to collect as many ideas as possible, making quantity much more important than quality at this initial stage. Brainstorming sessions are not the time or place to evaluate the merits of the ideas suggested.

Now That You've Got an Idea ...

22. **Check reality.** "Ideas are great, but how do they match up with marketplace realities?" asks Vance. In other words, don't become self-satisfied just because an idea seems good out of the box.

23. **Keep refining.** "A key lesson I've learned in interviewing many highly creative people is that they continually criticize their own ideas. Traditional brainstorming techniques taught us not to criticize, but really creative people do the opposite, looking for ways to make their ideas better," says Jack Ricchiuto, a Cleveland certified management consultant and author of *Collaborative Creativity.*

24. **Keep going.** "The creative process frequently involves going beyond the first idea. Uncreative people commonly marry the first good idea that comes along," says Ricchiuto. "But creative people detach from their ideas and refine them. They know that the more ideas, the better."

25. **Be patient.** In the end, the real secret to creativity is practice. "The more we do it, the better we get," says Ricchiuto. "The mythology is that creativity is a genetically determined trait. But it can be developed in all of us—if we keep questioning what we see and keep looking for creative solutions and ideas."

Source: "25 Ways to Innovate in Your Business," www.entrepreneur.com/article/0,4621,307942,00.html, compiled from Aubrey Daniels, "Generating Great Ideas From Employees" (www.entrepreneur.com/article/0,4621,279678,00.html)," April Pennington, "Innovation Expert Mark Rice" (www.entrepreneur.com/article/0,4621,291736,00.html), Robert J. McGarvey, "Turn It On" (www.entrepreneur.com/article/0,4621,226597,00.html), Kim T. Gordon, "Creative Brainstorming Techniques" (www.entrepreneur.com/article/0,4621,304962,00.html), Geoff Williams, "Innovative Model" (www.entrepreneur.com/article/0,4621,302457,00.html), and Juanita Weaver, "Ideas on Demand" (www.entrepreneur.com/article/0,4621,307255,00.html).

How to Use the VISPAC Method to Exceed Expectations

In today's increasingly competitive environment, it's important to not only meet but beat your customers' expectations. Paul Timm, from Brigham Young University's Marriott School of Management, uses the VISPAC method to stand out.

VISPAC stands for:

- **Value:** Give customers a bit more than they expected for the price.
- **Information:** Provide additional information so customers can easily use your products and services.
- **Speed:** Never miss a promised deadline, and deliver early whenever possible.
- **Personality:** Make sure your company projects a friendly image. Greet your customers and always, always smile.
- **Add-on:** Give customers something extra. Try credits toward free merchandise, discounts on their next purchase, or frequent buyer promotions.
- **Convenience:** Make it easy for people to do business with you.

Source: Rieva Lesonsky, *365 Tips to Boost Your Entrepreneurial IQ.*

Section 11

Seven Steps to Leaving Your Competition in the Dust

1. **Know your enemy.** Today, it's essential to understand all we can about our competitors. If you don't already have copies of your competitors' advertising and brochures—and can't recite from rote their key selling points and messages—how can you hope to successfully position against them?

2. **Market your specialty.** Once you know everything you can about your chief competitors, you can identify what your company offers its customers or clients that is unique or special. If necessary, alter your product or service itself, bundle in additional features, or find a way to deliver the same core product or service in a way that uniquely meets the needs of your prospects.

3. **Tackle new audiences.** If you've reached the maximum market share in a particular niche, why not try a new one? You may be able to add line extensions (variations of your product) that will stimulate sales from a whole new set of customers.

4. **Offer more value.** Some product and service providers traditionally compete based on discount pricing, but for many other types of businesses, cutting prices is often detrimental. A better idea is to offer something of additional value that your customers will find tempting.

5. **Add a sales channel.** Are you presently selling via one channel alone, such as exclusively through a brick-and-mortar store or by catalog only? Adding another channel, such as online sales, gives your customers more choices and allows them to shop more often and at their convenience. It's likely that most of your competitors offer sales through multiple channels.

6. **Tune into your customers.** To remain highly competitive, you must understand what your customers want. Unfortunately, your customers' needs and preferences can change on a dime, so you should have systems in place to regularly solicit their feedback. Be sure to initiate regular surveys as well as solicit ongoing feedback via your web site.

7. **Ask for the business.** Complacency is the enemy of small-business success. If you're not continually asking your best prospects and customers for their business, you can be sure your competitors are. The key to success is to have a consistent marketing message and select a mix of media and tactics that "touch" prospects and customers with sufficient frequency.

Source: Kim T. Gordon, "Competition, Beware," www.entrepreneur.com/article/0,4621,317204,00.html.

Section 11

Chapter 70

Negotiating

Section
11

Tips for Winning Negotiations

Winning at negotiations may be simpler than you think. But first, give up the idea that you must come out the winner. That's the advice of Ron Shapiro, sports agent for legendary baseball stars like Cal Ripken. Here are some of his words of wisdom:

- Shapiro believes successful negotiators leave both sides happy and use the process to build future relationships.

- If you try for a win-lose scenario, Shapiro says, you'll end up with a case of lose-lose. Instead, go for a win-win situation.

- Shapiro teaches a 3-P negotiating strategy:
  - Prepare
  - Probe
  - Propose

- Entrepreneurs, he claims, often have trouble with the preparation and probing, simply because they talk too much and don't listen.

So next time you're negotiating, take Shapiro's advice: "Get all you can, but also try to accommodate the other side's needs."

Source: Rieva Lesonsky, *365 Tips to Boost Your Entrepreneurial IQ.*

Tips to Sharpen Your Negotiating Aptitude

Negotiating is one of the most important skills entrepreneurs can have. Use these tips to sharpen your negotiating aptitude:

- First, know what you want. Establish a goal and consider what it will take for your to achieve it. Then know what the other party needs. Remember: it takes two to tango, so ask open-ended questions to gather information.

- Listen emphatically. What you hear is just as important as what you say.

- Remember that the other side is not the enemy. They are your ally and should be treated as such.

- Be patient. The negotiating process takes time; like that legendary tortoise, slow and steady wins the race.

- Finally, be flexible. As Mick Jagger says, "You can't always get what you want," so make sure you have a contingency plan.

Source: Rieva Lesonsky, *365 Tips to Boost Your Entrepreneurial IQ.*

Going Global

Section
11

Dos and Don'ts When Finding a Global Partner

Once you find a global partner, here are some dos and don'ts to guide you:

Don't:

- Make a commitment you can't keep.

- Assume your partner understands your expectations. Spell them out. And make sure you have a clear understanding of your partner's requirements.

- Go without a contract. Use it to lay the groundwork for your relationship.

Do:

- Find a customs broker. This person will help ensure that your foreign shipments meet proper regulations.

- Conduct research. If you learn how business is conducted in specific countries, you can minimize potential problems.

- Be prepared to pay upfront. Most international shipments are paid in advance.

- Keep strengthening your relationship. If you don't get cooperation from your foreign partner, you're not going to succeed.

Source: Rieva Lesonsky, *365 Tips to Boost Your Entrepreneurial IQ.*

Four Most Common Exporting Mistakes

As the globe shrinks, more and more smart entrepreneurs are preparing to do business overseas. You'll want to avoid the four most common exporting mistakes:

1. **Failing to plan a strategy:** Small businesses are particularly vulnerable to this lack of planning. But remember: it's harder to solve problems after the fact.

2. **Chasing inquires all over the world:** Patience is key to international marketing. Experts say to expand one nation at a time. And do your homework on each country you plan to do business in.

3. **Assuming that if it works in America, it will work anywhere:** Sales and marketing efforts need to be tailored to each country you're expanding to. You cannot ignore the cultural differences that shape each market.

4. **Assuming business will be conducted in English:** You should at least be familiar with the local language, and always take your own translator.

Source: Rieva Lesonsky, *365 Tips to Boost Your Entrepreneurial IQ.*

20 Factors to Consider Before Going Global

Factor 1: Get company-wide commitment. Every employee should be a vital member of your international team, from the executive suite to customer service through engineering, purchasing, production, and shipping. You're all in it for the long haul.

Factor 2: Define your business plan for accessing global markets. An international business plan is important in order to define your company's present status and internal goals and commitment, but it's also necessary if you plan to measure your results.

Factor 3: Determine how much you can afford to invest in your international expansion efforts. Will it be based on ten percent of your domestic business profits or on a pay-as-you-can-afford process?

Factor 4: Plan at least a two-year lead-time for world market penetration. It takes time and patience to build a great, enduring global enterprise, so be patient and plan for the long haul.

Factor 5: Build a web site and implement your international plan sensibly. Many companies offer affordable packages for building a web site, but you must decide in what language you'll communicate. English is unarguably the most important language in the world, but only 28 percent of the European population can read it and even fewer in South America and Asia. Over time, it would be best to slowly build a site that communicates sensibly and effectively with the world.

Factor 6: Pick a product or service to take overseas. You can't be all things to all people. Decide on something. Then stick with it.

Factor 7: Conduct market research to identify your prime target markets. You want to find out where in the world your product will be in greatest demand. Market research is a powerful tool for exploring and identifying the fastest-growing, most penetrable market for your product.

Factor 8: Search out the data you need to predict how your product will sell in a specific geographic location. Do you want to sell a few units to a customer in Australia or ten 40-foot containers on a monthly basis to retailers in France? Research will enable you to find out how much you'll be able to sell over a specific period of time.

Factor 9: Prepare your product for export. You should expect to adapt your product to some degree for sale outside your domestic markets before you make your first sale. Packaging plays a vital role in enabling international connections.

Factor 10: Find cross-border customers. There is no business overseas for you unless you can locate customers first.

Factor 11: Establish a direct or indirect method of export. It all boils down to export strategy and how much control you wish to exercise over your ventures. On the other hand, readiness to seize an opportunity is more important than having your whole strategy nailed down beforehand.

Factor 12: Hire a good lawyer, a savvy banker, a knowledgeable accountant, and a seasoned transport specialist, each of whom specializes in international transactions. You may feel you can't afford these professional services, but you really can't afford to do without them.

Factor 13: Prepare pricing and determine your landed costs. (Landed costs are the costs incurred in making goods available for sale: insurance, transportation, customs duties and taxes, other governmental charges, handling fees, and warehousing.) Be ready to test out your price on your customer. See what reaction you get and then negotiate from there.

Factor 14: Set up terms, conditions, and other financing options. Agree on terms of payment in advance, and never, ever sell on open account to a brand new customer. No ifs, ands, or buts. Just don't.

Factor 15: Brush up on your documentation and export licensing procedures. If you find it too time-consuming, hire a freight forwarder who can fill you in on the spot. Ask a lot of questions. Use their expertise to your advantage.

Factor 16: Implement an extraordinary after-sales service plan. The relationship between your company and your overseas customer shouldn't end when you make a sale. If anything, it should be just the start of a long relationship, which requires more of your attention. The "care and feeding" of your customers will determine if they keep coming back for more.

Factor 17: Make personal contact with your new targets, armed with culture-specific information and courtesies, professionalism, and consistency. Your goal should be to enter a different culture, adapt to it, and make it your own.

Factor 18: Investigate international business travel tips. The practical aspects of international business can make or break the success of your trip. In preparing to go boldly where you've never gone before, plan accordingly.

Factor 19: Explore cross-border alliances and partnerships. In charting your global strategy, consider joining forces with another company of similar size and market presence that's located in a foreign country where you're already doing business or would like to. Gauge how ready—or willing—you are to take on a 50/50 partnership and what it can and cannot do for you.

Factor 20: Enjoy the journey. Never forget that you are the most important and valuable business asset you have, and that the human touch is even more precious in our age of advanced technology. Take the best possible care of yourself, your employees, your suppliers, and your customers, and your future will be bright, prosperous, and happy.

Source: Laurel Delaney, "20 Factors to Consider Before Going Global," www.entrepreneur.com /article/0,4621,319156,00.html.

Tips to Prepare for Going Global

Sure, everyone's talking about going global, but can entrepreneurs actually do it? Yes, here's how:

- **Do research.** There's tons of free information out there. Start by contacting the Department of Commerce.

- **Develop an international pricing strategy, taking into account fluctuating foreign currencies**. And know upfront how you will be paid.

- **Learn the laws—all of them.** This includes the U.S. regulations as well as the ones of the nations where you will be doing business. Look for opportunities everywhere, not just in the countries you learned about in school.

- **Remember: entrepreneurship is hot worldwide.** Global entrepreneurs are looking for you as well. There's a lot of value in the words "Made in America."

Source: Rieva Lesonsky, *365 Tips to Boost Your Entrepreneurial IQ.*

Tips to Avoid Common Global Partnership Meeting Mistakes

Looking to expand overseas? Many businesses that do so fail, so be sure to prepare for meeting with your potential partners. To avoid making costly mistakes in your overseas meeting, follow these tips:

- Build a relationship before you get down to business. This entails making small talk before business talk.

- Don't impose time limits. Keep the meeting as open as possible; this will add strength to your negotiating position.

- Do your homework. Learn at least a bit about the country you're in; this shows respect for your potential partner's culture.

- Bring your own interpreter. Their interpreter will have their interests at heart.

- Understand everyone's body language. Americans think body language is universal—it's not.

- Dress with authority and respect. Make a good impression with your attire as well as your preparation.

Source: Rieva Lesonsky, *365 Tips to Boost Your Entrepreneurial IQ.*

Tips on Expanding the Family Business Overseas

Worry #1: How will increased capital demands affect the family shareholders' needs for liquidity?

It's expensive to do business abroad. "But because some family businesses are jeopardized by international corporations making incursions into their markets, they have little choice but to expand into international markets," says François de Visscher, a family business consultant in Greenwich, Connecticut.

"If management sees a need to market abroad, it must develop a thorough business plan to present to family and other shareholders highlighting the strengths, weaknesses, opportunities, and trends of the markets abroad. That will point out the need to broaden markets."

Worry #2: How can family businesses compete with large corporations that are expanding internationally?

Capitalize on the resources to which most businesspeople in other countries pay a lot of attention in business relationships: trust and stability.

The mentality behind family businesses is that they take a little more pride in their products and the way they do business. They can't point the finger when someone makes a mistake. They're the ones!

Search out family businesses in other countries. "Two family businesses that understand and respect each other's cultures can forge wonderful alliances," says Ernesto J. Poza, a consultant in Chagrin Falls, Ohio, who specializes in helping family businesses form alliances abroad, who has seen these relationships bloom into fast friendships that transcend business deals.

"A commonality of interests and mentalities exists between family businesses of different countries," agrees de Visscher. "They certainly feel more comfortable dealing with each other than having to deal with a [giant corporation] where it's harder to establish a trusted relationship."

Insist on win–win agreements with partners in foreign countries. Craft an agreement that's profitable to both parties and gives the overseas partner an incentive as the business grows.

Worry #3: How can we get family members used to the idea of globalization?

Develop an appreciation and understanding of a particular culture and language. Some family businesses look to their roots as a place to start learning more about a particular market. Others go where family members have spent time or have a particular interest. Poza tells of one family business that developed a business interest in Chile after a daughter did social work there. Sending potential successors overseas for travel and study might be one of the best investments a family business can make.

Source: Patricia Schiff Estess, "Growing Global," www.entrepreneur.com/article/ 0,4621,226777,00.html.

Top Tips for Global Packaging Materials and Mailings

Perhaps you truly can't judge a book by its cover, but consumers can—and do—judge a product by its package. And if you're trying to peddle your wares overseas, your packaging is even more crucial.

While what works in one country will not necessarily have the same effect in another, there are some universal truths:

- Color is a package's more important element.
- Worldwide, red is generally considered a positive color, and gold signifies quality.
- In Asia, packages should have an American and imported feel.
- In Europe, you should go with an upscale, elegant look.
- Warm, bright colors connect in Latin America.
- What sells in the United States works just as well in Canada.
- Overseas, storage in homes and stores is an issue, so keep your packages small.
- Avoid clutter, and limit your use of numbers and words.

Most important: do research! Remember: think globally but act locally.

Source: Rieva Lesonsky, *365 Tips to Boost Your Entrepreneurial IQ.*

Checklist for Becoming an Entrepreneur in China

1. **Visit beforehand.** Do you really want to live in China? Cities are crowded (traffic cops die at about age 40 on average due to bad air) and real estate in Shanghai is as pricey as in some cities in the U.S.

2. **Learn the language.** English may be the language of commerce everywhere else, but not in China. You can survive without Mandarin, but negotiating through translators is a major disadvantage.

3. **Partner with the locals.** Join up with the native Chinese who possess the skills you lack. Local partners should serve not as window dressing but as real contributors to your enterprise and its public face.

4. **Follow the rules.** The Chinese government is swift and effective when offended, State officials won't hesitate to shut down a foreign-owned business for infractions, especially if it is owned by an individual.

5. **Don't bring the family at first.** Starting a business in China is all-consuming; don't expect to see much of your spouse and children. School-age kids can be especially costly: a top private elementary school in Shanghai costs more than $20,000 a year.

6. **Be prepared for a long haul.** Most successful American entrepreneurs in China spend years building their business, View China as a three- to five-year investment, giving yourself time to deal with setbacks.

Source: G. Pascal Zachary, "Making It in China," *Business 2.0*, Volume 6, Issue 7, August 2005, p. 61.

Tips on Negotiating in Asia

- **Preparation**—Prepare your sales approach well, focusing on product features rather than pricing. If you are an operator dealing direct and negotiating rates, do not lead with your lowest offer. Instead, start high and negotiate to a point you are comfortable with. Never go below your lowest predetermined cutoff level. Walk out of any negotiations amicably. Non-agreement at any point does not necessarily mean failure!

- **Homework**—Check the credit standing and credit terms of your potential client. Assess business volume and commitment to your product.

- **Business Cards**—Pack a good supply. If possible, have your card details translated into the language of your destination on the reverse side of the card.

- **Promotional Material**—If possible, have your promotional material or at least a flier of your product printed in the language of your destination.

- **Appointment**—Always arrive at your meeting slightly early or at least on time.

- **Greeting**—Shake hands and present your business card with both hands, face up and right way round for the receiver. Do not fiddle with, bend, or deface the client's business card. When it is presented to you, take time to look at it and never put it in your back pocket. This is seen as a mark of disrespect to the owner.

- **Meeting**—Speak clearly and slowly. If your client is in doubt, say it again with a different expression. Listen well and do not make any off-hand remarks. Be patient. By maintaining and retaining emotional control, demonstrating patience, and not too aggressively pushing your position, not only do you leave further negotiations open, but you also importantly retain 'face' and subsequently earn respect. Be accurate with information and advice.

Source: Tourism Queensland, "Principles of Negotiation," www.tq.com.au/industry/international/understanding-asia/negotiation.cfm.

Finances

Section 11

Common Financial Mistakes Entrepreneurs Make During Growth

One of the biggest potential trouble spots for entrepreneurial businesses is when they're experiencing rapid growth. Larry Dondon, Managing Director of Entrepreneur's Re$ource Group, warns entrepreneurs to avoid the following mistakes:

- Failing to borrow funds
- Overlooking available financial resources
- Underestimating financial risks
- Ignoring the downside of investors
- Overestimating your borrowing potential
- Neglecting to manage lender relationships
- Preparing a loan application under pressure
- Failing to forecast cash needs

Source: Rieva Lesonsky, *365 Tips to Boost Your Entrepreneurial IQ.*

Avoiding the Cash Flow Drought

Even the most successful businesses can encounter a cash flow crisis. Since a cash crunch could cripple your business, it's good to be prepared.

- Establish a rainy-day fund. Set cash aside in an interest-bearing account you can draw on in an emergency.
- Review your current cash-management techniques. Don't pay bills until you have to, but take advantage of early-payment discounts. Ask your banker about special programs to help you better manage your money.
- Control your overhead. Keep your fixed costs low and your variable expenses tied to revenue, so if your income drops, so will your expenditures.
- Establish and maintain good credit. If you have a good track record, creditors may be more willing to work with you in times of crisis.
- Finally, find a financial advisor you trust. Chances are he or she will know what to do even when you don't.

Source: Rieva Lesonsky, *365 Tips to Boost Your Entrepreneurial IQ.*

Tips for Boosting Your Cash Flow

Facing a cash crunch? Most entrepreneurs do at some point. Cash flow problems often stem from slow-paying customers. If this sounds like your problem, you need to accelerate your income.

- Demand deposits upfront.
- Include bills with deliveries or submit them as soon as you're finished with a job.
- On long-term projects, submit interim invoices.
- Track the payment cycles of your regular clients and customers. Then be sure to bill them in time to be paid in their next cycle.
- Offer discounts for prompt payment or prepayment.
- Don't let past-due accounts slide. Make sure you collect, even if you need to hire a collection service.

There are other ways to increase your business's income. Consider broadening the scope of your business, adding complementary products or services, or raising prices or fees.

Source: Rieva Lesonsky, *365 Tips to Boost Your Entrepreneurial IQ.*

Tips on Using Invoices and Billing Statements

You probably think invoices and billing statements exist only to help you collect money. Actually, they can help you grow your business too. Here's how:

- Why not turn your invoices into marketing communications tools? Since you have to send out invoices anyway, use them to your advantage.
- On your invoices, try adding computer-generated messages to promote upcoming events, new products or services, or seasonal announcements.
- Plan your invoice messages three months in advance so you can promote different events and programs during each billing cycle.
- Printing directly on the invoice ensures your messages get read. This simple act enables your customers to understand more about your company and how they can more effectively do business with you.

Source: Rieva Lesonsky, *365 Tips to Boost Your Entrepreneurial IQ.*

Section 11

SCORE's Five Tips for Successful Debt Collections

1. Assume that most people are honest and want to pay you. Treat customers with respect during the collection process.

2. Try to find out why a customer is not paying. Has he or she fallen on hard times—a lost job or ill health? Or, is he or she withholding payment because your product was faulty or your service was poor?

3. Keep a customer's total payment history in mind. If a customer has paid on time over the years, don't jump on him or her with a collection call the first time a payment is late.

4. Be a good listener. When you understand the situation, you can come up with solutions that will help the customer get you paid.

5. Remember that friendliness will help a customer want to pay you first.

Source: SCORE, www.score.org/business_tips.html.

Advice on Debt Collection Protection

Do you have collection protection? Your ability to collect from past-due clients may depend on the language in your sales documents.

- Have an attorney—preferably one who specializes in creditors' rights—review your documents, including credit applications, sales contracts, invoices, and statements, to be sure they conform to state regulations.

- Make sure your invoices state when the payment is due.

- If you offer terms, you must clearly state the interest rate and conditions under which interest accrues.

- In some states, customers must agree to this in writing; find out if this applies to you.

- Stipulate that if there is a problem, the debtor is responsible for paying any attorney and collection fees.

Do yourself a favor: protect yourself now and collections will be much easier later.

Source: Rieva Lesonsky, *365 Tips to Boost Your Entrepreneurial IQ.*

Section 11

SCORE's Five Tips on Factoring

1. Know what the term "factoring" means. It's a way to turn your accounts receivable into cash by selling them to a finance company called a factor.

2. Make sure you understand the fees you will pay for this service. They typically include the cost of funds and making the collections.

3. Balance the cost against the gain. Factoring can be expensive but it may fuel your growth, improve cash flow, or enable you to take advantage of supplier discounts.

4. Ask your bank or CPA to recommend factors. Check their references.

5. Visit www.cfa.com, the web site of the Commercial Finance Association, and the International Factoring Association at www.factoring.org for a list of factors. The CIT Group site, www.cit.com, provides information on factoring. (Click on "Business Financing," then "Commercial Finance," to access the search feature.)

Source: SCORE, www.score.org/business_tips.html.

Seven Cash Flow Secrets Your Accountant Never Told You

1. **Shoeboxes are for shoes, not business records.** Pardon my candor, but you will never have a successful business if you don't systematically track your income and expenses, who owes you money, and who you owe money to. You don't have to have a big expensive computerized system, although a computer program like QuickBooks certainly does a beautiful job. But you've got to track basic information in a systematic manner.

2. **Getting your customers to "show you the money."** The best way to get your customers to pay what they owe is to remove every possible excuse for nonpayment. Don't extend credit unless it's absolutely necessary. Establish credit policies to help determine who will get credit. Get an invoice into the bill payer's hand as quickly as possible after the work is done or the product is delivered. Don't be afraid to send a letter or statement or make a phone call reminding your customer his or her bill is due. Always be firm. Focus on preserving the relationship. If a customer has a legitimate gripe about your business, do whatever you can to fix the problem.

3. **Budget is not a four-letter word.** A budget is a plan. It helps you stay focused on what you need to achieve. For example, you can use your budget to help you achieve sales goals and to determine how much you need to spend on advertising, how much you'll need for materials, and if you can afford to pay overtime.

4. **A customer in the hand is worth two in the bush.** It's easy to get caught up in the search for new customers. But never forget the ones you already have. What other

services or products can you offer to them? How can you get them to refer their friends and colleagues to you? You can build a successful business around a small number of customers by providing them with excellent customer care and a range of solutions. Loyal customers are money in the bank, they're easier to work with, and it's less expensive to keep them happy than to find new customers.

5. **The most powerful number in your business.** If you know only one number in your business, it ought to be your breakeven point. Your breakeven point is the moment in time when your income equals your expenses. If your income is higher than your expenses, you have a profit. If your expenses are higher than your income, you have a loss.

   First, to find your breakeven point you need to know what all of your expenses are. How much does it cost you to produce your product or deliver your service? That includes how much you need to pay yourself. If your business isn't able to support you, you're not breaking even. What do you need to do to achieve a level of sales high enough to cover your expenses? How many customers do you need to serve? How many products do you need to sell? If you can't reach that income level, what can you do to cut your expenses?

   Your whole business plan can flow from that one number. You can use your breakeven point as a powerful business tool to make decisions about marketing, strategy, plans for expansion, hiring a new employee, etc.

6. **How to make friends and influence check cutters.** Take the time to get to know the folks that cut the checks. Don't be afraid to build bridges and establish relationships. You meet lots of interesting people and your cash flow will improve.

7. **Why paying taxes is a cause for rejoicing.** The strategic approach of many small business owners is to have as little profit as possible at the end of the year. Otherwise, you'll have to pay taxes. So year after year, small business owners make decisions in their businesses based on intentional reducing profitability.

   Now, for the majority of small business owners, what the IRS considers to be profit is in actuality your paycheck. Are you working to lower your paycheck? Would you put up with that from an employer? If you put up with it from your own business, you condemn yourself to a life of poverty just to avoid having to pay taxes.

   If you're paying taxes, it means your business is making money. Don't let the thought of taxes hold you back. Think about it this way: even if you're paying 50 cents of every dollar to the government, that's 50 cents more in your own pocket. A word of caution: don't boost your earnings and spend it all. Make sure you plan ahead for the tax bill.

Source: Caroline Grimm Jordan, "7 Cash Flow Secrets Your Accountant Never Told You," morebusiness.com/running_your_business/financing/Estory-5663.brc.

SCORE's Five Tips on Conserving Capital

1. Determine your primary business of units sold, customers sold, average order, hours billed, etc. Know what drives your business.

2. Pricing should be determined by the sum of product costs, service costs, image of the business, direct and indirect costs, and a reasonable profit.

3. Conserve capital. Do not commit cash or capital until necessary. Don't buy services before you need them.

4. Lease instead of buy when it makes sense.

5. Look for office equipment that can do double duty, such as a fax machine that can also make copies.

Source: SCORE, www.score.org/business_tips.html.

Chapter 73

Hitting That Growth Point

Section 11

Is Your Current Location Too Small?

Heed this advice on searching for new digs from Jack Gold, president of Sterling Management, a relocation consulting company:

1. **Figure out how much space you really need.** Don't guess; miscalculations can be costly.

2. **Establish a budget.** Don't forget to add relocation costs into your plan.

3. **Check out the building's power supply.** Older structures might not have enough power for today's equipment-laden businesses.

4. **Ask about the office's services and access.** Can you get in 24 hours a day, 7 days a week? Is the building heated or cooled in the evenings or weekends?

Source: Rieva Lesonsky, *365 Tips to Boost Your Entrepreneurial IQ.*

Four-Point Test: Time for a Second Location?

When is the right time to expand your business into a second location? Take this four-point test to find out:

1. Are you ready to make the effort and take the risk of owning a business you don't personally operate? Realize it's impossible for you to be "hands-on" in two businesses as you are in one.

2. Is your company financially sound? If you're not doing well in your first location, chances are your second won't make it either.

3. Is your existing business running smoothly? How much time does your current business require? Can you realistically take time and energy away from it to focus on launching a second location?

4. Do you have the money? You'll not only need the initial start-up capital, but you'll need operating funds as well.

Before you grow, make sure you have sufficient resources—in time, energy, and cash—to meet the increased demands.

Source: Rieva Lesonsky, *365 Tips to Boost Your Entrepreneurial IQ.*

Section 11

Tips for Teaming up with a Corporate Giant

One of the smartest ways for small businesses to grow is to team up with a corporate giant. Being a subcontractor or regular supplier to a big business can really boost your bottom line.

1. Look at your track record. Many of the big guys shy away from start-ups and expect you to be in business for about five years. Your experience should also reflect an upscaling of your client base.

2. Make sure you have references.

3. Be sure you are capable of fulfilling what you say you can. If you mess up once, you may not get another chance.

4. Work on building a solid financial base so you don't run short of cash.

5. Don't start by trying to determine what a big business might need. Instead, define what you can offer a big business and then find a company that needs what you can offer.

Source: Rieva Lesonsky, *365 Tips to Boost Your Entrepreneurial IQ.*

SCORE's Five Tips on Preparing for Change

1. Examine your corporate culture to discover any impediments to change. Some traditions and practices may need to be revamped to meet new needs.

2. Keep talking about change so that employees think in terms of change and help make it happen.

3. Make expectations clear. Key employees should know that embracing change is part of their responsibility.

4. Monitor company procedures and systems to be sure they support change.

5. Plan far ahead for the biggest change of all: your retirement or exit from the company. Develop new leadership.

Source: SCORE, www.score.org/business_tips.html.

Favorite Mergers and Acquisitions Resources and Newsletters

American Institute of Certified Public Accountants: This organization, founded in 1887, is an information source for all accounting matters and issues (www.aicpa.org). A search of this site for Mergers & Acquisitions produced over two hundred results, including Adventures in Mergers/Acquisitions & Joint Ventures and Differences Between Mergers and Acquisitions.

M&A Databank: CNN Money provides a listing of the most recent deals on this web site (money.cnn.com/news/deals/mergers/dealchart.html), arranged with the most recent at the top, with target and acquiror names and the dollar value of the deal, with a link to a report on each deal. See also its related Top 25 Deals year-to-date list, arranged by the dollar value of the deal (money.cnn.com/news/deals/mergers/biggest.html). Coverage for these lists is worldwide.

M&A Insider: The International Network of M&A Partners (www.imap.com/resources/) is a "global partnership of leading Merger & Acquisition Advisory firms." Each quarter IMAP publishes the *M&A Insider,* "a newsletter dedicated to world of global middle-market M&A," with recent editions of the *M&A Insider* and other middle-market M&A resources available in PDF format.

Merger & Acquisitions Dictionary: This InvestorsEdge.Com dictionary entry (www.investorsedge.com/dictionary/Mergers_and_Acquisitions_dictionary_category.html) covers terms used in mergers and acquisitions, from Absorbed through Poison Pill to Zombie.

Mergers & Acquisitions: This Wikipedia entry (en.wikipedia.org/wiki/Mergers_%26_acquisitions) can be a good starting point for a brief orientation. It covers financing a merger or acquisition, motives behind this activity, levels and flows, types of mergers, major mergers and acquisitions since 1990, and more.

Mergers and Acquisitions Announced: This site, from the Online Investor, provides weekly compilations of merger and acquisition announcements (investhelp.com/mergers.phtml).

investopedia.com

Weekly insight on what's really going on in the markets from Investopedia co-founders. They also have Investing Basics, where they explain stocks, bonds, mutual funds, etc. from the perspective of a new investor.

CorporateAffiliations.com

Whether you're researching public or private firms, tracking down manufacturers of specific products or services, or even looking for individual executives, this exhaustive coverage from the LexisNexis Group (corporateaffiliations.com) makes it simple—from type of business, net worth, and sales data to contact information of key personnel and outside firms.

U.S. Mergers & Acquisitions Calendar: Yahoo! Finance provides monthly compilations of U.S. merger and acquisition announcements, with execution dates, acquiring and target companies, and brief information on terms (biz.yahoo.com/me/).

U.S. Securities and Exchange Commission: The primary mission of this organization (www.sec.gov) is "to protect investors and maintain the integrity of the securities markets," in part by requiring public companies to disclose financial and other information to the public. This site provides brief information on mergers (www.sec.gov/answers/mergers.htm). A site search for this topic produced over 1,500 documents. It is also possible at this site to search EDGAR (www.sec.gov/edgar.shtml), by company name, for SEC filings related to mergers, such as forms S-4, 14D9, 14D6, and 8-K, from 1993 to present.

Google Scholar: This version of Google (scholar.google.com) allows searches throughout the full text of a wide range of scholarly literature, including peer-reviewed papers, theses, books, preprints, abstracts, and technical reports from academic publishers, professional societies, preprint repositories, and universities. Search results, in some cases, may point to texts that can be viewed only for a fee or with a subscription. A search for "Mergers and Acquisitions" produced over 13,000 documents.

Google Book Search: A search (books.google.com) results in references to books that contain relevant content and provides the text of some. Over 18,000 books contain content on the topic of "Mergers and Acquisitions."

Source: University of Washington Libraries, "Mergers & Acquisitions Resources," www.lib.washington.edu/business/guides/mergers.html.

Why Mergers and Acquisitions Can Fail

It's no secret that plenty of mergers don't work. Those who advocate mergers will argue that the merger will cut costs or boost revenues by more than enough to justify the price premium.

Flawed Intentions

For starters, a booming stock market encourages mergers, which can spell trouble. Deals done with highly rated stock as currency are easy and cheap, but the strategic thinking behind them may be easy and cheap too. Also, mergers are often attempts to imitate: somebody else has done a big merger, which prompts top executives to follow suit.

A merger may often have more to do with seeking glory than business strategy. The executive ego, which is boosted by buying the competition, is a major force in M&A, especially when combined with the influences from the bankers, lawyers, and other assorted advisors who can earn big fees from clients engaged in mergers. Most CEOs get to where they are because they want to be the biggest and the best, and many top executives get a big bonus for merger deals, no matter what happens to the share price later.

The Obstacles of Making It Work

Coping with a merger can make top managers spread their time too thinly and neglect their core business, which spells doom. Too often, potential difficulties seem trivial to managers caught up in the thrill of the big deal.

The chances for success are further hampered if the corporate cultures of the companies are very different. When a company is acquired, the decision is typically based on product or market synergies, but cultural differences are often ignored. It's a mistake to assume that people issues are easily overcome. For example, employees at a target company might be accustomed to easy access to top management, flexible work schedules, or even a relaxed dress code. These aspects of a working environment may not seem significant, but if new management removes them, the result can be resentment and shrinking productivity.

Merging companies can focus on integration and cost cutting so much that they neglect day-to-day business, thereby prompting nervous customers to flee. This loss of revenue momentum is one reason so many mergers fail to create value for shareholders.

But not all mergers fail. Size and global reach can be advantageous, and strong managers can often squeeze greater efficiency out of badly run rivals. But the promises made by dealmakers demand the careful scrutiny of investors. The success of mergers depends on how realistic the dealmakers are and how well they can integrate two companies together while maintaining day-to-day operations.

Source: Investopedia.com, "The Basics of Mergers and Acquisitions: Why M&As Can Fail," www.investopedia.com/university/mergers/mergers5.asp.

Section 11

Tips on Reverse Mergers

What It Is: In a reverse merger, a privately held company buys a publicly traded, but usually dormant company. By doing so, the private company becomes public.

Appropriate for: Reverse mergers are appropriate for companies that do not need capital quickly and that will experience enough growth to reach a size and scale at which they can succeed as a public entity. Minimum sales and earnings to reach this plateau are $20 million and $2 million, respectively.

Best Use: Reverse mergers can be used to finance anything from product development to working capital needs. However, they work best for companies that do not need capital quickly. Not that reverse mergers take long to consummate, but the initial transaction is usually just the halfway point. Once public, a company generally must still find capital. Also, this financing technique works better for companies that will experience substantial enough growth to develop into a "real" public company.

Cost and Funds Typically Available: Expensive. Compared with a conventional initial public offering (IPO), fees and expenses are not that high for a reverse merger. Deals can be completed for $50,000 to $100,000, which might be 25 percent of the out-of-pocket costs that come with a full-blown IPO. In the process of making the deal, however, the acquiring company might give up ten percent to 20 percent of its equity. This is very expensive. After all, it means a company is surrendering ownership just for the privilege of being public. More equity will probably disappear when the company actually raises money. Funds typically available are $500,000 and greater.

Ease of Acquisition: Difficult but not as difficult as a conventional IPO. Perhaps the most challenging aspect of a reverse merger is trying to create a real trading market for the company's shares once the deal is done.

Source: "Reverse Merger," www.entrepreneur.com/article/0,4621,300886,00.html.

Steps to Take if Interested in a Reverse Merger

If a reverse merger sounds like a good idea to you, here are the steps you need to take.

- Find a shell company. That's a company that exists in name only and has ceased to trade. You can find one by contacting the usual suspects. As a first stop, ask an attorney. Every metropolitan area has a law firm with a securities practice. Often, these firms have a dormant public company sitting on one of the partners' bookshelves.

- Another alternative is an accountant. People who control shell companies tend to keep the financial statements, such as they are, up-to-date. This brings accountants into the loop. Like attorneys, they know where the bodies are.

- Another source is financing consultants. In fact, many actually have a couple of shell corporations and, upon request, can manufacture a clean public shell. A made-to-order shell without the baggage of a business failure in its background can sometimes be the way to go.

- Devise your financing strategy. A reverse merger is an indirect route to raising capital. Entrepreneurs must first consider how additional capital will be raised after the deal is done.

- A public company can issue and exercise warrants. Some public shell companies already have warrants issued and outstanding; some have previously registered the underlying common stock shares with the Securities and Exchange Commission, which is a significant benefit. This is much easier and much more valuable to a company that wants to raise capital with warrants. If the newly public company must create and issue warrants, the road to getting them exercised will be trickier but still possible. In short, exercising warrants where the underlying common shares are not registered requires the assistance of a brokerage firm and must occur in a state where there is no registration requirement for issuance of shares of up to $1 million.

- If you are going the private-offering route (i.e., an offering sold to select individuals rather than through a sale directly to the public at large), the deal must be carefully structured. Specifically, the amount of stock owned by investors whom the new owners do not know and cannot influence must be diminished so that a stable quote can be established. Usually, this is done by reducing the percentage of the total number of shares these investors own. By doing so, as an added incentive, the private investors can be offered stock at a discount to the market price.

- Clean up your act. Unfortunately, there's a stigma attached to reverse mergers. At LVA-Vision, a company that owns free-standing centers offering laser refractive eye surgery, founder Jerry Stephens, used the technique to brilliant effect. Although it worked for his company, Stephens says, "there's definitely another side to these deals. If it wasn't for my long-standing reputation in the medical community, our deal might have been perceived differently." Largely, he says, the bad rap stems from the fact that reverse mergers are not understood.

- Entrepreneurs contemplating such a transaction can and should take steps to elevate the profile of their "new" company, specifically:

  1. Hire a national accounting firm. One of the reasons the Big Four fees are high is because they inspire a lot of comfort among investors, traders, and regulators. If you saved a lot on fees at the front end, this might be worth investing in on the back end.

  2. Hire a prestigious law firm. It's almost a certainty that the attorney who initially helps you with your reverse merger transaction, if he or she is an expert in these kinds of deals, will not be with a prestigious downtown law firm. However, after the offering is completed, you should consider retaining one of these firms. Why? When deciding whether to get involved in your offering, many investors and brokers will judge your firm by the company it keeps. An unknown law firm makes a neutral to negative impression. But a well-known and powerful law firm sends an unmistakable message.

- Start with a clean shell. As was mentioned, many shells are created for the express purpose of merging with a private company. These shells have no predecessor entities and, as a result, little baggage in the way of a business failure or other skeletons in the closets.

- Check your greed. The great rallying cry of the 1980s, popularized by the Hollywood oily takeover artist Gordon Gekko, "Greed is good," doesn't apply with a reverse merger. It's possible to structure a reverse merger so that at the end of the day, the public owns two percent of the company and the remaining 98 percent is controlled by the owners of the private company that acquired the shell. Unfortunately, there's

Section 11

almost no incentive for any other investors to become involved if the only people who truly benefit are the insiders. The lesson: if you plan to involve the public with the intention of engaging in a truly symbiotic relationship, you simply must leave some value on the table.

Source: "Reverse Merger," www.entrepreneur.com/article/0,4621,300886,00.html.

Chapter 74

Growing Pains

Section
11

Four Smart Ways to Grow Your Business

Often new businesses experience growing pains. But that doesn't mean you have to suffer. Here are four smart ways to painlessly help your business grow:

1. **Develop a business plan that maps out your company's growth—and then follow it.** Don't forget to update it as you grow.

2. **Buy as you grow.** Don't load up on expensive equipment until you need it. But don't be afraid to buy what you need, either.

3. **Outsource.** Almost all businesses have busy times. To get through them, try outsourcing or subcontracting some work.

4. **Know when to expand.** Compare your current level of business with past performance. Are the numbers telling you it's time to hire a permanent employee or expand to a second location? Then do it. Don't be afraid to grow.

Source: Rieva Lesonsky, *365 Tips to Boost Your Entrepreneurial IQ.*

SCORE's Five Tips to Help You Prepare for Growth Spurts

1. **Get outside help.** Growth is tricky and stressful, so smart business owners rely on outside assistance—such as consultants or SCORE volunteers—to get them through it.

2. **Hire ahead of the need.** If you're growing fast, add a chief operating officer and/or chief financial officer—even if only on a part-time or consulting basis.

3. **Change your own role.** Stop doing everything yourself. Delegate day-to-day operations to others and become the leader, the strategic thinker, and the planner—in other words, the CEO.

4. **Weed out customers who don't contribute sufficiently to your bottom line.** Let go of those who distract you from your goal—for example, because they are outside the area in which you want to work or take too much of your time.

5. **Have reserve capital to weather growth's inevitable bumps.** Reserves don't have to be all cash—they can be excellent receivables or something else that can be turned into cash quickly.

Source: SCORE, www.score.org/business_tips.html.

Section 11

Tips for Building to Last

Try these tips from James Collins and Jerry Porras, authors of *Built to Last: Successful Habits of Visionary Companies*:

- **Be a clock builder, not a time teller.** Time tellers are charismatic leaders with great ideas, but clock builders build a "clock" that runs even in their absence. Most entrepreneurs are time tellers. To succeed, you must make the switch.

- **Build your company on core values.** All great companies, large and small, are built on a solid set of core values. Most have a clear sense of purpose beyond just making money.

- **Be willing to change everything—except your core values.** Small companies stay small when they're fixated on their first products or strategies. Small businesses become big businesses when they're willing to change and progress, yet remain true to their basic value system.

Source: Rieva Lesonsky, *365 Tips to Boost Your Entrepreneurial IQ*.

SCORE's Five Tips for Creating an Innovative Environment

1. Show your employees that you think of innovation as an ongoing process. Some ideas will work and many won't. Keep experimenting.

2. Listen, listen, listen. Innovation is a collaborative process.

3. Be open to "accidents," the unexpected connections that spark new ideas. Inspiration comes from everywhere—often from outside your own field.

4. Draw on your own employees—they know the company's problems and goals best. This is probably one time you don't need outside consultants.

5. Be patient. Creativity can't be hurried.

Source: SCORE, www.score.org/business_tips.html.

Tips for Creating a Job-Training Program

One of entrepreneurs' most common complaints is they can't find properly trained employees. One solution is to do on-the-job training. Here are some suggestions for starting a training program at your company:

- Determine your training goals. Make sure they are specific.

- Honestly assess your current training program, if you have one. Then identify the area, if any, that works well in your in your business, and try to duplicate those efforts.

- If you have any stand-out employees, enlist their aid in training others. And if they are going to be training others, it might help to send them to training themselves.

- Finally, the task may seem overwhelming, but on-the-job training is really four steps: tell, show, do, and follow up.

Source: Rieva Lesonsky, *365 Tips to Boost Your Entrepreneurial IQ.*

Tips for Using Big-Company Strategies

No matter the size of your business, sometimes it's smart to adapt big-business strategies to your company. Try these on for size:

- Use organizational charts and job descriptions. Even if you only have one employee, that person needs a detailed job description to do his or her best work.

- Schedule regular staff meetings. No matter how small your staff, the best way to keep everyone informed and on task is to meet regularly.

- Form an advisory group. This could consist of friends, former colleagues, your accountant, your lawyer, or even your banker. Make sure you meet regularly and ask for their objective opinions and guidance.

- Stay organized. This is the best way to make sure things don't fall through the cracks.

Remember: large companies can often absorb mistakes that could devastate a smaller business, so it's imperative you work smart.

Source: Rieva Lesonsky, *365 Tips to Boost Your Entrepreneurial IQ.*

Five Tips for Listening to Criticism Objectively

1. Remember what it's like being on the other side of criticism. When you must step out on a limb and share a well-intended criticism with someone, how do you want that person to respond to your critique? Picture the ideal response to a criticism you might offer, and make that your response the next time you are on the receiving end.

2. Ask questions to clarify your critic's position. Don't assume you know exactly what your critic means until you have asked questions. Asking questions not only helps you understand what the person is saying; it also indicates that you want to under-stand.

3. Acknowledge whatever truth there is in the criticism. There will almost always be

some truth to what your critic is saying. Make sure you hear it and respond to it.

4. Problem-solve with your critic. After listening fully to the complaint and clarifying precisely what it is about, explore solutions with your critic. All of this must be explored without sarcasm or condescension. Remember: you are solving a problem, not expressing what you ultimately think of this person.

5. Thank your critic for giving you the opportunity to correct or improve your behavior. This confirms your ability to be objective and professional. It also tells an honest critic that you are open to improving your performance and lets a manipulative critic know he can't get to you through criticism.

Source: Scott Miller, "More Tips for Turning Criticism into Praise," www.entrepreneur.com/article/0,4621,298872,00.html.

Tips for Turning Criticism into Praise

1. Consider criticism part of the process of doing your job. This helps you drop the emotional reaction to being criticized and enables you to use your problem-solving skills. Put in perspective, criticism is very positive.

2. Understand that it is very possible you have been misunderstood. It is inevitable that your intentions will be misconstrued, your end product misused, your words taken out of context. This gives you the opportunity to explore how what you said and did went awry and enables you to straighten things out, solve the problem, adjust your behavior, and regain the respect you deserve.

3. Use your listening skills to fully understand the criticism. When someone begins to criticize you, turn off your ego and crank up your objectivity. Hold your fire and let the other person talk. Don't interrupt. Make eye contact and think intently about what he or she is saying.

4. Don't defend yourself. It is pointless to try to defend yourself, and it interferes with your learning process. It is pointless because it signals a tendency to make excuses instead of solve problems. No matter how valid your self-defense, it comes off as a sign of weakness, insecurity, and unwillingness to take responsibility for your actions.

Source: Scott Miller, "How to Turn Criticism into Praise," www.entrepreneur.com/Your_Business/YB_SegArticle/0,4621,298065,00.html.

Section 11

Family Business and the Succession Plan

Section 11

Five Tips to Consider Before Bringing Your Spouse into the Business

If your partnership turns into a power struggle, you can put both your business and marriage at risk. Follow these five steps for creating a home-based business that will provide you and your spouse with fun and profit for many years to come:

1. **Divide your roles and responsibilities.** Even though both of you may possess the skills to do the work and serve your clients, it's important to divvy up your company's roles and responsibilities so that you don't step on each other's toes. In many small businesses, one partner is the "front of the house," handling sales and business development and preparing proposals and job estimates, and the other partner acts as the "back of the house," handling the day-to-day operations and taking care of the bookkeeping, payroll, and general office duties. While big decisions such as investing money in a new computer system or hiring an employee should be made together, this can be an excellent way to share power and minimize arguments.

2. **Develop an effective way of airing differences and resolving disputes.** While good communication is essential to any marriage, it's just as important in a business relationship. One way to clear the air is to hold weekly management meetings—on Monday morning, for example—to review the company's performance during the previous week and to put in place plans for improvement. If disputes erupt during the week, you and your spouse can either address them on the spot or wait until the next weekly meeting. It doesn't matter which approach you choose, as long as you and your spouse agree to it.

3. **Put a child-care plan in place.** Just because you'll be working from home now doesn't mean that you don't need daycare or babysitting—quite the opposite! If kids are running through your home office demanding attention, you're not going to be able to get much work done. One option is for you and your spouse to switch off child-care responsibilities (every other day or mornings and afternoons) so that the other spouse can focus on the business. Another option is to find a part-time or full-time babysitter or child-care program.

4. **Make sure both of you have enough room to work.** While some people have no problem working in a noisy office with lots of commotion, others need quiet and privacy in order to concentrate. While this isn't always possible in a home office with limited space, you can turn one room—say, the dining room—into the "sales and marketing" office while reserving the den or spare bedroom as the "tech room" where your spouse can focus on writing software and documentation.

5. **Agree on an exit strategy before you begin.** While it's hard to think about the company's future before you've even launched it, it's important to sit down with your spouse and decide where you want the business to go in terms of goals and objec-

tives. You could also run into problems if you want to bet the house and the kids' college fund on building the business and your spouse feels uncomfortable taking even the smallest financial risk. While it may not be necessary to have a lawyer draft a formal shareholders' agreement, it's a good idea for you and your spouse to agree on an annual budget for your business.

Source: Rosalind Resnick, "Starting a Business with Your Spouse," www.entrepreneur.com/article/0,4621,312642,00.html.

SCORE's Five Tips on Avoiding Conflicts of Interest

1. Be aware that, in a small or family-owned business, special favors to family members and friends de-motivate employees and set a bad example.
2. Think twice about offering a contract to a supplier who is a relative. Award contracts on merit.
3. Avoid letting family members borrow company vehicles, and don't allow your sister to ask the company computer wizard to set up her home office.
4. Don't put family members on the payroll if they're not working in the company or can't make a real contribution to the business.
5. Think of the future. If you hope to seek investors or go public, dealings with family members outside the business will be questioned.

Source: SCORE, www.score.org/business_tips.html.

Section 11

Seven Development Stages of Succession

Attitude preparation
Important attitudes toward work and the family business are formed during the first 25 years of life, including part-time work, occasional business-related trips, and outside work experience.

Entry
This usually occurs when the successor is between 20 and 30 years of age and takes an existing and necessary job in the business. Important elements include training, orientation, and developing relationships with other employees.

Business development
This usually occurs between the ages of 25 and 35, when the successor should be cultivating necessary skills and abilities.

Leadership development

This occurs between the ages of 30 and 40, when the successor's plans stretch beyond any one job to the time when he or she will be responsible for the entire business. Skills developed during this stage include team building and shared decision making.

If more than one successor candidate exists, this is the time when a natural leader emerges and self-selection or conflict may occur.

Selection

If multiple candidates exist selection would occur at this stage. Methods of making a choice include the following:

- An early choice by the incumbent
- Selection by the outside board
- Selection by the family executive team
- Consensus among family board and executives

Transition

During this period, authority and responsibility are transferred to the successor. This is the time when the successor becomes involved in the strategic decision making and in developing his or her management team.

The next round

Succession planning should always be on the agenda and a new leader of the business should begin talking about developing the next generation of leaders.

Source: Grant Thornton International, "The Seven Development Stages of Succession," www.familybizz.net/fam_bus_issue_sp.asp.

Where to Seek Counsel for Your Family Business

Section 11

Alfred University: Center for Family Business

business.alfred.edu/cfb.html

The Center for Family Business aims to provide distinctive educational networking opportunities for students, faculty, and alumni of Alfred University involved in the growth and development of family-owned businesses. The Center also strives to develop and sustain a complementary blend of academic and outreach activities that are conducive to achieving professional distinctiveness and success for Alfred University's students and business and community partners. Located in Alfred, New York.

Auburn University: College of Business: Lowder Center for Family Business and Entrepreneurship

www.business.auburn.edu/departments/bus_outreach/lowder.cfm

The Lowder Center for Family Business and Entrepreneurship combines outreach programming and academic studies in the area of family business. Efforts are directed at being responsive and proactive to the needs of family businesses, and to students interested in studying the dynamics of families in business. Located in Auburn, Alabama.

Babson College: Arthur M. Blank Center for Entrepreneurship: The Institute for Family Enterprising

www3.babson.edu/Eship

The Institute for Family Enterprising exists to educate members of the Babson community about the unique challenges that family businesses face and assist family businesses in meeting those challenges associated with operating, growing, and revitalizing organizations. Located in Wellesley, Massachusetts.

Bond University: School of Business: Australian Centre for Family Business

www.bond.edu.au/bus/centres/ACFB/acfb.htm

The Australian Centre for Family Business was formed to enhance the prospects for profitable continuity of family businesses for the benefit of family members, shareholders, and non-family staff, and in this way contribute to the economic and social development of Australia. The overriding mission of the Centre is to facilitate research into, and disseminate knowledge of, family business issues. Located in Gold Coast, Queensland, Australia.

Boston College: Wallace E. Carroll Graduate School of Management: Center for Work and Family

www.bc.edu/centers/cwf

The Center for Work and Family is a research organization dedicated to improving the quality of life of working families by promoting the responsiveness of communities to their needs. The guiding vision of the Center is the strengthening of families, broadly defined to reflect the diversity throughout our communities today. Located in Boston, Massachusetts.

Bryant College: Graduate School: Institute for Family Enterprise

web.bryant.edu/business/int_fam_ent.html

The Institute for Family Enterprise helps family-owned firms meet the unique managerial challenges associated with operating and sustaining a successful family enterprise. By working with the Institute, principals in these companies learn to identify and overcome family dynamics that often adversely affect business decisions. The Institute sponsors educational seminars and workshops that bring together academic and business experts to address a variety of topics, such as succession planning and conflict management. Located in Smithfield, Rhode Island.

California State University, Fresno: Sid Craig School of Business: Institute for Family Business

www.cvifb.org

The Institute for Family Business (IFB) provides educational outreach programs and resources to assist family business throughout the Central Valley. IFB conducts such outreach through regularly offered seminars, workshops and its annual conference. The Board of IFB is composed of family business owners.

California State University, Fullerton: School of Business Administration & Economics: Family Business Council

cbeweb-1.fullerton.edu/centers/fambusiness

The Family Business Council was formed to assist family businesses in recognizing their common problems and in finding solutions to the unique issues that confront them. The Council's mission is to use education to help family businesses in our region grow and prosper and to keep harmony in the family. Located in Fullerton, California.

Canadian Association of Family Enterprise

www.cafemembers.org/cafeuc

The Canadian Association of Family Enterprise (CAFE) is a non-profit organization dedicated to the well-being of the family in business. CAFE provides its members with educational programming on such issues as succession and continued personal support through its Advisory Groups. CAFE currently has chapters in Calgary, Edmonton, Halifax, Kelowna, Lefroy, Mississauga, Montreal, Ottawa, Saskatoon, Victoria, Vancouver, and Winnipeg.

Fairleigh Dickinson University: Rothman Institute of Entrepreneurial Studies: Family Business Forum

view.fdu.edu/default.aspx?id=1218

The Forum is a membership-based educational program for family-owned businesses. The Forum presents six programs a year that feature national and regional experts, panel discussions, and other interactive activities for its members. Members may also participate in Peer Group Discussion meetings scheduled several times throughout the year. Located in Madison, New Jersey.

Fambiz.com

fambiz.com

Fambiz.com is the internet's dominant web site for owners of family-controlled companies. The site enables visitors to search against a database of several hundred articles on a variety of family business topics, ranging from compensation and communications issues to asset protection and estate planning. Also published on the site is a weekly News & Comment feature, a family business calendar of events, and online archives.

Family Business Resources

www.massmutual.com/mmfg/business/solutions/additional/family_bus_centers.html

This site serves as a source of assistance for family businesses, advisors, and educators. In addition, the site offers statistics on family businesses, research, and the latest articles, as well as information on awards and support groups/workshops.

Section 11

George Washington University: Center for Family Enterprise

www.gwu.edu/~business/research/centers/CFE/

The primary mission of the Center for Family Enterprise is to ensure the survival and growth of family firms and develop a long-term relationship with the family business community. The Center provides an environment for family enterprises to learn, develop, and increase their awareness of effective methods to continue the health of the enterprise. Located in Washington, D.C.

Goshen College: Business Department: Family Business Program

www.goshen.edu/familybusiness

The Family Business Program is designed to meet the educational, informative, and interactive needs of the principals of family businesses. The focus is on enabling these persons to more effectively address issues involving perpetuation of the business and the succession of management to the next generation. Located in Goshen, Indiana.

Kennesaw State University: Cox Family Enterprise Center

www.kennesaw.edu/fec/

The Family Enterprise Center offers the finest family business expertise available. Family businesses regularly experience opportunities and problems that traditional business education does not address. Located in Kennesaw, Georgia.

Louisiana State University: E.J. Ourso College of Business: Louisiana Institute for Entrepreneurial Education and Family Business Studies

www.bus.lsu.edu/academics/entrepreneurial

The Louisiana Institute for Entrepreneurial Education and Family Business Studies was formed to address the issues and challenges of entrepreneurship, family business, and franchising. The Institute offers programs and activities such as educational seminars and workshops in an executive education format; university course work; business planning, marketing, and management consultation; and venture funding assistance, to give entrepreneurs effective management tools and problem-solving skills with a prime goal of creating jobs in Louisiana. Located in Baton Rouge, Louisiana.

Loyola College: Center for Closely Held Firms

www.loyola.edu/chf

The Center for Closely Held Firms was founded to help closely held and family businesses to survive, grow, and prosper. The Center offers members access to an extensive network of business contacts, including experts in finance, law, accounting, marketing, and insurance. The Center also pools resources from the private, professional, and academic areas to give companies assistance from a variety of perspectives. Located in Baltimore, Maryland.

Loyola University Chicago: Family Business Center

www.sba.luc.edu/centers/fbc

The Family Business Center is an internationally recognized pioneer and leader in family business program development and research, serving as a resource to family businesses in the Chicago region and throughout the nation. Located in Chicago, Illinois.

Montana State University: College of Business: Family Business Program

www.montana.edu/cob/FamilyBusiness/FamilyBusiness.html

The purpose of the Family Business Program is to provide educational opportunities and resources to family-owned businesses. In addition, the Program provides educational opportunities and resources to service providers of family businesses. Located in Bozeman, Montana.

Northeastern University: Center for Family Business

www.cba.neu.edu/portal/index.cfm?page=285&nav=260

The Center for Family Business covers a range of issues facing family businesses—how to avoid some of the major pitfalls and how to be proactive and prevent problems. Located in Boston, Massachusetts.

Oregon State University: Austin Family Business Program

www.familybusinessonline.org

The mission of the Austin Family Business Program at Oregon State University is to foster healthy family businesses through hands-on learning opportunities—workshops, checklists, videos, and academic courses. Located in Corvallis, Oregon.

Regent University: Center for Business Innovation
www.regent.edu/acad/schbus
This Family Business program teaches family business management techniques from the inside out: from creating and communicating a vision for the family and for the business to succession planning. Located in Virginia Beach, Virginia.

South Dakota: Family Business Association
www.usd.edu/fambus/index.html
The Family Business Association was founded in 1993 as the Family Business Initiative with the express mission of enhancing the long-term survival and success of its family business members. Located in Vermillion, South Dakota.

Tulane University: Levy-Rosenblum Institute for Entrepreneurship
www.freeman.tulane.edu/lri
The Levy-Rosenblum Institute offers a Family Business Forum designed to help family business owners understand and manage the challenges of family-owned and/or -operated businesses. The Forum offers seminars providing access to nationally recognized family business experts in a solution-oriented setting. Located in New Orleans, Louisiana.

University of Cincinnati: Goering Center for Family & Private Business
www.business.uc.edu/centers/goering.asp
The Center develops curricula to address issues unique to family and privately held businesses, sponsors research into these issues, and provides opportunities for education and information to the community at large. Located in Cincinnati, Ohio.

University of Connecticut: School of Business Administration: Family Business Program
www.sba.uconn.edu/page.asp?id=1.8.6
The Family Business Program serves the educational needs of families in business, with services ranging from seminars and workshops to individualized consultation for family businesses in crisis. The program provides a network of problem-solving resources, using the expertise, skills, and savvy of business owners, university faculty, corporate leaders, and other professionals. Located in Storrs, Connecticut.

University of Louisville: Family Business Center
inside.cbpa.louisville.edu/fbc
The Family Business Center is specifically designed to address the challenges and conflicts associated with family business, including managing the stress-related issues of a family-owned business. Located in Louisville, Kentucky.

University of Massachusetts Amherst: Family Business Center
www.umass.edu/fambiz
The Family Business Center helps family businesses recognize their common problems and find solutions to the unique challenges confronting them. The Center offers members a series of educational, interactive, and entertaining forums led by experts in family business

consulting, advising members in relevant areas of the law, accounting, estate planning, and banking. Located in Amherst, Massachusetts.

University of St. Thomas: Graduate School of Business: Center for Family Enterprise

www.stthomas.edu/cob/centers/cfe

The Center for Family Enterprise was created in 1990 as a learning community for families and professionals committed to the growth and continuity of family enterprise. The major thrust of the family business program is lifelong learning activities. This includes work-shops, leadership breakfasts, action seminars, and continuing education for lawyers, finan-cial planners, accountants, bankers, insurance brokers, estate planners, psychologists, and family counselors and mediators. Located in Minneapolis, Minnesota.

University of the Pacific: Eberhardt School of Business: Institute for Family Business

www1.pacific.edu/esb/ifb/index.html

The Institute for Family Business helps family-owned businesses find and develop solutions to their unique business challenges and concerns by providing educational opportunities, consulting and research services, and access to regional and national expertise. Located in Stockton, California.

University of Toledo: Center for Family Business

www.utfamilybusiness.org

The Center serves the unique needs of area family businesses and promotes greater incor-poration of family business issues into curriculum and research in the College of Business Administration. Located in Toledo, Ohio.

University of Tulsa: College of Business Administration: Family-Owned Business Institute

www.cba.utulsa.edu/Centers/FamilyOwned

The objective of the Institute is to develop programs to promote effective family business management, secure the health of family relationships, disseminate relevant information, and create a network for family business members. The goal of the Institute is to promote recognition of the economic significance of the family business sector and to provide a voice in society for family-owned businesses. Located in Tulsa, Oklahoma.

Wake Forest University: Babcock Graduate School of Management: Family Business Center

www.mba.wfu.edu/fbc

The Family Business Center is designed to help family businesses succeed and create stronger family ties. Located in Winston-Salem, North Carolina.

Source: EntreWorld (Ewing Marion Kauffman Foundation), www.entreworld.org.

Tips on How to Decide Who Gets the Family Business

Whether or not the candidates for the top job are family or not, the process for choosing your successor is basically the same: find the best person for the job. Although this can be very difficult if you want family to take over, it's even more difficult if the family member(s) expect to be immediately anointed to fill the top spot.

Family or outsider: Who will be chosen? I'd advise any business owner to be objective and honest in selecting, training, and coaching a replacement.

First, identify just what the mission and goals of your company are. The current leader usually knows this down in his or her soul, but it needs to be objectively translated and written out since everything that occurs in corporate life is a function of mission and goals.

Second, the business owner and a team of other key senior officers need to determine the exact role for the new replacement. Succession planning, downsizing, and expanding all present unique opportunities to take a hard look at what the current leader will do in both the near and long term.

Third, given the responses to the first two factors, the task force of execs needs to clearly identify the exact knowledge bases, skills, and abilities a successful replacement will have. They can start this process by examining just what factors have led to the success of the current chief executive. After that analysis, the task force needs to objectively determine if the current set of traits, attitudes, skills, knowledge, and abilities will be necessary and sufficient to carry the company into the future.

Armed with this critical data—these "factors for success"—the task force must next create specific questions, role-plays, and action scenarios to use during the interview process. And all candidates applying for the chief position must be interviewed by a series of current employees who've been trained to be objective in their questioning and in their evaluation.

After all candidates have gone through the interview process, the task force should then meet to evaluate the results of each round of interviews and select the candidate—whether family or not—who best embodies the qualifications needed to ensure the company's future success.

Source: David G. Javitch, "Successful Succession Planning," www.entrepreneur.com/article/0,4621,321648,00.html.

Section 11

Strategic Planning Steps for the Family Business Succession

So what is business strategic planning? It is a deliberate search/determination of the business' goals and objectives, and planning of courses of actions, including allocation of resources to develop and take control of the business's competitive advantage and unique attributes. It gives the business direction. It needs to be structured and includes:

- an environmental analysis
- strategic diagnosis (SWOT)
- values, vision, and mission building
- setting of specific measurable goals, objectives, strategies with specific action items, time frame (three to five years), responsibilities, resource requirements, and skills
- development of structures—including good corporate governance
- implementation and monitoring of the plan
- regular review and revision

Non-family executives and outside advisors are needed to challenge and stimulate the strategic planning process. They provide a constructive voice of reason and create a new dimension of experience, objectivity, and candor, and can help in anticipating new challenges.

It is most important that the plan is clearly communicated within the business and with the family to ensure understanding, ensuring commitment and buy-in from all parties. Family businesses that wish to be successful in the 21st century must preserve the values of the past, whilst creating a culture of change, innovation, and flexibility for the future.

Source: Grant Thornton International, "So What Is Strategic Planning for Family Businesses?," 67.96.180.115/fam_bus_issue_stp_process.asp.

Tips on Choosing an Advisor for Your Family Business

Here are some tips on choosing an outside family business advisor:

- Make sure the person is not affiliated with any family business members.
- Make efforts to keep the relationship professional, beginning with the hiring process.
- Do not allow the mediator to be drawn into family relationships; his or her involvement must be kept to the business level alone.
- Choose a person that all parties can trust.

- Set clear expectations at the beginning of what you want the counselor to accomplish.
- Make sure everyone involved is open to change.
- Let the consultant act as a confidant to business. He or she must understand the family relationship dynamics, but not get involved in them.
- A consultant should serve as a window on the outside world, a mirror to the activities of the business, and a catalyst for change.

Source: Jane Applegate, "Seeking Counsel for Your Family Business," www.entrepreneur.com/Your_Business/YB_SegArticle/0,4621,295160,00.html.

Tips on Managing Employees Who Happen to Be Family

No matter what your business is—selling, buying, servicing, or producing—the challenges of working with family members are the same. And they're not often easy to deal with.

David Javitch is an organizational psychologist and president of Javitch Associates, an organizational consulting firm in Newton, Massachusetts. With more than 20 years of experience working with executives among various industries, he outlines some familiar family problems and them offers advice on how to avoid future problems.

Common Family Problems:

1. **Birth order:** The "older brother" or "older sister" syndrome involves people viewing the eldest child as more powerful, more "special," or more entitled due to his or her birth order at the head of the pack.

2. **Position nepotism:** The sons or daughters of the founder or of the eldest founder get special treatment due to their relation to the founder.

3. **Teacher's pet:** Mommy's or Daddy's favorite, used to getting his or her own way, continues to be favored. Siblings often become jealous or angry.

4. **Inner-family fraternizing:** Some relatives and their spouses have favorite relatives with whom they socialize and interact outside the workplace. Or the opposite occurs: some relatives and their spouses never get along well with other members of the family. These feelings, both positive and negative, invariably spill over into the work setting.

5. **Family feud:** Family rivalry to succeed and be "the best" in order to gain favor with or praise from powerful or otherwise important relatives is intense, non-collaborative, and, at times, destructively competitive.

Remedy the Family Problems:

- First, make sure that everything that occurs—including the delegation of authority and responsibility, decision-making, promotions, rewards, demotions, praise, and salary increases—is based on concrete and clearly stated knowledge, skills, abilities, and personality traits.

- Second, leave your family issues at home. The workplace is not an environment in which you and your relatives should play out or resolve your childhood or adult dramas.

- Third, establish clear channels for communication.

The best way to avoid these and similar experiences is to drop interpersonal dislikes and deal directly with the individual involved. Based on our earlier rule, the goal is to treat family and non-family alike in all situations.

Source: David G. Javitch, "When Family Members Work Together," www.entrepreneur.com/article/0,4621,319309,00.html.

Tips on Preventing Feuds in the Family Business

You must avoid taking actions that could not only wreck the company, but also destroy family relationships. Many times, it's a great idea to start the process by enlisting the help of either a trusted business advisor (such as the business's accountant or lawyer) or a specialist in family business mediation to provide you with guidance and a level of objectivity along the way.

Succession Planning

Once you have a handle on how best to approach the family issues, the next level is to develop a succession plan that not only is a good plan from a business standpoint, but also has a good chance of being acceptable to family members who play a key role in the business.

Meeting both goals may at first appear contradictory or even a waste of time. Just as every business has its own corporate culture that it lives by, every family business has a complex set of dos and don'ts that have evolved over the years that must be reckoned with in establishing a "saleable" succession plan.

To have a "saleable" succession plan in this case, you may have to factor in the cost of continuing the employment of the other family members, while privately showing your main business relative (probably your dad) how this extra cost will impact the amount that he can receive for his fair share of the business. The key to selling this type of succession plan may be to let your dad decide whether or not he wants to take less money for his fair share of the business in order to continue to support the other family members after he's gone.

In any event, keep in mind that a good or even great succession plan that violates the unwritten rules of the family business is unlikely to be accepted by the family and can even be counterproductive to any future discussions.

Tax Planning

Tax planning must deal with the only two certain things in life: death and taxes.

In the transfer of ownership of a family business, your family must consider not only estate taxes, which may be imposed upon your parents' death, but also the income or capital gains taxes that Uncle Sam and the states will want to impose when your dad cashes out of the business while he is alive.

A word of caution at this point. While it's a great idea to work with professionals to help you handle other family and succession planning issues, it is mandatory that you have a knowledgeable tax advisor to help and your family successfully navigate the stormy waters of tax law.

Let's look at just one tax trap that you and your family could innocently fall into. Let's assume that you and the other family members decide that the best way to take care of your parents is to give your dad a lump sum payment for his stock in the company. Your dad will then take this lump sum money and invest it in order to comfortably live off the investment income.

Sounds like a plan, right? Wrong. When your dad starts to complete his tax return for the year after the sale, he quickly finds out that the lump sum payment he received has resulted in his owing a huge tax bill that wipes out a significant amount of his portfolio. Worse yet, his tax advisor then tells him that the family may incur an enormous estate tax bill after both he and your mom die.

Fortunately, there are many legally sound and acceptable tax-planning strategies that family businesses can adopt that will allow the transfer the ownership of the business from one generation to the other while at the same time minimizing income taxes, capital gains taxes, and estate taxes.

The main point to remember when dealing with tax-planning issues regarding your family business is that seeking sound tax advice isn't everything—it's the only thing.

Successful transitions of family businesses can be difficult and, at a minimum, require careful consideration of family, succession planning, and tax-planning issues and typically require the advice of trusted and knowledgeable advisors to help the family members reach a win-win plan that not only rewards the founding generation for a job well done, but also gives the next generation the opportunity to take the family business to the next level.

Source: Chris Kelleher, "Tax Planning," www.entrepreneur.com/article/0,4621,315884-3,00.html.

Tips on Resolving Feuds in the Family Business

Guidelines to Help Resolve Major Decisions

■ Remain true to the mission, philosophy, and values that have been agreed by the firm.

Section 11

- Use the policy and procedures that were established to guide work with employees and staff.

- When questions arise about growth and development as a firm, refer to the strategic plan.

- In policy disagreements, strive to achieve consensus. If all fails, a unanimous vote can be used to decide the issue.

- If unanimity cannot be achieved, hire a skilled facilitator to assist the process.

- Disputes over procedures such as screening job applicants or collection of overdue accounts can be decided by majority vote.

- Family members who have conflicts deal with problems themselves, and not through parents, spouses, family, and non-family members.

- Keep the focus on what is best for the family rather than for any individual.

Resolving Conflict Within Families

Establish a safe environment. A safe environment is where the individual feels comfortable to open and take the risk of bringing up conflicting or controversial points. The presence of an advisor can help create a safe environment where difficult issues can be explored. The following methods should help create ease:

- Listen respectfully and don't interrupt.

- Focus on the issue, not the person or personality.

- Leave titles outside the door and address one another as peers.

- Offer feedback with consideration and kindness; avoid making attacks.

Follow a systematic conflict resolution approach:

- Identify the issues. People often falsely assume that everyone understands the issue; sometimes issues stated clearly eliminate the problem.

- Determine each party's motivation to address the issue.

- Outline the positions and options suggested by all.

- List the characteristics of an ideal outcome that would address each party's needs.

- Consider a list of options. What are the pros and cons of each?

- The family should select an option that addresses their description of an ideal outcome.

- Allow the opportunity to reflect: decisions should not be rushed.

- Monitor the implementation. The family should evaluate how the solution is working and how they feel about the entire conflict resolution process.

Source: Grant Thornton International, "How to Resolve Conflict," 67.96.180.115/fam_bus_issue_rc_resolve.asp.

Chapter 76

Selling Your Business

Section 11

SCORE's Five Tips on Exit Strategies

1. Plan your exit when you start the business. Will you sell your company, pass it on to children, or take it public?

2. Take time to understand how your chosen exit affects business planning. Will family members need to be trained to replace you, for example?

3. Consider the cost of each strategy—loss of the ability to keep financial information private if you sell or go public, for example.

4. Be aware that your investors will have their own exit strategies. Be prepared to discuss their desired timetable for exiting your business, how they see it happening, and their expected return on investment.

5. Plan well ahead for a satisfying life when you leave your current business. Consider starting another business, teaching, volunteering—or becoming a philanthropist.

Source: SCORE, www.score.org/business_tips.html.

Six People Who Must Be at the Negotiating Table

On the Buyer's Side:

1. **CEO:** The chief executive needs a vision for how the new company fits into the existing organization. He or she wants to add revenue, products, or strategic capabilities, and also wants to brag about the purchase to board members.

2. **CFO:** This is the detail person and a professional skeptic. Taking a long-term view, the CFO knows he or she will take the heat if reality doesn't live up to expectations.

3. **CPA:** The buyer's CPA or accounting firm will validate the seller's numbers. The CPA will probably argue for a lower purchase price based on historical profits.

On the Seller's Side:

4. **Investment banker:** The investment banker keeps both teams moving toward the goal. He or she keeps one eye on the sale price and the other on the strategic best interests of the business owner.

5. **Transaction attorney:** The attorney is there to make sure no one gets hurt. The transaction attorney's focus is the sale contract, but he or she can also handle communication with the buyer.

6. **CPA:** The seller's CPA should be advising the seller on the personal tax consequences of the deal and how to handle the after-tax proceeds.

Source: David Worrell, "The Starting Lineup," www.entrepreneur.com/article/0,4621,317054-2,00.html.

Tips on Selecting a Business Broker

To find a business broker to help you sell your business, take these steps.

- Check newspaper ads under "Business Opportunities." Look in your local and regional papers, as well as *The Wall Street Journal*.
- Look in the Yellow Pages under "Real Estate" or "Business Brokers." Make sure to find a broker who specializes in selling businesses, not simply real estate.
- Ask for referrals. Ask other business owners who've sold businesses who they worked with. You local chamber of commerce can also provide referrals to business brokers, as can your banker, CPA attorney, and financial planner.

Source: Andi Axman, *Entrepreneur Magazine's Ultimate Small Business Advisor.*

Ten Steps to Take While Preparing to Sell Your Business

1. **Get a business valuation.** Obtain a realistic idea of what your business is worth from an objective, outside source. A professional valuation will give you a basis for gauging buyer offers and will give you an idea of what you can expect to net from the sale. It will also tell you your business's market position, financial situation, strengths, and weaknesses

2. **Get your books in order.** Buyers evaluating your business generally require at least three years' worth of financial information. The more formal your statements (accountant-reviewed or -prepared vs. internally generated statements), the better the impression you'll make—and the easier the due diligence for a buyer. Tax returns may suffice.

3. **Understand the true profitability of your business.** Most privately held businesses claim a variety of nonoperational expenses. Make sure you have supporting documentation for these expenses.

4. **Consult your financial advisor.** It's wise to speak to your tax advisor for help planning your financial future. Understanding your personal and corporate tax situation may also help you recognize your options with regard to deal structure.

5. **Make a good first impression.** Will a buyer visiting your shop for the first time see order or chaos? Buyers look for companies that show well, as an orderly shop is often indicative of an orderly management team and back-room operations.

6. **Organize your legal paperwork.** Review your incorporation papers, permits, licensing agreements, leases, customer and vendor contracts, etc. Make sure you have them readily available, current, and in order.

Section 11

7. **Consider management succession.** If you're absolutely vital to your business, to whom will a buyer be able to turn for help running the business after you leave? You should have a succession plan in place before going to market.

8. **Know your reason for selling.** Buyers are always curious as to why a seller wants to exit a business. (If it's so great, why are you leaving?) Be prepared to articulate your reasons.

9. **Get your advisory team in place.** Start interviewing attorneys and accountants who are proficient in mergers and acquisitions. Strongly consider hiring an intermediary, either a business broker or an investment banker, to represent you and help you through the selling process.

10. **Keep your eye on the ball.** Don't let your business performance decline because you're too focused on the sale of your business. This will only give buyers additional negotiating power to lower their offers.

Source: Loraine MacDonald, "Preparing to Sell Your Business," www.entrepreneur.com/article/0,4621,289171,00.html.

Section 12

Personal

Section
12

Taking Care of Your Body

Section 12

Tips for Long Hours of Work on the Computer

Here are some tips for staying connected to your body while you're working at your computer:

- To protect your wrists (and avoid developing carpal tunnel syndrome), get a wrist pad to place in front of your keyboard. Or simply use a rolled-up towel to support and elevate your wrists. Shake out your hands every now and then when you're typing for long periods of time.

- To protect your eyes, be sure to blink hard several times at regular intervals. This will help prevent eye dryness, a common computer-related problem. Exercise your eye muscles by occasionally looking away from the screen and focusing on objects farther away and in different directions. Then do a few eye rolls. Imagine that you are looking at a huge clock. Slowly roll your eyes straight up to 12 o'clock, then around to each number on the face of the clock till you're back where you started. Do this several times clockwise, then counterclockwise.

- To protect your back, check into ergonomically designed chairs, back support pillows, and footrests. (Office product catalogs and health product catalogs often carry them.)

- Do slow neck and shoulder rolls occasionally while you're sitting. Then get up and stretch at regular intervals.

- Make sure your monitor is raised to eye level, so your neck isn't angled as you look at the screen. (Test: sit in a "perfect posture" position, with your spine and shoulders straight, head centered, and look straight ahead. Your eyes should now be focused on the center of the screen.) If they aren't, buy a monitor stand from a computer store or office products catalog. These stands typically range in height from four to eight inches.

Source: MoreBusiness.com, "Staying Healthy in Front of the Computer Screen," morebusiness.com/running_your_business/businessbits/d912806095.brc.

Five Tips for Keeping Your Job from Making You Fat

1. **Ban the vending machines.** It's 3 o'clock and that old familiar afternoon hunger kicks in. Keep yourself away from the office vending machines by packing healthy and tasty snacks to get you through the day. Try options like yogurt, carrots and light dressing, low-fat or fat-free pudding snacks, or even peanut butter and crackers to get you through the afternoon.

2. **Order smart menu options.** Those who travel often or are required to eat a lot of business lunches can find that eating out every day begins to add up. Try ordering a

salad or soup rather than a filling burger and fries or heavy pasta dish. Eating a lighter lunch, even a soup and half-sandwich combo, will work wonders for your waistline and also keep you from your typical post-lunch "food coma."

3. **Make exercise a priority.** Many people think that they do not have the time during or before work to exercise. However, postponing exercise often means that it gets dropped because you had to work late, were too hungry, or were too tired after a long day. Try working out in the morning or during your lunch hour. If you travel for work, pack your workout clothes. Most hotels have exercise equipment on site and this is a good way to blow off steam after a tiring day of travel.

4. **Don't let the office party sabotage your diet.** If you don't have the willpower to pass on the latest office treat, you might have to pass on joining the party altogether. Bring a bottle of water to sip on while others consume as much as 1,000 calories in a single slice of fat-laden birthday cake and ice cream.

5. **Get up and move.** If you work at a computer, get up and take walking breaks to get your blood flowing. If you drive a lot of miles for work, stop at a rest area and stretch out. Walk up the stairs instead of taking the elevator. Moving more through-out the day will not only make you feel and look better, it will probably make you more productive, too.

Source: Kate Lorenz, "Is Your Job Making You Fat?," msn.careerbuilder.com/Custom/MSN/CareerAdvice/viewarticle.aspx?articleid=461&sc_cmp1=js_461_wihub_more5.

Tips for Sticking to Your Fitness Goals When Traveling

Busy entrepreneurs often don't take the time when traveling to stick to their fitness programs. But just because you're out of town doesn't mean you should abandon keeping fit. Try these tips:

- **Walk whenever possible.** During breaks at meetings and conventions, take a walking break. Remember: you don't want to break out in a sweat; a brisk five- to ten-minute stroll should do.

- **Stretch for two to three minutes every hour or so.** You can even do a simple stretch routine while sitting in your chair.

- **Avoid sugar.** Sure, those sweet rolls, doughnuts, and cookies often found at conferences taste great but they provide only a short-term energy boost. In the long run, the sweets will act as a depressant.

- **Limit caffeine and alcohol.** These drinks dehydrate you and limit your ability to focus.

- **Drink water—lots of it.** Take a water bottle with you and fill it regularly.

Source: Rieva Lesonsky, *365 Tips to Boost Your Entrepreneurial IQ.*

Section 12

Taking Care of Your Mind and Heart

Tips for When You're Losing Your Enthusiasm

Remember how motivated you were before you started your business? Enthusiasm often wanes as new businesses fight to get established. But there are ways to rekindle your entrepreneurial fire.

1. Create a motivating office environment. Surround yourself with positive reminders of how far you've come.

2. Give speeches. Sharing your story with others can refresh your spirits, and you may even learn a thing or two.

3. Surround yourself with positive people. Avoid those toxic people who drain you and poison your attitude.

4. Don't forget to reward yourself. Create deadlines, offer yourself an incentive to help sweeten the pot, and make sure you take the time to celebrate your victory.

Source: Rieva Lesonsky, *365 Tips to Boost Your Entrepreneurial IQ.*

Tips for Rekindling the Entrepreneurial Fire

Sometimes even the most enthusiastic entrepreneur needs a boost. When you feel the fire in your gut start to flicker, try these tips from sales and motivational guru, Barry Farber:

- Make a commitment. If you tell yourself you're simply not going to fail, then you'll stop trying to find excuses to quit.

- Never stop learning. Whether you prefer to read, listen, or watch, you should always seek more information. Use books, audiotapes and CDs, videos, and, of course, your computer to stretch your imagination and challenge your knowledge.

- Accentuate the positive. Hang out only with positive people. Negative people tend to douse your own enthusiasm; you can't afford to be brought down.

- Follow the golden rule. If you're there for other people, chances are they'll be there for you. Building and maintaining strong relationships is key to most successful entrepreneurs.

Source: Rieva Lesonsky, *365 Tips to Boost Your Entrepreneurial IQ.*

SCORE's Five Tips for Renewing Yourself as a Leader

1. Take a time-out each day. Put a "Gone Thinking" sign on your door and don't let anyone disturb you.

Section 12

2. Pursue hobbies and interests outside your business. They'll provide relaxation and may inspire creative ideas that you can feed back into the business.

3. Take a vacation or a sabbatical. (But first, make sure you leave the company in good hands!)

4. Spend time with your family. Kids provide a refreshing perspective.

5. Do something you've always wanted to do but never did—learn to build a house, take a course in acting.

Source: SCORE, www.score.org/business_tips.html.

SCORE's Five Tips on Knowing When You're Getting Stale

1. If you've been running your business ten years or more, it's probably time for fresh leadership. Consider bumping yourself up to chair and getting a new CEO.

2. Recognize that fatigue and boredom are signs you've been at the helm too long.

3. Answer honestly: Are you resistant to new ideas and risks? It so, you may be impeding your company's progress.

4. Ask yourself if you are still growing and learning. If not, that's another sign of personal stagnation as a leader.

5. If you think you're becoming too set in your views, surround yourself with people who challenge your thinking.

Source: SCORE, www.score.org/5_tips_l_8.html.

Section 12

Chapter 79

Getting the Most from Your Time and Effort

Section 12

Six Tips for Making the Most of Your Time

What do all entrepreneurs have in common? Too much to do and not enough time to do it all. Here are some smart tips to help you make the most of your time.

1. At the start of the week, try to forecast any problems that might arise and come up with a tentative plan to deal with them.

2. Each morning, ask yourself what tasks you absolutely must accomplish that day and focus on these objectives.

3. Realize that you are in control of your schedule. Don't let other people get you off track.

4. Plan ahead. Try to piggyback some tasks and group other activities.

5. Don't forget to take a break. You'll accomplish much more if you are mentally refreshed.

6. Most important, learn to say no! You have to realize sometimes you just can't do it all.

Source: Rieva Lesonsky, *365 Tips to Boost Your Entrepreneurial IQ.*

SCORE's Five Tips for Stopping the Work Pile-Up

1. Discard old magazines, books, and articles. The information is probably stale by now anyway.

2. Maintain a list of sources (actual and potential) by topic. If you need the information again, you can contact your source and get updated information.

3. Minimize duplicates of documents. Keep the original in a plastic sleeve to prevent damage and one copy on hand for easy circulation.

4. Keep files current. Retain only the final version of letters and proposals. After all, the old versions primarily contained material you decided not to use!

5. Streamline supplies. Get rid of bulky, space-taking supplies you don't use. Post a list of basic supplies on the inside drawer or cabinet door to remind you of what you do need.

Source: SCORE, www.score.org/business_tips.html.

SCORE's Five Tips for Being More Efficient

1. Don't start your office organizing by shopping for containers. Survey what files and books you need to store, measure them, then go to the store.

2. File, act, or toss papers and e-mails instead of letting them pile high on your desk. You should be able to make a decision immediately as papers cross your desk.

3. Take advantage of electronic devices such as e-mail, PDAs, and database file management to categorize work.

4. Choose the calendar system that's best for your organizational style, and stick with it. If it is computer-based, back up, back up, back up!

5. Manage your time ruthlessly. In a sense, it is what you are selling.

Source: SCORE, www.score.org/business_tips.html.

Memory-Enhancing Techniques

How's your ... umm ... memory? Are you on top of things, or are you starting to forget what you easily used to remember? Memory expert Harry Lorayne offers these memory-enhancing techniques:

- **Write it down.** Get your thoughts on paper or in your computer. Making lists allows you to focus on more important tasks and gives you a record of what you need to do.

- **Use technology.** Leave yourself voice-mail messages. Try a personal digital assistant to help you keep track of phone numbers, schedules, and lists.

- **Use word associations.** This is particularly helpful if you forget names. Associate the name with something unrelated so one thing reminds you of another, like favorite sports teams.

- **Listen carefully.** Perhaps you think your memory's slipping, while in reality you simply weren't paying attention.

- **Relax.** Don't feel guilty when you forget. Once you relax, you'll likely jog your memory.

Source: Rieva Lesonsky, *365 Tips to Boost Your Entrepreneurial IQ.*

Section 12

SCORE's Five Tips for Managing Yourself

1. Recognize when you've outrun your abilities. When one entrepreneur saw that her skills were not adequate to manage her company, she hired a president to handle day-to-day operations.

2. Get a CEO coach. Skilled consultants can help you learn how to take your company to the next level. SCORE can help.

3. Open yourself to being transformed. Listen, really listen, to employees. Let go of old notions of leadership (managing by fear, for example).

4. Be self-aware. Many business owners say self-awareness is essential to understanding what leadership style works for you.

5. Be a servant leader. Consider it your responsibility to serve employees and customers.

Source: SCORE, www.score.org/5_tips_1_9.html.

Buying a Business and Franchising

Chapter 80

Buying a Business

Section
13

Pros and Cons When Buying a Business

The pros of buying a business include:

- **Time savings and reduced risk.** Buying a business will reduce your overall risk by eliminating many of the tasks associated with starting a business from scratch. For instance, when you buy an established business, operational practices, supplier relationships, distribution channels, and key personnel have already been established, so you save time and money.

- **Easier planning.** Since you are buying a business with a cash flow, it will be much easier for you to project how much you will make in the future.

The cons of buying a business include:

- **Reduced reward.** With reduced risk comes reduced reward. Available cash flow will be burdened by the debt you must incur to buy the business.

- **Possible problems.** Always make certain that you are not inheriting any problems when you buy a business. Ask why the seller is selling. Has the company declined in revenue? If so, why? Are there personal reasons why it is necessary to sell the business now (e.g., divorce, health, etc.)? What marketplace changes may be affecting the business in the near future?

Source: American Women's Economic Development Corporation, "Buying a Business—Pros and Cons," www.sba.gov/test/wbc/docs/starting/buy.html.

Checklist for Buying a Business

❏ Why does the current owner want to sell the business?

❏ Does the business have high potential for future growth, or will its sales decline?

❏ If the business is in decline, will you be able to save it and make it successful?

❏ Is the business in sound financial condition? Have you seen audited year-end financial statements for the business? Have you reviewed the most recent statements? Have you reviewed the business's tax returns for the past five years?

❏ Have you seen copies of all of the business's current contracts?

❏ Is the business now, or has it been, under investigation by any government agency? If so, what is the status of any current investigation? What were the results of any past investigation?

❏ Is the business currently involved in a lawsuit, or has it ever been involved in a lawsuit? If so what is the status or the results?

❏ Does the business have any debts or liens against it? If so, what are they for and for how much?

❏ What percentages of the business's accounts are past due?

❏ How much does the business write off for bad debts?

❏ How many customers does the business serve on a regular basis?

❏ Who makes up the market for this business? Where are the customers located?

❏ Do sales fluctuate with the season?

❏ Does any single customer account for a large portion of the sales volume? If so, would the business be able to survive if it lost that customer?

❏ How does the business market its products or services? Does its competition use the same methods? If not, what methods does the competition use? How are they successful?

❏ Does the business have exclusive rights to market any particular products or service? If so, how has is it obtained this exclusivity? Is it making the best possible use of this exclusivity? Do you have written proof that the current business owner can transfer this exclusivity to you?

❏ Does the business hold patents for any of its products? Which ones? What percentage of gross sales do they represent? Would the sale of the business include the patents?

❏ Are the business supplies, merchandise, and other materials available from several suppliers, or are there only a handful that can meet the business's need? If the business lost its current supplier, what impact would that loss have on the business? Would it be able to find substitute goods for appropriate price and quality?

❏ Are any of the business products in danger of becoming obsolete or going out of style? Is it a fad business?

❏ What is the business's market share?

❏ What competition does the business face? How can the business compete successfully? Have the business's competitors changed recently? Have any of them gone out of business?

❏ Does the business have all of the equipment you think is necessary? Would you need to add or update any of the equipment?

❏ What is the business's current inventory worth? Would you be able to use any of this inventory, or is it inconsistent with your intended product line?

❏ How many employees does the business have? What are their positions?

❏ Does the business pay its employees high wages, or are the wages average or low?

❏ What benefits does the employer offer to their employees?

❏ Does the business experience high turnover? If so, why?

Section
13

❏ How long have the top managers been with the company?

❏ Will the change in ownership change the personnel?

❏ What employees are most important to the company?

❏ Do any of the business employees belong to any unions? If so, have they held any strikes? How long did the strikes last?

Source: Andi Axman, *Entrepreneur Magazine's Ultimate Small Business Advisor.*

Advice on Financing the Purchase of a Business

If you are short on cash and you want to buy a business, try these alternatives for financing your purchase:

- **Use the seller's assets.** As soon as you buy the business you will own the assets, so why not use them for financing? Make a list of all the assets you're buying and approach banks, finance companies, and factors.

- **Bank on purchase orders.** Factors, finance companies, and banks will lend money on receivables. Finance companies and banks will lend money on inventory. Equipment can also be sold and then leased back from equipment leasing companies.

- **Buy co-op.** Try and find someone to buy the business with you. An option is to ask the seller for a list of the people who were interested in buying the business and ask them to buy into the business as an investment. Be sure to write up a partnership agreement so they don't get the wrong idea and try to take the business from you.

- **Use an employee stock ownership plan (ESOP).** ESOPs offer you a way to get capital immediately by selling stock in the business to employees.

- **Lease with an option to buy.** Some sellers will let you lease a business with an option to buy. You make a down payment, become a minority stockholder, and operate the business as if it were your own.

- **Assume liabilities or decline receivables.** Reduce the sales price by either assuming the business's liabilities or having the seller keep the receivables.

Source: Rieva Lesonsky, *Start Your Own Business.*

Ten Commandments for Buying a Business

1. **Pay for the past, consider the present, but buy it for the future!** The past financials will help determine the purchase price, but they do not guarantee what the business will look like in the future. You must evaluate the business for what it can expect to provide you with after you buy it.

2. **Buy a good business and make it great!** All good businesses possess certain common features.

3. **Ingredients are nothing without a recipe.** Can you put all parts of the business together after the purchase into one cohesive unit poised for growth—and at what cost?

4. **Fall in love with the profit, not the product!** Many people get emotional about buying a business, which clouds their judgment. You must remain objective!

5. **Do what you do best and you'll manage the rest.** Make certain that you already possess what the business really needs.

6. **Put technology to work.** In order to grow any business, you must take advantage of technology. Can the business be put on "cruise control"? Can the business improve its systems and run on its own so you can focus your attention on driving the profits? Where can you access the technology and what are the costs?

7. **Determine what holds "the gold."** Nearly all businesses possess certain components that the current owner has not exploited.

8. **Make sure that the business has the essentials.** There are three personal things that every business must possess:

   - You must be able to explain it in simple terms to others.
   - You must be able to explain it with great enthusiasm.
   - You must be very proud of the business.

9. **Evaluate and identify what's not perfect yet.** No business is perfect. Every business needs attention. Sometimes the smallest improvements yield the greatest results.

10. **Think in terms of what it's worth to *you*.** Only you can truly evaluate the benefits of any venture.

Source: Diomo Corporation, "The Ten Commandments," www.diomo.com/-View#2.

Four Steps to Take Before Buying a Business

Step 1: Educate and prepare yourself fully for each stage of the buying process.

Step 2: Determine with absolute certainty what type of business is right for you and then focus your search strictly on businesses that make sense.

Step 3: Negotiate all of the details to ensure that you put together a deal that makes sense today and down the road.

Step 4: Investigate every aspect of the business for sale, the industry, the customers, the financials, the suppliers, the employees, and the competition to be sure that you learn everything before you buy!

Source: Diomo Corporation, www.diomo.com/index.asp?cat=excite.

# Chapter 81

Finding the Best Franchises

Top 50 New Franchises for 2006

1. Geeks on Call America
www.geeksoncallfranchise.com
On-site computer support services
Start-up costs: $53.4K–82.2K

2. Moe's Southwest Grill
www.moes.com
Quick-service fresh-Mex restaurant
Start-up costs: $350K

3. EmbroidMe
www.embroidme.com
Embroidery, screen printing, ad specialties
Start-up costs: $46.6K–222.3K

4. Chester's International LLC
www.chestersinternational.com
Quick-service chicken restaurant
Start-up costs: $98.4K–395K

5. ISold It
www.i-soldit.com
eBay drop-off stores
Start-up costs: $98.5K

6. United Shipping Solutions
www.usshipit.com
Transportation services
Start-up costs: $36K–75.5K

7. Super Wash
www.superwash.com
Coin-operated self-serve/brushless automatic
car washes
Start-up costs: $444K–1.1M

8. Handyman Matters Franchise Inc.
www.handymanmatters.com
Handyman services
Start-up costs: $59.8K–100.4K

9. Robeks Fruit Smoothies & Healthy Eats
www.rebeks.com
Fruit smoothies and healthy foods
Start-up costs: $184.5K–298.6K

10. 1-800-Water Damage
www.1800waterdamage.com
Water-damage restoration services
Start-up costs: $161K–172.5K

11. PremierGarage
www.premiergarage.com
Garage cabinetry, floor coatings, organizers
Start-up costs: $111K–396K

12. Express Tax
www.expresstaxservice.com
Tax preparation and electronic filing
Start-up costs: $13.6K–20.3K

13. Certified Restoration Dry Cleaning Network
www.restorationdrycleaning.com
Restoration dry cleaning services
Start-up costs: $37.4K–222K

14. Anytime Fitness
www.anytimefitness.com
Fitness centers
Start-up costs: $17.4K–209.3K

15. Max Muscle
www.maxmusclefranchise.com
Sports nutrition products and athletic apparel
Start-up costs: $175K

16. CHIP—The Child I.D. Program
www.chipfranchise.com
Children's ID and school safety program
Start-up costs: $23.5K–33.5K

17. Cuts Fitness for Men
www.cutsfitness.com
Circuit training for men
Start-up costs: $67.5K–104.7K

18. ComForcare Senior Services Inc.
www.comforcare.com
Nonmedical home-care services
Start-up costs: $42.5K–57.5K

19. Wireless Toyz
www.wirelsstoyz.com
Cellular phones, satellite systems, accessories
Start-up costs: $222.2K–400K

Section 13

20 QuikDrop
www.quikdropfranchise.com
eBay drop-off stores
Start-up costs: $100K

21. The Growth Coach
www.thegrowthcoach.com
Small-business coaching and mentoring
Start-up costs: $31.2K-49.4K

22. Affirmative Franchises Inc.
www.fedusa.com
Insurance and financial services
Start-up costs: $29K-74K

23. Real Living Inc.
www.realliving.com
Residential real estate
Start-up costs: $9.4K-107.5K

24 One Hour Air Conditioning & Heating
www.onehourair.com
HVAC replacement and services
Start-up costs: $31.3K-164.8K

25. CardSmart Retail Corp.
www.cardsmart.com
Card and gift stores
Start-up costs: $193.9K-263.6K

26. Mathnasium Learning Centers
www.mathnasium.com
Math learning centers
Start-up costs: $41.6K-65.2K

27. StrollerFit Inc.
www.strollerfit.com
Interactive fitness programs, classes, and products for parents and babies
Start-up costs: $3.95K-11.7K

28. Volvo Rents
www.volvorents.com
Construction equipment rentals
Start-up costs: $2M-5.2M

29. Educational Outfitters
www.educationaloutfitters.com
School uniforms
Start-up costs: $90.6K-194.7K

30. N-Hance
www.nhancefranchise.com
Wood floor and cabinet renewal system
Start-up costs: $27.5K-90.7K

31. System4
www.system4usa.com
Commercial cleaning
Start-up costs: $4.96K-22.3K

32. GarageTek Inc.
www.garagetek.com
Garage organization systems
Start-up costs: $201.5K-255K

33. Grout Doctor Global Franchise Corp.
www.groutdoctor.com
Ceramic tile grout repair and maintenance
Start-up costs: $13.3K-25.9K

34. Pump It Up
www.pumpitupparty.com
Children's party facilities
Start-up costs: $233.5K-583K

35. All About Honeymoons
www.aahfranchise.com
Travel agency specializing in honeymoons/destination weddings
Start-up costs: $11.1K-37.1K

36. Profit-Tell International
www.profit-tell.com
Audio marketing/advertising programs
Start-up costs: $30K-40.3K

37. WineStyles Inc.
www.winestyles.net
Wine store
Start-up costs: $148K-234.5K

38. Benjamin Franklin Plumbing
www.benfranklin.com
Plumbing services
Start-up costs: $44.3K-386.8K

39. Oxxo Care Cleaners
www.oxxousa.com
Dry cleaning and laundry services
Start-up costs: $224.5K-524K

40. Lyons & Wolivar Investigations
www.lwfranchise.com
Private investigation services
Start-up costs: $100K–200K

41. Instant Imprints
www.instantimprints.com
Imprinted sportswear, promotional products, signs
Start-up costs: $50.5K–187.1K

42. Liberty Fitness for Women
www.libertyfitness.com
30-minute women's fitness program
Start-up costs: $97.8K–149.6K

43. Save It Now!
www.saveitnow.com
Group buying program for businesses
Start-up costs: $77.4K–254.9K

44. National Water Surveying
www.findwellwater.com
Usable groundwater locating system
Start-up costs: $53.6K–85K

45. KidzArt
www.kidzart.com
Drawing-based fine arts educational programs
Start-up costs: $32.8K–45K

46. Abrakadoodle
www.abrakadoodle.com
Art education classes
Start-up costs: $40.7K–72.5K

47. New York NY Fresh Deli
www.nynyfreshdeli.com
Submarine sandwiches
Start-up costs: $116.8K–219.2K

48. Hometown Threads
www.hometownthreads.com
Personalized gift and retail embroidery service
Start-up costs: $165K

49. Haircolorxperts
www.hcx.com
Salons specializing in hair color
Start-up costs: $273.8K–421.2K

50. Strickland's
www.mystricklands.com
Homemade ice cream and related products
Start-up costs: $207.3K–295.8K

Source: Entrepreneur.com Franchise Zone, www.entrepreneur.com/franzone/rank/0,6584,12 -12-TP-2006-0,00.html.

Top 200 Global Franchises

Many can claim to be "king of the world," but who qualifies more than a company with 25,336 locations in 117 countries?

As we enter the 21st century, it's clear the world of international franchising has exploded. Franchises of all sizes, from all nations, and covering all industries have redefined business methods and even entire economies. A few years ago, McDonald's may have been the undisputed franchising king of the world, but today, many companies are vying for a piece of the universal crown, including Yogen Früz Worldwide, Subway, RadioShack, Snap-on Tools, and Kumon Math and Reading Centers.

These companies prove a diverse range of offer-ings can be successful in any country. Our 2000 ranking of the world's top 200 franchises includes companies representing the fast-food, cosmetics, hair-care, hotel, maintenance, and automobile-service industries, to name just a few. In the following ranking, you'll find compa-nies catering to every prospective franchisee's interest, from Jimmy John's Gourmet Sandwich Shops to Domino's Pizza, from Decorating Den Interiors to Blockbuster.

Entrepreneur International has compiled this list of the world's top 200 U.S. franchisors seeking international franchisees simply to assist you in your research. It's based on information from *Entrepreneur*'s January 2000 Franchise 500®,

Section 13

the most comprehensive list of franchise companies in existence.

This ranking is not intended to endorse, recommend, or promote any particular franchise. It's simply a tool you can use for comparisons. Before purchasing a franchise, it's crucial to conduct an in-depth, independent investigation, including visits to existing franchise locations and discussions with current franchisees as well as an attorney and an accountant.

Key: A: Africa, B: Asia, C: Australia/New Zealand, D: Canada, E: Europe (Eastern), F: Europe (Western), G: Mexico/Central America, H: Middle East, I: South America

1. McDonald's
(630) 623-5645, www.mcdonalds.com
Hamburgers, chicken, salads
franchises in the U.S./outside the U.S.:
10,678/8,929
Where seeking: worldwide

2. Yogen Früz Worldwide
(905) 479-5235, www.yogenfruz.com
Frozen yogurt and ice cream
Franchises in the U.S./outside the U.S.:
1,765/3,477
Where seeking: G, I

3. Subway
(203) 876-6688, www.subway.com
Submarine sandwiches and salads
Franchises in the U.S./outside the U.S.:
11,840/2,052
Where seeking: worldwide

4. RadioShack
(817) 415-8651, www.radioshack.com
Consumer electronics
Franchises in the U.S./outside the U.S.: 1,957/197
Where seeking: worldwide

5. Snap-on Tools
(414) 656-5088, www.snapon.com
Professional tools and equipment
Franchises in the U.S./outside the U.S.:
3,187/1,136
Where seeking: B, C, D, F

6. Kumon Math & Reading Centers
(201) 928-0044, www.kumon.com
Supplemental education
Franchises in the U.S./outside the U.S.:
1,000/23,256
Where seeking: B, C, D, E, F, G, I

7. Mail Boxes Etc.
(858) 546-7488, www.mbe.com
Postal/business/communications services
Franchises in the U.S./outside the U.S.:
3,099/712
Where seeking: worldwide

8. Domino's Pizza Inc.
(734) 668-1946, www.dominos.com
Pizza
Franchises in the U.S./outside the U.S.:
3,907/1,806
Where seeking: worldwide

9. GNC Franchising Inc.
(412) 288-2033, www.gncfranchising.com
Vitamin and nutrition stores
Franchises in the U.S./outside the U.S.:
1,289/234
Where seeking: A, B, C, D, H

10. Dunkin' Donuts
(617) 963-3942, www.dunkin-baskin-togos.com
Donuts and baked goods
Franchises in the U.S./outside the U.S.:
3,594/1,550
Where seeking: worldwide

11. ServiceMaster
(901) 684-7580, www.svm.com
Commercial/residential contract cleaning
Franchises in the U.S./outside the U.S.: 2,801/1,567
Where seeking: worldwide

12. Jani-King
(972) 991-5723, (972) 239-7706
www.janiking.com
Commercial cleaning
Franchises in the U.S./outside the U.S.:
6,018/1,432
Where seeking: worldwide

13. Blockbuster Video
(214) 854-3788, www.blockbuster.com
Videotape sales and rentals
Franchises in the U.S./outside the U.S.: 681/397
Where seeking: worldwide

14. Re/Max International Inc.
(303) 796-3884, www.remax.com
Real estate
Franchises in the U.S./outside the U.S.:
2,509/803
Where seeking: worldwide

15. Coldwell Banker Real Estate Corp.
(973) 496-5908, www.coldwellbanker.com
Real estate
Franchises in the U.S./outside the U.S.:
2,774/224
Where seeking: worldwide

16. Dairy Queen
(612) 830-0450, www.dairyqueen.com
Soft-serve dairy products and sandwiches
Franchises in the U.S./outside the U.S.:
5,027/806
Where seeking: B, D, F, G, H

17. Tim Hortons
(614) 791-4235, www.timhortons.com
Donuts and baked goods
Franchises in the U.S./outside the U.S.:
102/1,630
Where seeking: D

18. Chem-Dry
(435) 755-0021, www.chemdry.com
Carpet, drapery, and upholstery cleaning
Franchises in the U.S./outside the U.S.:
2,519/1,352
Where seeking: worldwide

19. Jazzercise Inc.
(760) 434-8958, www.jazzercise.com
Dance/exercise classes
Franchises in the U.S./outside the U.S.:
4,169/1,000
Where seeking: worldwide

20. Budget Rent A Car
(630) 955-7811, www.budget.com
Auto and truck rentals
Franchises in the U.S./outside the U.S.:
433/1,957
Where seeking: worldwide

21. Arby's Inc.
(954) 351-5222, www.arby.com
Roast beef sandwiches, chicken, subs
Franchises in the U.S./outside the U.S.: 3,001/177
Where seeking: D, F, G, H

22. TCBY Treats
(501) 688-8246, www.tcby.com
Frozen yogurt, ice cream, and sorbet
Franchises in the U.S./outside the U.S.:
2,807/226
Where seeking: worldwide

23. Jiffy Lube International Inc.
(713) 546-3656, www.jiffylube.com
Fast oil change
Franchises in the U.S./outside the U.S.: 1,390/0
Where seeking: D

24. Choice Hotels International
(301) 592-6205, www.choicehotels.com
Hotels, inns, suites, and resorts
Franchises in the U.S./outside the U.S.:
3,057/1,031
Where seeking: worldwide

25. Baskin-Robbins USA Co.
(818) 243-1429, www.dunkin-baskin-togos.com
Ice cream and yogurt
Franchises in the U.S./outside the U.S.:
2,316/1,934
Where seeking: worldwide

26. Novus Windshield Repair
(612) 944-2542, www.novuswsr.com
Windshield repair/replacement
Franchises in the U.S./outside the U.S.: 451/2,068
Where seeking: worldwide

27. Sonic Drive-In Restaurants
(405) 290-7487, www.sonicdrivein.com
Drive-in restaurant
Franchises in the U.S./outside the U.S.: 1,699/0
Where seeking: G

28. Papa John's Pizza
(502) 261-4031, www.papajohns.com
Pizza
Franchises in the U.S./outside the U.S.: 1,536/17
Where seeking: B, C, D, E, H

29. Blimpie International Inc.
(770) 980-9176, www.blimpie.com
Submarine sandwiches and salads
Franchises in the U.S./outside the U.S.: 2,043/54
Where seeking: worldwide

30. CleanNet USA Inc.
(410) 720-5307, www.cleannetusa.com
Commercial office cleaning
Franchises in the U.S./outside the U.S.: 2,042/0
Where seeking: worldwide

31. Merle Norman Cosmetics
(310) 337-2370, www.merlenorman.com
Cosmetics studios
Franchises in the U.S./outside the U.S.:
1,886/102
Where seeking: D

32. Taco Bell Corp.
(949) 863-2246, www.tacobell.com
Mexican quick-service restaurant
Franchises in the U.S./outside the U.S.:
3,541/227
Where seeking: B, C

33. KFC Corp.
(502) 874-2283, www.kfc.com
Chicken
Franchises in the U.S./outside the U.S.:
3,583/3,619
Where seeking: Worldwide

34. Super 8 Motels Inc.
(973) 496-2305, www.super8.com
Economy motels
Franchises in the U.S./outside the U.S.: 1,771/69
Where seeking: worldwide

35. Pizza Hut Inc.
(972) 338-7689, www.pizzahut.com
Pizza
Franchises in the U.S./outside the U.S.: 4,277/0
Where seeking: worldwide

36. Days Inns of America Inc.
(973) 496-7658, www.daysinn.com
Hotels and inns
Franchises in the U.S./outside the U.S.:
1,764/102
Where seeking: worldwide

37. The Medicine Shoppe
(314) 872-5500, www.medicineshoppe.com
Pharmacy
Franchises in the U.S./outside the U.S.:
1,084/193
Where seeking: worldwide

38. Thrifty Rent-A-Car System Inc.
(918) 669-2061, www.thrifty.com
Vehicle rentals, leasing, and parking
Franchises in the U.S./outside the U.S.: 540/717
Where seeking: worldwide

39. Management Recruiters International
(216) 696-6612, www.mrinet.com
Personnel placement/search/recruiting services
Franchises in the U.S./outside the U.S.: 760/150
Where seeking: A, B, C, E, F, G, H, I

40. Denny's Inc.
(864) 597-7708, www.dennys.com
Full-service family restaurant
Franchises in the U.S./outside the U.S.: 823/55
Where seeking: D, G

41. Merry Maids
(901) 537-8140, www.merrymaids.com
Residential cleaning
Franchises in the U.S./outside the U.S.: 769/396
Where seeking: worldwide

42. Church's Chicken
(770) 512-3920, www.churchs.com
Southern fried chicken and biscuits
Franchises in the U.S./outside the U.S.: 653/304
Where seeking: worldwide

43. Popeyes Chicken & Biscuits
(404) 459-4533, www.popeyes.com
Fried chicken and biscuits
Franchises in the U.S./outside the U.S.: 943/220
Where seeking: worldwide

Section 13

44. Fantastic Sams
(714) 779-3422, www.fantasticsams.com
Hair salons
Franchises in the U.S./outside the U.S.: 1,246/94
Where seeking: B, C, D, F, G

45. Supercuts
(612) 947-7301, www.supercuts.com
Family hair care
Franchises in the U.S./outside the U.S.: 812/3
Where seeking: D

46. Coverall Cleaning Concepts
(954) 492-5044, www.coverall.com
Commercial cleaning
Franchises in the U.S./outside the U.S.:
4,786/181
Where seeking: worldwide

47. Orion Food Systems Inc.
(605) 336-0141, www.orionfoodsys.com
Fast-food systems for non-traditional markets
Franchises in the U.S./outside the U.S.: 961/7
Where seeking: D, F, H

48. Rent-A-Wreck
(410) 581-1566, www.rent-a-wreck.com
Auto rentals and leasing
Franchises in the U.S./outside the U.S.: 624/24
Where seeking: A, B, C, E, F, G, H, I

49. Curves for Women
(254) 399-9731, www.curvesforwomen.com
Women's fitness and weight-loss centers
Franchises in the U.S./outside the U.S.: 701/7
Where seeking: C, D, E, F, G, I

50. Heel Quik! Inc.
(770) 933-8268, www.aquik.com
Shoe repair, clothing alterations, miscellaneous
services
Franchises in the U.S./outside the U.S.: 168/562
Where seeking: worldwide

51. The Quizno's Corp.
(720) 359-3399, www.quiznos.com
Submarine sandwiches, soups, and salads
Franchises in the U.S./outside the U.S.: 482/53
Where seeking: B, C, D, G

52. Cash Converters International
(847) 330-1660, www.cashconverters.com
Pre-owned merchandise stores
Franchises in the U.S./outside the U.S.: 12/532
Where seeking: A, B, C, D, E, F, H, I

53. Sylvan Learning Centers
(410) 843-8717, www.educate.com
Supplemental education
Franchises in the U.S./outside the U.S.: 611/54
Where seeking: worldwide

54. Minuteman Press International Inc.
(516) 249-5618, www.minuteman-press.com
Full-service printing center
Franchises in the U.S./outside the U.S.: 734/128
Where seeking: A, C, D, F

55. Sbarro
(516) 715-4183, www.sbarro.com
Quick-service Italian restaurant
Franchises in the U.S./outside the U.S.: 192/86
Where seeking: worldwide

56. Schlotzsky's Deli
(512) 236-3700, www.schlotzskys.com
Sandwiches, soups, salads, and pizza
Franchises in the U.S./outside the U.S.: 717/20
Where seeking: worldwide

57. Sign-A-Rama Inc.
(561) 478-4340, www.sign-a-rama.com
Full-service sign business
Franchises in the U.S./outside the U.S.: 91/83
Where seeking: worldwide

58. The Haagen-Dazs Shoppe Co. Inc.
(612) 330-7074, www.haagendazs.com
Ice cream and yogurt
Franchises in the U.S./outside the U.S.: 214/452
Where seeking: A, B, C, E, F, G, H, I

59. The Athlete's Foot
(770) 514-4903, www.theathletesfoot.com
Athletic footwear and related sports accessories
Franchises in the U.S./outside the U.S.: 179/279
Where seeking: worldwide

60. The Second Cup Ltd.
(416) 975-5207, www.secondcup.com

Section 13

Gourmet coffees, teas, related accessories
Franchises in the U.S./outside the U.S.: 0/377
Where seeking: worldwide

61. Jan-Pro Franchising International Inc.
(843) 399-9890, www.jan-pro.com
Commercial cleaning
Franchises in the U.S./outside the U.S.: 585/80
Where seeking: D, F, G

62. Kwik-Kopy Corp.
(281) 373-4450, www.kwikkopy.com
Printing, copying, and related services
Franchises in the U.S./outside the U.S.: 367/406
Where seeking: A, C, D, F, G, H, I

63. Furniture Medic
(901) 820-8660, www.furnituremedic.com
Furniture restoration and repair services
Franchises in the U.S./outside the U.S.: 468/126
Where seeking: worldwide

64. One Hour Martinizing Dry Cleaning
(513) 731-0818, www.martinizing.com
Dry cleaning and laundry services
Franchises in the U.S./outside the U.S.: 551/208
Where seeking: worldwide

65. Molly Maid
(734) 975-9000, www.mollymaid.com
Residential cleaning
Franchises in the U.S./outside the U.S.: 263/249
Where seeking: B, C, E, F

66. Liberty Tax Service
(757) 340-7612, www.libertytax.com
Income-tax preparation services
Franchises in the U.S./outside the U.S.: 74/213
Where seeking: D

67. Great Clips Inc.
(612) 844-3443, www.greatclipsfranchise.com
Family hair salons
Franchises in the U.S./outside the U.S.: 1,205/43
Where seeking: D

68. Maaco Auto Painting & Bodyworks
(610) 337-6176, www.maaco.com
Automotive painting and body repair
Franchises in the U.S./outside the U.S.: 504/49
Where seeking: D, G

69. Precision Tune Auto Care
(703) 777-9190, www.precisionac.com
Auto maintenance and engine performance
Franchises in the U.S./outside the U.S.: 446/118
Where seeking: worldwide

70. America's Maid Service-The Maids
(402) 558-4112, www.maids.com
Residential cleaning
Franchises in the U.S./outside the U.S.: 359/13
Where seeking: worldwide

71. Realty Executives
(602) 224-5542, www.realtyexecutives.com
Real estate with 100% commission
Franchises in the U.S./outside the U.S.: 450/39
Where seeking: worldwide

72. Fastsigns
(972) 248-8201, www.fastsigns.com
Computer-generated vinyl signs and graphics
Franchises in the U.S./outside the U.S.: 358/68
Where seeking: B, C, D, F, G, I

73. ProForma
(216) 520-8474, www.proforma.com
Commercial printing and promotional products
Franchises in the U.S./outside the U.S.: 383/28
Where seeking: D

74. Express Services Inc.
(405) 773-6442, www.expresspersonnel.com
Staffing and P.E.O. services
Franchises in the U.S./outside the U.S.: 368/25
Where seeking: A, C, D, F

75. Sir Speedy Inc.
(949) 348-5010, www.sirspeedy.com
Printing, copying, digital network
Franchises in the U.S./outside the U.S.: 640/127
Where seeking: worldwide

76. Signs Now Corp.
(941) 750-8604, www.signsnow.com
Computerized 24-hour sign-making services
Franchises in the U.S./outside the U.S.: 255/56
Where seeking: worldwide

77. Travel Network
(201) 567-4405, www.travelnetwork.com
Travel agency

Franchises in the U.S./outside the U.S.: 453/60
Where seeking: worldwide

78. Auntie Anne's Inc.
(717) 442-4139, www.auntieannes.com
Hand-rolled soft pretzels
Franchises in the U.S./outside the U.S.: 435/38
Where seeking: worldwide

79. U-Save Auto Rental of America
(601) 713-4330, www.usave.net
New and used auto rentals
Franchises in the U.S./outside the U.S.: 450/10
Where seeking: D, H

80. Hungry Howie's Pizza & Subs
(248) 414-3301, www.hungryhowies.com
Pizza, subs, and salads
Franchises in the U.S./outside the U.S.: 414/1
Where seeking: worldwide

81. Meineke Discount Mufflers
(704) 372-4826, www.meineke.com
Exhaust systems, shocks, brakes, struts
Franchises in the U.S./outside the U.S.: 852/9
Where seeking: G

82. RemedyTemp Inc.
(949) 425-7999, www.remedystaff.com
Temporary staffing services
Franchises in the U.S./outside the U.S.: 148/0
Where seeking: D

83. Candy Bouquet
(501) 375-9998, www.candybouquet.com
Designer gifts and confections
Franchises in the U.S./outside the U.S.: 319/67
Where seeking: worldwide

84. AAMCO Transmissions Inc.
(610) 617-9532, www.aamco.com
Transmission repair and services
Franchises in the U.S./outside the U.S.: 683/29
Where seeking: D

85. Play It Again Sports
(612) 520-8501, www.playitagainsports.com
New and used sporting goods
Franchises in the U.S./outside the U.S.: 551/67
Where seeking: D

85. Golden Corral Franchising
(919) 881-5252, www.goldencorralrest.com
Family steakhouse, buffet, and bakery
Franchises in the U.S./outside the U.S.: 298/2
Where seeking: G

86. Cottman Transmission Systems
(215) 643-2519, www.cottman.com
Transmission repair and services
Franchises in the U.S./outside the U.S.: 256/4
Where seeking: A, D, I

87. Togo's Eatery
(781) 963-3942, www.dunkin-baskin-togos.com
Specialty sandwiches, soups, salads, catering
Franchises in the U.S./outside the U.S.: 249/1
Where seeking: D

88. Pak Mail
(303) 957-1015, www.pakmail.com
Packaging, shipping, mailboxes
Franchises in the U.S./outside the U.S.: 318/32
Where seeking: worldwide

89. Mrs. Fields' Original Cookies Inc.
(801) 736-5970, www.mrsfields.com
Cookies and bakery products
Franchises in the U.S./outside the U.S.: 348/80
Where seeking: worldwide

90. Comet 1 Hr. Cleaners
(817) 861-4779, www.comet-cleaners.com
Dry cleaning and laundry services
Franchises in the U.S./outside the U.S.: 336/12
Where seeking: D, G

92. Century Small Business Solutions
(949) 348-5126, www.centurysmallbiz.com
Accounting and business counseling
Franchises in the U.S./outside the U.S.: 613/64
Where seeking: worldwide

93. American Leak Detection
(760) 320-1288, www.leakbusters.com
Concealed water and gas leak-detection services
Franchises in the U.S./outside the U.S.: 223/73
Where seeking: B, C, D, E, F, G, I

94. Gymboree
(650) 696-7452, www.gymboree.com

Section 13

Parent-child play program
Franchises in the U.S./outside the U.S.: 275/107
Where seeking: worldwide

95. Pillar To Post
(905) 568-8137, www.pillartopost.com
Home inspection service
Franchises in the U.S./outside the U.S.: 149/83
Where seeking: A, C, D, G

96. Color-Glo International Inc.
(612) 835-1395, www.colorglo.com
Fabric dyeing and restoration
Franchises in the U.S./outside the U.S.: 121/109
Where seeking: worldwide

97. Postal Annex+
(619) 563-9850, www.postalannex.com
Packaging, shipping, postal, business services
Franchises in the U.S./outside the U.S.: 220/0
Where seeking: worldwide

98. AmeriSpec Home Inspection Services
(901) 820-8520, www.amerispecfranchise.com
Home inspection service
Franchises in the U.S./outside the U.S.: 259/63
Where seeking: D

99. A & W Restaurants Inc.
(248) 699-2019, www.awrestaurants.com
Burgers, hot dogs, and root beer
Franchises in the U.S./outside the U.S.: 623/176
Where seeking: A, B, C, E, F, G, H, I

100. Pizza Inn Inc.
(972) 960-7208, www.pizzainn.com
Pizza, pasta, and salads
Franchises in the U.S./outside the U.S.: 437/63
Where seeking: H

101. O.P.E.N. Cleaning Systems
(602) 468-3788, www.opencs.com
Office and commercial cleaning
Franchises in the U.S./outside the U.S.: 377/0
Where seeking: worldwide

102. Radisson Hotels Worldwide
(612) 212-3400, www.radisson.com
Hotels, inns, resorts, and cruise ships
Franchises in the U.S./outside the U.S.: 222/165
Where seeking: worldwide

103. T.J. Cinnamons Ltd.
(954) 351-5282, www.tjcinnamons.com
Cinnamon rolls and gourmet bakery products
Franchises in the U.S./outside the U.S.: 338/2
Where seeking: D, E, F

104. CD Warehouse Inc.
(405) 949-2566, www.cdwarehouse.com
New and used CDs
Franchises in the U.S./outside the U.S.: 248/16
Where seeking: C, D, F, G

105. Huntington Learning Centers Inc.
(201) 261-3233, www.huntingtonlearning.com
Educational services
Franchises in the U.S./outside the U.S.: 151/0
Where seeking: D

106. AlphaGraphics Printshops
(520) 887-2850, www.alphagraphics.com
Quick printing, design, related business services
Franchises in the U.S./outside the U.S.: 265/80
Where seeking: worldwide

107. The HomeTeam Inspection Service
(513) 469-2226, www.hmteam.com
Home inspection service
Franchises in the U.S./outside the U.S.: 308/5
Where seeking: D

108. Gateway Cigar Store/Newstands
(905) 886-8904, www.gatewaynewstands.com
Newsstand and sundry store
Franchises in the U.S./outside the U.S.: 70/215
Where seeking: D

109. First Choice Haircutters
(905) 567-7000, www.firstchoice.com
Full-service family hair care
Franchises in the U.S./outside the U.S.: 12/164
Where seeking: D

110. Unishippers
(801) 487-0623, www.unishippers.com
Discounted transportation services
Franchises in the U.S./outside the U.S.: 295/2
Where seeking: D, F

Section 13

111. New Horizons Computer Learning Centers
(714) 432-7676, www.newhorizons.com
Computer training and support
Franchises in the U.S./outside the U.S.: 116/83
Where seeking: worldwide

112. Mr. Rooter
(254) 745-5098, www.mrrooter.com
Plumbing, sewer, and drain cleaning services
Franchises in the U.S./outside the U.S.: 181/84
Where seeking: worldwide

113. Bennigan's Grill & Tavern
(972) 588-5806, www.mrg.net
Casual-theme restaurant
Franchises in the U.S./outside the U.S.: 48/9
Where seeking: worldwide

114. Moto Photo Inc.
(937) 854-0140, www.motophoto.com
Film processing and portrait studios
Franchises in the U.S./outside the U.S.: 289/91
Where seeking: worldwide

115. Mr. Electric
(254) 745-5098, www.dwyergroup.com
Electrical services and repairs contracting
Franchises in the U.S./outside the U.S.: 78/30
Where seeking: worldwide

116. Kitchen Tune-Up
(605) 225-1371, www.kitchentuneup.com
Wood restoration, cabinet refacing, custom cabinets
Franchises in the U.S./outside the U.S.: 314/7
Where seeking: C, D

117. Home Instead Senior Care
(402) 498-5757, www.homeinstead.com
Nonmedical senior-care services
Franchises in the U.S./outside the U.S.: 197/0
Where seeking: worldwide

118. Coustic-Glo International Inc.
(612) 835-1395, www.causticglo.com
Ceiling and wall maintenance and building restoration
Franchises in the U.S./outside the U.S.: 143/55
Where seeking: worldwide

119. Country Inns & Suites by Carlson
(612) 212-1338, www.countryinns.com
Hotels
Franchises in the U.S./outside the U.S.: 162/21
Where seeking: worldwide

120. Fastframe USA Inc.
(805) 498-8983, www.fastframe.com
Custom picture framing and art sales
Franchises in the U.S./outside the U.S.: 177/10
Where seeking: B, C, D, F, G, H, I

121. Great Earth Vitamins
(909) 941-3472, www.greatearth.com
Vitamins and nutritional supplements
Franchises in the U.S./outside the U.S.: 135/8
Where seeking: worldwide

122. Gloria Jean's Gourmet Coffees
(831) 633-3726, www.greatbeans.com
Gourmet coffee, teas, and accessories
Franchises in the U.S./outside the U.S.: 213/36
Where seeking: B, C, E, F, G, H, I

123. Ziebart
(248) 588-1444, www.ziebart.com
Auto appearance services and accessories
Franchises in the U.S./outside the U.S.: 236/217
Where seeking: worldwide

124. The Mad Science Group
(514) 344-6695, www.madscience.org
Science activities for children
Franchises in the U.S./outside the U.S.: 6/31
Where seeking: worldwide

125. Once Upon A Child
(612) 520-8510, www.ouac.com
Children's clothing, equipment, furniture, toys
Franchises in the U.S./outside the U.S.: 203/16
Where seeking: D

126. PostNet Postal & Business Services
(702) 792-7115, www.postnet.net
Postal, business, and communications centers
Franchises in the U.S./outside the U.S.: 275/218
Where seeking: worldwide

127. HouseMaster
(732) 469-7405, www.housemaster.com

Home inspection service
Franchises in the U.S./outside the U.S.: 274/35
Where seeking: worldwide

128. Pretzelmaker Inc.
(801) 736-5970, www.mrsfields.com
Gourmet pretzels
Franchises in the U.S./outside the U.S.: 170/39
Where seeking: D

129. Microtel Inn & Suites
(404) 235-7460, www.microtelinn.com
Budget hotels
Franchises in the U.S./outside the U.S.: 161/1
Where seeking: worldwide

130. Sunbelt Business Brokers Network
(843) 853-4135, www.sunbeltnetwork.com
Business brokerage
Franchises in the U.S./outside the U.S.: 207/11
Where seeking: worldwide

131. Great Harvest Franchising
(406) 683-5537, www.greatharvest.com
Specialty whole-wheat bakery
Franchises in the U.S./outside the U.S.: 136/0
Where seeking: D

132. Music-Go-Round
(612) 520-8501, www.musicgoround.com
Musical instruments and sound equipment
Franchises in the U.S./outside the U.S.: 63/0
Where seeking: D

133. Handyman Connection
(513) 771-6439, www.handymanconnection.com
Home repairs and remodeling services
Franchises in the U.S./outside the U.S.: 80/20
Where seeking: D, G

134. Maid To Perfection
(410) 944-6469, www.maidtoperfectioncorp.com
Residential and light commercial cleaning
Franchises in the U.S./outside the U.S.: 152/2
Where seeking: D

135. Gingiss Formalwear
(630) 620-8840, www.gingiss.com
Men's formal wear rentals and sales
Franchises in the U.S./outside the U.S.: 198/0
Where seeking: D, G

136. The Great Steak & Potato Co.
(513) 896-3750, www.thegreatsteak.com
Cheesesteaks, grilled sandwiches, and salads
Franchises in the U.S./outside the U.S.: 167/17
Where seeking: worldwide

137. SuperGlass Windshield Repair
(407) 240-3266, www.sgwr.com
Windshield repair
Franchises in the U.S./outside the U.S.: 75/17
Where seeking: B, G, I

138. Knights Franchise Systems Inc.
(973) 496-1359, www.knightsinn.com
Hotels
Franchises in the U.S./outside the U.S.: 235/1
Where seeking: worldwide

139. Rainbow International Carpet Care/Restoration
(254) 745-5098, www.rainbowintl.com
Indoor restoration and cleaning
Franchises in the U.S./outside the U.S.: 295/131
Where seeking: worldwide

140. American Speedy Printing Centers
(248) 614-3719, www.americanspeedy.com
Printing center
Franchises in the U.S./outside the U.S.: 354/62
Where seeking: B, D

141. House Doctors
(513) 469-2226, www.housedoctors.com
Handyman services, home repairs
Franchises in the U.S./outside the U.S.: 142/1
Where seeking: D, G, I

142. Wild Birds Unlimited
(317) 571-7110, www.wbu.com
Bird-feeding supplies and nature gift items
Franchises in the U.S./outside the U.S.: 236/14
Where seeking: D

143. Stork News of America Inc.
(910) 426-2473, www.storknewsusa.com
Newborn announcement services and products
Franchises in the U.S./outside the U.S.: 131/2
Where seeking: D

144. Hilton Inns Inc.
(310) 205-7655, www.hilton.com
Hotels and resorts
Franchises in the U.S./outside the U.S.: 201/8
Where seeking: D, G

145. The Interface Financial Group
(905) 475-8688, www.interfacefinancial.com
Invoice discounting
Franchises in the U.S./outside the U.S.: 17/43
Where seeking: worldwide

146. Crestcom International Ltd.
(303) 267-8207, www.crestcom.com
Management, sales, office personnel training
Franchises in the U.S./outside the U.S.: 34/82
Where seeking: worldwide

147. Craters & Freighters
(303) 393-7644, www.cratersandfreighters.com
Specialty freight-handling service
Franchises in the U.S./outside the U.S.: 53/0
Where seeking: worldwide

148. Atlanta Bread Co.
(770) 444-1991, www.atlantabread.com
Bakery/cafe
Franchises in the U.S./outside the U.S.: 78/0
Where seeking: B, C, D, F, G, H, I

149. Help U-Sell Real Estate
(516) 364-9650, www.helpusell.net
Real estate
Franchises in the U.S./outside the U.S.: 168/0
Where seeking: worldwide

150. Ponderosa Steakhouse
(972) 588-5806,
www.metromediarestaurants.com
Family steakhouse
Franchises in the U.S./outside the U.S.: 304/47
Where seeking: worldwide

151. Maid Brigade USA/Minimaid Canada
(770) 391-9092, www.maidbrigade.com
Residential cleaning
Franchises in the U.S./outside the U.S.: 166/81
Where seeking: worldwide

152. Dr. Vinyl & Associates Ltd.
(816) 525-6333, www.drvinyl.com
Mobile vinyl, leather repair, windshield repair
Franchises in the U.S./outside the U.S.: 127/3
Where seeking: worldwide

153. Swisher Hygiene Franchise Corp.
(704) 364-1202, www.swisheronline.com
Restroom hygiene services
Franchises in the U.S./outside the U.S.: 97/17
Where seeking: worldwide

154. Wingate Inn International Inc.
(973) 496-1354, www.wingateinns.com
Hotels
Franchises in the U.S./outside the U.S.: 70/0
Where seeking: worldwide

155. Metal Supermarkets International
(905) 459-3690, www.metalsupermarkets.com
Retail metal supplier
Franchises in the U.S./outside the U.S.: 21/34
Where seeking: D, F

156. Jimmy John's Sandwich Shops
(847) 888-7070, www.jimmyjohns.com
Gourmet sandwiches
Franchises in the U.S./outside the U.S.: 50/10
Where seeking: worldwide

157. The BrickKicker Home Inspection
(630) 420-2270, www.brickkicker.com
Home and property inspection service
Franchises in the U.S./outside the U.S.: 115/0
Where seeking: D

158. Altracolor Systems
(504) 454-7233, www.altracolor.com
Mobile auto painting and plastic repair
Franchises in the U.S./outside the U.S.: 86/0
Where seeking: D, G, I

159. Pizzeria Uno Chicago Bar & Grill
(617) 218-5376, www.pizzeriauno.com
Full-service restaurant
Franchises in the U.S./outside the U.S.: 73/7
Where seeking: B, C, D, F, G, H, I

160. Bath Fitter
(802) 862-7976, www.bathfitter.com

Section 13

Acrylic bathtub liners, bath and shower walls
Franchises in the U.S./outside the U.S.: 52/16
Where seeking: D

161. Cinnabon Inc.
(770) 353-3093, www.cinnabon.com
Cinnamon rolls
Franchises in the U.S./outside the U.S.: 152/16
Where seeking: worldwide

162. Rocky Mountain Chocolate Factory
(970) 259-5895, www.rmcf.com
Chocolate and confections
Franchises in the U.S./outside the U.S.: 159/26
Where seeking: B, D

163. Cash Plus Inc.
(714) 731-2099, www.cashplusinc.com
Check cashing and related services
Franchises in the U.S./outside the U.S.: 46/1
Where seeking: D

164. Children's Orchard
(734) 994-9323, www.childorch.com
Children's products resale stores
Franchises in the U.S./outside the U.S.: 88/0
Where seeking: D

165. Howard Johnson International Inc.
(973) 428-7307, www.hojo.com
Hotels
Franchises in the U.S./outside the U.S.: 418/71
Where seeking: worldwide

166. The Steak Escape
(614) 224-6460, www.steakescape.com
Grilled sandwiches, baked potatoes, and salads
Franchises in the U.S./outside the U.S.: 146/5
Where seeking: A, B, C, D, E, F, G, I

167. Fabutan Sun Tan Studios
(403) 640-2116, www.fabutan.com
Tanning salon
Franchises in the U.S./outside the U.S.: 1/70
Where seeking: D

168. The Fourth R
(425) 828-0192, www.fourthr.com
Computer training solutions
Franchises in the U.S./outside the U.S.: 63/148
Where seeking: worldwide

169. Heaven's Best Carpet/Upholstery Cleaning
(208) 359-1236, www.heavensbest.com
Carpet and upholstery cleaning
Franchises in the U.S./outside the U.S.: 380/8
Where seeking: worldwide

170. Decorating Den Interiors
(301) 272-1520, www.decoratingden.com
Interior decorating services
Franchises in the U.S./outside the U.S.: 435/88
Where seeking: D, F

171. The Taco Maker
(801) 476-9788, www.tacomaker.com
Mexican fast food
Franchises in the U.S./outside the U.S.: 134/5
Where seeking: worldwide

172. Charley's Steakery
(614) 847-8110, www.charleyssteakery.com
Grilled subs, fries, and salads
Franchises in the U.S./outside the U.S.: 61/8
Where seeking: worldwide

173. Wetzel's Pretzels
(626) 432-6904, www.wetzels.com
Hand-rolled soft pretzels
Franchises in the U.S./outside the U.S.: 53/28
Where seeking: worldwide

174. High Touch-High Tech
(954) 755-1242, www.hightouch-hightech.com
Science activities for schools and kids' parties
Franchises in the U.S./outside the U.S.: 62/7
Where seeking: worldwide

175. National Property Inspections Inc.
(402) 333-9780, www.npiweb.com
Home and commercial property inspections
Franchises in the U.S./outside the U.S.: 97/2
Where seeking: D

176. Country Clutter
(707) 451-0410, www.countryclutter.com
Country gifts, collectibles, and home decor
Franchises in the U.S./outside the U.S.: 42/0
Where seeking: D

177. Big Apple Bagels
(773) 380-6183, www.babholdings.com

Section 13

Bagels, sandwiches, gourmet coffee, muffins
Franchises in the U.S./outside the U.S.: 123/8
Where seeking: worldwide

178. Sonitrol
(703) 684-6612, www.sonitrol.com
Electronic security services
Franchises in the U.S./outside the U.S.: 165/10
Where seeking: D

179. Talking Book World
(248) 945-9606, www.talkingbookworld.com
Audiobook rentals and sales
Franchises in the U.S./outside the U.S.: 18/0
Where seeking: D

180. Aire Serv Heating/Air Conditioning Inc.
(254) 745-2546, www.dwyergroup.com/aireserv
Heating and air conditioning services
Franchises in the U.S./outside the U.S.: 54/2
Where seeking: B, C, D, F, G, H, I

181. Pizza Factory Inc.
(559) 683-6879, www.pizzafactoryinc.com
Pizza, pasta, and sandwiches
Franchises in the U.S./outside the U.S.: 98/1
Where seeking: worldwide

182. Norwalk—The Furniture Idea
(440) 871-6057, www.norwalkfurniture.com
Custom furniture and accessories
Franchises in the U.S./outside the U.S.: 73/6
Where seeking: D

183. Pressed4Time Inc.
(978) 443-0709, www.pressed4time.com
Dry cleaning pickup/delivery and shoe repair
Franchises in the U.S./outside the U.S.: 107/26
Where seeking: D

184. Payless Car Rental System Inc.
(727) 323-3529, www.800-payless.com
Auto rentals and sales
Franchises in the U.S./outside the U.S.: 61/21
Where seeking: worldwide

185. Carvel
(860) 677-8211, www.carvel.com
Soft-serve ice cream and ice cream cakes
Franchises in the U.S./outside the U.S.: 417/31
Where seeking: B

186. Mister Money-USA Inc.
(970) 490-2099, www.mistermoney.com
Pawnshops
Franchises in the U.S./outside the U.S.: 25/0
Where seeking: G

187. Paper Warehouse Franchising Inc.
(612) 936-9800, www.paperwarehouse.com
Discount party supplies and cards
Franchises in the U.S./outside the U.S.: 45/0
Where seeking: D

188. Hawthorn
(404) 235-7460, www.hawthorn.com
Extended-stay suite hotels
Franchises in the U.S./outside the U.S.: 71/1
Where seeking: worldwide

189. Tutor Time Child Care Systems Inc.
(561) 994-2778, www.tutortime.com
Child-care learning center
Franchises in the U.S./outside the U.S.: 118/2
Where seeking: worldwide

190. Crown Trophy Inc.
(914) 963-0391, www.crownfranchise.com
Award and recognition items
Franchises in the U.S./outside the U.S.: 65/0
Where seeking: D

191. Worldsites
(905) 678-7242, www.worldsites.net
Internet services
Franchises in the U.S./outside the U.S.: 29/203
Where seeking: worldwide

192. Lady of America
(954) 492-1187, www.ladyofamerica.com
Fitness centers
Franchises in the U.S./outside the U.S.: 214/2
Where seeking: worldwide

193. Keller Williams Realty Network
(512) 328-1433, www.kellerwilliams.com
Real estate
Franchises in the U.S./outside the U.S.: 88/1
Where seeking: D

194. Faces
(905) 569-8998, www.faces-cosmetics.com
Cosmetics

Section 13

Franchises in the U.S./outside the U.S.: 0/79
Where seeking: worldwide

195. Cousins Subs
(414) 253-7705, www.cousinssubs.com
Hot and cold subs, salads, soups, and desserts
Franchises in the U.S./outside the U.S.: 106/0
Where seeking: D

196. Atwork Personnel Services
(423) 674-8778, www.atworkpersonnel.com
Temporary-help and permanent-placement services
Franchises in the U.S./outside the U.S.: 52/0
Where seeking: worldwide

197. Damon's International
(614) 538-2517, www.damons.com
BBQ ribs and casual dining
Franchises in the U.S./outside the U.S.: 111/2
Where seeking: worldwide

198. Shred-It America Inc.
(905) 855-0466, www.shredit.com
Mobile paper shredding and recycling
Franchises in the U.S./outside the U.S.: 38/9
Where seeking: worldwide

199. Tropik Sun Fruit & Nut
(847) 234-3856, www.tropiksun.com
Candy, nuts, popcorn, gifts
Franchises in the U.S./outside the U.S.: 106/0
Where seeking: D

200. Critter Control Inc.
(231) 947-9440, www.crittercontrol.com
Urban and rural wildlife management
Franchises in the U.S./outside the U.S.: 71/1
Where seeking: D

Source: Liza Potter, "America's Top 200 Global Franchises," www.entrepreneur.com/article/0,4621,232857-2,00.html.

Top Fastest-Growing Franchises in 2005

1. Curves
100 Ritchie Road
Waco, TX 76712
Phone: (800) 848-1096, (254) 399-9285
Fax: (254) 399-9731
www.buycurves.com
Began in 1992, franchising since 1995
Headquarters size: 50 employees
Franchising department: 40 employees
U.S. franchises: 7,860
Canadian franchises: 726
Other foreign franchises: 800
Costs:
Total investment: $36.4K–42.9K
Franchise fee: $39.9K
Ongoing royalty fee: 5%
Term of agreement: 5 years, renewable
Qualifications:
Net worth requirement: $75K
Cash liquidity requirement: $50K
Business Experience:
- Financially stable

2. Subway
325 Bic Drive
Milford, CT 06460
Phone: (800) 888-4848, (203) 877-4281
Fax: (203) 783-7329
www.subway.com
Began in 1965, franchising since 1974
Headquarters size: 650 employees
Franchising department: 20 employees
U.S. franchises: 18,280
Canadian franchises: 2,032
Other foreign franchises: 2,742
Costs:
Total investment: $70K–220K
Express/kiosk option available
Franchise fee: $12.5K
Ongoing royalty fee: 8%
Term of agreement: 20 years, renewable
Qualifications:
Net worth requirement: $30K–90K
Cash liquidity requirement: $30K–90K
Business Experience:
- General business experience

3. Jan-Pro Franchising International Inc.
Commercial cleaning
383 Strand Industrial Drive
Little River, SC 29566
Phone: (866) 355-1064
Fax: (843) 399-9890
www.jan-pro.com
janpro1@aol.com
Headquarters size: 10 employees
Franchising department: 6 employees
U.S. franchises: 3,940
Canadian franchises: 188
Costs:
Total investment: $5K-50K+
Franchise fee: $950-14K
Ongoing royalty fee: 8%
Term of agreement: 10 years, renewable
Qualifications:
Net worth requirement: $1K-14K+
Cash liquidity requirement: $1K+
Business Experience:
- Management skills

4. Coverall Cleaning Concepts
Commercial cleaning services
5201 Congress Avenue, #275
Boca Raton, FL 33487
Phone: (800) 537-3371, (561) 922-2500
Fax: (561) 922-2424
www.coverall.com
Began in 1985, franchising since 1985
Headquarters size: 73 employees
Franchising department: 185 employees
U.S. franchises: 7,992
Canadian franchises: 201
Other foreign franchises: 258
Costs:
Total investment: $6.3K-35.9K
Franchise fee: $6K-32.2K
Ongoing royalty fee: 5%
Term of agreement: 20 years, renewable
Qualifications:
Net worth requirement: $6K-32K
Cash liquidity requirement: $1.5K

5. Quizno's Franchise Co.
Quick-service sandwich shop
1475 Lawrence Street, #400

Denver, CO 80202
Phone: (720) 359-3300
Fax: (720) 359-3399
www.quiznos.com
Began in 1981, franchising since 1983
Headquarters size: 300 employees
Franchising department: 15 employees
U.S. franchises: 2,961
Canadian franchises: 289
Other foreign franchises: 50
Costs:
Total investment: $208.4K-243.8K
Franchise fee: $25K
Ongoing royalty fee: 7%
Term of agreement: 15 years, renewable
Renewal fee: $1K
Qualifications:
Net worth requirement: $125K
Cash liquidity requirement: $60K
Business Experience:
- Industry experience
- General business experience

6. Jackson Hewitt Tax Service
7 Sylvan Way
Parsippany, NJ 07054
Phone: (800) 475-2904
Fax: (973) 496-2760
www.jacksonhewitt.com
franchisedev@jtax.com
Began in 1960, franchising since 1986
Headquarters size: 322 employees
Franchising department: 19 employees
U.S. franchises: 4,330
Costs:
Total investment: $51.7K-85.4K
Express/kiosk option available
Franchise fee: $25K
Ongoing royalty fee: 15%
Term of agreement: 10 years, renewable
Qualifications:
Net worth requirement: $100K-200K
Cash liquidity requirement: $50K

7. Jani-King
Janitorial Services
16885 Dallas Parkway
Addison, TX 75001

Section 13

Phone: (800) 552-5264
Fax: (972) 991-5723, (972) 239-7706
www.janiking.com
info@janiking.com
Began in 1969, franchising since 1974
Headquarters size: 100 employees
Franchising department: 100 employees
U.S. franchises: 9,023
Canadian franchises: 540
Other foreign franchises: 1,369
Costs:
Total investment: $11.3K–34.1K+
Franchise fee: $8.6K–16.3K+
Ongoing royalty fee: 10%
Qualifications:
Net worth requirement: Varies
Cash liquidity requirement: Varies

8. Liberty Tax Service

Income-tax preparation services
1716 Corporate Landing
Virginia Beach, VA 23454
Phone: (800) 790-3863, (757) 493-8855
Fax: (757) 493-0169
www.libertytaxfranchise.com
sales@libtax.com
Began in 1972, franchising since 1973
Headquarters size: 150 employees
Franchising department: 15 employees
U.S. franchises: 1,404
Canadian franchises: 292
Costs:
Total investment: $40.5K–50.9K
Express/kiosk option available
Franchise fee: $28.5K
Ongoing royalty fee: Varies
Term of agreement: Perpetual, renewable
Qualifications:
Cash liquidity requirement: $50K
Business Experience:
- General business experience
- Marketing skills
- Customer service experience

9. CleanNet USA Inc.

Commercial cleaning service
9861 Broken Land Parkway, #208
Columbia, MD 21046

Phone: (800) 735-8838, (410) 720-6444
Fax: (410) 720-5307
www.cleannetusa.com
Began in 1988, franchising since 1988
Headquarters size: 45 employees
Franchising department: 32 employees
U.S. franchises: 2,963
Costs:
Total investment: $3.9K–35.5K
Franchise fee: $2.95K–32K
Ongoing royalty fee: 3%
Term of agreement: 20 years, renewable
Renewal fee: $5K
Qualifications:
Net worth requirement: $10K–300K
Cash liquidity requirement: $5K–100K
Business Experience:
- General business experience

10. The UPS Store

6060 Cornerstone Court W.
San Diego, CA 92121
Phone: (877) 623-7253
Fax: (858) 546-7492
www.theupsstore.com
usafranchise@mbe.com
Began in 1980, franchising since 1980
Headquarters size: 300 employees
Franchising department: 84 employees
U.S. franchises: 4,201
Canadian franchises: 271
Other foreign franchises: 1,213
Costs:
Total investment: $138.7K–245.5K
Franchise fee: $29.95K
Ongoing royalty fee: 5%
Term of agreement: 10 years, renewable
Renewal fee: 25% of current franchise fee
Qualifications:
Net worth requirement: $150K
Cash liquidity requirement: $50K
Business experience:
- General business experience
- General computer skills

Source: "Top 10 Fastest-Growing Franchises for 2005," www.entrepreneur.com/franzone/list-ings/fastestgrowing/0,5844,,00.html.

Chapter 82

Low-Cost Franchises

Section 13

Top Ten Low-Cost Franchises

1. Curves
100 Ritchie Road
Waco, TX 76712
Phone: (800) 848-1096, (254) 399-9285
Fax: (254) 399-9731
www.buycurves.com
Began in 1992, franchising since 1995
Headquarters size: 50 employees
Franchising department: 40 employees
U.S. franchises: 7,860
Canadian franchises: 726
Other foreign franchises: 800
Costs:
Total investment: $36.4K–42.9K
Franchise fee: $39.9K
Ongoing royalty fee: 5%
Term of agreement: 5 years, renewable
Qualifications:
Net worth requirement: $75K
Cash liquidity requirement: $50K
Business Experience:
- Financially stable

2. Jackson Hewitt Tax Service
7 Sylvan Way
Parsippany, NJ 07054
Phone: (800) 475-2904
Fax: (973) 496-2760
www.jacksonhewitt.com
franchisedev@jtax.com
Began in 1960, franchising since 1986
Headquarters size: 322 employees
Franchising department: 19 employees
U.S. franchises: 4,330
Costs:
Total investment: $51.7K–85.4K
Express/kiosk option available
Franchise fee: $25K
Ongoing royalty fee: 15%
Term of agreement: 10 years, renewable
Qualifications:
Net worth requirement: $100K–200K
Cash liquidity requirement: $50K

3. Jani-King
Janitorial services
16885 Dallas Parkway
Addison, TX 75001
Phone: (800) 552-5264
Fax: (972) 991-5723, (972) 239-7706
www.janiking.com
info@janiking.com
Began in 1969, franchising since 1974
Headquarters size: 100 employees
Franchising department: 100 employees
U.S. franchises: 9,023
Canadian franchises: 540
Other foreign franchises: 1,369
Costs:
Total investment: $11.3K–34.1K+
Franchise fee: $8.6K–16.3K+
Ongoing royalty fee: 10%
Qualifications:
Net worth requirement: Varies
Cash liquidity requirement: Varies

4. RE/MAX International Inc.
P.O. Box 3907
Englewood, CO 80155-3907
Phone: (800) 525-7452, (303) 770-5531
Fax: (303) 796-3599
www.remax.com
Began in 1973, franchising since 1975
Headquarters size: 350 employees
Franchising department: 10 employees
U.S. franchises: 3,614
Canadian franchises: 580
Other foreign franchises: 1,285
Costs:
Total investment: $20K–200K
Franchise fee: $10K–25K
Ongoing royalty fee: Varies
Term of agreement: 5 years, renewable
Renewal fee: Varies
Qualifications:
Business Experience:
- Industry experience
- General business experience
- Marketing skills

5. ServiceMaster Clean

3839 Forest Hill Irene Road
Memphis, TN 38125
Phone: (800) 255-9687, (901) 597-7500
Fax: (901) 597-7580
www.ownafranchise.com
brwilliams@smclean.com
Began in 1947, franchising since 1952
Headquarters size: 134 employees
Franchising department: 8 employees
Costs:
Total investment: $28.2K-99.9K
Franchise fee: $16.9K-43K
Ongoing royalty fee: 4-10%
Term of agreement: 5 years, renewable
Qualifications:
Net worth requirement: $50K-75K
Cash liquidity requirement: $15K-25K
Business Experience:
- General business experience

6. Liberty Tax Service

Income-tax preparation services
1716 Corporate Landing
Virginia Beach, VA 23454
Phone: (800) 790-3863, (757) 493-8855
Fax: (757) 493-0169
www.libertytaxfranchise.com
sales@libtax.com
Began in 1972, franchising since 1973
Headquarters size: 150 employees
Franchising department: 15 employees
U.S. franchises: 1,404
Canadian franchises: 292
Costs:
Total investment: $40.5K-50.9K
Express/kiosk option available
Franchise fee: $28.5K
Ongoing royalty fee: Varies
Term of agreement: Perpetual, renewable
Qualifications:
Cash liquidity requirement: $50K
Business Experience:
- General business experience
- Marketing skills
- Customer service experience

7. Kumon Math and Reading Services

After-school educational program specializing
in math and reading
300 Frank W. Burr Boulevard, 5th Floor
Teaneck, NJ 07666
Phone: (866) 633-0740, (201) 928-0444
Fax: (201) 928-0044
www.kumon.com
franchise@kumon.com
Began in 1958, franchising since 1958
Headquarters size: 400 employees
Franchising department: 12 employees
U.S. franchises: 1,352
Canadian franchises: 341
Other foreign franchises: 21,800
Costs:
Total investment: $10K-30K
Franchise fee: $1K
Ongoing royalty fee: $30+/student/mo.
Term of agreement: 2 years, renewable
Qualifications:
Business Experience:
- General business experience
- Marketing skills
- Good math, reading, and communications
skills

8. Chem-Dry Carpet Drapery & Upholstery Cleaning

Carpet-cleaning service
1530 N. 1000 West
Logan, UT 84321
Phone: (877) 307-8233
Fax: (435) 755-0021
www.chemdry.com
charlie@chemdry.com
Began in 1977, franchising since 1978
Headquarters size: 75 employees
U.S. franchises: 2,502
Canadian franchises: 117
Other foreign franchises: 1,296
Costs:
Total investment: $24.95K-86.95K
Franchise fee: $11.95K
Ongoing royalty fee: $213/mo.
Term of agreement: 5 years, renewable
Renewal fee: $750

Section 13

9. Jan-Pro Franchising International Inc.
Commercial cleaning
383 Strand Industrial Drive
Little River, SC 29566
Phone: (866) 355-1064
Fax: (843) 399-9890
www.jan-pro.com
janpro1@aol.com
Began in 1991, franchising since 1992
Headquarters size: 10 employees
Franchising department: 6 employees
U.S. franchises: 3,940
Canadian franchises: 188
Costs:
Total investment: $5K–50K+
Franchise fee: $950–14K
Ongoing royalty fee: 8%
Term of agreement: 10 years, renewable
Qualifications:
Net worth requirement: $1K–14K+
Cash liquidity requirement: $1K+
Business Experience:
- Management skills

10. Merle Norman Cosmetics
Cosmetic studio
9130 Bellanca Avenue
Los Angeles, CA 90045
Phone: (800) 421-6648, (310) 641-3000
Fax: (310) 337-2370
www.merlenorman.com
ypadilla@merlenorman.com
Began in 1931, franchising since 1989
Headquarters size: 464 employees
Franchising department: 10 employees
U.S. franchises: 1,816
Canadian franchises: 91
Costs:
Total investment: $33.1K–156K
Franchise fee: $0
Ongoing royalty fee: 0
Term of agreement: Open-ended
Qualifications:
Business Experience:
- General business experience
- Experience in retail, cosmetics, and customer service

Source: "Top 10 Low-Cost Franchises for 2005," www.entrepreneur.com/franzone/listings/lowinvest/0,5839,,00.html.

Low-Cost Automotive Franchises to Buy

Altracolor Systems
Ranked 480/500
Mobile auto painting and plastic repair
113 23rd Street
Kenner, LA 70062
Phone: (800) 727-6567
www.atracolor.com
Began in 1988, franchising since 1991
Headquarters size: 5 employees
U.S. franchises: 60
Costs:
Total Costs: $37.5K–53.95K
Franchise fee: $8K–19.5K
Royalty fee: $95/wk
Terms of agreement: 15 years renewable at no charge

Financing:
In-house: Equipment
3rd-party: None
Qualifications:
Cash liquidity: $11.7K

Affiliated Car Rental LC
Ranked 119/500
Car rentals
96 Freneau Avenue, #2
Matawan, NJ 07747
Phone: (800) 367-5159
Fax: (732) 290-8305
www.sensiblecarrental.com
Began in 1987, franchising since 1987
Headquarters size: 7 employees
U.S. franchises: 245

Costs:
Total Costs: $46.5K–69.5K
Franchise fee: $6–10.8K
Royalty fee: Varies
Terms of agreement: Perpetual
Financing:
In-house: franchise fee
3rd-party: Equipment, inventory
Qualifications:
Cash liquidity: Varies
Experience: General Business Experience

Priceless Rent-A-Car

Ranked 485/500
Car rentals and leasing
10324 S. Dolfield Road
Owings Mills, MD 21117
Phone: (800) 662-8322
Fax: (410) 581-1566
www.pricelesscar.com
Began in 1997, Franchising Since 1997
Headquarters size: 10 employees
Franchising department: 2 employees
U.S. franchises: 120
Costs:
Total Costs: $37.2K–216K
Franchise fee: $8K–26K
Royalty fee: $30/ car/mo
Terms of agreement: 10 years renewable at no charge
Financing:
No financing available
Qualifications:
Experience: General business experience and marketing skills

Rent-A-Wreck

Ranked 370/500
Auto rentals and leasing
10324 S. Dolfield Road
Owings Mills, MD 21117
Phone: (410) 581-5755
Fax: (410) 581-1566
www.rentawreck.com
Began in 1970, franchising since 1977
Headquarters size: 35 employees
Franchising department: 7 employees

U.S. franchises: 350
Foreign franchises: 26
Costs:
Total Costs: $36.6K–$211K
Franchise fee: $8K–26K
Royalty fee: $30.car/mo
Terms of agreement: 10 years renewable at no charge
Financing:
No financing available
Qualifications:
Experience: General business experience and marketing skills

Oil Butler Int'l Corp

Ranked 488/500
Mobile oil change, quick lube, windshield repair
1599 Route 22 W.
Union, NJ 07083
Phone: (908) 687-3283
Fax: (908) 687-7617
www.oilbuterinternational.com
Began in 1987, franchising since 1991
Headquarters size: 6 employees
Franchising department: 4 employees
U.S. franchises: 142
Foreign franchises: 19
Costs:
Total Costs: $28K–40.7K
Franchise fee: $15K
Royalty fee: 7%
Terms of agreement: 10 years renewable at $1K
Financing:
In-house: None
3rd-party: Equipment, franchise fee, inventory, start-up costs
Qualifications:
Cash liquidity: 15K

Novus Auto Glass

Ranked 154/500
Windshield repair/replacement
12800 Highway 13 S #500
Savage, MN 55378
Phone: (800) 944-6811
Fax: (952) 946-0481
www.novuglass.com

Section 13

Began in 1972, franchising since 1985
Headquarters size: 40 employees
U.S. franchises: 344
Foreign franchises: 2,013
Costs:
Total Costs: $38K–175K
Franchise fee: $7.5K
Royalty fee: 5–8%
Terms of agreement: 10 year renewable at $2.5K

Financing:
No financing available
Qualifications:
Cash liquidity: $50K/100K
Experience: General business experience and marketing skills

Source: Rieva Lesonsky and Maria Anton-Conley, *Entrepreneur Magazine's Ultimate Book of Low-Cost Franchises 2005/2006.*

Low-Cost Business Services Franchises

Coffee News
Ranked 236/500
Weekly newspaper distributed at restaurants
P.O. Box 8444
Bangor, ME 04402-8444
Phone: (207) 941-0860
Fax: (207) 941-1050
www.coffeenewsusa.com
bill@coffeenewsusa.com
Began in 1988, franchising since 1994
Headquarters size: 7 employees
Franchising department: 2 employees
U.S. franchises: 285
Canadian franchises: 105
Other foreign franchises: 275
Costs:
Total investment: $6K
Franchise fee: $5K/3K
Ongoing royalty fee: $20–75/wk.
Business Experience:
- General business experience
- Marketing skills
- Sales and advertising experience

Magnetsigns Advertising Inc.
Ranked 459/500
Permanent and portable sign rentals
4802 50th Avenue
Camrose, AB T4V 0R9 Canada
Phone: (780) 672-8720
Fax: (780) 672-8716
www.magnetsigns.com
Began in 1995, franchising since 1996

Headquarters size: 10 employees
Franchising department: 5 employees
U.S. franchises: 8
Canadian franchises: 82
Costs:
Total investment: $24K–80K
Franchise fee: $5K
Ongoing royalty fee: 10%
Term of agreement: 10 years, renewable
Renewal fee: $3K
Qualifications:
Net worth requirement: $50K
Cash liquidity requirement: $10K
Business Experience:
- General business experience

Profit-Tell international
Ranked 469/500
Audio marketing/advertising programs
201 E. Ogden Avenue, #208
Hinsdale, IL 60521
Phone: (888) 366-4653
Fax: (630) 655-4542
www.profit-tell.com
Began in 1993, franchising since 2001
Headquarters size: 7 employees
Franchising department: 7 employees
U.S. franchises: 17
Costs:
Total investment: $30K–40.3K
Franchise fee: $24K
Ongoing royalty fee: 0
Term of agreement: 20 years, renewable

Renewal fee: $1K
Qualifications:
Net worth requirement: $125K
Cash liquidity requirement: $23.7K
Business Experience:
- General business experience
- Sales experience

Rezcity.com Plus

Ranked 269/500
Online local city guides, travel store, eBay auction store
560 Sylvan Avenue
Englewood Cliffs, NJ 07632
Phone: (800) 669-9000, (201) 567-8500
Fax: (201) 567-3265
www.rezcity.biz
Began in 2002, franchising since 2002
Headquarters size: 18 employees
Franchising department: 8 employees
U.S. franchises: 249
Costs:
Total investment: $6.7K-61.2K
Franchise fee: $4.5K-50K
Ongoing royalty fee: 0
Term of agreement: 5 years, renewable
Qualifications:
Cash liquidity requirement: $5K-25K
Business Experience:
- General business experience
- Marketing skills

RSVP Publications

Ranked 365/500
Direct-mail advertising
1156 N.E. Cleveland Street
Clearwater, FL 33755
Phone: (800) 360-7787, (727) 442-4000
Fax: (727) 441-1315
www.rsvppublications.com
Began in 1985, franchising since 1998
Headquarters size: 10 employees
Franchising department: 2 employees
U.S. franchises: 77
Costs:
Total investment: $29.3K-142.95K
Franchise fee: $15K-100K+

Ongoing royalty fee: 7%
Term of agreement: 10 years, renewable
Renewal fee: $5K
Qualifications:
Net worth requirement: $50K
Business Experience:
- General business experience
- Marketing skills

The Alternative Board

Ranked 466/500
Peer advisory boards and business coaching
1640 Grant Street, #200
Denver, CO 80203
Phone: (800) 727-0126, (303) 839-1200
Fax: (800) 420-7055, (303) 839-0012
www.tabboards.com
Began in 1990, franchising since 1996
Headquarters size: 25 employees
Franchising department: 5 employees
U.S. franchises: 110
Canadian franchises: 11
Other foreign franchises: 1
Costs:
Total investment: $37.3K-98.7K
Franchise fee: $17K-47K
Ongoing royalty fee: Varies
Term of agreement: 10 years, renewable
Renewal fee: $1.5K
Qualifications:
Net worth requirement: $75K+
Cash liquidity requirement: $25K-50K
Business Experience:
- Industry experience
- General business experience
- Marketing skills
- Minimum 10 years' business executive experience

United Shipping Solutions

Ranked 404/500
Transportation services
6985 Union Park Center, #565
Midvale, UT 84047
Phone: (866) 744-7486, (801) 352-0012
Fax: (801) 352-0339
www.usshipit.com

Section 13

Began in 2002, franchising since 2002
Headquarters size: 6 employees
Franchising department: 1 employee
U.S. franchises: 174
Costs:
Total investment: $25K–86K
Franchise fee: $25K–30K
Ongoing royalty fee: 6%
Term of agreement: 5 years, renewable
Qualifications:
Net worth requirement: $100K
Cash liquidity requirement: $50K
Business Experience:
– General business experience
– Marketing skills

Worldwide Express

Ranked 256/500
Discounted air express services
2501 Cedar Springs Road, #450
Dallas, TX 75201
Phone: (800) 758-7447
Fax: (214) 720-2446
www.wwex.com
Began in 1991, franchising since 1994
Headquarters size: 12 employees
Franchising department: 7 employees
U.S. franchises: 162
Costs:
Total investment: $41.2K–295.7K
Franchise fee: $23.8K–266K
Ongoing royalty fee: 6%
Term of agreement: 5 years, renewable
Qualifications:
Net worth requirement: $50K
Cash liquidity requirement: $50K
Business Experience:
– General business experience
– Marketing skills

Leadership Management Inc.

Ranked 275/500
Executive and management training
4567 Lake Shore Drive
Waco, TX 76710

Phone: (800) 568-1241
Fax: (254) 757-4600
www.lmi-bus.com
Began in 1965, franchising since 1965
Headquarters size: 10 employees
Franchising department: 2 employees
U.S. franchises: 226
Costs:
Total investment: $33.5K–37.5K
Franchise fee: $30K
Ongoing royalty fee: 6%
Business Experience:
– General business experience

Proforma

Ranked 76/500
Printing and promotional products
8800 E. Pleasant Valley Road
Cleveland, OH 44131
Phone: (800) 825-1525, (216) 520-8400
Fax: (216) 520-8474
www.connectwithproforma.com
Began in 1978, franchising since 1985
Headquarters size: 120 employees
Franchising department: 10 employees
U.S. franchises: 578
Canadian franchises: 43
Costs:
Total investment: $52K
Franchise fee: $39.5K
Ongoing royalty fee: 6–8%
Term of agreement: 10 years, renewable
Renewal fee: $1K
Qualifications:
Net worth requirement: $200K
Cash liquidity requirement: $52K
Business Experience:
– General business experience
– Marketing skills
– Sales background helpful

Source: Rieva Lesonsky and Maria Anton-Conley, *Entrepreneur Magazine's Ultimate Book of Low-Cost Franchises 2005/2006.*

Low-Cost Children's Businesses Franchises

Kinderdance International Inc.
Ranked 268/500
Children's movement and educational programs
1333 Gateway Drive, #1003
Melbourne, FL 32901
Phone: (800) 554-2334, (321) 984-4448
Fax: (321) 984-4490
www.kinderdance.com
Began in 1979, franchising since 1985
Headquarters size: 7 employees
Franchising department: 3 employees
U.S. franchises: 109
Canadian franchises: 1
Other foreign franchises: 2
Costs:
Total investment: $12.95K–27.1K
Franchise fee: $10K–21K
Ongoing royalty fee: 6–15%
Term of agreement: 10 years, renewable
Renewal fee: 10% of current fee
Qualifications:
Net worth requirement: $10K+
Cash liquidity requirement: $6.4K+
Business Experience:
- Seeking energetic individuals who enjoy working with children

Stretch-N-Grow International Inc.
Ranked 239/500
On-site children's fitness program
P.O. Box 7599
Seminole, FL 33775
Phone: (727) 596-7614
Fax: (727) 596-7633
www.stretch-n-grow.com
Began in 1992, franchising since 1993
Headquarters size: 4 employees
Franchising department: 4 employees
U.S. franchises: 178
Canadian franchises: 6
Other foreign franchises: 49
Costs:
Total investment: $19.3K

Franchise fee: $18.6K
Ongoing royalty fee: $150/mo.
Term of agreement renewable
Qualifications:
Cash liquidity requirement: $20K–25K
Business Experience:
- Must have desire to work with children

Stollerfit Inc.
Ranked 482/500
Interactive fitness programs, classes, and products for parents and babies
100 E-Business Way, #290
Cincinnati, OH 45241
Phone: (866) 222-9348
Fax: (513) 489-2964
www.strollerfit.com
Began in 1997, franchising since 2001
Headquarters size: 4 employees
Franchising department: 6 employees
U.S. franchises: 38
Costs:
Total investment: $3.95K–11.7K
Franchise fee: $2.5K
Ongoing royalty fee: 15%
Term of agreement: 2 years, renewable
Qualifications:
Cash liquidity requirement: $5K
Business Experience:
- General business experience
- Marketing skills

Ident-A-Kid Services of America
Ranked 215/500
Children's identification products and services
2810 Scherer Drive, #100
St. Petersburg, FL 33716
Phone: (727) 577-4646
Fax: (727) 576-8258
www.ident-a-kid.com
Began in 1986, franchising since 2000
Headquarters size: 6 employees
Franchising department: 2 employees
Costs:

Total investment: $29.5K–64.96K
Franchise fee: $29.5K
Ongoing royalty fee: 0
Term of agreement: 10 years, renewable
Business Experience:
- General business experience
- Marketing skills

Computertots/Computer Explorers
Ranked 414/500
Tech training for schools, kids, and adults
12715 Telge Road
Cypress, TX 77429
Phone: (888) 638-8722, (281) 256-4100
Fax: (281) 256-4178
www.computertots.com
Began in 1983, franchising since 1988
U.S. franchises: 100
Foreign franchises: 3
Costs:
Total investment: $47.7K–66.3K
Franchise fee: $30K
Ongoing royalty fee: 8%
Term of agreement: 15 years, renewable
Renewal fee: 5% of franchise fee
Qualifications:
Cash liquidity requirement: $25K
Business Experience:
- General business experience
- Marketing skills

Drama Kids International Inc.
Ranked 388/500
After-school children's drama program
3225-B Corporate Court
Ellicott City, MD 21042
Phone: (410) 480-2015
Fax: (410) 480-2026
www.dramakids.com
Began in 1979, franchising since 1989
Headquarters size: 8 employees
Franchising department: 3 employees
U.S. franchises: 28
Foreign franchises: 114
Costs:
Total investment: $36.2K–43.2K
Franchise fee: $27.5K

Ongoing royalty fee: 10%
Term of agreement: 5 years, renewable
Renewal fee: $2K
Qualifications:
Net worth requirement: $50K
Cash liquidity requirement: $25K
Business Experience:
- General business experience

High Touch-High Tech
Ranked 473/500
Science activities for schools/children's parties
12352 Wiles Road
Coral Springs, FL 33076
Phone: (800) 444-4968
Fax: (954) 755-1242
www.hightouch-hightech.com
Began in 1990, franchising since 1993
Headquarters size: 9 employees
Franchising department: 3 employees
U.S. franchises: 70
Canadian franchises: 9
Other foreign franchises: 11
Costs:
Total investment: $20.1K
Franchise fee: $15K
Ongoing royalty fee: 7%
Term of agreement: 10 years, renewable
Renewal fee: $2.5K
Business Experience:
- General business experience
- Marketing skills
- Education or teaching experience

Kidzart
Ranked 494/500
Drawing and art education for all ages
1327 Dime Box Circle
New Braunfels, TX 78130
Phone: (800) 379-8302
Fax: (830) 626-0260
www.kidzart.com
Began in 1997, franchising since 2002
Headquarters size: 2 employees
Franchising department 2 employees
U.S. franchises: 43
Canadian franchises: 1

Costs:
Total investment: $32.8K–40K
Franchise fee: $25.5K
Ongoing royalty fee: 7%
Term of agreement: 10 years, renewable
Qualifications:
Net worth requirement: $100K
Cash liquidity requirement: $30K
Business Experience:
- General business experience
- Marketing skills
- Some teaching, creativity-oriented

The Mad Science Group
Ranked 230/500
Educational demonstrations for preschools, in-class and after-school programs, community centers, and scout programs
8360 Bougainville Street, #201
Montreal, PQ H4P 2G1 Canada
Phone: (800) 586-5231
Fax: (514) 344-6695
www.madscience.org
Began in 1985, franchising since 1995
Headquarters size: 30 employees
Franchising department: 3 employees
U.S. franchises: 133
Canadian franchises: 25
Other foreign franchises: 27
Costs:
Total investment: $37.3–39K
Franchise fee: $10K–23.5K
Ongoing royalty fee: 8%
Term of agreement: 20 years, renewable at no cost

Qualifications:
Net worth requirement: $50K
Cash liquidity requirement: 23.5K

Young Rembrandts Franchise Inc.
Ranked 368/500
Art classes for children
23 N. Union Street
Elgin, IL 60123
Phone: (847) 742-6966
Fax: (847) 742-7197
www.youngrembrandts.com
Began in 1988, franchising since 1997
Headquarters size: 15 employees
Franchising department: 8 employees
U.S. franchises: 46
Costs:
Total investment: $39.5K–48.8K
Franchise fee: $31.5K
Ongoing royalty fee: Varies
Term of agreement: 15 years, renewable
Qualifications:
Cash liquidity requirement: $75K
Business Experience:
- Industry experience
- General business experience
- Marketing skills
- Teaching and art skills; experience working with children

Source: Rieva Lesonsky and Maria Anton-Conley, *Entrepreneur Magazine's Ultimate Book of Low-Cost Franchises 2005/2006.*

Section 13

Low-Cost Financial Services Franchises

Econotax
Ranked 354/500
Tax services
5846 Ridgewood Road, #B-101, Box 13829
Jackson, MS 39236
Phone: (800) 748-9106, (601) 956-0500
Fax: (601) 956-0583
www.econotax.com
Began in 1965, franchising since 1968
Headquarters size: 6 employees
Franchise size: 6 employees
U.S. franchises: 66
Costs:
Total investment: $15.4K–33K
Franchise fee: $10K
Ongoing royalty fee: 12%
Term of agreement: 5 years, renewable
Qualifications:
Net worth requirement: $50K
Cash liquidity requirement: $10K
Business Experience:
- General business experience
- Customer service experience, computer skills

Express Tax
Ranked 320/500
Tax preparation and electronic-filing services
3030 Hartley Road, #320
Jacksonville, FL 32257
Phone: (888) 417-4461
Fax: (904) 262-2864
www.expresstaxservice.com
Began in 1997, franchising since 2002
Headquarters size: 11 employees
Franchising department: 5 employees
U.S. franchises: 238
Costs:
Total investment: $9.9K–16.6K
Express/kiosk option available
Franchise fee: $5K
Ongoing royalty fee: $12/return
Term of agreement: 10 years, renewable
Renewal fee: $1K
Qualifications:

Cash liquidity requirement: $9.9K–16.6K
Business Experience:
- General business experience
- Marketing skills

Jackson Hewitt Tax Service
Ranked 4/500
Tax preparation services
7 Sylvan Way
Parsippany, NJ 07054
Phone: (800) 475-2904
Fax: (973) 496-2760
www.jacksonhewitt.com
franchisedev@jtax.com
Began in 1960, franchising since 1986
Headquarters size: 322 employees
Franchising department: 19 employees
U.S. franchises: 4,330
Costs:
Total investment: $51.7K–85.4K
Express/kiosk option available
Franchise fee: $25K
Ongoing royalty fee: 15%
Term of agreement: 10 years, renewable
Qualifications:
Net worth requirement: $100K–200K
Cash liquidity requirement: $50K

Liberty Tax Service
Ranked 15/500
Income-tax preparation services
1716 Corporate Landing
Virginia Beach, VA 23454
Phone: (800) 790-3863, (757) 493-8855
Fax: (757) 493-0169
www.libertytaxfranchise.com
sales@libtax.com
Began in 1972, franchising since 1973
Headquarters size: 150 employees
Franchising department: 15 employees
U.S. franchises: 1,404
Canadian franchises: 292
Costs:
Total investment: $40.5K–50.9K

Express/kiosk option available
Franchise fee: $28.5K
Ongoing royalty fee: Varies
Term of agreement: Perpetual, renewable
Qualifications:
Cash liquidity requirement: $50K
Business Experience:
- General business experience
- Marketing skills
- Customer service experience

Fed USA Insurance/Financial Services
Ranked 400/500
Insurance and financial services and tax preparation
8960 Taft Street
Pembroke Pines, FL 33024
Phone: (888) 440-6875
Fax: (954) 583-3205
www.fedusa.com
Began in 2000, franchising since 2001
Headquarters size: 120 employees
Franchising department: 5 employees
U.S. franchises: 45
Costs:
Total investment: $49.1K-71.1K
Franchise fee: $19.95K
Ongoing royalty fee: $500/mo.
Term of agreement: 10 years, renewable
Renewal fee: $3K

Qualifications:
Net worth requirement: $75K
Cash liquidity requirement: $20K
Business Experience:
- General business experience
- Ability to manage finances, must enjoy dealing with the public

Property Damage Appraisers
Ranked 233/500
Auto and property appraisals for insurance
6100 Southwest Boulevard, #200
Fort Worth, TX 76109-3964
Phone: (817) 731-5555
Fax: (817) 731-5550
www.pdahomeoffice.com
Began in 1963, franchising since 1963
Headquarters size: 35 employees
Franchising department: 3 employees
U.S. franchises: 282
Costs:
Total investment: $18.3K-35.95K
Franchise fee: $0
Ongoing royalty fee: 15%
Term of agreement: 3 years, renewable
Business Experience:
- Industry experience

Source: Rieva Lesonsky and Maria Anton-Conley, *Entrepreneur Magazine's Ultimate Book of Low-Cost Franchises 2005/2006.*

Low-Cost Food Business Franchises

Candy Boutique
Ranked 111/500
Bouquets of candies and chocolates, sometimes also cookies, balloons, and stuffed animals
423 E. Third Street
Little Rock, AR 72201
Phone: (877) 226-3901
Fax: (501) 375-9998
www.candybouquet.com
yumyum@candybouquet.com
Began in 1989, franchising since 1993
Headquarters size: 30 employees

Franchising department: 30 employees
U.S. franchises: 600
Canadian franchises: 41
Other foreign franchises: 42
Costs:
Total investment: $7.5K-50K
Express/kiosk option available
Franchise fee: $3.6K-29K
Ongoing royalty fee: 0
Term of agreement: 5 years, renewable
Renewal fee: 25% of original fee
Qualifications:
Business Experience:

- Industry experience
- General business experience
- Marketing skills

Carvel

Ranked 125/500
Formulas and equipment for creating and serving ice cream, distribution of line of ice cream, cakes, pies, and other treats
200 Glenridge Point Parkway, #200
Atlanta, GA 30342
Phone: (404) 255-3250
Fax: (404) 255-4978
www.carvel.com
Began in 1934, franchising since 1947
Headquarters size: 18 employees
Franchising department: 17 employees
U.S. franchises: 488
Canadian franchises: 3
Costs:
Total investment: $30K-280K
Express/kiosk option available
Franchise fee: $30K
Ongoing royalty fee: $1.82/gal.
Term of agreement: 20 years, renewable
Renewal fee: Then current fee
Qualifications:
Net worth requirement: $250K+
Cash liquidity requirement: $80K
Business Experience:
- General business experience

Pizza Inn Inc.

Ranked 334/500
Restaurant serving pizza, pasta, and salads
3551 Plano Parkway
The Colony, TX 75056
Phone: (469) 384-5000
Fax: (469) 384-5059
www.pizzainn.com
Began in 1960, franchising since 1963
Headquarters size: 75 employees
Franchising department: 5 employees
U.S. franchises: 377
Foreign franchises: 72
Costs:
Total investment: $34K-697K
Express/kiosk option available
Franchise fee: $5K-20K
Ongoing royalty fee: 4-5%
Term of agreement: 10 years, renewable
Renewal fee: Depends on initial contract
Qualifications:
Net worth requirement: $75K-200K
Cash liquidity requirement: $25K-125K
Business Experience:
- General business experience

Source: Rieva Lesonsky and Maria Anton-Conley, *Entrepreneur Magazine's Ultimate Book of Low-Cost Franchises 2005/2006.*

Low-Cost Home Improvement Franchises

Archadeck

Ranked 289/500
Specializing in wooden decks, screened porches, gazebos
2112 W. Laburnum Avenue, #100
Richmond, VA 23227
Phone: (800) 789-3325, (804) 353-6999
Fax: (804) 358-1878
www.archadeck.com
Began in 1980, franchising since 1984
Headquarters size: 20 employees
Franchising department: 2 employees
U.S. franchises: 84

Canadian franchises: 8
Other foreign franchises: 1
Costs:
Total investment: $62K-107.5K
Franchise fee: $33.5K
Ongoing royalty fee: 3.5-5.5%+
Term of agreement: 10 years, renewable
Qualifications:
Net worth requirement: $150K
Cash liquidity requirement: $40K-75K
Business Experience:
- General business experience

Kitchen Solvers Inc.
Ranked 290/500
Kitchen and bath remodeling and cabinet refacing, flooring, closets
401 Jay Street
La Crosse, WI 54601
Phone: (800) 845-6779, (608) 791-5518
Fax: (608) 784-2917
kitchensolvers.com
Began in 1982, franchising since 1984
Headquarters size: 7 employees
Franchising department: 7 employees
U.S. franchises: 125
Canadian franchises: 7
Costs:
Total investment: $40.3K–73K
Franchise fee: $25K–29.5K
Ongoing royalty fee: 4–6%
Term of agreement: 10 years, renewable
Qualifications:
Net worth requirement: $200K
Cash liquidity requirement: $50K

Kitchen Tune-Up
Ranked 169/500
Specialize in custom cabinets, refacing, and restoration
813 Circle Drive
Aberdeen, SD 57401
Phone: (800) 333-6385, (605) 225-4049
Fax: (605) 225-1371
www.kitchentuneup.com
Began in 1986, franchising since 1988
Headquarters size: 10 employees
Franchising department: 9 employees
U.S. franchises: 314
Canadian franchises: 3
Costs:
Total investment: $18.6K–50.1K
Express/kiosk option available
Franchise fee: $25K/10K
Ongoing royalty fee: 4.5–7%
Term of agreement: 10 years, renewable
Qualifications:
Net worth requirement: $75K
Cash liquidity requirement: $15K–25K

Business Experience:
- General business experience

United States Seamless Inc.
Ranked 413/500
Specializes in seamless steel siding, gutters, windows, and doors
2001 1st Avenue N.
Fargo, ND 58102
Phone: (701) 241-8888
Fax: (701) 241-9999
www.usseamless.com
Began in 1992, franchising since 1992
Headquarters size: 6 employees
Franchising department: 6 employees
U.S. franchises: 87
Costs:
Total investment: $49.5K–147K
Franchise fee: $8.5K
Ongoing royalty fee: Varies
Term of agreement: 15 years, renewable
Qualifications:
Cash liquidity requirement: $4.5K–18.5K
Business Experience:
- Industry experience
- General business experience

Christmas Decor Inc.
Ranked 160/500
Holiday and event decorating services
P.O. Box 5946
Lubbock, TX 79408-5946
Phone: (800) 687-9551
Fax: (806) 722-9627
www.christmasdecor.net
Began in 1984, franchising since 1996
Headquarters size: 20 employees
Franchising department: 4 employees
U.S. franchises: 338
Canadian franchises: 16
Other foreign franchises: 1
Costs:
Total investment: $19.2K–42.4K
Franchise fee: $10.9K–17.5K
Ongoing royalty fee: 2–4.5%
Term of agreement: 5 years, renewable
Renewal fee: $2K

Section 13

Business Experience:
- General business experience

Decor & You Inc.

Ranked 379/500
Interior decorating services and products
900 Main Street S., Building 2
Southbury, CT 06488
Phone: (203) 264-3500
Fax: (203) 264-5095
www.decorandyou.com
info@decorandyou.com
Began in 1994, franchising since 1998
Headquarters size: 4 employees
Franchising department: 2 employees
U.S. franchises: 63
Costs:
Total investment: $34K-125K
Franchise fee: $14.5K/75K
Ongoing royalty fee: 10%
Term of agreement: 10 years, renewable
Renewal fee: 10% of franchise fee
Qualifications:
Net worth requirement: $50K
Cash liquidity requirement: $25K/50K
Business Experience:
- Marketing skills preferred but not required; interest in decorating

Interior by Decorating Den

Ranked 121/500
Interior decorating services and products
8659 Commerce Drive
Easton, MD 21601
Phone: (410) 822-9001
Fax: (410) 820-5131
www.decoratingden.com
victoriaj@decoratingden.com
Began in 1969, franchising since 1970
Headquarters size: 38 employees
Franchising department: 6 employees
U.S. franchises: 420
Canadian franchises: 30
Other foreign franchises: 9
Costs:
Total investment: $39.9K
Franchise fee: $24.9K

Ongoing royalty fee: 7-9%
Term of agreement: 10 years, renewable
Qualifications:
Net worth requirement: $50K
Cash liquidity requirement: $40K
Business Experience:
- Decorating skills; people skills

Miracle Method Surface Restoration

Ranked 332/500
Specializing in bathtubs, sinks, countertop, and tile repair/refinishing
4239 N. Nevada, #115
Colorado Springs, CO 80907
Phone: (800) 444-8827, (719) 594-9196
Fax: (719) 594-9282
www.miraclemethod.com
Began in 1977, franchising since 1980
Headquarters size: 4 employees
Franchising department: 4 employees
U.S. franchises: 88
Foreign franchises: 25
Costs:
Total investment: $26.5K-46.5K
Franchise fee: $20K
Ongoing royalty fee: 5%
Term of agreement: 5 years, renewable
Renewal fee: 5%
Qualifications:
Net worth requirement: $40K
Cash liquidity requirement: $25K
Business Experience:
- Marketing skills

Re-bath LLC

Ranked 255/500
Installation of bathtub and shower base liners
1055 S. Country Club Drive, Building 2
Mesa, AZ 85210-4613
Phone: (800) 426-4573, (480) 844-1575
Fax: (480) 833-7199
www.re-bath.com
Began in 1979, franchising since 1991
Headquarters size: 13 employees
Franchising department: 3 employees
U.S. franchises: 150
Canadian franchises: 4

Other foreign franchises: 3
Costs:
Total investment: $33.9K–200K
Franchise fee: $3.5K–40K
Ongoing royalty fee: $25/liner
Term of agreement: 5 years, renewable
Renewal fee: $1K
Qualifications:
Net worth requirement: $250K
Cash liquidity requirement: $100K
Business Experience:
- Industry experience
- General business experience
- Marketing skills

Humitech Franchise Corp.
Ranked 486/500

Humidity control products
15851 Dallas Parkway, #410
Addison, TX 75001
Phone: (972) 490-9393
Fax: (972) 490-9220
www.humitechgroup.com
Began in 2001, franchising since 2002
Headquarters size: 14 employees
Franchising department: 4 employees
U.S. franchises: 56
Canadian franchises: 1
Other foreign franchises: 7

Source: Rieva Lesonsky and Maria Anton-Conley, *Entrepreneur Magazine's Ultimate Book of Low-Cost Franchises 2005/2006.*

Low-Cost Maintenance Franchises

American Asphalt Sealcoating Co.
Ranked 496/500
Asphalt maintenance services and protective coating
P.O. Box 600
Chesterland, OH 44026
Phone: (888) 603-7325, (440) 729-8080
Fax: (440) 729-2231
www.american-sealcoating.com
Began in 1987, franchising since 1998
Headquarters size: 11 employees
Franchising department: 6 employees
U.S. franchises: 10
Costs:
Total investment: $35K–45K
Franchise fee: $15K
Ongoing royalty fee: 5–7%
Term of agreement: 15 years, renewable
Renewal fee: Administrative costs
Qualifications:
Net worth requirement: $50K
Cash liquidity requirement: $50K
Business Experience:
- Aggressive and outgoing personality preferred

Jet-Black Int'l Inc.
Ranked 347/500
Asphalt maintenance services.
25 W. Cliff Road, #103
Burnsville, MN 55337
Phone: (888) 538-2525, (952) 890-8343
Fax: (952) 890-7022
www.jet-black.com
Began in 1988, franchising since 1993
Headquarters size: 10 employees
Franchising department: 4 employees
U.S. franchises: 105
Costs:
Total investment: $49K–150K
Franchise fee: $20K
Ongoing royalty fee: 8%
Term of agreement: 15 years, renewable
Qualifications:
Total investment: $49K–150K
Franchise fee: $20K
Ongoing royalty fee: 8%
Term of agreement: 15 years, renewable

Section
13

Chem-Dry Carpet Drapery & Upholstery Cleaning

Ranked: 18/500
Carpet, drapery, and upholstery cleaning
1530 N. 1000 West
Logan, UT 84321
Phone: (877) 307-8233
Fax: (435) 755-0021
www.chemdry.com
charlie@chemdry.com
Began in 1977, franchising since 1978
Headquarters size: 75 employees
U.S. franchises: 2,502
Canadian franchises: 117
Other foreign franchises: 1,296
Costs:
Total investment: $24.95K–86.95K
Franchise fee: $11.95K
Ongoing royalty fee: $213/mo.
Term of agreement: 5 years, renewable
Renewal fee: $750

Heaven's Best Carpet and Upholstery Cleaning

Ranked 113/500
Carpet and upholstery cleaning
247 N. First East, P.O. Box 607
Rexburg, ID 83440
Phone: (800) 359-2095
Fax: (208) 359-1236
www.heavensbest.com
Began in 1983, franchising since 1983
Headquarters size: 6 employees
Franchising department: 3 employees
U.S. franchises: 866
Canadian franchises: 5
Other foreign franchises: 11
Costs:
Total investment: $24.9K–47.4K
Franchise fee: $5.9K
Ongoing royalty fee: $80/mo.
Term of agreement: 5 years, renewable
Qualifications:
Net worth requirement: $20K
Cash liquidity requirement: $9K
Business Experience:

- Industry experience
- General business experience
- Marketing skills

Anago Franchising Inc.

Ranked 105/500
Commercial cleaning
3111 N. University Drive, #625
Coral Springs, FL 33065
Phone: (800) 213-5857
Fax: (954) 752-1200
www.anagousa.com
Began in 1989, franchising since 1991
Headquarters size: 10 employees
Franchising department: 10 employees
U.S. franchises: 564
Costs:
Total investment: $8K–350K
Franchise fee: $2K–350K
Ongoing royalty fee: 5%
Term of agreement: 10 years, renewable
Qualification:
Net worth requirement: $10K–50K
Cash liquidity requirement: $2K–50K
Business Experience:
- General business experience
- Marketing skills are helpful

Bonus Building Care

Ranked 178/500
Commercial cleaning
P.O. Box 300
Indianola, OK 74442
Phone: (918) 823-4990
Fax: (918) 823-4994
www.bonusbuildingcare.com
Began in 1996, franchising since 1996
Headquarters size: 30 employees
U.S. franchises: 1,011
Costs:
Total investment: $7.6K–13.3K
Franchise fee: $6.5K
Ongoing royalty fee: 10%
Term of agreement: 20 years, renewable
Renewal fee: $2K

Buildingstars Inc.

Ranked 303/500
Commercial cleaning
11489 Page Service Drive
St. Louis, MO 63146
Phone: (314) 991-3356
Fax: (314) 991-3198
www.buildingstars.com
Began in 1994, franchising since 2000
Headquarters size: 18 employees
Franchising department: 3 employees
U.S. franchises: 167
Costs:
Total investment: $1.9K
Franchise fee: $995
Ongoing royalty fee: 10%
Term of agreement: 5 years, renewable

Cleannet USA Inc.

Ranked 29/500
Commercial office cleaning
9861 Broken Land Parkway, #208
Columbia, MD 21046
Phone: (800) 735-8838, (410) 720-6444
Fax: (410) 720-5307
www.cleannetusa.com
Began in 1988, franchising since 1988
Headquarters size: 45 employees
Franchising department: 32 employees
Costs:
Total investment: $3.9K-35.5K
Franchise fee: $2.95K-32K
Ongoing royalty fee: 3%
Term of agreement: 20 years, renewable
Renewal fee: $5K
Qualifications:
Net worth requirement: $10K-300K
Cash liquidity requirement: $5K-100K
Business Experience:
- General business experience

Jan-pro Franchising International Inc.

Ranked 19/500
Commercial cleaning
383 Strand Industrial Drive
Little River, SC 29566
Phone: (866) 355-1064

Fax: (843) 399-9890
www.jan-pro.com
janpro1@aol.com
Began in 1991, franchising since 1992
Headquarters size: 10 employees
Franchising department: 6 employees
U.S. franchises: 3,940
Canadian franchises: 188
Costs:
Total investment: $5K-50K+
Franchise fee: $950-14K
Ongoing royalty fee: 8%
Term of agreement: 10 years, renewable
Qualifications:
Net worth requirement: $1K-14K+
Cash liquidity requirement: $1K+
Business Experience:
- Management skills

Jani-King

Ranked 7/500
Commercial cleaning
16885 Dallas Parkway
Addison, TX 75001
Phone: (800) 552-5264
Fax: (972) 991-5723, (972) 239-7706
www.janiking.com
info@janiking.com
Began in 1969, franchising since 1974
Headquarters size: 100 employees
U.S. franchises: 9,023
Canadian franchises: 540
Other foreign franchises: 1,369
Costs:
Total investment: $11.3K-34.1K+
Franchise fee: $8.6K-16.3K+
Ongoing royalty fee: 10%
Term of agreement: 20 years, renewable
Qualifications:
Net worth requirement: Varies
Cash liquidity requirement: Varies

Jantize America

Ranked 360/500
Commercial cleaning
15449 Middlebelt
Livonia, MI 48154

Section 13

Phone: (800) 968-9182
Fax: (734) 421-4936
www.jantize.com
Began in 1985, franchising since 1988
Headquarters size: 4 employees
U.S. franchises: 30
Costs:
Total investment: $9.8K–16.8K
Franchise fee: $3.5K–8.5K
Ongoing royalty fee: 6–9%
Term of agreement: 10 years, renewable
Qualifications:
Net worth requirement: $25K
Cash liquidity requirement: $10K

OpenWorks
Ranked 141/500
Office and commercial cleaning
4742 N. 24th Street, #300
Phoenix, AZ 85016
Phone: (800) 777-6736
Fax: (602) 468-3788
www.openworksweb.com
Began in 1983, franchising since 1983
Headquarters size: 52 employees
Franchising department: 11 employees
U.S. franchises: 406
Costs:
Total investment: $15K–150K+
Franchise fee: $14K–67.5K
Ongoing royalty fee: 5–10%
Term of agreement: 10 years, renewable
Qualifications:
Cash liquidity requirement: $7K–150K+
Business Experience:
– General business experience

Servicemaster Clean
Ranked 12/500
Commercial, residential cleaning, and disaster restoration
3839 Forest Hill Irene Road
Memphis, TN 38125
Phone: (800) 255-9687, (901) 597-7500
Fax: (901) 597-7580
www.ownafranchise.com
brwilliams@smclean.com

Began in 1947, franchising since 1952
Headquarters size: 134 employees
Franchising department: 8 employees
Costs:
Total investment: $28.2K–99.9K
Franchise fee: $16.9K–43K
Ongoing royalty fee: 4–10%
Term of agreement: 5 years, renewable
Qualifications:
Net worth requirement: $50K–75K
Cash liquidity requirement: $15K–25K
Business Experience:
– General business experience

Tower Cleaning Systems
Ranked 363/500
Office cleaning
P.O. Box 2468
Southeastern, PA 19399
Phone: (610) 278-9000
Fax: (610) 275-8025
www.toweronline.com
Began in 1988, franchising since 1990
Headquarters size: 175 employees
Franchising department: 8 employees
U.S. franchises: 465
Costs:
Total investment: $1.9K–23.8K
Franchise fee: $1.5K–13.5K
Ongoing royalty fee: 3%
Term of agreement: 10 years, renewable

Vanguard Cleaning Systems
Ranked 175/500
Commercial cleaning
655 Mariners Island Boulevard, #303
San Mateo, CA 94404
Phone: (800) 564-6422, (650) 594-1500
Fax: (650) 591-1545
www.vanguardcleaning.com
Began in 1984, franchising since 1984
Headquarters size: 20 employees
Franchising department: 3 employees
U.S. franchises: 600
Costs:
Total investment: $2.2K–33.7K
Franchise fee: $1.9K–32.8K

Section
13

Ongoing royalty fee: 5%
Term of agreement: 10 years, renewable
Qualifications:
Cash liquidity requirement: $2.8K–9K
Business Experience:
- General business experience

Aire Serv Heating & Air Conditioning Inc.
Ranked 436/500
Heating and air conditioning services
1020 N. University Parks Drive
Waco, TX 76707
Phone: (800) 583-2662
Fax: (254) 745-5098
www.aireserv.com
Began in 1993, franchising since 1993
Headquarters size: 110 employees
Franchising department: 30 employees
U.S. franchises: 70
Foreign franchises: 12
Costs:
Total investment: $31.6K–119.5K
Franchise fee: $17.5K
Ongoing royalty fee: 3–5%
Term of agreement: 10 years, renewable
Renewal fee: $750
Qualifications:
Net worth requirement: $150K+
Cash liquidity requirement: $35K
Business Experience:
- Industry experience

Andy Oncall
Ranked 283/500
Handyman services
921 E. Main Street
Chattanooga, TN 37408
Phone: (423) 242-0401
Fax: (423) 622-0580
www.andyoncall.com
Began in 1993, franchising since 1999
Headquarters size: 7 employees
Franchising department: 2 employees
U.S. franchises: 45
Costs:
Total investment: $30.6K–49.2K
Franchise fee: $23K

Ongoing royalty fee: 5%
Term of agreement: 10 years, renewable
Qualifications:
Net worth requirement: $150K
Cash liquidity requirement: $40K
Business Experience:
- General business experience
- Sales and people skills desired

Furniture Medic
Ranked 150/500
Furniture restoration and repair services
3839 Forest Hill Irene Road
Memphis, TN 38125
Phone: (800) 255-9687, (901) 597-8600
Fax: (901) 597-8660
www.furnituremedicfranchise.com
furnmedic@attglobal.net
Began in 1992, franchising since 1992
Headquarters size: 24 employees
Franchising department: 8 employees
U.S. franchises: 407
Canadian franchises: 70
Other foreign franchises: 103
Costs:
Total investment: $35.5K–78.9K
Franchise fee: $22K
Ongoing royalty fee: 7%
Term of agreement: 5 years, renewable
Qualifications:
Net worth requirement: $60K–80K
Cash liquidity requirement: $15K–25K
Business Experience:
- Industry experience
- General business experience
- Marketing skills

House Doctors
Ranked 209/500
Handyman services and home repairs
575 Chamber Drive
Milford, OH 45150
Phone: (800) 319-3359
Fax: (513) 831-6010
www.housedoctors.com
info@housedoctors.com
Began in 1994, franchising since 1995

Headquarters size: 23 employees
Franchising department: 12 employees
U.S. franchises: 202
Foreign franchises: 2
Costs:
Total investment: $31.5K–60.6K
Franchise fee: $15.9K–35.9K
Ongoing royalty fee: 6%
Term of agreement: 10 years, renewable
Business Experience:
- General business experience

Mr. Appliance Corp.
Ranked 324/500
Household appliance services and repairs
1020 N. University Parks Drive
Waco, TX 76707
Phone: (800) 290-1422
Fax: (800) 209-7621
www.mrappliance.com
Began in 1996, franchising since 1996
Headquarters size: 110 employees
Franchising department: 30 employees
U.S. franchises: 81
Canadian franchises: 1
Other foreign franchises: 2
Costs:
Total investment: $32.2K–68.9K
Franchise fee: $15.9K
Ongoing royalty fee: 3–7%
Term of agreement: 10 years, renewable
Renewal fee: $2.5K
Qualifications:
Net worth requirement: $100K
Cash liquidity requirement: $25K
Business Experience:
- Industry experience

U.S. Lawns
Ranked 208/500
Landscape maintenance services
4407 Vineland Road, #D-15
Orlando, FL 32811
Phone: (800) 875-2967
Fax: (407) 246-1623
www.uslawns.com
Began in 1986, franchising since 1987

Headquarters size: 9 employees
Franchising department: 3 employees
U.S. franchises: 134
Costs:
Total investment: $48.5K–70K
Franchise fee: $29K
Ongoing royalty fee: 3–4%
Term of agreement: 10 years, renewable
Qualifications:
Net worth requirement: $100K
Cash liquidity requirement: $25K
Business Experience:
- General business experience
- Marketing skills

Weed Man
Ranked 103/500
Lawn care
11 Grand Marshall Drive
Scarborough, ON M1B 5N6 Canada
Phone: (888) 321-9333
Fax: (416) 269-8233
www.weed-man.com
Began in 1970, franchising since 1976
Headquarters size: 8 employees
Franchising department: 4 employees
U.S. franchises: 174
Canadian franchises: 118
Other foreign franchises: 1
Costs:
Total investment: $48.6K–70.3K
Franchise fee: $20K–33.8K
Ongoing royalty fee: 6%
Term of agreement: 10 years, renewable
Renewal fee: 50% of original fee
Qualifications:
Net worth requirement: $60K
Cash liquidity requirement: $30K
Business Experience:
- General business experience

Critter Control
Ranked 323/500
Urban and rural wildlife management
9435 E. Cherry Bend Road
Traverse City, MI 49684
Phone: (800) 699-1953

Fax: (231) 947-9440
www.crittercontrol.com
Began in 1983, franchising since 1987
Headquarters size: 10 employees
Franchising department: 4 employees
U.S. franchises: 98
Canadian franchises: 2
Costs:
Total investment: $25.5K–69K
Franchise fee: $18–36K
Ongoing royalty fee: 6–16%
Term of agreement: 10 years, renewable
Business Experience:
- Marketing skills
- Customer service and interpersonal skills

Truly Nolen
Ranked 475/500
Pest and termite control and lawn service
3636 E. Speedway
Tucson, AZ 85716
Phone: (800) 458-3664, (520) 977-5817
Fax: (520) 322-4010
www.trulynolen.com
Began in 1938, franchising since 1996
Headquarters size: 35 employees
Franchising department: 2 employees
U.S. franchises: 9
Foreign franchises: 60
Costs:
Total investment: $3.6K–300.5K
Express/kiosk option available
Franchise fee: $1.5K–45K
Ongoing royalty fee: 7%
Term of agreement: 5 years, renewable
Qualifications:
Net worth requirement: $50K
Cash liquidity requirement: $10K
Business Experience:
- General business experience
- Marketing skills
- Industry experience is preferred

Benjamin Franklin Plumbing
Ranked 383/500
Plumbing services
2 N. Tamiami Trail, #806

Sarasota, FL 34236
Phone: (800) 695-3579, (941) 552-5111
Fax: (941) 552-5130
www.benfranklinplumbing.com
Began in 2000, franchising since 2001
Headquarters size: 23 employees
Franchising department: 3 employees
U.S. franchises: 141
Costs:
Total investment: $34K–381.5K
Franchise fee: $25K
Ongoing royalty fee: 4–5%
Term of agreement: 10 years, renewable
Renewal fee: 50% of franchise fee

Rooter-Man
Ranked 187/500
Plumbing, drain, and sewer cleaning
268 Rangeway Road
North Billerica, MA 01862
Phone: (800) 700-8062
Fax: (978) 663-0061
www.rooterman.com
Began in 1970, franchising since 1981
Headquarters size: 28 employees
Franchising department: 5 employees
U.S. franchises: 146
Canadian franchises: 4
Other foreign franchises: 1
Costs:
Total investment: $46.8K–137.6K
Franchise fee: $3.98K
Ongoing royalty fee: Varies
Term of agreement: 5 years, renewable
Renewal fee: $2.5K
Qualifications:
Net worth requirement: $25K
Cash liquidity requirement: $10K
Business Experience:
- Mechanical ability

Home Cleaning Centers of America
Ranked 375/500
House, office, carpet, and window cleaning
10851 Mastin Boulevard, #130
Overland Park, KS 66210
Phone: (800) 767-1118

Section 13

Fax: (913) 327-5272
www.homecleaningcenters.com
Began in 1981, franchising since 1984
Headquarters size: 2 employees
Franchising department: 2 employees
U.S. franchises: 38
Costs:
Total investment: $25.8K-32.5K
Franchise fee: $9.5K
Ongoing royalty fee: 3-5%
Term of agreement: 10 years, renewable
Business Experience:
- Management skills

Maidpro

Ranked 329/500
Professional home and office cleaning
180 Canal Street
Boston, MA 02114
Phone: (888) 624-3776, (617) 742-8787
Fax: (617) 720-0700
www.maidpro.com
Began in 1991, franchising since 1997
Headquarters size: 9 employees
Franchising department: 5 employees
U.S. franchises: 41
Costs:
Total investment: $39.4K-75.9K
Franchise fee: $7.9K
Ongoing royalty fee: 3-6%
Term of agreement: 10 years, renewable
Renewal fee: $500
Qualifications:
Net worth requirement: $100K
Cash liquidity requirement: $50K
Business Experience:
- General business experience
- Franchisees should be computer literate

Maid to Perfection

Ranked 183/500
Residential and light commercial cleaning
1101 Opal Court, 2nd Floor
Hagerstown, MD 21740
Phone: (800) 648-6243, (301) 790-7900
Fax: (301) 790-3949
www.maidtoperfectioncorp.com

maidsvc@aol.com
Began in 1980, franchising since 1990
Headquarters size: 8 employees
Franchising department: 8 employees
U.S. franchise: 271
Canadian franchises: 23
Costs:
Total investment: $41K-49K
Franchise fee: $11.99K
Ongoing royalty fee: 4-7%
Term of agreement: 5-10 years, renewable
Qualifications:
Net worth requirement: $80K
Cash liquidity requirement: $50K
Business Experience:
- General business experience
- Marketing skills

Maids to Order

Ranked 319/500
Residential and commercial cleaning
4000 Embassy Parkway, #430
Akron, OH 44333
Phone: (800) 701-6243, (330) 666-9460
Fax: (330) 666-9710
www.maidstoorder.com
Began in 1988, franchising since 1992
Headquarters size: 6 employees
Franchising department: 5 employees
U.S. franchises: 45
Foreign franchises: 4
Costs:
Total investment: $35.1K-101.5K
Franchise fee: $12.5K-57.5K
Ongoing royalty fee: 5%
Term of agreement: 15 years, renewable
Qualifications:
Cash liquidity requirement: $18K-24K

Merry Maids

Ranked 45/500
Residential cleaning
P.O. Box 751017
Memphis, TN 38175-1017
Phone: (800) 798-8000
Fax: (901) 597-8140
www.merrymaids.com

Began in 1979, franchising since 1980
Headquarters size: 60 employees
Franchising department: 25 employees
U.S. franchises: 777
Canadian franchises: 69
Other foreign franchises: 433
Costs:
Total investment: $23.4K–54.5K
Franchise fee: $19K–27K
Ongoing royalty fee: 5–7%
Term of agreement: 5 years, renewable
Qualifications:
Net worth requirement: $32.5K–49.5K
Cash liquidity requirement: $28.7K–43.3K
Business Experience:
- General business experience
- Management experience

Duraclean Int'l
Ranked 170/500
Disaster restoration, mold remediation, and carpet cleaning
220 Campus Drive
Arlington Heights, IL 60004
Phone: (800) 251-7070, (847) 704-7100
Fax: (847) 704-7101
www.duraclean.com
Began in 1930, franchising since 1945
Headquarters size: 20 employees
Franchising department: 3 employees
U.S. franchises: 213
Canadian franchises: 12
Other foreign franchises: 146
Costs:
Total investment: $38.99K–71.5K
Franchise fee: $10K
Ongoing royalty fee: 2–8%
Term of agreement: 5 years, renewable
Qualifications:
Cash liquidity requirement: $50K

Aerowest/Westair Deodorizing Services
Ranked 342/500
Restroom deodorizing services
3882 Del Amo Boulevard, #602
Torrance, CA 90503
Phone: (310) 793-4242
Fax: (310) 793-4250
www.westsanitation.com
Began in 1943, franchising since 1978
Headquarters size: 20 employees
Franchising department: 10 employees
U.S. franchises: 52
Costs:
Total investment: $14.8K–44.2K
Franchise fee: $6K
Ongoing royalty fee: 8%
Term of agreement: 5 years, renewable
Qualifications:
Net worth requirement: $25K+
Cash liquidity requirement: $10K
Business Experience:
- General business experience
- Marketing skills
- Sales and service skills to facilitate management is an asset

Aire-Master of America Inc.
Ranked 428/500
Restroom deodorizing and maintenance services
1821 N. Highway CC
P.O. Box 2310
Nixa, MO 65714
Phone: (800) 525-0957, (417) 725-2691
Fax: (417) 725-8227
www.airemaster.com
Began in 1958, franchising since 1976
Headquarters size: 66 employees
Franchising department: 2 employees
U.S. franchises: 60
Canadian franchises: 2
Costs:
Total investment: $40.6K–110.9K
Franchise fee: $23K–50.5K
Ongoing royalty fee: 5%
Term of agreement: 20 years, renewable
Qualifications:
Net worth requirement: Varies
Cash liquidity requirement: Varies
Business Experience:
- Marketing skills

Section 13

Swisher Hygiene Franchise Corp.

Ranked 412/500
Restroom hygiene, commercial pest control
services and products
6849 Fairview Road
Charlotte, NC 28210
Phone: (800) 444-4138, (704) 364-7707
Fax: (800) 444-4565
www.swisheronline.com
Began in 1983, franchising since 1989
Headquarters size: 70 employees
Franchising department: 70 employees
U.S. franchises: 88
Canadian franchises: 8
Other foreign franchises: 37
Costs:
Total investment: $44.2K–170.1K
Franchise fee: $35K–85K
Ongoing royalty fee: 6%
Term of agreement: 5 years, renewable
Renewal fee: Varies
Qualifications:
Net worth requirement: $50K–150K
Cash liquidity requirement: $15K–50K
Business Experience:
- General business experience

Cartex Limited

Ranked 232/500
Leather, vinyl, plastic, and cloth repair
42816 Mound Road
Sterling Heights, MI 48314
Phone: (586) 739-4330
Fax: (586) 739-4331
www.fabrion.net
Began in 1987, franchising since 1988
Headquarters size: 10 employees
Franchising department: 3 employees
U.S. franchises: 119
Canadian franchises: 1
Costs:
Total investment: $34.5K–95.2K
Franchise fee: $23.5K–36.5K
Ongoing royalty fee: 7%
Term of agreement: 5 years, renewable
Qualifications:

Net worth requirement: $50K
Cash liquidity requirement: $35K

Creative Colors Int'l Inc.

Ranked 439/500
Mobile plastic, vinyl, leather restoration and
repair
5550 W. 175th Street
Tinley Park, IL 60477
Phone: (800) 933-2656, (708) 614-7786
Fax: (708) 614-9685
www.creativecolorsintl.com
Began in 1980, franchising since 1991
Headquarters size: 10
U.S. franchises: 54
Canadian franchises: 1
Other foreign franchises: 2
Costs:
Total investment: $37.5K–71.4K
Franchise fee: $19.5K+
Ongoing royalty fee: 6%
Term of agreement: 10 years, renewable
Renewal fee: up to 20% of current fee
Qualifications:
Net worth requirement: $50K+
Cash liquidity requirement: $20K+
Business Experience:
- General business experience
- Marketing skills

Dr. Vinyl and Associates Ltd.

Ranked 385/500
Leather and vinyl repair, bumper repair, and
dent removal service
821 NW Commerce
Lee's Summit, MO 64086
Phone: (800) 531-6600
Fax: (816) 525-6333
www.drvinyl.com
Began in 1972, franchising since 1981
Headquarters size: 14 employees
Franchises: 9 employees
U.S. franchises: 220
Foreign franchises: 53
Costs:
Total investment: $44K–69.5K
Franchise fee: $32.5K

Ongoing royalty fee: 7%
Term of agreement: 10 years, renewable
Qualifications:
Net worth requirement: $50K
Cash liquidity requirement: $15K
Business Experience:
- General business experience
- Marketing skills

Window Gang
Ranked 241/500
Window and pressure cleaning services
1509 Ann Street
Beaufort, NC 28516
Phone: (877) 946-4264
Fax: (252) 726-2837
www.windowgang.com
Began in 1986, franchising since 1996
Headquarters size: 6 employees
Franchising department: 3 employees
U.S. franchises: 138
Canadian franchises: 20
Costs:
Total investment: $40K-125K
Franchise fee: $25K-100K
Ongoing royalty fee: 6%
Term of agreement: 10 years, renewable
Renewal fee: $2.5K
Qualifications:
Net worth requirement: $50K
Cash liquidity requirement: $10K
Business Experience:
- Marketing skills

Window Genie
Ranked 351/500
Residential window cleaning and pressure washing
10830 Millington Court
Cincinnati, OH 45242
Phone: (800) 700-0022
Fax: (513) 412-7760
www.windowgenie.com

Began in 1994, franchising since 1998
Headquarters size: 9 employees
Franchising department: 3 employees
U.S. franchises: 47
Costs:
Total investment: $44.7K-55.4K
Franchise fee: $19.5K
Ongoing royalty fee: 6%
Term of agreement: 10 years, renewable
Qualifications:
Net worth requirement: $75K
Cash liquidity requirement: $30K
Business Experience:
- General business experience

Duct Doctor USA Inc.
Ranked 401/500
Residential and commercial air-duct cleaning
5555 Oakbrook Parkway, #660
Atlanta, GA 30093
Phone: (770) 446-1764
Fax: (770) 447-4486
www.ductdoctorusa.com
Began in 1985, franchising since 2000
Headquarters size: 12 employees
Franchising department: 2 employees
U.S. franchises: 11
Foreign franchises: 1
Costs:
Total investment: $41K-64K
Franchise fee: $25K
Ongoing royalty fee: 5-8%
Term of agreement: 10 years, renewable
Renewal fee: 10% of initial franchise fee
Qualifications:
Net worth requirement: $100K
Cash liquidity requirement: $50K
Business Experience:
- General business experience

Source: Rieva Lesonsky and Maria Anton-Conley, *Entrepreneur Magazine's Ultimate Book of Low-Cost Franchises 2005/2006.*

Section 13

Low-Cost Personal Care Franchises

Merle Norman Cosmetics

Ranked 23/500
Cosmetic studios
9130 Bellanca Avenue
Los Angeles, CA 90045
Phone: (800) 421-6648, (310) 641-3000
Fax: (310) 337-2370
www.merlenorman.com
ypadilla@merlenorman.com
Began in 1931, franchising since 1989
Headquarters size: 464 employees
Franchising department: 10 employees
U.S. franchises: 1,816
Canadian franchises: 91
Costs:
Total investment: $33.1K-156K
Franchise fee: $0
Ongoing royalty fee: 0
Term of agreement: Open-ended
Business Experience:
- General business experience
- Experience in retail, cosmetics, and customer service

Contours Express

Ranked 100/500
Women-only fitness center
156 Imperial Way
Nicholasville, KY 40356
Phone: (877) 227-2282
Fax: (859) 241-2234
www.contoursexpress.com
Began in 1998, franchising since 1998
Headquarters size: 5 employees
Franchising department: 5 employees
U.S. franchises: 325
Canadian franchises: 30
Other foreign franchises: 25
Costs:
Total investment: $35K-50K
Franchise fee: $12.5K
Ongoing royalty fee: $395/mo.
Term of agreement: 10 years, renewable
Qualifications:

Net worth requirement: $50K
Cash liquidity requirement: $15K

Curves

Ranked 2/500
Women-only fitness center
100 Ritchie Road
Waco, TX 76712
Phone: (800) 848-1096, (254) 399-9285
Fax: (254) 399-9731
www.buycurves.com
Began in 1992, franchising since 1995
Headquarters size: 50 employees
Franchising department: 40 employees
U.S. franchises: 7,860
Canadian franchises: 726
Other foreign franchises: 800
Costs:
Total investment: $36.4K-42.9K
Franchise fee: $39.9K
Ongoing royalty fee: 5%
Term of agreement: 5 years, renewable
Qualifications:
Net worth requirement: $75K
Cash liquidity requirement: $50K
Business Experience:
- Financially stable

Jazzercise Inc.

Ranked 26/500
Dance-fitness program
2460 Impala Drive
Carlsbad, CA 92008
Phone: (760) 476-1750
Fax: (760) 602-7180
www.jazzercise.com
Began in 1977, franchising since 1983
Headquarters size: 125 employees
Franchising department: 4 employees
U.S. franchises: 4,912
Canadian franchises: 95
Other foreign franchises: 918
Costs:
Total investment: $3K-33.1K

Franchise fee: $500/$1K
Ongoing royalty fee: to 20%
Term of agreement: 5 years, renewable
Business Experience:
- Movement skills; knowledge of health and fitness

Source: Rieva Lesonsky and Maria Anton-Conley, *Entrepreneur Magazine's Ultimate Book of Low-Cost Franchises 2005/2006.*

Low-Cost Recreation Franchises

Carlson Wagonlit Travel
Ranked 184/500
Travel agency
Carlson Parkway, P.O. Box 59159
Minneapolis, MN 55459-8207
Phone: (866) 248-3499
Fax: (734) 495-1413
www.carlsontravel.com
Began in 1888, franchising since 1984
Headquarters size: 775
Franchising department: 140
U.S. franchises: 778
Costs:
Total investment: $2.5K-10.4K
Franchise fee: $1.5K
Ongoing royalty fee: $950/mo.
Term of agreement: 5 years, renewable
Renewal fee: $1K
Business Experience:
- Industry experience
- General business experience
- Marketing skills

Cruiseone Inc.
Ranked 188/500
Cruise-only travel agency
1415 N.W. 62nd Street, #205
Fort Lauderdale, FL 33309
Phone: (800) 892-3928
Fax: (954) 958-3697
www.cruiseonefranchise.com
Began in 1989, franchising since 1993
Headquarters size: 50 employees
U.S. franchises: 460
Costs:
Total investment: $9.8K-11K
Franchise fee: $9.8K

Ongoing royalty fee: 3%
Term of agreement: 5 years, renewable
Qualifications:
Cash liquidity requirement: $20K

Cruise Planner/American Express Travel Service
Ranked 118/500
Cruise/tour travel agency
3300 University Drive, #602
Coral Springs, FL 33065
Phone: (888) 582-2150, (954) 227-2545
Fax: (954) 755-5898
www.beacruiseagent.com
franchising@cruiseplanners.com
Began in 1994, franchising since 1999
Headquarters size: 30 employees
Franchising department: 3 employees
U.S. franchises: 505
Costs:
Total investment: $9.99K-20.5K
Express/kiosk option available
Franchise fee: $9.99K
Ongoing royalty fee: 3-0%
Term of agreement: 3 years, renewable
Qualifications:
Net worth requirement: $17.1K
Cash liquidity requirement: $8.99K

Travel Network
Ranked 325/500
Travel agency
560 Sylvan Avenue
Englewood Cliffs, NJ 07632
Phone: (800) 669-9000, (201) 567-8500
Fax: (201) 567-4405
www.travelnetwork.com

Section 13

Began in 1982, franchising since 1983
Headquarters size: 18 employees
Franchising department: 9 employees
U.S. franchises: 264
Canadian franchises: 3
Other foreign franchises: 61
Costs:
Total investment: $34.2K–99K
Franchise fee: $3.95K–29.9K
Ongoing royalty fee: $250–750/mo.
Term of agreement: 15 years, renewable

Renewal fee: $500
Qualifications:
Net worth requirement: $15K
Cash liquidity requirement: $15K–30K
Business Experience:
- General business experience
- Marketing skills

Source: Rieva Lesonsky and Maria Anton-Conley, *Entrepreneur Magazine's Ultimate Book of Low-Cost Franchises 2005/2006.*

Low-Cost Service Franchises

Dry Cleaning To-Your-Door
Ranked 500/500
Dry cleaning pickup and delivery
1121 N.W. Bayshore Drive
Waldport, OR 97394
Phone: (800) 318-1800
Fax: (541) 563-6938
www.dctyd.com
Began in 1994, franchising since 1997
U.S. franchises: 99
Costs:
Total investment: $39.99K
Franchise fee: $24.5K
Ongoing royalty fee: 4.5%
Qualifications:
Net worth requirement: $75K
Cash liquidity requirement: $24.5K

Pressed 4 Time Inc.
Ranked 284/500
Mobile dry cleaning pickup and delivery
8 Clock Tower Place, #110
Maynard, MA 01754
Phone: (800) 423-8711, (978) 823-8300
Fax: (978) 823-8301
www.pressed4time.com
Began in 1987, franchising since 1990
Headquarters size: 5 employees
Franchising department: 2 employees
U.S. franchises: 172
Canadian franchises: 2

Other foreign franchises: 7
Costs:
Total investment: $24K–32.9K
Franchise fee: $21.5K
Ongoing royalty fee: 4–6%
Term of agreement: 10 years, renewable
Renewal fee: 10% of current franchise fee
Qualifications:
Net worth requirement: $50K
Cash liquidity requirement: $35K
Business Experience:
- Marketing skills

Allstate Home Inspections and Environmental Testing
Ranked 372/500
Home inspections and household environmental testing
2097 N. Randolph Road
Randolph Center, VT 05061
Phone: (800) 245-9932
Fax: (802) 728-5534
www.allstatehomeinspection.com
Began in 1989, franchising since 1996
Headquarters size: 5 employees
Franchising department: 5 employees
U.S. franchises: 49
Canadian franchises: 1
Costs:
Total investment: $29.7K–49.2K
Franchise fee: $23.9K

Ongoing royalty fee: 7.5%
Term of agreement: 6 years, renewable
Renewal fee: $2K
Qualifications:
Cash liquidity requirement: $7.9K–24K
Business Experience:
- Industry experience
- 4 hours marketing skills training, 5 supervised inspections, 5 independent inspections, 40+ hours home inspection training

Brickkicker Home Inspection
Ranked 235/500
Home inspection services
849 N. Ellsworth Street
Naperville, IL 60583
Phone: (888) 339-5425
Fax: (630) 420-2270
www.brickkicker.com
Began in 1989, franchising since 1994
Headquarters size: 19 employees
Franchising department: 6 employees
U.S. franchises: 185
Costs:
Total investment: $14.3K–53.7K
Franchise fee: $7.5K–25K
Ongoing royalty fee: 6%
Term of agreement: 7 years, renewable
Qualifications:
Net worth requirement: $50K
Cash liquidity requirement: $20K
Business Experience:
- General business experience
- Marketing skills

The Hometeam Inspection Service
Ranked 171/500
Home inspection
575 Chamber Drive
Milford, OH 45150
Phone: (800) 598-5297
Fax: (513) 831-6010
www.hometeaminspection.com
info@hmteam.com
Began in 1991, franchising since 1992
Headquarters size: 25 employees
Franchising department: 13 employees

U.S. franchises: 342
Canadian franchises: 8
Costs:
Total investment: $19.5K–49.1K
Franchise fee: $11.9K–29.9K
Ongoing royalty fee: 6%
Term of agreement: 10 years, renewable
Qualifications:
Cash liquidity requirement: $7.5K
Business Experience:
- Industry experience
- General business experience
- Marketing skills

HouseMaster Home Inspection
Ranked 223/500
Home inspection
421 W. Union Avenue
Bound Brook, NJ 08805
Phone: (800) 526-3939
Fax: (732) 469-7405
www.housemaster.com
Began in 1971, franchising since 1979
Headquarters size: 24 employees
Franchising department: 24 employees
U.S. franchises: 335
Canadian franchises: 38
Costs:
Total investment: $31K–67K
Franchise fee: $18K–30K
Ongoing royalty fee: 5–7.5%
Term of agreement: 5 years, renewable
Qualifications:
Net worth requirement: $50K
Cash liquidity requirement: $20K
Business Experience:
- Marketing skills
- Management skills

Inspect-It 1st Property Inspection
Ranked 403/500
Inspection Company
8541 E. Anderson Drive, #102
Scottsdale, AZ 85255
Phone: (800) 510-9100, (480) 355-3250
Fax: (480) 355-3255
www.inspectit1st.com

Section 13

Began in 1991, franchising since 1998
Headquarters size: 7 employees
Franchising department: 3 employees
U.S. franchises: 60
Costs:
Total investment: $33K–51K
Franchise fee: $24.9K–27.9K
Ongoing royalty fee: 6–7%
Term of agreement renewable
Qualifications:
Net worth requirement: $75K
Cash liquidity requirement: $30K

National Property Inspections Inc.
Ranked 185/500
Home and commercial property inspection
service
9375 Burt, #201
Omaha, NE 68114
Phone: (800) 333-9807
Fax: (800) 933-2508
www.npiweb.com
info@npiweb.com
Began in 1987, franchising since 1987
Headquarters size: 15 employees
Franchising department: 7 employees
U.S. franchises: 249
Canadian franchises: 13
Costs:
Total investment: $28.5K–31K
Franchise fee: $21.8K
Ongoing royalty fee: 8%
Term of agreement: 5 years, renewable
Qualifications:
Cash liquidity requirement: $23K
Business Experience:
– Industry experience
– Marketing skills

Pillar to Post
Ranked 86/500
Home inspection franchise
13902 N. Dale Mabry Highway, #300
Tampa, FL 33618
Phone: (877) 963-3129
Fax: (813) 963-5301
www.pillartopost.com

jmajirsky@pillartopost.com
Began in 1994, franchising since 1994
Headquarters size: 18 employees
Franchising department: 11 employees
U.S. franchises: 390
Canadian franchises: 90
Costs:
Total investment: $28.7K–46.5K
Franchise fee: $18.9K–28.9K
Ongoing royalty fee: 7%
Term of agreement: 5 years, renewable
Qualifications:
Net worth requirement: $100K
Cash liquidity requirement: $50K
Business Experience:
– General business experience
– Marketing skills

World Inspection Network
Ranked 176/500
Home inspection services
6500 6th Avenue N.W.
Seattle, WA 98117
Phone: (800) 967-8127
Fax: (206) 441-3655
www.winfranchise.com
Began in 1993, franchising since 1994
Headquarters size: 12 employees
Franchising department: 3 employees
U.S. franchises: 204
Costs:
Total investment: $41.7K–49.5K
Franchise fee: $25K
Ongoing royalty fee: 7%
Term of agreement: 5 years, renewable
Renewal fee: 5% of franchise fee
Qualifications:
Net worth requirement: $40K
Cash liquidity requirement: $13K
Business Experience:
– Marketing skills
– Working knowledge of Windows-based soft-
ware, comfortable selling and service, some
familiarity with construction/remodeling a plus

Lil' Angels Photography

Ranked 348/500
Preschool and day-care photography
4041 Hatcher Circle
Memphis, TN 38118
Phone: (800) 358-9101
Fax: (901) 682-2018
www.lilangelsphoto.com
Began in 1996, franchising since 1998
U.S. franchises: 99
Foreign franchises: 2
Costs:
Total investment: $30.7K–35.2K
Franchise fee: $17K
Ongoing royalty fee: 0
Term of agreement: 10 years, renewable
Qualifications:
Cash liquidity requirement: $32K
Business Experience:
- Sales experience preferred

The Sports Section
Ranked 191/500
Youth and youth sports photography
2150 Boggs Road, #200
Duluth, GA 30096
Phone: (866) 877-4746
Fax: (678) 740-0808
www.sports-section.com
frandev@sports-section.com
Began in 1983, franchising since 1984
Headquarters size: 130 employees
Franchising department: 35 employees
U.S. franchises: 215
Canadian franchises: 2
Other foreign franchises: 10
Costs:
Total investment: $24.7K–61.6K
Franchise fee: $12.9K–33.9K
Ongoing royalty fee: 0
Term of agreement: 10 years, renewable
Renewal fee: $1K
Qualifications:
Cash liquidity requirement: $16.4K–51K
Business Experience:
- Marketing skills
- Sales experience

Assist-2-Sell
Ranked 78/500
Discount real estate services
1610 Meadow Wood Lane
Reno, NV 89502
Phone: (800) 528-7816, (775) 688-6060
Fax: (775) 823-8823
www.assist2sell.com
Began in 1987, franchising since 1993
Headquarters size: 20 employees
Franchising department: 20 employees
U.S. franchises: 477
Canadian franchises: 6
Costs:
Total investment: $35K–62K
Franchise fee: $19.5K
Ongoing royalty fee: 5%
Term of agreement: 5 years, renewable
Renewal fee: $2.995K
Qualifications:
Cash liquidity requirement: $25K+
Business Experience:
- Industry experience
- Minimum two years' real estate sales experience

Avalar Real Estate and Mortgage Network
Ranked 389/500
Real estate and mortgage services
2911 Cleveland Avenue, #A
Santa Rosa, CA 95403
Phone: (800) 801-4030
Fax: (707) 546-7800
www.avalar.biz
Began in 1999, franchising since 1999
Headquarters size: 14 employees
Franchising department: 6 employees
U.S. franchises: 55
Costs:
Total investment: $31K–315.5K
Franchise fee: $4.4K–12.5K
Ongoing royalty fee: 5%
Term of agreement: 5 years, renewable
Qualifications:
Net worth requirement: $250K/500K
Cash liquidity requirement: $50K–100K

Section 13

Business Experience:
- Industry experience
- General business experience
- Marketing skills

Reality Executives International Inc.
Ranked 73/500
Real estate
2398 E. Camelback Road, #900
Phoenix, AZ 85016
Phone: (800) 252-3366, (602) 957-0747
Fax: (602) 224-5542
www.realtyexecutives.com
Began in 1965, franchising since 1973
Headquarters size: 15 employees
Franchising department: 4 employees
U.S. franchises: 778
Canadian franchises: 36
Other foreign franchises: 34
Costs:
Total investment: $18.6K–88.1K
Franchise fee: $1K–26K
Ongoing royalty fee: $50/licensee
Term of agreement: 5 years, renewable
Qualifications:
Cash liquidity requirement: $20K
Business Experience:
- Industry experience
- General business experience
- Marketing skills

Weichert Rea Estate Affiliates Inc.
Ranked 213/500
Real estate
225 Littleton Road
Morris Plains, NJ 07950
Phone: (973) 359-8377
Fax: (973) 292-1428
www.weichert.com
Began in 1969, franchising since 2000
Headquarters size: 1200 employees
Franchising department: 17 employees
U.S. franchises: 131
Costs:
Total investment: $45K–254K
Franchise fee: $25K
Ongoing royalty fee: 6%

Term of agreement: 7 years, renewable
Renewal fee: $1K
Business Experience:
- Industry experience
- General business experience
- Marketing skills

Interquest Detection Canines
Ranked 346/500
Drug detection using dogs
21900 Tomball Parkway
Houston, TX 77070-1526
Phone: (281) 320-1231
Fax: (281) 320-2512
www.interquestfranchise.com
Began in 1988, franchising since 1999
Headquarters size: 12 employees
Franchising department: 9 employees
U.S. franchises: 42
Costs:
Total investment: $46.5K–85.3K
Franchise fee: $30K
Ongoing royalty fee: 6%
Term of agreement: 10 years, renewable
Renewal fee: $3K
Qualifications:
Net worth requirement: $250K
Cash liquidity requirement: $50K
Business Experience:
- General business experience
- Marketing skills

Comforcare Senior Services Inc.
Ranked 384/500
Nonmedical home-care services
2510 Telegraph Road, #100
Bloomfield Hills, MI 48302
Phone: (800) 886-4044
Fax: (248) 745-9763
www.comforcare.com/franchise
Began in 1996, franchising since 2001
Headquarters size: 15 employees
Franchising department: 7 employees
U.S. franchises: 57
Costs:
Total investment: $40K–55K
Franchise fee: $16.5K

Section
13

Ongoing royalty fee: 3–5%
Term of agreement: 10 years, renewable
Renewal fee: $1.5K at most
Qualifications:
Net worth requirement: $100K
Cash liquidity requirement: $30K

Comfort Keepers
Ranked 116/500
Nonmedical in-home senior care
6640 Poe Avenue, #200
Dayton, OH 45414
Phone: (800) 387-2415
Fax: (937) 264-3103
www.comfortkeepers.com
admin@comfortkeepers.com
Began in 1998, franchising since 1999
Headquarters size: 23 employees
Franchising department: 6 employees
U.S. franchises: 512
Canadian franchises: 8
Other foreign franchises: 2
Costs:
Total investment: $41K–68K
Franchise fee: $23.2K
Ongoing royalty fee: 5-3%
Term of agreement: 10 years, renewable
Qualifications:
Net worth requirement: $75K+
Cash liquidity requirement: $44.5K–67K

Griswold Special Care
Ranked 331/500
Nonmedical home care
717 Bethlehem Pike, #300
Erdenheim, PA 19073
Phone: (215) 402-0200
Fax: (215) 402-0202
www.griswoldspecialcare.com
Began in 1982, franchising since 1984
Headquarters size: 70 employees
U.S. franchises: 79
Foreign franchises: 2
Costs:
Total investment: $15K–39K
Franchise fee: $9K
Ongoing royalty fee: 3-4%

Term of agreement: 7 years, renewable
Business Experience:
- Industry experience
- General business experience
- Marketing skills
- (Qualifications helpful but not required)

Visiting Angels
Ranked 193/500
Nonmedical home-care agencies
28 W. Eagle Road, #201
Havertown, PA 19083
Phone: (800) 365-4189, (610) 924-0630
Fax: (610) 924-9690
www.livingassistance.com
info@visitingangel.com
Began in 1992, franchising since 1998
Headquarters size: 13 employees
Franchising department: 10 employees
U.S. franchises: 225
Canadian franchises: 5
Costs:
Total investment: $25.99K–47.2K
Franchise fee: $25.99K–47.2K
Ongoing royalty fee: 2.95-2%
Term of agreement: 10 years, renewable
Renewal fee: $2.5K
Qualifications:
Net worth requirement: $30K–50K
Cash liquidity requirement: $15K

Complete Music
Ranked 302/500
Disc jockey service for weddings, parties, and other events
7877 L Street
Omaha, NE 68127
Phone: (800) 843-3866, (402) 339-0001
Fax: (402) 898-1777
www.cmusic.com
Began in 1974, franchising since 1983
Headquarters size: 10 employees
Franchising department: 6 employees
U.S. franchises: 161
Canadian franchises: 2
Costs:
Total investment: $19.8K–33K

Section 13

Franchise fee: $12K–20K
Ongoing royalty fee: 6.5–8%
Term of agreement: 10 years, renewable
Qualifications:
Net worth requirement: $50K
Cash liquidity requirement: $10K
Business Experience:
– General business experience

Protocol LLC

Ranked 477/500
Personal-care product vending machines
1370 Mendota Heights Road
Mendota Heights, MN 55120
Phone: (800) 227-5336, (651) 454-0518
Fax: (651) 454-9542
www.protocolvending.com
Began in 1987, franchising since 1996
Headquarters size: 60 employees

Franchising department: 10 employees
U.S. franchises: 47
Costs:
Total investment: $10.2K–22K
Franchise fee: $500
Ongoing royalty fee: 0
Term of agreement: 2 years, renewable
Qualifications:
Net worth requirement: $500K
Cash liquidity requirement: $50K
Business Experience:
– General business experience
– Marketing skills

Source: Rieva Lesonsky and Maria Anton-Conley, *Entrepreneur Magazine's Ultimate Book of Low-Cost Franchises 2005/2006.*

Chapter 83

Franchising Advice and Help

Section
13

Top Five Characteristics of Successful Franchisees

1. **Risk aversion:** Successful franchisees are risk-averse. They are willing to take some risk but want that risk to be as small and controlled as possible. Any business start-up involves some risk of failure, but a strong franchise with a proven track record of success will minimize this risk. Successful franchisees do their homework, so they know what they're getting into.

2. **System orientation:** Entrepreneurs have an almost uncontrollable urge to reinvent the wheel based on their incredible confidence in their ability to figure out how things should be done to maximize results. Successful franchisees, on the other hand, want proven systems. They don't want to have to figure out the best way to do something. They want a system of operation that tells them the best way to do anything associated with the business. They are willing to learn from others to avoid making mistakes, so they can be more successful more quickly.

3. **Coachability:** The motto of franchising is "In business for yourself, not by yourself." Successful franchisees look for opportunities to learn from others in their franchise system. Their philosophy is "When in doubt, ask." They constantly ask advice of the franchisor support staff and other successful franchisees and follow the advice they get. They understand that they don't know all the answers and are willing to ask for help when they need it.

4. **Hard-work affinity:** Successful franchisees have a willingness to do whatever it takes to get the job done. This attitude shows in their every action—putting in long hours, handling multiple tasks. No matter what franchise you're interested in, you can be sure it's going to take work to make it successful. The best franchisees know and accept that fact.

5. **Strong people skills:** Successful franchisees always have excellent interpersonal skills and can effectively interact with their employees and customers. They use these skills to create loyalty, value, and trust. Though this characteristic is listed last, it's probably the most important of all.

As you review this list, be honest with yourself. Do you already have each of these characteristics? If not, can you focus on applying yourself to developing and effectively portraying these characteristics through your actions?

If the answer to either of these questions is yes, you're on your way to becoming a successful franchisee. As always, take the time to thoroughly investigate any franchise opportunity to make sure the track record is strong and dependable, and you'll be set.

Source: Jeff Elgin, "Top 5 Characteristics of Successful Franchisees," www.entrepreneur.com/article/0,4621,307790,00.html.

The Six Steps to Franchising

Preface

The first thing you need to keep in mind in your investigation is that it is a process of mutual elimination for both you and the franchisor. You might find exactly the franchise you're looking for on the first try, but that is highly unlikely unless you are using a consultant like FranChoice (www.franchoice.com) to narrow the search for you. You should also understand that it is unlikely that any one person contacting the franchisor will turn out to be a great match for the franchise. Therefore both of you are trying to determine if the fit seems right from the beginning of the investigation. If either party comes to the realization that this is not the right match, he or she simply informs the other party and moves on.

Step One—General Information

The franchisor will begin by providing you with overview information on the company (typically a brochure and video package). He or she will then ask you to provide additional information on yourself (by filling out a questionnaire) to determine if you have the general characteristics that he or she is looking for. If each party is still interested, based on this information exchange, you will proceed to the next step.

Step Two—The Uniform Franchise Offering Circular

This document, commonly referred to as the UFOC, is the FTC-mandated disclosure document that gives you a wealth of information about the franchisor. The form and composition of the document are standard with any franchisor and must include information on a variety of topics of interest to you.

Step 3—Franchisee Calls and Visits

The most valuable source of information on any franchise system is the current franchisees. You need to plan on calling or visiting a number of the franchisees during your investigation. It sounds almost trite, but whatever you find the prevailing attitude of the franchisees on any issue to be, it will almost certainly be your attitude on the issue as well if you decide to become a franchisee. Visit with a sufficient number of the current franchisees to ensure you have a sense of the prevailing attitudes of the group.

Step 4—Review the System Documentation

A strong franchise company will have documented its systems, operations, and marketing programs in a concise and easy-to-use format for the reference of franchisees. Make sure that such documentation exists.

Step 5—Meet the People

At some point in the process of investigation, you will want to have personal meetings with key personnel of the franchise company. This might be possible in your local market or you may need to travel to the headquarters of the franchisor. Many franchisors facilitate this need by holding what are referred to as "Discovery Days." These are struc-

Section 13

tured events: you can go to a specified location and know that all of the key people from the franchisor will be available.

Step 6—Make a Decision

If you have been diligent, the entire process outlined above should have taken about two to four weeks to complete. You have now finished your investigation and have all the information you need to determine if this franchise is right for you.

Source: Franchise-Consultation.com, "Franchise Company Investigation Procedure," www.franchise-consultation.com.

The Pros and Cons of Buying into a Franchise

Pros

- Reduction of risk
- Turnkey operation
- Standardized products and systems
- Standardized financial and accounting systems
- Collective buying power
- Supervision and consulting readily available
- National and local advertising programs
- Point-of-sale advertising
- Uniform packaging
- Ongoing research and development
- Financial assistance
- Site selection guidance
- Operations manual provided
- Sales and marketing assistance

Cons

- Loss of control
- A binding contract
- The franchisor's problems are also your problems
- Very time-intense in the beginning

Source: Laura Tiffany, "Franchise Basics," www.entrepreneur.com/article/0,4621,285725,00.html.

Questions to Ask Yourself Before Deciding to Buy a Franchise

Financial

1. Have you and your spouse and knowledgeable family members discussed the idea of buying a franchise?

2. Are you in complete agreement?

3. Do you have the financial resources required to buy a franchise? If not, where are you going to get the capital?

4. Are you and your spouse ready to make the necessary sacrifices in the way of money and time in order to operate a franchise?

5. Will the possible loss of company benefits, including retirement plans, be outweighed by the potential rewards in terms of money and pride that would come from owning a franchise?

6. Have you made a thorough written balance sheet of your assets and liabilities, as well as liquid cash resources?

7. Will your savings provide you with a cushion for at least one year after you have paid for the franchise, allowing one year to break even?

8. Do you have additional sources of financing, including friends or relatives who might be able to loan you money in the event that your initial financing proves inadequate?

9. Do you realize that most new businesses, including franchises, generally do not break even for at least one year after opening?

10. Will one of you remain employed at your current occupation while the franchise is in its initial, pre-profit stage?

Personal

11. Are you and your spouse physically able to handle the emotional and physical strain involved in operating a franchise, caused by long hours and tedious administrative chores?

12. Will your family members, particularly small children, suffer from your absence for several years while you build up your business?

13. Are you prepared to give up some independence of action in exchange for the advantages the franchise offers you?

14. Have you really examined the type of franchise or business you desire and truthfully concluded that you would enjoy running it for several years or until retirement?

15. Have you and your spouse had recent physicals?

16. Are the present state of your health and that of your spouse good?

Section 13

17. Do you and your spouse enjoy working with others?

18. Do you have the ability and experience to work smoothly and profitably with your franchisor, your employees, and your customers?

19. Have you asked your friends and relatives for their candid opinions of your emotional, mental, and physical suitability to running your own businesses?

20. Do you have a capable, willing heir to take over the business if you become disabled?

21. If the franchise is not near your present home, do you realize that it would not be beneficial to sell your home and buy one closer until the new venture is successful?

22. Do you and your spouse have past experience in business that will qualify you for the particular type of franchise you desire?

23. Is it possible for either you or your spouse to become employed in the type of business you seek to buy before any purchase?

24. Have you conducted independent research on the industry you are contemplating entering?

25. If you have made your choice of franchises, have you researched the background and experience of your prospective franchisor?

26. Have you determined whether the product or service you propose to sell has a market in your prospective territory at the prices you will have to charge?

27. What will the market for your product or service be five years from now?

28. What competition exists in your prospective territory already?

29. From franchise businesses?

30. From non-franchise businesses?

Other Considerations

31. Do you know an experienced, business-oriented franchise attorney who can evaluate the franchise contract you are considering?

32. Do you know an experienced, business-minded accountant?

33. Have you prepared a business plan for the franchise of your choice?

Source: Erwin J. Keup, *Franchise Bible* (Entrepreneur Press).

Questions to Ask Yourself Before Approaching a Franchisor

To test your instincts, answer each of the following 24 questions. If your answer to any of the questions is no, or if you're simply not sure how to answer, further investigation of the franchise is definitely a good idea.

The Franchise Organization

- Does the franchisor have a good track record?
- Do the principals of the franchise have industry expertise?
- Is the franchisor's financial condition strong?
- Does the franchisor thoroughly screen its franchisees?
- Are the franchisor and its franchisees profitable?

The Product or Service

- Is there demand for the product or service?
- Are industry sales strong?
- Does the franchise's product or service fare well against competitors' offerings?
- Is the product or service priced competitively?
- Is there a lot of potential for growth in the industry?

The Market Area

- Does the franchisor offer exclusive territories?
- Does the territory you're considering have sales potential?
- Is the competition strong in this area?
- Are the other franchises near this area successful?

The Contract

- Are the fees and royalties reasonable?
- Are the renewal, termination, and transfer conditions reasonable?
- If the franchisor requires you to purchase proprietary inventory, is that inventory useful?
- If the franchisor requires you to meet annual sales quotas, are those quotas reasonable?

Franchisor Support

- Does the franchisor help with site selection, lease negotiations, and store layout?
- Does the franchisor provide ongoing training?
- Does the franchisor provide financing?
- Does the franchisor sponsor an advertising fund to which franchisees contribute?
- Are the franchisor's promotional programs strong?
- Does the franchisor have favorable national contracts for goods and services?

Source: "Franchisor Checklist," www.entrepreneur.com/article/0,4621,285409,00.html.

Section 13

Top Ten Money Questions to Ask Before Buying a Franchise

Before you decide to invest your time into a franchise, do some research and make sure you have the funds ready available before making the commitment.

1. **How much total investment will this franchise require?** This is a key question, since the Uniform Franchise Offering Circular (UFOC) document normally expresses this information in terms of a very large range of possible answers. In your calls to current franchisees and your research concerning your local market, make sure to narrow down these answers to provide as accurate an answer as possible. If you aren't completely sure, be sure to err on the high side.

2. **How much will I need in operating capital reserves to cover losses until the franchise reaches the breakeven point in cash flow?** You're not going to have any customers or revenue on the morning of your first day in your new business, but you will have expenses. Until your revenue grows enough to cover these expenses, you're going to have to feed additional cash into the business to pay the bills. Make sufficient allowance for this factor in your plans and, when in doubt, guess high. No one has ever gotten into trouble on a business start-up because he or she had put too much into financial reserves.

3. **How much extra cash do I need to cover living expenses while starting my franchise?** This is one of the critical areas many new franchisees fail to consider. After becoming a franchisee, there's a gap in time before your new business begins operating and typically another gap before it starts making enough profit to cover your living expenses. You need to carefully budget your living expenses to understand how much you'll need on a monthly basis and then make sure you've got sufficient cash—in addition to your business investment—to cover your expenses during this period. Then add a significant reserve on top of this amount—it'll help you sleep better at night.

4. **How long will it take my new franchise to reach breakeven?** This is one of the most important money-related questions you'll need to answer. It's no fun to feed extra money into a business to cover operating losses, but that's the reality in most start-ups. You'll normally find the answer to this question is a potential range of time for the franchise you're considering. Always plan that it'll take the longest time within this range to reach breakeven, so you're as safe as possible.

5. **How much of my total investment (including capital reserves) do I need to have in cash?** This answer can range from zero to 100 percent, depending on the franchise business you're contemplating. There's no right or wrong answer—just make sure you know what applies to you and that you easily have that amount of cash on hand.

6. **What standard financing options exist for me?** The most common forms of standard financing are bank loans and/or commercial leases. Any bank loan to start a new business will probably have to be secured either by your personal collateral (such as the equity in your home) or through an SBA guarantee program, and the

banks may require both forms of security. Most new franchisees find that securing an open line of credit against their home equity is the easiest and least expensive form of bank financing available to them. Leases can also be a favorable option, since they are typically fast to procure and secured by the assets that are being leased (though they sometimes require a personal guarantee as well).

7. **What alternative financing options exist for me?** In addition to standard sources, there's always the standby financing source: family and friends. There are also a number of companies that help people access retirement dollars in IRA or 401(k) accounts, without early withdrawal penalties, to use as a funding source for a franchise business.

8. **How much money can I make in this franchise?** This is the $64 question. You will normally find the answer is related to the amount of time the business has been open. The first year will probably be a loss, but by the third year the business should be making good money. Ask a lot of current franchisees about their experience at these levels. Make sure you know what your probable income will be by the time you complete that critical third year.

9. **What are the ranges in financial performance of the current franchisees?** Though we've previously referred to the fact that there is going to be a range in franchisees' answers, this point is so important that it bears repeating. Don't stop your research until you are completely confident you know both the high and low ends of the range. Two answers are not sufficient to establish a range you can have confidence in; ten or even more would be much better.

10. **How financially strong is the franchise company?** The franchise company is required to provide you with a copy of its audited financial statements in the UFOC document. You obviously want to work with a franchise company that not only is strong enough to survive, but also has the resources to reinvest in training and support of the franchisees. Make sure you review their financials and ask for help from a competent advisor if you're not comfortable doing this yourself.

Source: Jeff Elgin, "Top 10 Money Questions to Ask Before Buying a Franchise," www.entrepreneur.com/franzone/article/0,5847,322596,00.html.

Ten Warning Signs to Spot a Franchise Scam

1. **The Rented Rolls-Royce Syndrome.** The overdressed, jewelry-laden sales representative works hard to impress you with an appearance of success. These people reek of money—and you hope, quite naturally, that it will rub off on you. (Motto: "Don't you want to be like me?") Antidote: Check the financial statements in the Uniform Franchise Offering Circular; they're required to be audited.

2. **The Hustle.** Giveaway sales pitches: "Territories are going fast!" "Act now or you'll be

shut out!" "I'm leaving town on Monday afternoon, so make your decision now." They make you feel that you'd be a worthless, indecisive dreamer not to take immediate action. (Motto: "Wimps need not apply.") Antidote: Take your time and recognize The Hustle for the crude closing technique that it is.

3. **The Cash-Only Transaction.** An obvious clue that companies are running their programs on the fly: they want cash so there's no way to trace them and so you can't stop payment if things crash and burn. (Motto: "In God we trust; all others pay cash.") Antidote: Insist on writing a check—made out to the company, not to an individual. Better yet, walk away.

4. **The Boast.** "Our dealers are pulling in six figures. We're not interested in small thinkers. If you think big, you can join the ranks of the really big money earners in our system. The sky's the limit." And this was in answer to your straightforward question about the names of purchasers in your area. (Motto: "We never met an exaggeration we didn't like.") Antidote: Write your own business plan and make it realistic. Don't try to be a big thinker—just a smart one.

5. **The Big-Money Claim.** Most state authorities point to exaggerated profit claims as the biggest problem in business opportunity and franchise sales. "Earn $10,000 a month in your spare time" sounds great, doesn't it? (Motto: "We can sling the zeros with the best of 'em.") If it's a franchise, any statement about earnings (regarding others in the system or your potential earnings) must appear in the Uniform Franchise Offering Circular. Antidote: Read the UFOC and find five franchise owners who have attained the earnings claimed.

6. **The Couch Potato's Dream.** "Make money in your spare time .... This business can be operated on the phone while you're at the beach .... Two hours a week earns $10,000 a month." (Motto: "Why not be lazy and rich?") Understand this and understand it now: the only easy money in a deal like this one will be made by the seller. Antidote: Get off the couch and roll up your sleeves for some honest and rewarding work.

7. **Location, Location, Location.** Buyers are frequently disappointed by promises of services from third-party location hunters. "We'll place these pistachio dispensers in prime locations in your town." (Motto: "I've got 10 sweet locations that are going to make you rich.") Turns out all the best locations are taken and the bar owners will not insure the machines against damage by their inebriated patrons. Next thing you know, your dining room table is loaded with pistachio dispensers—and your kids don't even like pistachios. Antidote: Get in the car and check for available locations.

8. **The Disclosure Dance.** "Disclosure? Well, we're, uh, exempt from disclosure because we're, uh, not a public corporation. Yeah, that's it." (Motto: "Trust me, kid.") No business-format franchisor, with very rare exceptions, is exempt from delivering a disclosure document at your first serious sales meeting or at least 10 business days before the sale takes place. Antidote: "Disclosure: don't let your money leave your pocket without it."

9. **The Registration Ruse.** You check out the franchisor with state authorities and they respond, "Who?" (Motto: "Registration? We don't need no stinking registration!") In 15 states, franchisors are required to register; in Florida, Nebraska, and Texas, franchisors may file for exemption. Antidote: If you are in a franchise registration state (California, Hawaii, Illinois, Indiana, Maryland, Michigan, Minnesota, New York, North Dakota, Oregon, Rhode Island, South Dakota, Virginia, Washington, and Wisconsin) and the company is not registered, find out why. (Some companies are legitimately exempt.)

10. **The Thinly Capitalized Franchisor.** This franchisor dances lightly around the issue of its available capital. (Motto: "Don't you worry about all that bean-counter hocus-pocus. We don't.") Antidote: Take the UFOC to your accountant and learn what resources the franchisor has to back up its contractual obligations. If its capitalization is too thin or it has a negative net worth, it's not necessarily a scam, but the investment is riskier.

Source: Andrew A. Caffey, "How to Spot a Scam," www.entrepreneur.com/article/0,4621,287579,00.html.

Five Questions Not Answered in the Uniform Franchise Offering Circular

Don't make the mistake of assuming that the UFOC will tell you everything you need to know about the franchise investment. It is designed by regulators to deliver information that they consider important to the investor. However, here are five of the most important missed areas.

1. **Pricing/Product Distribution.** The guidelines for franchisors to follow in preparing this section are complex and cumbersome, resulting in confusing disclosures that are not particularly helpful. After all, smooth product sourcing, the savings on prices available based on large group purchases, and carefully considered product specifications are all fundamental business reasons for buying a franchise. Make a point of exploring product dynamics with the franchisees you meet. Check the franchise agreement and any other paperwork from the franchisor describing product matters.

2. **Franchisee Associations.** Nowhere in the UFOC is a franchisor required to disclose the existence of a franchisee association or advisory council. Yet this is an important aspect of the franchise program for a new investor. The presence of a strong association that is well attended and governed by franchisees is an attractive asset of any franchise program. Some associations are created by the franchisor and promoted by the company; others are "renegade associations" created by the franchisees and resented by the franchisor. Ask current franchisees about the role they play through an association or a franchisee council.

Section 13

3. **Training.** One of the keys to franchisee success is solid training. The UFOC will give you some of the basic facts; however, you need assurances about the program that cannot be delivered in a disclosure document. Is the training effective? Do franchisees feel that they are well prepared to run a successful business upon completing it? Is the training based on current thinking? Is it the best available in the field? Is it complete? How much of it is hands on, under supervision? Be sure you explore these ideas with franchisees and your franchisor representatives.

4. **Market for Product/Service.** This is a basic but intangible question that is difficult to address in a disclosure document. Is the market for the product or service a strong one? Is the growth of the market for the business on the rise or decline?

5. **Franchisor Support.** The language in a franchise agreement that describes the level of the franchisor's continuing support may be surprising. You are likely to find something like "The franchisor will provide such continuing advice and support as it deems appropriate in its absolute discretion." How's that for reassurance?! Even though the promises might be modest, the practice is important. Find out exactly— from franchisees and franchisor's representatives—what the company does for its new franchisees when they are planning to locate the business, when they are hiring staff, and during the opening and start-up phase. Is help available? Is it responsive? Will the franchisor be there to help if and when things go wrong?

Source: Andrew A. Caffey, "Information Not Included," www.entrepreneur.com/article/ 0,4621,299163,00.html.

Checklist for Interviewing Current Franchisees

Use this questionnaire when trying to investigate franchise opportunities by interviewing current franchisees.

Financial

1. Are you satisfied with the franchisor?

2. Is your franchise profitable?

3. Have you made the profit you expected to make?

4. Are your actual costs those stated in the offering circular?

5. Is the product or service you sell of good quality?

6. Is delivery of goods from the franchisor adequate?

7. How long did it take you to break even?

8. Was the training provided to you by the franchisor adequate?

9. What is your assessment of the training provided?

10. Is your franchisor fair and easy to work with?

11. Does your franchisor listen to your concerns?

12. Have you had any disputes with your franchisor? If so, please specify.

13. If you have had any disputes, were you able to settle them?

14. How was your settlement accomplished?

15. Do you know of any trouble the franchisor has had with other franchisees? If so, what was the nature of the problem?

16. Do you know of any trouble the franchisor has had with the government?

17. Do you know of any trouble the franchisor has had with local authorities?

18. Do you know of any trouble the franchisor has had with competitors?

19. Are you satisfied with the marketing and promotional assistance the franchisor has provided?

20. Have the operations manuals provided by the franchisor helped you?

21. What do you think of the manuals?

22. Are the manuals changed frequently? If so, why?

23. Would you like to make any other comments?

Checklist of Information to Secure from a Franchisor
Use this checklist when investigating and gathering information.

24. Is the franchisor a one-person company or a corporation with experienced managers who are well trained?

25. Does the franchisor operate a business of the type being franchised?

26. Is the franchisor involved in other business activities?

27. Is the franchisor offering you an exclusive territory for the length of the franchise or can the franchisor sell a second or third franchise in your market area?

28. Do you have the right of first refusal to adjacent areas?

29. Will the franchisor sublet space to you or will the franchisor help you find a location for franchise operation?

30. Must you lease fixtures, signs, or equipment from the franchise? If so, are the prices reasonable?

31. Does the franchisor provide financing? If so, what are the terms?

32. Does the franchisor require any fees from the franchisee other than those described in the offering circular? If so, what are they?

33. Has the franchisor given you information regarding actual, average, or forecast sales?

34. Has the franchisor given you information regarding actual, average, or forecast profits?

35. Has the franchisor given you information regarding actual, average, or forecast earnings?

36. What information have you received?

37. Will the franchisor provide you with the success rates of current franchisees?

38. Will the franchisor provide you with their names and locations?

39. Are there any restrictions on what items you may sell? If so, what are they?

40. Does your prospective franchisor allow variances in the contracts of some of its other franchisees? What is the nature of the variances?

41. In the event you sell your franchise back to your franchisor under the right of first refusal, will you be compensated for the goodwill you have built into the business?

42. Does the franchisor have any federally registered trademarks, service marks, trade names, logotypes, and/or symbols?

43. Are you, as a franchisee, entitled to use them without reservation?

44. Are there restrictions, exceptions, or conditions? If so, what are they?

45. Does the franchisor have existing patents and copyrights on equipment you will use or items you will sell?

46. Does the franchisor have endorsement agreement with any public figures for advertising purposes? If so, what are the terms?

47. Has the franchisor investigated you carefully enough to feel sure that you can successfully operate the franchise at a profit both to the franchise and to yourself?

48. Has the franchisor complied with FTC and state disclosure laws? Are there any regulations specific to the industry in which your franchise business will operate? (Include any special licenses or legal restriction on operations set by statutes.)

49. Does the franchisor have a reputation for honesty and fair dealing among the local firms holding its franchises?

Other Questions

50. How many years has the firm offering you a franchise been in operation?

51. What is a description of the franchise area offered you?

52. What is the total investment the franchisor requires from the franchisee?

53. How does the franchisor use the initial franchise fees?

54. What is the extent of the training the franchisor will provide for you?

55. What are your obligations for purchasing or leasing goods or services from the franchisor or other designated sources?

56. What are your obligations in relation to purchasing or leasing goods or services in accordance with the franchisor's specifications?

57. What are the terms of your agreement regarding termination, modification, and renewal conditions of the franchise agreement?

58. Under what circumstances can you terminate the franchise agreement?

59. If you decide to cancel the franchise agreement, what will it cost you?

60. What are the background experience and achievement records of key personnel (their "track records")?

61. How successful is the franchise operation? (Use D&B reports or magazine articles to supplement information the franchisor gives you.)

62. What is the franchisor's experience in relation to past litigation or prior bankruptcies?

63. What is the quality of the financial statements the franchisor provides you?

64. Exactly what can the franchisor do for you that you cannot do for yourself?

Source: Erwin J. Keup, *Franchise Bible* (Entrepreneur Press).

Negotiating Your Franchise Agreement

There are a number of reasons franchise companies refuse to negotiate, including:

- The issue of fairness. Why should a better negotiator get a better deal on the terms of the franchise, rather than every franchisee getting the same deal?

- The issue of legal requirements. A franchise company must comply with laws requiring it to disclose special deals or terms it negotiates under certain circumstances or with selected parties. This requirement protects other prospective franchisees through full disclosure, but compliance is cumbersome for a franchise that's executing many different terms.

- The issue of administration. It's a nightmare for a franchise system if every franchisee is on a different contract form with various terms and provisions. There's a significant cost to doing business this way, because every question that comes up requires a contract review before an opinion can be given.

Preparing for Your Negotiation

- Get an attorney to review the contracts. There are lawyers who specialize in franchise agreements.

- Even though good franchises are unwilling to negotiate terms, as mentioned above, many other franchise companies are willing to negotiate their franchise agreements. In fact, many of them will negotiate virtually any provision other than the initial, upfront fees you pay them. If you give this fact a little thought, you'll see the potential risk this situation represents for you.

- Call as many current franchisees as possible and find out what deal they got. In many cases, they might be willing to send you copies of the addendum with the changes they negotiated, so you can get a quick feel for what's available and make sure you're not missing anything.

Source: Jeff Elgin, "Negotiating Your Franchise Agreement," www.entrepreneur.com/article/ 0,4621,304524,00.html.

Section 13

List of Top Franchise Attorneys

Michael R. Liss
Edwards, Liss & Murray
Oak Brook, IL
(630) 571-5626
www.ibusinesslaw.org

Robin Day Glenn
Franchise Law Team
Rancho Santa Margarita, CA
(949) 459-7474, (888) 276-2976 (toll-free)
www.franchiselawteam.com

Javad Heydary
Heydary Garfin Hamilton LLP
Toronto, Ontario
(416) 972-9001, (866) HEYDARY (439-3279)
(toll-free)
www.heydary.com

Daniel Kaplan
Kaplan & Greenswag LLC
Northfield, IL
(847) 501-5300
www.kaplangreenswag.com

Steven Feirman, Partner
DLA Piper Rudnick Gray Cary
Washington, DC
(202) 861-3950, (703) 773-4240
www.dlapiper.com

Carmen D. Caruso, Partner
Schwartz, Cooper, Greenberger & Krauss
Chicago, IL
(312) 346-1300
www.schwartzcooper.com

Christopher Smith
Sonnenschein Nath & Rosenthal LLP
Washington, DC
(202) 408-9231, (202) 408-6400
www.sonnenschein.com

David Holmes
Holmes & Lofstrom
San Luis Obispo, CA

(805) 547-0697
www.holmeslofstrom.com

Margaret Narodick
Holmes & Lofstrom
Long Beach, CA
(562) 596-0116
www.holmeslofstrom.com

Stephen E. Story
Kaufman & Canoles
Norfolk, VA
(757) 624-3257, (757) 624-3000
www.kaufmanandcanoles.com

Genevieve A. Beck
Larkin, Hoffman, Daly & Lindgren, Ltd.
Minneapolis, MN
(952) 896-3293
www.lhdl.com

Pamela Mills
Sonnenschein Nath & Rosenthal LLP
Chicago, IL
(312) 876-7547, (312) 876-8000
www.sonnenschein.com

Jon Swierzewski
Larkin, Hoffman, Daly & Lindgren, Ltd.
Minneapolis, MN
(952) 896-3280, (952) 835-3800
www.lhdl.com

Harold Kestenbaum
Farrell Fritz, P.C.
Uniondale, NY
(516) 745-0099, (516) 227-0700
www.farrellfritz.com

Stephen A. Colley
Stephen A. Colley, APC
San Diego, CA
(858) 259-0888
www.stephenacolley.com

Thomas Oppold
Larkin, Hoffman, Daly & Lindgren, Ltd.
Minneapolis, MN
(952) 896-3397
www.lhdl.com

Alan Silberman
Sonnenschein Nath & Rosenthal LLP
Chicago, IL
(312) 876-8000
www.sonnenschein.com

Katherine Funk
Sonnenschein Nath & Rosenthal LLP
Washington, DC
(202) 408-6400
www.sonnenschein.com

John Baer
Sonnenschein Nath & Rosenthal LLP
Chicago, IL
(312) 876-8000
www.sonnenschein.com

James Goniea
Sonnenschein Nath & Rosenthal LLP
San Francisco, CA
(415) 882-5000
www.sonnenschein.com

Rochelle (Shelley) Spandorf
Sonnenschein Nath & Rosenthal LLP
Los Angeles, CA
(213) 623-9300
www.sonnenschein.com

Kenneth Costello
Jenkens & Gilchrist
Los Angeles, CA
(310) 442-8844, (310) 820-8800
www.jenkens.com

John Sotos
Sotos Associates
Toronto, Ontario
(416) 977-0007, (416) 977-5333 x 303
www.sotoslaw.com

Bret Lowell
DLA Piper Rudnick Gray Cary

Reston, VA
(703) 773-4242
www.dlapiper.com

Sandy Tucker
Williams Mullen
Richmond, VA
(804) 783-6418
www.williamsmullen.com

Stuart Hershman
DLA Piper Rudnick Gray Cary
Chicago, IL
(312) 368-2164
www.dlapiper.com

Charles S. Modell
Larkin, Hoffman, Daly & Lindgren, Ltd.
Minneapolis, MN
(952) 896-3341
www.lhdl.com

Stephen Rovak
Sonnenschein Nath & Rosenthal LLP
St. Louis, MO
(314) 241-1800
www.sonnenschein.com

Curtis Woods
Sonnenschein Nath & Rosenthal LLP
Kansas City, MO
(816) 460-2434, (816) 460-2400
www.sonnenschein.com

Brian Schnell
Faegre & Benson LLP
Minneapolis, MN
(612) 766-7472, (612) 766-7000
www.faegre.com

Srijoy Das
Archer & Angel
New Delhi, India
91-11-26261302
www.archerangel.com

Joseph Fittante
Larkin, Hoffman, Daly & Lindgren, Ltd.
Minneapolis, MN
(952) 896-3293, (952) 896-3256
www.lhdl.com

Section
13

Michael Millerick
Massie, Berman & Millerick
San Diego, CA
(619) 239-7790
www.mbmlaw.com

Michael Einbinder
Einbinder & Dunn, LLP
New York, NY
(212) 391-9500
www.ed-lawfirm.com

Rob Vinson
Vinson Franchise Law Firm
Incline Village, NV
(775) 832-5577
franchiselaw.net

Ann Hurwitz
DLA Piper Rudnick Gray Cary
Dallas, TX
(214) 743-4521
www.dlapiper.com

Martin Mendelsohn
Eversheds
London, UK
44-20-7919-4500
www.eversheds.com

Ritchie Taylor
Manning Fulton & Skinner, P.A.
Raleigh, NC
(919) 787-8880, (919) 510-9270
www.manningfulton.com

Henri-Xavier Ortoli
Eversheds
Paris, France
33 1 55 73 41 32
www.eversheds.com

Robert King Jr.
Sonnenschein Nath & Rosenthal LLP
Chicago, IL
(312) 876-8000
www.sonnenschein.com

Andrew F. Perrin
Larkin, Hoffman, Daly & Lindgren, Ltd.

Minneapolis, MN
(952) 896-3394
www.lhdl.com

Thomas M. Pitegoff
Pitegoff Law Office
White Plains, NY
(914) 681-0100
www.pitlaw.com

Kevin J. Collette
Ryan, Swanson & Cleveland, PLLC
Seattle, WA
(206) 654-2252
www.ryanlaw.com

Robert Joseph
Sonnenschein Nath & Rosenthal LLP
Chicago, IL
(312) 876-8000
www.sonnenschein.com

Al Mohajerian
Mohajerian Law Corp.
Los Angeles, CA
(310) 289-9625, (310) 556-3800
www.mohajerianlaw.com

James Cobb
Wyrick Robbins Yates & Ponton, LLP
Raleigh, NC
(919) 781-4000
www.wyrick.com

Lori Lofstrom
Holmes & Lofstrom
Long Beach, CA
(562) 596-0116
www.holmeslofstrom.com

Jeff Brown
J. Brown & Associates, LLC
Denver, CO
(303) 228-2177
www.jbrownlegal.com

Gary R. Duvall
Dorsey & Whitney, LLP
Seattle, WA
(206) 903-8800
www.dorsey.com

Eric Sternberger
Eric Sternberger, Attorney at Law
San Rafael, CA
(415) 459-3180
www.sternberger-law.com

Steven Feirman
DLA Piper Rudnick Gray Cary
Reston, VA
(703) 773-4240
www.dlapiper.com

Debra S. Hill
The Hill Law Firm
Jacksonville, FL
(904) 346-0140
www.smithhilllaw.com

Source: Franchise.com, www.efranchise.com/en/
us/template/buyer,AttorneyDirectory.vm.

Tips for Buying a Foreign-Based Franchise

Jeff Elgin, Entrepreneur "Buying a Franchise" coach, explains that buying a foreign franchise "is an exciting business dynamic, as it gives franchisees a fantastic way to take advantage of business concepts that may not exist in the domestic market or that have a unique twist. That said, this dynamic also raises a number of questions in the minds of many prospective franchisees."

"How safe is investing with a foreign-based franchise?"

The same disclosure requirements that apply to a domestic franchise also apply to any foreign company that comes into the United States to offer franchise opportunities. The franchise must provide you with a UFOC disclosure document containing information on key mandated factors. It is also subject to the same consumer protection rules in terms of the behavior of its representatives during the process of selling their franchise.

"What corporate structure do foreign-based franchises typically use in the United States?"

Most successful international franchising, in either direction, uses a "master licensing" arrangement. In this scenario, the franchisor finds a domestic partner that it contractually agrees will develop the franchise in the selected country. In the case of foreign-based franchises, this is the most typical structure we see. The foreign-based company will research the franchise business in the United States, then interview and select a master licensee that will own and control the franchise rights in this market.

"What extra research do I need to undertake?"

It's always a good idea to check out the past results of any franchise company. In the case of foreign-based franchises, you effectively have two companies you should research: the U.S. master licensee and the foreign-based main franchise company. You want to make sure the U.S. master has a track record of performance sufficient to demonstrate that the people know what they are doing and can help you be successful. You also need to know that they are strong enough financially to last and support your efforts long term.

"What if I am the first U.S. franchisee?"

There's an old adage used in relation to smart money investing in franchises: "When in doubt, send a scout." The simple fact is that being the first franchisee, or even part of

Section 13

the first group of franchisees, in any system under any circumstances always involves far more risk than waiting until later. Until they are tested in the real world, the company simply doesn't know how well its operating systems, marketing, training, and brand are going to work. If you do decide to be a test subject for them in their new U.S. operation, one advantage you may have relates to bargaining power. The very least you should do is negotiate for some form of an early-bird discount of costs, such as the initial franchise fee.

"What are the red flags I should be on the lookout for with a foreign-based franchise company?"
There is really just one, and that involves the transition of the opportunity into a different culture. There are many examples of U.S.-based franchises that have struggled when they brought their concepts into a foreign country because of cultural or language barriers. Make sure you have taken this into consideration prior to making any investment. If the company has not been operating in the domestic U.S. market long enough to prove the effectiveness of its concept, you have exactly the same risk as with any other start-up franchise—you don't know for sure that it's going to work well and you should therefore be cautious.

Investing in a franchise concept that has been developed and proven in another country before entering the U.S. market can be a wonderful opportunity ... or a train wreck. The only way to know for sure is to conduct a complete and thorough investigation of the franchise. This includes researching the people operating the franchise, the capital structure of the U.S. entity offering the franchises, and the track record of success they've achieved with other U.S. franchisees.

One final piece of advice: when in doubt about anything, ask the franchisor. Don't be bashful about this, since they have probably been asked the same thing by many others before you and should have the answers to your tough questions all ready to go. Research thoroughly, take the time to do this right, and you should be fine.

Source: Jeff Elgin, "Buying a Foreign-Based Franchise," www.entrepreneur.com/article/0,4621,321056,00.html.

List of Franchising Resources

Entrepreneur.com
Entrepreneur.com offers a free, no-obligation franchise consultation. With the help of our partner FranChoice, a leading franchise information company, you can find the franchise business that is your "perfect match." If you are looking to start a franchise or business, use this free service to save time and money, make an informed decision, and find a franchise that fits you.
www.franchise-consultation.com

Affordable Franchising

This company offers a combination of unique talent from business and franchise consultants and creative and technologically savvy professionals. They have over 25 years of experience in all areas of business management, office automation, marketing, and business consulting.
Phone: (888) 849-5390 (toll-free)
www.affordablefranchising.com

American Association of Franchisees and Dealers

The AAFD is a national non-profit trade association representing the rights and interests of franchisees and independent dealers throughout the United States. The AAFD was formed in May 1992 with the mission of "Bringing Fairness to Franchising." As the AAFD has expanded and evolved and as many franchising companies have contractually embraced the promise of win-win franchising, the AAFD's mission has expanded, but can be stated succinctly as "To define, identify and to use marketplace solutions to promote Total Quality Franchising."
P.O. Box 81887
San Diego, CA 92138-1887
Phone: (800) 733-9858
www.aafd.org

Franchise Chat

Franchise-chat.com was established in 1999 with two key objectives: to bring franchise news stories and resource articles from around the world to one convenient location and to provide a forum where prospective or current franchisees and franchisors and other interested parties, could interact, ask questions, and discuss franchise-related issues.

Franchisefind Limited

P.O. Box 37604
Parnell
Auckland, New Zealand
www.franchise-chat.com

Source: Compiled by author.

Chapter 84

Franchising Your Business

Section 13

Tips on How Fast Should You Grow

Once a business owner makes the decision to franchise, the new franchisor faces some basic "design" considerations. Franchisors can expand aggressively with more risk and more expense—or they can expand more conservatively and with less risk and less expense.

Starting with the End in Mind: Goal-Oriented Planning

When counseling new franchisors on their development options, my first question is always the same: "Where do you want to be in five years?" It is vitally important to start with the end in mind.

But when I ask them about their growth plans, many new franchisors tell me their goal is to "grow as fast as possible," sometimes adding, "as long as we maintain quality." Unfortunately, they're all missing the point.

Growth does not come without a cost. And faster growth comes at a greater cost. That cost is measured in dollars, commitment, time, and risk.

More important, success in franchising, like any other business endeavor, is the result of careful planning that starts with goals systematically reduced to tactics. So new franchisors should be specific about their goals and design their tactics around achieving very specific objectives.

Assuming the franchisor wants to achieve the "hockey stick" growth curve that leads to maximum valuation, he or she might attempt to sell ten franchises in year one, 20 in year two, 30 in year three, 50 in year four, and 75 in year five (assuming not all the year-five stores will open in year five). This plan can now be used to develop specific tactics to meet these goals.

Based on industry averages, this franchisor should now be able to calculate a specific budget for franchise marketing activities and know precisely whom he or she needs to hire and when he or she needs to hire them. In fact, every step of this process can be mapped out so the franchisor can develop a series of specific tactics and budgets to attain each year's specific objectives.

But what if this franchisor does not have the resources to achieve the year-one plan?

In that case, our budding franchisor has four basic choices:

1. Revise the goal downward.
2. Extend the timeframe for achieving that goal.
3. Bring in outside capital—and simultaneously increase goals to offset equity dilution.
4. Implement more aggressive franchise structures in order to accelerate growth.

Strategies for Speeding Growth

One strategy that is increasingly favored by new franchisors looking for accelerated growth is the use of *alternative franchise structures*. In most franchise systems, franchises are awarded for a single location. While the franchisee may later be granted the right to one or more additional locations, the process of continued growth is controlled solely by the franchisor.

Some franchisors in highly fragmented markets choose *conversion franchising* as a means of accelerating growth. A conversion franchise is granted when a franchisor awards a franchise on different (usually preferable) terms than an individual franchise, based on the fact that the franchise prospect has an established business, established clientele, and/or requires less training.

Franchisors who go the *conversion* route find their prospects are generally easily identified, reducing marketing costs substantially. And since these franchise prospects generally have established business relationships, they begin paying royalties sooner—and the early royalties tend to be larger. Moreover, these franchisees require less training and initial support.

Conversion franchising presents some significant challenges. As entrepreneurs, conversion franchisees can be more difficult to control than start-up operators. And since the best operators are already successful, they tend to be difficult to convert, while the astute franchisor still needs to avoid the worst operators, who may be desperate to convert. Finally, post-term restrictive covenants (i.e., noncompete agreements) are more difficult to enforce if the conversion franchisee is operating within the franchisor's industry before joining the franchise program.

Another structure used to accelerate growth is *area development franchising*. An area development franchise is similar to an option agreement in which the area developer is granted an exclusive option to open an established number of franchises in a defined geographical territory according to a defined opening schedule.

From the franchisor's perspective, an area development strategy is often attractive, because it enables the franchisor to work more efficiently with a limited number of area developers in larger markets that would otherwise be dominated by multiple start-up franchisees. Area developers are often better capitalized than start-up franchisees, and more experienced in terms of business ownership. On the negative side, however, a franchisor often assumes greater risk by awarding large markets to area developers before they demonstrate to the franchisor that they will be strong operators and contributors within the franchise system. Moreover, while area development contracts can be responsible for large numbers of franchise sales, the need for each area developer to open sites according to a development schedule that allows them some time between unit openings (combined with the fact that many area development contracts go unfulfilled) can mean the franchisor's market penetration is, in fact, slower, not faster.

Some franchisors have adopted an *area representative strategy* to supercharge franchise sales and growth. Area representative franchising involves the grant of a territory in which the area representative is subsequently allowed to sell individual franchises. In essence, the subfranchisee becomes a smaller version of the franchisor-selling franchises and providing a predetermined set of services (training, support, etc.) in return for a fee-splitting arrangement relative to franchise fees and royalties.

While providing the franchisor with the fastest form of growth, *subfranchising* done improperly can lower the level of quality in a system (since a third party is involved in quality control) and is generally responsible for lower levels of profits per franchisee, because the subfranchisee is an intermediary who requires additional "compensation." Adding this extra layer between the franchisor and individual franchisee can also result in less control within the franchise system.

The Risk of Slow Growth

I believe that new franchisors are more likely to fail from over-aggressive expansion than from a more conservative approach. It's much easier to expand more aggressively once a franchisor has established and proven its basic systems for supporting the initial group of franchised locations.

The key to success in franchising is successful franchisees. If your early franchisees are successful, you are on your way. But if early franchises fail, it is almost impossible to recover.

So while franchises can be sold as fast as we can line up qualified prospects, the real question to be addressed is whether or not we can adequately support this influx of franchisees.

Source: Mark Siebert, "How Fast Should You Grow?," www.entrepreneur.com/article/0,4621,318426,00.html.

List of Things to Include in the Uniform Franchising Offering Circular

- The history of the franchise and its officers and directors.
- A complete description of the business to be franchised.
- All costs and fees to which you will be subject under the agreement.
- All obligations of either party to the other during the term of the agreement and thereafter.
- Any relevant litigation history of the company or its officers.
- Any business failures, ownership transfers, franchise agreement terminations, or other potentially adverse information relating to the success rate of the existing units in the system.
- Audited financial statements for the previous three years for the franchise company.
- A list of the existing franchisees.

Section
13

- A complete copy of the actual franchise agreement document, which is usually attached to the UFOC but may be provided under separate cover at the option of the franchisor.

Source: Franchise-Consultation.com, "Franchise Company Investigation Procedure," www.franchise-consultation.com/how_to_choose_a_franchise.html.

Franchisee Bill of Rights

The franchisees of America, representing the best of the American entrepreneurial spirit, hereby recognize and demand a basic minimum of commercial dignity, equity and fairness. In recognition thereof, the franchisees of America do proclaim this Franchisee Bill of Rights as the minimum requirements of a fair and equitable franchise system:

- The right to an equity in the franchised business, including the right to meaningful market protection.
- The right to engage in a trade or business, including a post-termination right to compete.
- The right to the franchisor's loyalty, good faith and fair dealing, and due care in the performance of the franchisor's duties, and a fiduciary relationship where one has been promised or created by conduct.
- The right to trademark protection.
- The right to full disclosure from the franchisor, including the right to earnings data available to the franchisor which is relevant to the franchisee's decision to enter or remain in the franchise relationship.
- The right to initial and ongoing training and support.
- The right to competitive sourcing of inventory, product, service and supplies.
- The right to reasonable restraints upon the franchisor's ability to require changes within the franchise system.
- The right to marketing assistance.
- The right to associate with other franchisees.
- The right to representation and access to the franchisor.
- The right to local dispute resolution and protection under the laws and the courts of the franchisee's jurisdiction.
- A reasonable right to renew the franchise.
- The reciprocal right to terminate the franchise agreement for reasonable and just cause, and the right not to face termination, unless for cause.

Source: American Association of Franchisees and Dealers, "Franchisee Bill of Rights," aafd.org/index.php?option=com_content&task=view&id=7&Itemid=55.

Working from Home

Section
14

Business Matters

Licenses and Permits for Home-Based Businesses

Following are some of the most common licenses and permits that owners of home-based small businesses may need and where to go for more information.

Business License

Contact your city's business license department to find out about getting a business license, which essentially grants you the right (after you pay a fee, of course) to operate a business in that city. When you file your license application, the city planning or zoning department will check to make sure your area is zoned for the purpose you want to use it for and that there are enough parking spaces to meet the codes.

You can't operate in an area that is not zoned for your type of business unless you first get a variance or conditional-use permit. To get a variance, you'll need to present your case before your city's planning commission. In many cases, variances are quite easy to get, as long as you can show that your business won't disrupt the character of the neighborhood where you plan to locate.

Because you're planning to start a business in your home, you should investigate zoning ordinances especially carefully. Residential neighborhoods tend to have strict zoning regulations preventing business use of the home. Even so, it's possible to get a variance or conditional-use permit. In many areas, attitudes toward home-based businesses are becoming more supportive, making it easier to obtain a variance.

Fire Department Permit

You may need to get a permit from your fire department if your business uses any flammable materials or if your premises will be open to the public. In some cities, you have to get this permit before you open for business. Other areas don't require permits but simply schedule periodic inspections of your business to see if you meet fire safety regulations. If you don't, they'll issue a citation. Businesses such as restaurants, retirement homes, day-care centers, and anywhere else where lots of people congregate are subject to especially close and frequent scrutiny by the fire department.

Air and Water Pollution Control Permit

Many cities now have departments that work to control air and water pollution. If you burn any materials, discharge anything into the sewers or waterways, or use products that produce gas (such as paint sprayers), you may have to get a special permit from this department in your city or county. Environmental protection regulations may also require you to get approval before doing any construction or beginning operation. Check with your state environmental protection agency regarding federal or state regulations that may apply to your business.

Sign Permit

Some cities and suburbs have sign ordinances that restrict the size, location, and sometimes the lighting and type of sign you can use outside your business. To avoid costly mistakes, check regulations and secure the written approval of your landlord (if you rent a house or apartment) before you go to the expense of having a sign designed and installed.

County Permits

County governments often require essentially the same types of permits and licenses as cities. If your business is outside any city or town's jurisdiction, these permits apply to you. The good news: county regulations are usually not as strict as those of adjoining cities.

State Licenses

In many states, people in certain occupations must have licenses or occupational permits. Often, they have to pass state examinations before they can get these permits and conduct business. States usually require licensing for auto mechanics, plumbers, electricians, building contractors, collection agents, insurance agents, real estate brokers, repossessors, and anyone who provides personal services (e.g., barbers, cosmetologists, doctors, and nurses). Contact your state government offices to get a complete list of occupations that require licensing.

Federal Licenses

In most cases, you won't have to worry about federal licences. However, a few types of businesses do require federal licensing, including meat processors, radio and TV stations, and investment advisory services. The Federal Trade Commission can tell you if your business requires a federal license.

Sales Tax License

You need a certificate of resale for two reasons. (In other states, this may be called a seller's permit or a certificate of authority.) First, any home-based business selling taxable goods and services must pay sales taxes on what it sells. The definition of a taxable service varies from state to state. Depending on individual state rulings, both the parts and labor portions of your bill may be taxable.

Sales taxes vary by state and are imposed at the retail level. It's important to know the rules in the states and localities where you operate your business because if you're a retailer, you must collect state sales tax on each sale you make.

Health Department Permits

If you plan to sell food, either directly to customers as in a restaurant or as a wholesaler to other retailers, you'll need a county health department permit. This costs about $25 and varies depending on the size of the business and the amount and type of equipment you have. The health department will want to inspect your facilities before issuing the permit.

Source: Rieva Lesonsky, *Start Your Own Business.*

Section 14

Tips on Using Your Home Office Space

Is your desk a mess? This is a particular problem for home-based entrepreneurs, for whom space is usually at a premium. Try these organization tips from expert Lisa Kanarek, author of *Home Office Solutions: Creating the Space That Works for You*, *Organizing Your Home Business*, *101 Home Office Success Secrets*, and *Everything's Organized*.

- The only items on your desk should be the stuff you use regularly. Anything else is clutter.
- Stacking trays are good organizational tools, but in-and-out baskets work only if you clear your trays daily.
- If you're left-handed, keep your phone on the right side of your desk and vice versa, so you don't have to write over a phone cord.
- Add shelves near your desk and use it to store items you use less often, like dictionaries, three-hole punches, and extra supplies.
- Use drawer dividers to organize the items in your desk. This saves you from having to hunt through messy drawers looking for the items you need.

Source: Rieva Lesonsky, *365 Tips to Boost Your Entrepreneurial IQ.*

Should You Tell Your Clients You Work from Home?

Some home-based business owners wonder if keeping their home-based status a secret is really all that important anymore. Do clients really care? And if they do, what can you do about it?

- The chances are, your clients and customers really don't care, as indicated by the fact that a majority of people who work from home now use their home address for both personal and business mail. And with gasoline prices going up and up, we suspect that it will be increasingly important to have a location nearby.
- Of course, the internet is blind to location, so if you operate a business on the web, whether your business is in an abandoned school building in North Dakota or your apartment in Manhattan makes no matter.
- Unfortunately, there are some exceptions when it's preferable to use a separate address for your business. While cities and counties have liberalized their zoning laws to allow most home-based businesses, it's not uncommon for the covenants, codes, and restrictions (CC&Rs) of common-interest developments—those with homeowners' associations—to forbid home occupations within their walls. So if that applies to you and what you do doesn't involve people coming to your home, noise, or other activities that would irritate and draw attention from neighbors, you may wish to use a different address for your home-based business.

- Using a different address for your business also makes sense if you live on a street with a name like "Easy Jacks" or "Slowpoke Lane" and don't like the business image it conveys. And there are certain industries, such as cosmetics, whose suppliers won't sell products to businesses in home locations, so again an outside address would be important.

If, for whatever reason, using your home address for your business isn't desirable, here are two things you can do:

- Use a mail-receiving service such as those offered by the UPS Stores. This provides you with a street address to use in correspondence or on your web site, a decided advantage over using a plain old post office box, which automatically creates suspicion about a business's status in some people's minds.

- Work out an arrangement with a related business to use its address. You can usually do this for a nominal amount of money.

Source: Paul Edwards and Sarah Edwards, "Should You Tell Clients You Work From Home?," www.entrepreneur.com/article/0,4621,321028,00.html.

Time Management Tips for Home-Based Businesses

Many experts say time is the most important commodity for new home-based entrepreneurs. But it's a limited resource, so these tips will help you use yours wisely.

- Organize your workspace to streamline your operation. Make it as clutter-free as possible and keep frequently used items in front of you.

- Use lists to keep track of tasks. Ask yourself, "What is the most important thing to do?" and establish a priority list.

- Do your most vital tasks at your peak time of the day. Everyone has times when his or her energy and focus are highest. Figure out when yours are, and give yourself an uninterrupted two hours to accomplish your most important tasks.

- Make every minute count. A cordless phone is a must here: you can talk and do other things at the same time. Double up whenever possible.

Source: Rieva Lesonsky, *365 Tips to Boost Your Entrepreneurial IQ.*

Section 14

Tips for Protecting Your Home-Based Business

Of course you need insurance to protect your business from losses. But there are some things you can do to help prevent problems. Home-based entrepreneurs should take particular note of the following tips:

- Install and check surge protectors, smoke detectors, fire extinguishers, deadbolt locks, and motion-sensitive outdoor lights.
- Keep your office equipment out of view from the street.
- Store all money and important documents in a fireproof safe.
- Develop a disaster recovery plan and review it quarterly.
- Don't overload your electrical circuits.
- Keep stairs and walkways free of ice and debris.
- Set safety rules and enforce them all.

Source: Rieva Lesonsky, *365 Tips to Boost Your Entrepreneurial IQ.*

Advice for Preparing for Natural Disasters

Natural disasters—whether tornado, flood, earthquake, or fire—can be devastating both personally and professionally. Although you can't control disasters, you can take steps to prepare for the unexpected.

- Make a video record of your belongings. Buy, rent, or borrow a video camera and videotape everything in your home office. (While you're at it, film the rest of your home as well.) While taping, describe in detail everything you see. As they say, "A picture is worth a thousand words." In this case, your video record could mean several thousand dollars extra in insurance claims. Store the video in a safe place where it will be accessible if you need it: in your safe deposit box, at your spouse's off-site office, or out of town with friends or relatives.
- Keep a written record of your belongings with accompanying photographs. This is another option. Then store the record in your safe deposit box.
- Keep receipts and warranty information from large purchases in a hanging file folder labeled "Purchases." Within the file, label interior folders "Electronic," "Appliances," and any other general category of purchases. Before filing a receipt, staple it to the corresponding warranty booklet.
- Back up your data regularly and keep at least two copies (three is ideal). Store one copy in your office and two off-site. It's easy to purchase another computer, but data is difficult and time-consuming to replace.
- Store important business and personal documents in your safe deposit box or in a fireproof file cabinet. Information ranging from insurance policies to investment information can be time-consuming to replace. You may not need to refer to this kind of information often, but when you need it, you know it will be safe.
- Start a file labeled "Emergency Information" and keep it in the top drawer of your file cabinet. Inside, keep copies of your insurance papers, credit card numbers, and other

vital information that you would need easy access to in the event of an emergency.

- Make sure your home office equipment is insured. Don't assume your homeowner's insurance covers everything in your home. You may need to purchase additional coverage. The time to find out about coverage is before you need it.

Unfortunately, there is very little you can do to avoid natural disasters. By being prepared, however, you can make the impact more bearable.

Source: Lisa Kanarek, "Preparing for Natural Disasters," www.entrepreneur.com/article/ 0,4621,278076,00.html.

Tips for Shipping from Home

Shipping products from home involves satisfying your customers, maximizing the use of your time, and, of course, minimizing your costs. To make sure you get this right, we interviewed eBay PowerSeller and author Skip McGrath to discover the secrets to successful shipping.

Volume

- If you ship only three or four items a day, says McGrath, you can easily handle your shipping manually—that is, hand-addressing labels, taking items to the post office, and standing in line to arrange delivery confirmation.

- If you ship ten or more items a day, however, you'll want to invest about $300 in a label printer and postage scale that connects to your computer's USB or serial port so you can weigh your packages. Then using a service like Endicia, you can type in a ZIP code and your postage will be automatically calculated for you. The advantage of using a label printer instead of a regular printer is saving time because regular printers require that you insert labels sheet by sheet, which most likely means you'll be getting up from your desk for each batch.

- There are numerous sources for this type of equipment. Endicia, for example, sells a starter kit that includes a postage meter and label printer that complement its services. Stamps.com offers a free postage scale with its $15.95 monthly service. And you can almost always find postage scales and label printers for sale on eBay.

- When you get to the point where you're shipping 30 or more packages a month, it's also time to think about getting an account with UPS or FedEx Ground, so that you can schedule them to pick up your packages as needed.

Shipping Choice

- For most items, shippers still generally choose to use the Priority Mail option from the U.S. Postal Service because it's usually faster than other standard delivery options (for example, two to three days via the Postal Service vs. five to six days with UPS Ground).

■ For packages under five pounds and weekend delivery, Priority Mail is also cheaper. But for packages over five pounds, you'll do better with UPS or FedEx Ground.

Value

■ If you ship high-priced items like artwork or jewelry collectibles, McGrath says you should probably use overnight or two-day air freight: your merchandise will arrive sooner than via the U.S. Postal Service, and you'll increase the certainty of your deliveries.

■ Despite the post office's delivery confirmation option, it's simply not as reliable as UPS, FedEx, or DHL. And with valuable merchandise, you just don't want to take any chances.

Supplies

■ If you ship via the Postal Service, the post office's Priority Mail supplies—including boxes, envelopes, tape, and labels—are free. Another free source of supplies is retail stores, because most cities have ordinances requiring stores to recycle their shipping materials.

■ If what's available for free doesn't meet your needs, entering the phrase "packaging supplies" or "shipping supplies" into a search engine will generate results for suppliers offering thousands of shipping material options.

■ To keep your shipping process orderly, it's a good idea to set up a special area of your home office or garage for shipping activities. This way, you'll have an organized area where you can keep your tape guns, boxes, and other supplies conveniently available so you can efficiently box things up.

Cost

■ While customers love free shipping—some even search for it—if you decide to go this route, you'll still need to either charge for handling or build a handling cost into your product price.

Source: Paul Edwards and Sarah Edwards, "Shipping Products from Home," www.entrepreneur.com/article/0,4621,317058,00.html.

Hiring Employees for Your Home-Based Business

Rule 1. Provide full disclosure. Prior to an interview, you should let each candidate know about your home office base. In my case, one of the things I couldn't help but wonder was whether the company was trying to hide something from me. That's not the greatest foot to put forward to potential hires.

Rule 2. Ask potential candidates how they feel about working in a home office. This should be one of the first questions you ask—and you'll want to listen carefully to the answers you get. If you're not satisfied with their answers, follow up with some behavioral questions to find out what they're really thinking. You should give the candidates time to voice any misgivings they may have. If you've followed Rule 1, this question won't come as a surprise to your candidates and you'll be more likely to receive an honest answer.

Rule 3. Before an employee starts work, set up an appropriate workspace for him or her. You need to find a way to balance the limited space in your home with your employee's need for privacy. Let's face it, nobody wants to be in a situation where the boss can hear every single word he or she says on the phone. It just breeds discontent and puts more pressure on your employees. Over time, that pressure will build up and create a situation that isn't likely to end well.

Rule 4. Establish a separate space for meetings. At the very least, you should invest in a table you can sit around to hold meetings. In theory, using your desk as a place to sit around during a meeting is a decent idea. In practice, however, it will be difficult to set a professional tone for the meeting if you and your employee are crowded around your desk, trying to work in the midst of all your paperwork.

Rule 5. Take bathroom facilities into account. If you don't have a bathroom dedicated primarily to the office space and your employees, you might want to reconsider your plans to hire someone. Enough said.

Rule 6. Have an appropriate exit/entrance to your home office. The path to your home office should ideally not interfere with what goes on in the rest of the house. This rule isn't as critical as the restroom issue, but it helps lend a feeling of professionalism to the entire endeavor if you have an entrance that's as direct as possible.

Rule 7. Make the office off-limits to your family. You need to make sure your family understands that your office space—and in particular, the desk and computer of your employee—is a no-go zone. Sure, the office is in your house, but if you want your employee to feel comfortable, this is a line that must not be crossed.

Rule 8. Provide generous vacation time. More vacation rather than less. A home office is an intense work environment, and your employees are much more apt to burn out here than in a standard work environment. An extra week of vacation—and three should be the minimum—is a great way to minimize burnout.

Rule 9. Be flexible. Be open to your employees' ideas and needs. Suggest flex time or working remotely: your employees will thank you for it.

Section 14

Rule 10. Try and laugh a little. The close quarters of a home office can be stifling, and if you have only one employee, there are no co-workers around to whom he or she can vent. So figure out how to keep the mood light and learn to laugh about life's daily little annoyances.

Source: Tom Candee, "Hiring Employees for Your Homebased Biz," www.entrepreneur.com/article/0,4621,319278,00.html.

Tips for Staying in Touch with the Office While Traveling

Busy home-based entrepreneurs on the go know it's hard to stay in touch with the office while on the road. But it's vital to do so. Here are some smart ideas:

- Before you leave, let your most important clients know you're leaving—and when you're coming back.

- Leave a message on your answering machine stating how long you'll be gone, when you'll be back, and how often you'll be checking your messages. If possible, try to return important call the same day you receive them.

- Take advantage of e-mail. It's an efficient and relatively inexpensive way to keep in touch.

- Check ahead with your hotel to find out what kinds of business services it offers. Make sure you give your important clients all your contact numbers. This not only keeps your customers happy, but it makes your life less hectic when you return.

Source: Rieva Lesonsky, *365 Tips to Boost Your Entrepreneurial IQ.*

Chapter 86

Personal Issues

Tips for Beating the "Home-Based Blues"

Try these ideas to fight off the isolation:

1. Join your local chamber of commerce or a home-based or industry association—and attend the meetings. Networking is critical to growing businesses.

2. Get out of the house. Schedule some meetings with clients over a meal. Or make sure your meet your friends or former co-workers for lunch or drinks at least once a month.

3. Take a class.

4. Attend conferences or trade shows.

5. Give speeches about your business. Not only will you establish your expertise, but it's also a great way to market your business.

6. Join forces with another home-based business owner. This is a great way to expand your client base.

7. Finally, reward yourself. Take some time off—but spend it outside your home.

Source: "Fighting the 'Home-Alone Blues,'" www.entrpreneur.com/article/ 0,4621,301812,00.html, from Rieva Lesonsky, *365 Tips to Boost Your Entrepreneurial IQ.*

Recommendations for Balancing Your Business and Family

Home-based entrepreneurs often struggle to balance their business and family environments. The following ideas may help you walk that fine line.

- Whenever possible, create a separate workspace for your business. And always use at least two separate phone lines.

- Fight the temptation to work all the time. Establish regular work hours and keep them

- Set boundaries, both physical and psychological. Tell your family what you expect from them and what they can expect from you.

- Establish rituals. As silly as they may appear—I knew a man who walked around the block so he could tell himself he was on his way to work and then reversed the process in the evening—do whatever it takes to draw the line.

- Try to give yourself a cushion when setting deadlines. It's easier for home-based entrepreneurs to get off schedule.

Source: Rieva Lesonsky, *365 Tips to Boost Your Entrepreneurial IQ.*

Tips for Maintaining the Balance Between Work and Business

Home-based businesses often find it difficult to maintain the boundaries between work and business. Here are some smart ways to maintain control:

- Set business hours—and keep them. Let your clients know when you're open for business and that when it's 5 or 6 o'clock, the office is closed.

- Get a dedicated business phone line that routes unanswered calls into voice mail or an answering machine. After hours, even if you're still working, let the equipment take the call.

- Use a pager, especially if you travel or have a number of clients outside the local area. Tell your clients to page you, and then you control when to return the call.

- Encourage your clients to use faxes or e-mail whenever possible. That means always keep your fax machine on and check your e-mail regularly.

Source: Rieva Lesonsky, *365 Tips to Boost Your Entrepreneurial IQ.*

Tips for Running a Home-Based Business with Kids

When home-based entrepreneurs have kids, it can be a disaster. How do you manage this tough situation? First, set the ground rules. Here are some tips to help you get started:

- Tell your kids, "This is your home, but it's also my office." That means the things that make the business run—computers, files, etc.—are off-limits to them.

- If possible, set office hours. This lets your kids know when it's OK to disturb you without taking you away from your work.

- Establish rituals. Even if you don't leave the house, when you're set to go into your office, tell your kids, "Bye, I'm leaving." And you can signal when you're ready for interruptions by saying, "Hi, I'm back."

- This is the most important rule: follow the other rules. They not only help you, but they help your kids draw the line between your workday and your home day.

Source: Rieva Lesonsky, *365 Tips to Boost Your Entrepreneurial IQ.*

Advice for Running Two Businesses out of a Home Office

One of the newest entrepreneurial phenomena is couples running separate businesses out of their homes. And many are sharing one space. But you don't have to be on each other's nerves. Here are some smart ways to avoid conflict:

- Use any and all available technology. Try virtual assistants, e-mail, cordless headsets, and voice mail to solve privacy problems.

- Live by the rule "separate but equal." When setting up your workspace, use partitions and make it as soundproof as possible.

- Share and share alike. You can both use the same conference space, fax machine, copier, or even printer. However, you should not share a phone.

- Respect each other's responsibilities. Don't expect your partner to set aside his or her business commitments to fix your computer, help with you mailing, etc.

- Communicate regularly about your schedules, both verbally and in writing. A calendar you both refer to can be a life—and relationship—saver.

Source: Rieva Lesonsky, *365 Tips to Boost Your Entrepreneurial IQ.*

Resources

Advice from Successful Home-Based Business Owners

Home-based entrepreneurs often have a tough time growing their business because they have to go it alone. So we asked some successful home-based business owners to share their best advice:

- Be a good neighbor. Make sure your neighbors know what you're doing and that it won't impact them negatively.

- Work hard to balance home and work. This is hard for all entrepreneurs, but it's particularly difficult if you work and live in the same place.

- Be patient. There are few true overnight successes. Make a plan and stick with it.

- Go that extra mile. Finding customers can be harder if you're home-based. So make sure you please the ones you have each and every time.

- Get out of the house! Meet your friends or former colleagues for lunch. Join a group or association, or form an informal advisory board.

Source: Rieva Lesonsky, *365 Tips to Boost Your Entrepreneurial IQ.*

Associations and Books

Associations

National Association of Home Based Businesses
3 Woodthorne Court
Owings Mills, MD 21117
Phone: (410) 581-1373, (410) 363-3698
www.usahomebusiness.com
nahbb@msn.com

American Association of Home-Based Business/Small Business Advocate, Inc.
Phone: (888) 823-2366
www.jbsba.com
dsb@jbsba.com

American Home Business Association
1981 Murray Holladay Road, Suite 225
Salt Lake City, UT 84117
Phone: (800) 664-2422
Fax: (801) 273-2399
www.homebusiness.com
info@homebusiness.com

Home Business Institute
P.O. Box 480215
Delray Beach, FL 33448
Phone: (561) 865-0865, (888) DIAL HBI (342-5424)
Fax: (561) 865-8448
www.hbiweb.com
info@hbiweb.com

Small Office Home Office America
www.soho.org

Books

The Home Team: How to Live, Love, and Work at Home
Scott Gregory and Shirley Siluk Gregory
Bookhome Publishing

The Perfect Business: How to Make a Million from Home with No Payroll, No Employee Headache, No Debts, No Sleepless Nights!
Michael Leboeuf
Fireside Publishing

Start and Run a Profitable Home-Based Business: Your Step-by-Step, First-Year Guide
Edna Sheedy
Self-Counsel Press

Working from Home: Everything You Need to Know About Living and Working Under the Same Roof
Paul Edwards and Sarah Edwards
Putnam Publishing

Owning and Operating an E-Commerce Business

Getting into E-Commerce

Section
15

Five Powerful Ways to Make Money Online with a Web Site

There are many ways to make money online. The best way for you is to simply be creative with your skills, knowledge, and abilities. However, the following five options are powerful ways to make money online with a web site that you should definitely consider.

1. **Knowledge.** You can always sell your knowledge, which many times is the best way if you are an "expert" of any type or on any subject. People are looking for your knowledge and input, regardless whether you acquired it on your own, learned it in college, or wherever. People are always looking for answers online, so if you sell your knowledge you can simply make money from what you know.

2. **Affiliate programs.** Become an affiliate for products based on your web-site theme and then simply promote these programs through which you earn money from referrals. It is easier than it sounds and you only have to create a web site full of rich content.

3. **Hard goods.** Selling hard goods is a traditional way of making money and it transfers to the online forum as well. No matter what hard goods you have to sell, you can certainly find a buyer online. Create a web site that focuses on your goods, have a good shipping plan in place, and then start selling online.

4. **E-books.** Selling e-books, articles, and other written materials is also a powerful way to make money online. If you are good at writing, it is certainly something you should consider. You can sell things you're written on your web site or you can also write on demand, whatever works best for you and your web business.

5. **Auction goods.** Auction web sites are also very powerful ways to make money. The reason for this is you can sell a wide variety of products, do not necessarily need your own web site (although it helps), and can change your products from time to time as you need to. Many people enjoy working and selling via auction sites because any number of things can be sold, from old personal items to new products.

The best way for you to make money online is to do something that you like and enjoy. When you do something you like and enjoy, you will be able to commit to doing it full time. Working online can be difficult at times; if you do not enjoy it, then it will be difficult for you to be successful making money via your web site.

Source: Michael Turner, "5 Powerful Ways to Make Money Online with a Website," ezinearticles.com/?5-Powerful-Ways-to-Make-Money-Online-with-a-Website&id=56459.

SCORE's Five Tips for Taking Your Small Business Online

1. You should be able to deliver your product line economically and conveniently through the mail or over the internet.

2. The web allows you to market to customers outside your geographical location. Your product should appeal to people throughout the nation or the continent.

3. Compare new "technology" costs with current bricks-and-mortar costs, e.g., rent, labor, inventory, and printing costs.

4. Realize that the World Wide Web levels the playing ground—you can look like a big company with a great web site.

5. Draw visitors to your site cheaply. Establish and grow alliances that will hotlink to your site for free.

Source: SCORE, "5 Tips for Taking Your Small Business Online," www.score.org /5_tips_eb_10.html.

SCORE's Five Tips for Meeting the Demand for Speed

1. Realize that the swiftest competitor, not necessarily the smartest, is often the winner in today's marketplace. Speed is increasingly of the essence, no matter what business you are in.

2. Respond to sales leads quickly. One small business requires staff members to follow up within the hour, by e-mail, fax, or phone.

3. Get comfortable with rapid, strategic decision-making. Five-year planning horizons are out the window.

4. Compress your timetables. One internet start-up rolled out its expansion efforts in a reduced time span of 45 days, instead of a year as originally planned, beating out competitors.

5. Make speed a part of your corporate culture. Reward employees' swiftness with stock options, bonuses, or other perks.

Source: SCORE, "5 Tips on Meeting the Demand for Speed," www.score.org/5_tips_eb_8.html.

Section 15

Chapter 89

Domain Names

Section 15

Four Tips on Selecting a Domain Name

1. Choose a domain name for your business and for your product.

Yes, that's right. Multiple domain names. For example, if your business is ABC Corporation and your product is called Maximize Your Sales, then get the domain names www.ABCCorporation.com and www.MaximizeYourSales.com. You can have both of these domain names pointing to different pages of your web site. This way, customers who know you only by your product name can find you easily by typing in the name of your product and ".com," and those who know you by your corporate name can find you easily by typing your corporation and ".com." (Hint: If you are an individual with a small business, you should register your personal name also.)

2. Get domain names with hyphens in them.

In the previous example, we used the company and product domain names. Now, go out and purchase www.ABC-corporation.com and www.Maximize-Your-Sales.com.

Why should you do this? Two reasons, really. The first is aesthetic appeal. Wouldn't you agree that it's easier to read the long domain names with the hyphens in them? However, it is much easier to type a name into your browser without the hyphens, and that makes it easier on your customers, which is why you purchase the domain name without the hyphens.

Additionally, domain names with hyphens sometimes rank a bit higher in the search engines. A higher ranking in the search engines will drive more customers to your web site. Search engine algorithms are ever changing, but buying multiple domains and pointing each of them to a specific, product-related page on your main site can ultimately help you make more sales in the future. Be sure not to point multiple domains at the same page, though—that will get you dropped from most search engines.

3. Purchase domains that are similar in spelling to yours.

Every day, someone misspells a word. Inevitably, they will still land on someone's web page. Why not yours? Using the example above, you might want to purchase www.abccorperation.com and www.maximiseyoursales.com, just to be safe. If you own these names, it's easy to reroute them to your main web page.

4. Use a top keyword in your domain name.

Let's use another example to illustrate. Suppose you are selling garden tools. Not just any garden tools; you sell low-cost, high-quality garden tools. The name of your company is Garden Tool World. Using the tips above, you will purchase the domain names for your company. But what about your product?

The key here is to look for names for your product domain that people will be searching for. When a potential customer goes to a search engine, will he or she look for "low-cost high-quality garden tools"? Or will the customer look for "cheap garden tools"? With a little research, you can find out what people are looking for.

I use two tools to see what people are looking for on the internet: Wordtracker (www.wordtracker.com) and Overture's Inventory (inventory.overture.com). Simply type in the word or phrase you are looking for and you will see instantly which phrases are most popular. So if people are looking for "cheap garden tools," then your domain name might be www.cheapgardentools.com.

Choosing a domain name is an important part of the overall marketing process and should not be taken lightly. Make sure your domain name represents your company, product, and image, and you'll be setting a great foundation for future sales.

Source: Stephanie Frank, "Is Your Domain Name Hurting Your Sales? Tips on Selecting a Domain Name," entrepreneurs.about.com/cs/marketing/a/uc071703.htm.

Eight Quick Tips for Choosing a Domain Name

Your domain name is the center of your internet identity. So what type of things should you take into consideration when choosing the name that will represent you on the web? Jumpline.com offers these eight handy tips.

1. Keep it short.
Although some places allow you to register a name with up to 63 characters, you have to keep in mind that people need to be able to remember it and easily type it into their browser. Try to register the shortest name that your customers and other site visitors will associate with your web site. The general rule of thumb is, keep it under seven characters if possible (not including the suffix).

2. Go with .com.
Dot what? There are many suffixes available now. For businesses, we recommend a .com suffix. It is the first extension that most people try when searching for a web site. Also, since it is one of the oldest extensions, .com shows that your business has been around for a while and that you have a well-established presence on the Web.

3. Avoid trademarked names.
There are two really good reasons for this. First, it's not very nice. We have all heard the stories about the zany guy who thought ahead and bought "some-huge-multimillion-dollar-company.com" and sold it to the company for enough money to retire on. But, remember that those companies, like yours, have spent lots of time and money creating their brand, and what goes around comes around. Also, companies are no longer opening their pocketbooks to get their names back. They are calling their lawyers.

4. Register your domain now.
Domain names are being snatched up faster than candy at the St. Patrick's Day parade. You must register soon unless you want to get stuck with "the-domain-name-that-no-one-wanted.net." You do not have to have a webmaster or an e-commerce department or a web design consultant or …. Heck, you don't even need a web page. Just get out there and register before you lose the opportunity to get the name you really want.

5. Consider getting more than one.

One domain name may not be enough. Sometimes, it isn't a bad idea to register several similar names. If you have "yourname.com," register "yourname.net" so no one else takes it. You can register your full company name and a shorter version that's easier to remember. Some people even register common misspellings of their company's name. (You don't need a separate web page for each. Several domains can point to the same web site.)

6. Don't use spaces or symbols.

Just a reminder. Domain names can use only letters, numbers, and dashes. Spaces and symbols are not allowed. Also, domain names are not case-sensitive.

7. Ask around.

When you have settled on several available name choices, see what your friends and clients have to say. A name that may make perfect sense to you may be too hard for other people to remember. Is your domain easy to say? Is it hard to spell? Do you have to explain why you chose the name?

8. Don't spend lots of money.

At one time, companies were able to get away with charging reservation fees plus a "mandatory" $70 InterNIC fee. Recently, it was decided that other companies should be able to compete to sell domain names. This has lowered prices dramatically.

And remember, if you think that if you have found the right domain name, but you're not quite sure if it's the one, ... register it anyway before someone else does!

Source: Jumpline.com, "8 Quick Tips to Choosing a Domain Name," www.sitepoint.com/article/tips-choosing-domain-name.

Top Seven Steps to Domain Name Success

1. Search for domain names that describe your product or service. Don't worry if the .com is unavailable. Go for .com or .org or .net. The important part is to get your keywords in the domain name.

2. Register variants on your company name. For example, for TAMBA Internet, register tamba.com and tambainternet.com. You don't want to lose any customers simply because they assume your domain name wrongly.

3. Finish every phone conversation with "If there's anything else you want to know, please take a look at our web site. It's at www ...." People won't find your web site unless you tell them about it.

4. Always use an e-mail account on your own domain name, not a free e-mail account such as Hotmail. This brands Hotmail and not your company.

5. If the domain name you want is unavailable, make a note of the date on which its

Section 15

registration expires. Lots of domain names are released after their initial registration period expires and you can pick it up from a registrar when it's expired.

6. Register as many domain names as possible. Use your company name, your slogan, and a description of your products and/or services. The more routes into your web site, the better.

7. Don't forget: domain names expire. Always note down when yours expire and remember to re-register them. Someone could be waiting to get your domain name!

Source: Kay Hammond, "Top 7 Steps To Domain Name Success," top7business.com/?Top-7-Steps-To-Domain-Name-Success&id=32.

11 Steps to Registering a Domain Name

One of the first steps in setting up an online business is to register your domain name. It's very easy to do and it takes about ten minutes, as long as you know where to go and understand the terminology.

Here's how:

1. First, make sure your domain name has not been registered by someone else, by doing a whois search. Most domain registration sites maintain a whois database, but I generally use VeriSign.com.

2. Enter the domain name you want to check into the online form. Do not enter "www."

3. Some whois search forms make you enter a code contained in an on-screen graphic. This is to prevent overuse of the system by automated systems. If you are asked for the code, enter it.

4. The results of the whois search will tell you if anyone already owns the name. If the name is taken, you will have to select another one. If it is unregistered, you can proceed.

5. Select a domain name registrar. This is the company that will manage the domain registration for you. I have put together a list of low-cost registrars (following this article). You can find others at ICANN (Internet Corporation for Assigned Names and Numbers), at www.icann.org.

6. Enter your desired domain name on your registrar's web site.

7. Select the number of years you want to pay for. Paying for more than one year in advance may save you a little money.

8. Enter your contact information. There are four types of contacts: the registrant or owner, technical, billing, and administrative. You may use the same name for all if you wish.

9. If your registrar offers you the option, select a private or public registration. A private

registration costs more, but will protect your identity and may cut down on the amount of spam you receive.

10. Point your new domain to a web server or "park" the domain. If you have not yet built a web site, you should park the name with the registrar. If you have built a site, you must tell the registrar on which web server the site is located. This information is provided by your web host.

11. At this point, you are probably done! It may take up to four to eight hours for .com and .net domains to become active and about 24–48 hours for other domain extensions.

Source: Ana Rincon, "How To Register a Domain Name," onlinebusiness.about.com/od/domains/ht/registerdomain.htm.

Top Ten Cheap Domain Name Registrars

If you're looking for a cheap domain name registrar, here is a list of ten registrars that charge less than $10 for an annual .com registration. Some may offer even lower prices if you transfer existing domains from another registrar. This is also a good source to find low-cost hosting.

1. NetFirms
www.netfirms.com
$4.95 for one-year .com registration

2. Yahoo
www.yahoo.com
$4.98 for one-year .com registration

3. EV1Servers
www.ev1servers.net
$5.99 for one-year .com registration

4. Hostway
www.hostway.com
$6.95 for one-year .com registration

5. Stargate
www.stargateinc.com
$6.95 for one-year .com registration

6. Interland
www.interland.com
$7.95 for one-year .com registration

7. Web.com
www.web.com
$7.95 for one-year .com registration

8. AIT Domains
www.aitdomains.com
$7.99 for one-year .com registration

9. Go Daddy
www.godaddy.com
$8.95 for one-year .com registration

10. RegisterFly
www.registerfly.com
$9.99 for one-year .com registration

Source: Ana Rincon, "Top 10 Cheap Domain Name Registrars," onlinebusiness. about.com/od/domains/tp/CheapDomains.htm.

Site Design

Questions to Ask When Building Your E-Commerce Web Site

When building your e-commerce web site, you need to ask the following questions.

1. Will you use an existing software package to handle your shopping cart/storefront or will you develop your own shopping cart application?

2. Do you need real-time credit card processing?

3. Do you have a merchant account set up?

4. Do you need to have secure web pages in order to accept credit card information from your customers? If so, will this be via a host web site or will you create it on your own web site?

Source: eWebcircle Web Solutions, "Ecommerce Overview," www.ewebcircle.com.au/ecommerce.asp.

11 Site Design Tips for Businesses

The most important thing to remember when designing an electronic commerce site is to make it easy for your customers to make a purchase. I'm in the midst of designing an e-commerce site as I write this article, and I've learned several tips that will help you succeed in e-commerce site design.

Tip 1: Make it easy to buy.
This tip may seem vague and ambiguous, but it truly is the most important recommendation. Put yourself in your customer's shoes and test your designs. Isolate issues that might block your users from making a purchase. Ask yourself questions, such as the following:

1. How many pages and clicks does it take to make a purchase?

2. How much information do users have to fill out initially, versus when they make a subsequent purchase?

3. Can a quick purchase be made directly from the home page?

4. Does the site provide clear instructions on how to store selected items before completing a transaction?

5. How well does the site communicate with the user?

6. Does the site acknowledge the users' actions and provide clear, concise feedback as users progress through the purchasing process?

7. Can users collect multiple items before checking out?

Tip 2: Make a strong first impression.

Your e-commerce home page must make a strong first impression. This is where users are grounded to your company and are persuaded to start shopping. It is extremely important to provide branding for your store. Next, it is important to provide a clear visual definition of your store's categories or departments. You can accomplish this through the use of tabs or within the navigation bar.

A search feature must also be prominent near the company branding or at the top and bottom of almost all pages. Consider promoting special sale products on the home page to encourage spontaneous purchases. Provide abstracts with links to stories about your products to provide educational information and added appeal.

Tip 3: Minimize distractions: advertising isn't always necessary.

You may want to consider not providing other companies' advertisements on your home page or in other places throughout the purchase process. Remember that the goal of your home page is to encourage shopping and purchasing. You don't want to deter or lose users by having them click on another company's advertisement.

If you want to advertise, feature your own products in a way that they can be added to the user's shopping basket. Ideally, those products would be tied into the personal information you have about the user, so a user would be more likely to purchase them—and they might be seen as an advantage to shopping at your site. Keep the user focused on what your company offers—unless you have a complementary relationship with the other company.

Tip 4: Make it personal.

Are you looking for a way to build strong rapport with your shoppers? Provide personalization for the user, after the user registers as a shopper or member. Use this information to provide a personalized greeting to your home page or various department pages.

To get an in-depth understanding of personalization for Microsoft Site Server 3.0 Commerce Edition, read *Site Server 3.0 Personalization and Membership* by Rob Howard (ISBN 1861001940).

Tip 5: Avoid long instructions.

If you need to include long instructions on how to use your site or about how to make a purchase, it is time to redesign! To complete a quick purchase, a user needs minimal instructions. Most users will not read long instructions and may turn away in confusion. The web site at www.urbandecay.com employs a unique interface to portray the image and statement it makes with its products.

Tip 6: Provide visual clues to the user's location.

For stores that have multiple departments, it is important to create a sense of varying location. This can be accomplished by changing colors on the navigation bar or the background page and by providing different titles with text or graphics.

Tip 7: Show off products.

If at all possible, provide images of individual products. Process the images in three sizes: thumbnail, medium, and large. A thumbnail image is best used in a list of several products. At the individual product level, provide a medium-size image and the ability to click to view the enlarged version of the product. The larger view is not necessary, but worth considering if your product has details that are not reflected in the medium or thumbnail image.

The more details you can provide about the product, the better. If you have a long page about the product, be sure to provide the option to purchase it or add it to your basket or cart from both the top and the bottom of the informational text.

Tip 8: Light on the graphics.

One way to keep each page light is to change all graphics that represent text into actual HTML text. Another consideration is to reduce the individual product-images file size. Most product images are continuous-tone photographs. Therefore, the product photographs should be saved as 24-bit JPEG. When saving JPEG files, experiment with the quality levels.

Tip 9: Encourage spontaneous purchases.

This can be accomplished in various ways. If a product is mentioned on the home page, place product images and details, the sale price, and a direct link to purchase the item on your home page. In a news or feature article, include direct links to purchase products discussed within the article. Or on the side column, where advertisements for other companies would traditionally appear, create intimate, focused advertisements for your products, with a direct links to purchase the items from the advertisement.

Tip 10: Alternate background colors in long lists.

One good visual trick to make a long table of items easier to read is to alternate a light color background for each row or item. You can see an example of this if you search on an author's name at barnesandnoble.com. The search results return in alternate item background colors of gray and white. This technique may be scripted as an array in an Active Server Pages (ASP) file (e.g., <% colr = array ("#FFFFFF","#CCCCCC") %>). The array is then called from the table cell (e.g., <TD BGCOLOR="<%=colr(x)%>">).

Tip 11: Allow users to collect items.

Provide a shopping basket or a place for your users to collect items before checking out. Never make your users fill out the lengthy payment, shipping, and other forms more than once in a transaction! At the product level, provide a link to check out and a link to add that product to the shopping cart while continuing to shop.

One storage feature that is currently becoming popular is called a wish list. This feature is similar to a shopping cart, but it does not provide purchasing features. Think of it as a place to store items as your customers are shopping. Perhaps when wish list items go on sale, your site can notify your customers.

Source: Nadja Vol Ochs, "Site Server–Easy-to-Buy E-Commerce Site Design Tips," www.microsoft.com/technet/prodtechnol/sscomm/reskit/sitedes.mspx.

Section 15

Seven Must-Have Scripts in Hosted E-Commerce Systems

When shopping for e-commerce hosting, there are a lot of things you need to keep in mind. When you know what to look for it is a lot easier to ensure you get exactly what you need and not leave any important information out. Consider these seven must-haves before you start shopping for e-commerce hosting so you will be prepared.

1. **Storefront.** Regardless of what software you are using, one of your main concerns should be the storefront. You want to be able to customize your storefront to your specifications, at least within reason, and certainly you want it to appear professional and well put together. This should be a main consideration when shopping for e-commerce hosting.

2. **Support.** Regardless of the hosting you are using, you will want support, 24/7 if at all possible, and support that is real, live, and will help you with your problems. In addition to this, you should look for some self-help support as well in the form of a FAQ area and support providing advice for when you find yourself in certain situations. Good hosts will provide you with a great deal of information so you can help yourself.

3. **Building.** With your e-commerce host you want to be able to build your site easily and to your specifications. So, you certainly want to use software that is easy to understand and implement. In addition, it is helpful if wizards are available to help you throughout the building process.

4. **Integrated.** You want to make sure the host is integrated and works well with all of the other systems that you need for your site to be successful. If it is not integrated, you should strongly consider other options.

5. **Tools and Functions.** This is important because you want as many functions available as possible, from multiple currencies to a log of purchases, so your e-commerce host will need to be able to provide you with the space and tools you need to keep up with all of this information.

6. **Software.** When it comes to e-commerce software, you can either buy from a physical store or online from your host or create your own. The best option is to find a host that offers software that is of high quality and will help you with e-commerce.

7. **Ease of Navigation.** Your e-commerce software as well as your host should allow you and customers to navigate easily through all of the pages and all of the links without getting confused or backtracking.

Shopping for e-commerce hosting requires you know what you are looking for as well as what you need. As long as you choose an experienced host who has verified experience, you'll have a much better chance at making a wise decision.

Source: Michael Turner, "7 Must Have Scripts to Look for When Shopping for E-commerce Hosting," ezinearticles.com/?7-Must-Have-Scripts-to-Look-for-When-Shopping-for-E-commerce-Hosting&id=56485.

Three Directories of Freelance Programmers

Freelance Auction
Post a project and price to find a programmer.
www.freelanceauction.com

DMOZ E-Commerce Software Developers Listing
dmoz.org/Business/E-Commerce/Consulting/Software_Developers/

GetaFreelancer.com
www.getafreelancer.com

Source: Compiled by Contributing Writer Ty Martin.

Ten Tips for Good Web Writing

Content

1. **Write relevant content.** It may be tempting to write about your brother's dog, but if it doesn't relate to your site or page topic, leave it out. Web readers want information; unless the page is information about said dog, they really won't care, even if it is a good metaphor for what you're trying to say.

2. **Put conclusions at the beginning.** Think of an inverted pyramid when you write. Get to the point in the first paragraph. Then expand upon it.

3. **Write only one idea per paragraph.** Web pages need to be concise and to the point. People don't read web pages, they scan them, so short, meaty paragraphs are better than long rambling ones.

4. **Use action words.** Tell your readers what to do. Avoid the passive voice. Keep the flow of your pages moving.

Format

1. **Use lists instead of paragraphs.** Lists are easier to scan than paragraphs, especially if you keep them short.

2. **Limit list items to seven words.** Studies have shown that people can reliably remember only seven to ten things at a time. By keeping your list items short, you help your readers remember them.

3. **Write short sentences.** Sentences should be as concise as you can make them. Use only the words you need to get the essential information across.

4. **Include internal sub-headings.** Sub-headings make the text more scannable. Your readers will move to the section of the document that is most useful for them; internal cues make it easier for them to do this.

5. **Make your links part of the copy.** Links are another way web readers scan pages. They stand out from normal text and provide more cues as to what the page is about.

6. **Always, always, always proofread your work.** Typos and spelling errors will send people away from your pages. Make sure you proofread everything you post to the web.

Source: Jennifer Kyrnin, "10 Tips for Good Web Writing," webdesign.about.com/od/writing /a/aa031405.htm.

Seven Suggestions for an I-Mom-Friendly Web Site

The internet began as a male-dominated medium, but those days are long gone and merchants are advised to make sure their web sites are female-friendly to facilitate the rising surge of busy i-moms shopping online for their family and friends.

Women now account for 51.7 percent of internet usage, according to a 2005 Lucid marketing study, but that's only the tip of iceberg. When it comes to online purchasing, women are clearly leading the way. According to a Bizrate survey, women accounted for 62 percent of online purchases in the fourth quarter of 2004!

The above statistic shouldn't be that surprising when we consider that women are busy household managers and make many financial decisions across the United States. According to the Small Business Administration, "Women currently make up 80 percent of consumer spending. They currently purchase more than half the automobiles that are sold in this country. They consistently purchase more groceries, apparel and durable goods than men and they have become the primary ones to make healthcare decisions in 75 percent of American households."

Other research shows that women are less likely than men to use the internet for entertainment purposes, but rather they are looking for information, household tips, low prices, and, especially, ease of use in purchasing online.

Merchant Strategy

The following seven recommendations will make your web site a friendly home for busy moms online.

1. **Make your web site easy to navigate.** A specific product should be found easily and be only a few clicks away from anywhere in the web site.

2. **Provide in-depth product information.** The more product comparisons, reports, and reviews you can add, the less likely they'll leave your web site to round out their research.

3. **Provide quality graphics.** Seeing and feeling are, of course, the best way to examine and test a product, but the shortage of time has trumped that luxury. A quality, fast-loading image is extremely desirable.

4. **Offer a maximum selection.** Whether in your store or on your web site, this always makes sense.

5. **Maintain competitive pricing.** The internet facilitates easy price comparisons; if your prices are too high, it won't be a secret. Check the prices of your competitors.

6. **Offer a variety of shipping options, including gift-wrapping.** Women buy the great majority of family gifts. Merchants who gift-wrap will get a lot of free advertising by word-of-mouth.

7. **Offer excellent customer service.** If there's a problem, a return, or a question, there's nothing like a friendly voice by telephone.

Source: Rick David, "7 Suggestions for an i-Mom Friendly Web Site," ezinearticles.com/?7-Suggestions-for-an-i-Mom-Friendly-Web-Site-(e-commerce-news-and-statistics)&id=57212.

SCORE's Five Tips for Checking Your Web Site

1. Simple, clear, and fast—think of your homepage as a billboard. Tell them exactly what they need to know upfront.

2. Leave plenty of white space around text. A simple font on a light background works best. Separate wide blocks of text into columns.

3. Subheadings make for quick reading. Make sure pages are easily skimmed.

4. Let your best customers sing your praises. Display their testimonials prominently on your site.

5. After each update, click through your entire site. Mistakes or broken links will only send visitors away.

Source: SCORE, "5 Tips to See if Your Web Site Is up to Snuff," www.score.org/5_tips_eb_11.html.

SCORE's Five Tips for Improving Your Web Site

1. Visit the sites of other companies to find out what you like and dislike. Do some sites seem to "work" while others don't?

2. Decide what objectives you want your site to meet. Do you want it to be fun, funny, educational, "cool," or all of those things?

3. Consider your corporate culture and your company image. Your site should support both.

4. Design or redesign the site to meet your objectives. Unless you have a real expert on staff, hire a consulting firm to do the job.

Section 15

5. Get feedback. Ask customers how your site can be made more useful to them, and keep making improvements.

Source: SCORE, "5 Tips for Improving Your Web Site," www.score.org/5_tips_eb_3.html.

Merchant Accounts and Payment Gateways

Section
15

Seven Things You Need to Know About Merchant Accounts

When considering opening an online merchant account to accept credit card orders, there are a lot of things you need to keep in mind. The best thing to do is learn all about credit card processing before you open your online merchant account so you can handle everything from the beginning rather than having to go back and make many changes. The following topics are things you need to know about credit card processing online before you open an online merchant account:

Topic #1—Security
When it comes to making online purchases, you need to be sure your customers feel as confident as possible that your site is secure and there is very little chance that any fraud will take place during their purchase. In general, the credit card processing software takes care of the security for the transactions; however, you can boost security on your web site to reduce the theft of credit card numbers, hackers, and general fraud. Also, consider using additional secure measures, like asking for the numbers on the back of their Visa card or the four numbers on the front of their American Express. Doing so ensures that the person ordering has the credit card in hand, so more than likely this is the owner of the card.

Topic #2—Fixed Rates
Before signing up with a credit card processing company, you want to make sure you will be receiving fixed rates for the life of the service. Many firms offer this, so don't feel that this is not an option. When you set this up, it is important that you get this in writing to ensure your rates stay the same. Of course, your rates will rise if Visa or MasterCard increase what they charge for credit card purchases, but this should be the only condition. Don't sign any contracts without addressing this issue!

Topic #3—Bundled Rates
Be careful with bundled rate offers. Frequently, credit card processing companies will mention bundled rates and how they will save you money. This may or may not be the case, depending on your products and the average selling price. Do some research on this topic in comparison with the types and prices of products you sell to see if it will save you money or not. For most businesses it costs more.

Topic #4—Confidence
Before you open an online merchant account, be sure you have complete confidence in the company that is handling the credit card processing. If for some reason you do not, even if you don't know why, keep moving on until you find one you do feel comfortable with.

Topic #5—Credit Cards and Debit Cards
You want credit card processing software that will allow you to accept a wide variety of credit cards as well as debit cards. Do not limit yourself to just Visa or MasterCard.

Also accept cards like American Express, Diners Club, and all bank debit cards. Doing this will only increase your business.

Topic #6—Accept Credit Cards

Before opening an online merchant account, you should know that most people are going to purchase from you using their credit or debit card. Sending personal checks and or money orders might be an option you provide for the small percentage without credit cards or who mistrust the internet, but most people are going to buy with their cards, so it is important to have secure software and an easy-to-use interface.

Topic #7—Save Payment Information

Many web sites offer the option to save payment information. This means that more than likely you will have a return customer who wants to save time when shopping next time by not having to type in all of their information again. Provide this option to shoppers on your web site!

Source: Michael Turner, "Credit Card Processing—7 Things You Need to Know Before Opening an Online Merchant Account," ezinearticles.com/?Credit-Card-Processing---7-Things-You-Need-to-Know-Before-Opening-an-Online-Merchant-Account&id=56605.

Eight Service Charges Related to Merchant Accounts

1. **Statement**—The charge each month for issuing you statements on all transactions.

2. **Application fee**—Some institutions will charge you for the privilege of applying for an account, regardless of whether your application is successful or not.

3. **Setup fee**—Once your application has been approved, there may be other fees associated with establishing the account.

4. **Discount Rate**—A percentage deducted for each product sold.

5. **Transaction**—Added to the discount rate, a flat rate on each transaction.

6. **Monthly minimum**—What you will be charged regardless of the level of sales each month.

7. **Reserve**—Some providers require you to maintain a certain level in the account to cover chargeback fees.

8. **Chargeback**—The killer fee that may cost you up to US$30 per fraudulent transaction (which includes any client disputing a transaction successfully).

Source: Michael Bloch, "Payment Gateways, Internet Merchant Accounts and 3rd Party Credit Card Processors," www.tamingthebeast.net/articles2/back-end-ecommerce.htm.

Four Popular Payment Gateways

#1 CheckOut.com
Real Time Solution Price = $49
Gateway Fee = 0
Monthly Minimum = 0
Rate = 5.05%
Trans Fee = $0 .45
Tech Support Fee = None
Options = Visa, MC, Discover, AMEX
Merchant Account = International

#2 PayPal
Real Time Solution Price = None
Gateway Fee = None
Monthly Minimum = None
Rate = 2.9%
Trans Fee = $0 .30
Tech Support Fee = None
Options = Visa, MC, Discover, AMEX
Merchant Account =Selected Countries

#3 Protx
Real Time Solution Price = N/A
Gateway Fee = £20/month (under 1000 transactions per quarter)
Monthly Minimum = N/A
Rate = 0
Trans Fee = 10p (only if over 1000 transactions per quarter)
Tech Support Fee = None
Options = Visa, MC, Delta, Switch, Solo, AMEX
Merchant Account = UK Only

#4 Authorize.net
Real Time Solution Price = $299
Gateway Fee = $20/month
Monthly Minimum = $20
Rate = 0%-2.4%
Trans Fee = $0.35
Tech Support Fee = Free Support
Options = Visa, MC, Discover, AMEX, JCB, Enroute, Diners, eCheck.Net
Merchant Account = US Only

Section 15

For a comparison listing of over 35 payment gateways, check www.x–cart.com/payment_gateways.html.

Source: QualiTeam, "Recommended Payment Gateways," www.x–cart.com/payment_ gateways.html.

Three Services That Act as Both Payment Gateway and Merchant Account

PayPal
www.paypal.com

2Checkout
www.2checkout.com

WorldPay
www.worldpay.com

Source: Compiled by Contributing Writer Ty Martin.

Chapter 92

Avoiding Fraud and Scams

Section 15

Ten Ways to Prevent Online E-Commerce Fraud

When the internet was booming, the media headlines were screaming about consumers' safety and the chance of their credit cards being stolen during the online purchasing process. With all the preventions that have taken place to ensure consumers' safety, it has neglected the risk of the merchants' safety from the consumer. Where is the protection from consumers defrauding merchants?

The last person in line of protection when it comes to internet fraud is the merchants. Listed below are ten helpful tips that you can take action on to prevent yourself from consumer fraud.

1. **Carefully review orders.** Whenever you receive an order, take some extra time and review the order carefully. Make sure the customer filled out all the information correctly and all of the information matches. If the order is fraudulent, in most cases you can catch anything that doesn't seem right by just carefully reviewing the entire order.

2. **Check contact, shipping, and credit card information.** The customer's contact information should match up with the information he or she used for the shipping address and the credit card. If this information doesn't match up, then you need to find out why the customer wants the products shipped to another address or is using a credit card with different contact information. This is a very good sign of a scamster, but not in all cases.

3. **Run the Address Verification Service (AVS).** Provided by most merchant processors, you can run the AVS service on all of your transactions to ensure that the information they gave you matches with the information on the file with the card-issuing bank. If this information doesn't match, then special precaution is encouraged.

4. **Beware of free e-mail addresses.** The majority of scamsters will use a free e-mail address to hide their identity. To find out if the e-mail address a customer is using is free, just visit the domain name (after the @). For example, if the address is consumer@thewebsite.com, you can go to thewebsite.com to see if that web site provides free e-mail like Hotbot or Yahoo. It might be a good idea for you to require an e-mail address from the customer's ISP on your order forms. This way, you can save yourself time with the free e-mail address. If a customer uses one, just e-mail to inform him or her of your requirement.

5. **Document all contacts.** To give yourself greater protection and a bigger fighting chance against fraud, document all contacts you have with customers. Use caller ID and a voice-mail box and keep all e-mails to show as proof in making your case.

6. **Check domain name records.** One unknown trick is to look up the records of the domain name a customer is using in his or her e-mail address to see if it matches with

what the customer provided in the order. This will work only if the customer has a web site and used his or her own domain in the e-mail address. Take the same procedure as explained in tip 4 and use Network Solutions' database to search for the records: www.networksolutions.com/cgi-bin/whois/whois. The customer's information might not match up completely, if something changed or if the customer is using a home address rather than a business address, but you can at least check the city and state.

7. **Be cautious about above-average order amounts.** Take special caution when receiving noticeably high orders, especially around holiday seasons. Also pay attention to orders for merchandise to be shipped overnight delivery. Scamsters don't pay for their orders, so they don't care how much they cost and want them as fast as possible.

8. **Post warnings.** Place notices on your order forms and your web site content warning against fraud. For example, "Any person who uses a credit card fraudulently on this web site will be prosecuted to the fullest extent of the law." Such notices will usually run off most scamsters.

9. **Do a reverse search on telephone numbers.** You can purchase a database of phone numbers on a CD or you can use services such as www.anywho.com to do a reverse search on a phone number. This will allow you to confirm the contact information for the phone number that the customer has provided.

10. **Call the customer.** The last and usually the most effective way to clear up all confusion is to call the customer at the phone number provided. If the number isn't good, then try contacting the customer via e-mail for a valid phone number.

Source: Curtis Stevens, "Prevent Online E-Commerce Fraud," www.merchantseek.com/article12.htm.

12 Potential Signs of Online Payment Fraud

Keep your eyes open for the following fraud indicators. When there's more than one of these signs in a card-not-present transaction, fraud might be involved. Follow up, just in case.

1. **First-time shopper:** Criminals are always looking for new victims.

2. **Larger-than-normal orders:** Because stolen cards or account numbers have a limited life span, crooks need to maximize the size of their purchases.

3. **Orders that include several of the same item:** Having multiples of an item increases a criminal's profits.

4. **Orders made up of big-ticket items:** These items have maximum resale value and therefore maximum profit potential.

5. **Rush or overnight shipping:** Crooks want items they obtain through fraud as soon as possible for the quickest possible resale and aren't concerned about extra delivery charges.

6. **Shipping to an international address:** A significant number of fraudulent transactions are shipped to fraudulent cardholders outside of the U.S.

7. **Transactions with similar account numbers:** This is particularly so if the account numbers used have been generated using software available on the internet.

8. **Shipping to a single address, but transactions placed on multiple cards:** This could involve an account number generated using special software or even a batch of stolen cards.

9. **Multiple transactions on one card over a very short period of time:** This could be an attempt to "run a card" until the account is closed.

10. **Multiple transactions on one card or a similar card with a single billing address, but multiple shipping addresses:** This could be a sign of organized activity, rather than one individual.

11. **In online transactions, multiple cards used from a single IP (Internet Protocol) address:** More than one or two cards could definitely indicate a fraud scheme.

12. **Orders from internet addresses that make use of free e-mail services:** These e-mail services involve no billing relationships and there's often neither an audit trail nor verification that a legitimate cardholder has opened the account.

Source: "12 Potential Signs of Card-Not-Present Fraud," www.emscorporate.com/ecommerce/fraudTips.asp.

Nine Ways to Protect Against Payment Fraud

One of the great things about the internet is anonymity. One of the worst things about the internet is anonymity—especially for e-commerce merchant. If you utilize payment gateways for credit card transactions or are considering doing so, it is important to ask the gateway provider about their prescreening procedures. (This precedes actual credit card payment processing.)

Many payment gateway providers use the Address Verification System (AVS). AVS provides some protection by comparing the billing address on the web order form with the address held by the cardholder's bank—but the transaction may be approved even if the address verification information does not match! The merchant faces the possibility of chargebacks if the payment gateway decides to continue with the transaction on a questionable match.

The following strategies are worthwhile considering if you sell goods and services directly from your site using your own in-house payment processing. Some of the strategies can also be used in conjunction with third-party credit card processing systems.

1. **Request information.** While consumers value their privacy and require quick web site ordering facilities, it is of the utmost importance that you gather sufficient customer

identity details during the ordering process. The customer's name, credit card number, and expiry date are not enough. Tell your customers why you need the information and what you will do with it—after all, it's in their best interests too. The fewer charge-back fees you have to pay, the cheaper you can offer goods and services.

It's important that each order processed from your site also contain information regarding the IP address of the person placing the order. This can then be matched up with the information from your server logs or web site traffic reporting applications (see below). An IP address is a unique network identifier issued by an internet service provider (ISP) to a user every time he or she is logged onto the internet. While this is a good anti-fraud mechanism and useful for tracking fraudsters, please be aware that IP addresses can also be forged.

2. **Be aware of e-mail addresses.** Fraudsters rarely use their own e-mail addresses. With the proliferation of free e-mail services, it is quite easy to provide false contact details. A false Yahoo e-mail address can be established within five minutes. Increasing numbers of internet retailers are refusing to process web site orders that list free e-mail address services as the primary point of contact, opting to request from customers their ISP or business e-mail addresses. You can check an e-mail address quickly by going to the originating domain and seeing if it provides a free e-mail service.

3. **Compare the shipping address and the billing address.** If the shipping address is different from the billing address, be wary. However, it is not uncommon for people to give a shipping address different from the billing address if they're sending gifts or if the billing address is a post office box.

You'll rarely find a fraudster sending goods to the legitimate cardholder's address. At the point of ordering, request a telephone contact number for your customer. State that you need this number in order to contact him or her if there are any problems. Many cardholders of compromised accounts have been alerted in this way. The fraudster definitely won't give you his or her own phone number! If you are unsure, e-mail or call the customer to verify the authenticity of the transaction. Fraudsters hate merchant contact of any kind.

4. **Analyze your log files.** There's a plethora of site traffic tracking services, such as WebSTAT (www.webstat.com), and software that not only will return very valuable demographic data, but can also assist you in pinpointing the origins of fraud.

Still one of the best ways to analyze your log files is manually. By examining your logs carefully, you will be able to find out a suspect order's originating internet address. This tracking is made easier if you include a time stamp on each submitted web site order form. For example, if you find that an order originating from Russia gives a billing address of Sydney, make further inquiries.

Most commercially hosted domains will have a server log available for your account. It's basically a text file that records every single request to the site, including images. Contained in every request is an originating IP, the ISP-issued address of the computer that requested the file.

If you aren't sure about how to access your raw server logs, inquire with your hosting service. Learn more about interpreting server logs here: www.tamingthebeast.net/articles/webtraffic.htm.

5. **Be wary of overseas orders.** Orders from abroad can be very risky, but an integral part of your online business. It is very difficult to retrieve goods or apprehend fraudsters once the goods have left the country. Make further inquiries with the credit card company if an order seems suspect.

Unfortunately, Eastern Europe is still a very high risk for credit card fraud; many online business owners refuse to process orders from Eastern Europe. Other high-risk regions are Indonesia, Egypt, Turkey, Pakistan, Malaysia, and Israel.

6. **Investigate unusual orders.** Unusually large orders requesting express delivery definitely warrant further investigation, especially if the customer has not purchased from you before. Customers are pretty cautious and will tend to place small orders first, to test the efficiency and integrity of your online business, or they'll make some sort of contact with you prior to ordering.

7. **When in doubt, call the company.** Call the credit card company before attempting to process the order if in doubt: that extra five minutes may save you big dollars! Even if the order has been processed through automated systems, it's not too late to follow up before shipping the goods or providing the services. The idea is to deal with the situation before the cardholder is issued a statement, notices something on it that he or she didn't purchase, and then contacts the bank.

8. **Make your anti-fraud policy visible.** Visual deterrents are still one of the most effective ways of minimizing crime. In a bricks-and-mortar store, signs and cameras prevent shoplifting to some degree. Why not use the strategy on your site?

Add bold notices to the checkout pages stating your stance on fraud and that systems are in place to monitor all transactions. Not only will this decrease attempts at fraud, but will also demonstrate to your clients that you take transaction security very seriously.

9. **Use specialist anti-fraud services.** Like so many online business owners, perhaps you don't have time to carry out rigorous screening. With the increase in fraudulent transactions, many companies have sprung up to act as screening services to help minimize credit card fraud risks to merchants.

Source: Michael Bloch, "Preventing Credit Card Chargebacks—Anti-Fraud Strategies," www.tamingthebeast.net/articles2/card-fraud-strategies.htm.

Section 15

Eight Safeguards Against Fraud

There are countless ways to safeguard your business from fraud. But here are some simple ways to help yourself.

1. **Held orders.** Create a "held orders" department where orders can be reviewed manually. Set certain guidelines for which orders will be held. An example might be orders over $250, which might be raised to $500 or higher at Christmas.

2. **In-house database.** Create an in-house database of all fraudulent orders by address. Take the time to run all orders through this database.

3. **Shared database/chain calls.** Establish a network with other e-merchants in the same business as yours. Share fraudulent order information with them.

4. **Telephone database.** You can purchase these on CD-ROM or use services such as Anywho.com's reverse telephone look-up. Use these databases to check phone numbers.

5. **Issuing bank.** Contact the credit-issuing bank (CIB) and they will contact the customer for you. The CIB will confirm the name and address given by the customer. Many times the phone number given to you on the order form is no good; the CIB can help you in this instance. Have your merchant ID ready when calling the credit card company. Here are phone numbers you can call.

   American Express
   (800) 528-5200

   Discover Card
   (800) 347-2000

   Visa/MasterCard
   (800) 228-1122

   CardService International Merchant Services
   (800) 456-5989

   E-Commerce Exchange Merchant Account Set-Up
   (800) 242-0363 x 2736

6. **Call the customer.** If you think you have the correct number, you can call the customer yourself. Otherwise, the CIB will contact the customer and have him or her call you.

7. **Document customer phone calls.** This is extremely helpful when you've lost merchandise to a fraudster. I recommend that you get caller ID and record incoming phone calls. Have your customer service employees document the calls in a log as well.

8. **Cyber shoplifting notices.** Almost every retailer has shoplifting notices posted. Why don't you? Let the shopper know that all fraudulent orders will be pursued to the fullest extent of the law. Since each prosecution will vary according to the fraudster's state of residence, it is best to keep this vague.

Source: Sharon Curry, "E-Commerce Fraud," www.scambusters.org/Scambusters39.html.

List of Places for Reporting Fraud

FBI Local Field Office
www.fbi.gov/contact/fo/fo.htm

Secret Service (Financial Crimes Division)
www.treas.gov/usss/financial_crimes.shtml

Secret Service, Cyber Thread/Network Incident Report
www.treas.gov/usss/net_intrusion_forms.shtml

Federal Trade Commission (online complaint)
www.ftc.gov

Securities and Exchange Commission (if securities fraud or investment-related spam e-mails)
www.sec.gov

Internet Fraud Complaint Center
www.ifccfbi.gov

Department of Justice, Criminal Division, Computer Crime & Intellectual Property Section
www.cybercrime.gov

SpamCop (to report spam e-mails)
www.spamcop.net

econsumer.gov (e-commerce complaints for 20 nations: Australia, Belgium, Canada, Denmark, Estonia, Finland, Hungary, Ireland, Japan. Korea, Latvia, Lithuania, Mexico, New Zealand, Norway, Poland, Sweden, Switzerland, United Kingdom, United States)
www.econsumer.gov

National Fraud Information Center/Internet Fraud Watch
(800) 876-7060

www.fraud.org (Online Incident Report Form)
68.166.162.20/repoform.htm

Phone Busters (Canadian Anti-Fraud Call Centre)
www.phonebusters.com

Reporting Economic Crime On-Line (National White Collar Crime Centre of Canada)
www.recol.ca

Identity Theft (Federal Trade Commission)
www.consumer.gov/idtheft/index.html

Section 15

Better Business Bureau Online
www.bbbonline.org

Fight Spam on the Internet! (to report spam abuse)
spam.abuse.net/spam

Source: Amir Ali Tayyab, "How to Report and Avoid Internet Fraud," www.webmasterlingo.com /t696-how-to-report-and-avoid-internet-fraud.html.

Four Sites to Help You Avoid Scams and Fraud

Global E-Commerce Scams
www.rpifs.com/ecommerce/ecomscams.htm

E-Commerce Best Practices
www.businessknowhow.com/money/ecombest.htm

Merchants Beware! Fraud Is Rampant
www.amcho.com/vp026.htm

Avoid Credit Card Fraud
www.merchantseek.com/article8.htm

Source: Compiled by Contributing Writer Ty Martin.

Four Things to Do if You've Been Scammed

Yes, there will be instances where you will hit a brick wall on any sort of recovery, but there are some things you can do once you've been scammed. Most law enforcement agencies want to help. The problem is that law enforcement needs tools to do their jobs. Tools in this case means laws. There are not many laws that are specific to this crime. Many agencies use identity theft, mail fraud, receiving stolen goods, and other standard laws currently on the books. Here are the steps you should take when someone has stolen from you.

1. **Document.** Pull together all documentation, including any phone records you may have accumulated. Include the original order, who the cardholder victim is (if applicable), date the order was sent, and identifiers for the merchandise (serial numbers, etc.).

   This is where you will want to take a deep breath and do some basic research on your con. Do the reverse phone number lookup if he or she has called in. Run the name of the fraudster through Anywho.com or other online phone books. Check TheUltimates.com to research e-mail addresses. If your loss is high, then it would benefit you to pay $30 to have a private investigator skip-trace the "Ship To" address for you. You can try to identify the e-mail address domain name at Network

Solutions. It can give you limited information about who owns the domain name.

2. **Follow the product.** Where was the merchandise sent? Hopefully you have established a firm policy against shipping to drop boxes and post office boxes. If you have, then the address will be a firm physical address. Don't give up if you find out that the address is a deserted house. The police may have an investigation established on that location.

3. **Check the shipping information.** Pull the shipping information to get documentation of who signed for the merchandise and the date and time it was received.

4. **Local police.** Contact the local police who have jurisdiction over the address where you sent the merchandise. To locate the appropriate law enforcement agency, you can use the area code and telephone information or internet sites like the police directory at search.officer.com/agencysearch. Explain to them what happened. Police are interested in "sexy" cases. When I call them, I usually tell them that, in the majority of cases, the fraudster has stolen from more companies than mine and it could result in a high-dollar case. It would amaze you how often this is true.

This is where it can get tricky. Some police will not go in after the fact, but others will. If the fraudster has another order on deck, offer to help the police conduct a controlled delivery. A controlled delivery is a delivery that the seller has complete control over in order to collect enough information from the fraudster to prosecute him or her. Let's say your company has an order pending for a $500 television set for a fraudster who has already received other pieces of merchandise. Contact the police and arrange to deliver the television under their supervision. In some cases I've had police dress up as UPS employees and make the delivery themselves. The moment the con signs for the package, the arrest is made on the spot. I enjoy controlled deliveries. Nine times out of ten the controlled delivery will net the law enforcement agency more than the fraud against your company.

Source: Sharon Curry, "E-Commerce Fraud," www.scambusters.org/Scambusters39.html.

Shopping Carts

20 Tips to Minimize Shopping Cart Abandonment

Industry research shows up to 75 percent of shoppers abandon their online shopping carts before completing the checkout process. I'm not sure how comfortable I am with that statistic, but shopping cart abandonment is a significant problem. Numerous factors influence this rate. Here are some considerations.

1. **How many steps are in your checkout process?** This is usually what most people focus on. Our clients' checkout processes range from one to seven steps. We've discovered the number of steps is not all that critical. One client was able to bring the checkout process from six steps down to one; we found no correlation between reduction of steps and reduction in abandonment rate. Once people found what they came for, they found the time to check out no matter how many steps were involved.

   Should you change the number of steps? Yes! But if you don't have an inexpensive and simple way to test, it may not be worth the time, effort, and expense of reducing the number of steps in the checkout process. Try some of these other ideas first.

2. **Include a progress indicator on each checkout page.** No matter how many steps in your checkout process, let customers know where they are in the process. Number the steps and label the task clearly for each step. Give shoppers an opportunity to review what they did in previous steps and a way to return to their current step if they go back.

3. **Provide a link back to the product.** When an item is placed in the shopping cart, include a link back to the product page. Shoppers can then easily jump back to make sure they selected the right item. I was shopping for a printer and wanted to know how many and what color cartridges come with the printer. It wasn't obvious where I should click to review the product description. I had to navigate using my back button until I got my questions answered.

4. **Add pictures inside the basket.** Placing a thumbnail image of the product increases conversions by as much as ten percent.

5. **Provide shipping costs early in the process.** If possible, provide an estimated cost while visitors browse. They want to buy but want the answers to all their questions when they want them. Total cost is one of those critical questions. Also, if the shipping information is the same as the billing information, include a checkbox to automatically fill in the same information.

6. **Show stock availability on the product page.** Shoppers should not have to wait until checkout to learn if a product is out of stock. Also, give an estimated delivery date. Deal with the "I want it now" mentality and let them know when they should expect to get their products.

7. **Make it obvious what to click next.** Include a prominent "Next Step" or "Continue

Section 15

with Checkout" button on each checkout page. Make the button you want them to click next the most obvious. One top-50 e-tailer mistakenly placed its "remove from cart" and checkout buttons next to each other. Neither stood out. Many people ended up clearing their carts. When they went to check out, they found nothing in there and immediately abandoned the site in frustration.

8. **Make editing the shopping cart easy.** It should be simple to change quantities or options or to delete an item from the shopping cart. If a product comes in multiple sizes or colors, make it easy to select or change values in the shopping cart.

9. **Make it your fault.** If information is missing or filled out incorrectly during checkout, give a meaningful error message that's obvious to see. It should clearly tell visitors what they need to correct. The tone should be "the system was unable to understand what was entered," not "the visitor made a foolish mistake."

10. **Show them you're a real entity.** People's concerns start to flare up during checkout. Let them know you're a real company by giving full contact info during the checkout process.

11. **Offer the option to call.** If visitors have a problem during checkout or feel uncomfortable using a credit card online, offer a phone number. Devote a dedicated toll-free line for tracking purposes. Also offer a printable order form so customers can complete orders by fax, if they prefer.

12. **Make the most of cross- and up-sell.** It isn't always effective to up-sell on a product detail page; sometimes this is best left for checkout. Recommend items based on what's already in the shopping cart. Look at how Wal-Mart (www.walmart.com) sells flowers and up-sells a vase, vs. how ProFlowers (www.proflowers.com) does. Try interstitials or pop-ups to capture up- and cross-sell options.

13. **It's about new customers.** Make the checkout process even easier for new visitors than registered customers. Acquiring new customers is much harder than selling to the loyal ones. Registered customers will find a way to sign in (if they don't have a cookie). Don't position registration and login as an obstacle between new visitors and checkout.

14. **Add third-party reinforcement messages.** VeriSign, Better Business Bureau, and credit card logos either greatly boost conversions or at least keep them neutral. In other words, they can't hurt. A HACKER SAFE® (www.scanalert.com) rating certification helps clients across the board, especially those with larger-than-average order sizes. Its maker, ScanAlert, claims the certification can increase average orders 15.7 percent.

15. **Handle coupon codes with care.** A friend decreased his conversion rate by 90 percent. Think carefully about where you present the option to enter codes and how you label it.

16. **Offer a price guarantee.** If you sell name-brand products and your store is price-competitive or truly provides better value, try a "Lowest Price Match" guarantee.

17. **Provide multiple payment options.** Follow Wal-Mart's lead and add more payment options. Allow visitors to pay by credit card, check, PayPal, or any other means you can.

18. **Reassure customers at the right time and place.** How often is critical information buried in tiny type at the bottom of the page or deep within a site? In a brick-and-mortar store, it's fairly easy to find product warranty information. Offer customers this same opportunity online, at the point of action (POA). Link to product warranties, shipping costs, return policies, testimonials, even optional extended service plans. Or, provide the information in a pop-up. Make the best use of your assurances at the right place and time.

19. **Track your mistakes.** Develop a system to keep notified of errors during the checkout process. One client noticed a portion of his visitors had cookies turned off. He developed a cookie-free checkout option. His conversion rate and sales jumped.

20. **Use an exit survey.** If a visitor abandons checkout, offer an incentive to complete an exit survey. You may find out why he or she didn't complete that order.

Now you have 20 ways to reduce shopping cart abandonment. Every site is different, of course, with its own environment and issues. Don't obsess about abandonment rates. Many people use shopping carts as placeholders for considering items. Help those who want to check out and may have questions, doubts, or obstacles holding them back.

Some of these tips will result in dramatic improvements; others may not do much at all. Test each one that's appropriate. Improve your conversion rate one step at a time.

Source: Bryan Eisenberg, "20 Tips to Minimize Shopping Cart Abandonment," www.clickz.com/experts/crm/traffic/article.php/2245891 and www.clickz.com/experts/crm/traffic/article.php/2248551.

Three Providers of Custom Shopping Carts

Design by Linda, Iowa Web Site Design Company
www.designbylinda.com/shoppingcart.htm

Tech Groups' Web Development
www.techgroups.com/web-programming.php

The Presence (The Web Presence Group)
www.webpresencegroup.net/products/ecommerce-E-Commerce.php

Source: Compiled by Contributing Writer Ty Martin.

Listing of ASP Shopping Carts

netSHIP
www.dotnetship.com
An ASP, real-time shipping calculator that returns rates from any combination of UPS, USPS, DHL, and FedEx. [commercial]

Absolute Shopping Package Solutions
www.aspsolutions.com.au
An ASP shopping script. Optional shopping cart hosting services. [commercial]

A-Cart
www.alanward.net/acart
Shopping cart and order processing system, composed of ASP pages and an Access database. [free for non-commercial use]

ASPPilot
www.aspilot.com
A shopping cart software with full inventory and customer order and shipping management.

CactuShop
www.cactushop.com
An ASP & VBscript ecommerce cart. Customizable. [commercial]

CyberMerchant
www.intlink.ca/products/Shopping_cart_software.htm
Advanced ASP shopping cart software. By IntLink Solutions.

CyberStrong eShop
www.cyberstrong.com/eshop/
Shopping cart software that maintains an online store directly from a browser interface. By CyberStrong Internet Services, Inc. Source available. [commercial]

Dealer Locator
www14.brinkster.com/aspcoders/dealer_locator/
An ASP Script that can locate sales reps, dealers, branch offices, and stores by asking the user his/her ZIP code. It returns a list of nearest dealers, with necessary contact information, mail, and web site link (if any). [commercial]

EasyStoreCreator
www.easystorecreator.com
The online e-commerce solution for small businesses. Create a site in minutes, automatically update stock, use the integrated shopping cart, and change the look instantly.

GoECart Shopping Cart Software
www.goecart.com
An ASP e-commerce solution. Allows a merchant to set up and operate an online store quickly and easily, including point-and-click layout authoring. [commercial]

Hypercart
www.hypercart.com
Shopping cart software with web hosting package.

Intersys
sourceforge.net/projects/intersys/
Advanced ASP/COM/MSSQL e-commerce system. Integrated cart, user management, checkout, uploading, content management, auctions, reverse auctions and fixed price sales. [open source, BSD license]

MMK Cart
www.mmkcart.com
Fully integrated shopping cart program with template driven design, built-in affiliate program, built-in gift certificates, MySQL, MS Access, SQL Server compatibility. [commercial]

OriEshop
www.orieshop.com
A shopping cart software and complete e-business solution with powerful inventory control and order management engine. Includes live demo. [commercial]

PdshopPro
www.pagedowntech.com/products/
A complete ASP online store with built-in shopping cart system for Internet Information Server. [commercial]

Q-Shop Storefront System

quadcomm.com

ASP storefront featuring a cart, dynamic catalog, purchase history, web-based catalog/order/user administration, shipping and taxes calculation. Source code included.

Rapid Classified

www.4u2ges.com

Dynamic and flexible ASP classified system. It can work with MS Access, MS SQL, MySQL databases. [free for non-commercial web sites]

RocketCart

www.rocketcart.com

Application built in ASP for operation in NT environment. Backend is Microsoft Access or SQL Server.

WebStores 2000

www.webcortex.com

ASP application with Access and SQL Server backend running in IIS. Marketed to developers and ISPs.

xcClassified

www.xcclassified.com

Turnkey classified ad management system for IIS web servers. [commercial]

Source: Open Directory Project, dmoz.org/Computers/Programming/Internet/ASP/Applications/E-Commerce.

Listing of PHP Shopping Cart Scripts

ABC eStore

www.abcestore.com

A powerful shopping cart software. It has a templates system that allows changing both design and structure of the e-store without interfering with the code. It is integrated with payment gateways (2CheckOut, PayPal, Skipjack).

Amazon Shop

www.ghostscripter.com/products.php

A shopping cart for Amazon Associates. PHP and MySQL. Demo available.

aMember

www.amember.com

Free PHP script to set up paid membership on your site with PayPal/Clickbank support.

Arena97

www.c97.net/arena_lite.php

A script based on PHP/MySQL solution for online rental shop with multi-skin and multilingual support. [commercial]

Associate-O-Matic

www.associate-o-matic.com

Build and customize a complete Amazon.com Associate Store. [commercial]

AuthorizeIt

www.phplabs.com/scripts/AuthorizeIt/

A PHP interface to the authorize.net merchant gateway, which lets you set up your site to take credit card payments. By PHP Labs. [commercial]

BAV—Bank Account Validator

bav.malkusch.de/en/

Classes for bank account validation. It may be easily integrated into an existing project. At the moment only (but all) German bank accounts are supported. [open source, GPL]

Clover Shop PHP Shopping Cart Software

www.clovershop.com/index_en.php

An online store that features a product catalog, a shopping cart, an orders and administration page. Databases are flat text files and you can edit them through a web browser or offline in a text editor. [commercial]

CodeThatShoppingCart

www.codethat.com/shoppingcart/

A shopping cart that can be easily customized and integrated into any site with the PHP and MySQL installed. Cart offers SSL support, e-mail notification system. [commercial]

Section 15

Deonix Scripts Templates Management

www.deonixscripts.com/index.php?view=products_templatesmng.html
A PHP script that supports selling single templates and membership based templates sites. Also it support templates uploaded, members subscription, files management. [commercial]

DH-MLM

www.dhmlm.com
Software designed to help manage affiliates and real-time commission payments.

digiSHOP

digishop.digisoft77.com
Fully self-administered shopping cart that works with PHP/MySQL. Pricing and online order.

Digisoft 77 E-Commerce Shopping Cart

www.digisoft77.com
PHP Shopping Cart. It uses MySQL and requires no knowledge of HTML or programming. Demo available. [commercial]

5th Avenue Software

www.5th-avenue-software.com
A template-driven customizable PHP shopping cart utilizing MySQL or PostgreSQL. Interfaces with numerous payment, tax, and freight methods. [shareware]

FishCart

www.fishcart.org
An open source catalog management system. Includes multi-lingual support, customer information tracking, close out items, audio or video clips for products, and encryption.

Gold-PHP

www.gold-php.com
Providing EXS software solution in the PHP programming language for e-currency trading businesses.

Idevspot PayDownloadPal

www.idevspot.com/index.php?page=p_detail~5
Digital download delivery automation with PayPal e-commerce integration.

Idevspot Pixie Professional

www.idevspot.com/index.php?page=p_detail~9
Download delivery, affiliate system, subscription automation, eBay download automation script.

iUser Ecommerce

www.intensivepoint.com
Shopping cart and product delivery system designed for merchants who sell software and e-book instant downloads. Includes time-sensitive options, software updates access, support, and a feature to bundle digital products. [commercial]

MiracleCommerce

www.miraclefruit.com/products_miraclecommerce_overview.html
A shopping cart software for Linux provides complete e-commerce functionality, including web-based online store, product catalog management, order management, customer management, order status update notification, order cancellation, customer credit issuance, and returns handling. [commercial]

MR ICT PayPal Download Script

www.mrict.co.uk/internet_solutions/digital_goods_store/
Script allows sale of digital products using a PayPal "Buy it Now" button. The file can be any digital media downloadable by a web browser, including zip, pdf, mp3, gif, and jpeg. [commercial]

1-2-3 Music Store

1-2-3-music-store.com
PHP- and mySQL-based online store for music downloads. Specially designed for independent musicians and record labels.

OrbitHyip

www.orbitscripts.com/orbithyip_overview.html
A MySQL/PHP based Professional High Yield Investment Program (HYIP) script that is very easy to use and allows manage members and E-gold/IntGold/EvoCash/E-Bullion deposits. The script supports unlimited payout plans. Flexible template system allows easily change design. [commercial]

Payment Processors Order Forms

www.pickadesign.com/orderscripts/
Payment processor forms that allows reception of "instant" payment for product or services. The forms are available for PayPal, 2Checkout, WorldPay, Authorize.net, and Paysystems. [commercial]

PaymentPal

www.phplabs.com/scripts/PaymentPal/
Allows acceptance of PayPal transactions through web site automatically, via PayPal's Instant Payment Notification system. By PHP Labs. [commercial]

PHP Invoice

www.phpinvoice.com
A PHP/MySQL-based account and automated invoice management program. It supports automated billing through Paysystems, 2Checkout, Worldpay, PayPal, and custom payment gateway. Features: Support Tax, pro-rated billing, revenue reports. [commercial]

PHP-IPN Monitor

www.withinweb.com
A PHP/mySQL application for selling digital goods via PayPal and IPN (instant payment notification). [commercial]

PHPAudit

phpaudit.us
PHP software distribution solution. It automates the distribution of software code from new orders to product download and licensing. [commercial]

phpMyCart

phpmycart.com
A PHP- and mySQL-based ready-to-use virtual shop with a template-based storefront, unlimited products and categories, and different options for delivery and payment.

phpShop

www.phpshop.org
A free online shop that includes a modular system, easy management, featured items, and searching.

SauSurePay

surepay.sauen.com
Implementation of SurePay's "classic" interface. Also includes a plug-in for ready use with PHPshop. Open source.

S.C.S.S (Shopping Cart Software Solution)

www.shopping-cart-software-solution.com
A full-featured shopping cart software with integrated payment solutions based on PHP and MySQL database. [commercial]

Shop Director

www.polyspaston.com/shopdirector.html
A shopping cart written in PHP. Every page is based around HTML templates to allow total customization of the appearance. By Polyspaston.

Shop Maker

www.shopmaker.co.uk
Display your products, receive payments, and send out the goods. With customer order tracking and automatic invoice generation. [commercial]

Shop-Script

www.shop-script.com
Application includes credit card processing, template-based design, and compatibility with mySQL, MS SQL, and Interbase. Online order.

Sysbotz SimpleData

www.sysbotz.com/products/simpledata
A PHP/MySQL-based invoice and inventory intranet application.

TemplateReseller

www.templatereseller.org
A complete reseller script for web site templates, flash templates, corporate logos, PHP-Nuke themes.

tplShop

www.tpl-design.com/tplshop/
PHP 4.1+ and MySQL required. Lots of features with handy administrator tools. A web-based interface. [commercial]

Section 15

TwoCheckout
www.phplabs.com/scripts/TwoCheckout/
Support for accepting credit card payments via 2Checkout.com; includes basic post-back script. By PHP Labs. [commercial]

VeriSignup
www.phplabs.com/scripts/Verisignup/
Allows integrating Verisign's PayFlowLink into web site. By PHP Labs. [commercial]

ViArt
www.codetosell.com
A PHP shopping cart. It supports MySQL and PostgreSQL databases and includes support for ODBC connections. [shareware]

Webforce Cart (wfCart)
www.webforce.co.nz/cart/
A free PHP shopping cart class. It's designed as a component for PHP developers who would rather write their own store than use a complete solution.

Whois Cart Pro
whoiscart.net
A PHP-based application that provides a simple-to-use shopping cart for users purchasing domain names and hosting services. [commercial]

Whois.Cart
whoiscart.net
A PHP- and MySQL-based domain and hosting sales and management system that solves most manual labor involved with running a hosting business. [commercial]

Zen Cart
www.zen-cart.com/modules/frontpage/
A user-friendly PHP-based shopping cart system. [open source, GPL]

Source: Open Directory Project, dmoz.org/Computers/Programming/Languages/PHP/Scripts/E-Commerce.

Listing of Hosted Shopping Cart Systems

Americart
www.cartserver.com/americart/
Service that can be implemented regardless of where site is hosted. Same-day setup.

Apple Pie Shopping Cart
www.applepiecart.com
Search engine-friendly e-commerce solution that includes site statistics, HTML newsletter and site designer. Features: reviews, demo, and price list.

BankLine Relay
www.banklinerelay.com
Offers cookie-free service with secure VeriSign gateway and real-time UPS rates.

Beanbasket
www.beanbasket.com
Shopping cart service for businesses needing a feature-rich, easy-to-use e-commerce solution at an affordable price.

BetterCart
www.bettercart.com
Low-cost system designed for the small to mid-sized business. Same-day setup. Customization available.

Biz Shopping Cart
www.bizshoppingcart.com
Offers web-based shopping cart solutions for building online stores. Includes information about products and customer resources.

BizStudio Site Manager
www.bizstudio.com/main/home.htm
Cart, SSL server, store manager, and order manager. Same-day setup.

BIZyCart Ecommerce Server
bizycart.com
Service allowing creation and management of online storefront.

Bush Services Group, Inc.

bushservices.evsholdingco.com
Cart and credit card processing services to copy and paste into existing web pages. Hosted options also available.

Cart 4 Checkout

www.4checkout.net
Remotely hosted service that allows a web site to be hosted anywhere.

CCI Ecommerce

www.ccieshop.com
E-commerce solutions for businesses, individuals, and corporate clients.

Create Your Shop

www.createyourshop.com
Creates online storefront with including web-based management tools, online store builder, and hosting. Free trial.

Creative Cart

www.creativecart.com
Provides an affordable secure service. Same-day setup.

Custom Cart

www.customcart.com
Application to create a storefront with same-day setup.

D&D Designs

dnd_design.evsholdingco.com
Includes hosting, merchant account, and a secure site. Build online store yourself or this service can build it.

DesignCart

www.designcart.com
Low-cost monthly service to facilitate an SSL secure storefront.

Earthstores

www.now-on-sale.com
Online store builder includes a full-featured shopping cart and catalog management system with extensive customization capabilities.

EasyCATALOG

www.easycatalog.net
Pay-as-you-go online catalog and shopping cart that integrates with PayPal, Nochex, and WorldPay. Includes demo.

Ecartsoft

www.ecartsoft.com
Turnkey, platform-independent system that can be installed with same-day setup for existing site. Reseller opportunities available.

EcoCart 2000

www.ecocart2000.com
Ordering system implemented on VPI.net server. Same-day setup.

E-Commerce Software, Inc.

www.ecommerce-software-inc.com
Various pricing options for service with SSL security. Merchant account not needed. Reseller program available.

EKM Powershop

www.ekmpowershop.com/ekmps/index.asp
A secure shopping cart that links into an existing web site.

EZStores.Net

ezstores.net
Low-cost monthly storefront can be integrated with existing web site or as standalone. Same-day setup.

FastCart UK

www.fastcart.co.uk
Free shopping cart for WorldPay users. Includes login area and technical support.

Free Shopping Carts Software

www.free-shopping-carts-software.com
Offers Java- and CGI-based e-commerce shopping cart software and online store builder.

GoEmerchant.com

www.goemerchant.com
Provides tools to create an online store. Secure credit card processing with shopping cart software, merchant account, and web hosting.

Section 15

Hamilton Associates

www.hamassoc.com
Low-cost service offering various merchant account options.

InstantShops.com

www.instantproducts.com
Offers off-the-shelf software with low-price options. Same-day setup. Customization available.

Luckenbooth Software

www.luckenbooth.com
Software to build and maintain web sites and shopping carts with unlimited product categories and a listings version for real estate agents, car dealers, and others.

Merchant CGI

www.merchantcgi.com
Low-cost system for online merchants. Option exists for software purchase only. Contains software demo.

MerchantBankCART

www.merchantbankcart.com
Customizable online storefront. Will assist in securing merchant account. Seven-day free trial.

MonsterCommerce

www.monstercommerce.com
Provides various turnkey options for new and existing web sites. Sample client sites demonstrate features.

NetStores

www.netstores.com
Offers software, server, processing solution designed for simple integration into an existing web site.

1ShoppingCart.com

www.1shoppingcart.com
Features completely hosted shopping cart software and e-commerce solutions. Offers merchant accounts, automatic responders, ad tracking, and marketing tools.

POSPlugin

www.posplugin.com
Hosted integration of shopping cart system and secure online credit card processing. Includes company profile and contact details.

Remote Cart

www.remotecart.com
Fully secure service with affiliate program, free domain name, and redirection. Seven-day free trial.

SecureNetShop

www.securenetshop.com
Low-cost service to implement an online storefront. Online Data provides fast-response merchant accounts.

Start My Store

www.startmystore.com
Customizable storefront builder with customer relationship module and advertising management module.

Store54 Ecommerce System

www.store54.com
Offers customizable cart application with search engine optimization features. Includes product description and a demo.

Total Merchandiser

www.totalmerchandiser.net
Application allows for browser-based web site creation, including e-commerce shopping cart functionality.

Veracart

www.veracart.com
Shopping cart and online e-commerce solutions for small business web sites.

VirtualCart Secure Shopping

www.vcart.com
Includes an overview of the services available, pricing plans, and a downloadable demo.

WebPeddleGold

webpeddle.net
Storefront application with an online manage-

ment console. Compatible with all ImagineNation back-office utilities for order management and credit card processing.

WebStore Inc.

www.webstoreinc.com
Offers customizable, order entry, and secure payment system for online storefronts.

Web-Store-Buddy

www.web-store-buddy.com
Cart application that integrates into an existing site. Includes product description, pricing, and account login.

World Wide Merchant

www.wwmerchant.com
Software and service for online stores or catalogs. Hosting available.

Zcntr.com

www.zcntr.com
Capability to create web stores with search engine and secure order form.

Source: Open Directory Source, dmoz.org/ Computers/Internet/Web_Design_and_Develop ment/Hosted_Components_and_Services/Shop ping_Carts.

Listing of Perl/CGI Shopping Carts

Agora Hacks

agorahacks.com
Custom Perl hacks for the Agora.CGI shopping cart. Also custom programming services.

Better Basket Pro

www.imediasoftware.com/products/bbpro/index .php
A CGI shopping basket solution, no code required.

BusyBeeCart.com

www.busybeecart.com
A feature-packed flexible shopping cart. [commercial]

CheckItOut E-Commerce Solutions

ssl.adgrafix.com/
Provides users with feature-rich e-commerce software. Features sales and support, demonstration store, online manual, and version information, among other content.

The CITY Shop

www.nightmedia.net
A shopping cart: an object-oriented code base, easy multiple-language and multiple-shop implementation, an easy-to-customize shop interface. [shareware]

ClickCartPro

www.clickcartpro.co.uk
Full-featured shopping cart software. It uses SQL and a relational database model, which allows tie-ins to many RDBMS (including MySQL, PostgreSQL, MS SQL Server). [commercial]

ClickCartPro

www.clickcartpro.com
E-commerce shopping cart solution. By Kryptronic. [commercial]

EDatCat

www.edatcat.com/cgi-bin/cgiwrap/edatcat/ EDCstore.pl
Customize the Perl or CGI shopping cart system.

Elite's CGI Script Center

www.siteinteractive.com
E-commerce software. [shareware and commercial]

Groundbreak.com

www.groundbreak.com
A collection of free and not-so-free CGI scripts written in the Perl programming language, focusing on e-commerce and web business.

Section 15

HTML-CART

html-cart.com

A shopping cart program, very easy to install with store manager application. Demo and download available. [freeware]

I-Shop Pro

www.softlinx2000.com

Shopping cart solutions. [commercial and freeware]

Marketing Intelligence Master

www.neumediatech.com/index.html

Software builds web sites, creates shopping carts, and tracks customers' buying habits. By Neu Media Technologies. [Commercial]

Mountain-Net

www.mountain-net.com

An inexpensive but full-featured shopping cart system that uses Perl, with a built-in database, store management, and statistics. Allows processing through AuthorizeNet, Anacom, CyberCash, and SecureBank.

PayPal Calculator

www.paypalshoppingcart.org

CGI script. Integrates price calculation and order submission from a site to a PayPal account or PayPal shopping cart.

PerlShop Resources

www.perlshop.org

Site for PerlShop e-commerce script. Includes updates, hacks, and fixes for the script, as well as support resources.

ShopCMS

www.expertwebinstalls.com/shopcms_paypal_shopping_cart.html

A mySQL-based content management system designed as an easy-to-use-and-configure shopping cart. [commercial]

TKI Cart

www.imediasoftware.com/products/tkicart/

A CGI shopping cart that makes setting up online store a quick and easy process. [commercial, demo]

uStorekeeper Online Shopping Cart Software

www.uburst.com/uStorekeeper/

A complete e-commerce solution to create, operate, and maintain an online store. Features include affiliate tracking, merchant account interfaces, image upload utility. [commercial, trial version]

WebGenie Shopping Cart Professional

www.webgenie.com/Software/Shopcart/

Shopping cart software to build catalogs and CGIs for online e-commerce store. [commercial]

WebMasterCart

www.webmastercart.com

Shopping cart software and a catalog manager for Unix/Linux and Windows web servers. [shareware]

WebStore 400CS Shopping Cart

www.ratite.com/400CS/demo/

Flexible, low-cost, Perl shopping cart by RDC Software. Easy to install and customize. Online web store demonstrations and support documentation. Script customization available.

Zaygo

www.zaygo.com

Information and demos of DomainCart, a shopping cart for domain name sellers with an integrated domain WHOIS script, and HostingCart, the shopping cart for domain names and hosting. [commercial]

Source: Open Directory Project, dmoz.org/ Computers/Programming/Languages/Perl/WW W/Scripts/E-Commerce.

Benefits of a Custom-Developed Shopping Cart System

The benefits of a custom-developed shopping cart system are:

1. Fully customizable and built to requirements
2. The store can be developed toward the different payment gateways
3. Built using the scripting environment of your choice
4. Complete knowledge of your store in case of problems

Source: eWebcircle, "Ecommerce Overview," www.ewebcircle.com.au/ecommerce.asp.

Benefits of a Vendor-Built Shopping Cart System

The benefits of a vendor-built shopping cart system are:

1. Quick web development time
2. A customized shopping cart to fit your web site
3. Easy upgrades without the need for further development work
4. A structure that supports many processing companies

Source: eWebcircle, "Ecommerce Overview," www.ewebcircle.com.au/ecommerce.asp.

Chapter 94

Additional Resources for Payments

Section 15

Three Guides to Accepting Payments Online

Accepting Payments Online: An E-Commerce Web Site Overview
www.marketingsource.com/articles/view/1564

Guide to Payment Gateways and Merchant Accounts
www.tamingthebeast.net/articles2/back-end-ecommerce.htm

Online Payments Guide
www.eshopfitters.co.uk/online_payments_guide.php

Source: Compiled by Contributing Writer Ty Martin.

The Process of Online Sales Using Credit Cards

1. Customer visits your site.
2. Customer clicks on a "buy me" button after reviewing sales copy.
3. The selection is added to the shopping cart.
4. Once at the "checkout," the customer's personal and financial details are recorded via a secure form.
5. Details submitted from the form are transmitted to a payment gateway service, which is separate from the cart. The gateway service securely routes the information through the relevant financial networks.
6. If the transaction is successful, the customer's credit card account is debited and your merchant account is credited.
7. Once all funds have cleared, you are then able to transfer money to your ordinary business checking account.

Source: Michael Bloch, "Payment Gateways, Internet Merchant Accounts and 3rd Party Credit Card Processors," www.tamingthebeast.net/articles2/back-end-ecommerce.htm.

Seven Ways a Credit Card Chargeback Can Occur

A chargeback occurs when a credit card processor charges the merchant (you) for the cost of returned items or incorrect orders that the customer claims were made to his or her credit card. Chargebacks can also be initiated by banks, often without consulting their customers. These chargebacks are usually for processing or authorization-related issues. As you might imagine, chargebacks are quite costly for merchants.

Section 15

Here are some common causes of chargebacks, all of which you need to be concerned about as an e-commerce merchant, along with possible preventive measures:

You are the victim of fraudulent mail-order/telephone-order or Internet transactions.

Solutions:

- Create a database to identify high-risk transactions and block specific credit card numbers within your system.

- Use the Address Verification Service (AVS) to verify the cardholder's address at the time of the sale and compare the address against the information in the card issuer's database.

- Submit your customer service telephone number to your credit card processor so it can be included with your merchant name on customers' billing statements.

- Know your customers: obtain their telephone numbers during a transaction and call to verify the order and the numbers given to you.

- If they're available, use CVC2 (MasterCard) and CVV2 (Visa). These two numbers are the three unique digits on the back of a MasterCard or Visa credit card. These are used in situations where the card is not present.

The customer claims not to have received the requested goods or services or that you've charged improperly for goods or services he or she hasn't received yet.

Solutions:

- Obtain your cardholder's signed proof of delivery for every credit card transaction in which the merchandise or service is not delivered immediately at the point of sale.

- Disclose to your customer in writing the terms of a transaction, including shipping and handling charges and any applicable taxes. The first payment installment must not be processed until the shipment date of goods.

- Use the appropriate wording on the transaction receipt, such as "delayed delivery," "deposit," or "balance." Note: you can process delayed-delivery transactions before delivery of the goods, but you cannot process a deposit or balance transaction before delivery.

- You can process a prepayment transaction if you advise your customer that he or she will be billed immediately and you can process a full prepayment for custom-order merchandise (goods manufactured to the customer's specifications).

A customer requests a copy of a transaction through his or her credit card company, and you are asked for copies of all your documentation, called a "retrieval request."

Solution:

- It's critical that you file all customer information in a manner so you can quickly retrieve it and prove the customer made a purchase from your site. To reduce confusion that could result in a dispute, have a copy of each transaction to support it.

The customer claims the credit for a refund was not processed.

Solution:

- Process refunds to your customers' accounts quickly, always using the same card number from the original sale. Never give a customer a refund by cash or check. Be sure your return or refund policy is clearly stated on all receipts to avoid any disputes.

You get tangled in a dispute over duplicate transaction processing.

Solution:

- Make sure you process only one transaction at a time. If your customer makes more than one purchase or two purchases for the same dollar amount on the same day, make sure you create a separate invoice for each transaction.

Authorization is declined.

Solution:

- Do not continue to seek authorization on a declined transaction, do not reduce the amount requested, and do not repeat the request. Simply do not process the sale.

A cardholder disputes the quality of the merchandise or service or indicates it was defective.

Solution:

- Ensure that your customers are aware of your return policy by displaying it prominently on receipts. If you want your return policy to be limited, say so.

- Be sure your merchandise suits the needs of the customer and ensure that the goods are packed properly for shipping.

Source: Tim Miller, "Chargebacks: A Huge Price to Pay," www.entrepreneur.com/article/0,4621,290530,00.html.

Custom Credit Card Processing Services

InstaMerchant Internet Merchant Accounts
www.instamerchant.com

Durango Merchant Services (USA/International)
www.durangomerchantservices.com

Merchant Express (USA)
www.merchantexpress.com

Source: Michael Bloch, "Payment Gateways, Internet Merchant Accounts and 3rd Party Credit. Card Processors," www.tamingthebeast.net/articles2/back-end-ecommerce.htm.

Section 15

Top Seven Accounting Software Packages

For companies with up to $5 million in revenue:

1. BusinessVision 32 (Best Software)
2. Small Business Manager (Microsoft)
3. M.Y.O.B. (M.Y.O.B. Software)
4. Peachtree Complete Accounting 2004 (Best Software)
5. QuickBooks Pro 2003 (Intuit)
6. Simply Accounting (Best Software)
7. Vision Point 2000 (Best Software)

Source: Carlton Collins, "The Top 40 Accounting Software Products," www.asaresearch.com/articles/top40.htm.

11 Attributes of Effective Accounting Software for Large Retailers

1. The product must have good, clean, stable code.
2. The product must have good underlying technology.
3. The product must have a good company and leadership behind it.
4. The product must have strong financial reporting capabilities.
5. The product must have a sizable customer base.
6. The product must have strong customization capabilities.
7. The product must have a well-developed and knowledgeable VAR (Value-Added Reseller/Retailer) channel.
8. The product must have a wide breadth of modules.
9. The product must have a well-developed offering of third-party add-on products.
10. There should be a minimal number of missing features.
11. There should be no significant problems (such as missing modules, etc).

Source: Carlton Collins, "The Top 40 Accounting Software Products," www.asaresearch.com/articles/top40.htm.

Section 15

Drop Shipping

Section 15

979

The Process of Drop Shipping

1. You open an internet store, with a shopping cart and the ability to accept credit cards.

2. You find a distributor who is willing to drop ship the products you want to sell. The best place on the internet for this is www.WorldwideBrands.com. This is our web site; our Drop Ship Source Directory and Light Bulk Wholesale Directory are recognized as the best sources for legitimate wholesale suppliers on the internet.

3. You establish an account as a retailer with the wholesale supplier you choose.

4. You receive images and descriptions of the products you want to sell from the wholesale supplier and post them on your internet store.

5. A customer surfs into your internet store and falls in love with a product that you have priced at, say, $80. She purchases the item with her credit card. Your store charges her credit card $80 plus your shipping fee.

6. You turn around and e-mail the order to your wholesale supplier, along with the customer's name and address.

7. The wholesale supplier sends the product directly to your customer, with your store's name on the package.

8. The wholesale supplier charges you the wholesale price of, say, $45, plus shipping.

9. Your customer gets a cool product from your store shipped to her door, she tells all her friends about you, and you make even more money.

Source: Chris Malta, "What is Drop Shipping?," www.doingsuccess.com/ articles_business_malta_ecommerce-what-is-dropshipping.html.

The Four Advantages of the Drop-Shipping Model over the Wholesale Model

The drop-ship model offers many unique advantages over the wholesale model.

1. You do not have to spend a fortune on the huge inventory of wholesale stocks before you start a retail business. This translates into a very low business start-up cost. There is no risk of purchasing large quantities of stock and finding that you cannot sell off your goods because they have become obsolete among consumers. Therefore, with the variety of products offered by your drop shipper, it becomes feasible to test which products have a strong demand over the internet without losing a fortune on each test.

2. Another prime advantage of a drop-ship business is that there is no need to worry

about shipping your products to your customers. You do not have to provide storage space for your goods, nor do you have to incur warehouse costs. Your drop shipper will take care of all the logistics and shipping of your drop-ship business. In fact, most drop shippers are willing to label their products with your company name, so it will appear as if you are the one who shipped the products to your customers. The shipping cost for each product is also reduced, because your drop shipper can ship your products directly to your customers. A higher profit margin is achieved because of the elimination of unnecessary shipping costs.

3. Drop shipping is also unique in that it allows you to "sell high, then buy low," instead of "buy low, then sell high." Your risk involved in your retail business is dramatically lowered as you get paid upfront for your products, making a profit on each sale.

4. There is no minimum quantity restriction on your orders. From your web site catalogue, you can sell as much of your products as you want and you can leave the indenting of stocks to your drop shipper. The quantity of products that you can sell over your web site is limited only to your market demand and your marketing efforts.

Source: Ray Yee, "Using Drop Shipping for E-Commerce," dev.twinisles.com/library/drop-ship1.html.

Six Questions to Ask a Drop-Shipping Partner

Most companies that you contact will be more than happy to speak with you—after all, you are going to be selling their products for them. When you call, simply ask to speak with someone about becoming a vendor for their products. Once the switchboard puts you through to the right person, he or she will be able to answer any questions you have, including:

1. **What is the wholesale price they can offer you on their products?**
   You'll need to make sure that the wholesale price they offer is low enough that you will be able to generate a good profit based on what you will be able to sell their products for.

2. **Do they charge a handling fee for drop shipping? If so, how much?**
   Most companies that drop ship will simply add the cost of UPS or FedEx shipping onto your wholesale price, but some will also charge you a handling fee (generally between $1 and $5). This is to offset their cost of picking, packing, and processing the order for you.

3. **Do they have a monthly minimum *or* maximum of products they will drop ship?**
   Some companies will require that you sell a minimum dollar amount of their products each month (usually around $100 per month). A few will also have a monthly maximum of units they will ship for you. If you think that you will be selling more than this number each month, they'll refer you to one of their distributors.

Section 15

4. How do they ship their products?

Almost every company that drop ships products will use a major nationwide delivery service like UPS or FedEx. Ask them to include tracking numbers with the order confirmations they send. This will save you many potential problems when customers ask, "Where is my order?"

5. How do they bill you?

Most drop shippers will bill your credit card the wholesale price of the product plus shipping and handling as soon as they receive an order from you. With others, you may be able to set up a monthly billing cycle where you submit payment for all orders at the end of each month.

6. How do they deal with product returns?

Be sure to find out what their policy is regarding returns. Most reputable companies will offer some kind of guarantee or warranty on their products and will deal with returns for you. This way, if customers contact you with returns, you can simply tell them that the manufacturer will be happy to speak with them directly. If your manufacturer doesn't accept returns, look out! You will be the one stuck replacing defective merchandise for your customers.

Source: Corey Rudl, "Use Drop Shipping to Set up a Successful Online Store Selling Name Brand Products ... Without Spending a Dime on Inventory!," www.doingsuccess.com/ articles_business_corey-rudl_ecommerce_dropshipping.html.

Four Common Drop-Shipping Problems and Solutions

No business model is without disadvantages—and drop shipping your products can lead to some serious problems if you aren't careful. Below are a few of the most common problems, along with some tried-and-true solutions to help you save some serious time and money:

Problem #1: Shipping Delays

The best thing about drop shipping is that you don't have to worry about shipping your products. Well, this can occasionally create issues.

Let's say you send an e-mail to your drop shipper asking them to send an order to your customer and it just so happens that they are sold out of that item at the moment. The longer it takes them to let you know that the item is unavailable, the longer it will be before you can pass that information on to your customer and the worse you'll end up looking.

Solution: Insist on prompt order confirmation from your drop shipper. Ask them to send confirmation e-mails or faxes to you when they've processed your order, letting you know that the order has been shipped. If they find that they're out of stock, make sure they let you know immediately.

Problem #2: Tracking Shipping Status

Your customer calls you up a week after ordering a product and asks what the status of their shipment is. Unfortunately, since you didn't ship the product, you have no idea what to tell them. And if your customer is demanding a refund for an order that has already been shipped, you'll be paying for it when your drop shipper sends you the invoice!

Solution: Most of the nationwide delivery services (like UPS or FedEx) now offer online tracking services. If customers call to check the status of their shipments, you can instantly tell them where their package is by entering their tracking number at the UPS or FedEx web site. Better yet, include the tracking number in your confirmation e-mails to your customers and let them track their orders themselves. Just be sure to ask your drop shipper to provide you with tracking numbers once your orders have been shipped!

Problem #3: Drop Shipper Backs Out

Occasionally, a manufacturer or distributor will simply back out of their drop-shipping agreement with you. They may decide that the work involved in packaging and shipping their products for you simply isn't worth the trouble.

Solution: Unfortunately, you'll never really know how reliable your partners will be until you've placed a few orders from them. When you are setting up your agreements with your drop shippers over the phone, you should be able to get a good sense of how reliable they are based on how they answer your questions. This is one of those areas of your business where you'll have to follow your instincts!

Problem #4: High Shipping Costs

Finally, you can run into problems with shipping costs if you work with a number of manufacturers and distributors. For example, let's say a customer orders six products from your web site, with each one being drop shipped by a different manufacturer or distributor. The customer will have to pay shipping and handling costs on each individual item, and that can add up to a lot of extra money. If your customers see that they'll have to pay $40 to ship $80 worth of goods, they'll abandon their order every time.

Solution: You'll avoid those abandoned orders by just using one manufacturer or distributor on your web site. Keep in mind that many distributors deal with thousands of products (usually related to each other), so you can usually source all of your products with one distributor. Of course, your site may never run into this problem.

If you take my advice and focus on selling one or two niche products (like toasters), you can reduce the likelihood of customers ordering more than one product in the first place. (Who needs six toasters?)

Section 15

Source: Source: Corey Rudl, "Use Drop Shipping to Set up a Successful Online Store Selling Name Brand Products ... Without Spending a Dime on Inventory!," www.doingsuccess.com/ articles_business_corey-rudl_ecommerce_dropshipping.html.

Marketing and Promotions

Section 15

Search Engine Result Relationships

The search engine landscape has undergone some incredible changes in recent years, not only in the refinement of technology, but also in various partnerships between search companies. You may be running your queries on search engine X, but who is actually supplying the results? It may be another company altogether! So who is feeding whom? The following is a breakdown, current as of August 2005, of various search companies and their relationships with other engines.

Yahoo
Provides primary search results to Yahoo Search, Alta Vista and AllTheWeb. Receives paid listings from Yahoo Search Marketing (formerly Overture).

Google
Provides primary search results to Google, AOL Search, and Netscape. Supplies paid listings to Lycos, Ask Jeeves, Teoma, Netscape, AOL Search, and HotBot. Supplies secondary search results to HotBot. Receives directory data from DMOZ.

Lycos
Receives directory search results from DMOZ, primary search results from Ask Jeeves, and paid listings from Google Adwords.

Hotbot
Receives directory search results from DMOZ, primary search results from Ask Jeeves, and paid search and secondary results from Google Adwords.

AOL Search
Receives primary and paid search results from Google, plus directory results from DMOZ.

Ask Jeeves
Provides primary search results to Ask Jeeves, Hotbot, and Lycos. Receives secondary search results from Teoma and directory results from DMOZ. Receives paid listings from Google Adwords. Rumor has it that Ask Jeeves is currently developing its own PPC platform.

DMOZ
Provides directory results to Lycos, Hotbot, AOL Search, Google, Teoma, and Netscape, plus thousands of other, less well-known directories and engines.

Teoma
Provides primary search results to Teoma and secondary results to Ask Jeeves. Receives directory results from DMOZ and paid listings from Google Adwords.

Netscape
Receives primary and paid results from Google and directory results from DMOZ.

Section
15

AllTheWeb
Receives primary search results from Yahoo and paid listings from Yahoo Search Marketing (formerly Overture).

AltaVista
Receives directory and primary search results from Yahoo and paid listings from Yahoo Search Marketing.

MSN
Supplies primary search results to MSN Search. Receives paid listings from Yahoo Search Marketing.

Source: Michael Bloch, "Search Engine Relationships," www.tamingthebeast.net/articles5 /search-engine-relationships.htm.

Three Elements That Can Disrupt Search Engine Indexing

1. Frames produce a navigation system where the menu on the left scrolls independently of the page content on the right. Unfortunately, frames can wreak havoc with search engines. Unless you are careful to include <NOFRAMES> tags, search engines may not be able to find the content pages. Even if search engines do find your content pages, these pages can show up in response to a search engine query all by themselves, without the navigation system and links necessary for a visitor to find the rest of your web site. Don't use frames. If your current site has frames, make plans to rebuild the site without them. A menu constructed from Server Side Includes (SSIs) is just as easy to maintain—even easier, once you learn how to do it.

2. JavaScript and Flash are programming languages that can make very classy, animated menu systems. For example, a menu item might have a drop-down sub-menu that will wow your visitors (you hope). The problem is that if JavaScript and Flash systems replace plain hyperlinks, the search engine may not be able to find the underlying pages. Most search engines have posters on their walls saying, "I don't do Flash." Stubborn creatures, these search engines. One solution: retain your fancy menus, but include hypertext links at the bottom of the page to your sectional pages, with links on your sectional pages to all the subpages in that section. You can also submit a site map web page to the search engines that contains a link to every page on your site.

3. Dynamically generated web pages, created "on the fly" from a database, are more difficult for search engines to index, since these web pages don't exist in real time. They appear when a visitor clicks on a link. Then the database whirrs and spits out a transient web page for that visitor and that visitor alone. Database-driven content management systems are the only way to keep your sanity if your site contains thousands of web pages, but they cause search engine problems.

Source: Ralph F. Wilson, "12 Website Design Decisions Your Business or Organization Will Need to Make," www.wilsonweb.com/articles/12design.htm.

Five Free Ways to Increase Traffic to Your Online Store

So you've finally created a web site for your small online store! Now you think, "How do I get people to visit my site?" If you're like most new web site owners, you wonder how to bring potential customers to your site without spending lots of money on expensive advertising. Here are some ways to increase traffic to your online store.

1. **Offer a freebie or a contest for your items.** One of main reasons that people use the internet is to find free (or cheaper) stuff. If you offer a freebie or contest for one of your items, then you are likely to attract potential customers. To get maximum exposure for your freebie or contest, you should register with as many "free stuff sites" as possible. Here are a couple of sites that would be good starting points: www.thefreesite.com and www.realfreesite.com.

2. **Link to similar web sites.** A popular method used by webmasters to increase web traffic is to swap links with comparable web sites. However, the trick to maximizing the effectiveness of linking is to find sites with a minimum Google PageRank (a system that Google uses to judge the importance of each web page) of 3 or 4. To find out more information about PageRank, click here: toolbar.google.com. To find good linking partners, check out these two link partner directories: www.links-pal.com and www.gotop.com.

3. **Join an internet discussion group.** People also frequently use the internet to find places where they share common interests with other individuals, which has led to the creation of internet discussion groups. You can use discussion groups to introduce yourself and your product. Find a group that is related to your store or personal interest, and make sure any topic that you post is tied into a current discussion. Don't spam any discussion group with an obvious sales pitch. Simply write comments applicable to both the group and your product; people will naturally want to know more about you! A great listing of potential starting points for discussion groups is groups.yahoo.com.

4. **Post your product or service on a free classified ad page.** Although many web sites have only paid inclusion into their classified ads, many offer a free place where you are allowed to advertise your merchandise. If you spend time developing an interesting headline or ad, you can bring in a steady amount of traffic from these sites. To get started on free classifieds, you can use my own free service, www.mizambar.com/classified.html. In addition, the following link has a directory of tons of free classified services: www.ecki.com/links.

5. **Write an article related to your web site and submit it to e-zines.** By writing an

article about your service or a topic related to your web site, you instantly become an authority on your issue. Although you might have some apprehension about writing, if you have a web site, then you probably have something to talk about. Two great directories on e-zines are freezineweb.com and www.ezinelocater.com.

Source: Scott Patterson, "5 Free Ways to Increase Traffic to your Online Store," www.online-storeexchange.com/5freeways.html.

SCORE's Five Tips for Getting Noticed Online

1. Get your web site listed on major search engines, such as Google or Yahoo! Two sites, Search Engine Watch at www.searchenginewatch.com and the Web Marketing Info Center at www.wilsonweb.com/webmarket, offer guidance.

2. Join a "banner exchange" and trade advertising banners with other web sites. Look under "banner exchange" on search engines.

3. Visit sites similar to or related to yours and offer to exchange links with them.

4. Write useful articles for other sites and include your web address.

5. Get more online marketing help from such sites as www.zdnet.com/eweek, workz.com, and www.bcentral.com.

Source: SCORE, "5 Tips for Getting Noticed Online," www.score.org/5_tips_eb_5.html.

SCORE's Five Tips for Marketing Your Web Site

1. Think strategically. Your web site should be a part of your overall marketing plan.

2. Choose a web site address (URL) that's intuitive and easy to remember. Your company's name (if it's short) or the name of your main product might work well.

3. Put your web address on all your printed material, including business cards, letterhead, press releases, and invoices. Include it in all your advertising.

4. Don't forget offline media and traditional publicity techniques. Send news releases promoting your site to newspapers, broadcasters, and magazines.

5. Speak at conferences and trade shows, and write informative articles for trade publications. When you do, mention your web address.

Source: SCORE, "5 Tips for Marketing Your Web Site," www.score.org/5_tips_eb_4.html.

Ten Tips to Increase Your Sales

Want to take your business to the next level? If so, take these actions. They're guaranteed to make a difference in your sales results.

1. **Clarify your value proposition.** Strong value propositions are essential for getting in to see the corporate buyer. Make sure you can clearly articulate the business outcomes customers get as a result of using your product or service.

   Be precise—numbers, percentages, and time frames make your value proposition even stronger.

2. **Target a specific market segment.** Don't chase every available opportunity. Focus. Focus. Focus. Increase your knowledge and expertise in a particular market segment.

   Learn as much as you can about their business needs, terminology, issues, and marketplace trends. This significantly increases your client desirability.

3. **Prepare ad infinitum.** Today's customers suffer no fools. Unprepared sellers are quickly escorted out the door. Before you meet with any new prospect, research their business.

   Read their annual report, check out their web site, interview their clients, review analysts' reports. Find out what's important to them, their challenges, goals, and strategic imperatives.

4. **Create seductive ideas.** Use your brain and think for your prospective and existing customers. They're so busy putting out fires, they lack time for problem-solving, strategic thinking, creative alternatives, or even reflection.

   A seller who consistently brings business ideas to the relationship becomes indispensable—winning contracts with minimal competition and at full dollar value.

5. **Slow down, lean back.** Don't try to rush sales—even if you're desperate. Customers feel your push and immediately erect a wall of resistance. On first sales calls do not lean forward.

   To maintain a consultative approach you must lean back. The minute you lean forward, you're "selling"—trying to get your customer to buy. Lean back. Slow down. And you'll get the business sooner.

6. **Pursue quality, not quantity.** Make fewer sales calls—but much better ones. Focus all your efforts on preparing for the call. Determine the logical next step for each meeting. Then, working backwards, think about what you need to do to make this outcome a reality.

   Test every idea you come up with from your customer's perspective. Think, "If I said or did this, how would my customer interpret it or react?" Only his or her perception is important—not what you meant. Make your changes before the call to increase your success.

Section 15

7. **Minimize opportunity leakage.** Unless customers can explicitly state the business value of your offering in concrete terms your opportunity can easily evaporate into thin air—even if they appear highly interested.

   To increase your order rate, ask questions such as "Why would this help you? What value would you get from this service? What are the primary benefits you would realize from my product/service?" This cements the value in their brain.

8. **Make follow-up meetings concrete.** Don't ever leave a meeting without scheduling your next one—or you may never catch up with your customer again. They're running from meeting to meeting, busy handling way too many projects.

   The longer it takes to reschedule, the more their desire for your offering fades. Get the meeting on both your calendars now—even if it's just to talk on the phone.

9. **Always debrief your sales calls.** This is the only way you can get better. Ask yourself, "What went well? Where did I run into problems? What could I do next time to get even better results?"

   This is absolutely the only way you will improve. Sales is a grand experiment—customers change, markets change, your offerings change, and so does your knowledge base. Unless you're continually learning, you're losing ground.

10. **Reframe your attitude.** Stop blaming the economy or anything else for your problems. There are many things totally within your control. Approach all tough sales situations with a "What's possible?" or "How can I?" mindset. If you're stuck, brainstorm with friends or colleagues.

    Accept 100-percent responsibility for your sales success and continually be on the lookout for creative approaches to take your business to the next level

Source: Jill Konrath, "10 Tips to Increase Your Sales," www.marketingsource.com/articles/view/1534.

Ten More Ways to Increase Your Sales

1. **Determine your current situation.** How are you currently positioned in the internet home business market? How do you compare with the competition? Where would you like to be in a year or in five years and how would you like to get there? Or, more appropriately, how can you get there, as it is not always the way that you want that works. Planning requires that you understand how you currently stand.

2. **Calculate your operational budget and determine how much you can afford to spend on an ad campaign.** Also, this is the stage to decide your campaign mediums and the effectiveness of different mediums of advertising as it applies to the specific nature of your product and or services. It also helps to retain a percentage of your earnings toward future ad campaigns on an ongoing basis.

3. **Develop a good rapport with your customers.** To keep your customers visiting, buying, and begging for more, let them know how much you appreciate their business. Do not spare any personal touch you can invest in the relationship. It will pay for your time and effort tenfold. Create an e-zine to communicate with your customers and to generate new leads. This can be achieved by offering an opportunity to your visitors to subscribe to your e-zine from your web site or purchasing leads from a leads company.

4. **Attract visitors to your web site.** You may not even have customers yet. If you are starting from scratch, your first order of business would be to start growing a customer base, within your budget, of course. Create or have a strong sales copy done for your promotions. Consider targeted ad campaigns through Google or other search engines. You may also consider some of the other "viral" marketing traffic exchanges out there. Online campaigns consist of generating traffic to your web site, as this would improve your ranking with the traffic exchanges. Your ultimate goal is to generate free traffic, which comes from a high ranking in the traffic exchanges. In other words, you need to generate traffic first and then you can work on converting the traffic into buying customers or, better yet, return customers.

5. **Hire, rent, or buy a coach/mentor.** If you cannot afford one, get some of the informative e-books and magazines out there. Your decision-making prowess would be much better with this kind of backbone. Take note that even with all the information you may acquire from books and magazines, nothing compares to experience. Now, if you have to go on your experience, then you are setting yourself up to learn the hard and costly way.

6. **Participate in forums.** This one is a must-do for all internet home business marketers. In fact, this whole article could have been written around link promotion. Only one other means compares to forums when it comes to promoting your link/web site and increasing your ranking. Join a forum that concerns your line of business. The forum would promote your link as a result of your participation in discussions and postings. The flip side is that it also provides you for free a knowledge base that compares to hiring a mentor.

7. **Position your business to benefit from other webmasters' traffic.** There are several ways to achieve this. The most prominent is link exchanges with other web sites that are similar or complementary in nature to your business. You can do this by writing to the owner or webmaster of other sites; you can buy a link exchange program or join a link exchange. Most are free to join and some charge very minimal fees.

8. **Acquire an auto-responder to manage e-mail campaigns and e-zine delivery.** Do this as your customer base grows and you start to reap the benefits of your actions. By now, your actions should start to show returns and you can complement your campaigns by purchasing a leads-building campaign if you do not have one in place from the start. It is common knowledge among the big hitters that a lot of sales come from e-mail campaigns. Use your sales copy ad to develop an e-mail cam-

paign and stay in touch with your existing customers. This can also be used to sell new subscribers you generated in step 3.

9. **Learn to relax and balance work and social responsibilities.** This is a very crucial step to achieving anything in life. If your head is spinning now, you are on the right track for success and should step back a little, so you can see more, refresh, and increase performance. Everything contained here would be useless if you cannot find balance. As you relax, in whatever way you choose, remember to build a support system and share your experiences with acquaintances. You just might increase your network while doing something that relaxes you. The country club offers recreation and relaxation, but also networking opportunities.

10. **Evaluate your performance.** How much are you on target or off? Go back to step 1 and reinvent the wheel again. By now you have some experience with your business and know what works best for your business. If at any point you feel too comfortable, go over your business plans with a fine toothcomb until you experience a little discomfort. This step would always keep you sharp, focused, and abreast of what needs improvement and adjustment. Remember: your goal is to increase sales and not to get too comfortable. Stay motivated and fairly dissatisfied.

Source: Robert Kempster, "10 Ways To Improve Your Sales," www.marketingsource.com/articles/view/2158.

Four Easy Ways to Boost Your Sales

1. **Focus on what your customers really want.** Your customers really don't want your products or services. They don't even want what those products or services do for them. What they really want is to gain the specific feeling they get after buying and using your products or services.

   Keep this in mind when you create web pages, sales letters, and other selling presentations. Emphasize the feelings produced by using your product instead of talking about what your product is or how it works.

   Tip: Convert the benefits delivered by your product or service into vivid word pictures. Then put your prospect into the picture by dramatizing what it feels like to be enjoying those benefits.

2. **Keep communicating with your previous non-buyers.** You've heard it before, but I'll say it here again. Most prospective customers will not buy the first time they see or hear about your product or service. You're losing a lot of sales if you do not persistently follow up with those prospects.

   Your follow-up procedure can be as simple as periodically contacting them with a new offer. Or it can be more complex, like distributing a newsletter or providing updated product information.

Tip: You cannot follow up with prospects if you don't know how to reach them. Set up a system for collecting the names and contact information of all prospects who do not buy from you.

3. **Encourage questions.** Questions from prospects may be a nuisance. But answering them can be very profitable.

Prospective customers take time to ask questions only when they have a high level of interest in your product or service. Providing a satisfactory answer to a prospect's question often leads directly to a sale.

Invite prospects to ask questions when in live selling situations. And make it easy for them to ask questions when they are not ..., such as at your web site. For example, list a phone number or e-mail address at which you or someone else can answer their questions.

Tip: Include a questions-and-answers page on your web site with answers to frequently asked questions. It will reduce the number of questions you have to answer individually.

4. **Make buying easier.** Every unessential action in the buying process is an opportunity for the customer to reverse his or her decision, ... causing you to lose the sale.

Look for ways you can make your buying procedure easier and faster. For example, many marketers use a multi-step shopping cart to get online orders when a simple online order form would do the job with just one or two quick clicks.

Tip: Don't ask for unnecessary information during the ordering process. Instead, send a personalized thank-you message after the sale and include a brief request for the information.

Source: Bob Leduc, "4 Easy Ways to Boost Your Sales," www.marketingsource.com/articles/view/1719.

Ten Power-Packed Ways to Spark Your Sales

1. Spend money on targeted advertising instead of mass media advertising. You don't want to waste your ad dollars on people who aren't interested.

2. Increase your profits by concentrating on small details. Improving small things like text size, color, or graphics can really make a positive difference.

3. Keep your offers flexible. If you put a set price on your product, you could offer the people who can't afford it an optional payment plan.

4. Offer your knowledge or consulting as a bonus product. You could offer a free 15- or 30-minute consultation. This will add value to your product.

5. Personalize all your e-mail messages so they get read. Include the recipient's name in

Section 15

the subject line. This will grab people's attention quickly.

6. Keep your web site consistent. You don't want to keep things on your web site that are unrelated to the theme of your web site.

7. Attract more subscribers to your free e-zine by giving them free bonuses like e-books, software, online services, and other incentives.

8. Sell advertising space in your e-zine and on your web site. This will create an extra income stream for your business.

9. Make your web site ready for the public. Have an "About Us" page and clear descriptions of what actions you want your visitors to take.

10. Plan out your marketing. Don't just start advertising everywhere. Locate places and publications that your target audience would congregate around.

Source: Rudy Cline, "10 Power-Packed Ways to Spark Your Sales," www.marketingsource.com/articles/view/1824.

Additional Resources

Section 15

Three Places to Save Money on Your E-Commerce Site

Here are three basic ways to save money on your e-commerce site and increase your profits. While they may be simple, we know they are overlooked time and time again, resulting in thousands of dollars in lost revenue.

1. Aborted Sales

While most modern shopping carts come with many features, they all involve the collecting of information from clients—name, address, telephone number, user name, password, e-mail address, and so on.

New customers have browsed your site and found a product they wish to buy. They begin the checkout process and input all the details above. Your cart then builds the order and transfers them to PayPal 2 checkout or whatever payment gateway you use. What happens next? "Please input your name, address, e-mail, telephone number ...." The result? Lost and aborted sales. Surfers are lazy creatures; we know that. In an ideal world, your cart would have passed all those variables to the gateway and the user would not have to input them again. However, because there are so many gateways and they all require different variables, this is difficult.

The solution is simple: fire up your e-mail program and send them an e-mail. "We noticed that you placed an order for our XXX. However, unfortunately we did not receive payment for that item, so were unable to dispatch it. Did you have difficulty with our ordering system? Is there anything we can do to help you? If so please contact us in one of the following ways ...."

Taking a few moments to send them an e-mail can recover the sale. If you have your own merchant account, you could have them call you and place their order by phone. Customers like to feel like customers, not numbers; the fact that you took the time to contact them to find out what was wrong will give them confidence in your store and you may recover the sale.

2. Chargebacks

The curse of any e-commerce store is the dreaded chargeback. First, make sure your payment gateway offers some sort of seller protection. PayPal, for example, has a full seller protection policy. This is useful to prevent fraud. It is totally unfair that some dishonest people initiate chargebacks after receiving goods; however, as long as your gateway has seller protection and you have saved order details and proof of dispatch, you can go some way toward protecting yourself against that.

Surprisingly, most chargebacks are not fraudulent; they happen because the customer has forgotten who he or she bought from, especially if your registered company name with your gateway is different from that of your site. This is very easy to avoid. Before customers get transferred to payment, state clearly in your cart, "Please remember you will be billed by Fred's Enterprizes, not WidgetsGalore.com." When they are returned to your site, thank them for the order and then remind them again, "Please remember you will be billed by Fred's Enterprizes, not WidgetsGalore.com."

When you send the customer an e-mail saying his or her order has been dispatched, tell him or her again, "Please remember you will be billed by Fred's Enterprizes, not WidgetsGalore.com." We recommend that you follow up your orders; a couple of weeks after the purchase, send the customer another e-mail. Thank him or her for the purchase, say you hope he or she is enjoying your product, and once again mention, "Please remember you will be billed by Fred's Enterprizes, not WidgetsGalore.com."

Repetition is the key: the more you tell them, the more chance customers have of recognizing your company name on their credit card statement.

3. Hosting

If you have your own store, this is what you should have.

- **Your own design.** Your store should not look like everyone else's, or be template built. If you used an online store designer to build your site, we guarantee there are 100 other stores that look just like yours only with different names. Hardly good for your online image.

- **Your own hosting.** Not a subfolder of some larger site or virtual hosting. You should be able to add things like a links directory, message boards, support forums, guest books, and whatever else you think would enhance your site. You should be able to have features added or removed from your cart so that it operates as you want it to. To find out if you have your own hosting, e-mail your host and ask them if you can add any of the above.

- **No fees payable by you, other than a monthly hosting fee.** Incredible as it sounds, we have seen sites charge a monthly fee, plus a per-item listing fee, a per-item maintenance fee, commission on sales, and other such ridiculous charges. Many e-commerce hosts charge inflated prices for what is nothing more than virtual hosting (a subfolder of someone else's site). Most online stores are paying upwards of $50 a month for a restricted and substandard service. E-commerce hosting is no different from regular quality web hosting. It requires only MySQL and PHP capabilities. Of course, stores can use up more space than an information site, for example; however, in our opinion you should not be paying more than $30 a month to host your store.

Source: Gary Mchugh, "Saving Money on Your E-Commerce Site," ezinearticles.com/?Saving-Money-On-Your-E-commerce-Site&id=44475.

SCORE's Five Tips for Ensuring Your Customers' Privacy

1. Understand that protecting customers' privacy is essential to maintaining and increasing sales and profits online.

2. Develop a privacy policy, post it on your web site, and live by your policy. For guidelines, visit three web sites: www.privacyalliance.org, www.respectprivacy.com, and www.privacyrights.org.

3. Put top-notch security systems in place to make sure that customer data is not lost, misused, altered, or stolen.

4. Require that third parties with whom you deal provide similar data security.

5. Don't provide personal information collected from customers to third parties unless you have explicit permission from the customers to do so.

Source: SCORE, "5 Tips for Ensuring Your Customers' Privacy," www.score.org/5_tips_eb_2.html.

SCORE's Five Tips for Managing Virtual Relationships

1. Make sure you're up to speed. Good hardware, software, and training are the tools you need to make virtual relationships work.

2. Structure your workday so information can be easily shared, discussed, and exchanged.

3. Don't let the technology get in the way. If e-mail technology isn't working, quickly default to the phone or a letter.

4. Remember: people do business with people—not machines. Always keep up with your networking contacts.

5. You'll need another set of skills when you use nontraditional means to communicate: writing must be concise and thoughts must be closely linked.

Source: SCORE, "5 Tips for Managing Virtual Relationships," www.score.org/5_tips_eb_7.html.

SCORE's Five Tips on Electronic Contracts

1. Take note: federal law now makes electronic contracts and electronic signatures as legal and enforceable as those on paper.

2. Consider what advantages e-contracts might have for your business. Some companies will be able to conduct their business entirely on line, often with great savings.

3. Be aware that if you start using e-contracts, you have to let customers know whether paper contracts are available and what fees might apply for the paper agreements.

4. Proceed with caution. The law does not define what an electronic signature is, and e-signature technology is still evolving.

Section 15

5. Visit these Web sites for more information: the American Bar Association at www.abanet.org and Nolo at www.nolo.com, a site that specializes in legal issues.

Source: SCORE, "5 Tips on Electronic Contracts," www.score.org/5_tips_eb_1.html.

SCORE's Five Tips on Running a Web Site

1. Find ways to attract customers. Link up with a variety of search engines so that when potential customers are searching for your product, they'll find your company listed.

2. Make it easy for people to navigate your site. Hire a good web site designer.

3. Help customers trust you. Provide information on the company's history, mission, and values.

4. Enable customers to get in touch with you easily—via e-mail, phone, and regular mail—and respond promptly.

5. Provide top customer service along with the speed and good prices that technology offers. Think about how you will keep customers coming back.

Source: SCORE, "5 Tips on Running a Web Site," www.score.org/5_tips_eb_9.html.

Ten Factors That Make People Buy Online

Most of the people who visit your site will still find the idea of ordering online unusual. So your site needs to inspire visitors with confidence. It should say that yours is the kind of company that does things right and that, if they order something from you, it will be a good experience.

Here are ten factors that will turn visitors into profits.

1. **Work works.** The web levels the corporate playing field. A high school student is bound to make a better web site than a large industrial company. On the web, how big you are matters less than how hard you work.

   Large corporations need a large amount of investment to stay on the web, but if you are willing to work hard, you don't need a lot of money to get started.

2. **Choose the right niche.** As a general rule, whatever sells in print catalog will also sell on the internet. If the customer has to see something before buying it, then you probably can't sell it in a print catalog or online. Otherwise, you should be able to sell almost anything.

   Someone who works with computers is almost certain to have web access, so anything computer-related is likely to do comparatively well. And internet users are richer and better educated than the population as a whole, so luxury items may do well.

Section 15

More important than the type of products you sell is the size of the niche you choose. In the physical world, niches are based on geography. Geography is almost irrelevant on the internet. Niches on the internet are based on what you sell, not where you are. So the key here is to choose a niche small enough that you can dominate it. Small manufacturers may be the biggest internet winners because they can dominate a niche.

3. **High production values.** In a print catalog, "production values" refers to the quality of the paper and printing process used. High production values convince consumers to buy in print catalogs; so it goes as well on the web. Consumers will not buy from an amateurish web site.

If your company is unable to put up a good professional web site, then it seems natural to assume that your company cannot deliver good products or services.

4. **Make your site easy.** If you want people who visit your site to order online, don't put any obstacles in their way. Whatever you do, don't force visitors to register. Most major sites have learned not to require registration.

Place your navigation system somewhere on top or on the left side, constantly displaying on your site. Make it easy for all kinds of people (both average and technically inclined) to find their way on your site. You might was well include a search engine of some sort to your products database. A small button leading to the home page would add to the friendliness of your site.

5. **Be real.** Don't play hide-and-seek from your visitors. Include your name, phone number, e-mail address, and street address to show that you are a real person with real products and services to sell.

One mark of a fly-by-night company is it doesn't have any labels. Show your visitors that you care by including your contact number and the time you wish to be called. Remember: anything you do to show that you are real will help increase orders.

6. **Emphasize service.** You have to reassure your visitors (many times) that you are determined to provide great customer service. Tell it straight on your site by simply placing a text that says, "We guarantee that you will be satisfied with our products and services or we will refund your money with no questions asked." Your site should offer secure online ordering.

When a customer sends you e-mail, respond promptly; customers who have taken the time to send you e-mail are like gold, so treat them well. You have to reply eventually, so why not do it right away?

7. **Promote your site.** Having a great web site is not enough; you also need to let the people know it. For a starter, try submitting your site to seven famous search engines: AltaVista, Excite, Web Crawler, InfoSeek, Lycos, Hotbot, and Yahoo.

Capitalize on a few keywords at first and then increase them. Reciprocal links are also a good traffic booster. If you have to place a link to your site, request that the other party link to you as well. Target banner ads are a big plus, too.

8. **Capitalize on sales, not on hits.** You might boastfully say, "I got half a million hits a day," but the question is "How many are turned into sales?" Imagine seeing a "sales counter" on a site instead of a "hit counter."

9. **Change your site.** Regular change in a web site is one way of telling that your web site is inhabited. Frequently changing sites means it's expensive and caters to "expensive" visitors. For example, major online stores are expensive because the site is maintained by web consultants who charge by the hour. Fortunately, there are tools to make life on the web easier.

   One easy (lazy) way to make your site "look" constantly updated is to list featured items on the front page and rotate them every few days. Implementing a weekly or monthly theme will also do the trick.

10. **Think globally.** There's no shortage of marketable consumers on the web: our pool of prospects is the entire world.

Source: William Nabaza, "10 Factors That Make People Buy Online," www.marketing-source.com/articles/view/1427.

Affiliate Program Glossary

Affiliate marketing has a language all its own. Below is a collection of frequently used terms.

Above the Fold: Part of a web page that is visible once the page has loaded. Normally it is the top part of a web page. This term is derived from the newspaper industry, referring to the portion of the front page that is visible with the paper folded.

Affiliate: A web site owner who earns a commission for referring clicks, leads, or sales to a merchant.

Affiliate Agreement: Terms between a merchant and an affiliate that govern the relationship.

Affiliate Information Page: A page on your web site that explains clearly and concisely what your affiliate program is all about.

Affiliate Link: A piece of code residing in a graphic image or piece of text placed on an affiliate's web page that notifies the merchant that an affiliate should be credited for the customer or visitor sent to the merchant's web site.

Affiliate Manager: The manager of an affiliate program who is responsible for creating a newsletter, establishing incentive programs, forecasting and budgeting, overseeing front-end marketing of the program, and monitoring the industry for news and trends.

Affiliate Program: Arrangement by which a merchant pays a commission to an affiliate for generating clicks, leads, or sales from a graphic or text link located on the affiliate's site. Also known as *associate, partner, referral,* or *revenue-sharing program.*

Affiliate Program Directory: Directory of affiliate programs, featuring information such as the commission rate, the number of affiliates, and the affiliate solution provider. Associate-It, AssociatePrograms.com, and Refer-it are among the largest affiliate program directories.

Affiliate Solution Provider: Company that provides the network, software, and services needed to create and track an affiliate program.

Associate: Synonym for *affiliate*.

Auto-Approve: Affiliate application approval process in which all applicants are approved for an affiliate program automatically.

Auto-Responder: An e-mail feature that automatically sends an e-mail message to anyone who sends it a message.

Banner Ad: An electronic billboard or ad in the form of a graphic image that comes in many sizes and resides on a web site's web page. Banner ad space is sold to advertisers to earn revenue for the web site.

Browser: A client program (software), such as Internet Explorer, Netscape, or Opera, that is used to look at various kinds of internet resources.

Charge Back/Chargeback: An incomplete sales transaction (e.g., merchandise is purchased and then returned) that results in an affiliate commission deduction.

Click & Bye: Refers to the process of an affiliate losing the visitor to a merchant's site once the visitor clicks on the merchant's banner or text link.

Click-Through: The action when a user clicks on a link.

Click-Through Ratio (CTR): Percentage of visitors who click through on a link to visit the merchant's web site.

Client: A software program that is used to contact and obtain data from a server software program on another computer, often across a great distance. Each client program is designed to work with one or more specific kinds of server programs and each server requires a specific kind of client. A web browser is a specific kind of client.

Co-branding: Situation in which affiliates are able include their own logo and branding on the pages to which they send visitors through affiliate links.

Collaborative Commerce Networks: Networks of merchants and web sites that work hand in hand as true business partners. Merchants treat their affiliates as sales and distribution channels worthy of any and all support that manufacturers would give to their resellers.

Commission: Income an affiliate receives for generating a sale, a lead, or a click-through to a merchant's web site. Sometimes called a *referral fee*, a *finder's fee*, or a *bounty*.

Context-Centric: Matching your product or service offer closely to the visitors of an affiliate's site. Place the product or service in context (closely related to the content it's next to) and more people will buy.

Contextual Link: Integration of affiliate links with related text.

Contextual Merchandising: Placing targeted products near relevant content.

Conversion Rate: Percentage of clicks that result in a commissionable activity (sale or lead).

Cookies: Small files stored on the visitor's computer that record information that is of interest to the merchant site. With affiliate programs, cookies have two primary functions: to keep track of what a customer purchases and to track which affiliate was responsible for generating the sale and is due a commission.

CPA (Cost per Action): Cost metric for each time a commissionable action takes place.

CPC (Cost per Click): Cost metric for each click on an advertising link.

CPM (Cost per Thousand): Cost metric for one thousand banner advertising impressions.

CPO (Cost per Order): Cost metric for each time an order is transacted.

Customer Bounty: Pays the affiliate partner for every new customer that he or she directs to a merchant.

E-Mail Link: An affiliate link to a merchant site in an e-mail newsletter, a signature, or a dedicated e-mail blast.

E-Mail Signature: Signature option allows for a brief message to be imbedded at the end of every e-mail that a person sends. Also known as a *sig file*.

E-zine: Electronic magazine. Some e-zines are simply electronic versions of print magazines, whereas others exist only in their digital format.

FAQ: Frequently asked questions. FAQs are documents that answer the most common questions on a particular subject.

HTML code: The lines of code that affiliates use to put links on their web sites. Affiliate solution providers often provide a tool with which affiliates can simply copy the code for an affiliate link and paste it into their own HTML pages.

Hybrid Model: Affiliate commission model that combines payment options (e.g., CPC and CPA).

Impression: Advertising metric that indicates how many times an advertising link is displayed.

In-house: Alternative to using an affiliate solution provider, building affiliate program architecture within a company.

Lifetime Value of a Customer: The dollar amount of sales that a customer in his or her lifetime will spend with a particular company.

Manual Approval: Affiliate application approval process in which all applicants are approved for an affiliate program manually.

Media Metrix: A company that measures traffic counts on all the web sites and digital media properties on the Net. It regularly publishes the names of the Top 50 sites in the U.S., the Global Top 50, and the Media Metrix Top 500 web sites.

Merchant: An online business that markets and sells goods or services. Merchants establish affiliate programs as a cost-effective method to get consumers to purchase a product, register for a service, fill out a form, or visit a web site.

Mini-site: Prefabricated HTML page for affiliates that displays new or specialized products with integrated affiliate links.

Pay-per-Click: Program in which an affiliate receives a commission for each click (visitor) that it refers to a merchant's web site. Pay-per-click programs generally offer some of the lowest commissions (from $0.01 to $0.25 per click) and a very high conversion ratio since visitors need only click on a link to earn the affiliate a commission.

Pay-per-Lead: Program in which an affiliate receives a commission for each sales lead that it generates for a merchant web site. Examples would include completed surveys, contest or sweepstakes entries, downloaded software demos, or free trials. Pay-per-lead generally offers midrange commissions and midrange-to-high conversion ratios.

Pay-per-Sale: Program in which an affiliate receives a commission for each sale of a product or service that it refers to a merchant's web site. Pay-per-sale programs usually offer the highest commissions and the lowest conversion ratio.

Residual Earnings: Programs that pay affiliates not just for the first sale a shopper form their sites makes, but all additional sales made at the merchant's site over the life of the customer.

ROAS: Return on Advertising Spending. This is the amount of revenue generated for every dollar spent on advertising. For instance, a ROAS of $1 means you're generating $1 in sales for every $1 in advertising spent, and a ROAS of $5 means you generate $5 in sales for every $1 spent.

ROI: Return on Investment. This is what all marketing managers want to see from the money they spend on their marketing and advertising campaigns. The higher the sales, the large the number of shoppers and the greater the profit margin generated by sales, the better the ROI.

Server: A computer or a software package that provides a specific kind of service to client software running on other computers. The term can refer to a particular piece of software, such as a WWW server, or to the machine on which the software is running, e.g., "Our mail server is down today; that's why e-mail isn't getting out." A single server machine could have several server software packages running on it, thus providing many different servers to clients on the network.

Spam (or Spamming): Electronic junk mail or junk newsgroup postings, generally e-mail advertising for some product sent to a mailing list or newsgroup.

Storefront: Prefabricated HTML page for affiliates that displays new or specialized products with integrated affiliate links.

Super Affiliates: That small percentage of sites—the top one percent of affiliates, based on performance and earnings—that generate the lion's share of the revenue for your program. They are born marketers and are very successful with the affiliate program they promote from their sites

Targeted Marketing: Making the right offer to the right customer at the right time.

Text Link: Link that is not accompanied by a graphical image.

Tracking Method: The way that a program tracks referred sales, leads, or clicks. The most common are by using a unique web address (URL) for each affiliate or by embedding an affiliate ID number into the link that is processed by the merchant's software. Some programs also use cookies for tracking.

Two-Tier: Affiliate marketing model that allows affiliates to sign up additional affiliates below themselves, so that when the second-tier affiliates earn a commission, the affiliate above them also receives a commission. Two-tier affiliate marketing is also known as *MLM (multilevel marketing)*.

Viral Marketing: The rapid adoption of a product or passing on of an offer to friends and family through word-of-mouth (or word-of-e-mail) networks. Any advertising that propagates the way viruses do.

Source: Shawn Collins, "Affiliate Program Glossary," www.affiliatetip.com/affiliate_glossary.php.

Seven Ways to Increase Your Affiliate Commissions

Suppose you could launch an online business in the next ten minutes? Suppose that this business did not require your own web site, dealing with customers, refunds, product development, or maintenance? This is the ideal world of affiliate marketing.

1. **Know what programs and products to promote.** Of course you will want to promote those programs that will bring you the greatest profits in the shortest time. There are several factors that play into selecting such a program. Choose programs that have a generous commission structure, products that fit in with your target audience and have a solid track record of paying their affiliates on time. If you cannot recoup your investment, then prune such programs and keep looking for better ones. There are tens of thousands of affiliate programs online, so you can afford to

Section 15

be picky. This is a case where you will want to choose just the cream of the crop and so reduce the risk of losing your advertising dollars.

2. **Write free reports or short e-books to distribute from your web site.** Most likely you will be competing with other affiliate marketers who are promoting the same program. If you write a short report on a topic related to the product that you are promoting, then you can distinguish yourself from all other affiliates. In this report you can provide valuable information for free with a "recommendation" of the product. This is often referred to as a "soft sell."

   The report or e-book allows you to develop credibility with your audience and your readers are more likely to follow your recommendation. There is less resistance to this type of selling because the prospect doesn't feel "sold," just informed. The next step is to make this e-book "viral" by allowing those who bought the product through your link to "brand" the e-book for their own promotional use.

3. **Collect the e-mail addresses of those who download your free e-book.** Research has shown that over 60 percent of the sales of any product are made after the fifth exposure to the sales message. In other words, most people do not make a purchase on the first solicitation. You may need to send your marketing message over six times before you make a sale. This is the reason why you should collect the contact information of those who download your report. You can then follow up on these contacts to gently remind them to make the purchase.

4. **Never send prospects directly to a vendor's web site without collecting their contact info first.** Affiliate marketing is ideal but not perfect. You must keep in mind that you are providing a free advertisement for the product owners. The merchants pay you only when you make the sale. If you send prospects directly to their web sites, then these prospects are lost to you forever. If you collect these names, however, then you can always send other marketing messages to them and earn an ongoing commission instead of making a one-time sale.

5. **Publish an online newsletter or e-zine.** It is always easier to recommend a product to a friend than to sell to a stranger. This is the philosophy behind publishing a newsletter. A newsletter allows you to build a subscriber list and develop a relationship of trust with the people on this list. Your subscribers will then trust you to recommend products that will benefit them.

   This strategy requires a delicate balance of providing useful information along with a "sales pitch." In other words, if you send out frequent advertisements to your list and little valuable information, you are likely to lose credibility with your readers. But if you write informative editorials, you will build a sense of reciprocity in your readers that will lead them to "support" you by purchasing your affiliate products.

6. **Ask merchants for a higher-than-normal commission.** If you are very successful with a particular promotion, you should approach the merchant and negotiate a higher percentage commission for your sales. If the merchant is smart, he or she will likely grant your request rather than lose you. Keep in mind again that you are a zero-risk investment to the merchant, so don't be shy in your requests. Just be reasonable.

7. **Learn to write strong pay-per-click (PPC) ads.** One of the most effective means of advertising online is through PPC search engines. As an affiliate, you can make a sizeable income by just managing PPC campaigns on services such as Google Adwords and Overture (now Yahoo Search Marketing). Monitor your campaigns to see which ads are pulling their weight and trim those that are not.

You can use the ClickBank™ Market Place, for example, and just choose a hot-selling product and start promoting. Once you are earning a decent return on your investment, then you are in profit! Just this strategy alone can make all the difference to your commission checks.

Affiliate marketing is an entrepreneur's dream come true. Minimum investment, zero inventory, no employees, no product development—just big checks!

Source: Chris Coffman, "7 Ways To Increase Your Affiliate Commissions," www.marketing-source.com/articles/view/2086.

12 Powerful Ways to Use Autoresponders

Autoresponders are an effective and powerful marketing tool, allowing you to make contact with thousands of potential customers.

Use your autoresponder to:

1. **Publish a newsletter.** Your newsletter can keep your visitors informed about your services or products, while building your reputation as a credible expert in your particular business.

2. **Publish a newsletter only for your affiliates.** Inform them of current sales you are running and of promotional material that your affiliates can use to increase their commissions. Include tips, advice, and techniques that your affiliates can use to go out and promote your business successfully.

3. **Write reviews.** Cover books, software, music, e-books, movies, etc., and put each review in an autoresponder. Review your affiliate programs, using a link to your affiliate's page in your autoresponder.

4. **Create mailing lists.** Inform subscribers to your articles when you've written new ones that they may want to publish in their own newsletters or on their web sites.

5. **Automate your sales process.** Use an ad to ensure repeated exposure of your message. In your ad, put your autoresponder address where a visitor will be exposed to numerous marketing materials. This multiplies the chances of converting visitors into customers. For example, if you're selling a particular product, put testimonials about how spectacular it is on your autoresponder and add a detailed, enticing description of your product.

Section 15

6. **Distribute advertising rates.** Let's say you sell advertising on your web site or in your newsletter. Set your autoresponder to send the information about rates and how to place an ad automatically to all prospects' e-mail addresses. Then have your autoresponder follow up. It can also send notification of any special deals you are currently offering.

7. **Distribute an e-mail course.** Just be sure that each lesson has quality content—not a sales pitch. Your content will do the selling for you—and much more effectively. You can include tips centered on a different topic for each lesson, illustrating how your product will benefit the reader. Include the tangible benefits the visitor will reap by purchasing your product. Make sure to include a paragraph or two at the end of each lesson enticing your prospect to consider making a purchase.

8. **Distribute free reports.** This gives your visitor an idea of the type of information you can provide and the quality of your product or service. Make sure these reports are not sales letters or you will be more likely to lose a potential customer than gain a sale.

9. **Create trivia quizzes on your site and place the answers in an autoresponder.** Your visitor will then be motivated to request your autoresponder. Or create a contest and have any visitors enter by sending their responses to your autoresponder. Your autoresponder can be set up to send them a confirmation of their entry.

10. **Link to hidden pages on your autoresponder.** For example, a hidden page could be your affiliate page that contains graphics, promotional articles, and text links that interested affiliates can use. Inform visitors that they may have free access to your affiliate page by simply requesting your autoresponder. You will then gather a list of visitors who may be interested in becoming your affiliates.

11. **Use an autoresponder on your order page.** Post a request form for visitors to be notified of special offers or discounts in the future. This creates a very effective mailing list that contains the names of people who are already your customers.

12. **Put your links page on your autoresponder.** It should contain up to 50 links that would be of particular interest to your visitors. Make sure to add your own promotional copy at the top or bottom of this page.

Source: Melanie Burns, "12 Powerful Ways to Use Autoresponders That Will Take YOU to the Top," ezinearticles.com/?12-Powerful-Ways-To-Use-Autoresponders-That-Will-Take-YOU-To-The-Top&id=55884.

Global E-Commerce Resource Listing

World Trade Magazine
www.worldtrademag.com
This is a publication "for global supply chain decision makers."

Export Hotline

www.exporthotline.com

A collaborative web-based software suite allows members to manage all activities among buyers, sellers, and their trade service providers, including partner qualification, compliance, financial settlement, logistics, and insurance.

Sovereign Society

www.sovereignsociety.com

The Society, through various publishing efforts and seminars, provides advice on asset-protection strategies, tax management solutions, elite global investment opportunities, second citizenship and residency, offshore structures, and privacy solutions.

Better Business Bureau International

www.bbb.org

Federation of International Trade Association Global Trade Portal

www.fita.org/index.html

This portal is the source for international import export trade leads, events, and links to 8,000 international trade (export-import) related web sites.

Goldhaven

www.goldhaven.com/profile.htm

This is an "offshore investment information resource."

Global Information Network

www.searchinfo.com

GIN provides background searches of people throughout the United States and in more than 170 other countries.

Electronic Embassy

www.embassy.org

This is "a resource of and for the Washington, D.C., foreign embassy community." It features business directories and other resources.

Export Zone U.S.A.

www.exportzone.com

ExportZone is "an information help center dedicated to the development of U.S.A. exports to the world."

Source: Offshore Press, Inc., "Offshore e-Commerce Links," www.rpifs.com/osecomlinks.htm.

Owning and Operating an Automotive Business

Chapter 98

Dealerships

How to Run a Dealership:
Four Automotive Investment Principles

1. **Circle of Competence.** It's important to know what you know and, more importantly, what you don't know. Invest in the things you know and ignore the rest.

   I get asked, quite often, "George, what kind of cars should I buy?" My basic response for beginners is to buy what you know. If you have driven Hondas your whole life, that's probably a good place to start. You know how they ride, what noises to listen for, what the common problems are, ... much better than a guy who has only driven Subarus. Right?

   My second suggestion is to always try to expand your circle of competence.

2. **Margin of Safety.** Always buy with a margin of safety. Never pay too much. Your rate of return on your investment will be determined by the price you pay. Never pay too much, because there are always things you don't know about the car. So use that margin of safety to work in your favor.

   If the car is worth $5,000, don't pay $5,500 just to own it. You see it is totally possible you don't everything about the car. In fact, I bet you don't know everything about the car. There is an associated risk with buying any car or truck. There might be unknown repairs that need to be made once you get it to your mechanic. If you bought the car with a margin of safety, say $4,500, you have $500 you can use for the unexpected repairs. Or, maybe, it will take longer to sell the car than you imagined and you will need that margin of safety for more advertising.

   Remember: buy with a margin of safety.

3. **Mr. Market.** Mr. Market is your paranoid schizophrenic partner in the car business—or more directly he might be your wholesaler, your local auction, or just the marketplace in general.

   Every day Mr. Market, with no thought or reason, makes available cars that can be bought at various prices. You can either take Mr. Market up on his offering price for the car or say no and wait for a better deal.

   Be mindful that you can always ignore Mr. Market and wait for the next car for a better deal!

4. **Resource Allocation.** Your ultimate power and most critical decision is where to allocate your resources. Your main resource is your time and money. If you buy a car for too much money or one that requires too much work, it drains your resources. Be wise where you allocate your resources.

Source: George Dean, "Automotive Investment Principles," www.cardollars.com/auinpr.html.

Advantages and Disadvantages of Retailing with a Dealer's License

Advantages:

1. High profit margin on inventory. Great return on investment based on a reasonable turnover in inventory. If you buy a $1,200 car and make a $500 profit in two weeks, that's a 41 percent return on your money in two weeks! (In a self-directed IRA that beats the stock market easily! Think about it.)

2. With a retail car dealer's license, you can still wholesale for profit as well.

3. Ability to make extra money on warranties, financing, repairs, trade-ins, and extended service plans.

4. Use of dealer's license and dealer's plates.

5. Attend dealer-only auctions. Purchase inventory for wholesale prices at other dealerships.

6. No limit on the number of cars you can sell per year.

7. Purchase cars tax-free—no sales tax!

8. Ability to use the draft system and drive cars interest-free!

Disadvantages:

1. Low public perception of "used car salesman."

2. Long hours on weekends, nights, and holidays.

3. Cost to get started and maintain an adequate inventory.

4. Dealing with the public.

5. Advertising, marketing, and personnel costs.

Source: George Dean, "Learn to Buy & Sell Used Cars for Profit! … Starting Today," www.usedcardealerslicense.com/yourowncarlot.html.

15 Steps to Successful Auto Brokering

What is an auto broker? An auto broker is a person who finds and negotiates a new or used car deal on the behalf of a client for a profit. Basically, a car broker acts as a one-person car dealership. With the right personality, you can make six figures with no problem.

1. The customer contacts you via your offline or online marketing or through a referral (whom you call and thank immediately).

2. Walk the customer through the buying process explaining the obvious benefits of dealing with you. Share information and listen. (Let the client talk!)

3. Invite the customer to come in and further discuss his or her options and to inspect the trade-in.

4. Write up the order and take a small refundable deposit. You also mention the benefits of a long-term extended service contract.

5. Hunt for the car via retail or wholesale channels.

6. Negotiate the deal and buy the car.

7. Get a buy bid on the trade-in.

8. Call the customer with the trade-in value and prices on the extended service contracts.

9. Call the client and update on your progress.

10. Get the car cleaned and/or inspected.

11. Facilitate financing through the customer's bank or credit union or through your sources.

12. Have the paperwork printed up.

13. Deliver the car to the customer at his or her home or office or at your office. Sign the paperwork on the trunk or on the kitchen table. Drive the trade-in back to the office.

14. Send a thank-you letter the next day.

15. Call one week, one month, one year, and each year thereafter.

Source: George Dean, *How to Be an Auto Broker*, www.usedcardealerslicense.com/autbrok-manfi.html.

List of Dealership Licensing Requirements by State

Alabama
Dealers must obtain a Regulatory Permit from the Sales, Use & Business Tax Division. The permit must be presented to the county license-issuing official for issuance of a Privilege License and to the Taxpayer Service Center for tag issuance.
Categories of Regulatory Licenses: New Car Dealer, Used Car Dealer, Dismantler, Wholesaler, Rebuilder, Reconditioner.
Dealers must fulfill the following requirements:

- Provide evidence that motor vehicle held for resale are covered by a blanket liability insurance policy.

- Display a sign designating the place of business.

- Describe and ensure permanency of the place of business.

- Provide display area for one or more vehicles and a place for maintaining books and records.

Motorcycle and trailer dealers are exempt from regulatory permit. Licenses are renewed annually in person or by mail.

Dealer License Fees: $10.00 per category, plus $45.00, or up to $210.00 for the Privilege License, depending upon the city or county of dealership

$225.00 for automotive dismantlers

Alaska

Anyone in the business of buying and selling vehicles (acting as a dealer) must be licensed. License must be renewed every two years. Application and proof of bonding required.

Dealer License Fee:

$50.00 for original application/renewal

Arizona

The state assigns a permanent four-digit code for new and used vehicle dealers. Renewal is annual.

Dealer License Fees:

Original license and annual fee, $100.00

Branch license, $50.00 per location within county

Filing fee per application, $15.00

Provisional license, $10.00

Background investigation (per individual), $24.00

Arkansas

License issued by the Arkansas Motor Vehicle Commission is required for franchised motor vehicle dealers (buying/selling three or more vehicles in a year).

Dealer License Fee:

$100.00 per year for each dealership

$10.00 per year for each salesperson

Used car dealers must be certified by State Police, display proof of liability insurance, and file a $25,000 surety bond with the State Police. Boat dealers have no license requirements; however, trailer dealers must be certified by local law enforcement officers. If a trailer dealer accepts a motor vehicle as a trade-in, the vehicle must be licensed and titled in the name of the dealership. Trailer dealers are not granted reassignment privileges for motorized vehicles.

California

All dealers must be licensed with the state. A dealer number and corresponding dealer plates are issued.

Dealer License Fee:

$150.00 application

$100.00 renewal

New auto, commercial, and motorcycle dealers must also pay the New Motor Vehicle Board a $100.00 fee.

Colorado

All car, truck, motorcycle, and trailer dealers must be licensed to conduct business in the state. A license is not required for boat, special mobile equipment, and off-road vehicle dealers. Applications must complete an application, submit a financial statement, post bond, pass a written exam, have an approved business location, and submit to criminal back-

ground investigation. Licenses must be renewed annually.
Dealer License Fees:
Fees are adjusted annually.

Connecticut

New and used vehicle dealers, manufacturers, repairers, wrecker services, and junkyards must be licensed. New vehicle dealers must be franchised by a licensed manufacturer. License issuance is subject to initial approval of local authorities. Upon approval, an application is submitted to the Dealers and Repairers Division of the Department of Motor Vehicles. Applications must be renewed biennially.

Delaware

Private individual may sell four vehicles per year before being required to become a licensed dealer. All dealers must be licensed by the state by Division of Revenue through the Division of Motor Vehicles. Application must include the franchise agreement. Prior to the issuance of a license, all dealer facilities must be inspected by a division representative (no inspection fee).
Dealer License Fee:
$100.00 upon application and renewal. Must be paid to the State Division of Revenue.

District of Columbia

Dealers must be licensed to sell vehicles in the District. License is required for new and used vehicle dealers, and a license is required for salespeople. Licenses are issued by the Department of Consumer Regulatory Affairs. An investigation is performed prior to the issuance of dealer and sales rep licenses.
Contact: (202) 442-4400

Florida

Motor vehicle dealers must be licensed. Individual or business selling three or more vehicles in one year must have a dealer's license. Licenses are renewed annually.
Dealer types: Franchise, Independent (Used), Wholesale, Auction, Mobile Home, and Recreational Vehicles
Applicants for a Franchised Dealer License must present a sales/service agreement and appointment letter or letters of intent from the manufacturer or distributor. All dealers must submit fingerprint cards upon initial application for a dealer's license.
Dealer License Fees:
$300.00 application fee for all dealers
$39.00 for each fingerprint card
$40.00 for each mobile home or recreational vehicle dealer license application
$75.00 renewal fee for Franchise, Wholesale, Independent, and Auction Dealers
$140.00 renewal fee for all MH/RV dealers

Georgia

A Dealer License may be required for new vehicle dealers. Issuance is handled by each municipality. Leasing Companies and Independent Dealers who deal in used vehicles must be registered with the Used Car Dealers and Sales Tax Division. Mobile Home Dealers must be registered with the Fire Marshal's Office. Motorcycle Dealers and Trailer Dealers are not required to be registered.

Hawaii

New and used vehicle dealers must be registered. Registrations are issued by the State of Hawaii, the Department of Commerce and Consumer Affairs, and the Motor Vehicle Industry Licensing Board. Dealers must be franchised to sell new vehicles.

Idaho

New dealers must submit an application and present the contract from the manufacturer. (See Dealer/Salesman's license, Exhibit "D.") New Dealer Code—permanent three-digit number. Dealer plates and numbers are transferred upon sale of the dealership. Used Dealer Code (permanent four-digit number) is issued. Motorcycle, ATV, and snowmobile dealer requirements (new and used) are the same as for other dealers. Dealer's license must be displayed. All applications are investigated.
Dealer License Fees:
$115.00 and $10.00 paid with picture I.D.
$100.00 renewal fee

Illinois

All dealers must be licensed. Dealer establishment must be inspected prior to licensing. New dealers must present a franchise letter and all dealers must obtain a tax number issued by the Department of Revenue.
Used Vehicle Dealer License Fees:
$50.00 for Certificate of Authority
$25.00 for each additional establishment
Annual renewal.

Indiana

Vehicle Dealer: Must be licensed. Dealer must have a lot, a building not attached to or part of a residence, a display area for at least ten vehicles, a permanent sign with name and hours displayed, garage liability insurance in prescribed limits, and retail merchant certificate number. All classifications of dealers, except wholesalers, must sell at least 12 vehicles per year. Upon application. the dealer must present proof of insurance, a photograph of the place of business, and the franchise agreement (required only for new vehicle dealers upon initial application).
Salvage License: Issued for recyclers, crushers, rebuilders, and used parts dealers. Dealer must have three or more inoperable vehicles on the lot. A Salvage License does not grant reassignment privileges. Salvage operators cannot be issued dealer plates unless they meet the required dealer qualifications.
Fee: $10.00 annually
Transfer Dealer: Sale of vehicles is incidental to the business. Transfer dealers have restricted dealer plate use.
Fee: $20.00 annually
Wholesaler: Issued for a dealer that sells at least 120 wholesale vehicles per year with no retail sales.

Iowa

Distributors, manufacturers, motor vehicle dealers, mobile home dealers, and travel trailer dealers must obtain a dealer license to conduct business. Licenses are issued by the Office of Vehicle Services, Customer Services Section, on a staggered system; issued for two-, four-, or six-year periods. All applicants for a dealer license must have a place of business with a telephone installed and listed in the dealer's name, repair and display facilities, and an onsite inspection.

Dealer License Fees: Dealers, manufacturers, distributors of travel trailers and mobile homes
$70.00 for 2 years
$140.00 for 4 years
$210.00 for 6 years
Phone: (515) 237-3110, (515) 273-3219

Kansas

New and used vehicle dealers must be licensed and issued a dealer number. (Individuals or businesses selling over five vehicles in one calendar year must be licensed as a dealer.) Manufacturers of vehicles must also be licensed.

Dealer License fees:
$200.00 for manufacturers
$50.00 for dealers

License expires annually on December 31.

New vehicle dealers require franchise agreement and an inspection of location(s), which must be zoned commercial, before license is issued.

Inspection Fee:
None for the primary location, $10.00 per secondary location(s)

Application must be made in person.

Dealers and salespersons are also investigated prior to license issue. Salespersons, distributors, and factory representatives must fulfill state examination requirements.

Exam Fee:
$15.00 for salespersons
$25.00 for distributors and factory representatives

Report of monthly sales activity must be filed.

Kentucky

Automobile, truck, and motorcycle dealers must be licensed with the state. Trail dealers are not licensed. Dealers must have an established place of business and a business name that identifies them as motor vehicle dealers.

Annual fee: $100.00

All dealers must have at least one licensed salesperson for each location for which a license was issued. Use tax must be paid for all new vehicles sold.

Louisiana

Dealers must be licensed by the state. Upon application, new vehicle dealers must submit the franchise agreement. Used vehicle dealers cannot sell new vehicles. Any person who sells five or more used vehicles in any 12-month period must be licensed as a used motor vehicle dealer.

Dealer License Fee:
$10.00 for new vehicle dealers
$200.00 for used vehicle dealers
$100.00 for each additional place of business (new and used)

Maine

A license is required for new and used vehicle dealers. An individual or business selling more than five vehicles in a 12-month period, displaying three or more vehicles within a 30-day period, or buying vehicles for purpose of resale qualifies as a dealer in Maine. Application is submitted to the Bureau of Motor Vehicles. The application must provide the following information: size and location of the lot and size of the building, display, office, and repair area. Applications must be signed by all parties and witnessed. The building lease must be valid for at least one year.

Dealer License Fees:

$150.00 filing fee and $150.00 licensing fee (both fees required upon application and renewal)

$150.00 annual renewal

Maryland

Motor vehicle dealers must be licensed if they have sold more than five vehicles during a year. Dealers must have a location approved by an authorized representative of the MVA and must complete an application to be approved by the Business License & Consumer Services Division of the MVA, and must submit a bond in the name of the dealership. Laminated dealer photo license issued; annual renewal by mail is required.

Dealer License Fees:

$500.00 new and used dealers

$300.00 for boat trailer dealers and trailers 15 feet or less

Massachusetts

Required for persons principally engaged as dealers. (See class listing for specific requirements.) Dealers must have a separate business office on the premises, maintain a Used Car Record Book approved by the Registry of Motor Vehicles, and post a sign displaying the type of business. Watercraft dealers must have a franchise letter from the manufacturer, a sign indicating the type of business, and a separate place of business. Dealer Licenses are issued from the local City Hall; the Boston Police Department issues licenses for dealers based in the city of Boston.

Licenses are issued for the following dealer classes:

Class I—New and/or used vehicle dealer (business license required)

Class II—Used vehicle dealer (business license required)

Class III—Salvage parts/junk (business license required)

Owner/Contractor—Must have ten vehicles (one of which is special mobile equipment, SME) and garage to work in (business license required). Owner/contractor plates may be issued to government agencies for public safety uses, persons engaged in leasing storage or mobile office trailers, and persons engaged renting or leasing vehicles or trailers to the public (fleets of 20 or more)

Michigan

An individual acquiring one or more vehicles with the intent of resale is considered a dealer and must be licensed. All dealers must include classification(s) on the application for annual license.

Dealer Classifications:

Class A—New Vehicle Dealer

Section 16

Class B—Used Vehicle Dealer
Class C—Used Vehicle Parts Dealer
Class W—Broker
Class E—Distressed Vehicle Transporter
Class F—Vehicle Scrap Metal Processor
Class G—Vehicle Salvage Pool Operator
Class H—Foreign Vehicle Salvage Dealer
Class R—Automotive Recycler

Minnesota

All dealers must be licensed. New and used vehicle dealer licenses must have a permanently enclosed commercial building on a permanent foundation, office space for records. Personal franchise agreement and means for repairing vehicles are required for new dealers only. Used vehicle dealers must have a person to answer the telephone or an answering machine. Lessors and wholesale dealers must have an office, records, and a person to answer the telephone or an answering service. Auctioneer requirements are the same as for new or used dealers, but may be based outside the state. A site inspection is required for all dealers prior to the approval of a dealer license. Dealer classes include new, used and broker, lessor, parts, scrap metal, wholesale, leasing, and auctioning. Boat, snowmobile, and motorized bicycle dealers are required to be licensed.
Dealer License Fees:
$153.50 application and annual renewal fee
$103.50 if application is made after July 1
$13.50 for boat, snowmobile, and motorized bicycle dealers

Mississippi

Applicants must have a place of business and an office, must display a sign, and must file a bond with the application. An 11-digit designated agent number is assigned to each dealer. The number is carried on any issued title and in the dealer record.
Dealer License Fees (initial and renewal):
$100.00 new and used vehicle dealers
$75.00 trailer dealers
$50.00 motorcycle dealers

Missouri

New, used, boat, wholesale, manufacturers, motorcycle, and trailer dealers are required to be licensed if they sell six or more vehicles or boats per year. Application, proof of a place of business, criminal record check, and registration fee must be submitted. Statement of insurance certification required. License expires December 31 annually.
Dealer License Fees:
$150.00 motor vehicle dealers
$80.00 marine dealers
Fees are prorated on date of application.
Body shop/rebuilder, used parts dealer, salvage/dismantler, or mobile scrap processor must register and have a bona fide place of business. Only salvage dealers and dismantlers can purchase vehicles from a salvage pool.
Fee: $65.00 per designation

Expiration is June 30 annually.
Out-of-state salvage dealers must register with the state.
Fee: $25.00

Montana

To apply for dealer license, franchised dealers must submit a copy of the franchise agreement from the manufacturer. All other dealers must submit only license application. Applications are investigated prior to license issuance.
Dealer License Fees: New or used vehicle dealer
$30.00 with $30.00 annual renewal.
For applications after July 1, fees are reduced by half.
Call Motor Vehicles Division, (406) 444-4536

Nebraska

All dealer branches, dealers, and salespersons must be licensed. If an owner sells more than eight registered vehicles, motorcycles, or trailers within one 12-month period, a license is required. New car dealers must be franchised. Place of business, repair facility, ten-car parking lot, and a surety bond are required for application. An inspection is made to verify fulfillment of requirements.
Dealer License Fee: $160.00 annually

Nevada

Nevada Department of Motor Vehicles
Occupational & Business Licensing
www.dmvnv.com/olbl.htm

New Hampshire

Dealers must be licensed with the state. Prior to license issuance, applicants are investigated by an agency inspector and must also be approved by local authorities. License renewal is March 31, annually.
Dealer License Fee: $125.00
Dealer classifications include New, Used, Junk, Repair, Transporter, Utility, Motorcycle, and Wholesaler.

New Jersey

All new and used car dealers, leasing companies, and auto body repair facilities must be licensed. Applications for license are submitted to the Dealer's Unit, Business License Compliance Bureau. Dealer plates and registrations are available only from Trenton. New car dealers must be franchised to sell new cars. A special license is required for used car dealers. Application packages include the application form, affidavit, signature card, security check authorization waiver form, and supplemental application form.
Dealer License Fees:
$100.00 for automobile dealers
$350.00 for two-year auto body repair license fee

New Mexico

A dealer license is required for wholesalers, manufacturers, wreckers, distributors, new vehicle dealers, used vehicle dealers, house trailer, and motorcycle dealers. An established place of business must be maintained and zoning and fencing requirements must be met. All dealers must have a display area except wholesaler. On-site inspection is conducted prior to license issuance.

Dealer License Fee: $50.00 upon application and renewal

Dealer licenses are renewed December 31 each year.

Call Motor Vehicle Division, (888) 683-4636 (toll-free).

New York

Dealers must be registered to do business in the State. Application and fees are submitted to Vehicle Safety Services Division in Central Office of DMV. Facility inspections are conducted prior to registration issuance.

Dealer License Fees: original registration

$325.00 for two years (includes $25.00 application fee)

$300.00 for renewal

Registrations are for a two-year period only.

Dealers purchase MV-50 Certificates of Sale from the Department.

North Carolina

New dealers must be licensed. Application requires inspection approving established place of business.

Dealer License Fees:

Dealer Certificate $50.00

Salesman License $10.00

Dealers selling trailers or semi-trailers less than 700 lbs. and not carrying more than 1500 lbs. are exempt from dealer requirements.

North Dakota

All dealers of new and used cars, mobile homes, motorcycles, snowmobiles, trailers, and all-terrain vehicles must maintain a dealer license. Dealer licenses expire on December 31 each year. Renewal notices are sent to licensed dealers each October. Dealers are required to have an office and repair facilities. Watercraft trailer dealers are not licensed.

Dealer License Fees:

$50.00 for new and used car dealers

$35.00 for mobile home

$25.00 for motorcycle dealers

$10.00 for ATV dealers

$20.00 for snowmobile dealers

$20.00 for trailer dealers

Ohio

New dealer must submit license application, statement(s) of contract from the manufacturer(s), personal credit report, police report, photographs of the establishment, and financial statement. All dealer locations are physically inspected. Card-size salesman's license issued.

Oklahoma

New: Must be franchised, licensed with the Motor Vehicle Commission, have a shop for working on vehicles, and a used car outlet. Salesmen must be licensed.

Dealer License Fees:

$200.00 initial application

$60.00 annual renewal

Used, Wholesale, Salvage, and New/Used Manufactured Home Dealers: Must be licensed with the Used Motor Vehicle and Parts Commission.

Dealer License Fees:

$200.00 initial application

$100.00 annual renewal

Used dealers and new/used manufactured home dealers must have a building, lot, sign, and lavatory facilities. Salvage dealers must have a telephone, a lot, and a sign. Vehicles must be out and on site (fenced). Wholesale dealers must have an office.

Watercraft Dealers: Must be licensed with the Oklahoma Tax Commission.

Fee:

$200.00 plus $10.00 per dealer franchise agreement

Renewal: $100.00 plus $10.00 per each dealer franchise agreement.

New/Used Trailer Dealers: Must be licensed with the Oklahoma Tax Commission.

Fee: $15.00 (includes one dealer license plate) for each type of dealer

Oregon

Dealers must be licensed by the state.

Dealer License Fees:

$329.00 for three-year registration

$327.00 for three-year renewal (includes plate).

Dealer plates are issued to be used for demonstration and delivery purposes. Personal use is also permitted.

Pennsylvania

Application for license must indicate type of license for which the application is being made. License must be renewed annually. Each approved dealer is assigned an eight-digit dealer identification number (DIN). The first two numbers correspond to the category of vehicle the dealer is licensed to sell.

Rhode Island

All dealers must be licensed through the Motor Vehicle Dealers License Commission. Applications are investigated prior to license issuance. Licenses are renewed annually on December 31.

Contact: Motor Vehicles, (401) 588-3020

South Carolina

State license is required for all new and used car dealers and camper/motorcycle dealers.

Dealer License Fee: $50.00

Issued for demonstration and delivery use only. New car dealers are not required to be franchised; used car dealers may sell new cars.

South Dakota

An individual in the business of selling or advertising sale of vehicles is considered a dealer and must be licensed. Dealer application requirements and renewal applications are filed through the County Treasurer. Investigation of the applicant and the described place of business is conducted by the state dealer inspector.

The place of business must be:

a) a commercial structure within the state of South Dakota, with a display area for five or more vehicles
b) in accordance with building codes and zoning laws
c) location where required books and records are kept
d) the principal business at the location (cannot be the residence of the applicant)

Dealer License Fees:
new/used vehicle dealer $250.00 ($100.00 renewal)
mobile home dealer $250.00 ($75.00 renewal)
motorcycle dealer $200.00 ($75.00 renewal)
snowmobile dealer $100.00 ($50.00 renewal)
trailer dealer $75.00 ($50.00 renewal)

Tennessee

When an individual sells more than five vehicles during a calendar year, he or she is considered in business and must be licensed by the state as a dealer.
When applying for license, new vehicle dealers must submit a franchise agreement.
New Vehicle Dealer License Fee: $100.00 for each branch upon application/renewal.
Used vehicle dealers may not sell new vehicles.
Used Vehicle Dealer License Fee: $100.00 upon application/renewal
A facility inspection is conducted for all dealers prior to license issuance.

Texas

Any person who is engaged in the business of buying, selling, or exchanging motor vehicles, motorcycles, travel trailers, or trailers/semi trailers is required to obtain a dealer license. The Motor Vehicle Division assigns a current, valid, general distinguishing number for locations in each city municipality. The main exception is for a person who sells fewer than five vehicles in a calendar year, provided the vehicles are titled and registered in such person's name.
New Franchise Dealer License Fees: $175.00 franchise fee plus $500.00 for each required general distinguishing number; annual renewal fee determined by number of cars sold in a calendar year.
Used Car Dealer License Fees: $500.00 for the first year; $200.00 renewal fee per year
Texas Motor Vehicle Board, (512) 416-4800

Utah

License is required for all dealers. A dealer is an individual selling or exchanging three or more new or used motor vehicles within a 12-month period. All applicants are investigated by the Motor Vehicle Enforcement Division. Application Form TC-301 must be completed.
Dealer License Fees:
New Vehicle $125.00
Used Vehicle $125.00

Vermont

Dealers selling 12 or more cars in a year must be licensed. Dealers must have real estate value of not less than $10,000. License renewals are on a staggered basis. A Dealer Audit is conducted by State Inspectors for approval of license renewal.
Dealer License Fee: $275.00 for new and used automobile dealers (five plates)

Virginia

Certification of Qualification required: each new dealer-operator and salesperson must pass written examination ($25.00 fee). If applicant is a dealer in new vehicles with factory warranties, a copy of service agreement with manufacturer or distributor is required. The dealer sales office must be inspected by a DMV investigator prior to issuance. Each dealer is assigned a permanent dealer code with up to five digits. Licenses are staggered, fees are prorated, each plate must be insured, and all licenses expire on the last day of the designated month. Preprinted renewal forms are mailed to licensed dealers for renewal purposes.

Dealer License Fee:

$100.00 upon application and renewal of dealer license

$10.00 for each salesman license

Additional fee for Recovery Fund

New dealership must pay $250.00 for three consecutive years without a bond or fund claim being filed.

Annual fee:

$100.00

$10.00 renewal for each salesperson

Multi-year licensing is optional.

Fee: $200.00 for dealership

$20.00 each salesperson

Washington

All dealers must be licensed. Washington has three dealer classifications: Motor Vehicle, Mobile Home/Travel Trailer, and Miscellaneous dealers

Dealer License Fee: $500.00 original dealer licenses

$250.00 renewal (staggered annual renewal)

West Virginia

All dealers must be licensed. If an individual sells five or more vehicles in a calendar year, a license is required. Dealer licenses are renewed annually on June 30. New car dealers must provide at time of application, proof of established place of business, display area, franchise agreement, and room for repairs. An on-site inspection of dealer facilities is conducted prior to the issuance of a dealer license. Periodic inspections of dealer facilities are also conducted.

New Car Dealer License Fee: $100.00 upon application and renewal

Used Car Dealer requirements are the same as for new car dealers, with the exception of a franchise agreement, for which posted hours of operation and outside display area are required.

Used Car Dealer Fee: $100.00 upon application and renewal

Wisconsin

Manufacturers, distributors, dealers, and mobile home dealers are required to obtain business license (not required for trailer dealers). Individuals buying and selling more than five vehicles are required to obtain a dealer's license. Issued for two-year period based on date of issuance.

Dealer License Fee: $40-$100, depending on type of vehicle sold

Section 16

Dealers are required to file $25,000 bond. Trailer plates issued to trailer dealers for the transportation of trailers exceeding 3,000 lbs.

Wyoming
An Application for a Wyoming Dealer License must be submitted each year. All applications are investigated prior to license issuance.
Dealer License Fee:
$25.00 or $100.00 upon application and annual renewal (fee depends on number of retail sales)
Watercraft dealers require only a Sales/Use Tax license, which is issued by the Wyoming Department of Revenue.

Source: George Dean, "Learn All My Secrets, Tips, Strategies, & Resources," cardollars.com/dealerlicense4.html.

Ten Commandments for Success in the Car Business

1. **Always inspect a car thoroughly.** Do not buy project cars. Do not buy TMU ("True Mileage Unknown"), frame damaged, salvaged, cars that smoke, cars with branded titles, police cars, and such.

2. **Know your local market.** The Golden Rule of the car business is "You lock in your profit when you buy the car, not when you sell it." A second Gold Rule might be "You secure your financial future by creating serviceable notes on cheap used cars." The only way to know the value of a car is to know your local market! Read the newspaper, attend local auctions, visit web sites, visit dealers, call other wholesalers or used car managers. Get out on the street and start learning.

3. **Remember that a car is worth what you can get.** A pricing guide is only a guide—not the bible. A car is worth only what someone locally will pay for it. Some cars are routinely worth more than book and some less than book. You will only know by learning your local market.

4. **Stand behind your word.** Your word is everything in the car business. Many deals are closed over the phone or with a handshake.

5. **Build a network of buyers and sellers.** If you are retailing, you need customers to come and buy from you again and to tell their friends. If you are wholesaling, you need as many avenues as possible to redistribute cars. Build your number of contacts every opportunity you get.

6. **Follow strict inventory turnover rules.** As inventory ages, your profits will drop. In retailing, do not hold inventory over 60 days for any reason (unless you own a note lot selling cars for under $5995). Some dealers will work on a 90 turnover; I think that's too long. In wholesaling, do not hold a car for over seven days. You can develop your own rules; this is just a generalization.

7. **Do not buy a car if you do not know its value.** If you break this rule, quit the business. Make decisions based on logic and knowledge of your local market.

8. **Trust but verify.** People will try to take advantage of you.

9. **Know the key to your business.** When retailing, location is the key. When wholesaling, visiting dealers daily is key to your success. When auto brokering, marketing is the key.

10. **Specialize, specialize, specialize at first.** Start with just one car. Do everything yourself. Keep it a one-person operation as long as possible.

Source: George Dean, "Ten Golden Commandments to Success in the Car Business," www.usedcardealerslicense.com/tipofweek.html.

Top Ten Reasons Why Car Dealerships Need Newsletters

Check out the top 10 reasons car dealerships include a newsletter as part of their overall automotive promotions, according to The Newsletter Company:

1. **Newsletters reinforce loyalty.** Dealerships have a unique opportunity to build customer relationships that last a lifetime. Satisfied customers service their cars with dealers they know and trust and they are loyal to that dealer when they purchase their next car.

2. **Newsletters sell cars.** A newsletter offers you a unique opportunity to let your customers know about the newest makes and models your dealership offers, all in the comfort of their home. Newsletters are seen as informative and have a higher "trust" rating than advertising.

3. **Newsletters generate high ROI (return on investment).** Dealerships that send custom newsletters generate astronomical ROI figures that range from ten to 50 times their investment from service coupons alone.

4. **Newsletters are prospecting tools.** We'll compile a mailing list to directly target your prospects. We can also access names and addresses of owners driving competing makes and models. Many of the auto dealers who've sent our custom newsletters have prospected successfully for many years.

5. **Newsletters separate you from the competition.** When your customers receive your newsletter, they'll instantly recognize your dealership as a cut above the rest. That's because most dealers don't include a customer newsletter in their marketing budget, believing there simply aren't the resources to produce a high-quality customer newsletter. With the help of The Newsletter Company, your customers will receive a newsletter the competition can only dream of.

6. **Newsletters establish regular communication.** You and your customers both benefit from regular communication. Your newsletter tells your customers what's new

with the brands you sell and your latest dealership news. Use the newsletter to offer new products and services, note changes in hours or staff, or invite customers to a clinic or special event.

7. **A well-produced newsletter establishes a bond with customers.** What other auto advertising medium gives your dealership the opportunity to promote your products and services and provide a forum to communicate one-to-one with customers? A newsletter is seen as informative communication—not an advertisement that gets tuned out.

8. **Newsletters are flexible.** Your newsletter offers you the opportunity to spotlight key employees and even highlight new services to keep your customers coming back. Use it to generate immediate revenue by offering attention-getting coupons. You choose what to feature. And don't hesitate to ask for guidance. After 22 years of creating successful automotive newsletters, we can give you plenty of creative ideas.

9. **Newsletters are the best value for your marketing and advertising dollars.** Newsletters focus on customer retention, and every dealer knows it's easier and less expensive to keep a customer than to acquire a customer.

10. **Newsletters provide maximum benefits for minimal costs.** Newsletters are referred to as a dealership's "workhorse." Review the list, because you can't get benefits like these from any other form of auto advertising, including your service reminder program. Get your dealership's newsletter going and leave your competition in the dust!

Source: The Newsletter Company, "A Customer Newsletter Is One of the Best Automotive Promotions a Car Dealership Can Do," www.automotivedirectmail.biz/automotivepromotions.html.

Chapter 99

Detailing

Six Things It Takes to Start a Detail Business

1. **Money.** Money is the most important ingredient for starting your detail business. Money is needed to make your initial investment and pay rent or for a trailer (if mobile), salaries, advertising, and other associated start-up costs, such as licenses and permits. Some experts say you should have enough money on hand to cover three to six months of operating expenses. This means you should have enough money to pay yourself and expenses for six months after you launch your business, should business start out slow—and they usually do. What do you do if after launching your business you have no customers? How will you weather the dry spells of the new launch? The answer is simple: money. And do not forget about an advertising budget. What if the ads fall on deaf ears or you've chosen the wrong type of or placement for advertising? You need enough money to see yourself through the first three to six months of operation. Not enough capital is the reason for almost all business failures.

2. **Aggressive Approach.** Be aggressive in your approach to marketing your new detail business. You'll need to use guerrilla tactics in the first few months. Get the word out any way you can. But you need to know your best target market—why they would use your service, where they are, how to reach them, and what to say. Never miss an opportunity to leave your business card anywhere. When dining out, leave one on your table at the restaurant and a few more at the other tables. Send a press release to every newspaper and automotive specialty magazine covering your business area. Pass out cards at body shops and auto repair shops, especially those that cater to luxury cars like Mercedes-Benz and BMW and Porsche. You need sufficient capital to cover three to six months of operating expenses, especially marketing and advertising. The aggressive approach should also extend to your employees. They must be as enthusiastic as you are. After all, they will benefit should your business be a success. When it comes to marketing your new business, there is almost no wrong way to get the word out. Just be aggressive, but pointed at your target market. For example, detail service buyers are not coupon clippers, so stay out of value packs.

3. **Knowledge.** It is important to know the detail business, inside and out, not just how to detail. For example, there are laws that can affect your business—EPA laws, OSHA, etc. What are the current market trends in the detail business? Are there any problems with supply or demand for the detail service in your area? If so, you need to consider this in your business plan. Basically, you need to know the detail business better than your competition. You'll also need to know your competitors and keep abreast of everything they do. Are they raising or lowering prices? Know your customers. What services do they buy? (Or, just as important, what don't they buy?) Where do they come from? How did they find out about you?

4. **Education.** Before you start your business, do your homework. What supplies, equipment, chemicals, and employees do you need to begin or successfully operate your

detail business? It's equally important to know what you don't need. Don't waste money on something that is unnecessary. Do you really need two extractors when one is sufficient? Are four employees necessary or will just three suffice? Are you better off buying small or buying in bulk? Here you may have to speak with other detailers or seek out advice from an expert. In the short term and in the long run, educating yourself on the business you are starting will save you money and may mean the difference between success and failure. Work to know what you don't know.

5. **Integrity.** You should constantly demonstrate integrity with your customers, suppliers, and advertisers. Your customers should be able to count on you to always do the right thing and deal with them fairly. Honor your guarantees or your return policy. It will pay off for you in the long run to have truly satisfied customers. This is also true for your suppliers also. Pay your bills on time and make a good name for yourself. Your suppliers will become valuable assets to your detail business. You may need them as a reference on a future loan or for dealing with another supplier. Your advertisers should be able to count on you to give them your ads on time and with the correct payment. Again, you may need them someday to help announce a new product line or help in suggesting an ad campaign. Most importantly, never let yourself down. Follow the rules. Get the required permits or licenses you need. Don't think you're saving money by not having them; the penalties are always higher than the original fee. And, of course, never let the idea of earning a quick buck cloud your judgment. You'll know what is right and what is wrong because you'll feel it.

6. **Toughness.** Be tough. Take the mental approach that you will succeed no matter what obstacle is blocking your path and no matter how difficult it seems. You'll be spending long hard hours in your detail business—and if you aren't, something may be wrong. You need to stay tough and fight through the hard times. There will be hurdles to jump over and gaps to build bridges across. Only the tough survive. Sometimes you'll feel like taking the day off. Don't. There may be others who can't wait to see you fail. Don't give them the satisfaction. Hang in there. Others may also be ready to throw in the towel and you'll need to be tough for them. Starting a detail business is a huge task. There is so much to learn and so much to do, and much of what happens to you won't be known until it happens. But with careful preparation and the right mindset, you can increase your chances of succeeding in the long run.

Source: Bud Abraham, "A Start-up Detail Business ... What It Takes to M.A.K.E. I.T," www.mobileworks.com/detail_business_start_up.html.

Finding Customers for Your Detail Business

Look for average-Joe consumers who are in love with their cars:

- White-collar professionals with high profiles—including physicians, lawyers, and corporate executives
- Sports car owners, to whom appearance is everything—including under the hood
- People who lease cars (since a professional detailing can reduce the chance of incurring ghastly end-of-lease wear-and-tear charges)
- Show car owners, classic car owners, and car buffs who show off their vehicles for love ... and money
- New and used vehicle dealers (the pace can be grueling and the work doesn't always pay top dollar, but there's usually a lot of work for a new detailer)
- People who are selling their own cars in the local classifieds (currently a huge untapped market)
- RV dealerships and their customers (still another gold mine of possibilities)
- Automotive centers like auto malls
- Car washes (usually as an express detailing operation)
- Auto repair shops, including collision shops)
- Limousine companies
- Hotels with concierge service that might want to offer detailing as a premium service to guests
- Gas stations and garages that offer complete automotive services

Source: Eileen Figure Sandlin, *Start Your Own Automobile Detailing Business* (Entrepreneur Press).

List of Basic Detailing Services

- hand wash (with particular attention to tree sap, bug remains, bird droppings, and rail dust—iron particles that settle on the paint during transport by train, from contact between the wheels and the tracks)
- hand dry, usually with chamois or an other soft, lint-free cloth
- claying to remove all surface contaminants from the paint after the vehicle is washed
- hand application of wax or sealant
- application of wax using an orbital buffer

- window and exterior mirror cleaning
- trim and tire dressing application and polishing
- wheel/rim waxing
- floor and seat vacuuming (including vacuuming with a crevice tool for deep penetration)
- floor and seat shampooing
- cleaning and dressing of dashboard, door panels, and center console
- vent, kick panel, pedal, doorjamb, and ashtray cleaning
- floor mat vacuuming and steam cleaning
- headliner cleaning
- leather seat and trim cleaning and conditioning
- vinyl seat cleaning and dressing
- window and mirror cleaning and polishing

Source: *Entrepreneur Magazine,* "How to Start an Automotive Detailing Business."

List of Add-on Detailing Services

These services can really beef up your bottom line. The services not only will maximize the amount you can earn on every vehicle you detail, but also can be very lucrative profit centers in themselves. However, some of these services require hands-on training before you go to town on someone's vehicle so you don't inadvertently cause damage. Among these popular add-ons are:

- custom paint touch-up, chip and scratch repair
- black trim restoration
- carpet and upholstery dyeing
- vinyl and leather repair
- windshield repair and tinting
- paintless dent repair
- overspray or cement removal

Source: Eileen Figure Sandlin, *Start Your Own Automobile Detailing Business* (Entrepreneur Press).

Section 16

Tips for Hiring and Managing a Pit Crew

1. It's usually better not to hire family or friends. If they don't work out, you'll have to fire them, and that could create a very uncomfortable situation around the dinner table. The sole exception might be your spouse, who's supposed to love you no matter what. Just don't let your marriage suffer as a result of your business.

2. There are two types of employees you're most likely to need as a new detailer.

   - A detailing technician. This person will do everything from emptying ashtrays to putting away new shipments of wax and tire dressing.

   - An assistant manager. You need to hire one only if your operation is so successful right away and you need to hire someone more experience to help with the flotilla of vehicles you detail.

3. When prospecting for employees at high school career events, bring informational brochures about your business, a business card with your web site address, and some advertising specialty items, like pencils imprinted with your business name. Even if the student doesn't come to you for a job, that pencil may get around and spark someone else's interest in your business.

Source: *Entrepreneur Magazine*, "How to Start an Automotive Detailing Business."

Power Tools and Accessories Needed to Run a Detail Shop

- detailing trailer
- air compressor
- random orbital polisher
- variable-speed rotary buffer/polisher
- pressure washer
- 125-gallon water tank
- five-gallon stainless-steel tank sprayer
- ozone odor remover
- odor fogger system
- carpet extractor
- wet-dry vacuum
- vapor steam cleaner
- interior dryer

- creeper
- temperature gauge
- digital electronic paint-thickness gauge
- magnifier loupe
- towels
- towel wringer
- generator
- portable fluorescent lighting
- portable space heater
- portable pop-up tent
- wastewater reclamation system
- miscellaneous detailing tools
- miscellaneous detailing products
- magnetic signage
- washer, dryer

Source: Eileen Figure Sandlin, *Start Your Own Automobile Detailing Business* (Entrepreneur Press).

Best Locations for Setting up an Automotive Detail Shop

Your shop should be located in a commercial area that's easily accessible by highway or byway, preferably one that has plenty of traffic because that gives you added visibility.

Another desirable location is an auto mall, both because the new- and used-car dealers that anchor such malls are often frequent consumers of detailing work themselves and because there will be a steady stream of car shoppers in the area who could be prospective detailing customers. Likewise, a location in a mini-mall that has noncompeting automotive businesses, like tire stores, brake shops, vehicle alarm installers, and so on, can bring you great visibility and increased sales.

Source: Eileen Figure Sandlin, *Start Your Own Automobile Detailing Business* (Entrepreneur Press).

Top Six Considerations When Obtaining Warehouse Space

- If you're interested in a start-up with the lowest possible costs, then mobile is the way to go because no facility is necessary.

- Your first decision concerning your detailing facility should be whether you're up to the challenge of renovating an existing building or whether you'd prefer to move into a garage or gas station that's either defunct or for sale.

- Leasing can be a good way to go if you don't want the hassles of qualifying for a mortgage. But remember that a lease is a virtually unbreakable contract, no matter what happens to your business.

- When negotiating a lease for a lot of money, don't go it alone. Hire an attorney to look over the terms so you don't get burned. Among the things you'll want to negotiate are which additions or renovations are needed before the property is acceptable and the timetable for getting them done.

- A bare concrete floor is acceptable for your waiting area if it's unstained, but a durable floor covering like indoor-outdoor carpeting or tile is a good alternative. Be sure to select flooring in a neutral tone that will conceal dirt and blend with the wall color.

- You'll need a large, professional-looking sign that announces to the world that you're in business. It should give the name of your detailing shop in letters that are large enough to be seen from the road.

Source: Eileen Figure Sandlin, *Start Your Own Automobile Detailing Business* (Entrepreneur Press).

Car Washes

Types of Car Washes and Their Niches

- full-service—high start-up costs, intensive time needed, high profit potential, mechanical and general business knowledge a must
- exterior-conveyor—high start-up costs (somewhat lower labor cost than full-service), intensive time needed (slightly lower than full-service), high profit potential, mechanical and general business knowledge required
- in-bay automatic—medium start-up costs, medium time needed (significantly less than a full-service or exterior-conveyor car wash), medium profit potential, mechanical knowledge and some basic knowledge of business practices required
- self-service—low to medium start-up costs, low to medium time needed, low to medium profit potential, mechanical knowledge and some basic knowledge of business practices required

Source: Chris Simeral, *Start Your Own Car Wash Business* (Entrepreneur Magazine).

Recommended Car Wash Equipment Checklist

Wash-Related Equipment
- power-wash units
- vacuums
- automatic dryers (conveyor systems only)
- water heater
- water reclamation/recycling
- water softener

Retail/Lot Equipment
- shaded vacuum area
- floor heater
- vending machines
- changing machines
- signage
- security system
- landscaping
- trash receptacles

Section 16

- bathroom fixtures
- cash register
- lighting (exterior)
- inventory

Source: Chris Simeral, *Start Your Own Car Wash Business* (Entrepreneur Magazine).

Market Research Checklist for a Car Wash

- Population within two miles of car wash site?
- Population within three miles of car wash site?
- Population within five miles of car wash site?
- Traffic flow: How many cars pass by your proposed site on an average day?
- Traffic patterns: What is the speed limit on the adjacent road?
- Housing: Composed mainly of single-family homes or apartment buildings?
- Street location: Corner or midblock?
- Competition: Number of car washes within three miles of your site?
- Amenities: Number of convenience stores or other businesses in the immediate area?
- Labor pool: Adequate source of labor in your neighborhood?
- Average household income within three miles of your site?

Source: Chris Simeral, *Start Your Own Car Wash Business* (Entrepreneur Magazine).

U.S. Car Wash Associations

Car Wash Operators of New Jersey (CWONJ)
P.O. Box 48
Maywood, NJ 07607
Phone: N/A
www.cwonj1@aol.com
www.cwonj.com

Chicagoland Carwash Association
P.O. Box 298
Lockport, IL 60411
Phone: (708) 301-3568
administrator@chicagocarwash.org
www.chicagocarwash.org

Connecticut Carwash Association
P.O. Box 230
Rexford, NY 12148
Phone: (800) 287-6604 (toll-free)
www.wewashctcars.com

Greater St. Louis Professional Car Wash Association
1700 Ford Lane
St. Charles, MO 63303
Phone: (314) 949-5000
Fax: (314) 949-5008

Heartland Carwash Association
P.O. Box 932
Des Moines, IA 50304
Phone: (515) 965-3190, (888) 873-9735 (toll-free)
Fax: (515) 965-3191
www.heartlandcarwash.org
info@heartlandcarwash.org

International Carwash Association
401 N. Michigan Avenue
Chicago, IL 60611-4267
Phone: (312) 321-5199
Fax: (312) 245-1085
ica@sba.com
www.carwash.org

Mid-Atlantic Carwash Association
780 Ritchie Highway, Suite 28-S
Severna Park, MD 21146
Phone: (410) 647-5780, (888) 378-9209 (toll-free)
Fax: (410) 544-4640
info@mcacarwash.org
www.mcacarwash.org

Midwest Carwash Association
3225 W. St. Joseph Street
Lansing, MI 48917
Phone: (517) 327-9207, (800) 546-9222 (toll-free)
Fax: (517) 321-0495
www.midwestcarwash.com

New England Carwash Association
The Association Advantage
591 North Avenue, Suite 3-2

Wakefield, MA 01880
Phone: (781) 245-7400
Fax: (781) 245-6487
www.newenglandcarwash.org

New York State Car Wash Association

P.O. Box 230
Rexford, NY 12148
Phone/fax: (518) 877-6779
www.nyscwa.com

Ohio Car Wash Association

P.O. Box 9113
Canton, OH 44711
Phone: (330) 492-8761
www.ohiocarwash.com

Southeastern Carwash Association

184 Business Park Drive, Suite 200-S
Virginia Beach, VA 23462
Phone: (800) 834-9706 (toll-free)
Fax: (757) 473-9897
secwa@secwa.org
www.secwa.org

Southwest Car Wash Association

4600 Spicewood Springs Road, Suite 103
Austin, TX 78731
Phone: (512) 349-9023, (800) 440-0644 (toll-free)
Fax: (512) 343-1530
info@swcarwash.org
www.swcarwash.org

Western Carwash Association

10535 Paramount Boulevard, Suite 100
Downey, CA 90241
Phone: (562) 928-6928
Fax: (562) 928-9557
wcarwa@aol.com
www.wcwa.org

Source: Chris Simeral, *Start Your Own Car Wash Business* (Entrepreneur Magazine).

**Section
16**

Repair Shops

15 Required Components of a Repair Estimate

1. The shop's name, address, and telephone number
2. The customer's name, address, and telephone number
3. Date and time of estimate
4. Year, make, model, odometer reading, and license tag number of vehicle
5. Proposed work completion date
6. Description of customer's problem or request
7. Labor charges based on a flat rate, hourly rate, or both
8. Estimated cost and charges for repair
9. Charges for shop supplies or for hazardous or other waste removal
10. Charges for making an estimate and the basis for the charge
11. The customer's intended method of payment
12. Name and telephone number of any alternate person the customer would allow to authorize repairs
13. Terms of the parts and service guarantee
14. Notation if customer wants replaced parts returned
15. Charge for daily storage (Shops notify customers after repair work is completed and customers then have three working days to pick up the vehicle before storage fees may be charged.)

Source: Florida Department of Agriculture and Consumer Services, Division of Consumer Services, "Auto Repair—Be a Winner!!!," www.800helpfla.com/autorepair_txt.html.

Six Requirements of a Repair Invoice

The invoice must include:

1. Date and odometer reading
2. Description of work
3. Labor, parts, and other merchandise costs
4. Nature of parts (new, used, rebuilt, etc.)
5. Guarantee, if any
6. Registration number from the certificate issued by the Department identifying your shop

Section 16

Source: Florida Department of Agriculture and Consumer Services, Division of Consumer Services, "Auto Repair—Be a Winner!!!," www.800helpfla.com/autorepair_txt.html.

Three Legal Requirements for Repair Shops

1. Post in a conspicuous location in the customer service area the registration certificate and a sign advising consumers of their rights under the Motor Vehicle Repair Act and giving the Department's toll-free telephone number for assistance or information.

2. Include in the sign a statement advising consumers they are entitled to the return or inspection of replaced parts, if they request it at the time the work order is placed.

3. Include the registration number in any advertisements, announcements, or listing relating to motor vehicle repair in any newspaper, magazine, or directory.

Source: Florida Department of Agriculture and Consumer Services, Division of Consumer Services, "Auto Repair—Be a Winner!!!," www.800helpfla.com/autorepair_txt.html.

Automotive Resources

Section
16

List of Automobile Producers in U.S.

Acura
www.acura.com

Alpha Armouring Germany
www.alpha-armouring.com

Alpine Armoring
www.alpineco.com

Alfa Romeo
www.alfaromeo.com

Aston Martin
www.astonmartin.com

Audi
www.audiusa.com

Autech
www.autech.co.jp

Avto-Lada
www.lada.ru

AvtoVAZ
www.vaz.ru

BMW
www.bmwusa.com

Bristol Cars
www.bristolcars.co.uk

Brooke Cars
www.brookecars.co.uk

Bufori
www.bufori.com

Bugatti
www.bugatti-cars.de

Buick
www.buick.com

Cadillac
www.cadillac.com

Callaway
www.callawaycars.com

Caterham
www.caterham.co.uk

Chevrolet
www.chevrolet.com

Chrysler
www.chrysler.com

Citroën
www.citroen.com

Daewoo Motors
www.daewoous.com

Daihatsu
www.daihatsu.com

Dodge
www.dodge.com

FBS Cars Online
www.fbs-eng.co.uk

Ferrari
www.ferrariworld.com

Fiat
www.fiat.com

Ford
www.fordvehicles.com

General Motors
www.gm.com

Ginetta Cars
www.ginettacars.com

GMC
www.gmc.com

Grinnall Cars
www.grinnallcars.com

Invicta Car Company
www.invictacar.com

Holden
www.holden.com.au

Honda
www.honda.com

Hummer
www.hummer.com

Hyundai
www.hyundaiusa.com

Infiniti
www.infiniti.com

Isuzu
www.isuzu.com

Jaguar
www.jaguarusa.com

Jeep
www.jeep.com

Kia Motors
www.kia.com

Lamborghini
www.lamborghini.com

Lancia
www.lancia.com

Land Rover
www.landroverusa.com

LDV
www.ldv.co.uk

Lexus
www.lexus.com

Lincoln
www.lincolnvehicles.com

Lola Cars International
www.lola-group.com

Lotus
www.lotuscars.com

Mahindra
www.mahindraworld.com

Maserati
www.maserati.com

Mazda
www.mazdausa.com

McLaren
www.mclarencars.com

Mercedes-Benz
www.mbusa.com

Mercury
www.mercuryvehicles.com

Merlin Motors
www.merlinmotorsusa.com

MG
www3.mg-rover.com

Mini
www.miniusa.com

Mitsubishi
www.mitsubishicars.com

Morgan
www.morgan-motor.co.uk

Noble
www.noblecars.com

Nissan
www.nissanusa.com

Oldsmobile
www.oldsmobile.com

Opel
www.opel.com

Packard
www.packardmotorcar.com

Panoz
www.panozauto.com

Peugeot
www.peugeot.com

Pontiac
www.pontiac.com

Porsche
www.porsche.com/usa

Section 16

Proton
www.proton.com

Renault
www.renault.com

Rolls-Royce & Bentley
www.rollsroycemotorcars.com
www.bentleymotors.com

Rover
www3.mg-rover.com

Saab
www.saabusa.com

Saturn
www.saturn.com

Scion
www.scion.com

Seat
www.seat.com

Shelby
www.shelbyamerican.com

SICAR-M
www.sicar-m.com

Skoda
www.skoda-auto.com

Smart
www.usa.smart.com

Subaru
www.subaru.com

Suzuki
www.suzukiauto.com

Tiger Racing
www.tigerracing.com

Toyota
www.toyota.com

Trasco
www.trasco-cars.com

TVR
www.tvr-eng.co.uk

Unique Motor Company
www.uniquemotorcompany.co.uk

Vauxhall
vauxhall.co.uk

Volkswagen
www.vw.com

Volvo
www.volvocars.us

Westfield
www.westfield-sportscars.co.uk

Source: AutoGuide.net, "Manufacturers,"
www.autoguide.net/manufacturers/manufactur-
ers.shtml.

Automotive Car, Truck, and Motorcycle Technical Trade Training Schools

Apex Technical School
635 Avenue of the Americas
New York, NY
(212) 645-3300
www.apexschool.com

ASE test prep.com
Automotion Inc.
145 Golfwood Drive

West Carrollton, OH 45449
(800) 437-7483 (toll-free)
www.asetestprep.com

Aspire
925 Lincoln Highway
Morrisville, PA
(800) 247-1099 (toll-free)
www.aspireinc.com

Atri
1322 Rankin Street
Troy, MI
(866) 287-4797 (toll-free)
www.atritech.com

Automotive Technology Skyline College
3300 College Drive
San Bruno, CA
(650) 738-4440
www.skylinecollege.com

Automotive Video Inc.
6280 Arc Way
Ft. Myers, FL 33912
(800) 718-7246 (toll-free)
www.auto-video.com

Baran Institute of Technology
611 Day Hill Road
Windsor, CT 06095-1719
(800) 243-4242 (toll-free)
www.baraninstitute.com
automotive, auto body, and diesel technical
training

Council of Advanced Automotive Trainers
632 Gamble Drive
Lisle, IL 60532
(800) 922-2834 (toll-free)
www.caat.org

Denver Automotive & Diesel College
460 South Lipan Street
Denver, CO 80223
(800) 347-3232 (toll-free), (866) 647-DADC
(3232) (toll-free)
www.dadc.com

Diesel Institute of America
4710 East 7th Avenue
Tampa, FL 33605-4702
(800) 572-4327 (toll-free)
www.dieselschool.com

Engine City Technical Institute
2365 Route 22 West
P.O. Box 3116
Union, NJ 07083-1916

(800) 305-2487 (toll-free)
www.enginecitytech.com
automotive diesel technical training

I-CAR Inter-Industry Conference on Auto Collision Repair
3701 Algonquin Road, Suite 400
Rolling Meadows, IL 60008
(800) 422-7872 (toll-free)
www.i-car.com

Lincoln Tech School Institute
200 Executive Drive
West Orange, NJ 07052
(800) 806-1921 (toll-free)
www.lincolntech.com

Louisiana Technical College
900 Youngs Road
Morgan City, LA 70381
(985) 380-2436
www.youngmemorial.com
automotive technology

M&M Training and Development
1130 Route 22 West
Mountainside, NJ 07092
(888) 780-8724 (toll-free)
www.mmtraining.com
paintless dent removal training and tools

Masters School of Autobody Management
124 East Carrillo Street
Santa Barbara, CA 93101
(805) 564-3436
www.masters-school.com

Mechanics College
3801 Campus Drive
Waco, TX. 76705
(800) 792-8784 (toll-free)
www.mechanicscollege.com

Melior Inc.
One Perimeter Park South, Suite 450 N
P.O. Box 381282
Birmingham, AL 35243-0435
(877) 224-0435 (toll-free)
www.meliortraining.com

Section 16

MotorCycle Mechanics Institute
2844 W. Deer Valley Road
Phoenix, AZ 85027
(623) 869-9644
motorcycle career training program

Motorsports Employment
2011 West Chapman Avenue
Orange, CA 92868
(714) 991-9500
www.motorsportsemployment.com
employment site and education

NASCAR Technical Institute
220 Byers Creek Road
Mooresville, NC 28115
(800) 859-1202 (toll-free)
www.ntieducation.com

Nashville Auto-Diesel College
1524 Gallatin Road
Nashville, TN 37206
(800) 228-NADC (toll-free)
www.nadcedu.com

Northwest Kansas Technical College
1209 Harrison
Goodland, KS 67735
(785) 890-3641, (800) 316-4127 (toll-free)
www.nwktc.org

Ohio Technical College
1374 East 51st Street
Cleveland, OH 44103
(800) 322-7000 (toll-free)
www.ohiotechnicalcollege.com

Pittsburgh Diesel Institute Trust
West Hills Shopping Center
910 Beaver Grade Road
Moon Township, PA 15108
(800) 833-3454 (toll-free)
www.pittsburghdiesel.com

Tools For Education, Inc.
140 N. Ridge Avenue
Ambler, PA 19002

(888) 404-8320 (toll-free)
www.toolsforeducation.com

Universal Technical Institute (UTI)
10851 N. Black Canyon Highway, Suite 600
Phoenix, AZ 85209
(800) 859-7249 (toll-free)
www.uticorp.com

Veejer Enterprises
3701 Lariat Lane
Garland, TX 75042-5419
(972) 276-9642
www.veejer.com

Vincennes University
1002 N. 1st Street
Vincennes, IN 47591
(812) 888-4313
www.vinu.edu
training, collision repair, auto repair, diesel
truck/heavy equipment repair, John Deere Ag
Tech Program

WyoTech
4373 North 3rd Street
Laramie, WY 82072
(800) 521-7158 (toll-free)
www.wyotech.com

York Technical Institute
1405 Williams Road
York, PA 17402
(800) 227-9675 (toll-free)
www.yti.edu
Motorcycle Mechanic Technology program

USAutoJobs.com
24 Ridge Street
Middletown, NY 10940
(845) 344-1917, (845) 551-7613
www.usautojobs.com

Source: AutoTechs.info, "Automotive Technician's Resource Directory," www.autotechs.info/
education.htm.

Automotive Franchise Opportunities

AAMCO Transmissions, Inc.
One Presidential Boulevard
Bala Cynwyd, PA 19004
(800) 223-8887 (toll-free)
www.aamco.com

Aero Colours
6971 Washington Avenue South, Suite 102
Minneapolis, MN 55437
(800) 696-2376 (toll-free)
www.aerocolours.com

All Night Auto
3872 Rochester Road
Troy, MI 48083
(248) 619-9020
www.allnightauto.net

Alta Mere Complete Auto Imaging
4444 West 147th Street
Midlothian, IL 60445
(800) 377-9247 (toll-free)
www.altamere.com

ATL International, Inc.
8334 Veterans Highway
Millersville, MD 21108
(800) 935-8863 (toll-free)
www.alltuneandlube.com

Big O Tires
12650 E. Briarwood Avenue, Suite 2D
Englewood, CO 80112
(800) 321-2446 (toll-free)
www.bigotires.com

Car-X Auto Service
8750 W. Bryn Mawr, Suite 410
Chicago, IL 60631
(800) 359-2359 (toll-free)
www.carx.com

Colors On Parade
642 Century Circle
Conway, SC 29526
(800) 929-3363 (toll-free)
www.colorsfranchise.com

Cornwell Quality Tools
667 Seville Road
Wadsworth, OH 44281
(800) 321-8356 (toll-free)
www.cornwelltools.com

Creative Colors International®
P.O. Box 552
Oak Forest, IL 60452
(800) 933-2656 (toll-free)
www.creativecolorsintl.com

Fas-Break, Inc.
1635 W. University Drive, Suite #127
Tempe, AZ 85281
(800) 777-5169 (toll-free)
www.fasbreak.com

Fibrenew International
P.O. Box 33, Site 16, RR8
Calgary, AB T2J 2T9
Canada
(800) 345-2951 (toll-free)
www.fibrenew.com

Glass Doctor Corp.
1020 N. University Parks Drive
Waco, TX 76707
(800) 280-9959 (toll-free)
www.glassdr.com

Glass Mechanix
4555 N.W. 103rd Avenue
Fort Lauderdale, FL 33351
(800) 826-8523 (toll-free)
www.glassmechanix.com

Jiffy Lube International
P.O. Box 2967
Houston, TX 77252
(713) 546-4100
www.jiffylube.com

Lee Myles Associates Corp.
140 Route 17, Suite 200
Paramus, NJ 07652
(800) 533-6953 (toll-free)
www.leemyles.com

LINE-X
2525 "A" Birch Street
Santa Ana, CA 92707
(800) 831-3232 (toll-free)
www.linexcorp.com

MAACO Enterprises, Inc.
381 Brooks Road
King of Prussia, PA 19406
(800) 296-2226 (toll-free)
www.franchise.maaco.com

Mac Tools
4635 Hilton Corporate Drive
Columbus, OH 43232
(800) MAC-TOOLS (622-8665) (toll-free)
www.mactools.com

Matco Tools
4403 Allen Road
Stow, OH 44224
(800) 433-7098 (toll-free)
www.matcotools.com

Meineke Discount Muffler Shops
128 S. Tryon Street, Suite 900
Charlotte, NC 28202
(800) MEINEKE (634-6353) (toll-free)
www.meineke.com

Mighty Distributing
650 Engineering Drive
Norcross, GA 30092
(800) 829-3900 (toll-free)
www.mightyautoparts.com

Milex Tune-Up Brakes & Air Conditioning
4444 West 147th Street
Midlothian, IL 60445
(800) 377-9247 (toll-free)
www.milextuneupbrake.com

Mr. Transmission
4444 West 147th Street
Midlothian, IL 60445
(800) 377-9247 (toll-free)
www.mrtransmission.com

National Tools
2003 Bison Court
Grand Junction, CO
(800) 944-7005 (toll-free)
www.nationaltools.com

Novus Glass
10425 Hampshire Avenue
Minneapolis, MN 55438
(800) 328-1117 (toll-free)
www.novusglass.com

Power Window Repair Express
1801 W. Atlantic Avenue, Suite B3
Delray Beach, FL 33444
(877) PWR-Express (797-3977) (toll-free)
www.pwrexpress.com

Rent-A-Wreck
10324 South Dolfield Road
Owings Mills, MD 21117
(410) 581-5755
www.rent-a-wreck.com

Snap-on Tools Co.
2801 80th Street
Kenosha, WI 53141-1410
(877) 4-SNAPON (476-2766) (toll-free)
www.snapon.com

Supply Master USA®
6c White Deer Plaza
Sparta, NJ 07871
(800) 582-1947 (toll-free)
www.supplymasterusa.com

U-Save Auto Rental
4780 I-55 N, Suite 300
Jackson, MS 39211
(800) 438-2000 (toll-free)
www.usave.net

Valvoline Instant Oil Change Franchising, Inc.
3499 Blazer Parkway
Lexington, KY 40509
(800) 622-6846 (toll-free)
www.viocfranchise.com

Ziebart International Corp.
1290 East Maple Road
Troy, MI 48007
(800) 877-1312 (toll-free)
www.ziebart.com

Source: AutoTechs.info, "Automotive Technician's Resource Directory," www.autotechs.info/franchises.htm.

15 Automotive Industry Publications

Automotive Journal
P.O. Box 455
Palmyra, NJ 08065
(215) 338-8492
coverage: Eastern Pennsylvania, New Jersey, and Northern Delaware

Automotive News
1400 Woodbridge Avenue
Detroit, MI 48207
(313) 446-6000
www.autonews.com

Automotive Week Publishing Co., Inc.
P.O. Box 3495
Wayne, NJ 07474-3495
(201) 694-7792
www.auto-week.com

Automotive Undercar Trade Organization
1006 Glenbriar Court
St. Charles, IL 60174
(800) 582-1359 (toll-free)
www.undercar.org

Brake & Front End
Babcock
3550 Embassy Parkway
Akron, OH 44333
(330) 670-1234
www.brakeandfrontend.com

Modern Tire Dealer
341 White Pond Drive
Akron, OH 44320
(330) 867-4401
www.moderntiredealer.com

Motor
645 Stewart Avenue
Garden City, NY 11530
www.motor.com

Motor Age
2000 Clearwater Drive
Oak Brook, IL 60523
www.motorage.com

Professional Tool & Equipment News
1233 Janesville Avenue
Ft. Atkinson, WI 53538
(800) 547-7377 (toll-free)
www.pten.com

Transmission Digest
MD Publications
P.O. Box 2210
Springfield, MO 65801-2210
(800) 274-7890 (toll-free)
www.transmissiondigest.com

Undercar Digest
MD Publications
P.O. Box 2210
Springfield, MO 65801-2210
(800) 274-7890 (toll-free)
www.mdpublications.com/ud

Underhood Service
Babcock
3550 Embassy Parkway
Akron, OH 44333
(330) 670-1234
www.underhoodservice.com

Source: AutoTechs.info, "Automotive Technician's Resource Directory," www.autotechs.info/publications.htm.

Section 16

Top 75 Motor Vehicle and Car Body Manufacturers

1. General Motors Corporation
3044 W. Grand Boulevard
Detroit, MI 48202
(313) 556-5000

2. Ford Motor Company
P.O. Box 1899
Dearborn, MI 48121
(313) 322-3000

3. Chrysler Corporation
1000 Chrysler Drive
Highland Park, MI 48326
(810) 576-5741

4. United Technologies Corporation
United Tech Building
Hartford, CT 06101
(203) 728-7000

5. Ford Body and Assembly Operation
17000 Oakwood
Dearborn, MI 48121
(313) 322-7715

6. Dana Corp.
P.O. Box 1000
Toledo, OH 43697
(419) 535-4500

7. Navistar International Transportation
455 N. Cityfront Plaza Drive
Chicago, IL 60611
(312) 836-2000

8. Freightliner Corporation
4747 N. Channel
Portland, OR 97217
(503) 735-8000

9. PACCAR Inc.
P.O. Box 1518
Bellevue, WA 98004
(206) 455-7400

10. Delco Chassis Division
P.O. Box 1042
Dayton, OH 45401
(513) 455-9204

11. Nissan North America Inc.
990 West 190 Street
Torrance, CA 90502
(310) 719-8000

12. Saturn Corporation
P.O. Box 7025
Troy, MI 48007
(313) 524-5000

13. Honda
24000 Honda Parkway
Marysville, OH 43040
(937) 642-5000

14. New United Motor Manufacturing Inc.
45500 Fremont
Fremont, CA 94538
(510) 498-5500

15. Nissan Motor Manufacturing Corporation USA
983 Nissan Drive
Smyrna, TN 37167
(615) 459-1400

16. Mitsubishi Motor Manufacturing
100 N. Mitsubishi
Normal, IL 61761
(309) 888-8000

17. Armco Inc.
1 Oxford Centre
Pittsburgh, PA 15219
(412) 255-9800

18. Hyundai Motor America
P.O. Box 20850
Fountain Valley, CA 92728
(714) 965-3000

19. MascoTech Inc.
21001 Van Born Road
Taylor, MI 48180
(313) 274-7405

20. Renco Corporation
30 Rockefeller Plaza
New York, NY 10112
(212) 541-6000

21. Volvo GM Heavy Truck Corporation
P.O. Box 26115
Greensboro, NC 27402
(910) 279-2000

22. Toyota Motor Manufacturing USA
1001 Cherry Blossom Way
Georgetown, KY 40324
(502) 868-2000

23. Federal Signal Corporation
1415 W. 22nd Street
Oak Brook, IL 60521
(708) 954-2000

24. AutoAlliance International Inc.
1 International Drive
Flat Rock, MI 48134
(313) 782-7800

25. Blue Bird Corporation
P.O. Box 7839
Macon, GA 31210
(912) 757-7100

26. Coachmen Industries Inc.
P.O. Box 3300
Elkhart, IN 46515
(219) 262-0123

27. Thor Industries Inc.
419 W. Pike Street
Jackson Center, OH 45334
(937) 596-6849

28. Motor Coach Industries International
1850 N. Central Avenue
Phoenix, AZ 85004
(602) 207-5000

29. Peterbilt Motors Co.
1700 Woodstock Street
Denton, TX 76205
(817) 591-4000

30. Subaru-Isuzu Automotive Inc.
P.O. Box 5689
Lafayette, IN 47903
(317) 449-1111

31. AM General Corporation
105 N. Niles Avenue
South Bend, IN 46617
(219) 237-6222

32. Blue Bird Body Corporation
P.O. Box 937
Fort Valley, GA 31030
(912) 825-2021

33. Thomas Built Buses Inc.
P.O. Box 2450
High Point, NC 27261
(910) 889-4871

34. Budd Co.
12141 Charlevoix
Detroit, MI 48215
(313) 823-9100

35. Pierce Manufacturing Inc.
P.O. Box 2017
Appleton, WI 54913
(414) 832-3000

36. Holiday Rambler LLC
P.O. Box 465
Wakarusa, IN 46573
(219) 862-7211

37. Spartan Motors Inc.
P.O. Box 440
Charlotte, MI 48813
(517) 543-6400

38. Emergency One Inc.
P.O. Box 2710
Ocala, FL 32678
(904) 237-1122

39. Collins Industries Inc.
421 E. 30th Avenue
Hutchinson, KS 67502
(316) 663-5551

Section
16

40. AmTran Corporation
P.O. Box 6000
Conway, AR 72033
(501) 327-7761

41. Louis Berkman Co.
P.O. Box 820
Steubenville, OH 43952
(614) 283-3722

42. Andover Industries Inc.
P.O. Box 459
Andover, OH 44003
(216) 293-5900

43. FWD Corporation
105 E. 12th Street
Clintonville, WI 54929
(715) 823-2141

44. Eastar Company
3130 W. Monroe Street
Sandusky, OH 44870
(419) 627-3200

45. Elgin Sweeper Company
1300 W. Bartlett Road
Elgin, IL 60120
(708) 741-5370

46. Superior of Ohio Inc.
P.O. Box 1981
Lima, OH 45802
(419) 222-1501

47. Wheeled Coach Industries Inc.
P.O. Box 677339
Orlando, FL 32867
(407) 677-7777

48. Collins Bus Corporation
P.O. Box 2946
Hutchinson, KS 67504
(316) 662-9000

49. Vactor Manufacturing Inc.
1621 S. Illinois Street
Streator, IL 61364
(815) 672-3171

50. Athey Products Corporation
P.O. Box 669
Raleigh, NC 27602
(919) 556-5171

51. Marmon Motor Co.
P.O. Box 462009
Garland, TX 75046
(214) 276-5121

52. Simon Ladder Towers Inc.
64 Cocalico Creek
Ephrata, PA 17522
(717) 859-1176

53. De Tomaso Industries Inc.
P.O. Box 856
Red Bank, NJ 07701
(908) 842-7200

54. Eagle Coach Corporation
2045 Les Mauldin
Brownsville, TX 78521
(210) 541-3111

55. Johnston Sweeper Co.
4651b Shaefer Avenue
Chino, CA 91710
(909) 613-5600

56. Chubb National Foam Inc.
P.O. Box 270
Exton, PA 19341
(215) 363-1400

57. Shoals Supply Inc.
P.O. Box 150
Bear Creek, AL 35543
(205) 486-9459

58. TNT Auto Warehousing
3715 E. West Road
Tacoma, WA 98421
(206) 922-0540

59. TPI Inc.
136 Market Street
Warren, RI 02885
(401) 245-1200

60. WS Darley and Co.
2000 Anson Drive
Melrose Park, IL 60160
(708) 345–8050

61. Wright-K Technology Inc.
2025 E. Genesee Street
Saginaw, MI 48601
(517) 752–3103

62. Schwartz Industries Inc.
1055 Jordan Road
Huntsville, AL 35811
(205) 851–1200

63. Alfa Leisure Inc.
13501 5th Street
Chino, CA 91710
(909) 628–5574

64. Blitz Corporation
4525 W. 26th Street
Chicago, IL 60623
(312) 762–7600

65. Classic Auto Replicars Inc.
16650 NW 27th Avenue
Opa Locka, FL 33054
(305) 625–9700

66. O'Gara Hess
9113 Le Saint Drive
Fairfield, OH 45014
(513) 874–2112

67. B and B Homes Corporation
P.O. Box 2349
Mills, WY 82644
(307) 235–1525

68. Fontaine Modification Co.
9827 Mount Holly
Charlotte, NC 28214
(704) 391–1355

69. Luverne Fire Apparatus Ltd.
1209 E. Birch Street
Brandon, SD 57005
(605) 582–2300

70. Trans-Aire International
P.O. Box 2178
Elkhart, IN 46515
(219) 262–3411

71. All American Racers Inc.
2334 S. Broadway
Santa Ana, CA 92707
(714) 540–1771

72. Road Rescue Inc.
1133 Rankin Street
St. Paul, MN 55116
(612) 699–5588

73. Tee Jay Industries Inc.
34272 Doreka Avenue
Fraser, MI 48026
(810) 296–5160

74. Lodal Inc.
P.O. Box 2315
Kingsford, MI 49801
(906) 779–1700

75. HME Inc.
1950 Byron Center Avenue
Wyoming, MI 49509
(616) 534–1463

Source: Cool Fire Technology, "Leading Motor Vehicle and Car Body Manufacturers," www.cftech.com/BrainBank/MANUFACTUR-ING/CarBody.html.

Section 16

Owning and Operating a Manufacturing Business

Chapter 103

Research and Development

Three Resources for Researching Inventions and Patents

InventHelp—Searchable List of Inventions
www.inventhelp.com/invention-search.asp

U.S. Patent and Trademark Office
www.uspto.gov/patft

U.S. Patent Search (patents issued since 1975)
patents.cos.com/cgi-bin/search/main

Source: Compiled by Contributing Writer Ty Martin.

Six Points of Good Product Design

Although good design is almost impossible to define, common themes hold true across industry sectors and product types. A well-designed product tends to combine the following qualities:

- **Useful.** It works well and functions as promised. It does what it is expected to and satisfies a minimum or appropriate level of performance.

- **Usable.** It has appropriate ergonomics and user interface, considering who will be using it, how, where, and how often.

- **Desirable.** It looks good! What looks good will depend upon the nature of the market, lifestyle, culture, age, gender, education, occupation, and place of use. What looks good also depends upon competitive and complementary products. In general, it is important for the product aesthetics to be appropriate for the market, users, and usage environment. A good test is if customers are prepared to pay a premium because they desire it.

- **Producible.** It must be capable of economical volume manufacture using appropriate production methods, considering the impact on the organization of new components, assemblies, and processes. Producible products combine optimization of assembly and manufacture with modularity and platform strategies.

- **Profitable.** It must result in sufficient business rewards, measured in terms of market share, gross margin, breakeven, turnover, or sales volume. Financial rewards may also be supplemented by other business benefits.

- **Differentiated.** The benefits of good design are seen in products that are clearly differentiated. Differentiation can be gained through satisfying core user benefits in new ways, by delivering excellence in one of the product's physical attributes, or by providing leading support services around the physical goods.

Source: "What Is Good Design?," www.betterproductdesign.net/WhatIs.htm.

20 Tips and Tricks Concerning Inventions

1. Get as much publicity as possible. But be clear which message you want to put out!
2. Never judge an invention before someone has tried it out.
3. Comments like "We don't need that!" are normal, even for very good inventions.
4. Read about inventions and inventors to become aware of their high failure rate.
5. If someone gives you business advice, check his or her credentials. Many people just like to sound clever.
6. Most of your ideas that you think are new have been around already for a long time.
7. But some ideas that seem very straightforward have never been thought of.
8. Many of your ideas, even if they are new and original, are not worth a cent. Accept it and enjoy them.
9. Everything is a prototype until you have sold at least ten of it.
10. Take feedback from customers very seriously.
11. Get feedback from independent people as well as from other inventors!
12. Think NLP (Neuro-Linguistic Programming): try to please touch, ear, and eye!
13. Before you test a prototype on someone, make it look as close to the finished product as possible. It pays.
14. In each step of the prototype cycle, make as many improvements as possible. Testers get bored otherwise.
15. Paying pieceworkers (homeworkers paid per piece) is often a good way to keep production costs low.
16. Don't be too shy to ask good money for a good product.
17. A one-off payment for a license is much less hassle than a contract for royalties you might never get. This might be the preferable option, especially for inventions of minor value.
18. Patenting is extremely expensive and can take years. If you do not get the patent, you have spilled the beans. Confidentiality agreements are free, immediately binding, and more practical, because nobody can copy your idea.
19. Patenting is not recommended by international experts for inventors or small companies, because you might have to go to another country to fight for it and sue a company for several years, easily spending a million dollars. Do you have that? And what if you fail? If you try to patent anyway, be clear about its limitations—and yours.
20. Games, puzzles, and books are automatically protected by copyright once you go public.

Source: "Tips & Tricks Concerning Inventions," karl.kiwi.gen.nz/invtips.html.

Top Seven Strategies to Set (and Get) the Right Prices

Which product feature of yours is every buyer keen to know about? Which sales tool closes prospects instantly? Your price. Yet, despite the far-reaching consequences of a company's pricing, I'm surprised at how little time small business owners spend on it. Here are a few ways to bring pricing to the forefront of your marketing plan.

1. **Price is a promise.** Let's say you're shopping for cereal and come across two varieties. One is a well-known brand in a resealable 20-oz. package, which comes with a toy and sells for $4.99. The other is a store brand, that's packaged in a nondescript plastic bag and sells for $2.99. Which do you buy?

   If price were your only factor, you'd buy the $2.99 brand. But there are other factors. In this example, the $4.99 box promises you the reputation of a well-known brand, a toy to entertain your kids, and the convenience of resealable packaging. Remember that a price guarantees all the promises wrapped up in your product or service.

2. **Determine your promises.** Before you ever touch a calculator, first take stock of all the value factors that are bundled into your price.

   If your company sells a product, these might include:

   - the performance of your finished good
   - your distribution capabilities
   - your service and installation services

   If yours is a service, value factors might include:

   - the bottom-line impact of your deliverable
   - your company's ability to meet tight timelines
   - your experience level

3. **Pricing financially.** After taking stock of all your value factors, grab a calculator. First, add up all your direct costs (those incurred as a result of delivering your service), which include labor and raw materials. Then, add up all your indirect costs (all other costs that aren't direct), like rent, insurance, and utilities. Now, identify the profit your company needs to attain in order to fuel new investment and reward your employees. Finally, forecast what your annual unit volumes will be. Now, divide the total of your costs and profit by annual units sold and you end up with a unit price. Sure, this is a simplified example, but the process is sound. This kind of analysis will help ascertain where your prices should be from a financial perspective.

4. **Pricing competitively.** It's important not to stop here. Instead, gather competitive pricing information from any of these sources:

   - intermediaries (distributors, brokers)
   - previous customers

- prospects
- ex-employees of your competitors
- trade associations

After digging around enough, you'll be able to generate a range of prices that your competitors fall into. Together with your financial prices, you'll now have two reference points.

5. **Pricing by position.** The last step is to ask this question: "How do we want to be perceived in our market?" In my book, *The Marketing Toolkit for Growing Businesses*, I identify 13 possible price strategies you could choose from, but to make this easy, consider just three:

- Premium Price: the most expensive third of your market
- Middle Market Prices: the middle third
- Budget Price: the least expensive third

Based on the value factors you've identified and your chief competitors, which of these three price levels best matches your product? The lesson in this exercise is that price positions your product.

6. **The worst pricing decision you can make.** "Because we're slow right now, we'll lower our prices. Then as business rebounds, we'll raise them." This is a bad marketing decision—because lowering your prices immediately positions your product differently to buyers. Plus very few companies make attendant cost reductions, so margins erode. And when you try to raise prices again, customers who bought at the lower prices will expect to get more value factors for the price increase. A better strategy is to maintain your prices while seeking cost reductions to maintain your margins.

7. **Another bad pricing decision.** "If I drop my price to $15, then will you buy?" Here, you signal to a buyer that your list prices are not final. Sensing this, buyers will negotiate harder and the resulting price reductions will cut into your margins. Instead, think about coupling price discounts to the buyer with equivalent reductions in your offering. For example, you could say, "OK I can lower my price to $15, but I'll have to reduce our warranty period from five years to two."

Sure, pricing is a financial decision. But it has a wide-ranging impact on your positioning, your selling efforts, and your product offering. Remember the words of Thomas Paine: "What we obtain too cheap we esteem too little; it is dearness only that gives everything its value."

Source: Jay Lipe, "Top 7 Strategies to Set (and Get) The Right Prices," top7business.com/?Top-7-Strategies-To-Set-(and-Get)-The-Right-Prices&id=569.

Top Seven Ways to Invent Something New in Your Field

1. Create a new buzzword. Can't love them, can't hate them. Make one up today and write a book about it. You're welcome to be silly about it, because all the others who have created some of today's greatest buzzwords were and are pretty crazy people.

2. The "something new" could be a new process, a better way to do something. Trick: borrow something from an unrelated field and see if it can be integrated into your field.

3. Remember that if you can't be number one in your niche, invent a new one. How to do that? Find out your customers' top seven pains when dealing with your product, and answer one of those in a new way. You thus create a new niche in which you are now the leader.

4. Your own frustration with something wrong with your product, company, customers, or employees is sometimes the best motivator to develop a new spin or new product.

5. What if you could invent a new cash flow? If you did, what would it look like? All business problems can be solved by increasing sales, and this might be the fun one to do.

6. Something new for you might be something old for someone else. My point: emulate someone who has already achieved what you want to do, to save an enormous amount of time and resources.

7. Get excited. Most firms are led by leaders and employees who are sleeping at the wheel. If you even give the perception that you are innovating monthly, you will lead your field in less than a year. Today's buzz phrase: Perceived Innovation = Value Delivered. (But eventually, you must deliver the innovation or your term will expire shortly.) That does not mean copy. It means look, study, adapt, add, change your current ways, but it does not mean you should do blatant copying of someone else's strategy.

Source: Christopher M. Knight, "Top 7 Ways to Invent Something New in Your Field," top7business.com/?Top-7-Ways-To-Invent-Something-New-In-Your-Field&id=449.

Two Resources for Product Design

New Product Design Development Tips
www.businessballs.com/productdesign.htm

Product Design Forums
www.productdesignforums.com

Source: Compiled by Contributing Writer Ty Martin.

Five Steps to Turning Your Idea into a Product

The light bulb above your head is glowing so bright that it's threatening to blind everyone around you. But what should you do with your great invention idea? Before you start blabbing about your invention to the wrong person or run to the first company that offers to buy it, you need to do one thing: protect it.

Whether you want to produce and market your invention yourself or license it to another company, the only way to make money from your invention and to guarantee that no one will steal your idea is to file a patent with the U.S. Patent and Trademark Office. This can be an intimidating process, so we've asked Andy Gibbs, CEO of PatentCafe.com, to break it down for you in five easy steps.

Step 1: Document It. Simply having an "idea" is worthless—you need to have proof of when you came up with the idea for your invention. Write down everything you can think of that relates to your invention, from what it is and how it works to how you'll make and market it. This is the first step to patenting your idea and keeping it from being stolen. You've probably heard about the "poor man's patent"—writing your idea down and mailing it to yourself in a sealed envelope so you have dated proof of your invention's conception. This is unreliable and unlikely to hold up in court. Write your idea down in a specially designed inventor's journal and have it signed by a witness. This journal will become your bible throughout the patent process.

Step 2: Research It. You will need to research your idea from legal and business standpoints. Before you file a patent, you should do the following:

- **Complete an initial patent search.** Just because you haven't seen your invention doesn't mean it doesn't already exist. Before you hire a patent attorney or agent, complete a rudimentary search for free at www.uspto.gov to make sure no one else has patented your idea. You should also complete a non-patent "prior art" search. If you find any sort of artwork or design related to your idea, you cannot patent it—regardless of whether a prior patent has been filed.

- **Research your market.** Sure, your brother thinks your idea for a new lawn sprinkler is a great idea, but that doesn't mean your neighbor would buy one. More than 95 percent of all patents never make money for the inventor. Before you invest too much time and money into patenting your invention, do some preliminary research of your target market. Is this something people will actually buy? Once you know there's a market, make sure your product can be manufactured and distributed at a low enough cost so that your retail price is reasonable. You can determine these costs by comparing those of similar products currently on the market. This will also help you size up your competition—which you will have, no matter how unique you think your invention is.

Step 3: Make a Prototype. A prototype is a model of your invention that puts into practice all of the things you have written in your inventor's journal. This will demonstrate the design of your invention when you present it to potential lenders and licensees. Do not file a patent before you have made a prototype. You will almost always discover a flaw in your original design or think of a new feature you would like to add. If you patent your idea before you work out these kinks, it will be too late to include them in the patent and you will risk losing the patent rights of the new design to someone else.

Here are some general rules of thumb when prototyping your invention:

1. **Begin with a drawing.** Before you begin the prototyping phase, sketch out all of your ideas into your inventor's journal.

2. **Create a concept mockup** out of any material that will allow you to create a 3-D model of your design.

3. **Once you're satisfied with the mockup, create a full working model of your idea.** There are many books and kits that can help you create prototypes. If your invention is something that will cost a lot of money or is unreasonable to prototype (like an oil refinery process or a new pharmaceutical drug), consider using a computer-animated virtual prototype.

Step 4: File a Patent. Now that you have all of the kinks worked out of your design, it's finally time to file a patent. There are two main patents between which you will have to choose: a utility patent (for new processes or machines) or a design patent (for manufacturing new, nonobvious ornamental designs). You can write the patent and fill out the application yourself, but do not file it yourself until you have had a skilled patent professional look it over first. If the invention is really valuable, someone will infringe on it. If you do not have a strong patent written by a patent attorney or agent, you will be pulling your hair out later when a competitor finds a loophole that allows them to copy your idea. It's best to get the legal help now to avoid any legal problems in the future.

When searching for a patent attorney or agent, remember one thing: if you see them advertised on TV, run away! Once you are far, far away, follow these steps to choosing the best patent professional:

1. **Do your homework.** Have your inventor's journal, prototype, and notes with you. This will save them time and you money. This will also help persuade them to work with you.

2. **Make sure they are registered** with the U.S. Patent and Trademark Office.

3. **Ask them what their technical background is.** If your invention is electronic, find a patent professional who is also an electrical engineer.

4. **Discuss fees.** Keep your focus on smaller patent firms. They are less expensive and will work more closely with you. Agree to the estimated total cost before hiring your patent professional.

Step 5: Market Your Invention. Now it's time to figure out how you're going to bring your product to market. Create a business plan. How will you get money? Where will you manufacture the product? How will you sell it? Now is a good time to decide if you will manufacture and sell the product yourself, or license it for sale through another company. When you license your product, you will probably receive only two percent to five percent in royalty fees. This often scares away inventors who feel they deserve more. But consider the upside: you will not have the financial burden associated with maintaining a business. This could end up making you more money in the long run.

Source: Sarah Pierce, "5 Steps for Turning Your Idea into a Product," www.entrepreneur.com/article/0,4621,321635,00.html.

Ten Objectives for Rating Your Product Idea

Give your idea between one (weak) and five (strong) on the following points:
1. How strongly will people "want" your idea?
2. How novel have you proved it to be?
3. How direct will its path to buyers be?
4. How low-cost and available are the skills needed for development?
5. How able and willing to help are inventor support groups?
6. How well can you (not "could you") "sell" the idea to a stranger in an elevator?
7. How sure are you of getting the money you need?
8. How much alpha and beta testing have you done with X prototypes?
9. How well have you protected your idea?
10. How well have you recorded all your steps in your journal, to document them?
   Scoring: 45 and up: "Go for gold!"

   35–44: "Don't hold your breath too long."

   25–34: "Make improvements or stir your pot and put out another idea."

Source: "How to Rate an Idea," karl.kiwi.gen.nz/invtips.html.

The Steps of Inventing

Document your idea. One of the first things you will want to do is to make a sketch of your idea. As you develop your invention, it is very important to document your progress. It is highly recommended that you purchase a notebook with bound pages, so no pages can be removed or added undetectably. You will want to number the pages and log your activities. Initial and date each page. Keep track of development, tests, purchase sales slips of materials for prototypes, and photos of your invention. The last page should contain a statement that relatives or friends sign and date that they understand your idea. If there is ever a dispute, this notebook will establish the invention as your original idea and the dates of the developments. A suitable notebook designed for inventors, The Idea Journal, is now available from the United Inventors Association (www.uiausa.com).

Build a prototype. It is important that you can show that your invention actually works. Therefore, it is recommended that you build a prototype. This will be especially helpful if you decide to obtain a patent and market your invention. Building a prototype will help work out bugs and further refine your idea.

Submit a disclosure document with the U.S. Patent and Trademark Office. When the prototype is sufficiently developed to satisfy you that the idea is viable, you may wish to submit a Disclosure Document (www.uspto.gov/web/offices/pac/disdo.html) with the United States Patent and Trademark Office. Forms are available for download from the USPTO (www.uspto.gov/web/forms/index.html). This does not offer protection but establishes a date of conception. Two duplicate documents are sent to the USPTO with a self-addressed, stamped envelope. These documents are dated and stamped with a number. One set is mailed to you and one is kept in the USPTO for two years. This two-year grace period allows you to show your invention and try to determine whether it is marketable. Within the two-year period you must file a patent application. If your invention has been offered for sale or otherwise been shown to the public, you are limited to a maximum of one year from that date.

Do a patent search. Before submitting your invention to a patent attorney or agent, you can do a preliminary patent survey to see if you are infringing on someone else's invention. A patent survey can be done at a patent depository library; check www.uspto.gov/web/offices/ac/ido/ptdl/ptdlib_1.html for a library in your state. A preliminary patent survey can now be done on the internet, through the USPTO patent database (www.uspto.gov/patft/index.html). The ease of doing a patent survey on your personal computer has several advantages. First, you can do the search by entering keywords relating to your invention. The subsequent list of patents that match your keywords can further be visited. The USPTO database contains the full text and figures of the patent. There are several programs that can display the images properly, which can be downloaded free of charge from the links specified (www.uspto.gov/patft/help/images.htm). The USPTO also has a trademark database. A trademark search is easily obtained following instructions on the web site. The aforementioned libraries can be very helpful in getting you started surveying your ideas and inventions. In the event your idea has been patented before, you can make your patent superior—i.e., cheaper, more environmentally friendly, more efficient, or however—to what has been done before.

Do a provisional application. The Provisional Application (www.uspto.gov/web/offices/pac/provapp.htm) was introduced by the GATT (General Agreement on Tariffs and

Trade) Treaty. It allows a grace period of one year to file the patent application. The application is less formal than a patent application and provides patent pending status, allowing earlier marketing of your product.

File a patent application. There are three options in filing a patent application: using a patent agent, using a patent attorney, or doing it yourself. It is generally recommended that you should not file your own patent application. Using an experienced agent or attorney to file for the patent will greatly increase your chances of getting the patent and will generally make the patent broader by including more claims then you may come up with on your own. If you wish to file your own application, help is available from several sources. Check the ads in Inventors' Digest (www.inventorsdigest.com) for books and/or software such as Patent It Yourself by David Pressman (Nolo Press, www.nolo.com). Once your patent application (www.uspto.gov/main/patents.htm) is accepted by the USPTO, you may mark your invention "Patent Pending."

There are three types of patents: utility, design, and plant. The utility patent gives protection for 20 years after filing. The utility patent generally applies to a new and useful process, machine, manufacture, or any new and useful improvements thereof. The design patent covers any new, original, and ornamental design. The design patent is effective for 14 years after issue. The plant patent applies to a new and distinct variety of plant and is effective for 20 years after filing.

Market your invention. You may get a manufacturer to build and market your product and pay a royalty. This is probably the most desired method, but it is sometimes very difficult to arrange. Another method is to build your own company and market the product yourself. If this works out and you establish a market, you can sell the company. One of the ways to find a company to manufacture and market your invention is to show it at invention shows, fairs, or other appropriate industrial, boat, travel, or home shows. Check the United Inventors Association home page (www.uiausa.com) for upcoming events. There are companies advertising on the television and in magazines that promise to take your idea to the market. Check with an attorney before using these companies. Many of these companies make their money through fees charged to the inventors rather than through inventions that have been successfully marketed. Check with the National Inventor Fraud Center (www.inventorfraud.com) for lists of companies to use or avoid.

Source: Inventors' Association of South-Central Kansas, "Steps of Inventing," www.inventkansas.com/content.php?cid=1003.

Top Seven Ways to Get New Product Ideas

1. **Solve problem for people.** There are thousands of problems in the world. Create a product that can provide a solution to one of those problems.

2. **Find out what the current hot trend is.** You can find out what the new trends are by watching TV, reading magazines, and surfing the net. Just create a product that's related to the current hot trend.

3. **Improve a product that is already on the market.** You see products at home, in ads, at stores, etc. Just take a product that's out there and improve it.

4. **Create a new niche for a current product.** You can set yourself apart from your competition by creating a niche. Your product could be faster, bigger, smaller, or quicker than your competitors' products.

5. **Add on to an existing product.** You could package your current product with other related products. For example, you could package a football with a team jersey and football cards.

6. **Reincarnate an older product.** Maybe you have a book that's out of print and is no longer being sold. You could change the title, design a new front cover, and bring some of the old content up to date.

7. **Ask your current customers.** You could contact some of your customers by phone or e-mail and ask them what kind of new products they would like to see on the market.

Source: Larry Dotson, "Top 7 Ways to Get New Product Ideas," top7business.com/?Top-7-Ways-To-Get-New-Product-Ideas&id=451.

# Chapter 104

Using Computer-Aided Design

Five Reasons People Start Using Computer-Aided Design (CAD)

1. **File Sharing:** Clients, equipment suppliers, contractors, lenders, regulators, and others may have requested that drawings be sent to them over the internet. Scanning hand-drawn designs with a scanner for transmission has limitations. Bitmaps resulting from scanners reduce the detail of drawings so that information may be lost. Pencil drawings and blueprints are particularly hard to scan due to the large amount of background information that clutters up the final image and may require long sessions of editing before the image is clean enough to send. Also, the bitmap image, depending on resolution, may become a huge file that takes forever to send and receive and takes up too much storage space.

   All good CAD programs have convenient file-sharing utilities that will translate drawings into standard formats such as DWG, DXF, and others that can be easily and conveniently sent and received on the net.

2. **Design Efficiency:** Designing in the real world often requires the use of repetitive images and standard drawings. Believe me, the computer can store, manipulate, and manage your graphics much better than a metal file cabinet. Also, as government regulations increase each year, officials often want only small changes to a series of complex drawings. The computer makes creating and changing drawings relatively simple with a series of standard drawings and mouse clicks rather than starting from scratch each time a new drawing is needed.

3. **Organizing Work:** At some point in your business, searching for a certain drawing or a special detail begins to take up time. Having ten years of drawings fit on one or two CDs has some advantages. Computerized drawings force the designer to constantly back up, organize, and simplify the products of the design process. Believe it or not, the computer can help in the organization and storage of drawings, for both the compulsive saver and the impulsive artist.

4. **Just Keeping Up:** As time goes on, the computer, the internet, and the cell phone force themselves on us and we give in. To keep fighting may help one's image as an independent thinker, but it will not help a bottom line. When tools such as CAD become industry standards, avoiding their use may isolate the holdout designer from others in the marketplace, favoring the competition.

5. **Improving Job Skills:** Many schools offer classes in CAD. There is a vast range of teachers and programs available. Many are not very useful. A term of several weeks of study will not be enough to prepare you for a job, but you will get to experience what CAD drawing feels like. Many new graduates from qualified CAD schools are not useful in a tech position without a lot of practical experience. You will have to learn a lot in any CAD job that is not taught in any school. The diploma may just get

you inside the door. Time spent at the computer solving problems on your own develops the skills you will need quicker than classes, in my opinion.

Source: John Glassco, "Getting Started in CAD," www.eco-nomic.com/indexthn.htm.

Seven Tips for CAD Managers

1. **Keep an informal log (diary).** You can keep this log as an electronic document (I like Microsoft Word) or in a stenographer's pad to keep everything in one notebook. The log serves as an aid to memory and it documents what types of problems keep coming up. For example, three months from now, during John Doe's performance review, you might want some proof that you've had to explain the same concept to him 14 times in the last three months. If you keep a log you'll have the proof.

   Make no mistake: a big part of management is keeping things in writing. An informal log goes a long way toward documenting what you're doing and when and to what extent you're experiencing problems. Your log may well become the basis for anything from performance reviews to information that supports litigation against vendors who don't perform.

   If you want to prove something later, write it down now.

2. **Assign yourself tasks and report on yourself weekly.** It you're not crossing items off your list each week, then it may mean that either you're scheduling too much or you need to apply more time management skills to prioritizing what you work on. In such cases, reprioritize your weekly list or even put in some extra hours to get caught up. You may even want to consider a training class in time management if you still feel lost. Either way you'll learn about your own capabilities by analyzing your own work habits (before somebody else does).

3. **Never stop budgeting.** Always keep a spreadsheet file of your CAD department budget on your desktop and continuously update it. If you happen to remember you need to budget for a new service contract next year, don't wait to add it to your budget—do it immediately. Budget time is quite often hectic and if these add-ons to next year's budget aren't already documented, they may get lost in the shuffle. And if you're continuously tracking your current budget, you'll avoid going over budget before year-end, a problem that, like it or not, reflects poorly on you.

   Your budget document is the most important written document you'll produce each year because it determines what you can and can't purchase. So give this document the important attention it deserves year-round, not just at budget time.

4. **Never stop reading and cataloging.** Like budgeting, reading trade information should be a year-round pursuit. You may not learn something from everything you read, but then again, maybe you will! Take your reading a step further and catalog the really good stuff by printing or scanning it into an electronic archive.

Section 17

5. **Stay up to date on software—no matter what.** Do whatever you need to do to stay up to date on your industry's software advances. Even if your company isn't using the latest version of a given software program, do your best to have at least one copy of the latest and greatest to use for your own research and learning purposes. I realize that money is tight in the current economy, but as a CAD manager you really need to be on top of the latest features and technologies.

   After all, how can you advise your company on software-related issues if you're not fully aware of what is out there? And if your company can't see the wisdom of having at least one copy of the latest software tools on their CAD manager's desk, that may signal a problem in how the CAD manager is viewed, right?

6. **Don't be afraid to build your staff.** While some managers have trouble letting go or delegating, others are simply afraid that if others know how to do their job, they'll be seen as less valuable.

   But consider this:

   - If you don't delegate some tasks, you'll never be able to deal with every task that comes your way and you'll eventually get bogged down. And if that continues, you may be seen as having peaked in your job performance and your future becomes limited.

   - How do you expect to be promoted to a higher level if you don't train the personnel who will follow behind you?

   - If you don't develop the staff you have, they'll become bored and feel that they're in a dead-end career path. Would you rather have a motivated staff or one that would prefer to be elsewhere? It has always been my experience that CAD managers who demonstrate effective staff-building and delegation skills get promoted. Those who don't, don't. Enough said.

7. **Network aggressively.** Be sure to network with other CAD managers whenever you can. The CAD manager position can be an isolated one because there tends to be only one CAD manager in any operation. You'll have to actively network with other CAD managers because you're simply not going to see them in the course of your normal workday.

   Some of the best ways to network are pretty obvious:

   - Autodesk University® (www.autodeskevents.com/au)

   - User groups

   - Autodesk User Group International (AUGI®) guilds (www.augi.com)

   - Dealer demonstrations

Source: Robert Green, "Tips and Tricks for CAD Managers," usa.autodesk.com/adsk/servlet/item?siteID=123112&id=2259899&linkID=2475176.

Five Points to Choosing the Right CAD System

It is obvious to me that many companies are contemplating moving to a 3-D CAD design system (think Inventor, SolidWorks, Pro/ENGINEER, Revit, Architectural Desktop, Solid Edge, and thinkdesign), but it is equally obvious that many companies have no clue as to how to pick the right system.

Recommending the right CAD system requires that an understanding of the company's needs, skills, and limitations. You wouldn't buy a car without considering what you need, what you can afford, and how it performs during test drives, so why should software be any different? Here are five suggestions on shopping for the best CAD system for your company, based on some good old-fashioned homework and straight-up comparisons.

1. **Understand market realities.** Every software company will tell you its product is the best and its competitors' are inferior. All software packages have strengths and weaknesses, but the marketing people aren't going to admit the weaknesses (they're motivated to sell, sell, and sell). Only aggressive shoppers who educate themselves and drive the sales process to their own advantage will get good deals from software vendors. After all, if you don't know what you're shopping for, you'll simply have to trust the sales guys.

   So rather than accepting a barrage of sales claims and slick marketing presentations, you must challenge the software vendors to actually prove why their products will work best for you and why you should spend your company's money with them. To do that, you'll have to tell them what you need so they can address your concerns, right?

2. **Be realistic about budgets.** Get a good idea of what you can afford on a CAD system. Often management might say, "We don't care what it costs; we want to get the right system for our needs." That means, "We have a cost limit in mind, but we won't tell you what it is, because we hope you'll spend less." Upper management teams radically underestimate the expense of CAD systems and are shocked when shown the price tag. Persuade your management team to disclose its budget.

3. **Assess your needs and wants.** First, determine what you need the system to do. Consider the following basic categories:

   - What type of geometry do you need to create: 2-D, basic 3-D, or advanced 3-D?
   - Do you need parametric (variable) software functionality?
   - What is your industry?
   - What level of automation do you expect?
   - What level of integration with other software do you expect?
   - Do you see your needs changing in the next two years? If so, how?

Your answers to these questions will become the baseline for evaluating the software packages. Some of your requirements will disqualify certain types of software. (For instance, you won't need SolidWorks if you design buildings.) You might also find that you don't need nearly as much software as you think.

4. **Distinguish between real and perceived needs.** As you build up your list, you'll undoubtedly determine that some things are truly needed and some are merely desirable. Decide what you really need. You may hear from your managers that they want to go from 2-D to 100 percent 3-D parametric in one year, but they secretly think they can achieve this for $1,000 per seat. If the perceived need doesn't match the budget, software selection will become tougher. If you find out you don't have the budget to purchase something that meets all the needs, definitely take the time to determine which needs can be postponed.

5. **Make preliminary phone calls.** You can now begin to call software vendors in your area and ask for basic budgetary quotes based on your needs list. Your goal in this phase of investigation is simply to get an idea of how much money you'll need to spend per seat to achieve what your company needs. Be prepared to spend some time with the vendors describing what you need. Make it clear that you're simply trying to get an estimate. The vendors will appreciate your candor. As you talk with the vendors, be equally clear that you'll be testing and comparing several software solutions. By taking these steps, you'll show the vendors that you are business-motivated, cost-conscious, and functionality-focused. They'll do their best to earn your business.

Source: Robert Green, "The Right CAD System: Choose Wisely," *Cadence*, July 2003.

Capabilities of Modern CAD Systems

- Reuse of design components
- Ease of modification of designs and the production of multiple versions
- Automatic generation of standard components of the design
- Validation/verification of designs against specifications and design rules
- Simulation of designs without building a physical prototype
- Automated design of assemblies, which are collections of parts and/or other assemblies
- Output of engineering documentation, such as manufacturing drawings and bills of materials
- Output of design data directly to manufacturing facilities
- Output directly to a Rapid Prototyping or Rapid Manufacture Machine for industrial prototypes

Source: Wikipedia, "Computer-Aided Design," en.wikipedia.org/wiki/Computer-aided_design.

# Chapter 105

Procurement and Supply Chain

Topic	Page

Three Steps to Optimizing the Supply Chain

Distribution centers cost millions of dollars to build and operate. Companies must buy land (or find a suitable existing facility), add utilities, install logistics equipment, and hire staff—all on the assumption that this facility will represent the best strategy for the ultimate goal—customer satisfaction.

The key to the supply chain challenge, said Carter & Burgess logistics specialist Norm Saenz, is to carefully go through a three-step process gathering current information, establishing future priorities and modeling different distribution network scenarios.

Step 1: Gather information. "You need a lot of data to determine an optimum distribution network," Saenz said.

Saenz begins the process by answering critical planning questions such as these: How many distribution centers optimize the network? Where should they be located? Which customers will the distribution center support? What inventory will it house? How much inventory?

Essential information includes the location of current distribution centers, their capacities, and the volume going in and out. Also critical are profiles and locations of suppliers and customers.

"For example, are they shipping to other distribution centers, as they might be for a manufacturer shipping to a large retailer?" Saenz said. "Are they a retailer, shipping to their stores, like for a grocery retailer? Or are they individuals, like you would have for an e-commerce or catalog business?"

Saenz generates inventory and order profiles for existing distribution centers to understand the nature of the products being distributed. Are there significant amounts of bulk goods? Are products very large (refrigerators, air handling units, furniture) or very small (pencils, books, computer hard drives)?

Step 2: Establish priorities and set constraints. The second step in developing the network strategy is to understand the priorities of the company.

"Generally companies come to us with very clear objectives," Saenz said. "They want to add one distribution center, or close three regional warehouses and open one larger distribution center facility. They also might have a location in mind that they want us to evaluate."

Other priorities might be more general, such as designing a network that minimizes freight costs and reduces delivery times.

"An e-commerce retailer might want to reduce outbound shipping costs, so their priority would be a location closer to their customers," Saenz said. "They might also want to be located closer to Federal Express or UPS hubs, if that's how they are distributing their products."

Section 17

Constraints are also identified at this point. For example, in an ideal world, a company might best achieve its goals by adding three distribution centers but it can afford only one. Geography can also come into play: while the ideal location for a distribution center might be in the middle of Idaho, if labor isn't available, the facility needs to be sited somewhere with a higher population density.

"At the strategic level, we look in a very general way at road accessibility, rail networks and labor markets," Saenz said. "Rail, for example, can be critical for some suppliers." Saenz continued, "Then, at the tactical level, more analysis can be performed on transportation optimization, labor market surveys, etc."

Step 3: Run models and consider scenarios. Once information has been gathered and the priorities have been identified, it's time to plug all of the data into computer modeling software and let it run the numbers. Saenz's team relies on CAST modeling software from Radical, which is specifically designed to model supply chain networks. The software provides fact-based answers to complicated questions by evaluating numerous data points.

"Generally we start by running a baseline model with all of the existing distribution centers, suppliers, and customers," Saenz said. "Then we optimize this network, assuming no constraints. This gives us an idea of the best-case scenario, with no limitations."

Then the team starts building in the priorities and constraints established by the company.

If several scenarios have been discussed, each is run through the program. Then scenarios can be compared and ranked, with the best alternative usually becoming clear immediately. Saenz added, "With smaller networks, we perform the analysis with MS Excel, MS Access, and simple map generators to provide the same, accurate results."

Source: Carter & Burgess, "3 Steps to Optimizing the Supply Chain," www.c-b.com/information%20center/distribution%20&%20warehouse/ic.asp?tID=4&pID=250.

Key Concepts of Lean Procurement

There are four key concepts in most lean processes—center on people, postponement, optimization, and eliminating waste:

- **Center on People:** Most current processes rely on narrowly focused employees who perform repetitive tasks. Lean thinking prescribes transferring the maximum number of tasks and responsibilities to those workers. This actually adds value to the process and usually incorporates some system for measuring the bottlenecks, enabling you to find the cause and ultimately the cure.

- **Postponement:** The idea behind this is simple: delay any efforts until they are absolutely necessary. Also referred to as *pull*, this concept is fundamental to lean efforts. If you do nothing but add value, then you should be able to add value in as rapid a flow as possible. If this is not the case, then waste builds up in the form of inventory or extra wasted steps in a process. Essentially, postponement means that nothing is done until an upstream process requires it.

■ **Optimization:** This is the process of looking at the value chain as a whole and measuring the contributions of each activity as it relates to the effectiveness of the entire chain, not just the output of one step in the process. Most business activities have dependents and dependencies; in other words, the output of one activity is typically the input of another. Most activities have customers, in the form of internal or external people who consume the output of the given activity. Most activities also have inputs that are dependant on the output of another activity before they can add value. Take, for example, the assembly line—the velocity of the output of the finished goods is equal to that of the slowest activity in the process. This concept was popularized in *The Goal: A Process of Ongoing Improvement*, by Eliyahu M. Goldratt and Jeff Cox.

■ **Eliminate Waste:** Also known as "adding nothing but value," this is one of the most essential aspects of lean processes. For service organizations, it is typically the result of altering your processes in accordance with the other principles. The other way to accomplish this is to understand what value is, and what activities and resources are absolutely necessary to create that value. Once you have identified what value the organization or department provides, you are on your way to eliminating everything that is not critical in delivering that value. Think through your current processes and ask yourself if every activity adds value or if it is in place because "it's always been done that way." As a way to think about this, ask yourself who is the consumer of the service you provide. Put yourself in the shoes of that person or those people and examine how "customer-friendly" your process is and what parts of your process actually provide value to those people.

Source: Jon Strande, "A Guide to Streamlined Procurement," www.darwinmag.com/read/100103/purchase.html.

Five Steps to an E-Synchronized Supply Chain

Like no previous breakthrough, internet technology offers the potential for a single, universal mechanism of cooperation among companies. For any business process, the resultant implications are vast. But for supply chain management, they are awesome. Experts believe that the average Fortune 1000 multinational could capture $100 million in added value by mastering the "e-synchronized" supply chain.

So far, no organization has assembled all the ingredients needed to make e-synchronization happen. And, ironically, those that have come close often are constrained by a shortage of trading partners with similar levels of sophistication. Yet companies that are figuring it out typically share several characteristics. They usually have a well-developed ability to collaborate within their own organization and have extended that ability to achieve similar levels of collaboration with other organizations. In addition, they are enthusiastic innovators—adopting web-based technologies to increase internal and external information sharing, and readily migrating to new technologies and processes that increase business effectiveness.

For the rest of the world, however, five basic steps must be taken before e-synchronization becomes an endemic part of their business:

Step 1: Master business fundamentals. The defining characteristic of sophisticated multinationals such as Cisco Systems, Dell, and Sun Microsystems is the excellence of their conventional operations. Unfortunately, this is not the strong suit of most traditional multinationals, not because they lack awareness of this requirement but because of their inability to force through change. By contrast, the more sophisticated multinationals are operationally superior, partly because they needed that superiority to grow and partly because they are less constrained by traditional ways of doing things.

Step 2: Learn to operate in the web-based world. Achieving e-synchronization has much to do with implementing on the web what the organization already has developed to achieve operational excellence. The caveat is that, without operational excellence, e-commerce and e-procurement are likely to achieve virtual chaos rather than enhanced performance.

Step 3: Build new capabilities and relationships. One direct consequence of the web's ubiquity will be a loosening of long-term relationships between and among organizations in favor of shorter-term liaisons. In the e-synchronized world—where organizations all subscribe to the same set of standards—multinational corporations will come together in a series of brief cooperative engagements as expediency dictates. The key to success in this environment will be an ability to attract and assemble a portfolio of best partners.

Step 4: Manage complexity in real time. No company can sidestep the challenges of increasing complexity and decreasing time scales. Although the e-synchronized world offers a solution in the form of sophisticated tools and processes, it also requires that traditional companies learn new ways of operating. Making the transition demands an ability to learn in teams rather than as individuals, to develop the skills required to collaborate with customers and suppliers, and to experiment liberally and learn from the experience.

Step 5: Embrace change. Management's traditional role was to plan around the expected and then deal with the unexpected. More and more, however, the expected has become rare and the ability to optimize around the unexpected has become paramount. E-synchronization requires that companies make that leap without misdirecting their resources or business goals.

Source: Andrew Berger, "Five Steps to an e-Synchronized Supply Chain," *Supply Chain Integrated Marketing* (Accenture).

Change Is Good: A Step-by-Step Path to Best Practices

To survive and prosper today, you have to be at the top of your game. Your supply chain has to be better than your competition's supply chain. If you are great today, tomorrow you will be good and soon you will be out of business.

The best way to keep improving is to embrace best practices. This means understanding your customers' ever-changing requirements, having your operations and your costs thoroughly under control, getting the best return on investment, and realizing that you are never done with the job of continuous improvement.

Best practices are not events or a one-time activity. Rather, best practices involve a never-ending process that encompasses:

- Providing the best customer service.
- Leveraging equipment to minimize labor.
- Having a healthy, safe, and trained work force.
- Using systems and processes to continuously track and control movement of materials.
- Developing processes that eliminate duplication of effort.
- Having specific operational methods to meet all operational requirements.
- Using a commonsense application of technology to meet changing needs while minimizing the impact of implementing new technology.
- Managing day to day to get the most out of all aspects of the operation.
- Meeting and exceeding all corporate and government regulatory requirements while being proactive in planning for future regulatory requirements.
- Having contingency plans for meeting future identifiable operation challenges.

Step 1—Establish the Baseline. The process of best practices begins with the recognition that we can improve only that which we can measure. The first step is to select an aspect of the operation that we need to improve. Then we need to identify the parameters we want to measure. In the case of customer service, we would typically want to measure four parameters:

1. The correct product, which covers all characteristics of the product, including customer required shelf life.
2. A complete order, including all paper work, labeling, electronic submittals, etc.
3. On-time delivery. The customer does not care when it is shipped, only that it is received on time.
4. Perfect condition: no damage from the pallet and shipping container to the individual pack.

For each of these factors, one has to develop analytical measures. For example, the correct product can be tracked by conducting statistically based auditing of orders. The baseline should be presented graphically and tracked to identify and quantify problems, as well as to track the impact of improvements.

Step 2—Understand the Goal. The goal of best practices is to improve the entire operation. It is critical that improvements do not negatively impact other operations. For example, it does little to no good if improvements are made in receiving and in turn these improvements make the picking and shipping of product more difficult. The implementation of best practices requires that all members of the organization act as a single coordinated unit to identify and implement improvements.

These are the characteristics of operational best practices in supply chain performance:

- Understanding the importance of customer requirements and satisfaction when considering any changes to the operation. Changes cannot reduce customer satisfaction, and ideally changes should improve customer satisfaction.

- Developing a strategic plan that defines the requirements of an efficient and effective distribution system for both the present and future.

- Periodically reviewing and revising the strategic plan to reflect changes in the marketplace. All changes should be made with strong consideration of the strategic plan

- Having proper utilization of supply chain providers, including suppliers, manufacturers, 3PLs, and wholesalers. Supply chain partners can provide support in areas and functions that are not within your company's core competencies. In addition, supply chain partners can be used to handle peaks and unusual circumstances. For some organizations, supply chain partners are the best choices for the entire distribution process. For other companies, providers can assist in the introduction of new products or the creation of special packs.

- Conducting economic and qualitative evaluation of all potential improvements based on specific, weighted criteria. Nothing can kill a best practices program faster than the implementation of a change that is not economically justified or a change that has undesirable qualitative effects. Thus, all proposed improvements have to pass not only stringent economic analysis, but also qualitative analysis.

- When it comes to selecting and implementing warehousing technology, the first step is to define mission-critical functions and key business processes. Then select the technology solution that meets these requirements with little or no modification. Always keep in mind that the most important requirement is meeting customer satisfaction, both long term and during implementation.

Step 3—Develop Best Practices. Once the goals for the operation and measurements are in place, the understanding of all aspects of best practices must be identified. Key questions must include:

- What is the best use for the existing equipment?

- What modification will result in improved equipment utilization?
- How can we improve customer satisfaction?
- How do we eliminate duplication of effort?
- How do we handle peak requirements and what can we do to smooth out peaks?
- What changes can our vendors make that will improve the operation?
- What changes can we make to reduce vendor costs and thus prices?
- Are there alternate packaging materials and supplies that will improve customer satisfaction, reduce cost, and or improve the operation?
- What can we do to reduce utility costs?
- What improvements can be made to current software systems?
- What systems should be replaced or upgraded?
- What training will improve operations?
- How do we better meet our company and regulatory requirements?
- What are the proper safety practices?
- How can we improve ergonomics?
- What improvements can be made to maintenance?
- How will changes in one function impact other operations?
- What is the best use of supply chain partners?
- Where should unused raw material partials be stored?
- Where should auxiliary operations be located?
- What physical constraints affect decisions?
- How do we improve lot integrity?

Step 4—Implement Best Practices. The critical factors in implementing best practices are selling, planning, training, and testing.

- **Selling.** The key to implementing any change is to get everyone involved in making it a success. It is natural to resist change. Fully recognize that some changes may well make it more difficult to perform some jobs. Management can always just institute changes, but this leads to resistance and a lack of trust. It is better to take the time to explain why the change is being made and to enlist the ideas of everyone in the details of the improvement. Often, something as simple as adding some lighting will create a feeling that the change is everyone's idea and everyone works toward success.

- **Planning.** Few changes are as simple as they first appear. It is rare that a change does not require support from other functions and areas. And it is not uncommon for a change to limit capacity during start-up. Thus it is critical to plan for all changes in advance. With proper planning, all affected parties have an opportunity to prepare. One can be more confident that all new requirements will be accounted for and all required actions have been taken. Planning will show the impact of preparing and implementing the change on the throughput of the operation. Understanding the impact of throughput then makes it possible to avoid impacting customer service during peak periods.

- **Training.** New ways of doing things require that everyone be trained. The first goal of the training is to make certain that everyone knows about the improvements, how they affect the operation, and—most important—how the people are affected. The training must then address how the new tasks are to be accomplished. It is highly critical that the training include what to do when the unexpected or unusual happens.

   The training program has to be developed with strong consideration of adult learning requirements. Operating personnel are best trained with less classroom work and more hands-on learning.

Conclusion. If you are standing still, your competition will surely pass you. The use of best practices is an excellent way to continuously improve your operation. To ensure success, the keys are the following:

- Have an analytical understanding of the current state of the organization.
- Use a teamwork approach to implementing changes.
- Consider the impact of changes on the entire facility and organization.
- Have an implementation plan that includes selling the change, planning for the change, and training affected personnel.

Source: Tompkins Associates, Inc., "Change Is Good: A Step-by-Step Path to Best Practices," www.tompkinsinc.com/publications/competitive_edge/articles/12-04-BestPractices.asp.

Four Best Practices in Lean Procurement

- **Center on People:** In purchasing, there are two distinct groups of people—employees and vendor/suppliers. When considering the employees, the most effective strategy used by lean organizations is to empower employees with strategic accountability to perform tasks themselves. With proper business rules in place, you can empower users to perform purchases with pre-set spending limits, release requests, and similar initiatives. With vendors/suppliers, relationships are key and you need to be able to measure the effectiveness of those relationships. You should have tools in place to measure the performance of these constituents.

- **Postponement:** The two most wasteful items in purchasing are ordering too early and ordering what's not needed. By centering on people and allowing them to make purchases, you've taken a big step in the right direction in correcting both these wastes—but only if the empowered users are also aware of the concepts behind lean thinking. Typically, companies without a process in place for purchasing will be the most wasteful. Organizations that have a purchasing process in place will be effective only if they educate their users on the best practices of purchasing. Automating the process also contributes to the effectiveness of postponement. By limiting the items and quantities available to be ordered, users must conform to the guidelines prescribed by the business. Another critical success factors is tying replenishment to inventory by integrating your procurement software with your inventory system so you can improve your inventory turn and limit the likelihood of building unnecessary and excessive inventories.

- **Optimization:** Even a world-class purchasing process can have bottlenecks. One of the most common is in the form of approvals. If every purchase requires the approval of a single person, that person can become a constraint on the process. Another common bottleneck is necessity of human intervention when suppliers/vendors submit responses to the RFQ/RFP process. By automating the submission process and eliminating the time-consuming effort of validating the incoming data, companies can streamline this very costly activity by providing online tools that allow trusted vendors to submit data that is validated through software. Yet another common bottleneck occurs when the purchasing department receives numerous inquiries requesting status information. By providing status information to requestors and vendors through a web site or e-mail, interested parties are kept in the loop and the number of inquiries will decrease substantially.

- **Eliminate Waste:** By focusing on people, postponement, and optimization, you can effectively eliminate waste throughout the entire procurement process. However, eliminating waste in purchasing is not limited to just the efficiencies derived from the other principles in lean thinking. You should also examine all the activities that make up procurement for your organization. Doing this will help you identify superfluous steps that don't add value to the consumers of the process.

Source: Jon Strande, "A Guide to Streamlined Procurement," www.darwinmag.com/read/100103/purchase.html.

Five Components of Supply Chain Management

Supply chain management is the combination of art and science that goes into improving the way your company finds the raw components it needs to make a product or service, manufactures that product or service, and delivers it to customers. The following are five basic components for supply chain management.

1. **Plan.** This is the strategic portion of supply chain management. You need a strategy for managing all the resources that go toward meeting customer demand for your product or service. A big piece of planning is developing a set of metrics to monitor the supply chain so that it is efficient, costs less, and delivers high quality and value to customers.

2. **Source.** Choose the suppliers that will deliver the goods and services you need to create your product or service. Develop a set of pricing, delivery, and payment processes with suppliers and create metrics for monitoring and improving the relationships. And put together processes for managing the inventory of goods and services you receive from suppliers, including receiving shipments, verifying them, transferring them to your manufacturing facilities, and authorizing supplier payments.

3. **Make.** This is the manufacturing step. Schedule the activities necessary for production, testing, packaging, and preparation for delivery. As the most metric-intensive portion of the supply chain, measure quality levels, production output, and worker productivity.

4. **Deliver.** This is the part that many insiders refer to as logistics. Coordinate the receipt of orders from customers, develop a network of warehouses, pick carriers to get products to customers, and set up an invoicing system to receive payments.

5. **Return.** This is the problem part of the supply chain. Create a network for receiving defective and excess products back from customers and supporting customers who have problems with delivered products.

Source: CXO Media Inc., "Executive Guides: Supply Chain," guide.darwinmag.com/technology/enterprise/scm.

Procurement in Seven Steps

Procurement life cycle in modern businesses usually consists of seven steps:

- **Information gathering:** If the potential customer does not already have an established relationship with the sales and marketing functions of the suppliers of needed products and services (P/S), it is necessary to search for suppliers that can satisfy the requirements.

- **Supplier contact:** When one or more suitable suppliers have been identified, Requests for Quotes (RFQ), Requests for Proposals (RFP), Requests for Information (RFI), or Requests for Bids (RFB) may be advertised, or direct contact may be made with the suppliers.

- **Background review:** References for product/service quality are consulted, and any requirements for follow-up services—including installation, maintenance, and warranty—are investigated. Samples of the P/S being considered may be examined or trials may be undertaken.

- **Negotiation:** Negotiations are undertaken, and price, availability, and customization possibilities are established. Delivery schedules are negotiated, and a contract to acquire the P/S is completed.

- **Fulfillment:** Supplier preparation, shipment, delivery, and payment for the P/S are completed, based on contract terms. Installation and training may also be included.

- **Consumption, maintenance, and disposal**: During this phase the company evaluates the performance of the P/S and any accompanying service support, as they are consumed.

- **Renewal**: When the P/S has been consumed and/or disposed of, the contract expires or, if the product or service is to be reordered, the company reviews its experience with the P/S and determines whether to consider other suppliers or to continue with the same supplier.

Source: Wikipedia, "Procurement," en.wikipedia.org/wiki/Procurement.

Ten Steps to Supply Chain Success

The move is on for enterprises of all sizes to collaborate, connect, and share information to improve supply chain efficiencies.

Customers, suppliers, and distributors are evaluating and deploying dozens of component solutions that address specific aspects of supply chain management—design, planning, sourcing, scheduling, and execution. The common goal of each of these elements: supply chain optimization.

Companies still sitting on the sidelines wonder whether optimization technologies are too complex or cost-prohibitive to implement. In truth, optimization solutions can be rolled out like any other new technology, with pilots that demonstrate a clear-cut path to return on investment (ROI).

These guidelines for delivering tangible results are based on dozens of real-world manufacturing experiences with supply chain optimization.

1. **Start at the source.** The best place to begin optimizing the supply chain is during design and sourcing, where 80 percent of a company's supply chain costs are irretrievably locked in.

   For example, a company considering two prequalified sources for a component often chooses the supplier with the lowest purchase price, irrespective of other dimensions like lead time and quality. Why are these other dimensions important? The inventory costs associated with an inflexible supplier can nullify any of the original "lowest cost per component" savings. These complex interactions must be considered when designing and sourcing the best possible supply chain.

2. **Keep your eye on the prize.** Understand which key strategic goals speak most closely to overall company objectives. Are the objectives to reduce total cost, cut cycle time, or improve customer service levels? Optimize the supply chain to achieve these goals.

3. **Remember that the whole is greater than the sum of its parts.** Focus on total system performance rather than functional or departmental performance, particularly in complex, multi-enterprise supply chains. The most compelling benefits come to the

company that treats its entire, end-to-end supply chain with a holistic—rather than local—optimization approach. Think of the supply chain as an interdependent network, not individual silos; enhancements will have a ripple effect that positively affects other areas of the company.

4. **Plan for the unexpected.** Factor in demand and supply uncertainty, and ensure the flexibility to test dynamic "what if" situations across the entire chain. Some of the more robust optimization models now accommodate this unpredictability, which is still outside the realm of daily planning and execution solutions.

5. **Use reality as the basis.** Make sure that the supply chain optimization strategy can handle real-world constraints, including policies, implementation barriers, or other organizational constraints. A solution that addresses 80 percent of inefficiencies in the supply chain and delivers benefits today is infinitely more practical than a "perfect" solution that, in reality, is impossible to deploy. Additionally, seek solutions that succeed with the data already on hand.

6. **Appreciate that one small step is a giant leap.** Understand the metrics for quantifying a rapid, demonstrable ROI. Build agreement about what "rapid" means at the outset. Pursuing shorter-term objectives that can significantly improve financial performance today drives endorsement for future initiatives and the savings to fund them. This tangible payback ensures visibility at the executive level, which increasingly considers supply chain performance as a strategic imperative because of its impact on the bottom line.

7. **Open the lines of communications.** Break down organizational barriers with online collaboration tools that enable more effective decision-making across the entire supply chain. An added benefit: this collaboration supports companywide sharing of transferable skills and knowledge.

8. **Keep it simple.** In order to deliver positive results, supply chain optimization solutions must be easy to use and implement. Ensure that the people who will use the system can understand it and are equipped to modify and update it as needs change. Leverage solutions that require minimal training and integration time; this yields faster results and frees up employees for higher-value projects.

9. **Check that it plays well with others.** The most effective supply chains ensure a comprehensive, integrated approach, from design through sourcing, ERP, and logistics. If beginning with a single best-of-breed solution, ensure that it will support other supply chain and enterprise applications already in place.

10. **Know that the time is now.** A poorly designed supply chain can be a real business risk to operations and to a company's position in the industry. The wrong inventory levels, suppliers, and contract terms can add unforeseen costs that multiply every day, severely damaging the bottom line.

Source: Marcus Ruark, "Executive Comment: Ten Steps to Supply Chain Success," www.my-esm.com/digest/story/OEG20010705S0060.

Chapter 106

Understanding Manufacturing Costs

Three Types of Manufacturing Costs

Manufacturing cost estimates can usually be organized as shown below.

1. **Upfront Costs**

   a. Development "Guestimate"—Usually this is only an order-of-magnitude opinion of how difficult it might be to develop a "production ready" technology.

   b. Product Design—This is the work needed to specify a component in such a way that it can be produced. This differs from development in that there is no unproven product or production technology involved. There is usually iteration among the product designer, the tool designer, and the production people to optimize the design.

   c. Tooling Design and Fabrication—This is usually done by the tool maker. Production levels and peak capacity have the biggest impact. Tool life must also be considered.

2. **Production Setup**—The cost to set up for a production run, this usually includes some amount for the waste generated while tuning and testing the process. It is often impractical to set up for less than 10,000 or 20,000 units with mass production techniques.

3. **Production Costs**

   a. Component Production Cost—This is the incremental cost to produce "one more item" after it is in production. This usually includes raw material, machine time cost, machine operator cost, supplies, and post-production finishing.

   b. Assembly Setup and Assembly Cost—This is similar to the corresponding items for component production cost.

   c. Quality Control—This addresses what sample testing might be needed to ensure that the units work as intended.

Source: O'Connor Technical Systems, "Manufacturing Cost Estimates for Inventions," www.octs.com/inventhelp/mfrcost.htm.

Seven Key Points for Estimating Manufacturing Costs

1. Comparing a product with others can give a rough idea of manufacturing cost when you know the markup.

2. The minimum order price is often the biggest start-up cost.

3. A sensible strategy helps manage risk. Cost depends on the strategy you choose.

4. If you cannot describe your strategy, an estimate will be a waste of time and money.

5. Estimates usually include upfront, setup, and incremental production costs.

6. Patents that are prepared before manufacturing issues are analyzed may be of little value.

7. A preliminary technical evaluation can get you pointed in the right direction when you need to develop a strategy.

Source: O'Connor Technical Systems, "Manufacturing Cost Estimates for Inventions," www.octs.com/inventhelp/mfrcost.htm.

The Hidden Costs in Management Software

I. **The Changing Business Landscape.** In today's ever-changing business environment, managing operations is like shooting the rapids of a raging river. Just as you've coped with one challenge, another crops up where you least expect it. You think you see a path to take clearly ahead, but in an instant the riverbed drops, rocks emerge, and it's all you can do to keep your head above water. This is the nature of today's unpredictable business landscape, and everyone's in the same perilous boat. Especially for those responsible for warehouse and logistics execution, survival depends on the ability to respond quickly and efficiently to what lies ahead—and out of immediate sight.

Industry analysts have been observing this turbulence for some time now. They are virtually unanimous in their assessment of the one constant factor in today's business environment: change—accelerating change. Coping with change is posing difficult challenges throughout enterprise operations, and traditional solutions are proving woefully ill equipped to deal with the problems.

The Sources of Change. Typically the internet is seen as the principal driver of business change today, and there is no denying that the advent of the internet and the emergence of e-business as a dominant business model have dramatically altered the nature of business relationships. But the changes businesses face go deeper and further than the means by which a company communicates with its customers and suppliers; they permeate virtually all processes within the supply chain.

Collaboration is critical to success. Ubiquitous connectivity has ended the idea of the monolithic enterprise or "functional silo." Silos are nothing if not dysfunctional in today's competition. This means that market competition is no longer among enterprises, but rather among supply chains. As such, supply chain execution is at the heart of an enterprise's commercial vitality. It also means that collaborative capabilities are increasingly critical, as companies have to give customers and partners access to their information and services in order to compete with the speed and responsiveness today's markets demand. Leading industry analyst Gartner Group has labeled the new business paradigm "collaborative commerce." Those who have difficulty in adopting collaborative processes will struggle to meet the demands of new and emerging business models.

Even when companies grasp these sweeping changes in dynamics, change poses a difficult challenge as they plan for the future. Why? Sometimes change is predictable, but very rarely so.

The Difficulty of Planning for Change. Just think back two years about all the changes that have occurred in your business—both planned and unexpected. You couldn't have imagined the business challenges confronting you today: escalating customer demands, increasingly complex distribution models, time-to-fulfillment pressures heretofore unimagined. Not surprisingly, trying to implement warehouse management systems (WMS) or supply chain execution (SCE) solutions in the face of such uncertainty has proved a costly and ongoing puzzle for most that have made the attempt.

Consider the business challenges that have emerged in the last two years:

- **Cost management.** While cutting costs can't be considered a new business challenge, the level of demand for cost reduction—and sources of that demand—have multiplied as supply chains have become more integrated and better understood as a source of competitive advantage. The emergence of e-business options such as online exchanges and e-procurement systems has given more leverage to buyers to make demands of their suppliers, not only for better rates but also for faster delivery.

- **Inventory management.** With new business models emerging around internet-based collaboration, traditional models of inventory management are rapidly being transformed as customers look to minimize or eliminate inventory. Customers today may demand that you manage your inventory for them in their warehouses. This is not only a logistical challenge, but also an intellectual one: warehouse managers now need to think beyond their four walls. With inventory being kept at the customer site—within customer-defined acceptable levels—new tools are needed for accounting, for replenishing and decrementing stocks, and for determining order cycles on a regular basis.

- **Order management.** Order cycle times are being condensed as order frequency has increased dramatically. Orders themselves are coming in smaller sizes, so goods once shipped in full pallets must now be handled in smaller parcel shipments.

- **Customer service management.** All of this is occurring in an environment in which superior customer service is an expectation. Errors are unacceptable to the customer—and cannot be tolerated in an organization that wants to compete effectively. Accuracy is an increasingly critical determinate of profitability, in terms of both cost savings and revenue generation. In addition, customers expect their suppliers not only to deliver goods, but to provide value-added services as well.

The Resulting Challenge. While such demands paint a far different picture than the one observed two years ago, we know today to expect new challenges that will constantly alter that picture with ever-increasing speed. HighJump is one of the most interesting supply chain execution solution providers because its technology empowers companies to modify the system without the use of custom code. This is a very rare thing in the world of supply chain execution. Retail DC implementations are extremely complex, and HighJump's successful implementation at Circuit City provides further proof of the company's high-volume, complex implementations.

—Steve Banker, Director of Supply Chain Research

II. Defining and Finding a Solution. The imperatives of today's competition make the nature of an effective SCE or WMS solution quite clear. It must fit the needs of your business today while providing the ability to rapidly and cost-effectively respond to change in the future.

To fit your business today, the solution must address your core business issues and integrate easily with existing systems. To rapidly and cost-effectively respond to change, the solution must be inherently flexible—allowing you to meet increasing customer demands, build competitive advantage over time, and leverage technological advance—rather than just try to keep up with it.

The Conventional Approach. Conventional SCE and WMS systems have typically failed miserably in meeting these critical requirements. This is because most SCE and WMS vendors force you to adapt your business to their software, rather than adapt the software to the unique needs of your business.

Custom code is expensive, time-consuming, and risky! Because no out-of-the-box solution can provide a 100 percent fit with the individual needs of every business, the conventional approach has focused on offering a predetermined set of configuration options to address a range of typical needs. However, this approach brings with it wasted investment in the form of unnecessary features and functionality gaps where needs are not met. These functionality gaps are bridged with custom code—a labor-intensive, time-consuming, and potentially exorbitant proposition. The situation is further complicated as any initial code-based modifications tend to make subsequent changes even more expensive, risky, and time-consuming, and because these solutions are not prepared for change in the first place.

More often than not a perilous spiral occurs. Companies establish finite requirements and solution providers encase their solutions around those requirements. Six months later—which may be before these initial changes have even been completed—business needs have changed again and the system must follow suit. This means more custom code has to be written, tested, and implemented in what becomes a perpetual exercise.

In addition, change in one part of the system may have unintended effects on other parts of the system, a likelihood that increases with the volume of custom code and the nature of its implementation. In this scenario, system upgrades become hugely problematic because all code changes must now be applied again to the new version. This threatens the very stability of the systems they are intended to improve. So what started as an effort to build a solution oftentimes becomes an effort to control a burgeoning nightmare—one with very real risks.

An Alternative Approach: Proven Adaptability. HighJump Software, a 3M company, has taken a different view of the process—one that focuses on the need to adapt quickly and easily to a changing business environment. This approach has led HighJump to build WMS and SCE solutions that meet the unique needs of your business today while providing the flexibility to change without extraneous costs or disruption to ongoing operations.

This new approach addresses business needs effectively by providing "adaptability tools" that eliminate the need for custom coding. This tools-based system provides building blocks based on business process components that can be easily reconfigured to respond to changing business requirements in a fraction of the time of conventional systems—and at a fraction of the cost.

The results of this approach are remarkable, including:

- **Dramatic cost savings.** Costs can be cut by a factor of two to 200, with system implementation and maintenance so efficient that HighJump upgrades can be less expensive than upgrades of legacy systems—and can be completed in as little as four hours.

- **More rapid development time.** New functionality can be developed two to 200 times faster than with conventional systems.

- **Better use of new technology.** New technology is easily leveraged without business disruption, avoiding the obsolescence that is built into many conventional systems. Software providers are continuously working to improve their technology so it can be quickly and inexpensively applied to your advantage.

- **Mitigation of risk.** By eliminating the need for custom coding, HighJump minimizes the risk associated with change. As proof, HighJump Software has one of the highest success rates in an industry where implementation failures are far too common.

III. The Challenge Ahead. Change is real. It is a fact of business life. With today's increasingly intense and globally extended economic competition, change is creating pain in operations. This is happening so rapidly that companies face unplanned expenses to cover the excessive cost of labor and development time to upgrade their existing code-based systems.

The challenge for those looking to implement efficient SCE and WMS solutions is to find a solution that is flexible enough to meet today's core business needs, yet can adapt quickly and cost-effectively as those needs change over time. If a solution cannot do that, it will change from a solution to a problem.

Section 17

In these times, customers must be more demanding of their solution providers. They must challenge them to prove they can accommodate change—and if they can provide such proof—demand to know what the costs of accommodation will be over time.

Source: HighJump Software, *Exposing the Hidden Costs of Supply Chain Execution and Warehouse Management Software*, www.highjumpsoftware.com/promos/supply-chain-execution-wms-costs.asp.

Information Needed for Manufacturing Cost Estimates

Beginners sometimes go directly to a manufacturer to get a price before consulting an expert in production methodology and strategy. This is a mistake, for three reasons. First, because it ignores the intermediate steps needed to justify investing in the project. Second, because there's a good chance you are approaching a manufacturer that is mismatched to the job you have in mind. And, third, because you may be considering the wrong production process. You could waste a lot of time and money getting tooling quotes for a part that an expert could tell you would be better suited to another method that uses less costly tooling.

Basic Information for Estimates

1. **A parts list (often called a bill of materials) with the quantities of each component needed for every unit produced.** Organize this list by the product styles and variations you want studied. Don't forget to consider packaging and containers. (Sometimes the box is the most expensive single component.) Group the component parts as follows:

   - **Off-the-shelf:** Provide as much detail as you now know—i.e., make and model. Even if you don't know the manufacturer, list the retailers you know.

   - **Custom designed and/or manufactured:** Provide a sketch and describe as much as you can about the part, including how you think it might be made and from what materials.

   - **Concepts (anything not completely tested and proven):** Describe and sketch how you envision the component or assembly might work. Elaborate regarding any tests that have been done to verify that it will work that way.

2. **Production levels ("units per year") to consider for each style.** Indicate where common parts may be used between styles and variations. This will increase the production volume for those parts, which will decrease their cost. Describe the intended use for the items made at each level—i.e., non-working models, engineering tests, in-house product tests, market tests, initial sales, and low-level, mid-range, or full production.

3. **Peak capacity ("units per day") desired.** Will your production be steady and predictable? Or, like some seasonal products, will a large number of units be needed in a short time?

4. **Reaction time to changes in demand.** How quickly should production increase if demand is greater than capacity? This may be closely related to peak capacity, but there are other considerations. Would you invest more in tooling that can be quickly modified to produce more parts? Or, do you want to gamble that you can obtain new, higher-capacity tooling in time to meet demand and avoid losing market share? Tool delivery time can often be many months.

5. **Labor cost.** Tools that produce parts that are nearly ready for use cost more than tools that produce parts that need some hand finishing. Also, automated equipment can reduce handling and packing labor. Your consultant will need to know what labor cost to consider to recommend tool cost vs. labor trade-offs.

All of this information will help your expert recommend tooling and production options. It will be hard for any inventor to know the answers with much certainty at the start. However, just knowing that you need to think about these questions will help.

Other factors to consider are the budget and how much should be bet on your market predictions. Do you want the optimum tools and the most expensive options so that you will save money in the long run if you are right about exactly what the market will want? Or do you want to take a less risky approach with conservative options in case you learn that some changes would increase sales and profits?

Source: O'Connor Technical Systems, "Manufacturing Cost Estimates for Inventions," www.octs.com/inventhelp/mfrcost.htm.

Six Ways Supplier Collaboration Can Help Reduce Supply Chain Costs

1. **Compressing Cycle Times.** The opposing forces of delivering "the perfect order"— having the right product in the right place at the right time—and cost containment through reduced inventory levels must be balanced in your inbound supply chain. Delivering the perfect order is a key metric all organizations are focused on achieving. It is a calculation of the error-free rate for all components of the fulfillment and distribution process, including order entry, warehouse picking, on-time delivery, shipping without damage, and final invoicing. The benefits of the perfect order are clear: increased customer satisfaction, higher customer retention, and lower cost of lost sales. Delivering the perfect order should be accomplished without excess inventory or increased costs in the form of expedited deliveries. Striking this balance requires collaboration and real-time coordination with your supplier network. Reducing your suppliers' cycle times is the best way to realize the benefits of delivering the perfect order without incurring additional inventory and delivery costs.

Supplier collaboration solutions can reduce cycle times by creating an environment in which communication is automated, timely, accurate, and certain. These solutions provide the ability to efficiently communicate both current and forecasted demand requirements with suppliers and receive responses in real time. Additionally, supplier collaboration accommodates both system-to-system integration and web-based portals to allow for the accurate flow of real-time information and best practices. This drives further reductions in transaction costs.

In an economic environment where the supply chain often extends to include international shipping, the impact on the order-to-cash cycle throughout the supply chain can be extreme. International and homeland security can introduce significant barriers to timely delivery in a process already complicated by multiple touch points and opportunities for delay. The ability to proactively monitor and effectively supervise the end-to-end process directly determines your ability to manage long replenishment times profitably.

2. **Reducing Inventory Costs.** Whether your supply chain extends next door or across the ocean, the goal is the same: to optimize inventory levels and reduce the costs associated with carrying unnecessary safety stock. Supplier collaboration solutions create a tighter link between customer demand and your supplier network, allowing you to maintain high service levels while safely reducing inventory levels. With supplier collaboration, all stakeholders can automatically monitor inventory and demand levels to help ensure that variability in demand does not result in an unanticipated shortage. Working collaboratively with your supplier network to meet common customer demand allows for true supply chain synchronization, where cost is not simply pushed back into the supply chain to be passed on later, but rather is pushed out of the supply chain by allowing all links in the chain to plan based on timely, accurate information.

Further reductions in inventory costs can be achieved through the ability to plan labor more accurately. Optimal staffing levels can be maintained based on actual quantities of inbound materials. Labor productivity can also be enhanced by using inbound visibility to plan the flow of inbound goods to require the least amount of handling possible, whether through cross-docking, flow-through, or sequencing for the shop floor. Likewise, supplier collaboration solutions minimize the cost of product obsolescence in the face of ever-shortening product lifecycles by regulating inventory levels according to demand.

Supplier collaboration solutions can also be key in the successful conversion of inbound freight from prepaid to collect. Accurate shipment information can easily be obtained from suppliers to create optimal inbound routing and carrier assignment. With new government hours of service (HOS) regulations, accurate pick-up appointment scheduling has become a critical component in this process. Unbundling inbound transportation costs from material costs can also generate further savings by creating an apples-with-apples comparison of suppliers. Supplier collaboration solutions can also drive savings by keeping inbound routing requirements up to date across your supplier network where freight is not converted to collect.

3. **Streamlining the Inbound Flow of Goods.** You are continually challenged with optimizing both resources and the flow of goods throughout your supply chain. Collaboration creates more accurate and automated receiving processes, which in turn reduce costs. Use of a supplier collaboration solution empowers all suppliers in your network with the ability to provide you electronic ASN information. This will significantly enhance your ability to accurately and efficiently receive inbound goods. Additionally, these solutions can automate receiving with support of supplier shipping, labeling, and bar coding. Supplier collaboration solutions support additional value-added services such as special packing and sequencing requirements.

> "Receiving ASNs from suppliers typically reduces time to receive a shipment at the distribution center between 30–40%, with a corresponding reduction in costs to receive while improving the physical flow of goods. Web-based supplier portals can enable companies to receive ASNs from suppliers much more easily, especially those without EDI capabilities. Many companies can justify their investment in a supplier portal from the savings in receiving costs alone." (*Supply Chain Digest,* September 27, 2003)

4. **Streamlining the Flow of Information.** A supplier collaboration solution functions as a single, central repository for all information related to the inbound flow of goods. With the ability to reach all members of your supplier network regardless of the level of technology each has implemented, your supplier collaboration solution can serve as the system of record for all inbound material transactions. By centralizing this information and making it available through a web interface, you empower all stakeholders with an equal ability to participate in managing their respective segments of the supply chain. Duplicate orders and costly shortages can be prevented because stakeholders have access to accurate, current information. Sales can be enhanced by the ability to provide firm commitments on demand based on accurate item availability and inbound cycle times.

5. **Facilitating Proactive, Automated Management by Exception.** Most companies are moving toward increasingly lean environments, with less need for buffer stocks. Production plans and customer service are dependent on the timely receipt of raw materials, components, and finished goods. Unfortunately, the unexpected often happens and causes problems with these dependencies. Suppliers are suddenly out of stock, trucks are delayed, and suppliers ship short or late. The list goes on.

The faster you are aware of these exceptions, the faster and more effectively you can react to assess the impact to your supply chain and take appropriate steps. These may include changing manufacturing schedules, expediting shipments, finding another supplier, and communicating with customers. Visibility, real-time notifications, and automated event management through the PO and in-transit process allow you to have this capability.

Supply chain visibility demands automation and intelligence. As cycle times are compressed, visibility to potential performance issues must be intelligently and effectively elevated. Supply chain events such as shortages and quality issues must be automatically identified and elevated to the attention of managers or others who can work quickly to resolve them.

Or better yet, they are resolved automatically. Supplier collaboration solutions should manage the tactical issues of goods and information moving through the supply chain, freeing managers to "scan the horizon" for larger issues.

6. **Evaluating Supplier Collaboration Solutions.** Now that you have learned why supplier collaboration solutions are beneficial for your business, it is important to understand the variety of offerings on the market today. These solutions range in both price and functionality. It is essential that you carefully evaluate the unique requirements of your business to get a strong understanding of what you actually need and the budget you can allocate to the project. The following are key points for consideration:

- **Adaptable connectivity and integration model.** A solution that offers the same level of connectivity to "Mom and Pop" suppliers as well as the largest organizations will help ensure that everyone in your network is operating with the same information. The materials coming from small suppliers are rarely less important than those arriving from large ones. Likewise, you will need to be able to support a variety of transports and protocols for your trading partners, including EDI, XML, flat file, and web.

- **Support for real-time collaborative process management.** A solution that offers real-time collaboration empowers all stakeholders to participate in the process with current and accurate information. This creates an environment where exception conditions are automatically identified and solutions are quickly and effectively negotiated, with all parties informed and in agreement.

- **Integrated supply chain event management.** As discussed previously, management by exception is a key way supplier collaboration solutions drive cost reductions throughout your supply chain. To maximize your ability to leverage this functionality, a solution featuring configurable, automated exception management is the best choice.

- **Rapid implementation and simple user adoption.** Understanding the time frame and cost involved in system implementation and training is a critical step—and one many companies overlook in selecting supplier collaboration software. One component of the implementation process is the ability to integrate with your existing systems and often those of your suppliers. A solution with a configurable architecture will facilitate this. Another consideration for the implementation process is whether your vendor utilizes a best practices-based methodology. Ask potential vendors about their approach to implementation and how it will impact your business operations.

The system should also be easy to use so that users can become proficient with its functionality easily and quickly. Check with your vendor to understand the training and technical support options available.

- **Ease of configuration to meet changing requirements.** As with ease of implementation and training, configuration is an important element when it comes to evaluating and selecting supplier collaboration solutions. Your business, customer, and trading partner requirements are unpredictable, and it's impossible to know what sort of demands you'll face a month from now, much less a year away. Because of this, a system that easily and cost-effectively accommodates your changes will empower you to save money by performing modifications in house without involving your vendor. This type of configurable system will ensure that your long-term total cost of ownership is low.

- **Secure, controlled access for all trading partners.** Ensuring the security of your information is a top priority for your company and your supplier network. Supplier collaboration solutions must provide multi-enterprise, role-based security to both functions and data. Each trading partner represents a unique relationship and level of authority that need to be reflected in its ability to access information.

Conclusion. Supplier collaboration is a fundamental component of supply chain optimization. It is essential to your ability to meet customer demands on an ongoing basis and maintain profitability through continual process improvements and cost reduction. Understanding the relevance of supplier collaboration solutions, the manner in which they should be evaluated, and the five ways they can help you immediately reduce costs within your supply chain is an essential foundation for long-term success.

Source: HighJump Software, *Five Key Ways Supplier Collaboration Solutions Can Reduce Supply Chain Costs*, www.highjumpsoftware.com/promos/supply-chain-execution-wms-costs.asp.

Ten Ways Going Paperless in Manufacturing Will Reduce Costs Immediately

1. **Increased Levels of on-Time and Complete Shipments.** Manufacturing execution solutions provide the workflow, visibility, and event notification required to ensure that manufacturing is meeting customer demand. Additionally, these systems reduce non-value-added activity, increase data accuracy, and provide ERP and MRP systems with the real-time data needed to maximize processing, planning, and scheduling activities. This results in your ability to increase levels of on-time and complete shipments.

Creating a "paperless shop floor" means putting information in the hands of those who actually produce your products. The manufacturing execution solution creates this paperless environment by giving operators instant access to work instructions and CAD drawings, so they always have the direction required to build products that meet customers' demanding specifications.

Section
17

More importantly, having information about events as they occur allows companies to more easily identify and prevent potential problems or bottlenecks. For example, you may already be well aware of the problems created by shortages of key manufacturing materials that halt production, shipments arriving late or incomplete, and back orders. Additionally, a lack of visibility into machines operating outside control limits or processes not meeting appropriate yields can ultimately delay customer shipments. With event management, you have real-time notification of events and exceptions—often before they occur—so you are able to take proactive steps to manage them. This will likely save you the cost of expediting shipments that were unexpectedly completed late. Ultimately, you're able to keep costs in check, production and shipments on schedule, and customers happy.

By streamlining data acquisition and execution for operators on the factory floor, companies create efficient processes that consist only of value-added activities. The result is a leaner environment. From mobile data terminals for material handlers to strategically placed WIP stations or touch screens on the factory floor, workers are directed to perform tasks and collect information in real time using intuitive and graphical user interfaces. In addition, new employee training time is significantly reduced, while event-driven notification and workflow via electronic communication provides cross-training opportunities for the existing workforce. Manufacturing execution solutions empower companies to easily implement and manage truly paperless manufacturing processes.

2. **Strengthened Decision-Making Based on Real-Time Information.** Using a leading manufacturing execution solution, key personnel are given the decision-making data necessary to optimize manufacturing performance. From any location, the technology will allow managers to make immediate decisions on staffing, maximize labor efficiencies, control order fulfillment, and monitor machine utilization. Real-time performance reports such as actual vs. plan, production unit cycle time, production efficiency, scrap, and downtime by machine or work cell can all be specifically configured for up-to-the-second review and action by management.

When unexpected events occur, a manufacturing execution solution also helps managers and lead operators take proactive steps by utilizing a broad set of alerts and alarms. Using alert/alarm notification mechanisms such as e-mail, reader boards, lights, pagers, and phones, key individuals are notified about potential issues—before they become costly problems. Manufacturing execution solutions do not stop after notifying operators of unexpected events. This type of system pairs event notification with appropriate workflow so operators take suitable resolution steps in real time without affecting operations.

Production order status and work in process are readily accessible via web browser. This empowers managers and other decision-makers to communicate information electronically to customers and other manufacturing locations. Ease of information access also smoothes the daily transition between shift managers and provides updated statistics on key performance indicators (KPI), wellness views, and other important reports.

3. **Continuous Improvement: "Adapt or Fail."** Manufacturers have learned that staying competitive means they must continually improve their processes or face the consequences of technological Darwinism—"adapt or fail." Whether the initiative is Six Sigma or kaizen, traditional manufacturing execution solutions are nearly impossible to change when needed because they require expensive, time-consuming custom code-based modifications. Because of this, they become a barrier to operational excellence. This usually means that improvement opportunities are lost or work-arounds are developed to accomplish tasks outside of the system. This results in poor data accuracy.

A new type of adaptable manufacturing execution solution has recently been built on the belief that software should be a catalyst for continuous improvement—not an obstacle. These adaptable manufacturing execution solutions not only provide a detailed view of plant history, but their flexible architecture also allows you to reconfigure processes quickly and cost-effectively as your manufacturing operations change. It also provides metrics needed to make fact-based decisions and adapt as manufacturing operations improve over time.

4. **Maximized Supplier Relationships.** In today's lean and just-in-time manufacturing environments, collaboration with key suppliers is essential. The best manufacturing execution solutions provide manufacturers with the capability to exchange information among trading partners and enable true collaborative execution up and down the supply chain. A secure web portal replaces time-consuming phone calls and faxes as the basis for real-time information sharing and improved inventory visibility—critical factors in enhancing collaboration and streamlining supply chain operations.

Some manufacturing execution solutions also provide both the communication and visibility necessary to facilitate the effective delivery of goods from supplier to buyer. From the point of purchase order (PO) release at the buyer's location through fulfillment, shipment, and receipt, processes that have historically been performed manually—or in some cases simply not performed—are automated. With improved communication regarding compliance and/or serialized labeling requirements, inventory is received at the dock door with the required bar codes already applied. Functionality can also be provided to allow suppliers to perform other value-added services for their customers, including demand-pull replenishment, advanced shipping notification (ASN), and supplier quality inspections.

5. **Rapid Product Recall Decisions.** Product safety and quality are paramount concerns for manufacturers. When there are concerns about safety or quality, it is essential for manufacturers to have traceability tools that assist them in making product recall decisions. Manufacturing execution solutions aid in this process by capturing detailed product genealogies. When suppliers communicate a product defect, it is possible to trace exactly which finished goods were manufactured using the supplier's defective

Section 17

component. This traceability can be achieved using lot number, serial number, or other product attribute such as version, revision, or "born-on date."

Product recalls often result in enormous costs for the company issuing the recall. In most cases, companies lack information about the affected products. This results in companies inspecting individual products or being overly cautious and recalling products that have no risk of quality or safety issues.

Manufacturing execution solutions bridge this information gap for many manufacturers. With detailed product and order history information, these systems help companies deal with recalls in a timely, cost-effective manor.

6. **Leveraged ERP Investment.** Manufacturers that have implemented an ERP system have invested significant effort (and money) creating an enterprise software solution. Despite these investments, manufacturers often find their ERP systems do not provide the results they expected on the shop floor. ERPs often fall short because they are overly complex, difficult for shop floor employees to use, and rooted in traditional MRP batch-based processing. A manufacturing execution solution is designed to leverage an ERP investment, not replace it.

Manufacturing execution solutions address these issues by providing intuitive execution capabilities based on a real-time, lean execution philosophy. This means manufacturers get the best of both worlds—easy-to-use execution tools for the shop floor that also support planning decisions by continuously feeding real-time transaction information to the ERP. Manufacturing execution solutions share information with the ERP in real time, allowing the ERP to have an accurate representation of shop floor activities. With real-time visibility to execution, the ERP makes intelligent decisions about supply/demand matching and order promising.

7. **Reduced Cost of Regulatory Compliance.** Manufacturing environments are becoming increasing regulated. Whether the compliance requirement is for the FDA or Sarbanes-Oxley, the costs associated with achieving compliant processes can be excessive. With a rich transaction history that provides detailed audit trails and electronic approval processes, a manufacturing execution solution will facilitate compliant processes without excessive paperwork and manual work-arounds. Additionally, a manufacturing execution solution is designed to be responsive to change over time. This means that new regulatory requirements are easily met without system upgrades or customizations.

8. **Personalized Manufacturing.** Customer-specific manufacturing is a trend driving increased complexity and cost for today's manufacturers. Customer specific bills of materials, routings, and test instructions are challenging to manage, but can be a source of competitive differentiation. Manufacturing execution solutions respond to this challenge by offering personalization capabilities that meet today's customer requirements and adapt to meet tomorrow's unforeseen demands.

The ability to personalize a manufacturing execution solution is a key benefit—but not one that all applications offer. The greatest level of benefit will be achieved through a solution that accommodates personalization via configuration tool sets. With this type of platform, configurations can be made easily and cost-effectively. This means the manufacturers—not the solution vendors—truly own the system. With a flexible manufacturing execution solution, there is no custom coding required for configuration; changes carry over, and workflow can be altered as needed after the system go-live. The result of this is that the system's total cost of ownership is greatly reduced over the lifetime of the application.

9. **Focused Technology Approach.** With the most robust manufacturing execution solutions, nearly any station or work cell in the facility can be integrated into the system and either monitored, controlled, or reported against. Machines, scales, gauges, statistical process control (SPC) systems, PLCs, label printers, serial devices, PDAs, automated material handling equipment, wired and wireless terminals, and RFID systems are integral parts of manufacturing execution—and the best manufacturing execution solutions will integrate seamlessly with all of them. Manufacturing execution solutions often feed multiple host systems and facilitate reporting beyond the current capabilities of many ERP systems.

Solving the problems inherent in today's manufacturing environment is best accomplished using a modular technology approach. Manufacturing execution solutions start with bar code or RFID data acquisition to improve order visibility and extend beyond basic data collection as appropriate in each company's individual situation. This allows for a right-sized application based on current business needs and areas requiring the most attention. Oftentimes, this provides self-funding for future projects because ROI is generated quickly.

10. **Increased Business Value with Collaborative Manufacturing.** In today's emerging global economy, seamless communication does not stop at the four walls of the plant. Sharing information in real time both within the enterprise and beyond is an essential component to maintaining information integrity and achieving operational excellence. This communication must also include supply chain-wide notification of status and events in real time to effectively link a global network of suppliers, manufacturers, and customers. The right manufacturing execution solution will empower manufacturers to achieve seamless integration across their business systems and software—while protecting IT investments and customer relationships. It will achieve this by integrating web-based solutions directly with enterprise and business-to-business applications. A manufacturing execution solution should also provide the platform for real-time information flow, eliminate process gaps, and deliver competitive advantage—eliminating the delays and errors caused by systems that cannot effectively share operational data.

Finding the Right Manufacturing Execution Solution for Your Unique Environment
As you move toward coupling your manufacturing operations tightly with logistics, transportation, and customer demand, finding the right solution is key. As with any enterprise-wide software evaluation process, there are a handful of important ques-

tions that must be answered prior to selecting a vendor. You must be able to find a solution that addresses your business's specific pain points at a cost that works within your budget. For each vendor involved in the selection process, it is essential that your selection team gather detailed responses to the following issues:

- **Breadth of technology**—Does the vendor offer a wide range of supply chain-related solutions that integrate easily on the same platform? Does it have experience integrating with a variety of software and hardware systems? Does it have a history of releasing product upgrades containing new functionality that demonstrates a commitment to excellence in the space?

- **Ability to adapt to change**—How does the vendor approach changes to your system as your requirements shift? Does it utilize costly custom code? Do these changes carry forward during an upgrade?

- **Company history**—Has the company been in business for a number of years? Does it have a track record of solving problems for manufacturers? Does the product line demonstrate progressively more complex technologies developed using the most advanced toolsets?

- **Financial stability**—Will the company be around in three years to support the system you have purchased? Are the vendor's sales growing? Does the company have a sufficient amount of emergency capital in case of an economic downturn?

- **Customer base**—Does the vendor have a long list of satisfied customers? Are the majority of these customers referenceable? Can the vendor prove it can keep customers happy over the long term?

- **Implementation success**—Has the company ever had a failed implementation? If so, how recently? What were the reasons?

Conclusion

By now the good news for manufacturers should be clear: manufacturing execution solutions offer a host of bottom-line benefits through the creation of a "paperless shop-floor environment." The most effective manufacturing execution solutions will provide you with the tools necessary to cost-effectively increase productivity, eliminate non-value-added activities, decrease operating costs, and eliminate the potential for errors and waste. By leveraging this type of solution to streamline your operations and "go paperless" on the shop floor, you'll have the information and processes in place to meet stringent customer demands on time, every time.

Source: HighJump Software, *10 Key Ways "Going Paperless" with Your Manufacturing Operations Will Drive Immediate Cost Reduction*, www.highjumpsoftware.com/promos/supply-chain-execution-wms-costs.asp.

Manufacturing Tax Tips

Manufacturing companies may be liable for manufacturer excise taxes as well as the federal highway vehicle use tax. These companies may also be eligible to claim an income tax credit or a refund for gasoline, diesel fuel, or kerosene that is used in nontaxable uses.

Manufacturers are responsible for manufacturer's taxes on the following items. (For more information on each item listed, see IRS Publication 510, *Excise Taxes*, www.irs.gov/publications/p510/index.html.)

- Sport fishing equipment—tax based on the sale price of the item
- Bows—tax based on the sale price of the item
- Arrow components—tax based on the sale price of the item
- Coal—tax based on either the sale price of the item or the weight of the item
- Tires—tax based on the weight of the item
- Gas guzzler automobiles—tax based on the fuel economy rating of the automobile
- Vaccine—tax is based per dose

For purposes of reporting and paying manufacturers' taxes, a manufacturer includes both producers and importers.

A manufacturer is any person who produces a taxable article from new or raw material, or from scrap, salvage, or junk material by processing or changing the form of an article or by combining or assembling two or more articles. If you furnish the materials and keep title to those materials, and to the finished article, you are considered a manufacturer even though another person actually manufactures the taxable article.

An importer is the person who brings an article into the United States, or withdraws an article from a customs-bonded warehouse for sale or use in the United States.

A sale is defined as the transfer of title to, or the substantial incidents of ownership in, an article distributed to a buyer for consideration, which may involve the receipt of money, services, or other things. A sale can include both use and lease of an article.

A manufacturer who uses a taxable article is liable for the tax in the same manner as if it were sold.

The lease of an article (including any renewal or extension of the lease) by the manufacturer is generally considered a taxable sale. However, for the gas guzzler tax, only the first lease (excluding any renewal or extensions) of the automobile by the manufacturer is considered a sale.

Credits or Refunds

A credit or refund of the manufacturers' taxes may be allowable if the tax-paid article is, by any person:

- Exported
- Used or sold for use as supplies for vessels (except for coal and vaccines)
- Sold to a state or local government for its exclusive use (except for coal, gas guzzlers, and vaccines)
- Sold to a nonprofit educational organization for its exclusive use (except for coal, gas guzzlers, and vaccines)

In addition a credit or refund of manufacturers taxes may be allowable for the following special cases:

- Taxable articles in which the price is readjusted by reason of return or repossession of the article
- Tax-paid articles for further manufacture of another article subject to the manufacturers taxes (except for coal)

Heavy Highway Use Vehicle Tax

A truck or truck tractor is subject to the highway vehicle use tax if it:

- Is a highway motor vehicle (generally, a vehicle moved by its own motor and designed to transport a load over the public highways, even if it is designed to do other things),
- Is registered or required to be registered for highway use,
- Is used on a public highway, and
- Has a taxable gross weight of at least 55,000 pounds (taxable gross weight means the weight of the vehicle plus the weight of the trailers and semi-trailers customarily used in connection with vehicles of the same type, plus the weight of the maximum load customarily carried on vehicles, trailers, and semi-trailers of the same type).

The tax applies to the first use of a taxable vehicle on a public highway during the taxable period, which is each July 1st through June 30th. The person in whose name a taxable vehicle is registered or required to be registered must pay the tax on Form 2290, *Heavy Highway Vehicle Use Tax Return* (PDF, www.irs.gov/pub/irs-pdf/f2290.pdf). The tax is due by the last day of the month following the month in which the vehicle is first used during the taxable period. Thus, if you use a taxable vehicle in July, you must file Form 2290 by August 31. See Form 2290, *Heavy Highway Vehicle Use Tax Return* (PDF), and Publication 378, *Fuel Tax Credits and Refunds* (www.irs.gov/publications/p378/index.html).

Fuel Tax Credits and Refunds

A federal excise tax is imposed on gasoline ($.184 per gallon), clear diesel fuel ($.244 per gallon), and clear kerosene ($.244 per gallon). The amount of these taxes may be credited or refunded if these fuels are used in many types of off-road uses. Common off-road uses include use as heating oil, use in stationary engines, use in non-highway vehicles, and use in separate engines mounted on highway vehicles.

Generally, refunds of $750 or more may be claimed quarterly on Form 8849, *Claim for*

Refund of Excise Taxes (PDF, www.irs.gov/pub/irs-pdf/f8849.pdf). Claims not made on Form 8849 may be claimed as income tax credit on Form 4136, *Credit for Federal Tax Paid on Fuel* (PDF, www.irs.gov/pub/irs-pdf/f4136.pdf). See the forms and their instructions for specific claim requirements.

Note that a credit or refund is not allowable for the following:

- Any use in the propulsion engine of a registered highway vehicle, even if the vehicle is used off the highway.
- Any fuel that is lost or destroyed through fire, spillage, or evaporation.
- Any use of dyed diesel fuel or dyed kerosene. In fact, you may be subject to a substantial penalty if you use dyed fuel as a fuel in a registered diesel-powered highway vehicle.

It is important to keep records to support your claim. Keep these records at your principal place of business. These records should establish the number of gallons used during the period covered by the claim, the dates of purchase, the names and addresses of suppliers and amounts bought from each in the period covered by the claim, the purposes for which you used the fuel, and the number of gallons used for each purpose.

Source: Internal Revenue Service, "Excise Taxes—Manufacturing Tax Tips," www.irs.gov/businesses/small/industries/article/0,,id=100265,00.html.

# Chapter 107

Patents and Licensing

Ten Costs Involved in Patents

Costs Involved in Patents (as of February 1, 2005)

Disclosure Document ... $10

Provisional Application ... $200

Utility Patent Filing Fee ... $300

Design Patent Filing Fee ... $200

Plant Patent Filing Fee ... $200

Utility Patent Issue Fee ... $1,400

Design Patent Issue Fee ... $800

Plant Patent Issue Fee ... $1,100

Printed Copy of Patent ... $3

Patent Renewal Costs

... After 3.5 years $900

... After 7.5 years $2,300

... After 11.5 years $3,800

Source: Inventors' Association of South Central Kansas, "Steps of Inventing," www.inventkansas.com/content.php?cid=1003.

SCORE's Ten Steps to Protect Your Great Idea

1. Put all your ideas, notes, and drawings in an inventor's journal, and have it signed, witnessed, and dated. Be careful about disclosing your ideas to anyone—use a confidentiality or non-disclosure document when discussing your ideas.

2. File a Disclosure Document Program with the United States Patent and Trademark Office (www.uspto.gov). This costs only $10 for two years of pursuit of patenting, but it's not a patent.

3. Conduct a Preliminary Patentability. Search to discover what patents exist like your ideas—and get a patent attorney to render you a Patentability Opinion. There are many ways to conduct the search, including the Patent Depository Libraries on the www.uspto.gov web site. File a PTO Provisional Patent Application for one year if all looks good.

4. Make a model, demo, or illustration and conduct preliminary market research with end users. Know the consumers of your product and listen to feedback. Use feedback to fine-tune your project.

Section 17

5. Investigate intellectual property filings such as utility and design patents in the United States and overseas. Also investigate copyrights, trademarks, service marks, and domain name registrations for web sites. Explore U.S. and international protection options and limitations.

6. Think about the two main pathways to inventing success: entrepreneurship or licensing. How do you want to be rewarded for your great ideas? The pathway you choose will dictate a lot of your actions—and budget.

7. Do not fall prey to invention development/promotion scams, which are prevalent. Check with the Federal Trade Commission (FTC, www.ftc.gov) for a list of these unscrupulous firms. If their promises sound too good to be true, they probably are. Get real professional help and seek the support of legitimate inventor organizations.

8. Investigate competitive products to make your product superior or better priced. Employ brainstorming techniques to evolve and accelerate the marketability of your ideas.

9. Find an inventor mentor—someone who's done this process before—to provide guidance.

10. Believe in your ideas and persevere—it takes some time and effort to do all this right. Be realistic about your goals and good luck.

Source: Alan Tratner, SCORE Counselor from Santa Barbara, CA, "10 Steps to Protect Your Great Idea: Got a Great Idea? Follow these First Steps," www.score.org/protect_ great_ idea.html.

Principles of a Patent License Agreement

Patent license agreements are based on two bodies of law—the law of contracts, which enforces the promises of people, and the law of torts, which enforces the reasonable conduct of people.

A typical agreement is outlined below. The headings shown are representative of the kinds of things you should think about (and cover) in a patent license agreement. Your actual agreement may have different headings, more or fewer, and the points mentioned may be covered in different order. It is important only that you give thought to these points and make certain they're covered somewhere.

Note that these points are generally applicable to license of other intellectual property rights. Note also that the main difference between a license and an assignment is that the former provides that the Licensor retains legal title of the property and the latter does not.

I urge you to retain an attorney in the preparation (and negotiation) of your agreement and, in particular, a patent attorney, i.e., one who understands the problems encountered under intellectual property law.

Heading—Parties—Date

This agreement is effective as of such and such a day, by and between you, your address (hereinafter referred to as Licensor), and ABC Company, a corporation of Michigan, their address (hereinafter referred to as Licensee).

Recitals—Background. Material to aid in interpreting the agreement. It's usually not a binding part of the agreement (but may be made so if the attorney desires). Construction is generally along the following lines:

Witnesseth,

Whereas John Doe is the inventor of such and such, and has patents related to such and such, and

Whereas ABC Company is in the business of manufacturing such and such, and is interested in obtaining a license, etc.

One can continue on with as many such recitals as deemed appropriate. This is generally followed by a statement such as:

Now therefore, in consideration of the mutual covenants and promises hereinafter set forth, it is mutually agreed by and between the parties hereto as follows:

Now we get to the main body of the agreement. These are the promises that the parties are making to each other. If these promises are not kept, then presumably there is a breech of contract. Under the law of contracts, there are remedies for the breech. The contact itself will provide some remedies; the law of contracts will provide others.

Definitions. Devote some time to the definitions. They make it easier to write the rest of the agreement in a form that's easier to understand. Generally, you'll want to identify the licensed patents, licensed products, territory covered, and such terms as Net Sales, Improvements, etc.

Grant of License. Is the license to be exclusive or non-exclusive? May the Licensee grant sublicenses? What rights do you reserve solely to yourself? Make sure these are clearly stated.

Payments. Are there to be minimum payments per period? How much (in dollars or units)? This is especially important for exclusive licenses. What is the royalty percentage and what is it based on? This is usually Net Sales. Who will pay the patent expenses, if it's still pending, and the patent maintenance fees?

Records and Reports. What reports will the Licensee provide to verify the base that your royalty is applied to? When? This is usually quarterly. What access do you have to Licensee's records for audit purposes, and what is the procedure? How long must the Licensee retain these reports after termination?

Improvements. What happens in the event you make improvements in the invention? What happens in the event Licensee makes improvements in the invention?

Infringement. Who's responsible for enforcing (i.e., prosecuting infringers of) the

Section 17

patent? Keep in mind there may occur situations in which it is in the Licensee's interest to let the patent fail. What happens if Licensee's product(s), based on your patent, infringes the patents of others? You should avoid taking on this responsibility.

Patent Markings. If a patent number can be put on a product, it's good practice to require that it be done.

Other Obligations of Licensee. Will Licensee promise to produce some quantity level of product? Some dollar level of sales? To use best efforts to commercialize? To maintain some quality level? Does Licensee indemnify you for product liability? If so, make sure that's clearly stated and that it survives termination of the agreement.

Disclaimer of Agency. Statement that the parties are independent contractors, i.e., the actions of one are not binding on the other.

Insolvency of Licensee. What happens if the Licensee goes out of business? Becomes insolvent? Declares bankruptcy? Be sure to include provisions that automatically return the rights to you and don't get tied up with Licensee's encumbered assets.

Waivers and Modifications. Statement that occasional waiving of your rights, e.g., acceptance of late payments, does not alter your contract rights. Statement that the contract can be modified only in writing.

No Warranties. Statement that you are providing no other warranties. Avoid warranting Licensee's freedom from infringement of patents of third parties. Try to avoid warranting that the patents is valid. Try to avoid being deemed a "merchant" under the Uniform Commercial Code—the UCC is stacked in favor of the buyer. Try to exclude any liabilities for consequential damages.

Notices. What notices are required? Where and to whom are they to be sent? When do they become effective?

Transfer of Interest. Can Licensee transfer its rights? You would typically prefer not.

Term. How long is the license to last? Generally it's to expiration of the patent (or the last expiring patent), except as provided under Termination.

Termination. This is an important section—it's your way out if things don't work out as expected. Include any defaults not covered elsewhere. What is the form of notices of default? How long has Licensee to correct defaults? What happens to Licensee's products in process? Orders in process?

Compliance with Law. What laws can be violated by Licensee? Import-export regulations? Anti-trust? EPA? FDA? Make sure Licensee agrees to obey and conform to such laws and regulations.

Entire Agreement. Statement that this is the entire agreement and that you're making no other representations. Try to exclude any liability for (your) misrepresentation.

Final Provisions. What law governs the agreement? Statement that the agreement is binding on heirs, successors, etc. Statement that headings are for convenience and not binding.

Execution of Agreement. In witness whereof, the parties have caused this agreement to be executed by the duly authorized officers at the places and on the dates indicated below.

Other Considerations. The following topics frequently come up in patent license negotiations. They are best dealt with by separate agreements.

Know-How and Technical Assistance. Licensee may wish certain services or materials from you in addition to the patent rights conveyed above.

Trade Secrets. Licensee may wish certain trade secret rights in addition to, or in place of, the patents rights conveyed above.

Options. Licensee may wish some time before executing the final agreement. This can be covered in an option agreement, attaching the license agreement. In return for some consideration, you give them an option, for a specified time, to acquire the license.

Royalties. As a general rule of thumb, at least as a starting point, you can expect a royalty of about 5 percent of net sales. Be aware that this varies considerably across industries—it's certainly not 5 percent in the auto industry.

Recognize that you are trying to combine your rights and the Licensee's resources in a way that will benefit both of you. The Licensee is looking at profitability. It's trying to balance its risk against its potential gain. In negotiations, try to quantify this. The general feeling is that the Licensor should get about 25 percent of the pre-tax profitability and the Licensee about 75 percent.

Above all, don't overprice—this is the worst deterrent to successful licensing.

Negotiations. The key to successful negotiation is thorough preparation. Know your own (reasonable) goals and understand, as best you can, where the other party is coming from.

During negotiations, remember that your objective is a win-win resolution. Be flexible. Control your impatience, your anger. Listen. Watch for communication gaps and resolve them. And above all, maintain a sense of humor.

Source: The Entrepreneur Network, "The Patent License Agreement" (summary of a talk by John Sobesky), tenonline.org/art/8905.html.

Ten Points to Consider When Conducting a Patent Search

1. **Introduction.** Many inventors conduct a preliminary patent search prior to enlisting a patent agent or patent attorney to file a patent. This search is usually conducted

solely to determine uniqueness. If they find no patents exactly like their invention, they are happy and continue on their merry way. This is a very poor approach. We encourage examining patents closely to find additional possible product features, identify other potential uses for products, identify companies recently receiving patents in the area (potential licensees), and closely study the background sections and any data presented in the background sections and any data presented in the patents. You can learn a great deal from those who have gone before.

This page contains a few links to non–U.S. patent information; however, all the comments apply only to searching U.S. patents.

This page does not address these questions: "How can I protect my idea? Is my invention patentable? Should I seek patent protection? What kind of patent protection should I seek? When should I patent my invention? How much does a patent cost? How do I license an invention? Which web site is best to use when searching patents? Does my invention infringe on someone else's patent(s)? Should I get more than one patent? Should I file foreign patents? How can I avoid being caught in an invention scam?" These questions are best left to patent attorneys, patent agents, licensing professionals, and reputable inventor organizations. *Do not* ask us these questions!!! The United Inventors Association (www.uiausa.com) and National Inventor Fraud Center (www.inventorfraud.com) are good national resources. *Inventors' Digest* magazine (www.inventorsdigest.com), an excellent source in its own right, provides an online list of inventors groups around the country where you can obtain meet other inventors and often receive assistance with your problems.

2. **General U.S. Patent Information.**

   A. We suggest you visit your local Patent and Trademark Depository Library (www.uspto.gov/web/offices/ac/ido/ptdl/ptdlib_1.html) if at all possible. Patent and Trademark Depository Libraries can answer many of your questions, expose you to the local resources, and teach you how to use their patent search system. Many require appointments; call ahead and make one if necessary.

   B. The U.S. Patent and Trademark Office (USPTO) Independent Inventor Resources site (www.uspto.gov/web/offices/com/iip/index.htm) provides a nice introduction to patents.

   C. Most free U.S. online patent databases cover patents issued during the last 20–25 years. If the device is based on older technologies, you need to use one of the fee-based databases or one of the Patent and Trademark Depository Libraries.

3. **Why Conduct a Patent Search?**

   A. Patent searches are conducted for many purposes. Among them are to do the following:

      1. Determine if a particular invention is unique.

      2. Identify potential features for a new product.

      3. Identify other possible uses for a new product.

4. Determine independent inventors or companies currently or historically obtaining patents in a particular area.

5. Find the patent(s) for a particular invention.

6. Determine the state of the art in a particular area.

7. Identify patents in a specific field for generating citation maps (a tool in determining the relative importance/value of a specific invention).

8. Study the rate of innovation in a particular area.

9. Determine the patent portfolio of a specific company.

10. Determine if an invention infringes upon the intellectual property rights of others.

11. Learn about an industry or a specific company.

12. Search for potential solutions to design or safety problems.

13. Identify potential licensees.

14. To identify additional reference materials (journal articles, books, product literature) of use to those working in this area. Patents often list printed reference materials.

15. Identify inventors working in a certain field.

4. Patent Search Databases. The primary free access to U.S. patent databases is through the following:

A. USPTO web site (www.uspto.gov)

B. esp@cenet site (ep.espacenet.com), which allows U.S. searching
   (The USPTO site requires a TIFF viewer to view the images.)

5. Patent Search Procedure. We normally search to determine uniqueness, identify potential additional features for the product, identify additional potential uses for a product, or identify potential solutions for a design or safety problem. After trial and error, we have settled into the procedure below. It will meet the needs of most patent searchers.

Whether you search online (in any site), on a CD-ROM database, in person at a Depository Library, or at the Patent Office, the same procedure is followed. Below is a very brief description of our U.S. patent search procedure.

Each site/database has its own version(s) of the tools and different means for accessing images, stores patents back to different dates, and stores different degrees of patent information (bibliography only, abstracts, full text, images in different formats or not at all). Some do not update class/subclass changes. All have different search tools for searching for multiple words, by class/subclass, inventor, assignee, patent number, etc. The sites are sometimes down or very slow. We usually find it faster to use them in the middle of the night. Most well-known patent databases are continually changing and changing their interfaces. You just need to remember the procedure, find the tools needed to conduct the procedure, make sure the database meets your needs, and follow the procedure.

The links to the tools below refer to the U.S. Patent and Trademark site. The same tools can be found on most major patent search sites or on independent sites and then applied on the major sites. Make sure you are using current tools; they are continuously being updated.

A. The Steps

1. We usually "shoot from the hip" to start with by searching for any specific patents we may be aware of in this area, patents of companies we know work in this field, patents invented by inventors we know in this field, etc. Then, we settle down into the procedure below.

2. We try a few relevant words in the word search engine and see what turns up. If we turned up any patents in the "shoot from the hip" step above, we examine them for possible search words. We record the search words on a page in a project notebook and add other words as they come to mind or we encounter them in other patents. Usually the word list becomes separated into groups of words covering different aspects of the invention.

3. Access the Classification Index (www.uspto.gov/go/classification/uspcindex/index-touspc.htm). (In paper it is about the size of a small town phone book.) Look up your topic and you will find a class number. The area you are interested in may have several class numbers. (For example, marine propulsion and propellers [impellers] are in two separate classes.)

4. Access the Manual of Classification (www.uspto.gov/go/classification/). (In paper it is a large, three-volume set of ring binders.) Turn to or click to the class you are interested in and identify the specific subclasses best relating to your topic. You may need some assistance in understanding the hierarchical listing of subclasses. Many are subclasses of subclasses.

5. Access the Classification Definitions (www.uspto.gov/go/classification/select-numwithtitle.htm). This used to be on microfiche, but now you can access it online. Look up the specific class and subclass under study. Make sure you are really hunting for items resembling the definition of this class/subclass. Often additional hints are given for other places to look, including classes no longer existing.

6. Keep cycling through the three tools (Classification Index, Manual of Classification, and Classification Definitions) until you identify the appropriate classes and subclasses.

7. Search the database to identify patents in the classes/subclasses identified.

8. Examine the abstract and image of these patents to identify those resembling your device. Make copies of the drawings, abstracts, and descriptions of patents closely resembling your invention and of inventions serving the same purpose.

Note: It is not convenient to rapidly view the abstract and image of patents using the online free access patent databases, but this needs to be done. Just reviewing the titles is not sufficient.

9. After completing Steps 1 through 7, examine the patents for the following:

   a. Companies frequently appearing as assignees (patents assigned to them). Search for other patents assigned to these companies in order to identify more patents in the area of interest.

   b. Inventors frequently appearing on the patents (both independents and those working for companies). Search for other patents listing these individuals as inventors in order to identify more patents in the area of interest.

   c. Look for words and combinations of words in the patents of interest. Sort the words into groups. Some will describe one aspect of the invention and some will describe another. Record the search words on the list started earlier. Search for other patents containing these words in order to identify more patents in the area of interest. Be aware of what portion of the patent you are searching: some search abstract only, front page only, full texts.

   d. Examine the patents cited as reference by the patents of interest to see if some of them are of interest as well.

   e. Examine the class and subclass info of the patents of interest in order to identify other classes and subclasses that may contain patents of interest. Search these new classes/subclasses for additional patents of interest.

10. Keep cycling through steps 1 through 8 over and over until no more patents of interest are identified.

B. Patent Searching—a Process, Not an Event!!

We encourage conducting a very brief patent search when an idea is conceived. As the idea becomes more defined, conduct more in-depth patent searches. You invest time and/or money in patent searches just like you invest time and/or money in other aspects of new product development. You invest a little in each aspect as the project develops. Projects gradually become more developed in all areas, including intellectual property rights. Before investing more than a few hundred dollars in an idea, we suggest conducting an in-depth patent search, especially if you plan on licensing the idea. You can do it yourself and you will learn a great deal about the area of your invention. You will probably need to conduct additional patent searches as the invention progresses and time passes (new patents being issued).

6. **Learning from the Patents Found**

A. Are there features of the products in the patents you can include in your product?

B. Are there any additional potential applications for your product mentioned in the patents?

C. Do they contain any design or test data?

D. Do they list any reference materials (books, articles, etc.)?

E. Were any of the patents assigned to the U.S. government? They often contain significant design and test information.

F. Are any companies patenting products in this area potential licensees for your product?

G. How does your product compare with the products found during the patent search (and with those found below in the market and emerging technology searches)? Why would someone purchase yours instead of theirs? Why would someone purchase theirs instead of yours? Construct a matrix to compare the products based on features. Which products have which features?

H. Does one company or a small group of firms lead the industry in patents in this area or especially in the more significant patents?

I. Does one person or a small group of individuals lead the industry in patents in this area or especially in the more significant patents?

J. Is the number of patents being granted each year in the industry increasing, decreasing, or remaining the same?

K. Are there a few very significant patents in the industry (such as drug patents)? When do these key patents expire? How might the industry change when they expire? Do licensing agreements currently allow others to make the product? What are the terms (lengths) of those agreements?

L. Look at the patents cited by the patents of most interest to you. Is one patent cited as a reference by most of them? Be sure to examine it closely.

7. **Examine Products**

A. If you find a patent for a product currently in production, find the product or literature about the product. Review the product using our How Learn More About a Company by Examining Its Products site (www.virtualpet.com/industry/howto/preview.htm).

B. Significant patents will be pointed out in the marketing literature describing the features of the product. If one company's product has a very important feature and no one else's product does, it has a competitive advantage. This competitive advantage may be due to intellectual property.

8. **Search the Marketplace.** If you are trying to prove uniqueness, do not stop with just a patent search. Search the marketplace for the product. It may already be on the shelves.

A. Check stores that might carry the product.

B. Check catalogs that might carry the product.

C. Use the internet search engines (www.rbbi.com/links/sengine.htm) to search for the product.

9. **Search Emerging Technologies.** Perhaps the product has been invented, but is not yet on the shelves.

A. Technologies-for-sale sites

1. UVentures (www.uventures.com)—university technologies

2. Yet2.Com (www.yet2.com)—corporate technologies

3. TechEx (www.techex.com)—biomedical technologies

B. Universities, federal labs, and the military

4. Dissertations Index (index of Ph.D. dissertations) available online (wwwlib.umi.com/dissertations/)

5. Federally funded research summaries (www.osti.gov/fedrnd/)

6. Federal Laboratory Consortium for Technology Transfer (www.federallabs.org)

7. Technology Administration—U.S. government technology news and reports (www.technology.gov)

8. USDA Technology Transfer Information Center (www.nal.usda.gov/ttic/)

9. National Technology Transfer Center (iridium.nttc.edu)

10. National Technical Information Service (www.ntis.gov)

11. Defense Technical Information Center—military (www.dtic.mil)

12. Technical Support Working Group—U.S. government terrorist technology site (www.tswg.gov)

13. Combating Terrorism Technology Support Office (CTTSO) Broad Agency Announcement (BAA) Information Delivery System (BIDS) (www.bids.tswg.gov)

14. QinetiQ—large European defense technology and security company (www.qinetiq.com)

C. White papers in your area of interest, such as ZDNet's White Paper Directory (whitepapers.zdnet.com) for IT areas.

D. The Association of University Technology Managers—promoting global academic technology transfer (www.autm.net)

E. Recent Small Business Innovation Research Awards:

15. SBIRworld.com (www.sbirworld.com)

16. Small Business Administration Small Business Innovation Research Program and Small Business Technology Transfer Program (www.sbaonline.sba.gov/sbir/indexsbir-sttr.html)

Section 17

10. **Miscellaneous Patent Links.** The links below represent some free and fee-based information sites for both U.S. and non-U.S. patents.

- U.S. Patent and Trademark Office (www.uspto.gov)
- USPTO Patent Application Information Retrieval (portal.uspto.gov/external/portal/pair)
- esp@cenet—access to European and Japanese patents by country and world patents (ep.espacenet.com)
- World Intellectual Property Organization Intellectual Property Digital Library (www.wipo.int/ipdl/en/)
- World Intellectual Property Organization information and resources, including International Patent Classification manual (classification numbers) (www.wipo.int/portal/index.html.en)
- MicroPatent —fee-based searching of U.S. and world patents on the internet (www.micropat.com)
- Delphion—fee-based source for finding and viewing patent information (www.delphion.com)
- Thomson Scientific—databases for every stage of research and development (scientific.thomson.com)
- DialogWeb—fee-based access to thousands of business, scientific, intellectual property, and technical publications (www.dialogweb.com)

Come back and search the patents again from time to time as your invention matures.

Source: Polson Enterprises, "How to Conduct a Patent Search," www.virtualpet.com/industry/howto/psearch.htm.

List of Things That Qualify for Patent Protection

Examples of Patentable Subject Matter

The following items are just some of the things that might qualify for patent protection:

- biological inventions
- business methods
- carpet designs
- chemical formulas or processes
- clothing accessories and designs
- computer hardware and peripherals
- computer software

- containers
- cosmetics
- decorative hardware
- e-commerce techniques
- electrical inventions
- electronic circuits
- fabrics and fabric designs
- food inventions
- furniture design
- games (board, box, and instructions)
- housewares
- Internet innovations
- jewelry
- laser light shows
- machines
- magic tricks or techniques
- mechanical inventions
- medical accessories and devices
- medicines
- musical instruments
- odors
- plants
- recreational gear
- sporting goods (designs and equipment)

Source: Nolo, "Qualifying for a Patent FAQ," www.nolo.com/article.cfm/ObjectID/B1EDE764–1F7D–472B–92E4197921C56A8E/catID/FD8C060B–5DD4–4809–A53ECCF6BBD87E32/310/FAQ.

Ten Make-or-Break Points in Any Licensing Agreement

Harvey Reese, who specializes in International Product Leasing (Harvey Reese Associates, Inc., www.money4ideas.com) shares with us some tips he has found in his business experiences in licensing.

1. **How large is the advance?** How high is up? How long is a length of string? Up is as high as people agree it is, and the string is as long as it is supposed to be. You and

the licensee might agree that there should be an advance, but you won't initially agree on how much. If you each wrote a number on a piece of paper, there's not one chance in a thousand that both of you will have written the same sum. Knowing this, you should never ask the licensee what he's prepared to offer as an advance. That would be like owning a clothing store and asking the customer what he'd be willing to pay for the new suit he's trying on. You're the seller; it's your job to put a figure on the table. I can't tell you what that figure should be because there are too many variables, but I can tell you what it should represent.

There are two purposes for the advance. The first is to establish the seriousness of the licensee. It's what we used to call "earnest money." The advance should be large enough to convince you that the licensee is serious, yet not so large as to cause him to have second thoughts about the deal. The other reason for the advance, since it is non-refundable, is to compensate you for your time if, say, six months down the road the licensee changes his mind and decides not to produce your product. As a purely arbitrary rule of thumb, I try to calculate what a year's royalty might be and ask for an advance that represents about 25 percent of that amount. That seems to work in my own negotiations and the sum that is finally agreed upon is usually not far from that amount.

2. **What percentage should the royalty be?** The reason these points are negotiable is that there are no hard-and-fast rules. If what you've licensed is a high-volume, low-profit type of product, you might be happy to get three percent. If it's a slow-moving but high-profit item, you might be entitled to ten percent. None of the products I've ever been involved with have strayed beyond either of these extremes, and most wind up in the five percent area.

I developed a wonderful negotiating strategy that you're free to use. Let's say I ask for six percent and the licensee complains that competition will be able to undersell him because of the high royalty. I tell him that if and when competition comes along, if he's not competitive, I'll cut the royalty. I even know from experience that if and when competition does come along, it is usually based on features rather than price—and even if it is price, this clause is long forgotten as time passes and the product has evolved into something entirely different. But my suggestion sounds good when offered at the negotiating table and shows a sense of willingness to cooperate.

3. **When do you get your royalty payments?** My contracts always state that I'm to be paid monthly. Company salespeople get their commissions monthly, so why shouldn't I get paid the same way? Some small companies might agree, but larger ones never will. There's too much bookkeeping involved and most will insist on quarterly payments. It's a reasonable request and I always agree. The only reason I don't change my contract to read "quarterly" is to offer the licensee a small victory.

4. **How long does the licensee have to bring your product to market?** I apply the same principle as with the royalty payment schedule. My contracts call for the

licensee to have the product on the market in six months. They always balk and I always change it. Six months is usually not enough time, particularly with a seasonal product, and I'm prepared to allow as much time as seems necessary. Nine months is usually a reasonable time for the kind of products I'm involved with. The only reason my agreement still says six months is to provide further proof of my flexibility and willingness to oblige. Your invention might be more complex, involving a year or more in production, so you have to give the licensee the amount of time that's reasonable and fair, but not so much time that he has no incentive to move ahead at a brisk pace.

The longer the delay, the less chance your idea will become a reality.

5. **What territory are you awarding?** My contract routinely award licensing rights to the United States, Canada, and Mexico, which is fine for some companies but not for others. A company with worldwide operations is going to want to sell your product all over the place. That should be all right with you—why not? However, many smaller companies may sell abroad without a really strong international presence. My suggestion is to structure two separate agreements with performance guarantees built into the international one. That way, down the road, you can remove the international rights for non-performance, without interrupting their domestic activities where, hopefully, they're going great guns. If they're not doing a job for you overseas, they won't care if you take it away.

6. **What performance guarantees should you ask for?** If you're licensing a product that is not patented, you can't ask for any guarantees. Once your product is on the market, it's fair game for any company that wants to knock it off. Since you can't re-license it elsewhere, you're stuck with the guy you gave it to in the first place. However, if your product is strongly patented, you can move it around and are entitled to ask for minimum royalty guarantees. How much should it be? Who knows? It's an arbitrary figure based on what would be a reasonable amount in sales. The licensee should be able to make an estimate based on experience in the business, and you should be able to judge his estimates based on sales of similar or competing products.

7. **How long are you entitled to receive royalties?** I take the position that as long as a company is selling my product, or variations thereof, I should get royalties. Fair is fair. Some companies disagree. They figure that, since they are taking all the risk and they'll be putting money into constantly changing, improving, and adding to the product, at some point in time enough's enough. Actually, years ago my accountant found a loophole in the law that gave me great tax advantages by using a finite time and calling it a sale rather than a license, but that loophole has since been closed. There may be others, so if a great deal of money is potentially involved, you may want to discuss this with a tax attorney or your accountant.

8. **Who pays the legal fees to complete patent work?** Let's assume your product is not patented, but that it could be, or that you have filed a Provisional Patent

Application. It's not unreasonable to negotiate with the company to pay for the application for a conventional utility patent. The patent would be issued in your name and you would assign marketing rights to the company. You have a good chance of doing this with large companies who have patent attorneys on retainer and less of a chance with small companies where the legal fees are a burden—but it's worth putting on the table for discussion.

9. **Who pays legal fees in the event of infringement?** If you've licensed a patented product, another company might ignore the patent and simply knock it off. Or, if your product is not patented, you may have innocently infringed on an existing patent. Who pays the legal fees to defend the patent or defend against the infringement issue? Presumably, as the licensor, that's your responsibility, but I urge you to never, never sign a contract that obligates you to take legal action. It will cost you a ton of money if you lose the case and will probably also cost you a great deal of money if you win. Duck the issue entirely if you can, but if it does come up, you have to simply tell the licensee that the two of you will deal with the issue if and when it arises. You cannot and should not obligate yourself to take legal action to defend a five percent royalty. If you do, I can almost guarantee you'll regret it.

10. **What about remaining inventory?** There's an old business axiom that you can never count your profits until the entire inventory is out of the warehouse. Products tend to have a natural life span; when it's over, the manufacturer is invariably stuck with merchandise he can't sell. If he has to dispose of this merchandise at a cut price, do you still get your regular royalty rate? Frankly, it would be mean-spirited of you to insist on receiving the regular percentage, and I believe it will come back to haunt you. My suggestion is to use this simple formula. If the licensee has to sell the remaining merchandise at a 25 percent discount, you should also take a 25 percent discount in the royalty percentage. If he sells at a 50 percent discount, then you should also take a 50 percent discount. And so on. There probably won't be a great deal of money involved, and the licensee will remember your fairness when the next deal comes along.

The overriding intent of a licensing agreement, aside from the obvious desire to get what's reasonably deserved, should be to have a friendly, equitable deal that makes the licensee as satisfied as you are. Listen to the other side's legitimate needs and be prepared to compromise when it's not too painful to do so. You're going to invent something else for this guy and something else again after that. Your reasonableness at this first negotiation will set the tone of your ongoing relationship; you'll be rewarded for it many times over as time goes by.

Professionals like to deal with other professionals. The less you allow emotion to dictate and the more businesslike your attitude in addressing these issues, the more assured of success you'll be.

Source: Harvey Reese, "Ten Make-or-Break Points in Any Licensing Agreement," www.money4ideas.com/article9c.html.

Production

Seven Types of Waste in Manufacturing

1. **Overproduction.** Waste from overproduction is one of the greatest wastes commonly found in manufacturing operations. It is created by producing more products than are required by the market. When the market is strong, this waste may not be very noticeable. However, when demand slackens, the overproduction creates a very serious problem with unsold inventory and all the by-products associated with it:

   - Extra inventory
   - Extra handling
   - Extra space
   - Extra interest charges
   - Extra machinery and equipment
   - Extra defects
   - Extra overhead
   - Extra people
   - Extra paperwork

   Overproduction usually begins by getting ahead of the work required. More raw materials are consumed and wages paid than necessary, resulting in extra inventory. This situation requires additional material handling, storage space, and interest paid on money used to carry the inventory. Additional staff, computers, and equipment may be needed to monitor the extra goods. But as serious as these problems are, even more critical is the confusion about what the priorities are (or should be). People are distracted and unable to focus on immediate goals, which results in additional production control staff. Since the overproduction causes the machinery and operators to seem busy, additional equipment may be purchased and labor hired, under the assumption that they are necessary.

   Since overproduction creates difficulties that often obscure more fundamental problems, it is considered one of the most serious types of waste and should be eliminated as promptly as possible. The elimination lies in the understanding that machines and operators do not have to be fully utilized to be cost-efficient, as long as market demands are met. Unfortunately, this concept is difficult for many people to grasp. It is helpful for the operator at each stage of production to think of the next stage of the process as his or her "customer." Only the amount required by this customer should be produced, meeting the requirements of high quality, lowest cost, and correct timing.

2. **Waiting.** Unlike waste from overproduction, waste from waiting is usually readily identifiable. Idle workers who have completed the required amount of work and employees who spend much time watching machines but are powerless to prevent problems are two examples of the waste of waiting and are easy to spot. By com-

pleting only the amount of work required, the capacity—both speed and volume—of each work station can be monitored. This will result in using only the machinery and personnel required for the minimum amount of time to meet production demands, thereby reducing waiting time.

3. **Transportation.** The transportation and double or triple handling of raw and finished goods are commonly observed wastes in many factories. Often the culprit of this type of waste is a poorly conceived layout of the factory floor and storage facilities, which can mean long-distance transportation and over-handling of materials. This situation is aggravated by such factors as temporary storage or frequent changes of storage locations. In order to eliminate transportation waste, improvements must be made in the areas of layout, process coordination, methods of transportation, housekeeping, and general organization of the operation.

4. **Processing.** The processing method may be another source of waste. In observing this type of waste, one often finds that maintenance and manufacturability are keys to eliminating it. If fixtures and machinery are well maintained, they may require less labor on the part of the operator to produce a quality product. Regular preventative maintenance may also reduce defective pieces produced. When the principles of design for manufacture (DFM) are employed and manufacturability is taken into consideration in product design, processing waste can be reduced or eliminated before production even begins.

5. **Inventory.** Inventory waste is closely connected with waste from overproduction. That is, the overproduction creates excess inventory, which requires a list of extras including handling, space, interest charges, people, and paperwork. Because of the often substantial cost associated with extra inventory, rigorous measures should be taken to reduce inventory levels.

- Disposal of obsolete materials
- Production only of the number of items required by the subsequent process
- Purchase of required amounts of materials—savings achieved through volume discounts must be carefully weighed against inventory and storage costs
- Manufacture of products in required size lots—measure setup and changeover costs against inventory carrying costs to achieve the most appropriate size

It is important to understand that in many operations, inventory covers a myriad of other problems. As levels are reduced, these problems will surface and they must be corrected before inventory levels can be reduced to their optimum levels:

- Poor scheduling
- Machine breakdown
- Quality problems
- Long transportation time of raw materials and/or finished goods
- Vendor delivery times

Section 17

- Line imbalance
- Lengthy set up time
- Absenteeism
- Lack of housekeeping or factory organization
- Communication problems within the organization, with suppliers and with customers

6. **Motion.** Waste of motion can be defined as whatever time is spent not adding value to the product or process:

Movement ≠ Work

This type of waste is most often revealed in the actions of the factory workers. It is clearly evident in searching for tools, pick and place of tools and parts kept out of immediate reach of the work station, and especially the walking done by one operator responsible for several machines. All of these can be eliminated by carefully planned layout and fixture selection.

7. **Product Defects.** Waste from product defects is not simply those items rejected by quality control before shipment, but actually causes other types of waste throughout the entire manufacturing process.

- Waiting time is increased in subsequent processes, increasing costs and lead times.
- Rework may be required to make the part usable, increasing labor costs.
- Additional labor may be required for disassembly and reassembly.
- Additional materials may be needed for replacement parts.
- Sorting the defective from acceptable parts requires additional labor.
- Scrapping the defective pieces wastes both the materials and the work already added.

All of the above are serious, but pale in comparison with the results when customers discover defects. Not only are extra warranty and delivery costs incurred, but customer dissatisfaction may result in loss of future business and market share.

To eliminate product defect waste, a system must be developed to identify the defects (or the conditions that cause the defects) so that anyone present may take corrective action. Without this preventive system in place, other time-saving efforts are futile.

There is no advantage in using a highly automated machine to make defective parts faster.

The first step to eliminating the seven deadly wastes is to identify each one within the operation. After that, measures can be taken to correct the situation and eliminate the problems. Such action may require simple, inexpensive solutions to a single work station or may involve changes as massive as a new layout of the factory floor with more efficient machinery. The appropriate solutions require careful study of the operation, clearly defined objectives, and thorough investigation of the benefits to be gained by each change.

Source: Wendell B. Leimbach, "The Seven Deadly Wastes (and How to Tame Them)," www.mle-consulting.com/mfgr/deadly_wastes.html.

Ten Ways to Improve Your Manufacturing Productivity

1. **Analyze causes for downtime and rejects.** Record and analyze machine downtime and reject events to minimize interruptions and poor productivity.

2. **Monitor machines in real time.** Detect problems before productivity and quality suffers: see real-time displays of efficiency, utilization, OEE, yield, rate, cycle time.

3. **Automate production reporting.** Implement automated production data collection and reporting from all types of production machines. Print standard and custom reports automatically and export data to Excel, 1-2-3, or your Enterprise systems.

4. **Automate production scheduling, job tracking.** Reduce time-consuming manual production scheduling and job-tracking chores to just a few clicks of a mouse.

5. **Schedule P.M. based on actual machine/tool use.** Don't wait for your machinery to break or produce scrap before you perform maintenance. Instead, be proactive: schedule preventive maintenance based on actual machine/tool/component usage.

6. **Analyze manufacturing process variable performance.** Monitor temperature, pressure, cushion, shot size, stroke, shut height, tonnage, inject/fill/hold time, etc. Chart as X bar and R or export it to SQC/SPC applications.

7. **Implement OEE/ISO/continuous improvement programs.** Develop real-world production standards to make your job costing accurate. Implement activity-based costing, continuous improvement, and OEE programs.

8. **Manufacturing data collection for ERP, MES, and CMMS systems.** Close the loop with your Enterprise systems: automatically download production schedules into System's Job Queue, then upload production/performance/productivity and usage data at shift and job end.

9. **Export cycle counts and run time to CMMS systems. Eliminate manual "meter" reading and data collection.** ProductionACE (from Production Process) can export actual runtime and cycle counts to any third-party CMMS/EAM software during the production shift: cycle counts and runtime "meters" are updated in a real-time file.

10. **Read and print bar code labels at each machine as parts are made.** Printed labels can contain your choice of information, such as Product Description, Work Order #, Operator Name, Date/Time, Lot Number, etc.

Source: Production Process, "10 Ways to Improve Your Manufacturing Productivity," www.productionprocess.com/screens.

Ten Steps to Six Sigma Quality Manufacturing

The Six Sigma methodology for solving problems is similar to many other approaches. The differences arise mostly from Six Sigma's emphasis on statistical techniques to isolate and quantify undesirable variations in process and product performance. The mathematical techniques and analysis are central to Six Sigma steps for problem solving. The general steps one would follow with Six Sigma are:

1. Identify a process or product variation that is creating undesirable performance results.
2. Define the scope and parameters of the problem.
3. Develop and apply initial measures of process or product variability.
4. Estimate the business performance impact.
5. Prioritize the project with other Six Sigma projects to establish when analysis begins.
6. Collect and organize the data needed to carry out a thorough analysis.
7. Analyze the data to pinpoint the cause or causes of variation.
8. Develop an action plan for improving the process or product and a time frame for full implementation of the action plan.
9. Implement the improvements.
10. Establish the control and feedback mechanisms for continuous improvement of the process or product.

Six Sigma dovetails nicely with performance improvement initiatives intended to transform a traditional manufacturing company into a lean supply chain operation. An effective Six Sigma program can help to improve customer response time, cut cycle times, and improve product quality in engineering and performance. These improvements appear not only in a narrow "reduction of defects" but can also generate revenue based on improved customer satisfaction. Customer satisfaction improves, not because goods are more reliable and have fewer defects but because the entire process that the customer experiences from start to finish, from the sales office all the way through delivery and post-sale servicing and technical support, is improved. In addition, companies that implement Six Sigma programs can get additional benefits just by advertising their commitment to Six Sigma, as many have done, thereby raising the company's public profile. There is one important caveat, however: Six Sigma's heavy reliance on mathematical and statistical techniques for determining process as well as product performance intimidates many managers, making it harder to sell as an approach to key people within the organization. Six Sigma has its advocates, but it also has its detractors.

Resistance to Six Sigma arises sometimes because managers see Six Sigma advocates as "blind zealots" wedded to a single performance improvement philosophy. Companies that are considering implementing a Six Sigma program should be prepared to understand and cope with such resistance.

Section 17

Source: R. Michael Donovan & Co., "Six Sigma Approach to Quality Manufacturing," www.rmdonovan.com/six_sigma.htm.

Distribution

15 Key Factors That Impact Your Distribution Network Effectiveness

Distribution professionals "see" their operations on a daily basis. Competitive pressures, mergers, acquisitions, new product lines, and greater customer expectations are just the tip of the change iceberg for the modern logistics leader. On the surface, this continuum of change is just a cost of doing business in the latest "new economy." However, for those intimately involved in a distribution process, how these changes are accommodated can mean the difference between survival and burnout and/or even extinction in today's rapidly changing supply chain. This article focuses on 15 key areas that are the roadmap to an effective, flexible, and proactively responsive distribution operation.

1. **Centralization vs. Regionalization**—In distribution network planning, there is a well-established relationship among the number of distribution points, transportation costs, and customer service targets. In a graphical sense, the point at which these three entities merge is the optimum balance of facility and transportation costs to develop a low-cost, high-service distribution network. Normally, as distribution networks become more centralized, so do the internal support structures, such as facility management, order entry, customer service, and data processing. Depending on the degree of centralization achieved in support staffs, it is not uncommon to see cost savings of 50 percent or higher over decentralized networks. However, service levels, limitations on total facility size, risk mitigation, and throughput peaks must be factored into the decision matrix.

2. **Energy**—Any significant shift in the cost of energy—electricity, fuel, etc.—could have an impact on operating costs and, therefore, on distribution. Many distribution projects that are otherwise viable fail once the cost of energy becomes a factor. This is especially true for energy-intensive facilities such as refrigerated warehouses. For this reason, it is crucial to work with all energy providers to determine the load that a prospective operation would put on the local energy system and develop solutions that conserve energy while achieving goals. Some interesting energy solutions are:

   - **Abatement programs:** Many energy providers provide incentives to users who cut back their usage during defined high-load periods. This could be as simple as running the facility on minimal power during off-shifts or as complicated as metering the use of the facility or using a secondary power source (high-power generator or solar power) to run normally on a reduced energy load.

   - **High-efficiency units:** Many companies install high-efficiency appliances and fixtures in a facility to conserve energy usage with no performance penalty. There is some investment required, but the payback is often reduced rates and/or a lower monthly bill.

   Rising fuel costs make this a very sensitive component of distribution costs, regardless of whether transportation is handled via third party carriers or a private fleet. Here are some strategies to consider to mitigate this factor:

- **Cube out containers:** When a trailer is partially cubed out, you are often paying to transport air. Utilizing the maximum cube ensures that more of the shipping costs are being used to ship product.

- **Mode assessment:** Depending on service requirements, it may be possible to move from LTL (less than truckload) services to truckload or from parcel to LTL. In general, each shift will result in reduced freight costs.

- **Transportation management systems** (TMS): Poor transportation performance often stems from poor transportation planning. A TMS can provide more efficient route planning and load tendering, and result in savings in the process.

- **Private fleet concerns:** Private fleets can benefit from an in-house fuel supply program to gain control over fuel costs and usage. The investment can be offset by the elimination of one or more fuel supply chain links, reducing operating costs and sometimes allowing fuel blends that are more efficient and economical.

- **Regional vs. centralized networks:** The costs of delivery using different modes of transportation, as well as service availability, can be directly impacted when fuel costs rise. Understanding the modes used most often, the customer expectation, and the risk associated plays into the network structure decision.

3. **Flexibility**—In today's unpredictable business climate, flexibility is a key to continued success for some and survival for others. When designing a distribution facility, specifying versatile equipment is a critical requirement. The latest technology may look nice at start-up, but if it can't keep pace with unpredictable events, it is simply a waste of money. Planning for likely (and unlikely) changes in the distribution profile should drive the warehouse design and equipment specifications. For the majority of distribution operations, flexible equipment is the more practical choice.

4. **Global Marketplace**—In the ever-changing supply chain, global impact must always be considered. This could be as minor as a domestic customer wanting direct shipments to an international location, or as major as an acquisition by a global company or addition of a key global account. Successful distribution operations are ready for this type of change. Transportation systems should be designed with exports in mind; there should be contingencies for customs documentation and international shipping paperwork. Operations should be designed in a manner that product relabeling or special packaging for international customers can be accomplished easily. Facilities may need to accommodate inbound or outbound airfreight or ocean freight containers. Customer service functions may need to operate in 24-hour mode to assist customers in all time zones. Preparedness is the critical element in a global marketplace. If you are not a global company today, your success will drive you into that marketplace sooner rather than later.

5. **Government Involvement**—Just as government involvement has an impact on distri-

bution, distribution leaders have an obligation to be involved and aware of legislation that involves their industry. Many decisions are made daily at local, state, and federal levels that impact distribution operations. Taxes, labor regulations, transportation restrictions, and infrastructure decisions are continually up for review and discussion at every level of government. Without proper input, uninformed decisions often have a dramatic effect on the distribution community.

In addition, involvement in professional societies (many of which conduct lobbying activities) is an effective way to track the pulse of legislative movement and also an ideal forum to make your concerns known. For some ambitious souls, a direct role in local or municipal government may be an effective and fulfilling way to make an impact. By being proactive, distribution leaders can ensure that distribution and government entities can collaborate to provide benefit to both sides without unpleasant surprises.

6. **Information Systems**—In today's e-enabled world, timely and accurate information is a requirement. The days of keypunching in daily distribution activity and nightly updates to host financial systems are becoming a distant memory for successful distribution operations. Today's reality is that distribution execution systems must be:

- **Real time:** Customer requirements are moving toward being able to instantly track an order through every step of the fulfillment process to delivery. Optimally, this information is linked to an internet front-end where a customer can easily log in and see the exact status of his or her order. Real-time interfaces and host system updates enable this customer-focused initiative.

- **Paperless:** The reality is that paper equates to errors. Language and educational barriers result in paper pick documents that are often misinterpreted, at best resulting in lost dollars within the distribution operation or, worse, lost customers due to fulfillment issues that escape even the best inspection processes. The solution is paperless systems requiring operator validation that the right steps were followed and that the correct product was picked and packed.

- **Standardized:** In the past, many companies developed proprietary, legacy systems to manage their distribution operations. With the high growth associated with a successful distribution operation, many of these companies are finding that the investment to develop and maintain an in-house system no longer is viable. Standardized, industry-tailored software is now the rule rather than the exception. Software companies leverage their client base to continually update their product, adding far more base functionality than inflexible legacy systems.

7. **Modularity**—As companies in the distribution space come and go, their business will typically move to a new distributor or distributors. The ability to quickly take on significant business volumes dictates that modularity is a necessity for a thriving distribution organization. Modularity must be evident in:

- **Assets:** Distribution assets must be modular, providing the ability to easily expand facilities, capacities, and equipment to meet increasing demands and diverse products. Many companies design this into a facility, while others are constantly tracking alternate local space that could be closed on quickly.

- **Work assignments:** The workforce must be able to handle new work assignments and transfer knowledge to new employees effectively. This is a key to a successful start-up of a new operation or an addition to an existing operation.

- **Labor management systems:** These systems must be able to handle the addition of new operations quickly and economically so that performance can be measured and costs kept under control.

8. **Off-Highway Vehicles**—In the United States, issues regarding the environment and air quality continue to be under scrutiny. The push for more stringent air-quality regulations will impact the warehouse. Electric vehicles will take over as the preferred models in the warehouse, displacing non-electric vehicles. As this evolution occurs, manufacturers of electric rolling stock will respond with higher-power, higher-efficiency vehicles to facilitate this process.

9. **Pace**—Anyone with access to an e-retailer web site can now order product, specify their service requirements, pay for their order online, and track the order right to their doorstep. For distributors, this means that the pace of distribution must increase significantly to account for the reduced lead times, shorter product lives, increased inventory turnover, and greater customer expectations that are considered standard in the modern business-to-business and business-to-consumer marketplace. If a customer places an order today with next-day delivery, a company that picks and ships the order the next day won't be competitive for long. The entire supply chain needs to keep pace, from vendor compliance to information and execution systems, in order to support the new economy that the internet has enabled.

10. **People**—Success demands a team-based, participatory organizational culture and a total dedication to customer satisfaction. There are many ways to achieve this, ranging from simple solutions such as employee celebration days, employee suggestion programs, and other simple programs to more structured approaches such as revised organizational designs, compensation/incentive/bonus plans, and other processes that directly tie the distribution associates on the floor to satisfied customers.

11. **Price**—While service and quality are key factors in selecting a distribution partner, for many companies, decisions still comes down to price. Successful past relationships are no longer a good indicator of the future. Modern free enterprise demands efficient, effective, and low-cost distribution. Competition is fierce and many low-cost providers will not be here tomorrow as they undercut the market to get short-term volumes at an operating loss. The goal of a successful distribution operation should be to operate within their core values at the lowest cost possible. The path to competitive pricing is to operate efficiently and flexibly at low cost—to offer low prices any other way is inviting failure.

12. **Accountability**—A successful distribution operation must have accountability.

Accountability is made possible by effective leadership, clear communications, and efficient systems and equipment to enable productive operations and a fulfilling work environment. Accountability requires that leaders make difficult decisions while maintaining the commitment of the organization. Accountability requires establishing standards, identifying improvement opportunities, and measuring performance. Also required is some form of a reward process that answers the inevitable question, "What's in this for me?" Care must be taken that any rewards are tied to something that can be quantified as a true benefit to the organization; rewards without a basis will result in lack of credibility and a process that will ultimately fail.

13. **Reverse Logistics**—How to handle the products that are coming back into the operation as well as any returnable packaging that must be accounted for on a regular basis is a challenge. The decision on whether to accept the product, whether a refused shipment, an authorized customer return, or an unexpected return, must be planned for and communicated with the distribution operation as well as the receiving and handling process for the product or chaos will likely ensue.

    For example, a Tompkins Associates client in the direct-to-consumer home goods industry was having a horrible experience with returns. An item would be returned and graded "return to stock." An order would come in for the same item and the returned item (which was first quality) would be shipped. The customer would receive the item and then return it with the comment that it appeared not to be new. The solution was to establish vendor-quality packaging that looked very similar to the original vendor packaging. By using the new packaging for returns, the client was able to realize a 75 percent decrease in second-pass returns, saving over $5 million annually in returns freight and reducing the size of its returns department.

    Another opportunity in reverse distribution is returnable packaging, either pallets or containers.

    Another Tompkins client moved from disposable corrugate containers in its retail store replenishment operations to returnable containers and used the freight backhaul to return the empty containers to the distribution center. Operations in the distribution center were far more efficient, as the plastic totes were much more reliable and were more easily conveyed and stored than their corrugate predecessors, and the retail stores did not have to break down and dispose of thousands of corrugate boxes every year.

14. **Third-Party Logistics** (3PL)—A growing number of companies are turning to 3PL organizations to handle the customer fulfillment portion of their supply chain. Companies that are accustomed to true partnering with customers and suppliers have less trouble migrating to the 3PL world and achieving the potential cost savings. The key steps are to conduct a comprehensive search for the right 3PL vendor, thoroughly review cost proposals and contracts to ensure there is financial benefit, and work with the 3PL to make their operation a seamless extension of your company. This may involve shared management, integrated execution systems, and a unified appearance to partners and customers.

15. **Variety**—Special packaging, unitizing, pricing, labeling, kitting, and delivery requirements are becoming the norm and must be addressed in any distribution plan. These tasks should be designed into the operation, not "tacked on" as a reactive afterthought. Many companies invest large amounts of capital setting up specialized packing or value-added services (VAS) lines with the mandate to gain competitive advantages and in hindsight gain little except increased costs and headaches. A few key questions need to be answered when setting up these operations:

- What is the benefit of the process?
- How will we recoup our investment?
- Can we charge the customer for these services?
- Is it better to outsource this operation?

A simple review process can often provide justification to move forward and establish key design parameters to ensure that any "extra" requirements are integrated into the operation responsibly. Properly planned, these services can be a profit center, providing differentiation in a competitive marketplace while boosting the bottom line at the same time.

Source: Mike Prince, "15 Key Factors That Impact Your Distribution Network Effectiveness," www.tompkinsinc.com/publications/competitive_edge/articles/07-04-Distribution_ Networks.asp.

Seven Ways to Customize Your Distribution Network and Reduce Costs

To balance customers' demands with the need for profitable growth, most supply chain managers have moved aggressively to improve their distribution networks. Based on analysis by Andersen Consulting of more than 100 manufacturers, distributors, and retailers, they are doing it successfully by combining the following seven ideas into their strategies.

1. **Segment customers based on the service needs of distinct groups and adapt the supply chain to serve these segments profitably.** This equips a company to develop a portfolio of services tailored to various segments. For instance, one manufacturer of home improvement and building products told surveyors that it bases segmentation on sales and merchandising needs and order fulfillment requirements.

   You can also determine the services valued by all customers, not just by certain segments, and create segment-specific service packages that combine basic services for everyone. Segmentation is meant to maximize profits. Analyze the profitability of segments, plus the costs and benefits of alternate service packages, to ensure a reasonable return on investment.

Section 17

2. **Customize the logistics network to the service requirements and profitability of customer segments.** This can be a source of differentiation in industries where the actual products are largely undifferentiated. For example, one paper company found radically different customer service demands in two key segments—large publishers with long lead times and small, regional printers needing delivery within 24 hours. To serve both segments well and achieve profitable growth, the manufacturer designed a multilevel logistics network with three full-stocking distribution centers and 46 quick-response cross docks, stocking only fast-moving items located near the regional printers. Return on assets and revenues improved substantially, thanks to the new inventory deployment strategy.

3. **Listen to market signals and align demand planning accordingly across the supply chain, ensuring consistent forecasts and optimal resource allocation.**

   A photographic imaging manufacturer recounts how it had to cope with a production operation that stuck to a stable schedule, while the revenue-focused sales force routinely triggered cyclical demand by offering deep discounts at the end of each quarter. The manufacturer realized the need to implement a cross-functional planning process supported by demand planning software.

   At first, the results were dismaying. Sales volume dropped sharply, as excess inventory had to be consumed by the marketplace. But today, the company enjoys lower inventory and warehousing costs and a greater ability to maintain price levels and limit discounting.

   Channel-wide supply chain planning can detect early warning signals of customer demand. This made all the difference to a laboratory products manufacturer. Uneven distributor demand unsynchronized with actual end-user demand made real inventory needs impossible to predict and forced high inventory stocks. Distributors began sharing information on actual demand with the manufacturer and the manufacturer began managing inventory for the distributors. This coordination of manufacturing scheduling and inventory deployment decisions paid off, improving fill rates, asset turns, and cost metrics for all concerned.

4. **Differentiate product closer to the customer and speed conversion across the supply chain.** Manufacturers striving to meet individual customer needs through mass customization have discovered the value of postponement. They delay product differentiation to the last possible moment.

   This can help overcome the problem of SKU proliferation that is common in fulfilling customer requirements. A hardware manufacturer determined the point at which a standard bracket turned into multiple SKUs, which was when the bracket had to be packaged 16 ways to meet particular customer requests. The manufacturer further concluded that overall demand for the brackets is easy to forecast, while demand for the 16 SKUs is more volatile. The solution was to make brackets in the factory but package them at the distribution center, within the customer order cycle. This improved asset utilization by cutting inventory levels by more than 50 percent.

According to the surveyors, the key to just-in-time product differentiation is to locate the leverage point in the manufacturing process where the product is unalterably configured to meet a single requirement. In addition, challenge cycle times: can the leverage point be pushed closer to actual demand to maximize the flexibility in responding to the demand?

5. **Manage sources of supply strategically to reduce the total cost of owning materials and services.** Excellent supply chain management requires an enlightened mindset, such as gain-sharing arrangements where everyone who contributes to greater profitability is rewarded.

   To do this, you need a knowledge of all commodity costs, not only on direct materials but also for maintenance, repair, and operating supplies, plus the money spent on temps, travel, utilities, and everything else. Only then can you approach suppliers in the most efficient way—soliciting short-term competitive bids or entering long-tern contracts.

   The savings that result can fund other initiatives. Consider how creating a data warehouse to store vast amounts of transactional and decision support data in annual negotiations consolidated across six divisions cut one manufacturer's operating costs. In one year it was able to pay for a redesigned distribution network and a new order management system.

6. **Develop a supply chain-wide technology strategy that supports multiple levels of decision making and gives a clear view of the flow of products, services, and information.** Today's enterprise-wide systems must share information across the supply chain so that all partners can attain mutual success.

   A leading beer manufacturer did not do this and learned a lesson the hard way. Tracking performance from plant to warehouse, the manufacturer was pleased: 98 percent fill rate to the retailers' warehouse. But looking all the way across the supply chain, the manufacturer saw a different picture. Consumers in some key retail chains found this company's beer out of stock more than 20 percent of the time due to poor store-level replenishment and forecasting. The manufacturer is now scrambling to implement real-time information technology to gain store-specific performance data, which is essential to improving customer service.

7. **Adopt channel-spanning performance measures to gauge collective success in reaching the end user effectively and efficiently.** First, service is measured in terms of the perfect order, as viewed by the entire supply chain, including the customer. Second, excellent supply chain managers determine their true profitability of service by identifying the actual costs and revenues of the activities required to serve an account.

   To facilitate channel-spanning performance measurement, many companies are developing common report cards. These help keep partners working toward the same goals by building a deep understanding of what each company brings to the partnership and showing how to leverage their assets and skills to the alliance's greatest advantage.

Source: "7 Ways to Customize & Reduce the Cost of Your Distribution Network," *Managing Logistics* (October 2000), www.fita.org/ioma/distribution.html.

Section 17

12 Tips for Starting an Import/Export Business

Thinking of starting an import/export business? Jennifer Henzel, a Certified Import/Export Trade Professional with Global Focus Consulting in Vancouver, British Columbia, offers these tips for getting started.

1. Many countries have set up offices (consulates or embassies) in foreign countries to promote the exporting of their goods. The consulates will supply you with industry directories and more. Embassies are located in a nation's capital and consulates in other cities. In many cases, the embassy web site will contain directories and lists of manufacturers, as well as an e-mail link that you can use for sourcing.

2. To import or export goods, communicate with that country's consulate situated in your own country. If you are uncertain what products the other country wants, you can obtain catalogues and lists of manufacturers.

3. Contact your country's taxation department to ask about registration numbers or other procedures that you must follow. For example, if you are Canadian, you will need a Registration Number, issued by the Canada Border Services Agency (CBSA, www.cbsa-asfc.gc.ca). When you inform the CBSA of your plans to import or export, it issues an extension to your business number. This number is used on all related documents. For the United States, start with U.S. Customs and Border Protection, www.cbp.gov.

4. Find out about licensing requirements, if any. Many countries do not have licensing requirements for most products. However, if you are importing or exporting high-risk products (pharmaceuticals, liquor, chemicals, arms, certain food items, and certain articles of apparel), you might need a license. "I strongly recommend that people start out with low-risk items that can be easily traded and have fewer barriers—like giftware and consumer items," said Henzel. "Certain industries, like dairy, are guarded by lobby groups in some countries. You will be faced with quotas and restrictions."

5. Embargoes are trade barriers set up against other countries. Many countries have embargoes against Cuba, for example. First, contact your own government to determine whether there are restrictions or embargoes against the country you are considering. Next, contact that country's consulate or embassy to see if there are restrictions against goods from your country.

6. Participate in the local Boards of Trades (Canada) or Chambers of Commerce (Canada and U.S.). In addition to networking, you have access to research libraries and other resources that will offer good trade information.

7. Use customs brokers. "Small businesses attempting their own paperwork can run into delays at borders. If you make a mistake, you can be fined," said Henzel. "A custom broker's service is well worth the fee you pay."

8. Understand that in exporting there is no one solution to shipping and customs han-

dling that will work in every situation. Every deal is different. Each company and each set of products will require a different set of services, or a combination of services. Engaging the services of a freight forwarder is one possibility. Freight forwarders arrange shipping and customs for goods going to other countries. "You have to shop for these services and do your research," Henzel explained. "Ask a lot of questions. It's no different than buying a piece of furniture. You shop around first."

9. Be familiar with Incoterms, as posted to the International Chamber of Commerce web site (www.iccwbo.org/index_incoterms.asp). Incoterms are standard trade definitions that dictate the shipping and payment responsibilities of each party. The two companies involved negotiate Incoterms for each deal. The best-known Incoterms include EXW (ex works), FOB (free on board), CIF (cost, insurance, and freight), DDU (delivered duty unpaid), and CPT (carriage paid to). "You negotiate according to the Incoterms," Henzel said. "You decide who pays for shipping, who pays for insurance, etc."

10. Consult your bank for information about letters of credit, the most common form of payment when trading internationally. With a letter of credit, you minimize your risk because the banks ensure that the goods are delivered before the money is exchanged. For an importer, a letter of credit reduces the risk of having to pay in advance for goods or to pay for goods that are inconsistent with the product description in the letter. For an exporter, there's the buyer's bank's assurance that you will receive payment provided you ship the goods as specified within an agreed-upon time.

11. Participate in trade missions. Consult your Board of Trade or local Chamber of Commerce to discover what is available.

12. Look to the web for information about international trade. Many web sites offer an array of information that you can access for no charge, including Henzel's site, The Import Export Coach.com (www.importexportcoach).

Source: June Campbell, "A Dozen Tips for Starting an Import/Export Business," www.night-cats.com/samples/import.html.

Six Export Labeling Tips

Effective labeling of your export goods can mean the difference between your goods reaching their export destination in one piece, reaching it damaged, or not reaching it at all. These labeling tips will give your packages a fighting chance on their journey abroad.

1. **Label boxes and containers with required information.** For export, this information includes, but is not limited to, country of origin, shipper's mark, weight and/or volume information, cautionary marks and handling instructions (for instance, the word "glass," the symbol of a glass, the words "this side up," or the symbol of arrows pointing upward), consignee's mark, destination and order number, and number of the package and size of the case if there are multiple boxes or containers.

2. **Do not label boxes with information that is not required.** If there is no need to specify the content of the box on a label, avoid doing so. Identifying valuable goods contained in a box is an invitation for thieves and vandals. Use coded marks to identify export goods unless local laws prohibit this practice.

3. **Do not use boxes or containers with old labels.** Recycling is admirable; however, all old marks, addresses, or advertising must be removed or permanently obscured to eliminate confusion for handlers and carriers of your export goods.

4. **Ensure labels are clear and permanent.** Labels must be large enough to read and information must be indicated in the appropriate language. Labels for your export goods must also be waterproof and resistant to the elements.

5. **Label more than one side of the box or container.** Consignee marks as well as destination and transfer point marks should be applied to at least three sides of the package. If the postal service is handling your export shipments, it is a good idea to confirm shipping requirements with them directly.

6. **Symbols have international appeal.** Exporters can purchase self-adhesive labels with international carriage symbols. These are cautionary symbols providing carriers and handlers with instructions on the correct manipulation of your packages. There are commonly seen symbols, such as the wine glass (fragile) and the umbrella with the raindrops (keep dry). There are also more obscure symbols, such as the penguin inside a box (keep frozen) or the penguin inside a box with a diagonal line intersecting it (do not freeze). When an export shipment involves transfers through countries with different languages, symbols may act as the universal language that protects your goods.

Labeling is a critical element in the export process. It is often the attention given to these mundane tasks that makes the difference between shipping success and failure.

Source: Curtis Cook, "Labeling Packages for Export Shipments," sbinfocanada.about.com/od/canadaexport/a/exportlabelcc.htm.

14 Tips for Successful Exporters

Exporting your firm's products or services can provide you a valuable opportunity for growth. It takes a special approach, however, to access foreign markets successfully.

Let's look at the basic steps in becoming an export business success:

1. **Research your market.** Learn about your competitors, their products, and their prices.

2. **Know the customers.** How can you customize your products to meet foreign customers' needs?

3 **Understand the concept of "many markets."** Every market has different demands.

4. **Know the market's style requirements.** Some customers don't mind premium prices, as long as quality is superior.

5. **Learn the sales system and master the distribution network.** Find the right sales and distribution channels. Be careful about requests for "exclusive rights."

6. **Don't expect your foreign customers to understand English.** Be ready to translate your packages, instructions, and manuals.

7. **Learn to write clear communications.** Make messages, letters, faxes, and e-mails clear, concise, and accurate.

8. **Visit the market. Learn firsthand!** See your products in use. Collect competitors' samples.

9. **Visit prospects.** Urge your distributor or representative to set up three or four appointments each day for you with prospective customers.

10. **Be responsive and responsible.** Answer questions promptly. Offer prices and delivery terms you can meet.

11. **Provide for local service.** Fix or replace products. Foreign customers don't want a cash credit.

12. **Arrange for export financing.** You'll have new needs for working capital, letters of credit, wire transfers, and currency exchange. You might want to utilize the SBA's Guaranteed Export Working Capital Loan Program and arrange for foreign receivables insurance.

13. **Discuss the business with a reputable freight forwarder.** You'll need assistance with shipping.

14. **Don't try too much at the beginning!** Start with a bit of your product line, in a well-defined geographic territory.

Source: Roger S. Cohen, "Tips for Successful Exporters," www.rogercohen.com/training/Ten_tips_for_exporters.shtml.

Publications and Organizations

Recommended CAD Magazines

AUTOCAD Magazin: Das CAD-Praxismagazin
www.autocad-magazin.de

CAD UserCAD User Magazine
www.caduser.com

CadalystCADALYST OnLine
www.cadalyst.com

CADInfo.Net—Automated Design, Documentation and Visualization
www. cadinfo.net

CADWire
www.cadwire.net

CATIA Community
www.catiasolutions.com

Computer-Aided Design
www.elsevier.com/wps/find/journaldescription.c
ws_home/30402/description

Desktop Engineering
www.deskeng.com

Digital Engineering Magazin—Engineering-Management Heute
www.digital-engineering-magazin.de

Engineering Automation Report Online
www.eareport.com

Multi-CAD Magazine
www.multi-cad.com
Pro/E Community—for the Pro/ENGINEER User
www.proe.com

Source: The Computer Information Center, "Computer-Aided Design (CAD)—Magazines and Ezines," www.compinfo-center.com/cad/cad.htm.

Manufacturing Trade Magazines

IndustryWeek
www.industryweek.com

Manufacturing Business Technology
www.mbtmag.com

Plastics News
www.plasticsnews.com

Advanced Manufacturing Magazine
www.advancedmanufacturing.com

Injection Molding Magazine
www.immnet.com

Manufacturing & Technology News
www.manufacturingnews.com

Ceramic Industry Magazine
www.ceramicindustry.com

CleanRooms
www.cleanrooms.com

Welding and Cutting
www.welding-and-cutting.info

Wire & Cable Technology
www.wiretech.com

thefabricator.com: complete online metal fabricating source
www.thefabricator.com

Powder and Bulk Engineering
www.powderbulk.com

The Journal: The Magazine for Manufactured & Modular Housing Professionals
www.journalmfdhousing.com

Findlay Publications (UK Manufacturing)
www.findlay.co.uk

Machinists' Exchange Online
www.machinist.com

Screw Machine World
www.screwmachineworld.com

Source: Yahoo! Inc., Small Business Directory: Manufacturing > Trade Magazines, dir.yahoo.com/Business_and_Economy/Business _to_Business/Manufacturing/Trade_Magazines.

Manufacturing, Training, and Development Companies

Tec-Ease
www.tec-ease.com
Offers technical training and materials for the manufacturing industry.

Intelitek
www.intelitek.com
Provides solutions for teaching manufacturing technology.

Manufacturing Management & Technology Institute (MMTI)
www.mmt-inst.com
Provides publications, courses, and consulting to support lean production implementation.

Productivity, Inc.
www.productivityinc.com
Provides lean manufacturing training, consulting, books, learning tools, workshops, and more.

Resource Engineering, Inc.
www.reseng.com
Self-paced SPC (Statistical Process Control) and FMEA (Failure Mode and Effects Analysis) CD-ROM training programs for manufacturing organizations.

CyMation Inc.
www.cymation.net
Provides training in troubleshooting, control systems, maintenance, and operations to optimize manufacturing. Also offers to create user manuals and training documentation.

Micro Manufacturing Systems
www.micromfgsys.com
Provides education, training, and consulting for Micro-MAX MRP and related programs.

Sheet Metal Training Center
www.sheetmetal-16.org
A contractor and union cooperative program to prepare industry workers.

Tooling University
www.toolingu.com
Offers web-based training focusing on industrial manufacturing training skills such as metal cutting and CNC machining.

TII Technical Education Systems
www.tii-tech.com
Provides industrial technology training.

John Klees Enterprise, Inc.
www.johnklees.com
Offers seminars on injection-molding technology.

MasterTask Training Systems
www.mastertask.com
Provides CD-ROM and video training courses for machinists, CNC, and machinery operators. Courses cover measurement and quality control, and are suitable for in-plant or vocational training.

Applied Performance Strategies
www.aps-online.net
Offers technical training for students and adults, documentation services, program design, and HR consulting and training.

Best Manufacturing Practices
www.best-manufacturing-practices.com
Manufacturing process specialists offering online training courses, on topics including ISO 9000:2000 quality compliance, supply chain management, and strategic planning.

Six Sigma Training

www.six-sigma-training.org
Features the eight basics of the Lean Six Sigma method of competitive manufacturing practices with self-paced CD-ROM seminars available.

Industry Educators

www.industryeducator.com
Provides educational classes to support a wide range of manufacturing businesses at the production level.

Eaton Fluid Power Training

apps.vickers-systems.com/training/index.html
Features certified hydraulics training instructors teaching industry-specific technology courses.

Source: Yahoo! Inc., Small Business Directory: Manufacturing > Training and Development, dir.yahoo.com/Business_and_Economy/Business_to_Business/Manufacturing/Training_and_Development.

Supply Chain Trade Organizations

Air Transport Association of America
www.air-transport.org

Alliance of Manufacturers & Exporters
www.the-alliance.com

American Association of Exporters and Importers
www.aaei.org

American Association of Port Authorities
www.aapa-ports.org

American Automobile Manufacturers Association
www.aama.com

American Forest and Paper Association
www.afandpa.org

American Furniture Manufacturers Association
www.afma4u.org

American Institute for Shippers' Associations Inc.
www.shippers.org

American Management Association
www.amanet.org

American Petroleum Institute
www.api.org

American Plastics Council
www.americanplasticscouncil.org

American Powder Metallurgy Institute
www.mpif.org

American Short Line and Regional Railroad Association
www.aslrra.org

American Society of Transportation and Logistics
www.astl.org

American Trucking Association
www.trucking.org

Association for Manufacturing Excellence
www.ame.org

Association for Manufacturing Technology
www.mfgtech.org

Association of American Railroads
www.aar.org

Association of Home Appliance Manufacturers
www.aham.org

Association of Steel Distributors
www.steeldistributors.org

Automatic Identification Manufacturers
www.aimglobal.org

Automotive Industry Action Group
www.aiag.org

Canadian Pallet Council
www.cpcpallet.com

Chemical Manufacturers Association
www.cmahq.com

Collaborative Planning, Forecasting, and Replenishment
www.cpfr.org

Components, Packaging, and Manufacturing Technology Society
www.cpmt.org

Compressed Air and Gas Institute
www.cagi.org

Conveyor Equipment Manufacturers Association
www.cemanet.org

Council of Logistics Management
www.clm1.org

Customer Relationship Management Association
www.crm-a.org

Data Interchange Standards Association
www.disa.org

Education Society for Resource Management (formerly APICS—American Production and Inventory Control Society)
www.apics.org

Equipment Manufacturers Association
www.cemanet.org

Federation of International Trade Associations
www.fita.org

Food Distributors International
www.fdi.org

Grocery Manufacturers of America
www.gmabrands.com

Hazardous Materials Advisory Council
www.hmac.org

Industrial Distribution Association
www.ida-assoc.org

Industrial Safety Equipment Association
www.safetyequipment.org

Industrial Truck Association
www.indtrk.org

Institute for Operations Research and Management Services
www.informs.org

Institute for Supply Management (formerly NAPM—National Association for Purchasing Management)
www.ism.ws

Institute of Logistics
www.iolt.org.uk

Institute of Packaging Professionals
www.packinfo-world.org

International Association of Lean Practitioners
ialp.org

International Association of Plastics Distributors
www.iapd.org

International Association of Refrigerated Warehouses
www.iarw.org

International Organization for Standardization
www.iso.ch/iso/en/ISOOnline.openerpage

International Society of Logistics Engineers
www.sole.org

International Standardization Organization
www.iso.ch

International Warehouse Logistics Association
www.warehouselogistics.org

Logistics Management Institute
www.lmi.org

Material Handling Equipment Distributors Association
www.mheda.org

Material Handling Industry of America
www.mhia.org

Michigan Trucking Association
www.mitrucking.org

National Association of Aluminum Distributors
www.naad.org

National Association of Manufacturers
www.nam.org

National Association of Pharmaceutical Manufacturers
www.napmnet.org

National Association of Printing Ink Manufacturers
www.napim.org

National Center for Manufacturing Sciences
www.ncms.org

National Electronic Distributors Association
www.nedassoc.org

National Industrial Transportation League
www.nitl.org

National Private Truck Council
www.nptc.org
National Safety Council
www.nsc.org

National Small Shipments Traffic Conference
www.nasstrac.org

National Wooden Pallet and Container Association

www.nwpca.com

Packaging Machinery Manufacturers Institute
www.pmmi.org

Paperboard Packaging Council
www.ppcnet.org

Powder Coating Institute
www.powdercoating.org

Society of Automotive Engineers
www.sae.org

Society of Manufacturing Engineers
www.sme.org

Steel Manufacturers Association
www.steelnet.org

Supply Chain Council
www.supply-chain.org

Transportation Consumer Protection Council
www.transportlaw.com/tcpc

Transportation Law Center
www.transportlaw.com

Truckload Carriers Association
www.truckload.org

United States Council for Automotive Research
www.uscar.org

Warehousing and Education Research Council
www.werc.org

Source: Council of Logistics Management–Michigan Roundtables, "Trade Organizations," www.mi-clm.org/links/trade/tradeorgs.htm.

CAD Associations

COE—CATIA Operators Exchange
401 N. Michigan Avenue, 24th Floor
Chicago, IL 60611
Phone: (800) 263-2255 (toll-free), (312) 321-5153
Fax: (312) 527-6636
E-mail: coe@coe.org
Web: www.coe.org

GCAUG—Greater Chicago AutoCAD Users Group
P.O. Box 101
Palatine, IL 60078-0101
Phone: (847) 272-0343, (847) 229-7468
Web: www.gcaug.com

SVAPU—Silicon Valley AutoCAD Power Users
P.O. Box 62515

Sunnyvale, CA 94086
Phone: (408) 395-0855
Fax: (408) 354-2496
Web: www.power.org

VAUS—Vancouver AutoCAD Users Society
Web: www.vaus.org

WTAUG—West Texas AutoCAD User Group
P.O. Box 5062
Midland, TX 79704-6062
Phone: (915) 756-4138
Fax: (915) 756-2866
Web: www.wtaug.cjb.net

Source: MotionNET.com, CAD/CAM Associations, www.motionnet.com/cgi-bin/search.exe?a=cat&no=4079.

Manufacturing Associations

Association for Manufacturing Excellence
3115 N. Wilke Road, Suite G
Arlington Heights, IL 60004
Phone: (224) 232-5980
Fax: (224) 232-5981
E-mail: info@ame.org
Web: ame.org

Association for Manufacturing Technology
7901 Westpark Drive
McLean, VA 22102-4206
Phone: (800) 524-0475 (toll-free), (703) 893-2900
Fax: (703) 893-1151
E-mail: amt@amt.org
Web: www.amtonline.org

Manufacturers' Agents National Association
One Spectrum Pointe, Suite 150
Lake Forest, CA 92630
Phone: (877) 626-2776 (toll-free), (949) 859-4040

Fax: (949) 855-2973
E-mail: mana@manaonline.org
Web: www.manaonline.org

MESA International (Manufacturing Enterprise Systems Association)
107 S. Southgate Drive
Chandler, AZ 85226
Phone: (480) 893-6883
Fax: (480) 893-7775
E-mail: info@mesa.org
Web: www.mesa.org

National Association of Manufacturers
1331 Pennsylvania Avenue, NW
Washington, DC 20004-1790
Phone: (202) 637-3000
Fax: (202) 637-3182
E-mail: manufacturing@nam.org
Web: www.nam.org

National Center for Manufacturing Sciences
3025 Boardwalk
Ann Arbor, MI 48108-3230
Phone: (734) 995-0300, (800) 222-6267 (toll-free)
Fax: (734) 995-1150
Web: www.ncms.org

National Electrical Manufacturers Association
1300 North 17th Street, Suite 1752
Rosslyn, VA 22209
Phone: (703) 841-3200
Fax: (703) 841-5900
Web: www.nema.org

Society of Manufacturing Engineers
One SME Drive
P.O. Box 930
Dearborn, MI 48121
Phone: (800) 733-4763 (toll-free), (313) 271-1500
Fax: (313) 425-3400
E-mail: info@sme.org
Web: www.sme.org

Tooling & Manufacturing Association
1177 S. Dee Road
Park Ridge, IL 60068
Phone: (847) 825-1120
Fax: (847) 825-0041
Web: www.tmanet.com

Source: MotionNET.com, Manufacturing Associations, www.motionnet.com/cgi-bin/search.exe?a=cat&no=4089.

Purchasing, Distributing, and Supply Associations

Electronics Representatives Association
444 N. Michigan Avenue, Suite 1960
Chicago, IL 60611
Phone: (312) 527-3050
Fax: (312) 527-3783
E-mail: info@era.org
Web: www.era.org

Industrial Supply Association
1300 Sumner Avenue
Cleveland, OH 44115-2851
Phone: (866) 460-2360 (toll-free)
Fax: (877) 460-2365
E-mail: info@isapartners.org
Web: www.ida-assoc.org

Institute for Supply Management
2055 E. Centennial Circle
P.O. Box 22160
Tempe, AZ 85285-2160
Phone: (800) 888-6276 (toll-free), (480) 752-6276
Fax: (480) 752-7890
Web: www.ism.ws

Manufacturers' Agents National Association
One Spectrum Pointe, Suite 150
Lake Forest, CA 92630
Phone: (877) 626-2776 (toll-free), (949) 859-4040
Fax: (949) 855-2973
E-mail: mana@manaonline.org
Web: www.manaonline.org

National Electrical Manufacturers Representatives Association
660 White Plains Road, Suite 600
Tarrytown, NY 10591-1504
Phone: (914) 524-8650
Fax: (914) 524-8655
E-mail: nemra@nemra.org
Web: www.nemra.org

Source: MotionNET.com, Purchasing, Distributing & Supply Associations www.motionnet.com/cgi-bin/search.exe?a=cat&no=4557.

Additional Resources

Ten Steps to Turn Your Ideas into Wealth

Step	Attitude	Action
1. Idea	There must be a better way	Create a product design
2. Market A$$e$$ment	Who will buy my product?	Quantify your market
3. Prototype	Proof of concept	Make it now, now
4. Refine Product	Get ready for market	Test and refine
5. Organizational	Think like a CEO	Prepare a business plan and get business cards
6. Vital Paperwork	Make it official	Drawings, brochures, patents
7. Initiate Production	Start slowly, gradually	Initiate mass production
8. $ales and Marketing	Target and $ell, $ell, $ell	Find market niche, prepare a sales plan
9. Engage Distributors	The power of volume	Find the biggest and the best
10. Manage	Plan, control, manage, lead	Develop growth strategies

Source: Joe Hipp, "10 Invention Secrets: 10 Steps to Turning Your Ideas / Inventions into Big Cash Wealth, www.1000ventures.com/business_guide/im_ideas2cash_10steps.html.

Top Ten to-Do's for Mid-Market Manufacturers Managing Supply

Procurement and sourcing "best practices" aren't just for the *Fortune* 500. Here is AMR Research's action list for mid-market manufacturers trying to improve business,

By Pierre Mitchell, Vice President of Research, AMR Research

As mid-market companies look for ways to ruthlessly reduce costs, especially as their large customers are mandating price reductions from them, procurement and supply chain departments are front-and-center in terms of delivering the savings and the operational improvements to support these increasingly stringent customer require- ments. Unfortunately, the lack of skills, systems, and real organizational support for improving supply processes has these groups caught between a rock and a hard place. While there are hundreds of possible interventions to address the root causes of these operational challenges, here's a top-ten list of actions that mid-market manufacturers can take to improve their business:

1. Have a clear performance measurement system to make sure everyone is on the

same page. Make sure you have some type of Program Management Office or other organizational process to see all your improvement projects, allowing everyone to be on the same page. Springfield Re-Manufacturing Corp. is a great example of this. Buy Jack Stack's book *The Great Game of Business* and adopt some of its key principles for open-book management.

2. **Organize yourself around supply.** Strategic sourcing is about organizing yourself to take best advantage of key supply markets that are critical to your customers. Supply management is not about renaming the Purchasing Department and seeking margin erosion from your suppliers, but about getting your internal departments and suppliers aligned around key commodities and then shaping demand and supply to take down total costs. Set up at least a few cross-functional teams in your most strategic spending categories to prove the concept and follow point 1 above to make sure you're changing performance measures—you won't get anywhere if it's viewed that purchasing effort and purchase price variance (PPV) are your key measure.

3. **Re-write your job descriptions to align with points 1 and 2.** The old role of buyer-planner working as expeditor is dead. As Theresa Metty, the CPO of Motorola, says, the most important thing you can do is separate the strategic function of supply from the tactical buying process. You will never realize impactful change by functional buyers doing process improvement as a bottoms-up, after-hours exercise. Becoming a real commodity manager is what buyers need to aspire to; you may have to bring in external staff from supply chain leaders to do so.

4. **Have a formal process and toolbox for continuous improvement.** Use Lean, Six Sigma, Theory of Constraints, and appropriate strategic sourcing techniques to empower your employees to drive out waste. Use this competency as a strategic weapon like plastics firm Nypro has.

5. **Have your CEO unite the purchasing and supply chain organizations.** If your VP of Purchasing is reporting to the CFO and not working jointly with the VP of Supply Chain who reports to the COO, you're in trouble. If you can't influence the CEO, have an external firm introduce him or her to a peer who has done so successfully (or show other benchmarking data that can incite the organization into meaningful change).

6. **Get visibility of your spending.** This is just like Statistical Process Control 101—you can't control and improve what you can't see and measure. If you want an immediate, no-risk ROI, bring in an A/P audit firm to mine your A/P data for savings owed to you as well as other savings opportunities. While PRG/Shultz is the gorilla here, APEX Analytix does this in conjunction with a software tool so you can do strategic sourcing analysis.

7. **Clean up your master data to make your analyses meaningful.** If your supplier master and item master data is less than clean, your analysis results will be so as well. Don't boil the ocean here. Use a provider like Austin-Tetra to help with your supplier master data and have your commodity teams roll up their sleeves with pragmatic item master cleanup efforts. Keep in mind that this cleanup is vital to

many improvement efforts, not just supplier re-sourcing, but also inventory consolidation and part reduction efforts.

8. **Automate opportunistically with procurement cards, e-procurement applications, and supplier connectivity services.** Focusing on higher-value activities includes automating lower-value-added tasks; using procurement cards is a great way to start reducing order/payment costs for low-value transactions. As you get more advanced, though, you'll want to transition and/or integrate the p-card to an e-procurement system (including support for travel and expense processing) that will provide you with the line item details you need for ongoing analysis and to eliminate the one to three percent charges that get placed on the suppliers.

9. **Automate your sourcing processes, too.** Even if you don't have massive spending leverage, automate your sourcing process to find better supply and to free yourself to do process improvement efforts. If you want to get started, there are many vendors to choose from, all the way from competitive bidding services firms oriented toward the mid-market to hosted e-sourcing tools and services. If you've never done it before, MfgQuote.com is a great place to start.

10. **Join a buying consortium.** A group purchasing organization (GPO) is by no means a core supply strategy, but it is a useful tool in the toolbox, and companies are saving money here. If you want leverage where you have little, take a look here.

In summary, improving procurement means not just buying cheaper, but also buying smarter (specification improvement, demand management, strategic supply market analysis, etc.) and more efficiently. Every pathway to supply management excellence varies, but the above tactics should provide some good places to get started.

Source: Katrina C. Arabe, "Top 10 To-Do's for Mid-Market Manufacturers Managing Supply," news.thomasnet.com/IMT/archives/2003/10/top_10_todos_fo.html.

Six Objectives of Just-in-Time Manufacturing

Defining the planning process for a JIT manufacturing system requires an understanding of the objectives of JIT and the goals and objectives of the JIT system. After the objectives are established for the manufacturing, the process of planning becomes one of determining what is required to meet those objectives.

The goal of a JIT approach is to develop a system that allows a manufacturer to have only the materials equipment and people on hand required to do the job. Achieving this goal requires six basic objectives:

1. **Integrating and optimizing every step of the manufacturing process.** The manufacturing system is a continual process of reducing the number of discrete steps required to complete a particular process rather than plateaus of steps. Removal of bottlenecks in the manufacturing process is a critical step in integration. One of the

best ways to achieve this objective is to plan for 100 percent defect-free quality. Integrating and optimizing will involve reducing the need for unnecessary functions and systems such as inspection, rework loops, and inventory.

2. **Producing a quality product.** Total Quality Control (TQC) is one of the fundamental goals in JIT manufacturing. TQC emphasizes the quality at every stage of manufacture, including product design, down to the purchase of raw materials. Quality control is carried out at every stage of the manufacturing steps, from the source to the final step, rather than relying on a single processing stage that implements quality control on the final product.

3. **Reducing manufacturing cost.** Designing products that facilitate and ease manufacturing processes helps to reduce the cost of manufacturing and building the product to specifications. One aspect in designing products for manufacturability is the need to establish a good employer-employee relationship. This is to cultivate and tap the resources of the production experts (production floor employees) and the line employees to develop cost-saving solutions.

4. **Producing product on demand.** The fundamental principle of JIT is the concept of producing a product only as needed or on demand. This implies that a product is not held in inventory and production is initiated only by demand.

5. **Developing manufacturing flexibility.** Manufacturing flexibility is the ability to start new projects or the rate at which the production mix can be adjusted to meet customer demand. Planning for manufacturing flexibility requires understanding the elements in the manufacturing process and identifying elements in the process that restrict flexibility and improving on these areas. The unique feature of JIT is the change from a push system to a pull system. The idea behind this concept is that work should not be pushed on to the next worker until that worker is ready for it. Manufacturing flexibility requires that production managers consider the following aspects in scheduling and improving manufacturing flexibility:

   - Supplier lead time

   - The need to ensure fast and reliable delivery of finished goods to the customer

   - Production process time

   - Process set up time

   - Bottlenecks in production process, which should be reduced, and resources (e.g., workers, machines), which should be fully utilized

6. **Keeping commitments and links made between customers and suppliers.** The corporate commitment to developing the internal structures and the customer and supplier bases to support JIT manufacturing is the primary requirement for developing the JIT system. Trust and commitment between the supplier and the customer is a must, because every JIT operation relies on it.

Source: Gihan Perera Galhenage, Michael Lazuardi, Arion Lee, Chin Teck Lim, and Henry Nyi Nyi Lwin, "What Is JIT Manufacturing?," www.supplychainplanet.com/e_article000233125.cfm.

Section 17

Top Seven Ways To Successfully Sabotage Your Great Idea

I'm sure that you can recall many times when you have had a brainwave, a bolt from the sky, a sudden idea, or an intrusion that you never brought to fruition for any number of reasons.

Maybe you initially thought the idea was so brilliant that it seemed to be the answer you had been looking for, but still nothing came of it.

Why is it that some people appear to be able to get novel ideas and create terrific success for themselves while others (the majority) seem to flounder before they ever get started?

Is it that they are more intelligent or more "lucky" than the average person or there's some mysterious secret?

The answer is no. We all have the same ability to create our own success using our own original ideas. It's just that most of us don't have the belief in those ideas or don't have the confidence to stick with them.

There are many ways to sabotage our ideas. Here are seven of them.

1. **Dissect the idea piece by piece, but not know when to stop.** If you are anything like me, you would examine the idea as if under a microscope, subjecting it to the "What if?" question until you find something minutely wrong that causes you to say, "Aha, I knew the idea won't work." Obviously, there is a certain amount of examination that needs to be done, but it shows a lack of commitment if your enthusiasm deflates at the first sign of a potential problem.

2. **Share the idea with others who are not qualified to pass comment.** This is dangerous territory if you are just starting out with a new idea. Many potential world-changing ideas have been shattered by well-meaning and "loving" criticism. It is best that you keep the idea to yourself until you have built up enough reserves to face all those Doubting Thomases.

3. **Become too intrigued with the idea.** It is so easy to "not see the forest for the trees," to become so close to the idea that you miss the obvious flaws that might exist. Develop a macro/micro vision: see the detail and also the overall picture.

4. **Dismiss the idea out of hand.** "Bah! It will never work!" How do you know until you've tried it out? Many of the greatest ideas seemed barmy at the time they were conceived. Learn to be open-minded and patient to see if the idea has potential.

5. **It's been thought of before!** You can bet your bottom dollar that someone somewhere has thought of your idea before. However, that does not mean that it's been acted upon. Therefore, you could be the first one to actually develop it into something tangible.

6. **Play devil's advocate with the idea.** Sometimes it is a good practice to think the idea over from a different perspective—but not to the extent that you destroy it

7. **Think that the idea is the best thing since sliced bread.** Maybe the idea is a world-beater, but you must be realistic in your thinking. Be careful not to let your ego get carried away or you will set yourself up for a fall.

Bonus Tips

- Think that the idea has no merit. This is the opposite of number 6 above. Humility is a powerful thing, but remember you are just as capable of thinking great ideas as the best of them.

- Go ahead with the idea without sufficient preparation first. Do your homework. Find out background information, do some research. Persevere and then, when you have a solid foundation, show it to the world. Who knows? People might even pay you for it!

The universe is full of great ideas just looking for someone to take and carry them though to fruition. If you learn to open your mind with an expectant heart, you will receive all the ideas that you desire.

Be very careful how you handle those gemstones, for in a flash they come, but equally in a flash they can go again.

Source: Malcolm Harvey, "Top 7 Ways to Successfully Sabotage That Great Idea of Yours," top7business.com/?Top-7-Ways-To-Successfully-Sabotage-That-Great-Idea-Of-Yours&id=453.

Five Critical Factors to Consider Before Upgrading Your Warehouse Management System

The Cost Factor

The simple fact that traditional warehouse management systems contain custom code is the reason they are so expensive to upgrade. A full system upgrade can push your total cost of ownership (TCO) to $1 million or more—which can surpass the cost of implementing an entirely new system. And worse, these upgrades perpetuate an already troublesome and expensive situation.

The complexity of modifying the code means that only the vendor or vendor-certified IT consultants can undertake the type of modifications that you need to keep current with customer needs. Businesses oftentimes find themselves "held captive" by their vendors because they have no other means of altering the code. This type of work typically requires three to six months in development time, which can accrue a hefty bill from your vendor for the necessary coding, testing, and debugging. Much of this is due to the fact that any previous code-based changes made to tailor the system's standard functionality to fit your particular business needs must be re-applied, re-tested, and re-implemented.

Your customer service could also be negatively affected by diminished efficiency in the event of unexpected system downtime during the upgrade process. Ultimately, you could lose revenue if shipments are lost, expectations are not met, and unhappy customers start exploring alternative distribution options. Worse yet, you haven't solved the root cause of this perpetual problem. In short, upgrading an antiquated code-based system keeps you tied to your vendor for costly modifications.

The Time Factor

Chances are, you're already short on time. With the speed of today's unpredictable business environment, you'd probably prefer to spend your day managing customer expectations instead of managing a lengthy upgrade to your WMS. Or perhaps the increasingly complex demands of your customers have compressed the timeframe in which you can implement the changes your business needs to increase efficiency and remain competitive.

Unfortunately, the complexity of modifying code-based processes not only requires you to wait until your vendor can schedule the appropriate resources to begin the project, but it also means that the modifications involved will likely require three to six months to implement. In some cases, the upgrade process can extend over a year due to the intricacy of altering the underlying code.

Although many vendors promise short implementation times, the actual process typically goes far beyond their estimates. This happens because business requirements are constantly changing, even while a company's system is undergoing an upgrade. Many companies find themselves in a situation where midway through the upgrade they have to make additional changes that require the vendor to rework what has just been upgraded, further delaying the completion date.

In essence, extended periods of time spent upgrading your WMS is time not spent focused on the efficient operation and continual improvement of your business.

The Risk Factor

Upgrading a typical WMS can pose a variety of threats to your core business operations. Once again, the prevalence of custom coding means that these types of systems are not architected to handle change. Therefore, the difficulty involved in code modifications represents a serious risk for lost data and disrupted business due to system debugging and other testing that may lead to unexpected downtime.

In addition, upgrades made to one part of the system can have unintended effects on related functions. The likelihood of this occurring increases with the volume of custom code. Moreover, the traditional upgrade process puts business operations at risk if the upgrade cannot properly support them. Equally risky is the prospect of maintaining a WMS infrastructure that has limited to no support from the suppliers of related equipment and software.

Ultimately, the potential risk to customer relationships must be considered in the upgrade decision. Customers today demand short order cycles and high degrees of

Section 17

accuracy throughout the fulfillment process. Shipping mistakes and other customer service errors that can result from glitches in the upgrade process can cost you dearly in lost customers and revenue. Ironically, the upgrade process for a code-based WMS can threaten the stability of the operations and customer service it is intended to improve.

The Adaptability Factor

Your present need to adapt your WMS to the changing business environment is evidence of the fundamental importance of system adaptability. Just think of the number of changes—both planned and unplanned—that have occurred in your business over the last 12 months. Evolving markets, emerging technologies such as RFID, changing customer preferences—the global economic climate advances so quickly that no software provider can predict what your business will need six months or a year from now. Therein lies the problem.

It is a serious mistake to assume that any software upgrade—no matter how comprehensive it may seem during the initial implementation—can provide all of the functionality your business will need down the road. That's why adaptability is so crucial. A system upgrade that does not meet new business requirements forces you to develop more custom code, which puts your organization at a competitive disadvantage as it diverts capital and resources away from core business goals. As discussed in examining the cost, time, and risk factors, modifying code is not an easy or risk-free task. In the end, your company will bear unnecessary expense and jeopardize operations in meeting the changing demands of your customers. The inherent inflexibility of code-based systems prohibits you from reacting quickly and cost-effectively as your business environment changes.

The Support Factor

Whether you require vendor support for incremental changes to your WMS, a new version upgrade, or the answers to frequent questions, the level of support your vendor provides is critical to your ability to operate efficiently. Oftentimes companies decide to postpone upgrading to the latest version of their vendor's WMS software due to the fact that their previous custom changes will need to be reapplied to the new version. Unfortunately, this is essentially forgoing an upgrade to the level of support they will receive. This occurs because the vendor's support staff is continuously trained to deal with issues pertaining to the most recent version of the software, and therefore becomes less knowledgeable about previous versions as time passes.

Similarly, delaying a potentially complex upgrade to your WMS can require you to maintain older versions of related infrastructure such as databases, operating systems, and other software. Again, this means that the support personnel trained to deal with these components are focused on providing assistance for the newest versions and not those that are several years old. In some cases, support for older infrastructure is transferred from the original provider to a third-party vendor, which can then charge a premium to support organizations that elect to maintain older software and infrastructure components.

Ultimately, running on an outdated WMS not only hinders efficient operations, but also decreases the level and quality of support you receive from your vendors.

Source: HighJump Software, *The Critical Factors You Must Consider Before Upgrading Your Warehouse Software*, www.highjumpsoftware.com/promos/supply-chain-execution-wms-costs.asp.

Seven Ways to Immediately Increase Order Fulfillment Speed

Start Your (Fulfillment) Engines

The steps suggested below are by no means exhaustive; they are simply the most obvious changes that an enterprise might make to accelerate its order-fulfillment operation. Before undertaking any such changes, however, a thorough and objective review should be made of your company's current order-fulfillment practices—in order to identify the issues that need to be addressed.

1. **Integrate your systems.** One of the most common impediments to rapid order fulfillment is the lack of integration between disparate computing systems used in the process. A recent survey revealed that more than 90 percent of all orders placed on the internet end up being rekeyed into at least one other system. The result is increased manual labor, a greater opportunity for error and inaccuracy, and a built-in "time gap" within the order-fulfillment process.

   By integrating all elements in the process, companies can reduce manual labor—or reallocate it to tasks that will further speed fulfillment—while eliminating input errors that are costly, time-consuming, and destructive to customer satisfaction. The return on integration investment is typically fast, and the ongoing improvement it affords in order fulfillment powerfully supports the company's relationship with new and existing customers.

2. **Automate your picking.** If a company's picking processes are paper-based, numerous methods are available to automate those processes for greater order-fulfillment speed. The two primary methods are material-handling automation and radio frequency (RF)-directed picking.

   Material-handling automation techniques such as carousel, conveyor, and sortation systems have been shown to effectively increase throughput by breaking up order-fulfillment work into more manageable steps. RF-directed picking saves time by instructing workers on where to find orders to be picked. It also allows more effective batch picking by enabling the picking of multiple orders simultaneously. In both cases, automation technologies appreciably speed the order-fulfillment process; they quickly pay for themselves in terms of increased throughput capacity and greater customer satisfaction—which, in turn, leads to repeat business and larger orders.

For those companies that choose to wait before incorporating automated picking technologies, forward picking processes offer a means of speeding order fulfillment without adding automation. By using existing systems to identify the items that are moving the fastest, companies can then move or "forward" such items closer to shipping areas—providing them with fixed locations for storage. This can cut down on travel time within the facility by shortening the distance between picks as well as the distance from the pick to the staging area for shipping.

A second forward picking option, one that incorporates a degree of automation, is dynamic forward pick slotting. With this technique, the day's orders are examined and analyzed at the beginning of a shift, and items with the highest number of touches are moved forward to slots nearer to the shipping area. Again, this can significantly reduce travel time and labor, thereby increasing throughput.

3. **Incorporate automated shipment planning** (ASP). For operations that commonly utilize mixed pallets and packing, automated shipment planning can yield huge gains in order-fulfillment speed. By using advanced fulfillment software to determine optimal stacking and packing arrangements in advance, ASP relieves workers from this complex and often tedious task—and saves the time that's often lost to reconfiguration and repacking as workers "find their way" to a workable stack-and-pack solution through trial and error.

   By accounting for the physical characteristics of the items to be picked, the physical fulfillment process can easily be optimized. With ASP, workers can pick to a predestinated container, thereby speeding the packing step and simplifying the pallet-building process. As a result, goods get out the door much faster.

4. **Automate shipment verification.** While automation of verification is commonly used to increase accuracy, it can also greatly enhance speed of execution. By using bar codes and scale weights rather than manual or visual verification, the checking step can easily be automated—validating that the containers actually contain what is expected, as well as eliminating both time and expense from the entire picking, packing, and shipping process.

5. **Reduce or eliminate paperwork.** Filling out paperwork is a tedious and time-consuming process. In operations that incorporate a high degree of sorting (e.g., to zones), companies often allocate armies of personnel just to sort things, a process that may also involve extensive paper documentation—adding hours or days to the fulfillment process.

   By leveraging IT systems to automate the sorting process, precious time and labor can be saved. For example, many warehouses still operate with a process that prints tomorrow's orders today, has those orders sorted tomorrow, and only then has the orders picked—often on the following day or even later. By tying the computing system into this process, orders can be generated, sorted, and picked the same day. Items like bills of lading are also much more effective when actual rather than theoreticals are used—thus improving efficiencies throughout the fulfillment process.

6. **Source orders based on facility workload.** If a company has multiple warehouses or distribution centers, technology should be used to optimize utilization of capacity. It should also be used to streamline workflow based on how overall demand impacts workload and capacity in individual storage and shipping centers. An item typically sourced and shipped from Warehouse A may in fact be more efficiently handled by Warehouse B if Warehouse A is approaching capacity limits and Warehouse B is slow. The idea is to view the enterprise's resources as a whole in order to maximize flexibility, improve responsiveness, and cut order-to-fulfillment cycle times.

7. **Incorporate sales and marketing into the process.** By collaborating with sales and marketing, a company can price or promote products in a way that speeds the fulfillment process and drives revenue. For example, a company may offer its customers the opportunity to order in any quantity. While customers clearly appreciate this convenience, it can result in efficiency problems in the fulfillment operation by creating extra work (e.g., breaking cases, shipping packages that are less than full, etc.) that causes the company to bear atypical labor and turnaround costs.

By working with sales and marketing to encourage orders that speed and simplify fulfillment (e.g., by offering price breaks at specific quantities), companies can appeal to customers in a way that facilitates fulfillment—saving time and labor while also improving responsiveness.

Source: HighJump Software, *Seven Ways to Immediately Increase Order-Fulfillment Speed*, www.highjumpsoftware.com/promos/supply-chain-execution-wms-costs.asp.

Seven Ways to Boost Order Accuracy to Near-Perfect Levels

1. **Work with your vendors.** Receiving is where accuracy starts. If items are not properly identified and counted upon receipt, accuracy in all downstream processes (putaway, movement, kitting, picking, and shipping) is imperiled. Your vendors can help by providing you with clear and simple product labeling. Ideally, this should include bar code identification. At a minimum, ask your vendors to include a bar-coded part number on an identification label. This will help prevent mistaken identity problems in receiving. For maximum results, ask your vendor to label each pallet or container with a unique identifier and transmit an advanced ship notice (ASN) with pallet- or container-level detail. With this approach, a pallet or container can be received with a single bar code scan.

2. **Validate receipts against purchase orders.** With items properly identified, you have the ability to validate received items against the originating purchase order. Comparing shipments against purchase orders at the time of receipt adds another

measure of item identification and quantity verification. Most businesses perform this validation manually. However, this is a time-consuming and error-prone process, especially when receiving similar items or items with long, complex identifiers. For best results, use bar-code verification and automatic and systematic quantity checks using computer systems integrated with your purchasing software. This will dramatically reduce human error and significantly speed up the validation process.

3. **Validate put-away bins.** If not recorded accurately, much of the effort of accounting for receipts can go to waste when items are put away into bin locations. Like the receiving process, clear and simple bin location identifiers are a must. A simple bin numbering scheme will help workers quickly locate and record put-away bin locations. Put-away locations recorded on paper must be entered into tracking systems manually. This presents three opportunities for error. First, when a worker records the location to paper. Second, when data entry personnel try to discern the handwriting of the material handler. Third, when the paper never reaches the data entry worker because it has been lost or run through the laundry. Again, technology can provide the greatest degree of accuracy when bin locations are bar coded and workers must scan put-away locations to record and/or validate the put-away bin location. With this approach, all three potential errors are virtually eliminated because put-away locations are recorded accurately with one scan of a bar code, particularly with systems that update an inventory database at the moment of scanning.

4. **Simplify picking.** In most cases, the majority of order accuracy errors result from picking errors. Thus, special attention must be given to clarifying and simplifying the picking process. First, if your workers pick using a paper document, make sure that the picking document is clear and provides the information that the picker needs. Do not use shipping paperwork as picking paperwork. It includes extraneous information designed to aid the customer's receiving function, not the picker. The information should be presented in the order it is required: location, stock number, description, unit of measure, and quantity required. Always use large, easy-to-read fonts with double-spaced lines and horizontal rulers. The picker should use the clear, top copy of any multipage form. Second, make sure that the picking document lists line items in pick route order, to save the picker time and avoid accidentally skipping line items. While these measures will help improve picking accuracy, there is still considerable room for human error. To completely eliminate confusion and guarantee that no line items are skipped, some form of automation technology must be applied. With radio frequency (RF)-directed picking, for example, workers do not have a need for paper. A warehouse management system (WMS) simply directs a worker to each bin location (in an efficient path) to pick items on an order by sending the worker instructions via a handheld RF terminal. With a bar-code scanner the worker can confirm the bin location and item picked, thereby eliminating the potential for errors.

5. **Validate picks.** To achieve high degrees of accuracy in the picking process, many businesses employ "checkers" to validate the quality of order picks by means of inspection and redundant effort. There are two basic approaches to more cost-effec-

tive picking accuracy. First, checkers should only be used as a short-term, stopgap measure. Long-term quality requires that the order picker be held accountable for picking the correct items, in the correct quantity, and delivering them to the correct warehouse location. Through both positive and negative reinforcement, pickers can be given strong incentives to improve accuracy. Again, this approach will generate improvement, but will not likely deliver near-perfect order accuracy. This kind of accuracy requires utilizing the latest WMS and/or automation technology to direct picking processes and reduce the likelihood of shipping the wrong product. Bar-code scanners, voice recognition systems, and RF data terminals are becoming commonplace tools for achieving near-perfect accuracy in the order-picking function.

6. **Avoid counting—if you can.** Where appropriate, measure instead of count. Let's face it: counting can be boring, especially when counting large quantities. Packaging can be designed to hold a reasonable quantity of product relative to the quantity ordered. If the packaging holds 1,000 units and the typical order quantity is 100 units, then the package is too large. Similarly, if the product is packaged in individual units and the typical customer order quantity is 100 units, the package count is too small. To solve the counting problem, measure instead. Electronic weight scales can be both accurate and enhance productivity, especially for very small items. Weight verification validates quantities.

7. **Seek adaptability.** In the strictest sense of order accuracy, customers must receive the items they desire. However, as many warehousing and fulfillment managers know, customers' desires are subject to change at a moment's notice. In order to correctly ship customers the items they requested, your business processes must support change at a moment's notice. Many systems in use today do not support rapid or frequent changes to customer orders because they are unable to provide customers (or customer service representatives) visibility into the fulfillment process, and because changes are not easily communicated to fulfillment operations. Visibility is important because it can provide a view into the cost of making an order change (i.e., change is inexpensive if no action has been taken on a given order). Communication is important—critical, really—to completing the desired change accurately and effectively. Communicating verbally presents many opportunities for error, while communicating systematically provides insurance against errors.

Source: HighJump Software, *Seven Ways to Boost Order Accuracy to Near-Perfect Levels,* www.highjumpsoftware.com/promos/supply-chain-execution-wms-costs.asp.

62 Manufacturing Businesses You Can Start

1. **Patio Furniture Manufacturing.** Launching a business venture that builds custom cedar patio furniture is a relatively inexpensive enterprise to establish. Check out www.scrollsaw.com, design plans for patio furniture.

2. **Online Manufacturers' Directory.** Manufacturers' directories in print have served as a valuable resource tool for many corporations and small businesses for decades. Start by selecting a segment of the industry you want to concentrate on, like machined fasteners or fabric.

3. **Kitchen Cutting Boards.** Once you have mastered the art of producing high-quality kitchen cutting boards, you can then move on to butcher block tables, as the market demand for this specialty product is huge.

4. **Bookends.** One idea may be to capitalize on the ever-increasing environmentally friendly theme and manufacture all the bookends out of recycled materials. Keep your product different and unique.

5. **Weather Vanes.** These functional and attractive features add charm to any home and hearken back to the days of old and can be made from a wide variety of materials.

6. **Waterbeds.** Simply design and construct the waterbed frames and assemble the other parts to fit. Check out www.waterbedreplaceparts.com, wholesale source of waterbed parts.

7. **Custom Picture Frames.** Ideally, make your picture frames out of a unique material, such as copper, molded clay, plastic, or wood. The more interesting the materials and unique the design, the better.

8. **Wooden Signs.** There are a few methods of manufacturing attractive and functional wood signs. One is to use a router to remove wood and leave the words raised or concave and the other method requires a design stencil and sandblasting equipment to remove the wood around the words to make them rise. Check out www.signsup-plyusa.com, distributors of wholesale sign-making equipment.

9. **Scratch Posts.** This enterprise requires virtually no special skills and only basic hand or power tools, with an ever-constant demand.

10. **Wooden Sash Windows.** The main qualification for launching this venture is to possess a good deal of carpentry experience and knowledge. The product can be marketed directly to homeowners or to renovation companies on a subcontract basis.

11. **Birdhouses.** The only requirement for starting this business is to have basic woodworking equipment and experience. Check out www.scrollsaw.com, design plans for birdhouse construction.

12. **Online Birdhouses Sales.** Develop a web site to sell your own birdhouse creations as well as other hobbyist birdhouse builders.

13. **Wind Chimes.** Seashells, glass, metal, or bells—wind chimes can be manufactured from almost any kind of material. It's a great way to turn spare time into extra income.

14. **Saunas.** Design, manufacture, and wholesale your custom-built, you-assemble sauna kits nationwide for a great business venture. Check out www.saunasite.com, sauna design plans and information.

15. **Prototype Design.** Designing and building prototypes is a highly specialized business that requires a great deal of construction knowledge, ability to work with various mediums, and all required equipment necessary for building a host of various products.

16. **Roof Trusses.** Most new home construction now uses pre-engineered and -built roof trusses. Check out www.woodtruss.com, the Wood Truss Council of America.

17. **Floating Docks.** Building floating docks and swim platforms is a manufacturing business that can be started by about anyone with construction knowledge and a well-equipped woodworking shop.

18. **Canoe Paddles.** A business that manufactures wooden canoe and kayak paddles can be established right from a home-based garage workshop and requires only a small investment in woodworking equipment to get going.

19. **CD Racks.** CD racks can be manufactured from wood, plastic, or iron in various shapes and sizes and storage capacities.

20. **Art Easels.** It's easy to run this business from home and sell the art easels to artist supply stores on a wholesale basis and once you've gotten established, approach various manufacturers of all-inclusive painting kits to check out the viability of including an art easel with these painting kits.

21. **Picnic Tables.** Building picnic tables only requires basic construction knowledge and can be readily done in a small home-based workshop. Check out www.toolcenter.com/JERs/picnic.html, distributor of picnic table construction plans.

22. **Wood Moldings.** Start a business that manufactures custom wood moldings with standard profiles as well as made-to-order wood moldings. It's a terrific business start-up for the skilled and well-equipped carpenter.

23. **Old English Telephone Booths.** Starting a business that manufactures replica antique English phone booths is a business opportunity that can earn an additional $20,000 or more part-time.

24. **Hide-a-Beds.** Beds can be sold directly to consumers by placing product advertisements in local newspapers and the Yellow Pages, as well as constructing a hide-a-bed display, which can be set up at furniture and home and garden trade shows to generate sales leads.

25. **Packing Crates.** Designing and building custom made-to-order packaging crates is a great business to initiate and has an almost endless supply of potential customers. Check out www.nwpca.com, the National Wood Pallet and Container Association.

26. **Store Display Cases.** Often merchants require display cases and store fixtures that have to be specially constructed to highlight or merchandise their inventory.

27. **Futons.** Futons are a functional, yet inexpensive piece of furniture that can serve a multitude of uses and can be set up and managed from a home office. Check out www.futonfurnitureplans.com, distributors of futon construction plans.

Section 17

28. **Woodturnings.** Fruit bowls, candlesticks, stair spindles, or baseball bats—there are literally hundreds of products that can be manufactured simply by purchasing a wood-turning lathe and mastering the art of wood turning. Check out www.wood-turner.org, the American Association of Wood Turners.

29. **Window Sash Mirrors.** This is an ideal business venture to be started by someone who is seeking a low-investment home-based business opportunity that can generate a fantastic part-time income and still allow you to maintain a full-time job.

30. **Magnetic Signs.** The signs that are often used as removable advertisements on their cars are easy to design and produce, making this an ideal business venture for anyone looking for a home-based business with little start-up capital.

31. **Specialty Soaps.** There are hundreds of soap-making recipes available or you can create your own recipes for making soap to make your product unique. Check out www.soapcrafters.com, soap-making recipes.

32. **Mailboxes.** The completed custom mailboxes can be sold on a wholesale basis to retailers or directly to consumers via a booth at a busy weekend flea market or craft show.

33. **Silk-Screening Mouse Pads.** Purchase silk-screening equipment and a few hundred blank mouse pads is all that is necessary for starting your own business that produces mouse pads emblazoned with printed images, logos, and slogans. Check out www.printusa.com, distributor of equipment and supplies for screen-printing mouse pads.

34. **Staircases.** Providing you have the necessary skills and equipment, you can build and install staircases made from various construction materials, such as hard and soft woods, steel, concrete, or any combination of the above.

35. **Porch Columns.** Manufacturing decorative porch columns can be a very profitable business once established, especially if the main focus of the manufacturing business is to design and build Victorian porch column replicas.

36. **Theme Bunk Beds.** The key to success in this type of manufacturing business is to choose the right theme and make the beds unique and colorful.

37. **First-Aid Kits.** First-aid kits can be assembled, packaged, and sold to retailers on a wholesale basis or they can be specially designed and marketed to specific industries.

38. **Christmas Ornaments.** Christmas ornaments such as tree decorations and door wreaths are very simple and inexpensive to make, and can be sold in various ways, including to retailers on a wholesale basis or directly to consumers at a sales kiosk in a mall or at craft shows.

39. **Custom Doorstops.** The key to success in this type of manufacturing venture is that the doorstops must be unique in design, and the marketing methods employed must be innovative and clever. Check out www.ahma.org, the American Hardware Manufacturers Association.

40. **Wood Clothes Hangers.** Typical clothes hangers can destroy expensive clothes, so the potential market for custom-made clothes hangers to specifically fit one particular item is huge.

41. **Mold Making.** A business that specializes in making manufacturing molds for clients is not hard to establish but you or one employee must be able to design and build numerous styles of molds.

42. **Trade Show Displays.** The best way to capitalize on the demand for trade show displays and off-the-shelf, mass-produced, generic trade show displays. Check out www.epda.com, the Exhibit Designers and Producers Association.

43. **Snowboards.** Manufacturing snowboards is not a difficult task but it all lies within the design and composition of the snowboard and this business is best suited to individuals with designing background.

44. **Rubber Stamps.** Follow these steps to start a business that manufactures predesigned rubber stamps:

    ■ Research the industry, market, and business.

    ■ Establish a manufacturing process, and secure retail accounts for the stamps.

    ■ Manufacture the stamps and ship to retailers.

45. **Clocks.** The components needed to build clocks can be purchased on a wholesale basis from manufacturers of these items, while housing for the clock can be manufactured by your business.

46. **Brooms and Brushes.** The brooms and brushes that can be manufactured can cater to one specific industry that uses a specialty broom or brush, such as the chimney sweep industry. Check out www.abma.org/industrial.htm, the American Brush Manufacturers Association.

47. **Window Shutters and Blinds.** The complete shutters can be sold to national home improvement center retailers on a wholesale basis or the window shutters can be sold directly to homeowners on a custom order and installation basis.

48. **Treehouse Kits.** Treehouse kits can be packaged and sold to retail outlets on a wholesale basis or directly to customers via advertising the treehouse kits for sale on the internet, in newspapers and other publications, and by establishing a display model that can be exhibited at trade shows.

49. **Store Directory Boards.** This is a very competitive segment of the manufacturing and sign industry, so be sure to take a unique and innovative approach to the manufacturing process and appearance in the finished product.

50. **Plastic Displays.** The market demand for custom-designed and -manufactured product and information display holders is gigantic, and starting a business that specializes in manufacturing plastic displays is very easy.

51. **Online Factory Direct.** Develop an online "factory direct" web site that features products for sale manufactured by these home-based manufacturers. This cyberven-

Section 17

ture is successful since "factory direct" pricing attracts consumers and securing manufactured goods to be featured on the site would be very easy.

52. **Office Dividers.** The latest trend in office layout is no walls, only dividers to create a
really communal workplace. The office divider designs could incorporate handy features, such as adjustable shelving, built-in wastebaskets, and built-in message
boards.

53. **Antenna Ornaments.** Some of the best aspects about this type of manufacturing
business start-up are that the business can be started on a part-time basis and easily
operated from a home-based workshop.

54. **Doghouses.** Consider incorporating recycled materials into the construction process,
as you can play upon the benefits of recycling for marketing purposes. Check out
www.woodcraftplans.com, distributors of doghouse construction plans.

55. **Jewelry Boxes.** Consider using materials that normally would not be used for building this product, like recycled items, seashells, glass, or plastic.

56. **Fence Panels.** Fence panels can be sold to fence installation companies, landscape
contractors, and do-it-yourself building centers or directly to homeowners by placing advertisements in your local newspaper.

57. **Garden Arbors.** If you don't have design talent, plans are readily available at most
building centers for constructing garden arbors and only a small workshop space
and basic tools will be required for this venture.

58. **Lattice Manufacturing.** There are many uses for lattice including decorative interior
partitions for residential and commercial applications, exterior garden partitions and
design features, and interior and exterior hand railing components, just to mention a
few.

59. **Driftwood and Log Furniture.** There are literally hundreds of household and patio
furniture products that can be manufactured from driftwood, rough-cut logs, or even
waste wood, such as coffee tables, benches, serving trays, side tables, chairs,
planters, storage boxes, bunk beds, and picture frames.

60. **Air Freshener Manufacturing.** It is best to stay away from using chemical com-
pounds for this business and stick to natural and organic ingredients and sell them
to retailers or directly to customers at home and garden shows.

61. **Aluminum Door and Window Manufacturing.** Aluminum storm windows and
doors are easy to manufacture as the material required is referred to as extrusions. It
is a simple process of cutting the window framing rails to length, wrapping the glass
in a rubber gasket, and attaching the rails that are screw-fastened in the corners. If
this sounds like something you can do, this is the venture for you. Check out
www.thebluebook.com, a directory service listing manufacturers and distributors of
aluminum extrusions, equipment, and supplies used in manufacturing aluminum
windows and doors.

62. **Awning Manufacturing.** Providing you have the workshop space and zoning per-mits, you can even manufacture awnings right from your home office. Check out www.thebluebook.com, a directory service listing manufacturers and distributors of awning manufacturing equipment and supplies.

Source: James Stephenson, *Entrepreneur Magazine's Ultimate Start-Up Directory.*